Tort Law

Third Edition

Nicholas J. McBride
Fellow of Pembroke College, Cambridge

and

Roderick Bagshaw
Fellow of Magdalen College, Oxford

Harlow, England • London • New York • Boston • San Francisco • Toronto
Sydney • Tokyo • Singapore • Hong Kong • Seoul • Taipei • New Delhi
Cape Town • Madrid • Mexico City • Amsterdam • Munich • Paris • Milan

Pearson Education Limited
Edinburgh Gate
Harlow
Essex CM20 2JE
England

and Associated Companies throughout the world

Visit us on the World Wide Web at:
www.pearsoned.co.uk

First published 2001
Second edition published 2005
Third edition published 2008

ISBN: 978-1-4058-5949-3

British Library Cataloguing-in-Publication Data
A catalogue record for this book is available from the British Library

Library of Congress Cataloging-in-Publication Data
McBride, Nicholas J.
Tort law / Nicholas J. McBride and Roderick Bagshaw. — 3rd ed.
p. cm.
Includes bibliographical references and index.
ISBN 978-1-4058-5949-3 (alk. paper)
1. Torts—England. I. Bagshaw, Roderick. II. Title.
KD1949.M38 2008
346.4203—dc22

2008026797

10 9 8 7 6 5 4 3 2 1
12 11 10 09 08

Typeset in 10pt Minion by 3
Printed and bound by Henry Ling Ltd., at the Dorset Press, Dorchester, Dorset

The publisher's policy is to use paper manufactured from sustainable forests.

Dedicated to the memory of

JANE VAULKS

19 June 1976 – 16 October 2003

The Lord bless you and keep you
The Lord make his face shine upon you
and be gracious to you
The Lord turn his face toward you
and give you peace

(Numbers 6:24–26)

Contents

Visit the Tort Law, third edition mylawchamber site at **www.mylawchamber.co.uk/mcbride** to access valuable learning material.

FOR STUDENTS

Do you want to give yourself a head start come exam time?

Companion website support

- Use the model answers and tips for answering a range of tort problem questions to test yourself on various topics and prepare for exam success.
- Use the updates to major changes in the law to make sure you are ahead of the game by knowing the latest developments.
- Use the case notes and case updates on over 100 tort law cases to improve your knowledge and understanding of the law of tort.
- Use the bibliography of books and articles on tort law to help you read more widely around the subject, and really impress your lecturers.

Worried about getting to grips with cases?

Case Navigator*

This unique online support helps you to improve your case reading and analysis skills.

- **Direct deep links** to the core cases in tort law.
- **Short introductions** provide guidance on what you should look out for while reading the case.
- **Questions** help you to test your understanding of the case, and provide feedback on what you should have grasped.
- **Summaries** contextualise the case and point you to further reading so that you are fully prepared for seminars and discussions.

Also: The regularly maintained Companion Website provides the following features:

- Search tool to help locate specific items of content.
- Online help and support to assist with website usage and troubleshooting.

For more information please contact your local Pearson Education sales representative or visit **www.mylawchamber.co.uk/mcbride**.

*Please note that access to Case Navigator is free with the purchase of this book, but you must register with us for access. Full registration instructions are available on the website. The LexisNexis element of Case Navigator is only available to those who currently subscribe to LexisNexis Butterworths online.

Acknowledgments

Nick McBride and Roderick Bagshaw write: We would first of all like to thank Rebekah Taylor, the commissioning editor in Law at Pearson Education, for commissioning us to write a new edition of this book, and for all her help and support in producing the book. We would like to thank everyone at Pearson for their efforts in helping to produce this book, especially: Christine Statham, Zoe Botterill, Tim Parker, Katherine Cowdrey, Barbara Massam and Jonathon Price.

Thanks are also owed to Hannah Varley, who helped with some of the mundane tasks associated with producing a new edition of a textbook, and Helen Stagg, who helped Nick McBride understand the facts of *Gregg* v *Scott* [2005] 2 AC 176. We would both like to acknowledge the great support we have each received from our respective colleges.

Roderick Bagshaw writes: I would like to thank my wife, Liz, for providing terrific encouragement and support. I owe her so much. And, although thanking a co-author may seem unusual – indeed a reviewer of the last edition identified such a gesture as a defect! – I would also like to thank Nick. Without his dedication to explaining tort law in a concise, accurate and accessible way, and his commitment to this book, I suspect I would still be reworking erudite footnotes for a first edition rather than publishing a third.

Nick McBride writes: My half of this book could not have been written without the help and support of a huge number of people, including: my mother and my brother, Ben; everyone at TLIG (especially Albert and Valerie Muller, and Anthippie Dimozantos); Ines Anoustis; the Sheltons; Amanda and Emile Perreau-Saussine; Rod Bagshaw and his wife, Liz; Hannah Varley; and Helen Stagg. I owe them all so much. I owe a special debt of gratitude to Hannah Bill (legendary!) and the totally awesome Gabi Rutherford. Their astonishing kindness really carried me in writing this edition. As great as the debt that I owe Hannah and Gabi is, it is easily outweighed by the debt I owe my best friend, Isabel Haskey, who has been one of the mainstays of my life for almost 20 years now. If this book were half as perfect as she is, it would be a fine thing indeed. Finally, I would like to thank my father for all the help he gave me with the writing of this book.

Preface: The tort wars

The current division

The academic community of tort lawyers is now divided into two rival camps.[1] Much the larger camp is made up of academics who take what we might call the *modern* view of tort law. According to this view of tort law,[2] in tort cases the courts determine whether A should be held liable to compensate B for some loss that A has caused B to suffer. According to this view, then, tort law is simply the law on compensation – it tells us when one person will be held liable to compensate another for some loss that he or she has caused that other to suffer.

Throughout the 1960s and 1970s, it was assumed without question among academic tort lawyers that the modern view of tort law was correct. There was universal agreement that, in the words of Lord Bingham, the 'overall object of tort law is to define cases in which the law may justly hold one party liable to compensate another'.[3] There were, of course, disagreements among the tort academics as to *why* people were held liable 'in tort' to pay compensation to someone else. Some argued that the object of such awards was to pass losses that were suffered by individuals onto business and insurance companies, so that those losses could then be spread throughout the community through price rises and premium increases, thus minimising the social impact of those losses. Others argued that in holding people liable to pay other people compensation, tort law was concerned to minimise the 'cost of accidents' by encouraging people who could most cheaply avoid an accident occurring to take the precautions required to stop that accident occurring. And a third group argued that in making compensation awards, tort law was simply concerned to protect those who had suffered a loss which they did not deserve to suffer. But these disagreements masked an underlying consensus – a universal agreement among tort academics that the modern view of tort law was correct.

That consensus began to break down in the mid-1980s – round about the time the authors of this book went to Oxford to study Law. In Canada, a legal philosopher called Ernest Weinrib wrote a series of articles arguing that tort law was concerned with *corrective justice* – which, for our purposes, can be taken as a fancy name for 'remedying *wrongs*'.[4]

[1] Or possibly three. There is a school of thought that, unlike any other area of law one can possibly think of (such as contract law, or family law, or company law, or international law), tort law does not actually refer to anything in particular. According to this *nihilistic* view of tort law, nothing unites the various legal rules and principles that are customarily discussed in tort law textbooks. For some reason, this view seems quite popular among academics from the University of Cambridge: see Weir 2006, ix ('Tort is what is in the tort books, and the only thing holding it together is the binding'); Howarth & O'Sullivan 2001, 1 ('[it is] particularly difficult to present a rational or logical classification of [tort law]'); M&D, 90 ('Expecting structure, order or theoretical consistency from our courts or any underlying theory for tort recovery is perhaps asking too much from them'). It is hard to know whether these authors intend such statements to be taken seriously: why would they spend their time writing about a subject which – according to them – does not exist?

[2] Stevens 2007, at 2, calls this view of tort law, the 'loss model' of tort law.

[3] *Fairchild* v *Glenhaven Funeral Services Ltd* [2003] 1 AC 32 at [9].

[4] See Weinrib 1995 for the most complete statement of Weinrib's views on tort law, and law generally.

At roughly the same time, the greatest modern scholar of English private law – Professor Peter Birks, Regius Professor of Civil Law at the University of Oxford – started to take an interest in the classification of legal obligations, as part of his work on the law of unjust enrichment. He began to argue that tort law, as a subject, is not centred around a particular *response* – that is, compensation.[5] Rather, tort law focuses on a particular *event* – the commission of a *civil wrong* – and describes the varying ways in which the law responds to that event.[6] Out of the work of these two academics emerged a very different view of tort law from that which held sway in the legal academy in the 1960s and 1970s, and one which is now endorsed by a significant minority of tort academics.[7] According to this view of tort law, in tort cases, the courts determine whether A has committed a wrong in relation to B, and if he has, they determine what remedies will be available to B. To put it another – exactly equivalent – way, in tort cases, the courts determine whether A has violated B's rights in acting as he did, and if he has, they determine what remedies will be available to B.

We can call this view of tort law, the *traditional* view of tort law.[8] Traditional, because up until about 40 years ago, it had *always* been thought that tort law was all about protecting people who had suffered a wrong, people whose rights had been violated.[9] Up until about 40 years ago, Lord Hope's statement in *Chester* v *Afshar* that 'the function of the law [of tort] is to enable rights to be vindicated and to provide remedies when duties have been breached'[10] would have been regarded as a statement of the obvious. But no longer: those who endorse the modern view of tort law would in all likelihood dismiss a statement such as Lord Hope's as narrow and naive.

Why this disagreement matters

It is as impossible for a tort law textbook to be neutral on the issue of whether the modern or the traditional view of tort law is correct as it is for a science textbook to be neutral on the issue of whether the Earth is flat or spherical. The issue is too fundamental for neutrality to be an option. Whether the modern or traditional view of tort law is correct affects:

(1) *The reach of tort law*. One of the reasons for the popularity of the modern view of tort law among tort academics is that it makes their subject so excitingly huge. On the modern view of tort law, tort law has the potential to intervene and provide a remedy in *any* situation where A has caused B to suffer some kind of loss. That is, after all, the function of tort law – to determine whether it would be 'fair, just and reasonable' to allow B to sue A for compensation, and if it would be, to allow B to sue A for compensation. So, on the modern

5 It is noticeable that the first part of the US Third Restatement of Tort Law is explicitly centred around a response: 'Liability for Physical and Emotional Harm'. (The second part, 'Economic Torts and Related Wrongs', also seems based on the response of compensation for economic harm.) It is not clear how successful this approach will be: Peter Birks regarded any response-based approach to describing the law of tort as doomed to be incoherent, repetitive, and incomplete.

6 See Birks 1983, 1989, 1995, 1997a.

7 See Goldberg & Zipursky 2001, 2006; Coleman 1993, 2001; Calnan 2005; Stevens 2007; Beever 2007.

8 Stevens 2007, at 2, calls this view of tort law, the 'rights model' of tort law.

9 For example, the full title of the 13th edition of Sir Frederick Pollock's *The Law of Torts* (published London, 1929) was 'The Law of Torts: A Treatise on the Principles of Obligations Arising From Civil Wrongs in the Common Law'. See also Goodhart 1938.

10 [2005] 1 AC 134, at [87] (endorsed by Baroness Hale in *Gregg* v *Scott* [2005] 2 AC 176, at [216]).

view of tort law, any situation where one person causes another to suffer some kind of loss is one which tort academics are entitled to discuss with a view to deciding whether a remedy should be granted or not in that situation.

In contrast, the traditional view of tort law places severe constraints on the scope of tort law's jurisdiction. On the traditional view, if A has caused B to suffer some kind of loss, B will not be entitled to sue A in tort for compensation for that loss unless she can first show that A violated her rights in acting as he did. If she cannot do this then tort law has nothing to do with her and it cannot be invoked to help her out. As we will see later on in this Preface, this hurdle – of having to show that A's conduct violated B's rights – can be very difficult to surmount. And if it cannot be surmounted, that is the end of B's case so far as tort law is concerned. No matter how beneficial it might be to grant B a remedy in this situation, there is nothing to talk about so far as tort law, and the tort academics, are concerned.

(2) *What goes into tort textbooks.* On the modern view of tort law, the task of a tort textbook is to set out *all* the situations where B is entitled to sue A for compensation for a loss that A has caused her to suffer. In contrast, if the traditional view of tort law is correct then a tort textbook need only concern itself with cases where B is entitled to sue A for compensation because A has violated her rights. On the traditional view of tort law, cases of what we will call 'compensation without wrongdoing' – that is, cases where B is entitled to sue A for compensation for a loss that A caused her to suffer without, however, violating B's rights – fall outside the scope of a tort textbook.

(3) *How we think about the way cases are decided.* As anyone who has ever read a few tort cases will know, the way judges decide cases supports the traditional view of tort law. In a case where A has caused B to suffer some kind of loss and B is seeking some remedy against A as a result, the judges do *not* say – 'Well, let's weigh up the pros and cons of awarding B a remedy here. On balance, we find that it would be desirable to allow B to sue A for some compensation here, so it is duly ordered that A should pay B £10,000.' Instead – just as the traditional view of tort law would lead us to expect – the judges first of all look to see if A violated B's rights in acting as he did. If he did then they will normally grant B a remedy; if he did not, B's claim will fail. *Ubi ius, ibi remedium* – where there is a right, there is a remedy. If there is no right, there is no remedy (so far as tort law is concerned).

This fact about the cases creates a problem for the modern view of tort law. How can the modern view of tort law be correct when the way tort law cases are decided makes it so obvious that the traditional view of tort law is correct? The preferred solution for those academics who adopt the modern view of tort law is to argue that when the judges *say* that they are granting B a remedy in a given case because A violated her rights, that is not the *real reason* for their decision. In order to discover the real reason, one must discard all the nonsense in the cases about 'rights' and 'duties' and 'unmask' the real 'policy concerns' that motivated the courts' decision.[11] This is another reason why the modern view of tort law is

[11] Two notable examples of this kind of thinking were provided in two consecutive issues of the *Cambridge Law Journal* by the tort academic turned politician, David Howarth. In *Gorringe* v *Calderdale MBC* [2004] 1 WLR 1057, the claimant was injured when she drove her car into a bus. Had she been driving more slowly, she would have avoided the bus. The claimant sued the defendant local authority for failing to put up a warning sign by the side of the road, telling her to slow down. Lord Hoffmann, giving the leading judgment, dismissed the

so exciting, and therefore popular among tort academics. It *is* exciting to think that you have found out what is really going on – that the courts are pursuing a secret agenda in the cases and you know what that agenda is. But it must always be remembered that exciting is not necessarily true. It may be exciting to think that President Kennedy was assassinated by the CIA and the Mafia. But it is not necessarily true.

At any rate, whether the traditional view of tort law is correct or not should have a big impact on the way we think about the way tort cases are decided. If the traditional view is correct, then we have no reason not to take the judges seriously when they deny a claimant a remedy in a tort case on the ground that the defendant did not violate her rights in acting as he did. If the traditional view of tort law is wrong, and tort law is not in fact concerned with vindicating a claimant's rights, then in tort cases where a judge denies a claimant a remedy on the ground that the defendant did not violate the claimant's rights in acting as he did, that cannot be the real reason for the judge's decision. The fact that the defendant did not violate the claimant's rights cannot be sufficient reason to deny her a remedy in tort. Something else must be going on – and we need to find out what it is.

(4) *How we judge whether a case was correctly decided.* Finally, whether the traditional or modern view of tort law is correct will have a big impact on how we approach the issue of judging whether a given tort case was correctly decided. For example, in *Bradford Corporation* v *Pickles*,[12] the defendant blocked off a stream of water flowing under his land so that the water could not flow into the claimants' reservoirs. The claimants sued the defendant in tort. They lost: as they had no right to receive the water that flowed under the defendant's land, the defendant did nothing wrong to the claimants in blocking that water off. Was this case correctly decided?

If we adopt the traditional view of tort law then we will approach this issue by asking whether the House of Lords in *Bradford Corporation* v *Pickles* was right to say that the claimants had no rights over the water flowing under the defendant's land. If the House of Lords' decision on this issue was correct, then *Bradford Corporation* v *Pickles* was correctly decided: the defendant did not violate the claimants' rights in acting as he did, and so the claimants could not have been entitled to a remedy in tort against the defendant. If, on the other hand, we adopt the modern view of tort law, then that cannot be the end of the matter. So what if the defendant did not wrong the claimants in acting as he did? The traditional view of tort law is wrong: recovery in tort is *not* conditional on its being shown that

---

claimant's case on the ground that the defendant local authority had not owed her a duty to save her from the consequences of her own foolishness. According to Howarth 2004, at 548, the real reason for the decision was Lord Hoffmann's 'extremist hostility to the very idea of negligence liability'. In *Sutradhar* v *Natural Environment Research Council* [2006] 4 All ER 490, the claimant was poisoned from drinking water contaminated with arsenic. He sued the defendants in negligence for compensation – they had surveyed the water in the area where the claimant lived but did not test it for arsenic; had they done so, the arsenic would have been detected and steps would have been taken to protect people like the claimant from suffering arsenic poisoning. The House of Lords upheld the Court of Appeal's decision to throw out the claim, on the ground that the defendants – not having had any kind of contact or developed any kind of relationship with the claimant – had not owed him a duty to take steps to save him from suffering arsenic poisoning. According to Howarth 2005a's note on the Court of Appeal's decision, at 25, 'The court's real worry in *Sutradhar* seems to have been the 699 other claimants waiting in the wings and that their success might put a large hole in Britain's international development budget.'

[12] [1895] AC 587.

the defendant violated the claimants' rights in cutting off the water to their reservoirs. Instead, we should look at the pros and cons of awarding a remedy here, taking *all* the circumstances of the case into account.

What we think

So it is simply impossible to write a tort textbook without endorsing either the modern view of tort law or the traditional view of tort law. Too much depends on which view is correct. So where do we stand? We endorse the traditional view of tort law, and wholly reject the modern view of tort law. We do so for two reasons.

(1) *Process.* As has already been observed, *the way* tort cases are decided supports the traditional view of tort law. In a negligence case, the courts ask: did the defendant breach a *duty* of care owed to the claimant? In a case where a claimant is suing a defendant in nuisance because the defendant blocked something from coming onto the claimant's land, the courts ask: did the claimant have a *right* to receive the thing that the defendant obstructed from coming onto the claimant's land? Admittedly, in other tort cases, the courts tend not to inquire into whether the claimant had a right that the defendant not act as he did, or whether the defendant owed the claimant a duty not to act as he did. However, that is because if the defendant did what the claimant is alleging he did ('He hit me'; 'He unjustly slandered me'; 'He lied to me'; 'He sold his goods pretending they were made by me') it will be so obvious that the defendant violated the claimant's rights in acting as he did that the issue is not worth going into. In tort cases where there *is* an issue whether the defendant violated the claimant's rights even if he did what the claimant alleged he did, the courts *always* ask, as a precondition of awarding the claimant a remedy: If the defendant did what he is alleged to have done, did the defendant's actions violate the claimant's rights/did the defendant breach a duty owed to the claimant? Of course, it is *possible* that all this talk of 'rights' and 'duties' in the tort cases is a fiction – a 'device' that the courts employ to achieve some goal that they would rather not tell everyone they are pursuing. But it is not *likely*.

(2) *Outcomes.* The traditional view of tort law explains the *outcome* of tort cases far better than the modern view. Take, for example, this imaginary case.[13] Suppose that John is a stockbroker and he secretly hates Paul because he wishes he could go out with Paul's girlfriend, Mary. One day John finds out that Biocorp – a public company – is about to announce that it is insolvent. John sees his chance to do Paul down. He rings Paul up and says, 'Paul – don't tell anyone I've told you this, but I hear on the grapevine that a company called Biocorp is about to announce that it has discovered a vaccine for AIDS. Buy as many Biocorp shares as you possibly can – the price will rocket as soon as this news gets out.' Paul instantly rings Mary up to tell her the good news. As a result, Paul invests £50,000 in Biocorp, and Mary invests £10,000. They both lose all their money when it is announced that Biocorp is insolvent.

Now – anyone who knows anything about tort law will be able to tell you that Paul will be able to sue John in tort for compensation for the fact that he has lost his £50,000; and that

[13] Zipursky 1998a can claim the credit for being the first to point out the huge hole in the modern view of tort law that the law's treatment of this case creates.

[14] It is so easy that it is very hard to find a case to demonstrate that Mary cannot sue John here.

Mary will *not* be able to sue John. This is not a matter of dispute: this is a very easy case.[14] The traditional view of tort law has no problem explaining this result. When John lied to Paul he violated Paul's rights, not Mary's. So Paul is entitled to a remedy in tort in this case – compensation for the loss that he suffered as a result of John's lying to him – but Mary is not. John did not violate Mary's rights in acting as he did, so tort law does nothing for her. On the modern view of tort law, the fact that Mary is not entitled to sue John for damages here is very hard to explain. John is a bad man, and the courts are not normally overly concerned to limit the liabilities of bad men. But here they do – they only allow Paul to sue John, not Mary. Why? At the very least, if the modern view of tort law were correct, one would not expect this to be such an easy case for tort lawyers to resolve. One would expect some voices to be raised in the decided cases in favour of allowing Mary to sue John. But there is nothing – for tort lawyers, nothing could be more obvious than that Mary cannot sue John here. Only the traditional view of tort law explains why it is so obvious to tort lawyers that Mary has no claim in this situation.

So – the traditional view of tort law explains *both* the way tort cases are decided, *and* the outcome of those cases. The modern view of tort law finds it difficult to cope with either task. Only one conclusion can be drawn: the traditional view of tort law is correct; the modern view of tort law must be rejected as heresy. As the great physicist Richard Feynman would tell his students, 'It doesn't matter how beautiful your theory is, it doesn't matter how smart you are. If it doesn't agree with experiment, it's wrong.' In judging whether a particular view of tort law is correct it is irrelevant how popular or unpopular that view is. The truth is not a matter of majority vote. The *only* way to determine whether a given view of tort law is correct is to ask: is it consistent with the reality of what happens in tort cases? The traditional theory of tort law passes this test; the modern view of tort law does not. In the war that now prevails among tort academics over the nature of tort law, we are firmly on the side of those academics who endorse the traditional view of tort law, and have written this textbook on that basis.[15]

The relevance of public policy to tort law

While we unequivocally reject the modern view of tort law, we disagree with those who have taken their dislike of the modern view of tort law to such an extreme that they deny that considerations of public policy should have any role to play in the operation of the tort law system.[16] To explain: those who endorse the modern view of tort law take the view that if A has caused B to suffer some kind of loss, A should be held liable in tort to compensate B for that loss if, all things considered, it would be desirable to make A pay B such compensation. On this view, considerations of what is in the public interest – or, in other words, considerations of public policy – have a crucial role to play in determining whether A should be held liable in tort to compensate B for the loss that she has suffered. If it would be contrary to the public interest to make A liable to compensate B, then it is obvious that

[15] Readers who are interested in pursuing this debate are referred to the opening pages of Chapter 3 ('Tort Law and Its Critics'), as well as the Appendix to this book, where we deal with Professor Jane Stapleton's criticisms of the traditional view of tort law. Student readers who are coming to tort law for the first time are advised not to read these passages until they have at least read Chapers 1 and 2 of this book and gained a bit more knowledge of tort law and its terminology.

[16] See, in particular, Beever 2007; and, to some extent, Stevens 2007.

A should *not* be held liable in tort to pay such compensation to B. If it would be in the public interest to make A compensate B, then it is equally obvious that A *should* be held liable in tort to compensate B.

So on the modern view of tort law, the courts *must* take into account considerations of public policy in determining whether A should be held liable in tort to compensate B for some loss that he has caused her to suffer. Some academics who are hostile to the modern view of tort law would like to argue that this is *wholly* wrong: considerations of public policy should not be taken into account *at all* by the courts in determining whether A should be held liable in tort to compensate B. Now – we *agree* that the mere fact that it would be in the public interest to make A compensate B is not enough to justify making A liable in tort to compensate B. If B's rights have not been violated in the situation we are considering, then A cannot be held liable *in tort* to compensate B for the loss that she has suffered. However, we cannot accept that considerations of public policy should have no role at all to play in how tort law cases are decided:

(1) *Determining whether someone's rights have been violated.* If B wants to argue that A violated her rights in acting in some way, it seems to us that one has to take into account considerations of public policy in determining whether B had a right that A not act in the way he did. For example, suppose that B argues: 'A said something offensive to me and that upset me a great deal. I have an ongoing right that A not do anything that might offend me, so A violated my rights in acting as he did.' In determining whether B has such a right against A,[17] it seems to us obvious that one has to take into account the impact on freedom of speech that recognising the existence of such a right would have, and that the adverse effect that recognising a 'right not to be offended' would have on freedom of speech is one of the most obvious reasons why no such right is recognised in English law.

(2) *Granting a remedy in a case where a wrong has been committed.* Let's assume that A has violated B's rights and B has suffered some kind of loss as a result. B is allowed to sue A in tort for compensation for the loss that she has suffered. As we will explain in more detail in Chapter 3, it seems to us that the reason why the law allows B to sue A for compensation in this case is because it is in the public interest that wrongs should be remedied. In the words of Lord Bingham, 'the rule of *public policy* that has first claim on the loyalty of the law [is] that wrongs should be remedied.'[18]

(3) *Denying a remedy in a case where a wrong has been committed.* Suppose that it is admitted that A violated B's rights in acting as he did. Let's assume, for example, that A hit B for no good reason. In this sort of case, there is a strong presumption that B should have some sort of remedy against A for his conduct. But it seems to us obvious that if it would be contrary to the public interest to allow B to sue A in this case, then no remedy should be granted to B. The Latin sentiment, 'Let justice be done, though the heavens fall'[19] is *not* one that appeals to us. As we will see – most obviously in Chapter 26 ('Limits on the right to sue') – English law frequently denies remedies to the victims of wrongs on the ground that it would be contrary to the public interest to allow such a remedy to be granted.

[17] See, generally, Duff & Marshall 2006.

[18] *D* v *East Berkshire Community NHS Trust* [2005] 2 AC 373, at [24]–[25] (emphasis added).

[19] '*Fiat justitia, ruat coelum*' (the statement is usually attributed to Julius Caesar's father-in-law, Lucius Calpurnius Piso Caesoninus).

(4) *Adding extra remedies onto the basic structure of tort law*. The basic rule that underlies tort law goes as follows: if A violates B's rights and B suffers loss as a result, then B will normally be entitled to sue A for compensation for that loss. However, as we will see, the law adds lots of extra rules to that basic rule, such as:

(i) If A violates B's rights and B dies as a result, and B's dependants suffer a consequent loss of support, B's dependants will normally be allowed to sue A for compensation for that loss of support.
(ii) If A was acting in the course of his employment by C when he violated B's rights, then B will normally be entitled not only to sue A for compensation for the loss she suffered as a result of A's wrong, she will also be entitled to sue C for such compensation.
(iii) If A violates B's rights in such an outrageous manner that he deserves to be punished for his conduct, then B may be entitled to sue A not just for damages to compensate her for the loss she has suffered as a result of A's wrong, but for extra damages designed to bring A's total liability up to a level sufficient to punish him adequately for what he has done.

As we will see when we look at these rules in more detail, it seems obvious that the law gives effect to all these extra rules because it is in the public interest to do so.

So we would reject the extremist position that considerations of public policy should not be taken into account at all in deciding tort law cases. The courts frequently take such considerations into account, and we see nothing wrong with their doing so.

Notes on style

Citation

We have, for the most part, used the Harvard system of citation in referring to books and articles in this edition. (Five textbooks on tort law are referred to using abbreviations: see the bibliography for details.) To explain: in the main text we refer to a particular book or article by referring to the author and the date of publication. A reader interested in finding out more about that book or article should turn to the bibliography where full details of the book or article in question are given. So, for example, Atiyah 1996 refers (turning to the bibliography and looking at the entries for 'Atiyah') to a paper called 'Personal injuries in the twenty-first century: thinking the unthinkable', which appears in Birks 1996b, at pages 1–46. Turning to the entries for 'Birks', we discover that Birks 1996b refers to a book edited by P.B.H. Birks, entitled *Wrongs and Remedies in the 21st Century*, and published by Clarendon Press, Oxford.

Plaintiff/claimant

Since 1999, a person who sues someone else in an English court has been known as a 'claimant', rather than a 'plaintiff'. As a result, we have used the word 'claimant' throughout the book to describe someone who is or was bringing an action against someone else. Overseas readers of this book who live in jurisdictions where 'claimants' are still described as 'plaintiffs' will simply have to make a mental bleep whenever they come across the word 'claimant' and substitute the word 'plaintiff'.

Footnotes

Inevitably, this book is very heavily footnoted. Some footnotes are more important than others – most, for example, will only be of interest to students writing a dissertation or a thesis, or professionals engaged in legal research. The most important footnotes are marked '*Important note*' and should be read by everyone who uses this book.

The McBride and Bagshaw tort law website

This textbook was up to date as of 1 January 2008. Updates on more recent developments in tort law can be obtained by going to the McBride and Bagshaw tort law website, at http://www.mylawchamber.co.uk/mcbride. The website is free to access and requires no password. As well as providing users with regular updates on recent cases and statutes affecting tort law, users are also able to access sample problem questions on tort law with model answers.

Table of cases

Visit the *Tort Law, third edition* **mylawchamber** site at **http://www.mylawchamber.co.uk/mcbride** to access unique online support to improve your case reading and analysis skills.

Case Navigator provides:

- **Direct deep links** to the core cases in Tort Law.
- **Short introductions** provide guidance on what you should look out for while reading the case.
- **Questions** help you to test your understanding of the case, and provide feedback on what you should have grasped.
- **Summaries** contextualise the case and point you to further reading so that you are fully prepared for seminars and discussions.

Please note that access to Case Navigator is free with the purchase of this book, but you must register with us for access. Full registration instructions are available on the website. The LexisNexis element of Case Navigator is only available to those who currently subscribe to LexisNexis Butterworths online.

Pages where a case is discussed in detail are underlined

Table of statutes, statutory instruments and conventions

STATUTES

STATUTORY INSTRUMENTS

CONVENTIONS

Part I

The province of tort law

1 What is a tort?

A tort is a form of civil wrong.[1] So if you want to understand what a tort is, you have first to understand what a civil wrong is. And in order to do that, you have first to understand some fundamental legal concepts.

SOME FUNDAMENTAL LEGAL CONCEPTS

Legal duty

Someone will have a legal duty to act in a particular way if he is required by law to act in that way. How can we tell what the law requires us to do? Well, we look to *statutes* enacted by Parliament and *cases* decided by the courts to tell us what the law requires us to do.

Under our legal system, A will have a legal duty to do *x* if: (1) a statute that was enacted by Parliament and not subsequently repealed says that A has a legal duty to do *x*; *or* (2) previous decisions of the courts that have not been subsequently overruled and are not likely to be overruled explicitly or implicitly say that A has a legal duty to do *x*.

If A has a legal duty to do *x* because (1) is true then we say that A has a *statutory duty* to do *x*. If A has a legal duty to do *x* because (2) is true then we say that A has a *judge-made duty* to do *x*. In order to make this book easier to read, we will from now on refer to legal duties simply as 'duties'.

Private duties and public duties

Duties may be divided up into duties that are owed to other people and duties that are owed to no one in particular. Let's call the first set of duties, 'private duties' and the second set of duties – duties that are owed to no one in particular – 'public duties'.

A given duty is owed to someone else if it was imposed for the benefit of that someone else. A given duty is owed to no one in particular if it was not imposed for the benefit of a particular individual but was imposed for the benefit of the community as a whole or for the benefit of some section of the community.

So, for example, under s 6 of the Police Act 1996 '[every] police authority . . . shall secure the maintenance of an efficient and effective police force for its area'. That duty is not owed to anyone in particular: it is imposed on each police authority for the benefit of the community served by that police authority. In contrast, if you take two given individuals, A and B, A will have a duty under the Protection from Harassment Act 1997 not to 'pursue a course of conduct – (a) which amounts to harassment of [B]; and (b) which he knows or

[1] The word 'tort' derives from the Latin *tortus* which means 'twisted, crooked, contorted, distorted' (Lewis & Short, *Latin Dictionary*).

ought to know amounts to harassment of [B]'. This duty of A's is owed to B – it is imposed on A for the benefit of a particular individual: B.

One of the marks of a duty that is owed to another is that it may be waived by that other.[2] A duty which is owed to no one in particular cannot be waived by a particular individual. This follows as a matter of logic from what has already been said as to the nature of duties owed to others and duties owed to no one in particular. Suppose, for example, that John has a duty to do *x* and that duty is owed to Mary. Given that John's duty to do *x* was imposed on him for Mary's benefit, there does not seem much point in the law's requiring John to do *x* if Mary makes it clear that she is happy for John not to do *x* – unless, of course, Mary is in no position to form rational wishes as to how she wants to be treated by others because she is, for example, too immature or not in her right mind or ill-informed. So, as John's duty to do *x* is owed to Mary, Mary may release John from that duty so long, of course, as she is in her right mind, aware of the full implications of what she is doing and mature enough to decide for herself whether or not she wants John to do *x*. And, obviously, if Mary does release John from that duty, John will do no wrong to Mary if he does not do *x*. A Latin tag expresses this point – *volenti non fit injuria*: no wrong will be done to the willing.

On the other hand, suppose that Gary has a duty to do *x* and that duty is owed to no one in particular because it was imposed on Gary for the benefit of the whole community. In such a case, no particular individual will have the power to release Gary from this duty – as the duty in question was imposed on Gary for the benefit of the whole community, Gary can only be released from that duty if the whole community, acting through its representatives, indicates that it wishes Gary to be released from that duty.

There is an important exception to the rule that a duty that is owed to another may be waived by that other. This is the case where A owes B a duty which requires him to stop B doing something that she knows is dangerous. So suppose that Beth wants to sniff some glue – she knows that sniffing glue is dangerous but she is willing to take the risk in order to experience the temporary high that results from sniffing glue. Accordingly, she attempts to buy some glue from Paul's shop. Suppose further that Paul has a duty not to sell Beth any glue because it is obvious that she wants to buy it for the purposes of sniffing it. The law will have imposed this duty on Paul in a paternalistic attempt to save Beth from herself – so Paul's duty is imposed on him for Beth's benefit and will therefore be owed to Beth. Beth will not be able to waive this duty, though she would obviously like to do so. The law's intentions in imposing a duty on Paul not to sell glue to Beth would be frustrated if Beth were free to waive that duty. Beth would inevitably waive the duty and Paul would then be free to sell her the glue, which is not what the law wants.

So if A owes B a duty to stop B doing something that she knows is dangerous, then B will not be able to waive that duty of A's. It is quite unusual for one person to owe another this kind of duty: if B wants to do something that she knows is dangerous, the law will generally allow her to get on with it and will not impose duties on other people to stop her doing what she wants to do. However, it has become increasingly common for someone who has

[2] This might account for why – if A has a duty to do *x* which was imposed on him for B's benefit – we say that A's duty to do *x* is *owed* to B. As B may waive A's duty to do *x*, we mentally associate A's duty to do *x* with a debt *owed* to B; the idea being that just as B may waive a debt that is owed to her, so she can waive A's duty to do *x*.

knowingly put herself in harm's way and suffered some kind of loss as a result to try and sue for compensation for that loss on the ground that someone else owed her a duty to stop her endangering herself. The courts have generally been hostile to such claims, only allowing that such a duty might have been owed in cases where the person who put herself in harm's way was incapable of thinking rationally because she was too immature or because she was not in her right mind.[3]

So it has been accepted that if a prisoner is a clear suicide risk, the prison authorities will owe him a duty to take steps to stop him committing suicide.[4] It has also been held that a petrol station manager will owe a child a duty not to sell him petrol if it is obvious that he wants to buy the petrol to get high by sniffing it.[5] And it has been accepted that a school will owe a child on a school skiing trip a duty to take reasonable steps to stop him skiing off-piste – and this is so even if the child is aware of the risks involved in skiing off-piste.[6] In contrast, a claim that the police owed a criminal a duty to stop him jumping out of a high window in an attempt to escape police custody, was rejected by two judges out of three in the Court of Appeal.[7] Similarly, in *Tomlinson* v *Congleton BC*,[8] the House of Lords unanimously *rejected* an argument that if a council knows or ought to know that some adults are knowingly endangering themselves on council property – by, for example, swimming in a lake or climbing trees on land controlled by the council – the council will owe those adults a duty to stop them endangering themselves. It may also be noted that in Australia, it has been held that a casino will not owe an inveterate gambler a duty not to allow him to lose his money at its tables.[9]

Rights and duties

Lawyers use the word 'right' in three different ways.

First of all, lawyers say that A has a 'right' to do *x* if the law either gives A the power to do *x* or the law takes steps to make sure that A is allowed to do *x*. Lawyers uses the term 'right' in this way when they say that A has the right to sue B for damages, or that A has a right of freedom of expression.

Secondly, lawyers say that A has a 'right' if he has some kind of legally recognised interest that is protected under the law from being harmed by other people. Lawyers use the term 'right' in this way when they say that A has a right to physical integrity, or some kind of right over property, or a right to her reputation.

[3] See *Tomlinson* v *Congleton BC* [2004] 1 AC 46, at [46] (per Lord Hoffmann): 'A duty to protect . . . self-inflicted harm exists only in cases where there is . . . some lack of capacity, such as the inability of children to recognise danger . . . or the despair of prisoners which may lead them to inflict injury on themselves . . .'

[4] *Reeves* v *Commissioner of Police of the Metropolis* [2000] 1 AC 360.

[5] *E (a child)* v *Souls Garages Ltd*, The Times, 23 January 2001.

[6] *Chittock* v *Woodbridge School* [2002] ELR 735 (although no breach of the duty was established in this case).

[7] *Vellino* v *Chief Constable of Greater Manchester Police* [2002] 1 WLR 218 (the House of Lords refused leave to appeal).

[8] [2004] 1 AC 46. The claimant in that case disregarded notices warning him that it was dangerous to swim in a lake controlled by the defendant council. The claimant suffered an injury as a result of diving into the lake and sued the defendant council for compensation, claiming that it had owed him a duty to stop him swimming in the lake. His claim was rejected (though the Court of Appeal had ruled 2:1 in his favour).

[9] *Reynolds* v *Katoomba RSL All Services Club Ltd* [2001] NSWCA 234 (discussed, Cane 2001b). For an account of the (similarly negative) position of American law in this area, see Wolfe 1995.

Thirdly – and most importantly for our purposes here – if B has a duty to do *x*, and that duty has been imposed on B for A's benefit, then lawyers will say that A has a right that B do *x*. So – as we have already seen – if you take two given individuals, A and B, B will owe A a duty not to harass her under the Protection from Harassment Act 1997. Another way of putting this is to say that A has a right that B not harass her under the 1997 Act. The two expressions – B owes A a duty not to harass her and A has a right that B not harass her – are exactly equivalent. They are two sides of the same coin.

In contrast, if B has a duty to do *x*, and that duty has not been imposed on him for the benefit of any particular individual, then no one can be said to have a right that B do *x*. So, for example, no one has a right that a police authority 'secure the maintenance of an efficient and effective police force for its area'. A police authority's duty to do this is not imposed on it for the benefit of anyone in particular, and so no one can be said to have a right that a police authority set up an efficient and effective police force in its area.

From this point on, we will use the word 'right' in its third sense unless the context makes it clear that we mean to use the word 'right' in some other sense – such as to describe a legal power, or a power or interest that is protected by law.

Civil wrongs and public wrongs

Someone will commit a 'civil wrong' if they breach a duty owed to another.[10] To put it another – exactly equivalent – way, someone will commit a 'civil wrong' if they violate someone else's rights. In contrast, we use the term 'public wrong' to describe the breach of a duty owed to no one in particular. So if Ruth harasses Vijay, she will commit a civil wrong. If a police authority fails to set up an effective and efficient police force in its area, it will commit a public wrong.

TORTS AND OTHER CIVIL WRONGS

Life would be very simple if we could just say that 'tort' is just another name for a civil wrong, and so all civil wrongs are 'torts'. However, this would be wrong. While most civil wrongs amount to torts, not all civil wrongs are torts. There are four types of civil wrong that cannot be classified as being torts.

Breach of contract

If A undertakes to do *x* in a binding contract with B, then A will owe B a duty to do *x*. If A fails to do *x*, A will commit what is called a 'breach of contract'. A breach of contract is a civil wrong, but it is not a tort.

Having said that a breach of contract is not a tort, it is important that we acknowledge that the same action can amount to a breach of contract *and* a tort. Suppose, for example, that Karen pays Ian, a minicab driver, to take her to the airport. If Ian carelessly crashes the cab and Karen is injured, Ian will have committed both a breach of contract and a tort. A breach of contract because when Karen got into the cab, she entered into a binding con-

[10] See Birks 1995.

tract with Ian under which Ian undertook, among other things, to drive the cab carefully. A tort because Ian also owed Karen a duty to drive the cab carefully because it was reasonably foreseeable that if he did not, Karen would be injured,[11] and in breaching that duty Ian committed a tort – the tort of negligence.

It is of considerable importance to the law to establish whether a person's conduct in a given case amounts to: (1) a breach of contract; *or* (2) a tort; *or* (3) a breach of contract *and* a tort. This is because the law treats people who break contracts very differently from the way it treats people who commit torts:

(1) *Exemplary damages.*[12] The law does not allow exemplary damages – damages awarded in order to punish someone for the way he has behaved – to be awarded against someone who commits a breach of contract;[13] but it does, in some cases, allow exemplary damages to be awarded against someone who commits a tort.[14]

(2) *Limitation.* The limitation period for obtaining a remedy against someone who commits a breach of contract runs from the moment the breach occurs;[15] the limitation period for obtaining a remedy against someone who commits a tort generally runs from the moment the victim of that tort suffers 'damage' as a result of that tort being committed.[16]

(3) *Remoteness.* Suppose Carl breaches a contract made with Nita and Nita suffers some kind of loss as a result. In this case, Nita will only be able to sue Carl for compensation for that loss if Carl knew or ought to have known, *at the time he entered into the contract* with Nita, that Nita was likely to suffer that loss if he breached the contract in question. On the other hand, if Carl has committed a tort X in relation to Nita and Nita has suffered some kind of loss as a result, Nita will usually be able to sue Carl for compensation for that loss if it was reasonably foreseeable, *at the time Carl committed tort X*, that Nita would suffer that kind of loss as a result – and Nita may be able to recover compensation for that loss even if it was *not* reasonably foreseeable, at the time Carl committed tort X, that she would suffer that kind of loss as a result.[17]

Equitable wrongs

There was a time in England when there were two distinct types of courts: Courts of Law (or Common Law) and Courts of Equity. The Courts of Equity acted as a corrective to the Courts of Law, granting remedies that were unavailable in the Courts of Law when it would be just and equitable to do so or setting aside remedies that were granted in the Courts of Law when it would be just and equitable to do so. This cut both ways. A claimant seeking a legal remedy for some grievance of his who had had no luck in the Courts of Law could

[11] See below, pp. 73–74.

[12] Another, and in many ways preferable, term for exemplary damages is 'punitive damages'.

[13] *Addis* v *Gramophone Co. Ltd* [1909] AC 488; *Perera* v *Vandiyar* [1953] 1 WLR 672; *Kenny* v *Preen* [1963] 1 QB 499. McBride 1995 criticises the law's refusal to allow exemplary damages to be awarded against someone who has deliberately committed a breach of contract.

[14] See below, pp. 688–700.

[15] Limitation Act 1980, s 5.

[16] See below, pp. 523–5.

[17] See below, pp. 569–77.

try and see if the more generous Courts of Equity would help him. A defendant who had lost in a Court of Law and had a remedy granted against him could ask a Court of Equity to see if they would grant an order requiring his adversary not to take advantage of that remedy.

Of course, this is all history now. By the end of the nineteenth century, the two sets of courts were 'fused' with the result that all cases were heard by one set of courts. However, the rules and principles that were given effect to by the old Courts of Equity are still regarded as a distinct part of our legal system and are taught in law schools under the name 'Equity' or 'Trusts Law'. In the same way, civil wrongs that were only recognised as being civil wrongs by the old Courts of Equity are still regarded as a distinct category of civil wrongs and given a special name – 'equitable wrongs' – to mark them off from other civil wrongs.

An example of an equitable wrong is provided by the case where John gives Tom £10,000 and instructs him to apply that money for the benefit of Sarah. (In legal parlance, John tells Tom to hold the money 'on trust' for Sarah.) Suppose that Tom subsequently spends the money on a round-the-world cruise for himself. The old Courts of Law would not have thought that Tom did anything wrong in using the money in this way: in the eyes of the old Courts of Law, the money was Tom's to dispose of as he liked. The old Courts of Equity took a quite different view of the matter. They would have held that, given the conditions on which Tom received the £10,000, he owed Sarah a duty to apply that money for her benefit. So when he spent the money on himself and his wife, he violated her rights. Because it was only the old Courts of Equity that would have thought that Tom's behaviour in this case amounted to a civil wrong, we say that Tom has committed an 'equitable wrong' here (in this case, a 'breach of trust').

An 'equitable wrong' is not a tort. So it would be wrong to say that Tom committed a tort in spending on himself the £10,000 that John gave him. Having said that, there does not seem to be any reason why Tom's wrong here should not be treated as a tort. It is, after all, just a matter of historical accident that Tom's wrong is classified as an equitable wrong, rather than a tort. Given this, the law should treat someone who commits an equitable wrong in the same way as it does someone who commits a tort. Sensibly, the law is starting to do so.[18] The result is that, increasingly, only writers of textbooks on tort law have any interest in answering the question – was the civil wrong in this case an equitable wrong, or was it a tort? More and more often, the answer to that question has little significance to the law and therefore to legal practitioners. Only writers of textbooks on tort law need concern themselves with this question because, by definition, someone who merely commits an equitable wrong cannot be said to have committed a tort and is therefore of no interest to someone writing a textbook on tort law.[19] This limitation on the concept of a tort has one

[18] See *United Scientific Holdings* v *Burnley Borough Council* [1978] AC 904, 924G–925B; *Tinsley* v *Milligan* [1994] 1 AC 340, 371A–C; *Target Holdings* v *Redferns* [1996] AC 421, 432F–H; *Bristol and West BS* v *Mothew* [1998] Ch 1, 17; Burrows 2002b. However, differences in the treatment of breaches of equitable and common law duties remain. A description of the more important ones may be found in Davies 1993; see also Meagher, Heydon and Leeming 2002, 831–41.

[19] *Important note.* Edelman 2002a offers two arguments in favour of the view that we should say that an equitable wrong is a tort. His first argument is that a tort involves the breach of a duty owed to another – and therefore the concept of a tort encompasses equitable wrongs (which also involve the breach of a duty owed to another). This argument does not stand up: we would not say that rape is murder because both involve committing a

useful side effect. If the concept of a tort embraced some or all equitable wrongs then a book on the English law of tort – dealing as it does with questions such as: In what situations will someone commit a tort? and What remedies will be made available if someone has committed a tort? – would become unmanageably large to write or read.

Failure to pay a debt

Suppose that Gary owes Vijay £100. Suppose, for example, that Vijay paid Gary £100 by mistake. In this case, Gary will owe Vijay a duty to pay him back an equivalent sum. If Gary fails to pay up, he will commit a civil wrong. However, this civil wrong will not amount to a tort. So it would be wrong to say that Gary – or anyone who fails to pay a debt – has committed a tort.

Most breaches of a statutory duty owed to another

By definition, the breach of a statutory duty that is owed to no one in particular cannot amount to a tort. But even the breach of a statutory duty that is owed to another will usually not amount to a tort. The breach of a statutory duty that is owed to another will only amount to a tort if when Parliament created that duty it intended that breach of that duty should be treated as a tort by the courts and therefore that all the remedies that are normally available when someone has committed a tort should apply to the breach of that statutory duty. As this is a bit of a mouthful, let's just say that the breach of a statutory duty owed to another will only amount to a tort if Parliament intended, when it created that duty, that breach of that duty should be 'actionable in tort'.

So, for example, if A is a public authority and B is any given member of the public, A will, broadly speaking, owe B a statutory duty under s 6 of the Human Rights Act 1998 not to violate any of B's 'human rights' as set out in the European Convention on Human Rights and the various Protocols to that Convention.[20] If A breaches this duty, A will *not* commit a tort.[21] This is because Parliament made it clear when it passed the 1998 Act that it did not intend that the remedies that are normally available when someone has committed a tort should apply to a public authority that breached its duty under s 6 of the Act not to violate someone else's Convention rights. Instead, in s 8 of the 1998 Act, Parliament created a special regime of remedies which would be available when a public authority violated someone else's Convention rights.

---

crime. His second argument is that the law responds to an equitable wrong in exactly the same way as it does to someone's committing a tort. Again, this argument does not stand up. We would not say that rape is murder even if the law responded to a rape in exactly the same way as it does to someone's committing a murder. The latest (19th) edition of *Clerk and Lindsell on Torts* includes sections on breach of fiduciary duty and breach of confidence (both equitable wrongs) but this is not because the editors of that book think that these equitable wrongs are torts (they expressly say that they are not: C&L, 5), but because some tort cases raise issues of breach of fiduciary duty and breach of confidence and it therefore makes sense for pragmatic reasons to deal with those topics in a book on tort law.

20 The official title of the Convention referred to here is 'The European Convention for the Protection of Human Rights and Fundamental Freedoms'. However, in this book we will simply refer to this Convention as 'the European Convention on Human Rights' (ECHR for short).

21 Contrast Stanton 2003, who argues (at 3) that 'it seems almost certain' that a breach of duty under the 1998 Act 'will be regarded as a tort'.

In contrast, suppose that Mary visits Fred in his house. Fred will usually owe Mary a duty under the Occupiers' Liability Act 1957 to take reasonable steps to see that she will be reasonably safe while she is in his house.[22] If Fred breaches this duty, he will commit a tort. This is because when Parliament passed the 1957 Act, it clearly intended that all the remedies that are normally available in the case where someone has committed a tort should be available against Fred if he breaches the duty he owes Mary under the 1957 Act to take reasonable steps to see that she is reasonably safe.

Parliament sometimes makes it clear when it creates a statutory duty owed to another that it intends that a breach of that duty should be actionable in tort. So, for example, when Parliament enacted the Sex Discrimination Act 1975 it created a raft of statutory duties owed to others not to discriminate against them on grounds of their sex. At the same time, it made it clear that the tort remedy rules should apply to determine what remedies will be available if one of those statutory duties is breached. Under s 66 of the 1975 Act, '[a] claim by any person ... that another person ... has committed an act of discrimination against [him or her] which is unlawful [under the Act] ... may be made the subject of civil proceedings in like manner as any other claim in tort'.

Parliament will also sometimes make it clear when it creates a statutory duty owed to another that it does *not* intend that breach of that duty should be actionable in tort. As we have seen, this is the case with the Human Rights Act 1998. Again, in s 2 of the Health and Safety at Work Act 1974, Parliament stipulated that an employer will owe each of his employees a 'duty ... to ensure, so far as is reasonably practicable, the health, safety and welfare at work of [that employee]' while making clear at the same time that '[nothing in this Act] shall be construed ... as conferring a right of action in any civil proceedings in respect of any failure to comply with [the] duty imposed by [s] 2'.[23]

More often that not, though, when Parliament creates a statutory duty owed to another, it will not make it clear one way or the other whether it intends that a breach of that duty should be actionable in tort. In such a case, it has to be *inferred* what Parliament's intention on this matter is.

Summary

So – if A has committed a civil wrong, A will have committed a tort if his civil wrong does not amount to: (1) a breach of contract; or (2) an equitable wrong; or (3) a failure to pay a debt; or (4) the breach of a statutory duty owed to another that was not intended to be actionable in tort when it was created by Parliament.[24] As we shall see, there are lots of civil wrongs that do not fall into categories (1), (2), (3) or (4) and therefore lots of civil wrongs that are classified by English lawyers as 'torts'. It is the task of a student studying tort law to

22 Occupiers' Liability Act 1957, s 2(2).

23 Health and Safety at Work 1974, s 47(1)(a).

24 Cf. the definition of a tort offered by Judge Toulmin QC in *R* v *Secretary of State for Transport, ex p Factortame Ltd (No. 7)* [2001] 1 WLR 942, at [150]: 'I define a tort as a breach of a non-contractual duty which gives rise to a private law right to the party injured to recover compensatory damages at common law from the party causing the injury.' This definition suffers from a couple of difficulties that make it inferior to our definition: (1) it does not make it clear that a breach of duty will only amount to a tort if the duty breached is owed to another; (2) it is possible for someone to commit a tort without being held liable to pay anyone else compensatory damages.

understand when these civil wrongs will be committed and what remedies will be available when they are committed.

The next chapter will provide you with an overview of the law on these issues. But before we can get started on this overview, a preliminary point of terminology needs to be settled. We need a term to describe a duty, the breach of which will amount to a tort. Andrew Burrows proposes that we should use the term 'tortious obligation' to describe this kind of duty.[25] 'Obligation' is fine – that is just a fancy word for a duty that is owed to another. But 'tortious'? To say that a duty which is owed to someone else is a 'tortious obligation' is, literally, to say that it is a *wrongful* obligation – which is nonsense. But we have been unable to come up with anything better and so from now on we will use the term 'tortious' to describe any duty owed to another, the breach of which will amount to a tort. By the same token we will use the term 'tortious right' to describe any right, the violation of which will amount to a tort.

Visit **http://www.mylawchamber.co.uk/mcbride** to access updates on recent cases, as well as model answers and tips for answering tort problem questions.

Use **Case Navigator** to read in full the key case referenced in this chapter:

- **Tomlinson *v* Congleton BC**

[25] Burrows 1994, 3; see also Waddams 2003, 44.

2 An overview of tort law

WHAT IS TORT LAW?

Tort law is, literally, the law relating to torts and tortfeasors (that is, people who commit torts). But this is too broad a characterisation of what tort law is. For instance, tort law does not tell us when a tortfeasor may be criminally punished for what he has done – the criminal law tells us that, not tort law.[1] So it would be more accurate to say that tort law tells us: (1) in what situations someone will commit a tort – that is, breach a tortious duty owed to another; *and* (2) what remedies will be available if someone has committed a tort or is committing a tort. Someone who studies tort law, then, is solely concerned to find out the answers to two questions. First, in what situations will someone commit a tort? Secondly, what remedies will people be able to obtain if someone has committed a tort or is committing a tort? In this chapter we will answer these two questions briefly before answering them in much more detail in Parts II and III of this book.

IN WHAT SITUATIONS WILL SOMEONE COMMIT A TORT?

The answer to this question depends, of necessity, on how the law stands on the issue of when one person will owe another a tortious duty: A will not have committed a tort by doing *x* in situation S unless he owed someone else a tortious duty not to do *x* in situation S. So, for example, suppose that Ruth – a child – fell into a deep pond and while she was drowning Eric saw her plight but did nothing to assist her. Did Eric commit a tort in this situation? It depends on whether Eric owed Ruth a tortious duty to try to save her from drowning. In fact, if you come across a stranger in danger, you will *not* owe him or her any kind of duty to do your best to rescue him or her. So in the situation we are considering, Eric will not have committed any kind of wrong – let alone a tort – in acting as he did.

So, in what situations *will* someone commit a tort? A typical – though by no means complete – list of the situations in which someone will commit a tort might run as follows. Someone, A, will commit a tort if:

(1) he breaches a tortious duty of care owed to another; *or*

[1] Sometimes someone who commits a tort will at the same time commit a crime and become liable to suffer criminal punishment for what he has done. This will be the case, for example, if A beats B up: A's conduct will amount both to a tort and to a crime. Someone who commits a tort innocently or unknowingly will, as a general rule, not commit a crime in so acting – the law generally requires the perpetrator of a crime not only to act wrongfully (that is, to commit an *actus reus*) but also to do so with a guilty mind (a *mens rea*). That is not to say that someone who knowingly commits a tort will necessarily commit a crime in so acting. For example, if a hiker deliberately takes a short cut across another's land when he has no right to do so, he will commit a tort but no crime. However, trespassing on another person's property will sometimes amount to a crime: see Theft Act 1968, s 9 (definition of the offence of burglary); Criminal Justice and Public Order Act 1994, s 68 (definition of the offence of aggravated trespass); Sexual Offences Act 2003, s 63 (definition of offence of trespass with intent to commit a sexual offence).

(2) he directly applies force to another's person when he has no lawful justification or excuse for doing so; *or*
(3) he tells damaging lies about someone else when he has no lawful justification or excuse for doing so; *or*
(4) he unreasonably interferes with another's use and enjoyment of land; *or*
(5) he induces someone else to break a contract when he has no lawful justification or excuse for doing so; *or*
(6) he intentionally interferes with someone else's business using unlawful means to do so; *or*
(7) he knowingly or recklessly tells lies to someone else in order to induce that person to act in some way; *or*
(8) he maliciously brings a criminal prosecution against someone else when he has no reasonable cause to do so; *or*
(9) he breaches a tortious statutory duty owed to another.

In Part II, we will present a far more detailed and expansive list of the situations in which someone will commit a tort but this rudimentary list will serve for the moment. Six points may be made about it.

(1) *The naming of torts*. Lawyers like to give names to the different ways in which a tort may be committed. So lawyers say that someone will commit 'the tort of negligence' if he breaches a tortious duty of care owed to another; 'the tort of battery' if he directly applies force to another's person when he has no lawful justification or excuse for doing so; 'the tort of private nuisance' if he unreasonably interferes with another's use and enjoyment of land; 'the tort of inducing a breach of contract' if he induces someone else to break a contract when he has no lawful justification or excuse for doing so; 'the tort of intimidation' if he intentionally interferes with another's business by unlawfully intimidating that business's employees or customers; 'the tort of deceit' or 'the tort of fraud' if he knowingly or recklessly tells lies to someone else to induce that person to act in some way; 'the tort of malicious prosecution' if he maliciously brings a criminal prosecution against someone else when he has no reasonable cause to do so; and 'the tort of breach of statutory duty' if he breaches a tortious statutory duty owed to another.

Lawyers like to give names to the different ways in which a tort may be committed because it is convenient to do so. Suppose, for example, that a lawyer wants to argue: 'A committed a tort because he directly applied force to another's person when he had no lawful justification or excuse for doing so.' This is very long-winded. However, the fact that lawyers have given the above names to the different ways in which a tort may be committed means that our lawyer can put his argument in a much shorter form. He can say: 'A committed the tort of battery.' Again, suppose a writer of a textbook on tort law wants to say: 'Aggravated damages[2] may be awarded against someone who commits a tort by directly applying force to another's person when he has no lawful justification or excuse for doing so; but they may not be awarded against someone who commits a tort by breaching a tortious duty of care owed to another.' This is *very* long-winded. Conveniently, the fact that lawyers have given the above names to the different ways in which a tort may be committed

[2] Damages designed to assuage the victim of a tort's sense of outrage at the way he or she has been treated.

allows our writer to make this point more succinctly. He or she can simply say: 'Aggravated damages may be awarded against someone who commits the tort of battery; but they may not be awarded against someone who commits the tort of negligence.'

It may also be noted at this juncture that lawyers also like to give names to *groups* of torts. This is usually for reasons of either history or convenience or just to make a point about a certain group of torts. So, for example, lawyers often group together the torts of battery, assault and false imprisonment, and dub all these torts, 'torts involving a trespass to the person'. This is for reasons of history: these torts, which are all committed by interfering with another's person, were traditionally remedied by obtaining a writ of *trespass*.[3] Again, s 1 of the Torts (Interference with Goods) Act 1977 uses the term 'wrongful interference with goods' to describe the torts of conversion, trespass to goods and other torts which result in 'damage to goods or to an interest in goods'. This is for reasons of convenience: the 1977 Act was designed to reform the law on what remedies would be available when someone's goods were damaged or misappropriated through someone else's committing a tort, and so – for the purpose of setting out what those remedies would be – the Act needed to invent a catch-all term to describe all the torts that could form the basis of an action where someone else's goods were damaged or misappropriated. Finally, the torts dealt with in Chapters 20–23 of this book (such as the torts of inducing a breach of contract, conspiracy, intentional infliction of harm by unlawful means, deceit and passing off) are often grouped together by lawyers and given the collective name of the 'economic torts'. The name makes two points about these torts: (1) they are usually committed by causing another to suffer economic loss; *and* (2) someone who has suffered a form of pure economic loss[4] will only usually be allowed to sue for compensation for that loss if he has been a victim of one of these torts.

(2) *Tort and duty*. The above list of situations where someone will commit a tort helps to conceal or obscure the fact that committing a tort involves breaching a tortious duty owed to another. Only the presence of items (1) and (9) on the list helps to remind us that committing a tort involves breaching a tortious duty owed to another. So, for example, the list says that A will commit a tort – the tort of battery – if he directly applies force to B's person when he has no lawful justification or excuse for doing so. It does not make clear that the

[3] A writ was an order, requiring the courts to hear someone's case. The writ of trespass was not available to every victim of a tort who wanted to obtain a remedy for that tort's having been committed. The victim of a tort would often have to obtain an alternative writ, called the writ of trespass *on the case*, to have his case heard. But in order to obtain such a writ, he had to prove that he had suffered some kind of loss. So torts that were *not* covered by the writ of trespass were only actionable on proof of damage. By contrast, a victim of a tort who could obtain a writ of trespass, ordering the courts to hear his case, did not have to prove that he had suffered any kind of loss as a result of that tort being committed. So torts which were covered by the writ of trespass were actionable *per se* – that is, actionable even if the claimant had not suffered any loss as a result of that tort's having been committed. (See, generally, Ibbetson 1999.) Even though we no longer require people to obtain or issue writs in order to sue other people in tort, it remains the case to this day that torts that were traditionally remedied through the award of a writ of trespass are usually actionable *per se* and torts that were traditionally remedied through the writ of trespass on the case are usually only actionable on proof of damage. Having said that, 'the old distinction between actions for trespass and actions on the case does not provide a clearcut solution in every case [where the question of whether a tort is actionable *per se* arises]': *Watkins* v *Secretary of State for the Home Department* [2005] QB 883, at [47]. For a complete account of which torts are actionable *per se* and which are not, see below, Chapter 34.

[4] 'Pure' economic loss is economic loss not consequent on someone's person or property being harmed. So, for example, a gambler who loses a bet suffers a form of pure economic loss.

reason *why* A will commit a tort if he does this is that A will owe B a non-contractual, common law duty not to act in this way. This is left unsaid or suppressed – and as a result can often be forgotten or overlooked.[5]

So, for example, it has been said that 'liability for deceit or trespass is so self-evident that we do not consider it as resulting from a breach of duty.'[6] But it does.[7] If A hit B when he had no lawful justification or excuse for doing so, the reason we hold A liable to compensate B for the resulting injuries suffered by B is that A acted *wrongfully* in hitting B – A owed her a duty not to beat her up and he breached that duty. Of course, if B wants to sue A for damages, all she has to do is show that A hit her and that A had no lawful justification or excuse for doing so. She does not have to show *in addition* that A owed her a duty not to hit her. But that does not mean that A's liability is not based on the fact that he breached a duty owed to B in acting as he did. The reason that B does not have to show that A owed her a duty not to hit her is that it is *self-evident* that A owed B a duty not to hit her if he had no lawful justification or excuse for doing so. The only issue is whether A breached that duty in acting as he did – that is, the only issue is whether A hit B when he had no lawful justification or excuse for doing so.

It might be argued that the House of Lords' decision in *Stubbings* v *Webb*[8] establishes that the view taken here is incorrect. In that case, the claimant sued the defendant in August 1987, claiming that between 1959 and 1971 the defendant had sexually abused her, thereby committing the tort of battery. Unfortunately, the law says that actions in tort have to be brought within six years of the time when the tort complained of first caused the claimant to suffer some kind of harm. As the defendant's last sexual assault on the claimant took place in 1971, the limitation period for suing the defendant in tort ran out for the claimant in 1977. The claimant sought to get round this point by taking advantage of the Limitation Act 1980, s 11 which provides that:

> (1) This section applies to any action for damages for negligence, nuisance or breach of duty . . . where the damages claimed by the [claimant] for the negligence, nuisance or breach of duty consist of or include damages in respect of personal injuries . . .
> (4) . . . [the limitation period applicable to this kind of action] is three years from – (*a*) the date on which the cause of action accrued; or (*b*) the date of knowledge (if later) of the person injured.

The claimant argued that her action arose out of a 'breach of duty' and that she only acquired knowledge of the fact that the defendant's sexual assaults on her had caused her to suffer some kind of personal injury in September 1984, when she started undergoing therapy and realised her mental problems were due to the fact that she had been sexually assaulted by the defendant. So, the claimant argued, she had had until September 1987

5 But not, curiously enough, by *restitution* lawyers, who readily acknowledge that committing a tort involves breaching a duty owed to another: see, for example, Burrows 1983; 1998, 9–10; Edelman 2002a. This is almost entirely due to the salutary influence of Professor Peter Birks, who was – until his recent and untimely death – the world's foremost restitution lawyer: see Birks 1983, 1995, 1997a, 2000b.

6 Weir 2001a, 30; quoted with approval by Lord Rodger of Earlsferry in *Standard Chartered Bank* v *Pakistan Shipping Corpn (Nos 2 and 4)* [2003] 1 AC 959, at [41]. It is not clear that Tony Weir agrees with this statement anymore: it does not appear in the corresponding section of the second edition of his *An Introduction to Tort Law*. See Weir 2006, 30.

7 Winfield 1931, 32: 'Tortious liability arises from the breach of a duty . . .'; also M&D, 30: '[E]very tort [involves] the breach of some legal duty . . .'

8 [1993] AC 498.

(three years from when she first acquired knowledge of the effect the defendant's sexual assaults had had on her) to bring proceedings against the defendant. She had therefore issued proceedings against the defendant just in time by suing him in August 1987.

The House of Lords rejected this argument, holding that the claimant's action against the defendant for sexually assaulting her did not arise out of a 'breach of duty' and that s 11 of the 1980 Act did not therefore apply to the claimant's claim. The claimant's action was therefore dismissed on the ground that proceedings against the defendant had been issued too late.[9] Lord Griffiths remarked, somewhat cryptically, 'If I invite a lady to my house one would naturally think of a duty to take care that the house is safe but would one really be thinking of a duty not to rape her?'[10] But it is quite clear from Lord Griffiths' decision in *Stubbings* v *Webb* – with which the other Law Lords agreed – that he ruled against the claimant because he thought that the *phrase* 'breach of duty' in s 11 of the 1980 Act was not *intended* to cover such torts as battery. Lord Griffiths did *not* mean to *deny* that if A beats B up and B later sues A for damages, A's liability to pay B damages arises out of the fact that A acted wrongfully in beating B up.[11]

(3) *Negligence and duty*. A lot of academics are so hostile to the idea that liabilities in tort arise out of the breach of a duty owed to another that they even deny that liability in *negligence* arises out of the breach of a duty of care owed to another. Let us call such academics, *duty-sceptics*.[12] According to the duty-sceptics, when the courts say that A will owe B a duty of care in a given situation, all they mean to say by that is that A will be held liable to pay damages to B if he carelessly harms B in that situation.[13] So – on this view – if A is held

[9] A subsequent claim that the claimant's rights to a fair trial under Art 6 of the European Convention on Human Rights had been violated because the law on limitation of actions prevented her making out her claim against the defendant was dismissed by the European Court of Human Rights: *Stubbings* v *United Kingdom* [1997] 1 FLR 105.

[10] [1993] AC 498, 508.

[11] To the same effect, Edelman 2002a, n. 55; also *Stingel* v *Clark* (2006) 226 CLR 442, where the High Court of Australia held that the phrase 'breach of duty' covers cases of trespass to the person, observing (at [17]) that 'it is clear that eminent judges may disagree about whether, upon jurisprudential analysis, the phrase "breach of duty" is apt in the case of trespass, but statutes of limitation are more concerned with practical justice than with jurisprudential analysis . . .'. The decision of the Court of Appeal in *A* v *Hoare* [2006] 1 WLR 2320 makes clear some of the practical problems that arise out of the House of Lords' decision in *Stubbings* v *Webb*. In that case, two claimants who had been sexually abused at school sued the defendants for psychiatric illnesses that they had suffered as a result of: (1) being 'groomed' for sexual abuse (for example, by encouraging the claimants to commit sexually indecent acts or to watch pornographic videos); and (2) being sexually assaulted. The Court of Appeal was forced to rule that s 11 did not apply to *either* set of claims even though claims for (1) could *only* be brought in negligence. This was because, the Court of Appeal ruled, allowing a claim for psychiatric illnesses arising out of (1) to proceed while barring a claim for psychiatric illnesses arising out of (2) on the ground of limitation of actions would bring the law into disrepute – (2) being much more serious conduct than (1) – and it would be difficult to disentangle claims (1) and (2) (for example, in determining how much of the claimants' psychiatric illnesses were due to (1) rather than (2)).

[12] The intellectual origins of duty-scepticism among tort academics are well explored in Goldberg 2002, 2003a.

[13] *Important note*. See, for example, Cane 2006, 69: 'To say that a person owes a duty of care in a particular situation means (*and means only*) that the person will be liable for causing damage by negligence in that situation' (emphasis added; though see n. 7 on the same page for a graceful qualification of this view). See, to identical effect, Weir 1998b, 242–3; Jones 2002, 41; M&D, 116; Morgan 2006, 218–19. Two thoughts occur on reading statements such as these. (1) It is striking how often academics who think like this go on to complain that the law of negligence is 'incoherent' or 'in a mess': see, for example, Hepple 1997; Ibbetson 2003, 475. They never seem to consider the possibility that the law of negligence is not *actually* incoherent or in a mess; and that it only seems that way to them because they refuse to take seriously the notion that liability in negligence arises out of the breach of a duty of care owed to another. (2) It is as well that tort textbooks and articles do not enjoy

liable in negligence to pay damages to B, he is not held liable because he breached a duty of care owed to B by acting in the way he did (for no such duty existed); rather, he is held liable because he carelessly harmed B in a situation where someone who carelessly causes another harm will be held liable for that harm.[14] This view of duties of care in negligence is simply wrong and should be rejected by all right-thinking students. It cannot survive the devastating criticisms that have been made of it, both by one of us writing elsewhere[15] and by Professors Goldberg and Zipursky.[16] We need waste no more time on it here.

(4) *Rights-based and duty-based torts.*[17] As we have seen, if A commits a civil wrong, we can characterise what A has done in two different ways. We could say that A has breached a duty owed to another. Or we could say that A has violated someone else's rights. If Nita has committed the tort of negligence, lawyers almost always talk about what Nita has done in terms of her breaching a duty (of care) owed to another. They almost never say that Nita violated someone else's rights (that Nita take care) in acting as she did. However, lawyers are much happier using rights-based language in talking about other kinds of torts. For example, suppose that Paul has committed the tort of trespass to land by going onto Beth's land without her permission. Lawyers will instinctively say that Paul committed a tort in acting as he did because he violated Beth's rights in going onto her land without her permission.[18] They will almost never say that Paul committed a tort in acting as he did because he owed Beth a duty not to go onto her land without her permission. The same is true of the other trespass torts – such as assault or battery or false imprisonment. Lawyers consistently use rights-based language to describe what is involved in committing those kinds of torts. It is important to realise that this variation in the language that lawyers use to describe different torts does not reflect any fundamental difference between these torts. All torts involve the breach of a duty owed to another. All torts involve the violation of someone else's rights. It is a purely a matter of taste which description one adopts of what has happened when someone commits a tort; no matters of principle are involved.

(5) *The birth and death of torts.* The list of situations in which someone will commit a tort is never fixed. This is because the law on when one person will owe another a tortious duty is constantly evolving in response to changes in social attitudes and values.

For example, it used to be the case that if a man was married, other men would normally owe him: (1) a tortious duty not to commit adultery with his wife;[19] (2) a tortious duty not to encourage his wife to leave him; (3) if his wife left him, a tortious duty not to harbour his wife.[20] So someone would normally commit a tort if he committed

---

a wide circulation outside legal circles. For example, would we really *want* doctors and nurses to think that the law does not actually require them to treat their patients with a reasonable degree of care and skill; that the *only* thing the law requires them to do is to pay their patients damages if they fail to treat them properly?

[14] So, according to the duty-sceptics, liability in negligence is not wrong-based but *fault-based*. Thus Howarth & O'Sullivan 2000, 2: 'Negligence is liability for *fault*' (emphasis in original). To similar effect, see Cane 2006, 35; Giliker & Beckwith 2004, 3; Burrows 1998, 123.

[15] See McBride 2004.

[16] See Goldberg 2000; Zipursky 1998b; Goldberg & Zipursky 1998, 2001.

[17] See Stevens 2007, at 291.

[18] See Weir 2006, at 30: '... in cases of trespass, where liability depends on the invasion of rights, we do not use the notion of duty ...'

[19] Matrimonial Causes Act 1857, s 33.

[20] *Winsmore* v *Greenbank* (1745) Willes 577, 125 ER 1330.

adultery with a man's wife or encouraged a man's wife to leave him or harboured a man's wife when she left him. As McCardie J frankly admitted in *Butterworth* v *Butterworth and Englefield*, the reason for this was that '[a] wife was in substance regarded by the common law as the property of her husband'[21] – so interfering with a man's wife was regarded as being akin to interfering with his property. Now that society has rejected the idea that a man's wife is his property, the idea that other men will owe a married man a duty not to interfere with his marriage has also been rejected. Nowadays, someone who interferes with a man's marriage will not commit a tort[22] – or, indeed, any other kind of legal wrong.

Again, as we have seen, the law says at the moment that if you come across a stranger who is in danger of being killed or injured, you will not owe him a duty to rescue him. In taking this position, the law reflects the liberal values currently prevalent in society – in particular, the idea that a man should be legally free to do what he likes, however wicked or immoral, so long as his doing what he likes does not actually *cause* anyone else to suffer any harm. However, it is conceivable that our society will come to value the promotion of collective welfare more than the preservation of individual liberty. Should that happen, Parliament may well change the law and enact a statute which provides that: (1) if someone comes across a stranger who is in danger of being killed or injured, he will have a duty to rescue that stranger if he can do so without endangering himself; and (2) the tort remedy rules will apply to determine what remedies will be available if someone breaches this duty. If Parliament does change the law in this way, then someone *will* commit a tort if he or she comes across a stranger in danger of suffering some kind of harm and does nothing to assist that stranger when he could easily have rescued him.

(6) *The number of torts.* The list set out above of the situations in which someone will commit a tort lists nine different torts. There are in fact *at least* 25 different kinds of torts – a complete list of the torts recognised in English law might in fact comprise about 40 different torts.[23] Why are there so many torts? Well, there are as many torts in English law as there are different kinds of tortious duties that we owe each other – so the more tortious duties that we owe each other, the more torts there will be. So, if you take two given individuals, A and B, there are at least 25 different kinds of tortious duties that A will owe B and, correspondingly, at least 25 different kinds of tort that A can commit.

But are these different kinds of duties all that different? Might they just be facets or instances of one or two or three 'master duties'? If they are then the various 'different' torts recognised in English law are just facets or instances of one or two or three 'master

21 [1920] P 126, 130.

22 Section 4 of the Law Reform (Miscellaneous Provisions) Act 1970 provides that 'no person shall be entitled to ... claim ... damages from any other person on the ground of adultery with the wife of the first-mentioned person'. Section 5 of the 1970 Act provides that '[no] person shall be liable in tort ... (a) to any other person on the ground only of his having induced the wife ... of that other person to leave or remain apart from [that person]; ... (c) to any other person for harbouring the wife ... of [that person] ...'. Section 2 of the Administration of Justice Act 1982 provides that '[no] person shall be liable in tort ... to a husband on the ground only if having deprived him of the services or society of his wife ...'. The last remaining traces of the idea that a man's wife is his property were removed from the law by the House of Lords in *R* v *R* [1992] 1 AC 599, ruling that a man is not allowed to have sexual intercourse with his wife without her consent.

23 Rudden 1991–1992 provides us with a list of over 70 torts which have been recognised at one time or another in the common law jurisdictions. But it is doubtful whether some of the listed 'torts' are actually torts – for example, 'homicide' or 'products liability'.

torts'.[24] Sir Percy Winfield, a very great tort lawyer, thought that all the various torts recognised in English law were all just facets or instances of *one* 'master tort' – the tort of causing someone else harm when one has no lawful justification or excuse for doing so.[25] However, the established authorities seem to indicate that there is no such 'master tort' recognised in English law: there are plenty of occasions when someone will be allowed to harm someone else even if he has no lawful justification or excuse for doing so.[26]

Others have sought to argue, in private conversation with the authors, that the various tortious duties that one person will owe another in English law can essentially be reduced to about three – and that, correspondingly, the various torts recognised in English law can be reduced to about three. On this view, if you take two given individuals, A and B, A will owe B: (1) a tortious duty to ensure that he does not *intentionally* cause B harm when he has no lawful justification or excuse for doing so; (2) a tortious duty to take *care* that he does not cause B to suffer some kind of serious harm such as damage to B's person or property; (3) a tortious duty to *ensure* that B does not suffer any serious harm which A has exposed B to an unusual risk of suffering. All the existing torts recognised in English law essentially involve the breach of one or other of these three duties.

So all the existing torts recognised in English law can therefore be seen as facets or instances of one or other of three 'master torts' – the first, a tort of intention, is committed by intentionally and unjustifiably causing someone else to suffer some kind of harm (however trivial); the second, a tort of negligence, is committed by carelessly causing someone else to suffer some form of serious harm; the third, a tort of strict liability, is committed by exposing someone else to an unusual risk of suffering some kind of harm and then failing to ensure that that risk does not materialise.

This view of English law is too crude to be sustainable. For example, what about the case where A commits a tort by carelessly *failing to save* B from suffering some kind of harm? A must in this case have breached a tortious duty owed to B – but it is not a duty which fits within the scheme of duties set out above. So there are not just three tortious duties that one person will owe another but at least four. And what about the case where A commits a tort by carelessly causing B to suffer some kind of harm which is not that serious – such as pure economic loss? Again, A must have breached a tortious duty owed to B in this situation – but it is again not a duty which fits within the scheme of duties set out above. So the number of tortious duties that one person will owe another will not be four but must be at least five. And with similar arguments, we could easily show that the number of tortious duties that one person will owe another is in fact at least 25 – which is the figure we started off with.

So suggestions that the various torts recognised in English law are just facets or instances of a small number of 'master torts' seem wide of the mark.[27] In fact there is an irreducibly

24 Cf. Sugarman 2002, criticising the common law (at 378) for having 'too many torts'.

25 Winfield 1927; Winfield 1931, 32–9.

26 For examples, see below pp. 435–40. See also Goodhart 1938; Williams 1939–1941.

27 Which is not to say that there are not *some* torts which can be seen as facets or instances of a wider tort. See, for example, Chapter 21, below, where we argue that a number of different nominate torts are instances of the 'master tort' of using unlawful means to cause another loss.

large number of torts recognised in English law – and this is merely a reflection of the complexity and diversity of the tortious duties that we owe each other under English law.

WHAT REMEDIES WILL BE AVAILABLE WHEN SOMEONE COMMITS A TORT?

Let us now turn to the second question dealt with by the law of tort – what remedies will be available if someone has committed or is committing a tort?

Remedies available to the victim of a tort

The importance of being a victim

The law on remedies draws a fundamental distinction between the *victim* of a tort and *third parties* to a tort. Let's explain this terminology with an example.

Suppose that Carl commits a tort by breaching a tortious duty owed to Lara. To put it another – exactly equivalent – way, suppose Carl commits a tort by violating Lara's rights. Lara is the victim of Carl's tort and we can say that Carl's tort is committed *in relation to* her. Anyone else is a third party to Carl's tort.

The importance of the distinction between the victim of a tort and a third party to a tort is that most of the remedies that are available when a tort has been committed, or is being committed, are only available to the victim of the tort, the person in relation to whom the tort has been, or is being, committed. The law on remedies does very little for a third party to a tort who wishes to obtain a remedy in respect of that tort. For example, the principal remedy that is available when a tort has been committed is *compensation* for loss suffered as a result of the tort's being committed. The victim of a tort is routinely allowed to sue for compensation for the losses that she has suffered as a result of that tort's being committed. In contrast, a third party to a tort who has suffered loss as a result of that tort's being committed will rarely be allowed to sue for compensation for that loss. A very famous American case illustrates this point best.

In *Palsgraf* v *Long Island Railroad Co.*,[28] a young man – let's call him John – attempted to get onto a train as the train started to move off. He was carrying a package at the time. A railwayman who was nearby – let's call him Tom – attempted to help John onto the train but in doing so carelessly knocked the package carried by John to the ground. Unfortunately the package contained fireworks and when the package hit the ground, the fireworks exploded. Helen Palsgraf was standing some way away, but the shock of the explosion caused some scales which she was standing beside to fall over and hit her. She sued for compensation for the injuries she suffered when the scales hit her.

The issue in the *Palsgraf* case boiled down to whether Helen Palsgraf was entitled to sue Tom for compensation for her injuries. It was held that she was not so entitled. Tom *had* committed a tort in acting as he did. He had owed *John* a tortious duty to take care not to knock John's package to the ground because it was reasonably foreseeable that doing so would damage the contents of the package; and Tom had breached that duty. So Tom, in acting as he did, committed a tort in relation to John. Helen Palsgraf suffered loss as a

[28] 248 NY 339, 162 NE 99 (1928).

result. However, this did not entitle her to sue Tom for compensation for that loss: in order to do that, she had to show that Tom had committed a tort *in relation to her* in acting as he did. In other words, she had to show that Tom had owed *her* a tortious duty to take care not to knock John's package to the ground. But this she could not do: as it was not foreseeable that she would be injured if the package was knocked to the ground (on the face of it, the package looked perfectly innocuous), there was no reason why Tom should have owed *her* a duty to take care not to knock John's package to the ground.

Compensatory damages

Let's go back to our original situation where Carl has committed a tort in relation to Lara. In such a case, Lara will usually be entitled to sue Carl for *compensatory damages* sufficient to compensate her for the *actionable* losses that Carl's tort has *caused* her to suffer.[29]

However, Lara may be barred from suing Carl for anything by way of compensatory damages.[30] If she is, we say that Carl has a *defence* to Lara's claim for compensatory damages. For example, if Lara provoked Carl into committing his tort by committing some serious criminal offence, Carl may be able to raise a defence of *illegality* to Lara's claim for compensatory damages. Again, if Lara delays too long before suing Carl for damages – usually, more than six years from the date she first suffered harm as a result of Carl's tort – Carl will be able to raise a *limitation* defence to Lara's claim for damages.[31]

Even if, in the situation we are considering, Lara is not barred from suing Carl for compensatory damages, the amount of compensatory damages payable by Carl to Lara *may* be reduced below the level necessary to compensate Lara for the actionable losses that his tort has caused her to suffer.[32] This may happen, for example, if Lara was partly to blame for the fact that she suffered those losses – in which case we say that the damages payable to Lara will be reduced on the grounds that she was *contributorily negligent*. Similarly, the damages payable to Lara may be reduced if Lara received some kind of benefit as a result of Carl's committing his tort.

Non-compensatory damages

Lara may also be entitled to sue Carl for damages not designed to compensate her for any losses she has suffered as a result of Carl's tort.

For example, if Carl acted in an arrogant or high-handed fashion in committing his tort (for example, suppose he shoved Lara out of the way in order to get into a lift ahead of her), then Lara may be entitled to sue Carl for *aggravated damages* – that is, damages designed to assuage Lara's feelings of outrage at the way in which she has been treated by Carl.[33]

Again, if Carl committed his tort deliberately and merely being held liable to pay Lara compensatory damages would punish him insufficiently for his outrageous conduct in disregarding his legal obligations to Lara, Lara may be entitled to sue Carl for *exemplary*

[29] It should be noted that Lara will usually also be entitled to sue Carl for damages in respect of the actionable losses that Carl's tort *may* cause her to suffer in the future: see below, pp. 598–9. This point will be disregarded in what follows.

[30] See below, pp. 503–30.

[31] See below, pp. 523–5.

[32] See below, pp. 611–25.

[33] See below, pp. 682–7.

damages, otherwise known as *punitive damages*. There are, however, strict limits on when such damages may be awarded in English law. For example, in order to bring herself within one of the situations where punitive damages may be awarded, Lara would probably have to show that Carl committed his tort in order to make a gain for himself. Merely showing that Carl acted out of pure spite in committing his tort would not be enough.

Moreover, if Carl *did* make a gain from committing his tort, Lara may be entitled to sue Carl for *restitutionary damages* – that is, damages designed to strip Carl of the gain he has made from committing his tort.

Finally, if Lara suffered no loss as a result of Carl's tort, she may still be entitled to sue him for a nominal sum (called *nominal damages*), which sum will be awarded to her by the courts as token of the fact that Carl wronged Lara in acting as he did. Such an award will only be available if the tort that Carl committed is 'actionable *per se*'. Not all torts are actionable *per se* – the trespass torts are, but negligence is not.[34]

Remedies designed to prevent a tort being committed

So far we have been looking at the remedies that are available to the victim of a tort when a tort has been committed. But what if a tort is being committed right now? In such a case, the victim of the tort may be entitled to sue for an injunction, ordering the person committing the tort to stop doing what he is doing. The issuing of an injunction is a very effective way of preventing someone from committing a tort. This is because someone who breaches an injunction may be found to be in contempt of court and sent to prison as a result.

Remedies available to third parties to a tort

As we have seen, the normal rule is that if A commits a tort in relation to B and C suffers loss as a result, C will *not* be entitled to sue A for compensation for that loss. However there are two important exceptions to this rule:

(1) *Fatal torts*. Suppose Gary has committed a tort in relation to Karen and Karen has died as a result. In such a case, Karen's husband (if any) or parents (if Karen was a minor and unmarried at the time she died) will normally be entitled to sue Gary for damages designed to compensate them for their bereavement.[35] Karen's dependants (if any) will also normally be entitled to sue Gary for compensation for the loss of financial support that they have suffered as a result of Karen's death.[36] Neither group of people will be entitled to sue Gary for such damages if Karen would not have been entitled to sue Gary for compensation for her injuries had she survived Gary's tort and merely been injured by it.

(2) *Subrogation*. Suppose Nita has negligently crashed into Fred's car and that Fred's car was insured with Easimind against its being damaged. In this case, Fred has two ways of recovering compensation for the damage done to his car: he could sue Nita or make a claim on his insurance policy with Easimind. Suppose he chooses to make a claim on his insur-

[34] For further discussion of the reason why some torts are actionable *per se* and some are not, see above, n. 3.
[35] See below, p. 638.
[36] See below, pp. 631–8.

ance policy. If he does this, then Easimind will be entitled to bring an action against Nita in Fred's name and sue her for compensation for the damage that she did to Fred's car. (In lawyer's language, Easimind will be *subrogated* to Fred's rights to sue Nita. Lawyers sometimes make the same point in a more colourful way by saying that Easimind will be allowed to 'stand in Fred's shoes' and sue Nita in Fred's name.) In this way, they will recoup the money they had to pay out to Fred for the damage done to his car.

At first sight, this is unsatisfactory. Easimind will have been well paid in the form of insurance premiums to take the risk that it would have to compensate Fred if his car was damaged. So when Easimind compensates Fred for the damage done to his car, why should Easimind be allowed to turn round and, using the law on subrogation, recover that money from Nita? It might be argued that if Easmind were not subrogated to Fred's rights to sue Nita, then Fred would be entitled to claim compensation for the damage done to his car from his insurance company *and* then sue Nita in his own right for compensation for the damage done to his car.[37] Fred would as a result be doubly compensated for the damage done to his car and would therefore enjoy an undeserved windfall.[38] But this problem could be addressed by making Fred hand over to Easimind any damages he recovered from Nita.[39] And if Fred has no intention of suing Nita – and there is therefore no prospect of Fred enjoying an undeserved windfall – why do we, on this explanation, still allow Easmind to be subrogated to Fred's right to sue Nita?[40]

In *Banque Financière de la Cité* v *Parc (Battersea) Ltd*,[41] Lord Hoffmann explained that Easimind will be subrogated to Fred's rights to sue Nita because there will have been a term in Easimind's contract of insurance with Fred, stipulating that if Easimind compensated Fred for damage done to his car, Easmind would be subrogated to any rights Fred had to sue for compensation for that damage. So, in subrogating Easimind to Fred's rights to sue Nita, the law is simply giving effect to the contract between Fred and Easimind.[42] However, this does not seem convincing:[43] Easimind will be subrogated to Fred's rights to sue Nita even if Fred's contract of insurance with Easimind was silent on this issue.[44] Probably the best explanation as to why Easimind will be subrogated to Fred's rights to sue Nita in this

37 For reasons that will be explained below at pp. 614–16, the compensation payable by Nita to Fred will not be reduced to take account of the fact that he has already been compensated by Easimind for the damage done to his car.

38 See Burrows 2002a, 109–12; Degeling 2003, 180–3, 191–230.

39 In fact, this *is* what will happen if Fred – having been compensated for the damage done to his car by Easimind – subsequently recovers compensation for that damage from Nita. Easimind will have a charge over the damages recovered from Nita: *Lord Napier and Ettrick* v *Hunter* [1993] AC 713.

40 See Cane 1996, 436–7.

41 [1999] 1 AC 221.

42 Ibid., at 231.

43 See Burrows 2002a, 108–9; Rotherham 2002, 138.

44 *Important note*. This will *not* be the case if Nita negligently *injured* Fred and Fred claimed compensation for his injuries under a personal injury insurance policy with Easimind. In this situation, Easimind will *only* be subrogated to Fred's rights to sue Nita for compensation for his injuries if Fred's contract of insurance with Easimind provided this should happen. Furthermore, Fred will – unless his contract of insurance with Easimind provides otherwise – be free both to make a claim on his insurance contract with Easimind *and* sue Nita for damages in respect of his injuries: see *Dalby* v *India and London Life Assurance Co.* (1854) 15 CB 365, 139 ER 465; *Bradburn* v *Great Western Railway Co.* (1874) LR 10 Ex 1. It is thought that allowing Fred to do this will not confer an undeserved windfall on him – 'it is difficult to assert that he [would] be overcompensated [if he were allowed to make a claim against Easimind and Nita] given that no precise market value can be placed upon his pain and suffering and loss of amenity': Lewis 1999, 29.

situation is that the public interest demands that people who commit torts should suffer some kind of loss as a result – so as to deter people from committing torts. So Easimind is allowed to sue Nita in Fred's name for compensation for the damage she did to Fred's car because if it were not allowed to do this, Nita would be able to escape any kind of sanction for negligently damaging Fred's car.[45]

Remaining issues

Before we leave our overview of the law on what remedies will be available when a tort has been committed, we should briefly deal with two remaining issues.

Vicarious liability

Suppose that Ian has committed a tort and Ruth has suffered some kind of loss as a result. As a general rule, Ruth will not be entitled to sue anyone but Ian for compensation for the loss that she suffered as a result of Ian's tort.[46] However, there is one very important exception to this rule: if Ian was employed by Dawn when he committed his tort and there was a 'close and direct connection' between Ian's tort and what he was employed to do, then Dawn may be held *vicariously liable* in respect of Ian's tort. What this means is that Dawn will be treated in law as though she committed Ian's tort along with him. The result is that if Ruth is entitled to sue Ian for compensation for the loss she has suffered as a result of his tort, she will also be entitled to sue Dawn for such compensation.

Contribution[47]

Suppose Paul, an 8-year-old boy, was regularly beaten up at school by Alan, the school bully. Beth, the school's headmistress, was aware that Paul was being bullied but took no action to deal with the problem. In this case, Paul will of course be able to sue Alan in tort for compensation for the injuries he suffered when he was beaten up by Alan. But Paul will also be able to sue *Beth* for compensation for the injuries he suffered. The reason is that Beth owed Paul a non-contractual common law duty to take reasonable steps to stop him being bullied at school; she breached that duty by doing nothing to protect Paul from being beaten up by Alan; and Paul would not have been beaten up had Beth discharged the duty she owed Paul and intervened to stop Alan beating him up.

So suppose that Paul sues Beth for compensation for the injuries that he suffered as a

[45] For criticisms of this explanation, see Lewis 1999, 44–6. It must be admitted that this explanation does not completely convince in the case we are considering. Even if Nita is held liable in this case, she will not ultimately have to foot the bill for the damage that she has done to Fred's car. When she crashed into Fred's car, she will almost certainly have been carrying liability insurance (otherwise known as 'third party' insurance – to be distinguished from 'first party' insurance where someone insures his person or property against the risk of it being damaged). So if she is held liable in this case, her liability insurer will pay the bill. However, it could be argued that even in this case Nita will face some kind of sanction for committing her tort – her liability insurance premiums will go up; and this is something that would not have happened had Fred's insurer not been subrogated to Fred's rights to sue Nita.

[46] It should be noted that if Ian is held liable to pay Ruth something by way of damages, Ian may be entitled to shift the cost of paying Ruth off onto a third party. This will be the case if Ian has insured against the possibility of being held liable to Ruth; in such a case, Ian will be able to require his liability insurer to indemnify him against the cost of compensating Ruth for the loss that she suffered as a result of his tort.

[47] No detailed account of the law on contribution will be given in this book. For such an account, the reader is advised to consult a standard textbook on the law of restitution.

result of being beaten up by Alan and that Paul succeeds in obtaining such compensation from Beth. In this situation, Beth will then be entitled to bring what is called a claim in contribution against Alan. In other words, she will be able to sue Alan for a proportion of the compensatory damages that she has had to pay out to Paul. This is the result of s 1(1) of the Civil Liability (Contribution) Act 1978, which provides that: '... any person liable in respect of any damage suffered by another person may recover contribution from any other person liable in respect of the same damage'. How much will Beth be able to recover from Alan? Section 2(1) provides that 'the amount of the contribution recoverable from any person shall be such as may be found by the court to be just and equitable having regard to the extent of that person's responsibility for the damage in question'.

What happens if Paul sues Alan, and not Beth, for compensation for the injuries that he suffered? The same analysis applies: Alan, having compensated Paul, will then be entitled to bring a claim in contribution against Beth and thereby recoup from Beth at least some of the damages that he has had to pay out to Paul. This seems less than satisfactory. Why should Alan be allowed to shift some of the cost of compensating Paul onto Beth's shoulders? After all, it was Alan who was primarily responsible for Paul's being injured in this case. However, it is clear that Alan will be able to make a claim in contribution against Beth in this case, though presumably he would not be allowed to sue Beth for very much.[48]

What happens if Paul waives any rights he might have to sue Beth for compensation before he sues Alan for such compensation? If Alan pays up, can he then bring a claim in contribution against Beth? One would have thought not: when Paul sued Alan for compensation, Paul – having waived his rights against Beth – could not *at that time* have also sued Beth for such compensation. But in fact this makes no difference: Alan will be able to make a claim in contribution against Beth even if, at the time Paul sued Alan, Paul no longer had any rights to sue Beth. This is because s 1(3) of the 1978 Act provides that: '[a] person shall be liable to make contribution by virtue of subsection (1) above notwithstanding that he has ceased to be liable in respect of the damage in question since the time when the damage occurred, unless he has ceased to be liable by virtue of the expiry of a period of limitation ... which extinguished the right on which the claim against him in respect of the damage was based.'

BEYOND TORT LAW

We have already seen that tort law contains a number of rules and doctrines which specify when one person will be allowed to sue another for compensation for some kind of loss that he or she has suffered. If B has suffered some kind of loss and is entitled to sue A for compensation for that loss under these rules and doctrines lawyers usually say that B is entitled to sue A *in tort* for compensation for that loss or, alternatively, that A is liable *in tort* to compensate B for the loss that she has suffered.

But even if B is not entitled to sue A in tort for compensation for the loss that she has suffered, she may still be entitled to sue A for such compensation under some other area of law. If B is entitled to sue A for compensation under some other area of law, we should say that she's entitled to bring a *non-tortious* claim for compensation against A. There are a

48 *K* v *P* [1993] Ch 140.

number of situations where someone will be entitled to bring a non-tortious claim for compensation against someone else.

Appropriation

Suppose the State lawfully appropriates John's land. In such a case, John will not be able to sue the State *in tort* for compensation for the loss of his land. The State could not have committed a tort in taking John's land as it was allowed to do so. But John will still be entitled to bring a *non-tortious* claim against the State to be compensated for the loss of his land.[49]

The rule in *Rylands* v *Fletcher*

Suppose Fred keeps a tank of oil on his land. He regularly has the tank checked for leaks but, in between inspections, the tank – against all expectations – develops a leak during a particularly hot summer and some of the oil in the tank leaks onto land owned by Mary, Fred's neighbour, and damages Mary's roses. In this situation, Mary may be entitled to sue Fred for compensation for the damage done to her roses under what's called 'the rule in *Rylands* v *Fletcher*'. According to this rule, 'the person who, for his own purposes, brings on his land, and collects and keeps there anything likely to do mischief if it escapes, must keep it at his peril, and, if he does not do so, he is prima facie answerable for all the damage which is the natural consequence of its escape'.[50]

Let us assume that Mary *is* entitled to sue Fred for compensation for damage done to her roses under the rule in *Rylands* v *Fletcher*. There are some academics who will explain this result in the following terms: 'There is nothing mysterious about why Mary is entitled to sue Fred in this situation: she is entitled to sue him *in tort* for compensation for the damage done to her roses. Fred owed Mary a tortious duty to *ensure* that his oil did not leak onto Mary's land. So when Fred's oil did leak onto Mary's land, he committed a tort in relation to her and became liable to compensate her in tort for the loss suffered by her as a result of the leak – namely, the damage done to Mary's roses.'[51]

However, the better view is that Fred did *not* commit any kind of tort in this situation – at best, Fred owed Mary a tortious duty *to take care* that his oil did not leak onto her land, and he did not breach that duty. So Fred is held liable to compensate Mary for the damage done to her roses not because he committed a tort in allowing oil to leak onto Mary's land but because it simply seems fair that he should.[52] As Carleton Kemp Allen explained:

[49] The State's liability to compensate B arises out of the fact that its appropriating B's property will not be lawful unless it compensates B. For an interesting philosophical discussion of when it will, and when it will not, be legitimate for the State to appropriate B's property and compensate her for the loss of that property, see Goodin 1989.

[50] *Rylands* v *Fletcher* (1866) LR 1 Ex 265, 279 per Blackburn J. For a full account of the rule, see below, pp. 754–64.

[51] See Burrows 1983, 226, n. 23; Birks 1995, 41–2; Gardner 2002, 112; Ripstein 2002, 657; W&J, 75.

[52] *Important note.* In *Transco plc* v *Stockport Metropolitan Borough Council* [2004] 2 AC 1, the House of Lords showed itself to be deeply confused as to the basis of liability under the rule in *Rylands* v *Fletcher*. On the one hand, their Lordships made it clear that they thought that liability under that rule arose under the law on private nuisance (ibid, at [9], per Lord Bingham; at [52] per Lord Hobhouse; at [92], per Lord Walker) and therefore (as someone who creates, authorises, adopts or continues a private nuisance clearly commits a tort) that liability under the rule in *Rylands* v *Fletcher* is a form of tort liability. On the other hand, when their Lordships sought to justify the existence of the rule, they did *not* do so on the basis that a defendant who was

> It is often said that in respect of peculiarly dangerous things, there is a 'duty' irrespective of negligence or wilful aggression, to 'insure' neighbours and others against damage. This use of the term 'duty' is unfortunate ... There is of course a duty of careful management of any material thing, whether it belong to the family of '*Rylands* v *Fletcher* objects' or not; but it is difficult to see that there is any 'duty' to prevent a dangerous thing escaping through causes which have nothing to do with the maintainer's fault ... The true situation seems to be that he who maintains for his own advantage a peculiarly dangerous thing in proximity to others, necessarily imposes upon those others a risk of injury ... greater than is to be reasonably expected in the ordinary circumstances of social life, and it is therefore just and expedient that he himself should bear the risk of making good any damage to others which results from the maintenance of the object. This is certainly a liability; but it is a confusion of ideas to [say that it arises out of the breach of] a duty.[53]

If this is correct, then – in the situation we are considering – Mary is not entitled to sue Fred *in tort* for the damage done to her roses; no such claim is available to her as Fred did not commit a tort in relation to Mary in this situation. Rather, Mary is entitled to bring a *non-tortious* claim for compensation against Fred for the damage done to her roses.[54]

The Consumer Protection Act 1987

Suppose Dawn manufactures a microwave oven, taking the utmost care to use the highest quality components in manufacturing the oven. Suppose further that Paul eventually acquires the oven and one of its components fails, with the result that the oven blows up and Paul is injured. In this case, Paul will be entitled to sue Dawn for compensation under the Consumer Protection Act 1987. No one could seriously say in this situation that Dawn,

---

held liable under it to pay damages to a claimant is held liable because he will have committed some kind of legal wrong in relation to the claimant (which would be the case if the defendant's liability was genuinely a form of tort liability) but on the basis that if a defendant has exposed a claimant's land to a risk of being harmed by using his land in a non-natural way, then it is only fair that if that risk materialises, the defendant should be held liable to compensate the claimant: ibid, at [6] (per Lord Bingham) and [29] (per Lord Hoffmann).

53 Allen 1931, 193–4. See also Holmes 1873, 653; Wright 1961, 86; Restatement Torts 2d (1965) §4 Comment b; Cane 1998, 165; Waddams 1998, 124–5.

54 *Important note.* Having said that, it is not as yet widely acknowledged that you can have a non-tortious claim for compensation for some loss that you have suffered. As a result, academics are liable for the foreseeable future to regard claims for compensation under the rule in *Rylands* v *Fletcher* as arising 'in tort'. Likewise claims for compensation in public nuisance or under the Consumer Protection Act 1987, which are dealt with below, are likely for the foreseeable future to be classified, incorrectly, by the academic community as arising 'in tort'. (It took about 350 years for it to be widely acknowledged that claims to recover money paid over by a mistake or claims to be paid a reasonable sum for work done at another's request did not arise 'in contract' – as *Slade's Case* (1602) 4 Co Rep 92a seemed to suggest – but rather arose 'in restitution'. Let's hope we won't have to wait a similar period of time for it to be recognised that one can have a non-tortious claim for compensation for loss that one has suffered.) This means that if, in an exam, you are asked to consider what 'claims in tort' are available to the parties in a particular problem situation, you should interpret the term 'claims in tort' very loosely, as not only covering claims in tort *stricto sensu* but also non-tortious claims for compensation. Another consequence of the fact that the existence of non-tortious claims for compensation is not yet widely acknowledged is that the procedural rules (such as the laws on limitation of actions and the rules on conflicts of law) which govern when claims can be brought and in what courts do not cover non-tortious claims for compensation. Such procedural rules only cover claims 'in contract', claims 'in tort' and (now) claims 'in restitution'. Until these procedural rules are updated to take account of the possibility that one can have a non-tortious claim for compensation, one should apply the procedural rules that govern claims 'in tort' to non-tortious claims for compensation. (The alternative – which is to say that there are *no* procedural rules governing non-tortious claims for compensation so that, for example, there is no period of limitation on when a non-tortious claim for compensation may be brought – is unthinkable.)

in manufacturing the microwave oven, committed a tort in relation to Paul.[55] At best, Dawn owed Paul a tortious duty to take care to see that the microwave oven would not be unreasonably dangerous to use – and she did not breach that duty. So Paul's right to sue Dawn for compensation for his injuries will be non-tortious in nature.

Public nuisance

Suppose Gary creates a public nuisance and Wendy suffers some kind of special loss as a result – that is, loss over and above that suffered by the rest of the community as a result of Gary's actions. In such a case, Wendy will be entitled to bring a non-tortious claim against Gary for compensation for the loss that she has suffered.

Why can't we analyse Wendy's right to sue Gary in this case as arising in tort? The reason is that someone who creates a public nuisance will not commit a tort. To explain: someone will create a public nuisance if he unlawfully interferes with a *public* good – a good which, when it exists, may be enjoyed by everyone. So an example of a public good is a highway. If a highway exists then everyone may use it. So if A unlawfully interferes with a highway – either by unreasonably obstructing it or by unreasonably endangering other people who use the highway – then he creates a public nuisance. It follows from this that someone who creates a public nuisance commits a *public wrong* – not a civil wrong. The duty not to create a public nuisance is not imposed on someone for the benefit of any particular individual but for the benefit of the community as a whole. And as the creation of a public nuisance does not amount to a civil wrong, it cannot amount to a tort.

The Human Rights Act 1998

Suppose a public authority breaches the statutory duty it owes Eric under s 6 of the Human Rights Act 1998 not to violate his human rights, as set out in the European Convention on Human Rights. We have already seen that such a breach will not of and in itself amount to a tort.[56] So if Eric is entitled to sue the public authority in question for compensation for violating his human rights, that claim will be non-tortious in nature.

Strictly speaking, a book on tort law need not concern itself with the issue of when one person will be entitled to bring a non-tortious claim for compensation against another. If it merely sets out the situations in which someone will commit a tort and explains what remedies will be available when someone commits a tort it will have done what it purports to do: provide the reader with a comprehensive guide to the current state of tort law in this country.

[55] The Act itself seems to acknowledge that someone who is held liable under it will not necessarily have committed a tort. Section 6(1) of the 1987 Act provides that 'Any damage for which a person is liable under [the Act] shall be *deemed* to have been caused . . . by that person's wrongful act, neglect or default' (emphasis added). This provision would not be necessary if, in the situation we are considering, Dawn's liability under the 1987 Act to compensate Paul for his injuries arose out of the fact that she had *actually* committed a tort in manufacturing the microwave oven that injured Paul. Surprisingly, Stanton 2003 argues (at 7) that claims brought under the 1987 Act 'may be stated to be for breach of statutory duty'. This is wrong: the Act does *not* impose a statutory duty on various individuals and then specify what should happen when that duty is breached. All it does is require certain individuals in certain circumstances to pay compensation to other individuals.

[56] See above, p. 9.

Yet, in Part IV of this book, we have chosen to set out – under the heading 'Alternative Sources of Compensation' – a number of situations in which one person will be entitled to bring a non-tortious claim for compensation against someone else. We have chosen to do this for the same reason that textbooks on contract law detail the circumstances in which someone will be entitled to bring a non-contractual claim to be paid for work that he has done for someone else.

Someone who wants to be paid for work he has done for someone else will want to know of *all* his possible avenues of redress – so a contract lawyer who only knows when someone will be entitled to bring a *contractual* claim to be paid for work he has done for someone else will not be of much help to him. A good contract lawyer will be in a position to advise someone who wants to be paid for work he has done of *all* his possible avenues of redress – he will not only be able to advise his client as to whether he can bring a *contractual* claim to be paid for the work he has done but he will also be in a position to advise his client as to whether he can bring a *non-contractual* claim to be paid for doing that work.

Similarly, someone who wants to be compensated for a loss that he has suffered will want to be advised of *all* his possible avenues of redress. So he will not want to be advised by a lawyer who can only tell him whether he is entitled to sue someone *in tort* for the compensation he wants. He will want to be advised by a lawyer who is also in a position to tell him whether he will be able to bring a non-tortious claim so as to be compensated for the loss he has suffered. So a good tort lawyer will not only be familiar with the situations in which someone who wants to be compensated for a loss that he has suffered will be able to bring a claim in tort for such compensation – he will also be familiar with the situations in which someone who wants to be compensated for a loss that he has suffered will be able to bring a non-tortious claim for such compensation. As the object of a tort textbook is to produce good tort lawyers, this textbook would be deficient if it did not make reference to at least some of the situations in which someone will be entitled to bring a non-tortious claim to be compensated for a loss that he has suffered. Thus the necessity for Part IV of this book.

Visit **http://www.mylawchamber.co.uk/mcbride** to access updates on recent cases, as well as model answers and tips for answering tort problem questions.

3 Tort law and its critics

Perhaps the most pernicious myth about tort law which has been popularised by tort lawyers over the past 30 or 40 years goes as follows: The function of tort law is to determine when someone who has suffered loss at another's hands may sue that other to recover compensation for that loss.

An early statement of this view of tort law may be found in Cecil Wright's article 'Introduction to the law of torts'.[1] In that article, Wright observed:

> Arising out of the various and ever-increasing clashes of the activities of persons living in a common society, carrying on business in competition with fellow members of that society, owning property which may in any of a thousand ways affect the persons or property of others – in short, doing all the things that constitute modern living – there must of necessity be losses, or injuries of many kinds sustained as a result of the activities of others. *The purpose of the law of torts is to adjust these losses and to afford compensation for injuries sustained by one person as a result of the conduct of another.*[2]

In fact, this is incorrect. The function of tort law is *not* to determine whether or not someone who has suffered loss at another's hands will be entitled to recover compensation for that loss from that other.

Tort law can be split up into two parts, corresponding to Parts II and III of this book. Each part serves a different function. The function of the first part – which we can call the *duty-imposing* part – is to help determine what duties we owe each other.[3] The function of the second part – which we can call the *remedial* part – is to help determine what remedies will be available when one of these duties is breached. In other words, the function of the remedial part of tort law is to determine what remedies will be available when someone commits a tort. So if A has caused B to suffer some kind of loss but he has done so *without committing a tort*, the law of tort takes *no view* – one way or the other – as to whether B should be entitled to sue A for compensation for the loss she has suffered at A's hands. The question of whether or not B should be entitled to sue A for compensation for the loss she has suffered at A's hands *has nothing to do* with either the duty-imposing part of tort law or the remedial part of tort law.

All this must seem very strange to those who learned their tort law in the 1960s, 1970s and 1980s. Sadly, Cecil Wright's view of the function of tort law has won almost universal acceptance in such quarters.[4] For example, *Prosser and Keeton on the Law of Torts* – the

[1] Wright 1944, 238.

[2] Ibid. (emphasis added).

[3] This function is of course not performed exclusively by tort law: contract law, the law of restitution, Equity and the criminal law also help to determine what duties we owe to each other.

[4] There are some honourable exceptions: see Weir 2004, 1: '... the prime function of the area of social regulation we call "tort" is to determine when one person must pay another compensation for harm *wrongfully* caused' (emphasis in original); GS&Z, 38: 'Tort law ... provides injured parties with redress from those who have wronged ... them'; also Oliphant 2007, at 28: '... tort law may be said to perform the functions of defining and

classic American textbook on tort law – tells us that '[the] law of torts ... is concerned with the allocation of losses arising out of human activities; and since these cover a wide scope, so does this branch of the law'.[5] It then goes on to quote with approval the above passage from Wright's article. The late John Fleming agreed with the view taken by the editors of *Prosser and Keeton*. In the ninth edition of his *The Law of Torts*, he wrote, 'The law of torts is ... concerned with the allocation of losses incident to man's activities in modern society.'[6] Once again, Wright's article was quoted with approval. Closer to home, the 17th edition of *Winfield and Jolowicz on Tort* observes that 'tort [law] is concerned with the allocation of responsibility for losses, which are bound to occur in our society ... It is the business ... of the law of tort to determine when the law will and when it will not grant redress for damage suffered or threatened ...'[7] Paula Giliker and Gillian Beckwith take the same view: 'Tort law determines who bears the loss which results from the defendant's actions.'[8] As do David Howarth and Janet O'Sullivan: 'The primary task of tort law is to define the circumstances in which a person whose interests have been harmed by another may seek compensation.'[9] As do the comparative lawyers Walter van Gerven, Jeremy Lever and Pierre Larouche: 'Tort law ... consists of a body of rules determining the circumstances, and conditions, under which harm suffered by a victim will be borne by another person, most frequently, the perpetrator of a harm ... Tort law is therefore about [the] (re-)distribution of losses ...'[10] As does the legal philosopher Jules Coleman: 'Tort law is about messes. A mess has been made, and the only question before the court is, who is to clean it up?'[11] Unsurprisingly, this view of tort law has become popular among judges – if only because judges read law books and tend to believe what they read in them. So, for example, Lord Bingham remarked in the case of *Fairchild* v *Glenhaven Funeral Services Ltd* that, 'The overall object of tort law is to define cases in which the law may justly hold one party liable to compensate another.'[12]

Why is this misconception about the function of tort law so pernicious? The reason is that its widespread popularity has given rise to an equally widespread perception that tort law is in dire need of reform. The point can be illustrated by reference to the case of *Roe* v *Minister of Health*.[13] In that case, two patients went into hospital for minor surgery and came out permanently paralysed. In both cases, the hospital surgeon had injected the patient's spine with nupercaine to anaesthetise him and in both cases paralysis had resulted because the nupercaine was contaminated. The nupercaine was contaminated because

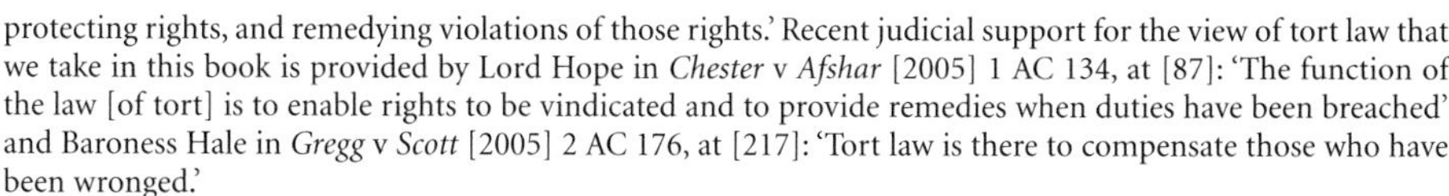

protecting rights, and remedying violations of those rights.' Recent judicial support for the view of tort law that we take in this book is provided by Lord Hope in *Chester* v *Afshar* [2005] 1 AC 134, at [87]: 'The function of the law [of tort] is to enable rights to be vindicated and to provide remedies when duties have been breached' and Baroness Hale in *Gregg* v *Scott* [2005] 2 AC 176, at [217]: 'Tort law is there to compensate those who have been wronged.'

5 Keeton 1984, 6.

6 Fleming 1998, 5.

7 W&J, 2, 4. See also Jones 2002, 1.

8 Giliker & Beckwith 2004, 2.

9 Howarth & O'Sullivan 2000, 1.

10 Van Gerven, Lever & Larouche 2000, 13. See also Zweigert & Kötz 1998, 597: '... it is the function of the law of tort to determine when the victim ought to be able to shift on to the shoulders of another the harm to which he has been exposed.'

11 Coleman 1998, 302.

12 [2003] 1 AC 32 at [9].

13 [1954] 2 QB 66.

before it was injected into the patients' spines it was stored in ampoules which were placed in phenol, a disinfectant. The ampoules had, unknown to everyone, tiny invisible cracks in them through which the phenol had percolated, contaminating the nupercaine. The patients in *Roe* sued the hospital in tort, seeking to obtain compensation for the losses they had suffered as a result of their paralysis. Their claims failed.

Now – if one thinks that the function of tort law is to determine when someone who has suffered loss at another's hands may sue that other for compensation for that loss, one would be entitled to think that tort law let down the patients in this case. There is a good case for saying that the patients in *Roe should* have been allowed to sue the hospital for compensation for the losses suffered by them. The hospital caused the claimants to suffer those losses and was in a much better position to bear those losses than the claimants. If the hospital had been ordered to compensate the claimants for the losses suffered by them, it would have passed on the costs of meeting the judgment against them to its insurers (who would have undertaken to meet the costs of any liabilities incurred by the hospital). The hospital's insurers would, in turn, have passed on the costs of indemnifying the hospital against its liabilities to the claimants in *Roe* to its customers in the form of fractionally higher premiums.

So – if the patients in *Roe* had been allowed to sue the hospital for compensation for the losses suffered by them as a result of their being paralysed, the two patients in *Roe* would not have had to shoulder the costs of the accident in *Roe*. Hundreds of thousands of people – the hospital's insurer's customers – would have borne those costs instead. Would it have been better if the costs of the accident in *Roe* had been borne by the two patients in *Roe* or by the hundreds of thousands of people who were the customers of the hospital's insurers in *Roe*? To ask the question is to answer it: it would of course have been better if the costs of the accident in *Roe* had been borne by the customers of the hospital's insurers. So it would have been better if the two patients in *Roe* had been allowed to sue the hospital in *Roe* for compensation for the losses suffered by them as a result of their being paralysed. It follows that if you think that the function of tort law is to determine when someone who has suffered loss at another's hands will be entitled to sue another for compensation for that loss, you will think that tort law failed the patients in the *Roe* case – it did not allow them to sue the hospital for compensation when it should have.

But the truth is more complicated. The reason why the patients' claims in *Roe* failed was that the patients could not establish that the hospital had committed a *civil wrong* in the way it treated the patients. True, the duty-imposing part of tort law imposed on the hospital a duty to treat the patients with a reasonable degree of care and skill; but the hospital fully discharged that duty. The patients were treated in accordance with best medical practice. No one could have foreseen that treating the patients in the way they were treated would expose them to a risk of paralysis. Of course, if the duty-imposing part of tort law had imposed on the hospital a duty to *ensure* that the patients did not suffer any kind of long-term harm as a result of being treated by the hospital, then the patients would have been allowed to sue the hospital in tort for compensation for their injuries. Each of the patients would have been able to argue, 'The hospital committed a civil wrong in relation to me in treating me the way it did – it owed me a duty to *ensure* that I did not suffer any kind of long-term harm as a result of being treated by the hospital, and it breached that duty.' So if any part of tort law was to 'blame' for the fact that the patients in *Roe* were not allowed to sue for compensation for their injuries, it was the duty-imposing part, which failed to impose on the hospital a duty to ensure that the patients in *Roe* did not suffer any long-term harm as a result of being treated in the hospital.

But was the duty-imposing part of tort law at fault for not imposing such a duty on the hospital? Would it be reasonable for the law to say that a hospital owes each of its patients a duty to *ensure* that that patient does not suffer any kind of long-term harm as a result of its treatment of that patient? Again, to ask the question is to answer it: of course it would not be reasonable for the law to impose such a duty on a hospital.[14] The most a hospital can reasonably be expected to do for its patients is to treat them with a reasonable degree of care and skill – and, as we have already seen, the duty-imposing part of tort law *does* impose a duty on hospitals to do exactly that. Unfortunately for the patients in *Roe*, they simply could not establish that *that* duty had been breached. So *tort law* did *not* let down the patients in *Roe*. The duty-imposing part of tort law would have acted in a wholly unreasonable fashion had it imposed on the hospital in *Roe* the kind of duty that would have allowed the patients in *Roe* to sue the hospital *in tort* for compensation for their injuries. The only duty that it was reasonable for the duty-imposing part of tort law to impose on the hospital was amply discharged by the hospital, thus making it impossible for the claimants to establish that the hospital had done anything *wrong* in the way it treated the claimants.

So it would have been quite wrong to allow the patients in *Roe* to sue the hospital *in tort* for compensation for the injuries they suffered. Of course, it may be they should have been allowed to bring some other kind of claim against the hospital – what we have called a claim for 'compensation without wrongdoing'.[15] So it may be that *the law as a whole* could be blamed for failing to provide the claimants with a means of obtaining compensation for their injuries; but *tort law* was blameless in this regard.

All of which is not to say that tort law is not in need of reform – it is merely to point out that critiques of tort law which attack tort law on the ground that it sometimes does not afford a remedy to someone who has suffered loss at another's hands when, in justice, that person ought to be allowed to obtain such a remedy rest on a false premise. They wrongly assume that the function of tort law is to determine when someone who has suffered a loss at another's hands will be entitled to sue that other for compensation for that

[14] Though see Gardner 2002 for a different view. Generally, the law will only impose on you a duty to *ensure* that *x* happens if you have promised in a *contract* to ensure that *x* will happen. If you do this, it is entirely reasonable for the law to impose on you a duty to ensure that *x* will happen – if you did not want to be subject to such an onerous duty, you should not have made the contract in the first place. The fact that only a contract can usually give rise to a duty to *ensure* that *x* happens led Stapleton 1997 to argue that the crucial difference between liability in contract and liability in tort is that all a claimant can sue for in tort are damages designed to put her in the position she would have been in had the defendant treated her reasonably (the 'normal expectancies' measure of damages), while a claimant can sue in contract to be put in the position that the other party to the contract contractually guaranteed to put her in (the 'entitled result' measure of damages) – whether or not it was reasonable to expect to be put in that position. This is to confuse an *accidental* feature of liability in tort and contract with an *essential* feature. For some trenchant criticisms of Stapleton's views, see Friedmann 1997 and Smith 1997.

[15] See above, p. xv. In fact, Kennedy 2001 recommended (at chapter 26, para 35) that patients who are injured in hospital should be able to recover compensation for their injuries without having to show that their injuries were due to anyone's acting negligently or doing anything else legally wrong. However, this proposal has been rejected on grounds of cost: Donaldson 2003, 15.

loss.[16] Criticising tort law on this ground is akin to criticising this book on the basis that it does not do a very good job of teaching people how to keep their motorbikes in good repair. As it is not the function of this book to teach people the art of motorcycle maintenance, the criticism is completely inappropriate. Given that the function of tort law is to help determine what duties we owe each other and to determine what remedies will be available when one of those duties is breached, tort law can only be judged according to how well or badly it does *that* job. A case for saying that tort law is in need of reform can only be made out by showing that the duty-imposing part of tort law operates in an oppressive, arbitrary or unduly permissive fashion in helping to determine what duties we owe each other; or by showing that the rules laid down by the remedial part of tort law that determine what remedies will be available when someone commits a tort are inadequate or unjust or irrational or undesirable.

Is tort law in need of reform? Almost certainly. We tend not, in this book, to go in for criticisms of the duty-imposing part of tort law, but a number of obvious criticisms can be made of the rules laid down by the remedial part of tort law that govern what remedies will be available when someone commits a tort; those criticisms are set out in Part III of this book.[17] One rule that is often the subject of criticism is the *compensation rule* – that is, the rule that says that if A commits a tort in relation to B, B will normally be entitled to sue A for compensation for the losses suffered by her as a result of A's tort. Many people think that the law should not give effect to this rule. For example, the legal philosopher John Finnis argues that 'our law is simplistic, unbalanced, and to some extent unjust and unjustifiable in maintaining a quasi-universal rule of full compensation for [the] ... losses caused by [A's] breach of [a] duty [that he owes] to [B], however minor that breach and whatever the relative resources of [A] and [B]'.[18] Is this criticism justified?

This is a very large question which we can perhaps reduce to manageable proportions by considering a homely analogy. Suppose that Wendy is thinking of going to Hawaii on holiday; the holiday will cost £2,500. She asks you whether, all things considered, she should go. In advising her, you would probably ask her three questions. First, why do you want to go to Hawaii – what will you get out of it? Suppose she says she'd like to go because she's heard it's a good place to get a good tan and eat good seafood. Once you know that, you would then ask her: Is there a cheaper way of getting a good tan and eating good seafood? If there is – say going to Marseilles on holiday is just as good in these respects and would only cost £1,000 – then you would advise her not to go to Hawaii, and to go to Marseilles instead. If there isn't, you would then ask Wendy: Is getting a good tan and eating good seafood so important that it's worth spending £2,500 of your hard earned money on

[16] For examples of such critiques of tort law see Abel 1994, 102–5; Cane 2006; Conaghan & Mansell 1999. For a critique of such critiques, which takes the same view of tort law as that taken here, see Goldberg 2002, 1519: '[W]e ... need to ask less ... of tort. In particular, we ... have to wean ourselves from the habit of treating tort as a means of devising *ad hoc* solutions to perceived social ills. By this I do not mean to say that tort ought not to address contemporary problems – it does and it should. Rather, I am suggesting that we must recapture the idea that tort cases are concerned with the focused task of identifying and remedying instances in which an actor has wronged another, as opposed to providing localized compensation or insurance schemes, regulating antisocial conduct for the good of society, or the like. Relatedly, we ... have to recapture a sense of tort as a body of law, rather than as an occasion for doing whatever seems right or practical at the time.' See, to the same effect, Klar 1998; Morgan 2004, 394–400; Stevens 2007, 326.

[17] See, for example, pp. 573–4, 617–18, 666, 694–7, below.

[18] Finnis 2002, 656.

it? If it isn't, then you would advise her not to go to Hawaii. But if it is, then you would conclude that she should go to Hawaii.

We can adopt the same procedure here to determine whether the law is justified in giving effect to the compensation rule. We begin by asking: Why does the law give effect to the compensation rule – what end or goal is it trying to achieve in giving effect to this rule? Once we have identified what this end or goal is – call it the *compensation goal* – we can then ask: Is giving effect to the compensation rule the most cost-effective way of achieving the compensation goal? Is there in fact a cheaper way of giving effect to the compensation goal? If there is, then we would conclude that Finnis is right: the law should not give effect to the compensation rule. But if there is not, we would then ask: Is achieving the compensation goal so important that the costs involved in giving effect to the compensation rule represent an acceptable price to pay to achieve that goal? If the answer is 'no', then we would again conclude that the law should not give effect to the compensation rule. But if the answer is 'yes', then we would conclude that the law should give effect to the compensation rule and criticisms of the rule such as Finnis's are misguided.

So – let's start with the first question. Why does the law give effect to the compensation rule? To help us out on this question, we can assemble a panel of tort scholars to discuss this issue. Call the members of the panel, John, Paul, Mary, Eric, Beth and Ruth. Their discussion as to the justifiability or otherwise of the compensation rule might go as follows:

John: It's very simple. The law holds tortfeasors liable to pay compensatory damages to the victims of their torts in order to *deter* people from breaching the tortious duties that they owe each other. If you know you are going to be held liable to pay damages if you breach a tortious duty owed to another, then you are less likely to breach that duty.[19]

Paul: That's too simplistic. I admit that *punitive* damages – damages designed to punish someone for committing a tort – are awarded to deter people from committing torts; but it seems strange to say that the law gives effect to the compensation rule for the same reason. If the law's only concern were to deter people from committing torts, it is hard to see why it would seek to do so by giving effect to the compensation rule. Why would it not simply hold a tortfeasor liable to pay a sum to the victim of his tort graduated according to the tortfeasor's means and his degree of fault in committing his tort? Indeed, why would the law hold the tortfeasor liable to pay damages to the *victim of his tort*? Why would it not hold him liable to pay damages to the State instead? And if awards of compensatory damages are made in order to deter people from committing torts, why is it that it is usually only the *victims* of torts who can claim such damages? Why does the law not say that *anyone* who has suffered loss as a result of a tort's being committed is allowed to sue for damages in respect of that loss? Furthermore, if the law gives effect to the compensation rule in order to deter people from committing torts, why does the law allow people to take out liability insurance to protect themselves against the consequences of being held liable to pay other people damages in tort under the compensation rule?

Mary: I agree – it is completely implausible to say that the law gives effect to the compensation rule in order to deter people from committing torts. My own view is that the law gives effect to the compensation rule because justice demands that if A commits a tort in relation to B, A should compensate B for the losses that she has suffered as a result of A's tort.

Paul: But I always thought justice related to the distribution of goods among a community: justice demands that they be distributed fairly among the members of the community.[20] So what's justice

[19] See Cane 2002, 34–5, 60–2.

[20] See Aristotle, *Nicomachean Ethics*, V.3.

got to do with the question of whether people should be held liable for the harm caused by their torts?

Mary: What you're talking about is one form of justice – distributive justice. But once all the goods have been shared out fairly, you've got to have some way of preventing people interfering with the distribution and taking more than their fair share. So if A takes goods which properly belong to B, justice demands that A be made to give the goods back. We call this form of justice, corrective justice. It's a kind of handmaiden to distributive justice – it ensures that fair distributions of goods aren't wrongfully disturbed.[21] So if A commits a tort and deprives B of a good that B was entitled to, the law holds A liable to compensate B for the loss of that good in order to restore the just distribution of goods that obtained before A committed his tort.

Paul: But the law holds A liable whether or not the good which B was deprived of was fairly distributed to her in the first place. And aren't there some goods, such as body parts, which *can't* be distributed but which *are* routinely the subject of tort actions – as when someone sues someone else for negligently breaking her leg or causing her brain damage? How can one say that *those* kinds of tort actions are concerned to restore a 'just distribution of goods'?

Eric: I agree. The problem with Mary's explanation is that her conception of corrective justice is far too narrow. In fact, corrective justice has nothing whatsoever to do with distributive justice: it stands on its own two feet. Corrective justice demands that if A wrongs B, A should put B back in the position she would have been in had A not wronged her. Once you realise that, it's easy to see that the law gives effect to the compensation rule because corrective justice demands that if A breaches a duty owed to B, A should be held liable to compensate B for the losses that she has suffered as a result of his breach, thereby putting her in the position she would have been in had the breach not occurred.[22]

Paul: Okay – but I don't see that really gets us very far in understanding why the law gives effect to the compensation rule. The law may give effect to the compensation rule because corrective justice demands that those who wrong others put those others in the position they would have been in had the wrong not occurred.[23] But why does the law give effect to the demands of corrective justice? And you can't say, 'Because corrective justice demands that it does' because that gets us nowhere.[24]

Beth: Exactly. I wonder if what we're missing at the moment is some sort of 'psychological' explanation of the compensation rule. It may be that the reason why the law gives effect to the compensation rule goes as follows. If A wrongs B, B is liable to feel extremely aggrieved and resentful towards A. If the law doesn't do anything to assuage that feeling, B may try and 'get her own back' on A, and a feud will develop between A and B – which is bad for everyone. So the law requires A to pay compensatory damages to B in an attempt to pacify B and preserve the social order.[25]

Paul: That seems to me a good explanation of why the law will sometimes award *aggravated*

21 See Gordley 1995.

22 See Weinrib 1995; Coleman 1993; Coleman 2001.

23 Though see Zipursky 2003 and Goldberg 2003b, at 577, pointing out that in a case where A has committed a tort in relation to B, the law – in giving effect to the compensation rule – does not actually *require* A to put B in the position she would have been in had A's tort not been committed; it merely gives B a *power* to sue A for damages that will have the effect of putting her in the position she would have been in had A's tort not been committed. Calnan 2005 argues effectively (at 1037) that this is not a fatal objection to the idea that the compensation rule gives effect to the demands of corrective justice.

24 Calnan 2005's response (at 1070) to Paul's demand is that corrective justice 'commands the state to give every citizen his "due" of freedom, and it commands citizens to give "due" respect to each other'. As both of these things are virtuous things to do, giving effect to corrective justice is a virtuous thing to do. But it might be argued against this that: (1) the compensation rule can sometimes have extremely harmful effects on individual liberty (for example, where it works to bankrupt a relatively blameless individual); and (2) respect for someone else cannot be commanded.

25 See Kelly 1967; Kelley 1990; Goldberg 2003c, 1341–2; Sherwin 2003.

damages to the victim of a tort, but not necessarily a good explanation of why the law will routinely award *compensatory* damages to the victim of a tort – after all some torts can be committed quite innocently and it's hard to see why, where a tort has been committed without any fault on the part of the tortfeasor, the victim of the tort should feel at all aggrieved or resentful towards the tortfeasor. Even a dog can distinguish between someone's carelessly tripping over him and someone's deliberately kicking him.

Ruth: I think there's something to Beth's explanation, but my explanation is slightly different. If A wrongs B, B has a natural right to take action against A to force him to make up for his wrong. However, the law can't tolerate the disturbance to the social order that this would involve. So it forbids B from taking direct action against A and instead provides B with a peaceful means of getting A to make up for his wrong by allowing B to sue A for compensation for the losses that she has suffered as a result of A's wrong. So the law gives effect to the compensation rule in order to provide the victim of a wrong with a peaceful means of obtaining redress from the person who committed that wrong.[26]

Paul: But it's not at all clear that if you wrong me I have a 'natural right' to force you to make up for your wrong[27] – after all, if it were, we would hardly be having this discussion, would we?

My own view is that a modified form of Beth's explanation provides us with a good explanation of why the law gives effect to the compensation rule. If A wrongs B, B won't necessarily feel aggrieved or resentful towards A for wronging her. But if A's wrong has resulted in B suffering some *uncompensated losses*, B *will* feel very resentful and aggrieved if A does not then offer to compensate her for those losses. The reason is quite complicated but it goes as follows. The duty A breached when he wronged B was imposed on A for B's benefit. In other words, it was imposed on A because B was – in the eyes of the law – important: someone worth going out of your way for.

Now – if A genuinely regrets having breached the duty he owed B, he will want to undo the effects of his breach. In other words, he will want to compensate B for any uncompensated losses that she has suffered as a result of A's breach. So if A does not offer to compensate B for those losses, he will signal to B that he does not regret his breach. But if he does not regret his breach, that must mean he does not think he should have been subject to the duty that he breached. In other words, if he does not regret his breach, he must not think that B is as important as the law thinks B is. So if A does not offer to compensate B for the uncompensated losses she has suffered as a result of A's breach, he will signal to B that he thinks that she is a person of little worth, certainly not worth the bother that the law demanded he take over her. Such a message is liable to make B very aggrieved and resentful.

So every time someone commits a tort and the victim of the tort suffers uncompensated losses as a result, a potential flashpoint is created in the relationship between the victim of the tort and the tortfeasor. Either the tortfeasor can offer to compensate the victim of the tort for the uncompensated losses that she has suffered as a result of his tort – in which case, all is well and good. Or the tortfeasor can refuse to do any such thing – in which case, the victim of the tort will feel very aggrieved and resentful towards the tortfeasor and attempt to get her own back, with deleterious consequences for the social order. In order to prevent this flashpoint arising, the law does not give the tortfeasor the opportunity to refuse to compensate the victim of his tort for the uncompensated losses that she has suffered as a result of his tort. Instead, it requires him to compensate her for those losses. So I agree with Beth that ultimately the law gives effect to the compensation rule in order to help preserve the social order – but I take a somewhat different view as to why someone's committing a tort has the potential to destabilise society.[28]

[26] See Zipursky 1998a; Zipursky 2002, 639–44.

[27] See Finnis 2002, 656.

[28] For an earlier attempt to present such an explanation as to why the law gives effect to the compensation rule, see McBride 2000.

Our view is that Paul's explanation of why the law gives effect to the compensation rule is the best on offer at the moment.[29] If Paul's account of what the law is trying to achieve in giving effect to the compensation rule is correct, we can then move on to ask – is there a cheaper way of preventing dangerous feuds arising between someone who commits a tort and the victim of a tort?

In order to answer this question, we must first have some idea of how much it costs us as a society to give effect to the compensation rule. Let's call this, the *social cost* of giving effect to the compensation rule. In calculating the social cost of giving effect to the compensation rule, we must not disregard the *incidental benefits* that we obtain by giving effect to the compensation rule. For example, while it cannot be said that the *purpose* of giving effect to the compensation rule is to deter people from committing torts, it cannot be

Costs involved in giving effect to the compensation rule	**Incidental benefits**[30]
(1) Costs of running courts to hear tort cases (2) Costs of employing lawyers to argue tort cases (3) Costs of recovering damages from a defendant against whom an award has been made in a tort case (4) Costs of taking out liability insurance to protect oneself against the possibility of being sued for damages in tort (5) Costs arising out of damages awards being made against defendants in tort cases (bankruptcies, etc.) (6) Costs arising out of defendants taking unnecessary precautions to avoid the slightest possibility that they might be sued in tort	(1) Relief to public purse from having cost of treating and maintaining victims of accidents borne by defendants and their liability insurers rather than by the State (through the NHS and social security payments) (2) Benefits arising out of damages awards being made to the victims of torts (minimisation of disruption caused to their life by tort being committed, etc.) (3) Benefits arising out of fact that people may be deterred by existence of the compensation rule from committing torts

Table 3.1 Calculating the social cost of giving effect to the compensation rule

[29] A couple of criticisms of it could be made. First, Paul's explanation seems inconsistent with the fact that if A commits a tort in relation to B and B dies as a result, B's estate will be allowed to sue A for compensation in respect of any actionable losses suffered by B as a result of A's tort before B died: Law Reform (Miscellaneous Provisions) Act 1934, s 1(1). If B is dead, then there is no potential flashpoint in the relationship between A and B that needs to be eliminated. However, the rule used to be that B's estate could *not* sue in this situation – which tends to strengthen Paul's explanation. Secondly, Paul's explanation does not explain why, if A commits a tort and damages B's property as a result, A will be held liable for the damage done to B's property even if B has already obtained full compensation for the damage done from her insurance company (see above, pp. 22–4). Paul's explanation, admittedly, does not account for why A is held liable in this case. It may be that A is held liable here so as to help ensure that people like A will be deterred from breaching the tortious duties they owe others (ibid.).

[30] For a lively and always interesting account of the incidental benefits of giving effect to the compensation rule – which does not, however, come anywhere close to dealing with the actual *purpose* of giving effect to the compensation rule – see Koenig & Rustad 2001.

denied that the existence of the compensation rule may *in fact* deter people from breaching the duties they owe other people. Incidental benefits like these help to keep down the social cost of giving effect to the compensation rule and must be taken into account in calculating that cost. So – in order to determine the social cost of giving effect to the compensation rule, we must first add up the costs involved in giving effect to the compensation rule and then make a deduction to take account of the value of the incidental benefits obtained by giving effect to the compensation rule.

Table 3.1 sets out in the left-hand column the costs involved in giving effect to the compensation rule and in the right-hand column the incidental benefits obtained by giving effect to the compensation rule. So the social cost of giving effect to the compensation rule equals the sum of the costs set out in the left-hand column *minus* the sum of the incidental benefits set out in the right-hand column.

It may be that the social cost of giving effect to the compensation rule will actually be a *negative* figure. In this case, the compensation rule 'pays for itself' – the incidental benefits obtained by giving effect to the compensation rule are so substantial that they outweigh the costs involved in giving effect to the compensation rule. If this is the case, then we should not abolish the compensation rule, anymore than someone who wants to go on holiday to Hawaii should turn down the offer of a free holiday to Hawaii. However, it is likely that the social cost of giving effect to the compensation rule will turn out to be a *positive* figure; in other words, the total costs involved in giving effect to the compensation rule will outweigh the incidental benefits obtained by giving effect to the compensation rule. If this is the case, then the compensation rule should be abolished if we can show that there is a cheaper way of preventing dangerous feuds arising between the victims of torts and tortfeasors.

One obvious alternative strategy would be to set up a *victims' loss compensation scheme*, under which victims of torts will be able to obtain compensation from the State for the losses suffered by them as a result of those torts being committed. If such a scheme existed, then if A committed a tort in relation to B, B would not suffer any uncompensated losses as a result of A's tort, and there would therefore be no need for A to do anything to 'undo' his tort – and so A would not have the opportunity to refuse to 'undo' his tort and thereby insult B. But would setting up such a loss compensation scheme represent a cheaper way of preventing tensions arising between victims of torts and tortfeasors than the current system, under which the law attempts to prevent those tensions arising by giving effect to the compensation rule?

In order to answer this question, we would need to calculate the social cost of giving effect to a victims' loss compensation scheme. This cost would be calculated in exactly the same way as we would calculate the cost of giving effect to the compensation rule: we add up the costs involved in giving effect to a victims' loss compensation scheme and subtract the incidental benefits involved in giving effect to such a scheme. Going back to Table 3.1, while costs (3)–(6) in the left-hand column would *not* be incurred under a victims' loss compensation scheme, costs (1) and (2) would be; and added to these would be the costs of raising the money needed to fund and run such a scheme. Turning to the right-hand column in Table 3.1, while incidental benefit (2) would also be obtained under a victims' loss compensation scheme, benefits (1) and (3) would not be obtained. So – it turns out – the social cost of running a victims' loss compensation scheme will be smaller than the social cost of giving effect to the compensation rule *if* the sum of costs (3)–(6) in Table 3.1

minus the sum of benefits (1) and (3) in Table 3.1 *exceeds* the cost of raising the money required to fund and run a victims' loss compensation scheme. It is beyond the scope of this book to make such a calculation – but it is unlikely that the social cost of running a victims' loss compensation scheme will be smaller than the social cost of giving effect to the compensation rule.

If this is the case, how about a *no-fault loss compensation scheme*? Under such a scheme, *anyone* who suffered a loss would be entitled to claim compensation for that loss. There would be three major differences between this kind of compensation scheme and a victims' loss compensation scheme, all arising out of the fact that an applicant for compensation under a no-fault compensation scheme would not need to show that he was the victim of a tort to qualify for compensation. First, the courts and lawyers would play a minimal role in the running of a no-fault loss compensation scheme. Secondly, the amount paid out in compensation under a no-fault loss compensation scheme would dwarf the amount paid out in compensation under a victims' loss compensation scheme. Thirdly, people generally would obtain a lot more protection against having their lives disrupted through the 'slings and arrows of outrageous fortune' than they would under a victims' loss compensation scheme – a lot more people would qualify for protection under a no-fault loss compensation scheme than would be the case under a victims' loss compensation scheme.

A no-fault compensation scheme would be just as efficacious as the compensation rule in preventing dangerous feuds arising between victims of torts and tortfeasors – but would the social cost of running such a compensation scheme be less than the social cost involved in giving effect to the compensation rule? To find out the answer to this, one must first add up costs (1)–(6) in Table 3.1 and then subtract the value of benefit (3) in Table 3.1. Let's say the resulting figure is £*x*. One must then find out how much it would cost to fund and run a no-fault loss compensation scheme and subtract from that the value of the benefits that will arise out of making compensation payments to those who would not qualify for compensation under the compensation rule. Let's say the resulting figure is £*y*. If £*x* is more than £*y*, then the social cost of running a no-fault loss compensation scheme will be *less* than the social cost of giving effect to the compensation rule, and the compensation rule should be abolished in favour of a no-fault loss compensation scheme. Again, it is beyond the scope of this book to make that kind of calculation – but it seems likely that £*x* will not be more than £*y*.

There is a third alternative that *may* provide a more cost-effective way of eliminating the tensions that arise when someone commits a tort in relation to someone else. That is to have a *mixed system* under which certain categories of people who have suffered loss are compensated for those losses under no-fault loss compensation schemes, while the compensation rule is given effect to in cases where the victim of a tort has suffered loss that is not covered by one of these no-fault compensation schemes. This is, for example, the system they have in New Zealand where those who suffer personal injuries in accidents are compensated under a no-fault compensation scheme, while victims of torts who suffer other kinds of losses are left free to claim compensation for those losses under the compensation rule.[31] Calculating the social cost involved in administering a mixed system such as this would be extremely difficult, but it is certainly very possible that the social cost of

[31] The New Zealand Accident Compensation Scheme is described in more detail below, at pp. 806–7.

running such a mixed system would be smaller than the social cost of giving full effect to the compensation rule. So it may be that the current state of affairs – under which the law gives full effect to the compensation rule when the victim of a tort suffers loss as a result of that tort being committed – cannot be justified. It may be that the law's aims in giving effect to the compensation rule could be more cheaply achieved if we switched to a mixed system, under which certain categories of people who suffer loss are protected under no-fault compensation schemes while the compensation rule is given effect to in cases where victims of torts suffered losses which are not covered by those schemes.

But equally it may be the case that giving full effect to the compensation rule is actually the cheapest way of eliminating the tensions that would otherwise arise when a tort has been committed. If this is the case, then our inquiry into the justifiability of the law's giving effect to the compensation rule can move on to the third stage – that of asking, 'Are the benefits of eliminating the tensions that would otherwise arise when a tort has been committed outweighed by the social cost of giving effect to the compensation rule?' To put the same question another way, 'If the compensation rule were abolished tomorrow, there might be a rise in revenge attacks on tortfeasors by the victims of their torts but is the social cost involved in giving effect to the compensation rule a price worth paying to ensure that these attacks do not occur?'[32] Again, it is beyond the scope of this book to answer this question – our purpose here is simply to identify the questions that have to be asked before we can come to a final verdict on the justifiability of the law's giving effect to the compensation rule.

However, it should also be noted that this discussion is, at the moment, of purely academic interest. Whether the law is justified or not in giving effect to the compensation rule, it looks like the compensation rule is here to stay. It is so deeply entrenched in our law that only an Act of Parliament could remove it and there is no sign that Parliament is interested in abolishing the compensation rule or narrowing its ambit. Indeed, as Tony Weir has pointed out, almost all legislative interventions in tort law over the past century have been designed to remove various limits that the courts had previously placed on the ambit of the compensation rule.[33]

Visit **http://www.mylawchamber.co.uk/mcbride** to access updates on recent cases, as well as model answers and tips for answering tort problem questions.

Use **Case Navigator** to read in full some of the key cases referenced in this chapter:

- **Fairchild *v* Glenhaven Funeral Services Ltd**

[32] This is assuming of course that the compensation rule does not 'pay for itself' and that there is a social cost attached to giving effect to the compensation rule.

[33] Weir 2006, 3.

Part II

Torts

A.

Negligence

Introduction

DEFINITION

A will commit the tort of negligence in relation to B if he breaches a duty of care owed to B.[1] The term 'duty of care', it should be noted, is ambiguous. We use the term 'duty of care' to describe at least three different kinds of duty that one person might owe another.

First, we say A owes B a 'duty of care' if A owes B a duty to take care not to act in some way.[2] Secondly, we say A owes B a 'duty of care' if A owes B a duty to perform some task with a certain degree of care and skill. Thirdly, we say that A owes B a 'duty of care' if A owes B a duty to take reasonable steps to ensure that some end or goal is achieved. Breach of any of these kinds of duty – being a breach of a 'duty of care' – amounts to negligence.

So a driver of a car owes other users of the road a duty of care – he owes them a duty to take care not to drive dangerously. If he breaches that duty he will commit the tort of negligence. Likewise, a doctor owes a patient of his a duty of care – he owes her a duty to treat

1 *Important note.* From now on, we will be using the term 'a duty of care' as shorthand for 'a *tortious* duty of care'. So when we say that A will commit the tort of negligence in relation to B if he breaches a duty of care owed to B, we are merely saying in shorter form that A will commit the tort of negligence if he breaches a *tortious* duty of care owed to B.

Of course, someone will not commit the *tort* of negligence if he breaches a *non-tortious* duty of care owed to another. So, for example, if A holds property on trust for B, A will owe B a duty to invest the trust property with reasonable skill and care. This duty of care will be non-tortious in nature as it is an equitable duty and breach of that duty will amount to an equitable wrong, not a tort. So if A breaches this duty of care he will not commit the tort of negligence.

Again, we have already seen that if A is B's employer, A will owe B a duty under s 2 of the Health and Safety at Work Act 1974 to take reasonable steps to ensure that B's health, safety and welfare at work is secured (see above, p. 10). This duty of care will be non-tortious in nature – s 47 of the 1974 Act makes it clear that breach of this statutory duty will not be actionable in tort. So if A is B's employer and he breaches the duty of care he owes him under s 2 of the 1974 Act, he will not commit the tort of negligence.

Another example of a non-tortious duty of care is provided by the Human Rights Act 1998. The decision of the European Court of Human Rights in *Osman* v *United Kingdom* [1999] 1 FLR 193 indicates that if the police *know* that C, a criminal on the loose, is *very likely* to kill B if he is not arrested, the police will violate B's right to life under Art 2 of the European Convention on Human Rights if they do not take reasonable steps to apprehend C. If this is right then, in the situation just described, the police will owe B a duty under the Human Rights Act 1998 to take reasonable steps to arrest C. This duty of care will be non-tortious in nature: a public authority which breaches a duty owed to another under the 1998 Act will not commit a tort (see above, p. 9). So if, in the situation just described, the police breach the duty of care they owe B and fail to take reasonable steps to apprehend B, they will not commit the tort of negligence. (For a discussion of what the legal position will be if a public authority breaches a duty owed to another under the 1998 Act, see below, pp. 743–53.)

2 If A owes B a duty to take care not to do *x* but *x* is the sort of thing that can only be done deliberately if it is done at all, we usually simply say that A owes B a duty not to do *x* – but the duty A owes B will still be a duty of care and breach of the duty will still amount to negligence. So, for example, suppose A is playing golf and is waiting to tee off at a particular hole. Suppose further that he knows that B is on the fairway in front of him. In such a case, A will owe B a duty to take care not to drive his ball down the fairway (see below, pp. 73–4). But as A's driving his ball down the fairway is the sort of thing that can only be done deliberately if it is done at all, we can simply say that, in the situation we are considering, A will owe B a duty not to drive his golf ball down the fairway.

her with a certain degree of care and skill; the sort of care and skill that a professional doctor would exercise in treating a patient. If he breaches that duty he will commit the tort of negligence. Similarly, an occupier of land will owe his visitors a duty of care – he will owe them a duty to take reasonable steps to ensure that they will be reasonably safe for the purposes for which they are on his land. If he breaches that duty he will commit the tort of negligence.

FURTHER POINTS

Before we plunge into the law on when one person will owe another a duty of care – a topic that will take up the next six chapters – we should make three general points about the tort of negligence.

Negligence and intention

Sir Percy Winfield once suggested that someone would commit the tort of negligence if, and only if, he 'breach[ed] a legal duty to take care by an *inadvertent* act or omission'.[3] This seems wrong.[4] Suppose Beth drives down a street at 80 miles an hour and as a result runs over Tom. Tom attempts to sue Beth in negligence for compensation. Could Beth really rebut Tom's claim that Beth committed the tort of negligence in driving as she did by arguing that while she admittedly owed Tom a duty to take care not to drive dangerously, she did not commit the tort of negligence in relation to Tom in driving as she did because she *deliberately* drove down the road at 80 miles an hour? The answer is 'no'. If Beth, in driving at 80 miles an hour down the street, breached the duty of care that she owed Tom not to drive dangerously, she will have committed the tort of negligence in relation to Tom – it will not matter whether she drove down the street at 80 miles an hour deliberately or inadvertently. Extrapolating from this, A will commit the tort of negligence in relation to B if he breaches a duty of care owed to B – and this is so even if A's breach is deliberate.

Perhaps acknowledging this point, Winfield later suggested that someone would commit the tort of negligence if: (1) he breached a duty of care owed to another *and* (2) when he breached that duty he did not intend to harm that other.[5] Again, there does not seem any reason for this limitation on the scope of the tort of negligence. Suppose, for example, that Gary's mother-in-law, Lara, visited him in his house. While she was in Gary's house, she put her foot through a rotten floorboard on Gary's staircase which Gary had neglected to replace and as a result twisted her ankle. Now suppose that Lara sues Gary in negligence, claiming that her injury happened as a result of Gary's breach of the duty of care that he owed her to take reasonable steps to see that she would be reasonably safe while she was on his premises. Could Gary really defeat Lara's claim by arguing that he did not commit the tort of negligence in relation to her when he failed to replace the rotten floorboard on his staircase because 'When I found out that the floorboard was rotten and liable to give way,

[3] Winfield 1926, 184 (emphasis added).

[4] It is also inconsistent with the House of Lords' ruling in *Wainwright* v *Home Office* [2004] 2 AC 406 that if A *deliberately* lies to B, telling her that her husband had been injured when he has not, and B is made physically sick as a result of hearing this, then B will be able to sue A for damages in negligence. See below, pp. 114–16.

[5] Winfield 1934, 41.

I deliberately left it untouched in the hope that when Lara came visiting she would put her foot through it'? Surely not[6] – the fact that Gary breached the duty of care he owed Lara as his visitor with the intention of harming her would not stop any court from concluding that Gary committed the tort of negligence in relation to Lara in this case.

Negligence and carelessness

'Negligence' is *not* to be equated with 'carelessness'. A number of different aspects of the law show that it would be an error to equate 'negligence' with 'carelessness'.

First, in the example we have just been considering, Gary's conduct in failing to replace his rotten floorboard in the hope that Lara would put her foot through it and injure herself amounts to 'negligence' – but we would hardly describe it as 'careless'.

Secondly, conduct we would characterise as 'careless' sometimes does not amount to 'negligence' because it does not involve the breach of a duty of care owed to someone else. For example, if the police carelessly fail to arrest a criminal who goes on to steal property from Paul's shop, the conduct of the police, while careless, is not 'negligent' – the police, in acting as they did, did not breach any duty of care owed to Paul.

Thirdly, a given defendant will sometimes be held to have committed the tort of negligence although *he* was not 'careless' in any way. So, for example, suppose an employer brought in a contractor to check the electrical appliances in his factory to ensure that none of the employer's workers were in danger of being electrocuted. Suppose the contractor failed to do a good job of checking the appliances and as a result failed to spot a defect in an appliance which later caused one of the employer's workers to suffer an electric shock. In such a case, the employer will be held to have breached the duty he owed the electrocuted worker to take reasonable steps to see that that worker would be reasonably safe in working for him – and this is so even if the employer took the greatest pains to ensure that the contractor was competent to check the electrical appliances in the employer's factory and did all he could to supervise the contractor to ensure that he did a good job.[7]

Negligence and damage

It is often said that 'damage is the gist of negligence' – that is, A will not commit the tort of negligence in relation to B by acting in some way unless B suffers some kind of harm as a result of A's actions. It seems to us that those who hold this view mix up two separate questions. First, when will someone commit the tort of negligence? Secondly, when will the victim of negligence be entitled to obtain a remedy in respect of that negligence?

Negligence is one of those torts (like slander, in most of its forms) where the courts will only give a remedy to the victim of that tort if he has actually suffered some harm as a result of that tort being committed. So if A has breached a duty of care owed to B, B will only be entitled to obtain a remedy in respect of A's conduct if she has suffered some kind of harm

[6] Cf. *New South Wales* v *Lepore* (2003) 212 CLR 511, at [162] (per McHugh J): '[a claimant] may, if he or she chooses, sue in negligence for the intentional infliction of harm'; also *Blake* v *Galloway* [2004] 1 WLR 2844, at [17] (per Dyson LJ): 'If the defendant . . . [had] deliberately aimed the piece of bark at the claimant's head, then [the claimant might have been able to sue the defendant in negligence].'

[7] See below, pp. 230–6.

as a result of A's breach. But whether or not she is entitled to obtain a remedy against A in respect of A's conduct has no bearing on whether or not A committed a tort in relation to her in acting as he did. We would say that when A breached the duty of care he owed B he committed the tort of negligence in relation to B – the issue of whether A's breach resulted in B suffering some kind of harm is only relevant to the question of whether B will be entitled to obtain a remedy in respect of A's breach.[8]

[8] Goldberg & Zipursky 2002 take a different view, arguing that the reason why negligence is only actionable on proof of loss is that if A owes B a duty of care of some description, A will not usually breach that duty if he is merely careless – A will only breach that duty if his carelessness results in B's suffering some kind of harm. See ibid., at 1652: 'The duty of care owed in most cases of actionable negligence is a duty to take care to avoid causing an ultimate harm . . . not a duty to take care to avoid [exposing someone to a] heightened risk [of suffering harm]. It is a duty to take care not to injure, rather than a duty to take care not to engage in . . . conduct that risks causing an ultimate injury . . .' We disagree. It seems to us that there are at least two problems with this view. (1) It seems likely that the fact that negligence is only actionable on proof of loss has more to do with historical accident (see above, p. 14, n. 3) than a point of principle about the nature of the duties of care we owe each other. (2) Goldberg & Zipursky concede that not all of the duties of care that we owe each other conform to their analysis – but why then should we accept that *any* of the duties of care that we owe each other conform to their analysis? They cannot argue that their analysis should be accepted because that accounts for why negligence is only actionable on proof of loss, because then their argument becomes circular. In effect, they would be arguing that the reason why negligence is only actionable on proof of loss is that most of the duties of care we owe each other are only breached when loss is suffered; and the proof that most of the duties of care we owe each other are only breached when loss is suffered is that negligence is only actionable on proof of loss.

4 Duties of care: an introduction

If we want to establish that A has committed the tort of negligence, the very first thing we have to show is that A owed someone else a duty of care.[1] How do we do this? What approach we adopt to this question will depend on whether A's case is a 'settled' case or a 'novel' case. A's case will be 'settled' if the decided cases or in-force statutes have already established whether or not a duty of care was owed in his case. A's case will be 'novel' if the decided cases or in-force statutes have not dealt with the issue of whether or not a duty of care was owed in his case.

THE APPROACH IN SETTLED CASES

In a settled case, one simply looks to the decided cases and in-force statutes to determine what they have to say about whether or not a duty of care was owed in that case. We say 'simply' but, in fact, it can be very difficult to determine what a given case establishes as to when a duty of care will be owed and when a duty of care will not be owed.[2]

Take, for example, the case of *Costello* v *Chief Constable of the Northumbria Police*.[3] In that case, the claimant was a woman police officer. She took a prisoner down to the cells at a police station. One Sergeant Hall accompanied her, just in case the prisoner attempted to attack the claimant. When they reached the cell area, Hall saw that there was a police inspector, an Inspector Bell, in attendance there. Thinking that Bell would intervene if there was any trouble, Hall went back upstairs. The prisoner then attacked the claimant and Bell did nothing to assist the claimant. The claimant sued the defendant chief constable for compensation, claiming that Bell breached a duty of care owed to the claimant when he failed to go to the claimant's assistance and that the defendant was vicariously liable in respect of Bell's negligence. The claimant won at first instance and the defendant appealed,

1 *Important note*. If you have occasion to consider whether a claimant can sue a defendant in negligence we would recommend that you characterise the duty of care that the defendant might have owed the claimant and breached in quite narrow terms. For example, suppose that Nita threw a snowball at Ian and it hit him in the face. Ian was injured as a result because a small stone had got caught up in the snowball when it was being made and the stone scratched Ian's face when the snowball hit him. Can Ian sue Nita in negligence? One *could* approach this issue by asking: (1) Did Nita owe Ian a duty to take care not to injure him? and (2) If so, did Nita breach this duty? But this would be inadvisable – the duty of care that Nita is supposed to have owed Ian and breached has been characterised at such a general level that it is hard to determine whether or not Nita did owe Ian such a duty and even if one can tell this, establishing a breach of the duty will involve a lot of work as well. Far better to ask: (1) Did Nita owe Ian a duty to take care not to throw a snowball at him which contained a small stone? and (2) If so, did Nita breach this duty? These questions are far easier to handle. As we will see, Nita *will* have owed Ian a duty to take care not to throw a snowball at him which contained a small stone: see below, pp. 73–4. But whether or not Nita breached the duty will depend on the particular circumstances of the case.

2 See, in addition to the text below, Stone 1946's discussion (at 187–8) of what the House of Lords' decision in *Donoghue* v *Stevenson* [1932] AC 562 established.

3 [1999] 1 All ER 550.

claiming that Bell had not owed the claimant a duty to take reasonable steps to save her from being attacked. The Court of Appeal found for the claimant. They held that Bell *had* owed the claimant a duty of care.

Now – what does this case establish? To answer that question, we need to know *why* the court found that Bell owed the claimant a duty of care. If the court found that Bell owed the claimant a duty of care because facts XYZ were established, then the decision in *Costello* indicates that one person will owe another a duty of care in a situation where facts XYZ hold true. However, the judgments in *Costello* do not make it clear *why* the court found that Bell owed the claimant a duty of care. May LJ handed down the only substantial judgment. He indicated that Bell owed the claimant a duty to take reasonable steps to save her from being attacked because he 'assumed a responsibility' to the claimant.[4] But the phrase 'assumed a responsibility' is so vague that the bare statement 'Bell owed the claimant a duty of care because he assumed a responsibility to her' tells us hardly anything about *why* Bell owed the claimant a duty of care.

So, if we want to know why the court found that Bell owed the claimant a duty of care in this case, we are going to have to make an educated guess. Suppose we reassemble the panel of legal scholars that we met in Chapter 3 to help us with this question. The discussion between them as to why Bell owed the claimant a duty of care in *Costello* might well go as follows:

> *John*: I can't see a problem with this case. Bell clearly owed the claimant a duty of care in *Costello* because he was a policeman and as such he had a responsibility to stop the criminal assault to which the claimant was subjected.
>
> *Paul*: No – that's too wide. Why would the court have placed such emphasis on what Bell *did* in finding that he owed the claimant a duty of care, if he owed her that duty of care simply because he was a policeman? The truth is, Bell owed the claimant a duty of care because he indicated to the claimant that she could rely on him to save her if she were attacked and she, in turn, probably relied on him by dropping her guard a bit.
>
> *Mary*: I agree with Paul that John's interpretation of the case is too wide, but Paul's explanation is just fantasy – there is no evidence in the case that the claimant dropped her guard or was even aware of Bell's presence in the room. The truth is, Bell owed the claimant a duty of care because they were both police officers, and police officers have a responsibility to go to each other's assistance if they are attacked. Otherwise, police officers will not be sure that they can depend on each other in going into dangerous situations and the efficacy of police operations will be substantially impaired.
>
> *Eric*: I agree with Mary that Paul's explanation is untenable; but I think Mary and John are making a mistake in thinking that Bell's status as a policeman was crucial to the finding of a duty of care here. The reason why Bell owed the claimant a duty of care here goes as follows. When the claimant walked down to the cells, Hall was ready to intervene if the claimant was attacked. But then Bell encouraged Hall to go back upstairs, thus depriving the claimant of her 'bodyguard'. As a result, Bell had a duty to go to the claimant's assistance if she was attacked.
>
> *Beth*: I agree with Eric that Mary and John are placing too much weight on Bell's status as a policeman. But the trouble with Eric's explanation is that Bell didn't really encourage Hall to go back upstairs; he merely *allowed* Hall to go back upstairs. I think we have to acknowledge that the real reason Bell was held to owe the claimant a duty of care here is that he was in a position to help her; the court, in finding a duty of care here, was simply giving effect to the moral principle that if you are in a position to help someone in need, you should.

[4] Ibid., 564.

Ruth: You're all wrong. The mistake you're all making is to focus on one or two elements in the factual matrix presented by the *Costello* case and say – *that's* the reason why the court found that a duty of care was owed in this case. So John focuses on the fact that Bell was a policeman and a criminal assault took place. Paul focuses on the fact of a possible understanding that existed between Bell and the claimant. Mary focuses on the fact that Bell and the claimant were both police officers. Eric focuses on the fact that had it not been for Bell's actions (or, as Beth points out, non-actions), Hall would have gone to the claimant's assistance. And Beth focuses on the fact that Bell was in a position to save the claimant. In truth, *all* these facts probably played a part in the court's decision in *Costello* to find that Bell owed the claimant a duty of care. Had any one of these facts not been present, then the decision may well have been different.

All these explanations of why the court in *Costello* found that a duty of care was owed in that case give rise to different accounts as to what the decision in *Costello* establishes.

On John's view, *Costello* establishes that if B is being beaten up and A, a police officer, comes on the scene, A will owe B a duty to take reasonable steps to rescue him.

On Paul's view, *Costello* establishes that if A indicates to B that he can be safely relied upon to go to her assistance if needs be, and B does so rely on A, A will owe B a duty to take reasonable steps to go to B's assistance if B needs such assistance.

On Mary's view, *Costello* establishes that if A and B are both police officers, and B is in some kind of danger, and A is in a position to help, A will owe B a duty to go to B's assistance.

On Eric's view, *Costello* establishes that if B is in some kind of danger and A discourages a third party from going to B's assistance, then A will owe B a duty to take reasonable steps to rescue B.

On Beth's view, *Costello* establishes that if B is in some kind of danger and A is in a position to help B, then A will owe B a duty to go to her assistance.

Finally, on Ruth's view, *Costello* simply establishes that in the factual situation presented in *Costello*, a duty of care will be owed.

So – just one case like *Costello* can give rise to (at least) six different accounts as to what that case establishes as to when one person will owe another a duty of care.[5] The same is true of a lot of 'no duty' cases – that is, cases in which it was held that no duty of care was owed. It can be very difficult to tell exactly what such cases establish as to when one person will *not* owe another a duty of care. Take, for example, the case of *Hill* v *Chief Constable of West Yorkshire*.[6] That case concerned a young woman, Jacqueline Hill, who was murdered by the serial killer, Peter Sutcliffe (otherwise known as the 'Yorkshire Ripper'). Jacqueline Hill's parents blamed the West Yorkshire police force for her death. They thought that if the police had been more effective in investigating Sutcliffe's earlier killings, he would have been arrested and jailed long before he killed Jacqueline Hill. So Jacqueline Hill's parents sued the police, claiming that they had owed Jacqueline Hill a duty to carry out their investigations into the Yorkshire Ripper killings with reasonable skill and care, and that Jacqueline Hill had died as a result of the police's breach of that duty of care.

[5] This is not to say that all these accounts are equally valid. Paul's explanation of the *Costello* case does seem far-fetched and John and Beth's explanations do seem to run counter to the tenor of May LJ's judgment in *Costello*.

[6] [1989] AC 53.

The House of Lords held that the police had *not* owed Jacqueline Hill a duty of care in investigating the Yorkshire Ripper killings. Lord Keith of Kinkel gave the leading judgment. Here are some excerpts from his judgment:

> The question of law which is opened up by the case is whether the individual members of a police force, in the course of carrying out their functions of controlling and keeping down the incidence of crime, owe a duty of care to individual members of the public who may suffer injury to person or property through the activities of criminals, such as to result in liability in damages, on the ground of negligence, to anyone who suffers such injury by reason of breach of that duty . . . [A] chief officer of police has a wide discretion as to the manner in which the duty is discharged. It is for him to decide how available resources should be deployed, whether particular lines of inquiry should or should not be followed and even whether or not certain crimes should be prosecuted. It is only if his decision upon such matters is such as no reasonable chief officer of police would arrive at that someone with an interest to do so may be in a position to have recourse to judicial review. So the common law, while laying upon chief officers of police an obligation to enforce the law, makes no specific requirements as to the manner in which the obligation is to be discharged. That is not a situation where there can readily be inferred an intention of the common law to create a duty towards individual members of the public . . .[7]
>
> It has been said almost too frequently to require repetition that foreseeability of likely harm is not in itself a sufficient test of liability in negligence. Some further ingredient is invariably needed to establish the requisite proximity of relationship between plaintiff and defendant, and all the circumstances of the case must be carefully considered and analysed in order to ascertain whether such an ingredient is present. . . .[8]
>
> It is plain that vital characteristics which . . . led to the imposition of liability [in the case of *Dorset Yacht* v *Home Office* [1970] AC 1004, where the Home Office was held liable in negligence for carelessly allowing some Borstal boys to escape custody with the result that – in an attempt to escape the island they were on – they commandeered a yacht belonging to the claimant and crashed it] are here lacking. Sutcliffe was never in the custody of the police force. Miss Hill was one of a vast number of the female general public who might be at risk from his activities but was at no special distinctive risk in relation to them . . . Miss Hill cannot . . . be regarded as a person at special risk simply because she was young and female . . . The conclusion must be that although there existed reasonable foreseeability of likely harm to such as Miss Hill if Sutcliffe were not identified and apprehended, there is absent from the case any such ingredient or characteristic as led to the liability of the Home Office in the Dorset Yacht case. Nor is there present any additional characteristic such as might make up the deficiency. The circumstances of the case are therefore not capable of establishing a duty of care owed towards Miss Hill by the West Yorkshire Police.[9]
>
> That is sufficient for the disposal of the appeal. But in my opinion there is another reason why an action for damages in negligence should not lie against the police in circumstances such as those of the present case, and that is public policy. . . . The general sense of public duty which motivates police forces is unlikely to be appreciably reinforced by the imposition of such liability so far as concerns their function in the investigation and suppression of crime. . . . In some instances the imposition of liability may lead to the exercise of a function being carried on in a detrimentally defensive frame of mind. The possibility of this happening in relation to the investigative operations of the police cannot be excluded. Further it would be reasonable to expect that if potential liability were to be imposed it would be not uncommon for actions to be raised against police forces on the ground that they had failed to catch some criminal as soon as they might have done, with the result that he went on to commit further crimes. While some such actions might involve

[7] Ibid., 59.
[8] Ibid., 60.
[9] Ibid., 62.

> allegations of a simple and straightforward type of failure – for example that a police officer negligently tripped and fell while pursuing a burglar – others would be likely to enter deeply into the general nature of a police investigation, as indeed the present action would seek to do. The manner of conduct of such an investigation must necessarily involve a variety of decisions to be made on matters of policy and discretion, for example as to which particular line of inquiry is most advantageously to be pursued and what is the most advantageous way to deploy the available resources. Many such decisions would not be regarded by the courts as appropriate to be called in question, yet elaborate investigation of the facts might be necessary to ascertain whether or not this was so. A great deal of police time, trouble and expense might be expected to have to be put into the preparation of the defence to the action and the attendance of witnesses at the trial. The result would be a significant diversion of police manpower and attention from their most important function, that of the suppression of crime.[10]

So – what does this case establish as to when one person will *not* owe someone else a duty of care? Let's reassemble three members of our panel of legal scholars to find out:

> *John*: It's very simple. *Hill* tells us that if the police are investigating a crime, they won't owe anyone a duty of care to catch the criminal who committed the crime.
>
> *Paul*: No – yet again you are taking a too simplistic view of the law. I think we need to distinguish between two kinds of cases. The first are cases where the police fail to catch a criminal because they have made an error of judgment – for example, they failed to catch a criminal because they did not devote enough resources to pursuing a particular lead. The second are cases where the police fail to catch a criminal because they have made an operational error – for example, they failed to catch a criminal because an operator failed to log a particular call that gave the police a valuable lead. *Hill* plainly indicates that the police will not owe anyone a duty of care not to make the first kind of mistake; but the question of whether the police might owe someone a duty of care not to make the second kind of mistake is left open by *Hill*.
>
> *Mary*: I think I agree with Paul, subject to one qualification. It's plain from Lord Keith's judgment that even in a case of operational error, the police will not have owed a duty of care to someone who was affected by that error unless the police knew that that kind of person was peculiarly likely to be harmed if the police made an operational error in investigating a particular kind of crime.
>
> *John*: What are you talking about? Lord Keith couldn't have been clearer that no duty of care would be owed either in the case of an error of judgment or in the case of an operational error. After all, he did mention a policeman negligently tripping and falling while chasing a burglar as an example of the sort of case where he did not think the police could be sued in negligence.
>
> *Mary*: But that was in the final section of his judgment where he said that no duty should be found in *Hill* because of the adverse effect such a finding might have on the police's ability to do their job. I'm sure Lord Keith would have agreed that if it could be clearly and quickly established in a given case that there was a clear operational error by the police, then there could be no policy objection to finding that the police were under a duty of care not to make such an error.

So there are at least three different readings of what a 'no duty' case like *Hill* establishes as to when one person will *not* owe someone else a duty of care.

So even in a settled case, there will often be room for debate between different people as to what the decided cases and in-force statutes say as to whether or not a duty of care was owed in that case, with the result that one lawyer will contend with utter conviction that the decided cases and in-force statutes establish that a duty of care *was* owed in that case, while another lawyer will argue with equal conviction that the decided cases and in-force statutes establish that a duty of care was *not* owed in that case.

[10] Ibid., 63.

Indeed, there will be times when there is room for debate as to whether a given case – say, the case of *Jones* v *Smith* – is a settled case or a novel case. One lawyer – let's call him Crusty – might take a very crabbed view as to what the decided cases establish as to when a duty of care will, and will not, be owed to another and as a result think that the decided cases and in-force statutes do not have anything to say as to whether or not a duty of care was owed in *Jones* v *Smith*. So Crusty will think that *Jones* v *Smith* is a novel case. Another lawyer – let's call him Hercules – might take a very expansive view as to what the decided cases establish as to when a duty of care will, and will not, be owed to another. Hercules will almost invariably argue that the decided cases and in-force statutes provide us with ample resources to decide whether or not a duty of care was owed in *Jones* v *Smith*. He will therefore think that *Jones* v *Smith* is a settled case.

We take the same view as Hercules. At the time of writing – late 2007 – there are simply so many cases on when one person will, and will not, owe another a duty of care that it is difficult to think of a genuinely novel case – that is, a situation where the decided cases and in-force statutes have absolutely *nothing* to say as to whether or not a duty of care was owed in that case. The next section of this chapter – which deals with how to find out whether or not a duty of care was owed in a novel case – is therefore of little practical interest. This is especially true of student readers of this book, who are highly unlikely ever to be asked in their exams to give an opinion on whether a duty of care was owed in a genuinely novel case. However, the following section *must* still be read by anyone interested in learning about the law of negligence. This is because all the decided cases that fill the law reports and tell us when one person will, and will not, owe another a duty of care were – at the time they were decided – novel cases. They were all cases where – at the time they were decided – it had not yet been settled whether or not a duty of care was owed in those cases.[11] So reading the next section will help you understand *why* those cases were decided the way they were.

THE APPROACH IN NOVEL CASES

For the sake of argument, let us assume that the following is a genuinely novel case: John constantly truanted from school and, as a result, he left school with no qualifications and few prospects. He now wants to sue the school authorities in negligence for compensation, claiming that they failed to take reasonable steps to stop him truanting and that had they done so, he would have done much better at school than he did and would now therefore have much better prospects than he does. So – did the school authorities owe John a duty to take reasonable steps to stop him truanting from school? As we are assuming this is a genuinely novel case, we must assume that the decided cases and in-force statutes do not have anything to say – one way or the other – on whether the authorities owed John a duty of care in this case. It has long been accepted that this fact is not necessarily fatal to John's claim. As Lord Wilberforce observed in *Anns* v *Merton LBC*, 'in order to establish that a duty of care arises in a particular situation, it is not

[11] If it had been clear at the time whether or not a duty of care was owed in that case, the issue of whether or not a duty of care was owed in that case would hardly have gone to court.

necessary to bring the facts of that situation within those of previous situations in which a duty of care has been held to exist'.[12]

The rise and fall of the *Anns* test

In the *Anns* case Lord Wilberforce went on to suggest a *two-stage test* that could be used to determine whether a duty of care was owed in a novel case such as John's. First, one would ask: Was it *reasonably foreseeable* that John would suffer some kind of harm if the authorities did not take reasonable steps to see that he did not truant from school? If the answer is 'no' then no duty of care was owed in the case we are considering. If the answer is 'yes', one then asks: Are there any reasons of *public policy* why we should *not* say that the school authorities owed John a duty to take reasonable steps to see that he did not truant from school? This time, if the answer is 'yes' then the authorities did *not* owe John a duty of care. But if the answer is 'no' then, under the *Anns* two-stage test for determining whether a duty of care was owed in a novel case, the school authorities *did* owe John a duty to take reasonable steps to see that he did not truant from school.

While the *Anns* two-stage test for determining whether a duty of care was owed in a novel case proved initially popular with the courts, it has now been disowned, largely thanks to the efforts of Lord Keith of Kinkel.[13] This was for two reasons. First, the two-stage test made the law on when one person will owe another a duty of care too uncertain. Secondly, the courts were too ready to find that the second stage of the two-stage test was satisfied in a given case. As a result there was a danger that the courts would find that one person owed another a duty of care in a given situation using the *Anns* two-stage test even though it was contrary to the public interest for them to find that such a duty of care was owed. In response to these concerns, the courts suggested a number of modifications that could be made to the *Anns* two-stage test for determining whether a duty of care was owed in a 'novel' case. Finally, in *Caparo Industries plc* v *Dickman*, the House of Lords adopted a new, *three-stage*, test for determining whether one person owed another a duty of care in a novel case.[14] This test has been used ever since by courts in England to determine whether one person owed another a duty of care in a novel case.[15]

The *Caparo* test[16]

The *Caparo* test for determining whether or not a duty of care was owed in a novel case such as John's works as follows. First, we ask: Was it *reasonably foreseeable* that John would suffer some kind of harm if the authorities did not take reasonable steps to see that he did

[12] [1978] AC 728, 751–2. See also *Donoghue* v *Stevenson* [1932] AC 562, at 619 (per Lord Macmillan): 'The categories of negligence are never closed.'

[13] Lord Keith criticised the *Anns* two-stage test in: *Peabody Donation Fund* v *Sir Lindsay Parkinson & Co. Ltd* [1985] AC 210, 240–1; *Yuen Kun Yeu* v *Att-Gen for Hong Kong* [1988] AC 175, 190–4; *Rowling* v *Takaro Properties Ltd* [1988] AC 473, 501; and *Hill* v *Chief Constable of West Yorkshire* [1989] AC 53, 60.

[14] [1990] 2 AC 605, 617–18 (per Lord Bridge of Harwich).

[15] The *Anns* test still enjoys some popularity in other common law jurisdictions: see, for example, the Supreme Court of Canada's decision in *Cooper* v *Hobart* [2001] 3 SCR 537 (noted, Neyers 2002). However, the version of the *Anns* test employed in *Cooper* v *Hobart* is so attenuated that it looks very much like the *Caparo* test.

[16] See Morgan 2006.

not truant from school? If the answer is 'yes' we then ask: Was there are a relationship of *proximity* between John and the school authorities at the time John was truanting from school? If the answer is 'yes' we then ask: Would it be *fair, just and reasonable* to find that the school authorities owed John a duty to take reasonable steps to see that he did not truant from school? If the answer is 'yes' then the school authorities did indeed owe John a duty to take reasonable steps to see that he did not truant from school. If, on the other hand, the answer to *any* of these three questions is 'no' then the school authorities did *not* owe John any such duty of care.

It is doubtful whether the second stage of the *Caparo* three-stage test for determining whether someone owed another a duty of care in a 'novel' case serves any useful purpose. To see why, consider John's case. Now: under the *Caparo* test, the authorities will only have owed John a duty to take reasonable steps to see that he did not truant from school if there was a relationship of 'proximity' between them. However, it is hard to imagine that any court would deny that there was a relationship of 'proximity' between John and the school authorities *if* it was reasonably foreseeable that John would suffer some kind of harm if the authorities did not take reasonable steps to see that he did not truant from school *and* it would be 'fair, just and reasonable' to find that the authorities owed John a duty to take reasonable steps to see that he did not truant from school. In other words, it is hard to imagine that any court would deny that the *second* stage of the three-stage *Caparo* test for determining whether the school authorities owed John a duty of care has been satisfied if the *first and third* stages of that three-stage test have been satisfied.

This impression is strengthened when one looks at the cases in which the courts have denied that one person owed another a duty of care under the *Caparo* test on the ground that there was no relationship of 'proximity' between the two parties. In all these cases, as Lord Oliver of Aylmerton observed in *Caparo Industries plc* v *Dickman* itself, the finding that there was no relationship of proximity between the defendant and the claimant 'can most rationally be attributed to the court's view that it would not be fair and reasonable to hold the defendant responsible'.[17] So it seems that the second stage of the *Caparo* three-stage test for determining whether one person owed another a duty of care in a 'novel' case is redundant: the second stage of the three-stage test will always be satisfied if the first and third stages of the three-stage test are satisfied.[18] If this is right, then the *Caparo* test for determining whether one person owed another a duty of care in a novel case really amounts *in substance* to a *two-stage* test. If we want to apply the *Caparo* test to determine whether the school authorities owed John a duty to take reasonable steps to see that he did not truant from school, all we *really* have to do is ask is: (*a*) Was it reasonably foreseeable that John would suffer some kind of harm if the authorities did not take reasonable steps to see that he did not truant from school; *and* (*b*) Would it be 'fair, just and reasonable' to find that the authorities owed John a duty to take reasonable steps to see that he did not

17 [1990] 2 AC 605, 633.

18 Indeed, in some cases, the second stage of the three-stage test will be satisfied if only the *first* stage of the three-stage test is satisfied. See, for example, Mann LJ's observation in *The Nicholas H* [1994] 1 WLR 1071, at 1085–6, that he was 'content to assume that the foreseeability of damage to the [claimants'] cargo [if the defendants failed to take care that they did not certify the ship carrying the claimants' cargo was seaworthy when it was not] was sufficient to constitute "a relationship of proximity" between them and the [defendants].'

truant from school? If the answer to both questions is 'yes' then the authorities *will* have owed John a duty of care under the *Caparo* test.[19]

As we have seen, all this is of little practical interest to student readers of this book, who will rarely – if ever – be called upon to apply the *Caparo* test to determine whether a duty of care was owed in a concrete situation. However, looking at the *Caparo* test for determining whether or not a duty of care was owed in a novel case does highlight one important point about the law on when one person will, and will not, owe another a duty of care. The decided cases that deal with this issue reflect the courts' evolving notions of when it would be fair, just and reasonable to find that one person owed another a duty of care. As we shall see below, even in a case – such as the *Palsgraf* case[20] – where a court refused to find that A owed B a duty of care because it was not reasonably foreseeable that B would suffer any harm as a result of A's actions, the court's *real* reason for refusing to find that a duty of care was owed in that case was that it would not be fair, just and reasonable to find that a duty of care was owed in that case. Similarly, in a case – such as the *Hill* case – where a court refused to find that A owed B a duty of care because there was no relationship of 'proximity' between the parties, the court's *real* reason for refusing to find that A owed B a duty of care will have been its perception that it would only be fair, just and reasonable to find that A owed B a duty of care if there existed a 'special relationship' between them, and as there was no 'special relationship' between them – no 'proximity' between them – it would not be fair, just and reasonable to find a duty of care here.

So what sort of factors will the courts take into account in deciding whether or not it would be 'fair, just and reasonable' to find that a duty of care was owed in a particular case? This is a list of the more important factors:[21]

Reasonable foreseeability of harm

As has just been observed, the courts will not find that A owed B a duty of care if it was not reasonably foreseeable that B would be affected by A's actions. This is because the law of negligence would become unduly uncertain if it simply said, 'You must not do *x* if someone somewhere will be harmed by your doing *x*.' If the law did say this then A would never know whether he was allowed to do *x* or not because he could never be certain whether or not someone somewhere would be harmed as a result of his doing *x*. Happily, the law does not say this. Instead, the law of negligence allows A to do *x* if it is not reasonably foreseeable that someone else will be harmed by A's doing *x*. So if A wants to know whether he is allowed to do *x*, all he has to do is take reasonable steps to check and see if anyone will be harmed by his doing *x*, and if it does not look as though anyone will be, he will know he is free to go ahead and do *x*.

Reasonableness

The law of negligence does not stop people acting reasonably, and it does not compel people to act unreasonably. So the courts will not find that A owed B a duty of care not to

[19] Compare: suppose there exists a rule that X will be true if A, B and C are true. If B will always be true if A and C are true, then if we want to know whether X is true all we have to do is ask: (*a*) Is A true? and (*b*) Is C true? If the answer to both questions is 'yes' then X will be true.

[20] Discussed above, pp. 20–1.

[21] See also Stapleton 1998.

act in a particular way if it was reasonable for A to act in that way; nor can A be said to have owed B a duty of care to act in a particular way if it would have been unreasonable for A to act in that way.

For example, in *Tomlinson* v *Congleton BC*,[22] the defendant local council maintained a park in which there was a lake, surrounded by some sandy beaches. The beaches were very popular and would attract as many as 2,000 sunbathers and picnickers a day during the summer. Swimming in the lake was not allowed because of the dangers involved and there were lots of notices around the lake telling people using the beaches that swimming was not allowed. The claimant ignored these notices and dived into the lake. Unfortunately, he hit his head on the bottom of the lake and was paralysed from the neck down. The claimant sought to argue that the defendant council had owed him a duty to do more than it had done to discourage him from swimming in the lake – and that he had been paralysed because the council had breached that duty. But what more could the council have done to stop the claimant swimming in the lake? The answer was: turn the beaches around the lake into marshland so no right-thinking person would want to go anywhere near the lake. The House of Lords rejected in the strongest terms the idea that the council had owed the claimant a duty to do something so ridiculous:[23]

> [I]t is not, and should never be, the policy of the law to require the protection of the foolhardy or reckless few to deprive, or interfere with, the enjoyment by the remainder of society of the liberties and amenities to which they are rightly entitled. Does the law require that all trees be cut down because some youths may climb them and fall? Does the law require the coastline and other beauty spots to be lined with warning notices? Does the law require that attractive waterside picnic spots be destroyed because of a few foolhardy individuals who choose to ignore warning notices and indulge in activities dangerous only to themselves? The answer to all these questions is, of course, no . . . In truth, the arguments for the claimant have involved an attack upon the liberties of the citizen which should not be countenanced. They attack the liberty of the individual to engage in dangerous, but otherwise harmless, pastimes at his own risk and the liberty of citizens as a whole fully to enjoy the variety and quality of the landscape of this country.[24]

Again, suppose that Beth applies for a job at Paul's firm and she asks her former employer, Mary, to supply her with a reference. Mary tells Paul that while Beth worked for her, Beth was frequently disciplined for being late and for stealing items from the office. This was true. In light of this information, Paul turns Beth down for the job. Now – in this case it was plainly foreseeable that Beth would suffer economic loss (failing to get the job working for Paul) as a result of Mary's reference, but the fact that it was reasonable for Mary to tell Paul the truth about what had happened when Beth worked for her means that we cannot find that Mary owed Beth a duty of care not to damage Beth's job prospects in the way she did.[25]

[22] [2004] 1 AC 46.

[23] While almost everyone would think it completely mad to turn the beaches around the lake into marshland, it should be noted that at the time of the accident in *Tomlinson*, Congleton BC had put in place plans to do exactly that because of a fear that it might be sued by someone who swam in the lake and was injured as a result. It is very likely that by the time the *Tomlinson* case was heard by the House of Lords, the beaches had already been destroyed, completely unnecessarily.

[24] Ibid., at [81] (per Lord Hobhouse). See also [46] and [48] (per Lord Hoffmann).

[25] *Lawton* v *BOC Transhield* [1987] 2 All ER 608.

The distinction between acts and omissions

This distinction is of fundamental importance to the law on when one person will owe another a duty of care. For our purposes here, we can say that an 'act' makes someone else worse off. An 'omission' fails to make someone better off. So if Gary pushes Eric – a drunk – into a lake, that is an act. By pushing Eric into the lake Gary has made Eric worse off than he was before he was pushed into the lake. Now suppose that after Eric has been pushed into the lake, Lara comes along, sees that Eric is face down in the lake and is in danger of drowning, and she fails to fish him out of the lake. That is an omission. Lara has not made Eric worse off in any way by her actions. She has merely failed to make him better off.[26]

The courts are far more willing to find that a duty of care was owed in an 'act' case than in an 'omission' case. To put it another way, the courts are far more willing to find that A owed B a duty of care not to make B worse off than they are to find that A owed B a duty of care to make B better off. We will fully explore the reasons for this in Chapter 9, but for the time being it suffices to point out that a duty not to do *x* is far less intrusive on individual liberty (because it leaves the person subject to it free to do anything but *x*) than a duty to do *x* is (because the person subject to a duty to do *x* is not free to do anything except *x*). The courts will usually only find that A owed B a duty of care to make B better off in some way if there existed some kind of 'special relationship' between A and B. If there was not, they will usually deny that A owed B a duty of care on the ground that there was no 'proximity' between the parties. The *Hill* case is an example of this. In the *Hill* case, the police failed to make Jacqueline Hill better off – they failed to save her from being killed by Peter Sutcliffe. But as there existed no special relationship between Jacqueline Hill and the police, the House of Lords found that the police did not owe Jacqueline Hill a duty to take reasonable steps to catch Peter Sutcliffe before he could kill again. There was not a sufficient relationship of 'proximity' between them to warrant finding that a duty of care was owed.

Seriousness of harm

In an 'act' case, whether the courts are willing to find that A owed B a duty of care not to act as he did will turn on a number of factors. One of the most important is the seriousness of the harm that B stood to suffer if A acted as he did. If it was reasonably foreseeable that B would suffer *physical injury* or *damage to his property* as a result of A's actions, then the courts will readily find that A owed B a duty of care not to act as he did.

[26] *Important note.* There are some cases where the distinction between an act and an omission can be difficult to apply. Take the case – considered *obiter* in *Candler* v *Crane, Christmas & Co.* [1951] 2 KB 164, at 183 and 194 – of the marine hydrographer who omits a reef from a map of the seabed. A ship's captain, using the map, steers his ship in such a way that it collides with the reef. This looks like an omission case – the hydrographer failed to save the ship from colliding with the reef because he failed to alert the captain to the existence of the reef. If it is then the members of the Court of Appeal who considered this case in *Candler* were right to think that the hydrographer did not owe the ship's owner a duty of care in preparing his map of the seabed: there was no 'special relationship' between the two that would justify finding that a duty of care was owed. But we might be able to say that this case is an act case if, had the map not been drawn up, the ship's captain would have relied on his own eyes or other charts, spotted the reef and steered the ship clear of it. If this is the case, then we can say that the marine hydrographer made things worse by drawing up his map – had he not drawn up his map, the ship would not have been damaged. If this is the case, then it could be said that the hydrographer owed the ship's owner a duty of care in drawing up his map, even in the absence of a 'special relationship' between the two, under the 'property harm principle' discussed below, pp. 73–4.

If, on the other hand, it was *merely* foreseeable that B would suffer *economic loss* as a result of A's actions, the courts will not find that A owed B a duty of care not to act as he did. The loss that B stood to suffer if A acted as he did was not serious enough[27] to warrant the law's intervening to require A to look out for B's interests.[28] This is not to say that the courts will always refuse to find that A owed B a duty of care in a case where he did something that made B economically worse off. It is merely to say that the *mere* fact that it was reasonably foreseeable that B would lose money as a result of A's actions will not be enough to justify a finding that A owed B a duty of care. Something more will be required, such as the existence of a 'special relationship' between A and B.

Similarly, if the only loss that it could be foreseen that B would suffer as a result of A's actions was that B would suffer *distress*, the courts will not find that A owed B a duty of care not to act as he did unless there existed some kind of 'special relationship' between

[27] For an interesting argument that cases of someone's suffering pure economic losses are always more trivial than cases of someone's suffering property damage (because property is more important to our personalities than stocks of wealth), see Witting 2001.

[28] *Important note.* Cases where a duty of care was denied because the only ground for imposing it would have been that it was foreseeable that the defendant would suffer economic loss as a result of the claimant's actions include: *Cattle* v *Stockton Waterworks Co.* (1875) LR 10 QB 453 (no duty of care owed to contractors not to delay them in their work, thereby making their contract to do that work less profitable); *Simpson & Co.* v *Thomson* (1877) 3 App Cas 279 (no duty of care owed to insurer not to damage insured property); *Société Anonyme de Remourquage à Hélice* v *Bennetts* [1911] 1 KB 243 (no duty of care owed by defendants not to sink ship being towed by tug, thereby preventing the tug earning a fee for towing the ship); *Weller & Co.* v *Foot and Mouth Disease Research Institute* [1966] 1 QB 569 (virus causing foot and mouth disease escaped from defendants' premises and caused outbreak of foot and mouth disease in area with the result that claimants' business as cattle auctioneers was temporarily suspended; no duty of care not to release virus owed by defendants to claimants); *Candlewood Navigation Corporation Ltd* v *Mitsui OSK Lines Ltd, The Mineral Transporter* [1986] AC 1 (no duty of care owed to claimants not to damage ship which claimants did not have proprietary interest in but which the claimants had to pay hire for even if the ship was damaged); *Leigh & Sillavan Ltd* v *Aliakmon Shipping Co. Ltd, The Aliakmon* [1986] AC 785 (no duty of care owed to claimant not to damage goods which the claimant had contracted to pay for but which he had not yet acquired ownership or possession of); *Simaan General Contracting Co.* v *Pilkington Glass Ltd (No. 2)* [1988] QB 758 (job of constructing building in Saudi Arabia given to claimant; building was to include a green glass curtain wall and the job of constructing the wall was subcontracted to F; job of constructing the glass that would make up the wall was sub-subcontracted to defendant; defendant's glass panels were not the right shade of green with the result that the fee payable to the main contractor for constructing the building was reduced; held, that defendant had not owed the claimant a duty of care in constructing the panels); *CBS Songs* v *Amstrad Consumer Electronics plc* [1988] AC 1013 (no duty of care owed to claimant recording company whose royalties might be reduced as a result of defendants' marketing tape-to-tape recording machine which would allow illegal copies of cassette tapes to be made); *Van Oppen* v *Clerk to the Bedford Charity Trustees* [1990] 1 WLR 235 (no duty of care owed by school to pupil to arrange insurance on his behalf against his being injured playing rugby at the school); *Pacific Associates* v *Baxter* [1990] 1 QB 993 (no duty of care owed by engineers employed to judge whether contractors should be paid for the work they have done to use reasonable skill and care in making those judgments); *Islington LBC* v *University College London Hospital NHS Trust* [2005] EWCA Civ 596 (no duty of care owed to local authority that foreseeably would have to spend money providing residential care to person who suffered stroke as a result of defendant hospital's negligence); *WBA* v *El-Safty* [2005] EWHC 2866 (doctor does not owe football club a duty of care to treat one of their footballer's injuries properly); *Customs and Excise Commissioners* v *Barclays Bank* [2007] 1 AC 181 (where A is suing B and has obtained a 'freezing order' over B's bank account to stop B transferring money from the account out of the country and beyond A's reach, B's bank will not owe A a duty of care to stop B withdrawing money from his account). It is customary to mention, alongside these cases, cases such as *D & F Estates* v *Church Commissioners* [1989] AC 177 and *Murphy* v *Brentwood DC* [1991] 1 AC 398 (held in both cases, no action maintainable in negligence against builders of a dangerously defective house for the cost of repairing the defects in the building). However, in those cases a duty of care *was* owed (see below, pp. 73–4): the real significance of those cases was that they set a limit on the losses that someone would be liable for if he or she breached that duty of care. Those cases are therefore more appropriately dealt with in Part III of this book, which deals with the remedies that will be available when someone commits a tort. An explanation of the House of Lords' rulings in *D & F Estates* and *Murphy* is set out below, at pp. 518–19.

A and B.[29] The mere fact that it was reasonably foreseeable that B would suffer distress as a result of A's actions will not be enough to warrant finding that A owed B a duty of care not to act as he did.[30]

So – if Mary is driving down the road she will owe nearby pedestrians a duty of care not to drive dangerously because it is reasonably foreseeable that they will be physically injured if she does drive dangerously. She will not owe a nearby pedestrian's employer a duty of care not to drive dangerously. This is because the only loss that it is foreseeable the pedestrian's employer will suffer if Mary drives dangerously and runs down the pedestrian is economic loss – the disruption his business will suffer as a result of his employee being run down – and there exists no 'special relationship' between Mary and the employer that would tip the scales in favour of a finding that Mary owes the employer a duty of care not to drive dangerously. Similarly, Mary will not owe the nearby pedestrian's uncles and aunts a duty of care not to drive dangerously – the only loss that it is foreseeable they will suffer if she drives dangerously and runs down the pedestrian is distress.

Fairness

One factor that the courts will always take into account in determining whether a duty of care was owed in a given situation is the need to be 'fair'. 'Fairness' is a slippery term, but best encapsulates the reason why the courts will sometimes refuse to find that a duty of care was owed in a particular case if doing so might expose a defendant to a 'liability in an indeterminate amount for an indeterminate time to an indeterminate class'.[31] If there is a danger that finding that A owed B a duty of care will result in A's liability for the harm he caused B getting out of all proportion to his fault in causing that harm, the courts may well refuse to find that a duty of care was owed. For example, in *The Nicholas H*[32] a certification society certified that a ship was fit to sail when it was not. When the ship sank with all its cargo on board, the cargo owners sued the certification society in negligence for compensation for the loss of the cargo, claiming that the defendant had owed them a duty of care not to certify the ship as being fit to sail when it was not. The House of Lords held that the certification society had not owed a duty of care to the cargo owners. This was so even though *The Nicholas H* was an 'act' case (without the certificate from the certification society the ship could not have sailed, so issuing the certificate made the cargo owners worse off than they were before the certificate was issued) and it was plainly foreseeable that the cargo owners would suffer property damage if the ship was certified as being fit to sail when it was not. Part of the reason for denying that a duty of care was owed in this case may have been that if a duty of care was found in this case, the certification society's liability could have run into millions of pounds – depending on the value of the cargo on board the ship – and got out of all proportion to the society's initial fault in approving the ship as being fit to sail.

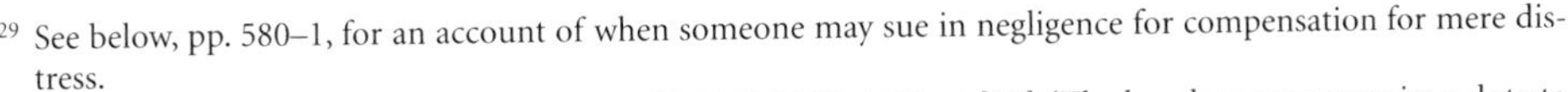

29 See below, pp. 580–1, for an account of when someone may sue in negligence for compensation for mere distress.

30 See *Rothwell* v *Chemical & Insulating Co. Ltd* [2006] 1 ICR 1458, at [63]: 'The law does not recognise a duty to take reasonable care not to cause anxiety.'

31 *Ultramares Corporation* v *Touche*, 174 NE 441 (1931), at 444, per Cardozo CJ.

32 [1996] AC 211.

Individual responsibility

If finding that a duty of care was owed in a particular case might tend to undermine people's sense of individual responsibility, then that is a factor which will weigh heavily (though not conclusively) against a finding that a duty of care was owed. There are two ways in which a finding of a duty of care might undermine people's sense of individual responsibility:

(1) *Spreading the blame for harm suffered by the claimant.* The first is where finding a duty of care might allow a responsible adult to escape some or all of the consequences of his own foolhardiness by giving him the right to sue someone else in negligence for compensation for self-inflicted injuries. We have already seen that the courts are usually unwilling to find that a responsible adult was owed a duty by a third party to stop him injuring himself.[33] For example, in *Vellino* v *Chief Constable of Greater Manchester Police*[34] the Court of Appeal held that the police had not owed a thief a duty to take reasonable steps to stop him harming himself in attempting to escape police custody. Similarly, in *Barrett* v *Ministry of Defence*,[35] a soldier died after he had too much to drink at a party held in his barracks. It was argued that the soldier's commanding officer owed the soldier a duty to take reasonable steps to ensure that he did not drink too much at the party. The Court of Appeal rejected this claim, holding that it would not be 'fair, just and reasonable' to find that the commanding officer had owed the soldier such a duty.[36]

(2) *Spreading the blame for harm suffered by someone else.* The second way in which finding that a duty of care was owed in a particular case might undermine people's sense of individual responsibility is if finding that a duty was owed might allow an admitted wrongdoer to use the law on contribution to make someone else bear some of the cost of compensating the victim of his wrong for the harm that he did her. For example, suppose Carl, a prison guard, rapes Mary, a female prisoner. Carl will be liable to pay Mary very substantial damages in such case. But Carl may claim that the prison authorities are liable, along with Carl, to compensate Mary for the harm she suffered as a result of being raped because she would not have been raped had the prison authorities not breached the duty of care they owed Mary to take reasonable steps to protect her from being raped by someone like Carl. If this were accepted, then Carl could make a claim in contribution against the prison authorities and make them bear some of the burden of compensating Mary for the harm she suffered as a result of being raped. As a result, Carl would be allowed to escape the full responsibility of compensating Mary for the harm he caused her. A concern not to allow this sort of thing to happen may account for why, in a case where A was harmed by B, and it is alleged that C was under a duty to take reasonable steps to save B from being harmed by A, the courts will refuse to find that such a duty was owed if B was not at 'special risk' of being harmed by someone like A.[37] The 'special risk' requirement helps ensure that C is

[33] See above, pp. 4–5.

[34] [2002] 1 WLR 218.

[35] [1995] 1 WLR 1217.

[36] However, once the soldier fell into a drunken stupor and the officers in charge undertook to look after him, they owed him a duty to look after him with a reasonable degree of care and skill: ibid., 1223. See below, p. 162.

[37] See below, pp. 165–6.

only held liable for the harm suffered by B in cases where C's blameworthiness for what happened to B is especially pronounced.

Parliament's intentions

The courts are subordinate to Parliament. It follows that the courts cannot find that A owes B a duty of care if to do so would undermine Parliament's intentions in passing a particular piece of legislation.

For example, imagine that Parliament placed the Identity and Passport Service (IPS, for short) under a statutory duty to process people's passport applications within eight weeks of their being submitted. Imagine also that Parliament provided that breach of this statutory duty should *not* be actionable in tort. So if B received a new passport 12 weeks after submitting her application for a new passport, she would *not* be able to bring an action for breach of statutory duty against the IPS. Could she instead argue that the IPS owed her a duty of care in negligence to process her application within eight weeks of its being submitted? The answer is, 'Without more – no. If the *only* basis for saying that the IPS owed B a duty of care in this case is the fact that it was under a statutory duty to process her application within eight weeks of its being submitted, then the courts cannot find that the IPS owed B a duty of care in processing her application.'

The reason why the courts cannot do this is that to do so would undermine Parliament's intention that the IPS's breach of statutory duty in B's case should not be actionable in tort. If the courts were to find that the IPS owed B a duty of care in processing her application based *only* on the fact that the IPS owed B a statutory duty to process her application speedily, then the courts would effectively be making the IPS's breach of statutory duty actionable in tort. The statutory duty that the IPS was under to process B's passport application speedily would give rise to a parallel duty of care, and B would be able to bring a claim in negligence against the IPS if the IPS breached its statutory duty to process her passport application speedily. It is for this reason that Lord Hoffmann, in particular, has repeatedly insisted that:

> If [a public authority's failure to perform a statutory] duty does not give rise to a private right to sue for breach, it would be unusual if it nevertheless gave rise to a duty of care at common law which made the public authority liable to pay compensation for foreseeable loss caused by the duty not being performed. It will often be foreseeable that loss will result if, for example, a benefit or a service is not provided. If the policy of the Act [imposing the statutory duty in question was] not to create a statutory liability to pay compensation, the same policy should ordinarily exclude the existence of a common law duty of care.[38]

The public interest

The courts will often refuse to find that a duty of care was owed in a specific case because

[38] *Stovin* v *Wise* [1996] AC 923, 952–3. See also Lord Hoffmann's judgments in *Gorringe* v *Calderdale MBC* [2004] 1 WLR 1057, at [23] ('If the statute does not create a private right of action, it would be, to say the least, unusual if the mere existence of the statutory duty could generate a common law duty of care'); and in *Customs and Excise Commissioners* v *Barclays Bank plc* [2007] 1 AC 181, at [39] ('you cannot derive a common law duty of care directly from a statutory duty'). To the same effect, see Lord Scott in *Gorringe* v *Calderdale MBC* [2004] 1 WLR 1057, at [71]: 'if a statutory duty does not give rise to a private right to sue for breach, the duty cannot create a duty of care that would not have been owed at common law if the statute were not there.'

doing so would harm the public interest. There are a number of different ways in which finding that a duty of care was owed in a given case might harm the public interest:

(1) *Overcautiousness*. First, finding that a duty of care was owed in a given case might cause a public body to become overcautious in discharging its functions. This is the reason why an officer will not owe a duty of care to the soldiers under his command in the heat of battle.[39] This is also the reason why, if the police suspect A of committing a crime, they will not owe A a duty of care in carrying out their investigations into whether or not he committed that crime.[40] If the police did owe A such a duty of care, they might become excessively cautious in charging him: they might only charge him when they were absolutely certain that there was no possibility that he might be innocent and therefore no possibility that he would ever have grounds to sue them.

A concern not to encourage overcautiousness by public bodies in the performance of their functions also caused the Court of Appeal to rule in *Harris* v *Evans*[41] that a health and safety inspector did *not* owe a duty of care to a claimant whose business was severely disrupted by the health and safety inspector making what turned out to be unjustified demands on the claimant. The Court of Appeal was fearful that if it found that health and safety inspectors owed duties of care to businesses affected by their findings and decisions, inspectors would – out of a desire to avoid being sued – become very cautious about making any decisions or findings that might adversely affect someone's business.[42] Similarly, in *D* v *East Berkshire Community NHS Trust*,[43] the House of Lords held that if the social services investigate allegations that A is abusing his children, the social services will *not* owe A a duty to carry out their investigations with a reasonable degree of care and skill.[44] Their Lordships feared that if the social services owed A such a duty of care, they would become excessively cautious about taking A's children into care, for fear that they might be sued by A if they made a mistake and took the children into care when they were not actually at risk.

In other cases, the courts have been unpersuaded that they should refuse to find that a duty of care was owed because (so it was claimed) finding that such a duty existed would make people working in the public interest excessively cautious in doing their jobs. For example, the courts have never hesitated to find that doctors owe duties of care to their patients in treating them, despite widely-expressed fears that doing so only encourages doctors to practise 'defensive medicine', giving patients excessive tests and treatments in an attempt to demonstrate publicly that everything has been done for the patient and avoid litigation.[45] Similarly, an argument that it would not be 'fair, just and reasonable' to find that firefighters owed owners of a property on fire a duty to take care not to make the fire

[39] See below, pp. 214–15.

[40] *Calveley* v *Chief Constable of Merseyside Police* [1989] AC 1228.

[41] [1998] 1 WLR 1285.

[42] Ibid., 1298 (per Sir Richard Scott V-C).

[43] [2005] 2 AC 373.

[44] The position is the same in Australia (*Sullivan* v *Moody* (2001) 207 CLR 562, at [62]) and New Zealand (*B* v *Attorney General* [2003] 4 All ER 833).

[45] American studies estimate the cost of defensive medicine in the United States as being in the tens of *billions* of dollars: see, for example, US Congress Office of Technology Assessment, *Defensive Medicine and Medical Malpractice*, OTA-H-602 (1994); Kessler & McClellan 1996.

worse because doing so would encourage firefighters to fight fires 'defensively' was rejected in *Capital & Counties plc* v *Hampshire CC*.[46]

Again, in *Spring* v *Guardian Assurance*,[47] the House of Lords dismissed fears that if they found that an employer will owe an ex-employee a duty to take care that he did not write the ex-employee an unfair reference, employers would become excessively cautious about saying anything negative about ex-employees in writing references for them – even though within the law of defamation, references are protected by qualified privilege precisely because it is feared that if they were not, referees would become unduly cautious about expressing themselves frankly in their references.[48] Finally, it used to be the law that a barrister would not owe a duty to his or her client to conduct that client's case in court with a reasonable degree of care and skill. One of the reasons for this was that it was feared that if barristers owed their clients such a duty of care, a desire to avoid 'the possibility of being sued in negligence would at least subconsciously lead some counsel to undue prolixity which would not only be harmful to [his or her] client but against the public interest in prolonging trials'.[49] However, the House of Lords in *Arthur J S Hall* v *Simons*[50] was less concerned about this and as a result swept away the no-duty rule in relation to barristers.

(2) *Diversion*. Finding that a duty of care was owed in a concrete case will harm the public interest if doing so will impede a public body from performing its primary function, and divert it into doing something else altogether. This is the reason why a judge deciding a civil case will not owe the parties to the case a duty to decide the case with a reasonable degree of care and skill.[51] The reason for this goes as follows:

> If we say that a judge deciding a civil case owes a duty to the parties in that case to decide the case with a reasonable degree of care and skill, then a judge in a civil case will decide that case with the threat hanging over him that if one of the parties to the case feels aggrieved by his judgment – and one of them always will – he might be sued by the aggrieved party. In order to avoid the threat of litigation, the judge may be tempted to ignore the law in deciding the case and instead attempt to 'split the difference' between the parties to the litigation in order to appease each of them. Or he might be tempted to avoid spelling out the reasons for his decision in too much detail so as to make it as difficult as possible for another court to find that he failed to decide the case with a reasonable degree of care and skill. It is obviously contrary to the public interest for judges to act in this way – but judges would be encouraged to act in this way if we found that a judge deciding a civil case owed a duty of care to the parties in that case.

Similarly, if A presents himself to the police as being a witness to a crime, the police will not owe A a duty of care to treat him properly as a witness, and a potential victim of crime.[52] If the police did owe crime witnesses such a duty of care, they might be encouraged to spend too much time interviewing witnesses and making sure that they were given

[46] [1997] QB 1004, 1043: 'It seems hardly realistic that a fire officer who has to make a split second decision as to the manner in which fire-fighting operations are to be conducted will be looking over his shoulder at the possibility of his employers being made vicariously liable for his negligence' (per Stuart-Smith LJ).

[47] [1995] 2 AC 296.

[48] For an account of the law on qualified privilege, see below, pp. 298–306.

[49] *Rondel* v *Worsley* [1969] 1 AC 191, 229 (per Lord Reid).

[50] [2002] 1 AC 615 (discussed, Seneviratne 2001).

[51] *Rondel* v *Worsley* [1969] 1 AC 191, 270 (per Lord Pearce); *Sirros* v *Moore* [1975] QB 118; *FM (a child)* v *Singer* [2004] EWHC 793.

[52] *Brooks* v *Commissioner of Police of the Metropolis* [2005] 1 WLR 1495.

adequate counselling and support instead of getting on with the job of investigating and solving crimes.

(3) *Waste of resources*. Finally, finding that a duty of care was owed in a concrete case will harm the public interest if doing so will encourage a lot of groundless litigation against a public body, which will take up valuable time and resources to fight. As we have seen, this was one of the reasons why, in the *Hill* case, the House of Lords thought that it would not be 'fair, just and reasonable' to find that the police owed potential victims of a criminal on the loose a duty to take reasonable steps to arrest him.[53] In other cases, this argument for finding that it would not be 'fair, just and reasonable' to find that one person will owe another a duty of care has been less successful. In *Phelps* v *London Borough of Hillingdon*, Lord Nicholls – with the agreement of Lord Jauncey of Tullichettle – suggested that the time had come to recognise that the teacher of a normal student will owe that student a duty to teach him with reasonable skill and care. He acknowledged some would be concerned that taking such a step would adversely affect the public interest:

> The principal objection [to recognising that the teacher of a normal student will owe that student a duty to teach him or her with a reasonable degree of care and skill] is the spectre of a rash of 'gold digging' actions brought on behalf of under-achieving children by discontented parents, perhaps years after the events complained of. If teachers are liable, education authorities will be vicariously liable, since the negligent acts and omissions were committed in the course of the teachers' employment. So, it is said, the limited resources of education authorities and the time of teaching staff will be diverted away from teaching and into defending unmeritorious legal claims. Further, schools will have to prepare and keep full records, lest they be unable to rebut negligence allegations, brought out of the blue years later. For one or more of these reasons [it is argued], the overall standard of education given to children is likely to suffer if a legal duty of care were held to exist.[54]

However, Lord Nicholls felt able to dismiss these concerns: 'I am not persuaded by these fears.'[55]

Novelty

The more novel a claim that a duty of care was owed in a particular case, the less likely it is that the courts will accept it. There are two reasons for this.

First of all, while the courts do sometimes act as legislators and create new law with their decisions, they do not like to advertise this fact for fear of attracting accusations that they are acting undemocratically and usurping the role of Parliament. So when the courts are invited in a particular case to create new law, they are unlikely to accept the invitation unless they can dress up the innovation that they will be introducing into the law as a marginal, or incremental, development of the existing law.

Secondly, just as Parliament can make mistakes in reforming the law, so can the courts. Indeed, the courts are more prone than Parliament in one respect to making mistakes in reforming the law. This is because when the courts are invited to reform the law in some way, they will often be unable to tell what the full effects will be of reforming the law in the

[53] See above, pp. 54–5.
[54] [2001] 2 AC 619, 667.
[55] Ibid.

way proposed. As a result, the courts will often find it difficult to tell whether a given reform of the law will be beneficial in the long run. Given this, the courts are rightly wary of using their powers to reform the law in radical ways, and are happier to make small changes in the law, where the effects of those changes can be more easily estimated and assessed.

The courts' unwillingness to develop the law on when one person will owe another a duty of care in radically new or unexpected directions was most memorably articulated by Brennan J, of the High Court of Australia, in *Sutherland Shire Council* v *Heyman*:

> It is preferable, in my view, that the law should develop novel categories of negligence incrementally and by analogy with established categories, rather than [as happened under the *Anns* two-stage test for finding a duty of care] by a massive extension of a prima facie duty of care restrained only by indefinable 'considerations which ought to negative, or to reduce or limit the scope of the duty of the class of the person to whom it is owed'.[56]

This *dictum* was subsequently referred to with approval by Lord Bridge in *Caparo Industries plc* v *Dickman*.[57] As a result of this, a lot of judges started to use an 'incremental test' to determine whether a duty of care was owed in a novel case. Under this test, the suggestion that a duty of care was owed in a novel case would be rejected unless it was possible to draw some analogy between that case and another case in which the existence of a duty of care had already been accepted.[58] However, this approach to determining whether a duty of care was owed in a novel case suffered from two problems. First of all, it placed too tight a constraint on the courts' ability to find a duty of care in a novel case. Secondly, as we saw with the conflict between Hercules and Crusty, above,[59] it is often arguable whether one case is genuinely analogous to another. For these reasons, in *Customs and Excise Commissioners* v *Barclays Bank plc*,[60] Lord Bingham dismissed the 'incremental test' for determining whether a duty of care was owed in a novel case as 'of little value as a test in itself'.[61]

It remains to be seen whether the *Customs and Excise Commissioners* case has killed off the 'incremental test' for determining whether a duty of care was owed in a novel case. However, the same case provides a great deal of support for Brennan J's view that the courts should be wary of making radical changes in the law on when one person will owe another a duty of care. So Lord Bingham conceded that, 'The closer the facts of the case in issue to those of a case in which a duty of care has been held to exist, the readier a court will be [to find a duty of care in the case in issue] . . . The converse is also true.'[62] And Lord Mance made it clear that he viewed 'incrementalism' as an 'important cross-check'[63] on finding a duty of care in a novel case, on the basis that 'caution and analogical reasoning are generally valuable accompaniments to judicial activity, and this is particularly true in the present area'.[64]

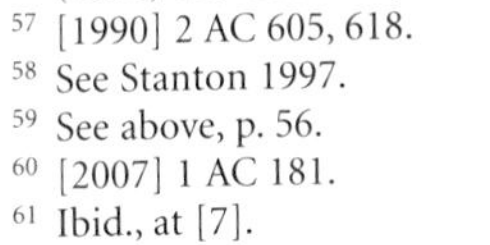

56 (1985) 127 CLR 424, 481.
57 [1990] 2 AC 605, 618.
58 See Stanton 1997.
59 See above, p. 56.
60 [2007] 1 AC 181.
61 Ibid., at [7].
62 Ibid., at [7].
63 Ibid., at [93].
64 Ibid., at [84].

The importance of remedying wrongs

In our list of factors that the courts will take into account in deciding whether A owed B a duty of care in a novel case, we have left to last a factor that some judges like to mention first in deciding whether a duty of care was owed in a novel case. This factor is: 'the rule of public policy that has first claim on the loyalty of the law: that wrongs should be remedied.'[65]

As a factor to be taken into account in judging whether A owed B a duty of care in a novel case, this is very puzzling. The very reason we want to know whether A owed B a duty of care is to find out whether or not A *wronged* B in acting as he did. So to say that one of the things we should take into account in judging whether A owed B a duty of care is the fact that A *did* wrong B, and that that wrong needs to be remedied by allowing B to sue A for damages, seems to be a fairly spectacular case of putting the cart before the horse. As Lord Rodger observed in the case of *D* v *East Berkshire Community NHS Trust*:[66]

> In [inquiring into whether a defendant owed a claimant a duty of care] I do not actually find it helpful to bear in mind – what is in any event obvious – that the public policy consideration which has first claim on the loyalty of the law is that wrongs should be remedied. Harm which constitutes a 'wrong' in the contemplation of the law must, of course, be remedied. But the world is full of harm for which the law furnishes no remedy. For instance, a trader owes no duty of care to avoid injuring his rivals by destroying their long-established businesses. If he does so and, as a result, one of his competitors descends into a clinical depression and his family are reduced to penury, in the eyes of the law they suffer no wrong and the law will provide no redress . . .

We agree, and do not think that this factor should play any part in a court's decision as to whether or not a duty of care was owed in a novel case.

Let's now go back to the case where John is suing his school for failing to take reasonable steps to stop him truanting. In the light of what has been said in the last few pages, would it be 'fair, just and reasonable' to find that a duty of care was owed in John's case? John's case is an 'omission' case – but that is no bar to a duty of care being found here as there was a 'special relationship' between John and the school here. Of course, it was foreseeable that John would merely suffer some kind of economic loss if he were allowed to carry on truanting and that fact on its own is not usually sufficient to ground a finding of a duty of care. On the other hand, it was foreseeable that John would suffer a very serious kind of economic loss if he were allowed to carry on truanting – he would have no prospects on the job market – and in any case there was a 'special relationship' between John and the school that might allow us to find that a duty of care to protect John's economic welfare was owed in this case. Against this, we have to weigh the prospect that finding that a duty of care was owed in this case might have an adverse effect on the way schools were run, with scarce resources being diverted away from pupils who actually want to learn and directed towards getting unwilling students into the classroom. In addition, finding that a duty of care was owed in John's case might undermine his sense of individual responsibility by allowing him to sue his school for compensation for the consequences of his own fecklessness.

So – there is something to be said on both sides of the case. This is often the case when

[65] See *X* v *Bedfordshire CC* [1995] 2 AC 633, at 663 (per Sir Thomas Bingham MR); *Gorringe* v *Calderdale MBC* [2004] 1 WLR 1057, at [2] (per Lord Steyn); *A* v *Essex CC* [2004] 1 WLR 1881, at [43]; *D* v *East Berkshire Community NHS Trust* [2005] 2 AC 373, at [24]–[25] (per Lord Bingham).

[66] [2005] 2 AC 373, at [100].

deciding whether it would be 'fair, just and reasonable' to find that a duty of care was owed. We just have to weigh the factors in favour of finding that a duty was owed against the factors militating against a finding that a duty was owed, and exercise our judgment to see which set of factors are more weighty in the particular case. So in a genuinely novel case there may be no clear answer as to whether a duty of care was owed under the *Caparo* test – different people will have different opinions as to whether it would be 'fair, just and reasonable' to find that a duty of care was owed. It is fortunate then that – as we have observed before – student readers of this book are highly unlikely ever to be asked to apply the *Caparo* test to determine whether or not a duty of care was owed in a concrete situation. They are far more likely to be presented with a settled case, where one can determine whether or not a duty of care was owed by simply referring to the decided cases and in-force statutes. In the next four chapters, we will set out our understanding of what the decided cases and in-force statutes establish as to when a duty of care will and will not be owed. Having done that, in Chapter 9, we will critically examine this area of the law and ask whether it needs to be reformed.

Visit **http://www.mylawchamber.co.uk/mcbride** to access udates on recent cases, as well as model answers and tips for answering tort problem questions.

Use **Case Navigator** to read in full some of the key cases referenced in this chapter:

- **Caparo Industries plc** *v* **Dickman**
- **Tomlinson** *v* **Congleton BC**
- **Marc Rich & Co AG** *v* **Bishop Rock Marine Co Ltd, The Nicholas H**
- **D** *v* **East Berkshire Community NHS Trust**
- **Phelps** *v* **London Borough of Hillingdon**
- **Customs and Excise Commissioners** *v* **Barclays Bank plc**

5 The legacy of *Donoghue* v *Stevenson*

In this chapter we will begin to set out what the decided cases and in-force statutes have to say on the issue of when one person will and will not owe another a duty of care. We start with probably the most famous case in English law dealing with that issue: *Donoghue* v *Stevenson*.[1]

THE DECISION IN *DONOGHUE* v *STEVENSON*

In *Donoghue* v *Stevenson*, a friend of the claimant bought her a 'ginger beer float' – a concoction made up of ice cream and ginger beer – at a café. The proprietor of the café opened a bottle of ginger beer and poured some of it over ice cream to make the float. There was some ginger beer left in the bottle and he handed that over to the claimant's friend. The claimant ate some of the float. Her friend then poured the rest of the ginger beer into a glass for her to drink. The decomposing remains of a snail floated out into the glass. Unsurprisingly, the claimant fell very ill. Now: the offending bottle of ginger beer had been bottled by the defendant and it was thought that the snail had managed to get into the offending bottle before it was filled with ginger beer and sealed in the defendant's factory. So the claimant sued the defendant in negligence, seeking to recover compensation for the illness she had suffered. The following question went to the House of Lords: Did the defendant owe the claimant a duty to take care that he did not bottle his ginger beer using bottles that contained noxious items such as snails? If he did not, then the claimant's claim in negligence was doomed to fail.

The House of Lords, by a bare majority, held that – other things being equal – the defendant *did* owe such a duty to the claimant. Why? Lord Atkin, delivering the leading judgment on the side of the majority, thought that the decided cases established that the following *neighbour principle* was part of English law and that, under this principle, the defendant owed a duty of care to the claimant:

> in English law there must be, and is, some general conception of relations giving rise to a duty of care, of which the particular cases found in the books are but instances. The liability for negligence, whether you style it such or treat it as in other systems as a species of 'culpa', is no doubt based upon a general public sentiment of moral wrongdoing for which the offender must pay. But acts or omissions which any moral code would censure cannot in a practical world be treated so as to give a right to every person injured by them to demand relief. In this way rules of law arise which limit the range of complainants and the extent of their remedy. The rule that you are to love your neighbour becomes, in law, you must not injure your neighbour; and the lawyer's question, Who is my neighbour? receives a restricted reply. *You must take reasonable care to avoid acts or omissions which you can reasonably foresee would be likely to injure your neighbour. Who, then, in law is my neighbour? The answer seems to be – persons who are so closely and directly affected by my*

[1] [1932] AC 562.

> *act that I ought reasonably to have them in contemplation as being so affected when I am directing my mind to the acts or omissions which are called in question.*[2]

As it was reasonably foreseeable that someone like the claimant would be injured if the defendant bottled his ginger beer with bottles containing noxious items such as snails, the defendant had owed the claimant a duty to take care that he did not bottle his ginger beer using such bottles. It would have been different, Lord Atkin held, if sellers of the ginger beer bottled by the defendant could have been expected to detect whether or not the ginger beer contained any noxious items or objects before allowing the general public to purchase it.[3] In such a case, it would *not* have been reasonably foreseeable that someone like the claimant – a consumer of the defendant's ginger beer – would be injured if the defendant used bottles that contained noxious items or objects such as snails to bottle his ginger beer. In such a case, it could have been expected that those charged with the task of selling the defendant's bottles of ginger beer would have intercepted any bottles which *did* contain noxious items such as snails before those bottles ever reached the lips of the general public.

Lord Atkin's neighbour principle is far too widely drawn to be acceptable as a statement as to when one person will owe another a duty of care under English law.[4] Under the neighbour principle no distinction is drawn – in determining whether a given defendant owed a given claimant a duty of care – between cases where the defendant has made the claimant worse off and cases where the defendant has failed to make the claimant better off. But English law does make a big distinction between these two kinds of case: as we have seen, it is far harder to establish a duty of care in the latter kind of case (an *omissions* case) than the former (a case involving a *positive act*). Moreover, under the neighbour principle, foreseeability of harm is the sole criterion to be taken into account in judging whether a given defendant owed a given claimant a duty of care. However, this is simply not the case in English law – even if it is foreseeable that A will suffer some kind of harm as a result of B's doing *x*, B will not necessarily owe A a duty to take care not to do *x*.

THE PHYSICAL DANGER PRINCIPLE

Donoghue v *Stevenson* is regarded as important nowadays because of Lord Atkin's judgment and its attempt to come up with a general statement as to when one person will owe another a duty of care.[5] However, the decision of the House of Lords in *Donoghue* v *Stevenson* was also important because it helped to establish that the following principle – a far narrower principle than Lord Atkin's neighbour principle – is part of English law. This

[2] Ibid., 580 (emphasis added).
[3] Ibid., 582.
[4] See Smith & Burns 1983a, 1983b.
[5] For an earlier attempt see the judgment of Brett MR (subsequently Lord Esher) in *Heaven* v *Pender* (1883) 11 QBD 503, 510. The attentive reader may have already gathered that we are deeply sceptical as to whether any such general statement can be made without lapsing into unintelligible language. There seems to be no justification for Lord Atkin's statement that '. . . in English law there must be, and is, some general conception of relations giving rise to a duty of care, of which the particular cases found in the books are but instances'. The better view, we would submit, is that there are many *different* kinds of situations and relationships in which one person will owe another a duty of care; to think that all these different situations and relationships have something in common which accounts for why they give rise to a duty of care is folly and can only lead to confusion. See, to the same effect, Tettenborn 2000a. Contra, Howarth 2006 (who sees all duties of care as instances of a general duty 'to act reasonably').

principle – we can call it the *physical danger principle* – goes as follows: If it is reasonably foreseeable that someone like B will suffer some kind of physical injury if A does x, then A will normally owe B a duty to take care not to do x. *Donoghue* v *Stevenson* itself provides an example of this principle at work. In that case, it was reasonably foreseeable that someone like the claimant – a consumer of the defendant's ginger beer – would be physically injured if the defendant bottled his ginger beer using bottles that contained noxious items such as snails. Accordingly, the defendant owed the claimant a duty to take care not to bottle his ginger beer using bottles which contained noxious items such as snails.

There are plenty of cases – in addition to *Donoghue* v *Stevenson* – which seem to support the idea that the physical danger principle is part of English law. They variously hold that:

(1) If A sells goods to B, A will normally owe B a duty to take care not to sell him goods that are unsafe to use or consume in the way they are intended to be used or consumed.

(2) If A is out driving, A will owe other users of the road a duty to take care not to drive dangerously; similarly, if A is parking his car, A will owe other users of the road a duty to take care not to park the car in a dangerous fashion.[6]

(3) If A and B are playing football and A attempts to tackle B, A will owe B a duty to take care not to execute the tackle in an unnecessarily dangerous manner.[7]

(4) If A is in possession of a dangerous chattel – such as a loaded firearm, a poison, or an explosive[8] – and B is incapable of handling that chattel properly, A will normally owe B and anyone else who might be harmed by the chattel's improper use a duty not to entrust it to B's care.[9]

(5) If A owns a car and B – who is obviously drunk – asks A for the keys to his car, intending to go for a drive in it, A will owe users of the highway a duty not to give B the keys to his car.[10]

(6) If A, a highway authority, places signs alongside a highway, A will owe each driver on that highway a duty to take care not to position those signs in such a way that that driver will be unreasonably endangered.[11]

(7) If A is building a house, A will normally owe any future occupants of that house a duty to take care not to build the house in such a way that it will become unreasonably dangerous to live in.[12]

[6] *Maitland* v *Raisbeck* [1944] KB 689; *Parish* v *Judd* [1960] 1 WLR 867.

[7] *Condon* v *Basi* [1985] 1 WLR 866.

[8] *Dominion Natural Gas Co.* v *Collins* [1909] AC 640, 646.

[9] *Dixon* v *Bell* (1816) 5 M & S 198, 199, 105 ER 1023, 1024; *Bamfield* v *Goole & Sheffield Transport Co.* [1910] 2 KB 94; *Oliver* v *Saddler & Co* [1929] AC 584, 599; *Burfitt* v *A & E Kille* [1939] 2 KB 743; *Donaldson* v *McNiven* [1952] 2 All ER 691; *Beckett* v *Newalls Insulation Co. Ltd* [1953] 1 WLR 8; *Philco Radio* v *Spurling* [1949] 2 All ER 882; *Newton* v *Edgerley* [1959] 1 WLR 1031; *Gorely* v *Codd* [1967] 1 WLR 19; *Attorney-General for the British Virgin Islands* v *Hartwell* [2004] 1 WLR 1273.

[10] *P Perl (Exporters) Ltd* v *Camden LBC* [1984] QB 342, 359.

[11] *Levine* v *Morris* [1970] 1 WLR 71.

[12] *Dutton* v *Bognor Regis United Building Co. Ltd* [1972] 1 QB 373, overruling *Bottomley* v *Bannister* [1932] KB 458 and *Otto* v *Bolton & Norris* [1936] 2 KB 46. The decision in *Dutton* was subsequently affirmed by the House of Lords in *Anns* v *Merton LBC* [1978] AC 728. The House of Lords has now disapproved both *Dutton* and *Anns*: *D & F Estates* v *Church Commissioners* [1989] AC 177; *Murphy* v *Brentwood DC* [1991] 1 AC 398. The better view of those decisions, we submit, is that they did *not* disapprove of the view taken in *Dutton* and *Anns* that if A builds a house he will owe B, a subsequent occupier of that house, a duty to take care to ensure that he does not build that house in such a way that it will become dangerous to live in. In *D & F Estates* and *Murphy*

(8) If it is reasonably foreseeable that C will be put in danger if A sets a building on fire, and that someone like B will attempt to rescue C if this happens, thereby putting himself in danger, A will owe B a duty to take care not to set that building on fire.[13]

(9) If B is married to C, A will owe B a duty to take care that he does not misinform her that C has been killed or injured if it is reasonably foreseeable that she will be made physically sick by this news.[14]

(10) If A is labelling bottles of medicine, he will owe B a duty to take care that he does not mislabel those bottles of medicine if it is reasonably foreseeable that someone like B will suffer some kind of physical injury if those bottles are mislabelled.[15]

(11) If B's mother asks A, a local authority, whether T would make a suitable child-minder for B, A will owe B a duty not to tell B's mother that T would make a suitable child-minder for B if A knows, or ought to know, that such advice will be acted on and that T has violent tendencies that mean that B will in fact be in danger of being killed or injured if she is looked after by T.[16]

(12) If B wants to adopt a child through A, an adoption agency, A will normally owe B a duty not to place with her a child which A knows or ought to know suffers from a personality disorder which means that the child is very likely to injure B if he is placed with B.[17]

(13) If A is asked to certify that an aircraft is ready to fly, he will owe those who are due to fly on the aircraft a duty not to say that the aircraft is ready to fly if he knows or ought to know that the aircraft is not fit to fly.[18]

Decisions like these – along with the decision in *Donoghue* v *Stevenson* – seem to show that the physical danger principle is well established in English law. This principle, it should be noted, is narrower than Lord Atkin's neighbour principle in two respects.

---

the House of Lords disapproved the view taken in *Dutton* and *Anns* that if (1) A builds a house and in doing so breaches the duty he owes B, a subsequent occupier of that house, to take care not to build the house in such a way that it will become dangerous to live in and (2) as a result, B is put to expense making the house safe to live in then, other things being equal, (3) B will be entitled to sue A in negligence so as to be reimbursed for the expense she was put to. For an explanation as to why B will not be entitled to sue A in negligence in this situation, see below, pp. 578–9. The fact that B will not be entitled to sue A *in negligence* to recover the money she spent on repairing her house does not, of course, mean that B will not be entitled to sue A *at all* to recover that money. She may have an action under the Defective Premises Act 1972 (on which, see below, pp. 492–3). For an interesting argument that she would be entitled to bring a claim in restitution against A to recover the expense incurred by her in making her house safe to live in, see Moran 1997.

13 *Ogwo* v *Taylor* [1988] AC 431. More difficult is the situation where A owes C a duty to save him from harm, A breaches that duty, and B attempts to save C instead, thereby endangering himself. One cannot use the physical danger principle here to establish that A owed *B* a duty to rescue C because A is merely guilty of an omission here and it is not clear why the fact that A owed *C* a duty to rescue her should mean that he also owed *B* a duty to rescue C. That A *will* have owed B a duty to rescue C in this situation is established by the decision of the Court of Appeal in *Baker* v *T E Hopkins* [1959] 1 WLR 966, though the Supreme Court of Canada took a different view in *Horsley* v *MacLaren, The Ogopogo* [1971] 2 Lloyd's Rep 410.

14 *Wilkinson* v *Downton* [1897] 2 QB 57, as reinterpreted by *Wainwright* v *Home Office* [2004] 2 AC 406, at [40] (per Lord Hoffmann): '. . . the law [is] able comfortably to accommodate the facts of *Wilkinson* v *Downton* . . . [within] the law of . . . negligence.' See below, pp. 114–16, for an account of the case of *Wilkinson* v *Downton* and its significance.

15 *Caparo Industries plc* v *Dickman* [1990] 2 AC 605, 636C.

16 *T* v *Surrey County Council* [1994] 4 All ER 577.

17 *A* v *Essex CC* [2004] 1 WLR 1881.

18 *Perrett* v *Collins* [1998] 2 Lloyd's Rep 255 (discussed, Witting 2000a).

First of all, the principle only covers *positive acts*, not *omissions*. If Fred and Lara are standing at the edge of a cliff then Lara will obviously owe Fred a duty to take care not to push him over the cliff edge under the physical danger principle because it is reasonably foreseeable that Fred will suffer some kind of physical injury if Lara pushes him over the edge. If, on the other hand, Fred is blind and is unknowingly walking towards a cliff edge, Lara – who is standing nearby – will *not* owe Fred a duty to shout out a warning to him under the physical danger principle.[19] True, it is reasonably foreseeable that Fred will suffer some kind of physical injury if Lara does not shout out a warning to him but her not shouting out a warning amounts to a failure to act, not an act – and, as we have already observed, the physical danger principle only applies to positive acts, not omissions.[20]

Secondly, the principle only applies in cases where it foreseeable that B will suffer some kind of *physical injury* as a result of A's doing *x* – where the term 'physical injury' covers death or lesser harms that any normal person would regard as forms of 'physical injury', such as wounds or bruises.[21] It should be noted that the term 'physical injury' does *not* cover any form of *psychiatric illness*.[22] So if it is reasonably foreseeable that B will suffer some kind of psychiatric illness if A does *x*, one cannot invoke the physical danger principle to say that A will owe B a duty to take care not to do *x* – and this is so even though many forms of psychiatric illness have a physiological origin.[23]

Interpretation

Let's now look at the physical danger principle in more detail. Suppose that Wendy has suffered some kind of loss as a result of Alan's doing *x* and we want to use the physical danger principle to establish that Alan owed Wendy a duty to take care not to do *x*. To do this, we will have to show that at the *time* Alan did *x*, a reasonable person in Alan's *position* would

[19] *Yuen Kun Yeu* v *Att-Gen for Hong Kong* [1988] AC 175, 192.

[20] *Important note*. In *Haseldine* v *Daw* [1941] 2 KB 343, A employed an engineer, B, to mend a lift on his premises. B failed to do the job properly, with the result that C was injured the next day when he used the lift and it fell to the bottom of the lift shaft. It was held that: (1) B had owed C a duty to mend the lift with a reasonable degree of care and skill; (2) B had breached that duty; and (3) B was therefore liable to compensate C for his injuries. Finding (1) cannot be supported by reference to the physical danger principle, as the principle does not apply to omissions (here, the failure to repair the lift properly). However, we *can* use the physical danger principle to justify the result in *Haseldine*. It was reasonably foreseeable that if B told A that the lift was fit to use when it was not, someone like C would be physically injured as a result. So B owed C a duty to take care not to tell A that the lift was fit to use when it was not under the physical danger principle. B breached this duty and C was injured as a result. So B was rightly held liable in negligence to compensate C for his injuries.

[21] It also seems to cover getting pregnant, which not many people would regard as a form of physical injury: see *Walkin* v *South Manchester HA* [1995] 1 WLR 1543; *Richardson* v *LRC Products* [2000] Lloyd's Rep Med 280; *Parkinson* v *St James and Seacroft NHS Hospital* [2002] QB 266; though the House of Lords was more equivocal in *McFarlane* v *Tayside Health Board* [2000] 2 AC 59, with Lords Steyn (at 81) and Millett (at 107) saying that pregnancy is a form of physical injury, Lord Slynn saying that it is not (at 74), and Lords Hope (at 86–87) and Clyde (at 102) saying that pregnancy is *analogous* to a physical injury. If pregnancy is a form of physical injury, then if John has sexual intercourse with Mary using contraception which he knows or ought to know is unreliable and Mary gets pregnant as a result and carries the child to term, will she be entitled to sue him for damages on the basis that he owed her, and breached, a duty to take care that he did not use unreliable contraception in having sex with her?

[22] Though the courts in other contexts do sometimes treat a psychiatric illness as though it were a form of physical injury: see *Page* v *Smith* [1996] AC 155, discussed below at pp. 573–5.

[23] For example, it is well established that most forms of depression are caused by chemical imbalances in the brain.

have realised that there was a *real risk* that *someone like* Wendy would suffer some kind of physical injury if the defendant did *x*.[24] The four italicised terms in the previous sentence all require some attention.

Someone like

It is not necessary to show – to invoke the physical danger principle in the above case – that at the time Alan did *x* a reasonable person in Alan's position would have thought 'If Alan does *x*, there's a real risk that *Wendy* will suffer some kind of physical injury.' It is enough if a reasonable person in Alan's position would have thought 'If Alan does *x*, there's a real risk that this kind of person will suffer some kind of physical injury' and Wendy turned out to be that kind of person. Two cases make the point.

In *Farrugia* v *Great Western Railway Co.*,[25] the defendant company loaded one of their lorries with a container that was too large for the lorry in question. The container was knocked off the lorry when it passed under a bridge and injured the claimant, who was running behind the lorry in order to hitch a ride on it. Let's say the name of the claimant was 'John Farrugia'.[26] The Court of Appeal held that the defendant company had owed the claimant a duty to take care that it did not overload its lorry. Of course, at the time the defendant company loaded its lorry, a reasonable person in the defendant company's position would not have been able to say, 'If this lorry is overloaded, there's a real risk that John Farrugia will be injured' because, before the accident, a reasonable person in the defendant company's position would never have heard of John Farrugia. But at the time the defendant company loaded the lorry, a reasonable person in the defendant company's position would have realised, 'If this lorry is overloaded, there's a real risk that a pedestrian walking near the lorry when it's on the road will suffer some kind of physical injury.' As things turned out, this description fitted the claimant – he was a pedestrian walking near the lorry when it was on the road – so it was reasonably foreseeable at the time the defendant company loaded its lorry that if it overloaded the lorry *someone like* the claimant would suffer some kind of physical injury. This was enough to establish that the defendant company owed the claimant a duty to take care not to overload its lorry under the physical danger principle.

In *Haley* v *London Electricity Board*,[27] the defendants, acting under a statutory power, dug a trench in the pavement. While they worked, they left a long handled hammer (called a punner) leaning against some railings at one end of the trench in order to help ensure

[24] *Important note*. This is subject to one very important qualification. Suppose that A does *x* and as a result a third party, T, physically injures B. Suppose further that B wants to invoke the physical danger principle to establish that A owed her a duty to take care not to do *x*. In this sort of *three-party case* the courts will *only* find that it was reasonably foreseeable that B would suffer some form of physical injury if A did *x* if a reasonable person in A's position would have realised that it was *very likely* (*Lamb* v *Camden LBC* [1981] QB 625, 642 (per Oliver LJ)) or *probable* (*Smith* v *Littlewoods LBC* [1987] AC 241, 258 (per Lord Mackay)) that T would injure someone like B if A did *x*. This is a higher standard than requiring B to show that a reasonable person in A's position would have realised that there was a *real risk* that T would physically injure B if A did *x*. So if Alan tells Eric that Wendy, Eric's wife, has been having an affair, and Eric is so angered by this news that he beats Wendy up, Wendy will probably *not* be able to establish that Alan owed her a duty not to tell Eric of her affair under the physical danger principle. While there was a real risk that Eric would beat Wendy up on being told that she was having an affair, it could not be said that it was very likely or probable that Eric would beat Wendy up.

[25] [1947] 2 All ER 565.

[26] The report does not make it clear what the claimant's first name was.

[27] [1965] AC 778.

that pedestrians would not unwittingly fall into the trench. They did not take any steps to fence off the trench. The claimant, a blind man called John Haley who was walking along the pavement, missed the punner with his stick, tripped over it and fell into the trench. The House of Lords held that the defendants had owed the claimant a duty not to dig the trench and then leave it unfenced. At the time the defendants dug the trench, a reasonable person in the position of the defendants would not have realised, 'If the defendants dig a trench on this street and then leave it unfenced, there's a real risk that John Haley will suffer some kind of physical injury' because a reasonable person in the position of the defendants would never have heard of John Haley before his unfortunate accident. But a reasonable person in the position of the defendants would have realised, 'If the defendants dig a trench and then leave it unfenced, there's a real risk that a blind man will fall into the trench and suffer some form of physical injury.' So, at the time the defendants dug the trench, it was reasonably foreseeable that *someone like* John Haley – a blind man – would be injured if the defendants dug the trench and then did nothing to fence it off. This was enough to establish that the defendants owed John Haley a duty not to dig the trench and then leave it unfenced.

Real risk

What if the trench dug by the defendants in *Haley* had not been on a public street but in a video arcade? Would a reasonable person in the position of the defendants have thought, 'If the defendants dig a trench here and leave it unfenced, there's a real risk that a blind man will fall into the trench and suffer some form of physical injury'?

Of course not – the possibility that a blind man might come into the vicinity of the trench would simply not have occurred to him, given the fact that the trench was being dug in a video arcade, a place which only sighted people would be interested in visiting. And if someone had suggested to him that a blind man might come near the trench, he would have dismissed the possibility as 'far-fetched or fantastic'.[28] So if a blind man did chance to approach the trench and fall into it, he would not be able to establish that it was reasonably foreseeable that someone like him would be injured if the defendants dug the trench and left it unfenced. He would not therefore be able to invoke the physical danger principle to establish that the defendants owed him a duty not to dig the trench and leave it unfenced.

It was different in *Haley* because the trench in *Haley* was on a public street and the House of Lords – much impressed by statistics offered by counsel as to the number of blind people in the country – did not think that a reasonable person in the position of the defendants would have dismissed the suggestion that a blind man might come into the vicinity of the trench and fall into it as being 'far-fetched or fantastic'. So in *Haley* a reasonable person in the defendants' position would have realised that there was a real risk that a blind man would be injured if the defendants dug their trench and then left it unfenced.

Position

Going back to the case of Alan and Wendy: in judging whether it was reasonably foreseeable at the time Alan did x that Wendy would suffer some kind of physical injury if Alan

[28] *Overseas Tankship (UK) Ltd* v *The Miller Steamship Co. Pty Ltd, The Wagon Mound (No. 2)* [1967] 1 AC 617, 642 per Lord Reid.

did *x*, we ask whether a reasonable person in Alan's *position* would have realised at the time Alan did *x* that there was a real risk that someone like Wendy would suffer some form of physical injury if Alan did *x*. In order to decide what a reasonable person in Alan's position would have realised at the time Alan did *x*, we must first give him or her some attributes – an age, a certain level of knowledge, possibly a gender. The fact that we are asking what a reasonable person in Alan's position would have realised means that he or she should share some of Alan's attributes – but which? If Alan was particularly stupid or thoughtless, we would *not* give that attribute to our imaginary reasonable person and ask whether a particularly stupid or thoughtless person would have realised at the time Alan did *x* that there was a real risk that Wendy would suffer some kind of physical injury if Alan did *x*.[29] So which of Alan's attributes do we give our reasonable person?

(1) *Knowledge*. In judging what a reasonable person in Alan's position would have realised at the time Alan did *x*, we give this reasonable person all the knowledge Alan had at the time Alan did *x*. So suppose Alan and Wendy were both in a laboratory and Alan had two beakers on his desk, each containing a different kind of chemical. Due to his researches and experiments, Alan knew that these two chemicals were liable to explode if they were mixed together – but nobody else in the world knew this at the time. Alan carelessly managed to knock the beakers over, the chemicals mixed, there was an explosion and Wendy was injured. There will be no problem establishing that Alan owed Wendy a duty to take care not to knock the beakers over when they were in the laboratory together – at that time, a reasonable person who knew what Alan knew would have realised that there was a real risk that Wendy would suffer some form of physical injury if Alan knocked the beakers over.

(2) *Age*. In judging what a reasonable person in Alan's position would have realised at the time Alan did *x*, we ask what a reasonable person of Alan's age would have realised. This follows from the decision of the Court of Appeal in *Mullin* v *Richards*.[30]

In that case, two 15-year-old school children – Teresa Mullin and Heidi Richards – were playfully fencing with plastic rulers when one of the rulers snapped and a fragment of plastic from the snapped ruler entered Mullin's right eye, blinding her in that eye. Mullin sued Richards in negligence, seeking to obtain compensation for the loss of her eye. Mullin claimed that, at the time they were fencing with the rulers, Richards owed Mullin a duty not to carry on the fencing match. Mullin further argued that Richards owed her such a duty because, at the time they were playing around, it was reasonably foreseeable that Mullin would be injured if Richards carried on fencing with Mullin. This argument was rejected in the Court of Appeal on the ground that at the time they were fencing, a *reasonable 15-year-old* would not have realised that there was a real risk that Mullin would be injured if Richards and Mullin carried on their fencing match – at the time Mullin and Richards were playing around, it simply would not have occurred to a 15-year-old, however reasonable, that the rulers used by Mullin and Richards in their fencing match would shatter. (Though presumably it would be different if the fencing match had been a particularly violent one.)

(3) *Mental age?* What if John and Paul, two 40-year-old men with a mental age of 15, started fencing playfully with some plastic rulers with the result that one of the rulers

[29] *Vaughan* v *Menlove* (1837) 3 Bing NC 468, 132 ER 490.
[30] [1998] 1 WLR 1304.

shattered and John's eye was damaged? Suppose John sued Paul, arguing that Paul owed him a duty not to carry on with the fencing match because a reasonable person in Paul's position would have realised that there was a real risk that John would be injured if Paul carried on his fencing match with John.

In judging what a reasonable person in Paul's position would have realised, do we ask – Would a reasonable person with a mental age of 15 have realised that there was a real risk that John would be injured if Paul carried on his fencing match with John? In which case, the answer seems to be 'no' and John's claim against Paul will fail, just as Mullin's claim against Richards failed in *Mullin* v *Richards*. Or do we ask – Would a reasonable person aged 40 have realised that there was a real risk that John would be injured if Paul carried on his fencing match with John? In which the case the answer may well be 'yes' and John's claim against Paul will succeed.

The consensus of academic opinion seems to be that in the above case the courts would disregard Paul's low mental age and ask whether a reasonable person of Paul's physical age (40) would have realised that there was a real risk that John would be injured if Paul carried on the fencing match.[31] To take any other line would open up the door to stupid and thoughtless defendants claiming that, like one's mental age, their stupidity or thoughtlessness is an inherited condition which should be taken into account in judging what a reasonable person in their position would have realised.[32]

(4) *Gender?* There is some evidence to suggest that, to some extent, men and women reason differently,[33] which creates the possibility that in judging what a reasonable person in a given defendant's position would have realised, it might be necessary to assign a gender to the reasonable person and ask whether a reasonable person with that gender would have realised that there was a real risk that the claimant would suffer some kind of physical injury if the defendant did what the defendant did. Presumably, if such a case were to arise, the reasonable person would be given the same gender as the defendant.

However, the effect of doing this could be to discriminate unfairly against women. If it is accepted that women, as a whole, are more caring and empathetic than men and therefore more likely to appreciate the consequences of their actions, then it follows the courts will be more likely to find that it was reasonably foreseeable that a claimant would be injured as a result of the defendant's actions – and therefore find that the defendant owed the claimant a duty to take care not to act in the way the defendant did – if the defendant is female.[34] Given this, it might be more satisfactory to determine whether it was reasonably foreseeable that the claimant would be injured as a result of the defendant's actions by asking, *in all cases*, whether a reasonable *male* in the defendant's position would have realised that there was a real risk that the claimant would suffer some kind of physical injury if the defendant did what the defendant did.

[31] See Moran 2003, 18–26.
[32] For criticism of this argument, see ibid., 28–31; also Mullender 2000.
[33] The classic work is Gilligan 1982.
[34] See Moran 2003, 92–130, 150–4.

Time

In *Roe* v *Minister of Health*,[35] it will be recalled, each of the claimants went into hospital for an operation. In both cases, their spines were injected with nupercaine at the start of the operation to anaesthetise them. Unfortunately, the nupercaine in question had been stored in ampoules which had, in turn, been stored in phenol, a disinfectant. Some of this phenol passed through tiny invisible cracks in the ampoules and contaminated the nupercaine which was injected into the claimants' spines. As a result, the claimants were permanently paralysed. Before the nupercaine was injected into the claimants' spines the ampoules had been inspected for cracks but none were visible and as a result the claimants' doctors thought that it was safe to inject the claimants' spines with the nupercaine; at the time, nobody realised that it was possible that ampoules of nupercaine might suffer from invisible cracks as a result of which the nupercaine contained in those ampoules might become contaminated.

It follows that, once the claimants' doctors had inspected the ampoules of nupercaine for visible cracks and found that there were none, the doctors did *not* owe the claimants a duty not to inject their spines with nupercaine under the physical danger principle. *At that time* (when the injections were administered), a reasonable person in the position of the claimants' doctors would not have thought that there was a real risk that the claimants would suffer some form of physical injury if their spines were injected with nupercaine. Of course, thanks to the experience of people like the claimants in *Roe* we now know better – we now know that if you inject someone's spine with nupercaine which comes from an ampoule which has no visible cracks, there is still a real risk that that nupercaine is contaminated and that that someone will suffer some form of physical injury as a result of being injected with that nupercaine. However, the crucial thing in *Roe* was that at the time the claimants were operated on, nobody realised this – as a result, it was not possible to argue that the claimants' doctors in *Roe* had owed the claimants a duty not to inject their spines with nupercaine under the physical danger principle.

Similarly, in *Abouzaid* v *Mothercare (UK) Ltd*,[36] the claimant was a 12-year-old boy who attempted to attach a sleeping bag to a pushchair. The sleeping bag was attached to the pushchair by passing two elasticated straps attached to either side of the sleeping bag around the back of the pushchair and buckling them together using a metal buckle attached to the end of one of the straps. Unfortunately, when the claimant attempted to buckle the straps together, they slipped from his grasp and the strap with the metal buckle at the end recoiled, hitting the claimant in his left eye. (Presumably the claimant was standing in front of or beside the pushchair when he let go of the straps; had he been standing behind the pushchair, the straps would have recoiled away from him when he let go of them.) The claimant's left eye was blinded as a result and he sued the defendants, who sold the sleeping bag through their stores, for compensation.

His claim in negligence was dismissed: he could not establish that the defendants had owed him a duty not to market the sleeping bag.[37] The reason was that *at the time the defendants marketed the sleeping bag*, a reasonable person in the position of the defendants

[35] [1954] 2 QB 66.

[36] The Times, 20 February 2001.

[37] The claimant was, however, allowed to sue for compensation under the Consumer Protection Act 1987: see below, p. 781.

would not have realised that there was a real risk that people like the claimant might suffer some form of physical injury as a result of the sleeping bag being designed the way it was. Before the claimant was injured, there was no reason for anyone to think that someone using the sleeping bag could suffer this kind of accident – presumably because everyone assumed that anyone attaching the sleeping bag to a pushchair would do so by standing behind the pushchair and pulling the straps attached to the sleeping bag towards them; not by standing beside or in front of the pushchair and pulling the straps away from them. Of course we now know better and, as a result, it may well be that stores nowadays owe their customers (and their customers' children) a duty not to market sleeping bags designed in the same way as the sleeping bag in the *Abouzaid* case.

Exceptions

If it is reasonably foreseeable that someone like B will suffer some kind of physical injury if A does *x*, A will *normally* owe B a duty to take care not to do *x*. It's not true to say that A will *always* owe B such a duty – there are a number of exceptional situations where such a duty will not be owed. They are as follows.

Reasonable conduct

Even if it is reasonably foreseeable that B will suffer some kind of physical injury if A does *x*, A will not owe B a duty to take care not to do *x* if – all things considered – it would be *reasonable* for A to do *x*.

There is an understandable temptation to think that if there is a real risk that B will suffer some kind of physical injury if A does *x*, it will always be unreasonable for A to do *x*. However, a moment's reflection will reveal that this cannot be true. Suppose, for example, that Gary and Vijay are playing football. Now there is a real risk that Vijay will suffer some kind of physical injury if Gary tackles Vijay – the possibility that Vijay will suffer such an injury cannot be dismissed as 'far-fetched or fantastic'. But no one would suggest that it would be unreasonable of Gary to tackle Vijay. Similarly, if you give a friend a lift down to the shops in your car, there is a real risk that your friend will suffer some kind of physical injury as a result: even if you take the utmost care in driving, there is always a possibility that you will have an accident while driving and that your friend will be injured as a result. But, again, no one would suggest that in driving your friend down to the shops, you are acting unreasonably.

Let's now look at some cases to see how this idea – that A will not owe B a duty to take care not to do *x* if, all things considered, it would be reasonable for A to do *x* – works in practice:

(1) *Bolton* v *Stone*.[38] In this case, the claimant, who was standing outside the defendants' cricket ground, was hit by a cricket ball that had been hit for six and cleared the seven-foot-high-fence around the defendants' cricket ground. The claimant sued the defendants in negligence but the House of Lords dismissed her claim. Why? The claimant argued that, at the time of her accident, a reasonable person in the defendants' position would have

[38] [1951] AC 850.

realised that there was a real risk that someone like her – a pedestrian walking outside the ground – would suffer some form of physical injury if the defendants played cricket at their ground. It was conceded that this was true. It was not unknown for cricket balls to be hit out of the defendants' ground – in the previous 28 years, a cricket ball had been hit out of the ground six times – so, at the time of the claimant's accident, the suggestion that 'If the defendants play cricket on their ground, someone outside the ground may be hit on the head and suffer some form of physical injury' could not have been dismissed as 'far-fetched or fantastic'.

So why did the House of Lords not find that the defendants owed the claimant a duty not to play cricket on their ground or, alternatively, that the defendants owed the claimant a duty not to play cricket on their ground without increasing the height of the fence around their ground to such an extent that it would be virtually impossible for someone to hit a cricket ball out of the ground? The reason was that while there was a real risk that someone like the claimant would suffer some form of physical injury as a result of the defendants' playing cricket on their ground, that risk was extremely small[39] and eliminating it would have put the defendants to a great deal of trouble – they would have had either to stop playing cricket on their ground or to increase the size of the fence around their ground.

Given this, the defendants acted quite reasonably in ignoring the risk and carrying on playing cricket without doing anything to increase the size of the fence around the ground. So it could not be argued either that the defendants owed the claimant a duty not to play cricket on their ground (because it was reasonable for the defendants to play cricket on their ground) or that the defendants owed the claimant a duty not to play cricket on their ground without increasing the size of the fence around the ground (because, again, it was reasonable for the defendants to play cricket on their ground without doing anything about the size of the fence around their ground).

(2) *Miller* v *Jackson*.[40] The situation was arguably very different in this case. A housing estate had been built next to a cricket ground which was owned by the defendants. About eight or nine times a season, a cricket ball would be hit out of the defendants' ground and would fall into the housing estate. The defendants tried a number of different schemes to stop this happening – they raised the fence around the ground as high as they could and instructed cricket players using the ground to try and hit balls for four, not six – but none of them worked completely. The only way of stopping balls being hit into the housing estate next to the ground completely was to stop using the ground as a cricket ground. And that is what the claimants – who owned one of the houses on the estate – demanded that the defendants do. They argued that the defendants owed them a duty not to play cricket on their ground because it was reasonably foreseeable that people like them – people living on the housing estate – would suffer some kind of physical injury if the defendants continued to play cricket on their ground.

There was no doubt that this was true. So the crucial issue in *Miller* v *Jackson* was whether the defendants could bring themselves within the exception discussed here: could

[39] In *Overseas Tankship (UK) Ltd* v *The Miller Steamship Co. Pty Ltd, The Wagon Mound (No. 2)* [1967] 1 AC 617, 642 Lord Reid estimated that the risk of someone being hit by a ball hit out of the defendants' ground was such that it would only happen once every thousand years or so.

[40] [1977] QB 966.

they show that, all things considered, it was reasonable for them to carry on playing cricket on their ground, despite the dangers involved for the inhabitants of the nearby housing estate? Of the three members of the Court of Appeal who had to deal with this issue, Lord Denning MR thought that it *was* reasonable for the defendants to carry on playing cricket.[41] The defendants provided a useful amenity in maintaining their ground as a place to play cricket and, besides, the ground had been used as a cricket ground long before the housing estate had been built up and it was hard to see why the defendants should have to stop playing cricket just because some developer had been selfish enough to build an estate on the defendants' doorstep. So Lord Denning took the view that the defendants did *not* owe the claimants a duty not to play cricket on their ground.[42]

Geoffrey Lane LJ took the opposite line. He held that, unlike the case in *Bolton* v *Stone*, the dangers to which people like the claimants were exposed as a result of the defendants' playing cricket on their ground were so serious that it could not be said that it was reasonable for the defendants to carry on playing cricket. So he took the view that the defendants' case did not fall within the exception discussed here. The defendants, then, owed the claimants a duty not to play cricket on their ground. The judge went on to hold that the claimants should be awarded an injunction, forbidding the defendants from playing cricket on their ground, albeit postponed for a year to give the defendants time to find another ground on which to play cricket.

Cumming-Bruce LJ's judgment is probably the most difficult to understand. He agreed with Geoffrey Lane LJ that the defendants owed the claimants a duty in negligence not to play cricket on their ground but he refused to award an injunction against the defendants requiring them not to play cricket on their ground. He thought that the public interest demanded that the defendants be allowed to continue playing cricket on their ground and so an injunction should be refused in this case.[43] But if the public interest in the defendants being allowed to continue to play cricket on their ground was so weighty, it was surely reasonable for the defendants to carry on playing cricket on their ground – so how could the defendants have owed the claimants a duty in negligence not to play cricket on their ground?

At any rate, the end result was that the defendants in *Miller* v *Jackson* were allowed to continue playing cricket on their ground and merely had to pay damages to the claimants.

(3) *Ward* v *London County Council*.[44] In this case, the defendant was driving a fire engine to a fire. He ran a stop-light at a light-controlled crossing and, in doing so, collided with the car which was proceeding over the crossing with the lights in its favour. The car was

[41] Ibid., 980.

[42] Confusingly, Lord Denning held that if a ball was hit out of the defendants' ground and hit one of the claimants, the defendants *would* be liable to pay damages to the affected claimant: ibid., 981–2. How can this be if the defendants did no wrong in playing cricket on their ground? It may be that the defendants' liability could be explained away as an example of compensation without wrongdoing (on which, see above, p. xv). A classic example of compensation without wrongdoing is, of course, liability under the rule in *Rylands* v *Fletcher* (on which, see above, pp. 26–7 and below, pp. 754–64) but it was assumed in *Bolton* v *Stone* that the rule does not apply to the case where someone is hit on the head by a cricket ball escaping from a cricket ground: [1951] AC 850, 857, 867.

[43] It has been held subsequently that the courts are not allowed to take considerations of the 'public interest' into account in deciding whether or not to award an injunction against an admitted wrongdoer: see below, pp. 730–1.

[44] [1938] 1 All ER 341.

being driven by the claimant at the time. Charles J held the defendant liable to the claimant, holding that the defendant had owed the claimant a duty not to run the stop-light: a reasonable person in the defendant's position would have realised at the time the defendant approached the stop-light that there was a real risk that someone like the claimant would be injured if the defendant ran the stop-light.

Why didn't the defendant come within the exception to the physical danger principle discussed here? Why wasn't it reasonable for the defendant to run the stop-light? Two reasons can be given. First, it is doubtful whether the defendant gained anything by running the stop-light – the delay involved in observing the stop-light could only have amounted to a few seconds, not enough to make any difference to the defendant's ability to fight the fire to which he was driving. Secondly, even if the defendant's running the stop-light had made some difference to his ability to put out the fire to which he was driving, life is more important than property and it was not reasonable for the defendant to endanger people like the claimant by running a stop-light in order to save someone else's property from being damaged.

In a case where we are attempting to see whether the defendant owed a claimant a duty to take care not to do *x* under the physical danger principle, it can often be difficult to tell whether or not the defendant acted reasonably in doing *x*. One often has to make difficult value judgments – one has to weigh the social benefit of the defendant's being allowed to do *x* against the dangers to which the defendant's doing *x* exposed other people and decide which is more important. To assist them in making these value judgments, the courts will often consult community and professional opinion as to what sort of risk-creating conduct is reasonable.

So, for example, suppose that a claimant was hit by a defendant driving down the road at 30 mph: the claimant walked out into the road and the defendant's speed was such that he was unable to avoid hitting her. The claimant sues the defendant, contending that under the physical danger principle he owed her a duty not to drive down the road at 30 mph: at the time, a reasonable person in the defendant's position would have realised that there was a real risk that someone like the claimant would be injured if he drove down the road at 30 mph. The defendant admits this but counters that he acted reasonably in driving down the road at that speed, seeking to bring himself within the exception to the physical danger principle discussed here. If the road was clear and visibility was good it is unlikely that the courts will disagree: it is generally accepted that it is reasonable for a driver to drive down a road at 30 mph if the road is clear and visibility is good.[45]

Again, suppose a surgeon operated on a patient using a general anaesthetic. When the operation finished, the patient failed to come round and slipped into a coma. Did the surgeon owe the patient a duty not to give her a general anaesthetic under the physical danger principle? Obviously, when the operation took place, it was reasonably foreseeable that the patient might suffer some kind of physical injury if she was given a general anaesthetic – there is always a risk that a patient who is operated on under a general anaesthetic

[45] *Moore* v *Poyner* [1975] RTR 127. If, on the other hand, the defendant had been driving in excess of the speed limit when he hit the claimant, the claimant should not have much difficulty establishing that the defendant owed her a duty to take care not to drive at the speed he was driving: see, on this, *Grealis* v *Opuni* [2003] EWCA Civ 177.

will not come round once the operation is concluded. But the surgeon may attempt to argue that the physical danger principle does not apply here because he acted reasonably in giving the patient a general anaesthetic.

In assessing whether it was reasonable for the surgeon to do this, the courts will consult expert medical opinion – if there is a body of medical opinion which says that operating on the patient using a general anaesthetic was a reasonable thing to do, the courts will *normally* find that the surgeon did not owe the patient a duty not to give her a general anaesthetic – and this is so *even if* there is another body of opinion which thinks that giving her a general anaesthetic was an unreasonable thing to do: normally the courts will be unwilling to take sides in medical disputes between different camps of responsible doctors.[46] However, the courts will only *consult* expert medical opinion on this matter – if there is a body of opinion which says that it was reasonable for the surgeon to operate using a general anaesthetic, the courts may still depart from that opinion and rule that it was unreasonable for the surgeon to give the patient a general anaesthetic if there is good reason to think that the contrary medical opinion is corrupt or illogical or anachronistic.[47]

Volenti non fit injuria

Of course, the surgeon in the above case would not normally have to show that it was reasonable for him to give the patient a general anaesthetic to defeat the claim that he owed her a duty not to give her a general anaesthetic under the physical danger principle. He could simply say – 'She agreed to my giving her a general anaesthetic – so the maxim *volenti non fit injuria* applies here.'

This will usually be a good answer to the claim against him: if it was reasonably foreseeable that B would suffer some kind of physical injury as a result of A's doing *x*, A will not have owed B a duty to take care not to do *x* under the physical danger principle if B agreed that A could do *x*. This assumes of course that B's consent was not vitiated – that is, that B was sane and understood what A's doing *x* involved, that B was not acting under pressure in agreeing that A could do *x*, and that B was old enough to decide for herself whether or not she wanted A to do *x*. If B's consent was vitiated, then the maxim that *volenti non fit injuria* will not apply.

So, for example, suppose two grown adults of sound mind, Carl and Nita, decide to re-enact William Tell's famous exploit of hitting an apple perched on a child's head with an arrow fired from a crossbow. Carl takes the part of William Tell; Nita takes the part of the child. In such a case, Carl will not owe Nita a duty not to fire the arrow at the apple on her head under the physical danger principle – even though there is clearly a risk that Nita will suffer some kind of physical injury if Carl fires the arrow. Similarly, if a customer asks a tattooist to inscribe a tattoo on his arm, the tattooist will not owe the customer a duty not to tattoo him – even though there is clearly a risk that the customer will suffer some kind of physical injury as a result of having his arm tattooed. The customer's consent to being tattooed releases the tattooist from the duty he might otherwise owe the customer not to tattoo him.[48]

[46] *Bolam* v *Friern Hospital Management Committee* [1957] 1 WLR 582.

[47] *Bolitho* v *City and Hackney Health Authority* [1998] AC 232.

[48] Of course, the tattooist will still owe the customer other duties, such as a duty to tattoo the customer with a professional degree of care and skill: see below, pp 133–4.

In *Johnstone* v *Bloomsbury Health Authority*,[49] the claimant was employed by the defendant health authority. Under the terms of his contract of employment the claimant was required to work 40 hours a week and the health authority had the power to require the claimant to work an additional 48 hours a week 'overtime'. Did this mean that the health authority was free to require the claimant to work 88 hours a week even if it was reasonably foreseeable that the claimant's health would suffer if he was asked to work such hours? The Court of Appeal said 'no': in agreeing that the defendant health authority *could* call on him to work up to 88 hours a week, the claimant did not agree that the defendant health authority could call on him to work such hours if it was reasonably foreseeable that doing so would make him ill.

But what if the claimant *had* agreed that the defendant health authority could call on him to work up to 88 hours a week – even if it was reasonably foreseeable that doing so would make him ill? Two members of the Court of Appeal (Leggatt LJ and Browne-Wilkinson V-C) seemed to think that, in such a case, the defendant health authority would have been free to require the claimant to work up to 88 hours a week – even if it were reasonably foreseeable that the claimant's health would suffer if he were asked to work such hours. But this is only true, we submit, if the claimant *willingly* agreed that the defendant health authority could call on him to work up to 88 hours a week even if it were reasonably foreseeable that doing so would make him unwell. It is very doubtful whether any doctor would *willingly* agree to this. It is far more likely that he would agree simply because the only alternative to doing so would be to leave his profession. As Stuart-Smith LJ pointed out, 'Any doctor who wishes to practise has to serve at least one year as a house officer in a hospital; the national health service (NHS) is effectively a monopoly employer.'[50] For this reason, Stuart-Smith LJ thought that if a doctor expressly agrees to work up to 88 hours even if it is reasonably foreseeable that making him work such hours will make him unwell, his employer will still not be free to require him to work up to 88 hours a week if it is reasonably foreseeable that the doctor's health will break down if he is made to work such hours.

The Road Traffic Act 1988, s 149 has made one important inroad on the principle of *volenti non fit injuria*. Under s 149(3) of the 1988 Act, if A takes B for a ride in a motor vehicle and B has willingly agreed that A can drive the vehicle dangerously, A will still owe B a duty to take care that he does not drive the vehicle in a dangerous manner. As s 149(3) provides: '[t]he fact that [B] has willingly accepted as his the risk of negligence on the part of [A] shall not be treated as negativing any [liability that A would otherwise incur to B].'

So, in *Pitts* v *Hunt*,[51] the claimant and defendant went for a ride on the defendant's motorbike. They were both very drunk and the claimant encouraged the defendant to drive the bike in a more and more dangerous fashion. Eventually, as a result of the defendant's reckless driving, the bike was involved in an accident and the claimant was injured. The claimant sued the defendant so as to be compensated for the injuries suffered by him. It was argued that the defendant did not owe the claimant a duty to take care not to drive the motorbike in a dangerous fashion because the claimant had agreed that the defendant

49 [1992] QB 333.
50 Ibid., 344–5.
51 [1991] 1 QB 24.

could drive the bike in such a way. This argument was dismissed: the claimant's agreement was of no effect under s 148(3) of the Road Traffic Act 1972 (the predecessor of s 149(3) of the Road Traffic Act 1988) and did not release the defendant from the duty that he owed the claimant under the physical danger principle to take care that he did not drive the bike in a dangerous manner.

Public policy

In *Mulcahy* v *Ministry of Defence*,[52] the claimant was a soldier serving with a British Army artillery unit during the Gulf War. While his unit was deployed in Saudi Arabia firing a howitzer into Iraq, his gun commander ordered him to fetch some water from in front of the howitzer. While the claimant was in front of the gun, the gun commander fired the gun. As a result the claimant's hearing was severely affected. The claimant sued the Ministry of Defence for damages, claiming that the gun commander had been negligent in firing the gun and that the Ministry of Defence was vicariously liable in respect of the gun commander's negligence.

In order to make out his claim, the claimant had to show that the gun commander owed him a duty to take care not to fire the gun while he was in front of it. Now – the claimant had a good case for arguing that the gun commander owed him such a duty of care under the physical danger principle: a reasonable person in the gun commander's position would have appreciated that there was a real risk that the claimant would suffer some form of physical injury if the commander fired the gun while the claimant was in front of it. Moreover, neither of the exceptions to the physical danger principle that we have already looked at applied here. It was not reasonable for the gun commander to fire the gun while the claimant was in front of it. And the claimant certainly did not agree that the gun commander could fire the gun while he was in front of it.

Despite this, the Court of Appeal refused to find that the gun commander had owed the claimant a duty of care. Why was this? The Court of Appeal's reasoning went something like this:

> We simply cannot allow the physical danger principle to apply to military officers operating in battle conditions. If we do, then officers will become unduly cautious in making decisions on the battlefield. An officer who is thinking about making some order which will put his men in danger of being killed or injured will think twice about making the order. He'll worry that if he gives the order and some of his men are killed and injured as a result, he could be sued by those men or their families – that those men or their families will argue that he owed his men a duty not to issue the order because it was reasonably foreseeable that some of his men would be killed or injured if he gave that order and the order was an unreasonable one to give. Of course, the officer will be confident that he would win any such litigation – he would be confident that he could show that any orders he gave were reasonable under the circumstances. But that's hardly relevant – being sued is an evil in itself which any rational person will try their best to avoid. So if we allow the physical danger principle to apply to officers acting in the heat of battle, we will only encourage them to become extremely cautious and timid in making decisions on the battlefield – only ordering their men forward, for example, when it is absolutely clear that it is safe to do so. Such an attitude is hardly conducive to winning wars. It would be better then not to apply the physical danger principle at all to military officers acting in the heat of battle – which means that we should

[52] [1996] QB 732.

rule in this case that the gun commander did not owe the claimant a duty to take care not to fire the gun while the claimant was in front of it.

So the Court of Appeal refused to find that the gun commander owed the claimant a duty of care in *Mulcahy*, not because there was no ground for finding that such a duty of care was owed, but because they thought that it was in the public interest to find that no such duty of care was owed.

In so doing, it should be noted, the Court of Appeal effectively gave the gun commander an *immunity* from being sued in negligence – and in so far as *Mulcahy* is a precedent which applies to all cases where a soldier is injured in battle as a result of something done by his superiors, the decision granted all military officers an *immunity* from being sued in negligence by soldiers injured in battle as a result of their actions. What do we mean when we say that the gun commander in *Mulcahy* was given an immunity from being sued in negligence?

A defendant will enjoy an immunity from being sued in negligence if a claimant would *normally* be entitled to sue the defendant in negligence but in fact she is prevented from doing so by some special legal rule.[53] This was the case in *Mulcahy*. The claimant would normally have been entitled to sue the gun commander in negligence for compensation for his loss of hearing – normally, he would have been able to invoke the physical danger principle to show that the gun commander owed him a duty to take care not to fire the gun while the claimant was in front of it; he would have been able to show that the gun commander breached that duty; that his loss of hearing was attributable to that breach of duty; and so on. But the normal rules did not apply in *Mulcahy* – the Court of Appeal created a special exception to those rules, holding that the physical danger principle did not apply to cases such as the claimant's, thereby ensuring that the claimant could not sue the gun commander in negligence.

Contrast this with the case where Alan, a blind man, unwittingly walks over the edge of a cliff and is severely injured. Wendy watched Alan approach the cliff edge but did not bother to call out a warning to him. On discovering this, Alan sues Wendy in negligence for compensation for his injuries. His case is dismissed on the ground that Wendy did not owe Alan a duty to warn him that he was in danger of walking over a cliff edge. In this case, it would be wrong to say that Wendy enjoys an immunity from being sued in negligence. She does not: it is impossible to say that Alan would *normally* be entitled to sue Wendy in negligence for compensation for his injuries. No special exception has been created to the basic rules governing when someone can sue someone else in negligence to protect Wendy from being sued here – Alan cannot sue Wendy here because according to those very rules he has no case against her.

It is important that one gets clear in one's head when it can be said that someone enjoys an immunity from being sued in negligence because it is becoming increasingly clear that if a claimant is prevented from suing a defendant because the defendant enjoys an immunity from being sued by the claimant, the claimant *may* be able to claim that his rights under Article 6(1) of the European Convention on Human Rights have been violated.

[53] This definition is in fact not wholly satisfactory (a more complicated definition of when someone will enjoy an immunity from being sued will be advanced below, at pp. 527–9) but it will serve for present purposes.

To explain: Article 6(1) provides that, 'In the determination of his civil rights and obligations ... everyone is entitled to a fair and public hearing within a reasonable time by an independent and impartial tribunal established by law.' This provision has been held to imply the existence of a right of *access to the civil courts*. The classic situation which is covered by this right is the situation where A has an *arguable* case against B but is prevented for some reason from taking B to court or making his case out against B once in court. So, for example, in *Golder* v *United Kingdom*,[54] a prisoner wanted to sue the governor of his prison for libel – his claim was that the governor had libelled him by putting him in solitary confinement for some infraction of the prison rules that he did not actually commit. However, the prisoner was denied access to a solicitor and was as a result prevented from taking the governor to court. It was held that his Article 6(1) rights had been violated.

What is of interest to us here is that the case law emanating from the European Court of Human Rights seems to suggest that Article 6(1) does not just cover this kind of situation but also the situation where A has *no* case against B because B enjoys an *immunity* from being sued by A.[55] In such a case, the Court has held, A will be able to claim that his Article 6(1) rights have been violated *if* giving B an immunity from being sued by A serves no legitimate purpose or giving B such an immunity serves a legitimate purpose but in a disproportionate way. It follows from this that the courts in future will have to be cautious about granting defendants immunities from being sued in negligence, as they did in *Mulcahy* – they will have to be careful that they only grant a class of people an immunity from being sued in negligence if doing so would serve a legitimate purpose and sacrificing the interests of those who might want to sue that class is an acceptable price to pay to achieve that purpose.[56] And all existing immunities, such as the immunity granted to military officers in *Mulcahy*, will have to be looked at again to ensure that their existence does not violate the Article 6(1) rights of potential claimants; if an existing immunity serves no legitimate purpose or serves a legitimate purpose but in a disproportionate way, it will have to be abolished.[57]

It seems likely that the immunity enjoyed by military officers from being sued in negligence for their actions on the battlefield will survive this process of scrutiny: the immunity serves a useful purpose and the test of whether an immunity is a 'proportionate' one seems a very relaxed one, if recent cases decided by the European Court of Human Rights are anything to go by. Of course, none of this has any relevance to the case where Alan wants to sue Wendy in negligence for the injuries sustained by him as a result of his walking off the edge of a cliff. As he has no case against Wendy, and not because she has an immunity from

[54] (1975) 1 EHRR 524.

[55] See below, pp. 527–9. It must be admitted, though, that the English courts have been unwilling to follow the example of the European Court of Human Rights and hold that Art 6(1) covers cases where someone enjoys an immunity from being sued. See, for example, the Court of Appeal's observation in *Matthews* v *Ministry of Defence* [2002] 1 WLR 2621, at [50] that it 'would be wrong to suggest that article 6(1) could be engaged by a provision of the substantive law of a member state which provides that certain groups will be under no liability in circumstances where others would be under such liability'. When *Matthews* was appealed to the House of Lords, their Lordships took a similarly restrictive view of the scope of Article 6(1): [2003] 1 AC 1163. The House of Lords' decision in *Matthews* is discussed in detail below: pp. 528–9.

[56] The courts are, of course, required not to violate claimants' Art 6(1) rights under the Human Rights Act 1998 (on which, see below, pp. 742–53).

[57] This has already happened with the immunity that barristers enjoyed from being sued in negligence by their clients: *Arthur J S Hall & Co. (a firm)* v *Simons* [2002] 1 AC 615.

being sued in negligence, but because he simply has no case, dismissing his claim cannot possibly violate his Article 6(1) rights.[58]

Beyond the physical danger principle

As we have already said, the decision of the House of Lords in *Donoghue* v *Stevenson* helped to entrench what we have called the physical danger principle in English law. But the decision in *Donoghue* v *Stevenson* had wider ramifications. The decision – and in particular Lord Atkin's neighbour principle – emboldened the courts to start finding that defendants owed claimants duties of care based only on the fact that it was reasonably foreseeable that the claimant would suffer some kind of harm as a result of the defendant's acting in the way he did.

Of course, there were limits as to how far the courts were willing to go in doing this. They never accepted, for example, that foreseeability of harm was a sufficient ground to impose a duty on a defendant to perform some positive act. And they never accepted that a defendant would owe a claimant a duty to take care not to act in a particular way if the only harm that it was foreseeable that the claimant would suffer as a result of the defendant's acting in that way was comparatively trivial, such as distress or anxiety or pure economic loss.[59] However, the courts have shown themselves willing to give at least partial effect to Lord Atkin's neighbour principle in two kinds of cases.[60]

[58] *Important note.* At one stage, the European Court of Human Rights (ECtHR) seemed to think that a defendant enjoyed an immunity from being sued in negligence *whenever* a claimant was prevented from suing her on the ground that she did not owe the claimant a duty of care: *Osman* v *United Kingdom* [1999] 1 FLR 193. It seemed to follow that *in any case* where A was prevented from suing B in negligence because B did not owe her a duty of care, A could claim that her Art 6(1) rights had been violated (whether they had been or not would depend on whether denying A's claim served a legitimate purpose and sacrificing A's interests was an acceptable price to pay to serve that purpose). The *Osman* case concerned the decision of the Court of Appeal in *Osman* v *Ferguson* [1993] 4 All ER 344. In that case, the police were sued in negligence for failing to arrest a deputy headmaster before he attacked and killed the father of a boy with whom the deputy headmaster was obsessed. The claim was dismissed on the ground that the police had not owed the father a duty of care. The ECtHR held that the Court of Appeal had violated the claimants' Art 6(1) rights in so ruling: the Court of Appeal had, in dismissing the claim, conferred an immunity from being sued in negligence on the police and they acted in a disproportionate way in conferring that immunity on the police. But, of course, the decision in *Osman* v *Ferguson* did *not* confer an immunity from being sued in negligence on the police – no sensible person could say that, 'One would normally expect the police to have been held liable in negligence for failing to arrest the deputy headmaster, but the Court of Appeal in *Osman* created a special exception for the police in this case to protect them from being sued.' Given this, it is hard to see how the Court of Appeal in *Osman* violated the claimants' Art 6(1) rights by throwing out their claim in negligence against the police. Subsequently, the ECtHR has recanted and confessed that its decision in *Osman* was based on a misunderstanding of the English law of negligence: *Z* v *United Kingdom* [2001] 2 FLR 612 at [100]. The *Z* case concerned the decision of the House of Lords in *X* v *Bedfordshire CC* [1995] 2 AC 633. In that case the claimants sued the social services in negligence for failing to protect them from being abused as children. The House of Lords dismissed the claims on the ground that the social services had not owed the claimants a duty of care. The ECtHR held that the House of Lords threw out the claimants' claim *not* because they wanted to give the social services an immunity from being sued in negligence but because, according to the well-established principles governing the law of negligence in England, the claimants simply had no case: [2001] 2 FLR 612 at [100]. So, the ECtHR held, it was impossible to argue that the House of Lords had violated the claimants' Art 6(1) rights in throwing out their claims.

[59] 'Pure economic loss' is economic loss suffered by a claimant which is not a result of the claimant's person or property being damaged.

[60] *Important note.* There is a third type of case where the courts may be willing to give effect to Lord Atkin's neighbour principle, and that is where A's actions are liable to have the effect of causing B to lose her *freedom*. See, for example, *Clarke* v *Chief Constable of Northamptonshire*, The Times, 14 June 1999 where the Court of Appeal

First, cases where a claimant has suffered a psychiatric illness[61] as a result of a defendant's doing *x*. (Let's call these *psychiatric illness cases.*) If the claimant can show that it was reasonably foreseeable at the time the defendant acted that someone like him would suffer a psychiatric illness as a result of the defendant's doing *x*, the courts may well find that the defendant owed the claimant a duty to take care not to do *x* – though, for reasons we will explore below, whether they will or not will often depend on how the claimant's psychiatric illness was triggered.

Secondly, cases where a defendant did *x* and an item of property P has been harmed as a result. (Let's call these cases *harm to property cases.*) If a claimant can show that it was reasonably foreseeable at the time the defendant acted that an item of property like P would be harmed if the defendant did *x* and the claimant had a sufficient interest in P at the time it was harmed, the courts will normally find that the defendant owed the claimant a duty to take care not to do *x*.

In the rest of this chapter we will look at when exactly the courts will find that a defendant owed a claimant a duty of care in these two kinds of cases. We will start with psychiatric illness cases.

PSYCHIATRIC ILLNESS CASES

We are concerned here with the situation where B has developed a psychiatric illness as a result of A's doing *x*; and B wants to sue A in negligence for compensation for that illness. To make out her claim, she will have to show that A owed her a duty to take care not to do *x*. When will B be able to do this?

Sometimes, she will be able to use the physical danger principle to establish that A owed her a duty to take care not to do *x*. This will be the case, for example, if A ran into B's car while she was in it and she was so frightened by the experience that she subsequently developed a psychiatric illness. In this case, B will be able to invoke the physical danger principle to establish that A owed her a duty to take care not to run into her car.[62] A similar analysis

ruled that the police will owe a prisoner a duty to take care not to misrecord the date on which he was taken into custody if the foreseeable effect of doing so would be to cause the prisoner to be detained for longer than he ought to be detained. Also *Al-Kandari* v *J R Brown & Co* [1988] QB 665, where the Court of Appeal ruled that if C has a proven record of attempting to kidnap B's children and A currently holds C's passport so as to prevent him attempting to leave the country with B's children, A will owe B's children a duty to take care that he does not do anything which would result in C getting his passport back.

[61] A mental condition will only amount to a psychiatric illness if it is recognised by the psychiatric profession as being such. On the distinction between psychiatric illnesses and lesser forms of mental distress, see *Reilly* v *Merseyside RHA* [1996] 6 Med LR 246 (apprehension, fear, discomfort and shortness of breath arising out of being trapped in a lift do not amount to a psychiatric illness) and *Group B Plaintiffs* v *Medical Research Council* [2000] Lloyd's Rep Med 161 (sleeplessness arising out of being told that one might contract the CJD virus in future is capable of amounting to a psychiatric illness).

[62] Note that in order to establish that A owed her a duty to take care not to run into her car, B will *not* have to show that it was reasonably foreseeable that she would suffer a psychiatric illness as a result of A's running into her car. In order to invoke the physical danger principle here, she merely has to show that it was reasonably foreseeable that she would be physically injured as a result of A's running into her car: *Page* v *Smith* [1996] AC 155. If, in crashing into B's car, A breached the duty of care he owed B under the physical danger principle to take care not to crash into her car, the usual rule is that B will only be able to recover for the reasonably foreseeable losses suffered by her as a result of the crash. However, *Page* v *Smith* created a special exception for people in B's position – it says that B will be able to claim for compensation for the psychiatric illness that she suffered as a result of A's negligence even if it was not a reasonably foreseeable consequence of A's negligence:

will apply in the case where – as happened in the case of *Group B Plaintiffs* v *Medical Research Council*[63] – A injects B with some hormone which may be contaminated with a deadly virus and B, on learning this, develops a psychiatric illness as a result of worrying about whether the hormone which was injected into her was contaminated or not. Provided that A knew or ought to have known that the hormone was potentially contaminated, B will be able to invoke the physical danger principle to establish that A owed her a duty not to inject her with the hormone.

But there are many cases where B has suffered a psychiatric illness as a result of A's doing *x* where B will *not* be able to invoke the physical danger principle to establish that A owed her a duty to take care not to do *x*. Let's call these *non-physical danger psychiatric illness cases*. Here are five such cases:

(1) *Psychiatric illness arising out of someone else's being killed or injured.* A does something which results in C's being killed or injured. B suffers a psychiatric illness as a result.
(2) *Psychiatric illness arising out of someone else's being maltreated.* A maltreats C – without killing or injuring C – and B suffers a psychiatric illness as a result.
(3) *Pyschiatric illness arising out of being given bad news.* A tells B some bad news – for example, that her daughter is dead. B suffers a psychiatric illness as a result.
(4) *Psychiatric illness arising out of being treated in a distressing or humiliating way.* A treats B in a distressing or humiliating way – such as making her undress in front of complete strangers. B suffers a psychiatric illness as a result.
(5) *Psychiatric illness arising out of being subjected to a stressful experience.* A makes B do some work which is extremely stressful. B suffers a psychiatric illness as a result.

B will not be able to invoke the physical danger principle in any of these cases to establish that A owed her a duty of care not to act in the way he did. But the courts may still find that A owed B a duty of care not to act in the way he did. In order to establish that A owed B such a duty of care, the *first* thing that has to be shown – in line with Lord Atkin's neighbour principle – is that it was *reasonably foreseeable* that someone like B would suffer a psychiatric illness as a result of A's acting in the way he did. But even if this is shown, that does not necessarily mean that A owed B a duty of care not to act in the way he did. The courts may require *something more* to be established before they will find that A owed B a duty of care not to act in the way he did. Let's now flesh this out by looking at each of the above non-physical danger psychiatric illness cases in detail and seeing what will have to be established before the courts will find that a duty of care was owed in those cases.

---

the fact that it was reasonably foreseeable that B would suffer some kind of physical injury as a result of A's negligence will be enough to make B's psychiatric illness actionable. There is little to be said in favour of this concession to claimants and the courts have subsequently shown themselves eager to confine *Page* v *Smith* to its own facts: see below, at pp. 573–5.

[63] [2000] Lloyd's Rep Med 161 (discussed, O'Sullivan 1999).

Psychiatric illness arising out of someone else's being killed or injured

Let's suppose that A has caused an accident x to occur in which various people were killed or injured.[64] Suppose further that B was not physically involved in the accident, but she still developed a psychiatric illness as a result of witnessing, or thinking about or hearing about the accident.[65] As we have already observed, if B wants to establish that A owed her a duty of care not to act as he did, the first thing she will have to show is that it was reasonably foreseeable that she would suffer a psychiatric illness as a result of A's causing that accident to occur.[66]

The requirement of reasonable foreseeability

It seems that B will only be able to satisfy this requirement of reasonable foreseeability in four situations.

(1) *Close and loving relationship.* Suppose that Carl accidentally ran Ian's fiancée, Dawn, down in his car and she was killed. Ian is so grief-stricken by the news of Dawn's death that he develops a psychiatric illness. Clearly in this case it will have been reasonably foreseeable that someone like Ian – someone who was in a close and loving relationship with Dawn – would develop a psychiatric illness if Carl ran Dawn down.

(2) *Rescue.* Continuing with the above case, suppose that Lara ran to Dawn's aid once she had been run over. She saw Dawn's injuries close up, heard Dawn's last words and Dawn died in her arms. Lara is so affected by this experience that she develops post-traumatic stress disorder, a form of psychiatric illness. Again, it will have been reasonably foreseeable that someone like Lara – who attempted to rescue Dawn after she was run down and witnessed at close quarters Dawn's condition having been run down – would develop a psychiatric illness if Carl ran Dawn down.

(3) *Feelings of responsibility.* Suppose that Dawn had been walking to the shops when she was run down. She had asked an acquaintance of hers, Gary to give her a lift to the shops in his car, but he had turned her down, saying he was too busy. When Gary heard the news

[64] The principles laid out here are not just confined to accident cases, but will also apply in a case where, for example, A *deliberately* killed or injured C and B developed a psychiatric illness as a result: see *W* v *Essex CC* [2001] 2 AC 592 (discussed below, at n. 72 and at p. 104, below).

[65] If B was involved in the accident, she would probably be able to invoke the physical danger principle to establish that A owed her a duty of care not to act as he did: see above, pp. 73–4.

[66] For a case where the claimant could not satisfy this requirement, see *Bourhill* v *Young* [1943] AC 92. In that case, a motorcyclist who was driving at an excessive speed drove into a motorcar and was killed. The claimant was 50 feet from the accident when it happened. She heard, but did not witness, the crash and developed a psychiatric illness as a result of the shock of hearing the crash. The claimant sued the motorcyclist's estate for compensation, claiming that the motorcyclist had owed her, and breached, a duty to take care not to run into the motorcar. The claimant's claim for compensation was dismissed by the House of Lords on the ground that the motorcyclist had not owed the claimant such a duty of care. It was simply not reasonably foreseeable that someone like the claimant – who was 50 feet away from the accident when it happened, who did not witness the accident occur, and who was unrelated to anyone involved in the accident – would develop a psychiatric illness if the motorcyclist ran into the motorcar. Of course, the claimant heard the crash occur, but the noise of the crash was not so horrific that someone of reasonable fortitude or 'phlegm' who heard it could have been expected to develop a psychiatric illness as a result – so the fact that the claimant heard the crash occur did not help her show that it was reasonably foreseeable that someone like her would develop a psychiatric illness if the motorcyclist ran into the motorcar.

of what had happened to Dawn, he was horrified and felt that he was, in part, responsible for Dawn's death. Overwhelmed by his feelings of guilt, Gary eventually developed a psychiatric illness. Again, it is clearly arguable in this case that it was reasonably foreseeable that someone like Gary – who felt responsible for Dawn's death – would develop a psychiatric illness if Carl ran over Dawn.

(4) *Witnessing an acutely horrific accident occur*. Suppose that Ruth saw Carl knock Dawn down. She did not know Dawn at all, she did not attempt to assist Dawn after she was knocked down and she did not feel at all responsible for Dawn's being run down. However, the impact of what she saw was such that she still developed a psychiatric illness. Here, Ruth will find it difficult to establish that it was reasonably foreseeable that someone like her – a mere bystander who saw Dawn being run down – would develop a psychiatric illness if Carl ran Dawn down. A bystander of reasonable fortitude or 'phlegm' could be expected to cope a little better with the experience of seeing a complete stranger being run down. But it is possible to conceive of accidents which are so acutely horrifying that a mere bystander witnessing the accident occur *could* be expected to develop a psychiatric illness as a result. In argument before the House of Lords in the case of *Alcock* v *Chief Constable of South Yorkshire Police*,[67] the example was given 'of a petrol tanker careering out of control into a school in session and bursting into flames'.[68] It does seem reasonably foreseeable that a passer-by witnessing this happen would develop a psychiatric illness as a result.

So – if A has caused an accident *x* to occur in which various people were killed and injured and B, who was not physically involved in the accident, developed a psychiatric illness as a result of witnessing, hearing about or thinking about the accident, B will *only* be able to establish that it was reasonably foreseeable that she would develop a psychiatric illness as a result of A's causing accident *x* to occur if:

(1) B was in a close and loving relationship with someone killed or injured in accident *x*; or
(2) B attempted to rescue people who were killed or injured in accident *x*; or
(3) B felt responsible for accident *x*'s occurring; or
(4) B witnessed accident *x* occur and the accident was so acutely horrifying that anyone of reasonable fortitude or 'phlegm' witnessing it occur could have been expected to develop a psychiatric illness as a result.

But, of course, it is important to remember that even if B falls into one of these categories, that does not necessarily mean that it *was* reasonably foreseeable that someone like B would develop a psychiatric illness as a result of A's causing accident *x* to occur. The reasonable foreseeability requirement might still not be satisfied. Two examples where this requirement will not be satisfied can be given.

First, Paul accidentally knocks Karen to the ground. Karen bruises her knee as a result. Sarah, Karen's mother, sees the bruise and develops a psychiatric illness as a result. Clearly, it was not reasonably foreseeable that someone like Sarah would develop a psychiatric

[67] [1992] 1 AC 310.
[68] Ibid., 403.

illness as a result of Paul's bruising Karen's knee. This is so even though Sarah was in a close and loving relationship with Karen.

Secondly, John accidentally runs Wendy down in his car. Fred sees the accident occur and calls an ambulance on his mobile phone, but otherwise does nothing to assist Wendy. He is subsequently so affected by the experience that he develops a psychiatric illness. Clearly it was not reasonably foreseeable that someone like Fred – someone who witnessed Wendy being run down and called an ambulance for her – would develop a psychiatric illness if John ran Wendy down. This is so even though, technically, one could say that Fred 'rescued' Wendy in the aftermath of the accident.

Reasonable foreseeability is not enough

The courts have not been willing to give *complete* effect to Lord Atkin's neighbour principle in this area. Even if B can show, in the situation we are considering, that it was reasonably foreseeable that she would develop a psychiatric illness as a result of A's causing accident *x* to occur, that will *not* be enough to establish that A owed B a duty of care not to act as he did. Something more will always be required to be shown before a duty of care will be found. What that 'something more' will be will depend on *how* B's psychiatric illness was triggered. Before we look at some of these cases that deal with this issue, let us sum up what they say:

(1) *Close and loving relationship.* Let's suppose that B developed her psychiatric illness because she was in a 'close and loving relationship' with C, who was killed or injured in accident *x*. In this sort of case, A will *only* have owed B a duty of care not to act as he did *if B's psychiatric illness was triggered by her witnessing accident x occur or its immediate aftermath.*

So, for example, suppose that C was so badly injured in accident *x* that B had to give up her job and look after C on a full-time basis. Suppose further that the strain of looking after C got too much for B and as a result she developed a psychiatric illness. In this sort of case, B will *not* be able to establish that A owed her a duty of care not to act as he did.[69] Even though it was perfectly foreseeable that she would develop a psychiatric illness as a result of A's causing accident *x* to occur, B's illness was not triggered by her witnessing accident *x* or its immediate aftermath.

This rule, it should be noted, gives rise to two points of difficulty. First of all, suppose that A caused an accident to occur in which B's son was badly injured. He was taken to hospital for treatment. B arrived at the hospital shortly afterwards and witnessed her son die. B subsequently developed a psychiatric illness. Before the courts will find that A owed B a duty to take care not to cause the accident in question, they will need to be satisfied that B's illness occurred because of what she saw when she saw her son in hospital in the immediate aftermath of the accident and that B's illness was not simply an abnormal reaction to the fact that her son died. So it must be shown that B's seeing her son in hospital amounted to a 'horrifying event, which violently agitated [her] mind'.[70]

[69] Ibid., 400 (per Lord Ackner).

[70] Ibid., 401. For criticisms of this requirement, see Teff 1996. This requirement was not satisfied in *Sion* v *Hampstead HA* [1994] 5 Med LR 170 where the claimant's son was involved in a motorcycle accident caused by the defendant that caused him to go into a coma and die after 14 days. The claimant attended his son's bedside

Secondly, suppose that A caused an accident to occur in which B's son was injured. Her son was taken to hospital and B came to the hospital some time later and developed a psychiatric illness as a result of what she saw and heard when she went to the hospital. Will B be able to claim that she witnessed the *immediate aftermath* of the accident when she went to the hospital? Obviously it will depend on how much time elapsed between the time the accident occurred and the time B went to the hospital. An hour's delay would not prevent B claiming that she witnessed the immediate aftermath of the accident[71] but a day's delay probably would.[72]

(2) *Rescue.* If B developed her psychiatric illness because she attempted to rescue some of the victims of accident *x*, A will only have owed her a duty to take care not to cause accident *x* if B put herself in physical danger in attempting to rescue the victims of the accident or she thought she was in danger when she attempted to rescue the victims of the accident.

(3) *Feelings of responsibility.* If B developed her psychiatric illness because she felt responsible for the fact that accident *x* occurred, A will only have owed her a duty to take care not to cause accident *x* if B witnessed accident *x* occur.

(4) *Witnessing an acutely horrifying accident occur.* If B developed her psychiatric illness merely because she witnessed accident *x* occur as a mere bystander, the decided cases seem to have taken the view that A will simply not have owed B a duty to take care not to cause accident *x* to occur. This is so even if accident *x* was so acutely horrific that anyone witnessing it as a mere bystander could have been expected to develop a psychiatric illness as a result.

Let's now look at some of the cases from which the above propositions of law are drawn.[73]

---

all that time and developed a psychiatric illness after his son died. It was held that the claimant's psychiatric illness was not triggered by his seeing his son in the aftermath of the accident – as he saw nothing particularly horrifying or shocking in the aftermath of the accident that could have triggered a psychiatric illness. The claimant's psychiatric illness simply amounted to an abnormal reaction to the loss of his son.

71 *McLoughlin* v *O'Brian* [1983] 1 AC 410.

72 *Alcock* v *Chief Constable of South Yorkshire Police* [1992] 1 AC 310. But regard must be had to the decision of the House of Lords in *W* v *Essex CC* [2001] 2 AC 592. In that case – an example of a trauma case which did not involve an accident – the defendants were a local authority who placed a 15-year-old boy with the claimants, two parents who acted as foster carers and who had four children of their own, then aged between 8 and 12. The 15-year-old boy – as the defendants well knew – had a history of sexual abuse. While he was fostered with the claimants, the 15-year-old boy sexually abused all of the claimants' children. When the claimants discovered this *four weeks later*, they each developed forms of psychiatric illness. The claimants sued the defendants in negligence, claiming that the defendants had owed them a duty not to foster the boy with them. The defendants applied to have the claims struck out, arguing that they had not owed the claimants such a duty. (It should be noted that the defendants almost certainly owed such a duty to the claimants' *children* under the physical danger principle.) The House of Lords refused to strike out the claims, holding that the claimants had an arguable case against the defendants. Foreseeability was clearly made out: the claimants were in a close and loving relationship with their children. But could they show that their psychiatric illness was triggered by their seeing that their children had been abused *in the immediate aftermath of that abuse*? Lord Slynn, giving the only judgment, held that it was arguable that this requirement was made out despite the long gap between the children's being abused and the claimants' finding out about it: 'it seems to me that the concept of "the immediate aftermath" of the incident has to be assessed in the particular factual situation. I am not convinced here that in a situation like the present the parents must come across the abuser or the abused "immediately" after the sexual incident has terminated': ibid., 601.

73 For a good, critical survey of the law in this area, see Butler 2002.

(1) *Alcock* v *Chief Constable of the South Yorkshire Police*.[74] This case arose out of the Hillsborough disaster where 95 football fans were crushed to death and hundreds more were injured at the Leppings Lane end of Hillsborough Football Stadium in Sheffield before an FA Cup semi-final between Liverpool and Nottingham Forest. The immediate cause of the disaster was the decision of the police to open an outer gate to the Leppings Lane end of the Hillsborough Stadium without cutting off access to spectator pens 3 and 4 at that end which were already full. Football fans rushed through the opened gate into pens 3 and 4 with the result that those at the front of those pens were crushed. The claimants in *Alcock* were relatives of the dead who had developed psychiatric illnesses – forms of post-traumatic stress disorder – in the aftermath of the disaster. None of the claimants whose cases were decided by the House of Lords in *Alcock* succeeded in their claims for compensation; none of them could establish that the police owed them a duty to take care not to cause the accident at Hillsborough.[75]

Most of the claimants in *Alcock* failed to establish that the police owed them a duty of care because they could not show that it was reasonably foreseeable that they would develop a psychiatric illness as a result of the accident at Hillsborough occurring. The only way they could show that it was reasonably foreseeable that they would develop a psychiatric illness as a result of the Hillsborough tragedy occurring was by showing that they were in a close and loving relationship with someone killed or injured at Hillsborough. But the House of Lords held that most of the *Alcock* claimants were *not* in a close and loving relationship with anyone killed or injured at Hillsborough. For example, Brian Harrison suffered post-traumatic stress disorder when he lost his two brothers at Hillsborough. His claim that the police owed him a duty to take care not to cause the accident at Hillsborough failed because there was nothing in the evidence before the House of Lords to suggest that he enjoyed a sufficiently close and loving relationship with his brothers as to make it reasonably foreseeable that he would develop a psychiatric illness as a result of their being killed and the House of Lords was not prepared to presume that Brian Harrison enjoyed such a relationship with his brothers.

It was different in the case of Mr and Mrs Copoc, who lost their son at Hillsborough and subsequently suffered post-traumatic stress disorder. In their case, the House of Lords *was* prepared to presume – in the absence of any evidence going the other way – that they enjoyed such a close and loving relationship with their son that it was reasonably foreseeable that they would develop a psychiatric illness in the aftermath of the Hillsborough disaster. Their claims that the police owed them a duty to take care not to cause the accident at Hillsborough failed because they could not establish that their psychiatric illnesses were triggered by their witnessing the Hillsborough disaster unfold or its immediate aftermath. They *did* see live pictures of the Hillsborough disaster unfolding on television but the fact that broadcasting guidelines forbade the transmission of live pictures showing scenes

[74] [1992] 1 AC 310.

[75] One claimant succeeded in his claim for compensation at first instance: William Pemberton, who went by coach with his son to the match. His son had a ticket to watch the match; Pemberton stayed on in the coach, intending to watch the match on the coach's television. Pemberton watched the disaster unfold on the television and then searched for his son. His son had in fact died in the disaster and Pemberton identified his body at around midnight. No appeal was made against the first instance judge's decision that the police had owed Pemberton a duty to take care not to cause the accident at Hillsborough: ibid., 339, 348, 351, 365.

of recognisable human suffering led the House of Lords to think that what the Copocs saw on television could not have accounted for their subsequently developing post-traumatic stress disorder. The pictures they saw were insufficiently shocking – they gave rise to anxiety, but nothing more. Nor could the Copocs establish that they developed their psychiatric illnesses as a result of witnessing the *immediate* aftermath of the Hillsborough tragedy. Only one of the Copocs – Mr Copoc – travelled to Sheffield after the disaster and he only saw his son's body the next day, long after the disaster had occurred. The real reason why the Copocs suffered post-traumatic stress disorder in the aftermath of the Hillsborough disaster was because of what they *imagined* their son had gone through – not because of what they *saw*.

The House of Lords was only prepared to presume that one other *Alcock* claimant enjoyed a close and loving relationship with someone killed or injured in the Hillsborough tragedy. This was Alexandra Penk. She lost her fiancé, Carl Rimmer, at Hillsborough and subsequently suffered post-traumatic stress disorder.[76] But again, Ms Penk's claim that the police owed her a duty to take care not to cause the accident at Hillsborough to occur failed because she could not establish that her psychiatric illness was caused by her witnessing the Hillsborough tragedy unfold or its immediate aftermath. All Ms Penk saw were live pictures of the tragedy unfolding – and they were insufficiently shocking for her post-traumatic stress disorder to be attributed to her witnessing them.

So – the House of Lords' decision in *Alcock* principally established two things. First, if B developed a psychiatric illness because she was in a close and loving relationship with someone killed or injured in an accident *x* that was caused by A, A will only have owed B a duty to take care not to cause accident *x* if B's pyschiatric illness was triggered by her witnessing the accident occur or its immediate aftermath.

Secondly, if a third party, T, was involved in an accident *x* that was caused by A, and B wishes to show that she was in a close and loving relationship with T for the purpose of establishing that A owed her a duty to take care not to cause accident *x* to occur, the courts will only presume that B was in such a close and loving relationship with T – in the absence of any evidence going the other way – if T was B's child, parent, fiancé or (presumably) spouse. If T was none of these things, then the courts will find that B did *not* have a close and loving relationship with T unless she can supply the courts with evidence tending to indicate that she did enjoy such a relationship with T.

Can either the first or second aspects of the House of Lords' decision in *Alcock* be supported?

We can understand the rationale behind the first aspect of the House of Lords' decision in *Alcock* by considering its effect in the following case. Fred participates in a live television show in which members of the public undertake various dangerous challenges. Fred's challenge is to undergo a bungee jump. Because Tom, a technician on the show, failed properly to attach Fred to the bungee rope, Fred fell to his death when he undertook the jump. Fred's fiancée, Beth, went with Fred to watch him undertake the bungee jump and saw him fall to

[76] Would the House of Lords have been prepared to presume that she was in a close and loving relationship with Carl Rimmer had they actually been married at the time of the Hillsborough tragedy? One would have thought so, but see Lord Keith's remarks in *Alcock*: '[the] kinds of relationship which may involve close ties of love and affection . . . may be present in family relationships or those of close friendship and may be stronger in the case of engaged couples than in that of persons who have been married to each other for many years': ibid., 397.

his death. She was so traumatised by what she saw that she developed post-traumatic stress disorder as a result. Fred's mother, Mary, saw Fred fall to his death because she watched Fred undertake the bungee jump at home on television. The shock of witnessing Fred's death resulted in her developing post-traumatic stress disorder. Fred's father, Eric, did not see Fred make his jump but he went to the mortuary two days after the accident to identify Fred's remains. He was so traumatised by what he saw that he subsequently suffered post-traumatic stress disorder. Ruth, Fred's daughter by his fiancée, did not see Fred make his jump. She suffered post-traumatic stress disorder when she was told that Fred had died and how he had died.

The decision in *Alcock* means that although it was reasonably foreseeable that Beth, Mary, Eric and Ruth would each develop some kind of psychiatric illness as a result of the occurrence of the accident involving Fred, Tom will only have owed Beth and Mary a duty to take care not to cause that accident to occur. No duty will have been owed to Eric because his post-traumatic stress disorder was not triggered as a result of his witnessing the *immediate* aftermath of Fred's death. No duty will have been owed to Ruth because her post-traumatic stress disorder arose because of how she reacted to the *news* of Fred's death, not because she *witnessed* Fred's death or its immediate aftermath.

Now: why do the courts artificially restrict the range of people to whom Tom owed a duty to take care not to cause the accident involving Fred in this way? Why will they say that Tom owed a duty of care in the situation we are considering to Beth and Mary but not to Eric or Ruth? It is hard to resist the impression that courts artificially restrict the range of people to whom Tom owed a duty of care so as to ensure that if Tom did carelessly cause Fred to fall to his death, he will not be held liable to compensate Beth *and* Mary *and* Eric *and* Ruth for the post-traumatic stress disorders that they each developed when Fred died. If Tom did carelessly cause Fred to fall to his death and was held liable to *that* extent, his liability would be out of all proportion to his fault. So, in the case just described, the courts will deny that Fred owed Eric and Ruth a duty to take care not to cause the accident that killed Fred as a rough-and-ready way of preventing Tom's liability in the event that he carelessly caused Fred to fall to his death getting out of all proportion to his fault. The way in which the courts limit Tom's liability is, admittedly, unprincipled – there is, for example, no real distinction between the situations of Fred's two parents, Mary and Eric, here and thus no reason why Mary should be allowed to recover from Tom if he carelessly caused Fred to fall to his death while Eric should not – but the desire to limit Tom's liability in the case just described is an intelligible one.

Less defensible is the second aspect of the House of Lords' ruling in *Alcock*. Suppose John caused an accident in which Nita's cousin was killed. Nita witnessed the accident and developed a psychiatric illness as a result. As a result of the second aspect of the House of Lords' ruling in *Alcock*, Nita will not be able to establish that John owed her a duty to take care not to cause the accident in which her cousin was killed unless she can come up with evidence that indicates that she was in a close and loving relationship with her cousin – and if Nita does advance evidence indicating that she was in a close and loving relationship with her cousin, John will be entitled to question the reliability of that evidence and, more broadly, cast doubt on whether Nita and her cousin were that close. It is obvious that both Nita and John will find this whole process immensely embarrassing, distasteful and unseemly. Moreover, the courts will have to undertake the grotesque and disreputable task of sifting the evidence presented by Nita and John to determine how close Nita actually was to her cousin. It is hardly likely that the courts will come out of this process with their dignity intact. Given this, it might be better if the House of Lords had held in *Alcock* that certain relationships will be conclusively presumed to have been close and loving relationships[77] and that all other relationships will be conclusively presumed not to have been close and loving relationships.

(2) *The rescue cases.* In *Chadwick* v *British Transport Commission*,[78] two trains crashed into each other at Lewisham. The defendants were responsible. The accident occurred about 200 yards from Henry Chadwick's home. He went to help the survivors of the accident and spent about nine hours crawling through the wreckage, administering injections to passengers who were injured and helping them to extricate themselves from the wreckage. As a result of what he saw and heard at the scene of the accident, Chadwick became psychoneurotic and had to spend six months in a mental hospital. Chadwick sued the defendants in negligence for compensation for his illness, claiming that the defendants had owed him, and breached, a duty to take care not to cause the Lewisham train crash. The court agreed on the basis that it was reasonably foreseeable that someone like Chadwick – someone who did what he did and saw what he saw in rescuing the victims of the Lewisham train crash – would develop a psychiatric illness in the aftermath of the Lewisham train crash. So *Chadwick* established that if A caused an accident *x* to occur and B developed a psychiatric illness as a result of what he saw and heard in helping and rescuing the victims of the accident and it was to be expected that B would develop such a psychiatric illness, then A will have owed B a duty to take care not to cause accident *x* to occur.

However, the decision in *Chadwick* was qualified by the House of Lords' decision in *Frost* v *Chief Constable of South Yorkshire Police*.[79] Again, the case arose out of the Hillsborough tragedy. This time the claimants were police officers who suffered post-traumatic stress disorder as a result of what they saw and heard when helping out in the aftermath of the Hillsborough disaster. Two of the claimants helped carry the dead, two of the claimants tried unsuccessfully to resuscitate injured spectators in the stadium and one of the claimants assisted at a mortuary to which the dead were taken. The claimants attempted to obtain compensation for their post-traumatic stress disorders, claiming that the senior police officers who were in charge of the policing of the Hillsborough semi-final had owed *them* a duty to take care not to cause the accident at Hillsborough. The House of Lords held that no such duty of care had been owed. In order to establish that the officers who were in charge at Hillsborough had owed them a duty to take care not to cause the accident at Hillsborough it was not enough for the claimant police officers to show that their post-traumatic stress disorders had arisen because of what they saw and heard in rescuing the victims of the Hillsborough disaster – they had also to show that they had put themselves in danger in rescuing the victims of the Hillsborough disaster or had thought they were in

[77] The Law Commission has proposed that if T was killed or injured in an accident caused by A and B developed a psychiatric illness as a result, the courts should conclusively presume that B was in a close and loving relationship with T if: (1) T and B were married at the time of the accident; (2) B was T's parent; (3) B was T's child; (4) T was B's brother or sister; (5) T and B had been living together as lovers for at least two years at the time of the accident. See Law Com. No. 249, *Liability for Psychiatric Illness* (1998).

[78] [1967] 1 WLR 912.

[79] [1999] 2 AC 455. The case is otherwise known as *White* v *Chief Constable of South Yorkshire Police*.

danger when they rescued the victims of the Hillsborough disaster. As neither of these things were true of the claimants in *Frost*, the officers who were in charge at Hillsborough had *not* owed the claimants a duty to take care not to cause the accident at Hillsborough.[80]

Why did the House of Lords qualify the effect of the decision in *Chadwick* in this way? It is hard to avoid the impression that the House of Lords decided *Frost* the way they did because they thought that the law would be brought into disrepute if the claimant police officers in *Frost* were allowed to claim compensation for the post-traumatic stress disorders that they suffered in the aftermath of Hillsborough when the relatives in *Alcock* had not been allowed to claim compensation for the post-traumatic stress disorders that they suffered in the aftermath of the Hillsborough disaster. Indeed, both Lord Steyn and Lord Hoffmann explicitly acknowledged as much in their judgments in *Frost*.[81] The easiest way of ensuring that the claimants in *Frost* would not be able to claim compensation for the post-traumatic stress disorders that they suffered in the aftermath of Hillsborough was, of course, to deny that the officers who were in charge at Hillsborough had owed those police officers a duty to take care not to cause the Hillsborough accident to occur and the House of Lords seized on the fact that the claimants in *Frost* were never in any physical danger and never thought they were in any physical danger as a 'reason' for finding that the officers who were in charge at Hillsborough had not owed the claimants in *Frost* such a duty.

In deciding *Frost* the way they did, the House of Lords did not overrule the decision in *Chadwick* that the defendants in that case *did* owe Chadwick a duty to take care not to cause the Lewisham train crash. This is because there was some evidence in Chadwick's case that he had put himself in danger of being killed or injured when he assisted in the aftermath of the Lewisham train crash. However, the decision in *Frost* does have an unfortunate implication, best highlighted by an 'extreme' case posited by Lord Goff, who dissented in *Frost*:

> Suppose there was a terrible train crash and that there were two Chadwick brothers living nearby, both of them ... distinguished by their courage and humanity. Mr A Chadwick worked on the front half of the train, and Mr B Chadwick on the rear half. It so happened that, although there was some physical danger present in the front half of the train, there was none in the rear. Both worked for 12 hours or so bringing aid and comfort to the victims. Both suffered [post-traumatic stress disorder] in consequence of the general horror of the situation.[82]

According to the decision in *Frost*, in this case, before the train crash, the defendants responsible for the train crash only owed Mr A Chadwick a duty to take care not to bring about the train crash. No duty was owed to Mr B Chadwick by the defendant before the train crash to take care not to bring about the train crash. Thus, as Lord Goff pointed out, if it were proved that the defendants carelessly brought about the train crash 'Mr A would recover but Mr B would not. To make things worse, the same conclusion must follow even

[80] See now *French* v *Chief Constable of Sussex Police* [2006] EWCA Civ 312 (police officers who suffered psychiatric illnesses as a result of their being investigated for their involvement in the shooting of an innocent man sued the defendant chief constable claiming that he had owed them a duty of care to protect them against the risk of suffering a psychiatric illness; held that the decision in *Frost* meant that police officers who witnessed the shooting and suffered a psychiatric illness as a result could not sue, and if this were the case then neither could the claimants).

[81] [1999] 2 AC 455, 499 (per Lord Steyn), 510 (per Lord Hoffmann).

[82] Ibid., 487.

if Mr A was unaware of the existence of physical danger in his half of the train. This is surely unacceptable.'[83] One can only agree.

Frost is a good example of the maxim that hard cases make bad law. The House of Lords in *Frost* found itself in a situation where it would have been politically unacceptable to allow the claimant police officers to recover compensation for the post-traumatic stress disorders suffered by them in the aftermath of the Hillsborough tragedy. But in order to dismiss the claimants' claims in *Frost* the House of Lords introduced an arbitrary and unjustifiable rule into English law – that if A has caused an accident *x* to occur and B has developed a psychiatric illness as a result of what she saw and heard in rescuing the victims of that accident, A will only have owed B a duty to take care not to cause accident *x* to occur if B either put herself in danger in rescuing those victims or thought that she was in danger in rescuing those victims.[84]

(3) *The responsibility cases.* In *Dooley* v *Cammell Laird & Co. Ltd*,[85] the claimant was a crane driver. The claimant was in his crane and was lowering a sling-load of materials into a hold when the rope which attached the sling-load to his crane snapped. The sling-load of materials fell into the hold where several of the claimant's colleagues were working. Fortunately, no one was injured. However, the claimant, sitting high up in his crane, did not know that and, thinking he was responsible for the accident that had occurred, developed a psychiatric illness at the thought of what he had done. In fact the accident was the fault of the defendants – the claimant's employers who had failed to check that the rope was strong enough for lifting purposes and the firm that had manufactured the rope – and the claimant sued the defendants, seeking compensation for the psychiatric illness that he had developed. The claimant's claim was allowed. It was held that the defendants had owed the claimant a duty to take care not to cause the accident that had occurred on the ground that because the claimant thought he was responsible for the accident that occurred, it was reasonably foreseeable that the claimant would develop a psychiatric illness as a result of that accident's occurring. So the decision in *Dooley* established that if A caused an accident to occur and B developed a psychiatric illness as a result because he mistakenly thought he was responsible for the fact that that accident had occurred, then A will have owed B a duty to take care not to cause that accident to occur.

However, just as the decision in *Chadwick* was substantially qualified by the decision of the House of Lords in *Frost*, so the decision in *Dooley* has been substantially qualified by the decision of the Court of Appeal in *Hunter* v *British Coal Corp*.[86] In that case, the claimant was employed by the defendants to work at their coal mine. He was driving a vehicle along a track when he became aware of a water hydrant protruding into the track. The claimant tried to manoeuvre the vehicle round the hydrant but the track was too narrow and the claimant managed to strike the hydrant, causing water to flow from it. The

[83] Ibid.

[84] The House of Lords might have dismissed the claimants' claims in *Frost* on the ground that they could not be allowed to seek compensation for harms that they voluntarily took the risk of suffering 'on the job'. (This is known as the 'fireman's rule' in some American states.) However, the House of Lords had previously ruled in *Ogwo* v *Taylor* [1988] AC 431 that a claimant's claim to be compensated for harm suffered by him could not be dismissed on the ground that he had voluntarily taken on the risk of suffering that kind of harm as part of his job and the House of Lords in *Frost* showed no inclination to overrule *Ogwo*. See below pp. 510–11.

[85] [1951] 1 Lloyd's Rep 271.

[86] [1999] QB 140.

claimant stopped his vehicle and got out and tried to stop the flow of water from the hydrant with the assistance of a fellow employee, one Tommy Carter. The claimant ran off, looking for a water hose that he could use to channel the flow of water from the hydrant, while Carter continued to attempt to shut the hydrant off. When the claimant was 30 metres away from the hydrant, it burst and Carter was killed in the explosion. The claimant only learned that Carter had died on his way back to the scene of the accident. Feeling responsible for Carter's death, the claimant developed a deep depression. In fact, the defendants were responsible for the accident that occurred: it was their fault the track down which the claimant had been driving had been too narrow with the result that the claimant's vehicle struck the hydrant with tragic consequences.

The claimant sued the defendants, seeking compensation for the depression that he had suffered in the aftermath of Carter's death. The Court of Appeal turned down the claimant's claim. They held that the defendants had not owed the claimant a duty to take care not to cause the accident that caused Carter's death. The claimant had to have witnessed the accident for such a duty to have been owed to the claimant. Not much can be said by way of justification or explanation of the Court of Appeal's decision. The Court of Appeal may have been motivated to decide *Hunter* that way because it was concerned that if it held that a duty of care was owed to the claimant in *Hunter* then it would follow that A, a motorist who ran down a child, would have to be found to have owed a duty to take care not to run down the child to anyone who developed a psychiatric illness because they felt responsible for the child's death whether they were on the scene of the accident when it occurred or not. If this were the law then a potentially large number of claims could be made against A (or, more accurately, his insurance company) and A's liability would grow out of all proportion to his fault in running down the child in question.

However, it should be noted that *Hunter* may not contain the last word on the issue of what has to be established before a duty of care will be found in this sort of case. In *W* v *Essex CC*,[87] the claimant foster parents each developed a psychiatric illness when a boy who had been placed with them sexually abused their children. They sued the local authority who had placed the boy with them in negligence. The House of Lords refused to strike out the claimants' claims, holding that it was arguable that the local authority had owed them a duty not to place the boy with them. The House of Lords thought that a duty of care might have been owed to the claimants in this case because they *felt responsible* for what had happened to their children.[88] If so, then the decision in *W* casts doubt on whether *Hunter* was correctly decided as, of course, the claimants were not present when their children were sexually abused.

(4) *The horrific accident cases.* Let us now consider what the authorities have to say about the following situation. A caused an accident *x* to occur in which a number of people were killed or injured. B developed a psychiatric illness as a result of witnessing this accident occur. B had no connection with anyone involved in the accident but it was still reasonably foreseeable that she would develop this psychiatric illness because the accident was so horrific that someone of reasonable fortitude or 'phlegm' who witnessed the accident occur

[87] [2001] 2 AC 592.
[88] Ibid., 601.

could have been expected to develop a psychiatric illness as a result. Will A have owed B a duty to take care not to cause accident *x* to occur?

Lord Ackner in *Alcock* thought that the answer may well be 'yes'.[89] Lord Oliver of Aylmerton agreed: 'I would not exclude the possibility . . . of a successful claim, given circumstances of such horror as would be likely to traumatise even the most phlegmatic spectator, by a mere bystander.'[90] Lord Keith took the same view.[91] However, since then, both the Court of Appeal, in *McFarlane* v *E E Caledonia Ltd*,[92] and the House of Lords, in *Frost* v *Chief Constable of South Yorkshire*,[93] have held that the House of Lords decided in *Alcock* that someone who suffers a psychiatric illness simply as a result of witnessing an accident occur will only be able to sue in negligence for compensation for that illness if he or she was in a sufficiently 'close and loving relationship' with someone involved in the accident. On this reading of *Alcock*, the decision of the House of Lords in that case establishes that in the situation we are considering, B will *not* be able to argue that A owed her a duty to take care not to cause accident *x* to occur: she was not in a sufficiently 'close and loving relationship' with anyone involved in the accident.

However, this reading of *Alcock* is simply wrong and completely inconsistent with the *dicta* from *Alcock* cited above. In fact, this reading of *Alcock* gets *Alcock* backwards. *Alcock* did *not* say that a bystander who develops a psychiatric illness as a result of witnessing an accident occur will only be able to sue in negligence for compensation for her illness if she was in a 'close and loving relationship' with someone involved in the accident. What *Alcock* said was that someone who develops a psychiatric illness because she was in a 'close and loving relationship' with someone who was involved in the accident will only be able to sue in negligence for compensation for her illness if her illness was triggered by her witnessing the accident or the immediate aftermath.

So the courts have tended to assume since *Alcock* that in the situation we are considering, A will *not* have owed B a duty to take care not to cause accident *x* to occur even though there is nothing in *Alcock* that compels that conclusion and indeed there are some *dicta* in *Alcock* that suggest that in the right circumstances A may well have owed B such a duty of care. The point, we would suggest, remains open to argument, though there may be valid reasons for denying the possibility of a duty of care being owed in this kind of situation.[94]

89 [1992] 1 AC 310, 403: 'while it may be very difficult to envisage a case of a stranger, who is not actively and foreseeably involved in a disaster or its aftermath, other than in the role of a rescuer, suffering shock-induced psychiatric injury by the mere observation of apprehended or actual injury of a third person in circumstances that could be considered reasonably foreseeable, I see no reason in principle why he should not, if in the circumstances, a reasonably strong-nerved person would have been so shocked. In the course of argument your Lordships were given, by way of an example, that of a petrol tanker careering out of control into a school in session and bursting into flames. I would not be prepared to rule out a potential claim by a passer-by so shocked by the scene as to suffer psychiatric illness.'

90 Ibid., 416.

91 Ibid., 397.

92 [1994] 2 All ER 1, at 14.

93 [1999] 2 AC 455, 462E–H (per Lord Griffiths), 472F (per Lord Goff), 496H–497B (per Lord Steyn), 502D–H (per Lord Hoffmann). Lord Browne-Wilkinson, the other judge in *White*, agreed with the judgments of Lords Steyn and Hoffmann: 462B–C.

94 For example, the Court of Appeal in *McFarlane* argued that it would be undesirable to allow that a duty of care might be owed to a mere bystander who had suffered a psychiatric illness as a result of witnessing a horrific accident occur: given that people's responses to horrific accidents are invariably subjective it would be difficult to determine whether or not the bystander's psychiatric illness was reasonably foreseeable: [1994] 2 All ER 1, at 14.

Self-harm: an exception to the rule?

In *Greatorex* v *Greatorex*,[95] C's son, S, was out driving in a friend's car when he crashed it and was injured as a result. C – acting in his capacity as a fire officer – attended the scene of the car crash and saw S unconscious, injured and trapped in the car. As a result of seeing this C developed a psychiatric illness. C then sued S for damages in respect of his psychiatric illness. (This was not as heartless as it seems. While S was not covered by liability insurance in driving his friend's car, the Motor Insurers' Bureau would have covered any judgment entered against S.) C argued that S owed him a duty to take care not to cause the car crash in which S was injured and that S's breach of this duty of care caused C to develop his psychiatric illness. Now, on the basis of what has already been said, one would expect the court to have ruled that S *did* owe C a duty to take care not to cause the car crash in which S was injured. C was in a close and loving relationship with S and developed his psychiatric illness as a result of attending the immediate aftermath of the accident in which S was injured. However, Cazalet J ruled that S had *not* owed C a duty to take care not to cause the car crash in which he was injured. Cazalet J gave two reasons why he thought it would be wrong to rule that S had owed C such a duty of care.

First of all, he thought that S's 'right of self-determination' would have been unacceptably limited if he had owed C a duty to take care not to crash the car he was driving.[96] It is not clear that this is correct. If someone *wants* to kill himself, there is a case for saying that he will *not* owe those members of his family who might be affected by his death a duty not to kill himself – the existence of such a duty would, it is true, completely take away his 'right of self-determination'.[97] But S was not trying to kill himself when he crashed his friend's car. Given this, it is not clear why his 'right to self-determination' would have been infringed if he had owed C a duty to take care that he did not crash his friend's car.

Cazalet J's second reason for denying that S owed C a duty of care in this case was that to allow that a duty of care will be owed in cases such as these is to 'open up the possibility of a particularly undesirable type of litigation between the family, involving questions of relative fault as between its members'. He continued:

> To take an example, A, while drunk, seriously injures himself. B his wife [develops a psychiatric illness as a result of seeing A injure himself]. What if A raises, by way of a defence, the fact that he had drunk too much because B had unjustifiably threatened to leave him for another man or had fabricated an allegation of child sexual abuse against him? Should the law of tort concern itself with this issue? In a case where A's self-harm is deliberate, the possibility that B's claim may be met by a defence of contributory negligence, alleging that B's behaviour caused A to harm himself, is an alarming one.[98]

Once again, this is not wholly convincing. Suppose, to take Cazalet J's example, A – in his drunken state – carelessly set fire to the family home and B only escaped the fire after she

[95] [2000] 1 WLR 1970.

[96] Ibid., 1984.

[97] The physical danger principle will still bind the would-be suicide – so he will owe other people a duty not to commit suicide in such a way that, it can reasonably be foreseen, will result in their suffering some kind of physical injury. So someone who wants to commit suicide will have a duty not to do it by taking a plane flight and blowing it up in mid-flight. Similarly, he will have a duty not to commit suicide by throwing himself off the top of a skyscraper if it is reasonably foreseeable that people walking around the base of the skyscraper will suffer some kind of physical injury if he does so.

[98] Ibid., 1985.

had been severely burned. In this case, the law will not prevent B from suing A in negligence in respect of her burns – even though allowing her to bring such an action will give rise to the same sort of difficulties as Cazalet J thought would arise if, in his example, B were allowed to sue A in negligence in respect of her psychiatric illness.

Primary and secondary victims

Suppose Alan has caused an accident *x* to occur and Lara has developed a psychiatric illness as a result. Judges and academics usually say that whether or not Alan owed Lara a duty to take care not to cause accident *x* to occur will depend on whether Lara was a 'primary' or 'secondary' victim of accident *x*. If Lara was a 'primary' victim of accident *x* then one set of rules will apply to determine whether Alan owed her a duty to take care not to cause accident *x* to occur. If Lara was a 'secondary' victim of accident *x* then a different set of rules will apply. We have avoided using language like this in discussing what has to be shown to establish that Alan owed Lara a duty to take care not to cause accident *x*. This is for two reasons.

First of all, the courts cannot seem to agree on when Lara will have been a 'primary' victim of accident *x* and when she will have been a 'secondary' victim of accident *x*. The distinction between 'primary' and 'secondary' victims of an accident was first introduced into English law in the *Alcock* case by Lord Oliver of Aylmerton. Lord Oliver said that Lara will have been a 'primary' victim of accident *x* if she 'was involved, either mediately or immediately, as a participant'[99] in accident *x* and held that she would be so involved if she was 'physically involved in [accident *x*], either through the direct threat of bodily injury to [herself as a result of the occurrence of accident *x*] or in coming to the aid of others injured or threatened [as a result of the occurrence of accident *x*]'[100] or if the occurrence of accident *x* 'put [her] in the position of being, or of thinking that [s]he is about to be or has been the involuntary cause of another's death or injury and [Lara's psychiatric illness] stemmed from the shock to [her] of the consciousness of this supposed fact'.[101] On the other hand, Lara will have been a 'secondary' victim of accident *x* if she 'was no more than the passive and unwilling witness of injury caused to others'.[102]

So, on Lord Oliver's view, the claimants in *Page* v *Smith*, *Chadwick* v *British Transport Commission* and *Dooley* v *Cammell Laird & Co. Ltd* were all 'primary victims' while the claimants in *Alcock* were 'secondary victims'. However, in *Page* v *Smith*,[103] Lord Lloyd proposed that in the case we are considering – where B developed a psychiatric illness as a result of A's causing accident *x* to occur – B will only have been a 'primary victim' of accident *x* if it was foreseeable that someone like B would suffer some kind of physical injury if accident *x* occurred.[104] On this view, the claimants in *Page* v *Smith* and *Chadwick* v *British*

99 [1992] 1 AC 310, 407.
100 Ibid., 408.
101 Ibid., 408.
102 Ibid., 407.
103 [1996] AC 155.
104 Lord Goff has questioned whether Lord Lloyd could possibly have meant to say this: see *Frost* v *Chief Constable of South Yorkshire* [1999] 2 AC 455, 478–80. However, Lord Goff assumed in *Frost* that a 'secondary victim' of an accident who developed a psychiatric illness as a result of the occurrence of that accident could only recover in respect of his illness if there was a close tie of love and affection between him and someone involved in the accident and he witnessed the accident occur or its immediate aftermath: ibid, 472F. (Note that this understanding of the law is flat contrary to what was said in the *Alcock* case: see above, p. 105.) If this is

Transport Commission were 'primary victims' while the claimants in *Dooley* v *Cammell Laird & Co. Ltd* and *Alcock* were 'secondary victims'. Lord Steyn endorsed Lord Lloyd's view of when someone will be a 'primary victim' of an accident in *Frost* v *Chief Constable of South Yorkshire*.[105] However, in *W* v *Essex County Council*, Lord Slynn remarked that 'the categorisation of those claiming to be included as primary or secondary victims is not as I read the cases finally closed. It is a concept still to be developed in different factual situations'[106] and seemed to endorse Lord Oliver's view in *Alcock* that the claimant in *Dooley* v *Cammell Laird & Co. Ltd* was properly to be classified as being a 'primary victim' of the accident in that case.[107]

Given this confusion over the meanings of the terms 'primary victim' and 'secondary victim' it seems to us better to dispense with these terms in discussing this area of the law: a clear understanding of the law can only be achieved if the law is stated in clear terms.[108] Our second reason for ignoring the fashionable distinction between 'primary' and 'secondary' victims is that the distinction is completely unnecessary. One can perfectly well discuss this area of the law without making use of this distinction at all – as we have attempted to do above.[109]

Psychiatric illness arising out of someone else's being maltreated

We are concerned here with the situation where A has maltreated C – without killing or injuring him – and B has as a result developed a psychiatric illness. Authority on when B will be able in this kind of situation to establish that A owed her a duty of care not to act

---

right and one takes Lord Lloyd's view that someone is only a primary victim of an accident if it was foreseeable that the occurrence of that accident would put him in danger of suffering some kind of accident, then that would mean *Dooley* v *Cammell Laird & Co. Ltd* [1951] 1 Lloyd's Rep 271 was wrongly decided. Hence Lord Goff's incredulity at Lord Lloyd's restrictive definition of when someone will be a 'primary victim' of an accident. But if one dispenses with Lord Goff's assumption as to when a 'secondary victim' of an accident will be entitled to recover in respect of a psychiatric illness that he has suffered as a result of the occurrence of that accident, then Lord Lloyd's view becomes unexceptionable.

105 [1999] 2 AC 455, 496H–B. Subject, presumably, to the qualification that someone will count as having been a 'primary victim' of an accident if he *believed* (incorrectly) that the occurrence of that accident put him in danger of suffering some kind of harm.

106 [2001] 2 AC 592, 601.

107 Ibid., 601.

108 Cf. Teff 1998, 113–14: '... preoccupation with a victim's "primary" or "secondary" status only adds a further layer of obfuscation, distracting attention from the central issue ... The primary/secondary divide ... is ... a recipe for more litigation and further confusion.'

109 *Important note.* Regrettably, the courts seem to be going in the opposite direction from that advocated in the text and have started to regard the distinction between 'primary' and 'secondary' victims as of crucial importance for the purpose of whether a duty of care was owed in *any* case where someone has suffered a psychiatric illness as a result of someone else's actions. See, for example, *Hatton* v *Sutherland* [2002] 2 All ER 1, at [19]–[22]. That case concerned the question of whether an employer owed an employee a duty not to make her do stressful work without giving her any assistance or counselling. It beggars belief that the courts think that the (vague) distinction between 'primary' and 'secondary' victims can be applied outside the context of a situation where a defendant's actions have resulted in someone's being killed or injured and a third party has suffered a psychiatric illness as a result. In *that* sort of context, one *might* distinguish between the person who was killed or injured (a 'primary' victim of the defendant's actions) and the psychiatric-illness-suffering third party (a 'secondary' victim of the defendant's actions). But in a case where A has made B do particularly stressful work which has resulted in B's suffering a psychiatric illness, it makes absolutely no sense whatsoever to ask whether B is a 'primary' or 'secondary' victim of A's actions.

in the way he did is currently thin on the ground.[110] Presumably, in order to determine whether A owed B a duty of care in this kind of case, the courts would apply by analogy the principles set out above that determine when a duty of care will have been owed in the case where A killed or injured C and B suffered a psychiatric illness as a result. So, for example, suppose Eric threatened to kill Wendy's girlfriend, Karen, and Wendy developed a psychiatric illness as a result. And suppose Wendy wanted to sue Eric for damages, arguing that he owed her a duty not to act as he did. Wendy would certainly first have to show that it was reasonably foreseeable that she would develop a psychiatric illness as a result of Eric's threats. If she sought to establish reasonable foreseeability on the basis that she was in a 'close and loving relationship' with Karen, she would presumably then have to show that her psychiatric illness was triggered as a result of her witnessing Eric threatening Karen or the immediate aftermath of Eric's threats.[111]

Psychiatric illness arising as a result of being given bad news

We are concerned here with the situation where A has given B some bad news and B has developed a psychiatric illness as a result. Say, for example, that A told B her daughter was dead and B developed a psychiatric illness as a result. She now wants to sue A in negligence for compensation, arguing that he owed her a duty of care not to act as he did.[112] Four different variations on this situation need to be distinguished.

(1) *B's daughter was dead and A acted responsibly in telling B this news.* In this case, B will *not* be able to establish that A owed her a duty of care not to act as he did: A acted perfectly reasonably and no one can be held to owe another a duty of care not to act reasonably.[113]

(2) *B's daughter was dead but A acted insensitively in telling B this news in the way he did.* The question of whether A will have owed B a duty in this situation to take care that he did not act insensitively in breaking the news to her of her daughter's death has not finally been decided. The issue came up in *AB* v *Tameside & Glossop HA*,[114] where a number of claimants claimed to have developed psychiatric illnesses because the defendant health authority had acted insensitively in telling them *by letter* (rather than face to face) that they might have been treated by a nurse who was HIV+. However, it was held that under the circumstances the defendant health authority had acted reasonably and that it could not therefore be argued that the defendant health authority had owed the claimants a duty of

110 Recent examples: *Duddin* v *Home Office* [2004] EWCA Civ 181 (claimant prisoner claimed to have developed a psychiatric illness as a result of a prisoner officer's making inappropriate remarks of a sexual nature to the claimant's wife; claim dismissed because no foreseeability of psychiatric illness established); *A* v *Leeds Teaching Hospital NHS Trust* [2004] EWHC 644 (claimant parents whose babies had died claimed to have developed psychiatric illnesses as a result of the defendant hospital's retaining body parts belonging to their babies without the claimants' consent; issue of whether the hospital owed the claimants a duty of care not to act in the way they did disposed of by holding that in the immediate aftermath of the babies' deaths, the claimants were the hospital's patients).

111 This is consistent with the approach adopted by the Court of Appeal in *Duddin* v *Home Office* [2004] EWCA Civ 181.

112 If B's daughter was killed as a result of C's actions, then whether or not B can sue C in negligence for compensation for her psychiatric illness, arguing that C owed her a duty to take care not to act as he did, will depend on the principles set out above, at pp. 94–105.

113 See above, pp. 59–60.

114 (1997) 35 BMLR 79 (noted, Dziobon & Tettenborn 1997).

care not to act as it did. What the position would have been had the defendant health authority been held to have acted insensitively was never therefore decided. It may be that in the case we are considering, the courts would simply give effect to Lord Atkin's neighbour principle and hold that A did owe B a duty to take care not to be insensitive in the way he broke the news to her or her daughter's death if it was reasonably foreseeable that A's being insensitive would cause B to develop a psychiatric illness.[115]

(3) *B's daughter was not dead, but A had good reason to think that she was and acted responsibly in telling B that her daughter was dead.* In this case, B will *not* be able to establish that A owed her a duty of care not to act as he did because A acted reasonably under the circumstances.

(4) *B's daughter was not dead and A had no good reason for thinking that she was.* In this case, A could not argue that he acted reasonably in telling B that her daughter was dead. Could B then argue that A owed her a duty of care not to act as he did? It seems to be the case that so long as it was reasonably foreseeable that B would develop a psychiatric illness as a result of A's misinforming her as to the fate of her daughter,[116] then the courts will find that A *did* owe B a duty of care not to act as he did.[117] So in this sort of case, the courts will give full effect to Lord Atkin's neighbour principle, and so long as A's conduct was unreasonable and it was reasonably foreseeable that B would suffer a psychiatric illness as a result of A's conduct, they will find that A owed B a duty of care not to act as he did.[118]

Psychiatric illness arising as a result of being subjected to a distressing or humiliating experience

In *Wainwright* v *Home Office*,[119] a man named Patrick O'Neill was arrested and taken into custody on a charge of murder. His mother and his brother went to visit him in prison. When they arrived at the prison they were strip-searched to check that they were not carrying any drugs that they could hand over to O'Neill. The strip-search was conducted by ordering the mother and the brother to undress; though the prison guards did touch the brother in the course of the strip-search. The mother was very distressed by the whole

[115] But even if the existence of a duty of care were allowed in this case, it would still have to be shown that A breached that duty of care and, more importantly, that A's breach triggered B's psychiatric illness; in other words, that B suffered her psychiatric illness because A was insensitive and not because her daughter had died.

[116] This might be hard to establish in the case where B was told by A that her daughter was dead but was told two minutes later that in fact her daughter was alive and well. One would expect B to feel overwhelming relief in this situation, and not to suffer a psychiatric illness. But see, on this, the case of *Farrell* v *Avon Health Authority* [2001] Lloyd's Rep Med 458, where a claimant who developed post-traumatic stress disorder after being told incorrectly that his newly-born son was dead was allowed to sue for compensation even though he was told five minutes later that there had been a mistake and his son was alive and well.

[117] *Allin* v *City & Hackney HA* [1996] 7 Med LR 167.

[118] The decision of the House of Lords in *Wainwright* v *Home Office* [2003] 3 WLR 1137 supports this point. That decision makes it clear that were the facts of *Wilkinson* v *Downton* [1897] 2 QB 57 (discussed below, pp. 114–16) to occur today – that is, were a claimant to be made physically sick as a result of a defendant's lying to her and telling her that her husband had been injured when he had not been – the claimant would be allowed to sue the defendant in negligence. The House of Lords' decision also makes it pretty clear that the same would be true if the claimant merely suffered a *psychiatric illness* as a result of the defendant's lies – she would be allowed to sue the defendant in negligence for compensation for her illness.

[119] [2004] 2 AC 406.

experience. The consequences of the strip-search for the brother were more serious: it was found that the strip-search had caused to him suffer a psychiatric illness.

The mother and the brother sued the prison authorities for damages. The mother could not sue the prison authorities in negligence because it is well established that you cannot normally sue in negligence for damages for pure distress.[120] And the brother did not need to rely on the law of negligence to sue the prison authorities: he could argue that the prison guards committed the tort of battery[121] in touching him, and sue them for damages on the basis that his psychiatric illness was triggered by their committing that tort. The interesting question for our purposes is whether the brother *could* have sued the prison authorities in negligence for compensation for his psychiatric illness, by arguing that they owed him a duty of care not to subject him to the distressing and humiliating experience of being strip-searched. Let's assume for the purposes of discussing this question that: (1) it was reasonably foreseeable that strip-searching the brother would result in his suffering a psychiatric illness (thus bringing *Wainwright* within the scope of Lord Atkin's neighbour principle); and (2) the prison authorities acted unreasonably in strip-searching the brother.

Given these two assumptions, could the brother have argued that the prison authorities owed him a duty of care not to order him to undress? The House of Lords' decision in *Wainwright* is frustratingly unclear on the issue.[122] In favour of the answer 'yes' is Lord Hoffmann's treatment in *Wainwright* of the case of *Janvier* v *Sweeney*.[123] In that case, the claimant was made physically sick as a result of the defendants' threatening her. She sued the defendants for damages and was allowed to recover on the ground that the defendants had committed a tort in relation to her in threatening her – the tort in *Wilkinson* v *Downton*.[124] Lord Hoffmann made it clear that he thought: (1) that the claimant in *Janvier* v *Sweeney* could have sued the defendants in negligence; and (2) that the claimant would have been entitled to succeed against the defendants even if she had merely suffered a psychiatric illness as a result of their threats.[125]

But if this is right, and the claimant in *Janvier* could have argued that the defendants in that case owed her a duty of care not to threaten her, then the claimant in *Wainwright* could equally well have argued that the defendants in that case owed him a duty of care not to order him to undress. However, there is a *dictum* in *Wainwright* which goes against this and indicates that the brother could not have sued the prison authorities in negligence, arguing that they owed him a duty of care not to order him to undress. In his judgment, Lord Scott observed, 'I agree with the Court of Appeal [in *Wainwright*], and with your Lordships, that if there had been no touching, as there was not in [the mother's] case, no tort would have

120 See below, pp. 580–1. Instead, the mother sought to sue the prison authorities on the basis: (1) that the common law recognises a tort of invasion of privacy and the prison authorities committed that tort when they ordered her to undress; and (2) that the prison authorities committed the tort in *Wilkinson* v *Downton* by ordering her to undress. The House of Lords dismissed the mother's claim, holding that: (1) the common law does not recognise a tort of invasion of privacy (see below, pp. 319, 338); and (2) that the tort in *Wilkinson* v *Downton* should be subsumed within the tort of negligence and that therefore a claim cannot be brought under *Wilkinson* v *Downton* where a claim in negligence would not be available (see below, pp. 114–16).

121 Discussed below, pp. 249–62.

122 This is perhaps understandable given the way *Wainwright* was argued.

123 [1919] 2 KB 316.

124 For an account of the tort in *Wilkinson* v *Downton*, see below, pp. 114–16.

125 [2003] 3 WLR 1137, at [40]: 'By the time of *Janvier* v *Sweeney* . . . the law was able comfortably to [deal with this kind of case] in the law of *nervous shock caused by negligence*' (emphasis added).

been committed.'[126] If this is right then if no one had touched the brother, the brother would not have been able to sue the prison authorities in negligence or anything else – and this is so even if the whole experience of being strip-searched caused the brother to suffer a psychiatric illness.

Our own view, for what it is worth, is that Lord Scott was wrong and that the brother in *Wainwright* could have sued the prison authorities in negligence had he chosen to do so.[127]

Psychiatric illness arising as a result of being made to do stressful work

We are concerned here with the situation where A makes B do some work which is very stressful and B develops a psychiatric illness as a result. In order to establish that A owed her a duty of care not to make her do that work, the very first thing that B has to establish is that it was *reasonably foreseeable* that she would develop a psychiatric illness if she were made to do that kind of work. But even if B can do this, that may not be enough to show that A owed B a duty of care not to make her do the work that triggered her psychiatric illness.

(1) *The requirement of reasonable foreseeability.* In *Walker* v *Northumberland County Council*,[128] the claimant was employed by the defendant local authority as an area social services officer from 1970 to 1987. He was responsible for managing teams of social services fieldworkers in an area which had a high proportion of child care problems. In 1986 the claimant had a nervous breakdown as a result of the stress his job was putting on him. When he came back to work he discovered that there was a considerable backlog of work waiting for him to clear up and within six months he had another nervous breakdown which led to his stopping work permanently. When he was dismissed by the defendant local authority on grounds of permanent ill health, the claimant sued the defendant local authority in negligence so as to be compensated for the loss of income resulting from his second, irremediable, nervous breakdown. The Court of Appeal allowed the claimant's claim, holding that when the claimant came back to work, the defendant local authority had owed the claimant a duty of care which required them to provide the claimant with some kind of assistance to perform his work. The basis for finding that the local authority

126 Ibid., at [60].

127 In support of this it may be observed that Lord Scott seemed completely to forget that the brother in *Wainwright* suffered a psychiatric illness: see ibid., at [57]: 'The essence of the complaint of each claimant is that he or she was subjected to conduct by the prison officers . . . that was calculated to, and did, cause humiliation and distress' (this was of course *not* the essence of the brother's complaint); and at [58]: '. . . there is an important difference between the case of [the brother] and that of [the mother]. In the course of, and as part of, the strip-search . . . one of the prison officers [touched the brother] . . .' (the other important difference, unnoted by Lord Scott, is of course that the brother suffered a psychiatric illness and the mother did not). The decision of Field J in *C* v *D* [2006] EWHC 166 also supports our analysis. In that case, when the claimant was a schoolboy, on one occasion the claimant's headmaster pulled the claimant's trousers down while he was in the school infirmary and stared at the claimant's genitals; the claimant developed a psychiatric illness as a result. Field J held that the headmaster was liable in tort to compensate the claimant for his psychiatric illness. Admittedly, the tort in question was the tort in *Wilkinson* v *Downton* (see below, pp. 114–16), but if it is right that a claim in negligence can be made whenever a claim under *Wilkinson* v *Downton* can be made, then Field J's decision implies that the headmaster owed the claimant a duty of care not to act in the way he did.

128 [1995] 1 All ER 737.

had owed the claimant such a duty of care was that it had been reasonably foreseeable when the claimant came back to work that he would suffer a second breakdown if the local authority insisted that he perform his duties without giving him any kind of assistance.

However, it was crucial to the outcome of the case that the claimant in *Walker* had *already* suffered a nervous breakdown. It was that first breakdown that made his second breakdown reasonably foreseeable. The decision of the Court of Appeal in *Hatton* v *Sutherland*[129] makes it clear that an employee who suffers a nervous breakdown as a result of being made to do particularly stressful work without any assistance or counselling will find it *very* difficult to show that her breakdown was reasonably foreseeable if nothing was done or nothing happened before her breakdown to alert her employers to the fact that she was having difficulty coping with the amount or type of work that she had to do. In that case, the Court of Appeal was hostile to the idea that the mere nature of an employee's work may be enough to make it reasonably foreseeable that she will develop a psychiatric illness if she is made to do that work without any kind of assistance or counselling.[130] The court went on to observe that, '*Unless he knows of some particular problem or vulnerability, an employer is entitled to assume that his employee is up to the normal pressures of the job*.'[131]

(2) *Reasonable foreseeability may not be enough*. The decision of the Court of Appeal in the *Walker* case seems to suggest that if it is reasonably foreseeable that an employee will develop a psychiatric illness if her employer makes her do some kind of work, then the employer will owe her a duty of care not to make her do that kind of work without giving her some kind of assistance. However, since *Walker* was decided, the courts have shown themselves uneasy at the idea that an employee can demand to be excused from, or given assistance to perform, some or all of her contractual duties merely because it is reasonably foreseeable that if she performs those duties without assistance, she will develop a psychiatric illness. For example, Lord Rodger observed in *Barber* v *Somerset County Council*,

> The contract of employment will usually regulate what is to happen if an employee becomes unable, due to illness or injury, to carry out his duties. There may be provision for a defined period on full pay, followed by a further defined period on reduced pay, followed by termination of the contract. At the end of the process the employer is free to make new arrangements. While the timetable is likely to be definite, the exact legal analysis of the employee's position when off work under such provisions is by no means free from difficulty. Whatever the position, however, the introduction of a tortious duty of reasonable care on the employer to provide assistance so that the employee can return to work and draw his normal pay, but do less than his full duties for an indefinite period, does not sit easily with such contractual arrangements. Nor does it seem likely to promote efficiency within the enterprise or department.[132]

In *Koehler* v *Cerebos*,[133] the High Court of Australia went further, holding that 'An employer may not be liable for psychiatric injury to an employee brought about by the employee's

[129] [2002] 2 All ER 1.
[130] Ibid., at [12] and at [24].
[131] Ibid., at [29] (emphasis in original). In *Barber* v *Somerset County Council* [2004] 1 WLR 1089, the House of Lords expressed broad agreement with this statement: ibid., at [5] (per Lord Scott: '[The Court of Appeal's decision in *Hatton* succeeds] in succinctly and accurately expressing the principles that ought to be applied') and, more tepidly, at [64] (per Lord Walker: '[The Court of Appeal's decision in *Hatton* provides] useful practical guidance, but it must be read as that, and not as having anything like statutory force').
[132] [2004] 1 WLR 1089, at [34].
[133] (2005) 222 CLR 44.

performance of the duties originally stipulated in the contract of employment ... Insistence upon performance of a contract cannot be in breach of a duty of care.'[134] If this is right, it severely narrows the scope of situations where an employee who has suffered a perfectly foreseeable psychiatric illness as a result of being made to do stressful work can sue in negligence for compensation for that illness. In effect, she would only be able to sue if she did not originally agree to do that kind (or level) of work when she started working for her employer, but her employer subsequently required her to do that kind (or level) of work.[135]

It is still unclear whether the English courts will follow these *dicta*. However, it may be suggested that, given the scope of the powers enjoyed by the courts to imply terms into contracts of employment to protect the interests of employees when it would be fair, just and reasonable to do so, this is one of those occasions when there is no point 'in searching for a liability in tort where the parties are in a contractual relationship'.[136] In other words, if the law of contract does not protect an employee who has developed a psychiatric illness as a result of the work she was made to do, it is hard to understand why the law of negligence should do any more for her. The reasons why the employee cannot bring a claim in contract for her psychiatric illness will apply with equal force to stop the employee bringing a claim in negligence for that illness.

WILKINSON v *DOWNTON*: THE REDUNDANT TORT

Before we go on to see how Lord Atkin's neighbour principle applies in cases where it is reasonably foreseeable that someone's acting in a particular way will harm someone else's property, we should briefly mention the tort in *Wilkinson* v *Downton*. This tort has been rendered redundant by the existence of the rules and principles set out so far in this chapter – but student readers of this book may still be expected to know about the tort in *Wilkinson* v *Downton* and mention it in their exams.

In *Wilkinson* v *Downton*,[137] the defendant played a joke on the claimant by telling her that her husband had met with a serious accident and that both his legs had been broken. In fact, as the defendant well knew, this was not true. The claimant was so upset to receive this news that she was physically sick. The claimant subsequently sued the defendant for compensation. At the time the case was decided, there existed a rule that you could not sue a defendant in negligence for compensation for some physical injury that you had suffered if the defendant had caused you to suffer that physical injury by making you distressed or upset.[138] Wright J, who decided *Wilkinson* v *Downton*, got round this rule by holding that the claimant was not confined to suing the defendant in negligence but could sue the defendant on the ground that he had committed a quite different tort in relation to her, which was subsequently dubbed 'the tort in *Wilkinson* v *Downton*'.

[134] Ibid., at [29].

[135] Ibid., at [37]. This was the case in *Daw* v *Intel Corporation (UK) Ltd* [2007] EWCA Civ 70, where the claimant worked for the defendants as a mergers and acquisitions payroll integration analyst and suffered a nervous breakdown when poor management resulted in her being loaded with more and more responsibilities with which she could not cope.

[136] *Tai Hing Cotton Mill* v *Liu Chong Hing Bank* [1986] AC 80, at 107 (per Lord Scarman).

[137] [1897] 2 QB 57.

[138] This rule was subsequently abolished in *Dulieu* v *White & Sons* [1901] 2 KB 669, discussed below, pp. 596–7.

Subsequent case law[139] has made it clear that A will be held to have committed the tort in *Wilkinson* v *Downton* in relation to B if:

(1) A deliberately did something unjustifiable to B; and
(2) A's actions caused B to suffer either a physical injury or a psychiatric illness; and
(3) at the time A acted – (i) A intended to cause B to suffer a physical injury or psychiatric illness; or (ii) A knew that his actions might cause B to suffer a physical injury or a psychiatric illness; or (iii) it was highly likely that A's actions would cause B to suffer a physical injury or a psychiatric illness.

However, if (1), (2) and (3) are established, then B will be able to sue A in *negligence*, claiming that A owed her a duty of care not to act in the way he did, and that he breached that duty of care, and she suffered a physical injury or a psychiatric illness as a result. So the tort in *Wilkinson* v *Downton* is completely redundant – no claimant will have to rely on it to sue a defendant in tort successfully.[140] If the claimant can bring a claim under the tort in *Wilkinson* v *Downton*, then he or she can also bring a claim in negligence. As a result, the Court of Appeal recently urged that claims that could formerly have been brought under *Wilkinson* v *Downton* should now be brought in negligence: 'It seems preferable for the law to develop along conventional modern lines rather than through recourse to this obscure tort, whose jurisprudential basis remains unclear.'[141] However, as Lord Hoffmann observed in *Wainwright* v *Home Office*, 'Commentators and counsel have . . . been unwilling to allow *Wilkinson* v *Downton* to disappear beneath the surface of the law of negligence'[142] and so it is as well for students to know about the existence of this tort, and to mention that it has been committed in answering any problem question where (1), (2) and (3), above, are established.

The tort in *Wilkinson* v *Downton* would still have some role to play if a claim for damages for mere distress could be made under it: as we have seen and will see, such claims cannot easily be made in negligence.[143] However, the Court of Appeal[144] and the House of Lords[145] have firmly rejected the idea that the claimant in *Wilkinson* v *Downton* could still have sued the defendant had she merely been distressed, and not been made physically sick, by the defendant's practical joke. In *Wainwright* v *Home Office*, Lord Hoffmann observed that because claims under the tort in *Wilkinson* v *Downton* can be made merely on the basis that it was *highly likely* that the claimant would suffer harm as a result of the defendant's actions, it would not be desirable to allow claimants to make claims for mere distress under the tort in *Wilkinson* v *Downton*. It cannot be a tort merely to do something that is *highly likely* to make someone else suffer distress.[146] Lord Hoffmann suggested that *at a minimum*

[139] *Wong* v *Parkside Health NHS Trust* [2003] 3 All ER 932, at [12]; *Wainwright* v *Home Office* [2004] 2 AC 406, at [41] and [44]; *C* v *D* [2006] EWHC 166, at [94] and [99].

[140] A former Professor of Law at Oxford University used to say that if A poisoned B's drink and B was made sick as a result of drinking the poison, the only tort B could sue A under was the tort in *Wilkinson* v *Downton*. But there seems no reason why B could not sue A in negligence here: A owed B a duty to take care not to poison her drink and he clearly breached that duty by putting poison in her drink. Negligence liability covers intentional acts, as well as careless acts: see above, pp. 48–9.

[141] *A* v *Hoare* [2006] 1 WLR 2320, at [136].

[142] [2004] 2 AC 406, at [41].

[143] See above, p. 63, and below, pp. 580–1.

[144] *Wong* v *Parkside Health NHS Trust* [2003] 3 All ER 932.

[145] *Wainwright* v *Home Office* [2004] 2 AC 406.

[146] Ibid., at [44]–[45].

it would have to be shown that: 'The defendant must actually have acted in a way that he knew [was] unjustifiable and [he] either intended to cause [distress] or at least acted without caring whether he caused [distress] or not.'[147] But even if this could be shown, he wished to reserve his position on whether in such a case a defendant would be liable for causing a claimant to suffer mere distress.[148]

HARM TO PROPERTY CASES

The property harm principle

The other type of case where Lord Atkin's neighbour principle has been applied to find that a defendant owed a claimant a duty of care is the case where A has done *x* and an item of property has suffered some kind of harm as a result. The basic principle that applies here is that A will normally have owed B a duty to take care not to do *x* if:

(1) at the time the property was harmed as a result of A's doing *x*, B had a sufficient interest in that property; *and*
(2) it was reasonably foreseeable at the time A did *x* that his doing *x* would result in that type of property being harmed.

Let's call this principle the *property harm principle*. A couple of examples can be given from the cases of this principle at work.

In *Spartan Steel & Alloys Ltd* v *Martin & Co. (Contractors) Ltd*,[149] the defendants – contractors who were employed to dig up a road – damaged an electric power cable that supplied power to the claimants' factory. The claimants were producers of stainless steel and were, at the time of the power cut, melting some metal in their furnaces to turn it into stainless steel ingots. The power cut caused the metal in the furnaces to be damaged. The claimants sued the defendants in negligence for compensation for damage done to the 'melts' that they were processing at the time of the power cut. The Court of Appeal allowed the claimants to recover, holding that the defendants had owed the claimants, and breached, a duty to take care not to damage any electric power cables running under the road on which they were working. The defendants had owed the claimants such a duty under the property harm principle: it was reasonably foreseeable at the time the defendants were working that if they damaged any electric power cables running under the road, the supply of electricity to nearby factories such as the claimants' would be interrupted and property being used or processed in those factories would be damaged as a result.[150]

In *Capital & Counties plc* v *Hampshire CC*,[151] the claimants were tenants of a modern commercial building called 'The Crescent'. The Crescent caught on fire and the fire brigade

[147] Ibid., at [45].
[148] Ibid., at [46]. The tort of intentional infliction of harm by unlawful means (dealt with below, Chapter 21) might have proved useful to claimants seeking some redress against a defendant who intentionally caused them to suffer distress. However, the courts seem to have ruled out the possibility that damages for mere distress might be recoverable under this tort: see below, p. 433.
[149] [1973] QB 27. See also *SCM (United Kingdom) Ltd* v *W & J Whittall & Son Ltd* [1971] 1 QB 337.
[150] The claimants were, however, *not* allowed to sue for damages in respect of the money they would have made had they been allowed to continue working during the time their power was cut off. For an explanation of this aspect of the *Spartan Steel* case, see below, p. 579.
[151] [1997] QB 1004.

was called to deal with the fire. Although the seat of the fire had not been located, the fire officer ordered that the building's sprinkler system be turned off. As a result, the fire spread rapidly and destroyed The Crescent. The claimants sued for compensation, claiming that the fire officer had owed them a duty not to switch off the sprinkler system. The Court of Appeal agreed that such a duty had been owed. The fire officer owed the claimants this duty under the property harm principle: it had been reasonably foreseeable at the time the fire officer attended the fire at The Crescent that The Crescent would burn down if its sprinkler system was turned off.

Let's now look at some of the key terms employed in the property harm principle in more detail.

What sort of harm?

What sort of harm to property has to have been done before this rule can be invoked? Two points can be made in response to this question.

(a) Destruction and damage

If A's doing *x* results in an item of property being destroyed or damaged,[152] then A's doing *x* will obviously have harmed the property for the purposes of the property harm principle. However, there are two very important qualifications to this.

(1) *Creating an item of property with a defect in it.* Suppose A creates an item of property which has a defect in it. The defect eventually results in the item of property being destroyed or damaged. In this sort of case, it cannot be said that A did anything to harm the item of property in question. A did not make the item of property in question worse in any way; he merely failed to make it better.

So, for example, suppose that Acme Products Ltd employed Megamix Construction Ltd to build a warehouse for them. Megamix gave Concreto Ltd the job of laying the floor of the warehouse. Unfortunately, Concreto used the wrong kind of concrete in laying the floor of the warehouse and, as a result, four years later the floor began to crack up. Acme attempts to sue Concreto in negligence for compensation for the fact that the floor of their warehouse has begun to crack up, claiming that Concreto owed them a duty to take care not to use the wrong kind of concrete in laying the floor. Now – it is well established, in England at least, that Acme's claim will fail. In the absence of any 'special relationship' between Acme and Concreto – which, let us suppose, did not exist here[153] – the courts will find that Concreto did *not* owe Acme a duty to take care not to use the wrong kind of concrete in laying the floor.[154]

152 *Important note.* Property will be 'damaged' if it is *physically changed in a way that makes it less useful or valuable*: *Hunter* v *Canary Wharf* [1997] AC 655, 676 (per Pill LJ). So in the *Hunter* case, the Court of Appeal held that the deposit of *excessive* dust on a carpet could constitute property damage for the purposes of negligence – but that the mere fact that it would cost money to remove a contaminant did not mean that there had been property damage. And in *Blue Circle Industries* v *Ministry of Defence* [1999] Ch 289, the Court of Appeal was willing to hold that the intermingling of plutonium with soil so that *it could not be removed* amounted to a form of property damage. See Weston 1999 for a very useful discussion of when someone who has lost computer data can argue that their property has been damaged.

153 Such a 'special relationship' did exist in *Junior Books Ltd* v *Veitchi Co. Ltd* [1983] 1 AC 520, discussed below, p. 135.

154 *Murphy* v *Brentwood DC* [1991] 1 AC 398; *Dept of the Environment* v *Thomas Bates & Son Ltd* [1991] 1 AC 499.

Why can't Acme use the property harm principle here to establish that Concreto owed them a duty of care in this case? Why can't they argue: (1) the floor belonged to us when it was harmed as a result of Concreto's using the wrong kind of concrete to lay the floor; *and* (2) it was reasonably foreseeable at the time Concreto laid the floor that the floor would suffer some harm in the future if they used the wrong kind of concrete in laying it? The reason why they can't use this argument is that (1) will not be true. The fact is, the floor was *never* harmed as a result of Concreto's using the wrong kind of concrete to lay the floor. Concreto's actions did not make the floor worse; Concreto merely failed to make it better.

(2) *Inflicting a defect on a previously sound item of property*. Suppose that there exists some sound item of property and A does something to make it defective. Suppose further that that defect destroys or damages that item of property at some time in the future. In this sort of case, A will be held to have harmed the item of property in question *when he made it defective*, *not* when the defect in the property destroyed or damaged the item of property.

So suppose that B puts a vase up for auction. The vase is displayed for inspection to potential bidders the day before the auction, along with all the other auction items. A looks at the vase but he puts the vase back on its stand a little roughly and as a result a small crack develops in the base of the vase. No one else notices the crack and at the auction C successfully bids for the vase. She takes the vase home. However, over time, the crack spreads and eventually the vase shatters. It is well established that in this sort of situation, C will *not* be entitled to sue A in negligence for compensation for the loss of her vase. She will not be able to establish that A owed her a duty to take care not to handle the vase roughly when inspecting it.[155]

But why can't she use the property harm principle here to establish that A owed her such a duty of care? Why can't she say – (1) the vase belonged to me when it was harmed as a result of A's rough handling of it; and (2) it was reasonably foreseeable at the time A inspected the vase that it would be harmed if he handled it roughly? The reason she can't say this is that (1) will not be true. The vase was not harmed as a result of A's rough handling *when it shattered* but when A's rough handling caused it to develop a crack – and the vase belonged to B at that time, not C.

So an item of property which is *already* defective will suffer no *further* harm if the defect subsequently destroys or damages that item of property. It follows that if B acquires an item of property that was already defective and the defect destroys or damages that item of property, B will not be able to claim that the item of property in question was harmed when it was in her hands. So she will not be able to use the property harm principle to establish that whoever was responsible for the property being defective owed her a duty to take care not to act as they did.

While this rule is easy to state, it is not easy to apply. That is because it can be difficult to tell – in a given case where B has acquired an item of property which has subsequently been damaged or destroyed – whether that item of property was damaged or destroyed by a defect which was present in that property before B acquired it (in which case B will not be able to claim that the item of property in question was harmed while it was in her hands) or whether that item of property was basically sound when B acquired it and it was

155 *The Aliakmon* [1986] AC 785, discussed below, pp. 121–2.

damaged or destroyed by an outside source (in which case B can claim that she had an interest in the property when it was harmed).

For example, suppose Paul buys a plastic bottle of lemonade from the supermarket, takes it home and places it in his fridge. The bottle of lemonade was produced by XYZ Ltd. Unfortunately, due to some fault in the manufacture of the plastic bottle, the bottle does not cope well with the cold of Paul's fridge and eventually shatters, spilling lemonade all over the place. Paul wants to sue XYZ in negligence, claiming that they owed him, and breached, a duty to take care not to bottle the lemonade using a plastic bottle that was liable to shatter in the cold.

Now – what has happened here? Did Paul, in buying the bottle of lemonade, acquire *one* item of property – a bottle of lemonade – which suffered from a defect? If so, he cannot claim that the bottle of lemonade was harmed when it burst in Paul's fridge. As it was always defective, XYZ did not ever do anything to harm the bottle of lemonade; they merely failed to make it better than it was. It follows that Paul will not be able to use the property harm principle to establish that XYZ owed him a duty to take care not to bottle the lemonade using a plastic bottle that was liable to shatter in the cold: XYZ did nothing to harm his bottle of lemonade.

But, on the other hand, could it be argued that Paul, in buying the bottle of lemonade, acquired *two* items of property – a plastic bottle, which was defective, and some lemonade, which was basically sound but was harmed when it spilled all over Paul's fridge and kitchen floor? If this analysis is correct, Paul could use the property harm principle to establish that XYZ owed him a duty to take care not to bottle the lemonade in a plastic bottle that was liable to shatter in the cold. He could argue: (1) I had an interest in the lemonade when it was harmed as a result of XYZ bottling it in a plastic bottle that was liable to shatter in the cold; and (2) it was reasonably foreseeable at the time XYZ bottled the lemonade that the lemonade would be harmed if XYZ bottled it using a plastic bottle that was liable to shatter in the cold.

So which is it to be? Did Paul acquire one item of property here or two? It is very difficult to say.[156] In *Aswan Engineering* v *Lupdine Ltd*,[157] Lloyd LJ (with whom Fox LJ agreed) took the 'provisional view'[158] that in this sort of case Paul would be able to argue that the

[156] Nolan 2007 suggests (at 984, referring to Tettenborn 2000b) that if a component part of a chattel can be removed without damaging the other parts of the chattel, the component and the rest-of-the-chattel should be regarded as being two separate items of property. But it is not clear how this test would apply in this case. In theory, the lemonade could be separated from the plastic bottle without damaging the lemonade (by pouring it into another container, for example). On the other hand, the lemonade will spill and be spoiled if it is suddenly deprived of its plastic container.

[157] [1987] 1 WLR 1. In that case, the claimants ordered some waterproofing compound from L. L, in turn, ordered some pails from the defendants to store the compound in when shipping it to the claimants. Having obtained the pails from the defendants, L filled them with compound and L shipped them to the claimants in Kuwait, where they were left in the blazing sun. Eventually the heat caused the plastic pails to collapse and the compound was lost. The claimants sued the defendants in negligence, claiming that the defendants had owed them a duty not to supply L with the pails that they did because it was reasonably foreseeable that doing so would result in the compound sold by L to the claimants being lost. Lloyd and Fox LJJ dismissed the claim on the ground that as the defendants had no idea the pails would be shipped to Kuwait, it was not reasonably foreseeable that the compound sold by L to the claimants would be lost if it was shipped to the claimants in the pails that the defendants supplied to L. Nicholls LJ dismissed the claim on the ground that the manufacturer of a container will not owe a duty of care in manufacturing the container to anyone who loses his or her property as a result of the container being insufficiently sturdy.

[158] Ibid., 21.

lemonade and the bottle were two separate items of property and that Paul could therefore invoke the property harm principle to establish that XYZ owed him a duty to take care not to bottle the lemonade in a bottle which was liable to shatter when cold.

The problem also crops up – to take some other examples offered by Lloyd LJ in the *Aswan* case – where a claimant's car is damaged because one of its tyres (which was supplied with the car) bursts and where a bottle of wine acquired by the claimant becomes undrinkable because its cork is defective. In both these cases we have to determine whether what has happened is that *an* item of property (a car complete with tyres, a bottle of wine) has been damaged because it suffered from a defect which affected the property long before it was acquired by the claimant or whether it would be more accurate to say that a sound item of property belonging to the claimant (a car minus one of its tyres, wine) has been damaged by a separate item of property (a tyre, a cork) which suffered from a defect. Lloyd LJ's provisional view was that the latter analysis is correct in both cases. If this is right, the claimant will be able to argue that the manufacturer of the car/bottle of wine owed him a duty to take care not to fit/plug the car/bottle of wine with a defective tyre/cork.[159]

(b) Loss

If a claimant's property has not actually been destroyed or damaged but merely lost, will it count as being harmed under the property harm principle? To get an easy case out of the way, if A's doing *x* has resulted in B's property being sunk at sea, B will have no problem establishing that A owed him a duty to take care not to do *x* under the property harm principle – so long, of course, as it was foreseeable that A's doing *x* would have the kind of effect it did.

But what about the case where A's doing *x* has resulted in B's property being stolen? Suppose, for example, that Gary and Fred are both in prison; Fred has been sentenced to five years in prison for a number of burglary offences. Gary happens to tell Fred one day that his aunt, Beth, has an extremely precious stamp collection but she does not bother to keep it in a safe or take any security precautions to ensure her house is not broken into. As soon as Fred is released, he tracks Beth down and steals her stamp collection. Can Beth sue Gary, arguing that he owed her a duty not to tell Fred about her stamp collection? It was, after all, reasonably foreseeable – here, very likely or probable[160] – that if he told Fred about her stamp collection, Fred would attempt to steal it from her. There is no authority on the issue but there seems little reason why, if the property harm principle applies to cases where property has been destroyed or damaged, it should not also extend to cases where property has been stolen. If it does, then Beth will probably be able to argue that Gary owed her a duty not to tell Fred about her stamp collection.

159 For another case raising this kind of problem, see *Bellefield Computer Services Ltd* v *E Turner & Sons Ltd* [2000] BLR 97, noted Duncan Wallace 2000. A wall separating a storage area within a building from the rest of the building was badly constructed with the result that when a fire broke out in the storage area, it spread to the rest of the building; held that this was a case of one item of property – a building divided up into different areas by a wall – being damaged because it suffered from a defect rather than a case of a sound item of property – the area of the building outside the storage area – being damaged because another item of property – the wall separating the storage area from the rest of the building – was defective. It might be different in the case where the electric wiring in a building is defective with the result that the building burns down: *Murphy* v *Brentwood DC* [1991] 1 AC 398, at 470, per Lord Keith. Also in the case where a defective boiler or 'electrical installation' in a house malfunctions and causes the house to burn down: ibid., at 478, per Lord Bridge. See also the discussion in *Payne* v *John Setchell Ltd* [2002] PNLR 146, at [26]–[41] (Humphrey Lloyd QC).

160 See above, p. 77, n. 24.

What sort of property?

The property harm principle applies, of course, in cases where *tangible* property – land, buildings, moveables – has been harmed. But what about *intangible* property? It seems the property harm principle will also apply to cases where intangible property has been destroyed as a result of a defendant's actions,[161] though such cases will necessarily be very rare, as intangible property – not taking a physical form – is very hard to destroy. However, one such case presented itself in *Ministry of Housing* v *Sharp*.[162]

In that case, the claimants had a charge on land owed by N. P proposed to buy the land from N and searched the land charges register to see who had an interest in the land. The defendant informed P that the register was clear – there were no encumbrances on the land. This meant that when P purchased the land from N – as it subsequently did – it took the land free from any encumbrances. The claimants therefore lost their charge over N's land when it was purchased by P. The claimants sued the defendant in negligence for compensation for the loss of their charge. The Court of Appeal allowed the claimants to sue, holding that the defendant had owed the claimants a duty to take care that he did not tell P that the register was clear of charges when it was not. It could be argued that the duty of care arose under the property harm principle. That is, it could be argued the defendant owed the claimant a duty to take care that he did not tell P that the register was clear of charges when it was not because it was reasonably foreseeable that if he did this any charges over the land owned by N would be destroyed.

What sort of interest?

If property has been harmed as a result of A's doing *x* and it was reasonably foreseeable at the time A did *x* that his doing *x* would have that sort of effect, B will only be able to invoke the property harm principle to establish that A owed her a duty to take care not to do *x* if she had a sufficient interest in the property that was harmed at the time it was harmed. What sort of interest will suffice?

This question was dealt with by the House of Lords in *The Aliakmon*.[163] The answer is B will have had a sufficient interest in the property that was harmed if, at the time the property was harmed, she had a *legal interest* in the property or *possession* of the property. But if she merely had an *equitable interest* in the property at the time it was harmed, then that will not be enough.[164]

In *The Aliakmon*, Leigh & Sillavan Ltd agreed to buy a quantity of steel coils from Kinso-Mataichi Corp. The steel coils were to be shipped to Leigh & Sillavan Ltd on *The Aliakmon*, a ship owned by the defendants. Because there were some doubts as to Leigh & Sillavan's ability to pay for the coils, Leigh & Sillavan would become liable to pay for the coils as soon as they were shipped but the coils would remain the property of Kinso-Mataichi until they were paid for. When the coils were placed aboard *The Aliakmon*, the defendant stowed them badly with the result that when Leigh & Sillavan received the coils, they were badly damaged.

161 Though the British Court of Columbia took a different view in *Esser* v *Brown* (2004) 242 DLR (4th) 112, holding that a notary who destroyed the claimant's interest in a ranch she owned with her husband when he executed a sale of the ranch to a third party which the claimant had not agreed to (her husband had forged her signature on the contract of sale) had not owed the claimant a duty of care not to destroy her interest in the ranch.

162 [1970] 2 QB 223.

163 [1986] AC 785.

164 Ibid., 812–13.

However, Leigh & Sillavan still had to pay for the coils because they had agreed with Kinso-Mataichi that they would pay full price for the coils on delivery, whatever their condition.

Leigh & Sillavan sued the defendants for compensation for the fact that the coils they had received and paid for were badly damaged as a result of the defendants' bad stowage. The defendants had had a duty to take care not to stow the coils badly under the basic rule discussed here – it had been reasonably foreseeable at the time the coils were shipped that they would be damaged if they were stowed badly. But was that duty owed to Leigh & Sillavan? Only if they had a sufficient interest in the steel coils at the time they were damaged – that is, during their voyage aboard *The Aliakmon*. The House of Lords held that they did not. Leigh & Sillavan did not legally own the coils at the time they were being transported and neither did they have possession of the coils. At most they had an equitable interest in the coils, but that was not enough.

Exceptions

The exceptions to the physical danger principle that have already been discussed will also apply to the property harm principle. So if A does *x* and as a result B's property is harmed, B will not be able to argue that A owed her a duty to take care not to do *x* if it was reasonable for A to do *x*, all things considered. So suppose A is on a mountain and he gets caught in a life-threatening snowstorm. In the blizzard, he comes across a locked and empty cabin, which belongs to B. In an attempt to save his life, A breaks a window of the cabin to gain access. As it is reasonable for A to do this, B will not be able subsequently to sue A for compensation for the loss of her window on the basis that A owed her, and breached, a duty not to break the window.[165] She might, however, be able to argue that A owed her, and breached, a duty to take care not to get caught on the mountain in inclement weather – because it was reasonably foreseeable that if he did so, he would be forced to break into her cabin to save his life.

Similarly, the *volenti* exception equally applies to the property harm principle, and the courts have shown themselves willing to set aside the property harm principle where

public policy demands. This was the case in *The Nicholas H*.[166] In that case, the eponymous ship, which was carrying the claimant's cargo, developed a crack in its hull while it was travelling from South America to Italy. The ship anchored off Puerto Rico and was inspected by the defendant classification society. The defendants told the shipowners that they would be willing to pass *The Nicholas H* as seaworthy – and thus allow it to continue on its way – if the shipowners temporarily repaired its hull and then repaired it properly as soon as possible after it discharged its cargo. The temporary repairs were done and *The Nicholas H* went on its way. However, it sank a week later when the temporary repairs failed. The claimant's cargo, which was worth $6,200,000, was lost. The claimant could recover only $500,000 from the shipowner by way of compensation for the loss of his cargo due to a limitation clause in the contract between the claimant and the shipowner.

The claimant sued the defendants for the balance of his loss, claiming that they had been

165 But even if A did not act wrongfully in breaking the window, he will probably still have to compensate B for the damage done to her window: an example of compensation without wrongdoing (on which, see above p. xv). See, for example, the American case of *Vincent* v *Lake Erie Transportation Co.*, 124 NW 221 (1910), discussed below at pp. 366, 711–12.

166 [1996] AC 211.

negligent in allowing *The Nicholas H* to proceed on its way. The House of Lords dismissed the claim, holding that the defendants had not owed the claimant a duty to take care not to approve the ship as seaworthy when it was not. This was so even though it had been perfectly foreseeable that the claimant's cargo would be destroyed if the defendants approved the *Nicholas H* as seaworthy when it was not. So why did the House of Lords not give effect to the basic rule discussed here?[167] The reason was that the House of Lords thought it would be contrary to the public interest to rule that a classification society will owe the owners of cargo aboard a ship a duty to take care not to say that a ship is seaworthy when it is not. Lord Steyn, giving the leading judgment, gave two reasons why such a ruling would be contrary to the public interest.

First, classification societies act in the general public interest in certifying whether or not ships are seaworthy – their doing so helps to save lives, ships and cargo at sea. If classification societies could be sued in negligence when their surveyors carelessly passed as seaworthy ships that were not seaworthy, then they would not – Lord Steyn thought – be able to carry out their functions as efficiently. They would be exposed to a wide number of claims; their surveyors would be overly inclined to label ships as unseaworthy if there was any doubt on the matter; classification societies' staff and resources would be tied up in dealing with claims made against them instead of being used for the main task of classifying ships.[168]

Secondly, Lord Steyn thought that if classification societies could be sued in negligence when their surveyors carelessly passed as seaworthy ships that were not seaworthy, then they would, before passing a ship as seaworthy, demand that the shipowner agree to indemnify them against any negligence liability they might incur as a result of passing the ship as seaworthy. So, in the end, any liabilities incurred by the classification societies in negligence would be passed on to shipowners – thus bypassing the limitations of liability that shipowners insert into their contracts of carriage with cargo owners. Shipowners would no longer be able to predict for insurance purposes the extent of the liabilities they would incur if their ships sank and merchant shipping would as a result be disrupted.

One further exception to the property harm principle is worthy of note. In *Stephens* v *Anglian Water Authority*,[169] the claimant, the owner of a cottage, complained that part of her land had collapsed because the defendant had extracted so much water from under his land that the water under her land had drained away. The claimant sued the defendant for compensation, arguing that the defendant had owed her a duty not to extract as much water from under his land as he had. The Court of Appeal rejected the claim, holding that the defendant had not owed the claimant a duty of care in extracting water from under his land.[170]

167 Lord Lloyd, dissenting, thought that the property harm principle should have been applied in the *Nicholas H* and a duty of care found: 'All that is required is a straightforward application of *Donoghue* v *Stevenson*' (ibid., 230). It seems likely that had anyone on board the *Nicholas H* been drowned when it sank, the House of Lords would not have hesitated to give full effect to the physical danger principle set out above and found that the defendants owed the people on board the *Nicholas H* a duty to take care not to approve the ship as being seaworthy when it was not – on the basis that it was reasonably foreseeable when the *Nicholas H* was in dock that those on board on the *Nicholas H* would suffer some kind of physical injury if the defendants approved it as being seaworthy when it was not.

168 For much the same reason, it has been held that the Civil Aviation Authority will not owe the owner of an aircraft a duty to take care that it does not certify the aircraft as being fit to fly when it is not: *Philcox* v *Civil Aviation Authority*, The Times, 8 June 1995.

169 [1987] 1 WLR 1381.

170 The House of Lords refused leave to appeal: [1988] 1 WLR 476.

Why didn't the Court of Appeal apply the property harm principle in this case? It was, after all, perfectly foreseeable that the claimant's land would collapse if the defendant extracted as much water from under his land as he did. The reason was simply that, under English law, an owner of land is free to extract as much water as he likes from under his land – regardless of what effect his extracting that water has on his neighbours.[171] It would have been different if the defendant had extracted so many *minerals* from under his land that minerals shifted out from under the claimant's land with the result that the claimant's land collapsed. A landowner is *not* free under English law to extract as many minerals from under his land as he likes regardless of the consequences that his doing so might have on his neighbours. So, if the defendant in *Stephens* had caused the claimant's land to collapse by extracting an excessive quantity of minerals from under his land, the defendant probably would have owed the claimant a duty not to act in the way he did under the property harm principle.[172]

THE LIMITS OF *DONOGHUE* v *STEVENSON*

As we have already observed, the courts have always refused to give full effect to Lord Atkin's neighbour principle. They have not accepted that A will have a positive duty to act if it is reasonably foreseeable that B will suffer some kind of harm if A does nothing. However, they have been prepared to accept that in certain limited situations one person will owe another a duty to act. We will look at these situations in Chapters 7 and 8.

The courts have also refused to accept that A will necessarily owe B a duty to take care not to do *x* if it is reasonably foreseeable that A's doing *x* will result in B suffering some kind of pure economic loss.[173] So in the great case of *Hedley Byrne & Co. Ltd* v *Heller & Partners Ltd*[174] – where the claimants suffered financial loss as a result of relying on the misleading advice of the defendant bankers as to the creditworthiness of one of the bankers' customers – the claimants could not rely on Lord Atkin's neighbour principle to help them establish that the defendants owed them a duty to take care not to mislead them as to that customer's creditworthiness. But they still came within an ace of establishing that such a duty of care was owed to them. In the next chapter we will look at what that case established as to when one person will owe another a duty of care.

Visit **http://www.mylawchamber.co.uk/mcbride** to access updates on recent cases, as well as model answers and tips for answering tort problem questions.

Use **Case Navigator** to read in full some of the key cases referenced in this chapter:

- **Frost *v* Chief Constable of South Yorkshire Police**
- **Wainwright *v* Home Office**
- **Barber *v* Somerset County Council**
- **Marc Rich & Co AG *v* Bishop Rock Marine Co Ltd, The Nicholas H**

[171] *Bradford Corporation* v *Pickles* [1895] AC 587, discussed below pp. 382–3.
[172] *Lotus* v *British Soda Ltd* [1972] Ch 123.
[173] See above, p. 62.
[174] [1964] AC 465.

6 The principle in *Hedley Byrne* and associated principles

THE PRINCIPLE IN *HEDLEY BYRNE*

The basic principle

In *Hedley Byrne & Co. Ltd* v *Heller & Partners Ltd*,[1] Hedley Byrne, a firm of advertising agents, wanted to find out whether a company called Easipower Ltd was creditworthy or not before they placed some advertising orders on Easipower's behalf. Hedley Byrne were personally liable for the cost of these advertising orders and were therefore understandably concerned to know whether they could recoup the cost of placing those orders from Easipower. Hedley Byrne's bankers approached Heller & Partners, Easipower's bankers, for a reference as to Easipower's creditworthiness. Heller gave Easipower a favourable reference, on the strength of which Hedley Byrne placed a number of advertising orders on Easipower's behalf. Soon afterwards, Easipower went into liquidation and Hedley Byrne were unable to recover from Easipower the money they had laid out on Easipower's behalf in placing those advertising orders.

Hedley Byrne sued Heller, claiming that Heller had owed them a duty to take care that it did not mislead them as to Easipower's creditworthiness and that Heller breached that duty when it supplied them with a positive reference as to Easipower's creditworthiness. The House of Lords dismissed Hedley Byrne's claim on the ground that Heller's advice to Hedley Byrne as to Easipower's creditworthiness had been given 'without responsibility'.[2] But the House of Lords made clear that had Heller not done this, it *would* have owed Hedley Byrne a duty to take care not to mislead them as to Easipower's creditworthiness.

But why would Heller have owed Hedley Byrne a duty of care? Their Lordships came up with a number of different explanations. Lord Reid: Heller would have 'accepted a responsibility' for the accuracy of their advice or would have 'accepted a relationship' with Hedley Byrne which required them to take care in advising Hedley Byrne.[3] Lord Morris: Heller would have 'assumed a responsibility' to tender Hedley Byrne 'deliberate advice'.[4] Lord Morris (with the agreement of Lord Hodson): Heller would have known or ought to have known that their advice would be relied upon by Hedley Byrne.[5] Lord Hodson: there would have existed a 'sufficiently close'[6] or 'special'[7] relationship between Heller and Hedley Byrne which would have given rise to a duty of care owed by Heller to Hedley Byrne. Lord Devlin: there would have existed a 'special relationship' between Heller and

[1] [1964] AC 465.
[2] Ibid., 492, 504, 511, 532–3, 539–40.
[3] Ibid., 486.
[4] Ibid., 494.
[5] Ibid., 503, 514.
[6] Ibid., 509.
[7] Ibid., 511.

Hedley Byrne that was 'equivalent to contract'; in other words, Heller would have 'assumed a responsibility' towards Hedley Byrne in circumstances where, if Heller had been paid by Hedley Byrne to assume that responsibility, there would have existed a contract between Hedley Byrne and Heller.[8] Lord Pearce: there would have existed a 'special relationship' between Heller and Hedley Byrne which gave rise to an 'assumption that care as well as honesty' was demanded when Heller advised Hedley Byrne.[9]

Given the vagueness and variety of these statements it is understandable that there has been a great deal of debate as to when exactly one person will owe another a duty of care under the decision in *Hedley Byrne*. Subsequent case law establishes that Lords Morris and Hodson's view that if A knows or ought to know that B will rely on some advice of his, A will owe B a duty of care in rendering that advice is too wide to be acceptable.[10] Something more is required before A will be found to have owed B a duty of care. But what is that 'something more'? The speeches of Lords Reid, Devlin and Morris in *Hedley Byrne* suggest that it needs to be shown that A 'assumed a responsibility' towards B for the quality of his advice. But when will A be held to have done this? There are essentially two schools of thought on this issue.

(1) *'Assumption of responsibility' is an empty concept.* According to this school of thought, the concept of an 'assumption of responsibility' is essentially meaningless. In other words, the courts will be free to find that A 'assumed a responsibility' towards B for the quality of his advice *whenever* they *want* to find that A owed B a duty of care in giving that advice.

This was the line taken by Lord Griffiths in the case of *Smith* v *Eric S Bush*: 'I do not think . . . assumption of responsibility is a helpful or realistic test of liability [under *Hedley Byrne*] . . . The phrase "assumption of responsibility" can only have any real meaning if it is understood as referring to the circumstances in which the law will deem the maker of the statement to have assumed responsibility to the person who acts upon the advice.'[11] In

Phelps v *Hillingdon LBC*, Lord Slynn made essentially the same point: 'The phrase ["assumption of responsibility"] means simply that the law recognises that there is a duty of care. It is not so much that responsibility is assumed as that it is recognised or imposed by law.'[12]

(2) *'Assumption of responsibility' is not an empty concept.* According to this second school of thought, the concept of an 'assumption of responsibility' is meaningful. In other words, it is only possible to say truthfully that someone has 'assumed a responsibility' to another in *certain definable circumstances*. Of course, the courts may have in the past found that a defendant 'assumed a responsibility' to a claimant outside those circumstances, but in those cases the courts were guilty of abusing the concept – in those cases the courts wanted to find that the defendant owed the claimant a duty of care for such-and-such a reason and

[8] Ibid., 528–9, 530.

[9] Ibid., 539.

[10] See, in particular, the decision of the House of Lords in *Williams* v *Natural Life Health Foods Ltd* [1998] 1 WLR 830, discussed below at pp. 131–2.

[11] [1990] 1 AC 831, 862.

[12] [2001] 2 AC 619, 654. See also the judgment of Lord Roskill in *Caparo Industries plc* v *Dickman* [1990] 2 AC 605 at 629; Stapleton 1998, 64–5; Barker 1993.

they simply *said* that the defendant 'assumed a responsibility' to the claimant in order to provide themselves with some legal justification for their finding that the defendant owed the claimant a duty of care.[13]

Lord Steyn took this view of the concept of an 'assumption of responsibility' in *Williams* v *Natural Life Health Foods Ltd*: 'There was, and is, no better rationalisation for [this] head of tort liability than assumption of responsibility ... There is nothing fictional about this species of liability in tort.'[14] Lord Bingham took the same view in *Customs and Excise Commissioners* v *Barclays Bank plc* when he remarked that 'there are cases in which one party can *accurately* be said to have assumed responsibility for what is said ... to another';[15] as did Lord Hoffmann in the same case when he said that, 'In ... cases in which the loss has been caused by the claimant's reliance on information provided by the defendant, it is critical to decide whether the defendant (rather than someone else) assumed responsibility for the accuracy of the information to the claimant (rather than to someone else) ...'[16]

We prefer the second view, not least because it seems that in *Hedley Byrne*, Lords Reid, Devlin and Morris must have had *something* in mind when they talked of a defendant owing a claimant a duty of care if he 'assumed a responsibility' to her. We would go further and say that if A takes on the job of advising B on a particular matter, A will 'assume a responsibility' to B for the quality of his advice if and only if *he indicates to B that she can safely rely on his advice*. If this is right then we can say that the House of Lords' decision in *Hedley Byrne* establishes that: If A takes on the job of advising B on a particular matter and he indicates to B that B can safely rely on that advice, then A will owe B a duty to take care that he does not give B any incorrect advice on that matter. Let us call this the *basic principle* in *Hedley Byrne*.[17] Let's now look at a number of different kinds of situations to see this principle in action.

(1) *Advice given 'without responsibility'*. The decision of the House of Lords in *Hedley Byrne* makes it clear that if A takes on the job of advising B on a particular matter but makes it clear that his advice is given 'without responsibility', he will normally not owe B a duty of care in giving that advice. By making it clear that his advice is given 'without responsibility', he is making it clear to B that his advice cannot be safely relied on.

It was necessary to say in the above paragraph that A will not *normally* owe B a duty of care in advising her if he has made it clear to her that his advice is given without responsibility. This is because under s 2(2) of the Unfair Contract Terms Act 1977, if A was acting

[13] See Lord Goff's judgment in *White* v *Jones* [1995] 2 AC 207 for a particularly transparent example of this happening. This is also what may have happened in the case of *Costello* v *Chief Constable of Northumbria Police* [1999] 1 All ER 550, discussed above at pp. 51–3 and below at p. 160.

[14] [1998] 1 WLR 830, 837. See also the judgment of Lord Browne-Wilkinson in *White* v *Jones* [1995] 2 AC 207, at 273–4.

[15] [2007] 1 AC 181, at [4] (emphasis added).

[16] Ibid., at [35].

[17] It is worth noting that this basic principle cannot explain the House of Lords' finding in *Smith* v *Eric S Bush* [1990] 1 AC 831 that a duty of care was owed in that case: see below, pp. 145–7. It is hardly surprising, then, that Lord Griffiths should have poured scorn in that case on the idea that an assumption of responsibility was a prerequisite to a duty of care being owed under *Hedley Byrne*: had he found that an assumption of responsibility *was* required, he would not have been able to rely on the decision of the House of Lords in *Hedley Byrne* as authority for the view that a duty of care was owed in *Smith* v *Eric S Bush*. For an explanation of the decision in *Smith* v *Eric S Bush*, see below, pp. 145–7.

'in the course of business' in advising B, and due to his carelessness in advising B she suffered some form of economic loss, A will not be allowed to rely on the fact that he gave his advice 'without responsibility' so as to deny that he owed B a duty of care in advising her, if it would be 'unreasonable' to allow him to rely on that fact to deny that he owed B a duty of care. So it is possible that if A was advising B 'in the course of business' he might still be held to have owed B a duty of care in giving her that advice even if that advice was formally given 'without responsibility'.

(2) *Advice given directly to advisee knowing that the advice will be relied on.* In *Hedley Byrne*, Lord Reid observed that:

> A reasonable man, knowing that he was being trusted or that his skill or judgment were being relied on, would, I think, have three courses open to him. He could keep silent or decline to give the information or advice sought: or he could give an answer with a clear qualification that he accepted no responsibility for it or that it was given without that reflection or inquiry which a careful answer would require: or he could simply answer without any such qualification. If he chooses to adopt the last course he must, I think, be held to have accepted some responsibility for his answer being given carefully, or to have accepted a relationship with the inquirer which requires him to exercise such care as the circumstances require.[18]

It follows from this that if B asks A to advise her on some matter, and A knows that B will rely on whatever he says, then if A undertakes to advise B on that matter, he will owe her a duty of care in giving her that advice. The reason for this is that when he takes on the job of advising B, A will *implicitly* indicate to B that she can safely rely on his advice. B will think – and will be entitled to think – that, 'A knew that I would rely on his advice unless I was discouraged from doing so. Given that he knew this, he surely would have discouraged me from relying on his advice if his advice could not be safely relied on. But he did not do this – he gave me his advice and did nothing to discourage me from relying on it. Surely, then, his advice can be safely relied on.'

This was the position in *Welton* v *North Cornwall District Council*.[19] In that case, the claimants owned a guest house which constituted food premises for the purpose of the Food Act 1984 and the Food Safety Act 1990. The claimants were visited by one E, a health inspector. E said that the claimants' kitchen was not up to scratch. He could have closed the claimants' kitchen down – effectively putting their guest house out of business – but instead took it upon himself to advise the claimants as to what they needed to do to their kitchen to bring it up to a satisfactory standard. Acting on this advice, the claimants made numerous alterations to their kitchen, 90 per cent of which – they subsequently discovered – were completely unnecessary. The claimants sued, claiming that E had owed them a duty of care in advising them as to what they needed to do to their kitchen to bring it up to scratch. The Court of Appeal allowed their claim. When E took on the job of advising the claimants as to what they needed to do, he knew that they would rely on whatever he said, and so by undertaking to advise the claimants, he implicitly indicated to them that his advice could be safely relied on.

It should be noted that in this kind of situation A will be held to have 'assumed a responsibility' to B, irrespective of whether or not he *subjectively* wanted to indicate to B

[18] [1964] AC 465, at 486.
[19] [1997] 1 WLR 570.

that she could safely rely on his advice. The duty of care that A will owe B in this situation will arise out of the fact that A gave B the impression that his advice could be safely relied upon. So whether or not the courts will find that A 'assumed a responsibility' to B will not depend on whether A *intended* to 'assume a responsibility' to B, but will instead depend on whether A *gave B the impression that he intended* to 'assume a responsibility' to B. As Lord Hoffmann observed in *Customs and Excise Commissioners* v *Barclays Bank plc*, 'The answer [to the question of whether the defendant assumed responsibility to the claimant] does not depend on what the defendant intended but . . . upon what would reasonably be inferred from his conduct against the background of all the circumstances of the case.'[20]

(3) *Advice given on a social occasion*. Suppose that A and B are drinking together in the pub, and B asks A whether he thinks she should invest her savings on the stock market. A says, 'Definitely – this is a good time to buy.' B acts on A's advice and invests all of her money in the stock market, and loses most of it when the stock market subsequently crashes. There is no doubt that A was careless in his advice: at the time he talked to B the stock market had reached a record high and there were widespread warnings that a correction in stock market levels was overdue. But did A owe B a duty of care in advising her whether or not to invest in the stock market? The answer will normally be 'no'. A did nothing to indicate to B that she could safely rely on his advice – that is, rely on his advice without seeking any further advice from anyone else. The casual context in which B sought A's advice meant that he had no reason to think that she would rely on whatever he said, and so B could not have been entitled to infer from the fact that A gave B his opinion on what she should do that he was indicating to her that she could rely on his advice without consulting anyone else.

So the normal rule is that someone giving advice on a social occasion will not owe a duty of care to the advisee.[21] However, the rule will be displaced if A gives B advice on a social occasion and in doing so explicitly assures B that she *can* safely rely on his advice. In such a situation, A will owe B a duty of care in advising her. This was the situation in *Chaudhry* v *Prabhakar*.[22] In that case, Chaudhry was thinking of buying a Golf car that her friend Prabhakar had spotted was for sale. Chaudhry obviously wanted to know whether the car was in good condition before buying it. Prabhakar advised her that the car was in good

[20] [2007] 1 AC 181, at [35]. See also [5] (per Lord Bingham): 'it is clear that the assumption of responsibility test is to be applied objectively . . . and is not answered by consideration of what the defendant thought or intended'; and *Henderson* v *Merrett Syndicates* [1995] 2 AC 145, at 181 (per Lord Goff): 'it must be expected that an objective test will be applied when asking the question whether, in a particular case, responsibility should be held to have been assumed by the defendant . . .'

[21] See *Hedley Byrne* & Co. *Ltd* v *Heller & Partners Ltd* [1964] AC 465, 482–3 (per Lord Reid); *Howard Marine & Dredging Co.* v *A Ogden (Excavations) Ltd* [1978] QB 574, 592–3 (per Lord Denning MR). The same will be true if John rang Mary out of the blue for her advice without making it clear that he was going to be relying on her advice: *Tidman* v *Reading Borough Council* [1994] Times LR 592; *Fashion Brokers Ltd* v *Clarke Hayes* [2000] PNLR 473. Or if the circumstances of John's inquiry were generally such as not to put Mary on warning that John was going to rely on her advice: see *James McNaughton Paper Group Ltd* v *Hicks Anderson & Co.* [1991] 2 QB 113 (held, no liability for an off-the-cuff statement made by accountant as to profitability of a company in the course of negotiations to take over the company). A different result would have been reached if it had been made clear to the accountant that his statement would be relied upon: *Galoo* v *Bright Grahame Murray* [1994] 1 WLR 1360; *Law Society* v *KPMG Peat Marwick* [2000] 1 WLR 1921. Puzzlingly, it has been held that a solicitor working for someone selling a house will *not* owe the purchaser of the house a duty of care in answering the purchaser's inquiries even if it is made abundantly clear to him that those answers will be relied upon by the purchaser: *Gran Gelato Ltd* v *Richcliff (Group) Ltd* [1992] Ch 560 (Nicholls V-C). For criticisms of the decision in *Gran Gelato*, see Reed 1996, 69–73; also Bernstein 1998, 642–4.

[22] [1989] 1 WLR 29.

condition and told her that she did not need to get a qualified mechanic to look at it. Chaudhry subsequently bought the car on the strength of this advice. The car subsequently proved to be unroadworthy and Chaudhry sued Prabhakar in negligence for compensation. The Court of Appeal held that Prabhakar had owed Chaudhry a duty of care in advising her as to the condition of the car: he had discouraged her from seeking anyone else's opinion on the condition of the car and had therefore explicitly indicated to her that his advice – that the car was in good condition – could be safely relied on.

(4) *Advice given by a non-expert.* It was suggested by the majority of the Privy Council in *Mutual Life and Citizens' Assurance Co. Ltd* v *Evatt*[23] that if A undertakes to advise B on some matter, A will not owe B a duty of care in giving that advice if A did not hold himself out as being an expert on the matter advised upon. This seems too strong, and the decision in the *Evatt* case – denying that a duty of care was owed by a defendant company advising the claimant investor on whether its sister company's finances were sound – has been criticised by the domestic courts.[24]

The better view, we would submit, is that if A makes it obvious that he is not an expert on the matter on which he is advising B, that is something that should be taken into account in deciding whether or not A indicated to B that his advice could be safely relied on. If A makes it clear to B – or B knows already – that he is not an expert on the matter on which B is seeking A's advice, then the courts will usually find that A did *not* indicate to B that his advice could be safely relied on.

But it would be different if B said to A, 'I know you are not a financial expert, but you're more of an expert than me, and I don't trust anyone else to give me good advice, so I'll do whatever you tell me to do – do you think I should invest in the stock market?' If A gives B his advice without urging B to seek out more opinions, then it will be hard not to find that A – in giving B his advice – implicitly indicated to B that she could safely rely on his advice. Similarly, it would be different if A said to B, 'I'm not a doctor, but even I know that you are as fit as a fiddle. You are going to look silly if you ask a doctor if you should be concerned about a silly lump on your arm. Take it from me – it's nothing.' In such a case, A will have explicitly indicated to B that she could safely rely on his advice as to the state of her health. So in both these alternative scenarios, the courts will – and should – find that A owed B a duty of care in advising her, even though A has no expertise in the matter on which he was advising B.

(5) *Advice given in a published work.* In *Candler* v *Crane, Christmas & Co.*, Denning LJ observed that, '. . . a scientist or expert . . . is not liable to his readers for careless statements made in his published works'.[25] This seems correct, even after the decision of the House of Lords in *Hedley Byrne*.[26] If A writes a textbook or an article, he cannot be taken to have invited his readers to think that the information in that article can be relied upon without seeking further advice.

[23] [1971] AC 793.

[24] See *Esso Petroleum Co. Ltd* v *Mardon* [1976] QB 801; *Howard Marine & Dredging Co.* v *A Ogden (Excavations) Ltd* [1978] QB 574; *Spring* v *Guardian Assurance plc* [1995] 2 AC 296, at 320 (per Lord Goff); *Commissioner of Police of the Metropolis* v *Lennon* [2004] 2 All ER 266.

[25] [1951] 2 KB 164, at 183.

[26] In fact, Denning LJ's (dissenting) judgment in the *Candler* case anticipated the judgment of the House of Lords in *Hedley Byrne* by 13 years.

(6) *Official registers.* Oftentimes, the law will require someone to be officially registered before they are allowed to trade, for example, as a child-minder. If A is in charge of maintaining such an official register, does A invite people looking at the register to think that they can rely on him to have taken care to ensure that C – someone who is on the register – is a fit and proper person to deal with? The Privy Council said the answer is 'no' in *Yuen Kun Yeu* v *Attorney-General for Hong Kong*.[27] The register in that case was a register of deposit-taking companies. The claimants lost the money they had deposited with a company that was on the register, but had been run fraudulently and with little regard for investors' interests. The claimants sued the defendant – who was in charge of maintaining the register – on the ground that by allowing the company's name to appear on the register, he had represented that people like the claimants could safely rely on him to have taken care to ensure that the company was a fit and proper company to accept deposits. The Privy Council rejected this argument: the existence of the procedure for registering deposit-taking companies did not 'warrant an assumption that all [registered] deposit-taking companies were sound and fully creditworthy'.[28]

(7) *Advice given by a third party.* Suppose that B wants some advice as to whether she should invest in a particular company, X plc. C – B's friend – asks A, an employee at X plc, whether it would be a good idea to invest in X plc. A assures C, 'Your friend should buy as many shares as possible. We are working on something at the moment that will quadruple the share price when it's announced.' C then goes to B and says, 'Take it from me – you won't go wrong if you invest in X plc.' B then invests a lot of money in X plc and loses all of it when X plc announces a few months later that it is insolvent. B then finds out from C that A was the source of his bad advice to invest in X plc. B sues A, claiming that he owed her a duty of care in advising C whether it was a good idea for her to buy shares in X plc. Her claim will fail. A did not 'assume a responsibility' to *B* in giving that advice – he never indicated to *B* that *she* could safely rely on that advice. There was, in fact, no kind of contact between A and B that could ground a finding that A 'assumed a responsibility' to B for the quality of his advice.

That this is correct is confirmed by the decision of the House of Lords in *Williams* v *Natural Life Health Foods Ltd*.[29] Natural Life Health Food Shops Ltd was a company which provided the following service. People who were interested in opening a health food shop could approach Natural Life for an assessment as to how successful the health food shop was likely to be. If, on the basis of that assessment, they were still interested in opening the shop, Natural Life would, for a fee, allow them to open their shop using the Natural Life Health Foods trade name and would advise them as to how to run their shop. The claimants approached Natural Life because they were interested in opening a health food shop in Rugby. The managing director of Natural Life, Richard Mistlin, prepared some reports which predicted that the health food shop the claimants were proposing to open would enjoy a healthy turnover. Even though he prepared the reports, Mistlin never actually had any dealings with the claimants – they dealt with another employee of the company, Ron Padwick. On the strength of Mistlin's reports, the claimants opened a health

27 [1988] 1 AC 175.
28 Ibid., at 197.
29 [1998] 1 WLR 830 (discussed, Armour 1999).

food shop in Rugby under the Natural Life trade name. However, the shop enjoyed less success than Mistlin's reports indicated it would and the claimants, after trading at a loss for 18 months, were finally forced to close the shop.

The claimants sued Natural Life in negligence. Unfortunately, Natural Life was not worth suing; it was wound up a couple of years after the claimants commenced proceedings against Natural Life. Mistlin, on the other hand, did have substantial assets – so the claimants then tried to sue him in negligence. They argued that he had owed them, and breached, a duty to take care that he did not mislead them as to how successful the Rugby health food shop was likely to be; and that had he not breached this duty, he would have told them that the Rugby health food shop was unlikely to be a success and they would never have invested their money in it.

The House of Lords rejected the claimants' claim. Lord Steyn, giving the only judgment, ruled that Mistlin had not owed the claimants a duty of care in preparing his reports as to how profitable the Rugby health food shop was likely to be under the basic principle in *Hedley Byrne*. While Mistlin *did* take on the job of preparing the reports given to the claimants on the potential profitability of the Rugby health food shop, the lack of contact between Mistlin and the claimants meant that *Mistlin* did not at any point indicate to the claimants that they could safely rely on his advice. In contrast, Natural Life – a separate person from Mistlin – *did* indicate to the claimants that they could safely rely on the advice Natural Life gave them as to how profitable the Rugby health food shop was likely to be. So Natural Life *did* owe the claimants a duty under the basic principle in *Hedley Byrne* to take care that they did not supply the claimants with any incorrect advice as to how profitable the Rugby health food shop was likely to be. However, as has already been observed, this was of little comfort to the claimants as Natural Life was not worth suing.

The extended principle

It is now well acknowledged that *Hedley Byrne* is not *just* authority in favour of the proposition that someone who takes on the task of advising another on a particular matter will, in certain circumstances, owe that other a duty of care in giving that advice. Certain *dicta* in *Hedley Byrne* suggest that if A has indicated to B[30] that B can safely rely on him to perform a particular task with a certain degree of care and skill and B has so relied on A, A will owe B a duty to perform that task with that degree of care and skill.[31]

Many cases, decided before and after *Hedley Byrne*, seem to support this suggestion. Most of them deal with the following kind of situation: (1) Paul is a professional – that is, he holds himself out as being able to perform a particular task T with a high degree of care and skill – a 'professional' degree of care and skill; (2) as a result, Karen is led to believe that

[30] By 'B' we mean either B or B's agent, acting on B's behalf.

[31] [1964] AC 465, at 502–3 (per Lord Morris): '. . . it should now be regarded as settled that if someone possessed of a special skill undertakes, quite irrespective of contract, to apply that skill for the assistance of another person who relies upon such skill, a duty of care will arise'; 531 (per Lord Hodson): '. . . those who hold themselves out as possessing a special skill are under a duty to exercise it with reasonable care'; 531 (per Lord Devlin): 'If a defendant says to a [claimant]: "Let me do this for you; do not waste your money in employing a professional, I will do it for nothing and you can rely on me", I do not think he could escape liability . . .'; 538 (per Lord Pearce): '. . . if persons holding themselves out in a calling or situation or profession take on a task within that calling or situation or profession, they have a duty of skill and care.'

Paul can be safely relied on to perform task T with a 'professional' degree of care and skill; (3) Karen asks Paul to perform task T for her; (4) Paul knows that Karen's request is made in the belief that Paul can be safely relied on to perform task T with a 'professional' degree of care and skill and Karen knows that Paul knows this; (5) Paul agrees to perform task T for Karen.

In such a case, Karen will think – and she will be entitled to think – 'Paul knew that I was only requesting him to perform task T in the belief that he could be safely relied on to perform task T for me with a "professional" degree of care and skill. Given that he knew this, he surely would not have agreed to perform task T for me if he could not be safely relied on to perform task T with a "professional" degree of care and skill. But he did not do this – he agreed to perform task T for me. Surely, then, Paul *can* be safely relied on to perform task T for me with a "professional" degree of care and skill.' In the case just described, then, Paul – by agreeing to perform task T for Karen – will have implicitly indicated to Karen that Karen can safely rely on him to perform task T with a 'professional' degree of care and skill. And Karen will have relied on Paul to perform that task with a 'professional' degree of care and skill by not asking anyone else to perform task T for her.

A lot of cases hold that, in this kind of situation, Paul will owe Karen a duty to perform task T with a 'professional' degree of care and skill. These cases therefore seem to support the suggestion that if A indicates to B that B can safely rely on him to perform a particular task with a certain degree of care and skill and B does so rely on A, then A will owe B a duty to perform that task with that degree of care and skill. These cases variously hold that:

(1) a doctor will owe his patient a duty to treat his patient with the care and skill that a reasonably competent doctor would exercise in treating a patient;[32] similarly,

(2) a dentist will owe his patient a duty to treat that patient with the care and skill that a reasonably competent dentist would exercise in treating a patient;[33]

(3) a vet who treats an animal at the owner's request will owe that owner a duty to treat that animal with the care and skill that a reasonably competent vet would exercise in treating that animal;[34]

(4) a solicitor who handles a case or transaction on behalf of a client will owe that client a duty to handle that case or transaction with the care and skill that a reasonably competent solicitor would exercise in handling that case or transaction;[35] similarly,

(5) a barrister who handles a client's case in court will owe that client a duty to conduct that case in court with the care and skill that a reasonably competent barrister would exercise in conducting that case;[36]

[32] *Gladwell* v *Steggal* (1839) 5 Bing NC 733, 132 ER 1283; *Pippin* v *Sherrard* (1822) 11 Price 400, 147 ER 512; *Barnett* v *Chelsea & Kensington Hospital Management Committee* [1969] 1 QB 428. The concept of a doctor–patient relationship was stretched *very* far by Gage J in *A* v *Leeds Teaching Hospital NHS Trust* [2004] EWHC 644, holding that the parents of a baby that had died in hospital enjoyed a doctor–patient relationship with the baby's doctor, so that the doctor owed the parents a duty to act towards them with reasonable skill and care – particularly in relation to explaining to them what the baby's post-mortem would involve and whether any of the baby's organs would be retained.

[33] *Edwards* v *Mallan* [1908] 1 KB 1002; *Fish* v *Kapur* [1948] 2 All ER 176.

[34] *Chute Farms* v *Curtis*, The Times, 10 October 1961.

[35] *Nocton* v *Lord Ashburton* [1914] AC 465; *Midland Bank* v *Hett, Stubbs and Kemp* [1979] Ch 383.

[36] *Arthur J S Hall* v *Simons* [2002] 1 AC 615 (not followed by the High Court of Australia in *D'Orta-Ekenaike* v *Victoria Legal Aid* [2005] HCA 12).

(6) a surveyor will owe a client of his who has asked him to value a house or piece of land that he is thinking of purchasing a duty to survey that house or land with the care and skill that a reasonably competent surveyor would exercise in surveying a house or a piece of land;

(7) an architect will owe a client who has commissioned him to design a building a duty to design that building with the care and skill that a reasonably competent architect would exercise in designing a building; moreover,

(8) an architect who has been commissioned by a client to supervise the construction of a building will normally owe that client a duty to supervise the construction work with the care and skill that a reasonably competent architect would exercise in supervising that sort of work; likewise,

(9) an engineer who has been engaged to undertake some building work by a client will owe that client a duty to execute that work with the care and skill that a reasonably competent engineer would exercise in doing that sort of work;[37]

(10) an accountant will owe a client who has commissioned him to draw up a set of accounts a duty to draw up those accounts with the care and skill that a reasonably competent accountant would exercise in drawing up a set of accounts;

(11) the referee of a game will owe the participants in the game a duty to referee the game with a reasonable degree of care and skill.[38]

It should be emphasised that if A – implicitly or explicitly – indicates to B that he can be safely relied on to perform a particular task T with a certain degree of care and skill and B did so rely on him, he will not owe B a duty to perform that task T with any *more* care and skill than he indicated he could be safely relied on to exercise in performing task T.[39]

So – in *Philips* v *William Whiteley Ltd*,[40] the claimant asked the defendants, a firm of jewellers, to pierce her ears. The claimant suffered some ill effects from the operation and sought to recover compensation for those ill effects by suing the defendants in negligence. The court dismissed the claimant's claim: it held that the defendants had owed the claimant a duty to pierce her ears with the skill and care that a reasonably competent jeweller would exercise in piercing someone's ears and that the defendants had not breached that duty. The claimant's claim that the defendant had owed the claimant a more stringent duty of care – a duty to pierce her ears with the skill and care that a reasonably competent surgeon would exercise in piercing someone's ears – was dismissed: the defendants had never indicated to the claimant that they could be safely relied on to pierce her ears with the skill and care that a surgeon would exercise in piercing someone's ears.

Similarly, in *Wilsher* v *Essex Area Health Authority*,[41] the Court of Appeal held that if A treats B, a hospital patient, A will owe B a duty to treat B with the skill and care that a reasonably competent person *in A's post* would exercise in treating that patient. It would be

[37] *Congregational Union* v *Harriss and Harriss* [1988] 1 All ER 15; *Ketteman* v *Hansel Properties* [1987] AC 189.

[38] *Vowles* v *Evans* [2003] 1 WLR 1607 (noted, Elvin 2003a).

[39] Ibid., at [28], holding that it is arguable that someone who volunteers to referee a game as a replacement for a referee who has not turned up will not be expected to referee the game with as much skill and care as someone who has been trained to act as a referee: 'the volunteer cannot reasonably be expected to show the skill of one who holds himself out [to be a] referee, or perhaps even to be fully conversant with the [l]aws of the [g]ame.'

[40] [1938] 1 All ER 566. See also *Shakoor* v *Situ* [2001] 1 WLR 410.

[41] [1987] 1 QB 730, reversed on other grounds by the House of Lords: [1988] 1 AC 1074.

unreasonable to take A as indicating that he will exercise any higher degree of care and skill in treating B. So a junior house officer who treats a patient will owe that patient a duty to treat that patient with the skill and care that a reasonably competent junior house officer would exercise in treating a patient; a level of skill and care which would, presumably, be lower than the level of skill and care that a reasonably competent consultant would exercise in treating a patient.[42]

It is worth noting at greater length two cases that seem to lend some support to the suggestion that if A indicates to B that B can safely rely on him to perform a particular task with a certain degree of care and skill and B does so rely on A, then A will owe B a duty to perform that task with that degree of care and skill.

(1) *Junior Books Ltd* v *Veitchi Co. Ltd.*[43] Junior Books Ltd engaged Ogilvie Builders Ltd to build a factory for them. The work of laying the floor was contracted out to Veitchi Co. Ltd, on the instructions of Junior Books' architect. Veitchi laid the floor of Junior Books' factory but did a poor job of it. Two years after the floor was laid, it began to crack up and needed to be completely replaced. Junior Books sued Veitchi in negligence so as to recover the cost of relaying the floor of their factory. In order to make out their claim, they had to establish that Veitchi, in laying the floor, owed Junior Books a duty to lay the floor with a certain degree of care and skill. The House of Lords held that Veitchi did owe Junior Books such a duty. The decision caused some consternation at the time; it was hard to see what principle underlay the House of Lords' decision and therefore how widely it applied. However – whatever the views were of the Law Lords who decided the case at the time – the decision is nowadays justified on the basis that Veitchi indicated, in negotiations with Junior Books' architect, that it could be safely relied on to lay the floor of Junior Books' factory with a certain degree of care and skill and Junior Books did so rely on Veitchi to take such care by causing Veitchi to be nominated as subcontractors by their architect.[44] Viewed in this way, the decision in *Junior Books* was an outgrowth of the *dicta* in *Hedley Byrne* referred to above.[45]

[42] Of course, one way in which a reasonably competent junior house officer might act negligently would be in failing to seek assistance from a more qualified physician when it ought to have been clear to a reasonably competent junior house officer that such assistance was necessary.

[43] [1983] 1 AC 520.

[44] In contrast, in *Simaan* v *Pilkington Glass Ltd (No. 2)* [1988] QB 758, the claimant contractors were appointed to construct a building in Abu Dhabi (the 'Al-Oteiba building', named after the sheikh who commissioned it). One of the main features of the building was to be a curtain wall, made out of green panels. The job of building the curtain wall was subcontracted to a company named Feal and the claimants instructed Feal to use glass panels manufactured by the defendants in constructing the building. The glass panels proved not to be suitable and the sheikh who commissioned the building refused to pay the claimants the full price due under their contract with the sheikh. The claimants sought to recover their loss from the defendants by suing them in negligence but it was held that the defendants had not owed the claimants a duty to construct the glass panels with reasonable care and skill. The crucial distinction between this case and *Junior Books* is that the defendants did not indicate to the claimants that they could be safely relied upon to do a good job of constructing the glass panels and the defendants had not so relied on them. In fact, the only reason why the claimants instructed Feal to use the defendants' glass panels in constructing the curtain wall was that the building's *architect* wanted the defendants' panels to be used.

[45] A view taken by Lord Oliver of Aylmerton (*D & F Estates* v *Church Commissioners* [1989] 1 AC 177, 215D: 'the decision of this House in *Junior Books* . . . rests . . . upon the *Hedley Byrne* doctrine of reliance') and Lord Keith of Kinkel (*Murphy* v *Brentwood DC* [1991] 1 AC 398, 466G–H: 'The case would accordingly fall within the principle of *Hedley Byrne* . . . I regard *Junior Books* . . . as being an application of that principle'). See also, to the same effect, Perry 1992, 302–8. However, others have found it difficult to see how *Junior Books* can be explained on this basis: see *Payne* v *John Setchell Ltd* [2002] PNLR 146, at [24] and references contained therein.

(2) *Henderson* v *Merrett Syndicates Ltd.*[46] In this case, the claimants were Lloyd's names who were members of syndicates managed by the defendants. Each syndicate was made up of a number of Lloyd's names. A syndicate's managing agent performed a number of functions. First, he would decide which risks should be insured by the syndicate. Secondly, in the case of risks which were insured by the syndicate, he would decide whether or not those risks should be reinsured with someone else. Thirdly, he would decide how to deal with claims against the syndicate – whether to settle those claims, and if so on what terms, and so on. Losses suffered by a syndicate were to be borne by the names who were members of that syndicate. A name's potential liability was unlimited – the greater the losses suffered by a syndicate of which he or she was a member, the greater would be his or her liability, without limit. The claimants suffered spectacular losses because (they claimed) the defendant managing agents had failed to run the affairs of their syndicates with the sort of care and skill that the claimants had expected them to when they joined those syndicates.

Each Lloyd's name, when he entered Lloyd's, signed an 'underwriting agency agreement' with an underwriting agent, whose job it was to place him with a syndicate. If the underwriting agent placed the name in a syndicate which he himself managed, the name was known as a 'direct name'. In such a case, the underwriting agency agreement between the underwriting agent and the name created a contractual relationship between the name and the underwriting agent *qua* managing agent of the member's syndicate. It was conceded that there was an implied term in the contract between a direct name and his underwriting agent *qua* managing agent that the latter would administer the affairs of the name's syndicate with a certain degree of care and skill.[47] If the underwriting agent placed the name in a syndicate which he did not manage himself, the name was known as an 'indirect name'. In such a case, there was no contractual relationship between the name and the managing agent of the name's syndicate.

The claimants in *Henderson* v *Merrett Syndicates Ltd* comprised a mixture of direct and indirect names. Obviously – assuming that the defendants did fail to take care to administer the affairs of their syndicates properly – the claimants who were direct names had an action in *contract* against the managing agents of their syndicates to recover compensation for the money they lost due to those agents' mismanagement. However, they wished to sue their managing agents in *negligence* to take advantage of the fact that the limitation periods for bringing actions in negligence expire later than the limitation periods for bringing actions for breach of contract. Of course, the claimants who were indirect names could not bring a claim in contract against the managing agents of their syndicates – even assuming that they could prove those managing agents did fail to take care to administer the affairs of their syndicates properly – and so could only seek redress against the managing agents of their syndicates by bringing an action in negligence against those agents. So each claimant in *Henderson* v *Merrett Syndicates Ltd* sought to establish – for the purpose of making out a claim in negligence against the managing agent of his syndicate – that the managing agent of his syndicate owed him a duty to administer the affairs of the syndicate with a certain degree of care and skill.[48] The House of Lords was of the opinion that every

[46] [1995] 2 AC 145.

[47] Ibid., 176.

[48] It is worth re-emphasising at this juncture that the word 'duty' is used here to refer to a *tortious* duty. It was obviously true that – in the case of a claimant who was a direct name – the managing agent of his syndicate

claimant in *Henderson* v *Merrett Syndicates Ltd* could establish that the managing agent of his syndicate owed him such a duty.

In the case of claimants who were *direct* names, this is easily explained by reference to the principle of law examined here: that if A indicates to B that he can be safely relied on to perform a particular task with a certain degree of care and skill and B does so rely on A, A will owe B a duty to perform that task with that degree of care and skill. When a name became a member of a syndicate which was managed by the name's underwriting agent – thereby becoming a direct name – the agent contracted with the name that he would run the affairs of the name's syndicate with a certain degree of care and skill and thereby indicated to the name that the name could safely rely on him to run the affairs of the syndicate with that degree of care and skill. The direct name would, in turn, rely on his underwriting agent to run the affairs of his syndicate with that degree of care and skill by agreeing to join the underwriting agent's syndicate and by staying on as a member of that syndicate while the underwriting agent administered its affairs.

In the case of the claimants who were *indirect* names, we can again explain the House of Lords' ruling by reference to the principle of law examined here. Before an indirect name became a member of a syndicate managed by a particular managing agent, the managing agent would expressly or impliedly indicate to the name, through the name's underwriting agent, that he could be safely relied on to manage the affairs of his syndicate with a certain degree of care and skill. The indirect name would in turn rely on the managing agent to run the affairs of his syndicate with that degree of care and skill by agreeing to join the managing agent's syndicate and by staying on as a member of the syndicate while the managing agent administered its affairs.

So the ruling of the House of Lords in *Henderson* v *Merrett Syndicates Ltd* that the claimant names could establish that the managing agents of their syndicates owed them a duty to administer the affairs of those syndicates with a certain degree of care and skill can be explained by reference to the principle of law examined here. Seen in this way, the decision in *Henderson* v *Merrett Syndicates Ltd* was, like the decision in *Junior Books*, an outgrowth of the *dicta* in *Hedley Byrne* that were referred to above – and that is, indeed, how the Law Lords who decided *Henderson* v *Merrett Syndicates Ltd* viewed their decision.

If it is the law (and it is)[49] that A will owe B a duty to perform a task with a certain degree of care and skill if he has indicated to B that he can be safely relied on to perform that task with that degree of care and skill and B has so relied on A, then it must be the law – by extension – that if A has indicated to B that he can be safely relied on to take reasonable steps to achieve some goal or end and B has so relied on A, A will owe B a duty to take reasonable steps to achieve that goal or end. There are a couple of cases that seem to indicate that this is true.

(who was also his underwriting agent) owed him a *contractual* duty to take care to administer the affairs of the syndicate properly.

49 Whittaker 1997 wishes it were not so, arguing that the extended principle in *Hedley Byrne* undermines the law of contract, which also makes 'assumptions of responsibility' binding, but only if they are made in a deed or if consideration is provided for them.

In *Welsh* v *Chief Constable of Merseyside Police*,[50] the claimant appeared before a magistrates' court charged with two offences of theft. He was remanded on bail to appear again on 19 August 1987. On 7 August the claimant was due to appear before the Crown Court to be sentenced for committing various criminal offences. Before his case was called, the claimant indicated to the Crown Prosecution Service (CPS) that he did commit the two theft offences for which he was due to appear before the magistrates on 19 August and he wanted the Crown Court to take into account those two offences in sentencing him. The Crown Court took those offences into account and the claimant – believing that the CPS would tell the magistrates that the Crown Court had already dealt with the two theft offences which they were due to try him for – failed to turn up to his hearing before the magistrates on 19 August. The magistrates, knowing nothing of the Crown Court hearing, issued a warrant for the claimant's arrest. The claimant was arrested under the warrant and held in custody for two days until the true facts came to light.

The claimant sued the CPS, claiming that they had owed him a duty to take reasonable steps to alert the magistrates to the fact that he had already been sentenced in the Crown Court for committing the two theft offences for which he was due to be tried in the magistrates' court. Tudor Evans J refused to strike out the claimant's claim, holding that it was strongly arguable that the CPS had owed him such a duty of care. It could be argued that the CPS indicated to the claimant that he could safely rely on them to take reasonable steps to inform the magistrates of what had happened in the Crown Court and that the claimant had relied on the CPS to take such steps by not turning up to his hearing on the 19 August.[51]

In *Swinney* v *Chief Constable of the Northumbria Police*,[52] the claimant passed on to the police information which indicated that T was involved in the killing of a police officer. The claimant gave the police this information in confidence and made it clear that she did not want T to find out that she had informed on him to the police. As the claimant gave her information to the police, it was written down on a document which named the claimant as the source of the information. This document was then left in an unattended police car which was broken into by criminals. The document was stolen and passed on to T. T then threatened the claimant with violence and arson and the claimant developed a psychiatric illness as a result. The claimant sued the police, arguing that the police had owed her, and breached, a duty to take reasonable steps to see that T would not find out that she had informed on him. The police sought to have the claimant's claim struck out on the ground that they had not owed her a duty of care. However, the Court of Appeal refused to strike out the claim: it thought it was strongly arguable that the police had owed the claimant a duty to take reasonable steps to ensure that T would not find out that she had informed on him. The reason why the Court of Appeal thought it was strongly arguable that the police had owed the claimant such a duty of care was that the police had indicated to her that they could be safely relied on to take reasonable steps to ensure that T would not find out that

50 [1993] 1 All ER 692.

51 It is quite clear that if the CPS had *not* indicated to the claimant that they could be safely relied on to take reasonable steps to inform the magistrates of his conviction, they would not have owed him a duty to take any steps to inform the magistrates of his conviction: *Elguzouli-Daf* v *Commissioner of the Police of the Metropolis* [1995] QB 335.

52 [1997] QB 464.

she had informed on him and the claimant did so rely on the police by giving them her information about T.[53]

To sum up this section then, the cases seem to establish that:

(1) if A indicates to B that he can be safely relied on to perform some task with a certain degree of care and skill and B does so rely on A, then A will owe B a duty to perform that task with that degree of care and skill; *and*

(2) if A indicates to B that he can be safely relied on to take reasonable steps to achieve some goal or end and B does so rely on A, then A will owe B a duty to take reasonable steps to achieve that goal or end.

Let's call this the *extended principle* in *Hedley Byrne*, to contrast it with the basic principle, which only applies to cases where A takes on the task of advising B on some matter. The extended principle applies to all kinds of tasks, not just the giving of advice.

The *SAAMCO* principle

The '*SAAMCO* principle' was introduced into our law in the case of *South Australia Asset Management Corp.* v *York Montague Ltd*[54] – hence, *SAAMCO*. The principle affects how much A can sue B for by way of damages if A breaches a duty of care owed to B under either the basic or extended principle in *Hedley Byrne*. Strictly speaking, then, we should not talk of it here. A discussion of the *SAAMCO* principle properly belongs in Part III of this book, which deals with what remedies will be available when someone commits a tort. However, it seems convenient for teaching purposes to mention it here rather than postponing discussion of the principle for a few hundred pages.

The *SAAMCO* principle has been described as being 'easier to formulate than to apply'.[55] This is not true: the *SAAMCO* principle is *both* extremely difficult to formulate *and* extremely difficult to apply.[56] The basic idea behind it seems to go like this.[57] Suppose B got A to perform some task for her or to give her some advice on a particular matter. Suppose further that A owed B a duty of care in performing that task or giving that advice and A breached that duty of care with the result that B suffered some kind of evil or failed to obtain some kind of good. The *SAAMCO* principle says that B will not be entitled to sue A in negligence for compensation for the fact that she suffered that evil or failed to obtain

53 When the case went to trial, the judge (Jackson J) found that the police had indeed owed the claimant a duty to take reasonable steps to see that T did not find out that she had informed on him. However, the claimant's claim was dismissed on the ground that the police had not breached that duty of care. See *Swinney* v *Chief Constable of Northumbria Police (No. 2)*, The Times, 25 May 1999.

54 [1997] AC 191 (noted, O'Sullivan 1997). The case is otherwise known as *Banque Bruxelles Lambert SA* v *Eagle Star Insurance Ltd.*

55 *Nykredit Plc* v *Edward Erdman Ltd* [1997] 1 WLR 1627, 1631 per Lord Nicholls.

56 A couple of cases illustrate the difficulties that the courts have experienced in applying the *SAAMCO* principle. See *Platform Home Loans* v *Oyston Shipways Ltd* [2000] 2 AC 190 (discussed below, pp. 622–3), where the House of Lords reversed a unanimous Court of Appeal's application of the *SAAMCO* principle, but not without dissent from one Law Lord (Lord Cooke); also *Aneco Reinsurance Underwriting Ltd* v *Johnson & Higgins Ltd* [2001] UKHL 51 where neither the House of Lords nor the Court of Appeal below could reach a unanimous decision as to how the *SAAMCO* principle applied in that case.

57 For more detailed treatments of the *SAAMCO* principle and how it operates, see Dugdale 2000, Evans 2001, Peel 2003a; Butler 2003. The originator of the *SAAMCO* principle talks about it extra-judicially at Hoffmann 2005, 596.

that good unless *B got A to perform the task or give her the advice in question in order to avoid that evil or obtain that good.*

In the *South Australia* case, Lord Hoffmann – the originator of the *SAAMCO* principle – gave an example of a situation where the principle would bite: 'A mountaineer about to undertake a difficult climb is concerned about the fitness of his knee. He goes to a doctor who negligently makes a superficial examination and pronounces the knee fit. The climber goes on the expedition, which he would not have undertaken if the doctor had told him the true state of his knee. He suffers an injury which is an entirely foreseeable consequence of mountaineering but has nothing to do with his knee.'[58] In this case, the doctor will have breached a duty of care owed to the climber under either the basic or the extended principle in *Hedley Byrne* and the climber has suffered injury as a result. But the climber will not be entitled to sue the doctor for compensation for that injury under the *SAAMCO* principle because he asked the doctor to advise him on the fitness of his knee in order to avoid suffering an injury as a result of his knee giving way – he did not ask the doctor to advise him on the fitness of his knee in order to avoid the kind of injury that he ended up suffering; that is, a non-knee-related injury.[59]

The *South Australia* case was concerned with the following kind of situation. C applies to B for a loan of £200,000 and offers certain properties – call them 'security properties' – as security for the loan. B gets A to value them and A values the properties as being worth £220,000. In fact, A failed to value the security properties with a professional degree of care and skill, thereby breaching the duty of care he owed B in valuing the properties. The security properties were in fact worth only £180,000. B – thinking that the security properties are actually worth £220,000 – loans C the £200,000 requested. Come the time for repayment, C defaults on the loan. B then seeks to get his money back by selling the security properties but – due to a fall in the market – the properties are now worth only £110,000. So B makes a net loss of £90,000 on the loan – the difference between the value of the loan and what he has managed to claw back by selling the security properties.

B discovers that A was negligent in valuing the security properties and he sues A for compensation for the £90,000 he lost on the loan to C. B argues that if A had not been negligent, A would have told B that the security properties were worth only £180,000 and so B would not have loaned C anything – C would have been unable to offer him sufficient security for the loan. It follows that had A not been negligent, B would not have lost £90,000. However, B will only be able to sue A for *£40,000* in damages under the *SAAMCO* principle. Why is this? The reason is that B got A to advise him as to the value of the security properties in order to ensure that he did not suffer a loss *as a result of lending money to C on inadequate security.*

Now – how much of the loss suffered by B here is suffered *because he lent money to C on inadequate security*? Well, the fact that B was willing to lend C £200,000 on security that was valued at £220,000 shows that he thought that security worth that much was adequate security for his loan. Had B lent C £200,000 on security worth that much, that security would have been worth £150,000 when the time came for C to repay. (We assume here that the security would have declined in value by £70,000 as a result of a fall in the market, just

[58] [1997] AC 191, 213.

[59] For an alternative explanation as to why there is no liability in this case, see below, p. 537, n. 22.

like the security properties that C actually offered to B as security for B's loan to him.) So had B lent money to C on adequate security, he would still have lost £50,000 on his loan to C. It follows that of the £90,000 loss suffered by B in this case, only £40,000 of that loss was suffered by him as a result of his lending money to C on inadequate security. So, under the *SAAMCO* principle, B will only be able to sue A for compensation for that £40,000 loss – B got A to value the security properties in order to help ensure that he did not suffer any loss as a result of lending money to C on inadequate security and, as things have turned out, B has lost £40,000, but no more than £40,000, as a result of lending money to C on inadequate security.[60]

A pre-*SAAMCO* case which can, in its result, be seen as giving effect to the *SAAMCO* principle is *Caparo Industries plc* v *Dickman*.[61] In that case, Caparo Industries plc were a company which held shares in Fidelity plc. Touche Ross, the defendants, audited Fidelity's accounts before they were circulated to Fidelity's shareholders. Touche Ross stated that the company's accounts gave a 'true and fair' representation of the company's financial position. This was not correct and Touche Ross should have known it. The accounts showed that Fidelity enjoyed a pre-tax profit of £1.3m. The true position was that Fidelity had suffered a loss of over £400,000. Caparo launched a takeover bid for Fidelity, relying on the fact that Touche Ross had given the company's accounts their seal of approval. The takeover bid was successful but when Caparo took a closer look at the books it discovered that it had paid too much for Fidelity.

Caparo sued Touche Ross in negligence, arguing that Touche had owed them, as one of Fidelity's shareholders, a duty of care in auditing the accounts and that Touche had breached that duty of care and that had they not breached that duty, Touche would have uncovered the truth about Fidelity's financial position and as a result Caparo would not have taken over Fidelity or Caparo would have paid a much smaller price for Fidelity. Caparo's claim for compensation was dismissed. It was conceded that Touche had owed Caparo a duty of care in auditing Fidelity's accounts – but Touche had only owed Caparo that duty in their capacity as shareholders. The loss that Caparo suffered as a result of

60 It would have been different if the fall in the property market had been more modest: say the security properties were actually worth £170,000 when C defaulted, having been originally worth £180,000. In that case, B's loss on the loan would have come to £30,000 and the loss he would have suffered had he lent C £200,000 on adequate security (that is, security worth £220,000) would have been £0 – the security properties would have declined in value from £220,000 to £210,000 but that would still have afforded enough security to allow B to get back all his money that he loaned C. So *all* of the £30,000 loss suffered by B in this scenario would have been attributable to the fact that he loaned C money on inadequate security and A would therefore be liable to compensate B *fully* for the loss suffered by him as a result of A's negligence.

61 [1990] 2 AC 605. Another pre-*SAAMCO* case which can be seen as giving effect to the *SAAMCO* principle is *Stevens* v *Bermondsey & Southwark Group Hospital Management Committee* (1963) 107 Sol J 478. The defendant's negligent diagnosis of the extent of the injuries suffered by the claimant as a result of a third party's negligence caused the claimant to settle his claim for damages against the third party for £125, when he would have been entitled to sue for much more. The claimant sued the defendant for the extra amount he would have demanded from the third party had the defendant not been negligent. Held that the claimant could not recover – the claimant had employed the defendant to diagnose his injuries in order to help him get better; not in order to help him determine how much he should sue the third party for compensation. See also *Reeman* v *Department of Transport* [1997] 2 Lloyd's Rep 648, where the claimant bought a boat which had been certified as being seaworthy by the defendant. In fact, the boat was not seaworthy and was, as a result, practically valueless. The claimant's action for damages was dismissed: the defendant had been employed to determine whether or not it would be safe for people to travel on the boat, not to ensure that the claimant did not make a bad bargain in buying a boat.

Touche's negligence was suffered by Caparo in a quite different capacity – in their capacity as corporate raiders. Given this, Caparo could not sue Touche for compensation for the loss, by analogy to the rule that if A commits a tort in relation to B and C suffers some kind of loss as a result, C will not normally be entitled to sue A for compensation for that loss. Touche committed a tort in relation to Caparo *qua* shareholders in auditing Fidelity's accounts but it was Caparo *qua* corporate raiders who suffered a loss as a result.

Nowadays, Caparo's claim for compensation could be dismissed by reference to the *SAAMCO* principle – Caparo's loss in this case arose out of the fact that it bid too much for Fidelity when it took it over, but the purpose of getting Touche Ross to audit Fidelity's accounts was *not* to help ensure that Caparo did not bid too much for Fidelity on taking it over. Touche were employed to audit Fidelity's accounts in order to help Caparo and the other shareholders in Fidelity decide whether to reward or punish Fidelity's board of directors for their performance over the previous financial year.[62]

Two common misconceptions about *Hedley Byrne*

Before concluding our discussion of the principle in *Hedley Byrne* we should briefly pause to note and dismiss two common misconceptions about *Hedley Byrne*.[63] Both arise out of the twin facts that: (1) in *Hedley Byrne* the claimants suffered a form of pure economic loss;[64] and (2) it was in *Hedley Byrne* that the House of Lords first countenanced the possibility that a claimant might be entitled to sue a defendant in negligence for compensation for some form of pure economic loss that she had suffered as a result of the defendant's actions.

(1) *Hedley Byrne only relevant in pure economic loss cases.* The first misconception is that *Hedley Byrne* is only ever relevant in establishing that a duty of care was owed in a case where a claimant has suffered a form of pure economic loss as a result of a defendant's actions. On this view, in cases where a claimant has suffered some other kind of harm – such as personal injury or psychiatric illness – as a result of a defendant's actions or non-actions, the decision in *Hedley Byrne* will be irrelevant to the inquiry as to whether or not

62 The *Caparo* case was distinguished in *Morgan Crucible Co. plc* v *Hill Samuel & Co. Ltd* [1991] Ch 295 where, it was claimed, the defendant representatives of a company made various representations to the claimants, who were thinking of taking over the company, as to the financial health of the company with the object of persuading the claimants to increase their bid for the company. The claimants subsequently discovered that they had bid too much for the company and sued for compensation. It was held that if these facts were made out, the claimants had an arguable claim against the defendants.

63 A third possible misconception which some students might entertain is that a duty to take care not to mislead others can only exist in a *Hedley Byrne*-type case. (This misconception may be encouraged by the discussion in W&J, at 485f, of 'Liability for Negligent Misstatement'; also McGregor 2003, 1507: 'For long English law resisted giving a remedy for negligent misrepresentation ... Not until *Hedley Byrne* ... was it held that negligent misrepresentation [could] constitute an actionable wrong.') This is obviously incorrect. In the right circumstances, the physical danger principle can operate to impose on someone a duty to take care not to mislead someone else. For example, if a blind man asks you if it is safe to cross the road, you will owe him a duty under the physical danger principle to take care that you do not tell him that it is safe to cross the road when it is not (it being reasonably foreseeable that if you do so, he will suffer some kind of physical injury as a result). See *Haseldine* v *Daw* [1941] 2 KB 343 (discussed above, p. 76, n. 20) for an example of a decision which could be explained on the basis that the defendant breached a duty to take care not to mislead someone else which arose under the physical danger principle.

64 That is, economic loss not consequent on the claimants' having suffered damage to their persons or their property.

the defendant owed the claimant a duty of care. This is nonsense: there is no sign that the Law Lords in *Hedley Byrne* meant their remarks as to when one person will owe another a duty of care to be confined to cases where a defendant has caused another to suffer a form of pure economic loss.[65]

(2) *Recovery for pure economic loss only allowed in Hedley Byrne cases.* The second misconception is that if a claimant has suffered a form of pure economic loss as a result of a defendant's actions, the claimant will *only* be able to establish that the defendant owed her a duty of care not to act as he did if the House of Lords' decision in *Hedley Byrne* covers her case.[66] So if *Hedley Byrne* does not cover the claimant's case, then the defendant will not have owed the claimant a duty of care.[67] This is, again, nonsense: there is no reason to think that the Law Lords in *Hedley Byrne* were seeking to lay down for all time an exhaustive set of rules as to when a duty of care will be owed in a pure economic loss case. As the House of Lords made clear in *Customs and Excise Commissioners* v *Barclays Bank*,[68] to establish that A owed B a duty of care in a case where B has suffered pure economic loss as a result of A's carelessness, it will be sufficient, *but not necessary*, to show that A assumed a responsibility to B not to be careless.[69]

Unfortunately, the misconception that a claimant can only recover in negligence for pure economic loss if *Hedley Byrne* covers her case is now quite widespread and has given rise to the further misconception that *any* pure economic loss case in the law reports in

[65] For examples of *personal injury* cases where a claimant will be able to invoke *Hedley Byrne* to establish that a defendant owed her a duty of care, see any medical negligence case that involves a failure to treat a patient with reasonable skill and care. For an example of a *property damage* case where the claimant was allowed to invoke *Hedley Byrne* to establish that the defendant owed her a duty of care see the Canadian case of *Densmore* v *Whitehorse* [1986] 5 WWR 708 (discussed, Bagshaw 1999). In that case, a fire started in the claimant's house. The claimant rang the fire department and was told a fire engine would be on its way; but none was actually sent and the claimant's house and its contents were destroyed. Held, that the fire department had owed the claimant a duty to take care not to mislead the claimant as to whether a fire engine would be sent under the basic principle in *Hedley Byrne* as it was made clear to them when she rang them that if they told her a fire engine was on its way she would not take any steps herself to save the contents of her house. See also *Stansbie* v *Troman* [1948] 2 KB 48 (discussed below, at p. 565) and *Bailey* v *HSS Alarms Ltd*, The Times, 20 June 2000 (failure to protect business from being burgled). A *psychiatric illness* case where *Hedley Byrne* could have been used to establish that the defendant owed the claimant a duty of care is *McLoughlin* v *Grovers* [2002] QB 1312, where the claimant developed a psychiatric illness as a result of being wrongfully convicted of robbery and causing grievous bodily harm; he sued his solicitors for compensation for his illness claiming that he would not have been convicted had they conducted his case with reasonable skill and care; held, that the claimant had an arguable claim against the defendants and his claim should not be struck out.

[66] See, for example, Murphy 2003, at 243: 'Outside the … *Hedley Byrne* principle, it seems that no duty to protect others from economic loss will arise, however predictable that loss may be…'; Jones 2002, at 141: 'unless a case can be brought under the umbrella of *Hedley Byrne* … there is generally no liability in respect of pure economic loss caused by a negligent act'; Howarth 2007, at 711: 'The rule that pure economic loss is not recoverable in negligence is subject to one substantial exception. Pure economic loss is recoverable if the defendant has assumed responsibility for the claimant's economic well-being.'

[67] For an example of this misconception at work, see the Court of Appeal's decision in *Phelps* v *Hillingdon LBC* [1999] 1 WLR 500, where the claimant sued for compensation for the harm done to her prospects as a result of the defendant's failure to diagnose her as being dyslexic while she was at school. As this was regarded in the Court of Appeal as being a pure economic loss case, it was conceded on all sides that the defendant could *only* have owed the claimant a duty of care in treating her if the decision in *Hedley Byrne* applied to the claimant's case: ibid., 513–14. It was found that it did not as the defendant had not 'assumed a responsibility' to the claimant. The claimant in *Phelps* appealed to the House of Lords, and their Lordships found that a duty of care *was* owed to the claimant: [2001] 2 AC 619. For an explanation of the House of Lords' decision in *Phelps*, see below: pp. 149–50.

[68] [2007] 1 AC 181.

[69] Ibid., at [4] (per Lord Bingham), [52] (per Lord Rodger), [73] (per Lord Walker), and [93] (per Lord Mance).

which the courts found that a duty of care was owed is a '*Hedley Byrne* case'.[70] Anyone labouring under this further misconception will find it quite impossible to come up with an intelligible account as to when one person will owe another a duty of care under *Hedley Byrne*. The reason is that while *most* of the pure economic loss cases in the law reports in which the courts have found that a duty of care was owed *are Hedley Byrne* cases, *not all of them are* – some of those cases rest on quite different principles, which we will explore below. So there is no *single* principle underlying all of the pure economic loss cases in the law reports in which the courts have found that a duty of care was owed and any attempt to discover such a principle will be doomed to failure.

THE DEPENDENCY PRINCIPLE

The following cases are often seen as being *Hedley Byrne* cases because they involve a claimant being allowed to sue a defendant in negligence for some pure economic loss that she has suffered. But it is in fact impossible to see the duties of care in these cases as arising under either the basic or extended principle in *Hedley Byrne*. The better view is that these duties of care arise under a quite different principle, which we will call the *dependency principle*. The dependency principle goes like this: if A takes on a task, knowing that B's future well-being is almost completely dependent on A's performing that task properly, then A will normally owe B a duty to perform that task with a reasonable degree of care and skill.

Before we go on to look at the cases which seem to give effect to this principle, three points about the dependency principle must be emphasised:

(1) *Acts, not omissions*. The dependency principle can *only* be invoked in a case where A has made B worse off than she would have been had A done nothing. It cannot be applied to find a duty of care in an omissions case was A has failed to save B from suffering some kind of harm. So, for example, suppose that Wendy and Gary are two strangers who are both sunbathing on an otherwise deserted beach. Wendy goes for a swim and starts drowning. Seeing this, Gary plunges into the sea to try and save Wendy. When Gary does this, he takes on the task of rescuing Wendy knowing that her future well-being is almost completely dependent on his performing that task properly. But it would be unfair to find that Gary owed Wendy a duty to rescue her with a reasonable degree of care and skill in this situation. To do so would penalise him for his act of kindness in trying to rescue her and leave him worse off – legally – than he would have been had he carried on sunbathing and simply left Wendy to her fate.[71]

(2) *Dependency has to be severe*. The dependency principle can *only* be invoked in a case where A takes on a task, knowing that B will be made *drastically* worse off if he fails to perform that task properly. So, for example, in *Spartan Steel & Alloys Ltd* v *Martin & Co.*

[70] One of the authors of this book has not been immune to this misconception in the past: see McBride & Hughes 1995. This second misconception seems to have originated in a misreading of some of the speeches in the House of Lords in *Murphy* v *Brentwood DC* [1991] AC 398. Lord Bridge, for instance, stated (at 475) that 'purely economic [losses are] . . . not recoverable in tort in the absence of a special relationship of proximity . . .' and some have misread this as meaning that 'purely economic losses are not recoverable in tort in the absence of a special relationship of the kind involved in *Hedley Byrne*-type cases'.

[71] See below, pp. 193–4.

(Contractors) Ltd,[72] when the defendant contractors in that case took on the job of digging up the road, they knew that if they failed to perform that task properly and severed a power cable running under the road, nearby businesses would suffer some disruption to their work. So nearby businesses were dependent on the defendant contractors in *Spartan Steel* doing their work properly. However, the degree of dependency was nowhere near serious enough to justify finding that the defendant contractors owed a duty of care to any nearby businesses that would have had their operations disrupted by a power cable being severed.[73]

(3) *Status of the principle*. No English court has ever explicitly endorsed the dependency principle as part of English law. In our view, the dependency principle provides the most satisfying explanation of why a duty of care was found in the cases gathered below. However, other people may interpret these cases as resting on an entirely different basis and therefore argue that there is absolutely no support in the decided cases for the idea that the dependency principle is part of English law. So it is debatable whether or not English law gives effect to the dependency principle and student readers of this textbook should be wary of too easily invoking the 'dependency principle' to find that a duty of care was owed in a particular situation that they have been asked to consider. With that said, let us now turn to the cases which, in our view, rest on the dependency principle.

The survey cases

These cases are concerned with the following kind of situation. B – who was not particularly well-off – wanted to buy a house. She managed to find a fairly cheap house at the bottom end of the property market and applied to C, a building society or a local authority, for a loan to help her buy the house. C appointed A – a surveyor – to survey the house for them to check that the house would provide them with adequate security for the loan. A surveyed the house and reported back that it was worth at least as much as the loan for which B was applying. Unfortunately, A failed to survey the house properly and failed to spot some defects in the house which meant that it was worth much less than B was proposing to pay for it. B was too poor to afford her own survey, but was reassured that the house was in good condition when C approved the loan to her – after all, she thought, if C's surveyor had spotted any problems with the house, C would hardly have agreed to loan her the money she needed to buy it. So B went ahead and purchased the house with the assistance of the loan from C. She then discovered that the house was worth much less than she agreed to pay for it.

It is now well established that in this sort of situation A will have owed B a duty to survey the house with a reasonable degree of care and skill. It is impossible to explain this result by reference to the extended principle in *Hedley Byrne* because the existence of the duty of care owed by A to B does not depend on A's having had any contact with B.[74] So

[72] [1973] 1 QB 27. See also *SCM (United Kingdom) Ltd* v *W & J Whittall & Son Ltd* [1971] 1 QB 337.

[73] Though see n. 95, below, for a different view.

[74] *Important note*. This has been made crystal clear by the decision of the Court of Appeal in *Merrett* v *Babb* [2001] QB 1174. In that case, the claimant, Merrett, lost a lot of money purchasing a defective house with the assistance of a loan from a building society. The building society asked a firm of surveyors to value the house for them and an employee of the firm, Babb, valued the house as being worth at least as much as Merrett was wanting to borrow to buy the house. Before Merrett had a chance to sue the firm of surveyors in negligence,

why will A have owed B a duty of care in this situation? Again the dependency principle seems to provide a good explanation of why A owed B a duty of care. When A took on the job of surveying the house he knew from the fact that the house was at the bottom end of the property market that B, the prospective purchaser, was not particularly well-off. This means he knew two further things.

First of all, he knew that it was likely that B would not commission her own survey of the house – so he knew that if he said the house afforded sufficient security for C's loan to B and C made a loan to B, B would probably buy the house without more ado. Secondly, when A took on the job of valuing the house, he knew that if B bought the house and it turned out to be worth much less than she paid for it, B would not be able easily to bear this loss. Already badly off, her buying the house would make her much worse off and bring her to the brink of destitution.

So when A took on the job of surveying the house, he knew – simply from the fact that the house was at the low end of the property market – that if he said the house was in good condition, B would certainly buy the house as a result and that if it turned out not to be in good condition, B would suffer a huge financial loss which she could ill afford to bear. So when A took on the job of surveying the house, he knew that B's future well-being was almost completely dependent on his surveying the house properly. As a result, he owed B a duty to survey the house with a reasonable degree of care and skill under the dependency principle.[75]

If this is right, then, in a case where B wants to buy a house with the assistance of a loan from C and C appoints A to survey the house to check that it will provide adequate security for the loan, A will only owe B a duty to survey the house with a reasonable degree of care and skill if A *knows* that B is going to rely on his survey and not commission her own survey

---

they went out of business. So instead she sued Babb – who had substantial assets – claiming that *he* personally had owed her a duty to survey the house with a reasonable degree of care and skill. By the time *Merrett* was decided, the decision of the House of Lords in *Williams* v *Natural Life Health Foods Ltd* [1998] 1 WLR 830 had made it clear that the existence of contact between a defendant and claimant is essential for a duty of care to arise between the defendant and claimant under *Hedley Byrne*. (See also, on this point, *Mills* v *Winchester Diocesan Board of Finance* [1989] Ch 428, *Mariola Marine Corp.* v *Lloyd's Register of Shipping* [1990] 1 Lloyd's Rep 547 and *A & J Fabrication (Batley) Ltd* v *Grant Thornton (a firm)* [1999] PNLR 811.) However, there had been absolutely no contact between Merrett and Babb at the time Babb surveyed the house that Merrett ended up purchasing; indeed, she was not even aware of his identity at that time. Despite this, the Court of Appeal still found that Babb *had* owed Merrett a duty of care in valuing the house and the House of Lords refused leave to appeal: [2001] 1 WLR 1859. So the duty of care in *Merrett* v *Babb* and the other survey cases *cannot* be explained by reference to the extended principle in *Hedley Byrne*. Of course, those who have fallen into the trap of thinking that *all* pure economic loss cases where a defendant has been held to have owed a claimant a duty of care are *Hedley Byrne* cases cannot but think that there is some conflict between the decisions in *Williams* v *Natural Life* and *Merrett* v *Babb*. There is, of course, no conflict: the *Williams* case was concerned with when one person will owe another a duty of care under *Hedley Byrne*; the duty of care in *Merrett* v *Babb* arose under a completely different principle.

75 Cf. Hoffmann J's explanation of *Smith* v *Eric S Bush* in *Morgan Crucible Co. plc* v *Hill Samuel & Co. Ltd* [1991] Ch 295, at 302. Stapleton 1991 seems to think (at 277–83) that it is hard to understand why A will have owed B a duty of care here when a builder of a house will *not* owe a subsequent purchaser of the house a duty to build that house with a reasonable degree of care and skill. In fact, as Stapleton 1995 seems to recognise (at 335–7) there is no contradiction here. The reason why a builder will not owe a subsequent purchaser of a house a duty to build that house with a reasonable degree of care and skill is that the builder – at the time he was building the house – will not *know* that if he does a bad job, a subsequent purchaser will definitely be made drastically worse off as a result. This is because there are ways that a subsequent purchaser of a house can protect herself against the risk that the house will turn out to be no good – for example, by having the house surveyed or by taking out insurance.

of the house. It is only in that situation that A will know that B's future well-being is dependent on his surveying the house properly. If A expects B to get her own survey of the house done then, in A's mind, nothing much will depend on A's survey. A will think that it will not matter if he fails to spot some defect in the house which affects its value in a big way; B's surveyor will probably see it instead and warn B against buying the house.

It *does* seem to be the case that A will *only* owe B a duty of care in surveying the house if he *knows* that B is not going to commission her own survey of the house.[76] Given this, it is highly unlikely that A will owe B such a duty if B is purchasing a house at the top end of the property market. A will expect B in such a case to commission her own survey of the house: if she is rich enough to buy a house at that end of the property market, she will be rich enough to afford her own survey. Similarly, if a company wants to buy a set of offices and it applies to a bank for a loan and the bank appoints a surveyor to value the offices, it is highly unlikely that the surveyor will owe the company a duty of care in surveying the offices; the surveyor will expect the company to commission its own survey of the offices.[77]

The reference cases

In *Spring* v *Guardian Assurance plc*,[78] Spring was employed as a sales director and office manager by Corinium Ltd. Corinium sold life assurance policies on behalf of Guardian Assurance, the defendants. When Corinium was taken over by the defendants, Spring was dismissed. Spring attempted to go into business on his own selling life assurance policies for Scottish Amicable. When he approached Scottish Amicable, that company asked the defendants to supply them with a reference for Spring. Scottish Amicable was obliged to do this under the rules of the Life Assurance and Unit Trust Regulatory Organisation (Lautro), of which Scottish Amicable was a member. The defendants supplied Scottish Amicable with a reference for Spring that stated, among other things, that Spring was 'a man of little or no integrity and could not be regarded as honest'. Unsurprisingly, Scottish Amicable declined to allow Spring to sell life assurance policies on its behalf. The same thing happened when Spring approached two other life assurance companies and for the same reason.

Spring sued the defendants in negligence, arguing that the defendants had owed him, and breached, a duty to use reasonable skill and care in supplying his prospective employers with references about him. The House of Lords found that the defendants had owed Spring such a duty of care. Why was this? It is impossible to explain this result on the basis that the defendants owed Spring such a duty under the extended principle in *Hedley Byrne*.[79] The defendants never indicated to Spring that he could safely rely on them to use reasonable skill and care in preparing references about him for prospective employers; and even if they did Spring never did anything in the expectation that they would act in that

[76] See *Smith* v *Eric S Bush*, *Harris* v *Wyre Forest District Council* [1990] 1 AC 831, 844 (per Lord Templeman), 865 (per Lord Griffiths), 871–2 (per Lord Jauncey); also *Caparo Industries plc* v *Dickman* [1990] 2 AC 605, 638–9 (per Lord Oliver); 661 (per Lord Jauncey).

[77] See *Omega Trust* v *Wright, Son & Pepper* [1997] PNLR 424; *Barex Brothers* v *Morris* [1999] PNLR 344. For a different view, see Todd 2007, 228.

[78] [1995] 2 AC 296.

[79] Admittedly, Lord Goff thought that this *was* a *Hedley Byrne* case (ibid., at 316) and Lord Lowry agreed with him (at 325). However, none of the other Law Lords agreed.

way. It would have been different if Spring had asked the defendants if he could give his prospective employers their name as a possible source of references and the defendants had agreed that he could. The defendants, by agreeing to supply Spring with a reference, would have implicitly indicated to him that he could safely rely on them to supply his prospective employers with references that were prepared with a reasonable degree of care and skill and Spring would have so relied on them by telling his prospective employers that they could ask the defendants for a reference about him. But this was not the case here. In *Spring*, the references supplied by the defendants were asked for, and supplied, over Spring's head.

So if this cannot be seen as being a *Hedley Byrne* case, why did the defendants owe Spring a duty of care in supplying his prospective employers with references for him? There are two possible explanations: one narrow, one wide. The narrow explanation of the case is that the defendants owed Spring such a duty of care because they were his *employers* and as such they had some responsibility not to endanger his future employment prospects unnecessarily, in the same way as, when Spring was employed by them, they had a responsibility not to unnecessarily endanger his person.[80]

The wide explanation sees the duty of care in *Spring* as arising under the dependency principle. When Spring's potential employers asked the defendants for a reference about him, the defendants knew that they held Spring's future career in their hands. If they supplied him with a bad reference, they would effectively terminate his career in the insurance industry and force him into a lengthy process of retraining to do something else. So they knew that Spring's future well-being was almost completely dependent on their doing their job as referees properly; as such they owed Spring a duty to do that job with a reasonable degree of care and skill.[81]

The Court of Appeal adopted the narrow explanation of *Spring* in *Kapfunde* v *Abbey National plc*.[82] In that case, the claimant applied for a job with the Abbey National. The Abbey National asked the defendant doctor to advise them as to the state of the claimant's health. Having inspected the claimant, the defendant advised that she was likely to have a higher than average level of absence from work. The claimant was turned down for the job as a result. She sued the defendant in negligence but the Court of Appeal dismissed her claim on the ground that the defendant doctor had not owed the claimant a duty of care in assessing her. It was held that the duty of care in *Spring* arose out of the fact that the claimant was once the defendant's employee and therefore the House of Lords' decision in *Spring* was of no assistance to the claimant here – there having been no pre-existing relationship of any kind, let alone an employment relationship, between the defendant and the claimant in *Kapfunde*.[83]

However, this narrow explanation of the decision in *Spring* seems untenable given that

[80] Ibid., 342 (per Lord Woolf); see also Cooke 1998, 47–51.

[81] Cf. Lord Lowry's reference in *Spring* to: 'the probability, often amounting to a certainty, of damage to the individual [resulting from a bad reference] which in some cases will be serious and may indeed be irreparable. The entire future prosperity and happiness of someone who is the subject of a damaging reference which is given carelessly but in perfectly good faith may be irretrievably blighted' (ibid., 326).

[82] [1999] ICR 1.

[83] In so ruling the Court of Appeal disapproved the first instance judgment in *Baker* v *Kaye* [1997] IRLR 219, holding that a doctor conducting a medical on a prospective employee for his prospective employers owed the prospective employee a duty to conduct the medical with a reasonable degree of care and skill. Why? Because when the doctor takes on the job of conducting the medical, he knows that whether or not the employee gets the job is 'wholly dependent on his assessment': ibid., 225.

Spring was *never actually an employee* of the defendants in *Spring*. In fact, there was *never any kind of contractual relationship between Spring and the defendants*.[84] Moreover, their Lordships thought it unnecessary to inquire into the nature of the relationship between Spring and the defendants to determine whether or not the defendants owed Spring a duty of care.[85] Given this, the better view of the decision in *Spring* is that the duty of care in that case arose under the dependency principle and that a duty of care may be owed by a defendant who supplies a reference about a claimant to a prospective employer even if there is no pre-existing relationship between the defendant and the claimant.[86]

If this is right, then if B applies for a job with C and A supplies C with a reference about B, A will owe B a duty to prepare the reference with a reasonable degree of care and skill – whatever the nature of the relationship between A and B. Of course such a rule goes well beyond what the dependency principle would demand: if B is applying for a job and A is asked to supply a reference, it is hardly the case that B's future well-being will be almost *entirely* dependent on A's writing the reference properly. If B does not get the job, she can always apply for another one. However, the interests of legal certainty demand that if the courts impose a duty of care in a *Spring* situation – where there was a very severe degree of dependency (Spring simply could not get a job anywhere in the insurance industry without the defendants' support) – they should also impose a duty of care whenever someone supplies a prospective employer with a reference about a prospective employee. The law would be intolerably uncertain if the law discriminated at all between different kinds of reference cases.

The *Phelps* case

In *Phelps* v *Hillingdon London Borough Council*,[87] the claimant suffered from (undiagnosed) dyslexia and as a result suffered severe learning difficulties at school. In an attempt to find out what was wrong, the claimant was sent at age 11 to an educational psychologist to be tested. The psychologist failed to notice that the claimant was dyslexic; she reported that the claimant suffered from no specific weaknesses and suggested that the source of the claimant's learning difficulties was a lack of confidence. She recommended that action be taken to boost the claimant's confidence in her abilities. With her dyslexia undiagnosed, the claimant continued to experience learning difficulties and left school at age 16 with no GCSEs.

Shortly after the claimant left school her parents paid for her to be tested again and this time around the claimant's dyslexia was diagnosed. The claimant sued the defendants, the psychologist's employers, claiming that the psychologist had owed her, and breached, a

[84] [1995] 2 AC 296, 315 (per Lord Goff).

[85] Ibid., 321 (per Lord Goff), 337 (per Lord Slynn), 340–1 (per Lord Woolf).

[86] Cf. the decision of the Ontario Court of Appeal in *Haskett* v *Trans Union of Canada* (2003) 224 DLR (4th) 419, extending the decision in *Spring* to find that a duty of care was owed in a case where the claimant was denied credit because a credit reporting agency wrongly reported that the claimant was a bad credit risk. The court's remarks at [29] ('Credit is an integral part of everyday life in today's society. Not only people seeking loans, mortgages, insurance or car leases, but those who wish, for example, to rent an apartment or even obtain employment may be the subject of a credit report ... Without credit, one is unable to conduct any financial transactions over the telephone or on the internet.') may be taken as suggesting that the source of the duty of care in the *Haskett* case was the dependency principle.

[87] [2001] 2 AC 619.

duty to test her with a reasonable degree of care and skill and that the defendants were vicariously liable in respect of the psychologist's negligence. The House of Lords held that the educational psychologist had indeed owed the claimant a duty to test her with a reasonable degree of skill and care.

It is pretty clear that the House of Lords' finding that such a duty of care was owed was based on the dependency principle. When the educational psychologist took on the job of testing the claimant, she knew that the claimant's future well-being was almost entirely dependent on her testing the claimant properly. She knew that if she misdiagnosed the source of the claimant's problems, the claimant would receive a completely inappropriate education and, as a result, her subsequent career prospects would look distinctly bleak. As Lord Slynn observed in *Phelps*: '[The psychologist] knew ... of the fact that her advice would be followed and of the importance of her assessment and advice to [the claimant's] future.'[88] Lord Nicholls also thought that this fact played a vital role in establishing that the psychologist owed the claimant a duty to test her with reasonable care and skill: '... [the claimant] was very dependent on [the psychologist's] assessment. [The claimant] was in a singularly vulnerable position ... This seems to me to be, on its face, an example *par excellence* of a situation [where a duty of care will be owed]'.[89]

THE PRINCIPLE IN *WHITE* v *JONES*

In *White* v *Jones*,[90] B quarrelled with his two daughters over his deceased wife's will. As a result, he made a will in which he left them nothing. Three months later – in June 1986 – he was reconciled with his daughters and resolved to make a new will under which his two daughters would receive £9,000 each. On 17 July 1986 he instructed the defendant solicitors to draw up a new will in those terms. By 14 September 1986, when B died, the defendant solicitors had still not got around to drawing up B's new will, so the daughters received nothing from B's estate. They sued the defendant solicitors in negligence, arguing that the defendants had owed them a duty to draw up B's new will with a reasonable degree of care and skill; that the defendants had breached that duty in taking so long over drawing up the will; and that had the defendants not breached that duty, they would have inherited £9,000 each from B's estate.

None of the principles of law examined so far in this chapter were of any assistance to the claimants in their attempt to argue that the defendants owed them a duty of care in drawing up B's will. The defendants of course owed *B* such a duty of care under the extended principle in *Hedley Byrne*: they had indicated to B that they could be safely relied on to draw up the will with a reasonable degree of care and skill and B had so relied on them by getting them, rather than anyone else, to draw up the will. But the defendants never indicated to the *claimants* that they could be relied on and indeed the claimants did not rely on the defendants to draw up the will with a reasonable degree of skill and care; the claimants, for example, did not both go out and buy new cars in the expectation that they would receive £9,000 each under B's will. There was in fact no contact between the

[88] Ibid., 655.
[89] Ibid., 666.
[90] [1995] 2 AC 207 (criticised, Weir 1995; also Klar 1998, 317–19).

defendants and the claimants. So the extended principle in *Hedley Byrne* did not apply here. Nor was the dependency principle of any assistance to the claimants – it could not be said that when the solicitors took on the job of drawing up B's new will, they knew that the claimants' future well-being was almost *entirely* dependent on their drawing up the will properly. It would have been nice for the claimants to receive £9,000 each under B's will but it would hardly have been devastating for them *not* to receive such a comparatively small sum.[91]

Despite all this, the House of Lords still held by a bare majority that the defendants *had* owed the claimants a duty to draw up B's will with a reasonable degree of care and skill. It was for a time thought that the decision was to be confined to its own facts – that is, to the case where A undertook to draw up a will for B, A failed to draw up the will properly and as a result C failed to receive an inheritance from B's estate. However, this view is no longer tenable. For example, in *Gorham* v *British Telecommunications plc*,[92] *White* v *Jones* was seen as authority for the proposition that a pensions adviser will owe not only the advisee a duty to advise him with a reasonable degree of care and skill; such a duty will also be owed to the advisee's family.[93] So how far does *White* v *Jones* go? To answer that question we need to know what principle or principles underlay their Lordships' finding that a duty of care was owed to the claimants in *White* v *Jones*. A number of alternatives suggest themselves:

(1) *The extended dependency principle.* In his judgment in *White* v *Jones*, Lord Browne-Wilkinson justified his finding that the defendants owed the claimants a duty of care in drawing up B's will in the following terms:

> The solicitor who accepts instructions to draw up a will knows that the future economic welfare of the intended beneficiary is dependent on his careful execution of the task. It is true that the intended beneficiary (being ignorant of the instructions) may not rely on the particular solicitor's actions. But . . . liability is not dependent upon actual reliance by the [claimant] on the defendant's actions but on the fact that, as the [defendant] is well aware, the [claimant]'s economic well-being is dependent upon the proper discharge by the [defendant] of his duty.[94]

[91] A subtle argument that might be made in favour of thinking that the dependency principle *does* apply here goes as follows: 'Had the claimants been left *a house* under the will, then the dependency principle *would* have applied to impose a duty of care on the solicitors to draw up the will with a reasonable degree of care and skill: the solicitors would have known *in that case* that if they performed the job of drawing up the will badly, the future well-being of the claimants would have been radically impaired. Now – the law would become intolerably uncertain if it said that a solicitor will owe a duty of care in drawing up a will to those who are due to inherit a "large" legacy under the will, but not to those who are due to inherit a "small" legacy. So the only practicable way the law can give effect to the dependency principle in a *White* v *Jones* situation is to say that if A is instructed to draw up a will under which B is due to inherit a legacy, A will owe B a duty to draw up that will with a reasonable degree of care and skill, whatever the size of the legacy B is due to receive under the will.' The problem with this argument is that it rests on an unjustified premise: even if the claimants in *White* v *Jones* had been due to receive a house under their father's will, it is hard to see why the claimants' future well-being would have been radically *impaired* had the solicitors done a bad job of drawing up that will. They would merely have missed out on a large bonus.

[92] [2001] 1 WLR 2129.

[93] See also *Goodwill* v *British Pregnancy Advisory Service* [1996] 1 WLR 1397 (held by the Court of Appeal that if A wants to be sterilised so as to avoid getting his wife B pregnant, and C undertakes the operation, C may owe B a duty of care under *White* v *Jones* to carry out the operation properly) and *Dean* v *Allin & Watts* [2001] 2 Lloyd's Rep 249 (held by the Court of Appeal that if A wants to borrow money from B and appoints C, a solicitor, to act for him and ensure that the loan is secured, C will owe B a duty of care under *White* v *Jones* to ensure that the loan of money from B to A is secured).

[94] [1995] 2 AC 207, 275.

Lord Browne-Wilkinson seems to be saying here that if A takes on a task, knowing that B's future economic well-being will be impaired if he fails to perform that task properly, A will owe B a duty to perform that task with a reasonable degree of care and skill. However, this is far too wide: it is not the law, and never has been the law, that A will owe B a duty of care in such a situation.[95] At a minimum, it would have to be shown that A knew when he took on the task in question that B's future economic well-being would be *severely* impaired if he failed to perform the task properly. Anything less than that – and the facts of *White* v *Jones* fell well short of that – will not be enough to warrant A's owing B a duty of care.[96]

(2) *The practical justice principle.* Lord Goff, in his judgment in *White* v *Jones*, said that 'practical justice' demanded that their Lordships find that the defendants owed the claimants a duty of care. Otherwise, 'the only person who might have a valid claim (i.e. the testator and his estate) [would] have suffered no loss, and the only person who has suffered a loss (i.e. the disappointed beneficiary) [would have] no claim'.[97] But this is only a problem if you accept that the defendants in *White* v *Jones* ought to have been held liable to *someone* for what they did. If the defendants ought to have been held liable to someone for what they did then it would indeed have been unjust for the defendants to escape liability for what they did because of the accident that the one party with a valid claim against the defendants suffered no loss.

So Lord Goff clearly thought that the defendants in *White* v *Jones* should have been held liable to someone for what they did. But why? There seems to be only one possible answer and it runs as follows. The defendant solicitors were professionals who acted unprofessionally. It can hardly be disputed that professionals who act unprofessionally deserve to have some kind of punishment or sanction inflicted on them – it is one of the main tasks of professional bodies such as the Law Society or the General Medical Council to punish those of its members who fail to live up to professional standards in their dealings with the public. The defendant solicitors in *White* v *Jones* therefore deserved to be punished for what they did – to be held liable to someone for what they did. On this analysis, then, Lord Goff was in favour of finding that the defendants owed the claimants a duty of care in *White* v *Jones* because if no such duty were found, the defendant solici-

[95] See Weir 2004, 76–80. For an alternative view, see Stapleton 2002a, 551–61 and references contained therein, suggesting that if A is 'vulnerable' to suffering harm at B's hands, that is a sufficient reason for the law to find that B will owe A a duty to take care not to harm B. To the same effect, see also McBride & Hughes 1995; Murphy 1996, 52–3; Witting 2000b, 631–4. A very strong High Court of Australia authority that seems to take this view is *Perre* v *Apand Pty Ltd* (1999) 198 CLR 180 (noted, Davis 2000). In that case, Sparnon – a farmer in South Australia – grew some potatoes on his land using seed supplied by the defendants. The potato crop turned out to be diseased because the seed supplied by the defendants was diseased. Legislation in Western Australia prohibited the importation of potatoes grown within 20 km of an infected crop for 5 years after the crop was discovered to be infected. This meant that the claimant – whose farm was 20 km away from Sparnon's – was not allowed to sell *his* potatoes in Western Australia for 5 years. The farmer sued the defendants in negligence and it was held that the defendants *had* owed the claimant a duty to take care not to supply Sparnon with diseased seed. Particular emphasis was laid on the fact that the defendants knew when they supplied the seed to Sparnon that if it was diseased, people like the claimant would be shut out of the Western Australian potato market and that there was nothing the claimant could do to protect himself against the effect of the defendants' supplying diseased seed to Sparnon.

[96] For an explanation why not, see below, pp. 208–14.

[97] [1995] 2 AC 207, 259.

tors would have been allowed to act unprofessionally without incurring any punishment or sanction in response.[98]

However, this analysis of the principle underlying the decision in *White* v *Jones* – if one can call it a principle – is weakened by the fact that the Court of Appeal has since made it clear that a solicitor who has failed to draw up a will properly will have owed the beneficiaries under that will a duty of care in drawing it up *even if* the deceased's estate is entitled to sue the solicitor for substantial damages for failing to draw up the will properly.[99]

(3) *The unhelpful assistance principle*. Probably the best analysis of the principle underlying the decision in *White* v *Jones* goes as follows. If A wanted to confer a benefit on B, and C undertook to assist A in conferring that benefit on B, but due to C's doing *x*, A was *prevented* from conferring that benefit on B, C will be found to have owed B a duty to take care not to do *x*.[100] The merit of this formulation is that it seems to fit all the available case law on when someone will and will not owe another a duty of care under *White* v *Jones*.

First of all, the formulation obviously fits the facts of *White* v *Jones* itself. In that case, B wanted to give each of his daughters £9,000 in his will. The defendants in that case undertook to assist B to confer that benefit on his daughters but due to their delay in drawing up B's will, B was prevented from conferring that benefit on his daughters. As a result, the defendants were held to have owed the daughters a duty to take care that they did not delay in drawing up the will.

Secondly, this formulation explains why a duty of care was owed under *White* v *Jones* in the *Gorham*[101] case. In that case, G, a married man with two young children, wanted to set up a pension which would provide some financial security for his wife and children should he predecease them. He went to Standard Life for some advice and they failed to advise him properly. They advised him to take out a Standard Life pension when in fact G's wife and children would have been far better off had G joined the occupational pension scheme run by his employer, British Telecom. When G died, G's wife and children sued Standard Life claiming that Standard Life had owed them, and breached, a duty to take care that they did not give G bad pensions advice. The Court of Appeal held that Standard Life had owed G's wife and children such a duty of care under *White* v *Jones*. Rightly so, if we accept the analysis of the principle underlying *White* v *Jones* advanced here. G wanted to provide his wife and children with as much financial security as possible after he died. Standard Life undertook to assist him in doing that but they in fact prevented him from doing that by giving him bad pensions advice. So – on the analysis of *White* v *Jones* advanced here – Standard Life owed G's wife and children a duty to take care that they did not give G bad pensions advice.

[98] Of course, the defendant solicitors were still liable to be disciplined by their professional body, the Law Society. Lord Mustill, in dissent, thought it inappropriate for the claimant daughters to be given a remedy against the defendant solicitors in order to ensure that the defendants' unprofessional conduct did not go unpunished: 'The purpose of the courts when recognising tortious acts and their consequences is to compensate claimants who suffer actionable breaches of duty, not to act as second-line disciplinary tribunals imposing punishment in the shape of damages' (ibid., 278). See, to the same effect, Klar 1998, 316–17.

[99] *Carr-Glynn* v *Frearsons* [1999] Ch 326.

[100] Lord Mustill thought that some such principle had to underlie the decision in *White* v *Jones* and on that basis condemned the majority decision as going 'far beyond anything so far contemplated by the law of negligence': [1995] 2 AC 207, at 291.

[101] [2001] 1 WLR 2129.

Thirdly, this formulation of the principle underlying *White* v *Jones* helps to explain why no duty of care will be owed under *White* v *Jones* in the following case.[102] A wants to transfer some land – Blackacre – to B. C undertakes to do the conveyancing but on his first attempt he fails to convey Blackacre properly. Before he makes a second attempt, A tells him that she has changed her mind: she no longer wants to give Blackacre to B. It seems to be generally acknowledged that B will not be entitled to sue C in negligence here. B will not be able to argue that when C attempted to convey Blackacre to him, C owed him a duty to take care not to botch the conveyance.[103] The reason why *White* v *Jones* will not apply here – on the analysis advanced here – is that C's failure to convey Blackacre to B at the first attempt did not *prevent* A from conveying Blackacre to B. But it might be different if A never changed her mind about conveying Blackacre to B but she died before C could make a second attempt at conveying Blackacre to B. In such a case, C's failure to convey Blackacre to B at the first attempt *will* have had the effect of preventing A from conveying Blackacre to B. So on the analysis of *White* v *Jones* advanced here, in this case, C may well have owed B a duty under *White* v *Jones* to take care that he did not fail to convey Blackacre the first time he tried to do so.

102 It also explains why no duty of care was owed under *White* v *Jones* to the claimant in *Goodwill* v *British Pregnancy Advisory Service* [1996] 1 WLR 1397, who became pregnant after having sex with M, who was supposed to have been sterilised by the defendants. Held, no duty of care was owed to the claimant by the defendants when they operated on M because it was hardly realistic to say that, in being sterilised, M was attempting to confer a benefit on women such as the claimant (the benefit of not getting pregnant): ibid., 1403. It might have been different though if the claimant had been M's wife – in such a case, it would have been possible to argue that M wanted to confer a benefit on the claimant in being sterilised. So if the claimant had been M's wife, it might have been possible to argue that the defendants owed the claimant a duty under *White* v *Jones* to take care that they did not botch M's operation: ibid.

103 [1995] 2 AC 207, 262, per Lord Goff. See also *Hemmens* v *Wilson Browne* [1995] Ch 223 (held: no duty owed by firm of solicitors to claimant in drawing up deed under which claimant would have had the right to call on A at any time to pay her £110,000); *Wells* v *First National Commercial Bank* [1998] PNLR 552 (held: bank which agrees to refinance company and, as part of the deal, agrees to pay off some of the company's debts will not owe the debtors a duty to pay off those debts); and *Briscoe* v *Lubrizol* [2000] ICR 694 (held: underwriters of company's health insurance scheme owe no duty of care to employee claiming under that scheme when they assess whether his claim is genuine or not; even if they turn down his claim when it is genuine, that will not prevent the employee obtaining what he is entitled to under the scheme).

7 Situations giving rise to a duty to act

THE GENERAL RULE

The general rule in English law is that there is no duty to save others from harm. The case of *Sutradhar* v *Natural Environment Research Council*[1] provides an example of this general rule at work. The claimant had been made ill as a result of drinking water from a well in Bangladesh that was contaminated with arsenic. The defendants had previously tested the water in the claimant's area as part of a geological survey designed to determine whether fish could be farmed in that area. They failed to test the water for arsenic. Had they done so, they would have detected the presence of arsenic, and the claimant would have been alerted to the dangers of drinking water from the well. The claimant sued the defendants in negligence, but his claim failed on the ground that the defendants had not owed the claimant a duty of care, either in testing the water or in reporting the outcome of their tests. Simply speaking, the defendants had not done anything to make the claimant worse off: they simply failed to save him from the danger of falling ill with arsenic poisoning. So strong was the case that no duty of care was owed by the defendants to the claimant that Lord Hoffmann was able to dismiss the claimant's claim as 'hopeless'.[2]

The general rule in English law that there is no duty to save others from harm applies just as much to public bodies as it does to private persons.[3] So, for example, in two of the four cases dealt with in the case of *Capital & Counties plc* v *Hampshire CC*,[4] firefighters failed to deal effectively with fires that started on the claimants' premises, with the result that the fires destroyed buildings on those premises.[5] The Court of Appeal held that the firefighters had not owed the claimants a duty to take reasonable steps to put the fires out

[1] [2006] 4 All ER 490.

[2] Ibid., at [2].

[3] See, in addition to the cases cited in the main text, *East Suffolk Rivers Catchment Board* v *Kent* [1941] AC 74 (river authority that takes on the job of repairing a sea wall owes no duty to repair the wall expeditiously to farmer whose land will be flooded until the sea wall is properly repaired); *Peabody Donation Fund* v *Sir Lindsay Parkinson & Co. Ltd* [1985] AC 210 (local authority which has powers to ensure that houses owned by claimants are being built in conformity to approved designs will not owe claimants a duty to exercise those powers); *Hill* v *Chief Constable of West Yorkshire* [1989] AC 53 (police authorities do not owe potential victims of criminal on the loose a duty to take reasonable steps to arrest the criminal); *Yuen Kun Yeu* v *Att-Gen for Hong Kong* [1988] AC 175 and *Davis* v *Radcliffe* [1990] 1 WLR 821 (banking authorities do not owe depositors with a bank a duty to take reasonable steps to see that the bank's affairs are properly run); *X* v *Bedfordshire CC* [1995] 2 AC 633 (local authority does not owe duty of care to children who are alleged to be victims of abuse in deciding whether or not to take those children into care); *Stovin* v *Wise* [1996] AC 923 (no duty owed by highway authority to motorists on road to remove line-of-sight obstructions that might endanger them, even when failure to do would be completely irrational); *Hussain* v *Lancaster City Council* [2000] QB 1 (victims of racial harassment by council tenants are not owed duty by council to take reasonable steps to bring harassment to an end). See also below, p. 193, n. 23, and accompanying text.

[4] [1997] QB 1004.

[5] The firefighters did, however, owe the claimants a duty to take care not to do something positive (such as switching off sprinkler systems) that would make the fires worse, and claims in negligence for breach of that duty of care succeeded in the other two cases dealt with in the *Capital & Counties* case: see above, pp. 116–17.

and as a result dismissed the claimants' claims in negligence for compensation for the loss of their buildings. As the Court of Appeal observed, 'In our judgment the fire brigade are not under a common law duty to answer the call for help, and are not under a duty to take care to do so. If, therefore, they fail to turn up, or fail to turn up in time, because they have carelessly misunderstood the message, got lost on the way or run into a tree, they are not liable.'[6]

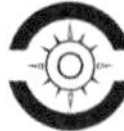

The House of Lords' decision in *Stovin* v *Wise*[7] was to the same effect. In that case Stovin was knocked off his motorcycle and severely injured when he was hit by an oncoming car at a junction. The junction was rendered dangerous by a raised bank adjoining it which interfered with Stovin's ability to see the car that hit him and the driver of the car's ability to see Stovin. A claim that the defendant highway authority had owed Stovin a duty to take reasonable steps to flatten the raised bank – which it had the statutory power to do – was rejected by the House of Lords. As the defendant highway authority had not made Stovin worse off in any way but had simply failed to save him from harm, there was no basis for finding that the defendant highway authority had owed Stovin a duty of care.

Stovin v *Wise* was subsequently followed by the House of Lords in *Gorringe* v *Calderdale MBC*.[8] In that case, the claimant driver argued that the defendant highway authority had owed her a duty to warn her to slow down when approaching a curve in the road, and that if it had warned her to do this she would have avoided crashing into a bus with the result that she was severely injured. The House of Lords rejected this argument. Lord Hoffmann strongly endorsed the general rule that there is no duty to rescue in English law, even when a public body is involved: 'Speaking for myself, I find it difficult to envisage a case in which a common law duty can be founded simply upon the failure (however irrational) to provide some benefit which a public authority has [a] power (or a public law duty) to provide.'[9]

So much, then, for the general rule. However, there are number of exceptions to this general rule. This chapter and the next will be devoted to setting out these exceptions.[10] In Chapter 8 we will look at a number of special statuses or positions, the occupation of which will give rise to a duty to rescue on the part of the person occupying that status or position. But before we get on to those, we will first set out in this chapter a number of different situations that will give rise to a duty to rescue. The first of these is where A has put B in danger of suffering some kind of harm to her person or property.

THE CREATION OF DANGER PRINCIPLE

A number of cases seem to establish that if it is reasonably foreseeable that A's doing *x* has had the effect of putting B in danger of suffering some kind of serious harm, A will owe B

[6] Ibid., at 1030.
[7] [1996] AC 923.
[8] [2004] 1 WLR 1057.
[9] Ibid., at [32].
[10] *Important note*. In addition to the exceptions set out in this chapter and the next, it almost goes without saying that A will owe B a duty to take reasonable steps to save her from harm if he has undertaken to take such steps and B has relied on A to do this. The duty will arise under the extended principle in *Hedley Byrne* (see above, pp. 132–9.)

a duty to take reasonable steps to ensure that B does not suffer that kind of harm.[11] So, to take an example from the American case law giving effect to this principle,[12] if Carl is driving along the road one night and he happens to hit and kill a large animal on the road he will owe other users of the road a duty to take reasonable steps to see that they do not crash into the obstacle he has created. While what we can call the *creation of danger principle* is easy enough to understand, it is unclear how far it goes. The following issues arise:

(1) *What sort of harm?* Clearly if A has created a danger that B will suffer some kind of personal injury, then A will have a duty to take reasonable steps to eliminate that risk. But what if A has just created a danger that B's property will be destroyed or damaged? Will he owe B a duty to take reasonable steps to eliminate that danger? For example, suppose Carl takes Beth's dog for a walk and he happens to throw the dog's favourite ball into a pond. The dog plunges into the pond to fetch it but it becomes clear to Carl that the dog cannot swim and is in danger of drowning. Will Carl owe Beth a duty to take reasonable steps to save her dog from drowning? One would have thought so.[13] However, it should be noted that the formulation of the creation of danger principle in the American Restatement 2d of Torts has

[11] This principle accounts for why (see *Ellis* v *Home Office* [1953] 2 All ER 149 and *New South Wales* v *Bujdoso* [2005] HCA 76) if A and B are imprisoned in the same jail and it is foreseeable that A will attack B if given the chance, the prison authorities will owe B a duty to take reasonable steps to see that A does not attack B. By confining B to the same jail as A, the prison authorities put B in danger of being attacked by A. The Court of Appeal has now ruled in *Butchart* v *Home Office* [2006] 1 WLR 1155 that the same principle applies in prison cases where it was foreseeable that A would act in a way that would cause B to suffer some kind of psychiatric illness (by, for example, committing suicide in front of B): the prison authorities will owe B a duty to take reasonable steps to protect him from suffering that illness. For other cases which can be interpreted as giving effect to the 'creation of danger' principle, see *E Hobbs (Farms) Ltd* v *Baxenden Chemicals* [1992] 1 Lloyd's Rep 54 (manufacturer of foam insulation installed in claimant's farm buildings held to have owed claimant a duty to warn him that the foam was combustible: 'a manufacturer's duty of care does not end when the goods are sold. A manufacturer who realises that omitting to warn past customers about something which might result in injury to them must take reasonable steps to attempt to warn them, however lacking in negligence he may have been at the time the goods were sold'; ibid., 65); *Watson* v *British Board of Boxing Control* [2001] 1 QB 1134 (defendants, who were – at a very general level – involved in the putting on of a boxing fight, thereby creating a danger that the boxers would suffer brain damage as a result, held to have owed the boxers a duty to take reasonable steps to see that they did not suffer such brain damage; which duty was breached by their failing to provide ring-side medical facilities to treat boxers who were knocked out in the ring); and *Kane* v *New Forest DC* [2002] 1 WLR 312 (defendant planning authority, which approved creation of right of way passing over main road at 'blindspot' for car drivers driving along main road, held to have owed users of the right of way a duty to take reasonable steps to see that they were not run over in crossing over the main road).

[12] *Hardy* v *Brooks*, 118 SE 2d 492 (1961).

[13] *Important note.* The clearest authority in favour of the idea that the creation of danger principle applies in the case where someone has created a danger of someone else's property being damaged is a criminal law case: *R* v *Miller* [1983] 2 AC 161. The defendant fell asleep in someone else's house. In so doing he dropped a lit cigarette onto the mattress on which he was lying. Soon after, the defendant woke up and realised that the mattress was on fire, but did nothing to deal with the problem. Instead he simply moved to another room. The fire subsequently spread to the rest of the house. The defendant was charged with the offence of arson, which is committed by intentionally or recklessly causing property to be destroyed or damaged by fire: Criminal Damage Act 1971, s 1. The defendant's act of dropping his cigarette could not give rise to criminal liability because while that caused the house to be burned down, he had not acted intentionally or recklessly in dropping the cigarette. While the defendant *had* acted recklessly when he woke up and failed to take steps to save the house from burning down, that failure could only be said to have *caused* the house to burn down if the defendant had had a *duty* to take such steps. The House of Lords held that the defendant *did* have such a duty. This was because the defendant had – albeit unwittingly – *created* the danger that the house would burn down; as a result, he had a duty, when he became aware of the danger, to take reasonable steps to deal with that danger. Accordingly, their Lordships held that the defendant had committed the offence of arson.

it applying only to cases where someone creates a danger that someone else will suffer a *physical injury*.[14]

(2) *Three party cases*. Suppose that John told Eric that he saw Eric's wife, Beth, at a nightclub the previous night. Eric was visibly maddened by this news: Beth had told him she was going out to play bingo. He subsequently went home and beat Beth up. Beth now wants to sue John for damages. Beth will not be able to invoke the physical danger principle to establish that John owed her a duty not to tell Eric that he had seen her at a nightclub: it was not reasonably foreseeable that Eric would beat her up on being told this news.[15]

But will Beth be able to invoke the creation of danger principle to establish that John owed her a duty to warn her that he had told Eric that he had seen her at a nightclub and to tell her to get out of her house until Eric had had a chance to calm down? It is hard to see why she should not be allowed to – so long, of course, as she can establish that Eric's reaction to John's news made it reasonably foreseeable that he would attack Beth as a result of John's disclosure. Whether or not the requirement is satisfied here will of course depend on how extreme Eric's reaction was to John's news: whether he uttered any threats against Beth, and so on.[16] But if it was reasonably foreseeable that Eric would attack Beth as a result of John's disclosure, there seems no reason why John should not be held to have owed Beth a duty to take reasonable steps to see that she was not attacked by Eric – by, for example, warning her that Eric was angry with her and that she should keep out of his way.

(3) *Self-harm*. If A's doing *x* has created a foreseeable danger that B will do something to harm himself, will A owe B a duty to take reasonable steps to stop B harming himself? The question has arisen in two contexts.

First of all, consider the case where the police or prison authorities have locked B up and it is reasonably foreseeable that their doing so has created a risk that B will attempt to kill himself. In this sort of case, it is well established that the police or prison authorities in question will owe B a duty to take reasonable steps to prevent him killing himself. This is so whether B is mentally ill[17] or completely sane.[18] It should be emphasised that it has to be

[14] §321: '[Someone who] does an act and subsequently realizes or should realize that it has created an unreasonable risk of causing physical injury to another . . . is under a duty to exercise reasonable care to prevent the risk from taking effect . . . even though at the time of the act [he had] no reason to believe that it [would] involve such a risk' (American Law Institute, 1965). See GS&Z, 99–100.

[15] It should be remembered that the test for reasonable foreseeability in these sorts of three party cases, where A does *x* and as a result C harms B, will only be satisfied if it was *very likely* or *probable* that C would harm B as a result of A's doing *x*: see above, p. 73, n. 24. This test is obviously not satisfied here.

[16] This requirement was not satisfied in *Topp* v *London Country Bus (South West) Ltd* [1993] 1 WLR 976. In that case, the defendants caused a minibus belonging to them to be left outside a pub, unlocked and with the keys in the ignition. Nine hours later an unidentified third party got into the bus, drove it down the road and knocked down and killed the claimant's wife. Held: the defendants did *not* owe the claimant's wife a duty to pick the bus up before anyone drove off with it. A reasonable person in the position of the defendants would *not* have thought that it was very likely or probable that someone would get in the minibus and drive off in it in a dangerous manner. It was not therefore reasonably foreseeable that leaving the minibus outside the pub, unlocked and with the keys in the ignition, would put people like the claimant's wife in danger of being killed or injured. So the creation of danger principle did not apply to impose on the defendants a duty to pick the bus up before anyone else drove off in it. The result may have been different had the defendants known that the pub outside which the bus was left was frequented by people who were 'particularly likely to steal vehicles and engage in joy-riding': ibid., 978.

[17] *Kirkham* v *Chief Constable of the Greater Manchester Police* [1990] 2 QB 283; *Knight* v *Home Office* [1990] 3 All ER 237.

[18] *Reeves* v *Commissioner of the Police of the Metropolis* [2000] 1 AC 360 (where the point was conceded without argument).

reasonably foreseeable that B is a suicide risk before any duty will be owed to him to save him from himself – and the mere fact that he has been locked up will not be enough to make it foreseeable that he will attempt to kill himself.[19]

Secondly, what is the position if A has served B a large amount of alcohol and B now proposes to drive himself home – and it is clear, from B's drunken state, that B will almost certainly crash his car and injure himself if he attempts to do any such thing? It seems clear enough that A will *owe other users of the road* a duty to take steps to stop B driving home under the creation of danger principle – A having helped to create the danger here that when B drives home he will injure other people.[20] But will A owe *B* such a duty of care? There is no English authority on the issue; the available Canadian authorities indicate that the answer is 'yes';[21] while the High Court of Australia has recently ruled that the answer is 'no'.[22]

(4) *Reasonable steps*. If A has created a foreseeable danger that B will suffer some kind of serious harm, with the result that he owes B a duty to take reasonable steps to ensure that B does not suffer that kind of harm, what will A actually be required to do? The question has received little attention in England, from either the courts or tort academics,[23] but it is possible to speculate a little.

Leaving aside for the moment cases where A has created a danger that B will harm himself, if the danger that A has exposed B to is one which B could avoid at no cost to himself if he were aware of it, then all A will be required to do is warn B of the danger. If the danger is one which B cannot easily avoid at no cost to himself, then A may be required to do more than just warn B of the danger. It is likely that A's duty in this case will be 'measured'[24] – so what A will be required to do will depend on how wealthy A is and how responsible A was for creating the danger to which B is exposed.

If A has created a danger that B will do something to harm himself, presumably a warning to B that he is in danger of harming himself will not be enough to discharge the duty A will owe B to take reasonable steps to see that he does not harm himself. A will have to do something more. Again his duty will be 'measured' but it seems unlikely that A will be required to do anything that would involve A violating B's 'rights'. So A will not be required to lay hands on B or take his property away from him in order to ensure that B does not harm himself if B has a 'right' that A not lay his hands on him or take his property away.[25]

19 *Orange* v *Chief Constable of West Yorkshire Police* [2002] QB 347.

20 See the Canadian cases of *Stewart* v *Pettie* [1995] 1 SCR 131 and *Prevost* v *Vetter* (2002) 100 BCLR (3d) 44.

21 *Jordan House Ltd* v *Menow* [1974] SCR 239; *Crocker* v *Sundance Northwest Resorts Ltd* [1988] 1 SCR 1186. See, generally, Dalphond 2002; also Solomon & Payne 1996 and Orr 1995.

22 *Cole* v *South Tweed Heads Rugby League Football Club Ltd* [2004] HCA 29.

23 For an American examination of the issue, see Matula 1996; also GS&Z, 926–52, 984–98.

24 On the concept of a 'measured' duty of care, see below, pp. 387–90.

25 If B is put into custody, the officers in charge of B *will* be permitted to remove his belt and shoelaces to prevent him committing suicide. As doing these things will not violate B's 'rights', a failure to do these things may amount to negligence if it is reasonably foreseeable that B will attempt to commit suicide in custody.

THE INTERFERENCE PRINCIPLE

A couple of cases seem to establish that *if*:

(1) A knows or ought to know that B is in danger of suffering some kind of serious harm H, *and*
(2) A knows or ought to know that:
either (i) he has done something that has had the effect of dissuading someone else from taking steps to save B from suffering harm H;
or (ii) he has done something positive[26] that has had the effect of preventing someone else from taking steps to save B from suffering harm H,
then
(3) A will owe B a duty to take reasonable steps himself to see that B does not suffer harm H.

We can call this *the interference principle* as the duty of care A will owe B in this situation arises out of the fact that he has interfered with someone else's taking steps to save B from suffering harm.

We have already set out the facts of *Costello* v *Chief Constable of the Northumbria Police*.[27] To recap: the claimant was a woman police officer who was attacked by a prisoner when she took the prisoner down to the cells in a police station. Another officer, H, accompanied the claimant in taking the prisoner down to the cells in order to help her out if there was any trouble. However, when H saw B – a police inspector – standing by the cells, H went back upstairs, assuming that B would assist the claimant if she was attacked by the prisoner. When the claimant was attacked, B – contrary to expectation – stood by and did nothing. The Court of Appeal found that B had owed the claimant a duty to take reasonable steps to save her from being attacked. While it is not clear why the court came to that conclusion, it can be inferred that they decided B owed the claimant a duty to take reasonable steps to save her from being attacked because, as B well knew, the claimant was in danger of being attacked by the prisoner and B dissuaded H from taking steps to ensure that the claimant would not be attacked by the prisoner.

In *Kent* v *Griffiths*,[28] the claimant suffered an asthma attack. Her doctor came to see her and decided that she had to be taken to hospital. She rang the London Ambulance Service – the LAS – and they told her they would send an ambulance along to take the claimant to hospital. No ambulance had arrived 13 minutes later so the claimant's husband rang the LAS to be told that the ambulance would be another seven or eight minutes. The ambulance still had not arrived 29 minutes after the original call so the claimant's doctor rang the LAS and was told the ambulance would be there in a couple of minutes. The ambulance

[26] So a mere *failure to assist* that has the effect of stopping a third party from saving someone else from harm will not engage the principle discussed here. Suppose, for example, that Beth is a diabetic child who is starting to go into a hypoglycaemic state due to lack of sugar. Beth's mother, Nita, rushes into a chocolate shop run by Fred and asks Fred for some chocolate that she can give to Beth. Fred refuses to give her any chocolate as Nita has forgotten her purse and cannot pay for it. Without any chocolate, Beth's condition rapidly worsens and she faints, smashing her head open on the pavement. Beth will not be able to establish that Fred owed her a duty to take reasonable steps to alleviate her condition under the principle discussed here: Fred did not do something *positive* to prevent Nita from helping Beth; Fred merely *failed to assist* Nita to help Beth.

[27] [1999] 1 All ER 550, discussed above, pp. 51–3.

[28] [2001] QB 36.

finally arrived 34 minutes after the original call. The claimant arrived in hospital 46 minutes after the original call and she promptly suffered a respiratory arrest which resulted in her suffering a miscarriage, a change of personality and serious memory impairment.

At first instance, Turner J held that the LAS had owed the claimant, and breached, a duty to take her to hospital as quickly as was reasonably possible and that had the LAS not breached that duty, the claimant would have reached hospital 32 minutes after the original call and would have received the treatment she needed to prevent her suffering a respiratory arrest. Accordingly, Turner J held the LAS liable to compensate the claimant for her arrest and the injuries that she had suffered as a result. The LAS appealed, claiming that it had not owed the claimant a duty of care. The Court of Appeal dismissed the appeal. Again, it is not clear why the court came to the conclusion that the LAS owed the claimant a duty to get her to hospital as quickly as was reasonably possible. However, it can be inferred that they reached this conclusion by the following chain of reasoning: (1) when the claimant suffered her asthma attack she was in danger of suffering a respiratory arrest; (2) the claimant's doctor and husband could have taken the claimant to hospital themselves in order to ensure that she did not suffer a respiratory arrest; however, (3) they were dissuaded from doing so by the LAS's repeated assurances that an ambulance was on the way to pick the claimant up;[29] as a result, (4) the LAS owed the claimant a duty to take reasonable steps to ensure that the claimant did not suffer a respiratory arrest – in other words, the LAS owed the claimant a duty to take her to hospital as quickly as was reasonably possible.

If the interference principle is part of English law, a number of issues arise as to how it applies.

(1) *The problem of identity*. The interference principle only applies where A dissuades or prevents *someone else* from attempting to save B from some serious harm that B is in danger of suffering. The interference principle will not of course apply where A dissuades or prevents *himself* from attempting to save B. But it can be difficult to determine in a given case whether a defendant prevented someone else from attempting to save the claimant or whether the defendant merely prevented himself from attempting to save the claimant.

The issue came up in *OLL Ltd* v *Secretary of State for Transport*.[30] In that case, a party of eight children and one teacher got into severe difficulty on a canoeing trip in the sea off Lyme Regis. The coastguard was mobilised but bungled the rescue operation, directing a lifeboat and a Royal Navy helicopter to search for the party in the wrong area. As a result, all the members of the party suffered severe hypothermia and four of the children died. It was claimed in the subsequent litigation that the coastguard had owed the members of the party a duty to take reasonable steps to rescue them. It was arguable that the interference principle applied here: it could have been argued that the coastguard prevented the lifeboat crew and the Royal Navy from rescuing the stricken party and as a result the coastguard owed the party a duty to take reasonable steps to rescue them. However, May J refused to find that a duty of care was owed by the coastguard here, holding that it would be 'artificial'[31] to distinguish between the coastguard and other rescue organisations that were

[29] Ibid., at [17]: 'But for the acceptance of the 999 call the [claimant] would have been driven to the hospital and would have arrived prior to her "arrest".'

[30] [1997] 3 All ER 897 (discussed, Bagshaw 1999).

[31] Ibid., at 907.

attempting to save the teacher and children at sea. This was a case of one person getting in his own way in attempting to rescue the canoeing party; not a case of one person getting in another's way in attempting to rescue the party.

(2) *Hypothetical third parties.* For the interference principle to apply, it seems it does not have to be shown that an *identifiable* third party was actually prevented or dissuaded from saving the claimant by the defendant; it merely has to be shown that it was very likely that *someone* would have tried to assist the claimant had the defendant not acted in the way he did.

The point is made by the American case of *Zelenko* v *Gimbel Bros.*[32] Mary Zelenko was taken ill in the defendant's store. The defendant took on the job of looking after her but failed to do anything for her for six hours. It could not be shown that any particular individual had been dissuaded or prevented from looking after Zelenko as a result of the defendant's taking charge of her. However, the court was satisfied that it was 'beyond doubt [that if the defendant had left Zelenko alone] some bystander . . . would have summoned an ambulance'[33] and as a result found that the defendant had owed Zelenko a duty to take reasonable steps to treat her illness.

The finding of a duty of care in *Barrett* v *Ministry of Defence*[34] may be similarly explained. In that case, a soldier got drunk at a barracks party. He eventually collapsed and the officer in charge of the party arranged for him to be taken back to his bunk. The soldier was then left there and eventually choked on his own vomit. The Court of Appeal held that no duty had been owed to the soldier to stop him getting drunk,[35] but that once the officer in charge had 'assumed responsibility'[36] for the soldier by having him taken back to his bunk, a duty had been owed to the soldier to take reasonable steps to see that he got through the night safely. While the language of 'assumption of responsibility' might be taken to suggest there was a *Hedley Byrne* relationship between the officer in charge and the drunk soldier, such a relationship could not arise on the facts as the drunk soldier was unconscious when the officer in charge took care of him. The better explanation of why there was a duty of care owed in *Barrett* is that the officer in charge probably discouraged other soldiers from taking responsibility for the drunk soldier's welfare by taking care of the drunk soldier himself.

(3) *The position of people who are employed to rescue others.* Suppose that Alan is employed to work as a lifeguard on a beach. Lara visits the beach and goes for a swim. However, she soon gets cramp and struggles to keep her head above water. Alan sees Lara's predicament but does nothing to assist her. Eventually, Lara drowns. Can we say that Alan owed Lara a duty to take reasonable steps to rescue her? The answer is obviously 'yes' if there were other people on the beach who saw that Lara was in trouble but did not go to her assistance because they thought Alan would rescue her – the interference principle would apply.

But suppose that, with the exception of Alan, the beach was deserted and so no one was discouraged from rescuing Lara as a result of Alan's presence. At first sight, it seems that it

[32] 287 NYS 134 (1935).
[33] Ibid., 135.
[34] [1995] 1 WLR 1217.
[35] Already discussed above, p. 64.
[36] [1995] 1 WLR 1217, 1223.

is not possible to argue that Alan owed Lara a duty to take reasonable steps to rescue her under the interference principle. But is this too quick? After all, when Alan was employed to work as a lifeguard on the beach, there must have been other people who applied for the job. Can we not say that Alan – by successfully applying for the job of lifeguard – has prevented these other people from rescuing Lara and, as a result, Alan owes Lara a duty to take reasonable steps to rescue Lara himself?

To apply the interference principle here would probably be a step too far – certainly, the available English authorities indicate that Alan would *not* owe Lara a duty to take reasonable steps to rescue her in this situation.[37] First of all, Alan has not really *prevented* any of the other applicants for his job from rescuing Lara in this situation – if they had wanted to work on the beach saving people for free, Alan would, presumably, have been grateful for the assistance. Alan has merely prevented the other applicants from earning the money that was on offer for working as a lifeguard on the beach; which is not the same thing. Secondly, if we want to hold that Alan owed Lara a duty here under the interference principle, we must be able to say who would have been given Alan's job had Alan not been available to take it and we must be able to show that that someone would have been in a position to rescue Lara when she started to struggle, that he would have had the inclination to rescue Lara at that time, and that he would have been able to rescue her before she drowned. It is unlikely that any of these things could be determined with any degree of certainty. So, in the interests of legal certainty and ensuring that the courts' time is not wasted on fruitless inquiries, it would be better if the interference principle were held not to extend to this kind of situation.

(4) *Prevention of self-help.* While the interference principle, as we have presented it above, only applies in cases where A dissuades or prevents a *third party* from going to B's assistance, there is no reason why the interference principle should not extend to cases where A dissuades or prevents *B* from saving herself from suffering some kind of harm. So, for example, it is well established that if Vijay is in prison and falls sick, the prison authorities will owe Vijay a duty to take reasonable steps to treat him.[38] The reason for this is that Vijay will be prevented, because he is in prison, from taking steps himself to obtain treatment for his illness.

Again, in *Mercer* v *South Eastern & Chatham Railway Companies' Managing Committee*[39] the claimant was hit by a passing train as he crossed a railway line. The gate to the path over the railway line was usually locked by the defendant when a train was due to come by, but

[37] *Alexandrou* v *Oxford* [1993] 4 All ER 328 (policemen investigating possible break-in at shop will *not* owe shopkeeper a duty to carry out their investigations with reasonable skill and care); *Capital & Counties plc* v *Hampshire County Council* [1997] QB 1004 (discussed above, pp. 155–6). On the other hand, see *Lowns* v *Woods* (1996) 36 NSWLR 344 (noted, Haberfield 1998; see also Williams 2001). The case concerned an 11-year-old boy who suffered from epilepsy. One day he suffered an epileptic fit and his sister was sent to fetch a doctor. She went to the local surgery and asked the doctor there – who was not the boy's doctor – to come and look at her brother. He refused, insisting that the boy should be brought to the surgery. As a result of the doctor's refusal to go and see the boy, there was a delay in treating his epileptic fit, with the result that the boy became quadriplegic. Held: the doctor had owed the boy a duty to take reasonable steps to treat him. There are also some *dicta* in in the case of *Barnett* v *Chelsea & Kensington Hospital Management Committee* [1969] 1 QB 428 which indicate that if A turns up to a casualty department seeking treatment, the doctor on call at the time will almost always owe A a duty to treat him: ibid., at 437.

[38] *Brooks* v *Home Office* [1999] 2 FLR 33.

[39] [1922] 2 KB 549.

the defendant had on this occasion left the gate unlocked and this had led the claimant to believe that it was safe to cross the railway line. It was held that the defendant had owed the claimant a duty to take reasonable steps to ensure that he locked the gate to the path over the railway line when a train was due to come by. The result can be justified by reference to the extension of the interference principle discussed here. The defendant's practice of locking the gate had had the effect of dissuading pedestrians from taking steps themselves to ensure that they were not run down by a passing train as they crossed the railway line: if the gate was unlocked they blithely assumed that it was safe to cross and crossed the railway line without a second thought. Given this, the defendant owed people like the claimant a duty to take reasonable steps to see that they were not run down by a passing train as they crossed the railway line. This, in turn, meant that he owed a duty to people like the claimant to take reasonable steps to ensure that he locked the gate when a train was due to go by.

THE CONTROL PRINCIPLE

It seems to be well established that if A is in control of a dangerous *substance* or *animal*, and it is reasonably foreseeable that someone like B will be harmed by that substance or animal if A allows it to escape his control, then A will owe B a duty to take reasonable steps to keep that thing or that animal under his control.[40] What is controversial is whether this principle – which we can call the *control principle* – extends to cases where A is in control of a *human being* and it is foreseeable that someone like B will be harmed if that human being escapes A's control. Whether or not A will owe B a duty to take reasonable steps to prevent the human being escaping his control seems to depend on what sort of human being it is.

(1) *Children*. It seems to be accepted that if A is in control of a child and it is reasonably foreseeable that someone like B will be injured if that child is allowed to escape A's control, A *will* owe B a duty to take reasonable steps to keep the child in question under his control.

For example, in *Carmathenshire County Council* v *Lewis*,[41] a four-year-old boy attending nursery school wandered off the school premises and onto the road running alongside the nursery school. The claimant's husband, who was driving along the road, swerved to avoid the boy and crashed into a tree and died. The claimant sued, claiming that the defendant county council – which owned the school – and the teachers at the school had owed her husband, and breached, a duty to take reasonable steps to keep control of the children at the school. The House of Lords agreed that the defendant county council and the teachers at the school had owed the claimant's husband such a duty of care. The defendant county council and the teachers at the school were jointly in control of the children at the school and it was, of course, eminently foreseeable that children at the school would wander into the road outside the school and cause accidents if the defendant county council and the teachers at the school did not keep control of them. It followed that the defendant county council and the teachers at the school owed people driving past the school – including the

[40] If the substance or animal escapes A's control without any negligence on his part and B is harmed as a result, B may still be entitled to sue A for compensation under either the rule in *Rylands* v *Fletcher* or the Animals Act 1971: see below, Chapter 42.

[41] [1955] AC 549.

claimant's husband – a duty to take reasonable steps to keep control of the children at the school.

(2) *Adults*. The position is more restrictive where A is in control of an adult – call him T – and it is reasonably foreseeable T will harm someone like B if he is allowed to escape A's control. In such a case, it seems that A will only owe B a duty to take reasonable steps to see that T does not escape his control, if B is *especially* at risk of being harmed by T if T is allowed to escape A's control. Let's call this requirement that must be satisfied before the control principle will apply to impose a duty on someone who is in control of a dangerous adult, the *special danger* requirement.[42]

So, for example, Lord Morris suggested in the case of *Dorset Yacht Co Ltd* v *Home Office* that 'If a person who is in lawful custody has made a threat, accepted as seriously intended, that, if he can escape, he will injure X . . . a duty [will be] owed to X to take reasonable care to prevent escape.'[43] In such a case, the special danger requirement will be satisfied: if the prisoner in question is allowed to escape, X will be at greater danger of being attacked by the prisoner than the rest of the population. If, on the other hand, A – a well-known psychopath – is in prison and the prison authorities allow A to escape and A goes on to attack and injure B, a random stranger, the special danger requirement will not be satisfied and the prison authorities will not be held to have owed B a duty to take reasonable steps to prevent A escaping.[44] While it was reasonably foreseeable that someone like B would be injured if A was allowed to escape custody – it was very likely or probable that A would attack a random member of the population if he were allowed to escape – B was at no greater danger of being attacked by A if A escaped custody than anyone else.

The special danger requirement was satisfied in the *Dorset Yacht* case itself. In that case, seven Borstal boys were on a training exercise on Brownsea Island in Poole Harbour. They were under the supervision of three officers. One night the Borstal boys escaped, taking advantage of the fact that all three officers had, contrary to instructions, gone to bed. They boarded one of the vessels in the harbour and set sail in it but it collided with the claimant's yacht. They then boarded the claimant's yacht and did further damage to it. The claimant sued the Home Office for compensation, arguing that the officers had owed him a duty to take reasonable steps not to let the Borstal boys escape. The House of Lords found that such a duty had been owed to the claimant. There was no problem showing that it was reasonably foreseeable that someone like the claimant would suffer harm if the Borstal boys were allowed to escape the officers' control. This is because it was reasonably foreseeable – very likely or probable – that if the Borstal boys were allowed to escape the officers' control, they would commandeer one of the boats in the harbour in an attempt to get off the island and make good their escape, and in so doing would damage the boat. It followed that it was reasonably foreseeable that someone like the claimant – someone who owned a boat in the harbour – would suffer harm if the Borstal boys were allowed to escape their officers' control.

42 For a possible explanation of this limit on the scope of liability under the control principle, see above, pp. 64–5.

43 [1970] AC 1004, at 1039.

44 See *Palmer* v *Tees Health Authority* [1999] Lloyd's Rep Med 351 (boy killed by psychopath in care of defendant medical authorities: held, the defendants did not owe the boy or the boy's mother a duty of care to control the psychopath).

The special danger requirement was satisfied here because people like the claimant – people who owned boats in the harbour – were at greater risk of suffering harm as a result of the Borstal boys' escape than other members of the population such as shopkeepers or owners of bikes on the island. Their boats would be especially valuable to the Borstal boys were the Borstal boys allowed to escape – so their boats were especially likely to be targeted by the Borstal boys on escape as compared with other items of property such as groceries or bikes. It follows that the result of the case would have been different had the Borstal boys, on escaping, robbed a shop on the island.[45] No duty would have been owed to the shopkeeper to take reasonable steps to prevent the Borstal boys escaping as there would have been no special risk that the shopkeeper's wares would be targeted by the Borstal boys on escape.

The special danger requirement was not satisfied in *K* v *Secretary of State for the Home Dept.*[46] In that case, M, a Kenyan citizen, was imprisoned for sexual assault and then for burglary. He was detained, awaiting deportation, but was released on order of the Home Secretary. M subsequently raped the claimant. The claimant sued the Home Secretary in negligence, claiming that he had owed her a duty not to release M. The Home Secretary applied to have the action struck out. For the purposes of hearing the striking out claim, it was assumed against the Home Secretary that he had acted unreasonably in ordering M to be released and that it was reasonably foreseeable that if M was released, he would attack someone like the claimant. It made no difference: the Court of Appeal still refused to find that the Home Secretary had owed the claimant a duty not to release M. The special danger requirement was not satisfied here. The claimant was at no greater risk of being attacked by M on release than the rest of the population or the rest of the female population.

Visit **http://www.mylawchamber.co.uk/mcbride** to access updates on recent cases, as well as model answers and tips for answering tort problem questions.

Use **Case Navigator** to read in full some of the key cases referenced in this chapter:

- **Sutradhar** *v* **Natural Environment Research Council**
- **Stovin** *v* **Wise**

[45] [1970] AC 1004, 1070 (per Lord Diplock).
[46] [2002] EWCA Civ 1983.

8 Statuses giving rise to a duty to act

There are a variety of cases where it is established that someone will have a duty to take reasonable steps to act in some way simply by virtue of the fact that he or she occupies some special status or position. In this chapter we will look at what these special statuses and positions are and the duties of care to which they give rise.

OCCUPIERS OF PREMISES

An occupier of premises – a term which we will use here to cover not only an area of land but buildings or parts of buildings as well – will normally owe a whole host of duties of care to other people by virtue of the fact that he is an occupier. Before we look at the duties of care that will be owed by an occupier of premises, we should first of all clarify what is involved in being an occupier of premises.

Who is an occupier?

When will it be true that a certain set of premises are 'occupied' by A? In *Wheat* v *E Lacon & Co. Ltd*, Lord Denning suggested: 'wherever a person has a sufficient degree of control over premises that he ought to realise that any failure on his part to use care may result in injury to a person coming lawfully there, then he is an "occupier" . . . In order to be an occupier it is not necessary for a person to have entire control over the premises. He need not have exclusive occupation. Two or more people may be "occupiers".'[1]

Given this test, it is clear that if, at a given time, a house is legally owned by A and A – or no one[2] – lives in it then, at that time, that house is occupied by A. Moreover, if, at a given time, a house is legally owned by A but A does not live in it because he has leased the house to B then, at that time, that house is occupied by B but not by A: B, as lessee, will have control over the premises, not A. What about the intermediate situation where, at a given time, a house is legally owned by A but A does not live in it because he is allowing B to live in it without, however, having formally leased the house to B? Is the house, at that time, occupied by A? Probably – the fact that A does not live in the house at that time because he is allowing B to stay in it as a licensee does not mean that A no longer has a sufficient degree of control over the house.

In *Wheat* v *E Lacon & Co. Ltd* itself, the defendants owned a pub which was run by a manager. The defendants allowed the manager to use the first floor of the pub as his private accommodation. A guest of the manager fell down some stairs on the first floor of the pub

[1] [1966] AC 552, 577.

[2] Cf. *Harris* v *Birkenhead Corporation* [1976] 1 WLR 279 (a house which was abandoned on being compulsorily purchased by the defendant local authority was occupied by the defendant local authority even though it never took possession of the house).

and was killed. It was held that at the time of the accident the first floor of the pub was occupied by the defendants and that the defendants therefore owed the deceased a duty to take care to see that he was reasonably safe for the purposes for which he was on the first floor. In *Ribee* v *Norrie*,[3] the defendant owned a hostel which contained a number of bedrooms which various people would rent from him. A fire started in the sitting room of the hostel which was set aside for the communal use of those using the hostel. The fire damaged a house adjoining the hostel. Whether the defendant was liable for the fire damage turned on whether he occupied the sitting room where the fire started. The court held that he did – he exercised a sufficient degree of control over the sitting room. As Ward LJ remarked, 'he had full power to regulate how that part of the hostel was to be used or not used as the case may be'.[4]

What about the case where A owns a house and he has engaged B to do some work on it? No doubt in such a case when B starts work the house will still be occupied by A – but what about B? It depends on how much *de facto* control over the house B exercises over it once he starts work on it. So if the work involves a major operation where no one is allowed to enter the house without B's say-so then there seems little doubt that the house will also be occupied by B once B starts work on it.

Having clarified when someone will be regarded as 'occupying' a certain set of premises, we can now turn to describe the duties of care that an occupier of premises will normally owe other people. We will begin with the duties of care that an occupier of premises will normally owe his 'visitors'.

Visitors

The 'common duty of care'

Section 2 of the Occupiers' Liability Act 1957 provides that if B enters premises occupied by A as A's 'visitor' – a term which we will shortly define – A will *normally* owe B a duty 'to take such care as is reasonable in all the circumstances of the case to see that [B] will be reasonably safe in using the premises for the purpose for which he is invited or permitted by [A] to be there'.[5] This duty is referred to by the Act as the 'common duty of care'.

There is a question whether the duty so owed by A to B is a duty to take reasonable steps to see that B is not injured by reason of the *state of the premises* occupied by A or whether the duty is, more broadly, a duty to take care to see that B is not injured by reason of the state of those premises *or* by reason of *things done* on those premises. Section 1(1) of the 1957 Act seems to indicate that the latter view is correct. It provides that the 1957 Act will 'regulate the duty which an occupier of premises owes to his visitors in respect of dangers due to the state of the premises *or to things done or omitted to be done on them*'.[6] However,

[3] (2001) 33 HLR 777.

[4] Ibid., at [20].

[5] *Important note.* A will also owe B a duty to take reasonable steps to see that any property B brings with him onto A's premises is reasonably safe; and this is so whether or not the property in question actually belongs to B: s 1(3)(b). There is a question whether A is merely required by this duty to take reasonable steps to see that B's property is not destroyed or damaged or whether he is *also* required to take reasonable steps to see that B's property is not *stolen*. On this issue, see *AMF International Ltd* v *Magnet Bowling Ltd* [1968] 1 WLR 1028, at 1050 (per Mocatta J).

[6] Emphasis added.

the Court of Appeal has now ruled in *Fairchild* v *Glenhaven Funeral Services Ltd* that the former view is correct.[7]

Who is a 'visitor'?

Not everyone who enters a given set of premises enters those premises as the occupier's 'visitor'. If B enters a set of premises occupied by A, B will enter those premises as A's 'visitor' *if*: (1) B was invited or permitted to enter those premises by A; *or* (2) B was invited or permitted to enter those premises by someone who had the ostensible authority to issue such an invitation or permission on A's behalf.[8]

In a case where B entered premises occupied by A, there is generally no difficulty about establishing whether or not A invited B to enter those premises.[9] It is more difficult to establish, in a case where B entered premises occupied by A without A's invitation, whether or not A *permitted* B to enter those premises. For example, in *Lowery* v *Walker*[10] members of the public had for about 35 years taken a short cut across the defendant's field to get to a railway station. In all that time, the defendant never started legal proceedings to try and get people to stop crossing his field. The House of Lords found that by acting in this way the defendant impliedly permitted members of the public to cross his land and, therefore, when they entered his land they did so as visitors and were owed a duty of care by the defendant. In contrast, in *Edwards* v *Railway Executive*,[11] the House of Lords found that the defendant railway company did not permit children to enter onto its land for the purpose of tobogganing down an embankment on its land even though children had been accustomed to entering the defendant's land for precisely that purpose for many years. In coming to its finding, the House of Lords emphasised that the defendant company had done its best to stop children from coming onto its land to play – it put a fence around its land and whenever it discovered that children had breached a hole in it, the defendant company sought to repair the fence.

A may invite or permit B to enter one set of premises occupied by him but not another set of premises occupied by him. In such a case, if B enters the latter set of premises, she will not enter those premises as a visitor and A will not owe her a duty under the 1957 Act to see that B is reasonably safe while she is on that latter set of premises. So, for example, if Wendy stays the night in a hotel managed by Alan and during the middle of the night Wendy breaks into the kitchens to make a sandwich for herself, Wendy will not enter the kitchens as a visitor and Alan will not owe Wendy a duty under the 1957 Act to take care to see that Wendy is not harmed in using the kitchens. By permitting Wendy to enter and use the hotel, Alan does not permit Wendy to enter and use the hotel's kitchens.

Exceptions to the rule

If B enters premises occupied by A as A's visitor, A will not *always* owe B a duty to take reasonable steps to see that B is reasonably safe in using those premises for the purpose for

[7] [2002] 1 WLR 1052, at [109]–[133]. The point was not raised when the case was appealed to the House of Lords.

[8] For a discussion of the concept of 'ostensible authority' in this context, see *Ferguson* v *Welsh* [1987] 1 WLR 1553, 1563, per Lord Goff.

[9] Though see the extraordinary facts of *R* v *Collins* [1973] QB 100, where the defendant climbed up to the window of a young lady's bedroom and she invited him in for sex, in the mistaken belief that he was her boyfriend.

[10] [1911] AC 10.

[11] [1952] AC 737.

which she is on the premises. There are two cases in particular where A will not owe B such a duty.

(1) *Exclusion of duty*. Under s 2(1) of the 1957 Act, A is free to 'restrict, modify or exclude' this duty owed to B 'by agreement [with B] or otherwise'.

So in *White* v *Blackmore*,[12] W attended a motor race with his family. At the entrance to the field where the races were held was a notice which said: 'Warning to the public, Motor Racing is dangerous . . . [it is] a condition of admission that all persons having any connection with the promotion and/or organisation and/or conduct of the meeting, including . . . the drivers of the vehicles . . . are absolved of all liabilities arising out of accidents causing damage or personal injury (whether fatal or otherwise) howsoever caused to spectators or ticketholders.' W was killed while watching one of the motor races. The Court of Appeal held that, on the day of the races, the chairman of the motor club that was holding the race and the racing organiser did not owe W any duty under the 1957 Act to take care to see that he was reasonably safe in watching the races. The notice was effective to exclude the duty that would otherwise have been owed to W under the 1957 Act as all reasonable steps had been taken to draw its existence to W's attention.

However, an important limit on the ability of *businesses* that occupy premises to exclude the duties of care they would otherwise owe their visitors has been created by the Unfair Contract Terms Act 1977. Section 2(1) of the Act provides that, 'a person cannot by reference to any contract term or notice given to persons generally or to particular persons exclude or restrict his [business][13] liability for death or personal injury resulting from negligence'.[14] Section 13 of the 1977 Act provides that, 'to the extent that [s 2 of the Act] prevents the exclusion or restriction of any liability it also prevents . . . (to the same extent) [the exclusion or restriction] of liability by reference to terms or notices which exclude [an] obligation or duty'.

So suppose that B visited A's business premises. Suppose further that she was injured on the premises and that she wants to sue A for damages. Suppose further that when B visited A's premises, he notified her that he was taking no responsibility for her safety. Now – the result of the above provisions in the 1977 Act is that, in deciding whether or not B is entitled to sue A for damages, the courts will *disregard* the notice that A gave B and decide the case on the basis that B was *not* notified that A was not assuming any responsibility for her safety. So they will find that A owed B a duty under the 1957 Act to take reasonable steps to see that she would be reasonably safe while she was on his premises. And if B can show that A breached that duty and that she was injured as a result, then B will be entitled to compensation from A. It may be, then, that *White* v *Blackmore* would be decided differently today were the same facts to occur. The courts would disregard the notice given by motor race organisers and hold that they owed W a duty to take reasonable steps to see that he

[12] [1972] 2 QB 651.

[13] Under s 1(3) of the 1977 Act, s 2 applies 'only to business liability, that is liability for breach of obligations or duties arising – (a) from things done or to be done by a person in the course of a business . . .; or (b) from the occupation of premises used for business purposes of the occupier'. Section 1(3) also makes it clear that the 'liability of an occupier of premises for breach of an obligation or duty towards a person obtaining access to the premises for recreational or educational purposes . . . is not a business liability of the occupier unless granting that person such access for the purposes concerned falls within the business purposes of the occupier'.

[14] A business is allowed to exclude or restrict its liability in negligence for harm that has been done to property or pure economic loss, but only if it would be reasonable to do so: s 2(2).

would be reasonably safe in watching the races. So – if W's dependants wanted to bring a fatal accidents claim against the organisers, all they would have to show is that the organisers failed to take reasonable steps to see that W would be safe watching the races, and that W was killed as a result.

(2) *Assumption of risk*. If B willingly takes the risk that she will be harmed in a particular way when she enters premises occupied by A, A will *not* owe B a duty to take reasonable steps to ensure that B is not harmed in that way while she is on those premises. The maxim *volenti non fit injuria* will apply.

This is the result of s 2(5) of the 1957 Act which provides that the 1957 Act 'does not impose on an occupier any obligation to a visitor in respect of risks willingly accepted as his by the visitor . . .'. So – in *Simms* v *Leigh Rugby Football Club*,[15] the defendant rugby club's ground had a concrete barrier running around the pitch, seven feet from the touchline, in order to keep the spectators from going onto the pitch. It was held that S, a rugby player who played on the defendant rugby club's ground, took the risk that he would be injured by being thrown against this concrete barrier when he stepped onto the pitch – the existence and location of the barrier being permitted under the byelaws of the game, as laid down by the Rugby Football League. So the defendant rugby club did not owe S a duty to take care to ensure that he was not injured by being thrown against the concrete barrier around the pitch.

It is clear that when B enters premises occupied by A in the *knowledge* that she might be harmed in a particular way as a result, B will not be held to have willingly taken the risk that she would be harmed in that way if she had no choice but to enter A's premises.[16] For example, in *Burnett* v *British Waterways Board*,[17] B was employed to work on a barge which was being towed into the defendant's lock when the rope towing the barge snapped and hit B. It was held that B did not take the risk that he would be injured in this way when the barge was being towed into the defendant's lock – even if at the time of the accident he knew he might be injured in this way as a result of the barge's being towed into the defendant's lock. This is because B had no choice but to stay on the barge as it was towed into the defendant's lock.

Trespassers

The basic rule

If B goes onto premises occupied by A, not as a visitor, but as a trespasser, then A may owe B a duty of care under the Occupiers' Liability Act 1984. This duty will require A to take reasonable steps to ensure that B is not killed or injured[18] by reason of a danger arising 'due to the state of the premises or to things done or omitted to be done on them' *if*: (1) A is, or ought to be, aware of the existence of the danger; *and* (2) A knows or ought to know that

[15] [1969] 2 All ER 923.

[16] Cf. Occupiers' Liability Act 1957, s 2(4)(a): 'where damage is caused to a visitor by a danger of which he had been warned by the occupier, the warning is not to be treated without more as absolving the occupier from liability, unless in all the circumstances it was enough to enable the visitor to be reasonably safe'.

[17] [1973] 1 WLR 700.

[18] Section 1(9). So A will *not* owe B a duty under the 1984 Act to take reasonable steps to see that any property that B has in his possession when he goes onto A's premises is not destroyed or damaged.

B is in, or may come into, the vicinity of the danger; *and* (3) A can reasonably be expected to offer B some protection against that danger.[19] Three points need to be made about this provision.

(1) *State of the premises*. The 1984 Act is plainly designed *only* to cover cases where B trespassed on A's premises and she was killed or injured because those premises had a dangerous *feature*. In such a case, A may have owed B a duty under the 1984 Act to take reasonable steps to see that she would not be killed or injured by that feature and may therefore be liable for B's being killed or injured. If, on the other hand, B trespassed on A's premises and was killed or injured on those premises *not* because those premises had a dangerous feature, her case will fall outside the scope of the 1984 Act.

For example, in *Revill* v *Newbery*,[20] Revill attempted to break into a shed on Newbery's allotment so as to steal some valuable items that Newbery kept there. Newbery – who had been subject to the repeated attentions of vandals and thieves in the area – was sleeping in the shed to protect his property. On hearing Revill's attempts to break in, Newbery took a shotgun, loaded it, poked the barrel through a hole in the door and fired the gun in order to scare Revill away. Revill was shot in the arm and sued Newbery. The Court of Appeal did not think that Revill could bring a claim against Newbery under the 1984 Act. It is submitted that this was correct. Revill was not injured because Newbery's premises had a dangerous *feature*; he was injured because Newbery shot him. It would have been different if Newbery had laid down man traps around his shed to deter thieves and one of these man traps had caught Revill. In such a case, Revill *would* have been injured as a result of Newbery's premises having a dangerous feature (the presence of the man traps) and he might therefore have been able to bring a claim against Newbery under the 1984 Act, claiming that Newbery owed him a duty under the 1984 Act to take reasonable steps to see that he would not be killed or injured as a result of the presence of the man traps.

Similarly, in *Tomlinson* v *Congleton BC*,[21] the claimant was injured when he went swimming in a lake on the defendant council's land. He had no permission to go swimming in the lake and so was trespassing on the council's land when he went into the lake. The claimant sued the council for compensation under the 1984 Act but his claim was dismissed: he could not show that he had been injured because the council's land had a dangerous feature. As Lord Hoffmann observed of the lake in the *Tomlinson* case, 'There was nothing special about [the lake]; there were no hidden dangers. It was shallow in some places and deep in others, but that is the nature of lakes. Nor was the council doing or permitting anything to be done which created a danger to persons who came to the lake. No power boats or jet skis threatened the safety of either lawful windsurfers or unlawful swimmers.'[22]

Could the claimant have argued that the lake *itself* was a dangerous feature of the land on which it was located and that he had therefore been injured because the council's land had a dangerous feature? Not on the facts of *Tomlinson*, where the claimant was a mature

[19] The quoted words come from s 1(1)(a) of the 1984 Act. The conditions for A's owing B a duty under the Act may be found in s 1(3) of the 1984 Act. Section 1(4) of the 1984 Act specifies what duty A will owe B if the conditions specified in s 1(3) are fulfilled.

[20] [1996] QB 567.

[21] [2004] 1 AC 46.

[22] Ibid., at [26].

adult: the mere existence of the lake did not pose any kind of danger to *him*.[23] However, it might have been different if the claimant in *Tomlinson* had been a small child who fell into the lake and was injured. The decision of the Court of Appeal in *Keown* v *Coventry Healthcare NHS Trust*[24] makes it clear that in such a case the lake *itself* would have counted as a dangerous feature of the land – with regard to the child – if the child was unaware of the danger of drowning that it was incurring by going near the lake. So if the child in our imagined case was too young to appreciate the danger posed by going near the lake on the council's land, the council would have owed the child a duty to take reasonable steps to protect him from that danger.[25] In the *Keown* case itself, the claimant was a child who was injured when he fell from a fire escape attached to the defendants' accommodation block; the claimant had been climbing the fire escape to impress his friends. The Court of Appeal held that the defendants had not owed the claimant a duty under the 1984 Act to take reasonable steps to protect him from the danger of falling from the fire escape. As the claimant well knew how dangerous it was to climb the fire escape, the mere presence of the fire escape did not pose any danger to *him*; it was what he chose to do on the fire escape that put him in danger.

(2) *The conditions for a duty to arise under the Act*. Suppose that B trespassed on land occupied by A. Suppose further that there was some quicksand on A's land and that B fell into the quicksand and died. A will only have owed B a duty to take reasonable steps to see that she would not fall into the quicksand if: (1) A knew or ought to have known of the existence of the quicksand; (2) *at the time B trespassed on A's premises*, A knew or ought to have known that someone like B might go into the vicinity of the quicksand; and (3) A could reasonably have been expected to do something to ensure that someone like B would not fall into the quicksand.

The italicised words do not appear in the 1984 Act but it follows from the decision of the Court of Appeal in *Donoghue* v *Folkestone Properties Ltd*[26] that they should be read into the Act. In that case, the claimant dived into the defendant council's harbour in the middle of winter. He hit his head on a submerged gridbed and was severely injured. He sued the council for compensation claiming that it had owed him a duty under the 1984 Act to take reasonable steps to see that he did not injure himself on the submerged gridbed.[27] The claimant's claim was dismissed on the ground that at the time the claimant dived into the harbour – the *middle of winter* – the defendants had no reason to think that anyone would try to dive into the harbour. So they had no reason to think at the relevant time that anyone would go anywhere near the submerged gridbed. It would have been different if the diver had executed his dive in the middle of *summer*. At *that* time of year it would have been reasonably foreseeable that trespassers *would* go near the

[23] See *Donoghue* v *Folkestone Properties Ltd* [2003] QB 1008, at [36]: 'An expanse of water, be it a lake, pond, river or the sea, does not normally pose any danger to a person on land.'

[24] [2006] 1 WLR 953.

[25] If the child had been allowed to come onto the council's land then the said duty would have been owed under the Occupiers' Liability Act 1957; if he had not been, then the duty would have been owed under the 1984 Act (assuming of course that all the other conditions required for a duty to have been owed under the 1984 Act were satisfied in this case).

[26] [2003] QB 1008.

[27] The claimant brought his claim under the 1984 Act because he was trespasser when he dived into the harbour.

submerged gridbed (by jumping into the harbour at a spot over the gridbed) and so the council in *Donoghue* would have come under a duty to provide trespassers with some protection against that danger by, for example, posting up warning signs telling people not to jump into the harbour.

(3) *The boundary between the 1984 Act and the 1957 Act.* Suppose that Sarah held a dinner party at her house. She told her guests, including Paul, that they could go anywhere they liked in the house, but not into the kitchen. Paul – suspecting that Sarah had prohibited her guests from going into the kitchen to prevent them discovering that she had not actually cooked the dinner herself but was instead serving takeaway food – walked into the kitchen and promptly slipped on the floor and suffered a severe spinal injury. Sarah had in fact told everyone not to go into the kitchen because she had had to clean up some food that she had spilled on the floor and as a result the floor was extremely slippery.

Paul now wants to sue Sarah in negligence for compensation for his injury. The only way his claim can succeed is if he can establish that Sarah owed him a duty to take reasonable steps to stop him going into the kitchen and that she breached that duty by, for example, not locking the kitchen door.[28] Now – which Occupiers' Liability Act will apply here to determine whether Sarah owed Paul such a duty? The argument for thinking that we must look to the 1957 Act is that we want to know whether Sarah owed Paul a duty to take reasonable steps to *stop* him going into her kitchen. That duty must have been owed to Paul *before* he went into Sarah's kitchen and *at that stage*, Paul enjoyed the status of being a 'visitor' on Sarah's premises.[29] So we should look to the 1957 Act – which 'regulate[s] the duty which an occupier of premises owes to his visitors' – to determine whether Sarah owed Paul a duty to take reasonable steps to stop him going into her kitchen.

The logic of this argument seems impeccable, but a majority of the House of Lords ruled in *Tomlinson* v *Congleton BC*[30] that we should in fact look at the *1984* Act to determine whether Sarah owed Paul a duty to take reasonable steps to stop him going into her kitchen.[31] On this view, the 1984 Act not only determines when you have a duty to protect a *trespasser* on your land from some danger arising on your premises but also when you have a duty to take reasonable steps to stop a *visitor* of yours from entering a dangerous area of your land which she is not permitted to enter.

Exceptions to the rule

Suppose B trespasses onto premises occupied by A. Suppose further that those premises have some dangerous feature. Even if conditions (1)–(3), above, are fulfilled, A will not necessarily owe B a duty to take reasonable steps to ensure that B is not killed or injured by that feature. For example, if B has voluntarily taken the risk that he will be killed or injured

[28] Paul will not be able to argue that *once he was in the kitchen*, Sarah owed him a duty to take reasonable steps to stop him falling over and injuring himself because once Paul was in the kitchen, Sarah could not reasonably have been expected to do anything to save him from falling over.

[29] Of course, as soon as he entered the kitchen, he became a trespasser: see above, p. 169.

[30] [2004] 1 AC 46.

[31] Applying the Act, the question of whether Sarah did owe Paul such a duty under the 1984 Act will largely turn on whether Sarah knew or ought to have known that despite her prohibition someone like Paul would attempt to enter the kitchen. If this condition is satisfied, then the courts may well find that Sarah owed Paul a duty to take reasonable steps to stop him going into the kitchen.

by that feature, then A will *not* owe B a duty to take reasonable steps to save him from being killed or injured.[32] The maxim *volenti non fit injuria* will apply.

So – in *Ratcliff* v *McConnell*,[33] R was a student who suffered serious injuries when he dived into his college's swimming pool at the shallow end. The pool was locked up for the winter and so when R used the swimming pool he did not do so as a visitor. R sued the college's governors, seeking to recover compensation for his injuries. He claimed that the governors owed him a duty under the 1984 Act to take reasonable steps to ensure that he would not be killed or injured if he dived into the swimming pool. The Court of Appeal dismissed R's claim, holding that when he dived into the swimming pool he willingly took the risk that he would be killed or injured as a result. He knew when he made his dive that there was a risk that the swimming pool would be too shallow to dive in but he nevertheless went ahead with his dive. Similarly, in *Titchener* v *British Railways Board*,[34] it was held that someone who walks across a railway line knowing that trains run along that line willingly takes the risk that he will be run down and killed or injured by a passing train.

What is the position if B trespasses on premises occupied by A and A has posted up notices outside the premises saying 'No responsibility accepted for the safety of trespassers'? Seemingly, those notices will be of no effect. A will still owe B a duty of care under the 1984 Act if there is some dangerous feature on the premises and conditions (1)–(3), above, apply. There is nothing in the 1984 Act to indicate that the duties of care arising under that Act may be excluded in the same way as the duties of care arising under the 1957 Act can be. However, this creates a paradox. Someone who occupies premises not used for business purposes can 'by agreement or otherwise' ensure that he owes his visitors *no* duty to take reasonable steps to ensure that they will not be harmed by some dangerous feature on the premises – but he may at the same time owe people who trespass onto the premises a duty, which cannot be excluded, to take reasonable steps to ensure that they will not be killed or injured by that feature. In such a case, the occupier's visitors will be worse off than people who trespass on his premises. It is not certain that this was intended by the legislature when it enacted the 1984 Act but only new legislation can remove the problem.

Persons entering premises by right

Now let's look at the position where B goes onto premises owned or occupied by A not because she has been invited or permitted to go onto those premises but because she has a *legal right* to do so. Obviously, B will be neither a 'visitor' nor a trespasser in this situation. So what duties of care will A owe her? The position is very complicated.

The *normal rule* is that B will be treated as though she were one of A's visitors. So A will normally owe her a duty under the Occupiers' Liability Act 1957 to take reasonable steps to see that she will be reasonably safe while she is on A's premises. This is the result of s 2(6) of the Occupiers' Liability Act 1957, which provides that, 'persons who enter premises for any purpose in the exercise of a right conferred by law are to be treated as permitted by the occupier to be there for that purpose, whether they in fact have his permission or not'. So

[32] Section 1(6): 'No duty is owed . . . to any person in respect of risks willingly accepted as his by that person . . .'
[33] [1999] 1 WLR 670.
[34] [1983] 1 WLR 1427 (decided under the Occupiers' Liability (Scotland) Act 1960).

a police officer who lawfully goes onto A's premises to conduct a search will be protected under the 1957 Act: A will owe her a duty to take reasonable steps to see that she is reasonably safe while she is on his premises.

However, the normal rule does *not* apply where there is a *right of way* over A's land and B uses that right of way to cross A's land.[35] This may be because it would be unduly burdensome to inflict on A a duty to take care to see that people using the right of way over his land are reasonably safe in using that right of way.[36] Whether or not A will owe B a duty of care in such a case, and what sort of duty A will owe B, will depend on what *sort* of right of way it is that B is using to cross A's land.

(1) *Where the right of way is a private right of way or arises under an access agreement or under the National Parks and Access to the Countryside Act 1949.* In such a case, B will be protected by the Occupiers' Liability Act 1984.[37] So if some dangerous feature exists on the right of way (such as a pot-hole) and A knows or ought to know about it and A knows or ought to know that someone like B is likely to come into the vicinity of that dangerous feature and that dangerous feature is one which A could reasonably be expected to do something about, then A will owe B a duty to take reasonable steps to see that she is not killed or injured by that feature.

(2) *Where the right of way arises under s 2(1) of the Countryside and Rights of Way Act 2000.* In such a case, B will again be protected under the Occupiers' Liability Act 1984.[38] However, ss 1(6A) and 1(6C) of the 1984 Act place an important limit on the duty that A would normally owe B under the Act. They provide that A will *not* owe B a duty to protect her against '(a) a risk resulting from the existence of any natural feature of the landscape, or any river, stream, ditch or pond whether or not a natural feature, or (b) a risk [that she will suffer injury] when passing over, under or through any wall, fence or gate, except by proper use of the gate or of a stile' unless he has intentionally or recklessly exposed her to such a risk.

(3) *Where the right of way amounts to a public highway.* In such a case, B will not be protected under the 1984 Act.[39] The only duties of care that A will owe B in such a case will arise under the common law. In such a case, A will of course owe B a duty of care under the *physical danger principle* to take care not to do something which will reasonably fore-

[35] The Occupiers' Liability Act 1957, s 1(4) provides that the normal rule will not apply where B crosses A's land using a private right of way or a right of way arising under – (i) an access agreement; or (ii) an order granted under the National Parks and Access to the Countryside Act 1949; or (iii) under the Countryside and Rights of Way Act 2000. The House of Lords ruled in *McGeown* v *Northern Ireland Housing Executive* [1995] 1 AC 233 that the normal rule will not apply where a highway crosses A's land and B uses it to pass over A's land.

[36] Cf. Lord Keith of Kinkel's remarks in *McGeown*: 'Rights of way pass over many different types of terrain, and it would place an impossible burden upon landowners if they had not only to submit to the passage over them of anyone who might choose to exercise them but also were under a duty to maintain them in safe condition' (ibid., 243).

[37] This is the result of the combined effect of s 1(4) of the 1957 Act and s 1(1) of the 1984 Act.

[38] See n. 37, above.

[39] Occupiers' Liability Act 1984, s 1(7). However, if the public right of way is maintainable at public expense, the highway authority in charge of the right of way will owe B a duty to 'maintain' it: Highways Act 1980, s 41. If B is injured because the right of way in question is not in a good condition, the relevant highway authority will have a defence to any action B might make against it for damages if it can show that it took 'such care as in all the circumstances was reasonably required to secure that the part of the [right of way] to which the action relates was not dangerous for traffic': s 58. See below, pp. 491–2.

seeably have the effect of injuring B. A may also owe B a duty to act to save B from some harm in using the highway if 'common humanity' would demand that he so act.[40]

Neighbours

Suppose that A occupies a set of premises and a dangerous situation arises on those premises that threatens to damage neighbouring land belonging to B. In such a situation, if A is aware of the danger to B's land that has arisen on his land, or ought to be aware of the danger, A will owe B a duty to take reasonable steps to eliminate the danger.

So in *Goldman* v *Hargrave*,[41] lightning struck a redgum tree on the defendant's land and set it on fire. The defendant cut down the tree but then did not do enough to put out the fire. The fire spread onto the claimant's land, causing much damage. The claimant successfully sued the defendant in negligence for compensation for the damage done to his land.[42] The Privy Council held that the defendant had owed the claimant a duty to take reasonable steps to put out the fire on his land, and that the defendant had breached that duty.[43] Decisions of the Privy Council are, of course, not binding on the English courts but the House of Lords has indicated that the decision in *Goldman* v *Hargrave* was correct.[44]

It is more uncertain whether A will owe a duty to his neighbour B to take reasonable steps to prevent his premises *becoming* a source of danger to B's land. The question was

40 *Herrington* v *British Railways Board* [1972] AC 877. The case was concerned with the question of when an occupier of land will owe a *trespasser* on the land a duty to save that trespasser from harm and was superseded in large part by the 1984 Act. However, if before the Act, occupiers of land owed trespassers on the land a duty of 'common humanity' then there seems no reason why occupiers of land should not owe the same duty in this day and age to people crossing their land via a public highway.

41 [1967] AC 645.

42 *Important note*. The claimant could have alternatively sued the defendant in *private nuisance* for compensation for the damage done to his land (see below, pp. 387–9) and, indeed, it is customary nowadays for claims for damage done to land as a result of dangerous situations arising on neighbouring land to be brought in private nuisance rather than negligence (see, for example, *Leakey* v *National Trust for Places of Historic Interest or Natural Beauty* [1980] QB 485 and *Holbeck Hall Hotel Ltd* v *Scarborough BC* [2000] QB 836). It is submitted that it makes no difference whether the claims in these sorts of cases are framed in either private nuisance or negligence (see *Leakey*, at 514–15 (per May LJ); also *Smith* v *Littlewoods* [1987] AC 241, at 274 (per Lord Goff)). This is because if a fire spontaneously starts on A's land, A will only owe people who own or have an interest in neighbouring land a duty to take reasonable steps to put out the fire and that duty will be imposed on A in order to help ensure that that neighbouring land is not damaged. So suppose that a fire started on A's land and A failed to take reasonable steps to put out the fire, with the result that it spread onto neighbouring land belonging to B. B was badly burned in the fire and C, a lodger staying on B's land with B's permission, had to move out because the fire damage done to B's land was so extensive. It is doubtful whether B could sue A in private nuisance for his injuries (see below, pp. 395–7, 581–2) and C would not be able to sue A in private nuisance for the inconvenience he has been put to because he did not have an interest in B's land when it was damaged (see below, pp. 394–5). It is submitted that neither party will be better off bringing a claim in negligence against A. B's claim for compensation for his burns will be dismissed because even though A owed him, and breached, a duty to take reasonable steps to put out the fire, the physical injuries suffered by B as a result of the fire spreading do not count as the 'right of kind of loss' – the kind of loss which the duty breached by A was imposed on him in order to avoid. (For an explanation of the 'right kind of loss' limit on the damages recoverable in a tort case, see below, pp. 577–8.) Any claim C might bring against A in negligence for the inconvenience he was put to as a result of A's allowing the fire to spread onto B's land will be dismissed on the ground that as C did not have an interest in B's land, A did not owe *C* a duty to take reasonable steps to put out the fire.

43 Had the fire been intentionally or carelessly started by the defendant, the claimant would have been entitled to sue the defendant for compensation for the damage done to his land without having to prove that the defendant was at all careless in allowing the fire to spread: see below, pp. 765–6.

44 *Stovin* v *Wise* [1996] AC 923, 930G–H (per Lord Nicholls), 944D–H (per Lord Hoffmann).

raised in *Smith* v *Littlewoods*.[45] The defendants purchased a cinema: they intended to knock it down and redevelop the land. For a few months the cinema was left unattended and unlocked. Vandals broke into the cinema and set it on fire. The fire spread to and damaged the claimants' premises. The claimants sued the defendants: they argued that the defendants had owed them a duty to take reasonable steps to keep the cinema secure, so as to prevent the cinema becoming a source of danger to their premises. The House of Lords dismissed the claimants' claim on the ground that it had not been reasonably foreseeable that the claimants' premises would be harmed if the defendants' cinema was not kept secure.[46]

In the course of deciding the case, Lords Brandon and Griffiths indicated that in the situation we are considering, A *will* owe B a duty to take reasonable steps to prevent his premises *becoming* a source of danger to B's land.[47] In contrast, Lord Goff thought that an occupier of land will *not* owe his neighbours a duty to take proactive steps to prevent his land *becoming* a source of danger to his neighbours' land: he will only owe his neighbours a duty of care in a *Goldman* v *Hargrave*-type situation where a danger *has* arisen on his land and he knows or ought to know of its existence.[48] Lord Mackay steered a middle path between these two extremes. He thought that if A occupies some premises and it is reasonably foreseeable that if those premises are not kept secure vandals will break into A's premises and start a fire which is liable to spread to B's land, then A *will* owe B a duty to take reasonable steps to keep his premises secure, thereby preventing them becoming a source of danger to B's land.[49] But Lord Mackay thought things would be different in the case where it is reasonably foreseeable that if A's premises are not kept secure, thieves will break into A's premises and use those premises to gain access to B's land and steal property from B.[50] While he did not go so far as to say that *no* duty of care would be owed in this situation,[51] he plainly thought this case more difficult than the 'fire' case just discussed. Puzzlingly, the fifth judge to decide *Smith* v *Littlewoods* – Lord Keith of Kinkel – expressed agreement with the judgments of Lord Mackay *and* Lord Goff, despite the clear differences between them.

So *Smith* v *Littlewoods* did not finally resolve the issue of whether an occupier of premises will owe his neighbours a duty to take reasonable steps to prevent his property becoming a source of danger to his neighbours' land. The most that can be said in light of the decisions in that case is that there was a clear majority in favour of the proposition that such an occupier *will* owe his neighbours a duty to take reasonable steps to keep his prem-

45 [1987] AC 241.

46 Ibid., at 250 (per Lord Brandon), 251 (per Lord Griffiths), 258–59 (per Lord Mackay).

47 Ibid., at 250: '[the defendants] owed to the [claimants] a duty to exercise reasonable care to ensure that the cinema ... did not become ... a source of danger to neighbouring buildings owned or occupied by the claimants' (per Lord Brandon); 'the duty of care owed [by the defendants] was a duty to take reasonable care that the condition of the premises they occupied was not a source of danger to neighbouring property' (per Lord Griffiths).

48 Ibid., at 272–4, 277–9.

49 Ibid., at 258.

50 Ibid., at 268.

51 He did think that if A came back home to find a thief boring a hole through one of his walls to gain access to B's house, then A would owe B a duty to take reasonable steps to stop the thief gaining access to B's house in this way: ibid., at 265. However, this result can easily be justified by reference to *Goldman* v *Hargrave*. In the case considered here a danger *will* have arisen on A's land which A knows about and therefore A will owe those of his neighbours who will be affected by that danger a duty to take reasonable steps to deal with it.

ises secure *if* it is reasonably foreseeable that if he does not vandals will break in and start a fire which is liable to spread to his neighbours' land.

Passers-by

Suppose A occupies premises that adjoin a highway. Suppose further that there is some fixture attached to those premises – such as a sign or a tree – which is liable to fall into the highway if it falls into disrepair. In such a case, A will owe people using the highway next to his premises a duty to take reasonable steps to see that the fixture in question does not fall into the highway and injure them.[52] So if the fixture in question is in an obviously dangerous condition, A will have a duty to take reasonable steps to repair the fixture or take it down.[53] And even if the fixture in question looks perfectly sound, A will have a duty from time to time to have an expert look at it to see that it does not suffer from any latent defects which mean that it is a danger to passers-by.[54]

OTHER OCCUPIERS

The regime of duties of care created by the 1957 and 1984 Acts also applies to occupiers of fixed or moveable structures[55] such as boats[56] or taxis or ladders.[57]

LANDLORDS

Section 4 of the Defective Premises Act 1972 provides that *if*: (1) A lets premises to someone else; and (2) A knows or ought to know the premises suffer from a defect;[58] and (3) under the contract of tenancy A would have an obligation to repair that defect were he

[52] If the fixture does fall into a state of disrepair and as a result falls into the highway, anyone injured as a result may be entitled to bring a claim in *public nuisance* for compensation for their injuries. See below, pp. 000–000, for a discussion of the availability of such a claim.

[53] *Tarry* v *Ashton* (1876) 1 QBD 314. The duty is non-delegable in nature. That is, if A employs someone else to repair the fixture, and that person fails to take reasonable steps to repair it properly, then A will be held to have breached his duty to take reasonable steps to repair the fixture: ibid.. For a discussion of non-delegable duties of care, see below, pp. 230–6.

[54] *Caminer* v *Northern and London Investment Trust* [1951] AC 88 (held: occupiers not liable in negligence for injuries caused as a result of an elm tree falling into a road from their premises because the tree was apparently healthy; and, while the occupiers had failed to get anyone in to inspect the tree, even if they had, no action would have been taken to repair the tree or take it down because inspection by an expert would not have revealed that there was a problem with the tree).

[55] Occupiers' Liability Act 1957, s 1(3)(a); Occupiers' Liability Act 1984, s 1(2).

[56] In *Horsley* v *MacLaren, The Ogopogo* [1971] 2 Lloyd's Rep 410, the Supreme Court of Canada ruled that if A invites B onto his boat and B falls overboard, A will owe B a duty to take reasonable steps to rescue him. Such a conclusion could not be reached under the Occupiers' Liability Act 1957. Under the 1957 Act, A's only duty would be to take reasonable steps to see that B was not injured as a result of the condition of the boat. Perhaps the Supreme Court's conclusion could be justified under the 'creation of danger principle', discussed above, pp. 156–9.

[57] If A gives B a ladder to stand on, can the ladder be said to be 'occupied' by A at the time B stands on it? The court thought not in *Wheeler* v *Copas* [1981] 3 All ER 405, holding that a bricklayer who was injured when a ladder given him by the defendant farmer collapsed had no claim against the farmer under the 1957 Act.

[58] Section 4(2). The Court of Appeal has made it clear that it need not be shown, for the purposes of this requirement, that A had actual knowledge of the existence of the defect or of facts which indicated that the defect existed: it is enough to show that a reasonable man in A's position would have discovered the existence of the defect. See *Sykes* v *Harry* [2001] QB 1014 (leave to appeal refused by the House of Lords: [2002] 1 WLR 2286).

aware of it;[59] then (4) A will *normally* owe 'all persons[60] who might reasonably be expected to be affected by defects in the state of the premises a duty to take such care as is reasonable in all the circumstances to see that they are reasonably safe from personal injury or from damage caused to their property by [that] defect'.[61]

By s 4(4) of the 1972 Act, if A lets premises to someone else and under the contract of tenancy he reserves the right to re-enter the premises to effect certain repairs to the premises, A is to be regarded for the purposes of s 4 of the 1972 Act as having an obligation under the contract of tenancy to effect those repairs to the premises. However, A cannot be treated by virtue of s 4(4) as having had an obligation under the contract of tenancy to repair a given defect in the premises if the responsibility for repairing that defect was clearly placed on the tenant under the contract of tenancy.

In *McAuley* v *Bristol City Council*,[62] M was a council tenant who fell from an unstable step in her garden and injured her ankle. She sued the council, arguing that she had sustained her injury because the council owed her, and breached, a duty to take care to see that she would not be injured by the unstable step in her garden. The council had not undertaken under the contract of tenancy to repair the unstable step in the garden.[63] However, the Court of Appeal *implied* a term in the tenancy agreement that the council had the power to enter the claimant's garden to inspect and repair any defective structures in the garden. This allowed the Court of Appeal to treat the council, for the purposes of applying s 4 of the 1972 Act, as though it *was* obliged under the contract of tenancy to repair the unstable step in the claimant's garden – and therefore to find that the council did owe the claimant a duty to take care to see that she would not be injured by that step.

It would have been different if *either* the council had expressly provided in the contract of tenancy that the responsibility for repairing defective structures in the claimant's garden fell on the claimant (in which case the council could not have been treated by virtue of s 4(4) of the 1972 Act as having had an obligation under the contract of tenancy to repair the unstable step in the claimant's garden) *or* the council had expressly provided in the contract of tenancy that it had no right to repair defective structures in the claimant's garden (in which case it would have been impossible for the Court of Appeal to have implied a term into the contract of tenancy that the council had the right to enter the claimant's garden to inspect and repair any defective structures there). However, the council did neither of these things.

EMPLOYERS

It has long been well established that if A employs B, A will *normally* owe B a duty to take reasonable steps to see that she is not killed or physically injured in working for him. So A will *normally* owe B a duty to take reasonable steps to ensure: (1) that B's fellow employees are competent and are therefore not likely to act in ways which would unreasonably

[59] Section 4(3).
[60] Including the tenant(s) of the let premises: *McAuley* v *Bristol City Council* [1992] 1 QB 134; *Sykes* v *Harry* [2001] QB 1014, at [21].
[61] Section 4(1).
[62] [1992] 1 QB 134.
[63] So no claim for breach of contract was available to the claimant.

endanger B's health and safety; (2) that B's place of work is reasonably safe to enter and work in; (3) that B and B's fellow employees will do their work in a way that will not unreasonably endanger B's health and safety; and (4) that B is provided with the necessary plant and equipment to enable her to do her work without unreasonably endangering her health and safety and that that plant and equipment is reasonably safe to use.

This duty will rarely be displaced on the grounds that *volenti non fit injuria*. For example, the mere fact that B goes to work every day knowing that her workplace is not a reasonably safe place to work in does not establish that she is willing to work for A in a place of work that is not reasonably safe for her to work in.[64] In such a case – where B's only alternative to turning up for work is to quit her job and seek alternative employment on an uncertain job market – it cannot be said that B *willingly* chooses to work for A in a dangerous workplace when she continues to turn up for work in the knowledge that her workplace is not a reasonably safe place to work in.[65] Similarly, if A warned B before employing her that her future place of work would not be reasonably safe to work in and B agreed to work for A on that basis, B cannot be said to have *willingly* chosen to work for A in a dangerous workplace if her only reason for agreeing to work for A in the knowledge that doing so would involve an unreasonable risk of her being killed or injured was that she needed a job. So, in the case just described, A, having employed B, will – despite his warning to B – still owe B a duty to take reasonable steps to ensure that B's workplace is reasonably safe for her to work in.

How far does the duty that A will owe B to take reasonable steps to see that she will not be killed or injured working for him go? For example, suppose that A employs B to do a particular kind of work and it becomes clear that B is very likely to suffer injury if she is made to carry on doing that kind of work. No doubt in such a case it would be good practice for A to reassign B to some other kind of work which is less dangerous. But what if there is no other work available? Will A owe B a duty to dismiss her? For a long time, the courts took the view that A could not owe B such a duty.[66] However, in *Coxall v Goodyear GB Ltd*[67] Simon Brown LJ took the view that if the risk that B will be injured if she carries on working for A is serious enough then A may well owe B a duty to dismiss her.[68]

So far we have discussed the duty an employer will owe his employee to see that she is not *killed or injured* while working for him. Will he also owe her a duty to take reasonable steps to see that she will not suffer *other kinds of harm*? The decision of the House of Lords in *Frost v Chief Constable of South Yorkshire*[69] seems to establish that an employer will not owe his employees a *general* duty to take reasonable steps to see that they do not suffer any

64 *McCafferty v Metropolitan Police District Receiver* [1977] 1 WLR 1073.

65 *Smith v Baker* [1891] AC 325.

66 See *Withers v Perry Chain Co. Ltd* [1961] 1 WLR 1314, at 1317 (per Sellers LJ): 'I cannot believe that the common law requires employers to refuse to employ a person who is willing to work for them simply because they think that it is not in the person's best interests to do the work. That would be imposing a restriction on the freedom of the individual which I think is foreign to the whole spirit of the common law of our country.'

67 [2003] 1 WLR 536.

68 Ibid., at [29]. In *Barber v Somerset County Council* [2004] 1 WLR 1089, Lord Rodger of Earlsferry took much the same view, acknowledging that in cases where an employee would be exposed to a substantial risk of injury if he carried on working, his employer might owe him a duty to sack him: ibid., at [30].

69 [1999] 2 AC 455.

kind of *psychiatric illness* in working for him.[70] However, we have already seen that it is well established that if it is reasonably foreseeable that an employee will suffer a nervous breakdown if she is made to do a certain kind of work without any kind of assistance or counselling, then the employer will owe his employee a duty to take reasonable steps to see that she gets that assistance or counselling.[71] Furthermore, the House of Lords has held that it is strongly arguable that if A employs B and A knows or ought to know that B is being harassed to such an extent by her fellow employees that there is a danger she will suffer a breakdown, A will owe B a duty to take reasonable steps to stop the harassment.[72]

Turning to harms to property and economic harms, it seems that an employer will not owe an employee a duty to take reasonable steps to see that her property is not harmed while she is working for him;[73] neither will he owe her a duty to take reasonable steps to see that she does not suffer some kind of pure economic loss in working for him.[74]

BAILEES

If A holds B's goods on a bailment for B,[75] A will *normally* owe B a duty to take reasonable steps to ensure that those goods are not harmed.[76] (In such a case, A is said to be a 'bailee' of B's goods and B is said to be a 'bailor'.) A will hold B's goods on a bailment for B if he is *voluntarily in possession*[77] of those goods.[78] So if B drops a wallet in the street, and A picks it up, he will hold it on a bailment for B.[79] If, on the other hand, B sends some unsolicited

70 See also *French* v *Chief Constable of Sussex Police* [2006] EWCA Civ 312 (no duty to give police officers adequate training in running operations involving firearms even if it was foreseeable – which it was not – that failure to do so would result in police officers who were involved in a wrongful shooting suffering psychiatric illnesses as a result being subjected to criminal and disciplinary proceedings).

71 See above, pp. 112–14.

72 *Waters* v *Commissioner of Police of the Metropolis* [2000] 1 WLR 1607 (held that it was strongly arguable that this principle applied in the case where the defendant commissioner occupied a status analogous to an employer in relation to the claimant policewoman, who suffered a breakdown as a result of being subjected to severe harassment from her fellow police officers for reporting that she had been raped by a fellow police officer).

73 *Deyong* v *Shenburn* [1946] KB 227 (no duty to prevent theft of clothes from dressing room). However, if an employee's property is destroyed or damaged while she is working in her employer's factory, she may be able to bring a claim in negligence against her employer under the Occupiers' Liability Act 1957. See above, n. 5.

74 *Reid* v *Rush & Tompkins Group plc* [1990] 1 WLR 212 (no duty to advise employee of advisability of taking out insurance when working for defendant abroad).

75 It is possible for A to hold *someone else's* goods on a bailment for B. This will be the case where C delivers goods to B to look after them, and B then hands those goods over to A to look after them. In this case – what is called a 'sub-bailment' – A will hold C's goods on a bailment for B and will owe B a duty to take reasonable steps to see that they are not harmed. (Whether A will *also* hold C's goods on a bailment for *C* – and therefore owe *C* a duty to take reasonable steps to see that they are not harmed – will depend on whether A was aware that the goods in question were not B's when they were handed over to him: *The Pioneer Container* [1994] 2 AC 324, 342 (per Lord Goff); *Marcq* v *Christie's* [2003] 3 WLR 980, at [49]–[50].) If he breaches this duty and C's goods are lost as a result, he can be sued by B for the value of the goods, even if B has not actually suffered any loss as a result of C's goods being lost: *The Sanix Ace* [1987] 1 Lloyd's Rep 465. However, B will hold any damages so recovered on trust for C.

76 By 'harmed' here, we mean destroyed, damaged or stolen.

77 For an account of when someone will be held to be in 'possession' of goods, see below, pp. 347–9.

78 There is an exception where C hands goods over to A to look after them and then sells the goods to B while they are still in A's possession. In such a case, A will only hold those goods on a bailment for B if he attorns to B (that is, if he acknowledges that he holds those goods on a bailment for B): Palmer 2000, 359, 398.

79 Similarly if A steals B's wallet: ibid., 359; though see Bell 1998, 470.

goods to A through the post, A will not hold those goods on a bailment for B because he will not have voluntarily taken possession of those goods.[80]

If A holds B's goods on a bailment for B, he will not necessarily owe B a duty to take reasonable steps to ensure that those goods are not harmed. For example, if B asks A to look after his watch and A makes it clear at the time he accepts the watch that he does not want to be responsible for its safety, then A will not owe B a duty to take reasonable steps to ensure that the watch is not harmed: *volenti non fit injuria*. What is the position if B handed over some goods to C to look after them, and then C asked A to look after those goods – and A took possession of the goods, but only on condition that he would not be responsible for their safety? The first point to be made is that A will not have held the goods in question on a bailment for B unless he was aware at the time he accepted them that they were not C's.[81] If A was aware that the goods were not C's at the time he accepted them, then he will have held the goods on a bailment for B and will have owed B a duty to take reasonable steps to ensure that they were not harmed – *unless* B authorised C to sub-bail his goods on terms similar to those that C agreed with A.[82] If B did not give such authorisation, then A's agreement with C that he would not be responsible for the safety of B's goods will have no effect on B.

CARRIERS

As we have seen,[83] if A gives B a lift in his car, A will normally owe B a duty under the Occupiers' Liability Act 1957 to take reasonable steps to ensure that the condition of his car is such that B will be reasonably safe in taking a lift in his car. But A will, in any case, owe B a more general duty to take reasonable steps to ensure that B will not be killed or injured in taking a lift in his car.

For example, in *Jebson* v *Ministry of Defence*,[84] the claimant was a soldier who went to Portsmouth with some fellow soldiers for a night out. Anticipating that the claimant and his companions would be in no condition to get back to their barracks after their night out, the defendants – the claimant's employer – sent a lorry to take them back home. The claimant – who was considerably the worse for wear after his night out – attempted to climb onto the roof of the lorry as it took him back to barracks. Unfortunately for the claimant, he failed in his attempt and fell off the lorry and into the road, suffering various injuries in the process. He claimed that the defendants had owed him a duty to take reasonable steps to ensure that he would not suffer any kind of injury in travelling in their lorry and that they had breached that duty in failing to have someone in the back of the lorry to supervise him and his companions and to make sure that they did not – in their

[80] In such a situation, A will still owe B a duty under the 'property harm principle' (above, pp. 116–24) to take care not to damage the goods in question. A will, however, be free to treat the goods as his own to dispose of if he remains in possession of them six months after first receiving them or 30 days after he notified B that they were unsolicited and invited B to arrange to pick them up: Unsolicited Goods and Services Act 1971.

[81] See above, n. 75.

[82] *Morris* v *C W Martin Ltd* [1966] 1 QB 716, 729 (per Lord Denning MR); *The Pioneer Container* [1994] 2 AC 324.

[83] See above, p. 179.

[84] [2000] 1 WLR 2055.

drunken state – try to climb out of the lorry while it was travelling along. The Court of Appeal allowed the claimant's claim.

PARENTS

It seems to be well established that a parent will owe his or her children a duty to take reasonable steps to ensure that they do not come to any harm.[85]

The point is for the most part academic. Suppose a child, Beth, suffered some kind of injury because of her father's carelessness. Beth will, generally speaking, have no incentive to sue her father for damages as suing him for such damages will usually only deprive him of money that he needs to raise Beth. However, the point made here becomes of great importance in the case where Eric, a car driver, carelessly runs down and injures Wendy, a child. If Mary, Wendy's mother, carelessly allowed Wendy to run into the road, Eric – on being sued for damages by Wendy – will be able to make a claim for contribution against Mary, arguing that Mary is just as liable as he is to compensate Wendy for her injuries. The end result is that Wendy will not be fully compensated for her injuries as, in practice, the claim in contribution against Mary will have to be satisfied out of the proceeds of Wendy's claim against Eric.

Section 2 of the Congenital Disabilities (Civil Liability) Act 1976 establishes that if Ruth is pregnant and is driving a car, Ruth will be 'under the same duty to take care for the safety of her unborn child as the law imposes on her with respect to the safety of other people'. So Ruth will owe her unborn child a duty to take care not to drive dangerously. It may be asked why this is. Why will Ruth owe her unborn child a duty of care *while she is driving* but not in other situations? For example, why will Ruth not owe her unborn child a duty to take care not to drink alcohol or smoke or fall down the stairs? The answer is that it would be pointless to hold that Ruth owes her unborn child a duty to take care not to do these things. Suppose, for example, that Ruth drinks heavily while she is pregnant and as a result her baby when it is born suffers from certain disabilities. And suppose we conceded that while the baby was in Ruth's womb, Ruth owed the baby a duty not to drink heavily. This concession would allow Ruth's baby to sue Ruth for compensation for the fact that he was born disabled – but why would he? He would only deprive Ruth of money that she needs to raise him.

It is different if Ruth drives her car while she is pregnant in such a dangerous manner that she ends up crashing the car, with the result that her baby is born disabled. In such a case, Ruth will have liability insurance that will cover her if she is held liable to compensate her baby for the fact that he has been born disabled as a result of her dangerous driving. So saying that in this case Ruth owed her unborn baby a duty to take care not to drive dangerously will serve a useful purpose. Ruth's baby will be able to sue her for the fact that he has been born disabled – but the damages payable will not come out of Ruth's pocket; rather they will come out of the pocket of Ruth's liability insurer.

[85] *Surtees* v *Kingston-upon-Thames Borough Council* [1991] 2 FLR 559.

TEACHERS

It seems well established that a teacher will owe the students in his charge a duty to take reasonable steps to see that those students do not come to any harm while on the school premises.[86] As Lord Clyde observed in the recent case of *Phelps* v *Hillingdon London Borough Council*: '[there] is no question that a teacher owes a duty of care for the physical safety of a child attending school under the charge of that teacher. The teacher has a duty to take reasonable care that the child does not come to any harm through any danger which may arise during the course of the child's attendance at the school.'[87]

It also seems to be accepted that if a student has 'special needs' or suffers from learning difficulties, his teachers will owe him a duty to take reasonable steps to ensure that that student is not disadvantaged as a result of the fact that he suffers from those special needs or learning difficulties. So in *X* v *Bedfordshire County Council*, Lord Browne-Wilkinson held – with the agreement of the other Law Lords deciding the case – that if 'it comes to the attention of [a] headmaster that a pupil is under-performing, he does owe a duty to take such steps as a reasonable teacher would consider appropriate to try to deal with such under-performance'.[88] In the *Phelps* case the House of Lords refused to strike out a number of claims which were premised on the basis that the teachers of a student who suffers from special needs or learning difficulties will owe him a duty to take reasonable steps to ensure that that student is not disadvantaged from the fact that he suffers from those special needs or learning difficulties. The House of Lords held it was arguable that the teacher of a student who suffers from special needs or learning difficulties would owe him such a duty of care. Lord Nicholls – with the agreement of Lord Jauncey of Tullichettle – went further and held that 'a teacher [will] owe a duty of care to a child with learning difficulties . . . A teacher must exercise due skill and care to respond appropriately to the manifest problems of such a child, including informing the head-teacher or others about the child's problems and carrying out any instructions he is given.'[89]

The cases do not go so far as to say that the teachers of a *normal* student will owe him a duty to teach him with reasonable skill and care. Lord Nicholls held that the teachers of a normal student would owe him such a duty of care in *Phelps*[90] but only one of the other six Law Lords who decided *Phelps* indicated that he agreed with Lord Nicholls on this point.

CHILD PROTECTION AND CHILD CARE AGENCIES

As we have just seen, the courts seem very willing to carve out special exceptions to the general rule that there is no duty to rescue when it is a child that is in need of rescue. This willingness is further reflected in two cases which impose on the social services special duties to help needy children.

[86] The duty does not extend to seeing that the child does not come to any harm off the school premises: *Bradford-Smart* v *West Sussex County Council* [2002] EWCA Civ 7 (discussed, Elvin 2003b).

[87] [2001] 2 AC 619, 670. See also *Van Oppen* v *Clerk to Bedford Charity Trustees* [1990] 1 WLR 235, at 250 (per Balcombe LJ). The same is true of educational authorities: see *New South Wales* v *Lepore* (2003) 212 CLR 511.

[88] [1995] 2 AC 633, 766.

[89] [2001] 2 AC 619, 667.

[90] Ibid.

In *D* v *East Berkshire Community NHS Trust*,[91] the Court of Appeal held that if the social services receive reports that a child is being abused and the social services decide to investigate those reports, the social services will owe the child in question a duty to investigate the reports with a reasonable degree of care and skill.[92]

In *Barrett* v *Enfield LBC*[93] the claimant had been taken into care by the social services when he was 10 months old. He stayed in care until he was 18 years old. In that time – the claimant alleged – he was placed with two foster families, and was moved into six different homes in 12 years. The claimant further alleged that the social services made no proper attempt to have someone adopt him, or to reunite him with his mother. The claimant sued the social services in negligence, claiming that they had owed him a duty to raise him with a reasonable degree of care and skill, and that he had developed psychological problems as a result of the social services' breaching that duty of care. The House of Lords unanimously held that it was arguable that the social services had owed the claimant a duty of care once they had taken him into care. Given the endorsement that the decision in *Barrett* subsequently received from the House of Lords in *Gorringe* v *Calderdale MBC*,[94] it may be that there is no longer any doubt that the social services will owe a duty of care to someone in the position of the claimant in *Barrett*.

Visit **http://www.mylawchamber.co.uk/mcbride** to access updates on recent cases, as well as model answers and tips for answering tort problem questions.

Use **Case Navigator** to read in full some of the key cases referenced in this chapter:

- **Fairchild *v* Glenhaven Funeral Services Ltd**
- **Tomlinson *v* Congleton BC**
- **Frost *v* Chief Constable of South Yorkshire**
- **Phelps *v* Hillingdon London Borough Council**
- **D *v* East Berkshire Community NHS Trust**

[91] *D* v *East Berkshire Community NHS Trust* [2004] QB 558.

[92] The position in New Zealand is the same: see *Attorney-General* v *Prince* [1998] 1 NZLR 262 (NZCA) and *B* v *Attorney-General* [2003] 4 All ER 833 (PC). In *X* v *Bedfordshire CC* [1995] 2 AC 633, the House of Lords refused to find that the social services would owe A such a duty of care, fearing that such a finding would induce the social services to become excessively cautious in investigating and acting on allegations of child abuse: ibid., at 650. However, it has since become clear that if the social services take a child into care who is not at risk of being abused, or fail to take a child into care when he is being abused, the child may be able to sue the social services under the Human Rights Act 1998 (in the first case, for violating his rights to privacy and family life under Art 8 of the ECHR; in the second case, for violating his rights to be free of cruel and degrading treatment under Art 3 of the ECHR): see *TP and KM* v *United Kingdom* [2001] 2 FLR 549 and *Z* v *United Kingdom* [2001] 2 FLR 612. Given this, the Court of Appeal in the *D* case thought there was little point in continuing to rule in *X*-type cases that no duty of care would be owed by the social services to a child whose case they were investigating: such a ruling would attempt to preserve for the social services an immunity from being sued that no longer existed.

[93] [2001] 2 AC 550.

[94] [2004] 1 WLR 1057.

9 Duties of care: evaluation of the current law

It is beyond the scope of this book to evaluate the whole of the law on when one person will and will not owe another a duty of care. Instead, this chapter will do two things.

The first part of this chapter will explain what factors the courts should take into account in determining whether or not one person will owe another a duty of care in a given situation.[1] This should give you a basis for judging whether or not the law is justified in saying that A will (or will not) owe B a duty of care in a given situation. All you have to do is say – would someone who took into account all the relevant factors that should be taken into account in determining whether A will or will not owe B a duty of care in that situation reach the same conclusion? If the answer is 'yes' then the law is *correct* to say that A will (or will not) owe B a duty of care in that situation. If the answer is 'no' then the law is *wrong* to say that A will (or will not) owe B a duty of care in that situation.

In the second part of this chapter, we will focus on ten situations where the law says that A will *not* owe B a duty of care. In each of these situations, either (1) A causes B to suffer some kind of pure economic loss; or (2) A fails to save B from suffering some kind of harm; or (3) A is a public body and B suffers harm as a result of A's acts or omissions. Some academics and judges take the view that the law is too restrictive in denying that a duty of care will be owed in these situations. We will see whether, taking into account all the relevant factors identified in the first part of this chapter, the law is in fact justified in refusing to say that a duty of care will be owed in these situations.

FACTORS RELEVANT TO AN INQUIRY INTO WHETHER A DUTY OF CARE WILL BE OWED IN A GIVEN SITUATION

The basic question

When the law says that A will owe B a duty of care in a given situation, it limits A's *liberty* in order to increase B's *security*. It declares that A ought to do something that he might not otherwise choose to do,[2] and it does so in order to protect B's interests.[3] So, for example, when the law holds that A, a driver, will owe a duty to B, a pedestrian using a nearby crossing, to drive his car towards the crossing at a reasonable speed, the law limits A's liberty to drive towards the crossing at a higher speed, and it does so in order to protect better B's person and property. It follows from this that in determining whether A will owe B a duty

1 This is a slightly different exercise from the one we engaged in above, at pp. 59–70, of describing what factors the courts *will* take into account in determining whether or not a duty of care was owed in a given situation. In this chapter, we explain what factors the courts *should* take into account in determining whether or not a duty of care was owed in a given situation. Of course, there will be a substantial overlap between the two lists.

2 For a detailed defence of this view, see McBride 2004.

3 Remember that we can only say that a duty of care is *owed* to a particular person if it was imposed for that person's benefit: see above, p. 3.

of care in a given situation the basic question the courts have to ask themselves is – Is limiting A's liberty in this situation a price worth paying to increase B's security? In addressing this issue, the following factors seem to us highly relevant:

The importance of A's freedom

Some freedoms are so important that the courts cannot justifiably place *any* limits on their exercise. An obvious example: suppose that A and B are engaged to be married. A breaks off the engagement. B is very distressed and sues A in negligence for compensation. The courts *cannot* say that A owed B a duty not to break up with her, because that would limit his freedom to choose who to marry.

Other freedoms are so important that the courts can only justifiably limit them if they have *very* good reason for doing so. An example is the freedom to choose who to work for, and on what terms. This freedom is so important that the courts will only usually place A under a duty to work for B if A has *agreed* to work for B *and* B has agreed to *pay* A to work for him. However, as we have seen, if A has told B that he will perform some task for B with a reasonable degree of care and skill and B relies on A to perform that task with that degree of care and skill, the courts will find that A owed B a duty under the extended principle in *Hedley Byrne* to do what he said he would do – and this is so even if B never offered to pay A a penny for his services. The fact that B is relying on A justifies the courts' limiting A's freedom to choose whether or not to work for her.

Whether subjecting A to a duty of care will effectively diminish his/her freedom

Suppose that the courts want to determine whether, in a given situation, A will owe B a duty of care to save B from being beaten up. If finding that A will owe B such a duty of care will not *effectively* diminish A's freedom, then obviously the courts will find it very easy to conclude that placing A under a duty of care to save B from being beaten up is a price worth paying to increase B's security.

Now – in what situations will finding that A owes B a duty of care to save B from being beaten up *not* effectively diminish A's freedom? Well, if A has already indicated that he will take care to save B from being beaten up (that is, he has already 'assumed a responsibility' to take care of B) then finding that A owes B a duty of care to save B from being beaten up will not effectively diminish A's freedom. A has already made clear that he wants to look after B, and you do not take away someone's freedom by making them do what they already want to do. Similarly, if A already owes someone else, or the public at large, a duty of care to save B from being beaten up, then finding that A owes *B* a duty of care to save B from being beaten up will not effectively limit A's freedom. A has already lost the effective freedom to choose not to save B from being beaten up.

The importance of B's interests

On the other side of the equation, the courts must – in deciding whether limiting A's freedom is a price worth paying to increase B's security – take into account the severity of the harm B will suffer if A is allowed to do what he likes. So it is easier to accept that limiting A's freedom is a price worth paying to protect B from suffering *physical harm* than it is to accept that limiting A's freedom is a price worth paying to protect B from suffering *pure distress*.

The harm that might be done to B as a result of subjecting A to a duty of care

If finding that A owes B a duty of care in a given situation will do B more harm than good, limiting A's freedom will not increase B's overall security and the courts should not find that A will owe B a duty of care.

For example, in *Barrett* v *Ministry of Defence*,[4] the Court of Appeal denied that officers in charge of a military barracks will owe the soldiers at the barracks a duty to stop them getting excessively drunk at a party because finding that such a duty is owed might actually encourage soldiers not to monitor their own alcohol intake and rely on their officers to stop them drinking when they have had enough.[5]

Again, in *White* v *Chief Constable of South Yorkshire*,[6] Lord Steyn suggested that one reason why the courts have been cautious about recognising the existence of duties to take care to protect someone else against suffering psychiatric harm is that the prospect of recovery of compensation for psychiatric harm that the recognition of such duties introduces may actually work to the long-term harm of the people to whom those duties are owed:

> Where there is generally no prospect of recovery, such as in the case of injuries sustained in sport, psychiatric harm appears not to obtrude often. On the other hand, in the case of industrial accidents, where there is often a prospect of recovery of compensation, psychiatric harm is repeatedly encountered and often endures until the process of claiming compensation comes to an end ... The litigation is sometimes an unconscious disincentive to rehabilitation. It is true that this factor is already present in cases of physical injuries with concomitant mental suffering. But it may play a larger role in cases of pure psychiatric harm, particularly if the categories of potential recovery are enlarged.[7]

Similar concerns led Lord Denning MR to deny that the defendant contractors in *Spartan Steel & Alloys Ltd* v *Martin & Co. (Contractors) Ltd*[8] owed a duty of care to the claimant factory owners not to cause them economic loss by interrupting the power supply to their factory. Lord Denning feared that recognising the existence of such a duty of care might have an adverse effect on factory owners like the claimants:

> [the] hazard [of suffering economic loss as a result of a power cut] is regarded by most people as a thing they must put up with – without seeking compensation from anyone. Some there are who instal a stand-by system. Others seek refuge by taking out an insurance policy against breakdown in the supply. But most people are content to take the risk on themselves. When the supply is cut off, they do not go running round to their solicitor. They do not try to find out whether it was anyone's fault. They just put up with it. They try to make up the economic loss by doing more work next day. This is a healthy attitude which the law should encourage.[9]

Adverse side effects

Suppose the courts are considering whether or not A will owe B a duty of care in a given situation. And suppose that – taking into account the above factors – the courts find that

[4] [1995] 1 WLR 1217.
[5] Ibid., 1224.
[6] [1999] 2 AC 455.
[7] Ibid., at 494.
[8] [1973] 1 QB 27.
[9] Ibid., 38.

limiting A's freedom would be a price worth paying to increase B's security. If this is the case then – in principle – the courts should recognise that A will owe B a duty of care. However, this is only in principle. It may still be wrong for the courts to find that A owes B a duty of care. This will be the case if such a finding would have some adverse side effect that will outweigh the benefit to B of finding that A owes B a duty of care. There are range of adverse side effects that might be caused by such a finding.

Damaging the rule of law

The first set of adverse side effects can be grouped together under the heading '*damaging the rule of law*'. The rule of law in England is damaged whenever something happens to make the English legal system work less effectively as a system for guiding and controlling people's behaviour. The legal philosopher Lon Fuller famously set out what ideals and principles would have to be observed by a legal system to make it work effectively as a system for guiding and controlling people's behaviour. He said that: (1) the legal system's laws must be public; (2) they must be clear and certain; (3) they must be prospective and not retroactive; (4) they must not contradict each other; (5) they must not place unreasonable demands on the people who are subject to them; (6) they must be stable; and (7) they must be followed, applied and enforced by those in charge of the legal system.[10] It follows from this that there are a number of different ways that recognising that A will owe B a duty of care in a given situation might damage the rule of law in England. The most important for our purposes are:

(1) *Making the law unclear or uncertain.* A concern to avoid uncertainty or lack of clarity in the law may be one of the reasons why the courts have so far been unwilling to recognise the existence of a general 'duty to rescue' in English law. As Richard Epstein points out, 'Once one decides that . . . an individual is required under some circumstances to act at his own cost for the exclusive benefit of another, then it is very hard to set out in a principled manner the limits of social interference with individual liberty.'[11] He asks, for example: If we admit that someone crossing a bridge has a duty to throw a rope to someone drowning in the waters below, would someone who is asked to donate a very small amount of money to charity to help save a life have a legal duty to make that donation? If a patient needed a life-saving operation which only one surgeon in the world could perform, would that surgeon come under a legal duty to travel to the patient's bedside and perform that operation – assuming of course that someone could be found who would be willing to cover his travel expenses?[12] Rather than confront these difficult questions, the English courts have preferred to adopt the *simpler, clearer and more certain* position that A is under no duty to attempt to rescue a stranger, B, from a danger if A played no role in creating the danger and is not otherwise responsible for it – and this is so no matter how easy the rescue might be and no matter how serious and imminent the danger B is in.

(2) *Making the law unduly onerous.* One of the reasons why it is *not* the law that if it is reasonably foreseeable that A's doing x will cause B to suffer some kind of pure economic

[10] Fuller 1964, 39.
[11] Epstein 1973, 198.
[12] Ibid., 198–9. The examples involving the bridge and the life-saving operation are both found in Ames 1908.

loss A will normally owe B a duty to take care not to do *x*, is that if this were the law, we would each be potentially subject to a huge and oppressive number of duties of care.[13] This is because it is impossible for an ordinary participant in modern life to avoid making a host of decisions every day which will bring about economic gains for some and losses for others. No doubt a person could, if pressed, demonstrate that most of these decisions were reasonable. But it can be argued that it would be intolerable for the law to impose such a burden of demonstration on each of us. People should not be told that it is their legal duty to take care of the economic interests of a host of others when making routine, everyday decisions. Such duties would subject too much of everyday life to legal regulation.

(3) *Making the law unstable.* One of the reasons why the *Anns* test for determining whether a duty of care was owed in a novel case[14] was abandoned by the courts was that it injected too much instability into the law of negligence. Because different judges have different views as to what is contrary to 'public policy' – just as different people have different views as to what is and what is not in the public interest – different judges would reach different conclusions as to whether A would owe B a duty of care in a given situation under the *Anns* test. So one set of judges – operating from a certain set of preconceptions as to what is contrary to 'public policy' – would rule that A would owe B a duty of care and then their rulings would be overturned by a different set of judges – operating from a different standpoint as to what is contrary to 'public policy' – who would rule that A would not owe B a duty of care. Stability in the law of negligence was impossible to attain because decisions as to whether a duty of care would be owed in a given case were based on shifting and unstable perceptions as to what was contrary to 'public policy'.

(4) *Making the law difficult to apply.* One criticism that has been made of the decision of the House of Lords in *Alcock* v *Chief Constable of South Yorkshire*[15] is that the House of Lords was only willing to recognise that the defendants owed a duty of care to the claimants in that case if the claimants could establish that they were in a 'close and loving relationship' with someone who was killed as a result of the defendants' actions. One understands the reason behind this aspect of the House of Lords' ruling: if the claimants were *not* in a 'close and loving relationship' with someone who was killed as a result of the defendants' actions, it was hardly reasonably foreseeable that the defendants' actions would result in the claimants developing a psychiatric illness. And yet it must be very difficult – in a case where A did something that resulted in C in being killed or injured and B, a relative or friend of C's, developed a psychiatric illness as a result – for the courts to determine whether B was in a 'close and loving relationship' with C. The issue is close to what lawyers call *non-justiciable*: an issue that is so far beyond the expertise of the courts that the courts cannot be asked to reach a conclusion on it. So the decision of the House of Lords in *Alcock* can be criticised for undermining the rule of law because it makes the law on when A will owe B a duty of care in the situation just set out very difficult to apply. It would have been preferable, some have argued, for the House of Lords to have ruled in *Alcock* that in this kind of situation A will *never* be found to have owed B a duty

[13] Cf. Goldberg & Zipursky 1998, 1833: 'To add ... [a] general [duty] to take care to avoid causing economic injuries [to all the other duties of care we owe others] would be enormously burdensome.'

[14] See above, p. 57.

[15] [1992] 1 AC 310.

of care not to kill or injure C.[16] Such a ruling would at least have had the merit of ensuring that the law in this area is easy to apply, which it is not at the moment.

(5) *Making the law difficult to enforce.* There is a natural limit on how many laws a legal system can effectively enforce. This limit is set by the number of courts a legal system employs and the resources that go into funding those courts. If this limit is breached then a number of a legal system's laws will effectively go unenforced – the legal system's courts will not have enough time or money to deal with breaches of those laws. Too many laws are as bad for a legal system in the same way that too much fat is bad for a human being – they slow the legal system down and make it unable to operate effectively as a legal system. So – like a doctor deciding what patients to treat in the limited time available to him – those in charge of running a legal system have to be *discriminating* about what laws to create. They can only create a limited number, and as a result have to ensure that the laws they do create are the ones that it is most pressing for people to observe.

Identical considerations apply to the courts when they decide what duties of care they will recognise. There is a natural limit to how many duties of care the English legal system can effectively enforce – and it is unlikely that it can effectively enforce all of the duties of care that it might, in principle, be desirable to recognise. So the courts have to prioritise and limit themselves to recognising the duties of care that it is most pressing that people observe. Doing more than this will fur up the arteries of the English legal system and severely impair its capacity to compel people to observe the duties of care that it recognises. This concern – a concern not to recognise 'too many duties' – may be one of the reasons why the courts are cautious about recognising duties to take care not to cause someone else to suffer pure economic loss.[17] Were such duties recognised, one would expect the courts to become clogged up with claims in negligence for pure economic loss, and the courts' ability to enforce more important duties of care – such as duties to take care not to cause other people to suffer physical injury or psychiatric illness – would be impaired as a result.

Bringing the law into disrepute

The second set of possibly adverse side effects that might result from recognising that A will owe B a duty of care in a given situation can be grouped together under the heading '*bringing the law into disrepute*'. The law is brought into disrepute when it is seen to run counter to the values of the ordinary people it is supposed to serve.

We have already seen one example of the courts' refusing to find a duty of care because to do so would have brought the law into disrepute. In *Frost* v *Chief Constable of South Yorkshire*,[18] the House of Lords refused to find that the senior police officers in charge at the Hillsborough tragedy had owed the claimant police officers a duty of care not to cause the tragedy. To do otherwise would have brought the law into disrepute given the outcome of the earlier *Alcock* case,[19] where the House of Lords denied that a duty of care had been owed to friends and relatives of those who died at Hillsborough who developed a psychi-

[16] See Stapleton 1994b.

[17] See, for example, Lord Denning MR in *Spartan Steel & Alloys Ltd* v *Martin & Co. (Contractors) Ltd* [1973] QB 27, at 38–9.

[18] [1999] 2 AC 455.

[19] *Alcock* v *Chief Constable of South Yorkshire Police* [1992] 1 AC 310.

atric illness as a result. The law could not be seen to be doing more for the police than it was willing to do for the friends and relatives of the deceased.

There are three very important ways in which recognising the existence of a duty of care might bring the law into disrepute:

(1) *Treating the bad more favourably than the good.* Suppose that Ian was on a deserted beach and he saw that Nita was drowning in the sea. Suppose further that he left Nita to her fate and lay down to sunbathe, with the result that Nita drowned. As we have seen, the courts will not find that Ian owed Nita a duty to take reasonable steps to save her from drowning: there existed no 'special relationship' between them that would warrant the courts' finding that Ian owed Nita a positive duty to make her better off and save her from drowning.

Now consider an alternative scenario. Suppose that Ian tried to rescue Nita but he botched his rescue effort and Nita still drowned. Should we say in this case that Ian owed Nita a duty to take reasonable steps to save her from drowning? Considerations of individual liberty might not apply here to demand that we find that Ian did not owe Nita a duty of care – after all, Ian of his own free will acknowledged that he should rescue Nita, and he attempted to save her. But the law would be brought into disrepute if we found that a duty of care was owed in this alternative scenario.[20] The reason is that if we find that a duty of care was owed in this case, we will be treating good Ian (who tried to rescue Nita but failed) more harshly than bad Ian (who never made any attempt at all to rescue Nita). We will subject good Ian to a duty of care – and a potential liability to pay other people damages – while letting bad Ian off scot-free. Fortunately, while there are some dangerous *dicta* to the contrary,[21] the balance of authority is in favour of the view that in the alternative scenario described above, Ian will *not* have owed Nita a duty to take reasonable steps to save her from drowning.[22]

This elementary point about the importance of not treating the bad more favourably than the good also explains why if Lara is being beaten up on the street Gary, a passing police officer, will *not* owe Lara a duty to take reasonable steps to save her from being harmed.[23] Again, considerations of individual liberty cannot explain why Gary does not

[20] McBride 2006b, 12–13.

[21] *Banbury* v *Bank of Montreal* [1918] AC 626, 689, per Lord Atkinson: 'It is well established that if a doctor proceeded to treat a patient gratuitously, even in a case where the patient was insensible at the time and incapable of employing him, the doctor would be bound to exercise all the professional skill and knowledge he possessed, or professed to possess, and would be guilty of gross negligence if he omitted to do so'; *Hedley Byrne & Co. Ltd* v *Heller & Partners* [1964] AC 465, 495, per Lord Morris: 'A medical man may unexpectedly come across an unconscious man, who is a complete stranger to him, and who is in urgent need of skilled attention: if the medical man, following the fine traditions of his profession, proceeds to treat the unconscious man he must exercise reasonable skill and care in doing so.' See also GS&Z, 100.

[22] *Horsley* v *MacLaren, The Ogopogo* [1970] 1 Lloyd's Rep 257, 263: 'even if a person embarks upon a rescue and does not carry it through, he is not under any liability to the person to whose aid he had come so long as discontinuance of his efforts did not leave the other in a worse condition than when he took charge' (per Schroeder JA, in the Ontario Court of Appeal; the case was appealed to the Supreme Court of Canada, but the Supreme Court found it unncessary to deal with the issue raised by Schroeder JA's *dictum*: [1971] 2 Lloyd's Rep 410); *Capital & Counties Plc* v *Hampshire CC* [1997] QB 1004, 1035 (per Stuart-Smith LJ): 'If [a passing doctor] volunteers his assistance [to help the victim of a traffic accident], his only duty as a matter of law is [to take care] not to make the victim's condition worse.'

[23] See *Osman* v *Ferguson* [1993] 4 All ER 344 (if A is very likely to be attacked by a criminal who is currently on the run, the police will not owe A a duty to catch the criminal before he attacks A); *Ancell* v *McDermott* [1993] 4 All ER 355 (a policeman who comes across a dangerous oil slick in the middle of a road will not owe a duty

owe Lara a duty of care in this case – Gary has, of his own free will, opted to become a police officer and one of his responsibilities as a police officer is to save people from harm. But the law would be brought into disrepute if Gary were found to owe Lara a duty of care here.[24] If Gary had not chosen to become a police officer but had instead made the selfish choice to become (say) a merchant banker, and had passed Lara by on his way home from work while she was being beaten up, the courts would not find that Gary owed Lara a duty to save her from being beaten up. So if the courts found that police officer Gary owed Lara a duty to save her from being beaten up, they would be effectively punishing him for his public-spirited choice to become a police officer. They would be guilty of treating the 'good' – that is, those who choose to work for the public good by entering the police force – less favourably than the 'bad' – that is, those use their talents exclusively for their own benefit.

(2) *Undermining democracy*. Suppose that a council decides to cut back on the funding it provides to pay for dyslexic children to be educated at specialist schools. As a result, B – a dyslexic child – is educated at a normal State school. On leaving school, B sues the council in negligence for compensation, claiming that her education suffered as a result of the council's decision to cut funds to people like her. The law would be brought into disrepute if the courts said that the council owed B a duty not to cut the funding available to people like her. This is because such a ruling would undermine democracy. The council (and, by extension, voters in the council's district) would no longer be in charge of decisions as to how to budget its money; instead, the courts would be in charge.

For the same reasons, the law would be brought into disrepute if the courts ruled that A will owe B a duty of care not to do *x* in a given situation when Parliament had already legislated to determine what duties of care would be owed by A to B in that situation and had *not* provided that A would owe B a duty of care not to do *x*. The courts' ruling would have the effect of undermining Parliament's decision as to what duties of care A should owe B in the situation at hand. So, for example, in *Murphy* v *Brentwood DC*[25] the House of Lords held that a builder will *not* owe future owners of a house he is building a duty to take care not to build the house in such a way that it will need to be repaired in future. One of the reasons they gave for so holding was that Parliament had already passed legislation – in the shape of the Defective Premises Act 1972 – to determine when a builder would owe duties of care to future owners of a house he was building and the House of Lords thought it improper to interfere with the scheme of duties of care created by that Act.[26]

Again, the law would be brought into disrepute if the courts ruled that, in a given situation, A will owe B a duty to exercise some statutory power that it has been given by

---

to oncoming motorists to warn them of the danger). It should be noted that English law is very much out on its own in taking this stance: other common law jurisdictions might well find that Gary *did* owe Lara a duty to take reasonable steps to save her from being beaten up. See, for example, *O'Rourke* v *Schacht* [1976] 1 SCR 53 (held, a policeman who becomes aware that there is an unprotected hole in the middle of the road will owe a duty to oncoming motorists to warn them of the danger).

24 Contra, Gray & Edelman 1998, arguing that because Gary *took on the job* of saving people like Lara, he *should* be held to owe people like Lara a duty to take reasonable steps to save them from harm. To the same effect, see Stevens 2007, 11–12. But why? Why should Spiderman be subject to duties that he would not be subject to were he to put away his costume and remain plain old Peter Parker?

25 [1991] 1 AC 398.

26 Ibid., at 457, 472, 480–1, 491–2 and 498.

Parliament when Parliament made it clear, in granting A that power, that it should be up to A to decide how and when to exercise that power. Such a ruling would tend to undermine democracy: the courts would be in the position of dictating to A what to do with the power granted it by Parliament when Parliament intended that A should be free to choose what to do with that power. It was for this reason – among others[27] – that the House of Lords in *Stovin* v *Wise*[28] declined to find that a duty of care was owed in that case by the defendant highway authority to users of a particular highway under the authority's control. It had been claimed that the highway authority owed users of the highway a duty to exercise its statutory powers[29] and demolish a raised bank that made it difficult for drivers joining the highway to see whether there was any oncoming traffic going down the highway. On the facts, the House of Lords found that Parliament intended that the highway authority should be free to choose whether to use the powers Parliament gave it to do anything about the raised bank,[30] and it would therefore be inappropriate for the House of Lords to find that the highway authority had actually owed users of the highway a *duty* to demolish the bank.

As we have already seen, if Parliament has imposed a statutory duty on A to do something for B but has made it clear that breach of that duty should not be actionable in tort, the courts will not find that A owes B a duty of care in negligence to help her out if the sole basis for doing so is the mere fact that A is subject to a statutory duty to assist B.[31] If the courts did otherwise, then they would undermine democracy and bring the law into disrepute. To find that A owes B a duty of care based solely on the fact that he is subject to a statutory duty to help her out would undermine Parliament's intention that any breach of that statutory duty should not be actionable in tort.

(3) *Disproportionate liability*. Although English law does not insist that awards of damages in tort are proportionate to the defendant's fault for causing the harm he did, most people would regard it as unfair if a defendant's liability in tort became wholly disproportionate to his fault. So, for example, most people would regard it as unfair if a defendant were held personally liable to pay millions of pounds to a claimant for some harm suffered by the claimant as a result of a momentary lapse of attention on the part of the defendant while

[27] *Important note*. As the House of Lords pointed out in *Gorringe* v *Calderdale MBC* [2004] 1 WLR 1057, the *major* reason for finding that no duty of care was owed in *Stovin* v *Wise* was that the defendant highway authority in that case had merely failed to confer a benefit on the claimant, and in the absence of any special circumstances or special relationship between the defendant authority and the claimant, it was impossible to find that the defendant authority had owed the claimant a duty to save her from suffering an accident on the road: see above, pp. 65, 156. For an explanation of the general 'no liability for omissions' rule as it applies to public bodies, see below, pp. 205–8.

[28] [1996] AC 923.

[29] Under s 79(1) of the Highways Act 1980, which provides that: 'When the highway authority ... deem[s] it necessary for the prevention of danger arising from obstruction to the view of persons using the highway to impose restrictions with respect to any land at ... any junction of the highway with a road ... the authority *may* ... serve a notice ... on the owner or occupier of the land, directing him to alter any wall ... so as to cause it to conform with any requirements specified in the notice' (emphasis added). Section 79(17) of the same Act defines 'wall' as including any 'bank'.

[30] Crucial to this conclusion was the majority's finding ([1996] AC 923, at 957) that it would *not* have been wholly unreasonable for the highway authority to leave the raised bank in place. Had it – as the minority contended (ibid., at 936) – been wholly unreasonable for the highway authority not to do anything about the raised bank, we can safely presume that Parliament intended that the highway authority *should* use its powers to demolish the bank when it granted the authority those powers.

[31] See above, p. 65.

driving.[32] We have already seen that this is the key reason why, if A has carelessly killed or injured B, with the result that C, D, E and F have all suffered psychiatric illnesses, the courts make it so difficult to find that A owed any of these 'secondary victims' a duty to take care not to kill or injure B.[33] Were the courts to find that A owed all of these 'secondary victims' such a duty of care, his liabilities arising out of B's being injured or killed would soon get out of all proportion to his fault.

Making the law overbearing

As we have seen, the basic question the courts have to ask themselves, in deciding whether to find that A owes B a duty of care in a given situation, is: Would limiting A's freedom be a price worth paying to increase B's security? If the answer is 'yes' then we can not only say that, in principle, the courts should find that A owes B a duty of care in the situation under discussion, but we can also say that *morally* A *should* take care to look out for B's interests in that situation. This is because if the answer to our basic question is 'yes' then A's freedom to choose what to do is less valuable than B's security – and so A should give up his freedom to choose what to do and instead seek to take care of B's interests.

It follows from all of this that when the courts impose a duty of care on any of us, they are in effect compelling us to do the right thing. It *also* follows from all of this that if, in a particular situation, taking care of B's interests would be the right thing for A to do, then, *in principle*, the courts *should* find that A owes B a duty of care in that situation. This is because if taking care of B's interests would be the right thing for A to do, then that shows that A's freedom to choose what to do is less important than B's security, and so limiting A's freedom is a price worth paying to increase B's security. So if the moral philosophers tell us that in a particular situation A *should* take care of B's interests, then it follows that *in principle* the courts *should* find that A owes B a duty of care in that situation.[34]

It is right to say, then, that the law on when one person will owe another a duty of care both *enforces* and *tracks* morality. But this does *not* mean that *whenever* A has a moral duty to take care of B's interests the courts should find that A owes B a duty of care.[35] This is not just because finding that A owes B a duty of care may have one of the adverse side effects listed above or below. It is also because – or so it seems to us – people must be given *some* leeway to do the wrong thing, or to act unreasonably, free from any kind of sanction from the State. If they are not given such leeway, then the law becomes oppressive and overbearing. There are two reasons why – or so it seems to us – the law needs to give people some room to do the wrong thing:

(1) *Fostering social relationships.* Tony Weir observes that, 'The understandable urge to bring legal standards up to those of delicate morality should be resisted, or there would be

[32] Of course, any incipient outrage at such an award would inevitably be defused by the fact that the driver's liability will always be covered by insurance.

[33] See above, pp. 98–100.

[34] Cf. Lord Atkin in *Donoghue* v *Stevenson* [1932] AC 562, at 583: 'I do not think so ill of our jurisprudence as to suppose that its principles are so remote from the ordinary needs of civilized society and the ordinary claims it makes upon its members as to deny a legal remedy where there is so obviously a social wrong.'

[35] Ibid., at 580: '. . . acts or omissions which any moral code would censure cannot in a practical world be treated so as to give a right to every person injured by them to demand relief. In this way rules of law arise which limit the range of complainants and the extent of their remedy.'

no room for generosity or for people to go beyond the call of legal duty.'[36] The conservative commentator Dinesh D'Souza explains why this is so important:

> [Suppose] that I am walking down the street, eating a sandwich, when I am approached by a hungry man [who] wants to share my sandwich. Now if I give him the sandwich, I have done a good deed, and I feel good about it. The hungry man is grateful, and even if he cannot repay me for my kindness, possibly he will try to help someone else when he has the chance. So this is a transaction that benefits the giver as well as the receiver. But see what happens [if the law *requires* me to give the hungry man my sandwich]. The government takes my sandwich from me by force. Consequently, I am a reluctant giver. The government then bestows my sandwich upon the hungry man. Instead of showing me gratitude, however, the man feels entitled to this benefit. In other words, the involvement of the [law] has utterly stripped the transaction of its moral value, even though the result is exactly the same.[37]

So compelling people to do the right thing gives people less space to engage in random acts of kindness that may result in them developing positive relationships with people that they do not otherwise know.[38] Of course, this does not mean that the law should be abolished and that everyone should be left free to choose in all circumstances whether or not to do the right thing. But it does mean that people need to be left *some* space to be left free to choose whether or not to do the right thing.

(2) *Preserving autonomy*. It is important that there are some areas in people's lives where they are left alone to do what they like, without having to convince any legal official that what they have done or what they are proposing to do is reasonable. If the law required people to act reasonably *all the time*, then people would be deprived of any sense that their lives were genuinely their own. Instead of feeling that they were in some respects authors of their own lives, people would instead feel that they were simply living out their lives along lines that had been pre-programmed according to someone else's dictates. So – in order that people retain some sense of themselves as autonomous beings – there are some areas of people's lives that simply have to remain private and free from legal regulation. It would seem to us that these areas should include: people's choices about who they spend social time with; people's choices about who they do business with; people's choices about what line of work they engage in; and people's choices about whether they live or die.

If all this is right, then in determining whether A will owe B a duty of care in a given situation, the courts should take into account whether, if A were found to owe B such a duty of care, the law would be impinging on the moral space A needs to be given to decide for himself what to do. If so, then the law would be acting in an overbearing way in imposing a duty of care on A, and that should count heavily against the courts' finding that A is subject to such a duty of care.

Disrupting the activities of public bodies

We have already talked a great deal about the fourth kind of way in which recognising that A will owe B a duty of care in a given situation may have an adverse side effect. This will be the case if recognising that A will owe B such a duty of care will *disrupt the activities of a*

36 Weir 2006, 1.
37 D'Souza 2002, 81–2.
38 See, further, McBride 2006a, 29–31.

public body – either because recognising that A will owe B such a duty of care will cause a public body to become *overcautious* about performing its functions; or because recognising that A will owe B such a duty of care will *divert* a public body away from performing its functions and cause it to do something else entirely; or because recognising that A will owe B such a duty of care will tend to result in a *waste* of public resources. We have already described at length how recognising the existence of a duty of care may result in such adverse side effects, and the interested reader is referred back to our discussion of this issue.[39]

These, then, are the four primary types of adverse side effects that may be caused as a result of recognising that a duty of care will be owed in a particular situation: the rule of law may be damaged; or the law may be brought into disrepute; or the law may become overbearing; or the activities of a public body may be disrupted. In determining whether a duty of care will be owed in a given situation, the courts must always be alive to the possibility that a positive finding on the duty front may have one or more of these types of adverse side effect and take that into account in their decision whether or not to recognise the existence of the duty of care under discussion.

Three final points

Those, then, are the factors that the courts should take into account in determining whether A will owe B a duty of care in a given situation. The courts should first of all ask whether depriving A of his freedom to choose what to do would be a price worth paying to enhance B's security. If the answer is 'no', they should refuse to find that A owes B a duty of care. If the answer is 'yes', the courts should then ask whether finding that A owes B a duty of care would have an adverse side effect that outweighs the benefit to B of having her security enhanced. If the answer to that second question is 'yes' then again the courts should refuse to find that A owes B a duty of care. If the answer to the second question is 'no' then, and only then, should the courts find that A will owe B a duty of care in the situation under discussion.

Before we go on to apply this method to evaluate the law's refusal to find a duty of care in the ten situations discussed below, we would like to make three final points about the factors that should be taken into account by the courts in determining whether one person will owe another a duty of care.

Deterrence

Let's go back to the situation where Gary, a police officer, fails to intervene to stop Lara being beaten up.[40] As we have seen,[41] as English law stands at the moment Gary will not owe Lara a duty of care to intervene to save her from being beaten up. It is tempting to criticise the law in this area along the following lines: 'We should find that Gary owes Lara a duty of care in this situation. If he did, then he could be sued for damages if he failed to

[39] See above, pp. 65–8.
[40] See above, pp. 193–4.
[41] Above, n. 23.

help Lara out, and the prospect of being sued would encourage him to peform his job as a police officer properly.'

Unfortunately, this sort of reasoning is upside down. If we find that Gary is liable to pay damages to Lara, we will do so because Gary violated Lara's rights in acting as he did. We do *not* find that Gary violated Lara's rights in acting as he did, in order to find that Gary is liable to pay damages to Lara. Tort law is no longer tort law if it simply becomes a device for sanctioning conduct that we find undesirable. Tort law exists to vindicate people's rights, and it is abused if we start *pretending* that Gary will violate Lara's rights if he fails to help her out so that we can threaten Gary that he will be held liable to pay damages to Lara if he fails to act like a responsible police officer and fails to save her from being beaten up.[42]

Having said that, the possibility that Gary may be encouraged to act like a responsible police officer if we find that he owes Lara a duty of care *may* be relevant to the inquiry into whether Gary owes Lara a duty of care in this situation. Suppose that we find that limiting Gary's freedom not to help Lara out is a price worth paying to increase Lara's security from physical attacks. If this is true then, in principle, the courts should find that Gary *does* owe Lara a duty of care in the situation we are discussing. But suppose someone then objects: 'If we find that Gary owes Lara a duty of care in this situation, that will have various adverse side effects. The law will be brought into disrepute: Gary will be treated more harshly under the law than he would have been had he been less public-spirited and become a merchant banker rather than a police officer. The law will also become more uncertain: if we find that a duty of care is owed in this situation, it will be difficult to know where we will stop in placing duties on police officers and the like to help those in need.' In assessing whether our finding that Gary owes Lara a duty of care will have an adverse side effect that outweighs the benefit of increasing Lara's security from physical attacks, it is legitimate to take into account the *positive* side effects that will result from finding that Gary owes Lara a duty of care. And one such positive side effect may be that finding that Gary owes Lara a duty of care may result in his doing a better job as a police officer. Taking this into account, we may conclude that, on balance, finding that Gary owes Lara a duty of care will not have an adverse side effect, or not enough of an adverse side effect to outweigh the benefit to Lara of having her security from physical attacks increased. If this is so we will conclude that the courts *should* find that Gary owes Lara a duty of care.

So the positive side effects that may result from our finding that Gary owes Lara a duty of care can be taken into account in determining whether or not to find that Gary owes Lara a duty of care – but not at the stage of determining whether, in principle, the courts should find that Gary owes Lara a duty of care. The only thing we should focus on at that stage is whether limiting Gary's freedom is a price worth paying to increase Lara's security. If we conclude that limiting Gary's freedom is *not* a price worth paying to increase Lara's security, then the courts should not find that Gary owed Lara a duty of care – and this is so

[42] So nothing we say should be taken as objecting to Parliament's instituting a new legal basis for suing public officers like Gary for compensation *outside* the law of tort, to ensure that people like Gary are encouraged to fulfil their public responsibilities. (At the time of writing, we understand that the Law Commission is about to issue a Consultation Paper recommending exactly this; whether there will be any political appetite to implement such a proposal is very doubtful.) What we object to is the law of tort being manipulated and abused in order to provide a way of redressing people's grievances about the way they have been treated by public officials.

no matter how overwhelming or attractive the side effects of finding that Gary owes Lara a duty of care would be.

Property rights

Suppose that Fred was a lorry driver and, in order to meet a deadline, he drove his lorry two days and nights continuously without sleeping. Eventually, he fell asleep at the wheel of his lorry and the lorry crashed into an electricity sub-station, producing a power cut that affected hundreds of businesses in the area. Wendy's factory was affected by the power cut and she estimates that the power cut cost her £10,000 in lost profits. She wants to sue Fred in negligence for compensation in respect of her loss. However, her claim will fail: she will not be able to establish that Fred owed her a duty to take care not to crash his lorry into the sub-station. And this is so even though it was reasonably foreseeable that if he did something like that, someone like Wendy – who ran a business in the area – would suffer economic loss as a result.[43]

Some writers on the law of negligence explain this result in the following way.[44] At the time Fred crashed into the power station, Wendy had *no* proprietary interest in the power station. This means that, as against Fred, Wendy had *no* right to exclude him from crashing into the power station. *Therefore* one cannot find that Fred owed Wendy a duty to take care not to crash into the power station – to find otherwise would give Wendy a right against Fred which only someone with a proprietary interest in the station could have had. However, this argument does not work.[45] Breaking it down, the argument goes as follows:

(1) Wendy *would* have had a right to exclude Fred from crashing into the power station had she had a proprietary interest in the power station; therefore,
(2) the fact that Wendy did *not* have a proprietary interest in the power station means that she *could not* have had a right to exclude Fred from crashing into the power station.

However, this is a *non sequitur*: (1) does *not* imply (2). Wendy *could* have had a right to exclude Fred from crashing into the power station based *not* on the fact that she had a proprietary interest in the power station (which she did not) but based instead on the fact that limiting Fred's freedom to crash into the power station was a price worth paying to enhance Wendy's security in the running of her business, and finding that Fred owed Wendy a duty of care in this situation would not have sufficent adverse side effects to outweigh the benefit of enhancing Wendy's security. So the fact that Wendy does not have a proprietary interest in the power station does not *automatically* mean that Fred did not owe Wendy a duty to take care not to crash into the power station.[46]

[43] *Spartan Steel & Alloys Ltd* v *Martin & Co. (Contractors) Ltd* [1973] 1 QB 27.

[44] See Benson 1995; Weinrib 2005, 159; Beever 2007, 237–46.

[45] In addition, were this argument correct, it is hard to understand why if Fred had *deliberately* crashed into the power station with the *intention* of disrupting Wendy's business, the courts would have no hesitation in finding that Fred committed a tort in relation to Wendy in acting as he did: see below, pp. 423–32.

[46] *Important note*. The fact that some people think it does may arise out of the fact that we use the term *right* in a number of different ways. (See above, pp. 5–6.) Another way of saying that Wendy does not have a proprietary interest in the power station is to say that Wendy has no *property right* (in technical terms, a right *in rem* – a right in a thing) in the power station. Because we say this, it is tempting to think that Fred did not violate Wendy's rights in crashing into the power station, and conclude as a result that Wendy cannot sue Fred in tort for crashing into the power station. But when we ask – Did Fred violate Wendy's rights in crashing into the power station? we are *not* asking (directly) – Did Wendy have a property right in the power station? We are

Having said that, there is no doubt that Wendy would find it *a lot* easier to establish that Fred owed her a duty to take care not to crash into the power station if she had a proprietary interest in the power station. As we have seen, English law says that if it is reasonably foreseeable that A's doing *x* will result in property in which B has a legal interest being damaged, then A will normally owe B a duty to take care not to do *x*.[47] In contrast, the mere fact that it is reasonably foreseeable that A's doing *x* will cause B to suffer some kind of pure economic loss will not be sufficient to give rise to a duty on A's part to take care not to do *x*. So if Wendy had a proprietary interest in the power station, she would find it very easy to establish that Fred owed her a duty to take care not to crash into the power station.

Why is this? Why does the law do more to protect people against the risk that their *things* may be damaged than that their *bank balances* might be harmed? Part of the reason is that some of the adverse side effects noted above that would result from recognising a duty to take care not to cause someone else economic loss tend not to arise, or arise in such a serious form, in cases where we impose a duty on someone to take care not to act in a way that will foreseeably result in someone else's property being damaged. So, for example, the law's telling us to take care not to do things that will foreseeably result in someone else's property being damaged does not, and will not, result in our being subjected to a ruinously oppressive number of duties of care. And the law's telling us to take such care does not, and will not, result in the legal system becoming overburdened with the task of enforcing a huge number of duties of care, thus impairing its ability to enforce very important duties of care such as duties to take care not to injure people or cause them psychiatric illness.

More fundamental, though, is the fact that enhancing people's security against their *things* being damaged is more important than enhancing people's security against their *bank balances* being harmed. This is for three reasons. First, people form emotional attachments to their things, whereas they do not – or do not normally – form emotional attachments to their bank balances.[48] So, for example, most people would not trade their pets or their homes for the price of a substitute. In contrast, we would regard it as a sign of mental imbalance in someone if they were emotionally attached to their bank balance being at a certain level. Secondly, while companies do not have any kind of emotional attachment to their physical assets, there seems little doubt that destroying a company's physical assets would be more disruptive to its operations and future profitability than damaging its balance sheet. Thirdly, society as a whole almost always loses out when property is damaged or destroyed; whereas the same is hardly ever true when someone suffers some kind of pure economic loss. This is because property that is damaged or destroyed is lost forever to all of us; whereas in most cases where someone has suffered some form of pure economic loss, someone else will have suffered a corresponding pure economic gain.

It follows from what has just been said, then, that in a case where it is reasonably foreseeable that A's doing *x* will result in B suffering harm X, we are far more likely to conclude

---

not asking whether Wendy had that *kind* of right. We are instead asking whether Wendy had a right (in technical terms, a right *in personam* – a right against a particular person) that Fred take care not to crash into the power station. In other words, we are asking whether at the time Fred was driving his lorry, the law imposed on him, for Wendy's benefit, a duty to take care not to crash his lorry into the power station. This is a wholly different question from the question of whether Wendy had a property right in the power station.

47 See above pp. 116–24 ('the property harm principle').

48 See Witting 2001.

that limiting A's freedom to do *x* is a price worth paying to increase B's security against suffering harm X if harm X consists in B's property being damaged than we would be if harm X consisted in B's bank balance being harmed.

Evaluating adverse side effects

The task of determining whether the courts' finding that A owes B a duty of care will have any adverse side effects, and if so, whether those side effects are serious enough to outweigh the benefits resulting from recognising that A owes B a duty of care is far from straightforward. This is for two reasons.

First, the courts will often find it hard to come by any reliable information about whether their finding that A owes B a duty of care will have any adverse side effects, and if so, what those side effects will be. As a result, it is all too easy for the courts to slide into relying on speculation and prejudice in addressing this issue.[49]

Secondly, if a court wants to judge whether an established adverse side effect of recognising that A owes B a duty of care is serious enough to outweigh the benefits of recognising that A owes B such a duty, the court first has to put a value on that adverse side effect and also put a value on those benefits so as to allow it to weigh the one against the other. There is no 'right' way of doing this. What values the court puts on that adverse side effect and on those benefits will depend on what is important to the court; in other words, it will depend on the court's political views. So one court may end up concluding that the established adverse side effect of recognising that A owes B a duty of care is not serious enough to outweigh the benefits of recognising that A owes B such a duty of care, when a different court – with a different set of political views – might have ended up reaching the opposite conclusion.

A couple of recent commentators on the law of negligence have concluded from this that the courts should adopt a method for determining whether one person owes another a duty of care that does *not* require them to ask themselves such questions as: Will our finding that a duty of care is owed in this case have any adverse side effects? If so, are those side effects serious enough to outweigh the benefits of finding that a duty of care is owed in this case?[50] So Allan Beever argues that if, *in principle*, the courts *should* recognise that A owes B a duty of care in a particular case,[51] then they should go straight on and *find* that A

[49] See Cane 2000b.

[50] Beever 2007, at 171–4, criticises those who would take 'policy concerns' into account in judging whether a duty of care is owed in a particular case on the ground that doing so: (1) 'requires judges to make open-ended political decisions'; (2) results in the 'courts involv[ing] themselves with concerns that lie beyond their institutional competence'; and (3) results in the courts 'balancing incommensurables'. (Two things are incommensurable if they are valuable/harmful for different reasons and so there is no common scale one can weigh them in to determine which is more valuable/harmful.) Stevens 2007 agrees, arguing at 308–10 that there are 'three reasons why the class of arguments which a judge can use to resolve a case [should be] restricted and exclude policy considerations': (1) 'unelected judges lack the political competence to weigh competing policy claims'; (2) 'judges lack the technical competence to assess all of the reasons which could, in theory, be taken into account in reaching a decision'; (3) admitting policy considerations into judicial decisions makes those decisions much harder to reach 'because of . . . the problem of incommensurability. When different possible policy goals are in play, the correct outcome will be impossible to determine'.

[51] Beever 2007 offers no elaborate account as to when, *in principle*, the courts should recognise that A owes B a duty of care but he insists at 69 that the rights we have against each other are based on 'a conception of interpersonal morality – a view of how we should treat each other as individuals'. He goes on to argue at 221 that the reason why a drowning child has no right to be rescued by a passing stranger – even in principle – is that 'the unilateral actions of one person cannot impose obligations upon another'.

owes B a duty of care and not worry about whether their doing so will have any adverse side effects.[52] Robert Stevens takes a different tack. He argues that if it is the case, *in principle*, that the courts *should* recognise that A owes B a duty of care in a particular case, but recognising that A owes B such a duty of care *will* have certain adverse side effects, the courts should simply refuse to find that A owes B a duty of care.[53] They should not attempt to judge whether recognising that A owes B a duty of care is still a worthwhile thing to do, despite the adverse side effects.

We disagree. We think that the courts can and should take into account the adverse side effects of their decisions in judging whether one person owes another a duty of care.

We admit that doing so will involve the courts in having to make difficult value judgments. However, the courts already make difficult value judgments when they determine, in principle, whether they should find that A owes B a duty of care. Simply determining whether sacrificing A's freedom of action is a price worth paying to enhance B's security involves making difficult value judgments. If the courts can be entrusted with the task of determining that issue of principle, then they can also be entrusted with the task of determining whether they should refuse to find that A owes B a duty of care because of the adverse side effects that will result from their doing so. If they get the judgment wrong – so that the value judgment they make is seriously at odds with the values of the community as a whole – then Parliament can always correct their decision.

We also admit that it can be difficult in some cases for the courts to determine whether a decision to find that A owes B a duty of care will have any adverse side effects, and if so, what. However, the solution to this problem is *not* for the courts to adopt a method of determining whether a duty of care will be owed in a particular case that is blind to all the possible consequences of that decision; the solution is, rather, *more information*. Moreover, there will be cases where it is *clear* that recognising that A owes B a duty of care will have disastrous side effects. In such cases, it is hard to understand why the courts should not take that into account in deciding whether or not to find that A owes B a duty of care.

TEN NO-DUTY SITUATIONS

Now that we have clarified what sort of factors should be taken into account by the courts in determining whether one person owed another a duty of care, we will look at ten situations where English law currently denies that a duty of care will be owed and see whether the law's refusal to find a duty of care in these situations is justified.

Omissions; physical harm; private person

Sarah's case

Suppose that Sarah is hurrying to work, talking on her mobile phone, when she sees that Carl, who is obviously very drunk, is staggering towards an open, unprotected manhole. She could easily interrupt her conversation and shout a warning to Carl that would save him from falling into the manhole. The courts have traditionally taken the stance that in

[52] Cf. Lord Scarman in *McLoughlin* v *O'Brian* [1983] 1 AC 410 at 430.

[53] Stevens 2007, 338.

the absence of some kind of special relationship between Sarah and Carl, Sarah will not owe Carl a duty to shout a warning to him[54] – and this is so even though it is highly foreseeable that if Sarah does not shout a warning, Carl will fall into the manhole and suffer severe, and possibly fatal, injuries.

A libertarian – someone who puts a high value on individual liberty – might well defend the law in this area on the ground that limiting Sarah's freedom to help Carl out is not a price worth paying to increase Carl's physical security. We would not put such a high value on Sarah's freedom. Limiting Sarah's freedom to help Carl out *might* be a price worth paying to increase Carl's physical security – particularly as this is an 'easy rescue' case, where Sarah can save Carl at no real cost or risk to herself. But there is an issue as to whether limiting Sarah's freedom in this case would actually increase Carl's physical security. If Sarah would in all probability call out a warning to Carl *whether or not* she owed him a duty of care to help him out,[55] then imposing such a duty on Sarah would not actually do very much to increase Carl's security. Indeed, it could be argued that imposing a duty of care on Sarah in this situation would actually make it *less* likely that Sarah would call out a warning to Carl and therefore *decrease* Carl's physical security. If Sarah did owe Carl a duty of care in this situation she might think, 'If I shout out a warning, and this guy still falls into the manhole, I'll have brought attention to myself and maybe I'll be sued for failing to do more to help him out. If I just look the other way and say nothing, then I can always pretend if someone asks me that I just didn't see him.'[56] None of these considerations would enter into Sarah's mind if she did *not* owe Carl a duty of care – she would just do the decent thing automatically and call out a warning to Carl.

So it may well be that, in principle, the courts should *not* find Sarah owes Carl a duty of care in this situation – but not because Sarah's freedom is particularly precious, but because finding that Sarah owes Carl a duty of care in this situation will not actually help Carl. Having said that, if it were the case that limiting Sarah's freedom in this case to help Carl out would be a price worth paying to increase Carl's physical security, the law's refusal to find that Sarah owed Carl a duty of care would still be justified because of the variety of adverse side effects that such a finding would have. First, and as we have already noted, finding that a duty to rescue is owed in these kinds of cases would inject a great deal of

[54] See, for example, *Yuen Kun Yeu* v *Attorney-General for Hong Kong* [1988] AC 175, 192; *Stovin* v *Wise* [1996] AC 923, 931. The law is similar in most common law jurisdictions: see Weinrib 1980, 247: 'No observer would have any difficulty outlining the current state of the law throughout the common-law world regarding the duty to rescue. Except when the person endangered and the potential rescuer are linked in a special relationship, there is no such duty.'

[55] Hyman 2005 investigated whether the absence of a general duty to rescue in American law had an adverse effect on people's willingness to help others out. He counted only 16 examples of bystanders failing to rescue (in the absence of a statutory duty) in the United States between 1994 and 2004. (He combed the accounts in law textbooks, over 100 relevant law review articles, and all newspaper and magazine stories on LexisNexis.) Hyman also sought to measure the relative incidence of voluntary rescue and non-rescue in the United States. Using data from organisations which provide awards for rescues he found that confirmed rescues outnumber non-rescues by about 740:1, and the risk of dying as a result of attempting a voluntary rescue is approximately 70 times higher than the risk of dying as a result of bystanders failing to offer assistance.

[56] To accommodate this objection, most states in the United States have enacted 'Good Samaritan laws', which typically provide that 'Any person who, in good faith, renders emergency medical care or assistance to an injured person at the scene of an accident or other emergency without the expectation of receiving or intending to receive compensation from such injured person for such service, shall not be liable in civil damages for any act or omission, not constituting gross negligence, in the course of such care or assistance.' See GS&Z, 100–1.

damaging uncertainty into the law.[57] Secondly, finding that a duty to rescue is owed in these cases may result in the law becoming overbearing, unjustifiably narrowing the space within which people are left free to choose to do the wrong thing. Thirdly, finding that Sarah owed Carl a duty of care might bring the law into disrepute. If others who were more immediately responsible for the harm suffered by Carl – such as the person who left the manhole open – were difficult to track down, or not worth suing, Sarah might end up being held liable in full to compensate Carl for his injuries when she was, in relative terms, the one least to blame for those injuries. Most people would regard this as unfair.[58]

Given this, we think the law is justified in refusing to find that a duty of care is owed in Sarah's case.

Omissions; physical harm or property damage; public bodies

Paul's case

Suppose that Siobhan is being attacked in the street by Alan. Paul, a police officer, sees this happening. As the law stands at the moment, the law will not find that Paul owes Siobhan[59] a duty to take reasonable steps to protect her.[60] This may not actually matter much to Siobhan: if Paul fails to intervene to protect Siobhan, she would almost certainly be able to sue Paul under the Human Rights Act 1998[61] on the ground that his failure to do more to protect her against Alan violated her right under Article 3 of the European Convention on Human Rights not to be subjected to 'inhuman or degrading treatment'.[62] However, for our

[57] See above, p. 190; also Tomlinson 2000 (demonstrating the uncertainty afflicting French law as a result of its recognising a general 'duty to rescue'). The law in Vermont states that a 'person who knows that another is exposed to grave physical harm shall, to the extent that the same can be rendered without danger or peril to himself or without interference with important duties owed to others, give reasonable assistance to the exposed person unless that assistance or care is being provided by others' (12 Vt. Stat. Ann. § 519). It is easy to think up hypothetical situations where it is very uncertain whether someone would have a duty of care under this provision. For example, suppose B has fallen in the street and is bleeding from his head. Some people gather round B and ask him whether he is okay. A, a doctor, comes along. Is B exposed to 'grave physical harm' in this situation? – perhaps he is: perhaps his bleeding will worsen and he will die unless he is given treatment. Is A able to give him that assistance without danger or peril to himself? – perhaps he can't: perhaps B has AIDS and A will expose himself to the risk of infection by treating B's wounds. Is B already being provided with assistance or care by others? – perhaps not, if the people around him are not doing anything effective to help him. Weinrib 1980 suggests (at 268–79) that a general duty to rescue can be recognised without making the law uncertain if it is limited to cases where the potential rescuer could not, or could not easily, *charge* the person in danger for rescuing him. However, this assumes that the law on when someone can charge someone else for rescuing him from danger is relatively clear; but it is not.

[58] Similarly, Stapleton 1995 argues that picking on 'peripheral parties', such as someone who fails to rescue another, may dilute the deterrent messages sent by tort law by distracting attention from the primary responsibility of those who created the dangerous situation in the first place.

[59] *Important note.* Of course, Paul may have owed a duty to the public at large to do more to protect Siobhan and may consequently have committed a *public wrong*. (The concept of a public wrong is explained above, pp. 3–4.) As a result, Paul could be subjected to criminal proceedings for doing so little to assist Siobhan. However, those who suffer loss as a result of the commission of a public wrong are rarely allowed to sue for compensation for that loss. In order to sue Paul, Siobhan would have to show that Paul committed a wrong *in relation to her* in failing to do more to protect her against Alan, and she will be unable to do this.

[60] See above, n. 23.

[61] See Chapter 41, below, for an account of when someone will be entitled to sue someone else under the 1998 Act.

[62] You might think that the only way a police officer could violate Siobhan's right under Art 3 of the European Convention on Human Rights (ECHR) was by *his* treating her in an inhuman or degrading way. However, the European Court of Human Rights takes a much wider view of the scope of people's rights under Art 3 of the

present purposes, it is worth asking whether the courts *should* find that Paul owes Siobhan a duty of care in this situation.

Intelligent discussion of this issue has long been impeded by the habit academics have of saying that Paul enjoys an *immunity* from being sued in negligence here.[63] Such language suggests that the courts give Paul *special treatment* when they refuse to find that Paul owes Siobhan a duty to take reasonable steps to stop Alan attacking her.[64] But it is clear that Paul is *not* being given any kind of special treatment here. A normal, private citizen would not owe Siobhan a duty to help her out.[65] So in finding that *Paul* does not owe Siobhan a duty of care, the courts are treating Paul in the same way they would a normal, private citizen.[66] Those who would like the courts to find that Paul owes Siobhan a duty of care in the situation we are considering are therefore really calling for the courts to treat Paul *differently* from how they would treat a normal, private citizen who was in a position to stop Alan attacking Siobhan.[67] So should they?

A libertarian would have no objection to the courts' finding that Paul owes Siobhan a duty of care in this case. This is because imposing such a duty on Paul would not have any adverse effect on his freedom: Paul is *already* under a duty (to the public, to his employers, and under the Human Rights Act 1998) to help Siobhan out in this situation. But it may be that adding yet another duty to assist Siobhan to the roster of duties to help her out that he is already subject to will not actually enhance Siobhan's security. If the prospect of being subject to criminal proceedings, being disciplined by his employers, and being sued by Siobhan under the Human Rights Act 1998 will not work to encourage Paul to save Siobhan from being attacked, then why should his being subject to a duty of care make any difference to him?

So it may be that there is no point in imposing a duty of care on Paul in this case. If this is right then, in principle, the courts should not find that Paul owes Siobhan a duty of care in this case. If this is wrong, and limiting Paul's (minimal) freedom not to help Siobhan out

---

ECHR. It has held that a public authority *may* violate someone's right under Art 3 if it *fails* to take reasonable steps to prevent that person being subjected to inhuman or degrading treatment *by someone else*: see, for example, *A* v *United Kingdom* (1999) 27 EHRR 611 and *Z* v *United Kingdom* [2001] 2 FLR 612. A similarly wide view is taken of the other rights set out in the ECHR. For example, the police will violate A's right to life under Art 2 of the ECHR if they know that A is in danger of being killed by B and they fail to take reasonable steps to save A from being killed by B: *Osman* v *United Kingdom* [1999] FLR 193. This approach to Art 2 was applied in *Van Colle* v *Chief Constable of the Hertfordshire Police* [2007] EWCA 325, where the police were held liable for violating the right to life of Mr Van Colle by failing to protect him from a person who he was due to give evidence against. This person had been intimidating Mr Van Colle to try to prevent him from giving evidence and eventually murdered him.

63 See, for example, Lunney & Oliphant 2008, 147; Jones 2002, 74; Howarth 2007, 673; Wright J 2001, 83; Giliker 2000, 373; Markesinis 1999, 96; Hoyano 1999, passim; Monti 1999, 758.

64 Cf. Hedley 2006, at 61, saying that the police are treated 'with special generosity by the courts'.

65 This follows from the discussion of Sarah's case, above pp. 203–5.

66 See Weir 2004, 17; McBride 2006b, 13–14. Contra, Bell 2002, at xviii, remarking that the fact that 'The public-private divide is less sharp than it once was ... [makes stark the] incongruity of [the law's applying] different rules for compensation between public and private sectors ...' (but English law does *not* apply one set of rules to the private sector and one set to the public sector: it applies the same rules across the board); Howarth & O'Sullivan 2000, at 91, asking 'Should public authorities be in a special position with regard to negligence actions?' (suggesting that they are, when in fact they are not); and Bowman & Bailey 1984 and Bailey & Bowman 2000, arguing that public bodies are unnecessarily given special protection by the law of negligence – that the 'policy concerns' underlying this special treatment can be easily accommodated within the normal rules governing liability in negligence (but public bodies enjoy no such special treatment at the moment).

67 See Feldthusen 1997, 24–9.

is a price worth paying to increase Siobhan's physical security, the courts' refusal to find that such a duty of care is owed to Siobhan may still be justified on the ground that such a finding would bring the law into disrepute. This is for two reasons. First, and as we have already noted, if Paul were found to owe Siobhan a duty of care in this situation, the law would treat Paul worse than if he had chosen to pursue a less public-spirited profession, such as being a merchant banker. Most people would regard this as unfair.[68] Secondly, if the law found that Paul owed Siobhan a duty of care in this situation, and it turned out that Alan was not worth suing, then Paul would end up being held liable in full for Siobhan's injuries when he was not the person who was immediately responsible for those injuries. Again, most people would regard this as unfair.[69]

The East Suffolk *case*

In *East Suffolk Rivers Catchment Board* v *Kent*,[70] the claimants' lands were flooded when a tidal river breached a protecting wall. The defendant authority took on the job of repairing the wall but incompetently chose the wrong method. By the time the authority used the right method the claimants' lands had been flooded for 178 days; if the right method had been selected initially, the flooding would have lasted only 14 days. The claimants sued the defendant authority, seeking to recover compensation for the extra damage done to the lands due to them remaining flooded longer than necessary. The House of Lords dismissed the claimants' claims: they held that the defendant authority had *not* owed the claimant a duty to repair the wall with a reasonable degree of care and skill.[71]

Was this right? It seems that limiting the defendants' freedom to do a bad job of repairing the wall would almost certainly have been a price worth paying to enhance the claimants' security over the enjoyment of their lands. So, in principle, the House of Lords should have found that the defendant authority *did* owe the claimants a duty of care in this case. However, the House of Lords ultimately refused to find that the defendants owed the claimants a duty of care in *East Suffolk* because they thought that to do so would – in effect – bring the law into disrepute. This is because had the defendant river authority done *nothing*, the House of Lords thought that the claimants could *not* have asserted that the authority owed them a duty to take reasonable steps to mend the wall.[72] Given this, the House of Lords thought that it would be paradoxical to find that once the defendants *decided* to do something about the sea wall, they owed the claimant a duty to mend it with

[68] See above, pp. 193–4.

[69] See above, pp. 64–6, 205.

[70] [1941] AC 74.

[71] Note that it again makes no sense here to say that the defendant authority enjoyed an 'immunity' from being sued in negligence. The defendant authority could straightforwardly have been sued in negligence if they had interfered with someone else's mending the wall or indicated to the claimants that they could safely rely on them to repair the wall with a reasonable degree of care and skill with the result that the claimants did so rely on them. Indeed, one of the side effects of the wrong method which the defendant authority chose was that debris was strewn across some of the lands, clogging and fouling them. If the claimants had sought compensation for the damage caused by this debris they probably would have succeeded in demonstrating that the defendant authority owed them a duty of care under the 'property harm principle'. But the claimants sought compensation for the damage caused by the flood water, not the debris.

[72] That this is correct has been made crystal clear by the decision of the House of Lords in *Gorringe* v *Calderdale Metropolitan Borough Council* [2004] 1 WLR 1057 (held: highway authority did not owe a motorist a duty to paint a warning telling her to slow down at a bend merely because it had a statutory power to paint such a sign on the road).

a reasonable degree of care and skill. To make such a finding would have made the defendants worse off than they would have been had they remained blithely indifferent to the claimants' plight and done nothing for them.[73] The old cynical saw that 'no good deed goes unpunished' would have become part of English law.

This argument, though sound on its face,[74] just begs the question – why, if the defendant river authority had done *nothing*, would the courts not have found that the defendants owed the claimants a duty to take reasonable steps to mend the sea wall? The reason is, again, that to find that the defendants were subject to such a duty of care would have brought the law into disrepute. Democracy would have been undermined, in that the courts would have taken over the job of deciding how the defendant authority's resources should be deployed. And even if this objection could have been overcome it is likely that imposing duties to act on the defendant authority in cases like the *East Suffolk* case would have disrupted the defendant authority's performance of its functions. The defendant authority might have started making decisions as to how it should deploy its resources based more on a desire to avoid litigation rather than an objective assessment of where there was most need of its services.

Acts or omissions; pure economic loss; private persons

As we have seen, absent the existence of a 'special relationship' between A and B, the courts will not usually find that A owes B a duty of care not to cause B to suffer some kind of pure economic loss. The four situations listed below correspond to four different ways that A could cause B, a stranger to him, to suffer some kind of economic loss:

(1) *relational economic loss*: A damages C's property, and B suffers some kind of pure economic loss as a result;

[73] Lord Atkin dissented on the ground that '[It is] established that a public authority whether doing an act which it is its duty to do, or doing an act which it is merely empowered to do, must in doing the act do it without negligence, or as it is put in some of the cases must not do it carelessly or improperly' (see *East Suffolk Rivers Catchment Board* v *Kent* [1941] AC 74, at 90). But the authorities relied on by him as establishing this were all cases where a public body in carrying out some works it was empowered to do *caused some damage to the claimant*, not cases where the public body, having decided to confer a benefit on someone else, failed to confer that benefit on him in an expeditious manner.

[74] Cf. Lord Hoffmann in *Stovin* v *Wise* [1996] AC 923, 949: 'If [a] public authority is under no duty to act, either by virtue of its statutory powers or any other basis, it cannot be held liable because it has acted but has negligently failed to confer a benefit on the [claimant] or to protect him from loss.' In light of this statement and the House of Lords' subsequent decision in *Gorringe* v *Calderdale MBC* [2004] 1 WLR 1057, it is hard to see how any part of the decision of the House of Lords in *Anns* v *Merton LBC* [1978] AC 728 can be said to be still good law. In that case, it was held that a local authority which decided to inspect the foundations of houses being built in its area in order to ensure that they were being safely constructed would owe future occupants of the houses a duty to carry out the inspections with a reasonable degree of care and skill. This aspect of the decision in *Anns* has *never* been overruled though it has been questioned whether it is correct: see *Murphy* v *Brentwood DC* [1991] 1 AC 398, 457H (per Lord Mackay), 463G (per Lord Keith of Kinkel); *Stovin* v *Wise* [1996] AC 923, 948H–951A (per Lord Hoffmann). The only retrenchment that has taken place in relation to *Anns* (other than the abandonment of the two-stage test for determining whether a duty of care is owed in a 'novel' case) is in relation to what can be sued for if the local authority carries out its inspections carelessly with the result that a house is built on inadequate foundations and subsequently becomes dangerous to live in. In *Anns*, it was held that: (1) anyone living in the house could sue for compensation for harm to his or her person or property caused by the house being in a dangerous condition; *and* (2) the owner of the house could sue for compensation in respect of the cost of having the house made safe to live in. It is highly doubtful whether (1) is still good law in England; (2) is certainly no longer true: see *Murphy* v *Brentwood DC* [1991] 1 AC 398.

(2) *negligent supply of defective goods*: A creates a defective item of property, and B suffers some kind of pure economic loss as a result;
(3) *negligent supply of defective services*: A performs some service for C and does so badly, and as a result B suffers some kind of pure economic loss;
(4) *incompetent business decisions*: A runs his business incompetently, and B suffers some kind of pure economic loss as a result.[75]

Fred's case

We have already come across Fred's case – Fred carelessly crashes his lorry into a power station, with the result that Wendy, who runs a business nearby, suffers a prolonged power cut and loses £10,000 profits. It is very clear that in this situation, the English courts will refuse to find that Fred owed Wendy a duty to take care not to crash into the power station.[76] In contrast, the High Court of Australia and Supreme Court of Canada have shown themselves willing to find that Fred owed Wendy a duty of care in this kind of situation provided it could be shown that Fred knew at the time he acted that Wendy was very likely to suffer pure economic loss if he carelessly damaged the power station.[77]

Who is right? Well, we would accept that limiting Fred's freedom to drive as he likes is a price worth paying to enhance the security of Wendy's profits; so, in principle, the courts *should* find that Fred owed Wendy a duty of care in this situation. This is because although Wendy's interest in the security of the profits she makes from running her business is not especially worthy of protection, the fact that Fred is *already* under a duty (owed to the owners of the power station) to take care not to crash into the power station means that

[75] Compare Feldthusen 1991, at 357–8 (cited by the Supreme Court of Canada in *Winnipeg Condominium Corp. (No. 36)* v *Bird Construction Co.* [1995] 1 SCR 85, at [12]), producing a fivefold categorisation of the various ways that someone may end up suffering some kind of pure economic loss: (i) through the acts or omissions of a public authority; (ii) through negligent misrepresentation; (iii) through the negligent performance of a service; (iv) through the negligent supply of shoddy goods or structures; (v) through relational economic loss. Our situation (1) corresponds with Feldthusen's category (v). Situations (2) and (3) corresponds with Feldthusen's categories (iv) and (iii), respectively. (We think there is no need to consider category (ii) separately from category (iii).) Situation (4) does not fit easily within Feldthusen's categories. We discuss a variety of situations that fall within category (i) below: pp. 214–19.

[76] *Spartan Steel & Alloys Ltd* v *Martin & Co. (Contractors) Ltd* [1973] 1 QB 27. Also *Cattle* v *Stockton Waterworks Co.* (1875) LR 10 QB 453 (no duty of care owed to contractors not to delay them in their work, thereby making their contract to do that work less profitable); *Simpson & Co.* v *Thomson* (1877) 3 App Cas 279 (no duty of care owed to insurer not to damage insured property); *Société Anonyme de Remourquage à Hélice* v *Bennetts* [1911] 1 KB 243 (no duty of care owed by defendants not to sink ship being towed by tug, thereby preventing the tug earning a fee for towing the ship); *Candlewood Navigation Corporation Ltd* v *Mitsui OSK Lines Ltd, The Mineral Transporter* [1986] AC 1 (no duty of care owed to claimants not to damage ship which claimants did not have proprietary interest in but which the claimants had to pay hire for even if the ship was damaged); *Leigh & Sillavan Ltd* v *Aliakmon Shipping Co. Ltd, The Aliakmon* [1986] AC 785 (no duty of care owed to claimant not to damage goods which the claimant had contracted to pay for but which he had not yet acquired ownership or possession of).

[77] See *Caltex Oil Pty Ltd* v *The Dredge 'Willemstaad'* (1976) 136 CLR 529 (High Court of Australia) (A negligently broke underwater pipeline that belonged to C and fed petrol to B's oil terminal; held, A owed B a duty of care not to break the pipeline based on the fact (at 555, per Gibbs J) that A knew or ought to have known that B 'individually, and not merely as a member of an unascertained class, [was] likely to suffer economic loss as a consequence of his negligence . . .') and *Canadian National Railway Co.* v *Norsk Pacific Steamship Co. Ltd* [1992] 1 SCR 1021 (Supreme Court of Canada) (A negligently damaged railway bridge belonging to C with the result that B, the railway company, incurred expense carrying freight to its destinations by alternative routes; held, A owed B a duty of care not to damage the railway bridge based on the fact (per McLachlin J at 1162) that B was the predominant user of the bridge).

limiting his freedom to drive as he likes by imposing a duty of care on him for Wendy's benefit will not effectively have any adverse effect on his freedom.

Having conceded that point, we would contend that the adverse side effects of finding that Fred owes Wendy a duty of care in this case justify the law's refusal to find that a duty of care was owed in this case.[78] First, if a duty of care were found in this case, the law would become very uncertain and unstable. The 'bright line' against a duty of care being found in cases of relational economic loss would have been breached and it would be very difficult to achieve a new and stable consensus as to when a duty of care will and will not be owed in cases where it is reasonably foreseeable that B will suffer some kind of pure economic loss as a result of A's damaging C's property (or person).[79] Secondly, this uncertainty and instability would invite claimants to bring a huge number of claims in negligence for compensation for relational economic loss to test the limits of when a duty of care would and would not be owed in such cases, and this would blunt the courts' abilities to enforce more important and pressing duties of care. Thirdly, the law would be brought into disrepute if the courts found that a duty of care was owed in cases like Fred's because doing so would give rise to a risk of exposing someone like Fred to liabilities (in Fred's case, to Wendy and anyone else who suffered a loss of profits as a result of the power cut) that were out of all proportion to his fault.[80]

Given these considerations, we think that the law is justified in refusing to find that a duty of care is owed in cases such as Fred's.

Peter's case

Suppose that Peter is constructing an office block. It is well established now that Peter will not owe future owners of the block a duty to construct it with a reasonable degree of care and skill.[81] So suppose, after Peter has finished the block, it is acquired by Rent-an-Office Ltd. They discover that the office block is subsiding because it was built on inadequate foundations, and are advised that if they do not underpin the foundations – at a cost of £30,000 – the subsidence will get worse and it will cost far more than normal to maintain

[78] *Candlewood Navigation Corporation Ltd* v *Mitsui OSK Lines Ltd, The Mineral Transporter* [1986] AC 1, at 16: 'the rule [against a duty of care being owed to third parties suffering relational economic loss] [is] a pragmatic one dictated by necessity'.

[79] Ibid., at 25: '[The rule against a duty of care being owed to third parties suffering relational economic loss] has the merit of drawing a definite and readily ascertainable line. It should enable legal practitioners to advise their clients as to their rights with reasonable certainty . . .'; also *Leigh & Sillavan Ltd* v *Aliakmon Shipping Co. Ltd, The Aliakmon* [1986] AC 785, at 817 (per Lord Brandon of Oakbrook): 'I do not think that the law should allow special pleading in a particular case within the general rule to detract from its application. If such detraction were to be permitted in one particular case, it would lead to attempts to have it permitted in a variety of other particular cases, and the result would be that the certainty, which the application of the general rule presently provides, would be seriously undermined. Yet certainty of the law is of the utmost importance . . .'

[80] Ibid., at 816 (per Lord Brandon of Oakbrook): 'the policy reason for excluding a duty of care [in cases of relational economic loss is] to avoid opening the floodgates so as to expose a person guilty of want of care to unlimited liability to an indefinite number of other persons whose contractual rights have been affected by such want of care'. See also *Cattle* v *Stockton Waterworks Co.* (1875) LR 10 QB 453, at 457–8.

[81] *D & F Estates* v *Church Commissioners* [1989] AC 177; *Murphy* v *Brentwood DC* [1991] 1 AC 398. For a survey of the authorities, see Todd 2007. Peter *will* owe any future occupants a duty to take care not to construct the building in such a way that it becomes *dangerous* to work in (see above, pp. 74–5) and will be held liable if a breach of that duty of care results in anyone in the building being killed or injured (though – so far as English law is concerned, at any rate – he will not be held liable *in negligence* for the cost of making the building safe to work in; for an explanation of this point, see below, pp. 578–9).

the building's appearance, avoid leaks, and keep the doors and windows in working order. In such a situation, Rent-an-Office Ltd will not be able to sue Peter in negligence for the losses they will suffer as a result of his failure to build the block properly: at the time he was building the office block, he will not have owed them a duty to construct it with a reasonable degree of care and skill.

If Peter was building the office block on his own behalf, planning to sell it off to the highest bidder once he was finished, then this aspect of the law is easily understood. Imposing a duty of care on him that was owed to future owners of the office block would unacceptably limit his freedom to choose who to work for. The law would basically be requiring him to work to a certain standard for those future owners without his having agreed with them that he would and without their having paid him a penny for his doing so. However, this objection to imposing a duty of care on Peter would disappear if Peter had been commissioned to build the office block by someone else (say, Eric). In such a case, Peter *would* owe Eric (either in contract or under the extended principle in *Hedley Byrne*) a duty to build the office block with a reasonable degree of care and skill. So imposing a similar duty on Peter for the benefit of *future* owners of the office block (and not just the first owner, Eric) would not deprive Peter of any liberty that he had not already surrendered in his dealings with Eric. Of course, any duty that was imposed on Peter for the benefit of future owners would have to be *identical* in content and conditions to the duty that Peter assumed to Eric in taking on the work of constructing the office block – if it were not, then Peter's freedom to choose who to work for, and on what terms, would again be unacceptably undermined. But provided that this requirement was satisfied, it might well be that curtailing Peter's freedom not to do a good job of constructing the office block might be a price worth paying to enhance the security of the businesses of future owners of the office block.

But it would still be wrong for the courts to find that Peter owed those future owners a duty of care. The law would be brought into disrepute if it did. The future owners of the office block would enjoy exactly the same rights as Eric, and this is so even though Eric *paid* Peter to do a good job of constructing the office block, while the future owners did not. Most people would think this unfair: the future owners of the office block should not get for nothing what Eric had to pay for.[82] Moreover, if Peter did owe future owners of the office block a duty to build it with a reasonable degree of care and skill, Peter would take into account the possibility that he might be sued by those future owners in determining how much to charge Eric for constructing the office block. So *Eric* would end up paying Peter a premium for the fact that the law had given *future owners* of the office block the same rights that Eric had to pay Peter to acquire. This would be extremely unfair on Eric. Finally, if Peter did owe future owners of the office block a duty to build it with a

[82] See Tettenborn 2000a. Also Lord Brandon of Oakbrook's remarks in *Junior Books Ltd* v *Veitchi Co. Ltd* [1983] 1 AC 520, at 551–2: 'The effect of [finding that Peter owes a future owner of the office block a duty to build the office block with a reasonable degree of care and skill] would be, in substance, to create, as between two persons who are not in any contractual relationship with each other, obligations of one of those two persons to the other which are only really appropriate as between persons who do have such a relationship between them.' Also Lord Bridge of Harwich in *Murphy* v *Brentwood DC* [1991] 1 AC 398, at 480: 'to hold that [a] builder owe[s] ... a duty of care [in respect of the quality of his work] to any person acquiring an interest in the product of the builder's work would be to impose upon him the obligations of an indefinitely transmissible warranty of quality.'

reasonable degree of skill and care, the consequence might be that Peter was exposed to liabilities that were disproportionate to his fault in constructing a faulty office block. He might be held liable to each successive owner of the office block for the running costs incurred by them as a result of the fact that the office block was constructed on defective foundations. Again, most people would regard this as unfair, particularly in the case of owners who acquired the office block knowing of its problems.

For all these reasons, then, English law is justified in refusing to find that Peter owes future owners of the office block a duty to build it with a reasonable degree of care and skill.

Ursula's case

Suppose that Simon, a management consultant, is considering hiring Tariq, an international expert on the coffee business, to form part of a team which will bid for a lucrative consultancy contract with Café Co. Ursula, Simon's lawyer, advises Simon that he cannot hire Tariq to form part of the team because he does not have a legal right to work in the United Kingdom. This advice is incorrect and incompetent, but Simon does not realise this. His team's bid for the lucrative contract is unsuccessful, but he is told that it would have succeeded if his team had included an expert such as Tariq. Could Tariq sue Ursula in negligence for compensation for the money he would have made had Ursula given Simon the correct advice, with the result that Simon would have obtained the consultancy contract and Tariq would have made a lot of money in consultancy fees from Café Co as a result of being part of Simon's winning team?

The answer, it seems, is 'no' – the courts would *not* find that Ursula owed *Tariq* a duty of care in the advice she gave Simon.[83] Despite the different setting, it should be clear after a moment's reflection that almost all of the reasons why a duty of care will *not* be owed by Peter to future owners of the office block he is building will also apply to deny that Ursula owed Tariq a duty of care in the advice she gave Simon. Ursula will have owed Simon a duty (both in contract and in negligence) to advise him with a reasonable degree of care and skill, but she will have been paid by Simon for assuming that duty. Given this, it would bring the law into disrepute if it awarded Tariq for free the same rights against Ursula that Simon had to pay Ursula to acquire. And the law would be brought into even more disrepute if the consequence of its awarding such rights to Tariq was that *Simon* had to pay Ursula *more* than her usual fees to cover the fact that the law had awarded such rights to *Tariq*. Moreover, finding that Ursula owed a duty to Tariq would create a risk of her being exposed to liabilities that were out of all proportion to her fault – if she were held liable to Tariq for the consultancy fees that he missed out on as a result of her failure to give Simon competent advice, then why not all the other members of the team?

We would therefore argue that the law is justified in refusing to find that Ursula owed Tariq a duty of care in this case.

[83] See, for example, *Williams* v *Natural Life Health Foods Ltd* [1998] 1 WLR 830. Despite Ursula's profession, the 'principle' in *White* v *Jones* (see above, pp. 150–4) would not apply in her case as Simon did not hire her in order to confer a benefit on Tariq, but for his, Simon's, own benefit.

Hector's case

Suppose that Gareth is a farmer who produces organic ducks at his farm in Norfolk. The market for organic ducks is relatively small and prices are good. Hector, who owns the farm next to Gareth's, hatches the idea of making some money by importing organic ducks from overseas.

Hector's first foray into the organic duck business is unsuccessful. He severely overestimates how many ducks consumers will want to purchase and ends up having to reduce his prices below his costs in order to dispose of his stock. Hector's prices are reduced so low that Gareth has to offer large discounts to keep his customers. After Gareth's prices have risen back to their previous level, Hector tries again to break into the organic duck business. But this time he fails to realise that the ducks that he is importing are very cheap because they are from a country which is regularly affected by outbreaks of a highly contagious poultry disease. Most UK poultry producers will not purchase stock from this country because of the risk of introducing the disease into the UK. Unfortunately the disease is detected in one of the ducks which Hector imports and the UK government bans all movement of poultry from farms within 10 km of Hector's for three months as a precautionary measure. The ban makes Gareth's ducks almost valueless; in three months' time they will be too old for sale as human food, and only suitable for pet food.

No doubt Gareth would like to sue Hector for the business losses that he has suffered due to his errors. But it is almost certain that English law would hold that Hector did not owe Gareth a duty to take care not to reduce the value of his ducks. Is this right? We think so. First of all, it is unlikely that placing a duty of care on Hector not to run his business in such a way as to harm Gareth's business unjustifiably would have enhanced the security of Gareth's business. If Hector's desire to make profits for himself was not incentive enough for him to take care not to make stupid business decisions, the fact that he owed Gareth a duty of care not to make such decisions would not have encouraged him to be any wiser in his decision-making. Secondly, even if limiting Hector's freedom to run his business as he wishes would be a price worth paying to enhance the security of Gareth's business, the adverse side effects that would result from imposing a duty of care on Hector in this case would make it wrong for the courts to impose such a duty of care on Hector. Finding that businesses owe their competitors a duty to take care not to make excessively risky decisions that unjustifiably harm those competitors would: (1) subject too many business decisions to legal regulation to be acceptable; (2) make the law extremely complex, uncertain and difficult to apply; and (3) flood the courts with negligence claims based on breach of the above duty, thus damaging the courts' abilities to enforce more important duties of care.

Despite these concerns, courts outside England have been tempted to recognise the existence of a duty situation that would cover the case where Gareth suffers business losses because Hector carelessly introduces disease into the vicinity of Gareth's farm. For instance, in *Perre* v *Apand Pty Ltd*[84] the High Court of Australia held that a defendant supplier of seed potatoes, which was aware that access to the lucrative Western Australian market would be lost to all local potato growers and processors if a potato disease was introduced into the area, owed a duty to local potato growers and processors not to introduce the disease into the area. The High Court argued that recognising the existence of such a duty

[84] (1999) 198 CLR 180.

was justified because the duty would not be owed to an indeterminate class[85] and that the members of the class to whom the duty would be owed were particularly vulnerable to such loss, in the sense that they could not protect themselves against it.[86] Some members of the High Court also attached significance to the fact that the claim seemed *close* to a private nuisance claim for unreasonable interference with the use and enjoyment of land, which would have been permitted.[87]

It seems likely that the English courts would refuse to follow the High Court's decision in *Perre*.[88] Recognising that simple 'vulnerability' to suffering some kind of pure economic loss is a sufficient basis for finding that other people owe you a duty of care not to cause you that harm is very likely to result in all of the adverse side effects identified in the last but one paragraph above.[89]

Acts or omissions; pure economic loss; public bodies

Harris *v* Evans

The 'Harris' of *Harris* v *Evans*[90] used a mobile telescopic crane to provide bungee jumping facilities to members of the public. The 'Evans' of *Harris* v *Evans* was a health and safety inspector who inspected the crane when it was on a site in Devon. Evans recommended to the local council that Harris not be allowed to use the crane until it had been certified as fit to be used for bungee jumping. The council acted on Evans' recommendation and forbade Harris to use his crane until he had obtained such a certificate. It was, in fact, impossible – and also completely unnecessary for the purposes of ensuring the public's health and safety – for Harris to obtain such a certificate, and so Harris found himself unable to offer bungee jumping facilities at the site in Devon. Nor could he do so anywhere else: on Evans's initiative, a neighbouring council warned Harris not to offer bungee jumping facilities at any site within their jurisdiction until he had obtained the right certificate for his crane; and when Harris tried to set up shop at another site, the local council that was in charge of that site forbade Harris from doing so (again, presumably at Evans's instigation). Harris went to court and it was held that Harris need not obtain a certificate saying that his crane was suit-

85 It seems to have been assumed by the majority that the duty would only be owed to farms and potato businesses physically based in the 20 km exclusion zone round any outbreak of disease. Kirby J, one of the majority judges, expressly distinguished the cases of the claimants from the situation of the trucking firm that used to drive their potatoes to Western Australia and the position of the Western Australian consumers who had to pay more for potatoes from elsewhere (ibid., at [298]).

86 McHugh J discussed the concept of 'vulnerability' most extensively (ibid., at [118]–[129]). He accepted that there are different degrees of 'vulnerability' and different ways of demonstrating it: 'The degree and the nature of vulnerability sufficient to found a duty of care will no doubt vary from case to case. Although each category will have to formulate a particular standard, the ultimate question will be one of fact.'

87 Ibid., at [14] (per Gleeson CJ), [196] (per Gummow J). An alternative analysis might have attached importance to the fact that the claimants were subjected to loss by precautionary measures designed to prevent the defendant's negligence causing an even greater amount of property damage: since the defendant would have been liable for such property damage it might seem only fair to hold that it also owed a duty to those whose economic interests would foreseeably be harmed in order to prevent such damage.

88 See, for example, *Weller & Co.* v *Foot and Mouth Disease Research Institute* [1966] 1 QB 569 (virus causing foot and mouth disease escaped from defendants' premises and caused outbreak of foot and mouth disease in area with the result that claimants' business as cattle auctioneers was temporarily suspended; no duty of care not to release virus owed by defendants to claimants).

89 For a more positive view of the decision in *Perre*, see Stapleton 2002a and 2003b.

90 [1998] 1 WLR 1285.

able to be used for bungee jumping in order to use the crane. At that stage, Harris had been put out of business for roughly three months. He sued Evans in negligence for compensation for the economic loss he had suffered as a result of Evans's incompetent advice. The Court of Appeal rejected his claim, holding that Evans had not owed Harris a duty of care.

We would argue that, *in principle*, the court *should* have found that Evans owed Harris a duty of care. On one side of the equation, Harris's business was his livelihood, and so the harm that he would suffer if his business were unjustifiably suspended as a result of the activities of a health and safety inspector was potentially very serious. On the other side, Evans enjoyed no effective freedom to interfere unjustifiably with Harris's business in the first place because, as a health and safety inspector, he was operating under a raft of statutory and contractual duties that regulated how and when he could interfere with someone else's business. Given this, we would argue that limiting Evans's freedom to interfere unjustifiably with Harris's business was a price worth paying to enhance Harris's business security.

Having said that, we would argue that the Court of Appeal was right to decline to find that Evans owed Harris a duty of care because of the adverse side effects that would result from such a finding. Evans's fundamental duty was to act in the interests of the public's health and safety. Finding that he owed Harris a duty of care in this situation may well have caused him to fail in that fundamental duty. If the law had said that Evans owed Harris a duty of care, Evans would have known that: (1) if he took steps to close down Harris's business, he might be sued in negligence by Harris; and (2) if he failed to close down Harris's business and a member of the public was harmed jumping off Harris's crane, that member of the public could *not* sue Evans in negligence for compensation for his or her injuries.[91] The combination of points (1) and (2) would have resulted in Evans's having a bias in favour of not closing down Harris's business when he went about his job of inspecting Harris's business. The existence of such a bias would be unacceptable in an officer whose sole focus should be on protecting the public. So in order to stop this bias arising, the Court of Appeal was right to find in *Harris* v *Evans* that Evans did not owe Harris a duty of care.

It would have been more difficult, we would suggest, to refuse to find that a duty of care was owed in *Harris* v *Evans* had the facts of that case been slightly different. Suppose that Harris could not have operated his business without getting a certificate from Evans saying that his crane was suitable to be used for bungee jumping. And suppose that Evans had refused to grant Harris such a certificate for no good reason. In such a case, finding that Evans owed Harris a duty of care in processing his application for a certificate would not – we would argue – have introduced an unacceptable bias into Evans's deliberations as to whether or not to grant Harris a certificate. This is because, had Evans owed Harris such a duty of care, Evans would have known that: (1) if he refused to grant a certificate, he might be sued in negligence by Harris; and (2) if he granted Harris a certificate and a member of the public was injured as a result, that member of the public could sue Evans in negligence.[92] Point (2) would have the effect of annulling any bias in favour of granting Harris

[91] Point (2) follows from the discussion of Paul's case, above.

[92] Unless the existence of such a duty of care was denied for public policy reasons, Evans would have owed the injured member of the public a duty of care in deciding whether or not to grant Harris a certificate under the physical danger principle (see above, pp. 73–4), it being foreseeable that if he granted Harris a certificate when his mobile crane was unsuitable to be used for bungee jumping, a member of the public would be injured as a result.

a certificate that would be created by point (1). However, it is probable that recognising that Evans owed Harris a duty of care in processing his application for a certificate would have had further adverse side effects which would have justified the courts in refusing to find that Evans owed Harris such a duty of care.[93] This seems to follow from our discussion of Mary's case, below.

Mary's case

Suppose that Richard has decided to set up a business selling air tickets to people going on skiing holidays and he is informed that he requires an Air Travel Organiser's Licence (ATOL) from the Civil Aviation Authority (CAA) before he can do this legally. One of the criteria which the CAA must be satisfied about before it can grant a licence is Richard's fitness to run such a business. Suppose further that Mary, an employee of the CAA, searches a computer database of people who have the sort of convictions which would make them unfit, but because she carelessly misspells Richard's name she wrongly concludes that Richard has several convictions for theft. Although this mistake is eventually realised the delay that it causes means that Richard receives his licence too late to launch his business for that year's ski season. Under English law it seems unlikely that Richard would be able to sue Mary in negligence for the economic loss he suffered as a result of missing a year's business. The courts would hold that Mary did not owe Richard a duty of care in processing his application for a licence.[94]

In principle, the courts *should* recognise that Mary owed Richard a duty of care here. Assuming that Mary had a contractual duty to the CAA to do a good job of processing Richard's application, she had no effective freedom not to process his application properly – so sacrificing that (non-existent) freedom would seem an acceptable price to pay for the purpose of enhancing Richard's security in running his business. Would recognising that Mary owed Richard a duty of care here have any adverse side effects that would be serious enough to override the beneficial effects of finding that Mary owed Richard a duty of care? Five possible adverse side effects can be identified:

(1) Finding that Mary owed Richard a duty of care in this case might result in a general

[93] *Important note.* If the Health and Safety Executive were under a statutory duty to take reasonable steps to ensure that business people like Harris were not unjustifiably denied a certificate to trade, but Parliament had made it clear that breach of that duty should *not* be actionable in tort, then a duty of care should still have been denied on our altered version of the facts in *Harris* v *Evans* on the ground that recognising such a duty would undermine democracy and bring the law into disrepute. This is because recognising that Evans owed Harris a duty of care in processing his application for a certificate to trade would mean that Evans could be held liable in negligence if he failed to process Harris's application correctly. This in turn would mean that the Health and Safety Executive would be vicariously liable for Evans's negligence, thus subverting Parliament's intention that the Health and Safety Executive should *not* be held liable in tort when someone was unjustifiably denied a certificate to trade. The only way of avoiding this result would be for the courts to refuse to find that Evans owed Harris a duty of care. For a closely analogous case decided on exactly these lines, see *Neil Martin Ltd* v *The Commissioners for Her Majesty's Customs & Excise* [2007] EWCA Civ 1041 (no duty of care on tax inspector properly to process contractor's application for a certificate that would allow him to claim payment for building work without deduction of tax even though without such a certificate the contractor would find it very difficult to obtain work (as employers are not generally happy to incur the inconvenience of deducting tax from payments to a building contractor and handing that tax over to the Revenue & Customs)), at [72].

[94] *Rowling* v *Takaro Properties Ltd* [1988] AC 473, at 500–3 (denial of licence to issues shares to Japanese company in return for company investing capital in New Zealand company); *Neil Martin Ltd* v *The Commissioners for Her Majesty's Customs and Excise* [2007] EWCA Civ 1041 (delay in issuing certificate to accept payments for building work without deduction of tax).

slowdown in the processing of applications for licences, as operators like Mary might be encouraged – in order to avoid any possibility of being sued in negligence – to do double and triple checks of people's names against their computer databases.

(2) Finding that Mary owed Richard a duty of care here might open the door to claims being brought against the CAA by people who claim that the CAA has wrongly judged them to be unsuitable to run a business. This might in turn have various adverse side effects, such as introducing an unacceptable bias into the CAA's deliberations in favour of granting applicants an ATOL. The courts might try and close this door by saying that people like Mary owe people like Richard a duty of care not to make 'operational' errors in processing their applications, but the CAA does not owe applicants for an ATOL a duty of care not to make 'judgmental' errors in considering whether they are suitable people to run a business. However, such a distinction would not protect the CAA from being sued in negligence for 'operational' errors in denying people's applications for an ATOL, and this in turn would create difficult and hard to resolve questions for the courts. Suppose, for example, the CAA refused to grant someone an ATOL because it gave so much weight in its deliberations to someone's past conviction for theft that it failed to give that person any credit for his subsequent charitable work. Would that count as an 'operational' or a 'judgmental' error?[95]

(3) Finding that Mary owed Richard a duty of care in this case would open a can of worms: a great deal of uncertainty would be created as to how far the precedent set in Mary's case went; and a lot of time would be consumed by the courts in attempting to resolve this uncertainty (possibly unsuccessfully), with the result that the courts' abilities to enforce more important duties of care would be blunted.

(4) If the CAA was under a statutory duty to process people's applications for an ATOL properly, but Parliament had made it clear that a breach of this duty should *not* be actionable in tort, finding that Mary owed Richard a duty of care might bring the law into disrepute on the ground that doing so undermines Parliament's intention that the CAA should not be held liable when people's applications for an ATOL were not processed properly.[96]

(5) If we characterise what Mary did as a *failure* to process Richard's application properly, the law would be brought into disrepute if it found that Mary owed Richard a duty of care in this case. People would rightly think that the law had a strange set of priorities if it found that a duty of care was owed in Mary's case – where her failure resulted in Richard suffering economic loss – when no duty of care is owed in Paul's case, above, where Paul's failure to intervene to stop Siobhan being attacked resulted in Siobhan being physically injured. Of course, it is possible to distinguish Mary's case from Paul's case on the ground that Mary did something *positive* to stop Richard's application for

[95] For similar reasons, the courts have been chary of adopting any bright line rule that public bodies cannot be sued in negligence for 'policy' decisions but can be sued in negligence for 'operational' errors. See, for example, the Privy Council's statement in *Rowling* v *Takaro Properties Ltd* [1988] AC 473 that the policy/operational distinction 'does not provide a touchstone of liability, but rather is expressive of the need to exclude altogether those cases in which the decision under attack is of such a kind that a question whether it has been made negligently is unsuitable for judicial resolution, of which notable examples are discretionary decisions on the allocation of scarce resources or the distribution of risks . . .'

[96] See above, n. 93.

an ATOL being granted; however, it is unlikely that the general public would be convinced by such fine distinctions.

Given these adverse side effects, we think that a good case can be made for saying that the law is justified in refusing to find that Mary owed Richard a duty of care in the above case.

The Yuen Kun Yeu *case*

In *Yuen Kun Yeu* v *Attorney General for Hong Kong*,[97] the claimants lost all the money they had invested with a deposit-taking company called the American and Panama Finance Co. Ltd (APF) when it went into liquidation. The claimants alleged that the company was run fraudulently and that the company had taken unacceptable risks with the money invested with it. The company was only allowed to accept deposits because it had been registered as a deposit-taking company by the defendant, the Commissioner of Deposit-taking Companies, under the Deposit-taking Companies Ordinance, which had been passed to protect members of the public depositing money with deposit-taking companies. The claimants sued the defendant, claiming that he should have known APF was being run fraudulently and that it was taking excessive risks with its clients' monies, and that he therefore owed them a duty of care either not to register APF as a deposit-taking company, or to take APF off the register once it was on it.

The Privy Council held that the defendant did not owe the claimants a duty of care. In our view, this was correct. Any other conclusion would have had numerous adverse side effects:

(1) *Damaging the rule of law*. Finding that a duty of care was owed in the *Yuen Kun Yeu* case would have made the law very uncertain – it would have been very difficult to know how far the precedent set by that decision went. Resolving that uncertainty would have taken up a great deal of the courts' time, thus blunting their abilities to enforce more important duties of care. Finally, finding that a duty of care was owed in cases such as *Yuen Kun Yeu* would have made the law very difficult to apply – given the delicacy of the issues involved and fine judgments required to resolve them, the courts would have found it very difficult to determine whether a banking authority had failed to take sufficient care to protect the interests of depositors in registering, or failing to deregister, a bank or investment company.

(2) *Bringing the law into disrepute*. Finding that the defendant owed the claimants a duty of care would have brought the law into disrepute in a number of different ways. First of all, democracy would have been undermined. When Parliament passed the Deposit-taking Companies Ordinance, it did not place the defendant under a statutory duty to take care in his decisions as to whether or not to register, or deregister, a deposit-taking company. Given this, the Privy Council would have been undermining Parliament's intentions by finding that the defendant owed the claimants a duty of care in negligence.[98] Secondly, the defendant would have been exposed to a potential liability far out of proportion to his fault in either registering, or failing to deregister, APF. Thirdly, it is likely that the defendant would have carried the major part of the bill for compensating the claimants for the fact that they

[97] [1988] AC 175.
[98] Ibid., at 195.

had lost their money when other people – that is, the managers of APF – were far more responsible for the fact that the claimants lost their money. Fourthly, if we characterise what the defendant did here as a *failure* to protect the claimants against the risk of losing their money, the law would be brought into disrepute if it found liability in this kind of case, but not in a case like Paul's, above.

(3) *Disrupting the activities of public bodies.* To find that the defendant owed the claimants a duty of care in deciding whether or not to register, or deregister, APF might have introduced into his mind a bias in favour of deregistering APF once it was on the register. Such a bias would have been undesirable given that the defendant also had to pay attention to the interests of existing depositors with APF in deciding whether or not to deregister APF.

10 Breach of duty

In the last six chapters we looked at the question: When will one person owe another a duty of care? In this chapter, we are concerned with the question: When will someone who owed another a duty of care be held to have breached that duty? The law in this area is far from straightforward to understand. We will begin by setting out the most basic principles that govern the inquiry into whether or not someone has breached a duty of care owed to another; later on, the picture will become more complex.

BASIC PRINCIPLES

Suppose A owed B a duty of care of some description – say, a duty to take reasonable steps to save B from harm. Obviously, A will be held to have breached that duty of care if A *personally* failed to take resonable steps to save B from harm. In judging whether or not A was guilty of such a personal failure, the courts will take a number of different considerations into account.

Degree and foreseeability of risk

Suppose A owed B a duty to take reasonable steps to ensure that B would be reasonably safe in doing *x*, say, visiting A's premises or working for A. If it is claimed that A breached this duty because he personally failed to take reasonable steps to eliminate some risk of harm that B was exposed to in doing *x*, the courts will, in evaluating this claim, first ask: Did A know or ought he to have known of the existence of this risk? If the answer is 'no', he will not have breached the duty of care he owed B.

If, on the other hand, the answer is 'yes', the courts will then ask: How serious was the risk?[1] If the risk was *non-trivial*, then A will have breached the duty of care he owed B to take reasonable steps to ensure that B would be reasonably safe in doing *x* if he did not take sufficient measures to eliminate the risk in question; whether the measures, if any, A personally took to eliminate the risk in question were 'sufficient' will depend on how serious the risk was.

If the risk was *trivial*, the courts will ask: How difficult or costly would it have been to eliminate the risk? If it would have been difficult or costly to eliminate the risk in question, then A will not have breached the duty he owed B to take reasonable steps to ensure that B would be reasonably safe in doing *x* even though he did nothing to eliminate the risk in question. If, on the other hand, it would have been easy for A to eliminate the risk in ques-

[1] The seriousness of a risk is measured by mutiplying the probability that that risk will eventuate by the size of the harm that will be done if that risk eventuates.

tion, then A's failure to eliminate that risk will have put him in breach of the duty he owed B to take reasonable steps to ensure that B would be reasonably safe in doing *x*.[2]

Let us illustrate these propositions by considering a few cases. In *Paris* v *Stepney Borough Council*,[3] the claimant was employed as a fitter in the defendants' garage. The claimant, who was already blind in one eye, lost the use of the other eye when, in removing a bolt on a rusty vehicle by striking it with a hammer, a chip flew up from the bolt and into his good eye. The claimant sued the defendants, claiming that the defendants breached the duty that they owed him to take reasonable steps to see that he would be reasonably safe in working for them when they failed to provide him with goggles to wear in doing 'bolt work' for them. The House of Lords allowed the claimant's claim. While the probability that the claimant would suffer an eye injury in doing 'bolt work' for the defendants was extremely low, the seriousness of the harm that would be suffered by the claimant if he did suffer an eye injury in doing 'bolt work' for the claimant was very high, given that he had only one good eye and would therefore be completely blinded if he suffered an eye injury in doing 'bolt work' for the defendants. Given this, the risk that the claimant would suffer an eye injury in doing 'bolt work' for the defendants could not be dismissed as trivial and the defendants, in failing to provide the claimant with goggles to wear when doing 'bolt work' for them, failed to take sufficient measures to eliminate that risk, given its seriousness.[4]

In *Hudson* v *Ridge Manufacturing Co. Ltd*,[5] the claimant was employed by the defendants and was injured when C, one of the claimant's fellow employees, tripped him up. It was held that the defendants were liable to compensate the claimant for his injuries: the claimant's accident had happened, in part, because the defendants had breached the duty they owed the claimant to take reasonable steps to ensure that he would be reasonably safe in working for them. C had for years been in the habit of engaging in this sort of horseplay which exposed his colleagues – including the claimant – to a very high degree of risk of suffering some kind of injury. When the defendants found out about C's behaviour they failed to take reasonable steps to prevent C from acting in this way. They did reprimand C for his behaviour when it occurred but, given the seriousness of the risk that C's behaviour posed for his colleagues, this was not sufficient. The defendants should have done more to deter C from engaging in horseplay when the system of reprimands plainly failed to work to cure his behaviour.

[2] We would submit that the law as stated in the preceding two paragraphs is unaffected by s 1 of the Compensation Act 2006, which provides that 'A court considering a claim in negligence . . . *may*, in determining whether the defendant should have taken particular steps to meet a standard of care (whether by taking precautions against a risk or otherwise), have regard to whether a requirement to take those steps might – (a) prevent a desirable activity from being undertaken . . ., or (b) discourage persons from undertaking functions in connection with a desirable activity' (emphasis added). Where the risk to which the claimant is exposed to was high then factors (a) and (b) will not and should not be taken into account in determining whether the defendant took reasonable steps to eliminate that risk; where the risk was trivial then factors (a) and (b) will be and should be taken into account in determining this issue.

[3] [1951] AC 367.

[4] It might have been different if the claimant had had *two* good eyes when working for the defendants. In such a case, the harm that he would have suffered if he had injured an eye in doing 'bolt work' for the defendants would not have been so serious and as a result the risk of him suffering an eye injury in doing 'bolt work' for the defendants would not have been so serious and might have even qualified as trivial – in which case, the defendants' failure to eliminate it by providing him with goggles that he could wear in doing 'bolt work' might have been excused on cost grounds.

[5] [1957] 2 QB 348.

In *Latimer* v *AEC*,[6] the claimant was employed by the defendants. He was injured when he slipped on an oily cooling mixture which had spread onto the floor of the defendants' factory where the claimant worked. The defendants had put down some sawdust to make the floor less slippery but the sawdust did not cover all the areas of the factory floor where the oil had spread. The claimant slipped on one of the untreated areas and sued the defendants, claiming that the defendants had breached the duty they owed him to take reasonable steps to ensure that the factory would be reasonably safe for him to work in. The claimant's claim was dismissed. The presence of the oily cooling mixture on the factory floor did, initially, expose the claimant – and other employees – to a serious risk of being injured in some way. However, by spreading sawdust on the floor, the defendants turned that risk into a trivial one. Once the sawdust was spread, the risk that the claimant would suffer some kind of injury by slipping on the floor became negligible. As it would have been costly and inconvenient for the defendants to take further steps – such as closing the factory down while the floor dried out – to eliminate the remaining risk that the claimant would suffer some kind of injury by slipping on the floor, the defendants did not breach the duty they owed the claimant to take reasonable steps to ensure that he would be reasonably safe in working for them when they failed to eliminate that remaining risk.

Personal circumstances

When will the courts take into account A's personal circumstances – such things as his wealth, health and physical skills – in judging whether A breached a duty of care owed to B? It depends on what kind of duty of care it was that A owed B.[7]

(1) *Negative duties.* If A owed B a duty to take care not to do *x* and A did *x* because he suffered from some kind of personal failing, the courts will find that A breached that duty if he knew or ought to have known that he suffered from that failing; on the other hand, if he did not know and had no reason to know that he suffered from that failing, the courts may well find that A did not breach the duty of care that he owed B.

So – in *Nettleship* v *Weston*,[8] the claimant gave the defendant, a friend's wife, some driving lessons. In the third lesson, he instructed her to turn left at a junction. She began to turn left but then she panicked and failed to straighten the car. The car mounted the pavement and struck a lamp post. As a result, the claimant's kneecap was smashed. The claimant sued the defendant, claiming that she had breached the duty she owed him to take care not to drive dangerously. At first instance, his claim was dismissed on the ground that the defendant had done her best to drive safely: it was her lack of experience that had resulted in her driving as dangerously as she did. The Court of Appeal reversed the decision at first instance. In the Court of Appeal's view, the defendant's lack of experience was not to be taken into account in judging whether or not she breached the duty she owed the claimant to take care not to drive dangerously.

In *Nettleship* v *Weston*, the defendant was aware that she was an inexperienced driver.

6 [1953] AC 643.
7 See, generally, Kidner 1991, 2–16.
8 [1971] 2 QB 691.

Mansfield v *Weetabix Ltd*,[9] on the other hand, was a case where the defendant lorry driver was unaware, and had no reason to be aware, of the personal failing that caused him to drive his lorry into the claimants' shop. The defendant in that case unknowingly suffered from malignant insulinoma – a condition which meant that, if he did not eat properly, his brain would be starved of the quantities of glucose necessary for it to function properly. On the day of the accident, the defendant had set out on a 40-mile journey without eating properly and, as a result, his driving became more and more erratic, culminating in his driving off the road and into the claimants' shop. The claimants sued the defendant, claiming that he had breached the duty he owed them to take care not to drive dangerously. The Court of Appeal dismissed the claim.[10] The defendant's malignant insulinoma meant that he could not have helped driving the way he did and so the defendant did not breach the duty he owed the claimants to take care not to drive dangerously. Of course, it would have been different if the defendant had been aware of his condition and gone out driving without taking care to eat properly. His failure to take reasonable steps to ensure that his driving would not be affected by his condition would have put him in breach of the duty he owed to all those on or near the roads used by him – including the claimants – to take care not to drive dangerously.

(2) *Extended* Hedley Byrne *principle*. If A owed B a duty to perform a task with a certain degree of care and skill under the extended principle in *Hedley Byrne*, the courts will hold that A breached that duty if he failed to perform that task with that degree of care and skill.[11] It will be irrelevant whether or not A was actually capable of performing that task with that degree of care and skill. This seems fair enough: if A was so inexperienced that he could not perform the task in question with the requisite degree of care and skill, he only has himself to blame for the fact that, in the end, he was fixed with a duty that he was incapable of fulfilling. If he was incapable of performing the task in question with the degree of care and skill required, he should never have taken the job on or encouraged B to think that he was capable of doing the job with that degree of care and skill.

(3) *Positive duties that were not voluntarily assumed*. If A owed B a duty to take reasonable steps to see that B did not suffer some kind of harm, and that duty of care was not voluntarily assumed,[12] then the courts will not hold that A breached that duty of care if A did his *best* – given his personal circumstances – to see that B did not suffer the harm in question.

So, for example, we have already seen that if a fire starts on land occupied by Eric and

[9] [1998] 1 WLR 1263.

[10] In so doing, they disapproved Neill J's judgment in *Roberts* v *Ramsbottom* [1980] 1 All ER 7, which suggested that a driver who drove his car dangerously due to the fact that he suffered some personal failing would be held to have breached the duty he owed others to take care not to drive dangerously if, at the time he was driving, he enjoyed some *limited* control of the car.

[11] See above, pp. 134–5, for a discussion of how much care and skill someone who takes on a task for another will be required to take under the extended principle in *Hedley Byrne*.

[12] Positive duties of care that are not voluntarily assumed are quite rare: the duty of care an occupier owes trespassers on his land and his neighbours would be an example; as is the duty of care that the police and prison authorities owe suicide risks in their custody. The duty of care that A will owe B to rescue B if A has discouraged other people from saving B is *not* an example: by discouraging those other people from rescuing B, A voluntarily assumed the duty of care that he owed B. Similarly, in the case where A owes B a positive duty of care under the extended principle in *Hedley Byrne*. The duty of care that an occupier will normally owe his visitors is more difficult to classify – in the case where the occupier chooses to invite a visitor onto his land, there is a case for thinking that the duty of care that he will owe the visitor is voluntarily assumed.

threatens to spread onto Wendy's land, Eric will normally owe Wendy a duty to take reasonable steps to put out that fire.[13] In judging whether or not Eric breached this duty, the courts will take into account Eric's personal resources:

> [L]ess must be expected of the infirm than of the able-bodied: the owner of a small property where a hazard arises which threatens a neighbour with substantial interests should not have to do as much as one with larger interests of his own at stake and greater resources to protect them: if the small owner does what he can ... he may be held to have done his duty: he should not be held liable unless it is clearly proved that he could, and reasonably in his individual circumstances should, have done more.[14]

The result is that Eric will merely be required to do the best he can, with the resources he has, to put out the fire. If he does that, then he will discharge the duty of care that he owes Wendy. Similarly, we have already seen that if Gary is imprisoned and it is reasonably foreseeable that he is a suicide risk, the prison authorities will owe Gary a duty to take reasonable steps to see that he does not commit suicide.[15] In judging whether the prison authorities breached this duty, the courts will take into account the prison authorities' resources – so the prison authorities will not necessarily be held to have breached the duty of care they owed A to see that he did not commit suicide if they, through lack of resources, were unable to give him the kind of supervision and treatment that he would have received on a psychiatric ward.[16]

Having said that, suppose A owed B a duty to take reasonable steps to eliminate some danger to which B was exposed, and that duty was not voluntarily assumed. Suppose further that A's resources were such that he could have paid for the services of a professional to come in and eliminate the danger in question. If A chose not to do this and instead attempted to deal with the problem himself, then he will be held to have breached the duty of care that he owed B if he failed to use the same degree of care and skill in dealing with that danger as a professional would have used. It will be no defence for A to say that he did the best he could to eliminate the danger given the abilities he had.

So, for example, suppose that there was some dangerous fixture on Ruth's land and Ruth owed Vijay a duty to take reasonable steps to make the fixture safe. Suppose further that Ruth could have paid for a professional to mend that fixture, but she chose instead to mend it herself. If Ruth did not mend the fixture with the sort of care and skill that a professional would have shown in mending it, Ruth will be held to have breached the duty of care that she owed Vijay – and this is so even if Ruth did the best she could, given her relative lack of expertise in the matter, to mend the fixture herself.[17] Similarly, if Carl falls sick in prison with the result that the prison authorities owe him a duty to take reasonable steps to treat him, if the prison authorities choose to treat him themselves instead of sending him to a proper hospital, they will be required to treat him with the degree of care and skill that he

[13] See above, pp. 177–8.

[14] *Goldman* v *Hargrave* [1967] AC 645, 663 (per Lord Wilberforce). If putting the fire out was beyond A, given his resources, he may still be held to have breached the duty of care that he owed B to take reasonable steps to put the fire out if he did not warn B of the danger and invite B to join with him in putting the fire out: see *Holbeck Hall Hotel Ltd* v *Scarborough BC* [2000] QB 836.

[15] See above, pp. 158–9.

[16] *Knight* v *Home Office* [1990] 3 All ER 237.

[17] *Wells* v *Cooper* [1958] 2 QB 265 (dangerous handle on door).

would have been treated with had he been sent to hospital. If the prison authorities' treatment falls short of that standard, then the prison authorities will breach the duty of care they owe Carl – and this is so even if they did their best to treat Carl properly, given the resources they had.[18]

Professional standards

Suppose A owed B a duty to perform some task with the skill and care that a reasonably competent professional would have exercised in performing that task. Say, for example, that A owed B a duty to perform an operation on her brain with the skill and care that a reasonably competent brain surgeon would have exercised in performing that operation.

As a general rule, in judging whether or not A's performance was up to scratch, the courts will allow themselves to be guided by the opinion of professionals in the field. So if there is a substantial body of opinion within the field of brain surgery that holds that A did nothing wrong in performing the operation on B in the way he did, then the courts will normally find that A discharged the duty of care he owed B in operating on her. If, on the other hand, no one can be found among the community of brain surgeons other than a few cranks and eccentrics to say that A acted properly in operating on B, the courts will normally find that A breached the duty of care he owed B by operating on her in the way he did.

The case of *Maynard* v *West Midlands Regional Health Authority*[19] illustrates the point.[20] In treating the claimant, the defendants subjected the claimant to a diagnostic procedure called a mediastinoscopy which damaged the claimant's vocal cords. The claimant sued the defendants, claiming that they had breached the duty they owed her to treat her with a professional degree of skill and care. The claim failed: the defendants could show that a substantial body of medical opinion would have supported the claimant's being subjected to a mediastinoscopy given her condition.

However, this general rule is subject to an important exception. Returning to the hypothetical example set out above, even if a substantial number of brain surgeons are of the opinion that it was quite proper for A to operate on B in the way he did, the courts will still hold that A breached the duty of care he owed B in operating on her if it was plainly illogical or unreasonable for A to have performed task T in the way he did.[21]

So in *Edward Wong Finance Co. Ltd* v *Johnson Stokes & Master*,[22] the claimants agreed to lend a company $1,355,000 to enable it to purchase a factory in Hong Kong. The loan was to be secured by, among other things, a mortgage of the factory. The defendant firm of solicitors acted for the claimants in the transaction. The factory was already subject to a

[18] *Brooks* v *Home Office* [1999] 2 FLR 33 (pregnant prisoner treated in prison rather than being sent to hospital).

[19] [1984] 1 WLR 634.

[20] The general rule traces its origin to the direction of McNair J in *Bolam* v *Friern Hospital Management Committee* [1957] 1 WLR 582, 587: 'A doctor is not guilty of negligence if he has acted in accordance with a practice accepted as proper by a responsible body of medical men skilled in that particular art... Putting it the other way round, a doctor is not negligent, if he is acting in accordance with such a practice, merely because there is a body of opinion that takes a contrary view.'

[21] *Bolitho* v *City and Hackney Health Authority* [1998] AC 232.

[22] [1984] 1 AC 296. See also *Lloyds Bank Ltd* v *E B Savory and Co.* [1933] AC 201 and *G & K Landenbau (UK) Ltd* v *Crawley & De Reya* [1978] 1 WLR 266.

mortgage which would have to be cleared by the time it was purchased. The defendant firm of solicitors followed the practice – usual in Hong Kong at the time – of forwarding to the sellers the purchase price in return for the sellers' giving them undertakings that they would apply the purchase price to clear the existing mortgage on the factory. The sellers did no such thing and absconded with the purchase money, leaving the claimants with a greatly reduced security for the money they had lent the company to purchase the factory. The claimants sued the defendant firm of solicitors in negligence. They won: it was held that the defendant firm had breached the duty of care it owed the claimants in relation to how it handled the purchase and mortgage of the factory. Given that the defendant firm could easily have secured the claimants' interests by paying off the existing mortgagee rather than relying on the sellers of the factory to do so, the defendant firm could not establish that it handled the purchase and mortgage of the factory with the skill and care that a reasonably competent solicitor would have handled it. The fact that most solicitors in Hong Kong would have acted – and would have thought it proper to act – in the same way as the defendants did was irrelevant.

Common sense

In determining whether or not A breached a duty of care that he owed to B, the courts will always take into account considerations of common sense such as the ones listed below.

Emergencies and other stressful situations

It is common sense that people tend to react sub-optimally in emergencies or in other stressful situations. So if A owed B a duty to take reasonable steps to see that B would be reasonably safe, A should not necessarily be held to have breached that duty of care if he, in an emergency or other stressful situation, failed to do as much as he might have done to ensure that B would be reasonably safe and his failure could reasonably be attributed not to any personal indifference on his part but to the situation in which he found himself.

In *Surtees* v *Kingston-upon-Thames Borough Council*,[23] it was alleged that a foster mother had breached the duty she owed the claimant, a child in her care, to take reasonable steps to ensure that the claimant did not come to any harm. The case was dismissed: there was no evidence that the foster mother had breached that duty. Sir Nicolas Browne-Wilkinson V-C warned that the courts:

> should be wary in its approach to holding parents in breach of a duty of care owed to their children . . . The studied calm of the Royal Courts of Justice, concentrating on one point at a time, is light years away from the circumstances prevailing in the average home. The mother is looking after a fast moving toddler at the same time as cooking a meal, answering the telephone, looking after the other children and doing all the other things that the average mother has to cope with simultaneously, or in quick succession, in the normal household. We should be slow to characterise as negligent the care which ordinary loving mothers are able to give individual children, given the rough-and-tumble of home life.[24]

[23] [1991] 2 FLR 559.
[24] Ibid., 583–4.

The House of Lords took a similar line in *Carmathenshire County Council* v *Lewis*.[25] In that case, it will be recalled, a four-year-old boy attending nursery school wandered off the school premises and onto the road running alongside the nursery school. The claimant's husband, who was driving a lorry along the road, swerved to avoid the boy, crashed into a tree and died. The claimant claimed – and the House of Lords accepted – that the teachers at the school had owed her husband a duty to take reasonable steps to ensure that children at the school did not wander into the road outside the school.

In determining whether any of the teachers at the school had breached this duty of care, their Lordships focused on the conduct of one Miss Morgan, who was supposed to be supervising the boy and one other child at the time the accident happened. She was supposed to take the pair for a walk and had briefly left them alone in a classroom. Having left them, she was then detained attending to a child who needed to have a bandage put on because he had hurt himself. The four-year-old boy took advantage of her absence to leave the classroom, walk across the playground and wander out into the road. The House of Lords refused to find that Morgan had breached the duty she owed users of the road to take reasonable steps to ensure that children at the nursery did not escape into the road. Lord Tucker noted, '[i]t is very easy after the event to think of several things she might have done which would have avoided the accident that resulted from her absence' but refused to find that she had failed to take reasonable steps not to allow the four-year-old boy to wander off the premises – in the circumstances, faced with the sudden need to bandage up another child's wounds, Morgan's conduct had been quite natural.[26]

Similarly, in *Wilsher* v *Essex Area Health Authority*, Mustill LJ held that, in considering whether or not a doctor or a nurse had failed in his or her duty to treat a patient with the degree of care and skill that a reasonably competent doctor or nurse occupying the same post would exercise in treating a patient, 'full allowance must be made for the fact that certain aspects of the treatment may have [had] to be carried out in what [one may call] "battle conditions." An emergency may overburden the available resources, and, if an individual is forced by circumstances to do too many things at once, the fact that he does one of them incorrectly should not lightly be taken as negligence.'[27]

Games

A similar principle applies in the case of games involving physical contact. If A and B are engaged in playing such a game, it is common sense that each of them is liable in the heat of the moment to do something that involves some kind of error of judgment or lapse, with the result that the other is injured in some way. So if A is guilty of such an error or lapse, he will not automatically be held to have breached the duty of care he owed B in playing

[25] [1955] AC 549.

[26] A claim against the council succeeded in the *Carmathenshire* case: it was held that they also owed people like the claimant's husband a duty to take reasonable steps to see that the children at the school did not escape into the road, and the council breached that duty because they did not take adequate steps to see that the school gates were kept locked.

[27] [1987] 1 QB 730, 749. To the same effect, in relation to soldiers conducting peace-keeping operations, see *Bici* v *Ministry of Defence* [2004] EWHC 786, at [46].

their game: it is only if his error or lapse involved a wanton or reckless disregard for B's safety that he will be held to have breached the duty of care he owed B.[28]

Self-help

It is common sense that adults can be expected to act in their own best interests. Given this, if A owes B, an adult, a duty to take reasonable steps to ensure that B is not harmed in some way, A can usually discharge that duty by putting B in a position to save himself from being harmed in that way. And if B is already in a position to save himself from being harmed in that way, A will not breach the duty of care he owes B if he takes no steps to ensure that B will not be harmed in that way.

So suppose Gary visited Dawn in her house. As we have seen, under the Occupiers' Liability Act 1957, Dawn will have owed Gary a duty to take reasonable steps to see that he was reasonably safe in visiting her. In determining whether or not Dawn breached that duty, the courts are enjoined by the Act to take the following considerations into account.

First, s 2(4)(a) of the Act provides that if Gary suffered harm because of a danger which he had been warned of by Dawn then Dawn should not be held to have breached the duty of care she owed Gary if the warning was 'in all the circumstances ... enough to enable [Gary] to be reasonably safe'. If Dawn warned Gary of the danger and the warning was sufficient to enable Gary to avoid the danger himself then Dawn, by giving the warning, will have discharged the duty she owed Gary to take reasonable steps to ensure that he would not be harmed by the existence of that danger. Dawn could reasonably expect, having equipped Gary with that warning, that Gary would act to save himself from being harmed as a result of the existence of that danger.[29]

Secondly, s 2(3)(b) provides that the courts, in assessing whether Dawn breached the duty of care she owed Gary, must take into account the fact that 'an occupier may expect that a person, in the exercise of his calling, will appreciate and guard against any risks ordinarily incident to it, so far as the occupier leaves him free to do so'. So if Gary visited Dawn's house to mend a defective light fitting and Dawn did not take any steps to ensure that Gary would not be electrocuted in mending the fitting, Dawn will not have breached the duty she owed Gary to see that he would be reasonably safe in visiting her premises – Dawn could reasonably have expected Gary to take steps to ensure that he would not be electrocuted in mending the fitting.

The same principles apply in the employment context. So, in *Qualcast (Wolverhampton)*

[28] *Wooldridge* v *Sumner* [1963] 2 QB 43 (spectator injured when defendant rode his horse too fast); *Condon* v *Basi* [1985] 1 WLR 866 (footballer injured as a result of foul tackle by defendant); *Caldwell* v *Fitzgerald* [2001] EWCA Civ 1054 (jockey injured in race as a result of actions of two other jockeys); *Blake* v *Galloway* [2004] EWCA Civ 814 (claimant struck in eye by piece of bark thrown at him by defendant in course of good natured horseplay).

[29] See *Roles* v *Nathan* [1963] 1 WLR 1117 (smoke from a boiler which heated the Manchester Assembly Rooms began to fill the boiler room; the claimants' husbands, chimney sweeps, were called in to clean the flues along which the smoke was supposed to travel before reaching a chimney; an expert was called in to inspect the problem and he warned the chimney sweeps not to work in the flues while the boiler was lit as there was a substantial danger that they would suffer carbon monoxide poisoning as a result; the sweeps disregarded the warning and died as a result; held – occupier of the Assembly Rooms did not breach the duty of care he owed the sweeps under the 1957 Act: the warning they had been given was enough to ensure that they would be reasonably safe from suffering carbon monoxide poisoning while working on the flues).

Ltd v *Haynes*,[30] the claimant spilled some molten metal onto his left foot and was injured as a result. The claimant claimed the accident happened because his employer, the defendant, had breached the duty it owed him to take reasonable steps to ensure that he did not do his work in a way that would unreasonably endanger his health and safety. It was held that the defendant had not breached this duty. The defendant had made available to the claimant a stock of protective spats which were designed to ensure that employees would not suffer any injury if they spilled molten metal on themselves. As the claimant was an experienced worker and knew of the need to wear spats when handling molten metal to protect himself from injury, the defendant, in providing the claimant with such spats, had done all he needed to do to ensure that the defendant would not do his work in a way that would unreasonably endanger his health and safety. It would have been different if the claimant had been inexperienced; in such a case, the defendant – in order to discharge the duty of care he owed the claimant – would have had not only to supply the claimant with protective spats but also to instruct him to put them on when handling molten metal.

In *James* v *Hepworth & Grandage Ltd*,[31] the claimant – like the claimant in *Qualcast* – spilled molten metal on himself and suffered injury because he was not wearing protective spats. In this case, the claimant's employer, the defendant, had made available to his employees a stock of protective spats and had posted warnings instructing his employees to wear spats when handling molten metal. The claimant was illiterate and therefore did not understand the warnings and the need to wear spats when handling molten metal. He sued the defendant, claiming that the accident occurred because the defendant had breached the duty it owed him to take reasonable steps to ensure that he did not do his work in a way that would unreasonably endanger his health and safety. The Court of Appeal held that the defendant did not breach this duty: the defendant had no reason to believe that the claimant was illiterate and was therefore entitled to expect that he would heed any warnings it gave him as to what he should wear in performing particular tasks. The defendant therefore discharged the duty of care it owed the claimant by supplying him with protective spats and warning him of the need to use them.

Children

It is common sense that, while adults can be expected to act in their own best interests, children cannot be expected to do the same. Given this, if A owes B, a child, a duty to take reasonable steps to ensure that B is not harmed in some way, A may be required to do more to ensure that B is not harmed in that way than he would if B were an adult. The Occupiers' Liability Act 1957 recognises this. Section 2(3)(a) of the Act provides that if an occupier of premises owes a child visiting those premises a duty under the Act to see that the visitor would be reasonably safe in using those premises for the purpose for which he was there, the courts should take into account – for the purpose of deciding whether or not the occupier breached that duty – the fact that 'an occupier must be prepared for children to be less careful than adults'.

So if Karen's premises contain a staircase which is dangerous to use and Karen posts a notice warning visitors of that fact, Karen's putting up that notice will discharge the duty

[30] [1959] AC 743.
[31] [1968] 1 QB 94.

she owes her adult visitors to take reasonable steps to ensure that they are not harmed as a result of the staircase being dangerous to use (so long as it is not necessary to use the staircase) but might not discharge the common duty of care that she will owe children who visit her premises. Children might be expected to disregard any warning notice and so taking reasonable steps to ensure that they will not be harmed as a result of the staircase being dangerous to use might require Karen to take some further steps to discourage children from using that staircase, such as cordoning it off.

While Karen must – in taking reasonable steps to ensure that child visitors to her premises will not be harmed as a result of using her premises for the purposes for which they are there – be prepared for children to be less careful than adults, if Paul, a child, visits Karen's premises under the supervision of his parents, Karen will be entitled to expect Paul's parents to take reasonable steps to ensure Paul's safety. So if it is reasonable to think that Paul's parents will take steps to ensure that Paul is not harmed as a result of the existence of some danger on Karen's premises, Karen will not breach the duty of care she owes Paul to see that Paul will be reasonably safe in using those premises for the purpose for which he is on those premises if she fails to take any steps *herself* to ensure that Paul is not harmed as a result of the existence of that danger.

So – in *Phipps* v *Rochester Corporation*,[32] a boy and a girl walked across a large open space of grassland which formed part of a building site which was occupied by the defendants. A long trench had been dug across the grassland for the purpose of laying a sewer and the boy fell into it, suffering injury as a result. It was held that the defendants *had* owed the boy a duty to take reasonable steps to see that he would not suffer injury crossing their land but they did not breach that duty when they failed to take any steps to ensure that the boy did not fall into the trench. The defendants could reasonably have expected that the boy's parents would accompany him on his trip across the grassland to ensure that he did not come to any harm or to have ascertained that the grassland had a long trench dug across it and forbidden him to walk in the vicinity of the trench.

BREACH THROUGH OTHERS

Suppose that A owed B some kind of duty of care – say, a duty to take reasonable steps to save B from some kind of harm. Now, normally, in judging whether or not A breached that duty of care, we will look to see what *A* did. However, this is not always the case. Sometimes *A* will be held to have breached the duty of care that he owed B because *someone else* failed to take reasonable steps to save B from harm. This will be the case in two situations.

Non-delegable duties of care

The basic idea

Suppose that A owed B a duty to take reasonable steps to save B from suffering some kind of harm. And suppose that A gave C the job of saving B from that harm. And suppose that C failed to take reasonable steps to save B from that harm. Will A be held to have breached the duty of care that he owed B? One's instinctive response would be to say:

[32] [1955] 1 QB 450.

> It depends on whether C appeared to be a fit and proper person to whom to give the job of saving B. If he was, then A took reasonable steps to save B by giving the job of saving B to C. If he was not, then A failed to take reasonable steps to save B when he gave the job of saving B to C. He should have done the job himself and not relied on C to do it for him.

And that is the correct answer *if* the duty of care owed to B was what is known as *delegable*. An example of a delegable duty of care is the duty that an occupier owes his visitors to take reasonable steps to see that they will be reasonably safe in visiting his premises.

So, for example, suppose that one of the stairs on the staircase in Mary's house was loose. Mary rang Vijay, a local carpenter, to repair the stair. Vijay came round and after half an hour's work appeared to have solved the problem. However, two days later Sarah came round to visit Mary and suffered a bad fall when she went upstairs and tripped on the defective stair, which suddenly came loose under her feet. If Vijay seemed like a reputable contractor and seemed to have solved the problem with the stair, it will not be possible to argue that Mary breached the common duty of care she owed Sarah to take reasonable steps to see that Sarah would be reasonably safe in visiting her. She *did* take such steps: she got a reputable contractor in to repair the dangerous stair on her staircase and only let him go when she was satisfied that he had repaired the problem.[33]

But – returning to the general example with which we began our discussion – our instinctive answer will be quite wrong if the duty owed by A to B to take reasonable steps to save B from harm was *non-delegable*. If it was non-delegable then *C's* failure to take reasonable steps to save B from harm will have put *A* in breach of the duty of care that he owed B. It's as if C's lack of care is transferred to A and A is held to have failed to take care to save B from harm. So even if A *personally* took reasonable steps to save B from harm by giving C the job of saving B – which will be the case if C seemed a fit and proper person to whom to give the job of saving B – A will *still* be held to have breached the duty of care that he owed B.

But note that if the duty of care that A owed B was non-delegable, C's failure will only have put A in breach of the duty of care that A owed B *because A gave C the job of saving B*. For example, it is well established that the duty of care that an employer owes his employees to take reasonable steps to see that they are not killed or injured working for him is non-delegable.[34] So if Carl employs Lara to work on a particular machine and he gives Tom the job of maintaining the machine to ensure that it is safe to work on, then if Tom fails to take reasonable steps to see that the machine is in good repair Tom's carelessness will put Carl in breach of the duty of care that he owes Lara as her employer. But if Fred, a fellow employee, carelessly bumps into Lara while she is working on the machine and she is injured as a result, then Fred's carelessness will not

[33] See the Occupiers' Liability Act 1957, s 2(4)(b): 'where any damage is caused to a visitor by a danger due to the faulty execution of any work of construction, maintenance or repair by an independent contractor employed by the occupier, the occupier is not to be treated without more as answerable for the danger if in all the circumstances he had acted reasonably in entrusting the work to an independent contractor and had taken such steps (if any) as he reasonably ought in order to satisfy himself that the contractor was competent and that the work had been properly done.'

[34] See below, p. 232.

put Carl in breach of the duty of care that he owes Lara. The reason is that Carl never gave Fred the job of seeing that Lara would not be killed or injured while she worked for him.[35]

Examples of non-delegable duties of care

So – how do we tell whether a given duty of care is delegable or non-delegable? There is no general test – either set out in the cases or emerging from the cases – that we can use to determine whether a given a duty of care is delegable or non-delegable.[36] We simply have to look at the cases to see whether the courts have *held* that the duty of care in question is delegable or non-delegable.[37] The following duties of care have been held to be non-delegable:

(1) *Employment.* As has just been observed, the duty of care that an employer owes his employees to take reasonable steps to see that they are not killed or injured in working for him is non-delegable.[38]

(2) *Bailment.* It is well established that the duty a bailee owes a bailor to take reasonable steps to safeguard the bailed property is non-delegable in nature.[39]

An example of the application of this principle is provided by the case of *Morris* v *C W Martin & Sons Ltd.*[40] In that case, the claimant gave her fur coat to a firm of furriers to be cleaned. They then sent the coat to the defendant cleaners. The defendants were bailees of the coat for the claimant and as such they owed her a duty to take reasonable steps to safeguard the coat. Unfortunately, the defendants gave the job of looking after the coat to one of their employees, who promptly stole it. Lord Denning MR held[41] that the employee's theft of the coat put the defendants in breach of the duty of care that they owed the claimant to safeguard her coat and accordingly held the defendants liable to the claimant

[35] See *Davie* v *New Merton Board Mills Ltd* [1959] AC 604 (employee injured by defective tool unable to sue employer on ground that manufacturer's negligence in manufacturing tool put employer in breach of non-delegable duty of care that he owed employee because employer never gave manufacturer job of ensuring that employees would be safe; note, however, employee would now be able to sue employer under s 1 of the Employers' Liability (Defective Equipment) Act 1969). Also *O'Reilly* v *National Rail & Tramway Appliances Ltd* [1966] 1 All ER 499 (employee injured as a result of fellow employees' negligence in handling live shell that was in a pile of scrap metal being processed by employees unable to sue employer on ground that employees' negligence put employer in breach of the non-delegable duty of care that he owed employee because employees not given job of ensuring employee's safety).

[36] Though see Murphy 2007, arguing (at 379–90) that non-delegable duties of care arise out of an assumption of responsibility to do something positive. There are some duties which are, of necessity, non-delegable. For example, if A is under a *strict duty* to *ensure* that outcome *x* does not occur, then if A gives B the job of seeing that that outcome does not occur and B fails to ensure that outcome *x* does not occur, A will have breached his duty: he was under a duty to ensure that outcome *x* did not occur and he failed to do this. A's duty is therefore non-delegable. Strict duties like this are rare in English law and, of course, are not relevant to the current discussion, which is concerned with duties of care.

[37] See *KLB* v *British Columbia* [2003] 2 SCR 403, at [31] (per McLachlin CJ). So if the duty of care in question has only recently been established and there is no authority on the issue of whether it is delegable or non-delegable, there is simply no way of knowing which it is.

[38] *Wilsons & Clyde Coal Co. Ltd* v *English* [1938] AC 57; *McDermid* v *Nash Dredging & Reclamation Co. Ltd* [1987] 1 AC 906.

[39] *Riverstone Meat Co. Pty Ltd* v *Lancashire Shipping Co. Ltd* [1961] AC 807; *Port Swettenham* v *T W Wu & Co.* [1979] AC 580, 591.

[40] [1966] 1 QB 716.

[41] Ibid., 725, 728.

for the loss of her coat.[42] The fact that it was the employee *who had been given the job* of looking after the coat who stole it was crucial to the finding that the defendants had breached the duty of care that they owed the claimant. Had it been some other employee who stole the coat, the defendants would not have been held liable unless they, or the employee who was given the job of looking after the coat, were personally at fault for the occurrence of the theft.[43]

(3) *Extended* Hedley Byrne *principle I.* A number of authorities indicate that if A owes B a duty to perform a certain task with a certain degree of care and skill under the extended principle in *Hedley Byrne*, that duty of care will be non-delegable.

So Denning LJ remarked in *Cassidy* v *Ministry of Health* that, 'when hospital authorities undertake to treat a patient, and themselves select and appoint . . . the professional men and women who are to give the treatment, then they are responsible for the negligence of those persons in failing to give proper treatment, no matter whether they are doctors, surgeons, nurses or anyone else'.[44]

Similarly, it was held in *Philips* v *William Whiteley Ltd*[45] that the defendant firm of jewellers in that case owed the claimant a non-delegable duty to pierce her ears with the degree of care and skill that a reasonably competent jeweller would exercise in piercing someone's ears. The defendants had summoned an employee of another firm to perform the operation but, fortunately for the defendants, the employee in question pierced the claimant's ears with the requisite degree of care and skill and did not therefore put the defendants in breach of the duty of care that they owed the claimant.

It may be that the decision in *Lloyd* v *Grace, Smith & Co.*[46] can also be explained on this basis. The claimant in that case consulted a firm of solicitors with a view to increasing the

[42] *Important note.* There is some dispute as to whether the true basis of the defendants' liability in this case was that: (a) the defendants' employee put them in breach of the non-delegable duty that they owed the claimant to safeguard her coat; or (b) the defendants were vicariously liable in respect of the tort committed by their employee (the tort of conversion) when the employee stole the coat. Lord Denning MR's judgment supports view (a). Diplock LJ's judgment in the same case supports view (b). Salmon LJ's judgment straddles both views. In *Lister* v *Hesley Hall Ltd* [2002] 1 AC 215 it was assumed without any debate that *Morris* v *C W Martin* was a vicarious liability case: ibid., at [19] (per Lord Steyn), [46] (per Lord Clyde), [57] (per Lord Hobhouse), [75]–[76] (per Lord Millett). In *Dubai Aluminium Co. Ltd* v *Salaam* [2003] 2 AC 366, Lord Millett once again assumed without debate that *Morris* was a vicarious liability case (at [129]). Lord Nicholls was less dogmatic (at [29]), noting that there was some debate over the basis of liability in *Morris*. However, he thought it unnecessary to express his views on the issue. The High Court of Australia was divided in *New South Wales* v *Lepore* (2003) 212 CLR 511 over the issue of how best to analyse the basis of liability in *Morris*. Gleeson CJ (at [48]) and Kirby P (at [312]) held that *Morris* was a vicarious liability case; Kirby P going so far as to deride alternative explanations of the case as 'feeble' (ibid.). However, Gaudron J (at [127]) and McHugh J (at [147], [161]) both viewed the defendants' liability in *Morris* as resting on the fact that their employee had put them in breach of a non-delegable duty of care that they owed the claimant. Tony Weir is in no doubt that the latter analysis is correct, pointing out that the defendants would have been just as liable in *Morris* to the claimant had they given her fur coat to an independent contractor to look after, which he then stole: Weir 2006, 112. (Had that happened, of course, there would have been no possibility of the defendants being held vicariously liable for the tort committed by the contractor in stealing the coat because one cannot ever be held vicariously liable in respect of torts committed by one's independent contractors: see below, pp. 650–1.) This seems to us the clinching argument and establishes that the liability in *Morris* is more satisfactorily viewed as arising out of the fact that the defendants' employee's actions put them in breach of the non-delegable duty of care that they owed the claimant to safeguard her coat.

[43] [1966] 1 QB 716, 740–1, per Salmon LJ.

[44] [1951] 2 KB 343, 362. See also *Gold* v *Essex County Council* [1942] 2 KB 293, at 301–2 (per Lord Greene MR).

[45] [1938] 1 All ER 566.

[46] [1912] AC 716.

income she received from her investments. Her affairs were entrusted to the care of the firm's managing clerk, who used his position to defraud the claimant of two cottages that she owned. The firm was held liable for the loss suffered by the claimant. The case is often viewed as one where the firm was held vicariously liable in respect of the managing clerk's deceit.[47] However, it is possible to argue that the true basis of the firm's liability in this case was that the firm owed a non-delegable duty to the claimant to handle her affairs with a reasonable degree of care and skill and that the managing clerk – who was given the job of handling the claimant's affairs – put the firm in breach of that duty of care when, far from handling her affairs with a reasonable degree of care and skill, he defrauded her of her cottages.[48]

(4) *Extended* Hedley Byrne *principle II.* It seems to follow from what has already been said that if A owes B a duty under the extended principle in *Hedley Byrne* to take reasonable steps to achieve some goal or end, then that duty of care will be non-delegable.[49]

So suppose that Mary owned a factory and she employed John to guard it at night, to see that no one broke into it. John will have owed Mary a duty to take reasonable steps to see that the factory was not broken into at night under the extended principle in *Hedley Byrne* – he indicated to Mary that she could safely rely on him to take reasonable steps to see that her factory was not broken into at night and she so relied on him. Furthermore, it follows from what has just been said that this duty of care will have been non-delegable in nature. Suppose now that John gave the job of looking after the factory to Fred and Fred allowed a gang of thieves to loot the factory. Fred's failure to take reasonable steps to see that the factory was not broken into will have put John in breach of the non-delegable duty of care that he owed Mary. Mary will as a result be allowed to sue John in negligence for the loss she has suffered as a result of her factory being looted.[50]

[47] *Lister* v *Hesley Hall Ltd* [2002] 1 AC 215, at [19] (per Lord Steyn), [73] (per Lord Millett).

[48] See *New South Wales* v *Lepore* (2003) 212 CLR 511, at [127] (per Gaudron J).

[49] This is perhaps the only way of justifying the result in *Rogers* v *Night Riders* [1983] RTR 324. The claimant in that case was injured when she took a trip in a minicab and a defective door on the minicab flew open. The claimant had summoned the minicab by ringing the defendant firm. The firm did not own any minicabs or employ any drivers itself – instead it had a list of drivers who were available to pick up customers and it would call drivers on that list when someone wanted a lift somewhere. (The drivers paid a fee for being placed on the list.) The Court of Appeal held that the defendant firm had owed the claimant a duty to take reasonable steps to check that the minicabs used by the drivers on its list were reasonably safe; that that duty was non-delegable; that the defendant firm had given the drivers on its list the job of checking their own minicabs for faults; that the claimant's driver had been at fault in failing to spot that the door on his minicab was defective and that his fault put the defendants in breach of the non-delegable duty of care that they owed the claimant. Accordingly, the claimant was entitled to sue the defendant for damages. It is difficult to know why the defendants owed the claimant a duty of care here. Conceivably, the extended principle in *Hedley Byrne* applied here – it is possible that the defendants implicitly indicated to the claimant that she could safely rely on them to take reasonable steps to see that her minicab was safe to travel in and that the claimant did so rely on the defendants. If this is right, then the finding that the duty of care owed by the defendants to the claimant here was non-delegable was unexceptionable.

[50] Cf. *Photo Production* v *Securicor* [1980] AC 827. The defendant security company in that case was employed to patrol the claimants' factory at night to see that it was not burned down or broken into during the night. The job of patrolling the factory was given to one of the defendants' security guards who, one night, deliberately started a fire in the factory with the result that the factory burned down. The defendant security company was held *prima facie* liable for the fire damage. (In fact, there was an exclusion clause in the contract between the defendants and the claimants that absolved the defendants of liability.) There are *dicta* in the case which indicate that the source of the defendants' *prima facie* liability in this case was that they were vicariously liable for the tort committed by their employee in starting the fire: at 846 (per Lord Wilberforce) and 852 (per Lord Salmon). However, it is possible to argue that the real source of the defendants' liability in this case was that

(5) *Danger*. It seems that if A owes B a duty to take reasonable steps to eliminate or minimise some serious hazard, then that duty of care is non-delegable.

So if a fixture attached to A's land is in obvious danger of falling into the highway and injuring someone, A will owe people using the highway a non-delegable duty to repair the fixture or take it down.[51] Similarly, if A creates an obstruction in the road which people are liable to run into at night. The duty A will owe users of the road to take reasonable steps to clear the road of the obstruction or warn them of its existence will be non-delegable.[52] Again, if A gets C to do something for him which is *inherently dangerous*[53] for B, then A will owe B a non-delegable duty to take reasonable steps to minimise the danger to which B will be exposed as a result of C's activities.[54]

(6) *Educational authorities*. As we have seen, an educational authority will owe children at a school under its control a duty to take reasonable steps to see that they do not come to any physical harm while they are at school.[55] The High Court of Australia has held in *New South Wales* v *Lepore* that that duty of care is non-delegable in nature[56] and there is no reason to think that an English court would come to any other conclusion if the question arose here.

Intentional misconduct

Suppose that A owed B a non-delegable duty to take reasonable steps to save B from harm. Suppose further that A gave C the job of seeing that B did not come to any harm. And suppose finally that C intentionally harmed B. Can we say that C – by intentionally harming B – put A in breach of the non-delegable duty of care that he owed B?

One would have thought so: C could hardly be said to have taken reasonable steps to save B from harm if he intentionally harmed B. However, three of the seven judges who decided *New South Wales* v *Lepore* argued that, in the case just described, C's actions will *not* have put A in breach of the non-delegable duty of care that he owed B.[57] C's actions,

---

their employee's lack of care put them in breach of a non-delegable duty of care that they owed the claimants: see *New South Wales* v *Lepore* (2003) 212 CLR 511, at [146]–[148] (per McHugh J).

[51] *Tarry* v *Ashton* (1876) 1 QBD 314. The question of what amounts to a 'serious hazard' is fraught with difficulty. However, it seems that a danger affecting users of the highway will amount to a serious hazard.

[52] *Saper* v *Hungate Builders Ltd* [1972] RTR 380.

[53] This requirement was not satisfied in *Salsbury* v *Woodland* [1970] 1 QB 324, where the claimant was injured as a result of the carelessness of a contractor in cutting down a tree on the defendant's land. The act of cutting down the tree was not inherently dangerous – 'The act . . . if done with ordinary elemental caution by skilled men, presented no hazard to anyone at all' (ibid., at 338, per Widgery LJ).

[54] *Honeywill & Stein Ltd* v *Larkin Brothers* [1934] 1 KB 191 (defendant had a third party set off a magnesium flash in theatre owned by the claimant, with the result that the theatre burned down; held, the defendant had owed the claimant a duty to take reasonable steps to see that the fire involved in setting off the flash did not spread; that he delegated the job of seeing the fire did not spread to the third party and the third party put the defendant in breach of the non-delegable duty that he owed the claimant by failing to take reasonable steps to see that the fire did not spread).

[55] See above, p. 185.

[56] (2003) 212 CLR 511. Callinan J dissented on this point: see [340].

[57] Ibid, at [31]-[37] (per Gleeson CJ) and at [264]–[267] (per Gummow and Hayne JJ). McHugh J disagreed: at [161]-[163]. Though it is not entirely clear, it seems that Gaudron J also disagreed, given the fact that she analysed both *Morris* and *Lloyd* v *Grace, Smith* as being cases where the defendants were put in breach of a non-delegable duty of care by the intentional actions of a third party: at [127]. Kirby P preferred to reserve his position on the issue: at [293]. As Callinan J did not think that the education authorities in the *New South Wales* case owed a non-delegable duty of care to the claimants, the issue did not arise for him.

they held, will only have put A in breach of the non-delegable duty of care that he owed B if C *carelessly* failed to save B from harm. So, they held, a teacher who commits a sexual assualt on a child at school will *not* put the education authority that is in charge of that school in breach of the non-delegable duty that they owe that child to take reasonable steps to see that that child does not come to any harm while he is at school. Such a teacher would only put the education authority in breach of its non-delegable duty of care if he or she *carelessly* failed to take steps to see that a child in his or her care did not come to any harm by, for example, failing to stop other children assaulting the child.

This is *not* the law in England, though it used to be. As Lord Salmon observed in *Port Swettenham Authority* v *T W Wu & Co.*, it used to be the law[58] that 'a master who was under a duty to guard another's goods was liable if the servant he sent to perform the duty for him performed it so negligently as to enable thieves to steal the goods, but was not liable if that servant joined with the thieves in the very theft'.[59] But, as Lord Salmon went on to say, 'This proposition is clearly contrary to principle and common sense, and to the law ... [as stated in] *Morris* v *C W Martin and Sons Ltd*'.[60] It is somewhat surprising, then, to see at least some members of the High Court of Australia attempting to revive this rule. But it is highly unlikely that any such attempt will be made here.

Companies and other artificial legal persons

A company is an artificial legal person. As such, as Lord Diplock remarked in *Tesco Supermarkets Ltd* v *Natrass*, 'it is incapable itself of doing any physical act or being in a state of mind'.[61] If a company is to act, then, it can only do so through natural persons – people who are, of course, capable of performing physical actions. This creates a problem when we want to determine whether or not a company breached a duty of care that it owed to someone else.[62] Whose actions should we look at in order to determine whether or not that duty of care was breached? The facts of the *Tesco Supermarkets* case illustrate the problem.

In that case, a customer at a Tesco store was charged 3s 11d for a packet of washing powder when posters in the window of the store advertised that brand of washing powder as being on special offer at 2s 11d per packet. The general manager of the store, one Mr Clement, was at fault for this: he had failed to take reasonable steps to ensure that the store was stocked with some packets with the lower price on them. Tesco was charged with committing an offence under s 11(2) of the Trade Descriptions Act 1968 which provided that 'if any person offering to supply any goods gives ... any indication likely to be taken as an indication that the goods are being offered at a price less than that at which they are in fact being offered he shall, subject to the provisions of this Act, be guilty of an offence'. In their defence, Tesco sought to rely on s 24(1) of the Act which provided that '[i]n any proceed-

[58] See *Cheshire* v *Bailey* [1905] 1 KB 237.

[59] [1979] AC 580, 591.

[60] Ibid.

[61] [1972] AC 153, 198.

[62] Of course, this issue only comes up if we want to establish whether a company is *personally* liable to compensate a claimant for some loss that he or she has suffered. If it is not personally liable to pay such compensation it may still be *vicariously liable* to pay such compensation if one of its employees caused the claimant to suffer the loss in question by committing the tort and there was a sufficiently close connection between what the employee was employed to do and the tort committed by the employee: see below, pp. 665–6.

ings for an offence under this Act . . . it shall be a defence for the person charged to prove – (a) that the commission of the offence was due . . . to the act or default of another person and (b) that he took all reasonable precautions and exercised all due diligence to avoid the commission of such an offence by himself or any person under his control'.

Tesco could establish that (a) was true – the offence was committed because of Mr Clement's 'default'. Could it establish that (b) was true – that it took all reasonable care to ensure that its goods were not sold at a price higher than the advertised price? Clearly, *Mr Clement* did not take such care – but did that mean that *Tesco*, Mr Clement's employer, did not take such care? More generally, whose actions should be looked at to determine whether Tesco took reasonable care to ensure that its goods were not sold at a price higher than the advertised price? The House of Lords' answer was that one should look at the actions of those who represented Tesco's 'guiding mind or will' – only if *they* failed to take care to ensure that Tesco's goods were not sold at a price higher than the advertised price would it be proper to say that *Tesco* failed to take care to ensure that its goods were not sold at a price higher than the advertised price. Mr Clement, the House of Lords held, did not 'function as the directing mind or will of the company. He was . . . being directed.'[63]

So *Mr Clement's* failure to take care to ensure that Tesco's goods were not sold at a price higher than the advertised price did not mean that *Tesco* failed to take such care. In fact, those who *did* represent Tesco's 'guiding mind or will' – the board of directors of Tesco and those to whom they had delegated the job of running Tesco – *had* taken reasonable care to ensure that Tesco's goods were not sold at a price higher than the advertised price. They had taken steps to instruct their store managers as to how their stores should be run; they had appointed a host of branch inspectors to go round the stores and make sure that the store managers were observing company policy in their running of the stores; and they had employed area inspectors to supervise the work of the branch inspectors. So Tesco – in the person of those who represented Tesco's 'guiding mind or will' – *had* taken reasonable care to ensure that Tesco's goods were not sold at a price higher than the advertised price and therefore had a defence under s 24(1) of the Trade Descriptions Act 1968 to the charge that they had committed an offence under s 11(2) of that Act.

The principle, endorsed in the *Tesco Supermarkets* case, that we ascertain what a company did at a particular time by looking at the acts of those who represented the 'guiding mind or will' of the company at that time is well established.[64] However, this principle has recently been brought into question at the highest level where it has been

[63] [1972] AC 153, 180 (per Lord Morris).

[64] It traces its origin to the judgment of Viscount Haldane LC in *Lennard's Carrying Co. Ltd* v *Asiatic Petroleum Co. Ltd* [1915] AC 705, 713: 'My Lords, a corporation is an abstraction. It has no mind of its own any more than it has a body of its own; its active and directing will must consequently be sought in the person of somebody who for some purposes may be called an agent, but who is really the directing mind and will of the corporation, the very ego and centre of the personality of the corporation.' Denning LJ found a characteristically colourful way to express the principle in *H L Bolton (Engineering) Co. Ltd* v *T J Graham & Sons Ltd* [1957] 1 QB 159, 172: '[a] company may in many ways be likened to a human body. It has a brain and a nerve centre which controls what it does. It also has hands which hold the tools and act in accordance with directions from the centre. Some of the people in the company are mere servants or agents who are nothing more than hands to do the work and cannot be said to represent the mind or will. Others are directors and managers who represent the directing mind or will of the company, and control what it does. The state of mind of these managers is the state of mind of the company and is treated by the law as such. So you will find that in cases where the law requires personal fault as a condition of liability in tort, the fault of the manager will be the personal fault of the company.'

suggested that *how* we ascertain what a company did depends very much on the *nature and purpose* of the legal rule which requires us to find out what that company did.

In *Re Supply of Ready Mixed Concrete (No. 2)*,[65] four companies which were engaged in the supply of ready mixed concrete entered into agreements with each other which fixed the prices at which they would supply ready mixed concrete to customers and determined what share each company would enjoy of the market for ready mixed concrete in the area in which the four companies operated. These agreements were unlawful under s 35(1) of the Restrictive Trade Practices Act 1976. The Director General of Fair Trading obtained injunctions against the four companies, requiring them not to enter into or give effect to any such agreements in future.

After the injunctions were obtained, employees of the four companies, without the knowledge of the management of those companies and contrary to their express instructions, started to operate a new agreement to fix prices and allocate work among the four companies. The Director General claimed that the companies had breached the injunctions and were therefore in contempt of court. In defence, the companies claimed that they had not entered into or given effect to any unlawful price fixing and work allocation agreement. The House of Lords dismissed the companies' claim – what the companies' employees did, the companies did. So if the companies' employees entered into and gave effect to an unlawful price fixing and work allocation agreement among themselves, the companies entered into and gave effect to such an agreement among themselves in breach of the injunction against them. This was so even though there was no way the companies' employees could be said to have represented the 'guiding mind or will' of the companies.

In a subsequent Privy Council case, *Meridian Global Funds Management Asia Ltd* v *Securities Commission*,[66] Lord Hoffmann – giving the only judgment – endorsed the result in *Re Supply of Ready Mixed Concrete (No. 2)* and sought to reconcile it with the decision in the *Tesco Supermarkets* case by arguing that: If applying a particular legal rule to a company requires the courts to find out what that company did, the courts should adopt the approach to finding out what that company did that the creators of the legal rule in question intended them to adopt for the purposes of applying that rule. 'This is always a matter of interpretation: given that [the rule in question] was intended to apply to a company, how was it intended to apply? Whose act ... was *for this purpose* intended to count as the act ... of the company? One finds the answer to this question by applying the usual canons of interpretation, taking into account the language of the rule (if it is a statute) and its content and policy.'[67]

So, in Lord Hoffmann's view, the *Tesco Supermarkets* case was decided the way it was because those who created the defence contained in s 24(1) of the Trade Descriptions Act 1968 did not intend the courts to treat Tesco as having failed to take care to ensure that its goods were not sold at a price higher than the advertised price if one of the Tesco store managers did not take such care. On the other hand, Lord Hoffmann argued, *Re Supply of Ready Mixed Concrete (No. 2)* was decided the way it was because an injunction against a company, requiring it not to enter into or give effect to unlawful price fixing and work allo-

[65] [1995] 1 AC 456.
[66] [1995] 2 AC 500.
[67] Ibid., 507.

cation agreements with other companies, would be of little use if a company that was subject to such an injunction could not be held liable for breaching that injunction if its employees set up and operated an unlawful price fixing and work allocation agreement without the knowledge of the company's management.

It is not true to say, then, that there is a *general* rule, good for *all* situations, that what a company did at a particular time is to be ascertained by reference to what those who represented the company's 'guiding mind or will' at the time did. However, the Court of Appeal has affirmed that the 'guiding mind or will' approach to determining what a company did should be adopted unless there is a good reason why a different approach should be adopted (such as that Parliament intended that a different approach should be adopted in the context of determining whether a company committed a particular statutory offence).[68] If this is right, then the 'guiding mind or will' approach should still be adopted when we have to determine whether or not a company breached a *duty of care* that it owed to someone else.

So, on the view taken here, if ABC plc manufactures bottles of ginger beer and Beth, an employee of ABC's, deliberately inserts a snail into one of ABC's bottles, Beth's actions will not necessarily put ABC in breach of the duty it owes each potential consumer of its ginger beer to take care that it does not put into general circulation ginger beer that is unsafe to consume. While *Beth* has failed to take such care, *ABC* will only be held to have failed to take such care if its management – its 'guiding mind or will' – failed to take care to ensure that its ginger beer would be safe to consume.[69]

In every case where an artificial legal person owed someone else a duty we are confronted with the problem – Whose actions should we look at to determine whether or not that person breached that duty? In the case of companies that problem is solved, we suggest, by adopting the 'guiding mind or will' principle according to which we ascertain what a company did at a particular time by looking at what those who represented that company's 'guiding mind or will' at that time did. The same approach should be adopted in relation to artificial legal persons that are not companies, such as local authorities.

BURDEN OF PROOF

Generally speaking, the burden is on the claimant in a negligence case to prove that the defendant breached a duty of care owed to her. So, for example, in *Knight* v *Fellick*,[70] the claimant was run down by the defendant driver. The claimant was so badly injured in the accident that she had no memory of how it happened. The claimant sued the defendant in negligence for compensation but her claim failed: she could not prove that the defendant was driving without due care and attention at the time he hit the claimant.

[68] *Attorney-General's Reference (No. 2 of 1999)* [2000] QB 796, 814, 816: 'the primary "directing mind and will" rule still applies though it is not determinative in all cases.'

[69] Of course, there is a possibility that ABC could be sued by anyone harmed by the snail on the ground that it is vicariously liable for Beth's negligence. Whether ABC is vicariously liable or not will depend on whether there was a 'sufficiently close connection' between Beth's negligence and what she was employed to do: see below, pp. 665–6. Also ABC might be held liable for any harm done by the presence of the snail in the bottle under the Consumer Protection Act 1987: see below, pp. 774–90.

[70] [1977] RTR 316.

It was significant that the accident in *Knight* happened at night, on a road which had no street lighting and that the claimant was wearing dark clothing at the time of the accident. Suppose that Gary ran Nita over in his car during the day when visibility was perfect and Nita wants to sue Gary in negligence. In such a case, Nita will find it very easy to convince a court that Gary was not driving with due care and attention at the time of the accident. She will be able to argue, 'Gary hit me in broad daylight. What more proof do you need that he wasn't driving with due care and attention at the time of the accident? Had he been driving carefully, he would have managed to avoid me. The facts speaks for themselves: *res ipsa loquitur*.' Of course, it may be that Gary *was* driving with due care and attention – it may be that he only hit Nita because she dashed out into the middle of the road right in front of his car. But if Gary cannot prove that that is what happened, the court will find that Nita has discharged the burden on her and find that at the time of the accident, Gary was in breach of the duty of care that he owed Nita to take care not to drive dangerously.

This way of arguing that a defendant breached a duty of care owed to a claimant – what's called by lawyers a *res ipsa loquitur* argument – only works if the facts of the case are such that the most natural explanation of what happened is that the defendant was careless.[71] So a *res ipsa loquitur* argument will be available to help establish that the defendant breached a duty of care owed to the claimant if: (1) the defendant performed a minor operation on the claimant's hand and after the operation was over the claimant lost the use of his hand;[72] (2) the claimant was working in the defendant's factory and an electrical panel fell on his head;[73] (3) the claimant was injured when a coach driven by the defendant suddenly veered across the road into the claimant's path;[74] (4) the defendant cleaned a suit belonging to the claimant and the claimant suddenly developed dermatitis on wearing the suit again.[75] But such an argument will not be available in the case where a door on a moving train operated by the defendant suddenly opens and the claimant falls out.[76] The fact that the door opened suddenly does not of itself indicate that the defendant was careless in operating the train: the door could just as well have opened because of the fault of another passenger.

As we have said, the burden of proof in a negligence case normally falls on the claimant to show that the defendant breached the duty of care that he owed her. However, there are a couple of exceptions to this general rule. In such cases, the *defendant* will be required to show that he was careful. If he cannot, then the courts will find that he breached the duty of care that he owed the claimant.

[71] The requirements that had to be satisfied before a *res ipsa loquitur* argument could be made in favour of the view that the defendant had breached a duty of care owed to the claimant were first set out by Erle CJ in *Scott* v *London and St Katherine Docks Company* (1865) 3 H & C 595, 601; 159 ER 665, 667: '... where the thing [which caused the accident complained of] is shewn to be under the management of the defendant ... and the accident is such as in the ordinary course of things does not happen if those who have the management use proper care, it affords reasonable evidence, in the absence of explanation by the defendants, that the accident arose from want of care.'

[72] *Cassidy* v *Ministry of Health* [1951] 2 KB 343.

[73] *Bennett* v *Chemical Construction (GB) Ltd* [1971] 1 WLR 1571.

[74] *Ng Chun Pui* v *Lee Chuen Tat* [1988] RTR 298 (note that no finding of negligence was ultimately made in this case – even though it looked at first as if the defendant had been careless in driving the coach, he had an explanation for his driving into the claimant's lane: he was trying to avoid a car that had cut in front of him).

[75] *Mayne* v *Silvermere Cleaners* [1939] 1 All ER 693.

[76] *Easson* v *London and North Eastern Railway Company* [1944] 1 KB 421.

(1) *Bailment*. If A holds goods on a bailment for B and those goods are lost, destroyed or damaged, it will be presumed – unless A can prove otherwise – that A breached the duty of care that he owed B to take reasonable steps to safeguard those goods.[77]

(2) *Criminal conviction*. If A owed B a duty of care and has been convicted of a criminal offence which A could not have committed had he fulfilled the duty of care that he owed B, in any civil proceedings between A and B it will be presumed – unless A can prove otherwise – that A breached the duty of care that he owed B.[78]

Visit **http://www.mylawchamber.co.uk/mcbride** to access updates on recent cases, as well as model answers and tips for answering tort problem questions.

[77] *Houghland* v *R R Low (Luxury Coaches) Ltd* [1962] 1 QB 694; *Port Swettenham Authority* v *T W Wu & Co.* [1979] AC 580.

[78] Civil Evidence Act 1968, s 11. On which, see *Stupple* v *Royal Insurance Co. Ltd* [1971] 1 QB 50.

B.

Rights-based torts

Introduction

The torts gathered in this section of the book are 'rights-based' in two senses.

First of all, it will be recalled that any time A commits a tort we can characterise what A has done in one of two, exactly equivalent, ways.[1] We could say that A has breached a duty owed to another. Or we could say that A has violated someone else's rights. If the tort committed by A was the tort of negligence, lawyers invariably characterise what A did in the first way, and say that A breached a duty (of care) owed to another. However, if A commits one of the torts gathered in this section of the book, lawyers will normally eschew the language of duty in characterising what A has done, and will instead say that A violated someone else's rights. So, for example, one of the torts we will look at in this section is the tort of *trespass to land*. A will commit this tort in relation to B if he goes onto B's land without B's permission. If A does this, lawyers will not normally say that A breached a duty owed to B in going onto B's land. Instead, lawyers will say that A violated B's rights by going onto B's land.

Secondly, it was observed above that lawyers use the word 'right' in three different ways.[2] One of the ways lawyers use the term 'right' is to describe a legally recognised interest that the law protects in some way. Each of the torts gathered in this section exists to protect a certain kind of legally recognised interest, such as a person's interest in their reputation, or their bodily integrity, or in property. Given this, we can say that each of the torts gathered in this section exists to protect some kind of legal right. So, for example, we can say that the torts of *assault* and *battery* exist to protect someone's right to bodily integrity. The tort of *false imprisonment* exists to protect someone's right to freedom of movement. The tort of *defamation* exists to protect someone's right to their reputation. The torts of *trespass to land* and *private nuisance* exist to protect a landowner's right to the peaceable and secure enjoyment of his or her land.

Nothing that has been said so far establishes that the rights-based torts that we discuss in this section of the book are distinct from the tort of negligence in any *fundamental* way. Just as is the case with the tort of negligence, someone who commits a rights-based tort commits a civil wrong. The fact that we use the language of 'rights' to describe this civil wrong, rather than the language of 'duty', indicates nothing important. Similarly, the duties of care recognised under the law of negligence can be said to be just as much 'rights-based' as the torts discussed in this section of the book. So duties of care arising under the 'physical danger principle' exist to protect people's rights to bodily integrity. Duties of care arising under either the basic or extended principle in *Hedley Byrne* exist to protect people's rights that they not be made worse off as a result of relying on another's word. Duties of care arising under the Occupiers' Liability Act 1957 variously exist to protect visitors' rights

[1] See above, pp. xiv, 17.
[2] See above, pp. 5–6.

to bodily integrity, and their rights to the secure enjoyment of their property. In contrast, duties of care arising under the Occupiers' Liability Act 1984 exist only to protect trespassers' rights to bodily integrity.

Having said that, there *are* some important differences between what we are calling 'the rights-based torts' and the tort of negligence:

(1) *Reasonable conduct*. No one can be held liable in negligence for acting reasonably. This is because it is not possible for the courts to find that A owed B a duty of care not to do *x* if it was reasonable for A to do *x*, all things considered.[3] In contrast, the fact that A acted reasonably will not always prevent him being held liable for committing a rights-based tort.

So, for example, suppose Eric is a police officer and suppose that Eric walked across Wendy's land searching for Gary, an escaped criminal. Suppose further that Wendy is now suing Eric for trespassing on her land. In such a case, Eric will *not* be able to defeat Wendy's claim merely by showing that it was reasonable, all things considered, for him to go onto Wendy's land in search of Gary. He will have to show that the law – in the shape of some in-force statute or a decided case – specifically authorised him to go onto Wendy's land in order to see whether Gary was on it. If he cannot show that this is the case then he will have committed the tort of trespass to land in going onto Wendy's land – and this is so no matter how reasonable it was for him to have walked across Wendy's land when he did.

Having said that, it should be acknowledged that this point about the rights-based torts – that no one can escape being held liable for committing a rights-based tort merely by showing that it was reasonable for them to do what they did, all things considered – is undermined by the courts' increasing willingness to allow defendants to escape being held liable for committing a rights-based tort by relying on a defence of *necessity*. So, for example, the courts are increasingly moving towards the position that it is not a tort to hit someone or lock someone up or go onto their land if it is *necessary* to do so. Those who think that protecting individual rights and liberties should come before promoting the general social welfare will regard this as a highly disturbing development; those with an opposite set of priorities will welcome it.

(2) *Strict liability*. Lawyers say that A is held 'strictly liable' to compensate B for some harm that she has suffered if A is held liable to pay compensation to B even though A was not personally at fault for B's suffering that harm.

There are some instances of strict liability within the law of negligence – as we have seen, someone who is subject to a non-delegable duty of care can be held to have breached that duty even though their own personal conduct was impeccable – but, for the most part, the rule is that you cannot be held liable in negligence to compensate someone else for some harm that they have suffered if you were not personally at fault for their suffering that harm.

In contrast, a lot of the torts gathered in this section of the book can be committed quite innocently. As a result, the existence of a lot of the torts discussed in this section gives rise to instances of strict liability in tort law. For example, suppose that Fred steals Nita's car. He

[3] See above, pp. 59–60.

subsequently pretends to Paul that the car is his and sells it to Paul. Paul then gives the car to his daughter, Beth, as an eighteenth birthday present. Beth subsequently wrecks the car in a crash and it is written off. In this situation, Paul will be held liable to pay Nita damages equal to the value of her car. This is because in both taking delivery of Nita's car and in subsequently handing it over to Beth, Paul committed the tort of *conversion*. Consequently, Nita is entitled to sue Paul for damages. This is so even though Paul was not at fault at all either for the theft of Nita's car or its subsequent destruction. So Paul is held strictly liable here to pay Nita damages equal to the value of her car.

It might be thought that this is unfair on Paul.[4] Perhaps in recognition of this, the law now sometimes provides people who have innocently committed some of the torts gathered together in this section with defences to being sued for damages. So, for example, s 1 of the Defamation Act 1996 provides, among other things, that if A, a shopkeeper, libels B by selling someone a newspaper which contains a defamatory statement about B, B will not be able to sue A for compensation for whatever losses she is presumed to have suffered as a result of A's libel if A can prove that he did not know and had no reason to know that the newspaper sold by him contained the defamatory statement complained of by B.

(3) *Recoverable harm*. The existence of the torts gathered together in this section of the book allows claims for compensation to be brought for harms which are hardly ever compensated for by the law of negligence. For example, if A has suffered *pure distress* (that is, distress not resulting from a physical injury or damage to A's property) as a result of B's actions, it is highly unlikely that A will be able to recover compensation for that distress by suing B in negligence.[5] However, if what B did was make A think that she was about to be killed or injured, then A can recover damages for the distress she suffered as a result of B's actions by bringing a claim in *assault* against B. Similarly, it is not clear whether the law of negligence currently allows claims to be brought for damages in respect of loss of liberty – but compensation for that kind of harm may be obtained by bringing a claim for *false imprisonment* against the person who was responsible for the claimant's being deprived of her liberty.

(4) *Need to prove harm*. Negligence is *not* a tort that is actionable *per se*. If a claimant wants to bring a claim in negligence against a defendant, it is not enough for her to show that the defendant breached a duty of care that he owed the claimant. She will have to show that she suffered some kind of actionable harm as a result of the defendant's breach. In contrast, almost all of the torts discussed in this section of the book are actionable *per se*. A claimant can bring a claim for damages against a defendant based on the fact that the defendant committed one of these torts without having to show that she actually suffered any kind of harm as a result of the defendant's tort. Of course, the damages recoverable if she cannot

[4] For a discussion of when strict liability might be justified, see below, pp. 653, 754–6, 774–5.

[5] The mere fact that it was foreseeable that A would suffer distress as a result of B's actions will not be sufficient to establish that B owed A a duty of care not to act as he did: see above, pp. 62–3. And if B did owe A a duty of care not to act as he did because – for example – it was reasonably foreseeable that A would suffer some kind of physical injury if B acted as he did, A's claim in negligence for compensation for the pure distress that she suffered as a result of B's actions will fail on the ground that she has suffered the 'wrong kind of loss' – not the kind of loss that B's duty of care was imposed on him in order to avoid: see below, pp. 577–82.

show that she suffered any kind of harm as a result of the defendant's tort will usually be very small – for that reason, they are called *nominal damages* – but it may still be worth the claimant's while to establish publicly that the defendant acted wrongfully in doing what he did.[6]

[6] For further discussion, see below, pp. 679–81.

11 Assault and battery

Let's start with some definitions. First, A will have committed the tort of *battery* in relation to B if: (1) he directly applied force to B's person; (2) he did so intentionally or carelessly; and (3) he had no lawful justification or excuse for acting in the way he did.

Secondly, A will have committed the tort of *assault* in relation to B if: (1) he intentionally or carelessly caused B to think that he was about to do *x*; and (2) if A had done *x*, he would have committed the tort of battery in relation to B.

The definition of when someone will commit the tort of assault is therefore parasitic on the definition of when someone will commit the tort of battery. It therefore makes sense in this chapter to begin with the tort of battery and explain in more detail when someone will commit that tort, before we turn our attentions to the tort of assault.

BATTERY

It follows from what has just been said that if B wants to sue A for committing the tort of battery in relation to her, she will have to show that A directly applied force to her person; that he did so intentionally or carelessly; and that he had no lawful justification or excuse for acting as he did. Let's now look at the key terms in this definition.

Direct application of force

There are a variety of ways of directly applying force to someone's person:

(1) *Touch*. A will directly apply force to B's person if he voluntarily *touches* B. So Paul will commit the tort of battery if he puts dye on Wendy's hair when he has no lawful justification or excuse for doing so.[1]

(2) *Projectiles*. A will directly apply force to B's person if B is hit by something which A *threw or propelled*.[2] It does not matter whether or not A directed the thing in question at B. In *Scott* v *Shepherd*,[3] the defendant threw a lighted squib into a marketplace where it was thrown from trader to trader, each seeking to get rid of the squib, until the squib exploded in the claimant's face and put out one of his eyes. It was held that the defendant had committed the tort of battery; the fact that the defendant had not thrown the squib at the claimant was immaterial.

(3) *Unseating*. A will directly apply force to B's person if he *applies force to something on which B is sitting* with the result that B is unseated and falls to the ground. So Gary will

[1] *Nash* v *Sheen*, The Times, 13 March 1953.
[2] *Pursell* v *Horn* (1838) 8 Ad & El 602 (boiling water).
[3] (1773) 2 Black W 892, 96 ER 525.

commit the tort of battery if Beth is sitting on a chair and Gary pulls it out from under her, causing her to fall to the ground. (It is assumed that Gary has no lawful justification or excuse for pulling Beth's chair out from under her.) Similarly, Nita will commit the tort of battery if Ian is sitting on a horse and Nita wilfully strikes the horse with the result that Ian is unseated and falls to the ground.[4] (Again, it is assumed that Nita has no lawful justification or excuse for wilfully striking Ian's horse.)

So, Carl will directly apply force to Lara's person if he wipes shoe polish on a towel and then rubs the towel in Lara's face; but he will not directly apply force to Lara's person if he leaves the towel in Lara's bathroom and Lara uses it, thus getting shoe polish all over her face. Similarly, Sarah will directly apply force to Eric's person if she pushes Eric into a hole; but she will not directly apply force to Eric's person if she digs a hole in the road and Eric falls into it. Likewise, Alan will directly apply force to Karen's person if he pulls Karen away as she attempts to enter a room; but Alan will not directly apply force to Karen's person if, when she attempts to enter a room, he stands in the doorway to the room, blocking Karen's way.[5]

What is the position if Sarah is standing on a train which suddenly comes to a halt with the result that Sarah falls over and crashes into John, a fellow passenger? In such a case, Sarah will not have directly applied force to John's person – while she touched John, she did not do so voluntarily. So Sarah will not have committed the tort of battery in this situation. Similarly, if Vijay pushes Fred into Dawn, Fred will not have directly applied force to Dawn's person – again, his touching Dawn was involuntary. On the other hand, Vijay *will* have directly applied force to Dawn's person in this situation – Dawn was hit by a thing (Fred) that was propelled by Vijay. So, in this situation, Fred will not have committed the tort of battery, but Vijay probably will have.

The requirement of intentional or careless conduct

Suppose A has directly applied force to B's person. If we want to show that A committed the tort of battery in acting as he did, we must show that A *intentionally or carelessly* applied force to B's person.[6] This is the result of the decision in *Fowler* v *Lanning*.[7]

In that case, the claimant sued the defendant. His statement of claim merely alleged that the defendant shot him. Diplock J held that the claimant's statement of claim was inadequate – it did not disclose any cause of action. If the claimant wanted to make out that the defendant had committed the tort of battery in relation to him, he had to allege and prove not only that the defendant shot him but also that the defendant intentionally or carelessly shot him.

So suppose Tom was out shooting birds in the woods one day when he accidentally shot Ian, a poacher, who had hidden in some bushes. In such a case, Tom will not have committed the tort of battery in relation to Ian. While he *did* directly apply force to Ian's person – Ian was hit by something (a bullet) which was propelled by Tom – Tom did not apply that force to Ian's person either intentionally or carelessly.

[4] *Dodwell* v *Burford* (1670) 1 Mod 24, 86 ER 703.
[5] *Innes* v *Wylie* (1844) 1 C & K 257, 174 ER 800.
[6] For more detail, see Trindade 1982.
[7] [1959] 1 QB 426.

It should be noted that in cases where A *carelessly* applied force to B's person, while in theory B might be able to make a claim in battery against A, B will almost always bring a claim in negligence against A for compensation for any harm that she suffered as a result of A's actions. So in practice, a claim in battery will only be brought where A *intentionally* applied force to B's person. For example, if A carelessly runs B down in his car, B will invariably bring a claim in negligence against A for compensation for the injuries suffered by her as a result of being run down by A. It is only if A intentionally runs B down that B will consider bringing a claim in battery against A.

Lawful justification or excuse

Let's now look at the main ways in which someone who has applied force to another's person can establish that he or she had a lawful justification or excuse for doing so.

Consent

Suppose that A has voluntarily touched B in some way. If B *validly consented* to A's touching her in the way he did, then A will not have committed a battery in this situation; he will have had a lawful justification or excuse for acting as he did.

In order to show that B validly consented to A's touching her in the way he did, it has to be shown that: (1) B agreed that A could touch her in the way he did; (2) at the time B agreed that A could touch her in the way he did, B's level of maturity, intelligence and understanding was such that B could be safely left to decide for herself whether or not A could touch her in the way he did; and (3) B did not agree that A could touch her in the way she did because she was forced to do so by anyone else. It does *not* have to be shown that: (4) B understood the risks, if any, that she would be exposed to if A touched her in the way he did. We will now look at each of these requirements in turn.

(1) *The need for agreement*. If A has touched B in some way, B will obviously not have validly consented to A's touching her in the way he did if B did not agree that A could touch her in the way he did. So suppose Ruth went to hospital for a tonsillectomy but her surgeon – due to an administrative mix-up – performed an appendectomy instead. In such a case, it could not be said that Ruth validly consented to her surgeon's touching her in the way he did.[8]

Even if B formally agreed that A could touch her in the way he did, it still cannot be said that she validly consented to A's touching her in that way, if, when she agreed, she did not really understand what A was proposing to do. So suppose Gary was a patient in a hospital and Lara, his doctor, proposed to Gary that they treat his condition by giving him an 'intrathecal injection of phenol solution nerve block'. If Gary agreed that Lara could do this but did not actually understand what Lara was proposing to do – because Lara did not bother to explain to Gary what such an injection involved – then it cannot be said that Gary validly consented to Lara's giving him such an injection.[9]

[8] *Chatterton* v *Gerson* [1981] 1 QB 432, 443.

[9] Ibid. Cf. *R* v *Williams* [1923] 1 KB 340 where the defendant – who had been engaged to give singing lessons to one Vera Howley – persuaded Howley to allow him to have sexual intercourse with her by pretending that he was performing a surgical operation on her to improve her voice. He was convicted of rape; she had not validly consented to the defendant's having sex with her as she did not really understand what he was proposing to do when she agreed that he could have sex with her.

A difficult issue is whether B has validly consented to A's touching her if she understood what A was doing in touching her, but had been misled as to A's *motives* in touching her. For example, in *KD* v *Chief Constable of Hampshire*,[10] the claimant became distressed while she was being interviewed by a police constable about her sexual history with a former boyfriend (who, it was alleged, had sexually abused the claimant's daughter). The constable hugged the claimant – but not, as the claimant thought, with the intention of cheering her up, but because he was attracted to her. It was held that the constable committed a battery in hugging the claimant – so while the claimant consented to being hugged by the constable, her consent must have been rendered invalid by her being misled as to the reasons why the constable was hugging her.

It should be noted that in the case of a continual touching which was *initially* agreed to, the touching can *become* unlawful if the person who is subject to it withdraws her consent to it. So suppose that Beth is incapacitated to such an extent that she requires continual medical treatment from Vijay to keep her alive. If, after a few months of being treated by Vijay, Beth loses her will to live and refuses any more treatment, Vijay will commit the tort of battery if he continues to treat Beth.[11]

(2) *The need for a sufficient degree of maturity, intelligence and understanding.* If A has touched B in some way with B's agreement, B will still not have validly consented to A's touching her in the way he did if, at the time B agreed that A could touch her in the way he did, B's level of maturity, intelligence and understanding was not such that B could be safely left to decide for herself whether or not A could touch her in the way he did.

If, at the time B agreed that A could touch her in the way he did, B was an adult (over 18) and not mentally unstable or acting under the influence of drugs or alcohol, it will be automatically presumed that B's level of maturity, intelligence and understanding was such that she could be safely left to decide for herself whether or not A could touch her in the way he did.

Section 8 of the Family Law Reform Act 1969 provides that 'the consent of a minor who has attained the age of sixteen years to any surgical, medical or dental treatment which, in the absence of consent, would constitute [a battery], shall be as effective as it would be if he were of full age . . .'. The effect of this is that if Tom medically treated Mary with Mary's agreement and Mary was between 16 and 18 when she agreed that Tom could treat her, it will be automatically presumed that Mary's level of maturity, intelligence and understanding at that time was such that she could be safely left to decide for herself whether or not Tom could treat her in the way he did – just as would have been the case if Mary had been over 18 when she agreed to being medically treated by Tom.

If, when B agreed A could touch her in the way he did, B was less than 16 years old then no fixed rules will apply – all the circumstances will have to be looked at to determine whether, when B agreed A could touch her in the way he did, B's level of maturity, intelligence and understanding was such that she could be safely left to decide for herself whether or not A could touch her in the way he did.[12]

[10] [2005] EWHC 2550.

[11] *B* v *An NHS Hospital Trust* [2002] 2 All ER 449.

[12] *Gillick* v *West Norfolk and Wisbech Area Health Authority* [1986] AC 112.

(3) *The need for an unforced agreement.* If A has touched B in some way with B's agreement, B will still not have validly consented to A's touching her in the way he did if B was forced or pressured into agreeing that A could touch her in the way he did. So suppose, for example, that Gary performed an abortion on Wendy and Wendy only agreed to the abortion because Fred, her father, threatened to kill her if she did not have it. In such a case, it cannot be said that Wendy validly consented to Gary's performing the abortion on her.

(4) *No need for 'informed consent'.* English courts have consistently rejected the notion that if A has touched B in some way with B's agreement, B will only have validly consented to A's touching her in the way he did if her consent was 'informed' – that is, B will only have validly consented to A's touching her in the way he did if, at the time B agreed that A could touch her in that way, B knew of the risks, if any, that she would be exposed to if A touched her in that way.[13]

So in *Chatterton* v *Gerson*,[14] the claimant had an operation which left her with an extremely painful scar. The claimant consulted the defendant – who was a specialist in treating pain – and he suggested that she have an operation to block the sensory nerve behind the scar which was transmitting pain signals to her brain. The claimant agreed and the defendant carried out the operation. After the operation, the claimant discovered that the area around her scar was numb and she had suffered a loss of muscle power in that area. The claimant sued the defendant, claiming that the defendant had committed the tort of battery in operating on her. She argued that she had not validly consented to the operation performed by the defendant because she had not been informed that there was a risk she would experience numbness and loss of muscle power if she had that operation. This argument was rejected: as the claimant had known perfectly well the nature of the operation the defendant was proposing to carry out on her when she agreed that the defendant could carry out that operation, she validly consented to that operation's being carried out. The fact that she was unaware that the operation involved some risk for her did not vitiate her consent in any way.

Belief in valid consent?

Suppose that Beth agreed that John could kiss her. Just before John kissed Beth, Beth changed her mind and decided that she did not want John to kiss her – but she did not tell John. Will John have committed a battery when he kissed Beth? It would seem harsh on John to say that he *did* commit a battery in this case because when he kissed Beth, he honestly and reasonably believed that Beth was consenting to his kissing her. However, if we say that John did not commit a battery in this situation because he honestly and reasonably believed that Beth was consenting to his kissing her, what should we say in the following alternative scenario?

Peter tells John that Beth – who is asleep in a nearby bedroom – told Peter before she fell asleep that she would love John to wake her up with a kiss. In fact, Beth knows nothing of this: Peter is playing a joke on both her and John. John goes into Beth's bedroom and kisses her awake. Beth is disgusted and wants to sue John for damages. Just as in the first scenario,

[13] *Chatterton* v *Gerson* [1981] 1 QB 432; *Sidaway* v *Board of Governors of the Bethlem Royal Hospital* [1984] QB 498, aff'd, [1985] AC 871; *Freeman* v *Home Office (No. 2)* [1984] 1 QB 524.

[14] [1981] 1 QB 432.

John honestly and reasonably believed that Beth had validly consented to his kissing her, but in this case it would be harsh on Beth if we said that John did *not* commit a battery in kissing her: we would be effectively saying that what Peter said to John deprived Beth of her rights not to be kissed by John while she was asleep.

Perhaps the best way out of these difficulties is to say that in the *first* scenario, Beth will be *estopped* – that is, Beth will be prevented – from denying in court that she validly consented to John's kissing her. This is because she encouraged John to believe that she consented to his kissing her, and he relied on that belief by kissing her. So because Beth will not be allowed to deny in court that she validly consented to John's kissing her, the court will find that Beth did consent to John's kissing her, and as a result the court will find that John did not commit a battery in kissing Beth. In contrast, in the *second* scenario, Beth will not be estopped from denying that she validly consented to John's kissing her. This is because *she* did nothing to encourage John to think that she wanted him to kiss her awake. So John will be unable to establish that Beth validly consented to his kissing her, and will as a result be held to have committed a battery in kissing Beth. If it seems harsh on John that he should have to pay damages to Beth in this case, it should be pointed that he will always be able to bring a claim in *deceit* against Peter and obtain compensation for any loss he has suffered as a result of relying on Peter's representation.[15]

Third party consent

Suppose that A touched B without B's consent but with the consent of a third party, C. As a general rule, C's consent will *not* make A's touching of B lawful. However, there are some exceptions to this general rule.

Suppose, for example, that Dawn medically treated Eric with the consent of Sarah, Eric's mother. Suppose further that Eric was under 18 when he was treated by Dawn and that Eric did not validly consent to his being treated by Dawn. In such a case, can it be said that Sarah's consent means that Dawn committed no battery in medically treating Eric in the way she did? The legal position is confused. On one view, Sarah's consent *does* mean that Dawn did *not* commit a battery in medically treating Eric – and this is so even if Eric or Eric's father objected to Dawn's treating Eric in the way she did.[16] On another view, Dawn will still have committed a battery in treating Eric *if* Eric objected to Dawn's treating him in the way she did *and* Eric was *either* over 16 when he was treated by Dawn *or* Eric was under 16 but his level of maturity, intelligence and understanding at the time he was treated was such that he could be safely left to decide for himself whether or not Dawn could treat him in the way she did – but if any of these conditions are not met, then Sarah's consent will have made Dawn's treatment lawful.[17]

The position is clearer if an under age patient is a ward of court at the time he is treated.[18]

[15] The tort of deceit is discussed below, at pp. 454–8.

[16] *Re R (a minor) (wardship: consent to treatment)* [1992] Fam 11, 23–5 (per Lord Donaldson MR); *Re W (a minor) (medical treatment)* [1993] Fam 64, 76 (per Lord Donaldson MR), 87 (per Balcombe LJ).

[17] *Re R (a minor) (wardship: medical treatment)* [1992] Fam 11, 27 (per Staughton LJ). This view rests heavily on some *obiter dicta* of Lord Scarman's in *Gillick* v *West Norfolk and Wisbech Area Health Authority* [1986] AC 112, 188H–189A: '. . . I would hold that as a matter of law the parental right to determine *whether* or not their minor child below the age of 16 will have medical treatment *terminates* if and when the child achieves a sufficient understanding and intelligence to enable him or her to understand fully what is proposed' (emphasis added).

[18] Adults cannot be made wards of court.

In such a case, the patient's doctors will commit no battery in treating him if they have a court's permission to do so – and this is so even if the patient does not want to be treated.[19] Obviously, a court will only permit doctors to treat a patient medically if it is in the patient's best interests to be so treated[20] and, in deciding whether or not such treatment is in the patient's best interests, the courts will take into account the patient's wishes.[21] However, an under-age patient who is a ward of court will possess no veto over how she is treated – whatever her age and whatever her level of maturity, intelligence and understanding.

Voluntary assumption of risk

It is not a tort to apply force to someone else's person if he or she has voluntarily taken a risk that such force will be applied to his or her person.

So, for example, it is well established that A will commit no battery if he brushes past B in the street.[22] The reason is that, in walking the streets, B will have voluntarily taken the risk that he will be touched by people brushing past him. Similarly, it is well established that if Tom plays football with Carl, Tom will commit no battery if he touches Carl in tackling him so long as the tackle is within the rules of the game. The reason for this is that, in agreeing to play football with Tom, Carl will have voluntarily taken the risk that Tom would subject him to tackles that are within the rules of the game. What if Tom's tackle was a foul tackle? In such a case, the courts draw a distinction between the case where Tom's tackle amounted to a mere 'error of judgment' or a 'lapse' and cases where Tom's tackle showed a 'wanton' or 'reckless' disregard of Carl's safety.[23] Carl can be taken to have voluntarily taken the risk that he would be subjected to the former kind of tackle, but not the latter. So if Tom tackled Carl in a way that showed a wanton or reckless disregard for Carl's safety, then Carl would be able to sue Tom for battery – but he would not if Tom technically committed a foul in tackling Carl, but the foul merely amounted to an error of judgment on Tom's part. Of course, if Tom punched Carl in the course of playing football with him, there is no doubt that Carl would be able to sue Tom for battery – it is not possible to argue that, in agreeing to play football with Tom, Carl voluntarily took the risk that he would be punched by Tom.[24]

Necessity

Suppose that A directly applied force to B's person. If it was *necessary* for A to do this to prevent a crime or protect someone from being physically harmed, then A *may* be able to argue that he acted lawfully in acting as he did.

19 *Re R (a minor) (wardship: consent to treatment)* [1992] Fam 11.

20 *Re B (a minor) (wardship: sterilisation)* [1988] 1 AC 199.

21 *Re W (a minor) (medical treatment)* [1993] Fam 64.

22 *Cole* v *Turner* (1704) 6 Mod 149, 87 ER 907; *Collins* v *Wilcock* [1984] 1 WLR 1172, 1177F.

23 *Condon* v *Basi* [1985] 1 WLR 866; *Blake* v *Galloway* [2004] EWCA Civ 814.

24 See *R* v *John William Billinghurst* [1978] Crim LR 553 where the defendant was held to have committed a battery in punching another player in an off-the-ball incident during a rugby football match. Willing participants in a fight will be held to have voluntarily taken the risk that they will be hit by their opponent, though if they are subjected to a blow that is particularly savage and unexpected, the defence of voluntary assumption of risk will not apply and the blow will amount to a battery: *Lane* v *Holloway* [1968] 1 QB 379. We speak here merely of *tort law*: in the interests of preventing disorder and unnecessary injury, under the *criminal law* a normal blow inflicted in the course of a fight between two willing participants will *normally* amount to a battery if the victim of the blow suffered actual bodily harm as a result: *R* v *Brown* [1994] 1 AC 212.

(1) *Self-defence*. Under the common law, A will be allowed to use reasonable force against B to protect himself from being attacked by B. The case of *Cross* v *Kirkby*[25] provides an example of a case where such a defence was successfully made out. In that case, Kirkby was a farmer who allowed the local hunt to ride over his land while hunting foxes. Cross was a hunt saboteur. While the local hunt was riding over Kirkby's land, Cross walked onto Kirkby's land in an attempt to disrupt the hunt. Kirkby attempted to remove Cross from his land with the result that Cross attacked Kirkby with a baseball bat, jabbing him in the chest and throat with the bat and eventually hitting Kirkby twice on the arm with the bat. Kirkby managed to grab the bat from Cross and hit Cross with it. Cross sustained a fracture of the skull as a result of the blow and sued Kirkby. Kirkby claimed that he had acted reasonably in self-defence in hitting Cross and had therefore done no wrong in hitting Cross.

The trial judge considered scientific evidence as to how heavy Kirkby's blow had been, found that the blow had been a 'heavy' one and held that Kirkby had used excessive force in striking Cross. He therefore found for Cross, awarding him £52,000 in damages. However, the Court of Appeal allowed Kirkby's appeal, finding that Kirkby *had* acted reasonably in self-defence. Beldam LJ – with the agreement of Otton LJ – thought that the correct test to apply, for the purpose of determining whether Kirkby acted reasonably in self-defence, was to ask: '[Did Kirkby] in a moment of unexpected anguish only [do] what he honestly and instinctively thought was necessary?' As Kirkby had only hit Cross in order to bring the attack on him to an end, the answer was 'yes'. All the Court of Appeal judges emphasised that the trial judge was wrong to find that Kirkby had used excessive force in hitting Cross because his blow was estimated to be 10 per cent harder than a blow delivered with average force. Beldam LJ remarked that 'the judge [in reaching such a finding] ... fell into the error ... [of] "using jeweller's scales to measure reasonable force"'. Judge LJ remarked that the victim of violence cannot be expected, when acting in self-defence, 'to measure [the force used by him in self-defence] with mathematical precision'.

What is the position if A hits B because he *mistakenly* believes that B is about to attack him? Will A be able to rely on the defence of self-defence to defeat any claim for battery that B might bring against A? The Court of Appeal has recently made it clear that the answer is 'Yes – *if* A *reasonably* believed that he was about to be attacked by B'.[26] So long, then, as A acts reasonably in defending himself from being attacked – both in assessing whether he is about to be attacked, and in the force he uses when he thinks that he is about to be attacked – he will be able to take advantage of the defence of self-defence to defeat any claim for battery that might be made against him. If, however, A acts unreasonably in defending himself – either in concluding that he is about to be attacked, when he was not, or in the force he used to counter an actual threat to his person – then the defence of self-defence will not be available to him.

(2) *Prevention of crime*. Section 3 of the Criminal Law Act 1967 provides that '[a] person may use such force as is reasonable in the circumstances in the prevention of crime, or in effecting or assisting in the lawful arrest of offenders or suspected offenders or of persons

[25] The Times, 5 April 2000.

[26] *Ashley* v *Chief Constable of Sussex Police* [2007] 1 WLR 398, at [78], [173], [206].

unlawfully at large'.[27] So if Alan attacks Helen, Helen will commit no battery if she uses reasonable force against Alan in an attempt to stop him attacking her. Similarly, if Sarah runs out of a store with some goods for which she has not paid, Vijay – one of the store's security guards – will commit no battery if he chases Sarah and wrestles her to the ground in an attempt to apprehend her.

(3) *Rescue of person to whom force is applied.* It is well established that if B is in danger of being hit by some moving object, A will commit no battery if he drags B out of the way. Similarly, it is well established that if B is brought *unconscious* into hospital, A, the attending doctor, will commit no battery if he gives B the medical treatment she needs to bring her back to good health.

In *Re F*,[28] the House of Lords gave formal expression to the principle underlying this last example and ruled that: if A has medically treated B, an adult, without her consent, A will *not* have committed a battery in so treating B if: (1) it was in B's best interests for A to treat her in the way he did; (2) B did not validly decline to be treated by A in the way he treated her; and (3) B was incapable of validly consenting to be treated by A in the way her treated her (either because she was drunk or because she was mentally unstable or because she was unconscious at the time she was treated by A).[29]

Parliament has now intervened to put the area of law governed by *Re F* on a statutory footing. Under s 5 of the Mental Capacity Act 2005,[30] D will have acted lawfully in doing an act 'in connection with the care or treatment of another person ("P") if': (1) 'before doing the act, D [took] reasonable steps to establish whether P [lacked] capacity in relation to the matter in question,' and (2) 'when doing the act, D reasonably believe[d] – (i) that P lack[ed] capacity in relation to the matter, and (ii) that it [was] in P's best interests for the act to be done' and (3) at the relevant time, P was not under 16.[31]

Under s 2 of the 2005 Act, 'a person lacks capacity in relation to a matter if at the material time he is unable to make a decision for himself in relation to the matter because of an impairment of, or a disturbance in the functioning of, the mind or brain'. And s 3(1) provides that, 'For the purposes of [s] 2, a person is unable to make a decision for himself if he is unable – (a) to understand the information relevant to the decision, (b) to retain

[27] See also the Education Act 1996, s 550A, which provides that 'A member of the staff of a school may use, in relation to any pupil at the school, such force as is reasonable in the circumstances for the purpose of preventing the pupil from doing (or continuing to do) any of the following, namely – (a) committing any offence, (b) causing personal injury to, or damage to the property of, any person (including the pupil himself), or (c) engaging in any behaviour prejudicial to the maintenance of good order and discipline at the school or among any of its pupils, whether that behaviour occurs during a teaching session or otherwise.'

[28] [1990] 2 AC 1.

[29] In *Re F*, F was a voluntary in-patient in a mental hospital. She was 36 years old but had the mental age of a small child. When she showed signs that she was about to become sexually active, F's mother sought to have her sterilised on the grounds that it would be harmful to F's mental health if she became pregnant. The House of Lords held that the hospital staff at F's mental hospital would commit no battery if they sterilised F without her consent: it would be in F's best interests to be sterilised; F had not validly declined to be sterilised; and F's mental age meant that F was incapable of validly consenting to be sterilised.

[30] The relevant provisions came into force on October 1, 2007: Mental Capacity Act 2005 (Commencement No. 2) Order 2007, SI 2007/1897.

[31] Point (3) is a consequence of s 2(5) of the 2005 Act, which provides that 'No power which a person ("D") may exercise under this Act – (a) in relation to a person who lacks capacity, or (b) where D reasonably thinks a person lacks capacity, is exercisable in relation to a person under 16.'

that information, (c) to use or weigh that information as part of the process of making the decision, or (d) to communicate his decision.'

Section 6 of the 2005 Act places an important limit on the scope of s 5. It deals with the situation where D 'restrained' P – where D will be held to have 'restrained' P if he 'use[d], or threaten[ed] to use, force to secure the doing of an act which P resist[ed], or' if he 'restrict[ed] P's liberty of movement, whether or not P resist[ed]'. Section 6 provides that if we want to establish that D acted lawfully in 'restraining' P, it will not be enough to show that conditions (1)–(3), above, were satisfied. It will also have to be shown that: (4) 'D reasonably believe[d] that it [was] necessary to do the act in order to prevent harm to P' and (5) 'the act [was] a proportionate response to – (a) the likelihood of P's suffering harm, and (b) the seriousness of that harm'.[32]

We can illustrate how the 2005 Act is likely to work by considering two cases that were decided under the old law, as set out in *Re F*.

In *B* v *An NHS Hospital Trust*,[33] the claimant suffered from spinal problems which resulted in her being paralysed from the neck down. This meant that she could not breathe without the assistance of a ventilator. The claimant had an operation to make her better, but it was unsuccessful. The claimant was bitterly disappointed with this and decided that she did not wish to live any more. She asked for her ventilator to be switched off. The claimant's doctors declined to do this, and so the claimant took them to court. It was held that *Re F* did not apply; and so the doctors were acting unlawfully in continuing to treat the claimant. Even if it were in the claimant's best interests to be kept alive, the claimant was old enough and intelligent enough to decide for herself whether she wanted to continue being treated, and so her refusal to be treated any more was perfectly valid.

It is likely that the same result would be reached under the 2005 Act. The claimant here did not lack capacity to decide for herself how she was to be treated: she was able to understand the information relevant to that decision; she was able to retain that information, use it and weigh it; and to communicate her decision about how she was to be treated. The fact that her decision may have been coloured by her bitter disappointment that her operation had not been more successful did not prevent her from having the 'capacity' to make that decision: under s 1(4) of the 2005 Act, 'A person is not to be treated as [being] unable to make a decision merely because he makes an unwise decision.'

In *Re T*,[34] T was injured in a car accident when she was 34 weeks pregnant. She was admitted into hospital where she went into labour. She was told that the baby would have to be delivered by Caesarian section and that it might be necessary to give her a blood transfusion to replenish her blood after the operation. After conversations with her mother, T told the hospital staff that she was a Jehovah's Witness and did not want to have a blood transfusion after her Caesarian. After the Caesarian was carried out – and before T had regained consciousness – T's condition suddenly deteriorated and she was transferred to an

[32] *Important note*. Even if conditions (1)–(5) are satisfied, this will not authorise D to do anything to P which would deprive P of his liberty: s 4A of the 2005 Act (as amended by the Mental Health Act 2007, s 50) provides that subject to certain narrow exceptions, 'This Act does not authorise any person . . . to deprive any other person . . . of his liberty'; and s 6(5) of the 2005 Act provides that 'D does more than merely restrain P if he deprives P of his liberty within the meaning of Article 5(1)' of the European Convention on Human Rights.

[33] [2002] 2 All ER 449.

[34] [1993] Fam 95.

intensive care unit where she was put on a ventilator and paralysing drugs were administered. She was then given a blood transfusion at the behest of T's father and boyfriend. The Court of Appeal had to decide whether the hospital had committed a battery in giving T a blood transfusion.

The court thought that the House of Lords' decision in *Re F* established that the hospital did *not* commit a battery in treating T in the way it did: the court thought that it had been in T's best interests to give her a blood transfusion (she might have died without it); T had not validly declined to be given a blood transfusion in the circumstances in which she was given it; and at the time the blood transfusion was administered T was incapable of validly consenting to its being given to her. The court gave two reasons for thinking that T had not validly declined to be given a blood transfusion in the circumstances in which she was given it. First, when T declined to be given a blood transfusion after her Caesarian she was simply declining to be given a blood transfusion in order to replenish her blood – she did not mean to indicate that if it was necessary for her to receive a blood transfusion to save her life, she still did not want to be given a blood transfusion. Secondly, when T declined to be given a blood transfusion after her Caesarian, she did so under pressure from her mother.

It is, again, likely that the same result would be reached under the 2005 Act. One important difference between the law under the 2005 Act, and the old law as stated in *Re F*, is that to establish that their treatment of T was lawful under the 2005 Act, her doctors would merely have to show that they *reasonably believed* that T lacked capacity at the time they gave her a blood transfusion, and that giving her a blood transfusion was in her best interests. There is no doubt that T lacked the capacity whether or not to decide to have a blood transfusion at the time it was administered, and it is highly likely that T's doctors would have been able to establish that they reasonably thought giving her a blood transfusion was in her best interests at the time it was administered. Section 4(6) of the 2005 Act does provide that in determining what is in a person's ('P's') best interests, the person making that determination ('D') must consider 'so far as is reasonably ascertainable – (a) [P]'s past and present wishes and feelings . . ., [and] (b) the beliefs and values that would be likely to influence his decision if [P] had [the] capacity [to make that decision] . . .'. However, even taking these factors into account, T's doctors would be able to argue convincingly that they reasonably thought that it was in T's best interests to have a blood transfusion: the fact that she did not want a blood transfusion to replenish her blood did not mean that she did not want a blood transfusion to save her life.

(4) *Rescue of persons other than person to whom force was applied.* If A has applied force to B's body in order to save *someone other than B* from being physically harmed, will A ever be entitled to claim that he acted lawfully in acting as he did? The law in this area is still developing.

In *Re S*,[35] the President of the Family Division, Sir Stephen Brown, ruled that a doctor who performs a Caesarian section on a pregnant patient in order to save the life of her foetus will commit no battery *even if* the patient has validly *declined* to undergo a Caesarian

[35] [1993] Fam 123.

section.[36] However, in *St George's Healthcare NHS Trust* v *S*,[37] the Court of Appeal held that Sir Stephen Brown was wrong: if a pregnant patient validly declines to undergo a Caesarian section, a doctor who performs such an operation on the patient will commit a battery even if it is necessary to perform the operation in order to save the life of the patient's foetus.

Re A[38] concerned a pair of conjoined twins, Jodie and Mary. Mary was much the weaker of the twins and relied on Jodie's heart and lungs to keep her alive. If an operation was not carried out to separate Mary from Jodie, Jodie's heart would fail within six months and they both would die. However, if such an operation were carried out, Mary would certainly die as a result. The Court of Appeal held that Mary and Jodie's doctors would act lawfully if they carried out the operation. The doctors were entitled to rely on a defence of necessity in this case as Mary posed a (passive) threat to Jodie's life and removing Mary from Jodie was the only way of saving Jodie's life. It is submitted that the decision is to be confined to its own facts – it does not, for example, authorise A to kill B if both are stranded in some wilderness and one needs to eat the other in order to survive; nor does it authorise a doctor to kill a terminally ill patient by removing his heart and lungs in order to give them to another patient who is in need of them.

Lawful chastisement

If A hits B to punish her for misbehaving, A will not usually be able to argue that he acted lawfully in hitting B. It used to be that there were two exceptions to this general rule. First, parents were allowed to use reasonable force to discipline their children. Secondly, a school-teacher, acting *in loco parentis*, was allowed to use reasonable force to punish the children in his care if they misbehaved.

The second exception no longer survives: s 548 of the Education Act 1996 provides that 'Corporal punishment given by, or on the authority of, a member of staff to a child ... cannot be justified in any proceedings on the ground that it was given in pursuance of a right exercisable by the member of the staff by virtue of his position ...'[39]

The first exception has now been qualified by s 58(3) of the Children Act 2004, which provides that 'Battery of a child causing actual bodily harm to the child cannot be justified in any civil proceedings on the ground that it constituted reasonable punishment.' So a parent, A, will have a committed a tort in using force to discipline his or her child, B, if – *either*: (1) in doing so, A caused B to suffer actual bodily harm;[40] *or* (2) A failed to use rea-

[36] In so holding he was following a suggestion of Lord Donaldson MR's in *Re T (adult: refusal of medical treatment)* [1993] Fam 95, 102: 'An adult patient who ... suffers from no mental incapacity has an absolute right to choose whether to consent to medical treatment, to refuse it or to choose one rather than another of the treatments being offered. The only possible qualification is a case in which the choice may lead to the death of a viable foetus.'

[37] [1999] Fam 26.

[38] [2001] Fam 147.

[39] In *R (Williamson)* v *Secretary of State for Education and Employment* [2003] QB 1300 (noted, Eekelaar 2003), the Court of Appeal rejected a claim that this provision violated the applicants' rights to manifest their religion or beliefs under Art 9 of the European Convention on Human Rights and Art 2 of the First Protocol to the Convention.

[40] Under s 58(4) of the 2004 Act, 'For the purposes of subsection (3) "actual bodily harm" has the same meaning as it has for the purposes of section 47 of the Offences against the Person Act 1847.' The courts have interpreted 'actual bodily harm' under the latter Act as meaning any hurt or injury that was 'not so trivial as to be wholly insignificant': *R* v *Chan-Fook* [1994] 1 WLR 689, at 696 (per Hobhouse LJ).

sonable force in disciplining B.[41] It is unlikely that this state of affairs will satisfy those who think it unacceptable for force ever to be used on children,[42] and further reform of this area of the law must be expected.

Acceptable contact

In *Collins* v *Wilcock*, Robert Goff LJ, as he then was, suggested that an application of force to another's person that is 'generally acceptable in the conduct of daily life'[43] will not amount to a battery.

So, on this view, if Beth touches Alan on the shoulder to get his attention, Beth will commit no battery – touching someone on the shoulder to get their attention is a generally acceptable thing to do. In *Collins* v *Wilcock* itself, a policewoman grabbed a prostitute by the arm to stop her from walking away while she was trying to question her. The Court of Appeal held that the policewoman committed the tort of battery in restraining the prostitute – the policewoman's conduct went some way beyond what is 'generally acceptable in the conduct of daily life'.

Further requirements?

A couple of cases have departed from the definition advanced here of when someone will commit the tort of battery.

In *Letang* v *Cooper*, Lord Denning MR – with the concurrence of Danckwerts LJ – suggested that in order to establish that A has committed the tort of battery in relation to B it had to be shown that A, in acting as he did, *intended to injure B*: '[if someone] does not inflict injury [on a claimant] intentionally, but only unintentionally, the claimant has no cause of action in [battery].'[44]

In *Wilson* v *Pringle*, the Court of Appeal held that if one wants to show that A committed the tort of battery in applying force to B's person, it must be shown that A acted in a *hostile* way in applying that force to B's person: 'for there to be ... a battery there must be something in the nature of hostility.'[45] In *Wilson* v *Pringle* itself the claimant and the defendant were both schoolboys. The defendant was walking down a corridor behind the claimant when, as a joke, he pulled at the claimant's sports bag – which the claimant was carrying over his right shoulder. The claimant fell and injured his left hip. The claimant sued the defendant, claiming he had committed the tort of battery. He obtained summary judgment; the judge taking the view that the defendant had obviously committed a battery. The Court of Appeal reversed the judge's decision, holding that it was not completely clear that the defendant had committed the tort of battery on these facts – a hearing would be required to determine whether the defendant, in acting as he did, acted with the requisite degree of hostility.

[41] In judging what amounts to reasonable force, the courts must 'consider the nature and context of the defendant's behaviour, its duration, its physical and mental consequences in relation to the child, the age and personal characteristics of the child and the reasons given by the defendant for administering punishment': *R* v *H (assault of child: reasonable chastisement)* [2001] 2 FLR 431, at [31].

[42] See, for example, Bitensky 1998.

[43] [1984] 1 WLR 1172, 1177G–H.

[44] [1965] 1 QB 232, 239G.

[45] [1987] 1 QB 237, 250C–D.

The suggestions in these cases as to what has to be established in order to show that someone has committed the tort of battery have *not* been followed by the courts. The Court of Appeal in *Wilson* v *Pringle* ruled that '[an] intention to injure is not essential to an action for [battery]',[46] thereby disapproving Lord Denning MR's statement to the contrary in *Letang* v *Cooper*. In *Re F*, Lord Goff of Chieveley disapproved the suggestion in *Wilson* v *Pringle* that an application of force to another's person must be 'hostile' before it can amount to a battery:

> I respectfully doubt whether that is correct. A prank that gets out of hand; an over-friendly slap on the back; surgical treatment by a surgeon who mistakenly thinks that the patient has consented to it – all these things may transcend the bounds of lawfulness, without being characterised as hostile. Indeed the suggested qualification is difficult to reconcile with the principle that any touching of another's body is, in the absence of lawful excuse, capable of amounting to a battery . . .[47]

ASSAULT

Less needs to be said here about when someone will commit the tort of assault. Only a couple of points need be emphasised.

(1) *The need to be put in fear of imminent attack*. A will only commit the tort of assault if he leads B to believe that he is *about* to commit a battery on B. So in *Tuberville* v *Savage*[48] it was held that Tuberville did not commit an assault when he reacted to something Savage said by drawing his sword while saying 'If it were not assize-time I should not take such language from you.' As it *was* assize time, Tuberville did not lead Savage to believe that Tuberville was about to strike him with his sword.

In *Thomas* v *National Union of Mineworkers (South Wales Area)*,[49] the claimants were coal miners who wished to go to work during the miners' strike. As they entered the colliery where they worked they suffered abuse and threats from massed pickets at the colliery gates. They sought to obtain an injunction against the massed picketing, claiming among other things that the pickets were committing the tort of assault in abusing and threatening them as they entered the colliery. This claim was rejected by Scott J on the ground that the claimants were always driven into the colliery and were separated from the pickets by ranks of policemen – given this, it could hardly be said that the abuse and threats the claimants received when they entered the colliery put them in fear that they were *about* to be beaten up by the pickets.[50]

46 Ibid., 249H.

47 [1990] 2 AC 1, 73B–C.

48 (1669) 1 Mod 3, 86 ER 684.

49 [1986] 1 Ch 20.

50 In *Mbasogo* v *Logo Ltd* [2006] EWCA Civ 1370, the Court of Appeal said of the *Thomas* case (at [75]) that: 'The threats made by pickets to those miners who sought to go to work were not an assault because the pickets had no capacity to put into effect their threats of violence whilst they were held back from the vehicles which the working miners were within.' This suggests that if A threatens to shoot B if B does not do as he says, then A's threat will *not* amount to an assault if A did not have the capacity to shoot B at the time he made his threat. This cannot be right. If A walks into a bank holding a gun and threatens to kill a cashier if she does not give him some money, A commits an assault whether or not the gun he is holding is real.

(2) *Silence*. In *R* v *Ireland*,[51] the House of Lords ruled that someone can commit the tort of assault through mere silence. The defendant in that case made a series of malicious telephone calls to three women – when they answered he would remain silent. The women all developed psychiatric illnesses as a result of their treatment at the hands of the defendant. The defendant was charged with committing the offence of assault occasioning actual bodily harm and was convicted. The House of Lords upheld the conviction, holding that his silent telephone calls could have led the women in question to believe they were about to be attacked by whoever was on the other end of the line.

[51] [1998] AC 147.

12 False imprisonment

A will commit the tort of false imprisonment in relation to B if he intentionally[1] 'imprisons' B when he has no lawful justification or excuse for doing so.

THE MEANING OF IMPRISONMENT

A will 'imprison' B if: (1) he completely restricts B's freedom of movement; or (2) he restricts B's freedom of movement to within a defined area. So Vijay will 'imprison' Beth if he grabs Beth's arm so that she cannot go anywhere. Similarly, Sarah will 'imprison' Eric if she locks Eric in a room – Eric will be free to move within the room but will not be free to move outside.

In *Bird* v *Jones*,[2] a public right of way ran through an enclosure created by the defendants for the purpose of viewing a boat race. The claimant, in an attempt to use the right of way, entered the enclosure. The defendants prevented the claimant from walking through the enclosure and instead instructed him to turn back and use another route to reach his destination. The claimant refused to move and stayed in the enclosure for half an hour. The claimant sued the defendants, claiming that they had committed the tort of false imprisonment. The claim was rejected: the defendant had done nothing that completely restricted the claimant's freedom of movement or restricted that freedom of movement to within a defined area. The claimant had been free at all times to leave the enclosure and find another way of getting to where he wanted to go.

If A restricts B's freedom of movement to within a defined area, he will 'imprison' B whether or not B knows that his freedom of movement is restricted to the area in question. So in *Meering* v *Grahame-White Aviation Company Ltd*, Atkin LJ remarked:

> It appears to me that a person could be imprisoned without his knowing it. I think a person can be imprisoned while he is asleep, while he is in a state of drunkenness, while he is unconscious and while he is a lunatic. Those are cases where it seems to me that the person might properly complain if he were imprisoned, though the imprisonment began and ceased while he was in that state. Of course, the damages might be diminished and would be affected by the question of whether he was conscious of it or not.[3]

These *dicta* were endorsed by the House of Lords in *Murray* v *Ministry of Defence*.[4] So if

[1] Though there is no authority on the matter, most scholars think that a defendant must have acted *with the aim of* imprisoning a claimant before the defendant can be held to have committed the tort of false imprisonment in relation to the claimant: see W&J, 100 n. 39; Lunney & Mitchell 2007, 458; GS&Z, 568. So – on this view – if A locks a room when he ought to have known that B was inside, that will not necessarily amount to false imprisonment; he must have locked the room with the aim of imprisoning B before he can be held to have committed that tort.

[2] (1845) 7 QB 742, 115 ER 668.

[3] (1920) 122 LT 44, 53–4.

[4] [1988] 1 WLR 692, 701C–703B.

Mary locks a room in which John is sleeping, Mary will 'imprison' John – the fact that John is completely unaware that he is in a locked room will be completely immaterial.[5]

What is the position if Ruth is in a particular room or building and Fred decides that if Ruth attempts to leave that room or building he will prevent Ruth from doing so but because Ruth has not yet attempted to leave the room or building in question, Fred has not actually done anything yet to prevent her from leaving that room or building? Has Fred 'imprisoned' Ruth? One would think the answer must be 'no': whether or not Fred has 'imprisoned' Ruth cannot merely depend on Fred's mental state.

The House of Lords confirmed that this view is correct in *R* v *Bournewood Community and Mental Health NHS Trust, ex parte L*.[6] That case concerned one L who had a history of mental health problems. Having spent 30 years being treated in Bournewood Hospital, L was discharged into the community in 1994 and looked after by paid carers. However, in 1997 after an incident in a day care centre, L became particularly agitated and voluntarily agreed to go back to Bournewood Hospital. Once there, he was kept in an unlocked ward and no attempts were made to restrain him from leaving. However, the staff there decided that if he attempted to leave, they would section him under the Mental Health Act 1983 and prevent him from leaving. L did in fact eventually attempt to leave and was sectioned under the Act. When L was eventually discharged, he sued the hospital, claiming that its employees had falsely imprisoned him in the period between his entering the hospital and his being sectioned. The House of Lords dismissed L's claim. By a majority of three to two, they held that the staff at Bournewood Hospital had not imprisoned L during that time: the fact that during that time they were prepared to section L if he attempted to leave did not mean that they had 'imprisoned' him.[7]

What is the position if A has caused a third party, C, to 'imprison' B? In such a case, can we say that *A* has 'imprisoned' B? The decision of the Court of Appeal in *Davidson* v *Chief Constable of North Wales*[8] indicates that the answer is 'yes' if A *persuaded, encouraged or requested* C to 'imprison' B, but otherwise the answer is 'no'. In that case, a store detective who was employed by the defendants thought that the claimant had left the store with a cassette for which she had not paid. The store detective reported his suspicions to the police and they arrested the claimant, thereby 'imprisoning' her. In fact the claimant did not steal the cassette in question – it had been paid for by a friend of hers. The claimant sued the defendants, claiming that the store detective, their employee, had falsely imprisoned her. The Court of Appeal dismissed the claimant's claim: the store detective did not persuade, encourage or request the police to arrest the claimant – all he did was report his suspicions to the police; he then left it up to the police to decide what to do.

[5] Most jurisdictions in the United States take the view that a claim for false imprisonment could *not* be made here: GS&Z, 571.

[6] [1999] 1 AC 458.

[7] The European Court of Human Rights subsequently ruled that L's rights under Art 5 of the ECHR not to be deprived of his liberty save in certain exceptional circumstances had been violated: *HL* v *United Kingdom* (2005) 40 EHRR 32 (noted, Pedain 2005). While the Court noted that the concept of 'deprivation of liberty' under Art 5 was wider than that of 'imprisonment' and did not as a result question the correctness of the House of Lords' decision that L had not been 'imprisoned', in truth the House of Lords' finding that L had not been 'imprisoned' was somewhat artificial given that the only reason L had not sought to leave the hospital was that he was being constantly drugged by staff at the hospital, who also discouraged relatives and friends of L from visiting him.

[8] [1994] 2 All ER 597.

LAWFUL JUSTIFICATION OR EXCUSE

If A has 'imprisoned' B, there are a number of different ways in which A could establish that he had a lawful justification or excuse for acting in the way he did.

Consent

Obviously, if A has imprisoned B with B's consent, then A will have had a lawful justification or excuse for acting as he did. So, for example, suppose that Peter is addicted to drugs and allows his parents to lock him in his room so that he can kick the habit that he has acquired. His parents will do no wrong in locking Peter up in his room. But what is the position if Peter is suffering such acute withdrawal symptoms that he begs his parents to let him out of his room? Will his parents commit the tort of false imprisonment if they do not let him out at that stage? It is hard to say. Perhaps the best analysis is that Peter is not in his right mind when he begs his parents to let him out of his room – so when he begs his parents to let him out, he does not withdraw the consent that he initially gave his parents to lock him up. On this analysis, Peter's parents will not commit the tort of false imprisonment if they do not let him out of his room in the situation we are considering.

In a case where A *does* validly withdraw his consent to being imprisoned by B, B must release A *within a reasonable period of time*. If B does not do so, he will commit the tort of false imprisonment. In *Herd* v *Weardale Steel, Coal and Coke Company Ltd*,[9] the claimant was a miner who descended to the bottom of a pit at the start of his shift. He then refused to do certain work and asked to be lifted up to the surface. The claimant was only allowed to go back up to the surface at the end of the morning shift and even then he was only permitted to go back up once all the miners on the morning shift had been taken to the surface. The claimant sued, claiming that he had been falsely imprisoned. The House of Lords dismissed his claim. One explanation of the decision is that the defendants had acted reasonably in not releasing the claimant from the bottom of the pit until the end of the shift: there was no reason why they should go to the trouble and inconvenience of arranging for the claimant to be taken back to the surface on his own.[10]

Voluntary assumption of risk

Another explanation of the decision in *Herd* is that it was lawful to keep the claimant at the bottom of the pit until the end of the shift because when he went down to the bottom of the pit at the start of the shift, he *voluntarily took the risk* that he would not be taken back up to the surface until the end of the shift. Another case which can be interpreted as supporting the idea that it is not unlawful to imprison someone who has voluntarily taken the risk that she will be imprisoned is *Robinson* v *Balmain New Ferry Company Ltd*.[11]

In that case, the claimant wanted to take a ferry across a river. In order to get to the wharf from which the ferry would depart, he had to go through a turnstile operated by the defen-

[9] [1915] AC 67.

[10] See Tan 1981 for this explanation of the decision in *Herd*, though he doubts whether the case was correctly decided on the facts.

[11] [1910] AC 295.

dants. As notices on either side of the turnstile made clear, the charge for using the turnstile to enter or exit the wharf was one penny. The claimant handed over a penny, went through the turnstile and waited on the wharf for the ferry to arrive and pick him up. The claimant then changed his plans and decided not to take the ferry at all. He attempted to go back through the turnstile but the defendants insisted that if he wanted to use the turnstile to leave the wharf, he had to pay them a penny – as was stipulated in the notices at the turnstile. When the claimant refused to pay the defendants the required penny, the defendants refused to let him use the turnstile, effectively trapping the claimant on the wharf. The claimant sued the defendants, claiming they had falsely imprisoned him, but his claim was dismissed by the Privy Council. One explanation of this decision is that when the claimant walked through the turnstile, he voluntarily took the risk that he would not be allowed to go back through the turnstile without paying a penny – he therefore voluntarily took the risk that if he did not pay a penny to go back through the turnstile, he would be imprisoned by the defendants on the wharf.

In *Sunbolf* v *Alford*,[12] the claimant ate a meal at the defendant's inn and attempted to leave without paying for it. The defendant forcibly restrained the claimant from doing so. The claimant sued the defendant, claiming that when the defendant prevented him from leaving the defendant's inn, the defendant falsely imprisoned him. The claimant's claim was allowed. However, the result might have been different if there had been a notice in the inn informing customers that they would be detained if they attempted to leave without paying for the food consumed by them in the inn. If this had been the case, the defendant could have argued that when the claimant chose to eat at his inn he voluntarily took the risk that if he did not pay for his meal he would be detained.[13]

Necessity

Suppose that A imprisoned B because it was *necessary* for him to do so. If B subsequently sues A for false imprisonment, will A be able to argue that he had a lawful justification or excuse for imprisoning B? The law on this issue is not terribly clear, but a number of different situations can be distinguished.

(1) *Prevention of harm to self.* Let us first of all consider the case where A needs to be locked up in order to stop him harming himself. The courts previously held that locking someone up to stop them harming themselves might be justified on grounds of necessity if the person who was in danger of harming themselves was mentally incapacitated. So, for example, in the case of *R* v *Bournewood Community and Mental Health NHS Trust, ex parte L*,[14] L – who was autistic, severely mentally retarded, and had a history of harming himself – became particularly agitated while attending a day centre for treatment and started banging his head on the wall. He was taken to hospital in an ambulance. The House of Lords held that L's being imprisoned in the ambulance on the way to the hospital was justified on the ground of necessity.

[12] (1838) 3 M & W 248, 150 ER 1135.
[13] For a different view, see Tan 1981, 167: 'a creditor cannot imprison his debtor in the absence of statutory authority' (quoting Glanville Williams).
[14] [1999] 1 AC 458.

However, the European Court of Human Rights subsequently held in *HL* v *United Kingdom*[15] that the way L had been treated violated his human rights under Article 5 of the European Convention on Human Rights. This provides that '[e]veryone has the right to liberty and security of person' save in certain exceptional cases such as where someone has been convicted of a criminal offence, or where someone has been lawfully arrested for the purpose of 'bringing him before the competent legal authority on reasonable suspicion of having committed an offence' or where 'persons of unsound mind, alcoholics, drug addicts or vagrants' have been lawfully detained 'for the prevention of the spreading of infectious diseases'.

L's case would now be governed by the Mental Capacity Act 2005, which – it will be recalled from the previous chapter[16] – sets out the conditions that need to be satisfied before one can do an act 'in connection with the care or treatment of another person' on the ground that they lack the capacity to decide for themselves how they should be cared for or treated. The UK government responded to the European Court of Human Rights' judgment in the *HL* case by inserting ss 4A and 4B into the 2005 Act.[17] Section 4A provides that, subject to three exceptions, the 2005 Act 'does not authorise any person ("D") to deprive any other person ("P") of his liberty'. The three exceptions are:

(1) if a court has ordered that P may be deprived of his liberty on the basis that P lacks the capacity to act in his own personal welfare, that depriving him of his liberty is in his best interests, and is a necessary and proportionate step to save him from harm;[18]
(2) if an application is being made to a court to authorise D to deprive P of his liberty, and it becomes necessary in the meantime to deprive P of his liberty in order to give P life-sustaining treatment;[19]
(3) D has been authorised to detain P in a hospital or care home under schedule A1 of the 2005 Act.[20]

Under these provisions, so long as L in the *Bournewood* case was in fact 'deprived of his liberty' by being kept in the ambulance, his being detained in the ambulance would not be lawful under the 2005 Act: his case did not fall within any of exceptions (1)–(3).

(2) *Prevention of harm to others*. There is no doubt that if A is going to kill B, or it reasonably looks like A is going to kill B, it is not false imprisonment to lock him up in a room to stop him killing B. Section 3 of the Criminal Law Act 1967 supports this view. That section, it will be recalled, provides that '[a] person may use such force as is reasonable in the circumstances in the prevention of crime . . .'.

The decision of the Court of Appeal in *Austin and Saxby* v *The Commissioner of Police of the Metropolis*[21] goes further and says that imprisoning innocent people who do not look as though they are about to commit an offence may be justified if that is the only possible

[15] (2005) 40 EHRR 32 (noted, Pedain 2005).
[16] See above, pp. 257–9.
[17] See Mental Health Act 2007, s 50.
[18] Sections 4A(3)–(4), 16(2)–(3).
[19] Section 4B.
[20] Section 4A(5).
[21] [2007] EWCA Civ 989.

way of preventing an imminent breach of the peace.[22] In that case, the police set up a cordon on Oxford Street on 1 May 2001, imprisoning within the cordon about 3,000 people, for about seven hours. They did this because they thought that some of the people within the cordon were 'May Day' protestors intent on wreaking havoc in central London. The Court of Appeal held that the police's action in this case was lawful because it 'was necessary to avoid an imminent breach of the peace'.[23]

The Court of Appeal added that it thought that the European Court of Human Rights would *not* find that the Article 5 rights of the people caught within the cordon had been violated by the police action: 'it would be surprising if [the police were found to have] infringed [their] rights under [A]rticle 5 [when a] judge has held that it was necessary for the police to take the steps they did.'[24] The Court of Appeal went on to suggest that the European Court would find that the police had not deprived the people within the cordon of their liberty – with the result that the facts of the *Austin* case would not fall under Article 5 at all.[25] This part of the Court of Appeal's decision seems very optimistic; it would not be at all surprising if the European Court of Human Rights found that the police action in the *Austin* case amounted to an egregious violation of the Article 5 rights of the people caught within the cordon.

(3) *Arrest under invalid byelaw.* In *Percy* v *Hall*,[26] the claimants were arrested over 150 times for trespassing on land in the vicinity of a military communications installation in North Yorkshire in breach of the HMS Forest Moor and Menwith Hill Station Byelaws 1986. These byelaws were actually invalid at the time the claimants were arrested because they were insufficiently precise. When this was discovered, the claimants sued the constables who had arrested them for breach of the byelaws, claiming that, as the byelaws were invalid, the constables had committed the tort of false imprisonment in arresting them. The claimants' claims were dismissed by the Court of Appeal. How can we explain this result? As the byelaws were invalid at the time the claimants were arrested, they could not have supplied the constables who arrested the claimants with a lawful excuse or justification for arresting the claimants. However, when the constables arrested the claimants 'they were enforcing what at the time appeared to be perfectly valid byelaws; to have done otherwise [namely, not to have arrested the claimants] would seemingly have involved them in a clear

22 The Court of Appeal based itself on *obiter dicta* in *R (Laporte)* v *Chief Constable of Gloucester Constabulary* [2007] 2 AC 105, at [82]–[85] (per Lord Rodger), and at [119]–[129] (per Lord Brown). They summed up these *dicta* as saying that: '(i) where a breach of the peace is imminent, or is reasonably thought to be imminent, before the police can take any steps which interfere with or curtail in any way the lawful exercise of rights by innocent third parties they must ensure that they have taken all other possible steps to ensure that the breach, or imminent breach, is obviated and that the rights of innocent third parties are protected; (ii) the taking of all other possible steps includes (where practicable), but is not limited to, ensuring that proper and advance preparations have been made to deal with such a breach, since failure to take such steps will render interference with the rights of innocent third parties unjustified or unjustifiable; but (iii) where (and only where) there is a reasonable belief that there are no other means whatsoever whereby a breach or imminent breach of the peace can be obviated, the lawful exercise by third parties of their rights may be curtailed by the police; (iv) this is a test of necessity which it is to be expected can only be justified in truly extreme and exceptional circumstances; and (v) the action taken must be both reasonably necessary and proportionate': [2007] EWCA Civ 989, at [35].

23 Ibid., at [68].

24 Ibid., at [93].

25 Ibid., at [104]–[105]. The Court of Appeal preferred not to express a view on whether the police action – if it did deprive the people within the cordon of their liberty – was justified under Art 5: ibid., at [108]–[117].

26 [1997] QB 924.

breach of their duties'.[27] This fact was crucial to the Court of Appeal's finding that the constables did not falsely imprison the claimants when they arrested them. The constables had a lawful justification or excuse for arresting the claimants because, at the time the constables arrested the claimants, it was *necessary* for them to do so. If they had not, they would have been in breach of their duties – they would have failed to enforce apparently valid byelaws.

(4) *Unduly prolonged detention in prison.* Suppose that A is convicted of committing a criminal offence and sentenced to spend some time in prison. Suppose further that someone makes a mistake in determining how long A should spend in prison and as a result A is imprisoned for three months longer than he ought to have been. Can A sue the prison governor on the ground that he was falsely imprisoned for those three months? If it was the courts that made the mistake in calculating A's sentence, then A will *not* be able to sue the prison governor for falsely imprisoning him.[28] The prison governor will be able to argue that he was duty-bound to imprison A for as long as he did, and that he therefore had a lawful justification or excuse for imprisoning A for the extra three months that A should not have served.

If, however, it was the prison governor who made the mistake in calculating A's sentence, then A *will* be able to sue the prison governor for falsely imprisoning him – and this is so even if the prison governor's mistake was an entirely reasonable one to make. This was established by the House of Lords' decision in *R* v *Governor of Brockhill Prison, ex parte Evans (No. 2)*.[29] In that case, the claimant was a woman named Evans who was sent to prison to serve several terms of imprisonment, running concurrently. At the time Evans was sent to prison, the Divisional Court had ruled – in a case called *R* v *Governor of Blundeston Prison, ex parte Gaffney*[30] – that the release date of a prisoner serving several concurrent sentences should be calculated in a certain way (call this 'Method X'). The governor, abiding by the decision in *Gaffney*, applied Method X to determine when Evans should be released. However, while Evans was still in prison, she went to court and persuaded the Court of Appeal to rule that the governor should have used a different method for calculating her release date – let's call this method 'Method Y'.[31] The Court of Appeal thereby overruled the decision of the Divisional Court in *Gaffney*. According to Method Y, Evans should have *already* been released and, accordingly, she was released on the same day as the Court of Appeal overruled *Gaffney*. In fact, according to Method Y, Evans should have been released 59 days before she was actually released. Evans sued the prison governor, claiming that she had been falsely imprisoned in being detained for those 59 days. The House of Lords allowed her claim.

It is, however, hard to see why the prison governor was not allowed to rely on a defence of necessity in this case to defeat Evans's claim. Until *Gaffney* was overruled, the governor

[27] Ibid., 945D–E.
[28] *Quinland* v *Governor of Swaleside Prison* [2003] QB 306. A will not be able to sue the *courts* for falsely imprisoning him by virtue of s 2(5) of the Crown Proceedings Act 1947, which provides that 'No proceedings shall lie against the Crown by virtue of this section in respect of anything done or omitted to be done by a person whilst discharging or purporting to discharge any responsibilities of a judicial nature vested in him, or any responsibilities which he has in connection with the execution of judicial process.'
[29] [2001] 2 AC 19 (noted, Cane 2001a).
[30] [1982] 1 WLR 696.
[31] *R* v *Governor of Brockhill Prison, ex parte Evans* [1997] QB 443.

of Evans's prison was *required* to calculate Evans's release date using Method X and to detain Evans in prison until that date. So the governor of Evans's prison was duty-bound to detain Evans for as long as he did.[32] It was therefore necessary for the governor of Evans's prison to detain Evans for as long as he did. Given this, it could be argued that the governor of Evans's prison had a lawful justification or excuse for detaining Evans for as long as he did. Indeed, if the constables in *Percy* v *Hall* had a lawful justification or excuse for arresting the claimants in that case based on the fact that they were duty bound to arrest the claimants when they did, it is hard to see why the governor of Evans's prison did not have a lawful justification or excuse for detaining Evans for as long as he did based on the fact that he was duty-bound to act in the way he did.[33]

Statutory authority

There are plenty of occasions when one person will be authorised or required by statute to imprison another. The most obvious example is provided by the Police and Criminal Evidence Act 1984, which sets out the rules governing when someone may be lawfully arrested for committing an offence.[34] Another example is provided by the Mental Health Act 1983, under which people suffering from mental disorders may in certain circumstances be arrested or detained in hospital.[35] A further example is provided by s 12(1) of the Prison Act 1952, which provides that '[a] prisoner, whether sentenced to imprisonment or committed to prison on remand or pending trial or otherwise, may be lawfully confined in any prison'.

This section does not, of course, authorise or allow the governor of a prison to detain a prisoner for longer than the period of his sentence or the time he is supposed to spend on remand.[36] So – as we have seen – the prison governor in *R* v *Governor of Brockhill Prison, ex parte Evans (No. 2)*[37] was held to have committed the tort of false imprisonment when he held the claimant in that case in prison for 59 more days than she was supposed to spend in prison. Section 12(1) of the 1952 Act *does* allow the governor of a prison to detain a convicted prisoner *whether or not* that prisoner was rightly or wrongly convicted. So suppose

32 Cf. Judge LJ's remarks in the Court of Appeal in *R* v *Governor of Brockhill Prison, ex parte Evans (No. 2)* [1999] QB 1043, 1071B–C: 'The governor was blameless. Indeed if he had not continued to detain [Evans] he would have been acting in defiance of the earlier decisions of the Divisional Court . . . So in detaining [Evans] for as long as he did the governor was responsibly performing his duties.'

33 All of which is *not* to say that Evans should not have been entitled to recover something for the extra days she was kept in prison. She should probably have been allowed to bring a *non-tortious* claim for compensation, just as people who are wrongly convicted of committing an offence and sent to prison are allowed to bring a non-tortious claim for compensation for the time they have spent in prison (see below, n. 38). See, to the same effect, Cane 2001a, 10.

34 For a detailed account of these rules, see any textbook on constitutional law.

35 See for example s 136 of the Mental Health Act 1983, which provides that if 'a constable finds in a place to which the public have access a person who appears to him to be suffering from mental disorder and to be in immediate need of care or control, the constable may, if he thinks it necessary to do so in the interests of that person or for the protection of other persons, remove that person to a place of safety . . .'.

36 Though see *Olotu* v *Home Office* [1997] 1 WLR 328. The claimant in that case was committed to custody for trial under a warrant that specified that she should be held in custody awaiting trial for a maximum of 112 days. The claimant was actually held in prison for 193 days. She brought a claim for false imprisonment against the governor of the prison in which she was detained. Her claim was dismissed on the ground that the prison governor was required by statute not to release her until ordered to do so by the courts.

37 [2001] 2 AC 19.

Nita was wrongly convicted of committing murder and was sentenced to life imprisonment. Suppose further that Nita's conviction was overturned three years later and she was released. In such a case, Nita could not sue the prison authorities, claiming that the prison authorities falsely imprisoned her during the three years she spent in prison before she was released. The authorities will have had a lawful justification or excuse under s 12(1) of the 1952 Act for detaining Nita for those three years.[38]

The House of Lords' decision in *R* v *Deputy Governor of Parkhurst Prison, ex parte Hague*[39] seems to suggest that s 12(1) of the 1952 Act not only authorises the governor of a prison to detain a prisoner within the confines of the prison but also authorises the governor of a prison to choose *how* that prisoner is to be detained. The decision actually dealt with two cases – the *Hague* case and *Weldon* v *Home Office*. In the *Hague* case, the claimant – a prisoner at Parkhurst Prison – claimed he had been falsely imprisoned because he had been kept in isolation for 28 days, contrary to the Prison Rules 1964. In the *Weldon* case, the claimant – a prisoner at Leeds Prison – claimed he had been falsely imprisoned because he had been detained in a strip cell. Lord Bridge remarked that the 'primary and fundamental issue' raised by the *Hague* and *Weldon* cases was: '[does] any restraint within defined bounds imposed upon a convicted prisoner whilst serving his sentence by the prison governor . . . but in circumstances where the particular form of restraint is not sanctioned by the prison rules, amounts for that reason to the tort of false imprisonment[?]'[40] The House of Lords answered this question in the negative and dismissed the claims of both the claimant in the *Hague* case and the claimant in the *Weldon* case. This result cannot be explained on the basis that a prisoner cannot be falsely imprisoned by the governor of his prison because he enjoys no liberty. The House of Lords was very clear that if A, a fellow prisoner of B's, locks B in a prison shed, then A will have committed the tort of false imprisonment.[41] Similarly, the House of Lords held that if A, a prison officer, locks B in a cell and does so in bad faith – knowing that he has no authority from the governor of the prison to do so – then A will have committed the tort of false imprisonment.[42] Both these findings presuppose that a prisoner *does* enjoy *some* liberty and *can* therefore be falsely imprisoned.

The reason the House of Lords gave for answering Lord Bridge's question in the negative was that if the governor of a prison detained a prisoner at that prison in some way (for instance, by putting him in a strip cell or an isolation unit), he could argue that he was allowed under s 12(1) of the 1952 Act to detain that prisoner in the way he did. So, in effect, the House of Lords took the view that s 12(1) of the 1952 Act permits the governor of a prison to determine how the prisoners in his charge will be detained. But this is patently untrue. If the governor of Parkhurst Prison breached the Prison Rules 1964 in keeping the claimant in the Hague case in isolation for 28 days, then he was plainly not authorised to detain that claimant in the way he did – whatever s 12(1) of the Prison Act 1952 says.

[38] Nita will, however, be entitled to bring a non-tortious claim for compensation for the years she spent in prison under s 133 of the Criminal Justice Act 1988 (restrictively interpreted in *R (Christofides)* v *Secretary of State for the Home Department* [2002] 1 WLR 2769 as applying only to cases where an innocent person was convicted of a criminal offence and not to cases where a guilty person was convicted of a more serious offence than he should have been with the result that he was held longer in prison than he should have been).

[39] [1992] 1 AC 58.

[40] Ibid., 162F-G.

[41] Ibid., 164C–D, 166H–167A, 178F.

[42] Ibid., 164D–E.

Similarly, if the governor of Leeds Prison was not allowed under the Prison Rules 1964 to put the claimant in the *Weldon* case in a strip cell, then he was plainly not authorised to subject the claimant to that sort of detention. Perhaps a better explanation as to why the House of Lords answered Lord Bridge's question in the negative is that they feared that if they said that a governor of a prison would commit the tort of false imprisonment if she subjected a prisoner to a form of restraint that breached the Prison Rules 1964, governors of prisons would be swamped by claims from prisoners, each arguing that he had been subjected to a form of detention that technically breached the 1964 Rules and that he had therefore been falsely imprisoned.

Visit **http://www.mylawchamber.co.uk/mcbride** to access updates on recent cases, as well as model answers and tips for answering tort problem questions.

13 Defamation

We are concerned in this chapter with two torts – libel and slander – both of which are committed by *defaming* someone else. We will discuss the difference between libel and slander in detail later on, but for the time being it is enough to know that if A makes a defamatory statement about B while *talking* to someone else, that is *slander* and B will usually have to prove that A's statement caused him some harm before he will be allowed to sue A. On the other hand, if A makes a defamatory statement about B to someone else in *writing*, that is *libel* and B will be allowed to sue A even if he cannot show that A's statement caused him harm.

So much for the difference between libel and slander – we'll now look at what they have in common. If B wants to sue A for libel or slander, B will have to show *in either case*: (1) that A published a statement to a third party that was defamatory of B; *and* (2) that B is the sort of person who can sue someone else for libel or slander. But even if (1) and (2) are true, B will *not* be entitled to sue A if A has a *defence* to B's claim. All this needs more explanation.

WHAT IS DEFAMATORY?

Suppose A made a statement S to a third party, C.[1] When will B be able to establish that that statement was defamatory of her? The answer is: statement S will have been defamatory of B if:

(1) an ordinary, reasonable person who heard or read statement S would tend as a result to think less well of B as a person;[2] *or*

(2) an ordinary, reasonable person who heard or read statement S would tend as a result to think that B lacked the ability to do her job effectively and efficiently;[3] *or*

(3) an ordinary, reasonable person who heard or read statement S would tend as a result to shun and avoid B;[4]

(4) an ordinary, reasonable person who heard or read statement S would tend as a result to treat B as a figure of fun or as an object of ridicule.[5]

[1] *Important note.* One can, of course, make a statement by *conduct* as well as by *words*. See, for example, *Monson* v *Tussaud's* [1894] 1 QB 671. In that case the claimant was someone who had been charged with shooting someone with a gun; a Scottish jury returned a verdict of 'not proven' and the claimant was released. The defendants subsequently featured the claimant in their waxworks exhibition, placing a model of the claimant with a gun in his hand near their 'Chamber of Horrors'. The claimant successfully sued the defendants for libel, arguing that they had, in their exhibition, represented that he was guilty of the shooting.

[2] *Sim* v *Stretch* [1936] 2 All ER 1237, 1240 (per Lord Atkin).

[3] *Drummond-Jackson* v *British Medical Association* [1970] 1 All ER 1094, 1104 (per Lord Pearson). Cf. *Cornwell* v *Myskow* [1987] 2 All ER 504 where a jury found that it is defamatory to say of an actress that 'she can't sing, her bum is too big and she has the sort of stage presence that jams lavatories'.

[4] *Youssoupoff* v *Metro-Goldwyn-Mayer Pictures Ltd* (1934) 50 TLR 581, 587 (per Slesser LJ).

[5] It has long been acknowledged that statements which expose someone to ridicule are defamatory: see *Parmiter* v *Coupland* (1840) 6 M & W 105, 108; 151 ER 340, 341–2.

So, for example, it is defamatory of B to say that she has committed adultery (in which case (1) would be true) or that her work is usually shoddy (in which case (2) would be true) or that she has a communicable disease (in which case (3) would be true) or that she always insists on wearing a Chelsea shirt when making love (in which case (4) would be true).[6] A couple of cases illustrate how this test for determining whether a given statement was defamatory works.

In *Byrne* v *Deane*,[7] the claimant was a member of a golf club which was run by the two defendants. The defendants kept some automatic gambling machines on the premises of the golf club for the use of the members. It was illegal of the defendants to do this and someone within the golf club reported the existence of the machines to the police. When the police removed the machines, someone else posted up a poem on one of the walls of the golf club which plainly indicated that the claimant had been responsible for telling the police of the existence of the machines. The claimant sued the defendants, claiming that the poem was defamatory of him and they were responsible for its publication. The Court of Appeal held, by a bare majority, that the poem was not defamatory: an ordinary, reasonable person who read the poem would not tend to think less well of the claimant as a result – he would think the claimant was to be congratulated on ensuring that the law was observed. Greer LJ dissented; he thought an ordinary, reasonable person who read the poem would draw the conclusion from it that the claimant had acted in a disloyal and underhand fashion and would therefore tend to think less well of the claimant as a result.

In *Charleston* v *News Group Newspapers Ltd*,[8] the *News of the World* published an article on a pornographic computer game which had superimposed the faces of the claimants – two stars of the television series *Neighbours* – on the bodies of two persons engaged in various sexual activities. The article had as its headline 'Strewth! What's Harold up to with our Madge?' and the article carried two large stills from the computer game. The text of the article made it clear that the claimants' faces had been used without their knowledge or consent. The claimants sued the owners of the *News of the World*, claiming that the photographs and the headlines were defamatory – the claimants claimed that an ordinary, reasonable person who looked at the photographs and the headlines would have thought that the claimants had willingly participated in the production of the pornographic computer game in question and would therefore think less well of the claimants as a result. The House of Lords dismissed the claimants' claim: an ordinary, reasonable person who saw the headline and photographs complained of would also have read the article below the headlines and the photographs and would have realised that the claimants had nothing to do with the production of the computer game in question.

Let us now look in more detail at what sort of statements are defamatory.

[6] *Important note.* It should be noted that a statement can be defamatory *even if it is true*. So if B *has* committed adultery it is still defamatory of her to say that she has committed adultery. Which is *not* to say that if B has committed adultery, she will be able to sue anyone who reports that fact to someone else. Anyone who says that B has committed adultery when she actually has committed adultery will be able to raise a defence of *justification* (discussed below, pp. 288–92) if B attempts to sue him or her for libel or slander.

[7] [1937] 1 KB 818.

[8] [1995] 2 AC 65.

Abusive words

It is often said that words of abuse are not defamatory if they are uttered and heard as such.[9] The reason is presumably that if an ordinary, reasonable person heard the words in question he would realise they were uttered in anger and merely to abuse and would therefore not take them seriously.[10] He would therefore not think less well of the person at whom the abuse was directed.

Offensive words

An offensive statement about B will not be defamatory *per se*; it will only be defamatory if an ordinary, reasonable person who heard the statement would tend either: (*a*) to think less well of B as a person; or (*b*) to think less well of B's ability to do his work; or (*c*) to shun and avoid B; or (*d*) to treat B as a figure of fun or an object of ridicule. Having said that, the courts have come close in a couple of cases to finding that words were defamatory *merely* because they were offensive.

In *Youssoupoff* v *Metro-Goldwyn-Mayer Pictures Ltd*,[11] the claimant sued the defendants, claiming that she had been libelled in a film released by the defendants. The film portrayed the life and death of Rasputin and suggested that Rasputin had enjoyed sexual relations with one 'Princess Natasha'. The claimant argued that an ordinary, reasonable person who saw the film would identify her with Princess Natasha and the suggestion that Rasputin had had sexual relations with the claimant/Princess Natasha would tend to make him think less well of the claimant. The defendants contended that there was nothing to associate Princess Natasha with the claimant and that there was therefore nothing in the film that would cause an ordinary, reasonable person to think less well of the claimant. The Court of Appeal rejected this claim, finding that an ordinary, reasonable person who watched the film would associate Princess Natasha with the claimant.

The defendants then contended that an ordinary, reasonable person who watched the film would gather from it that Rasputin *raped* the claimant/ Princess Natasha and his feelings towards the claimant would not therefore be adversely affected by the film. (It was conceded that if an ordinary, reasonable person who watched the film would gather from it that Rasputin *seduced* the claimant/Princess Natasha then the film would be defamatory of the claimant – an ordinary, reasonable person would conclude that the claimant was of low morals and would therefore think less well of her.) The Court of Appeal held that even if it were true that an ordinary, reasonable person who watched the film would gather from it that Rasputin raped the claimant/Princess Natasha, the film would still be defamatory of the claimant.[12]

Scrutton LJ evidently regarded the argument that 'to say of a woman that she had been

[9] *Penfold* v *Westcote* (1806) 2 B & P (NR) 335, 127 ER 656; *Fields* v *Davis* [1955] CLY 1543.

[10] For the same reason, Handley & Davis 2001 argue that 'words are not defamatory if they are spoken in a context where it is clear that they are in jest'. It is not clear whether the English courts would accept this. If they did not, comedians' freedom of expression would be seriously interfered with: almost all satirical depictions of public figures would be defamatory and *prima facie* actionable.

[11] (1934) 50 TLR 581 (discussed, Treiger-Bar-Am 2000).

[12] In fact both Greer LJ and Slesser LJ thought that an ordinary, reasonable person who watched the film would gather from it that Rasputin seduced the claimant/Princess Natasha (ibid., 586, 587).

[raped] by a man of very bad character when as a matter of fact she never saw the man at all and was never near him is not defamatory of the woman' as outrageous, remarking that he had 'no language to express my opinion of that argument'.[13] Slesser LJ based his finding that it would be defamatory to say of a woman that she had been raped on the ground that an ordinary, reasonable person who heard or read that statement would tend to shun and avoid the woman in question: 'a lady of whom it has been said that she has been [raped will suffer] in social reputation and in opportunities of receiving respectful consideration from the world.'[14] This does not seem convincing. The Court of Appeal in *Youssoupoff* therefore offered little by way of argument in support of its view that it will be defamatory to say of a woman that she has been raped. Of course, it is grossly offensive to say of someone that he or she has been raped when he or she has not been raped and that may have been one consideration which motivated the Court of Appeal in *Youssoupoff* to find that such a statement would be defamatory.

In *Berkoff* v *Burchill*,[15] Steven Berkoff, the well-known actor, sued the journalist Julie Burchill for libel after she called him, in one review, 'hideous-looking' and, in another review, compared his appearance unfavourably with Frankenstein's monster. The Court of Appeal held, by a bare majority, that Burchill's suggestion in these reviews that Berkoff was 'hideously ugly' was defamatory of Berkoff. The decision is very hard to explain and it is hard to avoid the impression that the Court of Appeal was led to find that Burchill's reviews were defamatory of Berkoff because they were so offensive. Of course, the Court of Appeal did not say as much – but the reasons that the majority in the Court of Appeal did offer in support of its decision are singularly unconvincing.

Neill LJ found that Burchill's reviews gave the impression that Berkoff was 'not merely physically unattractive in appearance but actually repulsive'. He went on to suggest that 'to say this of someone in the public eye who makes his living, in part at least, as an actor, is capable of lowering his standing in the estimation of the public and of making him an object of ridicule'.[16] It is hard to see why Neill LJ put such an emphasis on the fact that Burchill's reviews suggested that Berkoff was *repulsive* and the fact that Berkoff was, and is, an *actor*. Why should suggesting that someone is physically unattractive make him any the less an object of ridicule than suggesting that someone is actually repulsive would? And again – why should suggesting that an actor is repulsive make him any more an object of ridicule than suggesting that a painter or a teacher or judge is repulsive would? Turning to Phillips LJ's judgment, he expressly found that Burchill's reviews would *not* tend to cause ordinary, reasonable people to shun and avoid Berkoff. But, like Neill LJ, he found that Burchill's reviews could be defamatory of Berkoff because they could have the effect of making him an object of ridicule among ordinary, reasonable people. But such a finding shows a poor regard for ordinary, reasonable people – the suggestion that someone is 'hideously ugly' would surely *not* tend to cause ordinary, reasonable people to treat that someone as a figure of fun.

[13] Ibid., 584.
[14] Ibid., 587.
[15] [1996] 4 All ER 1008.
[16] Ibid., 1018f–g.

The repetition rule

Suppose Alan said to Karen, 'John thinks/John told me that Gary is a thief'. In such a case, it will be conclusively presumed that an ordinary, reasonable person who heard or read Alan's statement would have concluded that Gary was a thief. This rule of law is known as the 'repetition rule'. The repetition rule applies even if it would have been clear to an ordinary, reasonable person who heard or read Alan's statement that Alan was not necessarily endorsing John's opinion of Gary – as would be the case if Alan qualified his statement by saying that 'Of course, I have no way of knowing myself whether or not Gary is a thief.'[17] It follows that Alan's statement to Karen in the above case *will* be defamatory of Gary – it will be conclusively presumed that an ordinary, reasonable person who heard or read Alan's statement would have concluded from it that Gary was a thief and would as a result have thought less well of Gary.

A similar rule applies if Alan said to Karen, 'I think Gary is a thief'. Again, it will be conclusively presumed that an ordinary, reasonable person who heard or read Alan's statement would have concluded from it that Gary was a thief and would therefore have thought less well of Gary. It will therefore be conclusively presumed that Alan's statement to Karen was defamatory of Gary – and this is so even if an ordinary, reasonable person who heard or read Alan's statement could actually have been expected to think, 'Well, Alan thinks Gary is a thief, but his opinion is not necessarily correct and I should wait to make up my own mind about Gary instead of just blindly going along with Alan's opinions.'

Similarly, if Alan said to Karen, 'I have reasonable grounds to suspect Gary of being a thief', it will be conclusively presumed that an ordinary, reasonable person who heard or read Alan's statement would have concluded from it that there *were* reasonable grounds to suspect Gary of being a thief and would have thought less well of Gary as a result.[18] So, again, it will be conclusively presumed that Alan's statement to Karen was defamatory of Gary – and this is so even if an ordinary, reasonable person who heard or read Alan's statement could actually have been expected to think, 'Well, Alan may think he has reasonable grounds to believe that Gary is a thief – but what does he know? I should make up my own mind and judge Gary on the evidence presented to me.'

Community standards

In judging how an ordinary, reasonable person would react to a given statement about someone, one must take into account the current state of public opinion. So, for example, suppose Mary says of Fred that he is a homosexual. Is that defamatory? Thirty years ago, the answer would have been 'yes' – the state of public opinion at that time was such that an ordinary, reasonable person would have tended to think less well of someone if it were alleged that he was a homosexual.[19] Nowadays, it is more difficult to say – today, people

[17] *Stern* v *Piper* [1997] QB 123.

[18] *Shah* v *Standard Chartered Bank* [1999] QB 241.

[19] In *R* v *Bishop* [1975] QB 274, the Court of Appeal expressed the view (at 281) that if A said that B was a homosexual 'a submission that [A's] words were incapable of a defamatory meaning would be bound to fail and a jury would generally be likely to find them defamatory.'

generally are more tolerant of homosexuality and, given this, it is difficult to say that an ordinary, reasonable person would nowadays think less well of someone if it was alleged that he was a homosexual. This creates a problem for B if A says of him that he is a homosexual and B wants to sue A so as to establish publicly that he is in fact heterosexual – the courts may rule that A's allegation was not defamatory and thereby prevent B from suing A for libel or slander.

It follows from what has just been said that if B has higher standards of behaviour than the general public and A accuses B of engaging in conduct which is inconsistent with those high standards, B will find it difficult to show that A's words were defamatory for the purpose of suing A for libel or slander. So, for example, suppose Eric is a teetotaller but Sarah wrote to Wendy, saying that she saw Eric drinking a pint of lager in a pub at the weekend. Sarah's statement to Wendy will not be defamatory – an ordinary, reasonable person who read Sarah's statement about Eric would not think any the worse of Eric as a result. However, it would be different if Eric was well known to be a temperance campaigner. In such a case, an ordinary, reasonable person who read Sarah's statement would tend to think that Eric was a hypocrite and would tend to think less well of Eric as a result. On these facts, then, a case could be made out for thinking that Sarah's statement to Wendy was defamatory of Eric.

Innuendo

A statement which is innocent on its face will still be defamatory of B if:

(1) an ordinary, reasonable person *who was possessed of certain special knowledge* would tend on hearing or reading that statement to think less well of B; *and*
(2) the statement in question was published to one or more people who were possessed of that special knowledge.

If (1) *and* (2) are true of a particular statement, lawyers say that the statement in question gave rise to an *innuendo* which was defamatory of B.

So, to take a well-known example, suppose that Paul said to Beth that he saw Carl coming out of a particular house. Suppose further that that house happened to be a brothel. So an ordinary, reasonable person who knew the house in question was a brothel would, on hearing Paul's statement, tend to think less well of Carl as a person – he would tend to think that Carl used prostitutes. Now, if Beth *knew* that the house in question was a brothel, Paul's statement, while innocent on its face, will have been defamatory of Carl. Note that, so far as Beth is concerned, all that has to be proved – for the purpose of establishing that Paul statement was defamatory of Carl – is that Beth knew that the house in question was a brothel. It does *not* also have to be shown that Beth concluded from Paul's statement that Carl used prostitutes or that Beth thought any the less of Carl as a person when she heard Paul's statement. It is enough that an ordinary, reasonable person who was possessed of the knowledge Beth had when she heard Paul's statement would have tended to think less well of Carl if he had heard Paul's statement.

In *Cassidy* v *Daily Mirror Newspapers Ltd*,[20] the *Daily Mirror* published a photograph of one Cassidy with a lady companion. The caption accompanying the photograph informed the reader that Cassidy and his companion had announced their engagement. In fact, Cassidy was married to the claimant. The claimant successfully sued the *Daily Mirror* for libel. The Court of Appeal found that: (1) an ordinary, reasonable person who knew the claimant and knew that she purported to be Cassidy's wife would tend to think on the basis of the caption that she was a liar and was not Cassidy's wife at all; therefore (2) an ordinary, reasonable person who knew the claimant and knew that she purported to be Cassidy's wife would, on seeing the caption beneath the *Daily Mirror*'s photograph, tend to think less well of her as a person; (3) people who knew the claimant and knew that she purported to be Cassidy's wife had seen the photograph and its accompanying caption; therefore (4) the caption beneath the *Daily Mirror*'s photograph, while innocent on its face, gave rise to an innuendo – that the claimant was not married to Cassidy and was therefore a liar – which was defamatory of her.

Reference to claimant

Sometimes a statement is obviously defamatory, but there is an issue over whether the statement can be said to refer to the claimant. Two classes of statement need to be distinguished here. First, a statement that was not intended specifically to refer to the claimant but that could be read as referring to the claimant. Secondly, a statement that was intended specifically to refer to the claimant, but because the claimant was referred to under a common name or description, the statement could be read as referring to someone other than the claimant.

Statements not intended specifically to refer to the claimant

A defamatory statement which was not intended specifically to refer to B will still be defamatory of B if:

(1) an ordinary, reasonable person who *knew of B and her circumstances* would have, on hearing or reading the statement in question, thought that it referred to B and would, as a result, have tended to think less well of B; *and*
(2) the statement in question was published to one or more people *who thought that it referred to B*.

If (1) *and* (2) are true then the statement in question will be defamatory of B even though it was not intended specifically to refer to B.

We will usually have occasion to employ this test for determining whether a given statement was defamatory of a claimant in two kinds of situation. The first is the case where a defendant published a statement to another which defamed a particular individual (real or imaginary) and that statement could have been taken as referring to the claimant because people might have identified the claimant with the individual referred to in the statement. The second is the case where a defendant published a statement which defamed a particular class of people and that statement could have been taken as referring to the claimant because the claimant belonged to that class. Let us now look at how the courts have applied the above test in each of these situations.

[20] [1929] 2 KB 331.

(1) *Mistaken identity cases.* In *E Hulton & Co.* v *Jones*,[21] the *Sunday Chronicle* carried an article describing a motor festival at Dieppe. The article featured described various figures who attended the festival including one 'Artemus Jones'. He was described as being a 'churchwarden at Peckham'. The article alleged that while he was at the festival he had consorted with a woman who was not his wife and that he was, in general, 'the life and soul of a gay little band that haunts the Casino and turns night into day, besides betraying a most unholy delight in the society of female butterflies'. The claimant was a barrister called Artemus Jones. He sued the defendants, the publishers of the *Sunday Chronicle*, for libel. His claim was successful. It was found that friends of the claimant had seen the article in question and thought it referred to the claimant. Moreover, it was found that an ordinary, reasonable person who knew the claimant would have thought, on reading the article, that it referred to him and would have tended as a result to think less well of him as a person. The fact that the claimant was a barrister and not a churchwarden at Peckham did not affect the issue. No doubt the fact that the claimant and the person referred to in the article shared such a distinctive name as Artemus Jones played a large part in the finding that an ordinary, reasonable person who knew the claimant would have thought on reading the article in question that it referred to him.

In *Newstead* v *London Express Newspaper Limited*,[22] the *Daily Express* published an account of a trial for bigamy, referring to the accused as 'Harold Newstead, thirty-year-old Camberwell man'. The claimant – who was called Harold Newstead and who worked in Camberwell and was aged about 30 – sued the publishers of the *Daily Express* for libel. His claim succeeded. It was found that some acquaintances of the claimant had read the account in the *Daily Express* and thought that it referred to the claimant. Moreover, it was found that an ordinary, reasonable person who knew the claimant would have – on reading the report of the trial – thought that the report referred to the claimant and would therefore have thought less well of the claimant as a person. It might have been different if the name of the prisoner who was accused of bigamy had been 'John Smith' and the prisoner had simply been described as 'John Smith, a 30-year-old London man'.[23] In such a case, if another John Smith who came from London and was about thirty years old had sued the publishers of the *Daily Express* for libel, he would *not* have been able to establish that an ordinary, reasonable person who knew him would, on reading the report in the *Daily Express*, have thought that the report referred to the claimant and would therefore have tended to think less well of him: such an ordinary, reasonable person would have had no reason to identify the claimant with the prisoner named in the report in the *Daily Express* even though their names, ages and residences coincided.

In *Morgan* v *Odhams Press Ltd*,[24] the claimant took into his house a kennel girl who was helping a journalist with his inquiries into the activities of a dog doping gang. The claimant spent six days with the girl in his flat and in that period a few acquaintances of the claimant met him in the company of the girl. After the six days were up, the girl in question went to stay with the journalist she was helping. The journalist published his story about the dog doping gang in a Sunday newspaper and the story included a photograph of the kennel girl

[21] [1910] AC 20.
[22] [1940] 1 KB 377.
[23] Ibid., 391 (per MacKinnon LJ).
[24] [1971] 1 WLR 1239.

who had helped him break the story. The next day, *The Sun* published a story claiming that the kennel girl in question had been kidnapped by members of the gang. The claimant sued *The Sun* for libel, claiming: (1) that an ordinary, reasonable person who saw the kennel girl with the claimant during the six days that she spent with the claimant would, on reading the story in *The Sun*, think that the claimant was one of the dog doping gang who had kidnapped the girl and would therefore think less well of the claimant; and (2) that people who had seen the kennel girl with the claimant during the six days that she spent with the claimant had thought the story in *The Sun* referred to him. The claimant's claim was allowed: a jury found that (1) and (2) were true and the House of Lords declined to disturb the verdict, thinking that it was possible that an ordinary, reasonable person who read the story in *The Sun could* have thought, on the basis of having seen the claimant with the kennel girl, that the claimant had been involved in her kidnapping.

(2) *Defamation of a class.* Suppose Tom said or wrote to Dawn that 'All lawyers are corrupt'. Suppose further that Vijay is a lawyer. If Vijay sues Tom for libel or slander his claim will certainly fail. No court will find that an ordinary, reasonable person who heard or read Tom's statement would have thought that it referred to Vijay and would have tended as a result to think less well of Vijay.[25] Why is this? The answer is presumably that generalisations always admit of exceptions and an ordinary, reasonable person who heard or read Tom's statement would not have thought that Tom's statement applied to *all lawyers without exception*. An ordinary, reasonable person who heard or read Tom's statement would therefore have had no reason to think that Vijay *in particular* was covered by Tom's statement.[26]

It would be different if Tom said or wrote to Dawn that 'All the lawyers employed by the firm Sue, Grabbit and Run are corrupt' and Vijay was employed by Sue, Grabbit and Run. In such a case, Vijay will probably be able to establish that Tom's statement was defamatory of him. An ordinary, reasonable person who heard or read Tom's statement would be entitled to think that Tom, in making that statement, was not making a sweeping generalisation but was instead making a specific allegation against *each and every* lawyer employed at Sue, Grabbit and Run. So an ordinary, reasonable person who heard Tom's statement would be entitled to think that Tom's statement indicated that Vijay was corrupt and would tend to think less well of Vijay as a result.

So, in *Knupffer* v *London Express Newspaper Ltd*,[27] the *Daily Express* carried an article during the Second World War which accused members of the 'Young Russia' party of being willing to help Hitler by building up a pro-German movement within the Soviet Union. The claimant was the head of the British branch of the 'Young Russia' party. A number of people read the article and thought it referred to or reflected on the claimant. The claimant sued the publishers of the *Daily Express* for libel. His claim was dismissed by the House of

[25] *Eastwood* v *Holmes* (1858) 1 F & F 347, 349, 175 ER 758, 759: '[If] a man wrote that all lawyers were thieves, no particular lawyer could sue him unless there was something to point to the particular individual' (per Willes J).

[26] Cf. Lord Atkin's remarks in *Knupffer* v *London Express Newspaper Ltd* [1944] AC 116, 122: 'The reason why a libel published of a large or indeterminate number of persons described by some general name generally fails to be actionable is the difficulty of establishing that the claimant was, in fact, included in the defamatory statement, for the habit of making unfounded generalisations is ingrained in ill-educated or vulgar minds, or the words are occasionally intended to be a facetious exaggeration.'

[27] [1944] AC 116.

Lords: an ordinary, reasonable person who read the *Daily Express* article would not have thought it referred to the claimant in particular. The accusations against members of the 'Young Russia' party contained in the *Daily Express* article were far too generalised to make it reasonable to think that they applied to the claimant in particular.

In contrast, in *Riches* v *News Group Newspapers Ltd*,[28] the *News of the World* published a letter from a man who was holding his son and a woman hostage at gun point. The letter made various allegations against 'the Banbury CID' – including an allegation that members of the Banbury CID had raped his wife. Ten members of the Banbury CID sued the publishers of the *News of the World* for libel and were awarded substantial damages at first instance. The Court of Appeal held that the damages awarded to the claimants should be reassessed but did not question the propriety of awarding each of the claimants something by way of damages. Clearly, the Court of Appeal agreed with the court of first instance that the letter published in the *News of the World* was defamatory of *each* of the claimants. An ordinary, reasonable person who read the letter published in the *News of the World* would have thought that the allegations contained in the letter applied to *each and every* member of the Banbury CID – he would not have simply thought that those allegations merely amounted to sweeping generalisations which did not necessarily apply to each and every member of the Banbury CID.

Statements that were intended to refer specifically to the claimant, but under a common name or description

What would be the position if the *Daily Herald* published a story saying that 'A London-based labourer called Bob Jones has been arrested for terrorist activities'? No doubt there would be quite a few Bob Joneses who this statement could be taken as referring to, and as a result none of the Bob Joneses who this statement was *not* intended to refer to would be able to sue the *Daily Herald* for defamation. But what about *the* Bob Jones who the *Daily Herald did* intend to refer to – a London-based labourer of that name who was questioned by the police about an explosion on a site where he worked, but was not actually arrested by the police? Would *that* Bob Jones be able to sue the *Daily Herald* for defamation simply on the basis that the *Daily Herald*'s statement was intended to refer to him, or would he have to go to the trouble of showing: (1) that an ordinary, reasonable person who knew of him and his circumstances would have thought that the statement referred to him and would as a result have thought less well of him; and (2) that the statement in question was published to one or more people who thought that it referred to him? The question has not been much addressed, but we think in principle that *the* Bob Jones to whom the *Daily Herald* intended to refer should be able to sue the *Daily Herald* without having to establish that (1) and (2) are true. The fact that the claimant has a common name should not mean that he has fewer rights to protect his reputation than someone with a more distinctive name.[29]

[28] [1986] 1 QB 256.

[29] In *Jameel (Yousef)* v *Dow Jones & Co. Inc.* [2005] QB 946, the Court of Appeal said at [45] that: 'Where a common name is included in an article, the name itself will not suffice to identify any individual who bears that name.' However, it is submitted that this *dictum* is intended to apply only in cases where the article was not specifically intended to refer to the claimant.

THE REQUIREMENT OF PUBLICATION

If B wants to sue A for libel or slander, B will have to show that A *published* a statement that was defamatory of him to a *third party*. So, obviously, if Mary said to Ian, 'I think you're a thief', Ian would not be entitled to sue Mary for libel or slander: her statement was not published to a third party. A number of points may be made about when this requirement will be satisfied.

(1) *Spouses*. Suppose John told his wife, 'I think Ruth is a thief'. Ruth will not be able to sue John for libel or slander. The reason is that the courts will *not* find that John's statement in this case was published to a *third party*.[30] The courts' attitude is a throwback to the days when a husband and wife were regarded as having a common identity. While we have, of course, abandoned the idea that a husband and wife share a common identity, the courts still seem to think that someone who makes a defamatory statement to his or her spouse does not publish that statement to a third party.

(2) *Secretaries*. If John dictates a letter to Wendy, his secretary, that is defamatory of Eric, Eric may be able to sue John even if the letter is never sent. John will have published the defamatory statements contained in the letter to a third party, namely Wendy. But if Wendy hands back the letter to John for checking, Eric will not be able to sue *Wendy*. Wendy's handing back of the letter to John for checking will not amount to a publication by Wendy to a third party of the defamatory statements contained in the letter.[31] It would be different, of course, if Wendy showed the letter to someone other than John or Eric – in that case, Eric may well be able to sue Wendy for libel.

(3) *Misunderstanding*. It seems to be generally acknowledged that if John made a statement to Gary that was defamatory of Karen, John will not be held to have published that statement to a third party if Gary did not understand what John said because, for example, he was deaf or illiterate.

(4) *Private notes*. Suppose that John wrote down on a piece of paper 'Lara is a thief' and locked the piece of paper in a desk drawer. Suppose further that Carl, a burglar, subsequently broke into the desk drawer and read the piece of paper. Lara will not be able to sue John for libel.[32] John did not publish the defamatory material to Carl: he did not show Carl the piece of paper or allow him to read it.

(5) *Unintended recipients*. If John sent a letter to Alan that was defamatory of Sarah and Helen opened the letter and read it, the courts will not hold that John published the letter to Helen *unless* it was *reasonably foreseeable* when John sent the letter that it would be opened and read by someone like Helen.

So: in *Pullman* v *Hill & Co.*,[33] the defendant sent a letter to the claimants at their firm which claimed that they had obtained money under false pretences. The letter was opened by a clerk in the claimants' firm and was read by him and two other clerks. It was held that

[30] *Wennhak* v *Morgan* (1888) 20 QBD 635. The same rule will apply, of course, if a wife tells her husband something that is defamatory of another.
[31] *Eglantine Inn Ltd* v *Smith* [1948] NI 29, 33.
[32] *Pullman* v *Hill & Co.* [1891] 1 QB 524, 527.
[33] Ibid.

the defendant had published his defamatory letter about the claimants to the clerks because it was reasonably foreseeable that they would open and read the letter; it being normal practice for the clerks in a firm to open and read all the correspondence addressed to the firm.

Similarly, in *Theaker* v *Richardson*,[34] the defendant sent a letter to the claimant, a member of the local council, which accused her of shoplifting, of running a brothel, of being a prostitute and of having committed various acts of dishonesty in her position as a council member. The claimant's husband opened the letter and read it. The claimant sued the defendant for libel. A jury found for the claimant, holding that the defendant had published his letter to the claimant's husband – it had been reasonably foreseeable when the defendant sent his letter to the claimant that the claimant's husband would read the letter. The Court of Appeal declined to set aside the jury's verdict.[35]

In contrast, in *Huth* v *Huth*,[36] the defendant sent a letter to his estranged wife which, the claimants claimed, was defamatory of them. The claimants were the defendant's children – they claimed the defendant's letter suggested that they were illegitimate. In order to sue the defendant they had to show that the defendant had published the letter to someone other than his wife. (The fact that the defendant published the letter to his wife was not, of course, enough to allow the claimants to sue the defendant – as we have already seen, if someone publishes a defamatory statement to his wife, that statement will not be regarded as having been published to a third party.) In fact, the butler in the house where the defendant's wife was staying when she received the letter had opened and read the letter before he handed it over to the defendant's wife. The Court of Appeal held that the defendant had not published his letter to the butler as it was not reasonably foreseeable that the butler would open and read his letter. The claimants could not therefore show that the defendant had published his letter to anyone other than his wife and their claims were dismissed.

(6) *Platforms*. If John put a statement that was defamatory of Nita on an electronic bulletin board that was maintained by Vijay, the courts will hold that *Vijay* – as well as John – published that statement to whoever accessed the bulletin board and read John's statement.[37] What is the position if John posted up a statement that was defamatory of Nita on some premises which were owned or run by Vijay? In such a case, the courts will hold that *Vijay* – as well as John – published the statement to the people who read it *if* there is some evidence that Vijay *approved* of the posting up of that statement.[38] Similarly, it is suggested, if John made a defamatory statement about Nita in the course of a meeting held on premises owned or run by Vijay, *Vijay* – as well as John – will be held to have published that

[34] [1962] 1 WLR 151.

[35] Note that the old-fashioned view that husbands and wives share a common identity does not extend to cases where A makes a defamatory remark about B to B's husband. In such a case, the courts will hold that the remark *has* been published to a *third party*. They will not regard A's remark as having just been made to B.

[36] [1915] 3 KB 32.

[37] *Godfrey* v *Demon Internet Limited* [2001] QB 201.

[38] See *Byrne* v *Deane* [1937] 1 KB 818. An allegedly defamatory poem which was posted up on walls of golf club run by defendants held to have been published by defendants to whoever read the poem because there was some sign that they approved of its being posted up – the defendants had had the power to take the poem down, but none of them had. However, no claim could be made against the defendants because the poem was held not to be defamatory: see above, p. 275.

statement to the people who attended the meeting if there is some evidence that he approved of the making of that statement.

(7) *Chinese whispers*. Suppose John made a defamatory statement about Beth to Fred. Suppose further that Fred repeated that statement to Mary. If John authorised or instructed Fred to repeat his statement about Beth to Mary, then *John* – as well as Fred – will be held to have published Fred's statement to Mary.

However, if Beth suffered some kind of loss as a result of the publication to Mary, and wishes to recover compensation for that loss from *John*, she will not necessarily have to show that John – as well as Fred – published Fred's statement to Mary. Beth could choose to sue John for his statement to Fred. If she can sue him for making that statement, then she can recover compensation for all the *reasonably foreseeable* losses that John's statement to Fred has *caused* her to suffer.[39]

So if Beth *can* sue John for making his statement to Fred, all she has to do – if she wants to recover compensation for the losses she suffered as a result of the publication to Mary – is show that John's statement *caused* her to suffer those losses and it was *reasonably foreseeable* that she would suffer those losses if John made his statement to Fred.[40] The causation requirement will be satisfied if Fred acted *reasonably* in repeating John's statement to Mary. The reasonable foreseeability requirement will be satisfied if it was reasonably foreseeable when John made his statement to Fred that Fred would repeat it to Mary and Beth would suffer loss as a result.

Of course, if John's statement to Fred was privileged in some way so that Beth cannot sue John for making that statement to Fred, the only way Beth will be able to sue John for the loss she has suffered as a result of the publication to Mary is to show that John – as well as Fred – published Fred's statement to Mary. And, as we have said, John will only be held to have published Fred's statement to Mary if he authorised or instructed Fred to make that statement to Mary.

(8) *Shops*. If John sells a newspaper to Carl that contains a defamatory statement about Wendy, then John will be held to have published that statement to a third party. Similarly, if John helps print a newspaper that contains a defamatory statement about Wendy, the courts will hold that John published that statement to whoever read the newspaper once it was printed.[41]

[39] *Slipper* v *BBC* [1991] 1 QB 283.

[40] See *McManus* v *Beckham* [2002] 1 WLR 2982. In that case, it was held that it was possible that Victoria Beckham could be held liable for the losses suffered by the claimant as a result of the media reporting her claims that the David Beckham autographs on memorabilia sold by the claimant were forged. The Court of Appeal held (at [43], per Laws LJ) that whether she could be sued or not for those losses would depend on whether it was reasonably foreseeable at the time she made her claims (that is, very likely or probable: see above, p. 77, n. 24) that those claims would be reported in the media (ibid., at [43], per Laws LJ). With respect, it would also depend on whether it was *reasonable* for the media to report Victoria Beckham's claims: see *Ward* v *Weeks* (1830) 7 Bing 285, 131 ER 81 and *Weld-Blundell* v *Stephens* [1920] AC 956. The claim in *McManus* v *Beckham* was subsequently settled, with the Beckhams paying the claimant a substantial sum in damages as well as giving him some more signed memorabilia to sell in his shop.

[41] In each case, however, John may have a *defence* which would prevent Wendy from suing him for libel. See below, pp. 288–308.

TITLE TO SUE

If A has published a statement to another that was defamatory of B, B will only be entitled to sue A for libel or slander if B is the sort of person who can sue someone else for libel or slander.

If B is a *natural person* then there is no problem: a flesh-and-blood person may bring an action for libel or slander against a defendant if she feels that that defendant has defamed her. The case of *South Hetton Coal Company Ltd* v *North-Eastern News Association Ltd*[42] establishes that a *company* may be able to sue a defendant for libel or slander if the defendant publishes to another a statement that is defamatory of the company – but only if the statement in question has a tendency to damage the company's trading interests. What about a trade union? Section 10(1) of the Trade Union and Labour Relations (Consolidation) Act 1992 provides that a 'trade union is not a body corporate' – so a trade union does not enjoy sufficient personality to bring an action for libel or slander in respect of a statement that is defamatory of the trade union.[43]

If A publishes a statement to another that is defamatory of a *public body* – such as a local authority – the public body in question will *not* be entitled to sue A for libel or slander. This was established by the House of Lords' decision in *Derbyshire County Council* v *Times Newspapers Ltd*.[44] In that case, *The Sunday Times* printed a couple of articles which alleged that Derbyshire County Council had acted improperly in investing funds in its superannuation fund. Derbyshire County Council sued *The Sunday Times* for libel but its claim was dismissed by the House of Lords on the ground that an action for libel could not be maintained by a public body.

The House of Lords admitted that a public body could have a legitimate interest in bringing an action for libel or slander if it were the subject of a defamatory statement. As Lord Keith of Kinkel observed, the making of a defamatory statement about a public body 'might make it more difficult [for the body] to borrow or to attract suitable staff and thus affect adversely the efficient carrying out of its functions'.[45] However, the House of Lords felt that freedom of speech would be unreasonably infringed if the law did not assure people that they could criticise public bodies without fear of being made subject to actions for libel or slander as a result. Lord Keith remarked, 'it is of the highest public importance that a democratically elected governmental body, or indeed any governmental body, should be open to *uninhibited* public criticism. The threat of a civil action for [libel or slander] must inevitably have an inhibiting effect on freedom of speech.'[46]

The House of Lords did *not* go further in the *Derbyshire* case and say that a *politician* would have no right to sue for libel or slander if he felt that some criticism of his conduct in office was defamatory. Indeed, the House of Lords made it clear that if a defendant's criticism of a public body reflected badly on the people running the affairs of that body, those people might well be able to sue the defendant for libel or slander.[47] No doubt this can be

[42] [1894] 1 QB 133.

[43] *EETPU* v *Times Newspapers Ltd* [1980] 3 WLR 98. A trade union used to enjoy sufficient legal personality to bring an action for libel or slander: *National Union of General and Municipal Workers* v *Gillian* [1946] KB 81.

[44] [1993] AC 534.

[45] Ibid., 547E.

[46] Ibid., 547F–G.

[47] Ibid., 550D.

explained on the basis that politicians have more of an interest in vindicating their reputation than public bodies do – a politician, after all, has a life inside and outside politics which can be seriously affected by the publication of a defamatory statement about him – and this warrants giving politicians a higher degree of protection from being defamed than the House of Lords was willing to afford to public bodies.

It is now clear that the *Derbyshire* decision extends to *political parties* and that a political party which feels that it has been defamed by some statement made by someone else will not be able to bring an action for libel or slander in respect of that statement;[48] though, of course, if the statement simultaneously defamed a member of that party, he or she might be able to sue for libel or slander.

DEFENCES

Suppose A published a statement to a third party that was defamatory of B and B is the sort of person who can sue someone for libel or slander. In such a case, B will still not be entitled to sue A for libel or slander if A has some kind of *defence* to B's claim. The sort of defences that someone may be able to raise to an action for libel or slander are set out below.

Consent

First of all, *consent* is a defence to an action for libel or slander. B will not be able to complain about A's publishing a defamatory statement about her to a third party if B consented to that publication in the first place.

For example, in *Chapman* v *Lord Ellesmere*,[49] a stewards' inquiry held by the Jockey Club found that a horse trained by the claimant was doped when it ran a particular race. The Jockey Club disqualified the horse and 'warned' the claimant off the course where the horse ran. The Jockey Club's decision was published in the *Racing Calendar*, the Jockey Club's official journal. The claimant sued, claiming the publication was defamatory of him. The claimant's claim was dismissed – he had consented to that publication. He was held to have consented to the publication because when he obtained a trainer's licence, he agreed to abide by the rules of the Jockey Club, one of these rules specified that a decision of the Jockey Club could be published in the *Racing Calendar* if the Jockey Club thought it fit to do so.

Justification

Suppose A has published to another a statement that was defamatory of B because an ordinary, reasonable person who read or heard A's statement would have thought that *x* was true of B and would as a result have tended to think less well of B. In such a case, A will have a defence if B sues him for libel or slander if he can prove that *x was* true of B. If A can prove this, we say that he has a defence of *justification* to B's claim.

Notice that in order to raise this defence, it will *not* be enough for A to show that his

48 *Goldsmith* v *Bhoyrul* [1998] QB 459.
49 [1932] 2 KB 431.

words were *literally* true – he will have to show that the impression an ordinary, reasonable person would have gained of B from A's words was a correct one. So suppose John wrote a letter to Mary in which he remarked, 'I think Ian is a thief'. If Ian sues John for libel and John wants to raise a defence of justification to Ian's claim, it will not be enough for John to prove that *he actually did think* when he wrote the letter that Ian was a thief and therefore that his statement to Nita was literally true. It will be conclusively presumed that an ordinary, reasonable person who heard or read John's allegation would have thought on the basis of it that Ian *was* a thief[50] – given this, if John wants to raise a defence of justification to Ian's claim, he will have to prove that Ian *is* a thief.

Similarly, if Ian is suing John for libel because John wrote to Nita that 'Tom says that Ian is a thief', if John wants to raise a defence of justification to Ian's claim, it will not be enough for John to prove that *Tom actually said* to someone that Ian was a thief. As it will be conclusively presumed that an ordinary, reasonable person who heard or read John's allegation would have thought that Ian *was* a thief,[51] John will have to prove that Ian actually *is* a thief in order to raise a defence of justification to Ian's claim.

Again, suppose John wrote to Nita that 'I have reasonable grounds to suspect that Ian is a thief'. If Ian sues John for libel and John wants to raise a defence of justification to Ian's claim, it will not be enough for John to prove that he had reasonable grounds to suspect Ian of being a thief. So it will not be enough for John to prove that Tom told him that Ian was a thief and Tom had proved himself in the past to be honest and reliable so that Tom's statement to John gave John reasonable grounds for believing that Ian *was* a thief. As it will be conclusively presumed that an ordinary, reasonable person who heard or read John's statement would have thought as a result of hearing or reading that statement that there were reasonable grounds to suspect Ian of being a thief,[52] if John wants to establish a defence of justification to Ian's claim for libel, John will have to prove that there *are* reasonable grounds to suspect Ian of being a thief.

Sometimes there will be some dispute as to what impression an ordinary, reasonable man would have gained from hearing or reading a given statement. In *Lewis* v *Daily Telegraph Ltd*,[53] the defendants, the *Daily Mail* and the *Daily Telegraph*, both published front-page reports which alleged that the Fraud Squad was inquiring into the affairs of the claimant, Rubber Improvement Ltd. The claimant sued both newspapers for libel. It was admitted that the reports were defamatory: an ordinary, reasonable person who read the reports would have tended to think less well of the claimant as a result. The defendants sought to rely on a defence of justification to defeat the claimant's claim. The issue was: what would the defendants have to prove to raise such a defence? This turned on what impression of the claimant would have been gained by an ordinary, reasonable person who heard about or read the reports in the newspapers. The claimant argued that an ordinary, reasonable person who heard about or read the reports in question would have concluded from them that the claimant had operated in a dishonest or fraudulent manner – so the defendants would have to prove that the claimant *had* conducted its affairs in a dishonest way if they wanted to rely on a defence of justification to defeat the claimant's claim.

50 See above, p. 278.
51 Ibid.
52 Ibid.
53 [1964] AC 234.

The House of Lords disagreed. At best, an ordinary, reasonable person would have concluded from the stories in the defendants' newspapers that the claimant had conducted its affairs in such a way as to give rise to a *suspicion* that it was guilty of some dishonest or fraudulent conduct. As Lord Reid observed – if someone, on reading the stories in the defendants' newspapers had observed 'Oh, if the fraud squad are after these people you can take it they are guilty' an ordinary, reasonable person would have rounded on him 'with such remarks as – "Be fair. This is not a police state. No doubt their affairs are in a mess or the police would not be interested. But that could be because [someone] has been very stupid or careless. We really must not jump to conclusions. The police are fair and know their job and we shall know soon enough if there is anything in it. Wait till we see if they [bring charges]. I wouldn't trust [the people involved in this company] until this thing is cleared up, but it is another thing to condemn [them] unheard."'[54] So, in order to establish a defence of justification to the claimant's claim, the defendants did *not* have to show that the claimant had operated its affairs in a dishonest or fraudulent manner; at best, the defendants were required to show that the claimant had operated its affairs in such a way as to give rise to a suspicion that it had acted dishonestly or fraudulently in the way it operated.

In *Wakley* v *Cooke and Healey*,[55] the claimant, a former journalist, was a coroner in Middlesex. The defendants published an article in the *Medical Times* which contained an attack on the claimant. The article observed, 'There can be no court of justice unpolluted which this libellous journalist [meaning the claimant] ... is allowed to disgrace with his presidentship.' The claimant sued the defendants for libel. It was held that an ordinary, reasonable man would gather from this statement that the claimant had been in the habit of libelling others when he was a journalist. So the defendants could not raise a defence of justification to the claimant's claim by showing that the claimant had on *one* occasion been found to have libelled someone else as a journalist; they would have to show that the claimant had on *many* occasions libelled other people when working as a journalist. As the defendants could not show this, the claimant's claim was allowed.

A few more points may be made about the defence of justification.

Substantial justification

If A has published a statement to another that is defamatory of B, A does not have to prove – for the purpose of raising a defence of justification to any claim B might bring against him for libel or slander – that *every word* of what he said was correct; it is enough if he can show that what he said was *substantially correct*.

So in *Alexander* v *The North Eastern Railway Company*,[56] the defendant railway company reported that the claimant had been convicted of what would now be known as 'fare-dodging' and sentenced either to pay a fine of £9 or serve three weeks' imprisonment. In fact the claimant had actually been sentenced either to pay a fine of £1 or to serve two weeks' imprisonment. The claimant sued the defendants for libel. His claim was dismissed: while the defendants' report was inaccurate in its details, it was at the same time substan-

[54] Ibid., 259–60.
[55] (1849) 4 Ex 511, 154 ER 1316.
[56] (1865) 6 B & S 340, 122 ER 1221.

tially correct – the claimant *had* been convicted of fare-dodging and had been sentenced either to pay a fine or spend time in jail. Similarly, suppose Paul told someone else that Tom beat his wife three times a week but in fact Tom beat his wife twice a week. In such a case, Paul will be able to raise a defence of justification to any claim Tom might bring against him for libel or slander – what Paul said was substantially true, even though he got it wrong as to how many times Tom beat his wife a week. It is impossible to formulate a test to determine whether a given defamatory statement will be 'substantially correct' or not; in the end, one has to use one's common sense to resolve the issue.

Partial justification

Section 5 of the Defamation Act 1952 provides that '[in] an action for libel or slander in respect of words containing two or more distinct charges against the claimant, a defence of justification shall not fail by reason only that the truth of every charge is not proved if the words not proved to be true do not materially injure the claimant's reputation having regard to the truth of the remaining charges'. So suppose Karen said to someone else, 'John is a rapist and a thief'. Suppose further that John sues Karen for libel or slander for saying that he is, one, a rapist, and two, a thief. Suppose finally that Karen can prove that John is a rapist, but she cannot prove that John is a thief. In such a case, Karen will not only have a defence of justification to John's claim against her for saying that he is a rapist; Karen will *also* have a defence of justification under s 5 of the 1952 Act in respect of John's claim against him for saying that John is a thief. Now that it has been established that John is a rapist, Karen's statement that John is a thief could hardly further injure John's reputation in the eyes of ordinary, reasonable people – John's reputation in those people's eyes will have gone about as low as it possibly could go.

It would be different, of course, if Karen could prove that John is a thief but could not prove that John is a rapist. In such a case, Karen would have a defence of justification in respect of John's claim against her for saying that he is a thief, but she will *not* have a defence of justification in respect of John's claim against her for saying that he is a rapist. Section 5 of the 1952 Act cannot be invoked because it could hardly be said that now that it has been established that John is a thief, Karen's further charge that John is a rapist would not materially injure his standing among ordinary, reasonable people.

Staying with the above example but assuming again that Karen can prove John is a rapist but cannot prove that John is a thief – suppose John simply chooses to sue Karen for libel or slander in respect of her statement that he is a thief. Can Karen establish a defence of justification to John's claim by showing that John is a rapist? The answer, it seems, is 'no'.[57] However, if John leaves Karen's claim that he is a rapist unchallenged, he is not likely to be awarded much by way of damages to compensate him for the harm done by Karen's statement that he is a thief. The courts will take the view that a rapist does not have much of a reputation to lose and therefore suffers little harm if he is unjustly accused of being a thief.[58]

[57] *Polly Peck (Holdings) plc* v *Trelford* [1986] 1 QB 1000.

[58] See *Grobbelaar* v *News Group Newspapers Ltd* [2002] 1 WLR 3024 (£1 awarded in damages to Bruce Grobbelaar, the ex-Liverpool and Southampton goalkeeper, who – it was found – was justifiably accused by the defendant of taking bribes to 'throw' football matches but unjustifiably accused of acting on those bribes and actually throwing football matches).

Criminal conviction

Suppose Lara told Ian, 'Vijay burned down Sarah's house'. In such a case, Lara will *normally* have a defence of justification to any claim Vijay might bring against her for libel or slander if she can prove that Vijay was criminally convicted for burning down Sarah's house and Vijay's conviction was not subsequently overturned. Lara will *not* have to go further and prove that Vijay *actually did* burn down Sarah's house; that is, she will not have to prove that Vijay was rightly convicted.[59]

However, if Sarah made her allegation about Vijay 'with malice' and Vijay's conviction for burning down Sarah's house counts as 'spent' under the Rehabilitation of Offenders Act 1974, then Vijay will be treated as though he never burned down Sarah's house and, therefore, Lara's statement to Ian will be conclusively presumed to have been untrue.[60] The result is that Vijay will be able to sue Lara for libel or slander: Lara will not be able to raise a defence of justification to Vijay's claim.

Fair comment

If A has published to another a statement S that was defamatory of B and B wants to sue A for libel or slander, A may be able to raise a defence of *fair comment* to defeat B's claim. A will be able to raise this defence if:

(1) A was obviously expressing an *opinion*, rather than making a statement of fact, when he made statement S; *and*
(2) A was expressing an opinion on a matter of *public interest*, rather than private interest, when he made statement S; *and*
(3) A *honestly* held the opinion expressed by him when he made statement S and A *did not act maliciously* in expressing that opinion; *and*
(4) the opinion that A expressed in making statement S was *not based on facts which were untrue*.

All this needs more explanation.

Opinion and fact

The defence of fair comment only protects those who make defamatory statements that are, on their face, statements of opinion – the defence is not available to someone who makes a defamatory statement about another which is, on its face, a statement of fact.[61]

So – how do we tell whether a given statement is, on its face, a statement of opinion or a statement of fact? The key is to see whether the statement involves an *evaluative judgment*. Statements that involve evaluative judgments take a stand on whether something is good or bad, beautiful or ugly, funny or sad, right or wrong, admirable or despicable, tasty or

[59] Civil Evidence Act 1968, s 13(1): 'In any action for libel or slander in which the question whether the claimant did or did not commit a criminal offence is relevant to an issue arising in the action, proof that at the time when that issue falls to be determined, he stands convicted of that offence shall be conclusive evidence that he committed that offence . . .'

[60] Rehabilitation of Offenders Act 1974, ss 4(1), 8.

[61] For criticism of this limit on the defence, see Young 2000.

nasty, moral or immoral. Such statements are, on their face, statements of opinion. Statements that do not involve evaluative judgments are, on their face, statements of fact.

So if Helen says, 'Peter is having an affair with Ruth', that statement is, on its face, a statement of fact. Helen is not making any evaluative judgment in saying that Peter had an affair – she is simply reporting what he is supposed to have done. The same applies if Helen says, 'I think Peter is having an affair'. Again, no evaluative judgment is involved here – Helen is reporting her suspicions about Peter's conduct. So Helen will not be able to argue that her statement was, on its face, a statement of opinion – and this is so even though Helen preceded her statement with the words 'I think . . .'. In contrast, if Helen says, 'I think Peter is a despicable human being for having an affair with Ruth', that statement is, on its face, a statement of opinion because Helen is here making a judgment about Peter as a human being. She is judging him to be despicable, rather than admirable, because of his conduct in having an affair.

So in *London Artists Ltd* v *Littler*,[62] the defendant held a press conference in which he suggested that the claimants had attempted to force a play which he had been producing to close by persuading the four leading actors in the play to withdraw from it simultaneously. The claimants sued the defendant. The defendant attempted to defeat the claimants' claim by raising a defence of fair comment. He was not allowed to do so: his allegation that the claimants had plotted to close his play was, on its face, a statement of fact rather than a statement of opinion. This was quite right: the defendant was not making any evaluative judgment about the claimants in saying that they were trying to close his play down. He was reporting his suspicions about what the claimants were up to.

In contrast, in *Kemsley* v *Foot*,[63] *Tribune* published an article by Michael Foot which criticised a particular newspaper. The article carried the headline 'Lower than Kemsley'. Lord Kemsley was a well-known newspaper proprietor and the point of the headline was to indicate that while the newspapers controlled by Lord Kemsley were contemptible, the newspaper criticised in the article was even more contemptible. Lord Kemsley sued for libel, claiming that the headline defamed him. Michael Foot attempted to defeat his claim by raising a defence of fair comment, claiming that the statement implicit in the headline that Kemsley's newspapers were contemptible was, on its face, a statement of opinion. The House of Lords agreed. Again, this was correct: the statement that Lord Kemsley's newspapers were contemptible involved an evaluative judgment.

Public interest

The defence of fair comment only operates to protect people who utter defamatory opinions on matters of *public interest*. So suppose Gary behaved in an ungentlemanly way during a tennis match with Tom and Tom wrote to Beth that 'Gary is lower than vermin'. If Gary chooses to sue Tom for libel, Tom will not be able to raise a defence of fair comment – his statement did not express an opinion on a matter of public interest. On the other hand, suppose Fred observed of a particular politician that 'he is not fit to hold office'. If the politician in question chooses to sue Fred, Fred may well be able to raise a defence of

[62] [1969] 2 QB 375.
[63] [1952] AC 345.

fair comment to defeat the politician's claim. Fred's statement was a statement of opinion on a matter of public interest – the honesty and fitness for office of our politicians being a matter of public interest.

So what counts as a matter of public interest? In *London Artists Ltd* v *Littler*, Lord Denning MR offered a definition. According to Lord Denning, whenever 'a matter is such as to affect people at large, so that they may be legitimately interested in, or concerned, at what is going on; or what may happen to them or to others; then it is a matter of public interest on which everyone is entitled to make fair comment'.[64] So the quality of a West End play will count as a matter of public interest – people may be legitimately interested in how good the play is, so as to know whether or not to buy tickets for it. Given this, a critic's statements of opinion about the quality of a West End play may well be protected by the defence of fair comment.

Honesty and malice

If A has published to another an opinion which was defamatory of B, A will only be able to raise the defence of fair comment to defeat any claim made against him by B for libel or slander if: (1) A honestly held that opinion when he published it; *and* (2) A did not act maliciously in publishing that opinion.

Requirement (1) is probably a sub-requirement of requirement (2) in the sense that if requirement (1) is *not* satisfied, requirement (2) *cannot* be satisfied. Suppose, for example, that Paul wrote a review of a new play by Lara and said that he thought the play was terrible. Suppose further that Paul did not honestly think the play was terrible. If this is so then Paul *must* have been acting maliciously in saying that the play was terrible – if he did not honestly think the play was terrible then why did he say it was?

But even if requirement (1) *is* satisfied, requirement (2) may *not* be. Suppose, again, that Nita published an article criticising the food and service at a particular restaurant run by Fred. Suppose when Nita wrote the article she honestly thought that the food and service at Fred's restaurant was terrible. Nita may still have acted maliciously in publishing her article – she may, for example, have decided to expose the poor food and service at Fred's restaurant to get revenge on Fred for breaking up with her.

Lawyers usually sum up the above by saying that the defence of fair comment only protects those who express opinions that are 'fair'. Someone who has expressed an opinion which he did not actually hold or who has acted maliciously in expressing an opinion will not be able to establish that the opinion expressed by him was 'fair' and will as a result not be able to take advantage of the defence of *fair* comment if the opinion in question was defamatory and he is sued for stating it. However, this usage is liable to confuse – it may make one think, wrongly, that the defence of fair comment only protects people who express opinions that are *fair-minded* or *reasonable*. Given this, the reader should try to avoid adopting this usage and, instead of thinking that the defence of fair comment will only protect people who express opinions that are 'fair', he or she should try to remember that the defence of fair comment will protect expressions of opinion that are made hon-

[64] [1969] 2 QB 375, 391B–C.

estly and without malice – and this is so however unreasonable or outrageous or unfair the opinions in question happen to be.[65]

If A has expressed an opinion about B that is defamatory of B, it will usually be difficult to tell whether A *honestly* held that opinion when he expressed it. One way of determining whether this requirement is satisfied is to ask whether an honest man could *possibly* have held the opinion expressed by A.[66] If the answer is 'no' then it follows that A did *not* honestly hold the opinion that was expressed by him. If the answer is 'yes' then the matter remains open – it is possible that A honestly believed what he said, but it is, on the other hand, possible that he did not.

Turning to the question of when an expression of opinion will be held to have been published maliciously, the courts will find that A acted maliciously in expressing a defamatory opinion about B if he expressed that opinion out of spite or for some other evil or improper motive. Again, this will be hard to prove. In determining whether A acted maliciously in acting as he did, it will be legitimate to take into account A's general demeanour towards B,[67] the language A used in expressing his opinion about B and how necessary it was for A to publish his opinion about B as widely as he did.

The above principles as to when someone will be able to take advantage of the defence of fair comment to defeat a claim against him for libel or slander are modified somewhat in the case where a newspaper has published a letter or column which contained opinions which were defamatory of B. In such a case, if B sues the newspaper for libel, the newspaper will be able to raise a defence of fair comment even if *it* did not hold the opinions expressed in the letter or column in question. Of course, the newspaper will not be able to take advantage of a defence of fair comment to defeat B's claim if it acted maliciously in publishing the letter or column in question.

Untrue facts

The defence of fair comment will not protect someone who has expressed a defamatory opinion about someone else which was based on untrue facts. This rule of law is subject to two qualifications.

First, suppose Ruth said of Eric, 'I think Eric is a disgrace as a human being – despite all his wealth, he has never done anything to assist his estranged wife and child or his destitute mother.' Suppose further that Eric sues Ruth for libel or slander – arguing that Ruth defamed him when she said that he is a disgrace as a human being. Suppose finally that while Eric does nothing to support his destitute mother, he does actually help to support his wife and child. If Ruth can show that, had she known the true facts, she would honestly still have thought that Eric was a disgrace as a human being, Ruth will be able to raise a

[65] See Lord Nicholls's observations about the defence of fair comment in *Reynolds* v *Times Newspapers Ltd* [2001] 2 AC 127, 193: 'the time has come to recognise that in this context the epithet "fair" is now meaningless and misleading . . . The true test [to determine whether an expression of opinion is protected by the defence of fair comment] is whether the opinion, however exaggerated, obstinate or prejudiced, was honestly held by the person expressing it.' See also *Branson* v *Bower* [2002] QB 737.

[66] Cf. the tests for determining whether an expression of opinion will fall within the ambit of the defence of fair comment advanced in *Merivale* v *Carson* (1887) 20 QBD 275, 281 and *Turner* v *Metro-Goldwyn-Mayer Pictures Ltd* [1950] 1 All ER 449, 461C–F.

[67] *Thomas* v *Bradbury, Agnew & Co. Ltd* [1906] 2 KB 627.

defence of fair comment to defeat Eric's claim.[68] How can Ruth show that, had she known the true facts, she would honestly still have thought that Eric was a disgrace as a human being? One way is for Ruth to show that an honest man who knew the true facts *could* still have come to the conclusion that Eric was a disgrace as a human being. Of course, even if Ruth can defeat Eric's claim for damages arising out of her allegation that he is a disgrace as a human being, it will still be open to Eric to sue Ruth for libel or slander in respect of her allegation that Eric has never supported his estranged wife and child. As this is a statement of fact, not opinion, the defence of fair comment will not protect Ruth from being sued in respect of this allegation.

Secondly, if Vijay made an incorrect statement of fact about Mary on a privileged occasion and Wendy expressed an opinion on the basis of that statement of fact which was defamatory of Mary, the fact that Vijay's statement of fact was actually incorrect will not prevent Wendy from relying on the defence of fair comment to defeat any claim Mary might bring against her for libel or slander.[69]

Absolute privilege

If A has published a statement to C that is defamatory of B, B will *not* be entitled to sue A for libel or slander if the statement in question was *privileged*. Certain statements will *always* be privileged – such statements are said to be *absolutely privileged*. Other statements will only be privileged provided that certain conditions are met – these statements are said to be protected by *qualified privilege*. In this section, we will look at what sort of statements will be absolutely privileged; the following section is concerned with statements that will be protected by qualified privilege.

The reason why some statements are protected by absolute privilege is that the law sometimes places such a high priority on people being able to say what they want without fear of being sued that it assures such people that what they say will always be privileged.

So, for example, the law places such a high priority on Members of Parliament being allowed to say what they want to say in Parliament without fear of being sued that it assures Members of Parliament that what they say in Parliament will always be privileged.[70] So if Alan is a Member of Parliament he will be able to say what he wants about Karen in Parliament without fear of being sued by Karen for libel or slander – if Karen attempts to sue him, based on what Alan said about her in Parliament, Alan will always be able to raise a defence to Karen's claim. And this is so even if Alan knowingly tells complete lies about Karen in Parliament: he cannot be sued.

[68] See Defamation Act 1952, s 6, which provides that in 'an action for libel or slander in respect of words consisting partly in expressions of opinion, a defence of fair comment shall not fail by reason only that the truth of every allegation of fact is not proved if the expression of opinion is fair comment having regard to whether such of the facts alleged or referred to in the words complained of are proved'.

[69] *Grech v Odhams Press Ltd* [1958] 2 QB 275.

[70] This follows from Art 9 of the Bill of Rights 1688 which states that 'the freedom of speech and debates or proceedings in Parliament ought not to be impeached or questioned in any court or place out of Parliament'. An exception to this rule was created by s 13 of the Defamation Act 1996 which provides that where 'the conduct of a person in or in relation to proceedings in Parliament is in issue during defamation proceedings, he may waive for the purpose of those proceedings, so far as concerns him, the protection of any enactment or rule of law which prevents proceedings in Parliament being impeached or questioned in any court or place out of Parliament'.

In addition to statements made by Members of Parliament in Parliament, the following statements will also always be privileged:

(1) *Statements made in reports, papers and proceedings ordered to be published by Parliament.*[71]

(2) *Statements made in the course of judicial or quasi-judicial proceedings by anyone involved in those proceedings.* However, statements made in the course of judicial or quasi-judicial proceedings which have no relevance to those proceedings may not be privileged.[72] A court-martial will count as a 'judicial or quasi-judicial' proceeding;[73] as will disciplinary proceedings held by the Law Society.[74] So statements made in the course of either will be absolutely privileged. However, the holding of an industrial conciliation procedure will not count as a 'judicial or quasi-judicial' proceeding[75] and neither will an investigation by the European Commission into alleged breaches of European competition law.[76]

(3) *Statements made by a witness to his solicitor in preparing his testimony for court.*[77] While it is certain that such statements will always be privileged, it is uncertain whether other kinds of statements that a client may make to his solicitor will always be privileged. The House of Lords left the matter open in *Minter* v *Priest.*[78] There does not seem to be any reason why they should be: there does not seem to be any reason why the law should go further than it currently does to ensure that a client will be able to talk to his solicitor free from the fear that he might be sued as a result of what he says to his solicitor.

(4) *Statements made in the course of being questioned by someone investigating a crime; statements made at the request of someone investigating a crime.*[79] It is unclear whether a statement which is spontaneously made to the authorities for the purpose of encouraging them to start an investigation will be absolutely privileged. In *Hasselblad (GB) Ltd* v *Orbinson*,[80] the Court of Appeal thought that a letter sent to the European Commission complaining that a particular firm was engaging in anti-competitive practices would be protected by absolute privilege; their reason for so holding was that it was extremely important that people should be able to report these sorts of practices to the European Commission free from fear that their doing so would result in their being sued. However, in *Mahon* v *Rahn (No. 2)*,[81] Brooke LJ refused to decide whether an informant who spontaneously told the authorities that a particular investment adviser was guilty of fraud would always be able to claim that his statement to the authorities was privileged, preferring to leave the task of deciding that question to another day.[82]

71 Parliamentary Papers Act 1840, s 1.
72 *Seaman* v *Netherclift* (1876) 2 CPD 53, 56.
73 *Dawkins* v *Lord Rokeby* (1875) LR 7 HL 744.
74 *Addis* v *Crocker* [1961] 1 QB 11.
75 *Tadd* v *Eastwood* [1985] ICR 132.
76 *Hasselblad (GB) Ltd* v *Orbinson* [1985] QB 475.
77 *Watson* v *M'Ewan* [1905] AC 480; *Evans v London Hospital Medical College (University of London)* [1981] 1 WLR 184, 191G. See below, pp. 505–6.
78 [1930] AC 558.
79 *Mahon* v *Rahn (No. 2)* [2000] 1 WLR 2150.
80 [1985] QB 475.
81 [2000] 1 WLR 2150.
82 Ibid., at [195].

(5) *Statements made in a report prepared by an expert which may be used in later criminal proceedings.*[83]

(6) *Statements made by an investigator to someone else in the course of investigating a crime.*[84]

(7) *Statements made by one officer of state to another for the purpose of discharging some official business.* There is some authority in favour of the view that such statements will always be privileged. In *Chatterton* v *Secretary of State for India in Council*,[85] the claimant, a captain in the Indian Army, sued the Secretary of State for India for libel; he claimed the Secretary of State had, in a letter to his Under-Secretary of State, claimed that the Commander-in-Chief of the Indian Army had recommended that the claimant be put on half-pay on the grounds that keeping him as a full-time member of the Indian Army would be extremely undesirable. The claimant claimed that the Commander-in-Chief had made no such recommendation and that the Secretary of State had lied in his letter to the Under-Secretary of State so as to induce the Under-Secretary of State to besmirch the claimant's reputation in Parliament where questions were to be asked about the Secretary of State's treatment of the claimant. The claimant's claim against the Secretary of State was dismissed on the ground that his letter to the Under-Secretary of State was absolutely privileged. However, it is uncertain whether the same principle applies to statements made by one civil servant to another[86] or by one officer in the army to another.[87]

(8) *Statements made in an internal memorandum circulated within a foreign embassy.*[88]

(9) *Statements made in a fair and accurate and contemporaneous report of proceedings in public before a UK court or the European Court of Justice or the European Court of Human Rights or any international crime tribunal.* Section 14(1) of the Defamation Act 1996 provides that such statements will always be privileged. Section 14(2) provides that a 'report of proceedings which by an order of the court, or as a consequence if any statutory provision, is required to be postponed shall be treated as published contemporaneously if it is published as soon as practicable after publication is permitted'.

Qualified privilege

A statement which is protected by *qualified privilege* will be privileged so long as it was *not made maliciously*. For the purposes of this area of the law, A will be held to have acted maliciously in making a statement about B if: (1) he knew that that statement was untrue when he made it; *or* (2) when he made that statement, he did not care whether it was true or not; *or* (3) he made that statement for some improper or illegitimate reason.[89] The following kinds of statements will be protected by qualified privilege.

[83] *X* v *Bedfordshire County Council* [1995] 2 AC 633, 755G. See below, pp. 505–6.
[84] *Taylor* v *Director of the Serious Fraud Office* [1999] 2 AC 177. See below, p. 506.
[85] [1895] 2 QB 189.
[86] Henn-Collins J thought not in *Szalatnay-Stacho* v *Fink* [1946] 1 All ER 303.
[87] The Court of Queen's Bench thought it would in *Dawkins* v *Lord Paulet* (1869) LR 5 QB 94.
[88] *Fayed* v *Al-Tajir* [1988] 1 QB 712.
[89] *Horrocks* v *Lowe* [1975] AC 135. See also Mitchell 1999; Murphy 2003, 514–18.

The duty/interest test

If A has made a statement to C, that statement will be protected by qualified privilege if, *had the information contained in that statement been correct*, A would have had a moral or legal duty to pass that information on to C and C would have had an interest in receiving that information.

So: in *Watt* v *Longsdon*,[90] the claimant was the managing director of the Morocco branch of the Scottish Petroleum Company. The manager of the Morocco branch wrote to the defendant, a director of Scottish Petroleum, accusing the claimant of being drunk, dishonest and immoral. The defendant showed the letter to the chairman of the board and also the claimant's wife. The claimant sued the defendant for libel in respect of both publications of the letter.

The allegations contained in the letter were untrue so the defendant could not defeat the claimant's action by raising a defence of justification. However, the publication to the chairman of the board was held to be privileged. Had the information contained in the letter been correct, the defendant would obviously have had a duty to show the letter to the chairman of the board and the chairman of the board would have had an interest in seeing the letter. This established that the publication to the chairman of the board was protected by qualified privilege and, as the defendant had not been acting maliciously in showing the letter in question to the chairman of the board, the publication of that letter to the chairman of the board was privileged.

It was different with the publication to the claimant's wife. Obviously, had the allegations in the letter been true, the claimant's wife would have had an interest in seeing the letter. However, the defendant could *not* establish that had the allegations in the letter been true, he would have had a *duty* to show that letter to the claimant's wife. The Court of Appeal refused to be drawn on the question – If A has found out that B's husband has been cheating on her and generally engaging in disreputable activities, when will A have a duty to tell B of this fact? However, the Court of Appeal thought that the nature of the defendant's relationship with the claimant's wife was not such as to make it his place to tell the claimant's wife of what her husband was supposed to have been getting up to.

The common interest test

If A has made a statement to C, that statement will be protected by qualified privilege if it served A's interests to make that statement to C and it served C's interests to hear it.

For example, in *Watt* v *Longsdon*, the claimant also sued the defendant for libel in respect of a letter that the defendant wrote to the manager of the Morocco branch of Scottish Petroleum in which the defendant voiced his own suspicions about the claimant and asked the manager to obtain confirmation of the allegations contained in the manager's letter. The Court of Appeal held that the defendant's letter was protected by qualified privilege. This was because the defendant and the manager had a common interest in protecting the interests of Scottish Petroleum and this shared interest of the defendant and the manager's was served by the defendant's writing his letter to the manager and the manager's receiving it and acting on it. And as the defendant had not acted maliciously in writing to the manager, the letter was privileged.

[90] [1930] 1 KB 130.

Similarly, in *Hunt* v *Great Northern Railway Company*[91] the claimant worked as a guard for the defendant railway company. The defendants sacked the claimant on the ground that he had been guilty of gross neglect of duty. The defendants inserted a notice in the monthly circular which was distributed to the defendants' employees saying that the claimant had been guilty of gross neglect of duty and had been sacked as a result. The claimant sued the defendants for libel but his case was dismissed on the ground that the statement in the monthly circular was privileged. It was protected by qualified privilege, the court held, because the publication of the statement in the monthly circular served the interests of both the defendants and the people to whom the statement was published to, the defendants' employees – in both cases, because publication of the statement let the defendants' employees know that they would be sacked if they were guilty of gross neglect of duty. And as the defendants had not acted maliciously in publishing the statement in their monthly circular – they had not, for example, published the statement in order to make the claimant unemployable or published it in the knowledge that the claimant had not been guilty of a gross neglect of duty – that statement was privileged.

Lord Denning MR thought that what we might call the common interest test could be used to establish that statements made by an employer to his secretary in dictating a letter will be protected by qualified privilege. He argued in *Bryanston Finance* v *de Vries*[92] that as the employer and the secretary would both have an interest in getting the letter dictated by the employer written, any statements made to the secretary by the employer in dictating the letter would be protected by a qualified privilege. Such statements would therefore be privileged so long as the employer did not act maliciously in publishing them to his secretary. However, neither of the two other members of the Court of Appeal in *Bryanston Finance* agreed with Lord Denning MR on this point. They both thought the statements made in dictation would only be privileged if the publication to the intended recipient of the letter would also be privileged.

Statements made in self-defence

It is well established that if someone attacks or criticises A verbally or in print, then any statements made by A in order to rebut that attack or criticism will be protected by qualified privilege.

So in *Osborn* v *Thomas Boulter & Son*,[93] the claimant – a publican – wrote to the defendants to complain about the quality of their beer. The defendants wrote back suggesting that the source of the claimant's problems with their beer was that he watered it down once it was delivered to him. The claimant sued the defendants for slander on the basis that the defendants' letter had been published not only to the claimant but also to the defendants' secretary when it was dictated to her. His claim was dismissed on the ground that the defendants' rebuttal of the claimant's attack on the quality of their beer was protected by qualified privilege and the defendants had not acted maliciously in making the allegations that they did.

In *Watts* v *Times Newspapers Ltd*,[94] *The Sunday Times* published a story which accused

91 [1891] 2 QB 189.
92 [1975] 1 QB 703.
93 [1930] 2 KB 226.
94 [1997] QB 650.

the claimant, Nigel Watts, of plagiarism. However, they accompanied the story with a photograph of a quite different Nigel Watts, a property developer. This Nigel Watts complained and *The Sunday Times* printed an apology in its next edition which was dictated by Nigel Watts's solicitors, Schilling & Lom. The apology repeated the original defamatory story about the claimant. The claimant sued *The Sunday Times* for libel, claiming that the apology was defamatory of him. It was held that *The Sunday Times* could not claim that their apology was privileged as they were not publishing it to rebut an attack on themselves. *The Sunday Times* then sought to make a claim in contribution against Schilling & Lom on the ground that, having dictated the terms of the apology, they were also liable to pay damages to the claimant in respect of the publication of the apology. This claim was dismissed; it was held that, vis-à-vis Schilling & Lom, the apology was privileged as it had been dictated in order to rebut the attack which *The Sunday Times* had inadvertently made on their client.

The Reynolds *test*

The House of Lords' decision in *Reynolds* v *Times Newspapers Ltd*[95] established that statements made in an article published in a newspaper will be protected by qualified privilege if: (1) the article was on a matter of public concern or interest *and* (2) the newspaper acted responsibly in going ahead and publishing the article when they did and in the form that they did.[96] Such statements are said to be protected under the *Reynolds* test for qualified privilege.

In the *Reynolds* case, Lord Nicholls provided a list of factors which could be taken into account in determining whether a newspaper acted responsibly in publishing a particular article about someone when they did and in the form that they did:

> 1. The seriousness of the [allegations made in the article]. The more serious the charge, the more the public is misinformed and the individual harmed, if [the allegations in the report were] untrue. 2. The nature of the information [in the article], and the extent to which the subject matter is a matter of public concern. 3. The source of the information. Some informants have no direct knowledge of the events. Some have their own axes to grind, or are being paid for their stories. 4. The steps taken to verify the information. 5. The status of the information. [The allegations made in the article] may already have been the subject of an investigation which commands respect. 6. The urgency of the matter. News is often a perishable commodity. 7. Whether comment was sought from the [subject of the article]. He may have information others do not possess or have not disclosed. [However, an] approach . . . will not always be necessary. 8. Whether the article contained the gist of the [subject of the article's] side of the story. 9. The tone of the article. A newspaper can often raise queries or call for an investigation. It need not adopt allegations as statements of fact. 10. The circumstances of the publication, including the timing.[97]

95 [2001] 2 AC 127 (noted, Williams 2000).

96 See, now, *Jameel (Mohammed)* v *Wall Street Europe SPRL* [2007] 1 AC 359, at [31]–[32] per Lord Bingham, [55] per Lord Hoffmann, [107] per Lord Hope, [137] per Lord Scott.

97 [2001] 2 AC 127, 205. The decision of the Court of Appeal in *Loutchansky* v *Times Newspapers Ltd* [2002] QB 321 makes it clear that, in judging whether a newspaper acted responsibly in publishing a particular article when it did and in the form that it did, one should only take into account the information available to the newspaper at the time it published the article. (The House of Lords refused to grant leave to appeal this ruling: [2002] 1 WLR 1592.)

In the *Reynolds* case itself, *The Sunday Times* published an article which dealt with the resignation of Albert Reynolds, the Irish prime minister. The article alleged that Reynolds had deliberately and dishonestly misled the Irish Dáil on a particular matter and that Reynolds had been forced to resign when his colleagues found out about Reynolds's misconduct. In fact, this was not true: Reynolds never misled the Dáil and he resigned for other reasons. Reynolds sued *The Sunday Times* for libel and *The Sunday Times* claimed in its defence that its article was privileged. The House of Lords held that the article was not privileged. While there was no doubt that the article was on a matter of public concern and interest,[98] the House of Lords found that *The Sunday Times* did *not* act responsibly in publishing the article in the form that it did. The reason for this was that the article was unjustifiably one-sided in its presentation of the reasons why Reynolds resigned. No account was given of Reynolds's explanation of why he had resigned which Reynolds presented to the Irish Dáil on the day he resigned when, in fairness, one would have expected such an account to have been given. Indeed, the coverage of the story behind Reynolds's resignation had been much more balanced in the Irish editions of *The Sunday Times* and this must have counted against *The Sunday Times* in the eyes of the House of Lords in determining whether *The Sunday Times* acted responsibly in publishing its article about Reynolds's resignation in the form that it did.

Five points need to be made about the *Reynolds* test for qualified privilege:

(1) *Rationale.* Let's say that David is the editor of the *Daily Herald* and one of his reporters has come to him with a damaging story about Mary, a famous politician. The story is clearly on a matter of the public interest – it is alleged that Mary has been taking bribes – but it is not 100 per cent certain that the story is correct. So there is a risk that if David publishes the story, Mary might sue his newspaper for defamation and the newspaper will be unable to make out a defence of justification to defeat her claim. In formulating the *Reynolds* test, the House of Lords tried to provide David with some reassurance that he could safely go ahead and publish the story about Mary even though he was uncertain whether a defence of justification could be made out if the story went to court. The House of Lords essentially promised David, 'So long as you handle the story about Mary *responsibly*, then your newspaper will be immune from being sued successfully by Mary; and this is so even if the story about Mary turns out to be untrue.' In making this promise, the House of Lords was concerned to ensure that the law on defamation did not have a 'chilling' effect on legitimate freedom of expression by deterring editors like David from publishing stories like the story about Mary. Of course, if it turned out that Mary was *not* taking bribes, the effect of the House of Lords' ruling in *Reynolds* would have been to encourage David to publish an untrue story about Mary that unjustifiably besmirched her reputation. But the House of Lords thought that the risk of this happening was a price worth paying to ensure that other *true* but damaging stories on matters of the public interest were not suppressed by newspaper editors because they could not be certain that they would be able to prove that they were true in court.

[98] As Reynolds was one of the architects of the Northern Ireland 'peace' process, the reasons for his resignation were of public concern and interest in the UK.

(2) *Application*. In the very recent case of *Jameel (Mohammed)* v *Wall Street Europe SPRL*,[99] the House of Lords expressed concern that the *Reynolds* test was being applied too restrictively by the lower courts – that is, the courts of first instance and the Court of Appeal – and that the protection that it was intended to afford newspapers' freedom of speech was thereby being undermined. The House of Lords has now made it clear that while it is for the courts to decide whether a newspaper acted responsibly in handling a particular story in the way it did, the courts have to give newspapers some latitude in determining this issue. In particular, Lord Nicholls's list of factors that should be taken into account in determining whether a newspaper acted responsibly in handling a particular story should *not* be regarded as a series of hurdles *all* of which have to be cleared before the courts will find that the newspaper acted responsibly in handling that story.[100] Lord Hoffmann suggested that the newspapers' Code of Practice, as ratified by the Press Complaints Commission, could provide 'valuable guidance' as to whether a newspaper had acted responsibly in handling a particular story.[101] Lord Bingham went further and urged that in applying the *Reynolds* test, the courts should adopt something akin to the *Bolam* test for determining whether a professional acted negligently:

> editorial decisions and judgments made at the time, without the knowledge of falsity which is a benefit of hindsight, are [not] irrelevant. Weight should ordinarily be given to the professional judgment of an editor or journalist in the absence of some indication that it was made in a casual, cavalier, slipshod or careless manner.[102]

So – in the *Jameel (Mohammed)* case itself, the Wall Street Journal Europe (WSJE) published a story that suggested that the Saudi Arabian banking authorities were monitoring bank accounts held by, among others, Mohammed Jameel and the Abdul Latif Jameel Company, to ensure that they were not used 'wittingly or unwittingly' to help fund terrorist activities carried out by Al-Qaeda. Both Mohammed Jameel and the Abdul Latif Jameel Company sued the WSJE in defamation. The WSJE argued that the article in question was protected by qualified privilege under the *Reynolds* test. The Court of Appeal ruled that the *Reynolds* test was not satisfied in this case because the WSJE had not given Mohammed Jameel 24 hours to respond to the allegations in the article before publishing them. The House of Lords overruled the Court of Appeal, holding that it had adopted far too fussy an approach to the issue of whether the WSJE had acted responsibly in publishing its article. Looking at all the circumstances of the case, they held that the WSJE's article was plainly an example of the 'sort of neutral, investigative journalism which *Reynolds* privilege exists to protect'.[103]

(3) *Reportage*. *Reportage* is a 'fancy word'[104] for 'the neutral reporting without adoption or embellishment or subscribing to any belief in its truth of attributed allegations of both sides of a political and possibly some other kind of dispute'.[105]

[99] [2007] 1 AC 359.
[100] Ibid., at [33], per Lord Bingham; and at [56], per Lord Hoffmann.
[101] Ibid., at [55].
[102] Ibid., at [33]. To the same effect, see [51], per Lord Hoffmann.
[103] Ibid., at [35], per Lord Bingham.
[104] *Roberts* v *Gable* [2007] EWCA Civ 721, at [34] (per Ward LJ).
[105] Ibid., at [53] (per Ward LJ).

An example of *reportage* is provided by the case of *Roberts* v *Gable*,[106] where the defendant newspaper *Searchlight* – which exposes the activities of parties on the far right wing of British politics – published a story reporting that there had been a falling out in the aftermath of a London BNP (British National Party) rally with the claimants and two other individuals accusing each other of stealing the money collected at the rally. *Searchlight* did not take any sides in this dispute – its only desire was to report the fact that members of the BNP were feuding among themselves.

The claimants sued the defendant newspaper for libel, claiming that (under the repetition rule)[107] its article alleged that they *had* stolen the money collected at the BNP London rally. *Searchlight* claimed that the article was protected by qualified privilege under the *Reynolds* test. One problem with that claim was that *Searchlight* had not attempted to give the claimants an opportunity to respond to their article; nor had it attempted to find out the truth of what happened in the aftermath of the London BNP rally. However, the Court of Appeal held that this did not matter: *reportage* would be protected under the *Reynolds* test without there being any 'need to take steps to ensure the accuracy of the published information'.[108] So long as: (1) it was in the public interest to report the *fact* of the dispute being reported on; *and* (2) the newspaper reporting on the dispute reported it in a 'fair, disinterested and neutral way' without adopting any of the allegations made in that dispute as its own;[109] *and* (3) the newspaper acted responsibly in publishing the information about the fact of the dispute, *then* (4) the newspaper's report would be protected by qualified privilege under the *Reynolds* test.

(4) *Scope*. There is no reason to think that the category of statements that are protected by qualified privilege under the *Reynolds* test covers only statements made in articles published in newspapers. This category will also cover statements made in books, television documentaries or news programmes. It will also cover statements made in articles that have been posted in a newspaper archive on the Internet.[110]

(5) *Relationship with the duty-interest test*. One issue which divides the courts and affects the language in which they discuss the *Reynolds* test is the relationship between the *Reynolds* test for qualified privilege and the duty-interest test for qualified privilege, discussed above.[111]

On one view, the *Reynolds* test for qualified privilege is an outgrowth of, or application of, the duty-interest test. On this view, a newspaper that published an article on a matter of the public interest and that acted responsibly in publishing that article when it did and in the way it did can argue that it had a duty to publish that article and that its readers had an

106 [2007] EWCA Civ 721.
107 See above, p. 278.
108 [2007] EWCA Civ 721 at [61](2) (per Ward LJ).
109 Ibid., at [61](5).
110 *Loutchansky* v *Times Newspapers Ltd (Nos 2–5)* [2002] QB 783. The Court of Appeal held that a newspaper could not claim to have acted responsibly when it placed a defamatory article originally published in its print edition in an archive on the Internet without qualifying the article in any way to make it clear that its accuracy had been challenged. The House of Lords refused leave to appeal: [2002] 1 WLR 1552.
111 See above, p. 299.

interest in reading it, and that is why the article is protected by qualified privilege. On another view, the *Reynolds* test for qualified privilege is completely independent of the duty-interest test and stands on its own two feet.

In the recent *Jameel (Mohammed)* case, the House of Lords split 3:2 over this issue, with three Law Lords taking the view that the *Reynolds* test is an outgrowth of the duty-interest test,[112] while Lord Hoffmann and Baroness Hale took the view that the *Reynolds* test is a 'different jurisprudential creature' from the duty-interest test.[113] Our own view, for what it is worth, is that the *Reynolds* test cannot and should not be seen as an outgrowth of the duty-interest test for qualified privilege.

The *Reynolds* test *cannot* be seen as an outgrowth of the duty-interest test for qualified privilege because when we apply the latter test to determine whether a statement made by A to B is protected by qualified privilege we ask – *Had* the statement *been true*, would A have had a duty to make it to B, and did B have an interest in hearing that statement? We do *not* engage in this kind of exercise when we ask whether an article was protected by qualified privilege under the *Reynolds* test.[114] We do *not* ask: If the article *had* been true, would the newspaper have had a duty to publish the article, and would the newspaper's readers have had an interest in reading it?[115]

The *Reynolds* test for qualified privilege *should not* be seen as an outgrowth of the duty-interest test because asking whether a newspaper had a *duty* to publish a particular article and asking whether its readers had an *interest* in reading that article can – in the hands of a press-hostile judge – result in the bar for an article being protected by qualified privilege being set forbiddingly high.

Defamation Act 1996

The Defamation Act 1996 confers the protection of qualified privilege on a wide range of statements made on a matter of public concern or interest.[116] The Act splits these statements into two groups.

First, the Act provides that certain statements on matters of public concern or interest will be protected by qualified privilege 'without explanation or contradiction'. These include: (1) statements made in a fair and accurate report of proceedings in public of a legislature or a court or a public inquiry or an international organisation or an international conference located anywhere in the world; and (2) statements made in a fair and accurate copy of or extract from any matter published by a government or a legislature or an international organisation or an international conference located anywhere in the world.[117]

112 *Jameel (Mohammed)* v *Wall Street Europe SPRL* [2007] 1 AC 359, at [30] (per Lord Bingham); [107] (per Lord Hope); and at [130], [135] and [137] (per Lord Scott).

113 Ibid., at [46] (per Lord Hoffmann), and at [146] (per Baroness Hale), quoting *Loutchansky* v *Times Newspapers Ltd (Nos 2–5)* [2002] QB 783, at 806.

114 See *Kearns* v *General Council of the Bar* [2003] 1 WLR 1357.

115 Even if we did ask this, the answer would always be 'no' because it will not be true that each and every one of the newspaper's readers had an interest in reading the article. This is a further reason why the *Reynolds* test for privilege cannot be seen as an outgrowth of the duty-interest test.

116 Section 15(3) of the Defamation Act 1996 provides that the 1996 Act does not confer qualified privilege on matter published 'to the public, or a section of the public, . . . which is not of public concern and the publication of which [was] not for the public benefit'.

117 For a full list, see Part I of Sch 1 of the Defamation Act 1996.

Such statements will be privileged so long as the person who published it did not act maliciously in doing so.[118]

Secondly, the 1996 Act provides that certain other statements on matters of public concern or interest will be protected by qualified privilege 'subject to explanation or contradiction'. What this means is that if A, a newspaper, has published such a statement and the statement in question is defamatory of B, A will *not* be able to claim – if B sues it for libel or slander – that the statement was privileged if: (1) A acted maliciously in publishing that statement;[119] *or* (2) A refused or neglected to publish in a suitable manner a 'reasonable letter or statement by way of explanation or contradiction' of the statement published by A when it was requested to do so by B.[120]

The 1996 Act provides that statements that will be protected by qualified privilege 'subject to explanation or contradiction' include:[121] (1) statements made in a fair and accurate report of proceedings at any lawful meeting held in the EU on a matter of public concern;[122] (2) statements made in a fair and accurate copy of or extract from matter issued by any member state of the EU or by any organisation performing governmental functions in a member state of the EU[123] or by the European Commission; (3) statements made in a fair and accurate report of proceedings at any general meeting of a UK public company; (4) statements made in a fair and accurate copy of or extract from any document circulated to the members of a UK public company by its board or its auditors; (5) statements made in a fair and accurate report of any decision or finding made by an organisation concerned to promote a trade or a profession or a business or a game or a charitable object or general interest in art or science or religion or learning.

Innocent dissemination

Section 1(1) of the Defamation Act 1996 provides that if A has published to another a statement which was defamatory of B, A will have a defence to any claim for damages B might bring against A if: (1) A was not the 'author, editor or publisher' of the statement in question; (2) A took reasonable care in relation to its publication; *and* (3) A did not know, and had no reason to believe, that what he did would cause or contribute to the publication of a defamatory statement.[124]

118 Section 15(1).
119 Ibid.
120 Section 15(2).
121 For a full list, see Part II of Sch I of the Defamation Act 1996.
122 The House of Lords has held that a report which fairly and accurately summarises the contents of a press release issued to accompany a press conference will be protected by qualified privilege under this head: *McCartan Turkington Breen* v *Times Newspapers Ltd* [2001] 2 AC 277.
123 Defined in the Act as including 'police functions': Sch 1, Part II, para. 9(2).
124 It should be remembered that a statement can still be defamatory *even if it is true*. So suppose a bookseller sold a book which contained damaging allegations about Mary and Mary wants to sue the bookseller for libel. If we want to know whether the bookseller can take advantage of the defence set out in s 1(1) of the 1996 Act we ask – did the bookseller know, or have reason to know, that the book sold by him contained damaging allegations about Mary? If so, he will *not* be able to take advantage of the defence set out in s 1(1) of the 1996 Act. It will not matter whether or not the bookseller in question knew, or had reason to know, that the allegations in question were *untrue* – even if he did not know, and had no reason to know, that those allegations were untrue, he will still *not* be able to take advantage of the defence set out in s 1(1) of the 1996 Act if he knew, or ought to have known, that the book contained those allegations.

So the 'author, editor or publisher' of a defamatory statement will *not* be able to take advantage of the defence set out in s 1(1) of the 1996 Act. Section 1(2) makes it clear that the term 'author', as used in s 1(1) of the 1996 Act, 'means the originator of the statement [in question], but does not include a person who did not intend that his statement be published at all . . . "editor" means a person having editorial or equivalent responsibility for the content of the statement [in question] or the decision to publish it . . . [and] "publisher" means a commercial publisher, that is, a person whose business is issuing material to the public, or a section of the public, who issues material containing the statement [in question] in the course of that business'. Section 1(4) of the 1996 Act provides that an employee or agent of someone who was the 'author, editor or publisher' of a defamatory statement according to the above definition will *also* be held to have been the 'author, editor or publisher' of the statement in question if he was 'responsible for the content of the statement in question or the decision to publish it'.[125]

For the avoidance of doubt, s 1(3) goes on to provide that a person:

> shall not be considered the author, editor or publisher of a statement if he is only involved – (a) in printing, producing, distributing or selling printed material containing the statement; (b) in processing, making copies of, distributing, exhibiting or selling a film or sound recording . . . containing the statement; (c) in processing, making copies of, distributing or selling any electronic medium in or on which the statement is recorded, or in operating or providing any equipment, system or service by means of which the statement is retrieved, copied, distributed or made available in electronic form; (d) as the broadcaster of a live programme containing the statement in circumstances in which he has no effective control over the maker of the statement; (e) as the operator of or provider of access to a communications system by means of which the statement is transmitted, or made available, by a person over whom he has no effective control.

In *Godfrey* v *Demon Internet Ltd*,[126] the defendant was a company which ran an electronic bulletin board on the Internet. Someone posted a message on the Internet which was defamatory of the claimant and the message ended up on the defendant's bulletin board where it was accessed by various people. The claimant complained about the message to the defendant but even after he had done so the defendant failed to remove the message from its bulletin board. The claimant sued the defendant for libel on the ground that it had published the message on its bulletin board to other people. The defendant sought to take advantage of the defence set out in s 1(1) of the 1996 Act to defeat the claimant's claim. It was held that the defendant could not take advantage of this defence.

Admittedly, the defendant was *not* the 'author, editor or publisher' of the message complained of – that was made clear by s 1(3) of the 1996 Act. However, the defendant could not show that in running its bulletin board it was unaware it was contributing to the publication of a statement that was defamatory of the claimant. The claimant *did* draw the defendant's attention to the presence of the message on its bulletin board and it was obviously defamatory of the claimant. From that moment onwards, the defendant was aware that it was contributing to the publication of a statement that was defamatory of the claimant in running its bulletin board without removing the message complained of by the

[125] Section 1(4).
[126] [2001] QB 201.

claimant. Given this, s 1(1) of the 1996 Act did not operate to protect the defendant from being sued for libel in respect of any publications to third parties of the message on the defendant's bulletin board that took place after the presence of that message on the defendant's bulletin board was brought to the defendant's attention.

Offer to make amends

Suppose A has published to another a statement that was defamatory of B and B wants to sue A for libel or slander. If A cannot take advantage of one of the defences set out above to defeat B's claim, he may still be able to prevent B from suing him for libel or slander by making an 'offer to make amends' to B under s 2 of the Defamation Act 1996.

Section 2 of the Defamation Act 1996 provides that if A wants to make an 'offer to make amends' to B he *must* offer '(a) to make a suitable correction of the statement complained of and a sufficient apology to [B], (b) to publish the correction and apology in a manner that is reasonable and practicable in the circumstances, and (c) to pay [B] such compensation (if any), and such costs, as may be agreed or determined to be payable'.[127] If A only offers to do one or two of these things, then his offer will not amount to an 'offer to make amends' and will have no effect on B's right to sue A for libel or slander.

If A does make an 'offer to make amends' to B and B *accepts* the offer, B will be barred from suing A for libel or slander.[128] If B does *not* accept the offer, B will still be barred from suing A for libel or slander *unless*, when A published the statement which was defamatory of B: (1) he knew or had reason to believe that that statement referred to B or was likely to be understood as referring to B *and* (2) he knew or had reason to believe that the statement in question was both false and defamatory of B.[129] If (1) and (2) are true then A's 'offer to make amends' will have no effect on B's right to sue A for libel or slander – unless, of course, B accepts the offer.

THE DIFFERENCE BETWEEN LIBEL AND SLANDER

The distinction

Having reviewed what libel and slander have in common, we can now return in more detail to the question of what the difference between them is.

Broadly speaking, if A has published to another a statement which is defamatory of B, the tort – if any – committed by A in publishing that statement will be *libel* if the statement in question was published in *permanent form*; if, on the other hand, the statement in question was published in *impermanent form* then the tort – if any – committed by A in the case we are considering will be *slander*.

So, for example, if Karen *says* to Ian, 'Gary is a thief' then that is slander. However, if Karen sends Ian a letter saying, 'Gary is a thief', then that is libel. If Karen dictated a letter

[127] If B accepts A's offer but then they find themselves unable to agree on what should be paid to B by way of compensation, the courts will decide for them: Defamation Act 1996, s 3(5).

[128] Section 3(2).

[129] Section 4. *Milne* v *Express Newspapers Ltd* [2004] EWCA Civ 664 makes it clear that (2) will only be true if A acted *recklessly* in publishing the statement in question. Merely showing that a reasonable person in A's position would have realised that that statement was untrue and/or defamatory will not be enough.

to her secretary saying 'Gary is a thief' then that is slander. But if the letter is read out to a third party, that – it seems – will be libel.[130] It is submitted that if Karen records herself saying 'Gary is a thief' and then plays the recording back to Ian, that is libel; Karen's statement will have been published in a permanent form because it could be replayed.[131]

Some statutes provide that certain statements are to be treated as having been published in permanent form. So s 166 of the Broadcasting Act 1990 provides that for 'the purposes of the law on libel and slander . . . the publication of words in the course of any programme included in a programme service shall be treated as publication in permanent form'. So if John gives a speech in a public hall in which he makes various defamatory allegations about Nita, that will be slander. But if John makes the same speech on television, that will be libel. Similarly, s 4 of the Theatres Act 1968 provides that, subject to one exception, for 'the purposes of the law on libel and slander . . . the publication of words in the course of a performance of a play shall . . . be treated as publication in permanent form'. Section 7 of the 1968 Act makes it clear that this rule will not 'apply in relation to a performance of a play given on a domestic occasion in a private dwelling'.

The significance of the distinction

The principal[132] significance of the distinction between libel and slander is that if A has committed the tort of libel in relation to B, it will be presumed that A's libel caused B to suffer some kind of loss and so B will be entitled to sue A for compensatory damages without having to prove that she has suffered any kind of loss as a result of A's libel. The rule is different if A has committed the tort of slander in relation to B.

Generally speaking, it will *not* be presumed that B suffered some kind of loss as a result of A's slander. B will therefore have to prove that she suffered some kind of loss as a result of A's slander if she wants to sue A for compensatory damages. There are exceptions to this rule. If A has committed the tort of slander in relation to B, it will be presumed that B suffered some kind of loss as a result of A's slander if A had slandered B by suggesting: (1) that she had committed a serious criminal offence; *or* (2) that she had a communicable disease;[133] *or* (3) that she was no good at her job;[134] *or* (4) that she was unchaste or had committed adultery.[135] It should be noted that in each of these cases, B would find it very difficult to prove that A's slander caused her to suffer loss. This is because the tendency of each of these statements would be to encourage people to 'shun and avoid' B – but it would be very hard for B to demonstrate that but for A's statement, certain people would not have shunned and avoided B.

130 *Forrester* v *Tyrell* (1893) 9 TLR 257. However, in *Osborn* v *Thomas Boulter & Son* [1930] 2 KB 226, Scrutton and Slesser LJJ both thought that reading out a defamatory letter to a third party would amount to slander. Greer LJ disagreed.

131 Cf. the discussion in *Youssoupoff* v *Metro-Goldwyn-Mayer Pictures Ltd* (1934) 50 TLR 581 as to whether the tort – if any – committed in playing a film which contained a defamatory statement in its soundtrack would be slander or libel. The Court of Appeal expressed no firm view on the issue – merely saying the statement would be libellous if it served to amplify or explain the visual images presented in the film: ibid., 587.

132 Another difference between libel and slander is that libel will sometimes amount to a crime, whereas slander will not.

133 *Bloodworth* v *Gray* (1844) 7 Man & Gr 334, 135 ER 140.

134 Defamation Act 1952, s 2.

135 Slander of Women Act 1891, s 1.

The courts have recently addressed the issue of whether the rule that libel victims do not have to prove that they have suffered any loss before they can sue for libel is compatible with Article 10 of the European Convention on Human Rights, which provides that:

> (1) Everyone has the right to freedom of expression. This right shall include the freedom to hold opinions and to receive and impart information and ideas without interference by public authority and regardless of frontiers . . .
>
> (2) The exercise of these freedoms, because it carries with it duties and responsibilities, may be subject to such formalities, conditions, restrictions or penalties as are prescribed by law and are necessary in a democratic society . . . for the protection of the reputation or rights of others . . .

In *Jameel (Yousef)* v *Dow Jones & Co. Inc.*,[136] the Wall Street Journal (WSJ) published an article about a list – known as the 'Golden Chain' – of 20 people who provided financial backing for Al-Qaeda in its early years. The article was posted up on the WSJ's American website and a hyperlink was inserted into the Internet version of the article which allowed people reading the article on the Internet to see the 'Golden Chain' list. The fourth name on the list was 'Yousif Jameel'. Yousef Jameel – a Saudi businessman – sued for defamation in the UK. It was accepted that the name 'Yousif Jameel' referred to the claimant, but the defendants argued that Yousef Jameel's claim should be struck out because he had suffered no loss in the UK as a result of the existence of the hyperlink on the WSJ's American website. Only five people based in the UK had accessed the hyperlink: two of them had no idea who Yousef Jameel was, and the other three were all close associates of the claimant and did not therefore think any the worse of the claimant as a result of seeing the name 'Yousif Jameel' on the 'Golden Chain' document. The Court of Appeal held that the fact that an *individual* could sue for libel without having to prove that the libel had caused him any loss was not incompatible with Article 10 of the ECHR: 'We believe that circumstances in which a claimant launches defamation proceedings in respect of a limited circulation which has caused his reputation no actual damage will be very rare. We reject the suggestion that the fear of such suits will have a chilling effect on the media.'[137] However, the Court of Appeal *did* strike out Yousef Jameel's claim on the basis that to allow it to continue would serve no point and would therefore amount to an abuse of the process of the court.

In *Jameel (Mohammed)* v *Wall Street Europe SPRL*,[138] the House of Lords examined whether a *company* that was the victim of a libel should be able to sue in defamation without having to prove that the libel had caused it any loss. The House of Lords ruled that allowing the company to sue without proving that it had suffered any loss was not incompatible with Article 10. Crucial to its finding was the fact that a company can only sue for libel in respect of statements that tend to discourage people from doing business with the company.[139] The majority of their Lordships in the *Jameel (Mohammed)* case thought that if A made a statement about company B that had the tendency of discouraging people from doing business with B – say, for example, that A said that B's products were unsafe – requiring B to prove that it had actually suffered loss as a result of A's statement might be

136 [2005] QB 946.

137 Ibid., at [39].

138 [2007] 1 AC 359.

139 *South Hetton Coal Company Ltd* v *North-Eastern News Association Ltd* [1894] 1 QB 133. See above, p. 287.

too much to ask. Because the tendency of A's statement would be to cause people to 'shun and avoid' B's products, B might find it very difficult to show that but for A's statement, certain people would not have shunned and avoided B's products.[140]

EVALUATION OF THE LAW ON DEFAMATION

A complete evaluation of the law on defamation is beyond the scope of this book.[141] In this section we will confine ourselves to discussing some limited aspects of this area of the law.

Truth

If A has published to another a statement that is defamatory of B and B wants to sue A for libel or slander, B will *not* have to prove that A's statement was *untrue*. Should she have to?

One argument can be advanced in favour of the view that B *should* be required to prove that A's statement was untrue if she wants to sue A for libel or slander. Under the present law, B cannot clear her name by suing A for libel or slander. Even if she is successful in her claim against A, that will not be because the court found that A's statement was untrue. The court will merely have found that A could not prove that his statement was true – which is a very different thing. If B were required to prove that A's statement was untrue before she could sue A for libel or slander, then the question of the truth or untruth of A's statement would be placed firmly before the courts and a finding that A did libel or slander B would have the effect of clearing B's name – the courts could only reach such a finding if they first found that B had proved that A's statement about her was untrue.

At the same time, three arguments can be advanced in favour of the position currently taken by the law. First, it can be very difficult to prove a *negative*. Suppose that A's statement alleged that B once committed adultery. If B were required to prove that A's statement was untrue before she could sue A for libel or slander, how could B satisfy this requirement in this case? How could B prove that she has never committed adultery? Secondly, if the law did require the victim of a defamatory statement to prove that that statement was untrue before allowing her any remedy against the publisher of that statement, then the effect might be to encourage the press to become even less responsible in checking and sourcing stories which they publish than they are now. A newspaper which was proposing to publish a damaging story about B would no longer have to ask itself, 'Do we think we could prove this story was true in a court of law if B sued us for libel?' and have to think twice about publishing its story about B if it thought the answer was 'no'. Thirdly, if A attacks B physically, B will be allowed to sue A for damages unless *A* can prove that he had a lawful justification or excuse for attacking B – B will not have to prove that A did *not* have a lawful justification or excuse for attacking him before she will be allowed to sue A. Why should the rule be different if A attacks B verbally or in print? Why should B suddenly have to show that A's attack on her was unjustified before she will be allowed to sue A for libel or slander?

On balance, then, we would conclude that the law should *not* be changed so as to require

[140] [2007] 1 AC 359, at [26] (per Lord Bingham), [97] (per Lord Hope), and at [121] (per Lord Scott).
[141] For further discussion, see Gibbons 1996; Mahoney 1997; Barendt 1999.

the victim of a defamatory statement to prove that that statement was untrue before she will be allowed to obtain a remedy from the person who published that statement.[142]

The liability of distributors

The courts have consistently held that the law on defamation in the UK is compatible with Article 10 of the ECHR.[143] However, there is one aspect of the UK law on libel and slander which does, in our view, unnecessarily impinge on people's rights to freedom of expression.

Suppose Tom has written a book that obviously makes defamatory allegations about Mary. Suppose further that Eric, a bookseller, is considering whether to stock and sell copies of Tom's book. Eric may well think, 'Well – if I do stock and sell copies of Tom's book and the allegations in the book prove to be incorrect, I could well be sued for libel by Mary. Section 1 of the Defamation Act 1996 will not protect me because that only applies to people who unwittingly distribute material that is defamatory – and I won't fall into that category. I can't be sure that the allegations in Tom's book are correct so I will definitely be taking a risk of being sued for libel by Mary if I stock and sell copies of Tom's book. All in all, it might be best if I did not stock Tom's book.' Now – if all booksellers react in the same way as Eric, Tom will be unable to find a market for his book – and this is so even if all the allegations contained in the book are correct. This is hardly satisfactory.

Similarly, suppose Karen runs an electronic bulletin board on the Internet. Suppose further that Tom has posted a message on the board which is obviously defamatory of Mary. Mary complains to Karen about the message and requests her to withdraw it from the bulletin board. Again, Karen may well think, 'If I don't agree to Mary's request and the allegations made in Tom's message prove to be untrue, I could well be sued for libel by Mary. I won't be protected by section 1 of the Defamation Act 1996 because that only protects people who unwittingly distribute defamatory material – and I won't fall into this category of protected defendants if I keep Tom's message on the bulletin board now that my attention has been drawn to it and its defamatory nature. I have no idea whether the allegations contained in Tom's message are true or not so I will definitely be taking a risk of being sued for libel by Mary if I don't take Tom's message down. Given this, it might be better if I withdrew Tom's message from the bulletin board.' If Karen does think in this way, Tom's message will be withdrawn from Karen's bulletin board even if the allegations contained in that message were true. Again, this is hardly satisfactory.

In both these cases, the law on libel operates to 'chill' legitimate expression. In the first case, Tom's book will be rendered unmarketable by the law of libel even though it is perfectly accurate in what it says about Mary. In the second case, Karen will be encouraged by the law on libel to 'censor' Tom's message even though it is perfectly accurate in what it says about Mary. What can be done to ensure that the law on libel does not have this effect?

[142] In *Steel and Morris* v *UK* [2005] EMLR 15, the European Court of Human Rights ruled that this aspect of English law does not violate Art 10 of the ECHR (see at [93]–[94]).

[143] *Derbyshire County Council* v *Times Newspapers Ltd* [1993] AC 534, 551G (per Lord Keith of Kinkel); *Reynolds* v *Times Newspapers Ltd* [2001] 2 AC 127, 204 (per Lord Nicholls); *McCartan Turkington Breen* v *Times Newspapers Ltd* [2001] 2 AC 277, 300–1 (per Lord Cooke); *Loutchansky* v *Times Newspapers Ltd (Nos 2–5)* [2002] QB 783, at [74]; *Jameel (Mohammed)* v *Wall Street Europe SPRL* [2007] 1 AC 359, at [98] (per Lord Hope), [126] (per Lord Scott).

Probably the most satisfactory solution would be to change the law so that it says that someone who disseminates defamatory material which has been created by a third party will have a defence to being sued for libel if he did not know and had no reason to know that the allegations contained in that material were untrue.

If the law were changed in this way then, in the first case described above, booksellers could stock Tom's book confident in the knowledge that if the allegations in Tom's book proved to be untrue and they were sued for libel by Mary, they would have a defence to Mary's claim based on the fact that they did not know and had no reason to know that Tom's allegations were untrue. Similarly, in the second case described above, Karen could refuse to withdraw Tom's message from the bulletin board, confident in the knowledge that if the allegations contained in that message proved to be untrue and Mary sued her for libel, she would have a defence to Mary's claim based on the fact that she did not know and had no reason to know that the allegations in Tom's message were untrue.

Political speech

In the United States, statements about political figures are protected by qualified privilege.[144] Courts in the United States have taken the view that speech about politicians would be unreasonably restricted if the law did not say that someone who has made a false and damaging statement about a politician cannot be sued in libel or slander for making that statement unless he made that statement maliciously.[145] If the law did *not* say this, it is argued, then someone who wanted to make a damaging allegation about a political figure might be inhibited from making that allegation – he would fear that his making that allegation would result in his being sued for libel or slander.

In awarding qualified privilege to statements about political figures, the law in the United States allows people to make allegations about politicians free from the fear that they will be sued as a result. So long as they do not act maliciously in making those allegations they will have nothing to worry about – their allegations will be privileged and there will be no way of making them the subject of an action for libel or slander. By way of contrast, in the United Kingdom, statements about political figures are *not* automatically protected by qualified privilege. The House of Lords confirmed that this was the case in *Reynolds* v *Times Newspapers Ltd*.[146] Their Lordships advanced a number of arguments in support of the United Kingdom position.

144 *New York Times Co.* v *Sullivan* (1964) 376 US 254. In New Zealand, 'political speech' concerning past, present or prospective MPs is protected by qualified privilege: *Lange* v *Atkinson* [1998] 3 NZLR 424; *Lange* v *Atkinson (No. 2)* [2000] 3 NZLR 385. The position in Australia is much closer to that in England: *Lange* v *ABC* (1997) 189 CLR 520 establishes that a defamatory story about a political figure will be protected by qualified privilege so long as the publishers of the story took reasonable care to ensure that it was true and gave the subject of the story a chance to respond to it before publication. Loveland 2000 expresses a preference (at 181–4) for the Australian position. He criticises the *Sullivan* ruling on the ground that it gives a corrupt politician who is accused of acting corruptly by a newspaper an excuse for not suing the newspaper for libel – thereby avoiding having a court test the truth of the allegations against him. The corrupt politican can plausibly argue that there is no point in suing the newspaper as the *Sullivan* ruling means he will almost certainly lose his case.

145 A statement about any public figure – not necessarily a politician – will be protected by qualified privilege in the United States but in the section above we shall simply concentrate on the protection afforded by the law here and in the United States to 'political speech' – speech about politicians.

146 [2001] 2 AC 127.

Lord Nicholls observed that if statements about political figures were protected by qualified privilege, a politician whose reputation had been unjustly sullied by a newspaper acting in good faith would have no means of clearing his name – he would be barred from suing the newspaper for libel.[147] Lord Nicholls did not think that this was satisfactory – '[once] besmirched by an unfounded allegation in a national newspaper, a reputation can be damaged for ever, especially if there is no opportunity to vindicate one's reputation. When this happens, society as well as the individual is the loser . . . It is in the public interest that the reputation of public figures should not be debased falsely. In the political field, in order to make an informed choice, the electorate needs to be able to identify the good as well as the bad.'[148]

Lords Nicholls and Cooke both observed that if statements about politicians were automatically protected by qualified privilege, one could have no confidence that newspapers – especially the tabloid press – would act responsibly in using this new won freedom to make statements about politicians free from the fear that they would be sued as a result of what they said.[149] They did not elaborate on this point but they must have feared that the press would use this freedom to print damaging stories about political figures based on the slenderest of materials and to print damaging stories about politicians which were of no conceivable public interest.

Lords Cooke and Steyn observed that if political speech were protected by qualified privilege, a politician who was defamed by a story in a newspaper would find it very difficult to establish that the newspaper acted maliciously in publishing that story.[150] This is for two reasons. First, malice is in itself a difficult thing to prove. Secondly, English law makes it even more difficult to prove malice because it does not require newspapers to disclose the sources for their stories. So a politician who was defamed by a story in a newspaper and wanted to prove that the newspaper knew that the story was not true when it published it would not be able to get the newspaper to disclose the source of its story to see whether, given what the source said and his or her reliability, the newspaper could have believed its story to be true when it published it. Given these difficulties of proving malice, politicians would have very little protection against being defamed if political speech were protected by qualified privilege – such speech would be *de facto* absolutely privileged; a politician who was defamed by a particular story would in effect find it impossible to sue for libel in respect of that story.

Finally, Lord Steyn advanced another argument against holding that all statements about politicians are protected by qualified privilege. He thought that such a rule might violate the European Convention on Human Rights, under which the resolution of competing rights and interests – such as the right to freedom of speech and the interest in preserving one's reputation undamaged – is to be done on a case-by-case basis rather than by laying down general rules which apply in a wide variety of cases.[151]

While the law in the UK does not protect political speech *as such*, it does protect *some* statements about political figures. In particular, statements that amount to fair comment

[147] Ibid., 201.
[148] Ibid., 201.
[149] Ibid., 201–2 (per Lord Nicholls), 219 (per Lord Cooke).
[150] Ibid., 210 (per Lord Steyn), 219–20 (per Lord Cooke).
[151] Ibid., 211.

on a matter of public interest and statements that are protected by the *Reynolds* test for qualified privilege are protected under UK law. Given this, *in theory* most forms of political speech will be protected under the law in the United Kingdom and those forms of political speech which will not be protected – malicious speech, tittle-tattle and the publication of irresponsible and untrue stories about politicians – are perhaps not worthy of protection. However, *in practice* the UK law on defamation can still have the effect of chilling legitimate political speech if an editor like David – who, it will be recalled, was considering publishing a story alleging that Mary, a famous politician, was accepting bribes – is encouraged to 'sit on' a damaging story about a politician because he simply does not have any confidence that the courts will find that he acted responsibly in handling that story and consequently hold that that story was protected by qualified privilege. As we have seen, the House of Lords has attempted in *Jameel (Mohammed)* v *Wall Street Journal SPRL*[152] to reassure editors in this regard and has taken steps to ensure that the courts will in future adopt a more 'journalist friendly' approach to determining whether a story was handled in a responsible fashion than they have in the past. However, the fact that the House of Lords needed to do this in the first place indicates a worrying lack of respect and concern for journalistic free speech in the lower courts. It is also concerning that the UK is still the destination of choice for public figures 'forum shopping' for a set of courts that will assist them to suppress speech that damages their reputation.[153]

We are therefore undecided whether the UK courts can be trusted to administer the law on defamation in a way that does not chill legitimate political speech. The House of Lords' decision in the *Jameel (Mohammed)* case is a welcome development; but it remains to be seen whether the lower courts will follow suit and embrace the liberalisation of defamation law that the House of Lords' decision in *Reynolds* was intended to bring about.

Visit **http://www.mylawchamber.co.uk/mcbride** to access updates on recent cases, as well as model answers and tips for answering tort problem questions.

Use **Case Navigator** to read in full the key case referenced in this chapter:

- **Jameel (Mohammed)** *v* **Wall Street Europe SPRL**

152 [2007] 1 AC 359.
153 As happened in *Jameel (Yousef)* v *Dow Jones & Co. Inc.* [2005] QB 946, where the claimant brought a claim in a UK court against a US newspaper for publishing something on a US website that had only been accessed by five people in the UK.

14 Harassment

Section 1(1) of the Protection from Harassment Act 1997 provides that, 'A person must not pursue a course of conduct – (a) which amounts to harassment of another, and (b) which he knows or ought to know amounts to harassment of the other.' It is clear that anyone who breaches this duty will commit a tort. Section 3(1) of the 1997 Act provides that: '[an] actual or apprehended breach of section 1 may be the subject of a claim in civil proceedings by the person who is or may be the victim of the course of conduct in question.'

Five points need to be made about these provisions:

(1) *Course of conduct*. The duty created by s 1(1) of the 1997 Act can only be breached by someone who engages in a *course of conduct* which amounts to harassment. Section 7(3) of the Act provides that 'A "course of conduct" must involve conduct on at least two occasions.' The courts have not provided very much by way of clear guidance as to what amounts to a 'course of conduct'.

In *Pratt* v *DPP*,[1] it was held that losing one's temper with one's wife on Christmas Day and then again in March could amount to a 'course of conduct' that amounts to harassment. By contrast, in *Lau* v *DPP*,[2] the court refused to find that slapping one's girlfriend and then threatening her new boyfriend four months later amounted to a 'course of conduct'. Again, in *R* v *Hills*,[3] it was held that hitting one's live-in girlfriend once in April and then again in October could not be said to amount to a 'course of conduct'. Finally, in *Kelly* v *DPP*,[4] the court found that leaving three messages on someone's answering machine – all of which were listened to on the same occasion – could amount to a 'course of conduct' under the 1997 Act.

(2) *The meaning of harassment*. Section 7(2) of the 1997 Act provides that 'References to harassing a person include alarming the person or causing the person distress.' So the duty set out in s 1(1) of the 1997 Act will be breached if someone engages in a course of conduct which alarms or distresses someone else and he knows or ought to know that his engaging in that conduct is having that effect. Section 7(2) seems to imply that it is possible to harass someone without causing them alarm or distress, and this seems right – there is no reason why a course of conduct that is regarded by someone as simply an annoying nuisance should not be held to amount to harassment under the 1997 Act.

(3) *Limits on the scope of the Act*. Section 1(3) of the 1997 Act qualifies the effect of s 1(1), providing as it does that s 1(1) 'does not apply to a course of conduct if the person who

[1] [2001] EWHC Admin 483.
[2] [2000] 1 FLR 799.
[3] [2001] Crim LR 318.
[4] [2003] Crim LR 43.

pursued it shows – (a) that it was pursued for the purpose of preventing or detecting crime, (b) that it was pursued under any enactment or rule of law or to comply with any condition or requirement imposed by any person under any enactment, or (c) that in the particular circumstances the pursuit of the course of conduct was reasonable'.

So a policeman will commit no tort under the 1997 Act if he camps outside the house of a known car thief every day, with the object of deterring the car thief from going out and stealing cars. Similarly, if A has lent money to B and repayment is long overdue, A will commit no tort under the 1997 Act if he regularly rings B up and demands payment of his money – so long, of course, as A rings B at a reasonable time and does not do it unreasonably often. (A could not, of course, establish that his regularly ringing B up to demand payment of his money was reasonable if his telephone calls were made at 4 am or if he rang B every five minutes.)

In determining whether or not a given course of conduct was 'reasonable' the courts have to be careful that they do not violate people's rights to freedom of expression under Article 10 of the European Convention on Human Rights.[5] So in *Thomas* v *News Group Newspapers Ltd*, Lord Phillips MR explained that a newspaper which instituted a campaign against a particular individual would only be held to have acted unreasonably in running that campaign if the campaign amounted 'to an abuse of the freedom of the press which the pressing social needs of a democratic society require should be curbed'.[6] As a test for determining when a newspaper will be held to have acted unreasonably in running a campaign against a particular individual, this is unsatisfactory: it is likely to have a 'chilling' effect on people's legitimately exercising their right to freedom of expression. This is because the test is so vague that a newspaper which is thinking of running a campaign against an individual will find it hard to know whether it will or will not be held liable under the 1997 Act if it runs the campaign. As a result, it may well choose to 'pull' the campaign rather than run it and take the risk of being sued under the 1997 Act.

It would have been more satisfactory if the Court of Appeal in *Thomas* had adopted the test set out in the second American Restatement of Torts for determining when the infliction of severe emotional distress will be tortious, and ruled that a newspaper which ran a campaign against a particular individual could only be held to have acted unreasonably in so doing if its running that campaign was so 'extreme and outrageous' that it went beyond 'all possible bounds of decency ... and [was] utterly intolerable in a civilized society'.[7]

(4) *Companies are not protected.* In *Daiichi Pharmaceuticals UK Ltd* v *Stop Huntingdon Animal Cruelty*,[8] it was held that companies were not protected by the 1997 Act and could not seek an injunction in their own right to stop people attempting to disrupt the running of their businesses.[9]

5 Set out above, p. 310.
6 [2001] EWCA Civ 1233, at [50]. It was conceded in *Thomas* that this test would be satisfied if a newspaper campaign was calculated to stir up racial hatred.
7 Rest 2d, Torts, §46, Comment *d*. For a discussion of when this requirement will be satisfied, see GS&Z, 644–7.
8 [2004] 1 WLR 1503.
9 They would, however, probably be able to complain in their own right that the defendants' activities amounted to the tort of the intentional infliction of harm by unlawful means (discussed below, Chapter 21), the unlawful means in question being harassment of their employees (who are protected under the 1997 Act).

(5) *Vicarious liability*. In *Majrowski* v *Guy's and St Thomas's NHS Trust*,[10] the House of Lords confirmed that, unless Parliament provided otherwise, the principle that an employer will be vicariously liable in respect of an employee's torts that were committed in the course of his employment applied just as much to statutory torts as it did to common law torts, such as negligence or assault. So an employer will be held vicariously liable if one of his employees commits the tort of harassment in relation to someone else in the course of his or her employment.[11]

[10] [2007] 1 AC 224.

[11] On when someone can be said to have committed a tort in the course of his or her employment, see below, pp. 661–71.

15 Invasion of privacy

English law recognises privacy as a value which underpins various rules of tort law (for instance, parts of the torts of trespass to land, private nuisance, defamation, and malicious falsehood). However, English law has not elevated the protection of privacy to the status of a legal principle from which judges can directly derive conditions of tortious liability.[1] To put the same point another way, English law has *not* recognised a *general* 'over-arching, all-embracing cause of action for "invasion of privacy" '.[2] In the last decade, however, English law has developed a tort which deals with a *specific* form of invasion of privacy, and the first part of this chapter concentrates on this new tort which we will refer to as *the tort of wrongful disclosure of private information*. The remaining part of this chapter discusses whether English law ought to develop any further torts to deal with other specific forms of invasion of privacy.

WRONGFUL DISCLOSURE OF PRIVATE INFORMATION

The case of *Campbell* v *MGN*[3] concerned the publication in the *Daily Mirror* of the information that Naomi Campbell was a drug addict, was seeking treatment through Narcotics Anonymous, some details of her treatment, and a photograph of her at a place where a Narcotics Anonymous meeting took place. She conceded that the *Daily Mirror* was entitled to reveal that she was a drug addict and that she was seeking treatment, but contended that the defendant committed a tort in relation to her by publishing the other details and the photograph. The House of Lords unanimously confirmed that A will commit a tort[4] in relation to B if A unjustifiably discloses to C information which A knows or ought to know is private information about B. By a bare majority of three to two the House of Lords held that the *Daily Mirror* had committed this tort in publishing the details of Naomi Campbell's treatment and the photograph.

[1] In *Wainwright* v *Home Office* [2004] 2 AC 406, Lord Hoffmann suggested (at [31]–[33]) that English law should not give effect to a general principle such as 'the unjustified invasion of another's privacy is always actionable' because the detailed attention of a legislator would often be necessary in order to fashion conditions of liability and appropriate defences in the very different areas where the value of privacy might be invoked. He mentioned regulation of the use of images recorded by CCTV cameras as an example of an area where detailed legislation would be more appropriate than a judicial attempt to derive a solution from a broad principle.

[2] *Campbell* v *MGN Ltd* [2004] 2 AC 457, at [11] (per Lord Nicholls).

[3] Ibid. (henceforth, '*Campbell*').

[4] Strictly speaking only one of their Lordships refers to the wrong as a 'tort' (Lord Nicholls at [14]). But in the next subsection we explain why we think that the wrong should be acknowledged as a tort. Any reader who does not accept this explanation can instead treat the first part of this chapter as dealing with *part of* an equitable wrong for pragmatic reasons. See above, pp. 8–9.

The independence of the new tort

This new tort has its roots in the equitable wrong of breach of confidence. But while greater protection of privacy has been achieved *formally* under the cloak of this long-established wrong, it would be artificial to pretend that all that has happened is that breach of confidence 'has developed'. The traditional features of breach of confidence are not decisive in cases involving the wrongful disclosure of *private* information. For instance, the 'cause of action has now firmly shaken off the limiting constraint of the need for an initial confidential relationship'[5] and the narrow limits on the defences to the equitable wrong do not apply in cases protecting privacy.[6] Moreover, the principal influences on the future development of the civil wrong are likely to be human rights law and analogies with torts like libel and slander rather than any principles developed by the Courts of Equity. Thus we think that it makes most sense to treat the civil wrong committed in *Campbell* as a *new and independent tort* – the tort of wrongful disclosure of private information.[7]

One reason for treating wrongful disclosure of private information as an independent tort is that the equitable wrong of breach of confidence will continue to exist in its *original* form to deal with situations where abstract information – such as a trade secret – is disclosed to someone else on the condition that it will remain confidential.[8] But this raises the question how the courts will treat cases where the information is arguably private information within the scope of the new tort *and* an initial confidential relationship existed. In such cases a claimant may gain an advantage by demonstrating that a duty of confidence in the *original* form attaches to the information since this will add weight to the claim that it is appropriate to restrict a defendant's right to free expression.[9]

An important influence on the development of the new tort has been and will be the right to privacy contained in Article 8 of the European Convention on Human Rights (ECHR). Although s 6 of the Human Rights Act 1998 does not impose a duty to act compatibly with Convention rights on *private individuals*,[10] it does impose such a duty on public authorities, including the courts. Moreover, the European Court of Human Rights has held that in order to comply with Article 8, a State must do more than merely ensure that public authorities avoid violating privacy *themselves*. As the Court expressed the point

[5] Ibid., at [14] (per Lord Nicholls).

[6] *Theakston* v *MGN* [2002] EMLR 137, [66].

[7] Although the majority of the House of Lords in the *Campbell* case *refused* to treat wrongful disclosure of private information as an independent tort – and this refusal will have significant practical consequences, particularly in the field of remedies – two subsequent Court of Appeal decisions have referred to 'the rechristening of the tort as misuse of private information' as if Lord Nicholls's opinion (*Campbell*, at [14]) on this point was orthodox: *McKennitt* v *Ash* [2007] 3 WLR 194, at [8], *Lord Browne of Madingley* v *Associated Newspapers Ltd* [2007] 3 WLR 289, at [21]–[22].

[8] In *Douglas* v *Hello! Ltd (No. 3)* [2007] 2 WLR 920, a majority of the House of Lords accepted that a private event could be organised in such a way as to make the information that would be disclosed by a *photographic* image of the event into a commercial secret, which could be protected by the wrong of breach of confidence, and this could clearly cover what a particular person *looked like during the event*. The protection provided by this aspect of the wrong of breach of confidence is *separate* from the duty not to publish photographic images which disclose *private* information. The latter duty is discussed below, pp. 340–1.

[9] For instance, when considering the unauthorised publication of Prince Charles's travel journals the Court of Appeal stated that '[b]oth the nature of the information and of the relationship of confidence under which it was received weigh heavily in the balance in favour of Prince Charles': *HRH Prince of Wales* v *Associated Newspapers Ltd* [2007] 3 WLR 222, at [71].

[10] See below, pp. 743–6.

in *Von Hannover* v *Germany*: 'although the object of Article 8 is essentially that of protecting the individual against arbitrary interference by the public authorities, it does not merely compel the State to abstain from such interference: in addition to this primarily negative undertaking, there may be positive obligations inherent in an effective respect for private or family life. These obligations may involve the adoption of measures designed to secure respect for private life even in the sphere of the relations of individuals between themselves.'[11] The English courts have not resisted these positive obligations and have modelled the new tort on the assumption that 'the values underlying Articles 8 and 10 are not confined to disputes between individuals and public authorities'.[12] It is important to note, however, that the English courts have developed a *limited* new tort *of wrongfully disclosing private information* which corresponds to[13] Articles 8 and 10: they have *not* simply made *all* violations of Article 8 actionable against private individuals.[14]

The structure of the new tort

The new tort has an unusual structure because it exists at the meeting point of *two* human rights: A's disclosure to C of private information about B *may* infringe B's right to privacy, but a restriction on A making such a disclosure *may* infringe the right to free expression of both A and C.[15] Neither of these human rights is pre-eminent, so 'the proportionality of interfering with one has to be balanced against the proportionality of restricting the other'.[16]

The term 'balancing' is shorthand for a complex process, and one which requires an 'intense focus' on the particular facts of the case.[17] In order to impose tort liability only when that is appropriate given the competing rights at stake, the court is likely to find it convenient to proceed by asking the following questions:

(1) Is the information about B which A has disclosed[18] to C sufficiently *private* to come within the potential ambit of the tort?

[11] (2005) 40 EHRR 1, at [57].

[12] *Campbell*, at [18] (per Lord Nicholls). Article 10 is, of course, the provision which defines the right to free expression in the ECHR. See also at [50] (per Lord Hoffmann), 'I can see no logical ground for saying that a person should have less protection against a private individual than he would have against the state for the publication of personal information for which there is no justification.'

[13] The degree of correspondence is strong. Buxton LJ expressed the relationship as follows in *McKennitt* v *Ash* [2007] 3 WLR 194, at [11]: 'Those articles are now not merely of persuasive or parallel effect but . . . are the very content of the domestic tort that the English court has to enforce.'

[14] This point is important because Art 8 protects privacy in contexts beyond the scope of the new tort, and in some of these contexts there are good reasons for providing a person with more protection against a public authority than against a private individual. For instance, the compilation of records about individuals by public authorities requires justification under Art 8(2) but it is doubtful that the same can be said when private individuals keep diaries, scrap books or photograph albums. See, for example, *Amann* v *Switzerland* (2000) 30 EHRR 843, where the European Court of Human Rights held that there was an interference with an applicant's right to respect for his private life under Art 8 when a file card recorded that he had supplied a depilatory appliance to a customer in the Soviet embassy.

[15] It is important to remember that both *publisher* and *recipient* have a right to free expression.

[16] *Campbell*, at [140] (per Baroness Hale). See also [113] (per Lord Hope) and [167] (per Lord Carswell).

[17] *Re S (A Child) (Identification: Restrictions on Publication)* [2005] 1 AC 593, at [17] (per Lord Steyn).

[18] Or, where B is seeking a pre-publication injunction, 'is intending to disclose'. On pre-publication injunctions see below, pp. 725–6.

(2) If the information is sufficiently private, how important is it to protect this aspect of B's privacy?
(3) Was A's disclosure of the information to C *expression* within the ambit of Article 10?
(4) If so, how important is it not to restrict this sort of expression?[19]
(5) Given the answers to (2) and (4), will making A liable amount to a proportionate restriction on A's freedom of expression in order to protect B's privacy *or* will not holding A liable constitute a proportionate limit on the protection of B's privacy in order preserve freedom of expression?

It *may* also be necessary to ask a further question:
(6) Did A know, or ought A to have known, that the information was sufficiently private?

Private information

Suppose that A has disclosed information about B to C. When will that information be regarded as sufficiently private to come within the potential ambit of the tort discussed here?

The basic test

In answer to the question just posed, the basic test is whether B had a 'reasonable expectation of privacy' in relation to the information that A disclosed to C.[20]

Some simple points can be made about this test. First, in working out what this test means it is helpful to start by thinking of information as *private* if it is the sort of information which a person would expect to be able to control the dissemination of.[21]

Importantly, this means that B can have a 'reasonable expectation of privacy' even if the information is not totally *secret*. Usually[22] the information involved will have been known to *some* people other than B before A's involvement; for instance, because B permitted its disclosure to a *limited* circle[23] or because some class of people had a legitimate reason for obtaining the information.[24] Thus the relevant expectation is that B will be able to control whether, when and how the information is released beyond this circle.[25] Where, however,

[19] Importance must be assessed considering the interests of both *publisher* and *recipient.*

[20] *Campbell*, at [21] (per Lord Nicholls), [85] (per Lord Hope), [134] (per Baroness Hale).

[21] In *Campbell*, Lord Hoffmann said (at [51]) that the new tort 'focuses upon the protection of human autonomy and dignity – *the right to control the dissemination of information about one's private life* and the right to the esteem and respect of other people' (emphasis added).

[22] There are exceptions; for instance, where A takes a photograph of B and publishes it to C this may disclose information that *nobody* previously *knew* – *a fortiori* if A used a telephoto lens to photograph B while she was on her own in a private place.

[23] For instance to members of his close family or to close colleagues.

[24] For instance a doctor may have recorded his observations of B in B's medical records or the police may have obtained information about B in the course of a legitimate investigation.

[25] Difficult cases can arise where information is *available* to all, but onerous to obtain. It seems that a person *may* have a reasonable expectation that people will not make such information easily available. For instance, a celebrity may have a reasonable expectation that a newspaper will not publish his address: *Mills* v *News Group Newspapers Ltd* [2001] EWHC Ch 412. But we suspect that celebrities object to the publication of their addresses because this facilitates *intrusion* rather than because the *publication itself* threatens their dignity or autonomy. Consequently, such cases might be better dealt with under a form of privacy tort other than that dealing with *wrongful disclosure of private information*. See below, pp. 338–9, for discussion of the question whether English law should develop a tort of invasion of privacy by *unreasonable intrusion.*

information has already been widely or indiscriminately disclosed B may be unable to claim that she has any *reasonable* expectation of controlling its further publication.[26]

Secondly, the expectation of privacy must be *reasonable*: 'The law of privacy is not intended for the protection of the unduly sensitive.'[27] Thus a claim cannot be based on the publication by A of the sort of information about B that a reasonable person would not be worried about maintaining any degree of control over. For example, if B is inexplicably sensitive about other people finding out the date of her birthday this will not mean that A will commit a tort if he discloses the date to C. The sensitivity rule is qualified to an extent, however, by the further rule that the reasonableness of the expectation of privacy as to information about a particular feature is judged from the perspective of people who share the same feature. Thus in the *Campbell* case the question whether it was reasonable for Naomi Campbell to expect that the details of her treatment should be kept private was assessed from the perspective of a *reasonable drug addict receiving treatment*.[28]

One problem with the reasonable expectation test is that it seems to be circular: B's *privacy* can be protected when B *reasonably expects* her *privacy* to be protected. A related second problem is that it is unclear what the *nature* of the expectation must be. It is difficult to conclude that it must be a *factual* expectation because very few celebrities could claim that they *in fact expected* tabloid newspapers not to publish salacious details obtained from former lovers or photographs of them in embarrassing poses.[29] Thus it seems that when judges ask whether B had a 'reasonable expectation of privacy' they are really asking whether B *ought to be able to* expect privacy. But this, of course, is often a controversial question.

An analysis of the cases suggests that courts treat the following factors as relevant when considering whether the claimant had a 'reasonable expectation of privacy': (i) the nature of the information – certain types of information, for instance information relating to sexuality or health,[30] can be straightforwardly classified as *private*; (ii) the form

[26] The question often asked is whether the information is 'in the public domain', borrowing terminology from the equitable wrong of breach of confidence. But *private* information will only count as being 'in the public domain' if no useful purpose could be served by preventing further publication. In *Lord Browne of Madingley* v *Associated Newspapers Ltd* [2007] 3 WLR 289, at [61], the Court of Appeal identified 'an important distinction between information which is made available to a person's circle of friends or work colleagues and information which is widely published in a newspaper.' The Court cited Lord Goff's opinion in *A-G* v *Guardian Newspapers (No. 2)* [1990] 1 AC 109, 282, that the key question is whether the information has become 'so generally accessible that, in all the circumstances, it cannot be regarded as confidential'. There may *always* be a sufficient reason for preventing further publication of a photograph: 'In so far as a photograph does more than convey information and intrudes on privacy by enabling the viewer to focus on intimate personal detail, there will be a fresh intrusion of privacy when each additional viewer sees the photograph and even when one who has seen a previous publication of the photograph is confronted by a fresh publication of it. To take an example, if a film star were photographed, with the aid of a telephoto lens, lying naked by her private swimming pool, we question whether widespread publication of the photograph by a popular newspaper would provide a defence to a legal challenge to repeated publication on the ground that the information was in the public domain', (*Douglas* v *Hello! Ltd (No. 3)* [2006] QB 125, at [105]).

[27] *Campbell*, at [94] (per Lord Hope).

[28] Ibid., at [98] (per Lord Hope), [136] (per Baroness Hale).

[29] See below pp. 325–6 for discussion of whether these examples fall within the scope of the tort.

[30] The category of 'sexuality' includes information about a person's gender identification, sexual orientation and sexual life: *PG* v *United Kingdom* [2001] ECHR 546, at [56]. The category 'health' includes 'information about a person's health and treatment for ill-health', *Campbell* at [145] (per Baroness Hale), though *trivial matters* will not be protected: ibid., at [157] (per Baroness Hale), 'the privacy interest in the fact that a public figure has a cold or a broken leg is unlikely to be strong enough to justify restricting the press's freedom to report it'.

in which the information was kept – certain ways of storing information, such as in a private diary or a confidential file, support a claimant's assertion that he did not expect the contents to be *generally* published; (iii) the relationship between the claimant and the person who is disclosing the information, or who has disclosed it to the defendant – there is clearly a stronger expectation that information discovered in the course of a relationship will be kept private when the parties are priest and penitent, or doctor and patient, than when they are storekeeper and customer, or journalist and celebrity;[31] (iv) how the information was obtained – if the information had to be obtained by subterfuge or trickery this will suggest that it was *private*;[32] (v) the claimant's previous behaviour – if the claimant has given publicity to an aspect of his life then this may reduce the degree of privacy that he can reasonably expect in the future;[33] and (vi) the likely consequences of the disclosure.[34]

No doubt these factors are associated with different types of reasons for thinking that a defendant ought to be subject to a duty not to publish the information: the reasons why there should be a duty not to publish medical records which have blown out of a window are not identical to the reasons why there should be a duty not to publish photographs of people in their private gardens taken using a telephoto lens. But real cases often involve facts where more than one reason for imposing a duty can be identified, and in such cases the outcomes often – quite properly – reflect the *combination* of applicable reasons. Thus a claimant's reasonable expectation that a defendant will not publish particular information often derives from 'an interdependent amalgam of circumstances'.[35] For instance, when considering whether the Prince of Wales had a reasonable expectation of privacy with respect to a journal recording his impressions on a visit to Hong Kong, the Court of Appeal stated, 'It is not easy in this case, as in many others, when concluding that information is private to identify the extent to which this is because of the nature of the information, the form in which it is conveyed and the fact that the person disclosing it was in a confidential relationship with the person to whom it relates.'

Because of the difficulty of applying the reasonable expectation test in borderline cases some judges have advocated the use of a test based on a reasonable person's *reaction* to the

[31] For example, in *McKennitt v Ash* [2007] 3 WLR 194 at [14]–[18], [24], the Court of Appeal thought that the relevant information *might* have been private in *nature* anyway, but held that the conclusion that it should be protected from disclosure became irresistible once account was taken of the fact that the information had only become available to the defendant in the course of a close friendship between herself and the claimant.

[32] Lord Hoffmann suggested, in *Campbell* at [75], that it might be a violation of privacy to publish a photograph obtained by intrusion because to do so demonstrated that apparently private space was not inviolate.

[33] It will not often be the case that a claimant has acted in such a way as to make it wholly *unreasonable* for him to expect any measure of privacy in the future. The Court of Appeal in *McKennitt* v *Ash* [2007] 3 WLR 194, at [35]–[36] suggested that *Woodward v Hutchins* [1977] 1 WLR 760 might be a rare example of such a doctrine being applied: Bridge LJ, at 765, explained the outcome of that case as turning on the principle that 'those who seek and welcome publicity of every kind bearing upon their private lives so long as it shows them in a favourable light are in no position to complain of the invasion of their privacy by publicity that shows them in an unfavourable light'. But Buxton LJ described as 'cruelly insensitive' (at [54]) the suggestion that Loreena McKennitt's controlled disclosures about the effect on her of her fiancé's drowning prevented a claim based on the defendant's publication of a detailed description of her pitifully grief-stricken reaction.

[34] This factor is more likely to be significant when weighing the *importance* of respecting the claimant's expectation of privacy (see below, p. 330). But on occasion the likely consequences may establish the expectation, for example, where a defendant publishes which branch of a supermarket a celebrity claimant shops in each Thursday night or that the claimant has won the lottery.

[35] *HRH Prince of Wales* v *Associated Newspapers Ltd* [2007] 3 WLR 222, at [36] (per Lord Phillips CJ).

publication. For instance, in the *Campbell* case Lord Hope stated that 'the broad test is whether disclosure of the information about the individual ("A") would give substantial offence to A, assuming that A was placed in similar circumstances and was a person of ordinary sensibilities'.[36] This echoes the suggestion of Gleeson CJ in the High Court of Australia that a 'useful practical test' is whether the 'disclosure or observation of information or conduct would be highly offensive to a reasonable person of ordinary sensibilities'.[37] However, this test was criticised by some of the other Law Lords in the *Campbell* case. For instance, Lord Nicholls was concerned that the 'highly offensive' test raised the threshold of liability higher than the 'reasonable expectation' test, and that a person's reaction to a publication might reflect factors relevant to the later stages of an inquiry into whether a defendant could be held liable for disclosing private information (for instance, whether the publication was justified by free speech values) and not just whether the information was potentially *private*.[38] A further problem with a test based on a reasonable person's *reaction* to the publication is that such a test is unlikely to work when the information is about a disturbed adult[39] or a very young child.[40] Thus it seems likely that a test based on imagining a reasonable person's *reaction* will not generally be used *in place of* the basic test.

We will now consider how the basic test will be applied in some specific contexts.

Relationship cases

Where A, who was in a relationship with B, publishes information about B relating to events during the relationship then the *nature of the relationship* will be an important factor in deciding whether B had a 'reasonable expectation of privacy' with regard to the information. At one end of the spectrum of relationships are those where the expectation is strongest (and most likely to be protected by law), such as marriage, and other relationships intended to be permanent. Relationships where there is an express contractual agreement not to publish any information are also likely to be at the protective end of the spectrum. In *Campbell v Frisbee*[41] the Court of Appeal stated that it was at least arguable 'that a duty of confidentiality that has been expressly assumed under contract carries more weight, when balanced against the restriction of the right of freedom of expression, than a duty of confidentiality that is not buttressed by express agreement'. At the less protective end of the spectrum are relationships where the law is unlikely to treat any expectation as reasonable, such as 'a transitory engagement in a brothel'.[42] In *A* v *B* the Court of Appeal agreed with the opinion that the sexual relationship that Gary Flitcroft, a married footballer, had with a lap-dancer over the course of a year was at the 'outer limits of relationships which require the protection of the law'.[43] Some later courts, however, have expressed concern at the idea

[36] *Campbell*, at [92].

[37] *Australian Broadcasting Corporation* v *Lenah Game Meats Pty Ltd* (2001) 208 CLR 199, at [42].

[38] *Campbell*, at [22]. See also [135] (per Baroness Hale).

[39] In *T* v *BBC* [2007] EWHC 1683 (QB) the claimant was an 18 year old who was incapable of giving informed consent, and whose reactions to appearing in a television documentary were likely to be unpredictable and inconsistent, but on balance negative.

[40] In *Murray* v *Express Newspapers plc* [2007] EWHC 1908 (Ch) the claimant, the son of the author J.K. Rowling, was two years old at the time of the relevant publication.

[41] [2003] ICR 141.

[42] *Theakston* v *MGN Ltd* [2002] EMLR 137, [62].

[43] [2003] QB 195, at [47].

that no reasonable expectation of privacy attaches to a casual sexual encounter. For instance, in *Douglas* v *Hello! Ltd (No. 3)*, the Court of Appeal observed that 'to date the English courts appear to have taken a less generous view of the protection that the individual can reasonably expect in respect of his or her sexual activities than has the Strasbourg court'.[44]

Assessment of where the relationship between A and B lies on the spectrum is not the end of the matter. The court must also consider other relevant factors, such as the nature of the information,[45] and the connection between the relationship and the information that A proposes to publish. For instance, in *Lord Browne of Madingley* v *Associated Newspapers Ltd*[46] the claim was brought by Lord Browne, the group chief executive of BP plc, to restrain the defendants from publishing information received from Jeff Chevalier, who had been Lord Browne's homosexual partner for four years. Eady J, at first instance, held that the relationship was such that Lord Browne was entitled to expect that any comments he made to Jeff Chevalier about his business colleagues, and the content of conversations at dinner parties and the like, would remain private. But Eady J concluded, and the Court of Appeal upheld this, that Lord Browne could not expect the fact that he had provided Jeff Chevalier with assistance from BP plc's staff and resources, or the mere fact of the relationship, or the fact that he had discussed BP plc's business with his lover, to remain private.

Photographs

If a person goes to a public place then she clearly accepts that other people will be able to look at her and thereby obtain certain information about her. But a photograph taken of the person may capture *more* information than even a careful observer would perceive, will preserve that information in a potentially permanent form, and can be used to communicate *more* information *more* efficiently than mere words easily could. For instance, if John wanted to let Paul know about a dress that Mary wore to a child's birthday party (in order to criticise her for choosing to wear such a dress) then showing Paul a photograph of Mary wearing the dress would communicate more information about the dress more quickly and more convincingly than trying to describe it verbally.

If observers can *see* a person at a particular moment then how can she claim to have a reasonable expectation of privacy as to what would appear on a photograph taken at that moment? In the *Campbell* case Lord Hoffmann suggested that, '[t]he famous and even the not so famous who go out in public must accept that they may be photographed without their consent, just as they may be observed by others without their consent'.[47] But he

[44] [2006] QB 125, at [73]. This point was not related to the issues which were subsequently appealed to the House of Lords.

[45] Even when a relationship between A and B was 'transitory' there may be some types of information which B could reasonably expect A not to publish. For example, in *Theakston* v *MGN* [2002] EMLR 137, Ouseley J suggested that although the claimant would not be able to object to publication of details of his sexual activity during a visit to a brothel he could prevent publication of photographs showing his appearance during the activity.

[46] [2007] EMLR 19 (QB, first instance), [2007] 3 WLR 289, CA.

[47] *Campbell*, at [73]. In *Murray* v *Express Newspapers plc* [2007] EWHC 1908 (Ch), at [37], Patten J stated that 'A photograph taken by a member of the public which remains the property of that person and is at most shown to family and friends does not infringe any right of privacy because it does not lead to any real public exposure of the events portrayed.'

thought that they could object to *some* photographs taken in public being made available to the world at large.[48] He pointed to the case of *Peck* v *United Kingdom*,[49] where it was held that a person walking in the street with a knife could not object to being filmed by CCTV but could object to that film being broadcast on television.

Which photographs of people in public places is there a duty not to publish? In the *Campbell* case the House of Lords clearly suggested that it was not reasonable for a person to expect an *innocuous* photograph taken in public not to be published. This is because the information contained in such an image was unlikely to be the sort of information that a reasonable person would be worried about maintaining any degree of control over. Baroness Hale, for instance, stated that there was nothing essentially private about what Naomi Campbell 'looks like if and when she pops out to the shops for a bottle of milk'.[50] But where a photograph contains information that a reasonable person would want to maintain control over – for instance what the person looks like when in extreme distress or when eating messy food – then publication of a photograph of such an event might violate the person's privacy even though *looking at* the person during the event would not. Lord Hoffmann stated that 'the widespread publication of a photograph of someone which reveals him to be in a situation of humiliation or severe embarrassment, even if taken in a public place, may be an infringement of the privacy of his personal information'.[51]

The European Court of Human Rights, however, appears to hold a different view as to whether the publication of innocuous photographs taken in public can breach Article 8. In *Von Hannover* v *Germany*,[52] the Court held that the German state had violated Article 8 by permitting the publication in German magazines of photographs showing Princess Caroline of Monaco in the course of everyday activities such as visiting a market and riding a bicycle. An influential factor was that Princess Caroline had been subject to near-continuous observation by press photographers and it is easy to see how the innocuous nature of each photograph, judged individually, would not reflect the effect on a claimant's privacy of such a campaign. The Court's response was to treat the publication of each photograph, no matter how innocuous, as potentially violating Article 8: 'In the present case there is no doubt that the publication by various German magazines of photos of the applicant in her daily life either on her own or with other people falls within the scope of her private life.'[53]

In *Murray* v *Express Newspapers plc*[54] Patten J had to confront the apparent inconsistency between the *Campbell* and *Von Hannover* cases when faced with a claim arising from a photographic agency supplying a newspaper with a photograph taken in the street of the two-year-old son of the author J.K. Rowling being pushed in his pushchair. Patten J held that he was obliged to follow the House of Lords' decision in the *Campbell* case even if it was inconsistent with the decision of the European Court of Human Rights in *Von Hannover*. But he preferred the view that even after *Von Hannover* 'there remains an area

[48] *Campbell*, at [74]–[75]. See also at [122] (per Lord Hope).

[49] (2003) 36 EHRR 719.

[50] *Campbell*, at [154]. This was applied in *John* v *Associated Newspapers Ltd* [2006] EMLR 722, when Eady J refused to grant an interim injunction to prevent the defendant from publishing a photograph of Sir Elton John in the street, wearing a tracksuit and baseball cap, opening his front gate.

[51] Ibid., at [76].

[52] (2005) 40 EHRR 1.

[53] Ibid., at [53].

[54] [2007] EWHC 1908 (Ch).

of innocuous conduct in a public place which does not raise a reasonable expectation of privacy,'[55] noting that an unfettered application of an 'absolutist' reading of *Von Hannover* 'would herald a revolution in Britain's journalistic culture'.[56] Applying this understanding of the law he held that the claim by J.K. Rowling's son failed.[57]

Where the only way in which a defendant can obtain such a photograph is by taking it surreptitiously this tends to emphasise that the person was not accepting such a degree of access.[58] But the fact that a photograph was taken surreptitiously is not *sufficient* to establish that it depicts something private. For instance, the photograph of David Murray which Patten J held to be innocuous was taken surreptitiously.

What if a photograph is taken of someone in a private place? Clearly such photographs will often contain information that a reasonable person might want to maintain control over and will thus infringe the subject's reasonable expectation of privacy. But, in the *Campbell* case Lord Hoffmann went further than the other Lords and stated that 'the publication of a photograph taken by intrusion into a private place (for example, by a long distance lens) may in itself be [an infringement of the privacy of personal information], even if there is nothing embarrassing about the picture itself'.[59] No doubt most people would describe being spied on in a private place with a long-distance lens as an invasion of privacy regardless of whether the spy obtained and then published any information that a reasonable person would want to maintain control over. But this demonstrates that the essence of such a violation is *not* the *publication* of the information obtained. Thus we think that Lord Hoffmann's example involves a different form of invasion of privacy from *wrongful disclosure of private information* and the law would be more coherent if it treated it separately.[60] For the time being, however, so long as English courts continue to insist that the protection of privacy is linked to their capacity to *develop* the wrong of breach of confidence, it is likely that judges will be tempted to 'shoe-horn' cases involving different forms of invasion of privacy into the tort of *wrongful disclosure of private information*.

Sometimes a photograph may communicate information which is not contained in the image itself. For instance, in the *Campbell* case Baroness Hale thought that the photograph of Naomi Campbell outside the building where a Narcotics Anonymous meeting took place suggested that Naomi Campbell was being followed or betrayed.[61] However, although such a photograph might have communicated this to Naomi Campbell, and perhaps also to a shrewd tabloid reader, it is doubtful whether *this* was *private information* about Naomi Campbell which should have been withheld from the public.[62]

[55] Ibid., at [68].
[56] Ibid., at [47], citing Tugendhat & Christie 2006, para 6.52.
[57] A similar claim, involving a photograph of the 18-month-old twins of a television personality was rejected by the New Zealand court of Appeal: *Hosking v Runting* [2005] 1 NZLR 1.
[58] In *Campbell*, Lord Hope attached importance (at [121] and [123]) to the fact that the relevant photograph was obtained covertly.
[59] *Campbell*, at [76].
[60] We think that the example involves invasion of privacy *by intrusion*. See below, pp. 338–9.
[61] *Campbell*, at [155].
[62] No doubt in *some* contexts the fact that a person was being betrayed or followed might be private information that a reasonable person would not want others to know about.

Iniquity

The wrong of breach of confidence took the view that there could be no protection for 'iniquity'.[63] But it seems that a claimant can assert a reasonable expectation as to the privacy of *some* information relating to 'iniquitous behaviour', and that consequently a defendant will have to establish a justification for publishing such information. In the *Campbell* case, Lord Hoffmann said that 'use of drugs' was a matter in respect of which 'even a public figure would ordinarily be entitled to privacy'.[64] And in *CC* v *AB*,[65] Eady J concluded that there was no general rule that an adulterer could not obtain an injunction to restrain the publication of matters relating to his adulterous relationship. By contrast, in *X* v *Y* Mummery LJ held that a person's sexual activity in a transport café lavatory 'did not take place in his private life nor was it within the scope of application of the right to respect for it'[66] apparently because it amounted to a criminal offence.

Even where a person's behaviour is so iniquitous that he could have no *immediate* expectation of privacy with regard to it the experience of other jurisdictions warns against the stark position that such a person can never *develop* a right to control *further* publication of details of his behaviour. With the passage of time a person's legitimate interest in maintaining the benefit of successful rehabilitation may come to outweigh any possible public benefit to be gained by further publication.

Companies

Should a company be able to sue for invasion of privacy if, for instance, information about its private operations is published? The simplest way of answering this question would be to say 'yes' – tort law applies the same rules to claimants whether they are human beings or artificial legal persons.[67] But if we look deeper then it seems that many of the reasons for creating a privacy tort, such as protecting human dignity and facilitating love, friendship and community, do not apply to artificial legal persons.

In *R* v *Broadcasting Standards Commission, ex p BBC*[68] the Court of Appeal held that the Commission was entitled to uphold a complaint by Dixons (a company) that the BBC had infringed its privacy unjustifiably by carrying out covert filming in one of its stores. Lord Woolf MR pointed out that companies could engage in private activities which should be protected from unwarranted intrusion, such as board meetings. But both he and Hale LJ drew attention to the fact that Article 8 of the ECHR did not refer to a 'right to privacy' in general but only to a 'right to respect for his private and family life, his home and correspondence'. Thus the fact that Dixons succeeded in this case may not be a good guide to the scope of the new tort because its development has been strongly tied to Article 8.

Extending the new tort to protect companies would also be inconsistent with the opinion of three members of the High Court of Australia who expressly held in *Australian Broadcasting Corporation* v *Lenah Game Meats* that Australia's emergent tort of invasion of

[63] *Gartside* v *Outram* (1857) 26 LJ Ch 113.

[64] *Campbell*, at [36].

[65] [2006] EWHC 3083 (QB), at [30].

[66] [2004] ICR 1634, at [53]. See also [69]–[71] (per Dyson LJ). Brooke LJ dissented on this point.

[67] The wrong of breach of confidence, which the courts have purportedly developed in order to establish the tort of misuse of private information, clearly protects the interests of companies in preserving their industrial secrets and the like.

[68] [2001] QB 885.

privacy was for 'the benefit of natural, not artificial, persons'.[69] Similarly, companies are not protected under the United States Rest 2d, Torts, §652I: 'an action for invasion of privacy can be maintained only by a *living* individual whose privacy is invaded.'[70] By contrast, a rival textbook has argued that companies should be able to sue for invasions of privacy because they can sue for libel and slander, and allowing them to sue for invasions of privacy will prevent them from seeking to distort other torts in order to prevent unwanted publications about their private activities.[71] A further reason for allowing companies to sue may be that their interests in keeping information from being published will often be hard to separate from the privacy interests of their employees and clients. For instance, in *Green Corns Ltd* v *Claverley Group Ltd*[72] a claimant company sought to prevent the defendant from publishing the addresses of properties being used by the claimant company to house disturbed children and their carers and the weight of the privacy claim was treated as an aggregation of the weight of the claims that could have been brought by the company, the children and the carers.

Measuring the importance of protecting privacy

The importance of protecting particular private information from publication can be measured by reflecting on the reasons which are commonly given for such protection: to protect human dignity[73] and personality,[74] and to facilitate the formation of *special* relationships such as love, friendship and community.[75] Generally, the significance of an affront to dignity and personality can be measured by considering how *intimate* the information was. Similarly, it can be assessed how far *control* over the distribution of such information is important in forming particular *special relationships*. An alternative approach, which can be used alongside the first, ranks the importance of privacy interests by estimating the *intensity of the offence* that a reasonable person in the claimant's position might be expected to suffer on the publication of such information. A further relevant factor in measuring the importance of preventing the publication of particular material is the likelihood that the publication will cause *other significant harm* to the claimant beyond distress. In the *Campbell* case the majority in the House of Lords attached particular weight to the fact that publication of the details of Naomi Campbell's treatment might cause *harm* by disrupting her treatment.[76]

[69] (2001) 208 CLR 199, at [132].

[70] American Law Institute (1965), emphasis added. It seems that the protection offered by Art 8 of the ECHR does *not* end with an individual's death: see *Plon* v *France* (58148/00), 18 May 2004, unreported.

[71] Markesinis, Johnston & Deakin 2003, 699. Cf. the contrary view which appears in the most recent edition: M&D, 823.

[72] [2005] EWHC 958 (QB), at [51]–[52].

[73] See, for example, Bloustein 1964, 1003, 'The man who is compelled to live every minute of his life among others and whose every need and thought, desire, fancy or gratification is subject to public scrutiny, has been deprived of his individuality and human dignity.'

[74] *Von Hannover* v *Germany* (2005) 40 EHRR 1, at [50]: 'the guarantee afforded by Article 8 of the Convention is primarily intended to ensure the development, without outside interference, of the personality of each individual in his relations with other human beings.'

[75] See, for example, Fried 1968; also Feldman 1997.

[76] *Campbell*, at [98] and [119] (per Lord Hope), [130] and [165] (per Baroness Hale), [169] (per Lord Carswell).

Freedom of expression

What counts as expression?

Although it is *logical* to ask whether the defendant's disclosure of the information amounted to 'expression' within the ambit of Article 10 we might expect it to be rare for the answer to be 'no'. One situation where the defendant's behaviour may not count as 'expression' is where the defendant unintentionally permits C to obtain the information, for instance by forgetfully leaving B's medical records on a train. But this example raises the awkward question of what is meant by 'disclosure' in the context of the new tort. Because the cases considered so far in England have all involved deliberate publication the courts have not provided any guidance on whether the tort covers accidental or careless disclosures.[77]

Measuring the importance of preserving freedom of expression

The courts have provided more guidance on how to measure the importance of not restricting expression. In the *Campbell* case Baroness Hale said:

> There are undoubtedly different types of speech, just as there are different types of private information, some of which are more deserving of protection in a democratic society than others. Top of the list is political speech. The free exchange of information and ideas on matters relevant to the organisation of the economic, social and political life of the country is crucial to any democracy. ... This includes revealing information about public figures, especially those in elective office, which would otherwise be private but is relevant to their participation in public life. Intellectual and educational speech and expression are also important in a democracy, not least because they enable the development of the individuals' potential to play a full part in society and in our democratic life. Artistic speech and expression is important for similar reasons, in fostering both individual originality and creativity and the free-thinking and dynamic society we so much value.[78]

Expression which is not political, intellectual, educational or artistic, such as mere gossip, is still protected to an extent, because it may play an important role in preserving social networks and in making newspapers financially viable. But it will be far easier to justify a restriction on mere gossip[79] to protect privacy than a restriction on political debate.

Public interest

A potentially decisive factor in measuring the importance of preserving free expression is whether it is in the public interest for the information to be disclosed to the people to whom the defendant disclosed it. 'Public interest' is obviously a concept which cannot be

[77] A parallel could be drawn with the legal rules on what counts as 'publication' for the purposes of the torts of libel and slander (above, pp. 284–6). But these rules might be thought only to be tolerable from a free expression perspective because of the existence of the special statutory defence for 'innocent dissemination' and the 'offer to make amends' procedure (see below, pp. 306–8), and these provisions do not extend to liability for invasion of privacy.

[78] *Campbell*, at [148].

[79] In *Von Hannover* v *Germany* (2005) 40 EHRR 1, the European Court of Human Rights treated (at [65]) the preservation of freedom to publish photographs of Princess Caroline of Monaco's daily activities as relatively unimportant when 'the sole purpose was to satisfy the curiosity of a particular readership regarding the details of the applicant's private life, [and the photographs] cannot be deemed to contribute to any debate of general interest to society despite the applicant being known to the public'.

defined with any precision. In *A* v *B* the Court of Appeal suggested that 'in the majority of situations whether the public interest is involved or not will be obvious' and that where it is not obvious the factor is 'unlikely to be decisive'.[80] Perhaps in time courts will reach predictable decisions on what private information it is in the public interest to publish by drawing analogies with previous cases. But until a body of cases has been decided it may be helpful to quote the Press Complaints Commission's Code of Practice which states that the 'public interest includes: (i) Detecting or exposing crime or a serious misdemeanour. (ii) Protecting health and safety. (iii) Preventing the public from being misled by some statement or action of an individual or organisation.' It may also be worth drawing attention to some of the old breach of confidence cases which held that it could be in the public interest to publish information: about the dangerous teachings of a cult,[81] casting doubt on the safety of criminal convictions,[82] and to assist in the prevention of crime.[83]

Public figures

In *A* v *B* Lord Woolf CJ suggested that public figures must accept a greater degree of disclosure of information than ordinary individuals even when that disclosure is not justified by the public interest:

> because of his public position [a public figure] must expect and accept that his actions will be more closely scrutinised by the media. . . . Whether you have courted publicity or not you may be a legitimate subject of public attention. If you have courted public attention then you have less ground to object to the intrusion which follows. In many of these situations it would be overstating the position to say that there is a public interest in the information being published. It would be more accurate to say that the public have an understandable and so a legitimate interest in being told the information.[84]

In the *Campbell* case the Court of Appeal made it clear that Lord Woolf CJ was not intending to say that once *a person* was identified as a legitimate subject of public attention then *any information of any type* about that person could be published. Rather, the cases suggest that the public will have 'an understandable and so legitimate interest' where: (*a*) the information contradicts or clarifies information that C has published about the same aspect of his life; or (*b*) C is 'a role model whose conduct could well be emulated by others'.

With regard to (*a*), in *A* v *B* Lord Woolf CJ stated that, 'where a public figure chooses to make untrue pronouncements about his or her private life, the press will normally be entitled to put the record straight'.[85] This rule seems to be justified partly by the public interest in preventing the public from being misled, but also partly by the idea that if a person makes pronouncements about a particular aspect of his private life then it is fair to treat him as having waived his privacy to some extent. The second part of this explanation is important because it clarifies why courts do not seem to measure the benefit that the public might gain from avoiding being misled about some aspect of a celebrity's private life.

[80] [2003] QB 195, at [11](viii).
[81] *Hubbard* v *Vosper* [1972] 2 QB 84.
[82] *Lion Laboratories* v *Evans* [1985] QB 526.
[83] *Hellewell* v *Chief Constable of Derbyshire* [1995] 1 WLR 804.
[84] [2003] QB 195, at [11](xii).
[85] Ibid., at [43]. See also *Campbell*, at [58] (per Lord Hoffmann).

But with regard to (*b*), there are two grounds for doubting the fairness of a rule which tips the balance against 'role models' even in circumstances where the defendant cannot establish that the public interest will be advanced by publication of the information. First, this seems harsh when it is applied to persons who have never *projected* themselves as positive 'role models' for others. In *A* v *B* Lord Woolf CJ suggested that *all* footballers were 'role models' whether they liked this or not. Perhaps where a person has *chosen* to enter a particular sphere of life where he might be treated as a 'role model', for instance by becoming a vicar or a teacher, he can be fairly taken to have consented to information about particular aspects of his life being published. But where a person has become a 'role model' unintentionally, for instance by saving a drowning dog or making a scientific discovery, the consequences for his privacy seem harder to justify.[86]

The second ground for doubt is that the logic behind the rule is opaque: If 'role models' can influence young people then why should the law make it easier for the public to learn about their private misdeeds? In the *Campbell* case the Court of Appeal stated that it did 'not see why it should necessarily be in the public interest that an individual who has been adopted as a role model, without seeking this distinction, should be demonstrated to have feet of clay'.[87] The suggestion that publishing details of Gary Flitcroft's sex life or Naomi Campbell's drug addiction is useful in order to prevent members of the public being harmed by inappropriate 'role models' is unconvincing.[88] A more plausible explanation of the sentiment that leads (some) people to think that such publications are fair seems to be that where individuals are admired for their *distinctive* talents and gifts it is fair for the ways in which they are *undistinguished* to be revealed. The ordinary recipient of such information values it because it reassures him that neither Gary Flitcroft nor Naomi Campbell is such a *superior* being after all, rather than because it protects him against being unduly influenced by the examples they set. No doubt the ordinary recipient's reaction is as *natural* as other aspects of *envy*, but we are not convinced that 'the public have an understandable and so legitimate interest' in the satiation of this *jealous* impulse.

[86] The German courts have similarly argued that the public has a legitimate interest in being allowed to judge whether the personal behaviour of a 'figure of contemporary society *par excellence*' (*absolute Person der Zeitgeschichte*), the sort of person who might be treated as an idol or role model, convincingly tallies with his behaviour during official engagements. However, the European Court of Human Rights held in *Von Hannover* v *Germany* (2005) 40 EHRR 1, that the application of this doctrine to Princess Caroline of Monaco left her with insufficient protection for her right to privacy when 'the interest of the general public and the press is based solely on her membership of a reigning family whereas she herself does not exercise any official functions' (at [72]). The Court stated, at [77], that 'the public does not have a legitimate interest in knowing where the applicant is and how she behaves generally in her private life even if she appears in places that cannot always be described as secluded and despite the fact that she is well known to the public'.

[87] [2003] QB 633, at [41]. See also *Campbell*, at [151] (per Baroness Hale).

[88] Lord Justice Stephen Sedley was particularly cutting about this line of reasoning in his Blackstone Lecture 'Sex, Lies and Video-surveillance', 13.6.06: 'As for the customary claim, which the court seems to have accepted, that the revelations served the high purpose of exposing the flaws in a young persons' role model, one has to wonder what our moral custodians imagine goes on in young people's minds. Possibly – just possibly – a certain number of boys want to grow up playing football like Garry Flitcroft. Is the revelation in the family's Sunday paper that he has been sleeping with a lap dancer going to make them switch to, let us say, Wayne Rooney as their preferred role model? Or is it conceivably going to suggest to them that the great thing about being a professional footballer, or any other kind of media star, is that you can sleep with just about anyone?'

Striking the balance between the protection of privacy and freedom of expression

Suppose that A has disclosed to C information about B that is sufficiently private *potentially* to attract the protection of the tort considered here. How will the courts strike the balance between the desire, on the one hand, to protect B's privacy and the desire, on the other hand, not to limit disproportionately A's freedom of expression? It is hard to give any useful *general* guidance on this issue. However, two points can be made.

(1) *The dual perspective approach.* In deciding which right is to prevail in this case – A's right to freedom of expression or B's right to privacy – a court must take account of the fact that *neither* right should be subjected to a disproportionate restriction. So if the court is considering making A liable – thus restricting A's right of freedom of expression in order to protect B's privacy – it must ask if the restriction it is considering imposing on A's right to freedom of expression is rational, fair, not arbitrary and the minimum restriction necessary to protect B's right to privacy. In order to decide whether this is the case it will often be helpful for the court *also* to consider the case from the converse perspective; that is, to consider: If B's privacy is *denied* protection in order to protect A's right to freedom of expression, will this restriction on the protection of B's privacy be rational, fair, not arbitrary and the minimum restriction necessary to protect A's right to freedom of expression? The reason for this is that since one right must prevail, and neither right should be subject to any disproportionate restriction, the court will *only* be able to hold A *liable* if doing so amounts to a proportionate restriction on A's right to freedom of expression in order to protect B's privacy; while, at the same time, it will *only* be able to hold that A is *not* liable if turning down B's claim amounts to a proportionate limit on the protection of B's privacy in order to protect A's right to freedom of expression. Adopting a dual perspective approach allows the court to compare the *relative merits* of these two possible conclusions.[89]

(2) *Practical reality.* In striking a balance between protecting people's privacy and people's rights to freedom of expression, the courts must be careful to ensure that they are not devising standards which real journalists cannot be reasonably expected to meet. For instance, a real journalist cannot be expected to produce a justification for every choice of phrasing or supporting detail. In the *Campbell* case all of their Lordships recognised 'the importance of allowing a proper degree of journalistic margin to the press to deal with a legitimate story in its own way, without imposing unnecessary shackles on its freedom to publish detail and photographs which add colour and conviction'.[90] Thus a judge setting the balance must be careful not to hold a defendant liable merely because he or she would have presented the story in a different way, and must take account of the advantages which come with detailed argument and hindsight.

Having made these points, let's consider two concrete examples so as to get a better 'feel' for how the courts are likely to strike a balance between people's rights to freedom of expression and people's interests in having their privacy protected.

[89] A summary of the dual perspective approach is set out by Baroness Hale in *Campbell*, at [141], and it also seems to have been the approach used by Lord Hope, at [105], with the agreement of Lord Carswell, at [167]. Some subsequent cases have used the label 'parallel analysis' to refer to the same approach.

[90] Ibid., at [169] (per Lord Carswell). Lord Nicholls and Lord Hoffmann thought that this factor was decisive in favour of the defendants, but the majority disagreed.

(1) *The romantic politician.* Lara, a solicitor employed by Blandshire County Council, reveals to the *Daily Clarion* that she began a love affair with John, the Council leader, shortly before being appointed to her post. The *Daily Clarion* publishes this information in an article which also recounts Lara's recollections of John's performance as a lover.[91]

In this case, unless the relationship was intended to be casual and transitory, John is likely to be able to establish that the details of his affair with Lara are sufficiently private to qualify for potential protection. Moreover, regardless of the nature of the relationship, intimate information about his physical appearance and behaviour when love-making will be sufficiently private. At the same time the *Daily Clarion* will be able to establish that its publication is a form of 'expression'. Given this, whether John can sue the *Daily Clarion* or not will turn on what balance the court strikes between John's interest in having his privacy protected on the one hand and the *Daily Clarion*'s right to freedom of expression on the other.

Looking at the importance of protecting John's right to privacy first, John will point to the value of preserving the sanctity and security of intimate relationships of the kind he had with Lara, and to the value of protecting him from the loss of dignity and humiliation likely to be caused by the revelation of intimate information about his physical appearance and behaviour when love-making. John may seek to identify *other* damage that will be caused to him by publication, such as damage to his marriage.[92]

Turning now to the importance of protecting the *Daily Clarion*'s freedom of expression in this case, the *Daily Clarion* might argue that it is in the public interest to reveal information suggesting that inappropriate factors influenced a public appointment. This, however, raises the difficulty that it would be defamatory for the *Daily Clarion* to make this suggestion directly and to avoid liability for libel the newspaper would probably have to rely on the defence of justification or qualified privilege. In this context it is worth noting that to rely on the form of qualified privilege that attaches to publications relating to matters of public concern the newspaper would have to establish that it acted responsibly in going ahead and publishing the article when it did and in the form that it did.[93] Thus if the *Daily Clarion* seeks to rely on the public interest in revealing information which might lead readers to draw a defamatory inference it is *arguable* that the newspaper ought to demonstrate that it acted responsibly in not seeking further information as to whether such an inference was justified.

As an additional or alternative argument, the *Daily Clarion* may suggest that the moral integrity of an elected politician, a public figure, is a subject of legitimate interest to the public, and that information about John's extra-marital affair is relevant to his moral integrity. It must be noted, however, that this argument is unlikely to provide much support for publishing Lara's recollections of John's performance as a lover.

On balance, it seems that a court may regard treating the *whole* story as actionable as too great a restriction on the *Daily Clarion*'s freedom of expression and conclude that John

91 This example is based on one suggested by Lord Hoffmann in *Campbell*, at [60].

92 In *A* v *B* [2003] QB 195, at [43](v), Lord Woolf CJ instructed courts not to speculate as to whether it would be in a wife's interest to be kept unaware of the details of a husband's affair. But in *CC* v *AB* [2006] EWHC 3083 (QB), a claimant seeking to prevent a defendant from publishing that the claimant had been involved in an adulterous relationship with the defendant's wife was permitted to advance his case by pointing to the likely effect of general publication on his own wife and children (at [42]–[47]) *and* on the privacy rights of the defendant's wife (at [32]).

93 See above pp. 301–3, discussing *Reynolds* v *Times Newspapers Ltd* [2001] 2 AC 127.

must accept some invasion of his privacy in the interests of free expression because he is a public figure. But the court may also regard a duty not to publish Lara's recollections of John's performance as a lover as a proportionate limit on the *Daily Clarion*'s freedom of expression (and that of its readers) in the interests of protecting John's privacy.[94] In reaching this conclusion, the court will want to check that a reasonable newspaper editor can be expected to draw the line between the essential story which it should be free to publish and the salacious supporting details which invade John's privacy to an unacceptable extent.

(2) *The drunken student.* Sarah, a student, gets so drunk celebrating the end of her exams that she collapses in the street and has to be treated by paramedics. The incident is recorded by CCTV cameras belonging to Instown University, and the University later uses the images in a video it shows to students to warn them about the dangers of binge drinking.

Here, assuming that the case is argued as one of wrongful disclosure of private information,[95] Sarah will have to establish that the images contain information about her that a reasonable person would want to retain control over. If she is recognisable then it is likely that the images will convey what she looked like during a distressing and humiliating episode which is something that a reasonable person would want to retain control over, at least to the extent of preventing a permanent record of it being released to a wide audience. However, her willingness to expose this information about herself to those present in a public street will prevent her from claiming that her interest in maintaining control over the information is very weighty.

From the point of view of expression Instown University may seek to argue that the violation of Sarah's privacy is proportionate to the public interest in expressing an important social message in a graphic and effective manner. The court will want to investigate, however, whether it was *necessary* to violate Sarah's privacy in order to express this message effectively, or whether it was merely *convenient* to do so. In this context it will consider whether the same scene could have been equally well-presented using actors or by disguising Sarah's identity.[96] On balance it seems unlikely that Instown University will be able to justify using the images.

[94] This seems to have been the conclusion envisaged by Lord Hoffmann.

[95] If Instown University is a public authority within the Human Rights Act 1998 Sarah could claim under that statute and thereby seek to circumvent the limits on the new tort. In this example we assume that it is a *private* institution.

[96] In *Peck* v *United Kingdom* (2003) 13 BHRC 669, the European Court of Human Rights held that a local authority's disclosure to the media of CCTV footage showing the applicant in a public place with a large knife in order to increase the effectiveness of a new CCTV system 'pursued the legitimate aim of public safety, the prevention of disorder and crime and the protection of the rights of others' (at [67]), but interfered with the applicant's privacy to a disproportionate extent because no attempt was made to secure his consent and too little was done to ensure that his identity was properly masked (at [85] and [87]). Similarly, in *T* v *BBC* [2007] EWHC 1683 (QB), while Eady J recognised that there was a genuine public interest in the subject of adoption and that the BBC's proposed documentary intended to deal with the subject in a serious and informative way, he doubted whether it was necessary to *identify* T, a vulnerable young adult, when portraying her final meeting with her child.

The defendant's knowledge

Where a claim is brought against a publisher who has obtained the information *indirectly* the question may arise whether the publisher *knew or ought to have known* that the material it was publishing violated the subject's reasonable expectation of privacy.[97] Thus where A provides information about B to C, a newspaper, and C publishes this information, it will be C's knowledge which is in issue if B sues C.[98]

It seems, however, that the courts may define what a *media defendant* 'ought to know' so widely that the requirement will be rendered nugatory. In the *Campbell* case, the Court of Appeal held that 'the media can fairly be expected to identify confidential information about an individual's private life which, absent good reason, it will be offensive to publish'.[99] This suggests that a *professional* publisher will not be able to defend itself by relying on a misunderstanding as to what sorts of information the law potentially protects. But the court did not expressly consider the difficult situations which might arise where a defendant is misled as to the nature of the relationship between A and B or the circumstances in which a photograph was obtained.

The Court of Appeal in the *Campbell* case also said that, 'the media must accept responsibility for the decision that, in the particular circumstances, publication of the material in question is justifiable in the public interest',[100] meaning that a *professional* publisher cannot avoid liability by establishing an honest belief that publication was justifiable. But again, the court did not consider more difficult situations involving defendants who are understandably unfamiliar with the law or arguments relying on justifications other than the public interest, for instance a defendant's mistaken belief that the claimant had consented to the publication.

Evaluation of the new tort

Many torts are based on duties which reflect a balancing of the competing interests of potential claimants and defendants in the light of concerns about what sorts of distinctions courts can cope with in practice. But the new tort of wrongful disclosure of private information is unusual in that it requires the court to carry out this balancing process in every case. A major advantage of this structure is that it gives the tort the flexibility to respond to new factors that may be raised in future cases, and to new combinations of factors which may not have been anticipated. A major disadvantage, however, is that, at least until a significant number of cases have been decided, it will be difficult to predict what the law demands in borderline cases. In the light of this disadvantage it might have been preferable for Parliament to have produced detailed legislation on the protection of privacy. But in the light of Parliament's apparent unwillingness to undertake this task, and its apparent willingness at the time of passing the Human Rights Act 1998 for the courts to take it on, it is difficult to criticise the courts for usurping the legislative role. That said, having taken on the task the courts can be criticised for: (*a*) having built the new tort around the

[97] *Campbell*, at [85] (per Lord Hope), [134] (per Baroness Hale).
[98] Of course, if B only sues A then C's knowledge will be irrelevant.
[99] *Campbell* v *MGN Ltd* [2003] QB 633, at [68].
[100] Ibid.

unhelpfully circular concept of 'reasonable expectation of privacy'; (*b*) having provided no guidance on whether there will be liability for careless and accidental disclosures; (*c*) having developed a doctrine of 'legitimate interest in the behaviour of public figures' which seems to condone public pleasure at seeing the mighty humbled; (*d*) having given guidance on what must be shown as to the defendant's state of mind which is either inexplicably harsher than the law of libel or incomplete.

CASES NOT INVOLVING THE WRONGFUL DISCLOSURE OF PRIVATE INFORMATION

We have already mentioned that some aspects of privacy may be protected by torts dealt with elsewhere in the book (for instance, by the torts of trespass to land, private nuisance, defamation, and malicious falsehood). But these and the new tort discussed above do not between them provide comprehensive protection for privacy. For instance, most people would accept that being compelled to undress in front of a prison officer involves a violation of privacy, but the claimants in *Wainwright* v *Home Office*[101] were unable to establish that this behaviour fell within the ambit of any tort. Given that the House of Lords in the *Campbell* case confirmed their previous refusal in the *Wainwright* case to develop an 'over-arching, all-embracing cause of action for "invasion of privacy"',[102] it is worth asking whether they are likely to develop any further *limited* torts to protect against other *specific* forms of invasion of privacy.

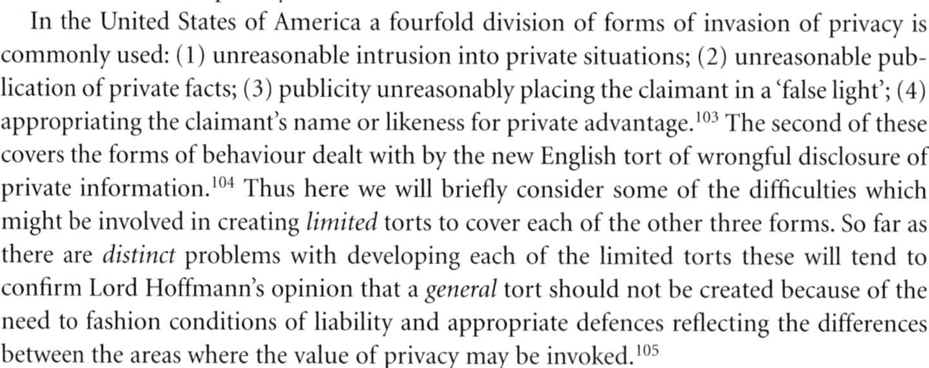

In the United States of America a fourfold division of forms of invasion of privacy is commonly used: (1) unreasonable intrusion into private situations; (2) unreasonable publication of private facts; (3) publicity unreasonably placing the claimant in a 'false light'; (4) appropriating the claimant's name or likeness for private advantage.[103] The second of these covers the forms of behaviour dealt with by the new English tort of wrongful disclosure of private information.[104] Thus here we will briefly consider some of the difficulties which might be involved in creating *limited* torts to cover each of the other three forms. So far as there are *distinct* problems with developing each of the limited torts these will tend to confirm Lord Hoffmann's opinion that a *general* tort should not be created because of the need to fashion conditions of liability and appropriate defences reflecting the differences between the areas where the value of privacy may be invoked.[105]

Unreasonable intrusion

A tort covering this form of invasion would extend over behaviour such as watching a stranger giving birth, compelling a person to remove his clothes in front of you, or taking a photograph of a person in a private place using a long-distance lens. The essence of this form of invasion of privacy is that the way in which the defendant behaves enables him to

[101] [2004] 2 AC 406 (discussed above, pp. 110–12).
[102] *Campbell*, at [11] (per Lord Nicholls).
[103] See, for instance, Prosser 1960; Rest 2d, Torts § 652A.
[104] Though as we have seen, above p. 328, some forms of behaviour which *properly* belong within one of the other headings are likely, for the time being, to be 'shoehorned' into the new English tort.
[105] *Wainwright* v *Home Office* [2004] 2 AC 406, at [31]–[33].

gather information about the claimant in violation of the claimant's asserted right to control when, how and to what extent such information is available to others. This can be usefully contrasted with the new tort of wrongful disclosure of private information where the essence is the defendant's *publication* of information about the claimant in violation of the claimant's asserted right to control when, how and to what extent such information is available to others.

It is at least arguable that if the claimant's right to control such information is to be protected at all then it ought to be protected against both unacceptable methods of *gathering* information and unacceptable *publication* of what has been gathered. In practice, however, it is easier to design liability rules dealing with *publication*. This is because rules relating to *publication* apply at a stage when we know what the information is and can measure the importance of it being kept private and of it being available to the public. By contrast, rules regulating methods of *gathering* information apply *before* we know what the defendant might discover by strip-searching the claimant or monitoring him in the street using a CCTV camera. Of course, it would not be impossible for the English courts to adapt the balancing approach at the core of the new wrongful disclosure tort in order to regulate intrusions. Thus the courts might ask if the likelihood of the defendant obtaining information by means of a particular gathering technique which it would be in the public interest to have available *outweighed* the extent to which use of such a technique would reduce the claimant's control over information which he might have a reasonable interest in maintaining control over. The outcome of such a balancing might be straightforward in many cases, in particular where the defendant was gathering information merely to satisfy prurient curiosity.[106] But there would also be controversial cases involving, for instance, the use of covert filming in investigating possible insurance fraud[107] and the use of 'ambush' interviews in journalism.

We noted above that in the *Campbell* case Lord Hoffmann seemed willing to develop a tort to cover the *publication* of a photograph taken of a person in a private place by using a long-distance lens even if the photograph contained no essentially private information.[108] It seems to us, however, that the essence of the wrong in such a case is the *intrusion* caused by *taking the photograph* and we will not be surprised if the courts develop a limited balancing-based tort to deal with such intrusions during the next decade.[109]

106 An example of a case which might be covered is provided by *Kaye* v *Robertson* [1991] FSR 62, where agents of the defendants entered a hospital room where the claimant, an actor, was recovering from brain surgery, took photographs, and purported to conduct an interview.

107 See *Jones* v *University of Warwick* [2003] 1 WLR 954, at [29], where the Court of Appeal apparently held that such filming violated Art 8.

108 *Campbell*, at [76].

109 Article 8 clearly entitles people to protection against *intrusions* into their privacy, and, as we have seen, the European Court of Human Rights has held that the article imposes a positive obligation on states which *may* require 'the adoption of measures designed to secure respect for private life even in the sphere of the relations of individuals between themselves' (see, e.g., *Von Hannover* v *Germany* (2005) 40 EHRR 1, at [57]). One way in which the United Kingdom could fulfil this obligation would be for the *courts* to create a new tort making unreasonable *intrusions* actionable.

False light

A tort covering this form of invasion would extend over behaviour such as publishing the false information that the claimant was romantically involved with a celebrity or a false version of a dramatic event involving the claimant. Clearly, if a newspaper published the information that Mary, a single woman, was dating Prince William, a single man, this would usually not be defamatory of Mary even if it was wholly false.[110] It would be likely, however, to subject Mary to a significant degree of unwanted public attention and it is easy to see why people might want to be protected from such attention. But the issue whether a tortious duty should be created to confer such protection raises two subsidiary questions. First, whether the degree of annoyance likely to be suffered by someone subjected to such attention is sufficiently significant to warrant such a step, given that there cannot be a duty to avoid all potentially annoying forms of conduct.[111] Secondly, whether the existence of such a duty might unduly restrict the activities of those who want to retell recent events in a dramatically engaging manner, such as the authors of docudramas and unauthorised biographies. It would certainly be a burden on modern historians and unauthorised biographers if they could be liable for non-defamatory factual errors, and we think that the complexity of the current law of libel – a product of both complex case law and detailed statutes – provides a good reason why courts should be cautious about presuming that they have the capacity to develop a new privacy tort in this area.

Appropriation of personality

A tort covering this form of invasion would extend over behaviour such as using a photograph of a person in an advertisement without his consent. For instance, if an airline published an advertisement for its flights using the picture of a person recently involved in a criminal case with the slogan 'for a quick getaway fly with our airline'[112] then the person depicted might be able to claim. Similarly, this tort might cover a case where a photograph of a teenager taken in a public place without obtaining her consent was used to illustrate a magazine article.[113] From a privacy perspective the utility of the tort is that it gives a person control over *how* her image and identity is used, and prevents that image and identity being treated as a mere tool by others. In practice, however, such a tort can play an important role in helping to preserve for celebrities the rewards they can gain by carefully licensing their images and identities for use in advertising.[114]

One difficulty with creating a tort to cover this form of invasion of privacy would be defining the scope of a claimant's protected interest. Where a photograph of the claimant

[110] It might be defamatory in unusual circumstances: for instance, if Mary was a nun.

[111] Such a duty would be unsatisfactory because it would impinge on so many aspects of ordinary social life. It would be extraordinarily ironic if many everyday encounters became subject to legal regulation in the interests of protecting *privacy*!

[112] EasyJet issued similar advertisements during 2003.

[113] *Aubry* v *Editions Vice-Versa Inc* [1998] 1 SCR 591.

[114] The extension of the tort of passing off in *Irvine* v *Talksport Ltd* [2002] 1 WLR 2355 (discussed below, p. 462) will protect the interest of a celebrity who has acquired a valuable reputation or goodwill from misrepresentations which enable a defendant to make use of or take advantage of that reputation (at [38], per Laddie J). The tort of passing off will not, however, protect an unknown teenager like the claimant in the *Aubry* case, above, and may not protect a claimant who has attained *notoriety*.

is used the matter is straightforward, but more difficult cases might involve use of a distinctive catchphrase, mannerism or vocal characteristic.[115] It might be possible to get round this problem by defining the tort so that it covered only *intentional* appropriation, but this would not avoid all difficulties.[116] A further difficulty would be defining the situations where use of a person's image without consent is legitimate. For instance, photographs are commonly used without the consent of those depicted to illustrate legitimate news stories, in protest and in satire.[117] In Germany a person's image is protected and in an important decision the Bundesgerichtshof had to determine when it was permissible for Greenpeace to use the name and picture of the president of a chemical company on a campaign poster.[118] No doubt English courts could solve similar disputes, but it is important to note that extending tort law to cover this form of invasion of privacy would be likely to involve a move away from the traditional preference for clear legal duties in commercial settings.[119]

In *Douglas* v *Hello! Ltd (No. 3)*[120] a majority of the House of Lords held that a private event, such as a wedding in a hotel, could be organised so that the information that would be disclosed by a *photographic* image of the event became a commercial secret, which could be protected by the wrong of breach of confidence. This may provide a person with some degree of control over exploitation of images of *what they looked like during such an event.* But the duty not to publish such confidential information is, naturally, far narrower than a *general* duty not to appropriate another's image would be.

Visit **http://www.mylawchamber.co.uk/mcbride** to access updates on recent cases, as well as model answers and tips for answering tort problem questions.

Use **Case Navigator** to read in full the key case referenced in this chapter:

- **Wainwright *v* Home Office**

[115] Cases from the United States have involved the use of a television presenter's catchphrase to market a portable toilet (*Carson* v *Here's Johnny Portable Toilets Inc.*, 698 F 2d 831 (1983)), the use of a singer who sounded like Bette Midler to advertise cars (*Midler* v *Ford Motor Co.* 849 F 2d 460 (1988)), and the use of a robot dressed like a gameshow hostess to advertise videorecorders (*White* v *Samsung Electronics America Inc.*, 971 F 2d 1395 (1992)).

[116] For instance, if the defendant argued that he intended to invoke a *generic* athlete of the 1970s and the claimant argued that his individual image was appropriated.

[117] The short phrase 'for private advantage' used in the summary of the tort clearly does not go very far towards answering the difficult issues raised, since newspapers and satirists generally seek to make a profit.

[118] BGH, 12 October 1993, NJW 1994, 124 (Federal Court of Justice, Germany).

[119] In *Von Hannover* v *Germany* (2005) 40 EHRR 1, the European Court of Human Rights held (at [72]) that states have undertaken a 'positive obligation under the Convention to protect private life *and the right to control the use of one's image*' (emphasis added). See also [57]. One way in which the United Kingdom could fulfil this obligation would be for the *courts* to create a new tort making appropriation of personality actionable.

[120] [2007] 2 WLR 920, HL (heard alongside *OBG Ltd* v *Allan*).

16 Conversion

MODES OF CONVERSION

It is notoriously difficult to define when someone will commit the tort of conversion.[1] There seem to be at least[2] six different ways of committing this tort. A will have committed the tort of conversion in relation to B if:

(1) *Taking possession.* B was in possession of certain goods, or had an immediate right to possess certain goods, and A took possession of those goods with the intention of keeping them[3] when he had no lawful justification or excuse for doing so.

So, for example, suppose Fred steals some jewellery from Karen, and then sells it to Eric, who takes possession of it. In this case, both Fred and Eric will have committed the tort of conversion in relation to Karen – Fred in stealing the jewellery from Karen and Eric in taking possession of the stolen jewellery with the intention of keeping it. Eric, it should be noted, will have committed the tort of conversion in this situation even if he bought the jewellery from Karen in perfect good faith and had no idea it was stolen.

In *Tear* v *Freebody*,[4] the claimant unlawfully erected a building and the defendant was given the job of tearing the building down. The defendant did so and then took the bricks and so on out of which the building was made to a stone yard, intending to retain them until he was paid for the work he had done in tearing down the building. The defendant was not entitled to do this. It was held that the defendant committed the tort of conversion in taking possession of the bricks.

It is essential to show – for the purpose of showing that someone has committed the tort of conversion under this head – that he took possession of an item of property *with the intention of keeping it*.[5] For example, in *Fouldes* v *Willoughby*[6] the defendant operated a ferry that ran between Birkenhead and Liverpool. The claimant took two horses on board the ferry, which the defendant refused to carry. The claimant refused to take the horses off

[1] See Bramwell LJ in *Hiort* v *The London and North Western Railway Company* (1879) 4 Ex D 188, 194: 'I have frequently stated that I never did understand with precision what was a conversion . . . I find it impossible to give an exhaustive description as to what was or was not a conversion.' Also Lord Nicholls in *Kuwait Airways Corpn* v *Iraqi Airways Co. (Nos 4 & 5)* [2002] 2 AC 883, at [39]: 'Conversion of goods can occur in so many different circumstances that framing a precise definition of universal application is well nigh impossible.'

[2] There may well be other ways of committing this tort. However, a student reader of this book need not be troubled with these.

[3] The expression 'keeping' here covers both the situation where A took possession of the goods with the intention of keeping them for himself and the situation where A took possession of the goods with the intention of giving them to a third party.

[4] (1858) 4 CB (NS) 228, 140 ER 1071.

[5] See Lord Nicholls in *Kuwait Airways Corpn* v *Iraqi Airways Co. (Nos 4 & 5)* [2002] 2 AC 883, at [42]: 'To constitute conversion detention . . . must be accompanied by an intention to keep the goods.' So someone who picks up a wallet in the street will not commit the tort of conversion if he picks it up with the object of restoring it to its rightful owner: *Isaack* v *Clark* (1615) 2 Bulstr 306, 312, 80 ER 1143, 1148.

[6] (1841) 8 M & W 540, 151 ER 1153.

the ferry so the defendant took hold of them and led them off the ferry and onto the shore where the defendant's brother took charge of them. The claimant stayed on the ferry which took him to Liverpool where he sent for the horses. The horses were never returned to him. The claimant sued the defendant, claiming that in taking the horses off the ferry he had committed the tort of conversion. The court doubted whether this was true: when the defendant took the horses off the ferry, he had no intention of keeping them.

(2) *Refusal to hand over goods.* B had an immediate right to possess certain goods that were in A's possession and A refused to hand them over to B when he had no lawful justification or excuse for making such a refusal.[7]

For example, in *Howard E Perry* v *British Railways Board*,[8] the members of the Iron and Steel Trades Confederation went on strike. In order to support this strike, the employees of the British Railways Board (BRB) were instructed by their union – the National Union of Railwaymen (NUR) – not to assist in the transport of any steel. The claimants had some 500 tonnes of steel located at various depots owned by the BRB which the BRB could not transport because of the action of the NUR. The claimants asked the BRB if they could collect the steel themselves and transport it by road but the BRB refused because it feared that if it agreed it would be subjected to further industrial action by the NUR. The claimants sued the BRB, claiming that it had committed the tort of conversion in refusing to hand over the steel to them. The claimants succeeded in their claim: the BRB had no lawful justification or excuse for refusing to hand over the claimants' steel to the claimants.

It was different in *Clayton* v *Le Roy*.[9] In that case the claimant bought a watch from the defendant's shop. A few years later the watch was stolen. The claimant informed the defendant and asked him to keep an eye out for it. The watch went through a few people's hands before it was purchased by one B. B sent the watch to the defendant to be valued. The defendant recognised the watch as being the one which had been stolen from the claimant. He wrote to both the claimant and B informing them of the position and asking them what they wanted him to do. A few days later a representative of the claimant's solicitors went to the defendant's shop and demanded that he hand over the watch. The defendant refused. It was held that the defendant did not commit the tort of conversion in refusing to hand over the watch. He had been justified in acting as he did: 'a man does not act unlawfully in refusing to deliver up property immediately upon demand made. He is entitled to take adequate time to inquire into the rights of the claimant.'[10]

[7] *Marcq* v *Christie's* [2004] QB 286, at [33]. A couple of authorities may be interpreted as contradicting this. In *Miller* v *Jackson* [1977] QB 966, at 978, Lord Denning MR remarked that it is not conversion to refuse to give back a cricket ball that has been hit into your back garden. (Though, as we will see, it is if you pick the cricket ball up and give it to someone else or start playing with it.) However, this may be explained on the basis that if a cricket ball is hit into your back garden, you are legally entitled to refuse to give it back, so as to encourage people not to hit cricket balls onto your property. In *British Economical Lamp Co.* v *Empire Mile End (Limited)* (1913) 29 TLR 386, the claimants hired out some electrical lamps to the tenants of a theatre which was owned by the defendants. When the tenants moved out of the theatre, they left the lamps behind. At the end of the period for which the lamps had been hired out, the claimants demanded their lamps back from the defendants. The defendants refused to hand over the lamps or to allow the claimants to come onto their land to remove the lamps themselves. It was held that the defendants did not commit the tort of conversion in refusing to allow the claimants to get their lamps back. This case *is* very difficult to reconcile with the position taken here and we are forced to suggest that it was wrongly decided.

[8] [1980] 1 WLR 1375.

[9] [1911] 2 KB 1031.

[10] Ibid., 1051 (per Fletcher Moulton LJ).

In order to show that A has committed the tort of conversion in relation to B under this head, it is essential to show that A *refused* to give B's property back to him. Merely showing that A failed to return B's property to him when he was supposed to is not enough. B must have demanded the property back and A must have refused to give it back or to allow B to get it back herself.[11]

(3) *Delivery into hands of third party.* B was in possession of certain goods, or had an immediate right to possess those goods, and A intentionally did something which resulted in their being delivered[12] into the hands of a third party when he had no lawful justification or excuse for doing so.

So, for example, Ian will commit the tort of conversion if he pledges[13] Ruth's property to Gary when he has no lawful justification or excuse for doing so.[14] Similarly, if B gives A some property to deliver to D and A gives it to C instead, A will normally be held to have committed the tort of conversion in relation to B.

In order to make out that A has converted B's property under this head it is not necessary to show that A *physically* handed over B's property to a third party – but it must be shown that a third party obtained possession of B's property as a result of something A did.

In *Ashby* v *Tolhurst*,[15] a thief stole the claimant's car from a private parking ground which was supervised by an attendant. It was claimed the attendant had committed the tort of conversion in allowing the thief to get away with the car. The claim was rejected. The thief did not obtain possession of the car as a result of anything the attendant did; all the attendant did was allow the thief to make good his escape once he had obtained possession of the claimant's car.

In contrast, in *Moorgate Mercantile Co. Ltd* v *Finch and Read*,[16] the hirer of a car under a hire-purchase agreement lent his car to the defendant who, unknown to the hirer, used the car to smuggle watches into the country. When the defendant's activities were discovered, the car was forfeited and sold by the Customs and Excise authorities. The owners of the car argued that the defendant had committed the tort of conversion. The Court of Appeal agreed: Customs and Excise had obtained possession of the claimant's car as a result of what the defendant did – that is, smuggling watches in the claimant's car.

Similarly, in *R H Willis & Son* v *British Car Auctions Ltd*,[17] the claimants leased a car to

[11] *Barclays Mercantile Finance Ltd* v *Sibec Developments Ltd* [1992] 1 WLR 1253, 1258 (per Millett J); also *Kuwait Airways Corpn* v *Iraqi Airways Co. (Nos 4 & 5)* [2002] 2 AC 883, at [37] (per Lord Nicholls): 'mere unauthorised possession or detention is not an act of conversion. Demand and refusal to deliver up are required . . .'

[12] It seems that for A to have committed the tort of conversion under this head, it is essential that his actions must have resulted in B's goods being *delivered* into the hands of a third party. So if A sells, or attempts to sell, B's goods to C, that will not *of itself* amount to conversion: it is only when the goods are actually handed over to C that the tort will have been committed. See, on this, *Lancashire Waggon Co.* v *Fitzhugh* (1861) 6 H & N 502, 158 ER 206; *Consolidated Company* v *Curtis & Son* [1892] 1 QB 495, 498; *Marcq* v *Christie's* [2004] QB 286, at [19]. *A fortiori*, if A goes about insisting that B's goods belong to A, that will not amount to conversion: see s 11(3) of the Torts (Interference with Goods) Act 1977 ('Denial of title is not of itself conversion').

[13] A will pledge B's property to C if he transfers possession of that property to C as security for a debt owed by A to C.

[14] Gary will also be held to have converted Ruth's property by accepting it as a pledge. See s 11(2) of the Torts (Interference with Goods) Act 1977, which provides that '[receipt] of goods by way of pledge is conversion if delivery of the goods is conversion'.

[15] [1937] 2 KB 242.

[16] [1962] 1 QB 701.

[17] [1978] 1 WLR 438.

Intangible property which does not take a corporeal form – such as a copyright – cannot therefore be converted. But cheques, insurance policies and negotiable instruments can be converted – while they represent forms of intangible property, they take a corporeal form.

Thirdly, even though land is an item of property that can be possessed, land cannot be converted.

TITLE TO SUE

We have already seen that, in most cases, A can only commit the tort of conversion in relation to B if he interferes with an item of property[28] which is in B's *possession* or which B has an *immediate right to possess*. This raises two questions. First, when can we say that an item of property is in someone's possession? Secondly, when can we say that someone has an immediate right to possess an item of property?

Possession

Suppose that B wants to show that an item of property[29] was in her possession on 1 January 2005. To do this, she will have to show that she *acquired* possession of that item of property at some time before 1 January 2005 and *she* did not subsequently *lose* possession of that item in the intervening period between that time and 1 January 2005.[30] This definition raises two issues. First, when can we say that someone has *acquired* possession of an item of property? Secondly, when can we say that someone has *lost* possession of an item of property?

Acquiring possession

B will acquire possession of an item of property if: (1) she takes control of that item of property with (2) the intention of preventing others from taking control of that item of property.

Someone will take control of an item of property if he takes as much control over that item of property as the nature of that item of property will admit. So, for example, in *Young v Hichens*[31] the claimant was fishing for pilchards and had almost encircled a shoal of pilchards with his nets when the defendant rowed through a gap in the nets and prevented the claimant from capturing the pilchards. The claimant sued the defendant, claiming that he had been in possession of the pilchards and that the defendant had disturbed his possession of the pilchards. The claim was rejected: at no time did the claimant have the pilchards completely under his control.

In contrast, in *The Tubantia*[32] the claimants attempted to salvage the cargo of a Dutch steamship which had been sunk in the First World War and lay under 100 feet of water. The

[28] From now on, the term 'item of property' will refer *only* to an item of property that is capable of being converted.

[29] It should be remembered that we are *not* referring to land here. The question of when someone can claim to be in possession of a piece of land is dealt with in Chapter 18, below.

[30] Harris 1961, 73–4.

[31] (1844) 6 QB 606, 115 ER 228.

[32] [1924] P 78.

claimants located the steamship in April 1922 and spent as many days exploring the ship and salvaging its cargo as the weather permitted until November 1922 when it became impracticable to continue exploring the ship during the winter. The claimants marked the location of the ship and returned in April 1923. They then spent about 25 days exploring the ship and salvaging the cargo until July 1923 when the defendants – encouraged by rumours that the ship had been carrying treasure at the time it was sunk – started to send divers down to the ship in an attempt to locate the treasure and take it for themselves. The claimants sued the defendants, claiming that they had possession of the ship and that the defendants were acting unlawfully in disrupting their possession of the ship. The claimants' claim was allowed: they had taken as much control over the Dutch steamship as the nature of the thing and its location allowed.

Someone who takes control of an item of property will not acquire possession of that item of property unless he intends, in taking control of that item of property, to prevent other people from taking control of that item of property. If he lacks this intention, he is said to have 'custody' of the item of property in question, not 'possession'. So, for example, if Sarah asks Fred to value a ring for her, when Sarah gives Fred the ring Fred will acquire custody but not possession of the ring.[33] When Fred takes control of the ring to inspect it he does not intend, in taking control of the ring, to prevent other people from taking control of it. Again, it is often said that employees only have custody of their work tools – they do not possess their work tools. When an employee takes control of some tools that he has been given to work with, he does not intend, in taking control of those tools, to prevent other people from taking control of those tools.[34] Of course, if an employee steals some work tools and takes them home he will acquire possession of those tools – he will have taken control of those tools with the intention of preventing other people from taking control of those tools.

Losing possession

If B has acquired possession of an item of property, B will lose possession of that item of property if: (1) someone else takes possession of that item of property; or (2) B intentionally abandons that item of property.

So B does *not* have to *retain control* of an item of property in order to retain possession of that item of property. For example, if Alan goes on holiday he retains possession of all the items of property in his house even though he does not have physical control over them while he is gone. Obviously, though, if someone breaks into Alan's house while he is gone and steals some items of property from Alan's house, Alan will lose possession of those items of property – someone else (the burglar) will have taken possession of those items of property. Again, suppose Alan employs Beth to perform some task for him and gives Beth

[33] *Armory* v *Delamirie* (1721) 1 Stra 505, 93 ER 664.

[34] While this works to explain the rule that an employee only has custody of his work tools and does not possess them, the rule, it should be noted, has its origins in the definition of the now defunct crime of larceny. Someone would commit the offence of larceny if he removed goods from the possession of their owner. Under this definition, an employee who had possession of his work tools would not commit the offence of larceny if he absconded with them – by definition, if he had possession of his work tools he would not remove them from the possession of their owner (his employer) if he absconded with them. In order to ensure that employees who absconded with their employer's tools *did* commit the offence of larceny in so doing, the idea grew up that employees did not possess their work tools – they only had custody of them.

the tools she will need to do the job. Alan will retain possession of the tools even after he has given them to Beth – and this is so even though Alan will not physically control the tools once he gives them to Beth. The reason why Alan will retain possession of the tools when he gives them to Beth is that when he gives the tools to Beth, Beth will merely acquire the custody of the tools: she will not possess them.

Immediate right to possess

Let us now answer the second of our two questions – When can we say that someone has an immediate right to possess an item of property? In order to answer this question, let us suppose that A is currently in possession of a watch. B will have an immediate right to possess the watch if she *currently* has a right to call on A to hand over possession of the watch to her. If she has no such right at the moment but will – other things being equal – acquire such a right in the future, that will not be enough: B will only have an immediate right to possess the watch if she *currently* has a right to call on A to hand over possession of the watch to her.

In *Gordon* v *Harper*,[35] the claimant leased a fully furnished flat to one B. B owed some money and the defendant sheriff – thinking that the furniture in the flat belonged to B – seized it and sold it in execution of the debt. The claimant sued the defendant in conversion. The claimant lost: he could not establish that at the time the defendant seized and sold the furniture in the flat he had a right to call on B to hand over possession of the furniture to him. At the expiry of the lease, he would have acquired such a right but the lease had not expired at the time the defendant seized and sold the furniture in question. B, on the other hand, being in possession of the furniture at the time it was seized and sold, could have sued the defendant for selling the furniture.

Let's now look at a few categories of situations in which someone *may* have an immediate right to possess an item of property.

(1) *Theft*. If B is in possession of an item of property and A takes the property off B when he has no lawful justification or excuse for doing so, B will acquire an immediate right to possess that property. So, for example, suppose Carl found a watch in the street and then Ruth took the watch off Carl when she had no right to do so. In this case, Carl will acquire an immediate right to possession of the watch. But Carl will lose this right if the watch finds its way into the hands of its rightful owner; once this happens, Carl will obviously have no right to call on the rightful owner to hand over possession of the watch to him.

(2) *Stolen property*. Suppose that A was in possession of stolen goods and that those goods were seized by the police in pursuit of a criminal investigation.[36] Suppose further that the true owner of the goods is untraceable and the police no longer have any statutory authority to retain those goods. In this situation, A will have an immediate right to possess the goods in question.[37] So if A demands that the police give him back the goods and the police

[35] (1796) 7 TR 9, 101 ER 828.

[36] Section 19 of the Police and Criminal Evidence Act 1984 grants the police a statutory power to do this: see below, p. 353.

[37] *Important note*. It must be emphasised that this will only be the case if the police remain in custody of the goods and the true owner of the goods cannot be traced. If the police have exercised a statutory power to transfer the

refuse to do so, they will commit the tort of conversion.[38] It seems that this will be the case even if A actually stole the goods in question.[39]

(3) *Lost property*. If A has found an item of property on B's land which had been lost by a third party, B will have an immediate right to possess that item of property if: (1) A is B's employee and A found the item of property in question in the course of his employment;[40] *or* (2) A is a trespasser on B's land;[41] *or* (3) the item of property in question was buried on B's land;[42] *or* (4) B has 'manifested an intention to exercise control over his land and the things which may be upon it or in it'.[43] If none of (1)–(4) are made out, B will have no right to possess the item of property found by A and A may keep it until, of course, the rightful owner turns up and claims the item of property in question.[44]

(4) *Bailment*. If A holds B's property as a bailee, B will have an immediate right to possess that property if the bailment on which A holds B's property is a bailment *at will* – that is, if B has reserved the right to reclaim her property from A at any time.

If A holds B's property on a fixed-term bailment, B will normally only acquire a right to call on A to hand over possession of the property once the fixed term has elapsed. But if A misuses B's property before the term has elapsed, B may immediately acquire a right at that stage to call on A to hand over possession of the property. So, for example, suppose Eric rented out a car to Mary for six months. Two months later, Mary gave the car away to Ian. In such a case, Eric will probably be able to establish that when Mary gave the car away to Ian, Eric acquired an immediate right to possess the car. As a result, Eric will probably be able to establish that Mary and Ian both committed the tort of conversion in relation to Eric when Mary gave the car away to Ian and Ian took possession of the car.

(5) *Trusts*. Suppose A holds an item of property on trust for B. Will B have an immediate right to possess that item of property? If the property is held *solely* on trust for B then B will have a right – under the decision in *Saunders* v *Vautier*[45] – to call on A to hand over possession of the property to her.[46] One would have thought, then, that if A held the trust property solely on trust for B and then disposed of that property to C in breach of trust, B would be able to sue both A and C in conversion – and indeed one case held exactly that.

However, if the law *did* say this, then the rule in Equity that a bona fide purchaser of

---

stolen goods to a third party, then A will no longer have any rights over the goods: *Buckley* v *Gross* (1863) 3 B & S 566. Similarly, if the stolen goods are still in the custody of the police, but the true owner can be identified, then A will have no right to demand that the goods be returned to him.

[38] *Costello* v *Chief Constable of Derbyshire Constabulary* [2001] 1 WLR 1437.

[39] Ibid., at [31].

[40] *City of London Corporation* v *Appleyard* [1963] 1 WLR 982; *Parker* v *British Airways Board* [1982] QB 1004, 1017G.

[41] *Hibbert* v *McKiernan* [1948] 2 KB 142; *Parker* v *British Airways Board* [1982] QB 1004, 1017E.

[42] *Waverley Borough Council* v *Fletcher* [1996] QB 334.

[43] *Parker* v *British Airways Board* [1982] QB 1004, 1018A–B.

[44] Of course, if A takes the property with the intention of keeping it for himself, that will be conversion – A is only allowed to take the property if his intention in so doing is to restore it to its rightful owner: see above, pp. 342–3.

[45] (1841) Cr & Ph 240, 41 ER 482.

[46] If A holds the property on trust for B and C, then B will only acquire a right to demand that A hand over the property to her if C agrees that she can do so. So B will not have an *immediate* right to demand possession of the property.

trust property disposed of in breach of trust cannot be sued for the value of that property[47] would be subverted.[48] A claim in conversion would lie against the bona fide purchaser. In order to prevent this happening, the Court of Appeal has ruled in *MCC Proceeds Inc.* v *Lehman Bros International (Europe)*[49] that if trust property which is held solely on trust for B is disposed of in breach of trust, a claim in conversion will *not* lie either against the trustee disposing of the property or the recipient of the property. While B might have an immediate right to possess the trust property, that right, being *equitable* in nature, is not sufficient to allow B to bring a claim in conversion. What has to be established is that B had an immediate right to posses the trust property *under the common law* – and this B cannot do, as she merely had an equitable interest in the trust property.

LAWFUL JUSTIFICATION OR EXCUSE

Let us now turn to the question of when someone will have a lawful justification or excuse for doing something that would otherwise amount to conversion. Such lawful justification or excuse will exist in the following situations.

Consent

Obviously, if B consents to A's interfering with an item of property which is in her possession or which she has an immediate right to possess, then A will have a lawful justification or excuse for doing so. So John will not commit the tort of conversion if he rides Karen's horse with her consent. Similarly, Wendy will not commit the tort of conversion if she takes some goods off the shelves of Ian's supermarket and puts them in her shopping basket (though she probably will if she puts them in her pocket).

The Animals Act 1971

The Animals Act 1971 authorises the occupier of land in certain cases to detain or destroy animals which trespass on his land. For example, s 7(2) of the 1971 Act provides that 'Where any livestock strays on to any land and is not then under the control of any person the occupier of the land may detain it.' Section 7(4) provides that 'Where livestock has been detained in pursuance of this section for a period of not less than fourteen days the person detaining it may sell it at a market or by public auction, unless proceedings are then pending for the return of the livestock . . .'

Section 9(1)(a) of the 1971 Act provides that in any civil proceedings against a person for killing or causing injury to a dog it shall be a defence to prove 'that the defendant acted for the protection of any livestock [on his land][50] and was a person entitled to act for the

47 See *Pilcher* v *Rawlins* (1872) LR 7 Ch App 259.

48 Though Tettenborn 1996 questions whether this is true (at 40–1). He argues that the real reason for maintaining that the beneficiary under a trust cannot bring a claim for conversion when the property is misappropriated is that to allow such a claim would expand the liabilities of: (1) innocent donees of trust property; (2) people who innocently assist a trustee to dispose of trust property; *and* (3) trustees who innocently commit a breach of trust by disposing of trust property to another.

49 [1998] 4 All ER 675, distinguishing *International Factors* v *Rodriguez* [1979] 1 QB 751.

50 Animals Act 1971, s 9(2).

protection of that livestock'. A defendant who has killed or injured a dog 'shall be deemed . . . to [have acted] for the protection of any livestock [on his land] if, and only if, either – (a) the dog [was] worrying or [was] about to worry the livestock and there [were] no other reasonable means of ending or preventing the worrying; or (b) the dog [had been] worrying livestock, [had] not left the vicinity and [was] not under the control of any person and there [were] no practicable means of ascertaining to whom it belongs'[51] or (c) the defendant reasonably believed (a) or (b) were true.[52]

Distress damage feasant

If an inanimate item of property of B's is on A's land without permission and is causing damage to A's land or disrupting the operation of A's business on that land, A will be allowed: (1) to take steps to move that item of property so that it no longer causes any damage or disruption, and then (2) to detain it until B fairly compensates him for the damage or disruption caused by the presence of that item of property on his land.[53] This remedy is known as 'distress damage feasant'.[54]

Recaption

If B is in possession of an item of property that rightly belongs to A, then A may be allowed to seize the item of property in question and take it into his possession.

This will be the case, for example, if Vijay steals Lara's goods and Lara arrests him while they are still on his person – Lara will be entitled to seize the goods and take them into her possession.[55] What if a watch that rightly belongs to Lara is on Vijay's land? When will Lara be allowed to go onto Vijay's land and seize the watch and take it into her possession? The position is unclear. If Vijay stole the watch from Lara, Lara will be allowed to go onto Vijay's land and reclaim it.[56] But where Vijay came by the watch innocently, the position is far more uncertain. In *Anthony* v *Haney*,[57] Tindal CJ suggested in some *obiter dicta* that if, in the situation we are considering, the watch came to end up on Vijay's land without any wrongdoing on his part, Lara will only be entitled to go onto Vijay's land and reclaim the watch if: (1) the watch ended up on Vijay's land by accident; *or* (2) someone stole the watch from Lara; or (3) Lara has already asked Vijay to return the watch to her and Vijay has wrongfully refused to comply with that demand.

51 Section 9(3).
52 Section 9(4).
53 See, for example, *The Ambergate, Nottingham and Boston and Eastern Junction Railway Company* v *The Midland Railway Company* (1853) 2 E & B 793, 118 ER 964.
54 The remedy of distress damage feasant also used to be available when an animal of B's strayed onto A's land and caused damage or destruction: see, for example, *Sorrell* v *Paget* [1950] 1 KB 252. But s 7(1) of the Animals Act 1971 provided that the 'right to seize any animal by way of distress damage feasant is hereby abolished'.
55 *Whatford* v *Carty*, The Times, 29 October 1960.
56 *Patrick* v *Colerick* (1838) 3 M & W 483, 150 ER 1235.
57 (1832) 8 Bing 186, 131 ER 372.

The Police and Criminal Evidence Act 1984

Under s 19 of the Police and Criminal Evidence Act 1984, any constable who is lawfully on any premises[58] 'may seize anything which is on the premises if he has reasonable grounds for believing – (a) that it has been obtained in consequence of the commission of an offence; and (b) that it is necessary to seize it in order to prevent it being concealed, lost, damaged or destroyed'.[59] Moreover, a constable who is lawfully on any premises may also 'seize anything which is on the premises if he has reasonable grounds for believing – (a) that it is evidence in relation to an offence which he is investigating or any other offence; and (b) that it is necessary to seize it in order to prevent it being concealed, lost, damaged or destroyed'.[60]

Returning goods

If A has B's goods and B has an immediate right to possess those goods, A will of course do no wrong if he returns the goods to B. What if A gives the goods to a third party, C, with instructions to return them to B? A will be allowed to do this so long as it is *reasonable* to give the goods to C for the purpose of returning them to B.

In *Elvin & Powell Ltd* v *Plummer Roddis Ltd*,[61] a conman approached the claimants – a firm of coat makers – and ordered about £350 worth of coats, asking them to be delivered to the defendants' shop. The coats were sent and the conman sent a telegram to the defendants in the claimant company's name, saying 'Goods despatched to your branch in error. Sending van to collect.' When the coats arrived at the defendants' shop, the conman turned up in a van and took the coats from them. He then disappeared. The claimants sued the defendants, claiming that they had committed the tort of conversion in handing the coats over to the conman. The claim was rejected – the defendants had only handed the coats to the conman because they wanted to return them to the claimants and it had been reasonable for them to hand the coats over to the conman for the purpose of returning them to the claimants.

This defence was not available to the defendants in *Hiort* v *Bott*.[62] In that case, the claimants mistakenly sent the defendants an invoice for barley together with a delivery order. The defendants had not in fact ordered any barley from the claimants but the invoice stated that the defendants had ordered the barley through one G. The defendants got in touch with G. He said there had been a mistake and asked them to endorse the delivery order to him so that he could have the barley delivered to the customer who actually ordered it. This the defendants did. G then used the delivery order to obtain the barley himself and absconded with it. The claimants sued the defendants, claiming that the defendants, in endorsing the delivery order, had committed the tort of conversion. The court agreed: the defendants had delivered the barley into G's hands without the claimants' consent and they had no lawful justification or excuse for doing so. They could not argue

[58] Police and Criminal Evidence Act 1984, s 19(1).
[59] Section 19(2).
[60] Section 19(3).
[61] (1934) 50 TLR 158.
[62] (1874) LR 9 Ex 86.

that they had delivered the barley into G's hands in order to return it to the claimants as the barley was already in the claimants' hands at the time they signed the delivery order.

The principle in *Hollins* v *Fowler*

In *Hollins* v *Fowler*, Blackburn J argued:

> I cannot find it anywhere distinctly laid down, but I submit to your Lordships that on principle, one who deals with goods at the request of the person who has the actual custody of them, in the bona fide belief that the custodier is the true owner, or has the authority of the true owner, should be excused for what he does if the act is of such a nature as would be excused if done by the authority of the person in possession . . . Thus a warehouseman with whom goods had been deposited is guilty of no conversion by keeping them, or restoring them to the person who deposited them with him, though that person turns out to have had no authority from the true owner.[63]

So if Carl steals Lara's dog and, pretending to Ruth that the dog is his, asks Ruth to look after it over the weekend, Ruth will not commit the tort of conversion in relation to Lara if she gives the dog back to Carl at the end of the weekend.[64] Again, suppose Fred steals Gary's painting and, pretending that the painting is his, hands it over to Sarah so that she can find a buyer for it. If Sarah cannot find a buyer and hands the painting back to Fred, she will not commit the tort of conversion in relation to Gary in so doing.[65]

Common currency

In the interests of ensuring the smooth running of the economy, the law provides that someone who accepts stolen money paid over to him as common currency will not be liable for conversion: 'Conversion does not lie for money, taken and received as currency . . .'[66] So if Tom steals some money out of Mary's wallet he will commit the tort of conversion. But if Tom takes that money and uses it to pay for some goods in Paul's store using that money, Paul will not commit the tort of conversion in accepting that money.

[63] (1875) LR 7 HL 757, 766–7.

[64] What would be the position if Carl instructed Ruth at the end of the weekend to give the dog to Tom? Would Ruth commit the tort of conversion in relation to Lara if she handed the dog over to Tom? The Privy Council's decision in *Maynegrain Pty Ltd* v *Compafina Bank* (1984) 58 ALJR 389 could be read as suggesting that the answer is 'no' (and W&J, at 773, also suggests that the answer is 'no'). However, that case may rest on technicalities of the law of agency which do not apply in Ruth's case. For further discussion, see W&J, 773 n. 3.

[65] *Marcq* v *Christie's* [2004] QB 286. There is an issue as to whether *Hollins* v *Fowler* goes even further and says that if Sarah found a buyer – Mary – for the painting, she would not be liable for conversion if she sold and delivered the painting to Mary. According to the terms of the test in *Hollins* v *Fowler*, she should not be liable, but as W&J observes, at 774, 'it is doubtful how far [that test] goes'.

[66] *Lipkin Gorman* v *Karpnale Ltd* [1991] 2 AC 548, 559 (per Lord Templeman). For similar reasons, the law provides that a bank that accepts a stolen cheque will not be liable in conversion so long as it acted in good faith and without negligence in accepting the cheque: Cheques Act 1957, s 4.

17 Trespass to goods

A will have committed the tort of trespass to goods in relation to B if: (1) he directly interfered with goods in B's possession; (2) he did so intentionally or carelessly;[1] *and* (3) he had no lawful justification or excuse for acting as he did. Only three points need to be made about this tort.

(1) *The requirement of direct interference.* It is easier to provide illustrations of situations in which someone's goods[2] will be directly interfered with than it is to define what directly interfering with someone's goods involves. So if Paul beats Ruth's cat, he will directly interfere with it;[3] but he will not if he kills Ruth's cat by laying down some poison which Ruth's cat eats. Ian will directly interfere with Mary's car if he places a wheel clamp on it;[4] but he will not if he finds Wendy's car on his land and he locks the gates to his land so that Wendy's car cannot be driven off his land.[5] If Lara gets on Eric's horse and rides away on it, she will directly interfere with the horse; but she will not if her dog escapes her control, runs up to Eric's horse and makes it run away by barking at it.

(2) *Lawful justification or excuse.* Suppose A has directly interfered with B's goods. Not much needs to be said on the issue of when A will be able to establish that he had a lawful justification or excuse for interfering with B's goods. The previous chapter on the tort of conversion will have given the reader a good idea as to the sort of situations in which such a lawful justification or excuse will exist. Only a couple of cases which deal with this issue need be mentioned here.

In *Arthur* v *Anker*,[6] the defendants wheel-clamped the claimants' cars, which were parked at the time in a private car park without the permission of the occupiers of the car park. The claimants sued the defendants, claiming that they had committed the tort of trespass to goods in clamping the claimants' cars. The claimants' claims were rejected: the defendants had had a lawful justification or excuse for clamping the claimants' cars. The claimants knew when they parked their cars in the car park without permission that there

[1] This seems to follow from *Fowler* v *Lanning* [1959] 1 QB 426. See *National Coal Board* v *J E Evans & Co. (Cardiff)* Ltd [1951] 2 KB 861, where the defendant contractors struck an underground cable belonging to the claimants when digging a trench on land belonging to the local county council. The claimants sued the defendants, claiming that they had committed the tort of trespass to goods in damaging the cable. Held: no trespass, even though the defendants had directly interfered with the claimants' cable – they had not intended to damage the cable and had not carelessly damaged the cable as they did not know and had no reason to know it was under the land on which they were digging.

[2] For the sake of convenience, in this chapter when goods are referred to as 'someone's goods' or some equivalent expression is used, what is meant is *not* that those goods belong to that someone but that that someone is in possession of those goods.

[3] *Slater* v *Swann* (1730) 2 Stra 872, 93 ER 906.

[4] *Arthur* v *Anker* [1997] QB 564; *Vine* v *Waltham Forest LBC* [2000] 1 WLR 2383.

[5] *Hartley* v *Moxham* (1842) 3 QB 701, 114 ER 675.

[6] [1997] QB 564.

was a risk that their cars would be clamped: there were very visible signs in the car park warning that cars that were not authorised to park in the car park would be clamped. So the claimants voluntarily took the risk that their cars would be clamped. As a result, the defendants had a lawful justification or excuse for clamping the claimants' cars.

It was different in *Vine* v *London Borough of Waltham Forest*.[7] In that case the claimant was driving her car along the road when she suddenly felt extremely ill. She pulled off the road, got out of the car and after she had walked a little way she was violently sick. After a few minutes she felt better and returned to her car only to find it had been clamped – she had parked in a parking space reserved for employees of Railtrack. The defendants were responsible for her car being clamped. The claimant sued them, claiming that they had committed the tort of trespass to goods in clamping her car.

The claimant succeeded in her claim. An attempt to justify the clamping on the ground that the claimant had voluntarily taken the risk that her car would be clamped failed: the claimant had not seen the sign which warned that her car was liable to be clamped if she parked where she did; it had been obscured by another car which had been parked nearby. What would have been the position if the claimant had seen the sign? In such a case, it would still have been difficult to establish that the claimant *voluntarily* took the risk that her car might be clamped given that the claimant only parked where she did because she was in great distress and needed to be sick. Given this, it is submitted that the claimant's claim should still have succeeded even if she saw the sign warning that cars parked where her car was would be clamped. These two cases raise a few issues which we will now deal with.

First, in *Arthur* v *Anker*, Sir Thomas Bingham MR suggested that a wheel-clamping firm would not be able to justify or excuse its clamping someone's car if it charged an exorbitant price for releasing the car.[8] This seems too strong. Suppose Dawn parked her car in a private car park, knowing that she had no authorisation to park there. Suppose further that the car park had very visible signs warning that 'Unauthorised vehicles will be clamped and may be towed away' and Dawn saw these signs. Suppose finally that John, someone who works for a wheel-clamping firm, clamped Dawn's car and charged her an exorbitant amount of money – say £2,000 – to release it. In such a case, John will *not* be able to excuse or justify his clamping Dawn's car. When Dawn parked her car, she did not expect that if her car were clamped she would have to pay £2,000 to release it – so it will not be possible to argue that Dawn voluntarily took the risk that her car would be detained until she produced £2,000 to release it.

But suppose that the signs in the car park warned that 'Unauthorised vehicles will be clamped and may be towed away – a fee of £2,000 will be charged for their release'. If this was the case, it *will* be possible to argue that when Dawn parked her car, she voluntarily took the risk that it would be detained until she produced £2,000 to release it. Given this, it *will* be possible to argue that John committed no trespass to Dawn's car in clamping it and charging Dawn £2,000 for its release. On the other hand, it might be argued that when Dawn saw the signs she did not seriously think that if her car were clamped she would *actually* be charged £2,000 to get her car back. In other words, it might be argued that Dawn

[7] [2000] 1 WLR 2383.
[8] [1997] QB 564, 573C.

thought that the warning that owners of clamped cars would be charged £2,000 for their release was for 'show' only, to deter people from parking in the car park without authorisation. If this were the case, it would be harder to establish, in the case we are considering, that Dawn voluntarily took the risk that her car would be clamped until she found £2,000 to release it.

Secondly, what is the position if Dawn parks her car in a particular place and, due to carelessness or stupidity, Dawn does not see the clearly visible signs nearby that warn that parking in the place where Dawn has parked is not permitted and cars parking in the place where Dawn has parked may be clamped and towed away? If John clamps Dawn's car will he be able to establish that he had a lawful justification or excuse for clamping her car? On the facts as we have presented them, it is hard to argue that Dawn voluntarily took the risk that her car would be clamped – as Dawn did not see the signs warning her that her car was liable to be clamped, she did not know she was taking a risk that her car might be clamped.

It might be thought that if, in this case, John's clamping Dawn's car will amount to a trespass to the car, then someone whose car had been clamped would find it very easy to establish that the clamping amounted to a trespass to his car: he could simply claim that he did not see any signs warning him that his car was liable to be clamped if it were parked where it was. However, he would find it hard to convince a court that he did *not* see any such signs if such signs were clearly visible in the area where he parked the car. As Roch LJ remarked in the *Vine* case: '[to] show that the car owner consented to or willingly assumed the risk of his car being clamped, it has to be established that the car owner was aware of the consequences of parking his car ... That will be done by establishing that the car owner saw and understood the significance of a warning notice or notices that cars in that place without permission were liable to be clamped. *Normally* the presence of notices which are posted where they are bound to be seen ... will lead to a finding that the car driver had knowledge of and appreciated the warning.'[9]

Thirdly, if John clamps Dawn's car and the clamping amounts to a trespass to Dawn's car, Dawn will be entitled to take reasonable steps to release her car from the clamp. However, if John proposes to charge Dawn a reasonable sum to release the clamp, Dawn will act unreasonably if, instead of paying the sum demanded and getting her car back that way, she releases her car from the clamp by breaking it.[10] So if John proposes to charge Dawn a reasonable sum to release the clamp, Dawn will not be entitled to break the clamp on her car and will commit the tort of trespass to goods *herself* if she does break the clamp on the car. But if John makes it clear that he will only release the car if Dawn pays him an exorbitant sum of money, then it might be reasonable for Dawn to break the clamp so as to free her car from the unlawful clamping – and if this is the case, Dawn will commit no trespass if she breaks the clamp.

(3) *The requirement of possession*. As we have said, A will commit the tort of trespass to goods in relation to B if he directly interferes with goods in B's *possession* when he has no lawful justification or excuse for doing so. But it is not always necessary for B to show that goods that have been interfered with were in her possession before she can sue for a trespass to them.

[9] *Vine* v *Waltham Forest LBC* [2000] 1 WLR 2383, 2390 (emphasis added).
[10] *Lloyd* v *DPP* [1992] 1 All ER 982, 992c–e.

First, if B held goods on trust for C and C was in possession of them at the time A, without lawful justification or excuse, directly interfered with them, A will have committed the tort of trespass to goods in relation to B as well as C.[11]

Secondly, if A, without lawful justification or excuse, directly interfered with a deceased's goods, A will have committed the tort of trespass to goods in relation to the deceased's executors or administrators even if they had not taken possession of the goods at the time A interfered with them.[12]

Thirdly, if B is the owner of a franchise (as will be the case, for example, if B has the right to the goods on a shipwreck), A will commit the tort of trespass to goods in relation to B if he, without lawful justification or excuse, directly interferes with the goods covered by that franchise – and this is so even if B has not yet taken possession of those goods.[13]

[11] *White* v *Morris* (1852) 11 CB 1015, 138 ER 778; *Barker* v *Furlong* [1891] 2 Ch 172.
[12] *Tharpe* v *Stallwood* (1843) 5 M & G 760, 134 ER 766.
[13] *Bailiffs of Dunwich v Sterry* (1831) 1 B & Ad 831, 109 ER 995.

18 Trespass to land

DEFINITION

A will commit the tort of trespass to land in relation to B if he crosses the boundary onto land possessed by B[1] when he has no lawful justification or excuse for doing so. A will also commit the tort of trespass to land in relation to B if he causes some object or matter to move directly onto land possessed by B when he has no lawful justification or excuse for doing so.

THE MENTAL ELEMENT REQUIRED TO COMMIT THE TORT

Suppose A at some time crossed the boundary onto land possessed by B. In order to establish that A committed the tort of trespass to land in so doing, B does *not* have to prove: (*a*) that when A crossed the boundary he intended to trespass on land possessed by B; *or* (*b*) that when A crossed the boundary, he knew or ought to have known that there was a risk he would trespass on land possessed by B. Indeed, A will have committed the tort of trespass to land in relation to B even if, when he crossed the boundary onto land possessed by B, he honestly believed that he was remaining on land where he was permitted to be. An honest mistake by A is not a defence to the tort of trespass to land.

We saw in Chapter 11 that it has been held that A cannot commit the tort of battery in relation to B unless he directly applied force to B *intentionally* or *carelessly*.[2] It has been argued that a similar rule should apply with regard to the tort of trespass to land.[3] Such a similar rule would mean that A would only commit the tort of trespass to land in relation to B if his movement – by which he crossed the boundary of B's land – was *intentional* or *careless*. It has not, however, been authoritatively settled that this is the law. The main reason why the point remains unsettled is that a defendant will not be held to have 'crossed' unless he had sufficient control over his own movements for the action which took his body across the boundary to be attributed to him. This means that even without a similar rule defendants will not usually be held liable for movements which were not intentional or careless.

The two previous paragraphs have discussed what state of mind A must have in order to commit the tort of trespass to land. It is important to distinguish this from the separate question of what state of mind A must have in order to make him liable to pay compensation for all the *consequences* of a trespass. The tort of trespass to land is actionable *per se*, which means that it is actionable regardless of whether B suffers any consequential

[1] The degree of connection that has to be established between B and the land is discussed in detail below, pp. 363–4.

[2] See above, pp. 250–1, discussing the result of the decision in *Fowler* v *Lanning* [1959] 1 QB 426.

[3] W&J, 619–20.

damage.[4] This means that A does not have to anticipate any consequential damage in order to commit the tort. But where the tort does lead to consequential damage A's state of mind *will* be relevant to whether A is held liable for that damage.

For instance, suppose that Ruth parked her car in a car park possessed by John without John's permission. Suppose further that while the car was parked there, the car – without any fault on Ruth's part – burst into flames and damaged the car park. On such facts, it is obvious that Ruth committed the tort of trespass to land, but this does not mean that Ruth will be held liable for all the *consequences* of her trespass. It is a matter of dispute what rule will be applied to determine whether Ruth is liable for the fire damage done to John's car park. On one view, Ruth will only be held liable if she intended the car to burst into flames or it was reasonably foreseeable that it would burst into flames when she parked it in the car park.[5] On another view, Ruth will be held liable for the fire damage done to John's car park (even if it was unintended and unforeseeable) *if* it was a direct result of Ruth's trespass and Ruth knew when she parked in John's car park that she did not have his permission to park there.[6] Whichever view one takes, it is clear that whether Ruth will be held liable for the fire damage done to John's car park will depend a great deal on what her state of mind was when she parked her car there. But her state of mind at the time she parked her car is *not* relevant to the issue of whether she committed the tort of trespass to land in relation to John when she parked her car.

THE DEGREE OF CONTROL REQUIRED TO COMMIT THE TORT

Control over physical movements

We noted above that a defendant will not be held to have 'crossed' the boundary unless he had sufficient control over his own movements for the action which took his body across the boundary to be attributed to him. In *Smith* v *Stone*,[7] the defendant pleaded that he had been carried across the boundary onto the claimant's land by the force and violence of others. Roll J held that this meant that the defendant had *not* committed the tort of trespass to land in relation to the claimant. The same judge later held that the defendant would have been liable if he had crossed the boundary under duress.[8] It might be different,

[4] See below, pp. 679–81.

[5] This is the normal rule that is applied to determine the extent of a defendant's liability when he or she has committed a non-intentional tort (that is, a tort which can be committed non-intentionally): see below, pp. 569–71.

[6] This was the view preferred by the New Zealand Court of Appeal in *Mayfair Ltd* v *Pears* [1987] 1 NZLR 459, from which our hypothetical example is drawn. (The court went on to find that the fire damage caused by the car bursting into flames in that case was *not* a *direct* result of the defendant's parking his car in the claimant's building. Consequently, it held that – in the absence of proof that the car's bursting into flames was intended or reasonably foreseeable at the time the defendant parked his car – the defendant could not be held liable for the fire damage suffered by the claimant.) Some support for the New Zealand Court of Appeal's approach comes from Lord Nicholls's judgment in *Kuwait Airways Corpn* v *Iraqi Airways Co. (Nos 4 & 5)* [2002] 2 AC 883. Lord Nicholls suggested that while the normal rule is that someone who converts another's goods should only be liable for the reasonably foreseeable consequences of his conversion, if A knowingly converts B's goods, A should be held liable for *all* the losses suffered by B that were a direct consequence of A's conversion: ibid., at [103]–[104]. There is no reason to think that he would apply a different rule if A knowingly trespassed on B's land.

[7] (1647) Style 65, 82 ER 533.

[8] Ibid.

however, if a threat caused A to leap across the boundary of B's land in an instinctive panic.[9]

Control over inanimate objects

With regard to the case where A has caused some object or matter to move directly onto land possessed by B, it is orthodox to distinguish between the movement of such a thing across the boundary which is a *direct* result of A's actions (and thus within the scope of the tort) and a movement which is an *indirect* consequence of A's behaviour (and thus outside the tort). The primary factor which the courts will use when trying to identify this distinction is the degree to which A's actions can be said to have *controlled* the crossing by the object or matter. Thus where A has thrown or fired an object across the boundary onto land B possesses A will have committed trespass to land in relation to B. But where A has released some substance into the atmosphere which has then emanated across the boundary (for instance, where A's operations release acid fumes which then drift on the breeze across the boundary) A will not have committed trespass to land, though B will still gain redress if he can establish that A committed the tort of private nuisance in acting as he did.[10] Similarly, if A loses control of a vehicle that he is driving so that it leaves the road and crosses onto land possessed by B this crossing will be considered an *indirect* consequence of A's actions.[11]

The distinction between crossings which are a *direct* result and those which are *indirect* consequences is *not* the same as the distinction between crossings which are *intentional* and those which are *unintended*. In some circumstances the connection between A's behaviour and an unintended crossing will be so close that A will be unable to deny that the crossing was a *direct* result of his behaviour. For instance, if Brian hits a golf ball towards land possessed by Chloe with the intention that it should stop just before the boundary then if, despite his intention, it bounces across the boundary it is unlikely that he will be able to claim that the crossing was merely an *indirect* consequence of his behaviour. The outcome might be different, however, if Brian is an excellent golfer who uncharacteristically slices a golf ball off a golf course and onto land possessed by Chloe.

A landowner is not generally treated as having sufficient control over things on his land so as to make him liable for trespass if they cross onto B's land as a result of ordinary natural processes. Thus where the roots or branches of a tree on A's land gradually grow so that they cross onto B's land no trespass will be committed but A may be guilty of committing the tort of private nuisance by encroachment.[12]

[9] *Braithwaite* v *South Durham Steel Co. Ltd* [1958] 1 WLR 986.

[10] For the tort of private nuisance, see below, Chapter 19.

[11] Thus A will not be liable in relation to B for trespass to land, but may be liable for the tort of negligence. The situation would be different if A *chose* to drive off the highway and onto B's land in order to avoid colliding with another vehicle or a pedestrian, though here A may be able to rely on the defence of necessity.

[12] *Lemmon* v *Webb* [1895] AC 1. See below, pp. 371–4.

Control over animals

The law on when A will commit a trespass to land in relation to B if his animals cross over onto land possessed by B is complicated. The possessor of livestock which strays onto another's land is strictly liable for *damage* done by that livestock to the land or that other's property which is on the land.[13] But this liability, although it is the statutory replacement for the common law wrong known as 'cattle trespass',[14] is best understood as part of the law relating to the keeping of dangerous things[15] rather than part of the law on when someone will commit the tort of trespass to land. The Animals Act 1971 also makes the keepers of *dangerous* animals liable for the damage that such animals cause[16] and consequently in such cases it is not usually necessary to determine whether the keeper is liable for having committed trespass to land through the animal.

In practice, then, the situations where it is most important to consider whether A has committed trespass to land as a result of an animal crossing onto land possessed by B are those involving animals which are neither 'livestock' nor 'dangerous animals'. In *Buckle* v *Holmes*,[17] the Court of Appeal held that where an animal did not fall within either the class of livestock or the class of dangerous animals, and was of a class not generally confined and unlikely to cause substantial damage on straying, such as dogs and cats, the owner of the animal would not commit the tort of trespass to land whenever the animal strayed onto someone else's land. But while this rule clearly applies to a dog or cat acting of its own volition, equally clearly it would be a tort for A to *send* such an animal onto B's land.

In *League Against Cruel Sports* v *Scott*,[18] Park J held that the master of a hunt would be liable for trespass to land if 'he either intended that the hounds should enter the land or by negligence he failed to prevent them from doing so'.[19] In so far as this makes a huntsman liable for *sending* hounds onto another's land it is uncontroversial. But the suggestion that a huntsman is liable for trespass if he negligently allows the hounds to stray is not easy to reconcile with *Buckle* v *Holmes*,[20] which was not drawn to Park J's attention. Our view is that an owner of a pet dog will not commit the tort of trespass to land if he negligently fails

13 Animals Act 1971, s 4. A claim can also be brought for expenses reasonably incurred in keeping the livestock and ascertaining the owner.

14 Section 1(1)(c).

15 See below, Chapter 42.

16 Section 2. Which animals are considered 'dangerous' is discussed below, p. 770.

17 [1926] 2 KB 125. (The defendant's cat strayed onto the claimant's property and killed the claimant's pigeons and poultry.) In *Tutton* v *A D Walter Ltd* [1986] QB 61 the judge refused to treat unwanted straying bees as trespassers for the purpose of deciding whether a landowner owed their owner a duty to take care not to harm them. Suppose Tom, a beekeeper, released bees which strayed onto Lara's land and Tom knew they were likely to do this when he released the bees. Will Tom have committed the tort of trespass to land in relation to Lara? The doctrine expounded in *Buckle* v *Holmes* indicates that the answer is 'no'. We think it *would* be trespass to land, however, to put bees through Lara's letterbox, or otherwise send them onto Lara's property.

18 [1986] QB 240.

19 Ibid., 251H–252A.

20 In a subsequent passage Park J confined his opinion to the case '[w]here a master of staghounds takes out a pack of hounds and deliberately sets them in pursuit of a stag or hind, knowing that there is a real risk that in the pursuit hounds may enter or cross prohibited land'. This makes the case far closer to that of the golfer who hits balls towards the claimant's land with the intention that they should stop just before the boundary. It must be doubtful whether Park J intended to hold that a master of hounds would be liable for trespass if he negligently lost control of the dogs but they then strayed to a place that he would not have expected them to go. In such a case it would be difficult to argue that the crossing of the boundary to such a place was a sufficiently *direct* consequence of the master's behaviour to constitute trespass to land by the master.

to prevent it from straying onto someone else's land,[21] but that Park J was correct to state that if such straying frequently happened and the owner was apparently indifferent to it, this might give rise to an inference that the owner intended the dog to cross the boundary.[22]

TITLE TO SUE

B will be able to sue someone for trespassing on a particular piece of land if she was in *possession* of the land at the time of the alleged trespass.[23] But it is important to note that possession of land is a legal concept, and is not synonymous with physical occupation. So if B's mother-in-law visits for a week then she will not take *possession* of the spare bedroom even if she physically occupies it. In *J A Pye (Oxford) Ltd* v *Graham* Lord Browne-Wilkinson confirmed that 'there are two elements necessary for legal possession: (1) a sufficient degree of physical custody and control ('factual possession'); (2) an intention to exercise such custody and control on one's own behalf and for one's own benefit ('intention to possess').'[24] Except in the case of *joint* possessors, only one person can be in possession of a piece of land at any one time,[25] and, while the necessary degree of 'physical custody and control' will vary somewhat in accordance with the nature of the land concerned, what is looked for is *dealing* with the land in the same way that 'an occupying owner might have been expected to deal with it'.[26]

An owner of land will generally be deemed to be in *possession* in the absence of evidence to the contrary. Where the owner has granted a lease, however, and the tenant has moved onto the premises, it will be the tenant who has exclusive possession and can sue for trespass.[27] Whether a licensee (someone with permission to be on land but not with an interest

[21] The owner might, however, be liable for any consequential damage, in the tort of negligence, or under Animals Act 1971, ss 2, 3 or 8.

[22] *League Against Cruel Sports* v *Scott* [1986] QB 240, 252E–F.

[23] Although the rule is that the claimant must be in possession *at the time of* the trespass, if a person who is entitled to possession *enters* land, and thereby gains possession, the law will treat him as if he was in possession from the date when he became entitled to enter *and* will allow him to sue someone who has trespassed after *that* time. This doctrine is known as *trespass by relation*. See, for example, *Ocean Accident & Guarantee Corp.* v *Ilford Gas Co.* [1905] 2 KB 493.

[24] [2003] 1 AC 419, at [40].

[25] It is possible, however, to *split* land so that, for instance, one person possesses the surface and another person possesses the subsoil. Furthermore, the holders of certain rights over land known as *profits à prendre* can also sue for trespass to land. Thus a holder of a right to herbage, a liberty of hunting or a fishery can sue for a trespass to the land which damages the right. This rule has been applied in a modern context to hold that the company which 'owned' a genetically-modified crop being grown on another's land was entitled to sue third parties for trespass to land: *Monsanto* v *Tilly* [2000] Env LR 313. By contrast, a person entitled to an easement, such as a right of way, will *not* be able to claim that A committed the tort of trespass to land in relation to her if A interfered with that right; but she may be able to claim that A committed the tort of private nuisance in relation to her in so acting: see below, pp. 371–2.

[26] *Powell* v *McFarlane* (1977) 38 P & CR 452, 471 (per Slade J), *approved* by the House of Lords in *J A Pye (Oxford) Ltd* v *Graham* [2003] 1 AC 419, [41] (per Lord Browne-Wilkinson).

[27] Nonetheless, a reversioner can sue where there is a trespass to land which causes either: (*a*) damage to the property which the reversioner will in time gain the right to possess; or (*b*) injury of such a permanent nature as to be necessarily prejudicial to the reversion: *Mayfair Property Co.* v *Johnston* [1894] 1 Ch 508 (trespass by foundations of wall); *Jones* v *Llanrwst UDC* [1911] 1 Ch 393 (trespass by deposit of faecal matter on riverbank). The right of a reversioner to bring an immediate action is useful because the reversioner might be more willing to take the risks of litigation than a tenant with a time-limited interest and there are occasions when it is desirable for a claim in trespass to be brought sooner rather than later, for instance when it is better for repairs to be effected immediately. Technically, the claim made by the reversioner in such cases is not identical to a claim for trespass to land since the reversioner will allege that the defendant has injured his reversion rather than his land.

in the land) is treated as being in possession for the purposes of suing a third party for trespass[28] depends on the terms of the licence.[29]

Where B is in possession of land, A cannot successfully defend an action for trespass to land on the basis that someone else has a title superior to B's,[30] unless A can establish that *he* has a superior title, or that he crossed the boundary with the permission of the person with a superior title.[31] This means that B can usually safely sue if *in fact* she is in possession, even if as a matter *of law* she has no title or formal interest in the land.

What counts as land

One question that has attracted some attention is how far B can claim to be in possession of the airspace above his property so as to be able to object to A's crossing that airspace or placing something in it. The original principle was often said to be that 'the man who has land has everything above it, or is entitled at all events to object to anything else being put over it'.[32] Thus possessors of land have successfully objected to, for instance, overhanging signs[33] and cranes.[34] Modern cases have suggested, however, that passing over land at a height at which there can be no interference with the ordinary use of that land is not a trespass, and that all members of the public have an equal right to use this airspace.[35] Thus the modern principle seems to be that the possessor of the surface's interest only extends to superjacent airspace which must be controlled if the possessor is to be able reasonably to enjoy the land and put it to purposeful use.[36] Even if the modern principle represents the law, it is merely a presumption, since often in a multi-storey building one owner's rooms on a higher floor will protrude over the rooms owned by another on the ground floor.[37]

Just as the tort of trespass to land can be committed by intruding into the airspace

[28] Where the licensor throws the licensee off the land, or tries to do so, the question is generally whether the licensee has become a trespasser (after failing to leave) and not whether the licensee can sue *for* trespass to land. The question often arises where the licensee sues for a trespass to the person committed in throwing him off the land and the licensor relies on the justification of using reasonable force to expel a trespasser. For when a licensee becomes a trespasser, see below, p. 365.

[29] In *Hill* v *Tupper* (1863) 2 H & C 121, 159 ER 51 the claimant was granted the 'sole and exclusive right or liberty' to put pleasure boats on the Basingstoke Canal, but this was held to be insufficient. By contrast in *Manchester Airport plc* v *Dutton* [2000] QB 133, the claimant was granted the right to enter and occupy the land concerned and this was held to be sufficient to allow it to obtain an order for possession against third parties who were squatting, partly on the basis that if the claimant had already entered under such a licence then it would have had sufficient possession to seek such an order. This strongly suggests that the claimant, although a licensee, would have had sufficient possession to sue for trespass. *Manchester Airport plc* v *Dutton* [2000] QB 133 was distinguished in *Countryside Residential (North Thames) Ltd* v *Tugwell* [2000] 34 EG 87, where a claimant seeking an order for possession against protesters who were camping on the site only had a licence to enter and carry out investigatory work and not one which granted 'effective control over the land'.

[30] This defence is commonly referred to as the defence of *ius tertii*.

[31] *Nicholls* v *Ely Beet Sugar Factory* [1931] 2 Ch 84, 86.

[32] *Wandsworth Board of Works* v *United Telephone Co. Ltd* (1884) 13 QBD 904, 919, Bowen LJ. This doctrine is often presented in Latin as *cujus est solum ejus est usque ad coelum*.

[33] *Kelsen* v *Imperial Tobacco Co.* [1957] 2 QB 334.

[34] *Anchor Brewhouse Developments Ltd* v *Berkley House Ltd* [1987] 2 EGLR 173.

[35] *Bernstein* v *Skyviews* [1978] QB 479. An overflight by a civil aircraft at a reasonable height is immune from liability under the Civil Aviation Act 1982, s 76(1).

[36] *Bernstein* v *Skyviews* [1978] QB 479. See also Gray 1991.

[37] *Corbett* v *Hill* (1870) LR 9 Eq 671.

immediately above B's land, it can also be committed by intruding into the ground beneath it.[38]

LAWFUL JUSTIFICATION OR EXCUSE

If A has crossed the boundary of B's land, there are many different ways in which A could establish that he had a lawful justification or excuse for crossing that boundary. We will not attempt to catalogue them here. A may, for instance, seek to establish that, in acting as he did, he was merely making lawful use of a highway[39] or private right of way, or that he had a licence to enter, or that statute[40] or common law[41] conferred on him a power to enter.[42] Here we will discuss only two instances where A might be able to establish that he had a lawful justification or excuse for crossing the boundary of B's land.

Licence (consent)

Suppose A enters B's land. A will not commit the tort of trespass to land in so doing if B has licensed him to enter. A may commit the tort of trespass to land, however, if he either exceeds the terms of the licence[43] or fails to leave within a reasonable time after the licence is withdrawn. Sometimes a contract will restrict B's power to withdraw a licence. But it is important to distinguish between cases where the withdrawal is wrongful (a breach of contract) but still effective and those where the withdrawal is ineffective.[44] If the withdrawal is effective, then A must leave B's land within a reasonable period of time – if he does not, then he will commit the tort of trespass to land in relation to B. If, on the other hand, the withdrawal is ineffective, A will *not* commit the tort of trespass to land if he stays on B's land.

38 For instance, by foundations or mining. As has already been observed (see above, p. 361), encroaching tree roots are treated as a form of private nuisance.

39 The public's right to use a highway is limited: In *DPP* v *Jones* [1999] 2 AC 240 the majority held that the public's right was not limited to passing, repassing and ancillary uses, and accepted that *at least some* other reasonable, peaceful and non-obstructive uses were lawful (at 257, per Lord Irvine; 281, per Lord Clyde; and 286–7, per Lord Hutton).

40 For example, police officers have statutory powers under ss 17 and 18 of the Police and Criminal Evidence Act 1984 to enter premises in order to make an arrest and to search after making an arrest.

41 For example, the common law confers powers to enter premises in order to reclaim wrongfully taken personal property, in order to abate a nuisance (though sometimes notice may be required), and in order to preserve person or property from immediate danger.

42 Where a person who is authorised by law to enter for a particular purpose afterwards abuses that authority he may be treated as a trespasser *ab initio*, that is, he may be treated as if the initial entry was unlawful. The doctrine is associated with *The Six Carpenters' Case* (1610) 8 Co Rep 146a, 77 ER 695. Although Lord Denning MR thought in *Chic Fashions Ltd* v *Jones* [1968] 2 QB 299 that the doctrine should be interred with the bones of the old forms of action, he later used the doctrine in *Cinnamond* v *BAA* [1980] 1 WLR 582.

43 The picturesque illustration commonly given is that a person licensed to walk down the stairs becomes a trespasser if he slides down the bannisters.

44 A textbook on tort is not the appropriate place to explore when licences cannot be revoked and when they will bind third parties. The interested reader should consult a standard textbook on land law.

Necessity

In *Southport Corporation* v *Esso Petroleum*,[45] the defendant shipowners dumped some oil from their ship into the sea when their ship ran aground. The defendants dumped the oil because they feared that the ship would break its back and the crew would be endangered if they did not. The oil washed up onto the claimants' foreshore. The claimants sued the defendants, claiming that they had committed the tort of trespass to land in dumping the oil.

Devlin J thought that the defendants could rely on the defence of *necessity* to justify their dumping the oil.[46] He also held, however, that the defendants would not be permitted to rely on the defence if the predicament was a result of their own negligence.[47] The defence is available only in cases of immediate danger or emergency. So in *Southwark LBC* v *Williams*,[48] the Court of Appeal held that the defence did not stretch to cover the case of homeless people who made an orderly entry into empty property.

The fact that in some circumstances necessity seems to make the defendant's decision to cause harm to the claimant justifiable does not mean that the defendant should necessarily be free from an obligation to pay compensation for the harm that he has caused. For instance, in *Vincent* v *Lake Erie Transportation Co.*[49] the defendant's boat was moored at the claimant's dock when a severe storm arose. The crew acted to prevent the boat from getting away from the dock and being lost, but with the result that the vessel was repeatedly thrown against the dock and damaged it. A majority of the Supreme Court of Minnesota held that the claimant was entitled to compensation for the damage done. One explanation for such an outcome is that there is an *incomplete* privilege to perform an act which would otherwise be a tort in a situation of necessity – that is, the act may be performed and the claimant cannot resist or prevent this, but liability is still imposed for any *material* harm done.[50] An alternative explanation is that while the availability of a defence of necessity meant that the defendant could not be held liable to compensate the claimant in *tort* for the damage done to the dock, the defendant could still be held liable in *restitution* for the damage done to the dock.[51]

[45] [1953] 2 All ER 1204. This judgment was reversed by the Court of Appeal but restored by the House of Lords: [1956] AC 218.

[46] See also *Cope* v *Sharpe (No. 2)* [1912] 1 KB 496.

[47] *Southport Corporation* v *Esso Petroleum* [1953] 2 All ER 1204, 1210A. See also *Rigby* v *Chief Constable of Northamptonshire* [1985] 1 WLR 1242.

[48] [1971] 1 Ch 734. See also *Monsanto* v *Tilly* [2000] Env LR 313.

[49] 124 NW 221 (1910).

[50] Bohlen 1926, 313; also Stevens 2007, 104. The reference to 'material' harm is intended to denote that the claimant cannot recover *simply* for the 'invasion of the right'. See also *Burmah Oil* v *Lord Advocate* [1965] AC 75, where the House of Lords treated a situation where oil installations were destroyed in wartime to prevent them falling into enemy hands as one where the acts were performed in the lawful exercise of the Royal prerogative but there was nonetheless an obligation to pay compensation.

[51] See below, pp. 711–12; also Weinrib 1995, 196–203.

19 Private nuisance

DEFINITION

A will commit the tort of private nuisance in relation to B if he creates, authorises, adopts or continues a state of affairs which unreasonably interferes with the use and enjoyment of land in which B has a sufficient interest. A will also commit the tort of private nuisance in relation to B if he creates, authorises, adopts or continues a state of affairs which unreasonably interferes with some natural right or easement that B enjoys. This needs a lot more explanation. However, before we go on to explain some of the key terms in the above definitions, it may be useful to distinguish the tort of private nuisance from the tort of trespass to land. Two points help to distinguish the two torts.

First, if A *directly* interferes with B's land,[1] the tort, if any, committed by A will be trespass to land. If, on the other hand, A *indirectly* interferes with B's land, the tort, if any, committed by A will be private nuisance.

Secondly, trespass to land does *not* cover cases where no person or physical object crosses the boundary onto B's land. Because of this second distinction, the tort of trespass to land does not cover situations where B's land is invaded by, for instance, noise, heat or vibrations. Further, where A's interference is with a natural right or an easement[2] the situation is covered by private nuisance and not by trespass to land.

These distinctions are not easy to apply in practice. It is easy to disagree over what counts as a *direct* interference and what counts as an *indirect* interference, and over what is a physical object and what is not. In borderline cases, however, it will rarely matter to a defendant if the claim is described as being for private nuisance rather than for trespass to land. From the defendant's perspective, if a claimant sues her for private nuisance instead of trespass to land, then the claimant will have to prove two additional things: (1) that the defendant's interference with the claimant's land was unreasonable and (2) that the defendant's interference caused damage.[3] Consequently, as a rule of thumb, where there is uncertainty about which tort is applicable it is safer for a claimant to sue for private

[1] When we use the phrase 'B's land' in this context we intend the word 'land' to include not just the earth itself but also things attached to it, such as buildings, which count as real property. The statement that the land must be 'B's' is shorthand for the fact that in order to claim B must have a particular relationship with the land. The precise nature of that necessary relationship is discussed below, pp. 394–5. At this stage an adequate summary may be that the land will count as 'B's land' if B has a legally-recognised interest in it, and usually it will be sufficient if B has exclusive possession of the land.

[2] These concepts are familiar to land lawyers, and we do not want to try to duplicate the discussions of them which will be found in textbooks devoted to that subject. Examples of natural rights and easements include: rights to the passage of light, rights to support from neighbouring land or buildings, and rights to use particular paths across another's land.

[3] It will be recalled from Chapter 18 that any crossing onto someone else's property, no matter how trivial, can be a trespass, and that trespass to land is actionable *per se*, that is, without proof of damage. The tort of private nuisance is not, generally speaking, actionable *per se*.

nuisance, because this will not be to the defendant's disadvantage.[4] We will now look at these two distinctions in more detail.

(1) *Direct and indirect*. The most important factor in drawing this distinction seems to be the defendant's degree of control over the thing which caused the interference. For example, if Eric crosses onto Mary's land this will be a direct interference and trespass, while if the roots or branches of Eric's tree cross over onto Mary's land this will be an indirect interference and private nuisance. The reason for the distinction between these two cases seems to be that Eric has direct control over how his own body moves but he does not have the same degree of control over how the roots or branches on his tree grow.

Similarly, if Eric throws rubbish onto Mary's land that is trespass, but if Eric releases acid smuts into the air which drift across onto Mary's land then that is private nuisance. Difficulties arise, however, where Eric releases something in a place where he knows that it will almost inevitably be carried onto Mary's land. Is the interference in that case *direct* or *indirect*? There are cases which suggest that if A puts something in a river where it will be carried by the flow onto B's land, A's interference with B's land will be sufficiently direct to amount to a trespass.[5]

(2) *Physicality*. All emanations for which A is responsible which do not involve the projection of a physical object onto B's land are treated as within the tort of private nuisance. Thus if A screams over B's garden fence or creates vibrations which rock B's house, B will have to try to show that A has committed the tort of private nuisance in so acting if she wants to sue A. She will not be able to claim that A's actions amount to a trespass to her land.

This second distinction can also be used to explain why some interests in land, in particular natural rights and easements, are *only* protected by private nuisance. The reason is that if B has an easement, for instance a private right of way over C's land, an interference with that right of way by A is not treated as involving any physical thing crossing onto *B's* land.[6]

USE AND ENJOYMENT OF LAND

An unreasonable interference with the claimant's activities will not amount to a private nuisance unless it is an interference with the usefulness or amenity of *land* (in which the claimant has a sufficient interest).

In order to understand what this means it may be helpful to contrast two situations. In the first, Judy produces thick clouds of smoke which drift into Henry's factory, with the result that work has to stop. In the second, Judy persuades Henry's suppliers to refuse to

[4] Although the modern rules of civil procedure relieve the claimant of the burden of *identifying* exactly which tort is supposed to have been committed, what facts have to be established for the claim to succeed depends on which tort is supposed to have been committed.

[5] See, for example, *Jones* v *Llanrwst UDC* [1911] 1 Ch 393.

[6] It might be thought obvious that nothing crosses onto B's land because the right of way is across C's land. But here we must remind ourselves that in some circumstances B will be able to sue A for trespass to land, even though the land belongs to C and B only has certain rights over it. Thus not only the person in possession of the soil but also those with certain rights over the land can sue for a trespass to land, e.g. the holders of hunting and fishing rights, and the owners of growing crops (see, above, p. 362 n. 25).

deliver the raw materials which his factory needs, with the result that work has to stop. Although the loss which Henry suffers in these two situations might, at first sight, appear to be the same, tort law regards the situations as *wholly* different. In the first situation Judy *may* have committed the tort of private nuisance in relation to Henry, because her activity has made the *land* which he uses for his factory less useful. But in the second case Judy will not be liable for private nuisance because she has not made the *land* less useful. In the second case Henry's land remains just as useful for running his business even though Judy's intervention means that *he* is unable to make use of the land because he cannot get the necessary raw materials for his business.

A defendant may commit private nuisance if he is responsible for a state of affairs which interferes with the usefulness or amenity of the claimant's land *even if* the claimant uses the land in a way which means that *he* is not inconvenienced. For instance, if Nigel's factory emits nauseating smells on weekdays which drift into Ingrid's neighbouring cottage, then Nigel *may* be committing the tort of private nuisance in relation to Ingrid *even if* Ingrid only uses the cottage at weekends. The fact that Ingrid suffers no 'consequential loss' will, naturally, affect the amount of damages she can claim for 'past loss'. But if she seeks a remedy to prevent any future unreasonable interference with her *right* to the use and enjoyment of land Nigel will not be able to claim that he is not committing a tort.[7]

Similarly, a claimant can base a claim on an unreasonable interference with the usefulness or amenity of land even if she *uses* the land by permitting others to use it. So Ingrid could base a claim on Nigel's interference even if she had never visited the cottage and used it by renting it out to holidaymakers. The fact that the holidaymakers would have been subjected to the nauseous smell, not Ingrid, would not prevent her from making a claim. Thus in *Andreae* v *Selfridge & Co. Ltd*,[8] where a defendant's building operations unreasonably interfered with the amenity of land used by the claimant as a hotel, the claimant did not have to establish that she had been *personally* disturbed by the noise or dust in order to recover damages covering the consequential loss of business. Indeed it would not have mattered if the claimant had been a company, and thus incapable of being woken up at night or choked with dust.

TYPES OF INTERFERENCE

It is useful to classify the types of interference which can amount to a private nuisance for two reasons. First, such a classification will help us to describe the *range* of situations which the tort of private nuisance can cover. Secondly, the tests which determine whether an interference is unreasonable vary depending on the type of interference involved. For example, it is far easier to establish that an interference is unreasonable when it involves an encroachment on someone's land than when it merely reduces the amenity value of someone's land.

Two systems of classification are worth discussing. The first classifies a given interference

7 *Price* v *Hilditch* [1930] 1 Ch 500, 509; *Nicholls* v *Ely Beet Sugar Factory Ltd (No. 2)* [1936] Ch 343.

8 [1938] Ch 1. These cases suggest that damages can be awarded for 'interference with the legal right' of the claimants. Another way of putting the matter, however, may be that unless a remedy is granted to prevent *future* interference the potential sale and rental values of the property will be depressed.

according to what *effect* it has on the land which is being interfered with. The second classifies a given interference according to *how* it arose.

Encroachment, physical injury, reducing amenity value

In *Hunter* v *Canary Wharf Ltd*, Lord Lloyd said that 'Private nuisances are of three kinds. They are (1) nuisance by encroachment on a neighbour's land; (2) nuisance by direct physical injury to a neighbour's land; and (3) nuisance by interference with a neighbour's quiet enjoyment of his land.'[9] Because this statement was given such prominence in a House of Lords' speech and has such an attractive simplicity, we feel that we must discuss it. Our opinion, however, is that it is dangerously misleading unless *five* modifications are made.

First, we think that the word 'another' should be substituted for 'neighbour' each time that it occurs. The word 'neighbour' in this context tends to suggest that the *defendant* must have an interest in neighbouring land, and, as we will explain below, we think that this is incorrect.[10]

Secondly, we think that the statement needs some reworking to make clear that (1), (2) and (3) are three forms of *interference*,[11] and that such interferences will only amount to private nuisances if they are *unreasonable*. We will explain in detail below how the courts decide whether a particular interference is *unreasonable*.[12]

Thirdly, we think that the word 'indirect' should be substituted for the word 'direct' in (2). As we have explained above,[13] one of the crucial distinctions between the torts of trespass to land and private nuisance is that in private nuisance the effect on the claimant's land is *indirect*. If A damages B's land *directly*, for instance by throwing a rock through B's greenhouse or taking an axe to her cherry tree, then the situation falls within the tort of trespass to land and not private nuisance.

Fourthly, we think that the phrase 'quiet enjoyment' is best avoided in (3) because it is a phrase which has a different meaning in landlord and tenant law. We would also prefer to avoid the word 'interference' because under our definition (1), (2) and (3) are *all* forms of interference. In its place we would substitute the phrase 'reducing the amenity value', a phrase Lord Lloyd used later in his speech[14] to explain (3). The phrase is intended to capture the key idea that this form of interference involves a state of affairs which makes the land *less useful* as land, but does not involve physical damage. Common examples of interferences falling within (3) include smells and noises, and consequently some cases refer to private nuisances of this form as involving 'interference with sensibilities'. We, however, prefer to highlight the fact that such interferences 'reduce the amenity value of the land' *because* claims can be brought by claimants which do not have 'sensibilities', like companies.

[9] [1997] AC 655, 695.
[10] See below, pp. 384–5.
[11] Lord Lloyd acknowledged this point later in his speech, ibid., 696: 'the essence of private nuisance is easy enough to identify, and it is the same in all three classes of private nuisance, namely, interference with land or the enjoyment of land.'
[12] See below, pp. 374–84.
[13] See above, p. 368.
[14] Ibid., 696.

Fifthly, we think that 'or his rights over land' should be added to (3) since otherwise the definition will not cover actionable interferences with natural rights and easements.

With these modifications the statement reads: 'Private nuisances can be divided into three kinds in accordance with the type of *unreasonable* interference involved. They are (1) nuisance by encroachment on another's land; (2) nuisance by indirect physical injury to another's land; and (3) nuisance by reducing the amenity value of another's land or his rights over land.' This modified version of Lord Lloyd's statement helpfully classifies the types of interference that can amount to a private nuisance according to their effect on the land which is being interfered with. It is also useful, however, to consider an alternative system for classifying the different kinds of interference that can amount to a private nuisance. This system divides up these kinds of interference according to *how* they arise.

Emanation, encroachment, obstruction and withdrawal, affront

If we divide types of interference according to *how* they arise then they fall into four categories. We will look at each category before considering a relevant aspect of the decision of the House of Lords in *Hunter* v *Canary Wharf Ltd*.[15]

(1) *Emanation*. Most cases of private nuisance involve interference caused by things that *emanate* onto a claimant's land. Thus typical cases involve the *emanation* of noise, smells, vibrations, acid smuts, and sewage onto a claimant's land.

(2) *Encroachment*. When the thing which crosses onto a claimant's land is something such as growing branches or tree roots lawyers tend to refer to the process as being one of *encroachment* rather than emanation.

(3) *Obstruction and withdrawal*. A more difficult category covers cases where the complaint is that A has *obstructed* or *withdrawn* some benefit which B could otherwise have expected to enjoy. For instance, A might obstruct the wind that would otherwise have passed over A's land and onto B's land and powered B's windmill. Or A might obstruct the groundwater that would otherwise have passed through A's land and percolated onto B's land, filling B's reservoir. Alternatively, A might withdraw the support that his land previously offered B's house. In these cases B must establish a *right* to the benefit passing to him free from unreasonable interruption before he can complain about A's obstruction or withdrawal.

Sometimes this is straightforward: B may be able to demonstrate that she has a private right of way across A's land and will then be able to complain if that right of way is unreasonably interfered with by A. But in some cases the need to show a right to the benefit will pose a considerable obstacle for B because English land law is so cautious about holding that landowners are subject to obligations to allow benefits to pass over, across or through their land. In particular, English land law is reluctant to recognise such obligations where they cannot be precisely defined. Saying that a defendant must not unreasonably interfere with a private right of way along a path or with the passage of a river which flows in a defined channel is one thing, but saying that he or she must not unreasonably interfere with the wind, or percolating groundwater, or invisible electromagnetic signals is another.

[15] [1997] AC 655.

Alongside the problem of defining such obligations with precision is the further difficulty that such benefits could easily be obstructed by activities that the law would not want to discourage. Thus almost any building might interfere with wind, groundwater and signals. The consequence of all this is that if B alleges unreasonable interference by obstruction of a benefit or withdrawal of support she may often lose simply because she can prove no entitlement to the benefit passing unobstructed or the support continuing.[16]

There are also two similar matters on which English land law has taken a firm view. First, a person cannot usually claim a right to an uninterrupted view across another's land, and consequently it is not a private nuisance to interfere with a claimant's view. In the United States some courts have been willing to draw a distinction between obstructing a view (which is not usually actionable) and positively creating an ugly sight (which can be treated as analogous to an emanation). But English law has not adopted this distinction. Nonetheless, although a claim cannot be based on obstruction of a view in certain circumstances it can be based on an obstruction of light.[17] Secondly, a person cannot automatically claim a right to his neighbour's land continuing to support his *building* (as opposed to his land) but must acquire an easement to gain such a right. This means that in the absence of such an easement a defendant is permitted to excavate on his own land even if the result is that the claimant's building collapses.[18]

(4) *Affront*. The fourth way in which A can commit the tort of private nuisance in relation to B is by *affront*. English law, however, has made only tentative moves towards accepting that this form of interference can amount to an actionable nuisance. Within this category the interference is caused by the mental disturbance – the affront – that comes from knowledge that nearby land is being used for a particular purpose, rather than by any emanation, encroachment or obstruction. In England this form of claim has been used principally against brothels, pornographic cinemas and sex shops.[19] But in practice such claims are rare because a claimant must demonstrate not only that he has suffered interference by affront but also that it was unreasonable for the defendant to create, authorise, adopt or continue the state of affairs which is causing the affront. This limits the number of claims because it will be difficult to persuade a court that it is *unreasonable* for a defendant to carry

[16] A famous example is the decision of the House of Lords in *Bradford Corporation* v *Pickles* [1895] AC 587 where because the Corporation could not establish any right to the percolating groundwater passing to them without interruption they could not complain even about Pickles's malicious interference with it.

[17] See below, p. 384.

[18] *Dalton* v *Angus* (1881) 6 App Cas 740, 804 (per Lord Penzance): 'It is the law, I believe I may say without question, that at any time within twenty years after the house is built the owner of the adjacent soil may with perfect legality dig that soil away, and allow his neighbour's house, if supported by it, to fall in ruins to the ground.' See also *Ray* v *Fairway Motors (Barnstaple) Ltd* (1969) 20 P & CR 261. Similarly, a landowner can extract percolating groundwater from beneath his own land even if this drains water from beneath another's land and causes damage: *Popplewell* v *Hodkinson* (1869) LR 4 Ex 248; *Langbrook Properties Ltd* v *Surrey CC* [1970] 1 WLR 161.

[19] See, for example, *Laws* v *Florinplace* [1981] 1 All ER 659, where ten residents of an area of Pimlico, London, which was claimed to enjoy an attractive village atmosphere, sought an injunction against the 'Victoria Sex and Video Centre'. Vinelott J held that even if the defendant changed the business's name and altered its signs and displays, it was still arguable that the 'profound repugnance' caused to the claimants by knowledge of nearby trade in hard pornography could amount to sufficient interference for the purposes of the tort. See also *Thompson-Schwab* v *Costaki* [1956] 1 WLR 335, where the Court of Appeal did not accept that the defendants could only be liable for using a house as a venue for prostitution if their activity had a *physical* effect on the claimant's enjoyment of his neighbouring house. In the United States 'nuisance by affront' has also been relied on against undertakers.

on a *lawful* business[20] which causes no interference more severe than affront. Despite its limited practical significance, the doctrine of private nuisance by affront is sometimes attacked for allowing the majority in a locality to impose its *moral* views on others.

A doctrine similar to nuisance by affront may explain a group of cases in which extreme dangers, such as warehouses of gunpowder, were held to be nuisances before they had caused any physical harm.[21] It might be said that in such cases there was an *immediate* nuisance from the fear and anxiety caused to people living in the vicinity.[22] There is a tension, however, between this explanation and the rule that a claimant can only obtain an injunction to restrain an *anticipated* tort when such a tort is 'highly probable' and 'imminent',[23] since a claimant might become fearful or anxious even when a risk is 'improbable' or 'remote'. It might also be objected that this sort of reasoning could allow a claimant to establish a tort where there was no rational basis for any fear or anxiety.[24] But this objection seems misplaced since a claimant would have to demonstrate that it was *unreasonable* for the defendant to have created, authorised, adopted or continued the state of affairs which caused the anxiety.

(5) *Interference with television reception.* One of the complaints in *Hunter* v *Canary Wharf Ltd*[25] was that the building of the Canary Wharf Tower interfered with the claimants' television reception because it stood between their homes and the Crystal Palace transmitter. In *Bridlington Relay Ltd* v *Yorkshire Electricity Board,*[26] Buckley J had suggested that interference with television reception could not constitute a legal nuisance because it was interference with a purely recreational facility, as opposed to interference with the health or physical comfort or well-being of the claimants. In *Hunter* the House of Lords expressed some doubts as to whether such reasoning was still convincing in the light of the increased social importance of television.[27] The majority held, however, that interference with television reception merely by building on one's own land was not actionable, relying on an analogy with the fact that interference with a view cannot give rise to a claim in private nuisance in the absence of an agreement.[28] Thus the case supports the proposition set out

[20] In *Laws* v *Florinplace* [1981] 1 All ER 659, 668, Vinelott J treated it as relevant to whether to grant an interim injunction that the defendant's business was 'at least near the boundary of the criminal law' and thought that at a full trial of the action it would be necessary to decide whether the business was lawful or not.

[21] *R* v *Lister* (1856–7) 7 Dears & B 209, 169 ER 979; *Hepburn* v *Lordan* (1865) 2 H & M 345, 71 ER 497; *R* v *Chilworth Gunpowder Co.* (1888) 4 TLR 557.

[22] In *R* v *Lister* (1856–7) 7 Dears & B 209, 227, 169 ER 979, 987, Lord Campbell CJ stated that, 'the well-founded apprehension of danger which would alarm men of steady nerves and reasonable courage, passing through the street in which the house stands, or residing in adjoining houses, is enough to show that something has been done which the law ought to prevent'. It is unclear whether a series of claims in the nineteenth century against smallpox hospitals and asylums are best explained as 'nuisance by anxiety', 'nuisance by affront', or both.

[23] The Court of Appeal in *Hooper* v *Rogers* [1975] Ch 43 treated this rule as requiring no more than that the degree of probability was sufficient to make an injunction just, and the application was not premature, but even this softened version of the rule seems more stringent than the approach taken in the gunpowder factory cases.

[24] The nuisance claim against the operators of a smallpox hospital which gave rise to the appeal in *Metropolitan Asylum District Managers* v *Hill* (1881) 6 App Cas 193 is often mentioned in this context. Although the claimants' evidence included allegations as to the emanation of smells from the morgue and of a disproportionate infection rate in the vicinity of the hospital it seems that many of the fears were exaggerated.

[25] [1997] AC 655.

[26] [1965] Ch 436.

[27] [1997] AC 655, at 684–5 (per Lord Goff), 708 (per Lord Hoffmann), 722 (per Lord Cooke).

[28] Ibid., at 685 (per Lord Goff), 699 (per Lord Lloyd), 709 (per Lord Hoffmann), 726–7 (per Lord Hope).

above that obstruction of a benefit that would otherwise pass onto a claimant's land is not actionable unless the claimant can establish a right to have the benefit come onto her land.[29]

UNREASONABLE INTERFERENCE

Our definition of private nuisance states that there must be an *unreasonable* interference. Consequently we must examine how the law determines whether a particular interference is *unreasonable*. The easiest point to make is that not all interferences are unreasonable. Nobody can expect that every noise, smell or vibration from their neighbours amount to a tort. Ordinary social living requires a degree of 'give and take'. Your neighbours have to put up with your singing in the shower; you, in turn, have to put up with their wailing baby. But this does not take us very far. Below we begin by discussing the general approach which the courts take in order to determine whether a particular interference is *unreasonable*, then move on to discuss some of the most influential factors.

Effect on the claimant

In order to determine whether a particular interference is *unreasonable* it is important to classify the *effect* on the claimant's land. This is because:

(1) It seems that all encroachments are unreasonable (though in practice many occupiers tolerate overhanging branches and straying roots).[30]
(2) Not all indirect physical damage is unreasonable. For instance, an interference which causes physical damage will not be unreasonable if it involved an emanation which was only capable of damaging unusually delicate property.[31]
(3) It is generally easier to establish that an interference causing indirect physical damage is unreasonable than an interference which only reduces amenity value. For instance, where an interference reduces amenity value an assessment of its reasonableness must take account of the nature of the locality where it occurs but this is not necessary in a case of indirect physical damage.[32]

Reasons and reasonableness

Clearly the degree of interference with a claimant's land will be a very influential factor when deciding whether the interference is unreasonable. But what a claimant must put up with does not turn only on the *degree* of interference. It is also relevant to ask *why* the interference was caused. Thus if I have builders in to replace the rotten floorboards in my house then my neighbour will be expected to put up with the inevitable loud noises. It would probably be unreasonable, however, for me to make exactly the same amount of noise by

[29] Consequently, the question whether an *emanation* of electromagnetic waves *onto* B's land which interferes with B's television reception can be actionable is still open.

[30] The question whether the occupier will be responsible for an encroachment is separate from the question whether the encroachment is an unreasonable interference.

[31] *Robinson* v *Kilvert* (1889) 41 Ch D 88. See below, pp. 377–8.

[32] See below, pp. 378–81.

banging on trays and kicking the furniture. In particular, it would almost certainly be unreasonable for me to make the same amount of noise if my purpose was to annoy my neighbour.[33] The point that the reason for the interference is relevant is sometimes made by saying that a defendant cannot be liable for interference stemming from a 'reasonable user'. It is important to note, however, that this is not the same as saying that the defendant cannot be liable for interference stemming from a 'careful user'. What is a 'reasonable user' does not turn wholly on the degree of risk to neighbours and the cost of precautions but on the extent to which the user is an ordinary part of social living.

Sometimes, for instance, a *gross* disturbance may not amount to an unreasonable interference. An example of this is provided by the case of *Southwark London Borough Council* v *Tanner*.[34] In that case, the claimants were tenants who lived in old houses with inadequate soundproofing. They could hear everything their neighbours did, 'their coming and going, their cooking and cleaning, their quarrels and their love-making.'[35] Lord Millett accepted that '[life] in these conditions must be intolerable'.[36] But the House of Lords unanimously found that there was not an actionable private nuisance. Despite the 'intolerable' effect of their everyday noises it was not unreasonable for the claimants' neighbours to make such noises – the interference resulted from those neighbours' reasonable and ordinary use of their property.

Lord Millett stated that there could be no liability if the acts causing the interference were *necessary for the common and ordinary use and occupation of land and conveniently done*.[37] The test of necessity is weak here: *common and ordinary* is the phrase which governs. Babies, televisions and washing machines are not strictly necessary for occupation of land, but they are all part of *common and ordinary occupation*, and they will not ordinarily be treated as involving unreasonable interference. *Conveniently done* is an important qualification here, however. The point seems to be that babies, televisions and washing machines must not be arranged so as to expose neighbours to maximum noise where it would be equally convenient to arrange them otherwise. Thus, if there was nowhere in his house that a defendant could put the washing machine without it disturbing his neighbours then the noise caused by the washing machine would not amount to an unreasonable interference with the neighbours' use and enjoyment of their land, but if it disturbed the neighbours only because he chose to put it in an alcove where the wall between the houses was particularly thin then the interference so caused might be unreasonable.

Reasonableness and reasonable care

Much academic ink has been spilled trying to explain the distinction between the test for unreasonableness in private nuisance and the test for unreasonableness in negligence. We think that this distinction can best be illustrated by thinking about a case where a chemical works operated by Vijay emits acid which causes a nauseous smell and damages the shrubs in the garden of Wendy's cottage, which she uses as a weekend country retreat. It seems

33 See below, pp. 382–3.
34 [2001] 1 AC 1.
35 Ibid., 7.
36 Ibid., 18.
37 Ibid., 21.

clear that it could be concluded that the operation of Vijay's chemical works is unreasonably interfering with Wendy's use and enjoyment of her land without any need to investigate whether the chemical works are being carelessly operated or not. No doubt if the chemical works are emitting the acid because Vijay is operating them in a careless[38] manner that would make it easy to show that the interference is unreasonable. But, to put the point firmly, it is *not necessary* to show careless operation in order to establish unreasonable interference.[39]

Most commentators agree with the analysis so far, but some say that nonetheless there is a *special type* of carelessness in such a case: carelessness not in the operation of the chemical works but in locating it in such a place that it can interfere with Wendy's use and enjoyment of her cottage. We think that this view is wrong and that the chemical works can be found to be causing an unreasonable interference even if there is evidence that it is located in by far the most sensible place. We think that even if everyone is agreed that such chemical works are valuable for society, and that this one has been located where it will interfere with the smallest number of people to the least extent, it can still be said that the interference that it causes is unreasonable. How can this be? How can what seems valuable and sensible be castigated as unreasonable and wrong? The answer we think is that the chemical works and its location is valuable and sensible *from the perspective of society as a whole*, but is unreasonable *from the perspective of Wendy*, who has had her garden made unpleasant and her shrubs damaged. Wendy can quite fairly argue that it is unreasonable to expect her to put up with *all* the consequences of the chemical works without any redress and the common law accepts this point of view.[40]

One way of thinking about what the common law is doing is to think of Wendy and Vijay as having *equal* rights to use and enjoy their land.[41] If both have bought their land then surely they both have equal rights to exploit it for uses which are ordinary in the locality. But if Vijay argues that the importance of his chemical works for society as a whole means that he should be able to continue operating in such a way as to render Wendy's land far less valuable for her ordinary purposes then he will not be respecting her *equal* right. Almost everyone would agree that Vijay should not be permitted to seize Wendy's cottage and evict

[38] It is worth noting that there is some ambiguity even in the word 'careless' in this context. Thus in the tort of negligence carelessness often refers to the degree of risk being created, whilst here one may just mean that Vijay is not meeting the standards of comparable chemical works operators.

[39] For instance, in *Dennis* v *Ministry of Defence* [2003] EWHC 793, it was found that the circuit flying of Harrier jump-jets from RAF Wittering caused a private nuisance to Mr Dennis, a neighbouring landowner, but it was not suggested that the jets were being flown carelessly or that the Ministry of Defence had carelessly chosen to train its pilots in an inappropriate way.

[40] The argument in this paragraph demonstrates why we would not want to adopt Conor Gearty's suggestion that *all* cases involving physical damage to land should be dealt with by the tort of negligence (or under the rule in *Rylands* v *Fletcher*, discussed below, pp. 754–64) rather than in private nuisance: see Gearty 1989. In contrast to Gearty, Lee 2003 argues that the label 'unreasonable' is 'unnecessary and misleading' in situations where a court is considering whether an interference which has caused physical damage to land is actionable because all that the court is really considering is whether strict liability should apply to a particular *activity*. But we do not believe that all that courts do in such cases is classify *activities*. For instance, they may also have to consider if an activity, although ordinary, was *conveniently done*, and whether the damage was merely trivial or a result of hypersensitivity.

[41] A defendant and a claimant will not have equal rights in *all* private nuisance cases. We argue below (pp. 384–5) that a defendant may be held liable even if he has no right to use the land where he creates the nuisance. We have merely chosen an example where a defendant and a claimant have equal rights in order to illustrate the necessity for compromise.

her without redress merely because it would be valuable and sensible to extend the chemical works onto the land occupied by the cottage. Seizing the cottage would clearly be a tort. Private nuisance exists to cover the situation where Vijay has not seized the cottage directly but is indirectly causing damage or reducing the extent that it can be used and enjoyed.

If we have identified the test for unreasonableness in private nuisance correctly then we can confront the difficult question of whether this test imposes *strict liability*. Here we run into trouble with the confusion surrounding the label *strict liability*. We can certainly say that the liability is strict in the sense that it is not a sufficient answer to Wendy's claim for Vijay to prove that he took reasonable care. The interference may still be unreasonable even if reasonable care was taken in siting and operating the chemical works. Liability is not strict, however, in the sense that the unreasonableness rule is just about the efficient absorption of loss and no moral opprobrium attaches to its breach. Even if it is valuable and sensible to locate a chemical works where it will damage a cottage owner's shrubs it is still *wrongful* to damage the shrubs. It is wrongful to treat a neighbour's shrubs as something which can be destroyed without redress just because it is convenient or expedient to destroy them.

Summary of the general approach

In summary, the standard of unreasonableness relies on a compromise between the competing interests of land users. Some elements of the compromise are relatively simple. For instance, an interference by encroachment will always be *unreasonable*. But other elements are more complicated. For instance, in cases where the interference causes a reduction in the amenity value of the claimant's land it is necessary to consider the nature of the locality and reasons why the interference is being caused as well as the degree of interference. In such cases, an interference can be *unreasonable* even if it is not a result of carelessness, and even if it is socially useful.

We will now discuss in more detail some of the factors which are most important when deciding if a particular interference was *unreasonable*.

Hypersensitivity

First, an interference will only be unreasonable if it would affect an ordinary occupier. If an interference would only harm a hypersensitive occupier then it will not be unreasonable.[42] According to the leading case, for an interference to be actionable it must be '[an] inconvenience materially interfering with the ordinary comfort . . . of human existence, not merely according to elegant or dainty modes of living, but according to plain and sober and simple notions among the English people'.[43]

[42] In *Network Rail Infrastructure Ltd* v *CJ Morris* [2004] EWCA Civ 172, the Court of Appeal suggested that it was no longer necessary to determine whether particular uses were hypersensitive since this issue had been subsumed in the more general question whether the defendant's behaviour was 'reasonable between neighbours'. We believe that the Court was wrong to say this since the general question is far too loose for lawyers to use in a predictable and consistent manner. Sub-rules have developed to foster predictability and consistency, and the hypersensitivity rule is one of these sub-rules which is used when deciding whether an interference for which the defendant is responsible is an *unreasonable* interference.

[43] *Walter* v *Selfe* (1851) 4 De G & Sm 315, 322, 64 ER 849, 852 (per Knight Bruce VC).

The principle applies to interference with 'dainty trades' as well as with 'dainty modes of living'. Thus in *Robinson* v *Kilvert*[44] the claimant complained that brown paper he had been storing had been damaged by the defendant's over-heating of the room below. The court held that there had not been an unreasonable interference because the heat could only have had a detrimental effect on an 'exceptionally delicate trade'.

It is important, however, to distinguish the test for liability from the question of the extent of a defendant's liability in a private nuisance case. This distinction means that once it has been established that a defendant is responsible for a state of affairs which would have unreasonably interfered even with a *reasonably robust* trade, a claimant can claim even though she actually operates a delicate trade.[45] Thus in *McKinnon Industries* v *Walker*,[46] the Privy Council held that the claimant could obtain a remedy for the noxious fumes and sulphur dioxide emitted from the defendant's plant. The fumes would have damaged any reasonably robust neighbouring trade so it did not matter that what had actually been interfered with was the claimant's delicate trade as an orchid grower.

The nature of the locality

A second factor, the nature of the locality, is important when the interference causes a reduction in amenity value rather than indirect damage to the land. The effect on the claimant's land was identified as a significant distinction in this context by the House of Lords in *St Helen's Smelting* v *Tipping*.[47] In that case Lord Westbury LC suggested that where there was an interference with personal sensibilities by, for instance, noise or smell, the question whether the interference was unreasonable would have to be judged taking into account the nature of the locality, while there would be no need to consider the nature of the locality if the interference resulted in material injury to the property.

Unfortunately, the *St Helen's* case left some loose ends. First, Lord Westbury LC at one point talks about 'material injury to property' being the condition for ignoring the locality, but later talks about 'sensible injury to the *value* of property' being the condition.[48] If the latter were right, then the distinction would virtually disappear, because most interferences with ordinary sensibilities will cause at least a temporary reduction in land value. Nobody is likely to pay as much for a bad-smelling house or for one with a noisy factory next door. This suggests that the distinction should be between interferences which cause indirect physical damage and interferences which reduce amenity value. The degree of noise, smell and the like which one should tolerate as part of the social rules of 'give and take' may vary with locality, but there is no *locality* where it is reasonable to do things which will physically damage the reasonably robust land of others.[49] Lord Hoffmann and Lord Cooke both mentioned *St Helen's Smelting* and the locality rule in *Hunter* v *Canary*

[44] (1889) 41 Ch D 88.

[45] Of course, any claim for damages for past losses will be subject to the rules relating to 'remoteness of damage'. See below, pp. 569–77.

[46] [1951] 3 DLR 577.

[47] (1865) 11 HLC 642.

[48] Ibid., at 650–1.

[49] There may, however, be *occasions* when it is reasonable to do things which may cause physical damage to the reasonably robust land of others. One example may be occasions where it is reasonable to take steps against a 'common enemy', discussed below, pp. 383–4.

Wharf,[50] and both expressed the distinction as between 'material injury to the property' and 'sensible personal discomfort'.[51] Lord Lloyd used a similar distinction, though he did not expressly link it to *St Helen's*.[52]

The second issue raised by Lord Westbury's distinction is that there are difficulties in identifying and classifying localities. The famously quotable observations on locality, such as that of Byles J, during argument in *Hole* v *Barlow*, that '[a] swine-style might not be considered a nuisance in Bethnal Green: but it certainly would be so in Grosvenor Square'[53] do not subdivide localities in any detail. *Gaunt* v *Fynney*[54] provides a fairly typical example of the 'broad brush' sometimes used by the judiciary in classifying localities: in this case Lord Selborne went no further than categorising Leek, Staffordshire, as a 'manufacturing town'. By contrast, in *Adams* v *Ursell*[55] the evidence suggested that most of Silver Street was 'in the lowest district of Dursley . . . but that the plaintiff's house and others near it were of a much better character'. In these circumstances Swinfen Eady J granted an injunction against the defendant preventing him from operating a fried fish shop in a building adjoining the claimant's, but refused to extend the injunction so as to prevent him from opening such a shop elsewhere on the street.

One suggestion that has gathered some momentum is that in classifying localities reference should be made to the opinions of planning authorities. The orthodox view, however, is that planning permission cannot authorise a nuisance. The right to bring an action in private nuisance is a matter of private right, and planning permission cannot remove private rights. Thus in *Wheeler* v *J.J. Saunders Ltd*, a case involving 'swine-styles' in the Mendips, Peter Gibson LJ stated, 'The court should be slow to acquiesce in the extinction of private rights without compensation as a result of administrative decisions which cannot be appealed and are difficult to challenge.'[56] This view also received some support from Lord Hoffmann in *Hunter* v *Canary Wharf*: 'It would, I think, be wrong to allow the private rights of third parties to be taken away by a permission granted by the planning authority to the developer. The Court of Appeal rejected such an argument in this case and the point has not been pursued in your Lordships' House.'[57]

This orthodox view had to be reconfirmed in *Wheeler* and *Hunter* because doubt had been cast on it by the case of *Gillingham BC* v *Medway (Chatham) Dock Co. Ltd*.[58] This case involved unusual facts in that the council which was claiming that the dockyard was a nuisance had previously authorised the development. The case is now taken to stand for the principle that while a grant of planning permission cannot directly authorise a nuisance, it may nonetheless have the effect of changing the character of the neighbourhood or locality. Thus *Gillingham* suggests that the decisions of planning authorities may help to define the

50 [1997] AC 655.
51 Ibid., 705H (per Lord Hoffmann), 712B (per Lord Cooke). Consistently with our previous view we would prefer to talk of interferences which 'reduce the amenity value of land' rather than interferences which cause 'sensible personal discomfort'.
52 Ibid., 695B–C.
53 *Hole* v *Barlow* (1858) 4 CB NS 334, 340, 140 ER 1113, 1116.
54 (1870) LR 8 Ch App 8.
55 [1913] 1 Ch 269.
56 [1996] Ch 19, 35.
57 [1997] AC 655, 710D. Similarly Lord Cooke said at 722C: 'compliance with planning controls is not itself a defence to a nuisance action.'
58 [1993] QB 343.

nature of a locality for the purposes of deciding whether an interference is unreasonable. If this is correct, then, for example, if planning permission was given for the development of an industrial park on a greenfield site, a neighbour would no longer be able to claim on the basis that the level of noise was inappropriate for a greenfield, but in order to establish private nuisance would have to show that the level of noise was inappropriate for an industrial park. Lord Cooke felt it necessary to apply the *Gillingham* principle to explain why an interference with television reception was not actionable in *Hunter* v *Canary Wharf*.[59] But none of the other Law Lords used this approach.

Although the *Gillingham* principle does not suggest that planning authorities can authorise a nuisance it may still be open to criticism because it allows an administrative decision *indirectly* to redefine and reduce private rights without compensation. If such decisions are sometimes made without all interested parties being represented, can be based on incomplete information and are difficult for third parties to challenge, then allowing them to redefine private rights is equally objectionable whether the effect is indirect or direct. Even if this fundamental criticism of the *Gillingham* principle is not accepted, two limits on its scope must always be borne in mind.

First, it seems that planning permission is only likely to 'change the nature of the locality' when it is permission relating to a major development. Even Lord Cooke suggested that the principle would only apply to a 'strategic planning decision affected by considerations of public interest'.[60] This suggests that a routine grant of small-scale planning permission will not trigger the principle. Secondly, it is important to remember what planning permission actually permits. If Alan applies for permission to build an extension on the back of his house, the planning authority will not consider how much noise Alan is going to make in the extension if he decides to practise his electric guitar in there, nor what pungency of smell Alan is going to emit if he uses the extension for making fibreglass sculptures. In simple terms, if Alan gets planning permission for building a particular structure, that does not mean that the planning authority regards it as reasonable in the locality for Alan to do whatever he may choose to do in the structure.

Joanne Conaghan and Wade Mansell have argued that the locality principle conceals judicial prejudice and is an essentially class-based exercise.[61] We think, however, that it is necessary to reflect carefully on what this criticism means. It is certainly true that the locality principle has been used to protect the well-heeled from fish and chip shops,[62] but it has also been used to protect blue-collar residential districts from industrial noise.[63] The core of the criticism is probably that the locality principle tends to lead to inhabitants of working-class housing areas having to put up with greater degrees of interference than inhabitants of more expensive areas. There is a risk here, however, of treating the social reality that the locality principle reflects as if it was a *consequence* of the principle.[64] Furthermore, it is worth noting that the locality principle applies equally to both claimants

59 *Hunter* v *Canary Wharf Ltd* [1997] AC 655, 722.

60 [1997] AC 655, 722E.

61 Conaghan & Mansell 1999, 137.

62 *Adams* v *Ursell* [1913] 1 Ch 269.

63 *Halsey* v *Esso Petroleum* [1961] 1 WLR 683.

64 To put the same point another way – housing is more affordable in such localities *because* they are areas which are understood to be noisy, etc., rather than the law allowing such areas to be subjected to additional noise, etc., because that is where the affordable housing is.

and defendants. Thus if it is established that Gary cannot use his property as a fish and chip shop because of the locality, then equally Gary is protected against others carrying on activities similar to fish frying which might reduce the amenity value of his land. Further, if it is found that in a particular locality it is reasonable for Ian to interfere with Nita's use and enjoyment of her land by using his land for light industry, then equally it will be reasonable for Nita to interfere with other people's use and enjoyment of *their land* by using *her* land for light industry. Thus while the locality principle means that there are inequalities between owners of property situated in different places, at the same time all owners in a particular locality have equal opportunities and restrictions on their use and enjoyment of land.

Time, duration, regularity

The third factor is largely a matter of common sense. In assessing whether an activity reduces the amenity value of a piece of land to an unreasonable extent, the courts will consider the time, duration and regularity of the interference in question. Night-time noise which interferes with sleep is far more likely to be held a nuisance than day-time noise. The unreasonableness of interfering with sleep was a major consideration in the case of *Rushmer* v *Polsue & Alferi*,[65] where a disgruntled resident persuaded North J to close down the printing presses of Fleet Street at night. When dawn breaks and when night begins are clearly matters of degree. In *Metropolitan Properties Ltd* v *Jones* Goddard LJ held that an electric motor which started at 8 am was a nuisance since 'after [that] hour an elderly gentleman is quite entitled to stay in bed, if he wants to, and have a restful time'.[66] On the other hand, in the case of *Vanderpant* v *Mayfair Hotel*,[67] the judge only granted an injunction against a hotel's noise-making between 10 pm and 8 am. Locality is probably a relevant factor. In agricultural areas no doubt the day begins rather earlier than it does in most student flats.

On duration, the courts have held that the temporary disturbances associated with building works are not a nuisance, provided that the works are carried on with reasonable care and skill. In *Andreae* v *Selfridge & Co. Ltd*,[68] the claimant's hotel on Wigmore Street, London, was affected by a major development by Selfridges. Lord Greene MR stated that reasonable care required restricting the hours of work, and 'using proper scientific means of avoiding inconvenience', but that it was not unreasonable to use pneumatic hammers for six days to break up reinforced concrete. Even the most innocent of noises may become a nuisance if it is repeated too often. Thus in the case of *Soltau* v *De Held*[69] the claimant succeeded in obtaining an injunction against a Roman Catholic church in Clapham which rang its chapel bell at 5 am and 6.45 am every morning, its steeple bell at 8.45 am, 6.45 pm and 7.15 pm every day, with occasional additional peals of all its bells at weekends.

[65] [1906] 1 Ch 234.
[66] [1939] 2 All ER 202, 204b.
[67] [1930] 1 Ch 138.
[68] [1938] Ch 1.
[69] (1851) 2 Sim NS 133, 61 ER 291.

Malice

An important, and much disputed, question is whether, if A reduces the amenity value of B's land *maliciously*, this will make the interference unreasonable.

In *Christie* v *Davey*[70] the defendant was unfortunate enough to live next door to a 'musical family' in Brixton.[71] Their musical activities disturbed his concentration and he responded by knocking on a party wall, beating on trays, whistling, shrieking and imitating what was being played. North J decided that this alternative symphony was an unreasonable interference and granted an injunction, stating that 'what was done by the Defendant was done only for the purpose of annoyance and in my opinion it was not a legitimate use of the Defendant's house to use it for the purpose of vexing and annoying his neighbours'.[72] It may be useful to compare this case with the *Southwark*[73] case where a comparable degree of disturbance was not actionable because it was a product of ordinary domestic living.

A similar conclusion to that in *Christie* was reached in *Hollywood Silver Fox Farm Ltd* v *Emmett*.[74] Here the claimant bred silver foxes and put up a sign advertising this fact. The defendant was developing one of his fields as plots for bungalows and took the view that people were less likely to buy a bungalow plot if they knew it was a mere 29 yards from where foxes were being bred. When the claimant refused to remove the sign the defendant carried out a threat to shoot with 'black powder' to frighten the foxes and disturb their breeding. Macnaghten J held that this firing had amounted to a nuisance, emphasising the use of bird-scaring cartridges and that the defendant's intention in firing the cartridges was to alarm and disturb the foxes. It is worth noting that in this case the defendant's malice meant that the interference was unreasonable *even though* the claimant's activity, breeding silver foxes, was arguably *hypersensitive*.[75]

The difficulty facing the suggestion that malice *is* a relevant factor is that it seems to be in tension with the decision of the House of Lords in *Bradford Corporation* v *Pickles*.[76] In this case it was alleged that Pickles had interfered with the groundwater percolating under his land principally because he wanted to force the Corporation, which used the water for its waterworks, to buy his land for an inflated price. In deciding the case against the Corporation their Lordships treated the question whether Pickles was malicious as irrelevant. Lord Watson, for instance, said that 'No use of property, which would be legal if due

[70] [1893] 1 Ch 316.

[71] Mrs Christie was a teacher of music and singing; her daughter was a medallist at the Royal Academy of Music and gave lessons on violin and piano; her lodger was also a medallist in music; and her son was in the habit of playing the cello in the kitchen up until 11 at night. Only Mr Christie was not musical. As North J observed, Mr Christie 'perhaps fortunately for himself, is very deaf' (ibid., 324).

[72] Ibid., 326–7.

[73] [2001] 1 AC 1.

[74] [1936] 2 KB 468.

[75] The defendant's barrister argued that 'the shooting would have caused no alarm to the animals which are usually to be found on farms in Kent', ibid., 474.

[76] [1895] AC 587. For suggestions that the decision in the *Bradford* case is inconsistent with the decision in the *Hollywood Silver Fox Farm* case, see MacDonald 1936–1938; Cross 1995, 453–5; Simpson 1995, 74; S&H, 62. Cane 1996 attempts to reconcile the two cases by arguing (at 265–6) that the defendant in *Bradford* was acting out of 'self-interest', while the defendant in *Hollywood* was acting out of 'spite'. This does not work: as our explanation of the facts in *Hollywood* shows, the defendant in that case was acting out of the plainest self-interest in attempting to disrupt the claimant's operations.

to a proper motive, can become illegal because it is prompted by a motive which is improper or even malicious.'[77]

It can be argued, however, that *Bradford* v *Pickles* can be distinguished from *Christie* and *Hollywood Silver Fox* because the *Bradford* case involved interference by *obstruction* of a benefit, while *Christie* and *Hollywood Silver Fox* involved interference by the *emanation* of noise.[78] It is important to remember that in an *obstruction* case a claimant can only sue if she can show that she has a *right* to receive the benefit that has been obstructed. Now – the claimants in *Bradford* v *Pickles* could not establish that they had a *right* to the water which the defendant obstructed.[79] Rather the law treated the defendant as having an absolute right to obstruct the water. Thus it did not matter that the defendant had acted maliciously in obstructing the water. If the claimants had no right to receive the water, they had no claim in private nuisance. So the House of Lords' broad statements about malice in *Bradford* v *Pickles* can be seen as being limited to situations where A prevents something going onto B's land which B had no right to receive. *By contrast*, in an *emanation* case the lawfulness of the defendant's activity can only be ascertained by considering whether the claimant should be expected to tolerate such interference, and obviously the fact that an interference is not a consequence of a 'common and ordinary use and occupation of land' – but rather a consequence of the defendant seeking to injure the claimant[80] – is *highly* relevant to the question whether the emanation involves an *unreasonable* interference. There is no reason why a claimant should be expected to put up with an interference created by a malicious emanation onto her land.

Defence against a common enemy

In *Arscott* v *The Coal Authority*[81] the Court of Appeal confirmed that it is reasonable for an owner or occupier of land to take convenient steps to protect her land against a 'common enemy', for instance flooding, even if the reasonably foreseeable consequence of these steps is to displace the problem onto a neighbour's land.[82] This rule is subject to three exceptions, however. First, a defendant is not permitted to protect her land by altering an established watercourse. Secondly, the rule only permits a defendant to take steps in *anticipation* of a threat from a 'common enemy' and does not permit a defendant to cure a

77 [1895] AC 587, 598.

78 See Taggart 2002, 189.

79 See, similarly, Steele 2007, 614; Stevens 2007, 22: 'it was held that the claimants had no (property) right to the percolating water. Without a right exigible against the rest of the world to the percolating water, no tort was committed when the supply was cut.'

80 Stevens 2007 suggests (at 23) that malice is relevant only because it demonstrates that a defendant's actions are 'pointless', or 'without social value'. We do not agree. The decision in *Hollywood Silver Fox* did not turn on whether there was greater 'social value' in fox-breeding or bungalow-development. It turned on the *unreasonableness* of intentionally reducing the amenity value of the claimant's land when it was not *necessary* for the defendant to do so in order to use his own land in a common and ordinary way.

81 [2004] EWCA Civ 892. The defendants were held not liable for raising the level of a playing field situated on a flood plain in order to protect it from flooding even though raising the field caused a flood to affect the claimants' houses more severely than it might otherwise have done.

82 The parties in the *Arscott* case were content to treat the 'common enemy' rule as existing independently of the question whether the defendant had *unreasonably* interfered with the use and enjoyment of land in which B has a sufficient interest. We believe, however, that the 'common enemy' situation is merely one where the courts have developed clear guidance as to what is reasonable; a view apparently shared by Laws LJ: ibid., at [40].

problem that has *already* arisen on her land by exporting the misfortune.[83] Thirdly, while a court will not seek to weigh up whether each and every protective measure was necessary and proportionate, it may still find that the defendant's actions were unreasonable if the protective measures were clearly excessive and the harm to the claimant was caused by their excess.

Incorporation of reasonableness into the definition of a right to receive a benefit

A special factor which is sometimes relevant in cases of interference by obstruction or withdrawal of a benefit is that sometimes an element of reasonableness is incorporated into the definition of the benefit that the claimant establishes a right to receive. For instance, a claimant cannot acquire by prescription a right to a continuance of present levels of light, but only a right to freedom from such obstruction of light as would interfere with the ordinary occupations of life.[84] In such a case *any* interference with the right, so defined, would be unreasonable. Usually, however, benefits are defined in more absolute terms. For instance, Beth may have a private right of way along a path across Carl's land. In such a case Beth would not be able to base a claim on any *reasonable* interference with her use of the path, but would have to show that the interference was *unreasonable*. For instance, if Fred also had a private right of way along the path and slowed Beth down by pushing a heavy cart up it, then Beth could not claim against him.

CREATING, AUTHORISING, ADOPTING OR CONTINUING

Everybody has a duty not to *create* a private nuisance or to *authorise* others to create a private nuisance. It is the duty of an occupier[85] of land who knows (or can be presumed to know) that a private nuisance has been created or has arisen on that land to take reasonable steps to eliminate the problem. This second duty is often referred to as the duty not to *adopt or continue* a private nuisance.

Creating

If A *creates* a state of affairs that causes an unreasonable interference with B's land then it seems straightforward that A should be liable.

One doubt, however, might stem from the common assertion that private nuisance is a tort committed between *neighbours*. This might be read as suggesting that only a neighbouring *landowner* can be held liable in nuisance, and not someone who creates an unreasonable interference but not on his own land. In *Hussain* v *Lancaster City Council*[86] the Court of Appeal relied on a thesis that Professor Newark was 'prepared ... to nail ... to the doors of the Law Courts and to defend against all comers'. The thesis states that 'the

[83] *Whalley* v *Lancashire and Yorkshire Railway Co.* (1884) 13 QBD 131.
[84] *Colls* v *Home & Colonial Stores Ltd* [1904] AC 179.
[85] In *L E Jones (Insurance Brokers) Ltd* v *Portsmouth City Council* [2003] 1 WLR 427 the Court of Appeal held that this duty was not limited to occupiers. We discuss this further below, pp. 390–1.
[86] [2000] QB 1. The facts of the case are discussed in more detail under the next subheading.

term "nuisance" is properly applied only to such *actionable user of land* as interferes with the enjoyment by the claimant of rights in land'.[87] Unfortunately, the Court of Appeal took this to mean that the essence of private nuisance required that 'the defendant's use *of the defendant's land* interferes with the claimant's enjoyment of the claimant's land'.[88] Thus the Court rejected the claim because the harassment of the claimants by the tenants of the defendant did not involve the tenants using their own premises. Rather the tenants were carrying out the harassment from the street and from open ground over which they had no rights.

The Court of Appeal's view is not orthodoxy. Indeed, in our opinion, it is nonsense. There are plenty of cases to suggest that a defendant can be held liable for creating an unreasonable interference with another's land even if he does not own or have a tenancy over the land that he creates it on. Thus a defendant can be liable if he creates the interference on a highway, or on land that he does not own but merely occupies or uses.[89] Quite apart from these cases, there is no reason in principle to make a claimant's degree of protection turn on the status of the person who creates the interference. A landowner deserves protection from an over-noisy neighbour regardless of whether that neighbour is owner, tenant, lodger or squatter. As Sir Christopher Staughton has pointed out,[90] it is not self-evident why a defendant who plays his stereo loudly at home may commit the tort of private nuisance in relation to his neighbour but a defendant who plays his car stereo loudly while parked outside his neighbour's house will not. Further, acceptance of the Court of Appeal's opinion in *Hussain* would lead to an undesirable distinction between this tort and the tort of trespass to land. Clearly a defendant can commit trespass to land without using his own land.[91]

Someone can *create* a nuisance even if he or she did not *intend* to bring about the situation which amounted to a nuisance. In *R* v *Moore*,[92] a gunmaker possessed land that he encouraged his customers to use for shooting at pigeons. Some of the pigeons were not brought down by his customers and a nuisance resulted from the large number of people

[87] Newark 1949, 489 (emphasis added). This thesis was approved by Lord Goff in *Hunter* v *Canary Wharf*, but, of course, in that case the focus was on the second part of the thesis – that the interference had to be with rights in land.

[88] [2000] QB 1, 23E (emphasis added). It will not have escaped the notice of the observant reader that Professor Newark only insists that nuisance must involve *user of land*, and not that it must involve *the defendant's use of the defendant's land*.

[89] Cases suggesting that the defendant does not have to possess or own the land that he creates the nuisance from include: *Halsey* v *Esso Petroleum* [1961] 1 WLR 683 (nuisance created from highway); *Hall* v *Beckenham Corp.* [1949] 1 KB 716 (nuisance created from public park); *Bernstein* v *Skyviews* [1978] QB 479 (nuisance created from air). There is also a series of cases supporting the view that picketing can be a private nuisance, at least if it involves obstruction, violence, intimidation, molestation or threats (*J Lyons & Sons* v *Wilkins* [1899] 1 Ch 255, 267, 271–2; *Hubbard* v *Pitt* [1976] QB 142, 177B–C, 183D–F, 189A; *Thomas* v *NUM (South Wales Area)* [1986] Ch 20, 65D), and none of these suggests that the pickets must be using their own land in order to commit the tort. For *dicta* pointing the other way, see *Esso Petroleum* v *Southport Corp.* [1954] 2 QB 182, 196–7 (per Denning LJ), [1956] AC 218, 242 (per Lord Radcliffe), suggesting that private nuisance cannot be committed from the sea.

[90] *Lippiatt* v *South Gloucestershire CC* [2000] QB 51, 65B.

[91] The inconvenience of the distinction can best be appreciated by remembering that it is a trespass to land to throw something directly onto B's land, and a private nuisance to release something so that it indirectly drifts onto B's land and causes an unreasonable interference. If the Court of Appeal's view was confirmed then B would seek, whenever A created an emanation from land other than his own land, to argue that the emanation was *direct* (and thus a trespass to land).

[92] (1832) 3 B & Ad 184, 110 ER 68.

who gathered outside his premises to shoot at the strays. In response to the argument that the gunmaker had not committed nuisance because he had not invited this crowd, Littledale J asserted that 'If the experience of mankind must lead any one to expect the result, he will be answerable for it.'[93]

Authorising

A1 can commit the tort of private nuisance by *authorising* A2 to create a state of affairs that causes an unreasonable interference with B's land. This principle can play an important role in attaching liability to owners of land who are not in occupation, for instance because they have granted a lease.

In *Hussain* v *Lancaster City Council*,[94] Malazam Hussain and his partner Linda Livingstone had bought a shop on the Ryelands estate in Lancaster. Thereafter they were subjected to over 2,000 racist attacks. Their claim listed several hundred attacks on their property (including use of petrol bombs), assaults and thefts, and named 106 alleged culprits. Many of these alleged culprits were tenants of Lancaster City Council on the Ryelands estate. Importantly, the council had power to evict these tenants from their homes if they were causing a nuisance to their neighbours, but had not done so. The claimants' case was that in these circumstances the council was liable for the state of affairs being created by its tenants.

One difficulty with the claim was that it sought to make the council liable for the racist attacks even though it was clearly not the council which was carrying them out. Can a landlord be held responsible for a state of affairs resulting from the deliberate misbehaviour of its tenants? The usual answer given by English law, found in cases such as *Rich* v *Basterfield*,[95] is that a landlord is *only* liable for a state of affairs created by his *tenants* if he has *authorised* its creation. In *Southwark London Borough Council* v *Tanner*, Lord Millett expressed the general rule when he said that, 'The person or persons directly responsible for the activities in question are liable; but so too is anyone who authorised them. Landlords have been held liable for nuisances committed on this basis. It is not enough for them to be aware of the nuisance and to take no steps to prevent it.'[96]

What will suffice for authorising? Lord Millett clearly asserts that knowing about a problem and not trying to solve it is insufficient. But what if the landlord knew when the lease was granted that the tenant was very likely to create a nuisance? In *Smith* v *Scott*,[97] Pennycuick V-C stated that this could be enough if the nuisance was certain to result from the purposes for which the property was let.[98] Subsequently, in *Tetley* v *Chitty*[99] Medway Borough Council was held liable for the noise nuisance caused by go-karts when they had

[93] Although *R* v *Moore*, above, was a case of public nuisance the same principle has been applied in cases of private nuisance, for example, *Walker* v *Brewster* (1867) LR 5 Eq 25 ('assemblage of idle and dissolute persons' outside a house used by defendant for twice weekly fêtes with fireworks).

[94] [2000] QB 1.

[95] (1847) 4 CB 783, 136 ER 715.

[96] [2001] 1 AC 1, 22.

[97] [1973] Ch 314.

[98] Ibid., 321. He stated that such a degree of 'high probability' was necessary in order to infer that the nuisance was impliedly authorised.

[99] [1986] 1 All ER 663.

leased land with (at least) implied permission to use the land as a go-kart track, and when noise nuisance was an ordinary and necessary consequence of such a use. In that case, however, McNeill J pointed out that there was some inconsistency in the previous cases as to what degree of knowledge or foresight a claimant would have to prove that the landlord had. McNeill J seemed attracted by the possibility that proving mere reasonable foreseeability of nuisance might be enough.[100] We think, however, that there is a significant gulf between foreseeing that something might possibly happen and *authorising* it. Nonetheless, even if later cases follow the generous view of McNeill J, this will not be enough to help claimants in the same position as those in *Hussain*. In that case it would have been difficult to prove that when Lancaster City Council granted tenancies to the alleged culprits it ought reasonably to have foreseen that they would pursue a campaign of racial persecution, still harder to prove that such a campaign was an ordinary and necessary consequence of the granting of the tenancies.

Adopting or continuing

Hussain can be contrasted with the case of *Lippiatt* v *South Gloucestershire CC*,[101] where a group of travellers allegedly set up camp on land belonging to the council and used that camp as a 'launching pad' for a series of damaging invasions of a neighbouring farmer's property. In this case the Court of Appeal held that the council was arguably liable for the nuisance resulting from the state of affairs on its land. A crucial distinction from *Hussain* is that in *Lippiatt* the travellers were *not* tenants of the council, and consequently the council continued to occupy the land. Orthodoxy holds that the responsibility of an occupier for a state of affairs which he did not create goes beyond responsibility for what he authorised, and extends to any state of affairs that he continued or adopted.[102] So what must B prove in order to establish that A continued or adopted a state of affairs arising on land A occupied that unreasonably interfered with B's use and enjoyment of his land?

In *Sedleigh-Denfield* v *O'Callaghan*,[103] the defendants owned and occupied land on which there was a drainage ditch. Middlesex County Council decided to use this ditch to drain water from a new residential development and substituted a culvert[104] for the ditch. The County Council's action was both lawless – it did not obtain permission from the owners – and incompetent – it failed to take the sensible precaution of putting in a grid to prevent the culvert becoming blocked. Three years later the culvert did block, and water which could not escape down it instead flooded the claimant's property. The House of Lords found that the defendant occupiers of the land were liable even though the state of affairs which led to the flood had been created by the trespassing and incompetent County Council. Viscount Maugham stated that an occupier in such a situation would be liable if he had 'continued' or 'adopted' the nuisance, and explained that, 'an occupier of land "continues" a nuisance if, with knowledge or presumed knowledge of its existence, he fails to take any reasonable

100 Ibid.

101 [2000] QB 51.

102 For criticism of this area of the law, see Bright 2001, arguing that a landowner should only be held liable for actions of people on his land if he authorised or encouraged those actions.

103 [1940] AC 880.

104 In less obscure language, a fifteen-inch pipe.

means to bring it to an end, though with ample time to do so. He "adopts" it if he makes use of the erection, building, bank or artificial contrivance which constitutes the nuisance.'[105] On the facts, Viscount Maugham found that the defendants had both 'continued' and 'adopted' the nuisance. The other Lords did not draw such a stern distinction between 'continuing' and 'adopting'. They did, however, stress the importance of 'knowledge' or 'presumed knowledge' of the nuisance or the potential for nuisance before the occupier could be liable.

In *Sedleigh-Denfield* the potential for interference with the claimant's land could have been easily and cheaply rectified by the defendants' putting a grid in front of the pipe's orifice. Moreover, the defendants might well have been able to obtain the cost of installing the grid from the County Council. More difficult questions are raised, however, where it will be costly to remove the potential for nuisance, and where those costs may not be recoverable from a third party, for instance because the potential for nuisance has been caused by an unidentified malefactor or by natural forces.

These more difficult questions had to be addressed by the Court of Appeal in *Leakey* v *National Trust*.[106] In this case the defendants owned and occupied a cone-shaped hill in Somerset called Burrow Mump. The claimants lived in converted cottages beneath the Mump. In 1976 the hot summer and wet autumn caused a crack which made it likely that the Mump would collapse onto the claimants' houses. Stabilising the Mump was likely to prove expensive and consequently the National Trust denied that it was responsible for a state of affairs created by the wondrous workings of nature. The Court of Appeal, however, held that the National Trust, as a landowner in occupation,[107] was responsible. Megaw LJ (with whom Cumming-Bruce LJ agreed) held that the *Sedleigh-Denfield* principle applied to a potential nuisance caused by the workings of nature,[108] and that if the defendant knew or ought to have known of the potential for nuisance, it was obliged to take reasonable steps to eliminate the problem. Importantly, however, the Court of Appeal also said that in judging whether particular steps were reasonably required, the defendant's capacity to find the money would be relevant; and alongside this could be considered the claimants' capacity to protect themselves from damage by erecting a barrier or providing funds for agreed works. While the duty to act reasonably is clearly subjective to this extent, Megaw LJ stressed that he did not envisage that it would be necessary to assess the wealth of the parties in anything other than an impressionistic manner.[109]

The nature of the occupier's duty with regard to natural forces was further explored in the case of *Holbeck Hall Hotel Ltd* v *Scarborough Borough Council*.[110] In this case a cliff on

105 Ibid., 894.

106 [1980] QB 485.

107 In fact there were some doubts as to whether the National Trust really occupied the Mump, but for the purposes of the litigation it conceded that it did: ibid., 509.

108 Ibid., 517–24.

109 Ibid., 526–7. In *Abbahall* v *Smee* [2003] 1 WLR 1472, in circumstances where defendant and claimant occupied different floors of a building beneath a leaking roof, and the defendant sought to argue that because of her relative poverty she should not have to contribute towards the repairs, the Court of Appeal held that such an approach would be 'unjust to the point of absurdity' [57] and that the costs should normally be divided in proportion to the benefit that each party would gain from the work [41]. The problems which may arise where a nuisance causes consequential damage while the parties are squabbling about contributions have not yet been addressed by the courts.

110 [2000] QB 836.

land belonging to the defendant council gave way and as a consequence a hotel on neighbouring land belonging to the claimant was destroyed. The case was particularly difficult because while the defendant ought to have foreseen some minor slips causing damage to the claimant's rose garden and lawn, there was no reason why it ought to have foreseen such an exceptional event as the massive slip which destroyed the hotel. In these circumstances, the Court of Appeal held that an occupier which failed to meet the measured duty to take reasonable steps to prevent a nuisance occurring on its land should only be liable to the extent of the damage that ought to have been foreseen.[111] Further, the Court of Appeal suggested that in the circumstances, where the hazard was a result of the forces of nature and the defendant would have gained little benefit from preserving its own land against the hazard, the defendant might well have fulfilled the duty to act reasonably by doing no more than informing the claimants of the risk and sharing information relating to it.

The case of *Marcic* v *Thames Water Utilities Ltd*[112] raised the difficult question whether a public authority responsible for sewers might be responsible for flooding incidents caused by the inadequate capacity of those sewers. The Court of Appeal held that the defendants were 'in no more favourable position than a landowner on whose property a hazard accumulates by the act of a trespasser or of nature', that they ought to have known of the hazard, and that consequently, following cases such as *Sedleigh-Denfield* and *Leakey*, they would be liable unless they took reasonable steps to avoid problems arising.[113] The House of Lords, however, disagreed because such a common law duty would conflict with the statutory scheme under the Water Industry Act 1991 for enforcing the statutory obligations of 'sewerage undertakers' and controlling their prices. Lord Hoffmann, in particular, doubted whether a claimant could determine the level of service that a public utility provider must provide by invoking the common law occupier's duty not to 'continue' a state of affairs on his land which might lead to a nuisance, because a judge would not be able to determine what 'reasonable steps' ought to be taken.[114]

The expansion of the rule that an occupier will be held to have continued a nuisance if he ought to have known of it and has failed to take reasonable steps to deal with it has led to some tension between the law of torts and established principles of land law. In particular, it is a basic principle of land law that a person whose land is subject to an easement is not obliged to undertake any repairs to the land so as to facilitate continued enjoyment of the easement, but instead the beneficiary of the easement has a right to enter the land to carry out works necessary to protect his right.[115] It seems that in light of the development of wider liability for adopting a nuisance this principle of land law can no longer be treated as an exhaustive summary of the law, at least when a failure to repair the land will lead to physical damage to the claimant's land.[116]

111 This contrasts with the usual rule of remoteness of damage (see below, pp. 569–71) that a defendant is liable for all damage of the same *type* as ought to have been foreseen, regardless of the *extent*.

112 [2004] 2 AC 42.

113 [2002] QB 929, [84].

114 [2004] 2 AC 42, [63]–[64], [70].

115 *Jones* v *Pritchard* [1908] 1 Ch 630, 637–8.

116 *Bradburn* v *Lindsay* [1983] 2 All ER 408.

Nuisance or negligence?

Given that the question whether an occupier will be liable for a state of affairs he did not create is answered by considering whether he has fulfilled a measured duty of care it is sometimes suggested that this group of cases properly forms part of the tort of negligence.[117] We would reject this suggestion. Such a suggestion is not merely one about the appropriate distribution of topics within textbooks. If the *Sedleigh-Denfield* doctrine was treated as *only* being part of the tort of negligence then this would make it difficult for a claimant to bring an action when a defendant occupier had failed to deal with a state of affairs which merely had the effect of reducing the amenity value of the claimant's land.[118] We think that the true position is that a breach of the duty can lead to a claim for continuing a private nuisance, but that there is also a parallel duty of care breach of which will amount to the tort of negligence.[119]

Non-occupiers

So far we have discussed when occupiers will be held to have 'continued' or 'adopted' a state of affairs existing on land which they occupy. The case of *LE Jones (Insurance Brokers) Ltd* v *Portsmouth City Council*[120] raised the question whether anyone other than the occupier might be held liable for a private nuisance if he did not take steps to abate a problematic state of affairs. The case involved damage caused by a tree which was situated on land vested in the highway authority but which the defendant council had agreed to maintain. Dyson LJ stated that 'the basis for the liability of an occupier for a nuisance on his land is not his occupation as such. Rather, it is that, by virtue of his occupation, an occupier usually has it in his power to take the measures that are necessary to prevent or eliminate the nuisance. He has sufficient control over the hazard which constitutes the nuisance for it to be reasonable to make him liable for the foreseeable consequences of his failure to exercise that control so as to remove the hazard.'[121] Dyson LJ's test, which focuses instead on *control* over the *hazard,* rather that *occupation* of the land, has the potential to catch not just occupiers, but also independent contractors managing hazards on land on behalf of occupiers, and possibly also non-occupiers, such as public officials, which have power to intervene and deal with hazards. We suspect, however, that the courts will be very cautious about extending liability much beyond those in occu-

117 This view is advanced by Gearty 1989, who writes of *Sedleigh-Denfield* (at 237): 'This was negligence pure and simple, confused by an ill-fitting and woolly disguise of nuisance.' See also Weir 1998a, 102–3: 'that the defendant's liability in nuisance [in *Sedleigh-Denfield*] [was] affected by considerations relevant in the tort of negligence seems beyond doubt.'

118 An example of such a case might be an occupier failing to deal with regular noisy trespassers, or with smelly rotting rubbish tipped onto his land by trespassers. In such a case the type of damage suffered by the claimant would not normally give rise to a claim in the tort of negligence but could give rise to a claim in private nuisance.

119 See above, pp. 177–9. The scope of the negligence duty may be important. Compensation for personal injuries can never be recovered in the tort of private nuisance (see below, pp. 395–7, 581–2), but can of course sometimes be recovered in the tort of negligence. Although Megaw LJ expressed the opinion that if an occupier breached a *Goldman* v *Hargrave*-type duty of care owed to his neighbour and his neighbour suffered a personal injury as a result, then the neighbour should be able to sue the occupier for damages in negligence (see *Leakey* v *National Trust* [1980] QB 485, at 523) there is currently no binding authority as to whether 'personal injury' suffered as a result of the breach of a *Goldman* v *Hargrave*-type duty of care will count as the 'right kind of loss' to be actionable in negligence. Our view is that it does not: see above, p. 177 n. 42.

120 [2003] 1 WLR 427.

121 Ibid., at [11].

pation.[122] Therefore, in the interests of simplicity, we have continued to use the phrase 'occupiers' to describe those who may be found to have adopted or continued a private nuisance.

Four defences

It is appropriate at this point to mention four defences which may prevent a defendant from being held responsible for a state of affairs or its consequences.

(1) *Necessity*. In the case of *Southport Corporation* v *Esso Petroleum Ltd*, a tanker got into difficulties and, fearing for the ship and the safety of his crew, the captain discharged his cargo of oil to make the tanker lighter. The oil polluted the claimant's beach. At first instance Devlin J suggested *obiter* that it would be a defence to create a nuisance in order to save human life, but that he was unwilling to hold that one could damage another's property in order to save one's own property without providing compensation.[123] The Court of Appeal split on the defence of necessity. Singleton LJ suggested that there was a defence of necessity to claims for creating a nuisance, and that the defendant could rely on it unless he was negligent in creating the necessity.[124] Denning LJ also suggested that there was a defence of necessity, but he felt that it was for the defendant to prove that the necessity was unavoidable.[125] In the House of Lords[126] the decision concentrated on the pleadings, but Lord Radcliffe suggested *obiter* that there was a defence of necessity in nuisance, unless it was the defendant's carelessness which brought about the necessity.[127]

One reason for the divergence in judicial opinion is that where the necessity was brought about by circumstances for which neither party was responsible the principal issue is which of two innocents should bear the cost. Had the ship been caught in freak weather which itself led to the spillage of the oil, the defendant would probably have been held not to have *created* the pollution. Should we treat the case differently if the defendant responds reasonably to freak weather and was not at fault in exposing himself to the risk in the first place? Whatever the final judicial answer to this question, it is already clear that the courts will not countenance the development of a wide defence of necessity. In *Andreae* v *Selfridge & Co. Ltd*, Bennett J was scathing about a plea that it was necessary for builders to create severe disturbance in order to complete the work swiftly. He referred to a line from *Paradise Lost*: 'So spake the Fiend, and with necessity, the tyrant's plea, excused his devilish deeds.'[128]

(2) *Statutory authority*. A defendant will not be liable if he can demonstrate that a statute authorised him to do what would otherwise amount to an actionable nuisance. In each case care must be taken to establish precisely what Parliament intended. In some cases it has

[122] Many of the principles applied, for instance that which relates contributions to the cost of dealing with the state of affairs to the degree of benefit that claimant and defendant will gain from the state of affairs being dealt with, are difficult to apply to defendants who are not occupiers.

[123] [1953] 3 WLR 773.

[124] [1954] 2 QB 182, 194.

[125] Ibid., 197. Strictly speaking, Denning LJ only discussed *public* nuisance, but his reasoning on necessity, which relied on a parallel with the tort of trespass to land, can be applied equally to *private* nuisance.

[126] [1956] AC 218.

[127] Ibid., 242.

[128] [1936] 2 All ER 1413, 1422.

been found that Parliament intended to authorise the defendant to conduct an activity *in a way which paid reasonable regard and care to the interests of others*, and did not intend to permit the defendant to cause any nuisance beyond that which would be an *inevitable* consequence of conducting the activity.[129] In other cases, however, it has been found that Parliament *assumed* that the authorised activity could be conducted somewhere and under some circumstances without creating a nuisance, and did not intend to permit the defendant to cause any nuisance whatsoever.[130]

(3) *Act of third party*. There seems little doubt that a defendant will avoid liability if he can prove that any unreasonable interference arising on his land was caused by a wholly unpredictable act of a trespasser. Where, however, a state of affairs created by a trespasser does not immediately cause an unreasonable interference, or continues to cause an interference over an extended period, an occupier of land may be held liable if he knew or ought to have known of the state of affairs and failed to take reasonable steps to rectify the situation.[131]

Further, where the trespasser's intervention was not wholly unpredictable a landowner may be held liable in negligence for failing to take reasonable precautions against the intervention. The question of how predictable an intervention must be before the landowner will be under a duty to take reasonable steps to prevent it is difficult to answer with confidence. The decision of the House of Lords in *Smith* v *Littlewoods Organisation Ltd*[132] provides no single clear answer. Lord Mackay LC stated that a landowner would only have had a duty to take reasonable steps to prevent a trespasser acting in some way if it was reasonably foreseeable that if he failed to take such steps then damage to the claimant would be probable, and that to establish that damage was probable it would be necessary to consider carefully both how likely the trespasser's intervention was and how likely it was that such an intervention would cause damage to the claimant.[133] By contrast, Lord Goff argued that a landowner would only owe his neighbour a duty to take reasonable steps to prevent a trespasser causing harm to his neighbour if: (1) the landowner had assumed a responsibility to his neighbour; *or* (2) the landowner was responsible for controlling the trespasser in question;[134] *or* (3) the landowner had negligently caused or permitted the creation of a source of danger which it was reasonably foreseeable that a trespasser might 'spark off';[135] *or* (4) the landowner knew or ought to have known that the trespasser in question had created a fire risk.[136]

(4) *Act of God*. A defendant will avoid liability in private nuisance if he can prove that any unreasonable interference was caused by a wholly unpredictable and uncontrollable natural force. In *Sedleigh-Denfield* v *O'Callaghan*, Lord Maugham stressed that the defendants had not tried to argue that the rainfall which caused the flood was so heavy as to give rise to a defence of 'Act of God'. He suggested that such a defence would, in any case, only

[129] See, for example, *Allen* v *Gulf Oil* [1981] AC 1001.
[130] See, for example, *Metropolitan Asylum District Managers* v *Hill* (1881) 6 App Cas 193.
[131] *Sedleigh-Denfield* v *O'Callaghan* [1940] AC 880. Discussed above, pp. 387–8.
[132] [1987] 1 AC 241.
[133] Ibid., 261.
[134] Ibid., 272.
[135] Ibid., 273-4. Lord Goff's example is the storage of a quantity of fireworks in an unlocked garden shed.
[136] Ibid., 274. Here the duty seems to be parallel to the measured duty of care that is considered in cases of *continuing* a private nuisance (see above, pp. 387–9).

have been available if the rain had been 'so exceptional in amount that no reasonable man could have anticipated it'.[137] A defendant may be liable if the force of nature was reasonably foreseeable, or if the state of affairs created by the force did not *immediately* lead to the interference. In the latter situation, if the defendant is an occupier, then he will be liable if he fails to take reasonable steps to deal with a known risk.[138]

A TORT TO LAND

In *Hunter* v *Canary Wharf Ltd*,[139] the House of Lords re-emphasised that the essence of private nuisance is that it is 'a tort to land'.[140] Lord Hoffmann, for instance, said that '[private nuisance] is a tort against land'.[141] The House of Lords did not, of course, mean by this that if A creates a private nuisance by unreasonably interfering with the use and enjoyment of a certain piece of land, he breaches a duty owed to that piece of land – that would be absurd. What they seemed to mean were two things.

First, A will only commit the tort of private nuisance *in relation to B* if he creates, authorises, adopts or continues a state of affairs which unreasonably interferes with the use and enjoyment of a piece of land with which B is linked by virtue of the fact that has *an interest* in that land. If, then, Mary created, authorised, adopted or continued a state of affairs which unreasonably interfered with the use and enjoyment of a piece of land in which Tom had *no* interest, Tom will not be able to establish that Mary – in acting as she did – committed the tort of private nuisance in relation to *him*. He will, in consequence, have to find some other ground to sue Mary if he wants to sue her for damages in respect of the harm suffered by him as a result of Mary's activities.

Secondly, if A has committed the tort of private nuisance in relation to B by unreasonably interfering with the use and enjoyment of Blackacre, a piece of land in which B has an interest, the duty breached by A in so acting will have been imposed on A to help ensure that B's *interest in Blackacre was not damaged*. So B will have to base his claim on the harm done by A's interference *to his interest in Blackacre*. He will not be entitled to base his claim on *any other type of harm* that he has suffered as a result of A's interference – for example, personal injury – though he may be entitled to seek damages for *some* other types of harm as '*consequential loss*'.[142]

We will now look at each of these propositions in more detail before considering some of the criticisms that have been made of this aspect of the House of Lords' decision in *Hunter* v *Canary Wharf*.

137 [1940] AC 880, 886.

138 This is another situation where the relevant duty is the measured duty of an occupier to take reasonable steps to prevent conditions on his land causing nuisance to his neighbour. *Goldman* v *Hargrave* [1967] AC 645 provides a good example of a state of affairs created by a uncontrollable force of nature (red gum set alight by lightning) only causing harm to a neighbour after the occupier had a reasonable opportunity to abate the risk.

139 [1997] AC 655.

140 This phrase comes from Newark 1949 where he wrote (at 482) that the essence of private nuisance was that 'it was a tort to land. Or to be more accurate it was a tort directed against the claimant's enjoyment of rights over land . . .' This passage was commended by Lord Goff in *Hunter* [1997] AC 655, at 687H as the clearest expression of the basic position.

141 Ibid., 702H.

142 See below, pp. 396–7, 581–2.

Title to sue

It seems to be correct, in English law at any rate, that A will only commit the tort of private nuisance in relation to B if he creates, authorises, adopts or continues a state of affairs which unreasonably interferes with a piece of land in which B has an interest. However, two difficult questions must be addressed. First, what counts as an interest *in land*? Secondly, if A has unreasonably interfered with a particular piece of land and B wants to sue A on the basis that A in so acting committed the tort of private nuisance in relation to her, does B have to *prove* that she has a legally-recognised interest in the land in question – and, linked with that, will B be barred from suing A if A can show that B did not have a legally-recognised interest in the land?

Interests in land[143]

English land law draws a distinction between interests *in land* and *personal* interests. The main distinction between these is that interests *in land* can bind third parties while *personal* interests generally do not. A person with a fee simple in possession over Greenacre has an obvious interest *in land* while a person who has purchased a ticket from the owner of Greenacre entitling him to visit Greenacre Hall for a guided tour has only a *personal* (contractual) interest. Consequently, if Greenacre Hall is blighted by intolerable noise created by Paul, the person with a fee simple in possession can sue for private nuisance but the visitor on the guided tour cannot. If Greenacre Hall is leased to a tenant then that tenant has an interest in land and is able to sue for private nuisance. The reversioner (that is, the person who will take back Greenacre Hall at the end of the tenancy) may also sue if the private nuisance has any effect on *his own* interest in land.[144] The interests of two classes of persons are particularly difficult to classify: (1) licensees, and (2) the spouses and children of people with interests in land. With regard to licensees, if the licence grants exclusive possession then the licensee will often be able to sue because of the *de facto* possession rule discussed in the next section. With regard to family members, it is clear that they will not be treated as having interests *in land* if they merely occupy the house as a home.[145]

De facto *possession*

A person who *in fact* enjoys or asserts exclusive possession over a piece of land will not be required to *prove* that he has a right to that possession in order to sue a defendant in private nuisance for unreasonably interfering with the use and enjoyment of that land. Moreover, the defendant will only be permitted to rely on the fact that the possessor has *no* right to possess the land in question[146] if either the defendant has the right to possession of that land, or the defendant created the nuisance with the authority of the person with the right to possession. This rule has several consequences.

First, a person enjoying exclusive possession in fact, but who has a defective title, will still

[143] We will not attempt to list *all* the interests which may qualify as interests *in land*. The interested reader should consult a standard textbook on land law.

[144] If, for instance, the noise is sufficiently loud to damage the windows, the tenant is not obliged to repair them, and the building will deteriorate if they are not repaired immediately, then the noise damages the reversioner's interest in the land.

[145] *Hunter* v *Canary Wharf Ltd* [1997] AC 655.

[146] This is often referred to as the defence of *ius tertii*.

be able to sue.[147] Secondly, a licensee enjoying exclusive possession may be able to sue without having to convince the court that a licence granting exclusive possession creates an interest *in land*. Thirdly, a person asserting exclusive possession over something which cannot be owned as land may be able to sue.[148]

Because most[149] of those who qualify as having a title to sue in nuisance under the first rule – on the ground that they have an interest *in the land* being interfered with – will also qualify under the second rule – on the ground that they enjoy *de facto* exclusive possession of the land interfered with, it might be thought to be a sensible simplification to treat the law as simply saying that a person who enjoys *de facto* exclusive possession of a piece of land can sue in nuisance if his use and enjoyment of that land is unreasonably interfered with.

Such a simplification is harmless as long as three points are borne in mind. First, by way of exception to the simplification, a reversioner can sue for interference with *his own* interest in land. Secondly, a defendant will have a good defence if he can demonstrate that *he* has the right to possession of the land in question or is acting on the authority of the person with that right. Thirdly, it may be necessary to investigate *interests* rather than *possession* when deciding what remedy to grant. In particular, if a court wanted to award damages compensating for *future* interferences in lieu of an injunction[150] it would be important to ascertain who would suffer those future interferences.[151]

Recoverable harm

Given that the test for liability is different in the torts of negligence and private nuisance it becomes important to consider whether there are any situations where there will be an awkward overlap. In *Hunter* v *Canary Wharf* the House of Lords limited the possibility of overlap by reasserting the traditional rule that only those with an interest in land can sue in private nuisance. Lord Lloyd and Lord Hoffmann went further, however, in eliminating the prospect of overlap and both stated that damages for personal injuries could not be recovered in private nuisance.[152] Lord Goff raised this issue but did not express any concluded opinion on it, preferring to say no more than that actions for interference with interests in land were the *typical* form of private nuisance.[153]

147 See, for example, *Pemberton* v *Southwark London Borough Council* [2000] 1 WLR 1672. In *Metropolitan Properties Ltd* v *Jones* [1939] 2 All ER 202 the claimant, Jones, had been a tenant of the flat affected by the nuisance, but he had assigned the tenancy (and hence the right to occupy) to a person called Storer, before returning to live in the flat when Storer disappeared, leaving him (Jones) still liable for the rent. Lord Hoffmann suggested in *Hunter* v *Canary Wharf Ltd* [1997] AC 655, 704E, that Jones should have been allowed to sue on the basis of his *de facto* possession.

148 In *Foster* v *Warblington UDC* [1906] 1 KB 648 the claimant sued for the pollution of oyster ponds on the foreshore.

149 The obvious exception is a reversioner.

150 For this remedy see below, pp. 729–32.

151 The fact that someone *presently* enjoys exclusive possession does not mean that such possession is likely to continue in the future.

152 [1997] AC 655, 696D, 707H. In *Transco plc* v *Stockport Metropolitan Borough Council* [2004] 2 AC 1, a majority of the House of Lords held that damages for personal injuries could not be recovered under the rule in *Rylands* v *Fletcher* (discussed in Chapter 42, below) because this was the rule in private nuisance: see [9] (per Lord Bingham), [35] (per Lord Hoffmann), [52] (per Lord Hobhouse).

153 *Hunter* v *Canary Wharf Ltd* [1997] AC 655, 692.

If damages for personal injuries could be recovered in private nuisance then the anomalous situation would arise that a person would find it easier to recover personal injury damages if injured when in a garden that she owned than if injured in the street or at work. Further, because only a claimant with an interest in land can sue in private nuisance, there would then be a second anomaly. A landowner who was injured in her garden by an emanation would be able to sue the creator of that emanation in nuisance for damages in respect of her injury without having to prove that the creator of the emanation acted carelessly; on the other hand, if the landowner's infant son (who would not have an interest in the land affected by the emanation) were injured by the same emanation, he would have to prove carelessness on the part of the creator of the emanation before he could sue for damages in respect of his injuries. One possible solution to the second anomaly would be to let those without interests in land sue in private nuisance. But the House of Lords rejected this solution, and ruled that it was inconsistent with the *function* of the tort which is to protect interests in land. The preferred solution to both anomalies was to deny that anyone could sue in private nuisance for compensation in respect of personal injuries.

It may be worth noting, however, that by excluding personal injuries from private nuisance a third apparent anomaly arises. If foul-smelling acidic smoke created by Gary drifts across land belonging to Lara, Lara will find it easier to sue Gary for the bad smell carried by the smoke than she will if the smoke physically burns her nostrils. If the bad smell reduces the amenity value of Lara's land then she will be able to sue Gary in nuisance for compensation for that without having to prove carelessness on Gary's part. On the other hand, carelessness must be established on Gary's part before Lara can sue him for compensation in respect of the harm to her nostrils.

A fourth anomaly might also arise, depending on how damage to chattels on the land is treated. Lord Hoffmann suggested that if Dawn committed the tort of private nuisance in relation to Carl by flooding Carl's land with the result that some cows belonging to Carl were drowned, Carl might be able to recover damages for the loss of those cows – in addition to damages for the injury to his land – as 'consequential loss'.[154] While it is easy to appreciate the convenience of such a rule, and its attraction in avoiding a need to distinguish between crops (which might count as part of the land itself) and cows (which would not), it would have the unattractive consequence of drawing a distinction between the level of protection given to cows and that given to people. Moreover, if some of the cows on the land were Carl's, and some belonged to his son, Craig, it seems that Carl would be able to claim in private nuisance for his cows as 'consequential loss' whilst Craig would have to try to bring a claim against Dawn for the tort of negligence.

A similar anomaly will also arise with regard to business losses consequential on an unreasonable interference with the use and enjoyment of land. A person with a sufficient interest in land can clearly recover for such losses in a private nuisance claim, provided that they really are *consequential*.[155] Thus if a defendant makes loud noises which unreasonably interfere with performances in a concert hall owned and occupied by Concert Promoters Ltd then this company will be able to sue for any consequential loss of business, subject to ordinary remoteness rules. But performers who lost business because of their perform-

[154] Ibid., 706.
[155] Ibid.

ances being disrupted would not be able to claim for their losses in private nuisance because they would not have a sufficient interest in the *land*.

Evaluation of the decision in *Hunter* v *Canary Wharf Ltd*[156]

The majority in *Hunter* v *Canary Wharf Ltd*[157] insisted that there had to be a clear distinction between the *function* of the tort of private nuisance and the *function* of the tort of negligence in order to explain the differences between the torts.[158] These differences were said to flow from the fact that private nuisance protects a claimant's interests in land, while negligence protects the personal safety of all persons regardless of whether they have interests in land. The argument, in summary, is that if those without interests in land were allowed to sue in private nuisance that would 'transform it from a tort to land into a tort to the person'[159] and blur the distinction between the two torts.

This transformation would also conflict with the way a majority of their Lordships thought that damages should be assessed for *past* harm[160] in private nuisance cases. Lords Lloyd, Hoffmann and Hope all insisted that the appropriate measure of damages for an interference with the use and enjoyment of land in cases not involving physical damage to the land is the diminution in the amenity value of the land caused by the nuisance.[161] This amenity value is an amount relative to the land, not relative to how many people live on it. Lord Hoffmann said, 'Damages for nuisance recoverable by the possessor or occupier may be affected by the size, commodiousness and value of his property but cannot be increased merely because more people are in occupation and therefore suffer greater discomfort.'[162]

Their Lordships also treated both the weight of the 'transformation' argument and the persuasiveness of the damages point as reinforced by the symmetry which would consequentially exist between the three different forms of interference which can constitute private nuisance: encroachment on land, indirect[163] physical damage to land and reduction in amenity value. Where interference is by encroachment on or physical damage *to land* it seems obvious that the person who should be able to sue is the person with the interest in the land. Equally it seems obvious that if that person claims damages then these should be calculated to compensate him for the diminution in the value of his interest in the land. Accepting that only those with interests in land can sue for interferences with sensibilities,

156 The ruling in this case relating to interference with television reception has already been discussed above, pp. 373–4.

157 [1997] AC 655.

158 Lord Hope pointed out one difference (ibid., at 724A–B), that 'the tort of nuisance is a tort of strict liability in the sense that it is no defence to say that the defendant took all reasonable care to prevent it' and Lord Hoffmann noted another (ibid., at 707H), that 'the law of negligence gives no remedy for discomfort or distress which does not result in bodily or psychiatric illness'.

159 Ibid., 693D–E.

160 Damages may be claimed for *past* harm. Further, where an injunction is claimed, a court may decide to award damages for anticipated *future* harm *in lieu* of an injunction. For more details, see Chapter 39, below.

161 [1997] AC 655, 696B–C (per Lord Lloyd), 706E–F (per Lord Hoffmann), 724G–H (per Lord Hope).

162 Thus both Lord Hoffmann (ibid., at 706D–707B) and Lord Lloyd (ibid., at 698D–699A) expressly disapproved of the suggestion in *Bone* v *Seale* [1975] 1 WLR 797 that damages for private nuisance by smell might be assessed by drawing an analogy with awards in personal injury cases for loss of the sense of smell. Lord Hope's views were less clear.

163 Their Lordship talked about *direct* physical damage instead of *indirect* physical damage, but we have explained above (at p. 370) why this was an error.

and that *all* they can sue for is reduction of the amenity value *of the land*, means that whatever the form of interference, only those with interests in land can sue and their damages should reflect the damage done to their interest.

Lord Goff provided two additional practical reasons why liability in private nuisance should only extend to those with interests in land. First, he pointed out that potential claimants often reach compromises with potential defendants, for instance permitting the nuisance to continue for a fixed period in exchange for payment. Lord Goff feared that the likelihood of such sensible arrangements would be reduced if potential defendants had to identify and deal with not just those with interests in the land but all the occupiers of each property affected by their activities.[164] Secondly, he suggested that if the range of liability in private nuisance extended beyond the clear category of those with interests in land it would prove impossible to find any other easily definable limit. Thus he raised the awkward cases of lodgers, au pairs, resident nurses, and employees.[165]

Of the Lords who heard the *Hunter* case, only Lord Cooke argued against the traditional rule. His dissent urged that there was no *logical* reason why those who had actually been enjoying the amenities of a home should be unable to sue for an unreasonable interference with those amenities and that consequently a judicial determination of the issue depended on a policy choice.[166] In approaching this choice he expressed a preference for utility and justice over symmetry and tidiness,[167] discounted Lord Goff's concerns about sensible compromises and au pairs,[168] and concluded, 'occupation of the property as a home is, to me, an acceptable criterion, consistent with the traditional concern for the sanctity of family life and the Englishman's home'.[169] A tolerable paraphrase of Lord Cooke's reasoning might be that in modern society a domestic house, a home, is more than just a piece of investment property. No doubt if the home is invaded by noxious fumes or bad vibrations the owner's investment is harmed, and only the owner should be able to claim for that damage *to the investment*. But equally without doubt is the fact that other occupants of the home will have suffered – their lives will have been rendered less restful and fulfilling – and, so far as they are concerned, they should be compensated for their loss. In doctrinal terms, Lord Cooke might be said to have been arguing that the interest that the tort of private nuisance should protect is not merely an interest in land but a wider 'interest in a home'.

We think that Lord Cooke is unfair to the majority when he portrays the divergence as turning on whether one prefers symmetry and tidiness or utility and justice. We think that the majority was motivated by the need to set down clearly who is protected by the law on private nuisance and for what harm damages can be recovered if A commits the tort of private nuisance in relation to B. Clarity on these issues is important for settling disputes and also for those who want, in advance of any dispute, to negotiate permission to develop and use land in ways which may inconvenience neighbours. It is important to remember that many private nuisance claims do not involve interference with 'homes' but with land used for various business purposes and it is unclear whether Lord Cooke would have also

164 [1997] AC 655, 692H–693C.
165 Ibid., 693C–F.
166 Ibid., 711C–D.
167 Ibid., 711B–C.
168 Ibid., 718A–D.
169 Ibid., 718B–C.

supported allowing those without *interests in land* to claim in such cases. On the other hand, we also think, that the majority's treatment of 'homes' as simply *investments in property* fails to reflect the way in which most members of our society value 'homes'. The question of who is protected by the law on private nuisance is part of a more general dispute in the law of torts between the desire to draw bright lines which will allow people to plan around the law and the desire to decide each case on its individual merits. There are no easy answers to the question of how to balance these two desires. In the area under discussion, it would be very helpful to have more evidence about whether those who carry out activities which *may* create a nuisance generally *try* to negotiate in advance, or not, before deciding whether the balance struck by the majority is preferable to the balance struck by Lord Cooke.[170]

Article 8 of the European Convention on Human Rights

Article 8(1) of the ECHR provides that 'Everyone has the right to respect for his private and family life, his home and his correspondence.' The European Court of Human Rights has held that this right can be violated by 'homes' being exposed to extreme noise or environmental pollution,[171] and that even when the State has not directly created the noise or pollution it may nonetheless be responsible for the violation if it has failed properly to regulate private industry.[172]

Several lawyers have argued that s 6 of the Human Rights Act 1998 obliges the English courts to develop the common law so as to make it compatible with the Convention,[173] and that they should fulfil this obligation by extending the tort of private nuisance so that *all* those who reside in a 'home' can sue (regardless of whether they have a sufficient interest in the land) if their use and enjoyment of the 'home' has been unreasonably interfered with and damages should be available for 'distress' caused by such interferences.[174] Two problems with this argument are worth mentioning here.

First, although the English courts are obliged to act compatibly with the Convention, the cases before the European Court of Human Rights have *not* established that a failure by a State to create *private law actions* for children and other non-owners to bring against polluters is incompatible with Article 8. The cases have established that a failure of the State to prevent such pollution by *regulation* is incompatible with Article 8, but that is not the same as saying that such regulation must be by the provision of private law actions.

Secondly, extending the tort of private nuisance may actually provide children and non-owners with *far more* protection than Article 8 requires. As we have seen, the tort of private nuisance allows the owner of a house in a luxurious residential district to sue when the

170 If such negotiating in advance is very rare we think this would strengthen the case for accepting Lord Cooke's views.

171 Though interference with a person's 'home' by noise or pollution can be justified under Art 8.2 if the interference is prescribed by law and necessary in a democratic society.

172 *Powell & Rayner* v *United Kingdom* (1990) 12 EHRR 355; *Lopez Ostra* v *Spain* (1995) 20 EHRR 277; *Guerra* v *Italy* (1998) 26 EHRR 357; *Hatton* v *United Kingdom* (2003) 37 EHRR 28.

173 See, for example, Hunt 1998.

174 Wright J 2001, 194. In *McKenna* v *British Aluminum*, The Times, 25 April 2002, Neuberger J thought that it was arguable that the English courts would accept this argument.

premises are subjected to the smell of frying fish,[175] but it seems highly unlikely that the European Court of Human Rights would regard such an owner's children as victims of a human rights violation.[176]

REMAINING POINTS

Three points remain to be made about the tort of private nuisance.

(1) *Some unusual forms of private nuisance.* There are some other torts which are treated as forms of private nuisance though they do not fit within the definition of what committing the tort of private nuisance involves which was advanced at the start of this chapter. For example: the tort of organising a rival market within 6½ miles of a franchise or statutory market;[177] or the tort of organising a ferry service which rivals that of a person with a franchise right to operate a ferry. Such torts have often developed their own esoteric rules, like that making the distance of 6½ miles significant, and consequently can claim to be treated as independent torts rather than forms of private nuisance. We think that it is likely, however, that a judge asked to resolve any uncertainty about the rules applying to these torts would draw strong analogies with the tort of private nuisance.

(2) *The relationship between private nuisance and public nuisance.* Although the word 'nuisance' is common to both wrongs it is important to remember that private nuisance and public nuisance are *separate* forms of unlawful conduct.[178] In some situations they may overlap, but not every defendant who commits the tort of private nuisance will create a public nuisance and not every defendant who creates a public nuisance will commit the tort of private nuisance.

At this stage in the chapter it will be clear that if A commits the tort of private nuisance in relation to B, he will usually do so by unreasonably interfering with the use and enjoyment of land in which B has an interest. In contrast, creating a public nuisance involves interfering with a *public right* or acting in a way which is generally *contrary to the public interest.* In many situations, such as when there is an actionable interference with the public right to free passage along a highway, there can be a public nuisance even though nobody's interests in land have been affected. Private individuals can seek redress, including damages, for public nuisances where they have suffered 'special damage'. But one can show that one has suffered 'special damage' without showing that land in which one has an interest has been unreasonably interfered with or damaged. Where a public nuisance *does* lead to a person suffering 'special damage' in the form of damage to land in which he has an interest there will be an *overlap* between private nuisance and a possible individual claim

[175] *Adams* v *Ursell* [1913] 1 Ch 269.

[176] In *Dennis* v *Ministry of Defence* [2003] EWHC 793 (QB), Buckley J held that the amount he was awarding a landowner for private nuisance caused by noise was sufficient to amount to 'just satisfaction' of the claim by the landowner and *his wife* that their rights under Art 8 had been infringed. It seems, however, that he reached this conclusion after using the wrong method to assess damages for private nuisance, and without considering whether the amounts would always coincide. See further, Bagshaw 2004a, 41.

[177] *Tamworth BC* v *Fazeley Town Council* (1978) 77 LGR 238; *Sevenoaks DC* v *Vinson Ltd* [1984] Ch 211; *Stoke-on-Trent City Council* v *W & J Wass Ltd* [1988] 1 WLR 1406.

[178] Public nuisance is discussed below, in Chapter 44.

for public nuisance. It seems, however, that it would not be to the private individual's advantage to sue for *public* nuisance in such a case.[179]

(3) *The relationship between private nuisance and the rule in* Rylands *v* Fletcher.[180] The rule in *Rylands* v *Fletcher* imposes liability on a defendant who has brought onto, or kept on, some land an exceptionally dangerous or mischievous thing in extraordinary or unusual circumstances, when the thing has escaped from that land and damaged the claimant's land.[181] There is some controversy over the relationship between the rule and the tort of private nuisance. Following the opinion of Lord Macmillan that '*Rylands* v *Fletcher* ... derives from a conception of mutual duties of adjoining or neighbouring landowners, and its cogenors are trespass and nuisance',[182] and the assertion of Lord Goff that '*Rylands* v *Fletcher* was essentially concerned with an extension of the law of nuisance to cases of isolated escape',[183] a majority of the House of Lords in *Transco plc* v *Stockport Metropolitan Borough Council*[184] stated that the rule in Rylands v Fletcher, like the torts of trespass to land and private nuisance, can only be relied on by those who have interests in land,[185] and cannot be used to claim compensation for personal injuries. Although this classification of the rule in *Rylands* v *Fletcher* is now authoritative, our view is that it is misguided and was adopted by the House of Lords without sufficient attention to the issues involved.[186] Consequently we will postpone discussion of liability under the rule in *Rylands* v *Fletcher* until Chapter 42, below.

Visit **http://www.mylawchamber.co.uk/mcbride** to access updates on recent cases, as well as model answers and tips for answering tort problem questions.

Use **Case Navigator** to read in full the key case referenced in this chapter:

- **Hunter *v* Canary Wharf Ltd**

179 A person choosing to sue in public nuisance instead of private nuisance would impose on herself the additional burdens of proving both that the state of affairs affected a sufficient proportion of the community and that she had suffered 'special damage'.

180 *Rylands* v *Fletcher* (1866) LR 1 Ex 265; (1868) LR 3 HL 330.

181 For what we mean by 'the claimant's land' in this context see above, n. 1.

182 *Read* v *J Lyons & Co.* [1947] AC 156, 173.

183 *Cambridge Water Co.* v *Eastern Counties Leather Plc* [1994] 2 AC 264, 304E.

184 [2004] 2 AC 1.

185 In practice those who have exclusive possession of land can often claim. See above, pp. 394–5.

186 We present our reasons for taking this view below, pp. 756–7. This view is shared by others: See, for example, Murphy 2004, Nolan 2005.

C.

The economic torts

Introduction

In this section of the book we will be talking primarily about seven different torts.

The first is the tort of *inducing a breach of contract*, which is primarily committed where A persuades C to breach a contract that C has with B. In such a case, A will normally be found to have committed the tort of inducing a breach of contract in relation to B, and will be held liable to compensate B for any losses that she has suffered as a result of C's breach. The second tort is the tort of *intentional infliction of harm by unlawful means*. As currently defined, this tort is committed where A intentionally harms B by committing (or threatening to commit) a civil wrong – a breach of contract, a tort, or an equitable wrong – in relation to C. The third and fourth torts we will be discussing are both *conspiracy* torts. The tort of *lawful means conspiracy* is committed where A and C combine together to inflict loss on B for no legitimate reason. The tort of *unlawful means conspiracy* is committed where A and C combine together to inflict loss on B using unlawful means to do so.

The final three torts that we will be discussing in this section all involve deceiving someone else. The first such tort is the tort of *deceit*, which is committed where A deliberately lies to B with the object of inducing B to do *x*, B is induced by A's lie to do *x*, and B suffers loss as a result. The second deception tort is the tort of *malicious falsehood*. This tort is committed where A deliberately tells a lie to C about B and B suffers loss as a result. The final deception tort is the tort of *passing off*. There are a variety of ways of committing this tort, but the principal way in which A will commit this tort is if people are induced to buy A's goods because he is selling them in a way that makes it look like they are made by B.

These seven torts do not, in truth, have that much in common. They are called 'the economic torts' because all of these torts are normally committed by one person causing another to suffer some form of pure economic loss. (The question of whether the 'economic torts' cover cases where one person has caused another to suffer a more serious form of loss than pure economic loss – such as physical injury or property damage – has not really ever been tested by the courts because anyone suffering physical injury or property damage as a result of someone else's actions will normally bring a claim in negligence for that harm. The question of whether the 'economic torts' can cover a less serious form of harm than economic loss, such as distress, has recently come up and the courts have ruled that they do not extend to cases where someone has caused another to suffer a form of harm less serious than economic loss.) However, the fact that these torts share a common name leads many to think that they must have something *more* in common than the fact that they all involve one person causing another to suffer some kind of pure economic loss. And so in books and articles we find wistful references to the fact that the economic torts have so far 'lacked their Atkin'[1] – some master genius who will finally discern the rule or

[1] See Wedderburn 1983, at 229.

principle that underlies all the economic torts and which will allow us to unify these torts into one single tort.

These tendencies to mono-mania must be resisted. There is absolutely no good reason to think that the torts gathered together in this section have anything in common except for the accidental fact of the kind of loss that tends to be suffered by someone who is a victim of these torts. All attempts to find a unifying rule or principle that underlies all of these torts have so far failed. For example, it has been suggested[2] that all of the economic torts give effect to a rule that A will commit a tort in relation to B if he intentionally causes B to suffer some kind of loss using unlawful means. So – according to this view – all of the economic torts are examples of, or species of, the tort of *intentional infliction of harm by unlawful means*. But this view is unsustainable. It does not have to be shown that A had an intention to harm B in order for it to be established that A committed the tort of inducing a breach of contract in persuading C to breach his contract with B. Nor does it have to be shown that A acted unlawfully in persuading C to breach his contract with B. The same is true of the deception torts. To establish that A committed one of those torts in relation to B, it does not have to be shown that A acted as he did because he was trying to harm B.[3]

Again, it has been suggested in some quarters that what the economic torts have in common is that they are all concerned with regulating *competition* between businesses.[4] So – it is argued – the economic torts reflect the courts' evolving notions of what businesses should, and should not, be allowed to do in obtaining a larger market share for themselves. Again, this attempt to unify the economic torts simply does not work. While it should be acknowledged that some of the landmark cases that have shaped the definition of the economic torts involve a business or a trader complaining about something a rival business or trader did, many cases involving the economic torts have nothing to do with regulating competition. Instead, they involve cases of employees trying to get a better deal from their employer by disrupting their employer's business, or cases of someone taking revenge on someone else for some past slight.

[2] See Weir 1997.

[3] See, in relation to the tort of deceit, *Polhill* v *Walter* (1832) 3 B & Ad 114, 110 ER 43. The fact that the tort of deceit can be committed without any intention to harm the victim of the deceit means that Weir 1964 (at 226), Cane 1996 (at 152, n. 9) and Sales & Stilitz 1999 (at 432) are *wrong* to suggest that deceit can be seen as an instance of the tort of using unlawful means to harm another.

[4] See Carty 2001, 3–4.

20 Inducing a breach of contract

ELEMENTS OF THE TORT

A will have committed the tort of inducing a breach of contract in relation to B *if*:

(1) B had a contract with a third party, C; *and*
(2) A induced C to breach that contract;[1] *and*
(3) A was in a certain state of mind – defined below – when A induced C to breach that contract; *and*
(4) A had no justification for acting as he did.

So, in *Lumley* v *Gye*,[2] Johanna Wagner, a well-known soprano, made a contract with Lumley to sing at Her Majesty's Theatre, and not to sing anywhere else. Gye, a rival opera impresario, was alleged to have persuaded Wagner to sing for him at the Royal Italian Opera – and therefore to break her contract with Lumley. The Court of Queen's Bench held that if Gye *had* persuaded Wagner to break her contract with Lumley then Gye would have committed a tort in relation to Lumley.[3]

The tort in *Lumley* v *Gye* is usually described as either 'the tort of procuring a breach of contract' or 'the tort of inducing a breach of contract'. At one time it was thought that the tort might extend beyond situations where A induced C to breach her contract with B, for instance, to situations where A made it *impossible* for C to perform her contract with B. In such situations C's failure to perform might not actually amount to a breach of contract: C's non-performance as a result of forces beyond her control might have been expressly excused under the contract or A's intervention might have had the effect of frustrating the contract. The apparent extension of the tort to cover situations where there was no breach led to it being renamed 'the tort of interference with contract'.[4] However, in *OBG Ltd* v *Allan*[5] the House of Lords held that it had been an error to think that the tort in *Lumley* v *Gye* extended to situations where A made it impossible for C to perform her contract with B. It is clear after the *OBG* case that A will *not* commit a tort in relation to B by making it impossible for C to perform her contract with B *unless* he uses *unlawful means* to make it impossible *and* he intends to cause harm to B. And then the tort A will commit in relation to B will be 'the tort of intentionally causing loss by the use of unlawful means' – the tort discussed in the next chapter[6] – *not* 'the tort of inducing a breach of contract'.

[1] *Important note*. The term 'induce' as used in this chapter does not bear its normal meaning of 'cause' or 'bring about'. We will discuss when someone will be held to have 'induced' a breach of contract below at pp. 411–15.

[2] (1853) 2 E & B 216, 118 ER 749.

[3] In fact, at the later trial of the facts, a jury found that Gye had not committed the tort because he had honestly believed that Wagner was at liberty to terminate her agreement with Lumley: for further details, see Waddams 2001.

[4] For instance, Fleming 1998, 756–7; W&J, 635–6.

[5] [2007] 2 WLR 920. Hereafter, '*OBG*'.

[6] See below, Chapter 21.

The state of mind necessary to commit the tort

Suppose A induced C to breach a contract that she had made with B. A will not have committed the tort of inducing a breach of contract in so acting unless he was in a *certain state of mind* when he brought about the breach. For example, if A merely *carelessly* brought about the breach by C, he will not have committed the tort of inducing a breach of contract. So what sort of state of mind does it have to be shown A was in before we will find that A committed the tort of inducing a breach of contract in inducing C to breach her contract with B?

The short answer is that when A induces C to breach the contract A must *know* that he is inducing a breach of contract *and* must *intend* to induce a breach of contract. But both of these elements require further discussion.

Knowledge that a breach is being induced

In *OBG* Lord Hoffmann explained the knowledge element in the following way:

> To be liable for inducing a breach of contract, you must know that you are inducing a breach of contract. It is not enough that you know that you are procuring an act which, as a matter of law or construction of the contract, is a breach. You must actually realize that it will have this effect.[7]

This means that if A mistakenly but genuinely believes that what he is procuring will *not* amount to a breach of contract then he will not be liable, even if that belief is unreasonable.[8] In one of the cases heard by the House of Lords alongside *OBG* – the case of *Mainstream Properties Ltd* v *Young* – two employees of the claimant had told the defendant that they were at liberty to purchase a particular plot of land for development. That was wrong; it was a breach of their contracts with their employer, the claimant, for them to divert the purchase to their joint venture with the defendant. But because the defendant believed what he had been told, that the two employees were at liberty to do what they did, he was not liable for inducing a breach.[9] Of course, the two employees were liable for breaking their contracts. Any mistake they made as to their contractual obligations, even if honest and reasonable, could not help them.

While a defendant who mistakenly believes that he is *not* bringing about a breach will not commit the tort, a defendant who makes a conscious decision not to find out how things stand will be liable. In *Emerald Construction* v *Lowthian*[10] the defendants, the officers of a building trade union, sought to persuade the main contractor building the Fiddlers Ferry power station to terminate a labour-only subcontract. The defendants knew of the subcontract but were not aware of its terms. The main contractor terminated the subcontract and committed a breach of contract in so doing; the subcontract did not

[7] *OBG*, at [39].

[8] *British Industrial Plastics* v *Ferguson* [1940] 1 All ER 479, HL.

[9] In *Meretz Investments NV* v *ACP Ltd* [2007] EWCA Civ 1303, the Court of Appeal dealt with a case where the defendant had received legal advice about the action which brought about a breach of contract; he had *not* been advised that the action would not induce a breach, but had been advised that he was *legally* entitled to act in this way. The Court concluded, at [124], that a defendant's honest belief that he was *legally* entitled to act in a particular way was sufficient to preclude his state of mind being held to have been an intention to induce a breach of contract. This seems doubtful, particularly since it might have the effect of protecting from liability a range of defendants who *mistakenly* believe themselves to enjoy a defence of justification.

[10] [1966] 1 WLR 691.

permit the main contractor to terminate it in the way that it did. The defendants were held liable for inducing a breach of contract even though they had not known for certain that the main contractor would commit a breach of the subcontract if it terminated it. Lord Denning MR remarked:

> Even if they did not know the actual terms of the contract, but had the means of knowledge – which they deliberately disregarded – that would be enough. Like the man who turns a blind eye. So here, if the officers deliberately sought to get this contract terminated, heedless of its terms, regardless of whether it was terminated by breach or not, they would do wrong. For it is unlawful for a third person to procure a breach of contract knowingly, or recklessly, indifferent whether it is a breach or not.[11]

This passage was quoted with approval by Lord Hoffmann in *OBG*.[12] He made clear that the crucial line was to be drawn between an honest belief – even if it stems from gross negligence – that a breach would not be induced, and a conscious decision not to confirm a suspicion that a breach would be induced.

Intention to induce a breach

A will only have committed the tort of inducing a breach of contract in relation to B *if* when A induced C to breach her contract with B he *intended to induce a breach of contract*. So we must ask what state of mind will count as 'intention' in this context. The simple answer to this is that A will be held to have intended to induce a breach of contract *if*:

(i) the *end* which A was seeking to achieve when he acted was inducing a breach of contract, *or*
(ii) inducing a breach of contract was the *means* which A was deploying to seek to achieve some other end.

But A will not be held to have induced a breach of contract if such a breach was merely a *consequence*, albeit one which A knew to be very likely to occur, of A's means or end. There are three points of detail that we must clarify.

(1) *A would have preferred not to have to induce a breach of contract*. Where a defendant sets out to achieve his end by means of inducing a breach of contract then he will be held to have intended to induce a breach of contract *even if* he would have preferred it to have been possible to achieve his end in some other way. Thus if Antville Football Club persuaded Conor to break his contract with Bugtown Football Club, by persuading Conor to refuse to play for Bugtown FC until they agree to transfer him to Antville FC, then it will not assist Antville FC for them to claim that they would have preferred the transfer to be arranged without such steps being necessary.

(2) *Uncertainty as to what means will be necessary*. A difficult issue concerns the position of a defendant who is determined to achieve a particular end but is unsure what means will be necessary to achieve it. For instance in *Emerald Construction* v *Lowthian*,[13] as we have seen, the defendants' end was to terminate a labour-only subcontract but they were not

[11] Ibid., 700H–701A.
[12] *OBG*, at [40]–[41].
[13] [1966] 1 WLR 691.

sure if the main contractor would have to breach the subcontract in order to achieve this. Lord Denning MR's comments, quoted above, suggest that he thought that defendants could commit the tort if they suspected that it might be necessary for a contract to be breached in order to achieve their end but went ahead without investigating whether this was the case because they did not care. Given that Lord Hoffmann cited these comments with approval in *OBG*,[14] it seems likely that a defendant will be held to have intended to induce a breach of contract by C if he intends to induce C to *take whatever means are necessary* to achieve a particular end, and he knows that it may be necessary for C to breach a contract with B, but he does not care. This is not, of course, to say that a defendant will be held to have intended to induce a breach of contract by C whenever he was recklessly indifferent as to whether *a consequence* of his conduct would be to persuade C to breach a contract with B. There is an important difference between being recklessly indifferent between different means of achieving your object and being recklessly indifferent as to the likely consequences of achieving your object.

(3) *'The other side of the same coin'*. In deciding what a defendant intends it is necessary to distinguish carefully between what is *part of* the defendant's end or means and what is a *consequence* of achieving that end or using those means. An outcome will count as *part of* the defendant's end if it is 'simply the other side of the same coin' *and* the defendant knows that this is the case.[15] An example of such a situation may be provided by the facts of *Lumley* v *Gye*: if Gye had known that Wagner had made a valid contract with Lumley not to sing elsewhere than at Her Majesty's Theatre then he must also have known that she could not sing for him at the Royal Italian Opera without breaching this contract. Thus he could *not* say that he intended to induce her to sing at the Royal Italian Opera but did not intend to induce her to break her contract with Lumley to sing nowhere except at Her Majesty's Theatre.

Intention to harm

We have explained that A will only be held to have committed the tort of inducing a breach of contract if, when A induced C to breach the contract, A *knew* that he was inducing a breach of contract *and* A *intended* to induce a breach of contract. It may be worth emphasising that it does *not* have to be shown that A *intended to harm* B when he acted as he did. This was confirmed by the House of Lords in *South Wales Miners' Federation* v *Glamorgan Coal Co. Ltd*[16] where the defendant miners' union had induced miners to break their contracts of employment in order to raise the price of coal (at the time the wages of miners were pegged to the price of coal) and argued that this would *benefit* the claimant colliery owners rather than harming them. The House of Lords held that the defendants' expectation that the claimants might benefit was irrelevant because to

[14] *OBG*, at [40]–[41]. At this point in his speech Lord Hoffmann is discussing 'knowledge' rather than 'intention', but there would be little point in holding that turning a blind eye to whether a contract would have to be broken is sufficient to constitute 'knowledge' if such reckless indifference could not also constitute 'intention'. Moreover, in a later passage in his speech, [69]–[71], Lord Hoffmann seems to assume that it would be actionable for A to encourage C to terminate a contract with B with reckless indifference as to whether C will have to breach this contract.

[15] *OBG*, at [134] (per Lord Hoffmann), [167] (per Lord Nicholls).

[16] [1905] AC 239. This case was cited with approval as authority for this point by Lord Hoffmann in *OBG*, at [8].

establish the tort it was sufficient to demonstrate an intention to induce the employees to breach their contracts.

Summary

So: before we can find that A committed the tort of inducing a breach of contract in inducing C to breach her contract with B, it will have to be established that when A acted as he did:

(1) he *knew* that he was inducing a breach of contract; *and*
(2) he *intended* to induce a breach of contract.

But (1) will also be satisfied if A *suspected* that he might have been inducing a breach of contract but he did not bother to find out. And (2) will be satisfied if A intended to achieve an end by whatever means were necessary, and A did not care that the necessary means might involve a breach of contract by C.

When will someone be held to have *induced* a breach of contract?

There is some uncertainty in the law as to when someone will be held to have *induced* someone else to commit a breach of contract. So, what guidance can be offered?

Persuasion

There is no doubt that if A has *persuaded* C to break a contract with B then A will be held to have induced C to breach that contract. Some commentators have argued that the tort should extend no further than this: 'liability should attach under *Lumley* v *Gye* only when the defendant has persuaded the [claimant's] contractor deliberately to break his contract.'[17] Persuasion in this context could involve either an enticing offer or an unattractive threat – either 'carrot or stick'.[18] However, there are some cases when A has been held to have induced C to breach her contract with B even though it would be difficult to describe the part he played in bringing about that breach as *persuasion*.

Advice

Suppose that Lara has contracted to sing at Paul's theatre in London and that Lara's aunt, Mary, has advised her not to go to London to sing because a wealthy relative is dying and this relative is likely to give bequests only to family members who pray at his bedside. If Lara takes this advice and breaks her contract, should Mary be held to have induced the breach?

Those who argue that Mary should not be held to have induced Lara to breach her contract assert that there is an important distinction between *creating* a reason to break a contract and *pointing out* that a reason exists.[19] But Winn LJ showed no sympathy for such a distinction when it was pressed in *Torquay Hotel* v *Cousins*, and suggested that a father

[17] Weir 1997, 35 (quoted approvingly by Carty 2001, at 61).
[18] Weir 1997, 34. Likewise, in *OBG*, [20], Lord Hoffmann treats persuasion to breach a contract by a threat of assault as falling within the tort of inducing a breach of contract *as well as* potentially falling within the tort of three-party intimidation.
[19] S&H, 353; Carty 2001, 47.

who told his daughter that her fiancé had been convicted of indecent exposure would have induced her to break her engagement even if the information was true.[20] Certainly there would be a risk, if the courts drew a distinction between persuasion and advice, that the line between making a soprano a generous offer to *persuade* her to break her contract and merely *advising* her that such an offer was likely to be available if she broke her contract would be difficult to draw in practice.

'Harbouring'

Can A be said to have induced a breach of a contract between B and C if C's breach of that contract happened *before* A became involved? Suppose, for example, that Beth, a soprano, contracted to perform exclusively for Ian. Suppose that Beth then walked out on Ian in breach of contract and was later engaged by Gary. Can Gary be said to have induced Beth to breach her contract with Ian? It seems that the English courts have taken the view that Gary *can* be held liable if Beth's breach of her contract with Ian was still 'retrievable'.[21] This is often referred to as liability for 'harbouring' – the idea being that in the case just described, Gary, by providing Beth with a 'harbour', made it less likely that Beth would return and perform for Ian.[22]

Facilitating

In *British Motor Trade Association* v *Salvadori*[23] C sold a car to A, in breach of a contractual undertaking that C had made with B that he would not sell the car to anyone within a year after purchasing it. A argued that C had been willing to sell the car and break his contract with B without any influence from him, and that consequently he could not be said to have induced the breach. Roxburgh J held, however, that C could not break the contract not to sell without *someone* being willing to buy, and that 'any active step taken by a defendant . . . by which he facilitates a breach' was sufficient to fall within the scope of the tort.[24] Some commentators, however, have expressed strong doubts about this statement because the courts have refused to adopt a general principle that anyone who assists another to commit a tort will be held liable.[25] It must be noted, however, that the cases which have rejected this principle have not involved defendants who both *knew* that they were bringing about a wrong and *intended* to do so.

Inconsistent dealing

If A has caused C to breach her contract with B by what is called 'inconsistent dealing' it can sometimes be very difficult to say whether A should be held to have induced C to

20 [1969] 2 Ch 106, 147D–E. Of course, in such a case the father might be able to rely on the defence of justification. See below, pp. 417–18. In *Camden Nominees Ltd* v *Slack (or Forcey)* [1940] Ch 352, Simonds J was equally clear that 'advice which is intended to have persuasive effects is not distinguishable from inducement', but also held that a person who provided advice could rely on the defence of justification if the law recognised a moral duty to give the advice.

21 *Blake* v *Lanyon* (1795) 6 TR 221, 101 ER 521; *De Francesco* v *Barnum* (1890) 63 LT 514.

22 If there was no doubt that Beth would never have returned to perform for Ian then Ian might be unable to sue Gary because Gary's wrong would not have caused him any actionable loss: *Jones Brothers (Hunstanton) Ltd* v *Stevens* [1955] 1 QB 275.

23 [1949] Ch 556.

24 Ibid., 565.

25 See below, p. 646.

breach her contract with B. Two examples may be given to illustrate the kind of problems that arise.

First, Wendy contracts with Carl that no building will be erected during Carl's lifetime on a particular plot of land ('Whiteacre') that Wendy owns. Wendy then sells Whiteacre to Karen. Would it be a tort for Karen to build on Whiteacre with the knowledge that to do so would bring about a breach of Wendy's contract with Carl?[26]

Secondly, Wendy owns a boat (the '*Prima Donna*') which she hires to Carl for two years. During this period, Wendy sells the *Prima Donna* to Karen. Would it be a tort for Karen to take possession of the *Prima Donna* before the two years for which Carl has hired the *Prima Donna* are up, with knowledge that she would thereby be bringing about a breach of the contract of hire that Wendy entered into with Carl?

It is important to note that if these matters came before the courts *before* Wendy had transferred Whiteacre or the *Prima Donna* to Karen then the central question might not be whether Karen's building on Whiteacre/repossessing the *Prima Donna* will amount to a tort. The issue might instead be: (1) Can Carl obtain a remedy to prevent *Wendy* putting herself in a position where she might be put in breach of her contract with Carl (such as an injunction ordering Wendy not to transfer Whiteacre/the *Prima Donna* to Karen)? (2) Can a court refuse to grant Karen specific performance of her contract with Wendy to purchase Whiteacre/the *Prima Donna* if the effect of granting such an order will almost certainly be that Wendy ends up in breach of her contract with Carl? The answer to both these questions is 'yes'.[27]

Even if Whiteacre or the *Prima Donna* has already been transferred to Karen, the first relevant question may not be whether Karen will commit a tort by building on Whiteacre or by claiming possession of the *Prima Donna*. Two other sets of rules must be considered. First, there is a special set of rules about when a covenant relating to land can be enforced against a subsequent owner of the land.[28] Secondly, where a contract between A and B creates an equitable interest in an item of property then this will bind a subsequent purchaser of the property unless he was a bona fide purchaser for value without notice.[29] A significant point to note about this second set of rules is that if the purchaser has *constructive notice* then he will be bound by the equitable interest, even though a stronger degree of knowledge – *and* intention – is necessary in order to commit the tort of inducing a breach of contract.[30] This has encouraged courts to be wary about recognising equitable interests in commercial settings.

[26] This example is similar to the situation in *Sefton (Earl)* v *Tophams* [1965] Ch 1140, where Stamp J found that the defendant would have committed the tort of inducing a breach of contract if he built. The Court of Appeal continued an injunction against the defendant, requiring him not to build, without finding that the defendant would commit the tort of inducing a breach of contract if he did build, and the House of Lords did not consider this point: *Sefton (Earl)* v *Tophams* [1967] 1 AC 50.

[27] For relevant case law on (1) see *Lumley* v *Wagner* (1852) 1 De G M & G 604, 42 ER 687; *Manchester Ship Canal Co.* v *Manchester Racecourse Co.* [1901] 2 Ch 37; *Sefton* v *Tophams* [1965] Ch 1140. For case law on (2) see *Willmott* v *Barber* (1880) 15 Ch D 96; *Warmington* v *Miller* [1973] QB 877.

[28] For these rules see, Smith 2006, chapter 21.

[29] *Swiss Bank Corp.* v *Lloyds Bank Ltd* [1982] AC 584, 598A–B, 613B–E. When such an equitable interest will arise is a controversial question. Compare *Lord Strathcona SS Co.* v *Dominion Coal Co.* [1926] AC 108 with *Port Line Ltd* v *Ben Line Steamers Ltd* [1958] QB 146.

[30] It was argued on pp. 408–9 above that a defendant could be liable if he 'turned a blind eye' to the existence of the contract, but it is commonly thought to be easier to establish 'constructive notice' than this 'Nelsonian knowledge'.

If neither of these special sets of rules applies then it becomes necessary to ask whether Karen may be liable for having induced a breach of the contract between Wendy and Carl by 'inconsistent dealing'. In determining whether there has been culpable 'inconsistent dealing' it seems particularly important to consider whether Wendy's *contracting* with Karen, or *performing her contract* with Karen, was *in itself* a breach of the contract between Wendy and Carl. If this is the case, as it would be if Wendy had, for instance, promised in a contract with Carl not to sell Whiteacre to anyone but Carl and then sold it to Karen, then Karen may be held to have committed the tort of inducing a breach of contract in relation to Carl if she had the requisite mental element when she contracted to buy Whiteacre from Carl or sought performance of it.[31]

Where neither the making of the contract between Wendy and Karen nor the performance of it was in itself a breach of the contract between Carl and Wendy, and the breach was instead the result of Karen later exercising the rights that she acquired as owner, then it seems correct that Karen should not be liable.[32] One possible explanation for this would be to treat Karen as *justified* in putting her own rights, as owner, ahead of Carl's right that Wendy fulfil her contract with him.[33] An alternative, however, would be to look at the claim that Karen, after becoming owner, should be obliged to act so as to enable Wendy to perform her contract with Carl as a claim that Karen should *assist* Wendy to fulfil that contract. As we will see below, there are good reasons for thinking that the law in this area does not extend so far as to impose on people a duty to *assist* others to fulfil their contracts.[34]

Preventing performance

Suppose A *prevented* C from performing a contract with B and B suffered some kind of financial loss as a result, and A did this knowing of the contract and intending that C should be unable perform it. In *OBG*[35] the House of Lords decided that A will *not* commit a tort in relation to B by making it impossible for C to perform her contract with B *unless* he uses *unlawful means* to make performance impossible *and* intends to cause harm to B. And then the tort A will commit in relation to B will be 'the tort of intentionally causing loss by the use of unlawful means' – the subject of the next chapter[36] – *not* 'the tort of inducing a breach of contract'.

Since A will not be held to have *induced* C to breach a contract if A takes steps which prevent C from performing, it follows that A will also not be held to have *induced* C to breach a contract if A *omits to take steps which would have enabled C to perform*. Thus if C

[31] This seems to follow from *British Motor Trade Association* v *Salvadori* [1949] Ch 556, discussed in the previous section.

[32] This view is also advanced by Bright 2000, 411–12. If this view is correct it follows that Karen should not be held liable for *inducing a breach of contract* in either of our two examples.

[33] Professor Treitel seemed to take this view: see Treitel 2003, 623. See also Smith 1977. For the defence of justification see below, pp. 417–18.

[34] See below, pp. 414–15.

[35] [2007] 2 WLR 920, HL. This point was expressed most clearly by Lord Nicholls, at [178]–[180]. Lord Hoffmann did not make the same point *explicitly*. But such a point is consistent with Lord Hoffmann's insistence that there can be no liability for inducing breach of contract unless there has been a breach of contract, because preventing performance will not always result in a breach. In *Meretz Investments NV* v *ACP Ltd* [2007] EWCA Civ 1303 the Court of Appeal confirmed that preventing performance could not amount to inducing a breach of contract and that Lord Hoffmann had not intended to disagree with Lord Nicholls on this point.

[36] This tort is discussed below, in Chapter 21.

agrees to sell a painting to B, and A, who currently owns the painting, refuses to sell it to C, then A will not have committed a tort in relation to B *even if* A's only reason for refusing to sell was because he wanted to cause C to be in breach of his contract with B. Indeed, even if A had already agreed to sell the painting to C *before* C made his contract with B, a failure by A to perform this contract will not be held to have *induced* C to breach his contract to sell it to B. In this latter case, however, A's breach of contract will amount to the use of 'unlawful means', so A may have committed the tort of 'intentionally causing loss by the use of unlawful means' in relation to B.

The two main arguments[37] in favour of fixing the limit on what counts as 'inducing' between persuading and preventing are that it is easier to draw this line than the principal alternative[38] and that there is a moral difference between seducing C into committing a wrong and merely rendering C unable to perform.[39] But the clarity of the persuasion/prevention distinction should not be exaggerated: there are some forms of behaviour which must be assessed, such as *harbouring*, *facilitating* and *inconsistent dealing*, which cannot be easily described as *either* persuasion *or* prevention. Similarly, the significance of the moral difference should not be overplayed: B may find it difficult to share the philosopher's view that if A persuades C to break her contract with B by threatening to have her tied up[40] he commits a different wrong from D who keeps C away by actually tying her up. But while B may think that he suffers the same harm – non-fulfilment of his contractual expectation – after the *OBG* case, English law treats A and D as having committed different torts in relation to B.

The necessary effect on a contract

Is an *actionable breach of contract* a necessary element of the tort discussed here? The answer after *OBG* is 'yes', since in that case the tort was explained as involving a form of

[37] A wider range of arguments for and against such a distinction are reviewed in Bagshaw 2000.

[38] The principal alternative is to draw a line between *direct* and *indirect* interferences with contract. But this distinction was not easy to draw and was expressly condemned as 'unsatisfactory' by Lord Hoffmann in *OBG*, at [38]. An attempt to identify the distinction was made in *Greig* v *Insole* [1978] 1 WLR 302, 334A–B, where Slade J said that 'the phrase "direct interference" covers the case where the intervener, either by himself or his agents, speaks, writes or publishes words or does other acts which communicate pressure or persuasion to the mind or person of one of the contracting parties themselves, while "indirect interference" refers to the case where, without actually doing any of these things, the intervener nevertheless procures or attempts to procure a situation which will result or may result in a breach of the contract'. A minor improvement might extend the phrase 'mind or person' to 'mind or person or property' in order to cover the case of *GWK Ltd* v *Dunlop Rubber Co.* (1926) 42 TLR 376, where the defendant prevented a car manufacturer from performing a contract to display the claimant's tyres by removing them. See also *The Nadezhda Krupskaya* [1997] 2 Lloyd's Rep 35 where the defendant shipowners 'withdrew' a ship and thereby prevented a charterer of it from performing its contract to sub-charter it to the claimants. Rix J held that this constituted the tort of inducing the breach of the sub-charter.

[39] Simester and Chan 2004 argue (at 152) that *persuading* C to break a contract is essentially different from *preventing* C from performing because only the former 'attacks the very status of [the contractual] undertaking as a reason-generating promise'. But while this argument identifies a way in which *persuasion* is different from *prevention* it does not explain why the law of torts ought to *use* the distinction. Similarly, Stevens 2007 (at 280) offers an explanation more likely to appeal to an outside observer than to the victim: 'Where the promisor has no choice [because he has been prevented from performing], the damage to the convention of promising, and consequently our ability to place trust in one another, is not undermined to the same degree [as it is when the defendant induces a voluntary breach by the promisor].'

[40] Recall that for Weir and Lord Hoffmann *persuasion* can involve 'carrot or stick': see above, n. 18.

secondary liability and, for A's liability to be secondary, C must also be liable: 'No secondary liability without primary liability.'[41]

(1) *Termination.* Will A have committed the tort discussed here if he persuaded C to terminate her contract with B in a *lawful* manner? The answer after *OBG* is 'no',[42] since there will be no primary liability in this situation.

This answer is consistent with the famous case of *Allen* v *Flood*,[43] which established that A will not commit a tort in relation to B if he persuades C by lawful means not to make a contract with B. So in that case, the defendant persuaded the employers of Flood and Taylor not to re-engage them the next morning. A majority of the House of Lords was clear that no tort was committed because the defendant did not induce a breach of contract and did not make use of unlawful means to harm Flood and Taylor. Without the defendant's intervention it seems certain that Flood and Taylor would have been re-engaged the next morning, but they had no contractual right to a new engagement. This seems very similar to the situation of a contract which one party can lawfully terminate. In such a situation there is *no right* that it should not be terminated.

(2) *Voidable contracts.* An analogous question is whether it is a tort to persuade someone to rescind a contract that is voidable.[44] In *Greig* v *Insole*, Slade J found that the authorities relevant to this question conflicted, but decided to assume that it was not a tort to induce a person who is entitled to rescind a contract to exercise that right.[45] Any other conclusion would clearly be inconsistent with the view of the House of Lords in the *OBG* case that the tort of inducing breach of contract is a form of *secondary* liability.

In *Proform Sports Management Ltd* v *Proactive Sports Management Ltd*[46] Judge Hodge QC had to consider the separate question whether it is a tort to persuade someone to *breach* a contract which *could have been* lawfully avoided by the party who was induced to breach it.[47] The judge decided that there was no good reason for imposing a duty not to induce a breach of any contract which *could be* lawfully avoided by the party who was induced to breach it.

[41] *OBG*, at [44] (per Lord Hoffmann). See also [5] (per Lord Hoffmann), [172] (per Lord Nicholls), [320] (per Lord Brown).

[42] The answer to this question was less clear before *OBG*. In *Torquay Hotel Co. Ltd* v *Cousins* [1969] 2 Ch 106, 147C, Winn LJ stated *obiter*, 'For my part I think that it can at least be said, with confidence, that where a contract between [B and C] exists which gives [C] an optional extension of time or an optional mode for his performance of it, or of part of it, but, from the normal course of dealing between them, [B] does not anticipate such postponement, or has come to expect a particular mode of performance, [inducing C] to exercise such an option should, in principle, be held actionable if it produces material damage to [B].' This view was contrary, however, to that expressed by Morris LJ in *DC Thomson & Co. Ltd* v *Deakin* [1952] Ch 646, 702. The High Court of Australia accepted in *Sanders* v *Snell* (1998) 196 CLR 329, at [23], that Morris LJ had correctly stated the law on this point.

[43] [1898] AC 1. This case is also discussed below, pp. 424–5.

[44] There is clear authority that someone will not commit the tort discussed here if he induces someone not to perform a contract which is void: *Joe Lee Ltd* v *Lord Dalmeny* [1927] 1 Ch 300.

[45] [1978] 1 WLR 302, 333A–G.

[46] [2007] 1 All ER 542, Ch.

[47] The party could have avoided the contract because he was a minor when he entered it and it did not fall into any of the exceptional classes of contract which are binding on minors. The contract concerned was one in which the footballer Wayne Rooney appointed the claimant company as his exclusive representative in contract negotiations and transfers for two years for a management fee calculated as a percentage of his earnings.

Justification

Suppose A has induced C to breach her contract with B. Suppose further that A acted with the requisite mental element when he induced C to breach that contract. If A had a *justification* for inducing C to breach her contract with B, the courts will *not* find that A committed the tort of inducing a breach of contract in acting as he did. It is important to note that the pivotal question is not whether *C's breach* was justified but whether *A's inducing C to breach* her contract was justified.

English law has recognised the validity of both legal and moral justifications for inducing a breach. A can claim to have had a legal justification if he had a legal right which was inconsistent with B's contractual rights and was superior or equal in status to those contractual rights. A simple example of this situation would be if Johanna Wagner had foolishly made two contracts with rival impresarios promising to sing exclusively for each. In such circumstances either impresario would be justified in seeking to persuade Johanna Wagner to break her contract with the other.

A more complex example was provided by *Edwin Hill* v *First National*.[48] In this case the defendant was a finance company which had loaned money to a property developer to enable him to purchase Wellington House for development. Unfortunately the project stalled and the developer became unable to repay. This meant that the defendant had the power to force the sale of Wellington House. Instead of exercising this power of sale, the defendant agreed to finance the project itself, but, as a condition of doing so, insisted that the property developer should break his contract with the architects who he had previously engaged. The architects then sued the defendant for inducing the developer to breach this contract. The defendant claimed that it had been justified in doing so.

The complexity in the case comes from the fact that although the defendant had a (superior) legal right in the form of its power to force the sale of Wellington House, it had not actually exercised *this* power. It had instead used the bargaining position that this power provided in order to put together a different deal (which included the breach of contract). Despite this complexity the Court of Appeal thought that the defendant could rely on the defence of justification. Two explanations were provided. First, the court identified the legal right which the defendant had which might justify it in interfering with the architects' contractual right as the right to receive payment of what was due. Given this, one could say that the defendant acted reasonably[49] to protect its right to be repaid the money it had lent the developer. Secondly, the court pointed out that the end result was no worse for the architects than if the power to force the sale had been exercised and that in such circumstances it made no sense for the law to prohibit a different deal which was better for both defendant and developer.

To establish a defence of moral justification the defendant must show that he was impelled to act by a sense of moral duty. It is not sufficient merely to claim that there were good reasons for inducing a breach or that the person breaking the contract might gain some valuable benefit from doing so: 'The fact that their motives were good in the interests

48 [1989] 1 WLR 225.

49 The reasonableness of changing architects was not considered in detail. But it should have been, because it is important to establish some inconsistency between the architect's right to the continuation of his contract and the defendant's right to be repaid.

of those they moved to action does not form any answer to those who have suffered from the unlawful act.'[50] In practice the defence of moral justification has been successfully deployed only rarely. An example is provided by *Brimelow* v *Casson*,[51] where the defendant induced theatre proprietors to break their contracts with a stage show producer in order to pressurise him into paying higher wages to the chorus girls he engaged. The supposed moral necessity was provided by the belief that the wages were so low that his employees were being forced into lives of immorality and prostitution.

IS INDUCING A BREACH OF CONTRACT A TORT?

In the *OBG* case the House of Lords held that liability for inducing a breach of contract is not an *independent* tort but is actually a form of *accessory* liability – the defendant is held liable because he participated in the contract-breaker's wrong.[52] This point has been used as a foundation for arguing that liability for inducing a breach of contract should be studied alongside liability for participating in torts committed by others, and should be reformulated to make it conform to a *general* model of *accessory* liability for torts.[53] The *general* model, however, treats a defendant who is an *accessory* to another's tort as if he *also* committed the same tort, and is *jointly* liable for it. Of course, if liability for inducing a breach of contract is a form of *accessory* liability it may remain convenient to *talk about it* as if it were a tort because it *sounds* so odd to say that a person who was never a party to a contract is *jointly* liable for breaching it. But there are at least three reasons for doubting whether a defendant who has induced a breach of contract will, even after the *OBG* case, *be treated* as if he is jointly liable for having breached a contract.

(1) *Different remedies.* Suppose that A has induced C to breach her contract with B. If A's liability to B in this situation is genuinely *secondary* in nature – and does not arise out of the fact that A committed a tort in relation to B in acting as he did – then it follows that the remedies available against A should be similar to those available against C. But the available evidence suggests that *different remedies* will be available against A and C.[54]

(2) *Different defences.* If a defendant's liability for inducing a breach of contract is genuinely *secondary* it seems odd that the defendant can rely on a defence of *justification* to escape being held liable even when the contract-breaker has undoubtedly committed the wrong of

50 *South Wales Miners' Federation* v *Glamorgan Coal Co. Ltd* [1905] AC 239, 252 (per Lord James). See also *Greig* v *Insole* [1978] 1 WLR 302, 341.

51 [1924] 1 Ch 302.

52 *OBG*, at [5] (per Lord Hoffmann), [172] (per Lord Nicholls), [320] (per Lord Brown). Similar views were expressed by academics before the *OBG* case: see Carty 2001, 272; Sales 1990, 503–4. The law on when someone will be held secondarily liable as an accessory to a tort committed by someone else is dealt with in Chapter 32, below.

53 Carty 1999, 506–10; Carty 2001, 272–3.

54 The cases where damages have been assessed do not seem to have proceeded by considering how much would be awarded in an action for breach of contract. See e.g. *Goldsoll* v *Goldman* [1914] 2 Ch 603, 615–16. Indeed, in *Lumley* v *Gye* (1853) 2 E & B 216, 230, one of the reasons that Crompton J gave for the existence of the tort was that the measure of damages might be different from that in an action for breach of contract. Moreover, as Stevens 2007 has pointed out (at 277), courts readily grant injunctions against defendants ordering them not to *induce* employees to breach their contracts of employment while they would not usually grant injunctions against the employees ordering them not to breach the same contracts.

breach of contract. In such a case, after all, the defendant may have knowingly and intentionally *persuaded* the contract-breaker to commit the wrong.

(3) *Vicarious secondary liability.* Suppose that A induces C to breach her contract with B – and that A, in so acting, was acting in the course of his employment by E. If A's liability for inducing C to breach her contract with B were genuinely secondary in nature then B could not sue *E* for damages in respect of the losses suffered by him as a result of C's breach.[55] But it seems likely that if A was an employee of the theatrical impresario, E, and in the course of his employment A persuaded C, a well known soprano, to breach her contract with B, a rival impresario, the courts *would* want to hold E vicariously liable.

Is there an alternative way of explaining the existence of the tort? Robert Stevens has written: 'The better view is that all contractual rights carry with them a right good against everyone else that they do not induce the infringement of the contractual right. The secondary right is accessory to the primary right and its infringement is a free-standing tort.'[56] This explanation insists that a defendant who induces someone to breach a contract is *not* jointly liable for committing the same wrong as the contract-breaker. It is not, however, an explanation that can draw any support from the *OBG* case.

EVALUATING THE TORT

Some legal commentators[57] have criticised the existence of the tort of inducing a breach of contract. The foundation for their criticisms is that if A has committed the tort by inducing C to breach her contract with B, B will be able to make a claim for breach of contract against C. Why, they ask, should B be given a claim against A as well?

Part of the answer may be that occasionally a claim against A will be more attractive than a claim against C. For instance, in *South Wales Miners' Federation* v *Glamorgan Coal Co. Ltd*[58] the defendant organisation had persuaded miners in South Wales to break their contracts with the coal companies which employed them and stop working for a one-day protest. Regardless of what we may think about such protests, we can easily imagine why the coal companies did not want to sue the people who had broken their contracts, the miners. It would not have been good for labour relations to have made legal claims against the miners as soon as they returned to work. There might also have been doubts about whether the miners would have had the money to pay for any losses suffered through stopping production for a day. Furthermore, from the point of view of the coal companies we can see why the defendant organisation might appear to have been 'the real authors of the mischief'.[59] The miners would not have stopped work for the protest without the encouragement of the defendant organisation. To use a biblical metaphor, the defendant organisation played a role similar to that of the serpent in the Garden of Eden.

[55] There is no precedent for an employer being held vicariously liable for an employee's breach of contract – whether that breach of contract was personally committed by the employee or whether the employee has been held to have committed that breach of contract because he was an accessory to it.

[56] Stevens 2007, 281. Bagshaw 2000, 132–7 identifies some reasons for recognising such 'a right good against everyone else'.

[57] See, for example, Howarth 1995, at 484: '*Lumley* v *Gye* was wrongly decided'; see also Howarth 2005b.

[58] [1905] AC 239.

[59] Ibid., 246 (per Lord Macnaghten).

But showing why victims of a breach of contract would like a tort of inducing a breach of contract to exist is not enough to satisfy all of its critics. One common criticism is that the tort fails to advance economic efficiency because it tends to discourage 'efficient breach' of contracts. A second common criticism is that the tort reduces the capacity of workers to organise effective industrial action and consequently facilitates oppression by powerful employers. Can these criticisms be answered?

Efficient breach

The notion of 'efficient breach' is based on the idea that it may be better for the wealth of society as a whole if particular contracts are broken.[60] Suppose, for example, that Tom owns the only widget in the world and he has contracted to sell it to Ruth, who will use it to generate 40 units of wealth each year. Tom discovers that Eric could use the widget to generate 50 units of wealth each year and is therefore willing to pay Tom more for the widget than Ruth is. In such a case, *it might be thought* that it would be better for Tom to break his contract with Ruth, pay her compensation for her expectation loss, and sell the widget to Eric instead.[61] But the existence of the tort of inducing a breach of contract means that it would be wrongful for Eric (or anyone else) to *persuade* Tom to break his contract with Ruth in order to ensure that the widget goes to the person who can make the most productive use of it.

So far it looks as if the critics of the tort have a good case. But we have ignored two things. First, the tort does not stop Eric negotiating with Ruth and Tom[62] to try to persuade them to cancel their contract so that it can be sold to him – and if Eric can make more money than Ruth using the widget then Eric should be capable of making very attractive offers to both Ruth and Tom. Secondly, in our discussion we have assumed that everyone knows how much Eric and Ruth can make with the widget. In real life such information is often not available. In particular, it is unlikely that Tom, if approached by Eric, will be in any position to know who is likely to make best use of the widget. Consequently, it might again be better to encourage Eric to negotiate with both Ruth and Tom. A further benefit of encouraging such negotiations rather than allowing Eric to persuade Tom to break his contract with Ruth is that it will avoid the courts having to spend valuable time and effort calculating how much by way of damages Tom should pay Ruth in the aftermath of his breaching his contract to sell the widget to her.[63]

[60] For a presentation of the doctrine of 'efficient breach' see Posner 2003, 119–21. But note that Posner has argued that the existence of the tort can be justified in most of the circumstances in which it is used: Landes & Posner 1987, 224.

[61] See, for example, Perlman 1982, at 128, 'In cases of [inducing breach of contract by] otherwise lawful acts, tort liability works at cross-purposes with contract policies. Contract remedies seem to promote efficiency, whereas the addition of inducer liability inhibits efficient outcomes.'

[62] If Eric wants the identical widget which Tom has contracted to supply to Ruth he may be able to negotiate solely with Ruth – but in other cases, where, for instance, Tom has contracted to supply the output of his widget factory to Ruth, and Eric instead wants Tom's factory to make slightly different widgets for him, all three parties will have to be involved in the negotiations.

[63] See Macneil 1982, at 957–60, for discussion of how it can only be determined whether a breach will be 'efficient' in the light of 'transaction costs' – that is, broadly speaking, the relative costs of negotiations and of sorting out breaches.

Industrial action and oppression

One answer to the second criticism advanced above might be that the tort of inducing a breach of contract has a role to play only where there is a contract between two parties. Now – an employee must have voluntarily (to the extent that the law of contract demands) agreed to the terms of his contract of employment. Given this, there is only limited scope for the employee to argue that it is oppressive to impose a duty on others not to *persuade* him to break his contract. But this argument only really works at a formal level. In practice, we know that in many circumstances employees (and others) have little control over the terms of the contracts that they enter. The South Wales miners had little opportunity when applying for jobs to influence the terms of any employment offered. Parliament has recognised that in practice employees are empowered by the possibility of collective industrial action and has provided a statutory immunity for economic torts committed in the furtherance of trade disputes.[64] There is no doubt, however, that the law in this area does still restrict liberty. The core issue is whether this restriction on liberty is justified by the protection that this area of the law provides for contractual rights. Our view is that for many people and companies their contractual rights are one of their most valuable assets, and that consequently it makes sense for the law to offer them some protection.[65]

TORTS ANALOGOUS TO THE TORT OF INDUCING A BREACH OF CONTRACT

If inducing breach of contract is a form of *accessory* liability which is *talked about* as a tort because it *sounds* odd to say that a person who was never a party to a contract is *jointly* liable for breaching it,[66] then we should ask whether there are similar torts covering the inducing of other similar wrongs.

English cases have recognised liability for inducing the violation of obligations which are somewhat similar to contractual obligations. For example, the Court of Appeal held in a case involving an employment relationship that was governed by statute rather than contract, that A could commit a tort in relation to B by inducing C to breach a statutory obligation to work provided that such a breach by C could give rise to a civil action by B.[67] It may also be a tort for A to persuade C to break a duty to grant a particular private law remedy to B.[68]

64 This immunity is now conditional on certain procedures being followed in the organisation of the industrial action: see below, p. 504.

65 See further, Bagshaw 2000, at 132–7.

66 Normally, where A had procured B to commit a tort against C the law holds that A and B are *jointly* liable for committing the tort against C. See below, Chapter 32.

67 *Associated British Ports* v *Transport and General Workers' Union* [1989] 1 WLR 939, 952E–F, 959H–960A, 964H–965B. Liability for inducing a breach of a statutory duty is not confined to statutory duties similar to employment obligations: *Meade* v *Haringey LBC* [1979] 1 WLR 637.

68 This was assumed by the Court of Appeal in *Law Debenture Corp.* v *Ural Caspian Ltd* [1995] Ch 152, although it went on to hold that there was no right to an equitable remedy until it had been granted. The matter is somewhat complicated, however, by the fact that the reasoning of the court invokes both (1) a *broader* version of the tort of inducing breach of contract than is authoritative after the *OBG* case, and (2) the case of *Acrow (Automation) Ltd* v *Rex Chainbelt Inc.* [1971] 1 WLR 1676, which was founded on a *broader* version of the tort of intentionally causing loss by the use of unlawful means than is authoritative after the *OBG* case.

By contrast, in *Metall und Rohstoff AG* v *Donaldson Lufkin & Jenrette Inc.*,[69] the Court of Appeal refused to recognise that it was a tort to induce someone to commit a breach of trust, principally to avoid any conflict with the well-developed equitable wrong of dishonestly assisting another to commit a breach of trust.[70] And in *Credit Lyonnais* v *Export Credit Guarantee Department*,[71] the House of Lords refused to find that it is a tort to assist someone else to commit a tort on the ground that there was no authority in favour of the existence of such a tort, and creating such a tort would be inconsistent with clear authority which stated that someone who assists someone else to commit a tort will not be held liable as an accessory to that tort.[72]

Visit **http://www.mylawchamber.co.uk/mcbride**
to access updates on recent cases, as well as model answers and tips for answering tort problem questions.

[69] [1990] 1 QB 391, at 481G–H.
[70] See *Royal Brunei Airlines* v *Tan* [1995] 2 AC 378.
[71] [2000] 1 AC 486.
[72] Ibid., at 500. See below, Chapter 32, for an account of when someone will be held liable as an accessory to a tort committed by someone else.

21 Intentionally causing loss by unlawful means

ELEMENTS OF THE TORT

A will have committed the tort of *using unlawful means to cause loss to another*[1] in relation to B if:

(1) A caused B to suffer some kind of loss;
(2) by interfering with the freedom of a third party, C, to deal with B; *and*
(3) the *means* by which A interfered with C's freedom to deal with B were *unlawful*; *and*
(4) A acted in the way he did with the *intention* of harming B.[2]

History

This tort developed as a *generalisation* of two more narrowly defined torts.

The first of these torts will be committed by A in relation to B if A makes use of unlawful threats in order to intimidate a third party, C, into not dealing with B, or ceasing to deal with B.[3] This tort is usually referred to as *three-party intimidation*.[4]

The second of these torts will be committed by A in relation to B if A makes use of unlawful means in order to interfere with a third party, C's, performance of a contract with B. For instance, in *Merkur Island Shipping Corp.* v *Laughton*,[5] the claimants owned a ship, the *Hoegh Apapa*, which docked at Liverpool. The defendant union officials made it impossible for the claimants to perform their charter-contract with C to 'prosecute ... voyages with the utmost despatch', and under the terms of the charter-contract C was not obliged to pay hire for the days when the ship was trapped in Liverpool. The defendant union officials achieved this by persuading the employees of a tug company to break their contracts of employment with the tug company by refusing to assist the tug company in fulfilling its obligation to tow the ship from its berth; in other words the means used by the defendants was commission of the tort of inducing breach of contract *in relation to the tug company*. The claimants sued the defendants, arguing that the defendants had committed

[1] In *OBG* v *Allan* [2007] 2 WLR 920 (hereafter *OBG*), this tort is referred to by Lord Hoffmann, Baroness Hale and Lord Brown as 'the tort of causing loss by unlawful means', but by Lord Nicholls as 'interference with a trade or business by unlawful means or, more shortly, the tort of unlawful interference'. We discuss below, pp. 432–5, whether the tort should cover only economic losses associated with 'trade or business' interests.

[2] Fridman 1993 suggests (at 113) that for this tort to be committed, 'It is only necessary to show that the defendant's acts caused the loss of which the [claimant] complains, and that the defendant knew, or presumably could have appreciated, that such would be the effect or consequence of his acts.' (To the same effect, see S&H, 346.) This is wrong: if it were right, then *Lonrho* v *Shell Petroleum (No. 2)* [1982] AC 173 (summarised below, p. 481) would have been decided differently.

[3] *Garret* v *Taylor* (1620) Cro Jac 567; *Tarleton* v *M'Gawley* (1790) Peake NPC 270.

[4] The qualifying term *three-party* is necessary because a tort of *two-party* intimidation *may* also exist. See below, pp. 433–5).

[5] [1983] 2 AC 570.

a tort in indirectly interfering with the claimants' ability to perform their charter-contract and that the defendants were therefore liable to compensate the claimants for the loss of hire suffered by them as a result of the defendants' interference. The House of Lords agreed, referring to the tort committed by the defendants as 'the common law tort of actionable interference with contractual rights'.[6] But the House of Lords also acknowledged that the case could fit within the general tort of 'interfering with the trade or business of another person by doing unlawful acts'.[7] Persuading the tug company's employees to break their contracts of employment was identified as the necessary 'unlawful means'. At one time this tort, 'actionable interference with contractual rights', was treated as an *extension* of the tort of inducing breach of contract.[8] But in the *OBG* case the House of Lords firmly stated that this had been an error.[9]

Between them, the two narrowly defined torts of *three-party intimidation* and *actionable interference with contractual rights* provided a good basis for recognising a more general tort. This is because the tort of *actionable interference with contractual rights* focused on a particular way in which a claimant might suffer loss – interference with his contractual rights – but could be committed by the use of any type of *unlawful means*, while the tort of *three-party intimidation* put no limit on the way in which a claimant might suffer loss, but focused on a particular type of *unlawful means* – unlawful threats. Thus the two narrowly defined torts suggested that it ought to be a tort to use *unlawful means* (including, but not limited to, unlawful threats) to cause loss (including, but not limited to, interference with contractual rights), though some features of this general tort of *using unlawful means to cause loss to another*, such as what might count as 'unlawful means', what the defendant's state of mind would have to be, and what loss it would protect against, remained to be settled. We will discuss each of these features below. But first we will explain why the use of 'unlawful means' is a central element in the tort.

Why are 'unlawful means' needed?

The requirement of 'unlawful means' was established in the important case of *Allen* v *Flood*.[10] In this case, Allen, a representative of the Ironworkers' Trade Union, went to an employer and said that unless the employer ceased to employ the claimants, Flood and Taylor, members of the Ironworkers' Trade Union would not work for the employer the next day. It is crucial that at the time all the employer's workers were employed on day-to-day contracts. Thus Flood and Taylor had no enforceable contractual right to be employed beyond the end of the day and equally the members of the Ironworkers' Trade Union were under no enforceable obligation to work for the employer the next day. So Allen's threat that his members would walk out if Flood and Taylor were not dismissed was not unlawful, and when the employer surrendered to the threat and failed to re-engage Flood and Taylor the next day it was doing nothing unlawful. Flood and Taylor argued, however, that Allen

[6] Ibid., 609.
[7] Ibid.
[8] This tort was the subject of the previous chapter. See, in particular, p. 407.
[9] See above, pp. 414–15, for an explanation of why the House of Lords thought that this was an error.
[10] [1898] AC 1.

had committed a tort in relation to them since he had maliciously caused them loss. Allen responded that there was no such tort.

Eventually,[11] a majority of the House of Lords concluded that Allen was correct and that a tort of 'maliciously causing loss' did not exist. The majority thought that the law would be too uncertain if liability turned solely on the question whether the defendant was malicious. In this corner of the law many claims arise from fierce competition between traders and from bitter industrial disputes, and it would clearly be difficult to draw the line between vigorous pursuit of self-interest and malice.[12] By contrast, the majority thought that there was a 'chasm' between lawful and unlawful means.[13] Competitors and participants in industrial disputes would know where they stood if the rule was simply that they could use any means to pursue what they perceived to be their interests provided that the means were not unlawful.[14] The justification based on certainty will only hold water, however, if 'unlawful means' is clearly defined.

Defining 'unlawful means'

In defining what amounts to 'unlawful means' for the purpose of the tort of *using unlawful means to cause loss to another*, the law draws on definitions of what is unlawful found in other areas of the law.

Tort

It is clear that if A has caused B to suffer some kind of loss by committing a *tort* in relation to C which interferes with C's freedom to deal with B, A will be found to have caused B to suffer that loss through unlawful means – with the result that A will be found to have committed the tort of using unlawful means to cause loss to another in relation to B if he acted as he did with the intention of causing loss to B.

In the *OBG* case Lord Hoffmann stated that A's behaviour would also amount to 'unlawful means' if the only reason that it did not amount to a *tort* in relation to C was that C did not suffer any kind of actionable loss.[15] An example of this extension of the meaning of 'unlawful means' may be provided by *Lonrho* v *Fayed*[16] where it was alleged that the defendant had caused loss to the claimant by using the unlawful means of making a deceitful statement to the Secretary of State for Trade and Industry, but it was not alleged that the Secretary of State had suffered any actionable loss as a result of this statement. It

[11] For an account of the litigation see Heuston 1986.

[12] A further concern at the time of *Allen* v *Flood* was that as the law then stood the question whether there had been malice would usually have been left to a jury.

[13] *Rookes* v *Barnard* [1964] AC 1129, 1168–9, per Lord Reid, 'I agree with Lord Herschell [in *Allen* v *Flood* [1898] AC 1, at 121] that there is a chasm between doing what you have a legal right to do and doing what you have no legal right to do.' See also *Allen* v *Flood* [1898] AC 1, 139, per Lord Herschell, 'In my opinion a man cannot be called upon to justify either act or word merely because it interferes with another's trade or calling; any more than he is bound to justify or excuse his act or word under any other circumstances, *unless it be shewn to be in its nature wrongful*, and thus to require justification' (emphasis added).

[14] See below, at pp. 438–40, for a more detailed account of the main arguments against the general proposition that A will commit a tort in relation to B if A intentionally harms B when he has no lawful justification or excuse for doing so.

[15] *OBG*, at [49]–[50].

[16] [1990] 2 QB 479.

seems that Lord Hoffmann thought that this extension was also wide enough to cover cases where A *threatened to commit a tort* in relation to C but did not have to go through with the threat because C 'gave in' and caused loss to B in the way which A sought.[17]

Breach of contract

The question whether a *breach of contract* will amount to 'unlawful means' for the purposes of the tort discussed here might seem to be more difficult. If A has breached a contract with C in order to harm B, one can clearly castigate what A has done as unlawful vis-à-vis C, but is there any reason to treat A's action as unlawful vis-à-vis B? The law of contract would not, after all, usually give B any right to insist on the contract being performed.[18] Nonetheless, it was decided in *Rookes* v *Barnard*[19] that a threat to break a contract was an unlawful threat for the purposes of the tort of three-party intimidation, which tort – as we have seen – forms part of the *general* tort. A major strand in the reasoning which supported this conclusion was that there was 'no difference in principle between a threat to break a contract and a threat to commit a tort'.[20] In *OBG* Lord Hoffmann also stated that 'In principle, the cases establish that intentionally causing someone loss by interfering with the liberty of action of a third party in breach of contract with him is unlawful.'[21] In other words, a *breach of contract* will count as 'unlawful means' for the purposes of the tort discussed here, and so will a *threat to breach a contract*.

Crime

Will the commission of a *criminal offence* count as 'unlawful means' for the purposes of the tort discussed here? This question does not cause any problems when the behaviour that constitutes the criminal offence could also be actionable as a tort, because we have already seen that all torts count as unlawful means. The question is difficult, however, when we think about minor crimes such as regulatory offences.[22] Here the main controversy flows from the fact that the definition of 'unlawful means' helps to determine what, for instance, traders can do to each other by way of competition, while Parliament may have defined certain things as minor crimes for reasons completely different from any considerations of what should be legitimate behaviour between competitors.

[17] *OBG*, at [49], 'In the case of intimidation, for example, the threat will usually give rise to no cause of action by the third party because he will have suffered no loss. If he submits to the threat, then, as the defendant intended, the claimant will have suffered loss instead. It is nevertheless unlawful means. But the threat must be to do something which *would* have been actionable if the third party had suffered loss.' There is a risk that this definition of which threats will count as 'unlawful means' will prove to be too narrow. For instance, if A threatens C that he will kill C's spouse unless C acts in a way which will cause loss to B, and C submits, then the threat which C will have used will *not* have been a threat of behaviour which would have been actionable by C if he suffered loss.

[18] For an exception, see the Contracts (Rights of Third Parties) Act 1999.

[19] [1964] AC 1129.

[20] Ibid., 1168 (per Lord Reid).

[21] *OBG*, at [48].

[22] An overlapping question is whether the breach of a statutory duty will count as 'unlawful means' for the purposes of the tort discussed here if the breach of the duty in question is *not* civilly actionable. (The breach of a statutory duty will be civilly actionable if: (1) its breach amounts to a tort, a breach of contract or an equitable wrong; *or* (2) its breach amounts to some kind of interference with a public right which causes someone to suffer special damage. See Chapter 25, below, for a discussion of when the breach of a statutory duty owed to another will amount to a tort. In Chapter 44, below, we discuss when an unlawful interference with a public right will be civilly actionable.)

For example, many competitors try to persuade each other's customers to switch allegiances by sending out small free gifts with advertising slogans. If John decided to try and take customers from Lara by sending Lara's customers free calculators, would we want to say that John committed the tort of using unlawful means to harm another in relation to Lara if it later turned out that the batteries in these calculators contained a chemical which can cause severe pollution so that it was a statutory offence to supply them? The dilemma here is that 'unlawful means' is meant to be a clearly defined concept and consequently there is an attraction to the answer that *all* criminal offences should count as 'unlawful means'. On the other hand, however, if the role of the tort is to define what methods it is wrongful for A to use against C in an attempt to cause loss to B, it makes nonsense of the tort to make it cover methods which nobody thinks are improper. Does anyone think if Tom sends Lara's customers defective calculators (instead of some other advertising gift) he is behaving wrongfully vis-à-vis Lara?

The question whether *criminal offences* should count as 'unlawful means' divided the House of Lords in the *OBG* case. Lord Hoffmann thought that they should not. He stated: 'In my opinion, and subject to one qualification, acts against a third party count as unlawful means only if they are actionable by that third party. The qualification is that they will also be unlawful means if the only reason why they are not actionable is because the third party has suffered no loss.'[23] By contrast, Lord Nicholls preferred the view that '[i]n this context the expression "unlawful means" embraces all acts that a defendant is not permitted to do, whether by the civil law or the criminal law'.[24] A majority in the House of Lords expressly adopted Lord Hoffmann's view, though Lord Walker predicted that the last word had not been heard on the matter.[25]

Interference with a third party's freedom

B's economic interests will often depend on third parties being willing and able to deal with him. For example, if B runs a business then he will clearly lose money if his customers take their business elsewhere or his employees resign or his suppliers refuse to sell him what he requires or if it becomes impossible for any of these groups to deal with him. But in such cases the customers, employees and suppliers *are likely* to be able to act in this way *without*

[23] *OBG*, at [49]. Lord Hoffmann explained that the qualification included cases where A had done everything necessary to commit a tort in relation to C but C had suffered no loss *and also* cases where A had threatened to use unlawful means on C but never had to go through with the threat because C surrendered to it and acted in a way which harmed B.

[24] *OBG*, at [162]. But in his discussion he seemed to qualify this by suggesting that a criminal offence might only be 'unlawful means' if it was a crime '*against*' the claimant. The relevant passage is not easy to follow. The House of Lords seems to have been concerned to define the tort of causing loss by the use of unlawful means so that it would not cover a delivery company gaining an advantage over its rivals by offering a faster service premised on its agents ignoring speed limits and traffic lights. With reference to a similar example Lord Nicholls states, at [160], that the reason that this would not be a tort is because '[t]he couriers' criminal conduct is not an offence committed against the rival company in any realistic sense of that expression'. The case is an unusual one because it involves a *promise* to third parties – potential customers – to commit crimes to their advantage, rather than the more familiar variation of a *threat* to commit crimes to their disadvantage. If we consider the more familiar variation – *threats* to commit crimes – it is not clear why the tort ought to cover only threats to commit crimes 'against' third parties. For instance, what if a defendant intentionally intimidated third parties into not trading with the claimant by *threatening* to commit blasphemy or to be cruel to animals?

[25] *OBG*, at [266]–[270] (Lord Walker), [302] and [306] (Baroness Hale), [320] (Lord Brown). We discuss below, at pp. 440–1, whether the House of Lords ought to have adopted Lord Nicholls's position.

committing any civil wrong to B. (The most obvious exception to this would be where by acting in this way the customers, employees or suppliers would be breaching a *contract* with B.)

In circumstances where B's economic interests depend on third parties remaining willing and able to deal with him, he will be potentially vulnerable to A taking steps to *interfere* with their willingness or ability. For instance, he will be potentially vulnerable to A scaring off his potential customers by threats of violence or preventing his suppliers from making deliveries by damaging their vehicles. A, of course, is likely to owe a duty *to the potential customers* not to act violently towards them and a duty *to the suppliers* not to damage their vehicles. But the tort of *using unlawful means to cause loss to another* is based on a further duty, owed *to B*, not to use such unlawful means with the intention of causing loss to him.

So, for example, if Dawn runs down a well-known footballer, Tom, with the intention of causing economic loss to the football club, Greatchester FC, which employs Tom, then Greatchester FC will be able to make a claim against Dawn on the basis that Dawn, in acting as she did, committed the tort of using unlawful means to cause loss to another in relation to Greatchester FC. Such a claim will be supplementary to Tom's claim for the wrong done *to him* when Dawn ran him down. Moreover, such a claim is permitted even though Greatchester FC could not claim for its losses if all that happened was that Dawn *negligently* ran down Tom. It is a crucial feature of the tort that Dawn must have acted as she did with the *intention* of causing loss to Greatchester FC.

In the *OBG* case Lord Hoffmann distinguishes between situations where A uses unlawful means to interfere with the freedom of a third party to deal with B and where A uses unlawful means to reduce the value to B of his freedom to deal with a third party.[26] For instance, in the case of *RCA Corpn* v *Pollard*[27] the claimant had the exclusive right to exploit records made by Elvis Presley and the defendant sold 'bootleg' recordings that had been made at concerts without the consent of Elvis. Lord Hoffmann stated that, assuming that this behaviour amounted to 'unlawful means',[28] *even if* the defendant had used such means with the intention of causing loss to the claimant he would still *not* have committed the tort of using unlawful means to cause loss in relation to the claimant. This is because the defendant's conduct did not interfere with the ability of Elvis's estate to perform its contract with the claimant.[29]

What forms of conduct will be regarded as 'interfering with the freedom' of a third party? The examples discussed by Lord Hoffmann in the *OBG* case suggest that the list includes:

(1) *making it impossible* for a third party to behave in a particular way towards B, including preventing a third party from performing a contract with B; and

[26] *OBG*, at [51], 'Unlawful means therefore consists of acts intended to cause loss to the claimant by interfering with the freedom of a third party in a way which is unlawful as against that third party and which is intended to cause loss to the claimant. It does not in my opinion include acts which may be unlawful against a third party but which do not affect his freedom to deal with the claimant.'

[27] [1983] Ch 135, CA.

[28] The behaviour was clearly criminal and might have also amounted to the tort of breach of statutory duty in relation to Elvis Presley: see *Lonrho Ltd* v *Shell Petroleum Co. Ltd (No. 2)* [1982] AC 173, at 187 (per Lord Diplock). For detailed discussion of what amounts to 'unlawful means' see above, pp. 425–7.

[29] *OBG*, at [53].

(2) *threatening* a third party to persuade him to behave in a particular way towards B; and
(3) *misleading* a third party to lead him to behave in a particular way towards B.

In situations (2) and (3) the threat or misleading statement can be used *either* to cause a third party to refrain from dealing with B *or* to take some *positive steps* which will cause loss to B.

Should the list also include:

(4) *making it less attractive* for a third party to behave in some way towards B which would be advantageous to B, with the result that the third party does not act in that way? and
(5) *making it more attractive* for a third party to behave in some way towards B which would be disadvantageous to B, with the result that the third party does act in that way?

Arguably, using unlawful means to *steer* a third party's behaviour should be covered because it is sufficiently similar to using a misleading statement or a threat of unlawful conduct to do so. For instance, if A used unlawful means to make it far more expensive for C to perform a contract with B, with the intention of causing C to terminate the contract lawfully and cause loss to B, it is hard to see why this would interfere with C's freedom *less than* misleading C as to the additional profits that he could make if he terminated the contract. Thus it is arguable that (4) and (5) should also be treated as situations which may involve *interference* with the freedom of a third party.

One curious consequence of the requirement for A's use of unlawful means to interfere with the freedom of a third party is that in certain circumstances A may be liable to B for threatening to do *x* to C, even though he would not have been liable if he had actually done *x* to C. For instance, if B has the contractual right to publish a book which C is about to complete, then if A seriously defames C by calling him a 'Nazi sympathiser', with the result that the contractual right is rendered valueless since no one is likely to buy the book until C clears his name, B will be unable to sue A even if A's intention when he defamed C was to cause loss to B. (The defamation will not have interfered with C's liberty to deal with B.) By contrast, if A *threatens* C that he will seriously defame him unless he terminates his relationship with B, then if C gives in to this threat B will be able to sue A if A's intention when he defamed C was to cause loss to B.

Intention to cause loss

B will only be able to base a claim on A's use of unlawful means to interfere with a third party's freedom to deal with him *if* A acted in the way he did with the *intention* of causing loss to B. So we must ask what state of mind will count as 'intention' in this context. The simple answer to this is that A will be held to have intended to cause loss to B *if*: (1) the *end* which A was seeking to achieve when he acted was causing loss to B, *or* (2) causing loss to B was the *means* which A was deploying to seek to achieve some other end. But A will not be held to have intended to cause loss to B if such loss was merely a *side effect*, albeit one which A knew to be very likely to occur, of A's means or end. There are four points of detail that we must clarify.

(1) *A would have preferred not to cause loss to B.* If causing loss to B was either A's end or the means by which he was seeking to achieve that end then A will be held to have intended to

cause loss to B *even if* he would have preferred not to have been put in a position where he had to adopt such an end or would have preferred not to have had to resort to such means to achieve his end.[30]

For instance, the defendants in the case of *Rookes* v *Barnard*[31] used unlawful means, a threat of a breach of contract, to persuade BOAC to dismiss the claimant, Rookes. The defendants might have preferred Rookes to have resigned his post voluntarily so that they did not have to persuade his employer to dismiss him, indeed they might have preferred to avoid the dispute that led to them targeting Rookes, but such preferences would not negate the fact that when they threatened BOAC they intended to cause loss to Rookes.

(2) *'The other side of the same coin'*. In deciding what a defendant intends it is necessary to distinguish carefully between what is *part of* the defendant's end or means and what is a *consequence* of achieving that end or using those means. An outcome will count as *part of* the defendant's end if it is 'simply the other side of the same coin' *and* the defendant knows that this is the case.[32] For instance, if A takes a horse which C was about to deliver to B, and A knows that C was about to do this, then A *cannot* simultaneously maintain that he intended to obtain the horse for himself but did not intend to prevent B from obtaining it: preventing B from obtaining the horse is *part of* his end of obtaining the horse for himself.

In *Douglas* v *Hello! (No. 3)*,[33] one of the appeals heard by the House of Lords alongside *OBG*, the defendants and claimants were respectively the publishers of two rival celebrity magazines, *Hello!* and *OK!* The claim resulted from the defendants' publishing unofficial photographs of the wedding of Michael Douglas and Catherine Zeta-Jones in *Hello!* shortly before the claimants were due to publish official photographs in *OK!* The trial judge found that the defendants had not intended to cause loss to the claimants on the basis of evidence from the controlling shareholder of *Hello!*'s Spanish holding company that his intention was only to avoid a loss of sales for *Hello!* and not to reduce sales of *OK!* But Lord Hoffmann identified this as a situation where the loss to *OK!* was necessarily intended because it was simply the flipside of the preserved sales of *Hello!*, presumably because a substantial proportion of the preserved sales would be to purchasers who would otherwise have bought *OK!* instead.[34]

Lord Hoffmann distinguished this situation from one where a customer suffered loss as a result of action directed against its supplier.[35] If, for instance, a defendant used unlawful

[30] *OBG*, at [165] (per Lord Nicholls).

[31] [1964] AC 1129.

[32] *OBG*, at [134] (per Lord Hoffmann), [167] (per Lord Nicholls).

[33] [2007] 2 WLR 920, HL. This appeal also contained discussion of the wrong of breach of confidence and the tort of conversion. These elements in the appeal are dealt with in Chapters 15 and 16 respectively.

[34] *OBG*, at [134]. It does not seem implausible that a substantial number of readers might usually buy only one magazine or the other, and that the defendants knew that. To establish that they did not intend to cause loss of sales to *OK!* the defendants would have to show that they honestly believed that any additional sales of *Hello!* resulting from the publication of the unofficial pictures would be to purchasers who would otherwise have bought no magazine or would nonetheless still buy *OK!*.

[35] *OBG*, at [64]. The case Lord Hoffmann cited, *Barretts & Baird (Wholesale) Ltd* v *Institution of Professional Civil Servants* [1987] IRLR 3, involved a strike in support of a pay claim by Fatstock Officers (FOs) employed by the Meat and Livestock Commission (MLC), which caused loss to private abattoirs because they could not get their meat certified for export. But the basic factual pattern is the same as that found in the more common scenario of action directed against a supplier which will almost inevitably harm the supplier's customers. Henry J described the defendants' state of mind in *Barretts & Baird* as follows, at [70]: 'Clearly, damage to the various plaintiffs was an unavoidable by-product of that withdrawal of labour and was a readily foreseeable

means to prevent trains from running with the intention of causing loss to a train operating company, although the defendant would probably know that some passengers would suffer loss as a result he would *not* be held to have intended to causes such losses because he could achieve his end – causing loss to the train operating company – even if all the passengers unexpectedly found cheaper and more convenient ways of travelling. In such a case any loss suffered by passengers would *not* be the flipside of the defendant's end. The situation would, of course, be different if one of the defendant's objectives was to inflict loss on the passengers *in order to* prompt them to put pressure on the train operating company.

(3) *Intending one type of loss and causing another.* In the *OBG* case Lord Hoffmann repeatedly states that what is required is *an intention to cause loss* to the claimant rather than *an intention to cause the particular type of loss to the claimant which the claimant suffers.* This might be significant if, for instance, A made threats of violence against B's potential customers with the intention of persuading them not to trade with B, but B avoided this type of loss either by paying for additional security for his potential customers or by reducing his prices so that his customers became convinced that the risk of violence was worth taking. It would be odd if in either of these circumstances the defendant could avoid liability by objecting that the type of loss which the claimant had suffered was not the type that he had intended to cause.

(4) *Believing that a claimant will be better off as a result of an interference with contractual rights.* The state of mind that the tort of intentionally causing loss by the use of unlawful means requires – an intention to cause loss to B – is different from the state of mind required in order to establish the tort of inducing a breach of contract. The latter tort requires the defendant merely to have intended to induce a breach of contract, and a defendant will not avoid liability by demonstrating that he honestly expected the claimant to *be better off as a result of the breach.* The distinction is potentially significant because where a defendant causes loss to a claimant by *preventing* a third party from performing a contract with the claimant the defendant's behaviour will only amount to a tort in relation to the claimant if it amounts to the tort of intentionally causing loss by the use of unlawful means.

The potential significance of the distinction may be easiest to grasp by considering an example. If Bryony is a film producer, Crystal is a film star who has contracted to appear in Bryony's film, and Alex is the novelist who wrote the book on which the film is based, then even if Alex honestly believes that Crystal has been miscast and that Bryony's film will be more successful with another star taking Crystal's role he will still commit the tort of inducing breach of contract in relation to Bryony if he *persuades* Crystal to break her

---

consequence and, perhaps, in the case of some FOs, a not undesired consequence on the basis that the greater the disruption caused the greater the pressure for a satisfactory settlement with the MLC and the sooner the return to normal working. But there is no evidence to suggest that the FOs would not have struck if their industrial action had not injured these plaintiffs. On the evidence the desire to strike was the cause of the injury to the plaintiffs rather than the desire to injure the plaintiffs being the cause of the strike.' Lord Hoffmann said, in *OBG*, at [64], 'I think Henry J was right ... when he decided a strike by civil servants in the Ministry of Agriculture in support of a pay claim was not intended to cause damage to an abattoir which was unable to obtain the certificates necessary for exporting meat and claiming subsidies. The damage to the abattoir was neither the purpose of the strike nor the means of achieving that purpose, which was to put pressure on the government.'

contract. But if Alex, with the same honest belief, *prevents* Crystal from performing her contract by unlawful means, for instance by imprisoning her in an isolated cottage, then he will *apparently* not commit a tort in relation to Bryony because he did not intend to cause any *loss* to her – he believed that his action would leave her better off. The most obvious way in which to make the outcomes consistent would be to insist that although Alex may have believed that the *net* consequence would be to make Bryony better off, he nonetheless intended to cause her some additional expenses, such as the extra cost of identifying and hiring a replacement star. An alternative way might be to define the *loss* which a defendant must intend to cause as 'loss of the benefit of the third party being free to deal with the claimant'. But if the courts decide that the tort requires an intention to cause a *net* financial loss to the claimant then the inconsistency will remain.

Types of loss

We have seen that the losses suffered by the victim of the tort discussed in this chapter sometimes flow from interference with the performance of a contract,[36] but that the tort can also protect claimants against economic losses *not* associated with existing contractual *rights*, such as where a defendant uses threats of violence to scare off a claimant's potential customers.[37] Clearly most of the cases involve claimants who have suffered economic losses associated with their occupation, trade or business. But we must ask whether the tort *only* protects claimants against such losses. In other words, we must consider whether the tort protects claimants against *non-economic* losses and against losses that are not associated with any occupation, trade or business.

With regard to non-economic losses it is difficult to see why using unlawful means to prevent deliveries of heating oil[38] should be actionable but not using unlawful means to prevent deliveries of veterinary or medical care with the intention of causing harm to the claimant's property or his health.[39] Nonetheless, many judicial discussions of the tort use language which *seems to assume* that the tort protects only *economic* interests.[40] One explanation for this assumption might be that intentionally causing personal injury to another is actionable in the absence of justification *regardless of whether unlawful means are used*, and regardless of whether the injury is inflicted through the instrumentality of a third

[36] An obvious example is the case of *Merkur Island Shipping Corp.* v *Laughton* [1983] 2 AC 570, discussed above, at pp. 423–4.

[37] In *J.T. Stratford & Son Ltd* v *Lindley* [1965] AC 269, Lord Reid said, 'In addition to interfering with existing contracts the respondents' action made it practically impossible for the appellants to do any new business with the barge hirers. It was not disputed that such interference with business is tortious if any unlawful means are employed' (ibid., p. 324).

[38] *Torquay Hotel Co. Ltd* v *Cousins* [1969] 2 Ch 106, CA, involved liability for using unlawful means to interfere with delivery of heating oil.

[39] In *Powell* v *Boldaz* [1998] Lloyd's Rep Med 116, the Court of Appeal noted that the claimants' barrister had *conceded* that compensation for personal injuries could not be obtained in a claim for the tort of *conspiracy* to use unlawful means, but did not reveal the reasoning behind this concession. In the next chapter, at p. 453, we will explain why we do not think that this concession was correct. We also discuss below, at p. 453, the relationship between the tort of conspiracy to use unlawful means and the tort of intentionally causing loss by the use of unlawful means.

[40] See e.g. *OBG*, at [47] per Lord Hoffmann, 'The essence of the tort therefore appears to be (a) a wrongful interference with the actions of a third party in which the claimant has an *economic interest* and (b) an intention thereby to cause loss to the claimant' (emphasis added).

party. Certainly it seems unlikely to be the law that A will commit no tort in relation to B if A deceives C, a surgeon, into believing that B's leg needs to be amputated, or A threatens C with death unless he amputates B's leg unnecessarily.

What if A uses unlawful means to cause *emotional distress* to B? In *Mbasogo* v *Logo Ltd*,[41] the Court of Appeal refused to extend the tort of 'intentional infliction of harm by unlawful means' to this situation because it believed that to do so would be tantamount to developing a *common law* tort of intentional harassment to supplement the Protection from Harassment Act 1997. It should be noted, however, that the *Mbasogo* case did not involve the use of unlawful means to persuade *third parties* to cause distress to the claimant, and much of the discussion concerned the desirability of finding that A will commit a tort in relation to B if he intentionally causes B to suffer distress using unlawful means to do so in a *two-party situation* – that is, a situation where A causes B to suffer distress without involving a third party.[42] Moreover, the court accepted that the tort of intimidation was a 'paradigm example' of a tort where compensation can be awarded for injury to feelings.[43]

With regard to economic losses that are not associated with any occupation, trade or business an obvious example might concern the value of a house. For example, if A threatened C with violence unless he erected a building on his land which blocked the sea view from B's holiday cottage, and A made this threat with the intention of causing loss to B, would the law really insist that this was only a tort in relation to B if he rented out the cottage as a business rather than using it for his own recreation? We do not believe that there is any good reason for confining the tort to the protection of economic interests associated with some occupation, trade or business.

RELATED TORTS

Two-party intimidation

We have seen that in the *OBG* case the House of Lords defined the tort of intentionally causing loss by unlawful means so that A could only commit it in relation to B if he interfered with C's freedom to deal with B. In other words, the tort was defined so as to cover only situations involving *three* parties.

It might be thought that there is no need for a similar tort in situations involving only *two* parties because the tort requires unlawful means, and, as we have seen, a defendant will only *usually* be held to have used unlawful means if he has committed a 'civil wrong'. Thus in situations involving only two parties the claimant can usually simply sue for this 'civil

41 [2007] 2 WLR 1062.

42 It might be thought that if A would not be liable for intentionally causing distress to B directly he equally should not be liable for using *unlawful means* to persuade C to cause such loss to B. But this view needs careful attention. The fact that the law might *not* hold A liable for treating B in a humiliating way does not mean that A should necessarily avoid liability to B for threatening C with violence unless he treats B in a humiliating way. (And the fact that C may commit no wrong in doing so is clearly not a reason for absolving A: *Rookes* v *Barnard* [1964] AC 1129.) The true comparison ought to be between the three-party situation and what the law would do if A used *unlawful means* intentionally to cause distress to B directly. But given the way in which *unlawful means* was defined by the majority of the House of Lords in the *OBG* case (see above, pp. 425–7) almost all such cases will involve A committing a civil wrong in relation to B *other than* intentionally causing loss by using unlawful means. (The sole exception, two-party intimidation, is discussed below, pp. 433–5.) And often those *other* civil wrongs in relation to B *will* permit recovery for distress.

43 *Mbasogo* v *Logo Ltd* [2007] 2 WLR 1062, at [97].

wrong'.[44] But we have also seen that a defendant will be held to have used unlawful means if he has *threatened* to commit a 'civil wrong', but has not had to do so because the person threatened *submits*. This means that there is one situation involving *two* parties where the claimant cannot simply sue for a 'civil wrong'. This is the situation where A threatens B that he will commit a civil wrong in relation to B unless B acts in some way that will cause him loss, and where A makes his threat with the intention of causing B to suffer loss. Would A commit a tort in relation to B in this situation if B submitted to the threat and acted in such a way as to cause himself some loss?

There is good evidence that such a tort of *two-party intimidation* exists. The Court of Appeal recognised the existence of the tort in *Godwin* v *Uzoigwe*[45] and awarded £20,000 to a teenager who had been coerced into working without pay for two and a half years by the defendant's violence and mistreatment. It was also recognised by Lord Devlin in *Rookes* v *Barnard*, who stated that 'an action will doubtless lie at the suit of a trader who has been compelled to discontinue his business by means of threats of personal violence made against him by the defendant with that intention'.[46] And although in the *OBG* case Lord Hoffmann defined the tort of intentionally causing loss by unlawful means so that cases of two-party intimidation would *not* fall within it, he expressly stated that he did not intend to say anything about 'the question of whether a claimant who has been compelled by unlawful intimidation to act to his own detriment, can sue for his loss'.[47]

One reason why Lord Hoffmann did not simply *confirm* the existence of the tort may have been the uncertainty which surrounds some elements of it. Three factors help to explain this uncertainty.

Firstly, threats are often made in two-party situations where there is a genuine dispute. For example, if A threatens to breach a contract with B unless B pays him a sum of money which is not due it may be the case that A *thinks* that all he is threatening is to exercise his right to refuse to perform until a sum that is owing is paid. If B pays the sum in this situation then the law may have an interest in treating the payment as the settlement of a dispute rather than a tort.

Secondly, and relatedly, where B makes a contract with A after a threat, or pays money to A after a threat, the doctrines of duress and economic duress determine whether A can enforce that contract, or will have to repay the money. Clearly it would be unsatisfactory if

[44] It has sometimes been suggested that a claimant might be able to obtain a greater measure of damages by framing his claim as one for a two-party version of the tort of intentionally causing loss by unlawful means rather than simply relying on the 'civil wrong'. For instance, if B could show that A intentionally caused loss to him by breaching a contract with him then perhaps he would be entitled to a greater measure of damages than would usually be awarded for a breach of contract. The measure of damages might be different because, for example, exemplary damages are not available for a breach of contract but are available for an intentional tort. It must be doubtful, however, whether the courts would be willing to establish a two-party version of the tort in order to allow a claimant to circumvent the rule that exemplary damages are not available for breach of contract. In an attempt to avoid such a consequence, Carty 2001 argues (at 111) that an actual breach of contract should only constitute 'unlawful means' in a case involving *three* parties. Similarly, Sales & Stilitz 1999 argue (at 424) that in a case only involving *two* parties, a threat to break a contract should constitute 'unlawful means' but an actual breach of contract should not.

[45] [1993] Fam Law 65, CA.

[46] [1964] AC 1129, 1205. Lord Devlin was quoting, with approval, from the contemporary edition of *Salmond on The Law of Torts*.

[47] *OBG* at [61].

these doctrines said that the contract was enforceable, or the money could be retained, but tort law insisted that B should be compensated by A for the loss caused by the threat.

Thirdly, in a two-party situation B has a better opportunity to protect himself, by refusing to submit, than in a three-party situation where C's response to the threat is out of B's hands. Thus a tort of two-party intimidation should *perhaps* be defined so as to require a claimant not to submit too readily to an insignificant threat. Cumulatively, these factors suggest that a two-party tort might not rely on elements precisely parallel to those found in the three-party tort. But because such matters have not been discussed by the courts they remain uncertain.

Conspiracy to cause harm using unlawful means

This tort is discussed in the next chapter.[48] Here it is sufficient simply to outline the fact that there are two views about its nature.

One view sees the tort as designed to extend a form of accessory liability to conspirators who do not commit civil wrongs themselves, but participate in an agreement that *others* should commit civil wrongs against an intended victim.

A second view sees the tort as a hybrid form of primary liability, where the wrongfulness derives from both participation in an agreement with at least one other to cause loss to an intended victim *and* the use of unlawful means, with that term defined *more broadly* than 'civil wrongs'.

Neither of these views, however, suggests that the tort of conspiracy to use unlawful means can *only* be committed when a defendant, or another conspirator, has interfered with a third party's freedom to deal with B. Thus, whichever view is correct, the tort of conspiracy to use unlawful means is not simply a *species* within the general tort of intentionally causing loss by the use of unlawful means.

ALTERNATIVES TO THE CURRENT LAW

The extreme position

As we have seen, an essential element in the tort discussed in this chapter is that A can only be held to have committed this tort if he has used *unlawful means* to cause B to suffer loss. Why have the courts not abolished this requirement and taken the *extreme position* that A will *always* commit a tort in relation to B if he intentionally causes B to suffer loss?[49] There are probably four reasons why the courts have not adopted this extreme position.

(1) *Justification*. First and foremost, the courts have refused to adopt the extreme position set out above because they recognise that there are occasions when A *ought* to act with the intention of harming B. So, for example, if Eric is attacking Wendy on the street, and Fred is in a position to use force to restrain Eric then Fred *ought*[50] to use force to restrain him.

[48] See below, pp. 450–3.

[49] The legal philosopher John Finnis seems to take this position: see Finnis 2002, 46: 'A sound tort law identifies as tortious every act *intended* precisely to cause harm to another person ...' (emphasis in original). It may be the case, however, that John Finnis did not intend his proposition to include all forms of *economic harm*.

[50] Morally, that is; the legal position is that Fred will have no duty to intervene absent special circumstances. See above pp. 203–7.

Similarly, if Tom has been tried and convicted of sexually abusing his daughter, then Karen – the judge presiding at Tom's trial – *ought* to send him to prison for a long time. Obviously, we would not want it to be illegal for Eric to hit Fred or for Karen to send Tom to jail – but it would be if the courts adopted the extreme position set out above.

(2) *Competition*. The courts have also refused to adopt the extreme position set out above because they have tended to think that competition in the marketplace would be unacceptably limited if they took this position. True, not all competition in the marketplace takes the form of one trader intentionally causing another trader to suffer harm. For instance, a trader may seek to stimulate demand for an innovative product without any intention to reduce the profits of traders selling other products.

However, some competition in the marketplace *does* take the form of one trader intentionally causing another trader to suffer harm. This is the case where John and Dawn are both in the business of selling mousetraps and Dawn, knowing that John is suffering from cash-flow difficulties, attempts to drive John out of business by deliberately cutting the price of her mousetraps to uneconomic levels. If Dawn succeeds in driving John out of business in this way – at which point Dawn, having captured John's customers, will raise her prices again to an economic level – Dawn will have intentionally caused John to suffer harm. If the courts took the extreme position set out above, this sort of competitive practice would be proscribed under the common law – Dawn would owe John a common law duty to ensure that she did not *intentionally* drive John out of business – and the courts have, rightly or wrongly,[51] thought in the past that the law would unacceptably limit competition in the marketplace if it made this sort of competitive practice illegal. More modern judicial discussions have suggested a different reason for not adopting the extreme position in the context of competition in the marketplace: it is better to leave Parliament to set limits on competitive behaviour.[52]

(3) *Legitimate reason*. There are other occasions – outside competition in the marketplace – when A may have a perfectly legitimate reason for wanting to harm B. If the courts took the extreme position set out above, A would not be permitted on these occasions to harm B. But the courts have taken the view that A *should be allowed* to harm B in these situations so long as his method of harming B is not independently unlawful, and have therefore rejected the extreme position set out above.

For example, suppose that Carl wants to stop ABC plc from testing the perfumes it makes on animals. Carl thinks that the best way of bringing pressure to bear on ABC to stop its testing is to cause economic loss to ABC by organising a boycott of its products. The courts take the view in this case that as Carl has a perfectly legitimate reason for wanting to organise a boycott of ABC's products and organising the boycott is not independently unlawful, Carl should be allowed to organise his boycott – something which he would not be allowed to do were the courts to adopt the extreme position set out above.

Again, when the case of *Allen* v *Flood* was being argued, one of the judges asked: If a

[51] Wrongly, in the view of Gronow 1995.

[52] *OBG*, at [56] (per Lord Hoffmann): 'The common law has traditionally been reluctant to become involved in devising rules of fair competition, as is vividly illustrated by *Mogul Steamship Co. Ltd* v *McGregor, Gow & Co.* [1892] AC 25. It has largely left such rules to be laid down by Parliament.' See the Competition Act 1998, as amended by the Enterprise Act 2002.

cook, wishing no longer to work alongside her master's butler because she did not get on with him, said to her master 'I will leave you at the end of my current engagement unless you dismiss the butler at the end of his' and the master, in consequence, dismissed the butler at the end of his engagement, will the cook have committed a tort?[53] The majority of the House of Lords thought the answer was 'no'.[54] The cook in this example had a perfectly legitimate reason for wanting to see the butler dismissed and the House of Lords thought that she should therefore be allowed to do what she could to get the butler dismissed so long as her means of doing so were not independently unlawful.

(4) *Freedom*. The courts have also been forced to reject the extreme position set out above because they have long recognised that people enjoy certain *absolute freedoms*. If A possesses an absolute freedom to do *x* then he is free to choose whether to do *x* irrespective of the consequences that his doing *x* will have for other people. Because the courts recognise that people enjoy certain absolute freedoms, they *cannot* take the extreme position set out above. The courts cannot at one and the same time say: (*a*) A has an absolute freedom to do *x*; *and* (*b*) A will commit a tort if he does *x* with the object of causing B to suffer some kind of loss. If A has an absolute freedom to do *x*, it follows that he must be allowed to do *x* even if his object in doing *x* is to harm B. In other words, if A has an absolute freedom to do *x*, his doing *x* cannot ever be said to be wrongful – and this is so even if his object in doing *x* is to harm B.

So, for example, the courts recognise that an owner of land has an absolute freedom to extract water that flows under his land in undefined channels. As a result the courts have always held that a landowner will do no wrong if he intentionally harms someone else by extracting water that flows under his land in undefined channels. This was the result in *Bradford Corporation* v *Pickles*[55] where, it will be recalled, the defendant, Pickles, intercepted water flowing under his land in undefined channels that would otherwise have flowed into the claimant's reservoirs. Pickles plainly intended by doing this to cause the claimant inconvenience – Pickles had no use for the intercepted water himself. By inconveniencing the claimant in this way Pickles hoped, it seems, to give the claimant an incentive either to buy his land or to pay him to restore the water supply. Either way, Pickles, in acting as he did, intentionally harmed the claimant. The House of Lords refused to find that Pickles had owed the claimant a common law duty not to act in the way he did. Pickles had an absolute freedom to extract the water from under his land even if his object in so doing was to harm the claimant. Pickles did not therefore commit a tort in acting as he did.

The American position

It is easy to see why the English courts have not adopted the extreme position set out above. But they also haven't adopted the *American position*, under which A will commit a tort in relation

[53] [1898] AC 1, 36 (per Cave J), 179 (per Lord James). Lord Herschell (at 138–9) and Lord Shand (165–6) had a different recollection of what was said in argument: they thought it had been asked what the position would be if a butler threatened not to renew his contract with his master unless the cook were let go.

[54] It would, of course, be different if the cook had encouraged the master to dismiss the butler *before* the end of his engagement and the master had acted on that encouragement. In such a case the cook would have committed the tort of inducing a breach of contract: see above, Chapter 20.

[55] [1895] AC 587.

to B if A intentionally harms B *when he has no lawful justification or excuse for doing so.*[56]

Suppose, for example, that Lara ran a corner shop selling newspapers and so on. Suppose further that Alan disliked Lara's political views so much that he resolved to ruin Lara by setting up a rival shop beside hers, selling the same goods that Lara sold but at much lower, and uneconomic, prices. Suppose finally that Lara soon went out of business under the pressure of this competition. The ruling in *Allen* v *Flood* makes it clear that because Alan used lawful means – selling goods at cheap prices – to drive Lara out of business, she will not be able to establish that Alan committed a tort in relation to her in acting as he did. But why don't the English courts adopt the American position and rule that Alan committed a tort in relation to Lara when he intentionally drove her out of business when he had no lawful justification or excuse for doing so? Four reasons can be given.

(1) *The difficulty of ascertaining someone's motives.* Whether A had a lawful justification or excuse for intentionally harming B can often turn on what his *motives* were for harming B.[57] So, for example, in the above case we say that Alan had no lawful justification or excuse for acting as he did because he acted as he did out of a dislike for Lara's political views. But it is often very difficult to ascertain what someone's motives were for acting as he did.

Take the example of the cook and the butler, considered above. In the example we stipulated that the cook secured the dismissal of the butler not out of spite but because she just didn't want to work with him any more. But if such a case were to occur in the real world it would be very difficult to tell whether the cook acted as she did because she disliked the butler and wanted to see him harmed (in which case, she would have had no lawful justification or excuse for procuring the butler's dismissal) or whether the cook acted as she did because she wanted to work alongside colleagues she liked and the butler did not fit the bill (in which case, she would have had a lawful justification or excuse for procuring the butler's dismissal).

Similarly with the case considered above where Carl wants to organise a boycott of ABC's products so as to put pressure on ABC to give up testing its perfumes on animals. In the real world, it would be very difficult to tell whether Carl's boycott is being organised for that reason (in which case Carl would have a lawful justification or excuse for organising the boycott) or whether Carl's boycott is being organised because Carl wishes to punish ABC for experimenting on animals (in which case Carl would not have a lawful justification or excuse for organising the boycott).

So if the courts adopted the American position, they would find it very difficult in a case where A has intentionally harmed B to determine *why* A set out to harm B, for the purpose of determining whether A had a lawful justification or excuse for harming B.[58] The ruling in *Allen* v *Flood* has the merit of ensuring that the law on whether A committed a tort in

[56] See Restatement 2d, Torts, §870: 'One who intentionally causes injury to another is subject to liability to the other for that injury, if his conduct is generally culpable and not justifiable under the circumstances' (American Law Institute, 1979). See also *Tuttle* v *Buck*, 119 NW 946 (1909) (defendant banker was held liable to the claimant when he set out, for malicious reasons, to drive the claimant out of business as a barber by setting up a barber's shop near the claimant's shop and undercutting the claimant's prices).

[57] See Restatement 2d, Torts, §870, Comment *i.*

[58] Had *Allen* v *Flood* [1898] AC 1 gone the other way, in any case where a defendant intentionally harmed a claimant, it would have been – at that time – up to a jury to determine why the defendant acted in the way he did. Undoubtedly one of the reasons why *Allen* v *Flood* was decided in the way it was, was that the House of Lords did not think that a jury could be trusted to act responsibly in determining why a defendant intentionally harmed a claimant. The fear was that a jury would be influenced by its own personal likes and dislikes to

this case is easy to apply – one simply looks to see whether A employed lawful or unlawful means to harm B. It is far from clear that this area of the law would be just as easy to apply if the English courts took the American position and said that it is a tort to harm someone else intentionally when you have no lawful justification or excuse for doing so.

(2) *The legitimacy of motives.* Suppose that A has intentionally harmed B and we know *why* A harmed B. If the courts adopted the American position, then they would hold that A committed a tort in harming B if he had no lawful justification or excuse for acting as he did. However, the question of whether A had a lawful justification or excuse for acting as he did given the reasons for which he acted will often be very difficult and controversial to resolve.[59] For example, suppose A drove B out of business because B beat up his son – would A have had a lawful justification or excuse for acting in the way he did? What if A acted as he did because B seduced A's wife, or offered A's daughter drugs? These are very difficult questions and it is not clear the courts are the right institutions to answer them.[60] Under the ruling in *Allen* v *Flood* these questions never arise. If A sets out to ruin B using unlawful means to do so he will commit a tort – the question of whether or not A has a lawful justification or excuse for doing this never arises because it cannot be justifiable or excusable to break the law in order to inflict harm on someone else.[61] If A sets out – on his own[62] – to ruin B using lawful means to do so then A will *not* commit a tort, and this is so whether or not A has a lawful justification or excuse for acting in this way.

(3) *Certainty.* The third reason why the English courts have not adopted the American position emerges out of the first two: if the law said that A will commit a tort in relation to B if he intentionally harms B when he has no justification or excuse for doing so, the law would become intolerably uncertain. Take the example of the cook and butler that we have already considered twice before. Were the law to take the American position, the cook would not be able to tell with any degree of certainty whether or not her procuring the butler's dismissal would amount to a tort or not. Maybe it would, maybe it wouldn't – it would all depend on how the courts, acting after the event, construed her motives and how much sympathy they had for the reasons why she acted as she did. This is unsatisfactory: as Tony Weir points out, 'Is it not important that people should be able to be told in advance what they may or may not do . . .?'[63]

(4) *Freedom.* In *Wainwright* v *Home Office*,[64] the House of Lords considered whether they should recognise that A would commit a tort in relation to B if he intentionally caused B dis-

put either the worst or best possible construction on a defendant's motives for intentionally harming a claimant. See ibid., at 26 (per Mathew J), 118 (per Lord Herschell).

59 See Weir 1997, 74–5.

60 Again (see above, n. 58) had *Allen* v *Flood* [1898] AC 1 gone the other way, it would have been – at that time – up to a jury to determine these issues, and the House of Lords' distrust of juries' abilities to determine correctly whether or not someone had had a lawful justification or excuse for intentionally harming someone else undoubtedly influenced the House of Lords' decision in that case.

61 Though Parliament has taken the view that a trade union official who uses unlawful means to inflict harm on an employer in the course of a trade dispute should not be held liable for so acting: see the Trade Union and Labour Relations (Consolidation) Act 1992, s 219 (summarised below, p. 504).

62 This qualification is required because on the existence of the tort of lawful means conspiracy, which is discussed in the next chapter.

63 Weir 1997, 68.

64 [2004] 2 AC 406.

tress when he had no lawful justification or excuse for doing so. Lord Hoffmann, delivering the leading judgment, thought that they should not take such a step: 'In institutions and workplaces all over the country, people constantly do and say things with the intention of causing distress and humiliation to others. This shows lack of consideration and appalling manners but I am not sure that the right way to deal with it is always by litigation ... [It] might not be in the public interest to allow the law to be set in motion for one boorish incident.'[65] The fear underlying Lord Hoffmann's judgment here is that were English law to take the step of recognising that it is a tort intentionally to cause someone else distress when one has no lawful justification or excuse for so doing, then our freedom to do and say what we like would be radically curtailed.[66] It seems likely that freedom would be similarly curtailed if any act which intentionally caused another person any additional cost or loss of profit amounted to a tort in the absence of lawful justification or excuse. Under the ruling in *Allen* v *Flood*[67] no such concern arises. If A intentionally causes B to suffer some kind of harm, A will only commit a tort in relation to B if the means he uses to inflict that loss are *already* means that are unlawful. So *Allen* v *Flood* does not have the effect of curtailing our liberties in any way at all.

So there is a lot to be said for the English courts' refusal to adopt the American position.[68]

Lord Nicholls's position

We have already seen that Lord Nicholls in the *OBG* case would have defined the tort of intentionally causing loss by unlawful means more broadly than the majority of the House of Lords. He would have treated 'all acts that a defendant is not permitted to do, whether by the civil law or the criminal law'[69] as 'unlawful means'. Moreover, in response to the argument that it would be odd to allow B to bring a claim when A commits a crime in such a way as to interfere with C's freedom to deal with B, while not allowing B to bring a claim when A commits a crime in such a way as *directly* to impede B's ability to pursue profitable endeavours, Lord Nicholls predicted that if A *intentionally* caused harm to B by committing some crime *against him* then the courts might well grant B a remedy.[70] Thus we can summarise the extent to which Lord Nicholls's position goes beyond the established law: he was of the opinion that it ought to be the law that A will commit a tort in relation to B if *either* (1) A intentionally causes loss to B by committing a crime against him, *or* (2) A intentionally causes loss to B by committing (or threatening to commit) a crime against C in order to cause loss to B 'through the *instrumentality* of' C.[71] So why didn't the majority of the House of Lords in the *OBG* case adopt Lord Nicholls's position? Three reasons can be given.

65 Ibid., at [46].

66 In the United States, where a tort of intentionally causing another emotional distress without lawful justification or excuse is recognised, this concern is addressed by requiring that the defendant's conduct has been so 'extreme and outrageous' that it goes beyond 'all possible bounds of decency ... and [is] utterly intolerable in a civilized community': see Rest 2d, Torts, §46, Comment *d*.

67 Strangely, *Allen* v *Flood* was not cited at all in *Wainwright* v *Home Office* even though, had the House of Lords declared that it is a tort intentionally to cause another distress without lawful justification or excuse, they would have created a large exception to the principles laid down in *Allen* v *Flood*.

68 For an alternative view, see Finnis 1995; also Dietrich 2000.

69 *OBG*, at [162]. See above, p. 427 n. 24, for discussion as to whether Lord Nicholls intended to qualify this proposition.

70 *OBG*, at [161].

71 *OBG*, at [159] (emphasis in the original).

(1) *Arbitrariness.* Above we considered the example of John trying to take customers from Lara by sending her customers free calculators, where this scheme involved a criminal offence because the calculators contained a chemical which can cause severe pollution. Lord Hoffmann thought that this sort of example demonstrated that it would be *arbitrary* to allow the question whether John had committed a tort in relation to Lara to turn on the question whether a criminal offence had been committed. In this example the aspect of John's scheme which is criminal has no effect on the likelihood of the free gifts influencing Lara's customers so that they cease to trade with her. Moreover, if it was possible to ask Parliament *why* it made supplying products containing this chemical into a criminal offence it is very unlikely that its reply would include the unfairness of traders using such products in attempts to lure away each other's customers.

Lord Nicholls might respond to this argument by claiming that he would not allow such criminal offences to trigger the tort, but only those that are crimes *against* the third party and enable the defendant to cause loss to the claimant 'through the *instrumentality* of' the third party. But this leads on to the second reason why the majority in *OBG* might have rejected Lord Nicholls's position.

(2) *Uncertainty.* If only *some* criminal offences count as 'unlawful means' – those that are crimes *against* the third party and enable the defendant to cause loss to the claimant 'through the *instrumentality* of' the third party – then it will be necessary to define what these qualifications mean. The requirement that the loss must be caused 'through the instrumentality of the third party' might be thought to be similar to, and no more uncertain than, the requirement that the unlawful means 'interfere with the freedom of a third party to deal with the claimant'. But it is not obvious which crimes are 'crimes against C' and which aren't. For instance, would contempt of court by ignoring a judicial order granted in litigation involving C be a 'crime against C'?

(3) *Constitutionality.* A third reason is that many crimes are created by statute and it would be undesirable to treat the fact that conduct contravenes a statutory provision as a reason for bringing it within the ambit of a tort in the absence of evidence that Parliament intended the provision to be used in this way. The proposition that A will commit a *tort* in relation to B if A intentionally causes loss to B by committing a crime against him seems capable of converting a large number of minor regulatory offences into *torts*, and it must be doubtful whether it would be appropriate for the judiciary to do this.

So there is a lot to be said for the refusal of the majority of the House of Lords in the *OBG* case to adopt Lord Nicholls's position.[72]

Visit **http://www.mylawchamber.co.uk/mcbride** to access updates on recent cases, as well as model answers and tips for answering tort problem questions.

Use **Case Navigator** to read in full the key case referenced in this chapter:

- **Wainwright** *v* **Home Office**

[72] For an alternative view, see Sales & Stilitz 1999.

22 Conspiracy

THE *MOGUL* DECISION

In the mid 1880s one group of shippers entered into an association in order to try to squeeze rival shippers out of the China tea shipping market. The association offered discounts on freight charges to shipping agents who only ever used ships owned by association members, and association members agreed between themselves that if a non-association ship tried to find a cargo of tea, they would immediately send association ships to the same port to offer to carry the cargo at a cheaper freight rate, even if they had to carry it at a loss. The defendants in the action were members of this association.

The claimants owned ships which had previously taken part in the China tea trade, and indeed had been part of the association in previous years, but had been excluded in 1885 because the claimants only sent their ships to China for the three-week tea season when shipping was most profitable while the other association members operated shipping links between China and Europe all year round. Despite being excluded the claimants sent their ships to China to load tea during the 1885 season, the association responded by sending ships to undercut their rates, and the claimants were forced to make their rates so low that they made a loss in order to get any cargo at all.

The claimants then sued the defendants, but the House of Lords held that the defendants had not committed a tort in relation to the claimants.[1] Lord Watson explained that although the defendants had agreed to band together and pursue the course of action which caused loss to the claimants, '[i]f neither the end contemplated by the agreement [between members of the association], nor the means used for its attainment were contrary to law, the loss suffered by the [claimants] was *damnum sine injuria*'.[2] (Damage which it is not a legal wrong to inflict.) This sentence reflects the fact that there are *two* forms of tort involving a conspiracy. One form depends on the *end* contemplated by the agreement being unlawful; the other form depends on the *means* used to attain the end being contrary to law. The claimants lost in the *Mogul* case because they could not establish that the defendants had committed either form of conspiracy tort.

Although the claimants *alleged* that the defendants had made use of unlawful means in conspiring against them, they failed to substantiate this: they failed to prove that unlawful threats had been made, and although the contract which held the association together might have been unenforceable the *making of* such an agreement was not, at that time, unlawful. With regard to the 'end contemplated', Lord Watson dismissed the suggestion that this had been unlawful: 'There is nothing in the evidence to suggest that the parties to the agreement had any other object in view than that of defending their carrying trade

[1] *Mogul Steamship Co.* v *McGregor, Gow & Co.* [1892] AC 25.

[2] Ibid., 42.

during the tea season against the encroachments of the [claimants] and other competitors, and of attracting to themselves custom which might otherwise have been carried off by these competitors. That is an object which is strenuously pursued by merchants great and small in every branch of commerce; and it is, in the eye of the law, perfectly legitimate.'

So – banding together to pursue a course of action which causes loss to a claimant is not *in itself* a tort, but there are *two* forms of tort involving a conspiracy. We will refer to these as 'lawful means conspiracy' and 'unlawful means conspiracy'. In the next section we will discuss when A will be held to have committed the tort of 'lawful means conspiracy' in relation to B, and in the subsequent section we will discuss when A will be held to have committed the tort of 'unlawful means conspiracy' in relation to B.

LAWFUL MEANS CONSPIRACY

Elements of the tort

It seems well acknowledged now that if A joins forces with a third party, C, and they together intentionally cause B to suffer harm for no good reason, then A will commit a tort. This tort is known as '*lawful means* conspiracy'[3] to distinguish it from the tort of '*unlawful means* conspiracy' which, as we will see, is committed where A and C join together and intentionally cause B to suffer some kind of harm, using unlawful means to do so.[4] So there are two differences between lawful means conspiracy and unlawful means conspiracy. For the tort of lawful means conspiracy to be made out, there is no need to show – as there is in an unlawful means conspiracy case – that the conspirators did anything unlawful in the course of causing loss to the claimant. And for lawful means conspiracy to be made out it is not enough to show – as it is in an unlawful means conspiracy case – that the conspirators intended to harm the claimant in acting as they did; it has to be shown that the claimants intended to harm the claimant for no good reason.

Let's now look at the various elements of the tort of lawful means conspiracy in more detail.

The need for agreement

So – A will have committed the tort of lawful means conspiracy in relation to B if: (1) A joined forces with C and they together intentionally caused B to suffer some kind of harm; *and* (2) they did so for no good reason.

(1) is established by showing that A and C *agreed* that they would take steps to harm B and that they put that agreement into effect. So (1) will *not* be established in the case where A sets out to cause B harm and orders his employees to engage in various actions which will have that effect – as there is no *agreement* between A and his employees that they will take steps to harm B, it cannot be said that A and his employees have joined forces against B.[5]

3 The tort is also sometimes known as 'conspiracy to injure'. Carty 2001 calls the tort 'simple conspiracy' (at 16). In *Rookes* v *Barnard* [1964] AC 1129, 1204, Lord Devlin referred to the tort as 'the *Quinn* v *Leathem* type [of conspiracy]', referring to the leading case (discussed below, pp. 446–7) on when this tort will be committed, and the label '*Quinn* v *Leathem* conspiracy' is also sometimes used.

4 See below, pp. 450–3.

5 See *Crofter Hand Woven Harris Tweed Co.* v *Veitch* [1942] AC 435, 468 (per Lord Wright). On the other hand, see Viscount Simon LC, at 441: 'It was argued that the [defendant] Mackenzie should not be regarded as acting

Good reason

Suppose that A and C joined forces and they intentionally caused B to suffer some kind of harm. When will the courts hold that they had no good reason for acting as they did? The following guidance can be gleaned from the cases:

(1) *Business*. If A and C were business persons, A and C will have had a good reason for acting in the way they did if they acted as they did in order to protect or promote their business interests.

In *Mogul Steamship Co.* v *McGregor, Gow & Co.*,[6] as we have seen, the defendants entered an agreement, and steps were taken to pursue it, with the intention of causing immediate loss to the claimants and preventing them from enjoying any portion of a lucrative market in the future. Nonetheless, the House of Lords held that the defendants had not committed the tort of lawful means conspiracy because excluding the claimants from the market served the legitimate business interests of the defendants.

In *Sorrell* v *Smith*,[7] a union of retail newsagents attempted to limit the number of retail newsagents operating in any given area by adopting a policy of refusing to deal with wholesalers who supplied retail newsagents who had opened for business without the union's permission. R, a wholesaler, fell foul of the policy when he supplied a particular retail newsagent with newspapers when the newsagent had not obtained permission to trade from the union. In accordance with the policy, S – a retail newsagent within the union – withdrew his custom from R and switched it to W, another wholesaler who was prepared to abide by the union's demands. The defendants were members of a committee representing the proprietors of newspapers. They took the view that the union – in attempting to limit the number of retail newsagents trading in a given area – was acting contrary to their interests and weighed in on the side of R in an attempt to disrupt the union from achieving its aims. The defendants threatened not to supply W with any newspapers unless S switched his custom back to R. The House of Lords held that the defendants committed no tort in acting in this way. While they may have set out to cause S to suffer harm in acting as they did – in the sense that they were trying to make S do something he did not want to do – they had a good reason for doing so: they were trying to protect their business interests.

(2) *Trade unions*. If A and C were trade union officials, A and C will *usually* have had a good reason for acting as they did if they acted as they did in order to further the interests of their trade union or its members.

In *Crofter Hand Woven Harris Tweed Co. Ltd* v *Veitch*,[8] the defendants were officials of the Transport and General Workers' Union. All the dockers at Stornoway, the main port of the Isle of Lewis, and the great majority of the workers employed in the spinning mills on

in combination with the [defendant] Veitch, so as to establish the element of agreement between them in the tort of conspiracy, because Veitch held the responsible position of Scottish area secretary to the union, whereas Mackenzie was only branch secretary for Stornoway. This, I think, is an unsound contention. The respective position of the two men in the hierarchy of trade union officials has nothing to do with it. *Even if Mackenzie could be regarded as only obeying orders from his superior, the combination would still exist if he appreciated what he was about*' (emphasis added).

[6] [1892] AC 25.

[7] [1925] AC 700.

[8] [1942] AC 435.

the Isle of Lewis, were members of the TGWU. The workers employed in these spinning mills would produce yarn that would be given out to the crofters on the Isle of Lewis. The crofters would weave the yarn into tweed cloth which would then be finished in the mills and sold as 'Harris tweed' by the mill owners. The claimant also sold 'Harris tweed' but he had a different method of manufacturing it. The claimant imported yarn from the mainland, handed it out to the crofters on the Isle of Lewis to weave into tweed cloth and then sent the tweed cloth back to the mainland for finishing. As a result, the claimant's 'Harris tweed' was cheaper than the mill owners' 'Harris tweed'. The mill owners resolved to do something about this and persuaded the defendants to order the dockers at Stornoway to refuse to handle yarn imported from the mainland – the intended effect being to drive the claimant out of business.

The House of Lords held that the defendants committed no tort in so acting. There was some ambiguity about why the defendants acted as they did. On one reading of the case, the defendants agreed to drive the claimant out of business in order to keep the mill owners' business competitive, thus guaranteeing that those of their members who were employed by the mill owners would not lose their jobs. On another reading of the case, the defendants struck a deal with the mill owners under which the mill owners would – in return for the defendants' assistance in putting the claimant out of business – allow the creation of a 'closed shop' in the spinning mills in the Isle of Lewis the effect of which would be that someone could only obtain employment in those mills if they were a member of the TGWU. On either reading, the defendants had a good reason for acting as they did: they did so in order to promote the interests of their members.

However, if A and C are officials of a trade union and they set out to cause B to suffer harm in order to promote the interests of their union or its members, it will *not* always be the case that they had a good reason for seeking to harm B.[9] In the *Crofter* case, Viscount Simon LC observed: 'If . . . the mill-owners in the present case had promised a large subscription to the trade union funds as an inducement to bribe the [defendants] to take action to smash the [claimant's] trade, I cannot think that the [defendants] could excuse themselves for combining to inflict this damage merely by saying that their . . . purpose was to benefit the funds of the union thereby.'[10]

In *Giblan* v *National Amalgamated Labourers' Union of Great Britain and Ireland*,[11] the claimant was once the treasurer of the defendant union. There were some irregularities in the way the claimant handled the union's finances and it was alleged that the claimant had kept for himself some money which he should have handed over to the union. The claimant agreed to pay the money over to the union but never did. As a result, officials of the union resolved to make life difficult for the claimant. Accordingly, whenever he found

[9] Contra, Gronow 1995, who takes an unduly pessimistic view of the current scope of this tort.

[10] [1942] AC 435, 446. This view was supported by Viscount Maugham (at 451). What if the defendants in the *Crofter* case *had* acted as they did because the mill owners had promised to allow the creation of a closed shop in the mills in return for the trade union's assistance in ruining the claimant? It is hard to see a distinction between that case and the case where a trade union assists in ruining a third party's competitor because the third party promised to give a handsome sum to the trade union's funds in return for such assistance. Viscount Simon LC did not have to confront this difficulty: he found, on the facts, that the defendants had not acted as they did because the mill owners had promised in return to allow the creation of a closed shop in the mills (at 439) but had instead acted 'to benefit their . . . members by preventing under-cutting and unregulated competition, and so helping to secure the economic stability of the island industry'.

[11] [1903] 2 KB 600.

employment, the union officials would threaten his employer with reprisals unless he discharged the claimant. In this way the union officials secured on four different occasions the claimant's dismissal from some job he had found.

It is difficult to tell whether the officials acted in this way to punish the claimant for acting as he did (in which case they would not have had a good reason for acting as they did – see (4), below) or because they wished to compel him to pay the debt he owed the trade union. However, the Court of Appeal was prepared to find that even if the latter was the case – and that therefore the trade union officials were acting as they did to protect and promote the interests of the trade union – the trade union officials had no good reason for acting as they did and therefore committed the tort of lawful means conspiracy in acting as they did.[12] Even if the trade union officials acted as they did to compel the claimant to pay his debt, they still had no good reason for doing what they did as they had a perfectly good legal remedy available to them to compel the claimant to pay the union what he owed it. They had no need to take the extra-legal measures they did to compel him to pay up.

(3) *Public interest.* In *Scala Ballroom (Wolverhampton) Ltd* v *Ratcliffe*,[13] the claimants were proprietors of a ballroom. They operated a colour bar, excluding coloured visitors from the dance floor. At the same time, they allowed coloured musicians to play in the orchestra. The defendants were officials of the Musicians' Union. They attempted to bring the colour bar to an end by warning the claimants that members of the Musicians' Union would not be allowed to play at the claimants' ballroom while the colour bar was in place. The Court of Appeal held that the defendants had committed no tort in so acting. While they had, in acting as they did, sought to harm the claimants – in the sense of seeking to make the claimants do something they did not want to do – they had had a good reason for doing so. The Court of Appeal found that the defendants had, in acting as they did, sought to promote the interests of the coloured members of their union. However, we would submit, even if the defendants' union had had no coloured members they would still have had a good reason for acting as they did. If the defendants honestly felt that what the claimants were doing was wrong, then there seems no reason why the defendants should not have been allowed to organise together to attempt to induce the claimants to give up their colour bar.

(4) *Punishment.* If A and C acted as they did because they wanted to punish B for something she did or for the fact that she held certain views, then A and C will *not* have had a good reason for acting as they did *unless* they thought that punishing B was necessary to safeguard their business interests or to protect the interests of their trade union.

In *Quinn* v *Leathem*,[14] Leathem was a butcher. The Belfast Journeymen Butchers and Assistants' Association was upset that Leathem did not exclusively employ men who belonged to that union. In fact, none of Leathem's employees belonged to that union and neither did Leathem. Leathem attended a meeting of the union and offered to make his employees members of the union. The union insisted that he dismiss his employees and

[12] The only tort that the trade union officials could have committed was the tort of lawful means conspiracy; the union officials had employed no unlawful means in their attempts to make life difficult for the claimant and they did not induce any of his employers to discharge him in breach of contract.

[13] [1958] 1 WLR 1057.

[14] [1901] AC 495.

employ existing members of the union instead. Leathem refused to do this. The defendants, officials of the union, resolved to punish Leathem for taking this stand and did so by threatening Leathem's customers that union members employed by those customers would walk out on their jobs if they continued to deal with Leathem. As a result, Leathem lost a lot of custom. On these facts, the House of Lords held that the defendants had committed a tort. They had organised together and intentionally caused Leathem to suffer loss and had no good reason for doing so – they did not act as they did to advance the interests of their union or the members of the union, but simply out of a vindictive desire to see Leathem punished for acting as he did.

In *Huntley* v *Thornton*,[15] the claimant was employed in a shipyard in Hartlepool when he received a notice from his union to stop work for 24 hours in support of a wage claim. The claimant refused to abide by this instruction and went to work as usual. The defendants, members of the Hartlepool district committee of the union, recommended that the claimant be expelled from the union (a recommendation not acted on by the union's executive council) and then embarked on a campaign to prevent the claimant finding alternative employment by threatening anyone who employed him, or thought of employing him, with industrial action. It was found, at first instance, that the defendants had committed a tort in so acting. They had intentionally harmed the claimant and had done so for no good reason. In acting as they did, Harman J held, the defendants were not acting to promote the interests of their trade union. Rather, the defendants sought to harm the claimant for showing 'an arrogant attitude' towards them; in acting as they did, the defendants 'entirely lost sight of what the interests of the union demanded, and thought only of their own ruffled dignity'.[16]

Some have sought to sum up the above by saying that if A and C join forces and intentionally cause B to suffer some kind of harm, they will have committed a tort if their *predominant purpose* in causing B to suffer that harm was to injure B.[17]

This formulation is apt to confuse. In all the cases we have looked at so far the defendants' purpose was to injure the claimant and in all the cases we have looked at so far the defendants' purpose was to injure the claimant to achieve some other end – either to advance the defendants' business interests (as in the *Mogul* case) or to advance the interests of the defendants' union (as in the *Crofter* case) or to assuage the defendants' sense of resentment or outrage towards the claimant (as in *Quinn* v *Leathem* and in *Huntley* v *Thornton*). How can one say, then, that in *Quinn* and *Huntley* the defendants' predominant purpose was to injure the claimant; but in *Mogul* and *Crofter* the defendants' predominant purpose was not to injure the claimant?

Moreover, the formulation under scrutiny here – that if A and C join forces and intentionally cause B to suffer some kind of harm, they will have committed a tort if their predominant purpose was to harm B – is apt to mislead. It may lead us to think that if trade union officials set out to cause – and succeed in causing – B to suffer some kind of harm they will not commit the tort of lawful means conspiracy so long as their primary intention

[15] [1957] 1 WLR 321.
[16] Ibid., 341.
[17] *Crofter Hand Woven Harris Tweed Co.* v *Veitch* [1942] AC 435, 445 (per Viscount Simon LC); *Lonrho plc* v *Fayed* [1992] 1 AC 448, 465H (per Lord Bridge of Harwich).

in so acting was to promote the interests of the officials' trade union. However, we have already seen that there may be cases where trade union officials who intentionally cause another person harm may be guilty of committing the tort of lawful means conspiracy even though their ultimate object in so acting was to promote the interests of their trade union. This was the case in the *Giblan* case and may be the case where trade union officials set out to ruin an individual in return for a promised contribution to trade union funds.

For these reasons, we would reject the view that if A and C join forces and intentionally cause B to suffer some kind of harm, whether or not they have committed the tort of lawful means conspiracy will depend on whether or not A and C's predominant purpose in so acting was to injure B. This view is confusing and misleading. The touchstone of liability in this context, we submit, is whether or not A and C had 'just cause or excuse for the action taken'.[18]

Mixed motives

So far we have been dealing with the situation where A and C join forces and intentionally cause B to suffer some kind of harm for no good reason – in such a case, A and C will commit the tort of lawful means conspiracy. We must now deal with two questions:

(1) Suppose A and C joined together and they intentionally caused B to suffer some kind of harm and A had a good reason for acting in the way he did but C did not? Will A have committed a tort in this situation?

(2) What is the position if A and C joined forces and intentionally caused B to suffer some kind of harm and C had a good reason for acting in the way he did but A did not? Will A have committed a tort in this situation?

The answer to question (1) is 'no' unless A *knew* of C's reasons for seeking to cause B to suffer harm.[19] So, in *Huntley* v *Thornton*,[20] when the claimant left Hartlepool and moved to Teesside in an attempt to escape the attentions of the Hartlepool district committee of the claimant's union and find work, the Hartlepool district committee persuaded two union officials in the Teesside district to join with them in helping prevent the claimant find work. However, the two union officials in question committed no tort in so acting – they had been led to believe that safeguarding the interests of the union required them to take steps against the claimant and had no idea that the Hartlepool district council was engaged in a petty and vindictive campaign against the claimant.

The answer to question (2) seems to be 'no' unless C knew of A's reasons for seeking to cause B to suffer harm. If C did know, then both A and C will have committed a tort in organising together to harm B. Why will *C's* ignorance – if he is ignorant of A's purposes – absolve *A*? The answer, it seems, is that an agreement – a conspiracy – to inflict harm on another cannot be unlawful unless *at least* two parties to it are acting unlawfully. So if C cannot be held to have acted unlawfully – committed a tort – in agreeing with A that they would seek to cause B to suffer some kind of harm, then that agreement with A could not have been unlawful. But if the agreement with A was not unlawful, then A could not have

[18] *Sorrell* v *Smith* [1925] AC 700, 712 (per Viscount Cave LC). See also *Crofter Hand Woven Harris Tweed Co.* v *Veitch* [1942] AC 435, 451–2 (per Viscount Maugham).

[19] Ibid., at 495 (per Lord Porter).

[20] [1957] 1 WLR 321.

acted unlawfully in being party to it. So A could not have committed a tort in agreeing with C that they would seek to cause B to suffer some kind of harm.

This line of reasoning, while superficially attractive, has nothing to recommend it. If A wishes for no good reason to cause B to suffer some kind of harm there is no reason why the law should not enjoin him from joining forces with someone else to cause B to suffer that harm – whatever the motivations of that someone else. According to the orthodox view summed up above, if A wishes for no good reason to cause B to suffer some kind of harm, the law only requires A not to join forces with a third party, C, to inflict that harm on B if C *also* has no good reason for wanting to harm B. It is hard to see why the law would take such an odd position.

Evaluating the tort

Two criticisms may be made of the tort of lawful means conspiracy:

(1) *Paradox*. The first is that the existence of this tort introduces a paradox into the law. The decision of the House of Lords in *Allen* v *Flood*[21]made it clear if A, acting alone, sets out to ruin B because he dislikes his political views he will commit no tort so long as his method of ruining B is lawful in nature. In contrast, the existence of the tort of lawful means conspiracy means that if A and C combine to ruin B because they dislike his political views, A will commit a tort even if A and C's chosen method of ruining B is lawful in nature. This, it might be thought, makes no sense: as Lord Diplock observed in *Lonrho Ltd* v *Shell Petroleum (No. 2)*, 'Why should an act which causes economic loss to [B] but is not actionable at his suit if done by [A] alone become actionable because [A] did it pursuant to an agreement between [A] and C?'[22]

(2) *Difficulty*. Whether or not the tort of lawful means conspiracy has been committed in a particular case will often depend on what the defendant's motives were for seeking to harm the claimant. However, it is often very difficult to determine what someone's motives were for acting as they did. For example, in *Quinn* v *Leathem*[23] it must have been very difficult to determine why the defendants victimised the claimant in that case. On the one hand, it was argued that the defendants acted as they did because they were outraged at the way the claimant had stood up to them and they wanted to teach him a lesson. On this reading of the case, the defendants had no good reason for seeking to harm the claimant and were liable for committing the tort of lawful means conspiracy. On the other hand, it could have been argued that the defendants had sought to harm the claimant in order to promote the interests of their trade union, by making it clear to everyone that anyone who failed to go along with their demands would incur severe sanctions. On this reading of the facts, the defendants in *Quinn* v *Leathem* had a good reason for acting as they did, and should not have been held liable for committing the tort of lawful means conspiracy. In the end, the House of Lords found that the defendants had acted as they did out of spite, rather than a desire to safeguard the interests of their trade union. However, it must have been a

[21] [1898] AC 1. Summarised above, pp. 424–5.
[22] [1982] AC 173, 188.
[23] [1901] AC 495.

close-run thing. It might be argued that a tort which requires us to peer into the windows of people's souls in this way has no place in English law.[24]

UNLAWFUL MEANS CONSPIRACY

Elements of the tort

If A joins forces with a third party, C, and they agree that unlawful means will be used with the intention of causing B to suffer some kind of harm, and this is carried into effect with the consequence that B suffers some kind of harm, then A will commit a tort in relation to B. This tort is known as '*unlawful means* conspiracy'.

Let's now look at the various elements of the tort of unlawful means conspiracy in more detail.

The need for agreement

This tort, like lawful means conspiracy, requires an agreement between A and C, and the taking of steps to put that agreement into effect.

Intention to harm the claimant

To be held liable, the conspirators must intend to cause B to suffer some kind of harm. But while conspirators can only commit lawful means conspiracy if they have 'no good reason' for acting as they did, they can commit unlawful means conspiracy *regardless of the quality of their reasons*, if they have agreed that unlawful means should be used to cause B loss and that has been done.

Unlawful means

The most controversial question concerning unlawful means conspiracy is what forms of behaviour will be classed as 'unlawful means' for the purposes of the tort. Two views have gained a measure of judicial support.

One view is that behaviour can only constitute 'unlawful means' for the purposes of the tort if it amounts to an independently actionable civil wrong to the claimant by at least one of the conspirators. Two arguments can be relied on to support this view. The first argument is that unlawful means conspiracy is effectively a form of *accessory* liability, which allows a defendant who has agreed with others that an actionable civil wrong should be committed against B to be held liable even if he has not committed that wrong himself, but has 'kept his hands clean'. If it is correct to characterise unlawful means conspiracy as a form of *accessory* liability then it follows that the unlawful means must be an independently actionable civil wrong to the claimant – otherwise there would be no *primary* civil wrong for the defendant to be an accessory to.

The second argument is that if behaviour which *does not* amount to an independently actionable civil wrong can constitute 'unlawful means' for the purposes of this tort then it

[24] In *Lonrho Ltd* v *Shell Petroleum (No. 2)* [1982] AC 173, 188–9, Lord Diplock stated that the tort 'must I think be accepted by this House as too well-established to be discarded however anomalous it may seem today' but 'unhesitatingly' chose to confine it to the 'narrow limits that are all that common sense and the application of the legal logic of the decided cases require'.

will raise the same paradox as the tort of lawful means conspiracy: if A had used the same means acting on his own to harm B intentionally he would not have committed a tort, but if he agreed with C that the means should be used to harm B then he will have committed a tort.

The rival view as to the meaning of 'unlawful means' is that it should cover all means that are contrary to law, including, in particular, behaviour that is contrary to the criminal law but will not amount to an independently actionable civil wrong. The principal argument in support of this view involves treating unlawful means conspiracy as a close relation to lawful means conspiracy, which is clearly *not* a form of accessory liability. If lawful means conspiracy and unlawful means conspiracy are closely related torts then they might be argued to both follow the pattern of requiring: (1) A to agree with C that action should be taken with the intention of causing loss to B; *and* (2) an additional element. As we have seen, the additional element required to establish a case of lawful means conspiracy is absence of a 'just cause or excuse for the action taken'. But on this view the unlawful means is merely an alternative additional element – the additional element required to establish a case of unlawful means conspiracy – and there is no *logical* reason why 'unlawful means' should be defined as requiring an independently actionable civil wrong. To put the point a different way, on this view 'unlawful means' is a shorthand for 'methods which it ought to be a wrong to the claimant for a conspiracy to use in order to harm the claimant'. If this is right there is no *logical* reason for insisting that independently actionable civil wrongs are the only methods which it is wrongful for a *conspiracy* to use.

Which view ought to be supported? In *Revenue and Customs Commissioners* v *Total Network SL*[25] the Court of Appeal confronted a case where the defendant was alleged to have been part of a conspiracy with other companies to commit a 'carousel fraud' on the Revenue. The conspiracy was designed to lead the Revenue to believe that a series of transactions had occurred which entitled one company to reclaim VAT from the Revenue and left another company obliged to pay a similar sum as VAT to the Revenue: but the transactions were circular, and if the plan succeeded then the company apparently entitled to reclaim money would obtain it but the company obliged to pay a similar sum would 'disappear' leaving the Revenue out of pocket. The Revenue sued the defendant for 'unlawful means conspiracy'[26] and identified the common law criminal offence of 'cheating the revenue' as the 'unlawful means'.[27] The Court of Appeal expressed the opinion that if the matter had not been governed by binding authority they would have held that 'unlawful means' for the purpose of the conspiracy tort did *not* require an independently actionable civil wrong.[28] The Court thought, however, that the opposite conclusion had been

[25] [2007] 2 WLR 1156.

[26] The Revenue expressly chose *not* to amend its claim to allege a lawful means conspiracy despite an invitation by the Court of Appeal to consider this option.

[27] As an alternative argument the Revenue suggested that the unlawful means requirement might have been satisfied by one of the conspirators having committed the tort of deceit, but the Court of Appeal held that this tort could not be established because it had been superseded in the particular context by a statutory scheme allowing for the recovery of an undeserved rebate. (The Revenue could not use this statutory scheme against the defendant because the defendant was not a UK taxpayer.)

[28] Ibid., [67]–[68]. A similar view was expressed by Davis J at first instance in *Mbasogo* v *Logo Ltd* [2005] EWHC 2034 (QB).

previously reached by the Court of Appeal in *Powell* v *Boldaz*,[29] and although the reasoning in that case was not flawless it constituted a binding authority.

The reasoning in *Powell* v *Boldaz* had claimed to draw support from the speech of Lord Diplock in *Lonrho Ltd* v *Shell Petroleum Co. Ltd (No. 2)*.[30] As we have seen,[31] Lord Diplock doubted whether there were good reasons for behaviour being actionable when A and C agreed that it should be carried out but not when A carried it out on his own. If one shares these doubts then it would be sensible to conceptualise the tort of unlawful means conspiracy as a form of accessory liability and insist that 'unlawful means' must be an independently actionable civil wrong to the claimant, because this will reduce the number of situations where two or more people banding together are subject to greater constraint than one powerful individual acting on his own.

A different argument that has sometimes been used is that 'unlawful means' should have the same meaning in the tort of 'unlawful means conspiracy' as it has in the tort of intentionally causing loss by the use of unlawful means. But, as we saw in the previous chapter, in the *OBG* case the House of Lords confined the tort of intentionally causing loss by the use of unlawful means to situations where A uses unlawful means to limit C's liberty to deal with B. Thus the role of 'unlawful means' in this tort is to define what A should not do to C as a way of harming B. By contrast, in the tort of unlawful means conspiracy the role of 'unlawful means' is to define what A and C should not agree to do to B directly. This difference in roles means that some elements of the definition of 'unlawful means' within the tort of intentionally causing loss by the use of unlawful means – such as the rule that behaviour will constitute 'unlawful means' if the only reason it did not amount to a tort to B was that B suffered no loss – would make no sense as part of a definition of 'unlawful means' within the tort of unlawful means conspiracy. That said, many of the arguments that might be relied on for excluding *crimes* from the definition of 'unlawful means' used by the tort of intentionally causing loss by the use of unlawful means[32] – such as that Parliament might have created crimes without any intention that they should be used as the basis for making claims in tort against other people – could also be used to support excluding *crimes* from the definition of 'unlawful means' used by the tort of unlawful means conspiracy. Thus it would be odd if the arguments were thought to be sufficient in the context of one tort but insufficient in the context of the other.[33]

[29] [1998] Lloyd's Rep Med 116, 126. The same conclusion was reached by Laddie J at first instance in *Michaels* v *Taylor Woodrow Developments Ltd* [2001] Ch 493.

[30] [1982] AC 173. The Court of Appeal in *Revenue and Customs Commissioners* v *Total Network SL* [2007] 2 WLR 1156 did not think that Lord Diplock's speech supported this conclusion (at [57]) but accepted that it *arguably* did (at [78]).

[31] See above, p. 449.

[32] These arguments are discussed above, p. 441.

[33] The Court of Appeal expressed its opinion in *Revenue and Customs Commissioners* v *Total Network SL* [2007] 2 WLR 1156 *before* the House of Lords decided *OBG Ltd* v *Allan* [2007] 2 WLR 920, but after the appeal in that case was argued.

The independence of the tort

Two points may be made about the independence of the tort of unlawful means conspiracy:

(1) *Accessory liability*. The first point to be made is that *if* the unlawful means requirement will only be satisfied when an independently actionable wrong has been committed in relation to the claimant then it is arguable that it is unnecessary to recognise an *independent* tort of unlawful means conspiracy: instead unlawful means conspiracy should simply be recognised as a further way in which accessory liability can be established.[34]

(2) *Intentionally causing loss by unlawful means*. Before the case of *OBG Ltd* v *Allan*[35] clarified when A will be held to have committed the tort of intentionally causing loss by the use of unlawful means in relation to B it was often asked whether the tort of unlawful means conspiracy was a *species* within the *general* tort of intentionally causing loss by unlawful means.[36] It is now clear, however, that A will only be held to have committed the tort of intentionally causing loss by unlawful means in relation to B when A has wrongfully interfered with the actions of a third party in which B has an economic interest.[37] Obviously, when A and another conspirator agree to use unlawful means to harm B they are not confined to means which interfere with the actions of a third party. For example, suppose A agrees with C and D that whenever one of them sees B in the street he will assault[38] her or damage her clothes, and this conspiracy is carried into effect. In this case, A ought to be held liable to B for unlawful means conspiracy, and it should not matter that none of A, C or D wrongfully interfered with the actions of a third party. If this is correct then the tort of unlawful means conspiracy is clearly *not* merely a species of the *general* tort of intentionally causing loss by unlawful means. This does not mean that the same facts can never give rise to claims for both torts. For instance, if A, C and D agree that whenever one of them sees a potential customer heading towards B's trading premises they will threaten that customer with violence in order to persuade him not to trade with B, and this conspiracy is carried into effect, then A, C and D should be held liable to B for unlawful means conspiracy, and at least one of them will *also* be liable for having committed the tort of causing loss by unlawful means to B by intimidating his potential customer.

[34] Accessory liability is discussed below in Chapter 32.

[35] [2007] 2 WLR 920.

[36] See McBride & Bagshaw 2003, 424.

[37] [2007] 2 WLR 920, at [47]. This tort is discussed in detail in Chapter 21.

[38] In *Powell* v *Boldaz* [1998] Lloyd's Rep Med 116, at 126, the claimant's counsel conceded that damages for personal injuries are not recoverable under the tort of unlawful means conspiracy. But if the tort is effectively a form of *accessory* liability it would be very peculiar if it only covered torts protecting economic interests.

23 Torts involving the deception of others

We are concerned here with three completely separate torts, united only by the fact that they all involve the defendant deceiving someone else: deceit, malicious falsehood and passing off.

DECEIT

A will have committed the tort of deceit (or fraud) in relation to B if:

(1) he made a representation of fact to B which was untrue; *and*
(2) when he made that representation to B he did not honestly believe that it was true;[1] *and*
(3) he intended, in making that representation to B, to induce B to act in a particular way; *and*
(4) B was induced to act in that way by A's representation.[2]

There are seven points worth making about this tort:

(1) *Conduct.* Someone can obviously make a representation of fact by words or writing, but they can also do so by conduct. If A has conducted himself in such a way that B *reasonably* inferred from A's conduct that *x* was true, then it is fair to say that A represented to B that *x* was true.[3]

(2) *Representation of opinion.* A representation of opinion always carries with it a representation of fact that can ground an action for deceit. This is because if A says to B, 'I think

[1] In *Derry* v *Peek* (1889) 14 App Cas 337, at 374, Lord Herschell observed that, 'in order to establish an action of deceit, there must be proof of fraud, and nothing short of that will suffice . . . [F]raud is proved when it is shewn that a false representation has been made (1) knowingly, or (2) without belief in its truth, or (3) recklessly, careless whether it be true or false.' But if (1) is true, (2) is true. And if (3) is true, (2) is true. So we can reduce Lord Herschell's statement down to: '[F]raud is proved when it is shewn that a false representation has been made . . . without belief in its truth' without losing anything.

[2] There is no further requirement that A's representation must have been made in a commercial context: see *P* v *B* [2001] 1 FLR 1041 and *Magill* v *Magill* (2006) 226 CLR 551 (both cases allowing a claimant to bring an action for deceit against his ex-partner, claiming that she lied to him in telling him that he was the father of her child).

[3] This requirement was not satisfied in *Ward* v *Hobbs* (1878) 4 App Cas 13. In that case, Hobbs sold pigs to Ward at the Newbury market. Ward later discovered that the pigs were suffering from typhoid fever; all but one of the pigs died and some other pigs of Ward's also died, having been infected by the pigs bought from Hobbs. Ward sued Hobbs claiming, *inter alia*, that Hobbs had committed the tort of deceit. The claim failed: Hobbs had made no representation that his pigs were free from illness and of good quality. Ward argued that Hobbs's act of driving the pigs to market when he had a statutory duty not to do so if they were suffering from a contagious disease meant that he represented to Ward that his pigs were free from disease. However, even if Ward inferred from Hobbs's driving his pigs to market that the pigs were free from disease, this was not a reasonable inference to draw; it was not *reasonable* to think that Hobbs would observe his statutory duty and not drive his pigs to market if they were suffering from a contagious disease. As Lord Selborne remarked (at 29): '[t]o say that every man is always to be taken to represent, in his dealings with other men, that he is not, to his knowledge, violating any statute, is a refinement which . . . would not I think appear reasonable to any man.'

that *x* is true' he makes a representation that it is a fact that he thinks *x* is true. So if A says to B 'I think that *x* is true' when he does not actually think *x* is true then A makes an untrue representation of fact to B – he represents to B that he thinks *x* is true when this is not true. Some judges have gone further and said that if A says to B 'I think that *x* is true' when A is in a much better position than B to know whether or not *x* is true, then A's representation 'I think that *x* is true' will amount to a representation of fact that there is *good reason* to believe that *x* is true.[4] Some judges have gone even further than this and said that in such a case, A's representation 'I think that *x* is true' will amount to a representation of fact that *x is* true.[5]

(3) *Representation of intention*. Similarly, a representation of intention always carries with it a representation of fact that can ground an action for deceit. This is because if A says to B, 'I intend to do *x*', he makes a representation that it is a fact that he currently has an intention to do *x*. So if A says to B 'I intend to do *x*' when he has no such intention, A makes an untrue representation of fact – he represents to B that it is currently his intention to do *x* when this is not true.

For example, in *Edgington* v *Fitzmaurice*,[6] the directors of a company issued a prospectus inviting subscriptions for debentures issued by the company. The prospectus stated that the object of the issue was to raise money to allow the company to complete alterations in the buildings of the company, to purchase horses and vans and to develop the company's trade. In fact the directors intended to use the money raised to pay off some of the company's debts. It was held that the directors had made an untrue representation of fact in the prospectus – they had represented that it was their intention to invest the money raised by the issue of debentures when it was actually their intention to use the money to pay off some of the company's debts. Bowen LJ put the point memorably: '[t]here must be a misstatement of an existing fact [for an action in deceit to be maintained]: but the state of a man's mind is as much a fact as the state of his digestion.'[7]

Similarly, in *East* v *Maurer*,[8] the defendant ran two hairdressing salons in neighbouring areas. The defendant decided to sell one of the salons and devote all his efforts to working in the other salon. The claimants were interested in purchasing the salon the defendant wanted to sell and, in order to encourage them to buy the salon, the defendant assured them that he did not intend to work regularly in the other salon. In so assuring the claimants, the defendant made an untrue representation of fact: he represented that he had no intention of working regularly in his other salon when, in fact, he had every intention of doing so.

(4) *Inducement*. The courts will hold that A's representation of fact to B induced B to do *x* if A's representation *played some part* in B's decision to do *x*.[9]

4 *Brown* v *Raphael* [1958] 1 Ch 636.

5 *Bisset* v *Wilkinson* [1927] AC 177.

6 (1885) 29 Ch D 459.

7 Ibid., 483.

8 [1991] 1 WLR 461.

9 It does *not* have to be shown that B would not have done *x but for* A's representation: *Downs* v *Chappell* [1997] 1 WLR 426 (action for deceit available when claimants bought bookstore having been shown a set of accounts for the bookstore which made the bookstore out to be a lot more profitable than it was: the fact that the state of the accounts played some part in the claimant's decision to buy the bookstore was enough to ground an action for deceit – it was irrelevant that the claimants might well have bought the bookstore anyway had they never seen the accounts).

In *Smith* v *Chadwick*,[10] the claimants claimed that they were induced to buy shares in a company because its prospectus falsely represented that G was a director of the company. This claim was dismissed. The claimants could not have been induced to buy shares in the company by the representation in the prospectus that G was a director of the company because, by their own admission, the claimants had never heard of G before the prospectus was issued. The representation in the prospectus that G was a director of the company could not therefore have played any part in the claimants' decision to take up shares in the company.

In *JEB Fasteners Ltd* v *Marks Bloom & Co.*[11] (*not* a deceit case) the claimants started negotiations to take over a company which had recently started trading in the same products as the claimants. In the course of negotiations, the defendants drew up and showed to claimants the company's accounts, which accounts gave a false picture of the financial health of the company. The claimants decided to take over the company. When the takeover proved unsuccessful the claimants sued the defendants, claiming that they had been induced to take over the company by the misrepresentations as to the company's profitability contained in the company's accounts. The claimants' claim was dismissed. The judge was satisfied that the company's accounts had played *no* part in the claimants' decision to take over the company. Two considerations played a large part in this finding. First, the claimants' main object in taking over the company was to secure the services of the company's two directors. Secondly, the claimants knew before they took over the company that its accounts were unreliable.

Sometimes it is very difficult to know whether a given person was induced to act in a certain way by a representation that was made to him or her. So, for example, suppose Beth bought a car from Vijay. Suppose further that, while Beth was inspecting the car before making up her mind whether or not to buy it, Vijay told Beth that the car had just passed its MOT. Did that representation induce Beth to buy the car? In other words, did that representation play any part in Beth's decision as to whether or not to buy the car? It is very hard to say. To assist them in resolving difficult questions like this, the courts have adopted a principle that if: (1) A made a representation to B with the object of inducing B to do *x*; *and* (2) it would have been reasonable for B to have taken that representation into account in deciding whether or not to do *x*; *and* (3) B did *x* after A made that representation to her; *then* (4) it is presumed that A's representation induced B to do *x*.[12] This principle allows us to presume in the situation just discussed that Beth *was* induced to buy the car from Vijay by Vijay's representation that it had just passed its MOT. Vijay made that representation in order to induce Beth to buy the car; it would have been reasonable for Beth to have taken Vijay's representation into account in deciding whether or not to buy the car; and Beth did buy the car.

(5) *Untrue representations that later come true*. Suppose that A made a representation of fact to B intending to induce B to do *x* and B was induced to do *x* by that representation. Suppose further that A's representation of fact was – to A's knowledge – untrue at the time he made it, but, by the time B came to do *x*, A's representation of fact was no longer untrue. What is

[10] (1884) 9 App Cas 187.
[11] [1983] 1 All ER 583.
[12] *Smith* v *Chadwick* (1884) 9 App Cas 187, 196 per Lord Blackburn: 'if it is proved that the defendants with a view to induce the claimant to enter into a contract made a statement to the claimant of such a nature as would be likely to induce a person to enter into a contract, and it is proved that the claimant did enter into the contract, it is a fair inference of fact that he was induced to do so by the statement.'

the position? The question came up in *Ship* v *Crosskill*.[13] In that case, a company issued a prospectus which said, *inter alia*, that more than half the capital of the company had been subscribed. At the time the prospectus was issued, this was not true. However, by the time the claimant applied for, and was sold, shares in the company, this was true. It was held that the claimant could not bring an action in deceit to recover the money he had paid for shares in the company. At the time he bought the shares in the company, he was not deceived.

(6) *Ambiguous representations*. In *Smith* v *Chadwick*,[14] a company's prospectus claimed that the 'present value of the turnover or output of the entire works is over £1,000,000 per annum'. This was ambiguous: it could have meant that the company's entire works had actually produced £1,000,000's worth of produce in one year (which was not true) or it could have meant the company's entire works were capable of producing £1,000,000's worth of produce in one year (which was true). The claimant was induced by this statement to buy shares in the company. He then sued the directors of the company in deceit, seeking to recover the money he had paid for the shares.

To succeed in his claim the claimant would have had to show: (1) that he understood the statement in the company's prospectus to mean that the company's entire works had actually produced £1,000,000's worth of produce in one year;[15] (2) that – by saying that the company's turnover was over £1,000,000 per annum – the directors intended to encourage people to think that the company's entire works had actually produced £1,000,000's worth of produce in one year; (3) the directors did not honestly believe that the company's entire works had actually produced £1,000,000's worth of produce in one year;[16] and (4) the directors intended, by encouraging people to believe that the company's entire works had actually produced £1,000,000's worth of produce in one year, to induce people to buy shares in the company. As things turned out, the claimant's claim failed: he could not prove that (1) was true.

(7) *Representations later discovered to be untrue*. Suppose that A made a representation of fact to B intending to induce B to do *x*, and B was induced to do *x* by that representation. Suppose further that at the time A made that representation, he honestly believed that it was true but before B did *x*, A discovered that his representation was untrue. What is the position?

The law, as it stands now, seems to say that if A did not warn B in time that his representation was untrue, then A committed the tort of deceit.[17] So, it will be recalled, in *East* v *Maurer*[18] the defendant assured the claimants – who were interested in buying one of his hairdressing salons – that he did not intend to work regularly at his other salon. This assurance induced the claimants to buy the defendant's salon, just as the defendant intended. The defendant was held to have committed the tort of deceit – at the time he gave the assurance he had every intention of working regularly at his other salon. The result would have been the same if the defendant had been telling the truth when he assured the claimants

[13] (1870) LR 10 Eq 73.

[14] (1884) 9 App Cas 187.

[15] The claimant's claim could not have succeeded if he had understood the statement in the company's prospectus to mean that the company's entire works were capable of producing £1,000,000's worth of produce in one year because, in that case, the claimant would not have been deceived when he bought shares in the company – just like the claimant in *Ship* v *Crosskill*.

[16] *Akerhielm* v *De Mare* [1959] AC 789, 805.

[17] *Brownlie* v *Campbell* (1880) 5 App Cas 925; *Briess* v *Woolley* [1954] AC 333.

[18] [1991] 1 WLR 461.

that he did not intend to work regularly at his other salon, but before the sale went through, he – without telling the claimants – changed his mind and decided that he would after all work regularly at his other salon.

MALICIOUS FALSEHOOD

As a general rule, A will commit the tort of malicious (or injurious) falsehood in relation to B if he maliciously makes a false statement to C that refers to B or B's property and B suffers loss as a result.

The term 'maliciously' needs some explanation. A will have acted maliciously in making a false statement to C if: (1) he knew the statement was untrue when he made it; *or* (2) he did not care whether or not the statement was true when he made it; *or* (3) he made that statement for some dishonest or improper reason.[19]

A couple of examples of this tort being committed can be given from the case law. In *Ratcliffe* v *Evans*,[20] the *County Herald*, a Welsh newspaper, incorrectly said that the claimant had ceased to trade as an engineer and boilermaker and that the claimant's firm had ceased to trade. As a result the claimant experienced a loss of business. He was held entitled to sue the *County Herald* on the ground that it had committed the tort of malicious falsehood. The *County Herald* had not acted in good faith in publishing its story about the claimant and the claimant had suffered loss as a result of its publication.

In *Khodaparast* v *Shad*,[21] the claimant was an Iranian woman who worked in an Iranian community school. She had an affair with the defendant and when she brought it to an end, the defendant sought to take some revenge by circulating photocopies of pages from pornographic magazines which appeared to contain photographs of the claimant advertising telephone sex services. In fact the claimant had nothing to do with telephone sex services; the defendant's photocopies were made by photocopying pages from pornographic magazines on which he had artfully superimposed revealing pictures of the claimant that he had taken during their affair. As a result of the defendant's circulating these photocopies, the claimant was dismissed from her job. The claimant successfully sued the defendant for committing the tort of malicious falsehood – the defendant had, through his photocopies, maliciously misled people into thinking that the claimant was involved in telephone sex services and the claimant had suffered loss as a result.[22]

Four points can be made about the tort of malicious falsehood:

(1) *Malicious falsehood and privacy*. In *Kaye* v *Robertson*,[23] Gorden Kaye, the well-known comic actor, was recovering in hospital from being hit on the head by a piece of wood during a big storm in 1990. Representatives of the *Sunday Sport* gained access to his room and conducted an interview with him, which interview the *Sunday Sport* proposed to publish in its next edition. Kaye's injuries were such that he was in no condition to grant an interview – Kaye had no recollection of talking to the *Sunday Sport*'s representatives 15 minutes after the interview ended – and he sought an injunction preventing the *Sunday*

[19] *Dunlop* v *Maison Talbot* (1904) 20 TLR 579.
[20] [1892] 2 QB 524.
[21] [2000] 1 WLR 618.
[22] The House of Lords refused leave to appeal: [2001] 1 WLR 126.
[23] [1991] FSR 62.

Sport from publishing the interview, claiming, *inter alia*, that the *Sunday Sport* would commit the tort of malicious falsehood if it published the interview. The Court of Appeal agreed and granted the injunction.

The Court of Appeal's reasoning was that in publishing the interview the *Sunday Sport* would implicitly represent that Kaye had chosen to give an 'exclusive' interview to the *Sunday Sport*; this was not true and the *Sunday Sport* knew that this was not true; and Kaye would suffer loss as a result of the *Sunday Sport*'s representation because other newspapers would be inclined to pay Kaye less for an interview with him about his accident if the *Sunday Sport* had already published an 'exclusive' interview with him on the same topic. So if the *Sunday Sport* published its interview with Kaye it would make a statement to its readers which it knew was untrue and Kaye would suffer loss as a result. The reasoning is a little strained and probably the true explanation of the case is that the Court of Appeal wanted to prevent the *Sunday Sport* from invading Kaye's privacy by publishing its interview with him and its finding that the *Sunday Sport* would commit the tort of malicious falsehood if it went ahead and published its interview was simply a means of giving it a legal basis for restraining the *Sunday Sport* from invading Kaye's privacy.

(2) *The difference between malicious falsehood and defamation.* The case of *Ratcliffe* v *Evans* illustrates one difference between the torts of libel and slander and the tort of malicious falsehood. A cannot commit either the tort of libel or the tort of slander by making a false statement to C that refers to B unless that statement is defamatory of B. In contrast, A *may* commit the tort of malicious falsehood by making a false statement to C that refers to B even if that statement is not defamatory of B. The statement in *Ratcliffe* v *Evans* was not defamatory of the claimant – right-thinking people would not think less well of the claimant on hearing that he had closed down his business – but that did not prevent a finding that the defendant had committed the tort of malicious falsehood in making that statement.

There are two other differences between the torts of libel and slander and the tort of malicious falsehood. First, to bring an action for malicious falsehood, you have to prove that the statement you are complaining of was untrue; to bring an action in defamation, all you need do is prove that the statement you are complaining of was defamatory – it is for the defendant to prove that it was true. Secondly, to bring an action for malicious falsehood, you have to prove that the defendant acted maliciously in making the statement which you are complaining about; in an action for libel or slander, you will not normally need to show that the defendant acted maliciously to succeed in your claim.

Of course, it is possible that you may be able to sue someone for malicious falsehood and defamation at the same time. This will be the case if a defendant maliciously published a false and defamatory statement about you to someone else and you suffered loss as a result. In such a case, you will be able to sue either for malicious falsehood or defamation, depending on which way of presenting your action is more advantageous.[24]

(3) *Presumption of loss.* The normal rule in a malicious falsehood case is that the claimant has to prove that the defendant's statement caused her to suffer some kind of loss. However, s 3(1) of the Defamation Act 1952 qualifies this rule. It provides that, 'In an action for malicious falsehood, it shall not be necessary to allege or prove . . . damage – (a) if the words

[24] *Joyce* v *Sengupta* [1993] 1 WLR 337.

upon which the action is founded are calculated to cause pecuniary damage to the claimant and are published in writing or other permanent form; or (b) if the said words are calculated to cause pecuniary damage to the claimant in respect of any office, profession, calling, trade or business held or carried on by him at the time of the publication.'

(4) *An exception to the rule*. There is one well-established exception to the rule that A will commit the tort of malicious falsehood if he maliciously makes a false statement to C that refers to B and B suffers some kind of loss as a result.

If Carl is a trader and he lures some business away from his rivals by making the groundless boast that his goods are superior to those of his rivals, he will *not* commit the tort of malicious falsehood. This is so even though Carl's boast refers to his rivals' goods, is unjustified, made maliciously and results in damage to his rivals' business. Why does Carl's conduct in this case not amount to a tort? The reason for this is as follows.

Suppose the law *did* say that a trader in the marketplace will owe his rivals a common law duty not to cause them loss by maliciously representing that their goods are inferior to his when they are not; in other words, suppose the law *did* say that a trader in the marketplace *will* commit the tort of malicious falsehood if he causes his rivals to lose business by maliciously boasting that his goods are superior to those of his rivals when they are not. If this *were* the law then if a trader boasted that his goods were superior to his rivals, and his rivals suffered loss as a result, the rivals would have grounds to sue the trader and the courts would be given the unenviable task of deciding whether or not the trader's goods *were* superior to those of his rivals – a question which would often be too difficult or too controversial for the courts to resolve.[25]

However, Carl *will* commit the tort of malicious falsehood if he lures some customers away from Lara, one of his rivals, by maliciously alleging that Lara's product suffers from defects *x*, *y* and *z* when it does not.[26] In taking this stand the law does not impose an impossible burden on the courts. If a trader lures business away from one of his rivals by alleging that the rival's product suffers from defects *x*, *y* and *z*, and the rival chooses to sue the trader for malicious falsehood, the courts should have no problem determining whether or not the trader's allegations were justified.

PASSING OFF

It is probably impossible to supply a general definition of when someone will commit the tort of passing off.[27] Two main forms of the tort can be identified.

[25] See the remarks of Lord Herschell LC in *White* v *Mellin* [1895] AC 154, 164–5: 'My Lords, I cannot help saying that I entertain very grave doubts whether any action could be maintained for an alleged disparagement of another's goods, merely on the allegation that the goods sold by the party who is alleged to have disparaged his competitor's goods are better either generally or in this or that particular respect than his competitors' are . . . I think it is impossible not to see that . . . a very wide door indeed would be opened to litigation, and that the Courts might be constantly employed in trying the relative merits of rival productions, if an action of this kind were allowed.'

[26] *De Beers Abrasive Products Ltd* v *International General Electric Co. of New York* [1975] 1 WLR 972.

[27] Characteristically, Lord Diplock attempted a general definition in *Erven Warnink Besloten Vennootschap* v *J Townend & Sons (Hull) Ltd* [1979] AC 731, 742D–E. For criticisms of the definition see McBride & Bagshaw 2001, at 385–6; also *Consorzio del Prosciutto di Parma* v *Marks & Spencer plc* [1991] RPC 351, at 368 (per Nourse LJ); and Carty 2001, 180. Lord Diplock himself admitted that his general definition did not quite cover all the situations that might give rise to an action for passing off: [1979] AC 731, 742F.

(1) *Appropriation of goodwill*. The first form of the tort is committed if A *appropriates* the *goodwill* attached to B's name or business when he was not entitled to do so. What is 'goodwill'? Lord Macnaghten supplied a definition in *Inland Revenue Commissioners* v *Muller & Co.'s Margarine Ltd*, observing that goodwill 'is a thing very easy to describe, very difficult to define. It is the benefit and advantage of the good name, reputation, and connection of a business. It is the attractive force which brings in custom.'[28]

So A will commit this form of the tort if he markets his goods or services in such a way as to create a substantial risk that people will purchase those goods or services in the belief that they are B's goods or services.[29] If he does this he will mislead people into thinking that his goods or services are supplied by B and in so doing appropriate the goodwill attached to B's name or business.[30] This is what happened in *Reddaway* v *Banham*.[31] The claimant had for some years made belting and sold it as 'Camel Hair Belting'. As a result, the name 'Camel Hair Belting' was used in the trade to refer to the belts manufactured by the claimant. The defendant began to manufacture belts made of the yarn of camel's hair and stamped the words 'Camel Hair Belting' on them. He was held to have committed the tort of passing off – in stamping 'Camel Hair Belting' on his belts he had created a substantial risk that people would purchase his belts in the belief that they were manufactured by the claimant.

Similarly, in *Reckitt & Colman Products Ltd* v *Borden Inc.*,[32] the House of Lords held that Borden would commit the tort of passing off if it sold its lemon juice in lemon-shaped bottles. Reckitt & Colman had been selling its Jif lemon juice in lemon-shaped bottles for 30 years and as a result consumers tended to think that lemon-shaped bottles contained Jif lemon juice. There was therefore a substantial risk that if Borden sold *its* lemon juice in lemon-shaped bottles, consumers would purchase Borden's lemon juice in the belief that it was Jif lemon juice. Borden could not, it was found, eliminate this risk by labelling its lemon-shaped bottles to make it clear that they did not contain Jif lemon juice; the House of Lords found that, when selecting a lemon juice from a range of bottles of lemon juice on

[28] [1901] AC 217, 223–4. Lord Macnaghten went on to say that goodwill is a form of property (albeit intangible): ibid. If this is right, there is a case for dealing with passing off alongside other torts involving an interference with property such as conversion, trespass to goods, trespass to land and private nuisance. However, we have chosen for the time being to continue to deal with passing off as a 'deception' tort.

[29] See, in addition to the cases cited in the text, *Parker-Knoll Ltd* v *Knoll International Ltd* [1962] RPC 265 (held it would be passing off to market furniture under the name 'Knoll International' because doing so would create a substantial risk that people would purchase that furniture in the belief that it was marketed by Parker-Knoll); *Norman Kark Publications Ltd* v *Odhams Press* [1962] 1 WLR 380 (held the defendants would not commit the tort of passing off in relation to the claimants – the publishers of a magazine called *Today* – if they published a magazine called *Today, the New John Bull*; there was no substantial risk that people would be confused into purchasing the defendants' magazine in the mistaken belief that it was the claimants'); *Alain Bernardin et Compagnie* v *Pavilion Properties Ltd* [1967] RPC 581 (held the defendants did not commit the tort of passing off in relation to the claimants when they opened a nightclub in London called 'The Crazy Horse Saloon'; while the claimants ran an identically named nightclub in Paris, the Paris nightclub was not so well known that people in London were liable to go the defendants' nightclub in London in the mistaken belief that it was run by the claimants).

[30] Note that it is essential to show that A appropriated the goodwill specifically attached to B's name or business. If B has spotted a gap in the market and moved to fill it, A will do nothing wrong if he copies B's example and attempts to corner that part of the market himself: while it is wrong for A to appropriate the goodwill that is specifically attached to B's products, there is nothing wrong in A's borrowing B's good ideas. See, on this, *Cadbury Schweppes Pty Ltd* v *Pub Squash Co. Pty Ltd* [1981] RPC 429 (held, no tort committed by defendant who marketed a sports drink aimed at the same kind of consumer as the claimant's sports drink); also Cane 1996, 80–1.

[31] [1896] AC 199.

[32] [1990] 1 WLR 491.

sale in a supermarket, shoppers tended not to look at the labels on the bottles of lemon juice in making their choice. So Borden's labelling its lemon-shaped bottles to make it clear that they did not contain Jif lemon juice would not eliminate the risk that shoppers would purchase Borden's lemon juice in the belief that it was Jif lemon juice.

It should be emphasised that this form of the tort may *also* be committed in situations *outside* the one we have just been considering: to establish that A committed this form of the tort it does *not* have to be established that he marketed his goods or services in such a way as to create a substantial risk that his customers would think those goods or services were B's. It merely has to be shown that A appropriated the goodwill attached to B's name or business when he was not entitled to do so.

So it has been held that if A markets his goods or services in such a way as to mislead people into thinking that they are of the *same quality* as B's goods or services, he will commit the tort of passing off[33] – if A markets his goods by making people think that his goods are as good as B's when they are not, A will appropriate the goodwill attached to the products marketed by B when he is not entitled to do so. It has also been held that a charity will commit the tort of passing off if it solicits donations under a name which is liable to make people think that they are donating money to a quite different, and well-established, charity.[34] It has further been held that a radio station committed the tort of passing off when it misled potential advertisers into thinking that Eddie Irvine, the Formula One driver, was a fan of the station, thereby appropriating the goodwill associated with Eddie Irvine's name when it was not entitled to do so.[35]

It should also be noted that this form of the tort can be committed quite innocently.[36] Suppose, for example, Paul opened a video shop in Bristol and decided to call it 'Videodrome' after the famous David Cronenberg film of that name. Suppose further that Karen had already had the same idea and had run for a number of years a well-regarded video shop in London, also called 'Videodrome'. In this situation Paul may well have committed the tort of passing off in relation to Karen – and this is so even if Paul had no idea Karen's shop existed and had no intention, in naming his shop 'Videodrome', of appropriating any of the goodwill that had become attached to Karen's shop.

33 See *J Bollinger* v *Costa Brava Wine Co.* [1960] 1 Ch 262 (held that the defendants committed the tort of passing off in relation to the claimant champagne manufacturers when they sold wine made in Spain or from grapes produced in Spain as 'champagne' or as 'Spanish champagne', thereby appropriating the goodwill attached to the claimants' business when they were not entitled to do so – the defendants' wine not being as good as genuine champagne); also *Erven Warnink Besloten Vennootschap* v *J Townend & Sons (Hull) Ltd* [1979] AC 731 (held that it was passing off for the defendants to manufacture a mixture of dried egg powder and Cyprus sherry under the name 'Keeling's Old English Advocaat'; if the defendants marketed their product under this name, they would appropriate the goodwill attached to genuine advocaat when they were not entitled to do so – genuine advocaat, which is made out of brandy, egg yolks and sugar, being far superior to the defendants' product).

34 See *British Diabetic Association* v *Diabetic Society Ltd* [1995] 4 All ER 812 (held that it would be passing off for a charity to solicit contributions under the name 'The Diabetic Society' because there was a substantial risk that people would make donations to the charity in the belief that they were donating money to the quite distinct British Diabetic Association).

35 *Irvine* v *Talksport Ltd* [2002] 1 WLR 2355.

36 It used to be a matter of debate whether someone who innocently committed the tort of passing off could be held liable to pay anything more than nominal damages to the victim of his tort, with the House of Lords reserving its position on the issue in *Marengo* v *Daily Sketch and Sunday Graphic* (1948) 65 RPC 242. However, in *Gillette UK Ltd* v *Edenwest Ltd* [1994] RPC 279, Blackburne J held that no special rule existed for defendants who innocently committed the tort of passing off: they would be held liable to pay damages to the victims of their torts in the same way as any other tortfeasors. See, on this, Carty 2001, 211–12.

(2) *Endangering goodwill.* The second form of the tort of passing off is committed if A markets his goods or services in such a way as to create a danger that the goodwill attached to B's name or business will be unjustifiably damaged.

This is what happened in *Associated Newspaper plc* v *Insert Media Ltd.*[37] In that case, the defendant inserted advertising material into the claimant's newspapers without the claimant's consent. The Court of Appeal held that the defendant, in so acting, had committed the tort of passing off. There was a substantial risk that people would think that the defendant's advertising material was inserted with the claimant's consent. There was therefore a substantial risk that people would associate the defendant's advertising material with the claimant and would hold it against the claimant if the advertising material proved to be dishonest or inaccurate.

Similarly, in *Mirage Studios* v *Counter-Feat Clothing Company Ltd*,[38] the claimants were owners in copyright of the Teenage Mutant Ninja Turtles. A major part of the claimants' income came from licensing other people to use images of the Teenage Mutant Ninja Turtles on products manufactured by those people. The defendants sought to cash in on the craze for the Teenage Mutant Ninja Turtles by drawing pictures of humanoid turtles and licensing various garment manufacturers to use those pictures on T-shirts and jogging clothes. It was held that the defendants had committed the tort of passing off in so acting. There was a substantial risk that people would mistake the defendants' drawings for images of the Teenage Mutant Ninja Turtles and would think that the claimants – the owners of the Teenage Mutant Ninja Turtle image – had licensed the use of those drawings on the items of clothing on which they appeared. There was therefore a substantial risk that people would associate the claimants with the items of clothing on which the defendants' drawings appeared and would therefore hold it against the claimants if those items of clothing proved to be of poor quality.

Again, in *Clark* v *Associated Newspapers Ltd*,[39] the *Evening Standard* was held to have committed the tort of passing off when it published a weekly column called 'The Secret Diary of Alan Clark MP'. The column was written in the same manner as Alan Clark's published diaries and amounted to a witty and exaggerated weekly fantasy as to what Alan Clark might have written in his diary that week. Although it was made clear that the diary entries were written by Peter Bradshaw, an *Evening Standard* journalist, it was held that there was a substantial risk that people would think that the diary entries were written by Alan Clark and that people would think less well of Alan Clark as a result.

Visit **http://www.mylawchamber.co.uk/mcbride** to access updates on recent cases, as well as model answers and tips for answering tort problem questions.

[37] [1991] 1 WLR 571.
[38] [1991] FSR 145.
[39] [1998] 1 WLR 1559.

D.

Other torts

24 Torts involving the misuse of power

INTRODUCTION

The torts gathered together in this chapter owe their existence to the fact that if A possesses power over B, A will *sometimes* owe B a tortious duty not to misuse that power. Such duties are in fact very rare.

The reason for this is that when we had separate Courts of Law and Courts of Equity, the Courts of Law were traditionally loath to interfere with the exercise of private powers, for the same reasons that the House of Lords ruled in *Allen* v *Flood* that intentionally harming someone else did not of and in itself amount to a tort unless unlawful means were used to inflict the harm. To take any other position would, in the view of the Courts of Law, unacceptably interfere with individual liberty, and create too much uncertainty over whether a given use of private power counted as a misuse. As a result, it was left up to the Courts of Equity to take steps to control the use of private powers. So, for example, if A gave Blackacre to B, making it clear that he expected B to use Blackacre for C's benefit, the Courts of Law regarded B – as the legal owner of Blackacre – as being free to do what he liked with the land. It was left up to the Courts of Equity to stop B misusing A's gift by imposing equitable duties on B to use the land for C's benefit. So if B used Blackacre for his own benefit, he would commit an equitable wrong, not a tort.

Having said that, the courts have been more willing to impose tortious duties on the holders of *public powers*, requiring them not to misuse those powers knowingly or maliciously.[1] Thus the torts of *malicious prosecution*, and *misfeasance in public office*, which are the subject of this chapter.

MALICIOUS PROSECUTION

Elements of the tort

A will have committed the tort of malicious prosecution in relation to B if:

(1) A prosecuted B for committing a criminal offence; *and*
(2) the prosecution ended in B's favour;[2] *and*
(3) A had no reasonable and probable cause to prosecute B for that offence; *and*
(4) A acted maliciously in prosecuting B for committing that offence.[3]

[1] For a discussion of whether the duty not to misuse public powers should be set at the level of a duty *to take care* not to misuse one's powers, rather than a duty not to misuse one's powers *knowingly or maliciously*, see above, pp. 205–8, 214–19.

[2] That is, B was not found guilty of committing that offence or B was found guilty of committing that offence but her conviction was subsequently reversed.

[3] For a general discussion of the tort, see Fridman 1963.

Four points should be made about this tort:

Prosecution

In order to show that A has committed the tort of malicious prosecution in relation to B, it is first necessary to show that A prosecuted B for committing a criminal offence. This requirement will obviously be satisfied if A is a private citizen and brings a private prosecution against B for committing an offence. Similarly, if A works for the Crown Prosecution Service and in that capacity prosecutes B for committing an offence.

Outside these simple cases, the House of Lords has made it clear that A will be held to have prosecuted B for committing a criminal offence if he was *directly responsible* for B's being prosecuted for committing that offence.[4] So, for example, suppose that A supplied information to the police which indicated that B had committed some offence and B was subsequently prosecuted for that offence. When will A be held to have prosecuted B for committing that offence? The Court of Appeal's decision in *Mahon* v *Rahn (No. 2)* makes it clear that A will only be held to have prosecuted B in this situation if: (1) A supplied his information to the police with the intention of persuading the police to prosecute B; *and* (2) the facts of B's case were such that it was impossible for the police to exercise any independent judgment as to whether or not B should be prosecuted for theft.[5]

Both these requirements were satisfied in *Martin* v *Watson*.[6] In that case, the defendant complained that the claimant had indecently exposed himself to her. The claimant was charged with committing the offence of indecent exposure but, when the case came to trial, no evidence was offered against the claimant; the defendant had declined to give evidence. The claimant was cleared and sued the defendant, claiming she had committed the tort of malicious prosecution. The House of Lords agreed. It held that the defendant was directly responsible for the claimant's being prosecuted for committing that offence. She had claimed that the claimant had committed the offence of indecent exposure with the intention of persuading the police to prosecute the claimant and only the defendant could know whether or not the claimant had committed that offence. As a result, it was virtually impossible for the police officers who charged the claimant to exercise their own judgment as to whether or not the claimant had committed the offence. Given this, it was fair to say that the defendant was responsible for the claimant's being prosecuted.

Termination of prosecution in claimant's favour

The courts will refuse to say that A committed the tort of malicious prosecution in prosecuting B for committing a particular criminal offence if B was found guilty of committing that offence and her conviction has not yet been reversed. This is to stop B from reopening the question of whether or not her conviction was valid by bringing an action for malicious prosecution against A.[7]

[4] *Martin* v *Watson* [1996] 1 AC 74.

[5] [2000] 1 WLR 2150, at [269].

[6] [1996] 1 AC 74.

[7] As a general rule, if B claims that A has committed a tort in relation to her by acting in some way, B will be barred from suing A for damages if her doing so would bring into question the correctness of an earlier judicial decision: see below, pp. 506–8.

In *Basébé* v *Matthews*,[8] the defendant claimed that the claimant assaulted her. He was found guilty and was fined 40s. He had no right to appeal against the decision and so when he sued the defendant for malicious prosecution – claiming that the defendant's claims had been false and made maliciously – his conviction had not been reversed. The Court of Appeal refused to find that the defendant committed the tort of malicious prosecution. Byles J remarked: 'there is [no] doubt that the criminal proceeding must be determined in favour of the accused before he can maintain an action for malicious prosecution. If this were not so, almost every case would have to be tried over again upon its merits ... [I]t makes no difference that the party convicted has no power of appealing.'[9]

Reasonable and probable cause

If A prosecuted B for committing a particular criminal offence he will not have had reasonable and probable cause to prosecute B for committing that offence if: (1) A did not think, in prosecuting B, that B probably committed that offence; *or* (2) A thought that B probably committed the offence for which he prosecuted B, but it was unreasonable for him to think this, given the evidence available to him at the time he prosecuted B.

It used to be thought that A would, in prosecuting B for committing a criminal offence, not have reasonable and probable cause to prosecute B if he did not think that B was guilty of committing that offence. So if A, in prosecuting B, lacked an honest belief in B's guilt, he would not have reasonable and probable cause to prosecute B.[10] However, we would submit, this is not the law. As Lord Denning observed in *Glinski* v *McIver*: 'in order to have reasonable and probable cause a man who brings a prosecution, be he a police officer or a private individual [need not] believe in the *guilt* of the accused ... [I]n truth he has only to be satisfied that there is a proper case to lay before the court.'[11] In an earlier case, Denning LJ, as he was then, remarked: 'There are many justifiable prosecutions where the prosecutor has not himself formed any concluded belief as to the guilt of the accused. If he is a very fair-minded man he may well say to himself "The case is so black against the man that I feel I must prosecute, but I am not going to believe him to be guilty unless the court finds him to be so." Such a man would, I should have thought, have reasonable and probable cause for instituting a prosecution even though he did not affirmatively believe the man to be guilty.'[12] The law is as we have stated it: If A prosecutes B for committing a particular criminal offence, A will not have reasonable and probable cause to prosecute B for committing that offence if he does *not* think, in prosecuting B, that B is *probably* guilty of that offence. So if A prosecutes B for committing a particular offence while thinking at the time that B is probably innocent of that offence, A will lack reasonable and probable cause to prosecute B for committing that offence.[13]

Even if A did think, when he prosecuted B for committing a particular criminal offence, that B was probably guilty of committing that offence, A will have lacked reasonable and

[8] (1867) LR 2 CP 684.

[9] Ibid., 687.

[10] *Hicks* v *Faulkner* (1878) 8 QBD 167, 171 (*per* Hawkins J), approved in *Herniman* v *Smith* [1938] AC 305.

[11] [1962] AC 726, 758.

[12] *Tempest* v *Snowden* [1952] 1 KB 130, 139.

[13] See Lindley J in *Shrosbery* v *Osmaston* (1877) 37 LT 792, 794: 'if a man believes that another is not guilty of a criminal charge, and prosecuted unsuccessfully, I confess I have the greatest difficulty in seeing that such a man can be held to have reasonable and probable cause for prosecuting.'

probable cause to prosecute B for committing that offence if A's view that B was probably guilty of committing that offence was, on the evidence available to him, an unreasonable one to take: 'there must [have been] cause (that is, sufficient grounds . . .) for thinking that [B] was probably guilty of the offence imputed.'[14] Whether or not A's view that B was probably guilty of committing the offence for which A prosecuted B was reasonable or not is judged by reference to the evidence available to him at the time of the prosecution – it does not matter if some of the evidence was flawed or incorrect: '[A must] be judged not on the real facts but on those which he honestly, and however erroneously, [believed]; if he [acted] honestly upon fiction, he can claim to be judged on that.'[15]

In *Hicks* v *Faulkner*,[16] the defendant sued one of his tenants for rent due under the lease. The claimant, the tenant's son, swore that before the rent became due the tenant had given up the lease by surrendering to the defendant the key to the premises let by the defendant to the tenant. The defendant did not remember this happening and charged the claimant with perjury. The claimant was acquitted of having committed this offence and he sued the defendant, claiming that the defendant had committed the tort of malicious prosecution. The claimant's claim failed; the court held that the defendant had had reasonable and probable cause to prosecute the claimant for perjury. The reason was that it had been reasonable for the defendant to think, given the state of his memory, that the claimant had perjured himself: '[i]f a man has never seen reason to doubt, but on the contrary, has ever had reason to trust, the general accuracy of his memory, and that memory presents to him a vivid apparent recollection that a particular occurrence took place in his presence within a recent period of time, is it not reasonable to believe in the existence of it?'[17] So it would have been different if, to the defendant's knowledge, his memory was generally faulty and unreliable: in such a case it would not have been reasonable for him to believe, on the basis of his memory of things, that the claimant had probably committed the offence of perjury.

In *Dawson* v *Vansandau*,[18] the defendant prosecuted the claimant on a charge of conspiring to defraud his creditors on the basis of a statement made to him by B, one of the parties to the alleged conspiracy. When the claimant was acquitted of the charge he sued the claimant for malicious prosecution. The claimant won his claim at first instance but the verdict was annulled on the basis that it might have been reasonable for the defendant to have thought – on the basis of B's statement – that the claimant had probably conspired to

[14] *Glinski* v *McIver* [1962] AC 726, 766 (per Lord Devlin). So it is enough for A – to establish that he had reasonable and probable cause to prosecute B for committing a particular offence – to show that he thought and that it was reasonable to think, on the basis of the evidence available to him, that B probably did commit that offence. Of course, for B to be convicted of committing that offence it has to be shown *beyond a reasonable doubt* that B committed that offence. This means that A might have had reasonable and probable cause to prosecute B for committing a particular offence even if the evidence available to him at the time he prosecuted B was not enough to secure a conviction. This would be the case where the evidence available to A at the time he prosecuted B was such that it would convince a reasonable man that B *probably* committed the offence for which A prosecuted him but not such that it would convince a reasonable man that B *definitely* committed that offence. See *Dawson* v *Vansandau* (1863) 11 WR 516, 518: '[There may be] evidence sufficient to make out a *prima facie* case, and warrant the preferring of a criminal charge, though it might not be sufficient evidence upon which to convict.'

[15] *Glinski* v *McIver* [1962] AC 726, 776 (per Lord Devlin).

[16] (1878) 8 QBD 167.

[17] Ibid., 172–3.

[18] (1863) 11 WR 516.

defraud his creditors: '[a]n accomplice, or a tainted witness, may give evidence sufficient to make out a *prima facie* case, and warrant the preferring of a criminal charge.'[19]

In *Abbott* v *Refuge Assurance Co. Ltd*,[20] the claimant took out an endowment policy with the defendants for his wife. A few years later, the defendants were tricked into handing over the surrender value of the policy (£2,415) to the claimant's secretary, who impersonated the claimant's wife and led the defendants to believe that she wanted to surrender the policy in return for its surrender value. The claimant's secretary confessed to what she had done and implicated the claimant in the plot. Counsel advised the defendants that the secretary's statement was sufficient evidence on which to prosecute the claimant. The defendants brought a private prosecution against the claimant for conspiracy to defraud – the Director of Public Prosecutions having declined to prosecute – but the prosecution failed. The claimant sued the defendants for malicious prosecution but his claim failed.

It was held, among other things, that the defendants, having taken the advice of counsel, had had reasonable and probable cause to prosecute the claimant. In the terms advanced here, it had been reasonable for the defendants to believe counsel's advice that the secretary's statement indicated that the claimant probably did conspire to defraud them and therefore it had been reasonable for the defendants to believe, given that advice, that the claimant probably did conspire to defraud them. However, while the opinion of counsel was a 'potent' factor in establishing that the defendants had reasonable and probable cause to prosecute the claimant, it was 'not ... conclusive'.[21] As a matter of common sense, it would not have been reasonable for the defendants to believe counsel's advice if it had been obviously incompetent or based on a desire to please the defendants; nor would it have been reasonable for the defendants to believe counsel's advice that the claimant probably committed the offence of conspiracy to defraud if that advice was based on an incorrect summary of the available evidence.[22] None of those possibilities were actually made out in the *Abbott* case and so the defendants *did* have reasonable and probable cause to prosecute the claimant.

Malice

It seems that A will act maliciously in prosecuting B for committing a criminal offence if his predominant purpose in prosecuting B for committing that offence is *not* to ensure that justice is done to B.[23]

So if A had no reasonable and probable cause to prosecute B for a particular criminal offence because, when he prosecuted B, he did not think that B was probably guilty of that offence, it may be inferred that A acted maliciously in prosecuting B for committing that offence. If A did not think that B was probably guilty of committing that offence then A probably did not prosecute B for committing that offence with the primary aim of ensuring

[19] Ibid., 518.
[20] [1962] 1 QB 432.
[21] Ibid., 450 (per Ormerod LJ).
[22] *Malz* v *Rosen* [1966] 1 WLR 1008.
[23] See Alderson B's observation in *Stevens* v *Midland Counties Railway* (1854) 10 Ex 352, 356; 156 ER 480, 482: 'Any motive other than that of simply instituting a prosecution for the simple purpose of bringing a person to justice, is a malicious motive on the part of the person who acts in that way.'

that justice would be done to B.[24] (Note that the reverse is not true: 'even from the most express malice, want of probable cause ... is not to be inferred.'[25] Even if A's primary aim in prosecuting B was not to ensure that justice would be done to B, A could still believe – and it could be reasonable for A to believe – that B probably committed that offence.)

It was suggsted in *Glinski* v *McIver* that the police prosecuted the claimant for conspiracy to defraud not 'in order to bring him to justice for that offence, but ... [in order] to punish the claimant for having a week before given evidence, which the police believed then to have been perjured, for the defence in the case of *Reg* v *Comer*'.[26] On another reading of the facts in *Glinski* v *McIver*, the police prosecuted the claimant in order to induce him to admit that he had perjured himself in the *Comer* case the week before. Even on this reading, the police acted maliciously in prosecuting the claimant: their object in prosecuting the claimant was not to ensure that justice was done to the claimant – if the claimant had admitted his perjury, they would have dropped the prosecution.

In *Heslop* v *Chapman*[27] it was alleged that the reason Heslop charged Chapman with perjury was to stop Chapman giving evidence for another person also indicted for perjury at Heslop's suggestion. If this were true then Heslop, we would submit, acted maliciously in prosecuting Chapman for perjury; Heslop's object in prosecuting Chapman would not have been to ensure that justice was done to Chapman: Heslop would not have cared whether or not Chapman was actually guilty of perjury but would only have prosecuted him to prevent him from acting contrary to Heslop's interests in another case.

It should be noted that even if A does not prosecute B with the predominant aim of ensuring that justice is done to B, A may still not act maliciously in prosecuting B if he is only prosecuting B because the law requires him to do so. In *Abbott* v *Refuge Assurance Co. Ltd*, the defendants prosecuted the claimant for conspiracy to defraud because it was a rule at the time that if A's property had been taken from him as a result of B's committing a felony, then before A could sue B to recover the value of his property from B, he had to prosecute B first for committing that felony. So the defendants prosecuted the claimant for conspiracy to defraud so as to put themselves in a position to launch civil proceedings against the claimant to recover the value of the money they lost as a result of the fraud practised on them. The Court of Appeal held that the defendants had not acted maliciously in prosecuting the claimant for this reason.[28] The Court of Appeal reasoned that while the defendants' predominant aim in prosecuting the claimant was to get their money back, they only prosecuted the claimant because the law made their doing so a precondition of

[24] This might not always be true. Suppose Vijay is suspected of murdering Carl. Vijay, in his defence, claims that Carl committed suicide. Sarah, the prosecutor in charge of the case, thinks – on the basis of Vijay's demeanour and history – that Vijay probably did not murder Carl. Nevertheless she acknowledges she might be wrong and decides to put Vijay on trial for Carl's murder in order to allow a jury to sort out the issue of Vijay's guilt. The jury acquit Vijay and Vijay sues Sarah for malicious prosecution. Sarah will have lacked reasonable and probable cause to prosecute Vijay by virtue of the fact that she thought that Vijay probably did not murder Carl. However, it is impossible to say that Sarah acted maliciously in prosecuting Vijay in this case. Sarah, in prosecuting Vijay, was actuated by a desire to see that justice was done to Vijay – to see that Vijay would be punished if he were (contrary to Sarah's belief) actually guilty of murdering Carl.

[25] *Glinski* v *McIver* [1962] AC 726, 744 (per Viscount Simonds).

[26] [1962] AC 726, 766 (per Lord Devlin).

[27] (1853) 23 LJ QB 49.

[28] [1962] 1 QB 432, 452–3, 461–2, 469.

their getting their money back from the claimant, and the defendants could not have acted maliciously in simply doing what the law required them to do.

Torts analogous to the tort of malicious prosecution

It seems well established that:

(1) *Arrest warrant.* A will commit a tort if he maliciously and without reasonable and probable cause procures the issue of a warrant for B's arrest.[29]

(2) *Search warrant.* A will commit a tort if he maliciously and without reasonable and probable cause procures the issue of a search warrant authorising the police to search B's premises.[30]

(3) *Liquidation proceedings.* A will commit a tort if he maliciously and without reasonable and probable cause starts liquidation proceedings against a trading company or bankruptcy proceedings against an individual.[31]

(4) *Disciplinary proceedings.* There is no tort of maliciously and without reasonable and probable cause instituting disciplinary proceedings against someone else. So if A maliciously and without reasonable cause institutes disciplinary proceedings against B and does not in doing so commit one of the torts mentioned in this book, he will not commit a tort.[32]

(5) *Civil proceedings.* There is no tort of maliciously and without reasonable and probable cause bringing a civil action against someone else. So if A maliciously and without reasonable cause brings a civil action against B and does not in doing so commit one of the torts mentioned in this book, he will not commit a tort.[33]

Does this make sense? Why will the law protect B from having arrest warrants issued against her for no good reason or from her being subject to unwarranted bankruptcy proceedings while it does not take any special steps to ensure that B is not subjected to groundless disciplinary proceedings or to ensure that B is not the victim of unjustified civil suits? The traditional explanation for the distinctions drawn by the law in this area is that the law in this area is designed to prevent people suffering three kinds of harm: damage to their reputation, damage to their person and damage to their property (or wallet).[34] So where B is liable to suffer one of these kinds of harm as a result of proceedings being taken against her, A will owe B a tortious duty to ensure that he does not maliciously start such proceedings when he has no reasonable and probable cause to do so.

So B's being subject to a criminal prosecution is liable to harm both her reputation and her person (if she might be imprisoned as a result of the prosecution). As a result, the law

[29] *Roy* v *Prior* [1971] AC 470.

[30] *Reynolds* v *Commissioner of Police of the Metropolis* [1984] 3 All ER 649.

[31] *Quartz Hill Consolidated Gold Mining Co.* v *Eyre* (1863) 11 QBD 674.

[32] *Gregory* v *Portsmouth City Council* [2000] AC 419, 432.

[33] *Metall und Rohstoff AG* v *Donaldson Lufkin & Jenrette Inc.* [1990] 1 QB 391, 471H–472D; *Gregory* v *Portsmouth City Council* [2000] AC 419, 432–3.

[34] The threefold division of the harms concerned to be prevented by the law in this area goes back to a *dictum* of Holt CJ's in *Savill* v *Roberts* (1698) 12 Mod Rep 208, 88 ER 1267.

protects B from being maliciously prosecuted for committing a criminal offence when there is no reasonable and probable cause to do so. Again, the issue of a warrant for B's arrest or to search B's premises is liable to harm her reputation and – in the case of a warrant for B's arrest – her person. So – again – the law protects B against the malicious procurement of an arrest warrant or search order without reasonable and probable cause. By the same reasoning, because B's being subject to bankruptcy proceedings is liable to damage B's reputation (her credit), the law will protect B against the malicious initiation of bankruptcy proceedings without reasonable and probable cause.

Given this, it is hard to see why the law does *not* protect people against the malicious initiation of disciplinary or civil proceedings without reasonable or probable cause. The bringing of disciplinary proceedings against B is liable to damage her reputation and her income. While being subject to civil litigation is, generally speaking, not liable to damage one's reputation, it *is* liable to injure one's property in the sense that it is liable to cost one a lot of money to defend. This was denied by Bowen LJ in *Quartz Hill Consolidated Gold Mining Co.* v *Eyre* who observed that: '[t]he bringing of [a civil] action does not as a natural or necessary consequence involve any injury to a man's property, for this reason, that the only costs which the law recognises, and for which it will compensate him, are the costs properly involved in the action itself. For those the successful defendant will have been already compensated, so far as the law chooses to compensate him.'[35] However, this is not true. The costs awarded to a successful defendant to a civil action will always be less than the true costs incurred by the defendant in defending that action.

In *Gregory* v *Portsmouth City Council*, the House of Lords expressed some unease at the state of the law in this area but refused to disturb it. It thought the jump from imposing common law duties on people not to start *legal proceedings* maliciously and without reasonable and probable cause to imposing common law duties on people not to start *private disciplinary proceedings* maliciously and without reasonable and probable cause was too large a jump for the law to take.[36] It thought that there was a stronger case for changing the law so as to protect people from being subjected to malicious and groundless civil actions but expressed the hope that other areas of the law such as the law on defamation, conspiracy and malicious falsehood would suffice to protect the interests of people who were subject to malicious civil actions without reasonable and probable cause.[37]

MISFEASANCE IN PUBLIC OFFICE

Public officials have a special capacity to cause harm by abusing their official powers or neglecting their official duties. 'The rationale of the tort [of misfeasance in public office] is that in a legal system based on the rule of law executive or administrative power "may be exercised only for the public good" and not for ulterior and improper purposes.'[38] In many situations a public official who abuses his or her powers will commit one of the other torts discussed in this book. For instance, if a public official physically detains someone when he

[35] (1863) 11 QBD 674, 690.
[36] [2000] AC 419, 431–2.
[37] Ibid., 432–3.
[38] *Three Rivers DC* v *Governor and Company of the Bank of England (No. 3)* [2003] 2 AC 1 (henceforth, *Three Rivers (No. 3)*), 190 (per Lord Steyn, quoting Nourse LJ in *Jones* v *Swansea CC* [1990] 1 WLR 54, 85F).

has no lawful authority to do so, he will commit the tort of false imprisonment. Similarly, a public official will commit the tort of conversion if she seizes someone else's property when she has no lawful authority to do so. But in some situations an abuse of power by a public official will not fall within the ambit of any other tort. This will be the case, for example, if a public official refuses to grant a licence to someone when such a licence would normally have been granted,[39] or orders someone not to carry out a profitable activity when such an order should not have been given, or neglects his or her official duties.[40] The tort of misfeasance in public office is normally the only tort which could have been committed in these situations.

Elements of the tort

A, a public official, will commit the tort of misfeasance in public office in relation to B if:

(1) in bad faith he misuses his powers or neglects his duties with the specific intention of injuring B *and* B suffers material damage; *or*
(2) in bad faith he acts in a way that he knows is beyond his powers or is inconsistent with his duties and he knows that his acting in that way is likely either to injure B or to injure a class of people of which B is a member *and* B suffers material damage.

In the case of *Three Rivers DC* v *Bank of England (No. 3)*[41] the members of the House of Lords expressed different views as to whether (1) and (2), above, amount to two different forms of the tort or not. Lord Steyn suggested that it was 'conducive to clarity to recognise' that (1) and (2) are alternative forms of the tort with a 'unifying element of conduct amounting to an abuse of power accompanied by subjective bad faith'.[42] By contrast, Lord Millett argued that 'the two limbs are merely different ways in which the necessary element of intention is established'.[43] On this question we prefer the view of Lord Steyn because we doubt whether anything properly called intention can be inferred from the proof of (2). We would describe the relationship between the two forms in this way – form (2) is an *extension* of the scope of the tort beyond form (1).

Several elements of the definition are worth further discussion.

[39] Many of the cases on misfeasance in public office involve abuses of licensing powers. For example, *Roncarelli* v *Duplessis* [1959] SCR 121 involved an abuse of the power to grant liquor licences to restaurants, *David* v *Abdul Cader* [1963] 1 WLR 834 involved an abuse of the power to licence cinemas, and *Three Rivers (No. 3)* involved allegations of abuse of the power to license banks. Another group of cases involve alleged abuses of planning powers: see, for example, *Dunlop* v *Woollahra MC* [1982] AC 158 and *Barnard* v *Restormel BC* [1998] 3 PLR 27.

[40] Some of the claims in *Three Rivers (No. 3)* involved allegations that the defendant had deliberately decided not to perform the duties imposed on it by the statutes which made it the regulator of deposit-taking institutions. In *Odhavji Estate* v *Woodhouse* [2003] 3 SCR 263, the Supreme Court of Canada expressly rejected the argument that the tort only covered the abuse of powers. The Court held (at [30]) that the tort should cover both abuse of powers and neglect of duty because they were 'equally inconsistent with the obligation of a public officer not to intentionally injure a member of the public through deliberate and unlawful conduct in the exercise of public functions'.

[41] [2003] 2 AC 1. The House of Lords dealt with the issues raised in two separate sets of speeches that are reported sequentially in [2003] 2 AC. Only the second set of speeches used numbered paragraphs. Thus our references to the first set of speeches use page numbers and our references to the second set use paragraph numbers.

[42] Ibid., 191–2.

[43] Ibid., 235.

Public official

This is defined broadly. Best CJ was of the opinion that 'every one who is appointed to discharge a public duty, and receives a compensation in whatever shape, whether from the Crown or otherwise, is constituted a public officer'.[44] Most cases involve officers who are members of the executive, but the Court of Appeal of New Zealand has held that the tort can also be committed by a judge.[45] Public bodies, such as local councils, can be liable, as well as individual public officials.[46] If A is a public official, he can commit the tort of misfeasance in public office by abusing any of the powers attached to his post. 'It is not the nature of the power which matters. Whatever its nature or origin, the power may be exercised only for the public good. It is the office on which everything depends.'[47] Thus an official who works for a particular public body can commit the tort by abusing the powers which come from the public body being a landlord,[48] or which come from the fact that the body has the capacity to make contracts, and not just by abusing the special statutory and prerogative powers that the public body may have. Indeed, it seems that a public official can also commit the tort by using his or her position to lay claim to powers that he or she does not legally have. In the Australian case of *Northern Territory* v *Mengel*,[49] the defendant public officials committed the tort of misfeasance in public office by asserting a power to stop the Mengels transporting their cattle to market when, in fact, they did not have such a power.

Acts and omissions

Obviously, a public official may commit the tort of misfeasance in public office if he performs a *positive act* that is unlawful, such as issuing an unlawful order. If B wants to claim that A committed the tort of misfeasance in public office by performing some kind of positive act, it will be important for B to identify the act in question since a pivotal issue will be A's state of mind in performing the act in question.[50]

A difficult question is whether the tort also covers situations where a public official *fails to act*, knowing that this is likely to lead to B suffering some kind of harm. Different members of the House of Lords gave different answers to this question in *Three Rivers (No. 3)*, where some of the claims were based on *failure* to revoke a licence.[51] Lord Hobhouse stated that 'If there is a legal duty to act and the decision not to act amounts to an unlawful breach of that legal duty, the omission can amount to misfeasance for the purpose of the

[44] *Henly* v *Mayor of Lyme* (1828) 5 Bing 91, 107, 130 ER 995, 1001. In *Stockwell* v *Society of Lloyd's* [2007] EWCA Civ 930, the Court of Appeal concluded that Lloyds was *not* a public officer for the purposes of the tort.

[45] *Rawlinson* v *Rice* [1998] 1 NZLR 454.

[46] Further, a public body may be held vicariously liable if one of its employees commits the tort of misfeasance in public office: *Racz* v *Home Office* [1994] 2 AC 45. For the rules governing when an employer will be vicariously liable in respect of a tort committed by one of his employees, see below, Chapter 33.

[47] *Jones* v *Swansea CC* [1990] 1 WLR 54, 85F, per Nourse LJ.

[48] As was the case in *Jones* v *Swansea CC* where the claimant alleged that the council had maliciously refused to allow a change of user of premises that she leased from the council.

[49] (1995) 185 CLR 307.

[50] *Calveley* v *Chief Constable of the Merseyside Police* [1989] AC 1228, 1240.

[51] *Three Rivers (No. 3)*, involved claims that the Bank of England, as regulator of deposit-taking institutions, was liable to compensate depositors who lost money on the collapse of the Bank of Credit and Commerce International (BCCI). The claims alleged that the Bank of England had acted unlawfully in licensing BCCI and in not intervening sooner to control its activities.

tort ... What is not covered is a mere failure, oversight or accident.'[52] This answer suggests that two separate conditions must be fulfilled before an omission can amount to misfeasance: there must be (1) a breach of a *legal duty* to act, and (2) a *decision* not to act. Lord Hutton also seemed to support (2) and said that where the claim was based on an omission it 'must be a deliberate one involving an actual decision'.[53] By contrast, Lord Hope stated 'I would reject the argument that proof of conscious decisions to act or not to act is required. In my view the tort extends to a deliberate or wilful failure to take those decisions.'[54]

There can be little doubt that condition (1) is required in a claim based on an omission because the tort of misfeasance requires *unlawful* behaviour and an omission will not be unlawful unless there was a duty to act. It is important to remember, however, that public law insists that where an official has a *power* to act: (*i*) that official will be under a legal *duty* to exercise the power if, in the circumstances, it would be utterly unreasonable[55] not to do so, and (*ii*) that official will be under a legal duty *to consider* whether to use that power or not. Lord Hope's reason for rejecting condition (2) was that he thought it would benefit a defendant who repeatedly procrastinated and refused to make a decision. But it is arguable that such a defendant could be described as having *decided* to breach legal duty (*ii*).[56]

State of mind

The state of mind which it must be proved a public official had at the time of his unlawful act or omission is different for the two forms of the tort. To prove that A has committed form (1) of the tort in relation to B, B must prove that A 'specifically intended' to injure B (or a class of persons of which B was a member) when he misused his powers or neglected his duty. It is probably also necessary to show that A knew that it was not lawful to injure B – otherwise the tort might cover cases where a public official honestly believed that punishing someone else was legally authorised.[57]

Suppose now that B wants to establish that A, in acting beyond his powers or inconsistently with his duties, committed form (2) of the tort of misfeasance in public office. What will B have to prove was A's state of mind when he acted in this way? In addressing this question, it is important to distinguish between what must be shown to have been A's state of mind towards the unlawfulness of his act and what must be shown to have been A's state of mind towards B. As to the first, in the *Three Rivers (No. 3)* case Lord Steyn said that 'only reckless indifference in a subjective sense will be sufficient'.[58] So, at the very least, B will have to 'prove that [A] acted with a state of mind of reckless indifference to the illegality of his

[52] *Three Rivers (No. 3)*, 230. See also 237, per Lord Millett.

[53] Ibid., 228.

[54] Ibid., [69].

[55] Those who have studied administrative law will be familiar with this concept being called '*Wednesbury* unreasonableness', after the case of *Associated Provincial Picture Houses Ltd* v *Wednesbury Corp.* [1948] 1 KB 223.

[56] The House of Lords in *Three Rivers (No. 3)* split 3:2 over whether the claims should be permitted to proceed to trial. The dissentients, Lord Hobhouse, at [172]–[173], and Lord Millett, at [191], regarded the claims based on omissions to revoke the licence as flawed by a failure to establish a legal duty to revoke. Lord Hope was willing to allow the case to proceed on the basis of the general allegation that 'the Bank deliberately ran away from its responsibility as the relevant supervisory authority' (at [68]).

[57] The formulation of the tort in *Three Rivers (No. 3)* does not mention this element, but both forms of the tort require 'bad faith' and in our opinion it is obvious that 'bad faith' requires not just an intention to injure but also knowledge that such injury is not lawful.

[58] Ibid., 193.

act'.[59] This means that B must show that A knew that the act was unlawful, or suspected that the act was unlawful but did not bother to check further because he or she did not care whether it was or not. As to A's state of mind towards B, Lord Steyn said that at the very least B must prove that A acted 'in the knowledge that his act would probably injure [B] or a person of a class of which [B] was a member'.[60] But again, proof of actual knowledge is not necessary and it would be sufficient for B to prove that A suspected that injury to B would probably be caused but did not bother to check further because he or she did not care.

In *Akenzua* v *Secretary of State for the Home Department*[61] the Court of Appeal had to consider whether Lord Steyn's statement that A must know that 'his act would probably injure [B] or a person of a class of which [B] was a member' meant that the tort could not catch a defendant who unlawfully acted in a way which imperilled people indiscriminately. The Court held that it did not matter whether the defendant could contemplate harm to a particular *group of persons* provided that the *way in which the harm was caused* was the same sort of way as the defendant had in contemplation at the time of his unlawful act or omission. Thus if A unlawfully released C knowing him to be an arsonist, A might be liable to B if she was injured by a fire started by C, but not if she was injured by C's negligent driving.

Bad faith

The speeches in *Three Rivers (No. 3)* have not settled the role of 'bad faith' in the context of the tort. Lord Hope suggested that 'bad faith' was *demonstrated* by proof of the relevant state of mind.[62] Thus, for him at least, 'bad faith' was not an *additional* ingredient. By contrast Lord Hutton treated 'bad faith' as requiring an evaluation of the defendant's *motive*.[63] If a bad motive is an additional ingredient then a public official who knowingly acted unlawfully, and knew of the risk of probable harm to the claimant, could nonetheless avoid liability if he acted for the purest of motives, for instance, because he believed that the unlawful behaviour was in the public interest. This has been criticised on the ground that 'there should be no encouragement given to [public officials] to dream up arguments as to why it was a good idea to deliberately choose not to comply [with legislation]'.[64] But Lord Hutton's view seems to give more weight to the function of the tort as being to control *abuse* of the official's position. The official's pure motive clearly cannot make his unlawful behaviour lawful, but we think that it may be sufficient to prevent it from falling within this tort.

Lord Steyn's error?

In *Three Rivers (No. 3)* Lord Steyn stated that 'in both forms of the tort the [state of mind] required *must be directed at the harm complained of*, or at least to harm of the type suffered

[59] Ibid.

[60] Ibid., 196.

[61] [2003] 1 WLR 741. The case involved the allegation that an immigration official had unlawfully arranged for a dangerous person to be released from custody so that he could become a police informer. The claimants were the personal representatives of a person who was subsequently murdered by the dangerous person.

[62] *Three Rivers (No. 3)*, [44].

[63] Ibid., [121]–[125].

[64] Stanton 2003, 134.

by the plaintiffs'.[65] If Lord Steyn's view is correct then what follows from it? Suppose A misused his powers intending[66] B to suffer a particular kind of harm – harm H – and thereby committed the tort of misfeasance in public office. Suppose further that in fact B did not suffer harm H as a result of A's misusing his powers but instead suffered a quite different kind of harm. For instance, suppose that A unlawfully released C from custody despite being aware that C would probably attack B, but in fact C stole a large sum of money from B and fled the country. In such a case, applying Lord Steyn's rule, A will not be held liable to compensate B for the harm suffered by her as a result of A's act of misfeasance. This result is contrary to the usual rules as to the extent of a defendant's liability where a defendant has committed an *intentional* tort.[67] Moreover, Lord Steyn did not expressly consider what the correct legal outcome should be in such a case. Consequently there are grounds for arguing that Lord Steyn made an error. In our opinion, he should have said that in order to commit the tort of misfeasance in public office in relation to B, A must, when misusing his powers, intend B to suffer harm, or know that B will probably suffer harm, or suspect that B will probably suffer harm and not care, but that if A has committed the tort, the separate and further question of what damages are recoverable should be governed by the usual rules governing the extent of an intentional tortfeasor's liability.[68]

Material damage

In *Watkins* v *Secretary of State for the Home Department*[69] the House of Lords considered whether three prison officers had committed the tort of misfeasance in public office in relation to Watkins, a serving prisoner, when they unlawfully and in bad faith opened his correspondence. The case was difficult because Watkins had suffered no 'material damage', that is, no economic loss or physical or mental injury,[70] as a result of these unlawful acts. Indeed the trial judge had found that he appeared 'to thrive on these conflicts'. The House of Lords concluded that the three prison officers had not committed the tort of misfeasance in public office in relation to Watkins *because* he had not suffered 'material damage'. One factor that seems to have particularly influenced the judges who decided the case is that they did not want the tort to be available as a vehicle for claimants whose sole object was to punish public officials through obtaining awards of punitive damages.

Visit **http://www.mylawchamber.co.uk/mcbride** to access updates on recent cases, as well as model answers and tips for answering tort problem questions.

[65] *Three Rivers (No. 3)*, 195–6 (emphasis added).

[66] Or knowing or suspecting that B would suffer a particular kind of harm – harm H.

[67] An intentional tort is one which can only be committed deliberately. On the rules governing the extent of an intentional tortfeasor's liability, see below, pp. 575–6.

[68] In *Watkins* v *Secretary of State for the Home Department* [2006] 2 AC 395, [72], Lord Rodger referred to these rules in connection with the tort of misfeasance in public office. He did not draw attention, however, to their inconsistency with Lord Steyn's statement in *Three Rivers (No. 3)*.

[69] [2006] 2 AC 395.

[70] In the subsequent case of *Karagozlu* v *Metropolitan Police Comr* [2007] 2 All ER 1055 the Court of Appeal held that a claim for misfeasance in public office could also be based on a 'loss of liberty', including the loss of residual liberty that a prisoner would suffer if he was unlawfully moved from an open prison to a closed prison.

25 Torts involving the breach of a statutory duty

OVERVIEW

We have already seen some examples of situations where someone will commit a tort if he or she breaches a statutory duty. For example, an occupier of premises will commit the tort of negligence if he breaches the statutory duty he owes his visitors under the Occupiers' Liability Act 1957 to take reasonable steps to see that they will be reasonably safe in visiting his premises. Again: A will commit the tort of harassment in relation to B if he breaches the duty he will normally owe her under the Protection from Harassment Act 1997 not to engage in a course of conduct that amounts to harassment of B and which he knows or ought to know amounts to harassment of B.

We are concerned in this chapter with situations where A has breached a statutory duty but A has not – in breaching that duty – committed one of the torts we have already come across. Three such situations can be distinguished.

(1) *Breach of duty owed to claimant.* If A has breached a statutory duty owed to B[1] and B has suffered loss as a result, B will be entitled to sue A for compensation for that loss if: (1) the duty breached by A was imposed on him in order to help ensure that B did not suffer that kind of loss;[2] *and* (2) A committed a tort in breaching that duty.

(2) *Breach of duty owed to third party.* If A has breached a statutory duty owed to C and B has suffered loss as a result, B will not normally be entitled to sue A for compensation for that loss.[3] For example, in *Wingrove* v *Prestige & Co. Ltd*,[4] the claimant was a clerk of works employed by Middlesex County Council to supervise the defendants as they built a school for the council. The claimant was blinded in both eyes as a result of an accident on the construction site. The accident occurred because the defendants committed a breach of a statutory duty: they had a statutory duty to ensure that 'suitable and safe scaffolds shall be

[1] That is, the duty breached by A was imposed on him for B's benefit.

[2] *Gorris* v *Scott* (1874) LR 9 Ex 125 (discussed below, pp. 577–8); *Bretton* v *Hancock* [2006] PIQR 1 (if A allows B to drive her car without insurance, in breach of the statutory duty she owes other drivers on the road to ensure that people who drive her car carry insurance, and B and C – another driver on the road – both drive their respective cars so badly that A's car is involved in an accident and A, a passenger in the car, is injured, with the result that C is liable to compensate A for her injuries but cannot bring a claim in contribution against B because B is impecunious, C cannot sue A for the money he would have been able to sue B for had B been insured; the statutory duty A breached in this case was imposed on her to help ensure that C could sue B for compensation for any injuries that C might suffer as a result of B's bad driving, not to help ensure that C could bring a claim in contribution against B).

[3] If A committed a tort in breaching the duty owed to C, then B may exceptionally be entitled to sue A for compensation for the losses suffered by her as a result of A's breach under the principles set out below in Chapter 31. Again, if A committed a tort in breaching the duty owed to C, and in breaching that duty, A intentionally harmed B, then A will have committed the tort of intentional infliction of harm by unlawful means (discussed above, Chapter 21) in relation to B, and B will be able to sue A for damages.

[4] [1954] 1 WLR 524.

provided for all work that cannot be safely done on or from the ground or from part of the building . . .'[5] The claimant sued the defendants for compensation for his injury but his claim was dismissed. The statutory duty that the defendants breached had been imposed for the benefit of the defendants' employees, not the claimant.[6]

(3) *Breach of duty owed to no one in particular.* If A has breached a statutory duty which was imposed on him for the benefit of the community as a whole and B has suffered loss as a result, B will only be entitled to sue A for compensation for that loss if A's breach amounted to a *public nuisance*[7] and B suffered *special damage* as a result of A's breach.[8]

For example, in *Lonrho Ltd* v *Shell Petroleum (No. 2)*,[9] the claimants in that case owned an oil pipeline which ran into Southern Rhodesia. Oil companies would pay the claimants to use the oil pipeline to transport oil into Southern Rhodesia. When Southern Rhodesia unilaterally declared itself independent of the UK, the UK government made it illegal to supply oil to Southern Rhodesia and the claimants' pipeline fell into disuse. The defendants secretly continued to supply oil to Southern Rhodesia, in breach of the sanctions applied by the UK government to Southern Rhodesia. Had they not, it was likely that the Southern Rhodesian government would have collapsed sooner than it did; that the sanctions against Southern Rhodesia would have been lifted earlier than they were; and that the claimants' pipeline would not have been out of use for as long as it was. Let us say that the defendants' unlawful conduct caused the claimants' pipeline to be put out of use for an extra nine months. The claimants sued the defendants for compensation for the profits they would have made had oil companies been allowed to use their pipeline during those nine months. The claimants' claim was dismissed. The statutory duty breached by the defendants in this case was imposed for the benefit of the UK as a whole, which had an interest in bringing down the Southern Rhodesian government through the use of sanctions. The duty breached by the defendants was therefore owed to no one in particular. So it followed that the claimants could only sue the defendants for compensation for the losses suffered by them as a result of the defendants' breach of statutory duty if the defendants' breach amounted to a public nuisance – which it did not.[10]

The statutory duty that was breached in *Lonrho* was clearly imposed for the benefit of the community as a whole, and not for any particular individual's benefit. However, not all cases are so clear-cut. For example, in *X* v *Bedfordshire County Council*,[11] the claimants were five children who suffered years of abuse at home. Despite being alerted to this, the relevant local authority failed to initiate proceedings to take the claimants into care, thereby breaching various statutory duties which required it to intervene to protect 'at risk'

[5] Building (Safety, Health and Welfare) Regulations 1948, reg 5.

[6] For further examples, see W&J, 352; Oliphant 2007, 827–8.

[7] For an account of the law on public nuisance, see Chapter 44, below.

[8] It was suggested in the Australian case of *Beaudesert Shire Council* v *Smith* (1966) 120 CLR 145, at 160 that B would *also* be able to sue A if A intentionally breached the statutory duty in question and the loss suffered by B was an inevitable consequence of that breach. However, the House of Lords ruled in *Lonrho* v *Shell Petroleum (No. 2)* [1982] AC 173, at 188 that this was *not* the law in England. (Nor is it now the law in Australia: *Northern Territory* v *Mengel* (1995) 185 CLR 307.)

[9] [1982] AC 173.

[10] Note that the claimants could not sue the defendants for compensation on the ground that the defendants had committed the tort of intentional infliction of harm using unlawful means in acting as they did. While the defendants knew perfectly well that their conduct would inevitably harm the claimants, their *aim* or *object* in breaking sanctions was not to harm the claimants.

[11] [1995] 2 AC 633.

children. The claimants sued the local authority for compensation in respect of the losses they had suffered as a result of the local authority's breaches of statutory duty. It follows from what has already been said that the claimant's claim for compensation could only succeed if the statutory duties breached by the local authority had been imposed on the local authority for the benefit of the claimants. One would have thought this requirement was easily satisfied in this case, but the House of Lords held that the statutory duties that were breached in *X* were 'all concerned to establish an administrative system designed to promote the social welfare of the community'.[12] So the statutory duties that the local authority breached in *X* were *not* owed to the claimants, but were rather owed to no one in particular. The claimants' claims for compensation were accordingly dismissed.

So – if A has breached a statutory duty and B has suffered loss as a result, and that breach does not amount to a public nuisance, B will normally only be able to sue A for compensation for the loss suffered by her as a result of A's breach if: (1) the duty breached by A was owed to B; *and* (2) the duty breached by A was imposed on him in order to help ensure that B did not suffer the kind of loss that she has suffered; *and* (3) A committed a tort in breaching that duty.[13]

Now – let's suppose that A has breached a statutory duty owed to B and B has suffered the right kind of loss as a result of the breach of that duty. How do we determine whether A's breach amounts to a tort? In Chapter 1, we said that the breach of a statutory duty owed to another would amount to a tort if Parliament intended that that breach should be treated as a tort by the courts – that is, if Parliament intended that all the remedies that are normally available when a tort has been committed should be available in respect of that breach. We said that if Parliament had created the duty with that intention, we could say that Parliament intended that breach of that duty should be 'actionable in tort'.[14] So – how do we determine whether Parliament intended that a breach of the statutory duty breached by A should be actionable in tort?

If Parliament has made its intentions clear on the matter, then there is no problem. If Parliament expressly said that a breach of the statutory duty breached by A should be actionable in tort then B will be entitled to sue A.[15] If Parliament expressly said that it should not be, then B will not be entitled to sue A.[16]

[12] Ibid., 747 (per Lord Browne-Wilkinson).

[13] For a *dictum* indicating that (1) and (2) must be satisfied before B can sue A see *South Australia Asset Management Corporation* v *York Montague Ltd* [1997] AC 191, 211 (per Lord Hoffmann): 'A plaintiff who sues for breach of a duty imposed by the law (whether in contract or tort *or under statute*) must do more than prove that the defendant has failed to comply. He must show that the duty was owed to him and that it was a duty in respect of the kind of loss which he has suffered' (emphasis added). There are plenty of *dicta* in favour of the view that (3) must also be satisfied before B will be allowed to sue A – that is, in favour of the view that B will not necessarily be allowed to sue A even if the duty breached by A was owed to B and B has suffered the kind of loss that the duty breached by A was imposed on him in order to avoid. See, for example, *Pickering* v *Liverpool Daily Post* [1991] 2 AC 370, 420 (per Lord Bridge).

[14] See above, p. 9.

[15] This will be the case if the statutory duty breached by A arose under s 17 of the Race Relations Act 1976 (which provides that an educational establishment will owe someone applying for a place to study at that establishment a statutory duty not to discriminate against him on the grounds of his race). Section 57 of the 1976 Act makes it clear that a breach of that duty will be actionable in tort: 'A claim by any person ("the claimant") that another person ("the respondent") . . . has committed an act of discrimination against the claimant which is unlawful by virtue of [s 17 of the 1976 Act] . . . may be made the subject of civil proceedings in like manner as any other claim in tort . . .'

[16] This will be the case if the statutory duty breached by A arose under s 9 of the Post Office Act 1969 (which

The difficulty arises if Parliament did *not* make it clear – when it created the statutory duty breached by A – whether or not a breach of that statutory duty should be actionable in tort. How do we ascertain Parliament's intentions in that kind of case? Lord Denning MR thought that in such a case it was impossible to tell what Parliament's intention was: 'you might as well toss a coin to decide.'[17] Others take the view that it *is* possible to discern Parliament's intention, but to do so one must consider 'the whole Act [that created the statutory duty breached by A] and the circumstances, including the pre-existing law, in which it was enacted'.[18] However, it is unlikely that this approach – which Keith Stanton calls the 'construction approach' – to discerning Parliament's intention will often be successful: in many cases the courts will be 'seeking to discover something which is not there'.[19] Given this, we favour a different approach to the question of whether Parliament intended that a breach of the statutory duty breached by A should be actionable in tort. Stanton calls this approach 'the presumption approach'.[20] It goes as follows.

We start off by making a basic presumption that Parliament intended, when it created the statutory duty breached by A, that it should be actionable in tort. The argument in favour of making this presumption has seven stages. It goes as follows:

(1) The law should be consistent – it should treat like cases alike.
(2) There is no fundamental difference between judge-made duties that are owed to others and statutory duties that are owed to others.
(3) Given this, the law should treat someone who breaches a statutory duty owed to another in the same way as it does someone who breaches a judge-made duty owed to that other.
(4) Someone who breaches a judge-made duty owed to another will be routinely ordered to pay compensation to the victim of his breach.
(5) Given this, someone who breaches a statutory duty owed to another should be ordered to pay compensation to the victim of his breach.
(6) We presume that Parliament, when it created the statutory duty breached by A, wished to respect the basic dictate that the law should treat like cases alike and therefore intended that if A breached that duty he should be held liable to pay compensation to the victim of his breach.
(7) We therefore presume that when Parliament created the statutory duty breached by A, it intended that a breach of that duty should be actionable in tort.[21]

---

provides that 'It shall be the duty of the Post Office . . . to provide throughout [the British Islands] . . . such services for the conveyance of letters . . . as satisfy all reasonable demands for them'). Section 9(4) of the Act makes it clear that a breach of this duty will *not* be actionable in tort: 'Nothing in this section shall be construed as imposing upon the Post Office . . . any form of . . . liability enforceable by proceedings before any court.'

[17] *Ex parte Island Records* [1978] 1 Ch 122, 135A.

[18] *Cutler* v *Wandsworth Stadium Ltd* [1949] AC 398, 407 (per Lord Simonds).

[19] Stanton 2003, 24. Students, in particular, are likely to find the 'construction approach' unhelpful in attempting problem questions involving the breach of a statutory duty owed to another. This is because the statutory duty in question is very likely to have been made up by the examiner. As a result, there simply will not exist any legislative history relating to that statutory duty for the student to consult in an attempt to determine whether Parliament intended that a breach of that duty should be actionable in tort.

[20] Ibid., 25–6.

[21] *Important note*. This argument only makes sense if it is accepted that (4) is true: that is, if it is accepted that someone who breaches a judge-made duty owed to another will be routinely ordered to pay damages to the victim of his breach. As we have seen (see above, pp. 14–17), many academics do *not* accept that a defendant

Having made this basic presumption, we then see if that presumption can be rebutted. That is, we see if there is some indication that Parliament did *not* intend that a breach of the statutory duty breached by A should be actionable in tort. How do we do this?

(1) *Did Parliament provide what should happen on breach of the statutory duty?* We first of all see if Parliament specified what should happen if someone breached the duty breached by A. If it did, and it did not specify that a breach of that duty should be actionable in tort, then that provides some indication that Parliament did *not* intend that a breach of the duty breached by A should be actionable in tort. The reason behind this is that if Parliament had intended that a breach of the duty breached by A should be actionable in tort, we would have expected Parliament to make that clear when it specified what should happen if someone breached the duty breached by A.

So, for example, in *Scally* v *Southern Health and Social Services Board*,[22] the question was raised: If an employer owes an employee of his a statutory duty under s 4(1) of the Contracts of Employment and Redundancy Payments Act (Northern Ireland) 1965 to give that employee a written statement detailing the particulars of his contract of employment, will the employer commit a tort if he breaches that duty? The House of Lords thought the answer was 'no'. In s 5(1) of the 1965 Act, Parliament specified what should happen in the situation we are considering – if an employer owed his employee a duty under s 4(1) of the 1965 Act to give that employee a written statement detailing the particulars of his contract of employment and he breached that duty, the employee would have a right to have the particulars of his contract of employment specified by a tribunal. The fact that Parliament did not at the same time make it clear that a breach of duty under s 4(1) of the 1965 Act should be actionable in tort tended to show that Parliament did *not* intend that a breach of a duty arising under s 4(1) of the 1965 Act should be actionable in tort.

However, if Parliament specified what should happen if someone breached the duty breached by A and did not in doing so specify that a breach of that duty should be civilly actionable, that does not provide a *conclusive* indication that Parliament did *not* intend, when it created that duty, that a breach of that duty should be actionable in tort. For example, in *Groves* v *Wimborne*,[23] the claimant was injured by some unfenced cogwheels. In leaving the cogwheels unfenced, the claimant's employer, the defendant, breached the

who is held liable to pay damages to another in negligence or deceit or private nuisance or defamation is held liable because he has breached a judge-made duty owed to another. Let's call such an academic, a *duty-sceptic*. A duty-sceptic will take a very restrictive view of what judge-made duties we owe each other: she will tend to think that the *only* judge-made duties we can be said to owe each other are duties to pay other people money in certain situations. Unfortunately, someone who breaches *that kind of duty* – a duty to pay money to another – will *not* be routinely ordered to pay damages to the victim of his breach. So a duty-sceptic will *not* accept that (4) is true and will therefore reject the presumption approach altogether. Moreover, a duty-sceptic will find it hard to understand why the breach of a statutory duty owed to another should *ever* give rise to liability in tort. This is because as soon as one starts denying that all the other causes of action in tort (in negligence, deceit, private nuisance, defamation and so on) are based on the fact that the defendant has breached a duty owed to the claimant, actions in tort which arise out of the fact that a defendant has breached a statutory duty owed to another will start to look anomalous and out of place. It is therefore unsurprising – given the current (and completely undeserved) popularity of duty-scepticism among tort academics – that so many of them should be hostile to the existence of the action for breach of statutory duty. See, for example, Fleming 1998, 134; and Davis 1998, applauding the Canadian Supreme Court's decision to abolish the action in *R* v *Saskatchewan Wheat Pool* [1983] 1 SCR 205.

22 [1992] 1 AC 294.

23 [1898] 2 QB 402.

statutory duty he owed the claimant under s 5 of the Factory and Workshop Act 1878 to ensure that all dangerous machinery used by the claimant was securely fenced. Section 82 of the 1878 Act provided that an employer who breached a statutory duty owed to one of his employees under s 5 of the 1878 Act would be liable to be fined. Parliament did not further specify that the breach of a statutory duty under s 5 of the 1878 Act would be actionable in tort. Despite this, the Court of Appeal still found that when Parliament created the statutory duty contained in s 5 of the 1878 Act, it intended that a breach of that duty should be actionable in tort. Vaughan Williams LJ observed that 'where ... a remedy is provided in cases of nonperformance of the statutory duty, that is a matter to be taken into consideration for the purpose of determining whether [Parliament intended that breach of that duty should be actionable in tort], or whether [Parliament] intended that there should be no other remedy than the statutory remedy; *but it is by no means conclusive or the only matter to be taken into consideration for that purpose*.'[24]

(2) *Common sense*. Secondly, we ask: As a matter of common sense, can it really be contemplated that Parliament intended that a breach of the duty breached by A should be actionable in tort? If the answer is 'no' then that provides a strong indication that when Parliament created the duty breached by A it did *not* intend that a breach of that duty should be actionable in tort.

For example, in *R* v *Deputy Governor of Parkhurst Prison, ex parte Hague*,[25] it was claimed that a prison governor would commit a tort if his treatment of a prisoner violated the Prison Rules 1964. So, for example, a prison governor will owe a prisoner of his a statutory duty under rule 43 of the Prison Rules 1964 not to put that prisoner into isolation for more than 24 hours without the authority of the board of visitors or the Secretary of State. It was claimed in *ex parte Hague* that a governor who breached this duty would commit a tort in so doing. This claim was rejected by the House of Lords. As a matter of common sense, it could hardly be supposed that Parliament intended, when it authorised the creation of the Prison Rules, that a prisoner who was the victim of a technical breach of the Prison Rules should be allowed to sue the governor of the prison in which he was held for compensatory damages, as would happen if breaches of the Prison Rules were actionable in tort.[26]

(3) *Does the duty depend on someone's having a certain state of mind?* Thirdly, we ask: Is the existence of the duty breached by A dependent on the state of mind of the person who is subject to that duty? If the answer is 'yes', that indicates that when Parliament created the duty breached by A it did *not* intend that a breach of that duty should be actionable in tort.

24 Ibid., 416 (emphasis added). See also *Phillips* v *Britannia Hygienic Laundry Co.* [1923] 2 KB 832, 841 (per Atkin LJ).

25 [1992] 1 AC 58.

26 Another possible reason for not allowing a prisoner to bring an action for breach of statutory duty if he was treated in a way that violated the Prison Rules is that the statutory duty that was breached in his case was not imposed for his benefit but for the benefit of the community as a whole, which has an interest in seeing that its prisons are well run. See ibid., at 172 (per Lord Jauncey of Tullichettle): 'The [Prison Rules] are wide-ranging in their scope covering a mass of matters relevant to the administration and good government of a prison ... The rules are regulatory in character, they provide a framework within which the prison regime operates but they are not intended to protect prisoners against loss, injury and damage nor to give them a right of action in respect thereof.'

For example, s 2(2) of the Child Care Act 1980 provided that: 'Where it appears to a local authority with respect to a child in their area . . . that his parents are . . . prevented . . . from providing for his proper accommodation, maintenance and upbringing . . . [and] that the intervention of the local authority . . . is necessary in the interests of the welfare of the child, it shall be the duty of the local authority to receive the child into care.' In *X* v *Bedfordshire County Council*,[27] the House of Lords had to decide – among many other things – whether a breach of this statutory duty would amount to a tort. The House of Lords thought that it would not: it thought that when Parliament enacted the 1980 Act it did not intend that a breach of this statutory duty should be actionable in tort. One of the reasons for this was that a local authority would only incur a duty under s 2(2) of the 1980 Act to take a child in its area into care if it *thought* that the child's parents were incapable of bringing the child up properly and that taking the child into care was necessary to protect the child's interests. Given this, if a breach of the statutory duty under s 2(2) of the 1980 Act *were* actionable in tort in tort the following paradoxical result would obtain.

A local authority that thought a child in its area needed to be taken into care but then failed to take that child into care would be liable to pay compensatory damages to that child: as soon as it thought the child needed to be taken into care, it would have incurred a duty to take the child into care under s 2(2) of the 1980 Act and it would have breached that duty by failing to take the child into care, thereby committing a tort in relation to that child. On the other hand, a local authority which perversely refused to acknowledge that a child needed to be taken into care would *not* be liable to pay compensatory damages to that child when it failed to take that child into care: it would never have incurred a duty to take the child into care under s 2(2) of the 1980 Act and would therefore have done no wrong in failing to take that child into care. When Parliament created the statutory duty contained in s 2(2) of the 1980 Act, it could not have intended to produce such a paradoxical result. It follows that when Parliament created the statutory duty contained in s 2(2) of the 1980 Act, it could not have intended that a breach of that duty should be actionable in tort.

Again, s 65 of the Housing Act 1985 provides that if a housing authority '[is] satisfied that [an applicant for accommodation] has a priority need and [is] not satisfied that he became homeless intentionally, [it] shall . . . secure that accommodation becomes available for his accommodation'. In *O'Rourke* v *Camden London Borough Council*,[28] Lord Hoffmann thought that when Parliament enacted this section, it could not have intended that a breach of this duty should be actionable in tort. If it *had* had such an intention then the following 'anomalous' result would obtain: 'a housing authority which accepts it has a duty to house the applicant but does so inadequately will be liable in damages, but an authority which perversely refuses to accept it has any such duty will not.'[29] As Lord Hoffmann observed, 'This seems to me wrong.'[30]

(4) *Oppressiveness*. Fourthly, we ask: Would finding that a breach of the duty breached by A is actionable in tort impose an oppressive burden on whoever is subject to that duty? If

[27] [1995] 2 AC 633.
[28] [1998] AC 188.
[29] Ibid., 196.
[30] Ibid.

the answer is 'yes' then that tends to indicate that when Parliament created the duty breached by A, it did *not* intend that a breach of that duty should be actionable in tort.

For example, in *Atkinson* v *The Newcastle and Gateshead Waterworks Company*,[31] the defendants supplied Newcastle and surrounding towns with water. Under the Waterworks Clauses Act 1847, they had a statutory duty to install fire hydrants and supply water to those hydrants at a certain pressure. They breached this duty with the result that firefighters could not obtain any water from one of the defendants' fire hydrants to put out a fire in the claimants' house. As a result, the claimants' house burned down. The claimants sued the defendants claiming that they had committed a tort in breaching their statutory duty under the 1847 Act. The claimants' claim was rejected. The Court of Appeal thought that when Parliament created the duty breached by the defendants it could not have intended that a breach of that duty should be actionable in tort:

> it certainly appears a startling thing to say that a company undertaking to supply a town like Newcastle with water, would not only be willing to be put under [a statutory] duty to supply gratuitously for the purpose of extinguishing fire an unlimited quantity of water at a certain pressure ... but would further be willing in their contract with [P]arliament to subject themselves to the liability to actions by any number of householders who might happen to have their houses burnt down in consequence [of the company's non-performance of this duty]; and it is, a priori, equally improbable that [P]arliament would think it a necessary or reasonable bargain to make ... [T]he company would virtually become gratuitous insurers of the safety from fire, so far as water is capable of producing that safety, of all the houses within the district over which their powers were to extend.[32]

(5) *Public interest*. We ask, fifthly: Would finding that a breach of the duty breached by A is actionable in tort seriously interfere with the performance of some important public function? If the answer is 'yes', then that again indicates that when Parliament created the duty breached by A it did *not* intend that a breach of that duty should be actionable in tort.

This was one of the considerations that led the House of Lords to conclude in *X* v *Bedfordshire County Council*[33] that when Parliament imposed duties on local authorities to safeguard the welfare of children in their jurisdiction in the Children and Young Persons Act 1969, the Child Care Act 1980 and the Children Act 1989, Parliament did not intend that the breach of those duties should be actionable in tort. As Lord Browne-Wilkinson observed:

> the Acts in question are all concerned to establish an administrative system designed to promote the social welfare of the community. The welfare sector involved is one of peculiar sensitivity, involving very difficult decisions how to strike the balance between protecting the child from immediate feared harm and disrupting the relationship between the child and its parents. Decisions often have to be taken on the basis of inadequate and disputed facts. In my judgment in such a context it would require exceptionally clear language to show a parliamentary intention that those responsible for carrying out these difficult functions should be liable in damages if, on subsequent investigation with the benefit of hindsight, it was shown that they had reached an erroneous conclusion and therefore failed to discharge their statutory duties.[34]

[31] (1877) 2 Ex D 441.
[32] Ibid., 445–6.
[33] [1995] 2 AC 633.
[34] Ibid., 747C–E.

Again, as we have seen, the House of Lords thought in *R* v *Deputy Governor of Parkhurst Prison, ex parte Hague*[35] that Parliament could not have intended that a breach of a statutory duty owed to a prisoner under the Prison Rules 1964 should be actionable in tort when it authorised the creation of the Prison Rules. It is hard to resist the impression – though it must remain an impression as the point was not explicitly acknowledged – that one of the main reasons the House of Lords reached this conclusion was that if a breach of a statutory duty owed to a prisoner under the Prison Rules were actionable in tort, prisoners could severely disrupt the conduct of prison life by making compensation claims on the ground that they had been the victims of technical breaches of the Prison Rules.

(6) *Useful purpose.* Sixthly, we ask: Would finding that a breach of the duty breached by A is actionable in tort serve some useful purpose? If the answer is 'no' then that indicates that when Parliament created the duty breached by A, it did *not* intend that a breach of that duty should be actionable in tort.

For example, in *McCall* v *Abelesz*[36] the claimant let a room in a house owned by the defendants. Through no fault of the claimant the authorities cut off the supply of gas and electricity to his room and the defendants did nothing to get the supply reconnected in the hope that if the gas and electricity supply to the claimant's room remained cut off, the claimant would be persuaded to take up alternative accommodation that they were offering him. The defendants owed the claimant a statutory duty under s 30(2) of the Rent Act 1965 not to act in this way and the claimant sued the defendants, claiming that in breaching this duty they had committed a tort.[37] The Court of Appeal dismissed the claimant's claim. They thought that when Parliament enacted the 1965 Act, it did not intend that a breach of the duty set out in s 30(2) of that Act should be actionable in tort. One of the reasons the Court of Appeal gave for reaching this conclusion was that little useful purpose would be served if a breach of the duty set out in s 30(2) of the 1965 Act were actionable in tort. If a breach of this duty were *not* actionable in tort, a tenant who was subjected to harassment from his landlord designed to induce him to give up his tenancy would still have a perfectly good set of remedies against that landlord because the harassment would amount to a breach of contract. So a tenant would not be afforded any greater protection against being harassed by his landlord if a breach of the duty set out in s 30(2) of the 1965 Act *were* actionable in tort.

In *Cullen* v *Chief Constable of the Royal Ulster Constabulary*,[38] the claimant was arrested under suspicion of being involved in an act of terrorism. During his time in police custody, the police denied him access to a solicitor and in doing so committed a breach of statutory duty. The claimant suffered no loss as a result of being denied access to a solicitor but still sued the police for nominal damages. A bare majority of the House of Lords held that the claim should be dismissed. The majority thought that Parliament had not intended that a breach of this kind of statutory duty should be actionable in tort even if the victim of the

35 [1992] 1 AC 58.

36 [1976] 1 QB 585.

37 Section 30(2) of the Rent Act 1965 provided that: 'If any person with intent to cause the residential occupier of any premises . . . does acts calculated to interfere with the peace or comfort of the residential occupier . . . or persistently withdraws or withholds services reasonably required for the occupation of the premises as a residence, he shall be guilty of an offence . . .'

38 [2003] 1 WLR 1763.

breach suffered no loss as a result of the breach. The best explanation of this decision is that no useful purpose would be served if denial of access to a solicitor were actionable *per se* – that is, actionable in tort without the claimant having to prove that he had suffered any loss as a result of the denial of access. Of course, if unlawfully denying someone access to a solicitor were actionable *per se*, then someone who was denied access to a solicitor could bring a claim in tort against the police straightaway, without having to wait for the denial of access to cause him some kind of loss. He would thereby be provided with a speedy means of getting a court to determine whether or not he was entitled to a solicitor. However, someone who is denied access to a solicitor while in custody *already* has a speedy means of getting a court to determine whether or not he is entitled to see a solicitor – he can make an application for judicial review of the decision to deny him access.[39]

Suppose, having looked at all these matters, we get the impression that when Parliament created the duty breached by A it did *not* intend that a breach of that duty should be actionable in tort. If this is the case, we will find that B is not entitled to sue A for compensation for the loss suffered by her as a result of A's breach. If, on the other hand, having taken everything into consideration, we do *not* get the impression that Parliament did *not* intend that a breach of the duty breached by A should be actionable in tort when it created that duty, our initial presumption that Parliament *did* intend that a breach of that duty should be actionable in tort when it created that duty will remain unrebutted and we will conclude that A committed a tort in breaching that duty. B will therefore be entitled to sue A for compensation for the loss suffered by her as a result of A's breach.

Let's now apply this method for determining whether a breach of a statutory duty amounts to a tort to a concrete case. In *Monk* v *Warbey*,[40] Warbey allowed one Knowles to drive his car when Knowles was not insured against third party risks (risks of being held liable to third parties) in driving that car. In doing so, Warbey breached the statutory duty that he was subject to under s 35(1) of the Road Traffic Act 1930, which provided that 'it shall not be lawful for any person ... to permit any other person to use a motor vehicle ... unless there is in force in relation to the user of the vehicle ... such a policy of insurance or such a security in respect of third-party risks as complies with the requirements of this Part of this Act'. Knowles negligently injured Monk in driving Warbey's car but because Knowles was uninsured he was not worth suing. Instead, Monk sued Warbey for compensation for the loss that he had suffered as a result of Warbey's breach of statutory duty in allowing Knowles to drive his car.

Monk had no problem showing that the duty breached by Warbey was imposed for his benefit. The duty was of course imposed for the benefit of other drivers on the road like

[39] Ibid., at [34]–[40] (per Lord Hutton). Lords Bingham and Steyn dissented, on the ground that someone who is denied access to a solicitor will hardly be in a position to make an application for judicial review to get a court to determine whether the denial of access is lawful or not: ibid., at [20]. However, it is hard to see how being allowed to sue for nominal damages would assist such a detainee – the lack of access to a solicitor would make it just as difficult for him to bring a claim in tort against the police. The only possible advantage of allowing claims for nominal damages to be made in cases like *Cullen* is that if such claims could be made, then a detainee who was denied access to a solicitor while in custody would be able to bring a claim in tort against the police months or years after he was detained for the *sole* purpose of having it established in a public forum whether or not the police acted lawfully in denying him access to a solicitor. But it is hard to see what *useful* purpose would be served in allowing him to do this.

[40] [1935] 1 KB 75.

Monk. Moreover, Monk had no problem showing that he had suffered the kind of loss which the duty breached by Warbey had been imposed on him in order to avoid. The duty was imposed on Warbey in order to help ensure that other drivers on the road did not suffer harm to their persons or property that were not covered by a liability insurance policy[41] – and Monk suffered exactly that kind of harm. So whether Monk could sue Warbey came down to whether Warbey committed a tort in allowing Knowles to drive his car. This, in turn, depended on whether Parliament intended – in creating the duty breached by Warbey – that a breach of that duty should be actionable in tort. The Court of Appeal concluded that it did: there was nothing to displace the initial presumption that Parliament intended that a breach of the statutory duty imposed by s 35(1) of the Act should be actionable in tort when it created that duty.

True, the 1930 Act specified that someone who breached the duty under s 35(1) could be fined or imprisoned and did not mention at the same time that his breach would be actionable in tort. But this did not conclusively indicate that Parliament did *not* intend that a breach of the statutory duty imposed by s 35(1) of the Act should be actionable in tort. And there was no other indication that Parliament did not intend that a breach of the statutory duty imposed by s 35(1) of the Act should be actionable in tort: (1) it was not silly or ludicrous to think that Parliament intended, when it created the statutory duty imposed by s 35(1), that a breach of that duty should be actionable in tort; (2) the duty's existence did not depend on Warbey's state of mind; (3) if a breach of the statutory duty imposed by s 35(1) were actionable in tort, an oppressive burden would not be imposed on car owners: it was quite easy for car owners to avoid breaching the duty; (4) finding that a breach of the statutory duty imposed by s 35(1) was actionable in tort would not have any detrimental effect on the performance of any valuable public functions; and (5) it was impossible to say that no significantly useful purpose would be served if a breach of the statutory duty imposed by s 35(1) were actionable in tort – if a breach of the statutory duty imposed by s 35(1) were actionable in tort then someone who was negligently knocked down by a car driven by someone other than its owner would have a remedy against the owner if the driver had no insurance against third party risks and was therefore judgment-proof.

EXAMPLES

Having seen how one determines whether or not the breach of a statutory duty owed to another will amount to a tort, let's now look at some specific examples of statutory duties, breach of which *will* amount to a tort.

Health and safety at work

We have already seen that an employer will not commit a tort if he breaches the general duty that he will owe all of his employees under s 2 of the Health and Safety at Work Act 1974 'to ensure, so far as is reasonably practicable, the health, safety and welfare at work of all his employees'. This is because s 47(1)(a) of the 1974 Act provides that '[nothing in this Act] shall be construed . . . as conferring a right of action in any civil proceedings in respect

[41] See, on this, *Bretton* v *Hancock* [2006] PIQR 1 (above, n. 2).

of any failure to comply with [the] duty imposed by [s] 2'. However, s 15 of the 1974 Act gave the government power to introduce statutory regulations governing health and safety in the workplace and s 47(2) of the 1974 Act provided that a breach of a duty arising under these regulations should be actionable in tort unless the regulations provide otherwise. Section 15 has been used to introduce a huge number of regulations governing health and safety in the workplace, such as the Workplace (Health, Safety and Welfare) Regulations 1992, the Personal Protective Equipment at Work Regulations 1992, the Construction (Health, Safety and Welfare) Regulations 1996, the Fire Precautions (Workplace) Regulations 1997, the Provision and Use of Work Equipment Regulations 1998 and the Control of Substances Hazardous to Health Regulations 2002.[42] Particularly significant are the Management of Health and Safety at Work Regulations 1999, which require an employer, among other things, to make a 'suitable and sufficient assessment of . . . the risks to the health and safety of his employees to which they are exposed whilst they are at work' and to take 'preventive and protective measures' to protect the health and safety of his employees on the basis of that risk assessment.[43] It used to be that a breach of duty under the 1999 Regulations was not actionable in tort[44] but the Management of Health and Safety at Work and Fire Precautions (Workplace) (Amendment) Regulations 2003 now provide that a breach of duty under the 1999 Regulations *will* be actionable in tort.[45] As virtually any accident at work can be said to be attributable to an employer's failure to implement a 'suitable and sufficient' risk assessment, it is likely that the 1999 Regulations will provide a fertile source of litigation in the future.

Highways

Under s 41(1) of the Highways Act 1980, the highway authority for a particular highway will owe the users of that highway 'a [statutory] duty to maintain the highway'.[46] Section 41(1A) provides that 'In a particular, a highway authority are under a duty to ensure, so far as is reasonably practicable, that safe passage along a highway is not endangered by snow or ice.'[47] A highway authority which breaches its duty to maintain the highway will commit a tort; the 1980 Act clearly contemplates that if a user of a highway is injured because the

[42] Most of these regulations have been introduced in response to EU Directives.

[43] Regs 3–4.

[44] This was by virtue of Reg 22(1), which provided that 'Breach of a duty imposed by these Regulations shall not confer a right of action in any civil proceedings.'

[45] The 2003 Regulations do this in a somewhat backhanded way, amending Reg 22 of the 1999 Regulations so that it says: 'Breach of a duty imposed on an employer by these Regulations shall not confer a right of action in any civil proceedings insofar as that duty applies for the protection of persons not in his employment.' Thus, but only by implication, a breach of a duty arising under the 1999 Act *will* be actionable if an *employee* was affected by the breach. The somewhat grudging wording of the new Reg 22 is no doubt attributable to the fact that the government was forced into changing the old Reg 22 on the ground that the old Reg 22 failed properly to implement EU health and safety directives.

[46] It has been held that this duty does not go so far as to require the highway authority to erect traffic signs along the highway to reduce the risk of accidents: *Lavis* v *Kent County Council* (1992) 90 LGR 416; *Gorringe* v *Calderdale MBC* [2004] UKHL 15.

[47] This provision was inserted by s 111 of the Railways and Transport Safety Act 2003 and has the effect of reversing the decision of the House of Lords in *Goodes* v *East Sussex County Council* [2000] 1 WLR 1356, which held that a highway authority will *not* be required under s 41 to keep the highways under its jurisdiction free from ice.

relevant highway authority breached the statutory duty it owed him to maintain the highway, he will be entitled to sue the highway for damages.

Section 58(1) of the 1980 Act provides that in 'an action for damages against a highway authority in respect of damage resulting from their failure to maintain a highway . . . it is a defence . . . to prove that the authority had taken such care as in all the circumstances was reasonably required to secure that the part of the highway to which the action relates was not dangerous for traffic'. So, in effect, a user of a highway who is injured or whose property has been harmed[48] because the relevant highway authority failed to ensure that the highway was properly maintained will not be able to sue the highway authority for damages in respect of his injuries if the highway authority can prove that it took reasonable steps to see that the highway in question would be reasonably safe to travel on.

Building work

Section 1(1) of the Defective Premises Act 1972 provides that:

> A person taking on work for or in connection with the provision of a dwelling (whether the dwelling is provided for by the erection or by the conversion or enlargement of a building) owes a duty – (a) if the dwelling is provided to the order of any person, to that person; and (b) without prejudice to paragraph (a) above, to every person who acquires an interest (whether legal or equitable) in the dwelling; to see that the work which he takes on is done in a workmanlike or, as the case may be, professional manner, with proper materials and so that as regards that work the dwelling will be fit for habitation when completed.[49]

It is quite clear that someone who breaches this duty will commit a tort: both ss 1(5) and 2(1) of the 1972 Act contemplate that someone who breaches this duty may be sued by a victim of the breach who has suffered loss as a result. Three points may be made about this statutory duty.

(1) *Approved scheme.* Section 2(1) of the 1972 Act provides that if someone breaches the duty set out in s 1(1) in doing work on a dwelling, no action may be brought against him for breaching the duty set out in s 1(1) if the dwelling in question is covered by an 'approved scheme' which protects people who acquire interests in houses which prove to suffer from structural defects. For a long time, most houses in the UK were covered by an approved scheme operated by the National House Building Council with the result that during that time most people who discovered they lived in houses which suffered from structural defects because of the way they were built were barred from suing for breach of the statutory duty owed to them under s 1(1) of the 1972 Act. However, the National House Building Council no longer submits its scheme for approval and so the existence of this scheme no longer stands in the way of an action being brought in respect of a breach of the duty set out in s 1(1) of the 1972 Act.

[48] It appears no action can be brought under the Highways Act 1980 for pure economic loss resulting from a highway authority's breach of its duty to maintain the highway: *Wentworth* v *Wiltshire CC* [1993] QB 654.

[49] Why did we not mention this duty when setting out the situations in which it has been established one person will owe another a duty of care? (See above, Chapters 4–8.) The reason is that the duty set out in s 1(1) of the 1972 Act is *not* a duty of care – it is much stricter than that. It requires someone who takes on work in connection with the provision of a dwelling to *ensure* that the work is done in a workmanlike manner, with proper materials and done in such a way that the house will be fit for habitation.

(2) *Who is subject to the duty?* Because the National House Building Council's scheme worked for a long time to prevent actions being brought for breach of the duty set out in s 1(1) of the 1972 Act, there is very little case law on this section. So it remains uncertain *who* is subject to the duty set out in s 1(1): the duty could apply not only to builders and engineers but also to architects and surveyors. Section 1(4) provides that a 'person who – (a) in the course of a business which consists of or includes providing or arranging for the provision of dwellings or installations in dwellings; or (b) in the exercise of a power of making such provision or arrangements conferred by or by virtue of any enactment; arranges for another to take on work for or in connection with the provision of a dwelling shall be treated for the purposes of this section as included among the persons who have taken on the work'.

(3) *Work done to order.* Section 1(2) of the 1972 Act provides that if A takes on work in connection with the provision of a dwelling on B's behalf and does so on the understanding that he is to do that work in accordance with B's instructions, A will be treated as having discharged the duty set out in s 1(1) of the 1972 Act if he does the work in accordance with B's instructions.

Equality

The law imposes a raft of statutory duties on employers, businesses and schools requiring them not to discriminate against people on grounds of their sex, race, disability, sexual orientation, religion or belief. Breach of *most* of these duties will amount to a tort.

The Sex Discrimination Act 1975

Part III of the Sex Discrimination Act 1975 provides that:

(1) *Education.* If B applies to study at an educational establishment, the educational establishment will normally owe B a statutory duty not to discriminate against him or her on grounds of his or her sex either in the terms on which it offers to admit B or by refusing to admit him or her.[50]

Moreover, if B studies at an educational establishment, the educational establishment will normally owe B a statutory duty not to discriminate against him or her on grounds of his or her sex 'in the way it affords [him or her] access to any benefits, facilities or services, or by refusing . . . to afford [him or her] access to them, or . . . by excluding [him or her] from the establishment or subjecting [him or her] to any other detriment'.[51]

(2) *Goods and services.* If A provides goods, facilities or services to the public which B wants to purchase, A will normally owe B a statutory duty not to discriminate against B on grounds of his or her sex *either* by refusing to deal with B *or* by refusing to provide B with goods, facilities or services of the same quality as he would provide to people of the opposite sex *or* by refusing to provide B with goods, facilities or services on the same terms as he would deal with members of the opposite sex.[52]

[50] Sex Discrimination Act 1975, s 22.
[51] Ibid.
[52] Section 29.

(3) *Land*. If A has the power to dispose of premises to other people and B wishes to acquire those premises, A will normally owe B a statutory duty not to discriminate against B on grounds of his or her sex 'in the terms on which he offers [B] those premises, or by refusing [B's] application for those premises, or in his treatment of [B] in relation to any list of persons in need of premises [fitting the description of the premises disposed of by B].'[53]

Section 66 of the 1975 Act makes it clear that a breach of any of these duties will amount to a tort: 'A claim by any person ("the claimant") that another person ("the respondent") . . . has committed an act of discrimination which is unlawful by virtue of Part III . . . may be made the subject of civil proceedings in like manner as any other claim in tort.'

The Race Relations Act 1976

Part III of the Race Relations Act 1976 imposes on people and institutions statutory duties not to discriminate against people on grounds of their race which are identical to the duties set out in Part III of the Sex Discrimination Act 1975.[54] Again, s 57 of the 1976 Act makes it clear that a breach of any of these duties will amount to a tort in terms identical to those employed by s 66 of the 1975 Act.

The scope of liability under the 1975 and 1976 Acts

Suppose A owed B one of the statutory duties we are discussing here – that is, a duty of some description not to discriminate against B on grounds of his or her sex or race. In determining whether A breached this duty, we do not just look at A's behaviour. We are also required by ss 41(1) of the 1975 Act and 32(1) of the 1976 Act to look at the behaviour of A's employees, if he has any. Section 41(1) of the 1975 Act provides that: '[a]nything done by a person in the course of his employment shall be treated for the purposes of this Act as done by his employer as well as by him, whether or not it was done with the employer's knowledge or approval.' Section 32(1) of the 1976 Act says the same thing. It seems that an employee will be taken to have been acting 'in the course of his employment' by A for the purpose of the 1975 and 1976 Acts when he did *x* if he did *x while he was working for A*.

So in *Jones* v *Tower Boot Co. Ltd*,[55] the claimant worked in the defendant's shoe factory. The claimant was of mixed parentage and this resulted in his being subjected to unremitting abuse from his fellow employees while he worked at the factory. He claimed that the defendant had subjected him to a detriment because of his race contrary to s 4(2)(c) of the Race Relations Act 1976. The claimant's claim was upheld. True, *the defendant* had not *personally* subjected the claimant to any kind of detriment because of his race. However, the defendant's *employees* had: they had subjected the claimant to abuse because of his race. And the defendant's employees were regarded, for the purposes of the 1976 Act, as having acted in the course of their employment when they abused the claimant: they were working for the defendant when they abused the claimant. The defendant was therefore treated

[53] Section 30.

[54] See Race Relations Act 1976, ss 17 (statutory duties not to discriminate on grounds of race owed by educational establishment to applicants and students at that establishment), 20 (statutory duty not to discriminate on grounds of race against a customer for goods, facilities or services offered to public), 21 (statutory duty not to discriminate on grounds of race owed by person disposing of premises to person seeking to obtain those premises).

[55] [1997] ICR 254. This was *not* a tort case but is illustrative of the point being made here.

under s 32(1) of the 1976 Act as though *he* had racially abused the claimant and had therefore subjected the claimant to some kind of detriment because of his race.

Duties arising under the Disability Discrimination Act 1995 and the Employment Equality Regulations 2003

The Disability Discrimination Act[56] 1995,[57] the Employment Equality (Religion or Belief) Regulations 2003[58] and the Employment Equality (Sexual Orientation) Regulations 2003[59] all work in the same way. They require certain classes of people not to discriminate or harass members of other classes of people on the ground that they are, respectively, disabled,[60] of a certain religious or philosophical persuasion,[61] or have a certain sexual orientation.[62] The relevant classes are: (*a*) employers – employees/applicants for jobs;[63] (*b*) employers – contract workers;[64] (*c*) appointments committees – potential office holders;[65] (*d*) barristers/barristers' clerks – tenants/pupils/applicants for a tenancy or pupillage;[66] (*e*) firms – partners/employees being considered for partnership;[67] (*f*) trade organisations – members of the organisation/potential members;[68] (*g*) qualifications bodies – those seeking to obtain a qualification;[69] (*h*) providers of vocational training – trainees/potential trainees;[70] (*i*) employment agencies – temps/potential temps;[71] (*j*) institutions of further and higher education – students/potential students.[72]

The Disability Discrimination Act 1995 also provides that: (1) it is unlawful for a provider of services to discriminate against a disabled person;[73] (2) it is unlawful for anyone who provides employment services to harass a disabled person on the ground that he is disabled;[74] and (3) it is unlawful for anyone with the power to dispose of any premises to discriminate against a disabled person.[75]

The 1995 Act and 2003 Regulations make it clear that a breach of one of the duties mentioned in the preceding paragraph will be actionable in tort[76] – and that damages for injury to feelings may be awarded.[77] The Act and the Regulations also provide that 'Anything done by a person in the course of his employment shall be treated for the purposes of this Act as also done by his employer, whether or not it was done with the employer's knowledge or

[56] Henceforth, 'DDA'.
[57] As amended by the Disability Discrimination Act 1995 (Amendments) Regulations 2003.
[58] Henceforth, 'ROBR'.
[59] Henceforth, 'SOR'.
[60] DDA ss 3A–3B
[61] ROBR, Regs 3–5.
[62] SOR, Regs 3–5.
[63] DDA, s 4; ROBR (and SOR), Reg 6.
[64] DDA, s 4A; ROBR (and SOR), Reg 8.
[65] DDA, s 4D; ROBR (and SOR), Reg 10.
[66] DDA, s 7A; ROBR (and SOR), Reg 12.
[67] DDA, s 6A; ROBR (and SOR), Reg 14.
[68] DDA, s 13; ROBR (and SOR), Reg 15.
[69] DDA, s 14A; ROBR (and SOR), Reg 16.
[70] ROBR (and SOR), Reg 17.
[71] ROBR (and SOR), Reg 18.
[72] ROBR (and SOR), Reg 20.
[73] DDA, s 19.
[74] Section 21A.
[75] Section 22.
[76] DDA, ss17A, 25; ROBR (and SOR), Regs 30–31.
[77] DDA, ss17A(4), 25(2); ROBR (and SOR), Reg 31(3).

approval.'[78] However, they also go on to provide that 'In proceedings . . . against any person in respect of an act alleged to have been done by an employee of his, it shall be a defence for that person to prove that he took such steps as were reasonably practicable to prevent the employee from – (a) doing that act; or (b) doing, in the course of his employment, acts of that description.'[79]

Intellectual property

Patents

If B takes out a patent on an invention of hers, A will owe B a statutory duty under the Patents Act 1977 not to infringe B's patent. Section 60 of the 1977 Act provides that subject to certain exceptions:

(1) *Product.* If B's invention is a product, A will infringe B's patent if he 'makes, disposes of, offers to dispose of, uses or imports the product or keeps it whether for disposal or otherwise' without B's consent.

(2) *Process.* If B's invention is a process, A will infringe B's patent if: (*a*) A, without B's consent, 'uses the process or he offers it for use in the United Kingdom when he knows, or it is obvious to a reasonable person in the circumstances, that its use there without [B's consent] would be an infringement of the patent' *or* (*b*) A, without B's consent, 'disposes of, or offers to dispose of, uses or imports any product obtained directly by means of that process or keeps any such product whether for disposal or otherwise'.

(3) *Product or process.* If B's invention is a product or a process, A will infringe B's patent if he, acting without B's consent, supplies someone who is not 'entitled to work [B's] invention with any of the means, relating to an essential element of the invention, for putting the invention into effect when he knows, or it is obvious to a reasonable person in the circumstances, that those means are suitable for putting, and are intended to put, the invention into effect in the United Kingdom'.

If A breaches the statutory duty he owes B not to infringe B's patent, he will commit a tort: s 61 of the Patents Act 1977 provides that 'civil proceedings may be brought in the court by the proprietor of a patent in respect of any act alleged to infringe the patent.' However, if A infringes B's patent when he 'was not aware, and had no reasonable grounds for supposing that [B's] patent existed', B will be barred from suing A for damages in respect of any loss suffered by her as a result of A's infringement of her patent or damages in respect of any profit made by A in infringing B's patent.[80]

Copyright

If B owns the copyright in some kind of work, A will owe B a statutory duty under the Copyright, Designs and Patents Act 1988 not to infringe B's copyright in that work. It is not possible to summarise the various ways in which someone can infringe another's copyright

[78] DDA, s 58(1); ROBR (and SOR), Reg 22(1).
[79] DDA, s 58(5); ROBR (and SOR), Reg 22(3).
[80] Patents Act 1977, s 62(1).

A.

Compensatory damages: Basic principles

Introduction

In the following five chapters, we will set out the principles that determine when the victim of a tort can sue the person who committed that tort for compensation in respect of the losses that she has already suffered or may suffer in the future as a result of that tort being committed – and if she can, how much she will be able to recover by way of damages.

Suppose that A has committed a tort in relation to B. If B wants to sue A for compensatory damages, she must first show that A's tort has *caused* her to suffer some kind of loss. She must next show that this loss is *actionable*. If she can do both these things, then she will usually be entitled to sue A for compensation in respect of that loss. However, A may be able to raise a *defence* to B's claim for compensation; if he does, then B will not be able to sue A. But if A's tort caused B to suffer some kind of actionable loss and A has no defence to B's claim for compensation in respect of that loss, then A will be held liable to pay B a *sum sufficient* to compensate her for that loss. However, the damages payable to B may in certain circumstances be *reduced* beneath the level necessary to compensate her for the loss she has suffered as a result of A's tort. This will happen if, for example, B was partly to blame for the fact that she suffered that loss or because B obtained a benefit as a result of A's tort which offset in part the loss she suffered as a result of that tort having been committed.

In Chapter 26, we will explain when someone who has committed a tort will have a *defence* to being sued for compensation by the victim of that tort. Chapter 27 explains when the victim of a tort will be able to establish that that tort *caused* her to suffer some kind of loss. Chapter 28 deals with the law on when a loss that has been suffered by the victim of a tort will be *actionable*. In Chapter 29 we will explain how the courts *assess* how much should be paid by way of compensation to the victim of a tort who has suffered various actionable losses as a result of that tort having been committed. Finally, in Chapter 30 we will set out the law on when the damages payable to the victim of a tort to compensate her for the actionable losses she has suffered as a result of that tort having been committed will be *reduced* below the level necessary to compensate her fully for the fact that she has suffered those losses.

26 Limits on the right to sue

If A has committed a tort in relation to B, B may – depending on the circumstances – be barred from suing A for compensatory damages. This will be true in the following situations.

SPECIAL DEFENCES

If A has committed a tort in relation to B and A has a *special defence* to being sued by B for compensatory damages, B will – obviously – be barred from suing A for such damages.

In Part II of this book – which dealt with when someone will be held to have committed a tort – we noted some occasions when a tortfeasor would have a special defence to being sued for damages by the victim of his tort. So, for example, if Paul runs a newsagents and has committed a tort in relation to Lara by selling a newspaper which contains a defamatory statement about Lara, Paul will be able to raise a defence to any claim Lara might make against him for damages if he can show that when he sold the newspaper he did not know, and had no reason to know, that it contained a defamatory statement about Lara.[1] Similarly, if John commits a tort in relation to Wendy by infringing the patent that she holds on some invention, Wendy will be barred under s 62(1) of the Patents Act 1977 from suing John for compensatory damages if, at the time John infringed Wendy's patent, he 'was not aware, and had no reasonable grounds for supposing that [her] patent existed'.[2]

DEATH

It used to be the rule at common law that if A committed a tort in relation to B and A subsequently died, B would be barred from suing A (or, more accurately, A's estate) for compensatory damages. Similarly, it used to be the rule at common law that if A committed a tort in relation to B and B subsequently died, B (or, more accurately, B's estate) would be barred from suing A for compensatory damages in respect of the losses suffered by B as a result of A's tort before she died. These rules were, for the most part, abolished by s 1(1) of the Law Reform (Miscellaneous Provisions) Act 1934. However, the 1934 Act left the old common law rules intact in one respect. Section 1(1) of the 1934 Act provides that 'this subsection shall not apply to causes of action for defamation'. So suppose that Ruth libelled Eric and shortly after this happened Eric died. In such a case, Eric's estate will be barred from suing Ruth for compensatory damages in respect of the losses suffered by Eric as a result of Ruth's libel before he died. Alternatively, suppose that Ruth died shortly after she libelled Eric. Again, Eric will be barred from suing Ruth's estate for compensatory damages.

[1] See above, p. 306.
[2] See above, p. 496.

CROWN IMMUNITY

It used to be the rule at common law that 'the Crown could do wrong'. So it was simply not possible to sue a body which exercised the powers of the Crown (such as a government department or a branch of the armed forces) in tort for damages. However, the Crown Proceedings Act 1947 abrogated this rule to some extent.

Suppose that the Ministry of Public Works – a public body which exercises the powers of the Crown – has committed a tort in relation to Gary and Gary has suffered some loss as a result. In this case, Gary will *not* be barred from suing the Ministry in tort for compensation for the loss he has suffered if: (1) the Ministry was Gary's employee and it breached one of the common law duties of care it owed Gary as his employer; *or* (2) the tort committed by the Ministry consisted in the breach of a common law duty that it owed to Gary by virtue of the Ministry's 'ownership, occupation, possession or control of property'; *or* (3) the tort committed by the Ministry consisted in the breach of a statutory duty which is binding on persons 'other than the Crown and its officers'.

If none of (1), (2) or (3) are true in the case we are considering, the old common law rule will still hold sway and Gary will be unable to sue the Ministry in tort for compensation for the loss he has suffered.[3]

TRADE UNION IMMUNITY

If A, a trade union member, has committed a tort in relation to B, B will be barred from suing A for compensatory damages under s 219 of the Trade Union and Labour Relations (Consolidation) Act 1992 Act *if*: (1) A committed that tort in the 'contemplation or furtherance of a trade dispute';[4] *and* (2) the tort committed by A was one of the following torts: inducing a breach of contract, interfering with the performance of a contract, interfering with B's business using the unlawful means of threatening a breach of contract, lawful means conspiracy; *and* (3) none of the qualifications to s 219 of the 1992 Act apply in A's case.[5]

3 Of course, if Gary can establish that it was not only the Ministry that committed a tort in relation to him in the situation we are considering, but also one of the Ministry's employees, Gary will still be able to sue the Ministry for compensation for the harm that he has suffered under the law on vicarious liability: Crown Proceedings Act 1947, s 2(1)(a).

4 Section 244 of the 1992 Act defines a 'trade dispute' as involving a 'dispute between workers and their employer which relates wholly or mainly' to such things as – the workers' terms and conditions of employment, the employer's actions in firing or refusing to engage one or more workers; matters of discipline; a worker's membership or non-membership of a trade union; facilities for officials of trade unions.

5 *Very broadly speaking*, s 219 will not work to protect A from being sued by B if: (1) A's tort was committed by him in the course of picketing which was not rendered lawful by s 220 of the 1992 Act (s 219(3)); (2) A's tort was committed because B proposed to employ a non-union member or refused to discriminate against a non-union member (s 222); (3) A's tort was committed because B dismissed an employee for unofficial trade union action (s 223); (4) B was not party to the trade dispute in the furtherance of which A's tort was committed (s 224, though A will still be protected if his tort was committed in the course of lawfully picketing B's premises); (5) A's tort was committed in order to pressure B into recognising a trade union (s 225).

WITNESS IMMUNITY

B will be barred from suing A for damages in respect of anything said by A about B as a witness in judicial proceedings. This immunity from liability – known in legal circles as *witness immunity* – applies even if A *knowingly* gave false testimony about B. Even in this case, B will be barred from suing A for libel or slander or malicious falsehood. Why is this? The reason is that the law regards it as supremely important that witnesses in judicial proceedings should be able to say what they want in court free from the fear that they might be sued for what they say. So the law makes witnesses completely immune from being held liable for what they say in court, thereby assuring witnesses that there is no prospect that they could be successfully sued for what they say in court.[6]

The policy underlying the existence of witness immunity means that its ambit has had to be extended to statements made *outside* court. After all, witnesses would hardly be encouraged to say what they want in court if someone who was displeased with what they said could sue them not for what they said in court but for what they said to their lawyers in preparing their testimony. So in *Watson* v *M'Ewan*,[7] Jessie M'Ewan brought divorce proceedings against Thomas M'Ewan. The defendant made various defamatory statements about Jessie M'Ewan to Thomas M'Ewan's barrister when he was collecting evidence about the case. These statements came to Jessie M'Ewan's attention and she sued the defendant. The House of Lords held that she was barred from suing the defendant – his statements to Thomas M'Ewan's barrister were protected by witness immunity.[8]

Again, the policy underlying the existence of witness immunity means that its ambit has had to be widened to protect witnesses from being sued not for what they have *said* but for what they are alleged to have *done*. For instance, a witness would hardly be encouraged to say what he wanted in court if he knew that someone who was displeased with his evidence could sue him, alleging that he had unlawfully conspired with his lawyers or some other third parties to injure the claimant by giving false evidence about him in court. Because of this, the law on witness immunity was extended by the Court of Appeal in *Marrinan* v *Vibart*[9] to say that a witness who has given testimony in court cannot be sued on the basis that in giving that testimony he was engaged in an unlawful conspiracy to injure the claimant.

Attempts have been made to extend the ambit of witness immunity to cover statements made by investigators in investigating possible offences on the basis that investigators must be able to feel free to say what they want in the course of investigating possible offences and investigators would feel inhibited in making statements in the course of their investigations

6 Witnesses who knowingly give false testimony in court are, of course, liable to be prosecuted for perjury. However, the prospect of a prosecution for perjury is not likely to have any 'chilling' effect on what (honest) witnesses say in court. Witnesses will know that prosecutions for perjury are very rare and are only brought in blatant cases of dishonesty, so there is little or no likelihood of a witness who gives his testimony in good faith being prosecuted for perjury.

7 [1905] AC 480.

8 What is the position if someone makes a statement to a lawyer in preparing his testimony for court but he is never actually called as a witness? It seems that he will still be immune from being sued for what he said in his statement: *Evans* v *London Hospital Medical College (University of London)* [1981] 1 WLR 184, 191G. Similarly, if one side in a civil case commissions an expert witness to prepare a report on the merits of their case, that report will be protected by witness immunity even if it is never used in court but is merely used as the basis for arriving at a settlement of the dispute: *Stanton* v *Callaghan* [2000] QB 75.

9 [1963] 1 QB 528.

if they thought that their statements could be used as the basis of making claims for libel or malicious falsehood or negligence against them. These attempts have proved largely successful. In *X* v *Bedfordshire County Council*, Lord Browne-Wilkinson held that a psychiatrist who was employed by the police to determine who had sexually abused a child could not be sued in negligence for mistakenly reporting that the child had been sexually abused by the child's mother's lover; her report was protected by witness immunity.[10] In *Taylor* v *Director of the Serious Fraud Office*,[11] the defendant was a lawyer in the Serious Fraud Office. She suspected that the claimant, a lawyer practising in the Isle of Man, was engaged in a major fraud with one F. She wrote to the Attorney-General of the Isle of Man, requesting his assistance in her investigation. When F was eventually charged and prosecuted, the Serious Fraud Office's files on him were disclosed to F. These files included a copy of the defendant's letter which F showed to the claimant. The claimant sued the defendant for libel. The claim was dismissed; it was held that the statements made in the letter were protected by witness immunity.

The protection given to investigators in making statements in the course of their investigations would be easily subverted if the law said that an investigator who made a statement in the course of his investigations could be sued on the ground that in making that statement he was engaged in a conspiracy to injure the claimant. If the law said this then an investigator – so the argument goes – would be inhibited in making statements in the course of his investigations; he would know that someone who was adversely affected by a statement made by him in the course of his investigations could sue him, alleging that in making that statement he was engaged in a conspiracy to injure the claimant. Given this, the law probably does protect investigators from being sued on the basis that *in making statements in the course of their investigations* they were engaged in a conspiracy to injure the claimant. But the recent case of *Darker* v *Chief Constable of the West Midlands Police*[12] makes it clear that the law does not go any further than this – it does not protect an investigator from being sued on the basis that he committed a tort *by encouraging other people to fabricate evidence or by concealing evidence*. So if Gary and Mary, two police officers, falsely alleged that they saw Ian steal jewellery from a store, Ian will be prevented from suing Gary and Mary for libel or conspiracy or misfeasance in public office; their statement will be protected by witness immunity. But if Gary and Mary induce a third party, Tom, to allege falsely that he saw Ian steal jewellery from a store, Ian will be able to sue Gary and Mary for conspiracy or misfeasance in public office. They will not be protected by witness immunity.

ABUSE OF PROCESS

If A has committed a tort in relation to B, B will sometimes be barred from suing A for compensatory damages on the ground that B will only be able to establish that she is entitled to sue A for such damages by bringing into question – in other words, by making a *collateral attack* on – the correctness of an earlier decision of the courts. In such a case, B

[10] [1995] 2 AC 633, 755G.
[11] [1999] 2 AC 177.
[12] [2001] 1 AC 435.

may be barred from suing A for compensatory damages on the ground that bringing such an action would involve an *abuse of process*. It is hard to tell *when* B will be barred from suing A on this basis but the following test may be suggested: B will be barred from suing A on the ground of abuse of process if it would not be legitimate to allow B to challenge the correctness of the earlier judicial decision by bringing a claim in tort against A.

For instance, in *Hunter* v *Chief Constable of the West Midlands Police*,[13] the claimants were the Birmingham Six. They had been convicted of causing two bomb explosions which killed 21 people and injured 161 others. They were convicted largely on the basis of written and oral confessions that they made while in police custody. At their trial, they had claimed that these confessions had been beaten out of them. The trial judge held a hearing on the matter and concluded that the claimants had not been beaten by the police and held that their confessions were admissible in evidence. After the claimants were convicted, they sued the police for assault. Their claims were struck out on the ground that they involved an abuse of process. The claimants' claims sought to challenge the correctness of the trial judge's decision that the claimants had not been beaten and, in the absence of any fresh evidence that was unavailable to the trial judge at the time he made his decision, it would not be legitimate to allow the claimants to attack the correctness of that earlier decision by bringing a claim in tort against the police.

Similarly, in *Smith* v *Linskills (a firm)*,[14] the claimant was convicted of aggravated burglary at the Crown Court and sent to prison. On his release, the claimant sued the defendants, the solicitors who had acted for him during his trial, claiming that they had breached the duty they owed him to represent him with a professional degree of care and skill. The claimant's claim was dismissed on the ground that it amounted to an abuse of process. The claimant's claim involved an attack on the correctness of his conviction – he could only show that the defendants' negligence had caused him to suffer some kind of loss by showing that 'if his criminal defence had been handled with proper care he would not, and should not, have been convicted'.[15] In the absence of any fresh evidence that was unavailable to the Crown Court when the claimant was convicted, it would not be legitimate to allow the claimant to cast doubt on the correctness of his conviction by bringing a claim in tort against the defendants.

In contrast, in *Walpole* v *Partridge & Wilson (a firm)*,[16] the claimant was convicted of obstructing a veterinary officer in the execution of his duty in that he tried to prevent the officer taking blood samples from the pigs at his farm. The claimant instructed the defendants, his solicitors, to appeal against the decision. He thought that as the officer had no reason to suspect that his pigs were diseased, he had not committed any offence in attempting to prevent the officer taking blood samples from them. The defendants failed to lodge an appeal in time and the claimant sued them in negligence. The Court of Appeal refused to strike out the claimant's claim on the ground that it amounted to an abuse of process. While the premise of the claimant's claim was that his conviction would have been overturned on appeal and therefore that he should not have been convicted in the first place, the claimant's claim that he should not have been convicted in the first place was

[13] [1982] AC 529.
[14] [1996] 1 WLR 763.
[15] Ibid., 768H–769A.
[16] [1994] QB 106.

based on a point of law which was not considered by the court which convicted the claimant. Given this, it was not illegitimate to allow the claimant to bring a claim in tort against the defendants even though the bringing of such a claim would inevitably challenge the correctness of his conviction.

All these cases concerned claimants who claimed to have been convicted of some *criminal* offence due to the negligence of their lawyers. What is the position if, say, A, a barrister, represented B in a *civil case* and B lost her case? Could B sue A in negligence for damages, alleging that A failed to conduct her case with a professional degree of care and skill and that had A conducted her case properly she would have won the case? The question was considered in *Arthur J.S. Hall* v *Simons*,[17] which established that a barrister who represented a client in court would owe that client a duty to represent that client with a reasonable degree of care and skill. Lord Hoffmann thought that in the situation just described, any claim by B would *not* normally be struck out as involving an abuse of process.[18]

VOLENTI NON FIT INJURIA

The general rule

If A has committed a tort in relation to B and B has suffered some kind of loss as a result, B will normally be barred from suing A for compensation for that loss on the ground that *volenti non fit injuria* if she willingly took the risk that *she would suffer that kind of loss in the way that she suffered it*.[19]

For example, in *Morris* v *Murray*,[20] Morris and Murray went drinking together. At the end of the evening Murray suggested that they go for a ride in his light aircraft. Both men were quite drunk at this stage but Morris agreed to Murray's suggestion. Once both men were inside the plane, Murray – in his drunken state – just managed to get the plane airborne but it crashed soon after. Morris was badly injured and Murray was killed. Morris sued Murray's estate for damages in respect of his injuries, claiming that Murray had been negligent in the way he had piloted the plane. The Court of Appeal dismissed Morris's claim.[21] In climbing into the plane he had willingly taken a risk that Murray would fail to

[17] [2002] 1 AC 615.

[18] Ibid., 706–7. He did suggest one exception. Suppose Carl represented Nita in a defamation case where Karen was suing Nita for defaming her. Suppose further that Nita admitted that her statements about Karen were defamatory but claimed that they were true. Suppose finally that Carl did not do a very good job of arguing Nita's case with the result that the court found that Nita's statements were not true and found for Karen. In such a case, Lord Hoffmann suggested, if Nita then sought to sue Carl in negligence, her claim might be struck out on the ground that it amounted to an abuse of process. In order to make out her claim against Carl, Nita would have to show that but for Carl's negligence, the courts would have accepted that her statements about Karen were true. So Nita's claim would amount to an attack on the correctness of the court's decision that her statements about Karen were not true. Lord Hoffmann thought it might be improper to allow Nita to attack this decision. This must be right: it would surely be wrong to allow Nita to bring an action against Carl which, if successful, would have the effect of blackening Karen's name without giving Karen any opportunity to defend herself.

[19] Jaffey 1985 takes a much narrower view of the defence, arguing that it will only be available if B expressly agreed that A's conduct would not be actionable before he did what he did. However, this view is too narrow; it is certainly not consistent with the authorities mentioned below.

[20] [1991] 2 QB 6.

[21] The House of Lords refused leave to appeal: [1991] 1 WLR 1362.

pilot the plane properly and that he would be injured as a result. It would have been different, it might be suggested, if – once Morris and Murray were airborne – Murray had suddenly been overcome by suicidal feelings and had deliberately targeted the plane at the ground. While Morris willingly took the risk when he climbed into the plane that he would be injured as a result of the plane being badly piloted, he did not willingly take the risk that he would be injured as a result of Murray's deliberately crashing the plane into the ground. Given this, in our alternative scenario, Morris would not have been barred from suing Murray's estate for damages on the ground that *volenti non fit injuria*.

That this is correct is confirmed by the decision of the Court of Appeal in *Slater* v *Clay Cross Co. Ltd.*[22] In that case, the defendants operated a railway which passed through a tunnel. For many years, local residents walked through the tunnel to get to a village. One day the claimant happened to be walking through the tunnel when she was hit by one of the defendants' trains and was injured. The claimant sued the defendants, claiming that the defendants' driver had been negligent in the way he had driven the train; he had not kept a proper look-out and so on. The defendants argued that the claimant's claim should be dismissed on the ground that when the claimant walked through the tunnel she had voluntarily taken a risk that she would be hit by an oncoming train. However, the Court of Appeal dismissed this argument, holding that when the claimant walked through the tunnel she did not willingly take a risk that a train driver would *negligently* run into her.[23]

It should be emphasised that for the *volenti* defence to be raised, it must be shown that the claimant – who is seeking compensation for some loss that she has suffered – *willingly* took the risk that she would suffer that loss in the way that she did. So in *Haynes* v *Harwood*,[24] the defendant negligently left some horses unattended in the street.[25] A boy threw a stone at the horses and as a result they bolted. The claimant, a nearby police constable, threw himself in the way of the horses and seized their reins and brought them under control – but in doing so he suffered various personal injuries. The claimant successfully sued the defendant in negligence for compensation for his injuries. The Court of Appeal held that the defence of *volenti non fit injuria* was not available here. While the defendant had taken the risk when he tried to stop the horses bolting that he would be injured, he did not *willingly* take that risk – he had only acted as he did because it was an emergency.

Exceptions to the general rule

A couple of exceptions to the general rule set out above are worth mentioning.

(1) *Paternalistic duties.* If A owes B a duty to stop B harming herself, then if A breaches that duty with the result that B harms herself, A will not be able to defeat B's claim for damages

[22] [1956] 2 QB 264.

[23] See also *Blake* v *Galloway* [2004] EWCA Civ 814: claimant who participated in a good natured game which involved friends throwing twigs and pieces of bark at each other willingly took the risk that he might be hit by a piece of bark; though not if the piece of bark was thrown with the intention of harming the participant or was thrown in such a way as to evince a reckless disregard for the claimant's safety.

[24] [1935] 1 KB 146.

[25] Why 'negligently'? Well, it was reasonably foreseeable that the horses might bolt and injure passers-by if they were left unattended in the street. As a result, the defendant owed those passers-by a duty to take care not to leave the horses unattended in the street under the physical danger principle set out above, pp. 73–4.

on the ground that *volenti non fit injuria*. While B – when she harmed herself – willingly took the risk that she would suffer that harm in the way she did, if the *volenti* defence were available to A here A's duty would become meaningless. A would be completely free to breach it, safe in the knowledge that if B took advantage of his breach to harm herself, he would be able to raise a *volenti* defence to any subsequent claim she might bring against him for compensation for the harm she had suffered.[26]

(2) *Traffic accidents*. In *Pitts* v *Hunt*,[27] the claimant and defendant stole a motorbike and took it for a joyride. The defendant drove the motorbike and the claimant rode in the bike's pillion car. The defendant – with the encouragement of the claimant – drove the bike faster and faster, and finally crashed the bike. The claimant was injured in the crash and sued the defendant for compensation. The defendant sought to raise a *volenti* defence to the claimant's claim. The Court of Appeal held he could not.[28] While the claimant had willingly taken a risk that he would be injured in the way he was when he encouraged the defendant to drive faster and faster, the equivalent of what is now s 149(3) of the Road Traffic Act 1988 applied to prevent the defendant from relying on a *volenti* defence to defeat the claimant's claim. Section 149(3) of the 1988 Act provides that, 'The fact that a [passenger] has willingly accepted as his the risk of negligence on the part of the [driver] shall not be treated as negativing any . . . liability of the user.'[29]

The 'fireman's rule'

Some American states have adopted what is known as the 'fireman's rule' under which someone whose job involves running the risk of suffering a particular kind of loss cannot seek to recover compensatory damages if he actually suffers that kind of loss in doing his job.[30]

So if A negligently starts a fire in his house and B, a fireman, is injured in the course of fighting the fire, then – under the 'fireman's rule' – B will be barred from suing A for compensatory damages in respect of the injuries suffered by him as a result of A's negligence. Again, the 'fireman's rule' would operate to bar a police officer who developed a psychiatric illness as a result of what he saw or heard in dealing with a particularly traumatic incident from suing for compensatory damages in respect of that illness.

The reason for the fireman's rule is clear enough: if you have been paid to run a particular risk, you should not complain if that risk materialises and you suffer loss as a result. However, in *Ogwo* v *Taylor*, the House of Lords refused to adopt the 'fireman's rule' in English law and allowed a fireman to sue a householder for damages in respect of injuries

26 *Reeves* v *Commissioner of Police of the Metropolis* [2000] 1 AC 360, 375–6 (per Lord Jauncey of Tullichettle).

27 [1991] 1 QB 24.

28 The claimant's claim for damages was, however, dismissed on the ground of illegality: see below, n. 75.

29 So the result in *Morris* v *Murrary* would have been different if Murray had invited Morris to come for a drive in his car and had driven the car so badly that it crashed with the result that Morris was injured. In such a case, s 149(3) of the Road Traffic Act 1988 would have applied to prevent Morris's claim being barred on the ground that *volenti non fit injuria*.

30 California: *Walters* v *Sloan*, 571 P 2d 609 (1977); Michigan: *Kreski* v *Modern Wholesale Electric Supply Co.*, 415 NW 2d 178 (1987) (though see also *Miller* v *Inglis*, 567 NW 2d 253 (1997) and *Gibbons* v *Caraway*, 565 NW 2d 663 (1997), holding that the 'fireman's rule' does not apply in cases where defendant wilfully and wantonly created a risk that the claimant would be injured).

suffered by him in fighting a fire negligently started by the householder.[31] The House of Lords had another opportunity to adopt the 'fireman's rule' in *Frost* v *Chief Constable of West Yorkshire Police*[32] where – it will be recalled – the claimant policemen sought to recover damages in respect of the psychiatric illnesses they claimed to have developed as a result of the work they did helping out in the aftermath of the Hillsborough tragedy. However, their Lordships again showed no sign that they were in any way inclined to adopt the 'fireman's rule'.

CONTRACTUAL EXCLUSION OF LIABILITY

Suppose A has committed a tort *x* in relation to B. Suppose further that, before A committed that tort, A and B entered into a contract under which B undertook not to sue A for compensation if she suffered loss as a result of A's committing tort *x* (in which case we say A and B's contract contained an *exclusion clause*).[33] In such a case, B will be barred from suing A for compensatory damages *so long as* A is not himself barred from taking advantage of the exclusion clause in his contract with B to prevent B from suing him for such damages. As a general rule, A *will* be entitled to take advantage of the exclusion clause in his contract with B. Parliament has, however, created a number of exceptions to this general rule:

(1) *Business liability for negligently inflicted death or personal injury*. Under s 2(1) of the Unfair Contract Terms Act 1977, 'A person cannot by reference to any contract term ... exclude or restrict his [business][34] liability for death or personal injury resulting from negligence.' Under s 1(1) of the Act, a person is 'negligent' if he breaches a 'common law duty to take reasonable care or exercise reasonable skill or care' or a duty of care imposed on him by the Occupiers' Liability Act 1957.

So suppose Tom agreed to perform some medical operation on Dawn for a substantial fee. Suppose further that, before performing the operation, Tom and Dawn contractually

[31] [1988] AC 431, 449C, approving *Salmon* v *Seafarer Restaurants Ltd* [1983] 1 WLR 1264.

[32] [1999] 2 AC 455.

[33] Of course, if A and B did enter into a contract with each other before A committed tort *x*, there may be a dispute over whether A and B's contract contained an exclusion clause. This will be the case, for example, if, when A contracted with B, he intended that his contract with B should contain an exclusion clause, but B had no intention of agreeing to such a clause. And if A and B did enter into a contract with each other before A committed tort *x* and that contract *did* contain an exclusion clause, there may be a dispute over whether that exclusion clause operated to exclude A's liability to pay compensatory damages to B in the event of his committing tort *x*. This will be the case, for example, if the exclusion clause in A and B's contract was drafted using such vague language that it is debatable whether it excludes A's liability to pay compensation to B in the event of her being harmed as a result of his committing tort *x*. It is outside the scope of this book to explain how the courts resolve these disputes. The interested reader should consult a specialist book on the law of contract for such an explanation.

[34] Unfair Contract Terms Act 1977 s 1(3): 'In the case of both contract and tort, sections 2 to 7 aply only to business liability, that is liability for breach of obligations or duties arising – (a) from things done or to be done by a person in the course of a business (whether his own business or another's); or (b) from the occupation of premises used for business purposes of the occupier; and references to liability are to be read accordingly but the liability of an occupier of premises used for business purposes of the occupier; and references to liability are to be read accordingly but the liability of an occupier of premises for breach of an obligation or duty towards a person obtaining access to the premises for recreational or educational purposes, being liability for loss or damage suffered by reason of the dangerous state of the premises, is not a business liability of the occupier unless granting that person such access for the purposes concerned falls within the business purposes of the occupier'.

agreed that if Tom negligently injured Dawn in the course of the operation he would not be held liable to compensate her for her injuries. Suppose finally that Tom performed the operation so negligently that Dawn suffered severe brain damage as a result. In such a case, Dawn would not be barred from suing Tom for compensatory damages; Tom would not be allowed to take advantage of the exclusion clause in his contract with Dawn to prevent her from suing him for such damages.

(2) *Business liability for negligently inflicted harm not resulting from death or personal injury.* Under s 2(2) of the Unfair Contract Terms Act 1977, 'in the case of [loss other than that resulting from death or personal injury] a person cannot exclude or restrict his [business] liability for negligence except in so far as the term [excluding or restricting that liability] satisfies the requirement of reasonableness.'

So suppose Karen, a professional car mechanic, agreed to repair Paul's car. Suppose further that under the terms of their agreement, Karen would not be held liable for any damage done by her to the paintwork of Paul's car in the course of repairing it. Suppose finally that Karen negligently damaged the paintwork of Paul's car while repairing it. In such a case, Paul would *only* be barred from suing Karen for compensation for the damage done to his paintwork if the exclusion clause in the contract between Paul and Karen was 'reasonable'.

How do we judge whether the exclusion clause in the contract between Paul and Karen was 'reasonable' or not? In *Smith* v *Eric S. Bush*, Lord Griffiths provided some guidance.[35] He suggested that we should ask the following questions. (1) Were Paul and Karen of equal bargaining power? Did Paul have the ability to object to this term and the bargaining power to get Karen to withdraw it? If so then the term might be 'reasonable' – Paul has only himself to blame if he did not use his bargaining power to insist that this term was not part of the contract. (2) Could Paul have gone elsewhere to have his car repaired? If so, the term might again be regarded as 'reasonable' – if Paul did not want to be subject to this term then he could have gone elsewhere and the fact that he did not might go to show that Paul regarded the term as fair. (3) How difficult was it for Karen to repair Paul's car without scratching the paintwork? If very difficult, it might have been 'reasonable' for Karen to make it clear that she would not be held liable if she scratched the paintwork while repairing Paul's car. (4) What would be the practical consequences of declaring this sort of term to be 'unreasonable'? Would car mechanics be exposed to liabilities which, being unpredictable in size, would be difficult to insure against? Would it make more commercial sense to throw the burden of bearing the cost of any damage done to the paintwork of a car while it is being repaired on the owner of the car (and his insurer) rather than the repairer? If the answer is 'yes' then, again, the term might be regarded as 'reasonable'.

However, Lord Griffiths emphasised that 'it is impossible to draw up an exhaustive list of the factors that must be taken into account when a judge is faced with [the] very difficult [task of deciding whether a given exclusion clause is "unreasonable"]'.[36] The four questions set out above were merely questions which he thought 'should . . . always be considered'.[37]

[35] [1990] 1 AC 831, at 858–9.
[36] Ibid., 858.
[37] Ibid.

(3) *Misrepresentation*. Under s 3 of the Misrepresentation Act 1967, 'If a contract contains a term which would exclude or restrict – (a) any liability to which a party to a contract may be subject by reason of any misrepresentation made by him before the contract was made; or (b) any remedy available to another party to the contract by reason of such a misrepresentation, that term shall be of no effect except in so far as it satisfies the requirement of reasonableness as stated in section 11(1) of the Unfair Contract Terms Act 1977;[38] and it is for those claiming that the term satisfies that requirement to show that it does.'

So if, for example, the defendant in *Saunders* v *Edwards*[39] had insisted that the contract for the sale of his flat to the claimants included a term to the effect that he would not be held liable for any misrepresentations, innocent or otherwise, made by him to the claimants in the course of negotiations over the sale of the flat, the claimants would only have been barred from suing the defendant for compensatory damages in respect of the losses suffered by them as a result of the fraudulent misrepresentation made by him in the course of negotiations (that a right to use the roof terrace which the flat overlooked came with the flat) if the defendant had been able to show that that exclusion clause was reasonable.

It is worth noting that s 3 of the Misrepresentation Act 1967 – unlike s 2 of the Unfair Contract Terms Act 1977 – does *not* just apply when someone seeks to rely on a contract term to exclude or restrict some 'business liability' of his. Section 3 of the 1967 Act applies even in cases (as in *Saunders* v *Edwards*) where a defendant made a misrepresentation outside the course of business.

(4) *Unfair terms*. Under the Unfair Terms in Consumer Contracts Regulations 1999, if a contract made between a consumer and a seller or supplier of goods or services acting in the course of business contains an 'unfair' term then that term is not valid and cannot therefore be relied on in any litigation between the consumer and the seller or supplier in question.[40]

So, for example, suppose Vijay employed Mary – a professional surveyor[41] – to value a particular house for him that he was thinking of buying. Suppose further that Mary's contract with Vijay specified that if Vijay suffered any loss as a result of Mary's valuation, Mary would not be held liable to compensate Vijay for that loss. Suppose also that Mary negligently overvalued the house because she failed to spot that the house suffered from certain structural defects and, as a result, Vijay, having bought the house on the basis of Mary's

[38] Section 11(2) specifies that 'In determining . . . whether a contract term satisfies the requirement of reasonableness, regard shall be had to matters specified in Schedule 2 of the Act . . .' Schedule 2 of the 1977 Act instructs the courts to take into account the following matters in judging the reasonableness of a term: (*a*) the relative strength of the bargaining power of the parties to the contract; (*b*) whether the customer received an inducement to agree to the term or could have entered into a similar contract with someone else without having to agree to that term; (*c*) whether the customer knew or ought to have known of the term; (*d*) if the term excluded a defendant's liability for acting in a particular way, how reasonable it was to expect the defendant to avoid acting in that way; (*e*) (in the case of a contract for the sale of goods) whether the goods were manufactured, processed or adapted to the special order of the customer.

[39] [1987] 1 WLR 1116 (see below, p. 519).

[40] Unfair Terms in Consumer Contracts Regulations 1999, Reg 8.

[41] The Regulations only apply to terms in contracts between consumers and sellers or suppliers (Reg 4) where a 'seller or supplier' is defined by the Regulations as meaning 'any natural or legal person who [in contracting with another] is acting for purposes relating to his trade, business or profession, whether publicly owned or privately owned' (Reg 3(1)).

valuation, suffered various losses. If, under the 1999 Regulations, the exclusion clause in Mary and Vijay's contract was 'unfair' then it would be invalid and Vijay would be allowed to sue Mary for compensation for the losses suffered by him as a result of Mary's negligence. (Of course, Mary may in any case be barred from relying on the exclusion clause in her contract with Vijay to defeat his claim against her for compensation under s 2(2) of the Unfair Contract Terms Act 1977.)

The exclusion clause in Mary and Vijay's contract will not be regarded as being 'unfair' if it was 'individually negotiated'.[42] If it was not – say it was a term which was included in Mary's standard form contract for doing surveying work – then it will be regarded as being 'unfair' if the term, contrary to the requirement of 'good faith', caused a 'significant imbalance' in Mary's and Vijay's rights and obligations under the contract to the detriment of Vijay.[43] The definition of what amounts to an 'unfair' term is so loose that it is hard to predict, in any given case, whether or not the courts will hold that an exclusion clause in a contract between two people is 'unfair' and therefore invalid under the 1999 Regulations.[44]

(5) *Traffic accidents.* Under s 149 of the Road Traffic Act 1988, if (1) A drives B in his car; *and* (2) A is required, under s 143 of the 1988 Act, to carry third party insurance (liability insurance) in driving that car; then (3) if A and B agree that A will not be held liable to compensate B if she is harmed as a result of A's driving that car negligently, the agreement between A and B will be of no effect.

Three party cases (1)

Let us now consider a more complex situation. Suppose that John employed XYZ plc to build an extension on his house. John's contract with XYZ specified that if XYZ or 'any subcontractor' employed by XYZ to help in the construction of John's extension unintentionally damaged John's house or its contents in doing such work, John would not seek to sue the person responsible. XYZ subcontracted the work of wiring the extension to Ruth. While Ruth was doing the wiring, she carelessly caused a fire to start which damaged John's house. John now wants to sue Ruth in negligence for damages to compensate him for the fire damage done to his house. Can Ruth take advantage of the exclusion clause in the contract between John and XYZ and thereby prevent John from suing her for such damages?

Until recently, Ruth would *only* have been able to take advantage of the exclusion clause in the contract between XYZ and John if she could show that she was a party to the contract between XYZ and John by, for example, showing that XYZ was acting as her agent in entering into the contract with John.[45] (Of course, even if this were true Ruth might still have been barred by statute from taking advantage of the exclusion clause in the contract

[42] Regulation 5.
[43] Regulation 5(1).
[44] Witness, for example, the history of the litigation in *Director General of Fair Trading* v *First National Bank plc* where a term requiring a defaulting borrower to pay interest on his loan until he had paid off the loan was judged to be unfair under the Regulations by the Director General of Fair Trading (who is given power under the Regulations to direct companies to remove terms which are unfair under the Regulations from their standard form contracts); fair by Evans-Lombe J at first instance ([2000] 1 WLR 98); unfair by the Court of Appeal ([2000] QB 672); and, finally, fair by the House of Lords ([2002] 1 AC 483).
[45] *Scruttons Ltd* v *Midland Silicones Ltd* [1962] AC 446.

between XYZ and John.) It is hard to understand why the courts should have taken such a position. John indicated in his contract with XYZ that if one of XYZ's subcontractors unintentionally damaged his house, he would be happy to forego any rights he might otherwise have to sue the responsible subcontractor for damages. Given this, it is hard to see why the courts should have gone out of their way to allow John to sue Ruth for damages in respect of the unintentional damage done by Ruth to John's house.[46]

The courts took the above position because they thought that the doctrine of *privity of contract* dictated that Ruth should not be allowed, in the situation we are considering, to take advantage of the exclusion clause in the contract between John and XYZ if she was not a party to that contract. However, the doctrine has now been reformed by the Contracts (Rights of Third Parties) Act 1999. Under that Act, if A and B have entered into a contract to which C is not a party, C may 'enforce' a term in the contract *if*:

(1) C is expressly identified by the contract – whether by name or as a member of a class or as answering to a particular description – as someone who may 'enforce' that term; *or*

(2) (*i*) the term purports to confer a benefit on C *and* (*ii*) C is expressly identified by the contract, whether by name or as a member of a class or as answering to a particular description *and* (*iii*) when A and B entered into the contract they did *not* intend that C should *not* be able to 'enforce' that term.[47]

So in the situation we were considering, Ruth would probably be able, under the provisions of the 1999 Act, to take advantage of the exclusion clause in the contract between John and XYZ, thereby preventing John from suing her for compensation for the fire damage done to his house. This term purported to confer a benefit on Ruth; Ruth – as a 'subcontractor' – was expressly identified in the contract between John and XYZ; and there is no evidence that John and XYZ did *not* intend that Ruth should be able to take advantage of that term in the situation under consideration here.

However, it should be noted that under s 3(6) of the 1999 Act, Ruth will *not* be allowed to take advantage of the exclusion clause in the contract between John and XYZ if, had Ruth been a party to that contract, she would *not* have been allowed, under the Unfair Contract Terms Act 1977 or some other statutory provision, to take advantage of that exclusion clause to prevent John from suing her for compensatory damages.

[46] Ibid., 488–9 (per Lord Denning, dissenting). Perhaps recognising this, the courts sometimes went out of their way to prevent people like John suing people like Ruth through such devices as: (1) finding that there was a contract, collateral to the ones between John and XYZ and XYZ and Ruth, under which John undertook not to sue Ruth in negligence if she unintentionally damaged John's house (see *New Zealand Shipping Co. Ltd* v *A.M. Satterthwaite & Co. Ltd, The Eurymedon* [1975] AC 154); or (2) finding that when Ruth worked on John's house, she did not owe him a duty to take care not to damage the house or its contents (see *Norwich City Council* v *Harvey* [1989] 1 WLR 828).

[47] Section 1(6) of the Act provides that, 'Where a term of a contract excludes or limits liability in relation to any matter references in [the 1999] Act to the third party enforcing the term shall be construed as references to his availing himself of the exclusion or limitation.'

Three party cases (2)

Now let us turn to see what the position is in another three party situation. Suppose that Fred committed a tort in relation to Lara by doing *x*. Suppose further that before Fred did *x*, Fred entered into a contract with Wendy under which they agreed that he would not be held liable if he did *x*. Suppose finally that Lara wants to sue Fred for damages to compensate her for the losses she has suffered as a result of Fred's doing *x*. Will Fred be able to take advantage of the exclusion clause in his contract with Wendy and prevent Lara from suing him for such damages?[48] As a general rule the answer to this question is 'no'. This is not surprising. It is hard to see why an agreement between Fred and Wendy should ever have the effect of prejudicing Lara's rights against Fred. However, there are some exceptions to the general rule just set out.

Bailment

Suppose that Lara bailed goods to Wendy and Wendy sub-bailed those goods to Fred, telling him that they belonged to Lara. Suppose further that Fred and Wendy agreed that Fred would not be held liable if Lara's goods were destroyed or damaged while in Fred's care. Suppose finally that Lara's goods *were* destroyed because Fred failed to take proper precautions to keep them safe from harm.

There is no doubt that Fred has committed a tort in relation to Lara here. In this situation, he owed Lara a duty to take reasonable steps to ensure that Lara's goods were not destroyed or damaged[49] and he breached that duty. However, if Lara authorised Wendy to sub-bail her goods to Fred on the terms which Wendy agreed with Fred, Lara will be barred from suing Fred for compensation for the loss of her goods: Lara will be bound by the exclusion clause in the contract between Fred and Wendy.[50]

[48] In posing this question we assume, of course, that Lara is not a party to the contract between Fred and Wendy. If she were then it would be straightforward to find that Fred could take advantage of the exclusion clause in his contract with Wendy and prevent Lara from suing him for compensatory damages. Lara, as a party to the Fred-Wendy contract, would be bound by the terms of that contract.

[49] See above, pp. 182–3. It is crucial that when Fred took the goods, he knew they were Lara's. If Fred had taken possession of the goods in the belief that they were Wendy's, it is doubtful whether he would have owed *Lara* a duty to take reasonable steps to keep the goods from harm. It is therefore doubtful that Fred would have committed a tort in relation to Lara in failing to keep her goods safe: see *The Pioneer Container* [1994] 2 AC 324, 342.

[50] *Morris* v *C.W. Martin* [1966] 1 QB 716, 729 (per Lord Denning MR); *The Pioneer Container* [1994] 2 AC 324. We assume of course that Fred is not barred by statute from taking advantage of the exclusion clause in his contract with Wendy to prevent Lara suing him. It is more difficult to know what the position is if: (1) Lara authorised Wendy to sub-bail the goods on the basis that the sub-bailee would not be held liable for the loss of the goods; *and* (2) Fred destroyed the goods in this case through an act of *positive carelessness*. In this case, Lara will not need to rely on the existence of any bailment relationship between her and Fred to sue Fred: she can simply say that Fred owed her a duty under the 'property harm principle' set out above (at pp. 116–24) to take care not to destroy her goods; that he breached that duty; and that he is liable for the loss that she has suffered as a result of Fred's breach. In such a case, will Fred be able to argue that Lara is bound by the exclusion clause in his contract with Wendy – or does the principle established in *Morris* v *C.W. Martin* apply only to cases where an owner of goods' claim against a sub-bailee for the loss of his goods is based on a claim that there existed a bailment relationship between her and the sub-bailee? It is very difficult to say. For a discussion of the point, see Treitel 1999, 135–7.

Other cases

Suppose that Fred took on the job of drawing up Wendy's will and that Lara stood to receive a substantial bequest under that will. Suppose further that Fred carelessly failed to draw up the will in such a way that it would be valid and this fact was only discovered after Wendy's death. The result was that Lara did not receive her bequest. It is well established now that Fred will have committed the tort of negligence in relation to Lara in this case and Lara will normally be entitled to sue Fred for damages to compensate her for the loss of the legacy that she would have received under Wendy's will had it been correctly drawn up.[51]

But what is the position if Wendy's contract with Fred specified that Fred was not to be held liable in the event of his carelessly drawing up an ineffective will for Wendy? In such a case, it seems that Lara will be barred from suing Fred for damages: she will be bound by the exclusion clause in Fred and Wendy's contract.[52] The reason for this is that any claim brought by Lara against Fred for compensatory damages in the situation we are considering will be founded on the fact that Fred took on the task of preparing Wendy's will. Elementary fairness dictates that if Lara wants to take advantage of this fact and sue Fred for damages in respect of the losses suffered by her as a result of the way Fred performed that task, Lara must make allowance for the fact that Fred only took on that task on the understanding that he would not be held liable at all if he carelessly drew up an ineffective will for Wendy. Given this, it would be unfair to allow Lara to sue Fred unless, of course, Fred is barred by statute anyway from relying on the exclusion clause in his contract with Wendy to defeat Lara's claim.

Now suppose that Lara wanted a house built for her and she engaged Wendy to build it for her. Lara – having been impressed by a presentation from Fred – ordered Wendy to subcontract the work of laying the floors of the house to Fred, which Wendy duly did. The contract between Wendy and Fred specified that he would not be held liable if the floors of the house started to crack up more than a year after they were laid. Fred failed to do a good job of laying the floors of Lara's house and after two years the floors began to suffer from serious cracks. Now – there is no doubt in this situation that Fred has committed the tort of negligence in relation to Lara. He owed her a duty to lay the floors of her house with reasonable skill and care under the extended principle in *Hedley Byrne* and he breached that duty.[53] However, Lord Roskill thought in *Junior Books Ltd* v *Veitchi Co. Ltd* that, in the case just described, Lara would be bound by the terms of the subcontract between Fred and Wendy 'in some circumstances'.[54] As that contract specified that Fred could not be held liable if Lara's floors cracked up more than a year after they were laid, Lara might therefore be barred from suing Fred for compensation for the losses she has suffered as a result of the floors cracking up *two* years after they were laid.[55]

Lord Roskill did not make it clear in *what* circumstances Lara would be bound by the terms of the Fred-Wendy contract. It seems to us that Lara would only be bound by those terms if Fred warned Lara before she ordered Wendy to subcontract the flooring work to

[51] See above, pp. 150–4.

[52] *White* v *Jones* [1995] 2 AC 207, 268 (per Lord Goff). Again, this assumes that Fred will not be barred under the Unfair Contract Terms Act 1977 or some other statutory provision from taking advantage of the exclusion clause in his contract with Wendy to prevent Lara from suing him for damages.

[53] *Junior Books Ltd* v *Veitchi Co. Ltd* [1983] 1 AC 520, discussed above, p. 135.

[54] Ibid., 546E–F.

[55] We assume of course that Fred is not barred by statute from taking advantage of the exclusion clause in his contract with Wendy to prevent Lara suing him.

him that he was only willing to lay her floors on the basis that he could not be held liable if the floors cracked up more than a year after they were laid.[56] If Lara was willing to take the risk that she would have no remedy against Fred if the floors of her house cracked up after a year, there seems little reason why the courts should assist Lara to obtain such a remedy.[57] However, if Lara had no idea that the Fred-Wendy contract would contain an exclusion clause under which Fred would be free from liability if the floors of Lara's house started to crack up more than a year after they were laid, it is hard to see why Lara's rights against Fred should be limited by such a clause.

ILLEGALITY

Suppose that A has committed a tort in relation to B and B has suffered various losses as a result. Suppose further that A's tort or B's losses arose out of, or in connection with, B's committing a criminal offence. In this case, A *may* be able to raise a defence of *illegality* (otherwise known as the defence of *ex turpi causa non oritur actio*)[58] to prevent B suing him for damages.

The law in this area has been complicated somewhat by the enactment of s 329 of the Criminal Justice Act 2003, which is intended to *supplement*[59] the common law (judge-made law) on when A will be entitled to rely on a defence of illegality to prevent B suing him for damages.[60] We will begin our discussion of this area of the law by explaining when A will be able to raise a defence of illegality under the common law to defeat B's claim. We will then discuss when A will be able to raise a defence under s 329 of the 2003 Act to defeat B's claim against him.

The position at common law[61]

Let's go back to the basic situation we were considering. That is, suppose that A has committed a tort in relation to B and B has suffered various losses as a result. And suppose further that A's tort or B's losses arose out of, or in connection with, B's committing a criminal offence. The courts have found it hard to agree in this situation on when *exactly* A will be entitled to rely on a defence of illegality to prevent B suing him in tort for damages. This is hardly surprising: *whatever* the exact circumstances of A and B's case, there will *always* be good reasons for *both* denying *and* allowing B's claim for damages here.

[56] Of course, if Fred warned Lara that he could not be relied on to do a very good job of laying the floors, Lara would probably not be able to sue Fred at all. Fred will only have owed Lara a duty to lay the floors with the degree of care and skill that he indicated to her that he could be relied on to lay them with (see above pp. 134–5). So if Fred warned Lara he could not be relied on to do a very good job of laying the floors, Lara will face severe difficulties showing that he breached the (minimal) duty of care that he owed her in laying the floors.

[57] The same reason explains why Lara will not be allowed to sue Fred if Wendy sub-bails Lara's goods to Fred and agrees – with Lara's consent – that Fred will not be held liable if he fails to take reasonable steps to keep Lara's goods safe from harm and they are destroyed or damaged as a result.

[58] No action will arise out of an illegal act.

[59] This is made clear by s 329(6), which provides that the defence made available by s 329(4) 'is without prejudice to any other defence'.

[60] Section 329 will only come into force when the government makes an order bringing it into force (see s 336) and at the time of writing no such order has been made.

[61] See, generally, Glofcheski 1999.

If the courts allowed B's claim here, they would offend people's sense of fairness. They would rightly say, 'Why should B be allowed to take advantage of our laws when she is not willing to abide by them? She should not be allowed to pick and choose. If she thought it was all right to break the law when she committed her criminal offence, she should not now be allowed to take advantage of the law and sue A for damages in respect of the losses she has suffered as a result of A's tort.' If, on the other hand, the courts did *not* allow B to sue A here, they might be seen to be winking at wrongdoing. They would treat A more leniently than other wrongdoers and in doing so might send out a message that what A did was 'not really' wrong, or not so wrong that A should be treated in the same way as other wrongdoers.

Given these competing imperatives, the courts have usually[62] attempted in illegality cases to steer a middle way between them, sometimes allowing the defence to be raised, sometimes not.[63] *Generally speaking*,[64] in the case we are considering, A *will* be allowed to rely on the defence of illegality to defeat any claim B might bring against him for compensation for the losses she has suffered as a result of his tort *if*: (1) the criminal offence committed by B was a serious one;[65] *and* (2) there was a very close connection between B's committing that offence *and* A's tort *or* the losses suffered by B as a result of A's tort.[66]

A case where this test was clearly *not* satisfied was *Saunders* v *Edwards*.[67] In that case, the defendant sold a second floor flat of his and all its contents to the claimants. The flat overlooked a flat roof which the defendant had converted into a roof terrace accessible from his flat. The defendant represented to the claimants that a right to use the roof terrace came with the flat. In fact, as the defendant knew, the defendant had no right to use the roof terrace and his landlord had frequently objected to his doing so. The defendant's fraudulent representation played a large part in the claimants' decision to acquire the flat. The defendant and the claimants agreed that the flat and its contents were worth £45,000. The claimants persuaded the defendant to agree to sell them the contents for £5,000 – far more than they were worth – so as to minimise the price paid by them for the flat. The claimants did this in an illegal attempt to avoid paying the higher rate of stamp duty on the flat which would have been payable had they purchased the flat for more than £40,000. After the

[62] Though see Sedley LJ's dissenting judgment in *Vellino* v *Chief Constable of Greater Manchester Police* [2002] 1 WLR 218, which suggests that in illegality cases a defendant should *never* be allowed to raise the defence of illegality to defeat a claim for damages that has been made against him. Instead, the damages payable to the claimant should be reduced for contributory negligence in appropriate situations: 'It is clear that since the passage of the Law Reform (Contributory Negligence) Act 1945 the power to apportion liability between claimant and defendant in tort actions of all kinds has afforded a far more appropriate tool for doing justice than the blunt instrument of [the defence of illegality]' (ibid., at [55]). It is significant that Sedley LJ is plainly contemptuous of public feelings that it would be unfair to allow a claimant in a tort case to sue for damages if the tort in question or the claimant's losses arose out of, or in connection with, the claimant's committing a criminal offence: 'The public conscience, an elusive thing, as often as not turns out to be an echo-chamber inhabited by journalists and public moralists' (ibid., at [60]). Such a judge will, of course, see little reason why a defendant in a tort case should ever be allowed to rely on the illegality defence.

[63] See *Saunders* v *Edwards* [1987] 1 WLR 1116, at 1134 (per Bingham LJ).

[64] *Important note*. There is one important exception to the rule set out in the text. This is that A will *not* be allowed to rely on the illegality defence if doing so would permit him to appropriate B's property in circumstances where he has no statutory authority to do so: *Webb* v *Chief Constable of Merseyside Police* [2000] QB 427.

[65] Defined by Sir Murray Stuart-Smith in *Vellino* v *Chief Constable of Greater Manchester* [2002] 1 WLR 218 as being one which is punishable with imprisonment (at [70]).

[66] Ibid.; see also *Cross* v *Kirkby*, The Times, 5 April 2000.

[67] [1987] 1 WLR 1116.

claimants moved in they discovered the defendant's fraud and sued him in deceit for the loss of wealth they suffered in paying too much for the defendant's flat. The defendant argued that the claimants' illegal attempt to avoid paying the correct rate of stamp duty on the purchase of the flat meant they were barred from suing him for compensatory damages. Unsurprisingly, this argument was dismissed. There was no real connection between the defendant's tort and the claimants' tax evasion.

Two cases where this test clearly *was* satisfied were *Clunis* v *Camden and Islington Health Authority*[68] and *Vellino* v *Chief Constable of Manchester Police*.[69] In the *Clunis* case, the claimant, who had a history of mental disorder and violent behaviour, stabbed Mr Jonathan Zito to death at a tube station. He pleaded guilty to manslaughter on grounds of diminished responsibility and was detained under the Mental Health Act 1983. The claimant sought to sue the defendant health authority in negligence so as to recover compensatory damages for the losses suffered by him in being detained under the 1983 Act. He claimed that the defendant health authority had owed him a duty to treat his mental health problems with a professional degree of care and skill and that had the defendant health authority not breached this duty – as he claimed it had – he would not have stabbed Mr Zito to death and been detained under the Mental Health Act. The Court of Appeal held that even if the defendant health authority had owed the claimant a duty of care and breached that duty, the claimant's claim for damages still could not succeed: it was barred on the ground of illegality.[70] There was obviously a very close connection between the serious criminal act committed by the claimant in this case – manslaughter – and the losses for which the claimant was seeking compensation – that is, the losses associated with the claimant's being imprisoned for manslaughter.[71]

In the *Vellino* case, it will be recalled, the claimant was a career criminal who was seriously injured when, in an attempt to escape police custody, he jumped out of the kitchen window of his flat. His claim for damages was dismissed on the ground that the police had not owed him a duty to stop him trying to escape. However, Sir Murray Stuart-Smith went on to hold that even if the police had owed him such a duty and breached it, the claimant would still have been barred from suing the police for damages in respect of his injuries on the ground of illegality. There was obviously again a very close connection between the serious criminal offence that the claimant committed in the *Vellino* case – that is, attempting to escape police custody – and the injuries for which the claimant was seeking compensation.

However, not all cases are as easy as these. The following cases are generally regarded as being more marginal: whether or not the defence of illegality can be pleaded in these kinds of cases will depend on all the circumstances.

[68] [1998] QB 978 (followed in *Worrall* v *British Railways Board* [1999] CLY 1413).

[69] [2002] 1 WLR 218.

[70] The House of Lords refused leave to appeal: [1998] 1 WLR 1093.

[71] The decision in *Clunis*, it should be noted, runs counter to that in *Meah* v *McCreamer* [1985] 1 All ER 367. In that case, the claimant was involved in a car crash that was caused by the defendant's negligence. The injuries sustained by the claimant in the car crash had the effect of changing the claimant's personality for the worse, with the result that he sexually assaulted two women. The claimant was imprisoned and recovered damages from the defendant for the losses suffered by him as a result of his being imprisoned. However, unaccountably, the judge in *Meah* v *McCreamer* was not invited to dismiss the claimant's claim on the ground of illegality. Had the judge been so invited, he would – one would hope – have accepted the invitation and dismissed the claimant's claim.

(1) *Provocation.* Suppose that Tom provoked Dawn to shoot him by burgling her house. Suppose further that Dawn's shooting Tom cannot be justified on the ground of self-defence. If Tom sues Dawn for damages in respect of the injuries he sustained as a result of Dawn's shooting him, will Dawn be able to raise a defence of illegality to his claim? The Court of Appeal made it clear in *Cross* v *Kirkby*[72] that Dawn will only be able to rely on the defence of illegality if there was a sufficiently close connection between Tom's burgling Dawn's house and Dawn's shooting him.

Such a connection was not made out in *Revill* v *Newbery*.[73] In that case, it will be recalled, the claimant was shot by the defendant when he attempted to break into a shed on the defendant's allotment. The Court of Appeal held that the claimant was *not* barred from suing the defendant for compensatory damages on the ground of illegality. The Court of Appeal explained this decision in *Cross* v *Kirkby* on the basis that there wasn't a sufficiently close connection between the claimant's attempting to break into the defendant's shed and the defendant's shooting him. In shooting the claimant, the defendant was guilty of a gross overreaction to the claimant's conduct.

It might have been different in *Revill* if the claimant had been breaking into the shed in order to beat up the defendant. In such a case, while it might have been unreasonable – and therefore tortious – for the defendant to have shot the claimant, one would still be able to understand why the defendant acted in the way he did. There would then have been a sufficiently close connection between the claimant's criminal act in breaking into the shed and the defendant's shooting him so as to allow the defendant to rely on the defence of illegality to defeat the claimant's claim for damages.

Some support for this comes from the case of *Cross* v *Kirkby* itself. In that case, it will be recalled, Cross – a hunt saboteur – attacked Kirkby – a farmer who was allowing the local hunt to ride across his lands – with a baseball bat. Kirkby seized the baseball bat and hit Cross with it on the head. When Cross sued Kirkby, the Court of Appeal dismissed Cross's claim on the ground that Kirkby had acted reasonably in self-defence in striking Cross. The Court of Appeal went on to hold that even if Kirkby *had* acted unreasonably in striking Cross, they would have still allowed Kirkby to rely on the defence of illegality to defeat Cross's claim for damages. There would still have been a sufficiently close connection between Cross's conduct and Kirkby's striking him.

(2) *Joint venture.* In *National Coal Board* v *England*, Lord Asquith considered what the position would be if 'A and B, agree to open a safe by means of explosives, and A so negligently handles the explosive charge as to injure B'.[74] His Lordship thought that, in this case, A would be able to raise a defence of illegality to any claim B might make against A for damages. In this case there would be a very close connection between A's tort and the illegal venture that A and B were engaged on at the time A committed his tort, as that tort was committed in the course of furthering the illegal venture.[75] Lord Asquith thought it would

[72] The Times, 5 April 2000.

[73] [1996] QB 567.

[74] [1954] AC 403, at 429.

[75] The decision of the Court of Appeal in *Pitts* v *Hunt* [1991] 1 QB 24 bears out Lord Asquith's point. The claimant and defendant in that case went joyriding on a motorbike – the defendant drove the bike and the claimant travelled in the pillion car attached to the motorbike. The claimant urged the defendant to drive faster and faster and when the defendant complied, he crashed the bike and the claimant was injured. The claimant's

be different if 'A and B are proceeding to ... premises which they intend burglariously to enter, and before they enter them, B picks A's pocket and steals his watch.'[76] In this sort of case there would be less of a connection between A's tort and the illegal venture that A and B were engaged on; accordingly, Lord Asquith thought that in this second case, A would *not* be entitled to rely on a defence of illegality to defeat B's claim against him for damages.

(3) *Illegal employment.* In *Hewison* v *Meridian Shipping Services Pte Ltd*,[77] the claimant worked for the defendant shipping company as a crane operator. The claimant suffered from epilepsy and should therefore not have been put in charge of a crane. However, the claimant concealed his epilepsy from the defendants, thereby committing a criminal offence under s 16 of the Theft Act 1968.[78] Due to the defendants' negligence, the claimant was injured on the job. The injuries suffered by the claimant caused him to have three epileptic fits. As a result, the defendants became aware of the claimant's condition and were forced to dismiss him. The claimant sued the defendants for damages in respect of the losses that their negligence had caused him to suffer.

The Court of Appeal allowed the claimant to sue for damages in respect of the physical injuries he had suffered as a result of the defendants' negligence. No defence of illegality could be raised to prevent the claimant suing for such damages – and this was so even though the claimant would not have suffered those injuries had he not committed a serious criminal offence in lying to the defendants about his medical condition.[79] The Court of Appeal obviously thought there wasn't a sufficiently close connection between the claimant's lies and either the defendants' negligence or the injuries suffered by the claimant as a result of the defendants' negligence.

But the Court of Appeal reached a different conclusion when it considered the claimant's claim to be compensated for the money he would have earned working for the defendants in the future had he not been negligently injured by the defendants. (Had he not been injured, he argued, his epilepsy would not have become known to the defendants and he would not have been subsequently dismissed by the defendants.) In order to earn that money, the claimant would have had to continue deceiving the defendants about his medical condition, and in so doing he would have committed a serious criminal offence. So the loss of (future) earnings suffered by the claimant as a result of the defendants' negligence was inextricably linked to his willingness to commit a serious criminal offence in the future. Given this, the Court of Appeal ruled by 2 to 1 that the defendants would be entitled to raise a defence of illegality to the claimant's claim to be compensated for that loss.[80]

---

claim for damages in respect of his injuries was thrown out on the ground of illegality – there was a very close connection between the defendant's negligent driving and the joint illegal venture which the claimant and the defendant were engaged on at the time the defendant negligently crashed the bike.

[76] [1954] AC 403, at 429.

[77] [2002] EWCA Civ 1821.

[78] The offence of obtaining a pecuniary advantage by deception.

[79] Had he not lied, he would not have been employed by the defendants and would therefore not have been in a position to be injured as a result of their negligence.

[80] It is hard to see why Ward LJ, who dissented, thought the claimant's claim for this loss of (future) earnings might have merit. After all if Ian beat up a burglar, Gary, so badly that Gary had to give up his 'career' as a burglar, he could hardly be allowed to sue for the money he would have made in the future had he been allowed to continue burgling people's houses. Perhaps the real reason for Ward LJ's dissent was that he did not think that the claimant's offence in lying about his health was actually that serious.

The position under s 329 of the Criminal Justice Act 2003

Section 329 of the 2003 Act provides that if:

(1) B is suing A for damages on the basis that A committed the tort of assault, battery or false imprisonment in relation to B by doing *x*;[81] *and*
(2) B's actions round about the time A did *x* resulted in B's being convicted of an imprisonable offence;[82] *and*
(3) A did *x* because he honestly believed at the time: (*i*) that B was about to commit an offence or had committed an offence or had just committed an offence and because he honestly believed that it was necessary; *and* (*ii*) that it was necessary to do *x* in order to protect himself or another person; or to protect or to recover property; or to prevent the commission or continuance of an offence; or to apprehend B or secure B's conviction of having committed an offence;[83] *and*
(4) A's doing *x* was not grossly disproportionate to whatever B did, *then*
(5) A will be able to raise a defence to B's claim against him.[84]

Two points may be made about this provision. First, it is unlikely that it adds anything to the existing law on when someone will be entitled to rely on a defence of illegality to defeat a claim in tort that has been made against him. Suppose, for example, that Lara wants to sue Eric in tort for damages for some loss that she has suffered. Suppose further that Eric is not entitled to rely on a defence of illegality under the common law to defeat Lara's claim because he cannot establish that there was a very close connection between Lara's committing a serious offence and Eric's tort or the losses suffered by Lara as a result of Eric's tort. In such a case, it is unlikely that Eric would be able to rely on s 329 to defeat Lara's claim against him for damages.

Secondly, the fact that s 329 operates only in cases where a claimant sues a defendant for damages on the ground that the defendant committed the tort of assault or battery or false imprisonment in relation to her makes s 329 very easy to evade. Suppose, for example, that Gary breaks into Karen's house and in order to defend her property Karen shoots Gary in the leg. Obviously, if Gary sues Karen for damages on the basis that she committed a battery by shooting him in the leg, then s 329 will come into play. However, Gary could easily evade the effect of s 329 by suing Karen in negligence, claiming that 'You owed me a duty not to discharge your gun in my direction.' The fact that Karen shot Gary *deliberately* would not of course stop Gary suing Karen in negligence – a deliberate action can amount to negligence.[85]

LIMITATION

Suppose A has committed a tort in relation to B and B has suffered various losses as a result. If B delays too long before suing A for damages to compensate her for the fact that she has suffered these losses, she may be barred on *grounds of limitation* from suing A for such

[81] Section 329(1)(a), (8)(a).
[82] Section 329(1)(b). If conditions (*a*) and (*b*) are satisfied, then B will have to secure a court's permission before he is allowed to sue A: s 1(2).
[83] Section 329(4)(a), (5).
[84] Section 329(4)(b).
[85] See above, pp. 48–9.

damages. There are two reasons B will be barred from suing A for damages if she delays too long before bringing an action against A. First, it would be unfair on A if B could sue him for damages in respect of the losses that he caused her to suffer many years after he caused her to suffer those losses. A would constantly have the threat of litigation hanging over his head and, as a result, would find it difficult to make long-term plans or decisions about the future.

Secondly, the interests of justice would not be served if B were free to sue A for damages in respect of the losses that A caused B to suffer many years after A caused B to suffer those losses. It is in the interests of justice that suits be brought promptly when witnesses with evidence relevant to the suit are still available, when documents relevant to the suit are still easily to hand and when the memories of all involved in the suit are still fresh and uncorrupted by the passage of time. The longer the period of time before a claim is brought to court, the more likely that relevant witnesses will have died or disappeared, that relevant documents will have been destroyed or lost and that the memories of those involved in the case will have become stale and unreliable. Thus: the longer the period of time before a claim is brought to court, the harder it is likely to be to decide correctly whether or not that claim has any merit.

A detailed account of when the victim of a tort will be barred on grounds of limitation from suing the person who committed that tort for compensatory damages is beyond the scope of this book. However, a brief summary of the law in this area can be given. The *general rule* is that if A has committed a tort in relation to B, B will be barred from bringing an action against A in respect of that tort if she does not sue A within *six years* of the date she was first entitled to obtain a remedy in respect of A's tort.[86]

However, this general rule is subject to various qualifications.

(1) *Ignorance*. What if B was first entitled to obtain a remedy in respect of A's tort on 4 July 2005 – but she only found out that she was entitled to obtain such a remedy on 1 August 2011? As a general rule, if it was A's fault that B did not know she was entitled to sue A for committing his tort until 1 August 2011, then the limitation period will be extended and B will have six years from 1 August 2011 to bring an action against A, not six years from 4 July 2005.[87]

If it wasn't A's fault that B was left in ignorance for so long that she was entitled to sue A, then B will normally be stuck – the limitation period for suing A having elapsed on 4 July 2011, she will be barred from suing A for damages. However, it is different if the tort committed by A was negligence and A's negligence caused B to suffer various actionable losses which B only found out about on 1 August 2011. In such a case, B will have three years to sue A from the date that she could first have reasonably been expected to find out

[86] Limitation Act 1980, s 2. Assume that A committed his tort on 1 January 2005. If that tort was actionable *per se* (that is, the tort committed by A was actionable even if it did not cause B to suffer any actionable loss), then B will *normally* have until 1 January 2011 to sue A for committing that tort. The reason for this is that because A's tort was actionable *per se* B was entitled to obtain a remedy in respect of that tort as soon as it was committed. If, on the other hand, A's tort was not actionable *per se* (that is, the tort committed by A was only actionable if it caused B to suffer an actionable loss), then B will *normally* have six years from the date she first suffered an actionable loss as a result of A's tort to sue A for committing that tort. So if A's tort was not actionable *per se* and B first suffered an actionable loss as a result of A's tort on 25 December 2010, B will *normally* have until 25 December 2016 to sue A for committing that tort. The reason for this is that because A's tort was not actionable *per se*, the first time B was entitled to obtain a remedy in respect of A's tort was on 25 December 2010.

[87] Limitation Act 1980, ss 32(1)(b), 32(2). It appears this qualification to the general rule does not apply to actions under the Defective Premises Act 1972: *Warner* v *Basildon Development Corp.* (1991) 7 Const LJ 146.

about those losses. So if B could only have been reasonably expected to find out about the actionable losses which A's tort caused her to suffer on 15 June 2009, she will have until 15 June 2012 to sue A.[88]

(2) *Physical injury*. If A has committed a tort in relation to B and B has suffered some kind of physical injury as a result, a special limitation regime will sometimes apply to B's action against A. This will be the case if A's tort involved 'negligence, nuisance or [a] breach of duty'.[89] If it did, then B will normally have three years from the date she was injured as a result of A's tort to sue A for damages in respect of that injury. There are two exceptions to this rule. First, if – once B was injured – it took some time for her to find out that A had caused her to suffer that injury, she will have three years from the date she found out that A had injured her to sue him.[90] Secondly, if the applicable limitation period for suing A in respect of B's injury has elapsed, the courts may nevertheless allow B to sue A for compensation for her injury if it would be 'equitable' to do so.[91]

(3) *Defamation, malicious falsehood and deceit*. If A has committed one of these torts in relation to B, a special limitation period will apply. In cases of defamation and malicious falsehood, B will normally have only a year to sue A from the moment she was first entitled to obtain a remedy in respect of A's tort.[92] In the case of deceit, B will have six years from the time A's deceit first came to light to sue A.[93]

THE IMPACT OF ARTICLE 6 OF THE EUROPEAN CONVENTION ON HUMAN RIGHTS

Thus stands the law at the moment on when the victim of a tort will be barred from suing the person who committed that tort for compensatory damages. However, for the sake of completeness we should note one further point. Suppose that A has committed a tort in relation to B but he has a defence to being sued for damages by B. Call the defence that A can raise to any claim B might make against him, *defence x*. In such a case, B may be able to argue that allowing A to rely on defence *x* to defeat her claim for damages will violate

[88] Limitation Act 1980, s 14A. This rule is not meant to prejudice the limitation period for suing A that B would enjoy under the general rule. So if A breached a duty of care owed to B on 1 January 2005 and B first suffered an actionable loss as a result of that breach on 1 April 2006 and she could have reasonably been expected to find out about that loss on 1 March 2008, B will have until 1 April 2012 to sue A for the losses suffered by her as a result of his negligence – she won't have to bring her action against A by 1 March 2011. It should also be noted that the extension of time for bringing an action in negligence afforded by this section is subject to a 'long stop' limitation period which will expire 15 years after the victim of another's negligence was first entitled to obtain a remedy in respect of that negligence: s 14B. So if A breached a duty of care owed to B on 1 January 2005 and B first suffered an actionable loss as a result of that breach on 1 April 2006, but B could not reasonably have been expected to find out about that loss until 1 February 2020, B will only have until 1 April 2021 to sue A – the limitation period for suing A will not be extended until 1 February 2023.

[89] Limitation Act 1980, s 11(1). The House of Lords held in *Stubbings* v *Webb* [1993] AC 498 (discussed above, pp. 15–16) that this provision does not cover cases where A has committed a tort involving a trespass to B's person.

[90] Limitation Act 1980, s 11(1).

[91] Section 33.

[92] Section 4A. However, the limitation period may be extended under s 14A, discussed above at pp. 524–5. If the applicable limitation period for B's suing A has expired, the courts may still allow B to sue A if it would be 'equitable' to do so: s 32A.

[93] Section 32(1)(a).

her rights under Article 6(1) of the European Convention on Human Rights.[94] If this is right, then the courts will be required under s 6 of the Human Rights Act 1998 not to allow A to rely on defence *x* to defeat B's claim.

If B wants to establish that her Article 6(1) rights will be violated if A is allowed to rely on defence *x* to defeat B's claim against him for damages, she will have to do two things. First of all, she will have to show that allowing A to rely on defence *x* to defeat B's claim *could* violate her rights under Article 6(1). If she can do this, let's say that her case is *covered* by Article 6(1). If she can show that her claim is covered by Article 6(1), she will then have to show *either* that allowing A to rely on defence *x* to defeat her claim will serve no legitimate purpose *or* that allowing A to rely on defence *x* to defeat her claim will serve a legitimate purpose but in a disproportionate way. If she can do this, then B's Article 6(1) rights *will* be violated if A is allowed to rely on defence *x* to defeat B's claim.

When will a claimant who wants to sue someone else but is unable to do so be able to establish that her case is covered by Article 6(1)? This is a very difficult question and the cases on this issue are currently in a state of some confusion. However the following points can be made.

(1) A claimant cannot argue that her Article 6(1) rights have been violated just because she has not been allowed to sue a defendant.[95]

(2) The law on the scope of Article 6(1) draws a distinction between cases where a claimant has been prevented from suing a defendant because the domestic law governing her case put a *procedural* bar in the way of the claimant suing the defendant and cases where a claimant has been prevented from suing a defendant because the domestic law governing her case put a *substantive* bar in the way of her suing the defendant.

(3) A claimant who has been prevented from suing a defendant will be able to argue that her case is covered by Article 6(1) if she was prevented from suing the defendant because the law put a *procedural* bar in the way of her suing the defendant.[96] So, for example, a prisoner who was prevented from suing his prison governor for libel because, under UK law, he was not allowed access to a solicitor was able to establish that Article 6(1) covered his case.[97] Similarly, the case of a claimant who was sexually abused by the defendant as a child and was prevented from suing him for damages on grounds of limitation was held to be covered by Article 6(1).[98] The law on limitation of actions created a procedural bar to her claim.[99]

(4) By contrast, Article 6(1) will not cover the case where a claimant has been prevented from suing a defendant because the law put a *substantive* bar in the way of her suing the defendant. If the claimant's claim against the defendant failed because she had *no right* to

[94] Article 6(1), of course, provides that 'In the determination of his civil rights and obligations . . . everyone is entitled to a fair and public hearing within a reasonable time by an independent and impartial tribunal established by law.'

[95] *Z* v *United Kingdom* [2001] 2 FLR 612, at [88].

[96] *James* v *United Kingdom* (1986) 8 EHRR 123, at [81].

[97] *Golder* v *UK* (1975) 1 EHRR 524, discussed above, p. 90. The prisoner's Art 6(1) rights were found to have been violated.

[98] *Stubbings* v *United Kingdom* [1997] 1 FLR 105. The European Court of Human Rights went on to find that the claimant's Art 6(1) rights had not actually been violated: the laws on limitation which prevented the claimant suing the defendant pursued a legitimate goal, and in a proportionate way.

[99] See *Matthews* v *Ministry of Defence* [2003] 1 AC 1163, at [128] (per Lord Walker): 'Bars arising from statutes of limitation are . . . generally regarded as procedural.'

sue the defendant under the law applicable to her claim, then we would *normally* say that there existed a *substantive* bar which prevented her from suing the defendant. However, it is clear from the decided cases that a claimant whose claim against a defendant has failed because she had no right to sue him will *sometimes* be able to argue that the bar on her suing the defendant that existed in her case was actually *procedural* in nature and *not* substantive.

(5) The European Court of Human Rights (ECtHR for short) has held in a number of cases that a claimant who has been prevented from suing a defendant because she had no right to sue him will be able to argue that a *procedural* bar stood in the way of her suing the defendant if the reason why she had no right to sue him was that the domestic law governing her claim conferred an *immunity* on the defendant from being sued by the claimant.[100] These cases take their inspiration from the following *dictum* of the ECtHR in *Fayed* v *United Kingdom*:

> it would not be consistent with the ... basic principle underlying Article [6(1)]... – namely that civil claims must be capable of being submitted to a judge for adjudication – if, for example, a State could, without restraint or control by the Convention enforcement bodies, remove from the jurisdiction of the civil courts a whole range of civil claims or confer immunities from civil liability on large groups or categories of persons ...[101]

(6) The ECtHR has never explained when exactly a defendant can be said to enjoy an *immunity* from being sued by a claimant. Some cases seem to suggest that a defendant will enjoy an immunity from being sued by a claimant if: (1) the claimant wants to bring an action against the defendant which is well recognised under the domestic law governing her case; *and* (2) the domestic law governing the claimant's case provides that the claimant has no right to bring such an action against the defendant, but it does so for reasons that have nothing to do with the merits of the claimant's case.[102] If (1) and (2) are made out then, according to these cases, the claimant will be able to argue that the domestic law governing her case has put a *procedural* bar in the way of her suing the defendant and that therefore her case is covered by Article 6(1).[103]

(7) The House of Lords has, however, taken a much narrower view as to when a claimant who has no right to sue a defendant can argue that the bar which the law places on her suing the defendant is procedural in nature, rather than substantive.

[100] *Tinnelly & Sons Ltd* v *United Kingdom* (1998) 27 EHRR 249, at [71]–[72]; *Al-Adsani* v *United Kingdom* (2001) 34 EHRR 273, at [46]–[48]; *Fogarty* v *United Kingdom* (2001) 34 EHRR 302, at [25]–[26]; *McElhinney* v *Ireland* (2001) 34 EHRR 322, at [23]–[25].

[101] (1994) 18 EHRR 393, at [65]. It may be that the ECtHR was, in saying this, attempting to transform Art 6(1) into a European equivalent of the Fourteenth Amendment to the Constitution of the United States, which provides that no State shall 'deny to any person within its jurisdiction the equal protection of the laws'.

[102] See the cases cited above, n. 100.

[103] It could be argued that our account of the scope of Art 6(1) is inconsistent with the decision of the ECtHR in *Powell and Rayner* v *United Kingdom* (1990) 12 EHRR 355. In that case the claimants were prevented from suing the defendants in private nuisance because of s 76(1) of the Civil Aviation Act 1982, which provides that no claims in private nuisance can be brought in respect of 'the flight of an aircraft over any property at a height above the ground which is ... reasonable.' It was held that the bar on the claimants' suing the defendants here was a substantive one and that Art 6(1) did not therefore cover the claimants' case. However, two points can be made in response to this. First, it is not clear that the bar which existed in *Powell and Rayner* had nothing to do with the merits of the claimants' case: if the flight of aircraft over the claimants' property was 'reasonable' that would weaken the strength of the claimants' claim that they were entitled to sue the defendants in private nuisance. Secondly, the decision in *Powell and Rayner* antedated the decision in *Fayed*, and it may well be that if a case like *Powell and Rayner* came up again today, the decision would be very different.

In *Matthews* v *Ministry of Defence*,[104] the claimant was a sailor who suffered various asbestos related injuries as a result of working in the Royal Navy between 1955 and 1968. He sued the Ministry of Defence for compensation. Under the law that was applicable to his claim, he would have had no right to sue the Ministry of Defence for compensation *if*: (1) his injuries were suffered as a result of the condition of any ship used by the armed services; *and* (2) the relevant Secretary of State issued a certificate to that effect.[105] Such a certificate was issued in the claimant's case and as a result his claim for damages was thrown out.[106]

The claimant argued that his rights under Article 6(1) were violated when his claim was thrown out. The House of Lords disagreed: they held the bar which prevented the claimant suing the Ministry of Defence in this case was substantive, not procedural, in nature and that therefore the claimant's case was not covered by Article 6(1). The House of Lords was prepared to admit that a *no right* case might in certain circumstances be covered by Article 6(1). At the same time, it is clear that their Lordships took a very narrow view of what those circumstances might be. Lord Hoffmann suggested that a *no right* case would be covered by Article 6(1) if the reason why the claimant had no right to sue a defendant was that the government had been given an 'arbitrary power' to declare that the claimant had no right to sue the defendant and thereby stop her case in its tracks.[107] Lord Millett took the view that a *no right* case would be covered by Article 6(1) if the reason why the claimant had no right to sue the defendant was that the government had passed a statute stripping people like her of the right to sue people like the defendant for reasons which were unrelated to the reason why people like her had a right to sue people like the defendant in the first place.[108]

In so ruling, the House of Lords took the view that the object of Article 6(1) is to prevent the government arbitrarily interfering with people's enjoyment of the rights that they are afforded under the law – either through using procedural tricks designed to prevent them getting a full hearing of their case or by using its legislative power to strip people of rights to sue that they would otherwise enjoy. Seen in this way, it was obvious that the claimant's case in *Matthews* was not covered by Article 6(1). Section 10 of the Crown Proceedings Act 1947 was not intended to deprive people of any rights that they previously enjoyed under statute or the common law. Instead it preserved, in part, the old rule that people had *no rights* to sue the Crown, while at the same time ensuring – through the certification procedure – that those prejudiced by the preservation of that rule would obtain an alternative means of compensation for the harm they had suffered through the award of a pension.[109]

(8) In *Roche* v *United Kingdom*,[110] the ECtHR had the opportunity to address the question of whether the bar to bringing a civil claim considered in the *Matthews* case was substantive

[104] [2003] 1 AC 1163.

[105] Crown Proceedings Act 1947, s 10. This provision was later repealed by the Crown Proceedings Act 1987, and therefore does not figure in our account of the scope of Crown immunity set out above, at p. 504. As the claimant's injuries in *Matthews* were suffered by him as a result of his working in the Royal Navy between 1955 and 1968, his claim for compensation for those injuries was governed by s 10.

[106] Though the issuing of the certificate meant that the claimant became entitled to a pension which would help compensate him for the injuries he had suffered.

[107] [2003] 1 AC 1163, at [35].

[108] Ibid., at [79].

[109] Ibid., at [73] (per Lord Hope).

[110] (2006) 42 EHRR 30.

or procedural in nature. Of the 17 judges who decided the case, nine agreed with the House of Lords in *Matthews* that the bar was substantive in nature and therefore the claimant in *Roche* could not complain that applying it to prevent him suing the Ministry of Defence for damages violated his Article 6(1) rights. The remaining eight judges took the position set out in point (6), above, and held that the bar was procedural in nature, with the result that applying that bar to stop the claimant suing the Ministry of Defence might have violated his Article 6(1) rights. The decision in *Roche* makes it difficult to know what position the ECtHR will take in the future as to when a *no right* case will be covered by Article 6(1).

(9) The difference between the position taken by the minority in *Roche* as to when a *no right* case will be covered by Article 6(1) and the position taken by the House of Lords in *Matthews* v *Ministry of Defence* may be better appreciated through the use of a concrete example. We have already seen that if Paul libels Karen and subsequently dies, Karen will not be allowed to sue Paul's estate for damages.[111] Whether or not Karen will be able to argue that this violates her rights under Article 6(1) will depend on whether the bar on Karen's suing Paul's estate here is procedural or substantive in nature.

It is not hard to imagine that the minority in *Roche* would rule that the bar here is *procedural* in nature: Karen wants to sue Paul's estate for damages in defamation – a cause of action which is well acknowledged in UK law – but she is prevented from doing so by s 1(1) of the Law Reform (Miscellaneous Provisions) Act 1934 and for reasons which have nothing to do with the merits of her claim. So the minority in *Roche* might well rule that Article 6(1) covers Karen's claim here.[112] Equally, it seems to follow from the decision in *Matthews* that the House of Lords would rule that there exists a *substantive* bar in the way of Karen's suing Paul's estate here. Section 1(1) of the 1934 Act does not deprive people like Karen of any rights that people like her previously enjoyed. Instead it preserves, in part, the old rule that the victim of a tort would have *no rights* to sue the person who committed that tort if he died after he committed that tort. So the House of Lords – if asked – might well rule that Article 6(1) does *not* cover Karen's case here, with the result that Karen will *never* be able to claim that the courts will violate her Article 6(1) rights if they throw out her claim, no matter how silly or disproportionate the rule embodied in s 1(1) of the 1934 Act is.

Now that we have a firmer grasp of what sort of cases are covered by Article 6(1), we can return to our original case – where A has committed a tort in relation to B but can raise a defence *x* to any claim that B might make against him for damages. When will B be able to argue that her claim against A is covered by Article 6(1)? It is clear that if the defence relied on by A to defeat B's claim is a limitation defence then B's case will be covered by Article 6(1). B will have no problem establishing that the bar on her suing A created by that defence is procedural in nature. It is much more uncertain what the position is in relation to the other defences that A might raise to defeat B's claim. Normally one would think that these defences create a substantive bar to B's suing A: if A is able to take advantage of any

[111] See above, p. 503.

[112] Of course, if Art 6(1) does cover Karen's case here, dismissing Karen's claim will not necessarily violate her Art 6(1) rights: it depends on whether dismissing her claim will serve a legitimate purpose and in a proportionate way. It is hard to think that it will. Given this, the issue of whether Art 6(1) covers Karen's claim becomes vitally important – it seems that if Art 6(1) covers Karen's claim, then dismissing Karen's claim against Paul's estate *will* violate her Art 6(1) rights.

of these defences, B will have *no right* to sue A. But, as we have seen, even some *no right* cases will be treated by the courts as cases where the law has placed a *procedural* bar in the way of a claimant suing a defendant. Can any of the defences considered here be treated as creating a procedural bar in the way of B's suing A?

If we follow the approach of the minority in *Roche* to the question of when a *no right* case will involve a procedural bar, then the following defences might well be regarded as creating a procedural bar to B's suing A if they are relied upon by A to defeat B's claim: Crown immunity, witness immunity, trade union immunity and abuse of process. All of these defences will operate to prevent B from bringing a tort claim for damages against A – a claim which is well acknowledged under UK law – and for reasons that have nothing to do with the merits of B's claim. The defences of *volenti*, exclusion of liability and illegality will also prevent B bringing a tort claim for damages against A but the defences in those cases will be centrally concerned with the merits of B's claim.

If, on the other hand, we follow the House of Lords' approach to this question, then trade union immunity is probably the only defence (other than the obvious one of limitation) that could be said to raise a procedural bar to B's suing A. It could be argued that Parliament, in creating this immunity, stripped people of rights they previously enjoyed under the common law. If this is right then, under the House of Lords' approach to the scope of Article 6(1), cases where a defendant is able to take advantage of the defence of trade union immunity may well be covered by Article 6(1). An employer who is prevented from suing a trade union for damages under s 219 of the Trade Union and Labour Relations (Consolidation) Act 1992 Act might therefore be able to argue that his Article 6(1) rights have been violated – though whether they have or not will depend on whether s 219 serves a legitimate purpose in a proportionate way.[113] By contrast, it is hard to argue that the existence of defences such as witness immunity, Crown immunity, *volenti*, exclusion of liability and illegality strip people of rights that they previously enjoyed before those defences were created. The defences came with the rights: they did not post-date them.

So it is still uncertain what effect Article 6(1) of the European Convention on Human Rights will have on the availability of the defences dealt with in this chapter. If the House of Lords' view as to the scope of Article 6(1) is correct, then the effect should be very small – Article 6(1) will not prevent a tortfeasor relying on most of the defences set out in this chapter. If the ECtHR follows the view of the minority in *Roche* – and the ECtHR case law that preceded the decision in *Roche* – then the impact of Article 6(1) should be more far-reaching.

Visit **http://www.mylawchamber.co.uk/mcbride** to access updates on recent cases, as well as model answers and tips for answering tort problem questions.

Use **Case Navigator** to read in full the key case referenced in this chapter:

- **Frost v Chief Constable of West Yorkshire Police**

[113] It is likely, though, that s 219 would survive this process of scrutiny, given that it is so severely qualified.

27 Causation of loss

Suppose that A has committed a tort in relation to B. If B wants to sue A for compensatory damages, the very first thing she will have to show is that A's tort *caused* her to suffer some kind of *loss*. Before we go on to describe the tests that the courts use to determine whether or not A's tort has caused B to suffer any kind of loss, it is worth cataloguing the different kinds of loss that A's tort might have caused B to suffer.

TYPES OF LOSS

There are many different kinds of loss that A's tort may have caused B to suffer.

(1) *Physical injury*. A's tort could have caused B to suffer some kind of physical injury. The term 'physical injury', as it is used here, is fairly straightforward.[1] B will suffer a form of physical injury if her leg breaks or she develops cancer. She will also – seemingly – suffer a form of physical injury if she becomes pregnant.[2] However, the concept of 'physical injury', as it is used here, does not cover *death*.[3] If A commits a tort in relation to B and B dies *instantaneously* as a result, B will not – for our purposes here – suffer a physical injury or, indeed, any other kind of loss. It makes no sense to say that B's dying means that she *has* suffered a loss as a result of A's tort – B is no longer around for her to experience her death as a loss. However, if A stabs B and B dies of her wounds six months later, then A's tort in stabbing B will have caused B to suffer a form of physical injury and associated losses such as distress; and an action can be brought for compensation for these losses even after B's death.[4]

(2) *Property damage*. A's tort could have caused property in which B had an interest to be destroyed or damaged.[5]

(3) *Psychiatric illness*. A's tort could have caused B to develop a psychiatric illness – that is,

[1] In *Rothwell* v *Chemical & Insulating Co. Ltd* [2007] 3 WLR 876, the House of Lords made it clear that a mere physiological change that does not have any kind of adverse effect on the health or welfare of the person will not count as a 'physical injury'.

[2] See above, p. 76 n. 21.

[3] It will be recalled that the term 'physical injury' *does* cover death in the context of the physical danger principle, which we identified as underlying the decision in *Donoghue* v *Stevenson* [1932] AC 562: see above, p. 76.

[4] See above, p. 503.

[5] The fact that property damage counts as a loss in its own right helps to explain why a claimant whose property has been wrongfully damaged will still be entitled to sue for substantial damages even if she has not actually suffered any loss *as a result* of the property being damaged: see *Mediana (Owners of Steamship)* v *Comet (Owners of Lightship)* [1900] AC 113 (the claimants' lightship was damaged as a result of the defendants' negligence and had to be taken out of service to be repaired, during which time its place was taken by a substitute lightship maintained by the defendants for exactly this purpose: the claimants were held entitled to sue the defendants for substantial damages to compensate them for the (temporary) loss of their lightship, even though they did not suffer any further loss as a result of suffering that loss).

a form of mental harm that is regarded as amounting to a psychiatric illness by the medical profession.

(4) *Damage to reputation.* A's tort could have caused B's good name to be impaired or ruined.

(5) *Imprisonment.* A's tort could have caused B to be locked up. This will obviously be the case if the tort committed by A was false imprisonment. But A could have caused B to be locked up by committing some other kind of tort. In *Meah* v *McCreamer*,[6] it will be recalled, the claimant was involved in a car crash that was negligently caused by the defendant. (The claimant was in the defendant's car and the defendant was drunk at the time of the car crash.) The claimant sustained serious head injuries in the accident that caused his personality to change for the worse. The claimant went on to attack two women and was sent to prison as a result. The court held that the defendant's negligence had caused the claimant to be locked up and the claimant (wrongly, in our view)[7] recovered damages for his imprisonment.

(6) *Distress.* A's tort could have caused B distress. We use the term 'distress' here to cover not only anxiety and upset but also pain and suffering. There are a variety of ways in which A's tort could have caused B distress. A's tort could have caused B to suffer some kind of personal injury with the result that B experienced some degree of pain and suffering. Similarly, A's tort could have caused B's property to be damaged with the result that B suffered a great deal of distress.[8] Alternatively, A's tort could have caused B to suffer a *pure* form of distress: that is, one which was not consequent on A's tort causing B to suffer some kind of personal injury or property damage. So, for example, suppose A upset B by repeatedly making aggressive telephone calls to her, thereby committing the tort of harassment. In this case, A's harassment will have caused B to suffer a pure form of distress.

(7) *Inconvenience.* A's tort could have caused B to suffer hassle or inconvenience. Again, the most obvious way in which A's tort could have caused B to suffer this kind of loss is if A's tort caused B to suffer some form of personal injury which made it difficult for B to get around. Another obvious way in which A's tort could have caused B to suffer hassle or inconvenience is if A's tort caused her to suffer some other kind of loss such as personal injury or property damage and B sued A for compensation for that loss. The very act of bringing litigation will involve hassle or inconvenience for B and B will reasonably be able to argue that A's tort caused her to suffer that hassle or inconvenience.[9]

(8) *Loss of amenity.* A's tort could have caused B to suffer a loss of amenity. This will be the case if A's tort has prevented B from enjoying some pleasurable experience that she would otherwise have experienced. So suppose A's tort caused B's leg to break with the result that

[6] [1985] 1 All ER 367.
[7] See above, p. 520 n. 71.
[8] Though in this case, B will not be able to claim damages for her distress; the distress suffered by her as a result of her property being damaged will not be an actionable loss: see below, pp. 593–4.
[9] However, B will not be able to claim damages for that hassle or inconvenience. It is regarded as non-actionable.

B could not go on holiday. In such a case, A's tort will have caused B to suffer a loss of amenity.[10]

(9) *Loss of a chance of obtaining a benefit.* A's tort could have caused B to suffer loss by depriving her of the chance of obtaining some kind of benefit. The claimant in *Chaplin* v *Hicks*[11] (*not* a tort case) suffered this form of loss. The claimant was a contestant in a beauty competition organised by a newspaper. She had passed the preliminary stages of the competition and the defendant had arranged to meet her to see if she should make the final of the competition. The defendant – in breach of contract – never turned up and the final went on without the claimant. The defendant's breach of contract deprived the claimant of the chance to win the beauty contest and, as such, caused the claimant to suffer a form of economic loss, for which she was entitled to claim compensation in an action for breach of contract.

(10) *Incurring a chance of suffering a harm.* A's tort will have caused B to suffer loss if, as a result of that tort being committed, there is a chance that B will suffer some kind of harm in the future. So, for example, suppose that B lost an arm as a result of A's tort being committed. Fortunately, this did not result in B losing her job. However, there is now a chance that if B becomes unemployed in the future – because, for example, her employer went out of business – she will find it difficult to secure alternative employment. So as a result of A's tort being committed, there is now a chance that B will suffer a prolonged period of unemployment in the future. This counts as a loss for which B may be entitled to be compensated.[12]

(11) *Economic loss.* A's tort will have caused B to suffer some form of economic loss if B has been made economically worse off as a result of that tort having been committed. An economic loss that B has suffered as a result of A's tort having been committed will be classified as *pure economic loss* if it does not result from B's person or property being damaged.

(12) *Wasted expenditure.* Of the different types of economic loss that A's tort could have caused B to suffer, this is the first: A's tort could have caused B to spend money on something which she would not otherwise have spent money on or had occasion to spend money on. So if A's tort caused B to lose the use of her legs with the result that B had to spend money on a wheelchair and having a lift installed in her house, A's tort will have caused B to suffer the form of economic loss discussed here: A's tort will have caused B to spend money on things that she would not otherwise have spent money on.

(13) *Loss of income.* Obviously, A's tort will have caused B to suffer a form of economic loss if B's earnings are now less than they would have been had A not committed that tort.

(14) *Interception of benefit.* A's tort will also have caused B to suffer some kind of economic

[10] One of the puzzling features of the law of tort as it stands at the moment is that a victim of a tort who is in an irreversible coma as a result of that tort being committed will be entitled to bring a claim for loss of amenity: see *Wise* v *Kaye* [1962] 1 KB 638; *H West & Son Ltd* v *Shepherd* [1964] AC 326; *Lim* v *Camden Area Health Authority* [1980] AC 174. It is difficult to see why such damages can be claimed: they can be of no earthly benefit to the victim of the tort.

[11] *Chaplin* v *Hicks* [1911] 2 KB 786.

[12] See below, pp. 594–6.

loss if it has prevented B from obtaining money that she would otherwise have obtained. The claimants in *White* v *Jones*[13] suffered this form of economic loss. In that case, it will be recalled, the defendants were instructed to draw up a will under which the claimants would have received £9,000 each. The defendants dallied too long over drawing up the will and the testator died before the will was signed and witnessed. The defendants' negligence – they had owed the claimants a duty to draw up the will with reasonable skill and care – caused the claimants to suffer a form of economic loss; the defendants' negligence prevented the claimants receiving the money which they would otherwise have received under the will.

The case of *H West & Sons Ltd* v *Shepherd*[14] provides a good illustration of the different kinds of loss that might be suffered by the victim of a tort. In that case, the claimant, then aged 41, was knocked down by a motor lorry that was driven negligently by the defendant. The claimant sustained severe head injuries resulting in cerebral atrophy and paralysis of all her limbs. She was unable to speak but could communicate by moving her eyes, face and hands. She was only expected to live for another five years after the accident and might have appreciated what sort of condition she was in.

We can isolate five different losses that the defendant's negligence caused the claimant to suffer in this case. First, physical injury: the defendant's negligence caused the claimant to sustain head injuries. Secondly, distress: the defendant's negligence caused the claimant to suffer distress in two ways: (1) the claimant experienced pain and suffering when she was knocked down; (2) the claimant suffered distress as a result of knowing what her condition was. Thirdly, inconvenience: the claimant had to put up with the hassle and inconvenience involved in trying to live her life in a paralysed condition. Fourthly, loss of amenity: as a result of the defendant's negligence, the claimant could not enjoy many of the pleasures of life that she would have enjoyed but for the defendant's negligence. Fifthly, economic loss: the defendant's negligence caused the claimant to suffer a loss of income.

ESTABLISHING CAUSATION: THE BASIC APPROACH

Suppose that A has committed a tort in relation to B and B wants to establish that A's tort has caused her to suffer some kind of loss – say, some form of physical injury. To do this, B will *almost always* have to show that A's tort *materially contributed* to her suffering that physical injury.[15] In order to do this, B will have to establish three things:

(1) B would not have suffered that injury in the way she did *but for* A's tort.
(2) A's tort *materially increased* the risk that B would suffer that injury in the way she did.
(3) That nothing happened *after* A committed his tort and *before* B suffered her injury to *break the chain of causation* between A's tort and B's injury.

If these three things are made out, then we can say that A's tort caused B's injury. Of course, all of this needs much more explanation.

13 [1995] 2 AC 207.
14 [1964] AC 326.
15 See Lord Reid in *Bonnington Castings* v *Wardlaw* [1956] AC 613, at 621: 'the real question is whether [the defendants' negligence] materially contributed to the [claimant's] disease.' See also Weir 2006, at 72.

The 'but for' test for causation

We cannot say that A's tort caused B to suffer a particular type of loss if B would have suffered that loss in the way she did[16] even if A's tort had not been committed. This is what is known as the 'but for' test for causation.

Examples of the application of the 'but for' test

In *Barnett* v *Chelsea & Kensington Hospital Committee*,[17] three nightwatchmen presented themselves at a hospital casualty department, complaining that they had started vomiting after drinking some tea. The casualty officer on duty told the men to go to bed and call their own doctors. The men followed his advice and five hours later one of them died from arsenic poisoning. It was held that the casualty officer's failure to treat the man who died (in breach of the duty of care he owed him to treat him with a reasonable degree of care and skill) did not cause his death; he would have died anyway, even if he had been treated by the casualty officer.

In *Jobling* v *Associated Dairies Ltd*,[18] the claimant was employed by the defendants in their butchers' shop. In 1973 he slipped on the floor of the shop because the defendants had failed (in breach of their duty under the Office, Shops and Railway Premises Act 1973) to keep the floor free from slippery substances. The claimant suffered a back injury which was somewhat disabling. In 1976 the claimant's back became completely disabled because he developed a condition called myelopathy. The myelopathy was completely unconnected with the claimant's accident in 1973. It was held that while the defendants' failure to keep

[16] *Important note*. The qualifier 'in the way she did' is important. In the case where B has suffered some sort of loss and it is alleged that A's tort caused her to suffer that loss, you have to look at *how* B suffered that loss and ask – would she have suffered that loss *in the way she did* but for A's tort? If you do not, your causal judgments will soon go awry.

For example, suppose that Karen is walking down the street and she is attacked by Paul, who breaks both her legs. Obviously in this case Paul's attack caused Karen's legs to be broken – *and this is so even if, had Paul not attacked Karen, John would have done so and broken both her legs*. Karen's legs would not have been broken *in the way they were* had Paul not attacked her. It is irrelevant – at any rate, when making judgments about causation – that Karen's legs would have been broken anyway by John had Paul not attacked her.

Of course, when it comes to assessing how much Paul should pay Karen by way of damages for the fact that he broke her legs, it would usually be highly relevant that Karen's legs were 'doomed' to be broken in any case. However, if the damages payable to Karen were reduced significantly in this case to take account of the fact that her legs were 'doomed', then she would be seriously undercompensated for the fact that her legs were broken. She could not sue Paul for substantial damages; and she could not sue John for anything, given that he committed no tort in relation to her (though he was going to do so). Given this, the courts could be expected to disregard the fact that Karen's legs were 'doomed' when Paul broke them, and allow Karen to sue Paul for substantial damages designed to compensate her *in full* for the pain and suffering and so on that she suffered as a result of her legs being damaged. See the discussion of *Baker* v *Willoughby* [1970] AC 467 below, at pp. 550–2.

Once it is understood that it has to be shown under the 'but for' test that B would not have suffered a particular type of loss *in the way she did* but for A's tort, the 'but for' test can be seen to provide a perfectly adequate starting point for determining whether A's tort caused B to suffer that loss. There is certainly no need (as Stapleton 2003a suggests, at 393) to abandon the 'but for' test in favour of some other test for causation such as the NESS test (propounded by Hart & Honoré 1985; R. Wright 1985, 1988, 2001), under which A's negligence will be held to have caused B's cancer if it was a *N*ecessary *E*lement in a *S*et of circumstances that would have been *S*ufficient to cause B to contract cancer. The NESS test for causation suffers from formidable difficulties of its own: for example, the NESS test produces false positives and false negatives when it is applied to determine whether a tort that was committed by *failing to act* in a particular way caused the victim of the tort to suffer some kind of harm: see Fischer 1992.

[17] [1969] 1 QB 428.

[18] [1982] AC 794.

the floor of their shop free from slippery substances had caused the claimant's disablement between 1973 and 1976, that failure had not caused any of the claimant's disablement after 1976. If the defendants had kept the floor of their shop free from slippery substances, the claimant would still have been completely disabled from 1976 onwards.

In *McWilliams* v *Sir William Arrol & Co.*,[19] the claimant's husband was working for the defendant, his employer, on a steel lattice tower when he fell to his death. It was found that the defendant's failure to provide the husband with a safety belt (in breach of his duty under s 36(2) of the Factories Act 1937) did not cause the husband's death. If the defendant had supplied the husband with a safety belt he would not have worn it so it could not be said that but for the defendant's failure to supply the husband with a safety belt, the husband would not have fallen to his death.[20]

Application of the 'but for' test in an Empire Jamaica *type case*

In *The Empire Jamaica*,[21] the defendants' ship collided with, and damaged, the claimants' ship. At the time of the accident, the defendants' ship was sailing in breach of regulations that said that the first and second mate of the ship should be certified: in fact only the first mate on the defendants' ship was certified. Did the defendants' breach of regulations cause the accident? Applying the 'but for' test to this question produces an ambiguous answer. This is because there were two ways the defendants could have complied with the regulations that they breached.

The first way of complying with the regulations was to ensure that when the ship sailed, the first and second mates on the ship were certified. The defendants failed to do this, but this failure did *not* cause the accident that damaged the claimants' ship according to the 'but for' test. The accident would still have happened, even if the second mate on the defendants' ship was certified. However, the second way of complying with the regulations was not to allow the defendants' ship to sail at all, given that the second mate on board was not yet certified. Again, the defendants failed to do this. Now – we can say that the accident which damaged the claimants' ship would not have happened but for this failure. Had the defendants' ship not sailed at all, it would never have been in a position to collide with the claimants' ship.

So – whether we say that the claimants' ship would not have been damaged but for the defendants' breach of regulations depends on how we characterise that breach. Do we say that the defendants' breach consisted in their sailing their ship without having a certified second mate on board? Or do we say that the defendants' breach simply consisted in their sailing their ship? It seems that the approach we should adopt in cases like this is to characterise the defendants' breach in the way that is most favourable to the defendants. This is what the House of Lords did in *The Empire Jamaica* case – they characterised the defen-

[19] [1962] 1 WLR 295.

[20] It might have been different if the defendant had owed the claimant's husband a duty not only to supply him with a safety belt but *also* to take steps to ensure that he wore it. In that case, it could have been argued that had the defendant supplied the claimant's husband with a safety belt *and* taken steps to ensure that he wore it, the claimant's husband would have worn a safety belt while he was working and would not have fallen to his death. It could therefore have been argued that the defendant's breach of the duty he owed the claimant's husband to supply the claimant's husband with a safety belt *and* to take steps to ensure that he wore it caused the claimant's husband to die. See, for example, *Nolan* v *Dental Manufacturing Co. Ltd* [1958] 1 WLR 936.

[21] [1957] AC 386.

dants' breach as consisting in their sailing their ship without having a certified second mate on board and consequently found that the defendants' breach of regulations did not cause the accident in which the claimant's ship was damaged.

We can apply the above statement of the law to solve a problem which is a favourite of tort examiners everywhere.[22] John – a learner driver – goes out for a drive without having a qualified driver sitting beside him in the car. While he is driving along – *and driving perfectly carefully* – Beth suddenly runs out into the middle of the road without looking to see if there is any oncoming traffic and is hit by John's car. The accident happened so suddenly that there was nothing John – or any other driver, however careful and experienced – could have done to avoid it. Beth is injured as a result of the accident and wants to sue John in negligence for compensation for her injuries. Now – there is no problem in finding that John owed someone like Beth a duty not to go out driving without having a qualified driver sitting beside him. This is because it was reasonably foreseeable that if he did this, someone like Beth – a nearby pedestrian – would be injured.[23] But John could have complied with this duty in one of two ways.

(1) He could have stayed at home and not gone out driving (in which case, Beth would not have been injured).
(2) He could have gone out driving with a qualified driver sitting beside him (in which case, Beth would still have been injured because the qualified driver would not have been able to do anything to avoid the accident, any more than John could have done).

So this gives us two different ways of characterising John's breach of the duty that he owed Beth in this case. We can say that John breached that duty by: (1) going out driving; or (2) going out driving without having a qualified driver sitting beside him. Characterising John's breach in the way that is most favourable to him, we will say that John's breach of duty to Beth consisted in his going out driving without having a qualified driver sitting

[22] *Important note.* The law on the application of the 'but for' test in an *Empire Jamaica* case also provides us with an alternative explanation of why there is no liability in the case put by Lord Hoffmann in *South Australia Asset Management Corp.* v *York Montague Ltd* [1997] AC 191, at 213: 'A mountaineer about to undertake a difficult climb is concerned about the fitness of his knee. He goes to a doctor who negligently makes a superficial examination and pronounces the knee fit. The climber goes on the expedition, which he would not have undertaken if the doctor had told him the true state of his knee. He suffers an injury which is an entirely foreseeable consequence of mountaineering but has nothing to do with his knee.' In this case, the doctor obviously owed the mountaineer a duty not to tell him that his knee was sound when it was not. But there were two ways the doctor could have discharged that duty: (1) he could have told the mountaineer that his knee was not sound (in which case, the mountaineer would not have gone on the expedition and would not have been injured); or (2) the doctor could have treated the knee and made it sound, before passing the mountaineer as fit to climb (in which case, the moutaineer would still have gone on the expedition and would still have been injured). Characterising the doctor's breach in the way that is most favourable to him, we say that the doctor breached his duty to the mountaineer in this case by failing to make his knee sound – and consequently find that the doctor's breach did *not* cause the mountaineer to be injured, as that injury would still have been sustained in the way it was even if the doctor had not breached his duty to the mountaineer. Having said that, it is not possible to explain the *SAAMCO* principle as resting on such reasoning. For example, in a case where a bank has employed a surveyor to value a property that is being offered as security for a loan of £1.4m, and the surveyor has carelessly valued the property as being worth £2m, when it was actually only worth £500,000, there is only one way of characterising the surveyor's breach: he failed to report that the property was only worth £500,000. It is not possible to say that the surveyor breached his duty of care to the bank by failing to take steps to inflate the property's value to £2m before reporting that it was worth that much. The surveyor simply could not have done this; and you cannot have a duty to do the impossible.

[23] See above, pp. 73–4 (the 'physical danger principle').

beside him – and consequently find that John's breach of duty did not cause Beth's injuries. Had John gone out driving with a qualified driver sitting beside him, Beth would still have been injured in the way she was.

Divisible losses

It is sometimes possible to divide up a loss that has been suffered by the victim of a tort and say in relation to one part of the loss that it would not have been suffered in the way it was had the tort not been committed; while holding in relation to the other part that it would still have been suffered in the way it was even if the tort had not been committed. In such a case, the person who committed the tort in question will be held to have caused the victim of his tort to suffer the first part of the loss she has suffered, but not the second.

So, for example, in *Holtby* v *Brigham & Cowan (Hull) Ltd*,[24] Holtby worked for 24 years as a marine fitter. For twelve of those years he worked for the defendants. Holtby's work meant that he was frequently exposed to asbestos dust. None of his employers – including the defendants – took any special precautions to protect him against the asbestos dust and Holtby eventually developed asbestosis. He sued the defendants and the trial judge found that Holtby's asbestosis would have been 75 per cent less severe if the defendants had provided him with proper protection against asbestos dust in the years that he worked for them. So had the defendants not been negligent, Holtby would still have suffered a quarter of the asbestosis that he was currently suffering from. Accordingly, it was held that the defendants only caused Holtby to suffer 75 per cent of the asbestosis he was suffering from and they were held liable to compensate Holtby for that loss – with the compensation being assessed by determining what sum would fully compensate Holtby for the asbestosis suffered by him and knocking 25 per cent off that figure. The Court of Appeal upheld the trial judge's award.[25]

It may seem a little unreal that Holtby's asbestosis could have been divided up in this way. Indeed, the courts sometimes seem overeager to divide up a loss that the victim of a tort has suffered and hold the person who committed that tort liable for a portion of that loss. For example, in *Rahman* v *Arearose Ltd*,[26] the claimant was attacked by some thugs while he worked in a burger bar. One of his eyes was injured in the attack and needed to be operated on. He was taken to the defendants' hospital but the operation on the eye was so

[24] [2000] 3 All ER 421.

[25] See also *Allen* v *British Rail Engineering Ltd* [2001] ICR 942, where an employee who contracted Vibration White Finger (VWF) condition as a result of using vibrating tools in the course of his employment by the defendant was allowed to recover damages in respect of that part of his condition that he would not have suffered from had the defendant not wrongfully failed to assess his employees for the incidence of VWF among them. The decisions in *Holtby* and *Allen* implicitly cast doubt on the correctness of the decision of the House of Lords in *Bonnington Castings Ltd* v *Wardlaw* [1956] AC 613. In that case the claimant's employer exposed the claimant to excessive quantities of silica dust at work, in breach of a statutory duty that he owed the claimant. The claimant later developed a lung disease and sued his employer for compensation for the disease, claiming that the employer's breach of statutory duty had caused him to develop that disease. The House of Lords held for the claimant, finding that the employer's breach of statutory duty had 'materially contributed' to the disease – by which, presumably, they meant the employer's breach had made the claimant's lung disease more serious than it would otherwise have been. But if this is right, then the claimant should only have been awarded damages to compensate him for the 'extra' lung disease that he was suffering from that was attributable to the employer's breach of statutory duty. However, the claimant was actually awarded damages to compensate him for the *whole* of his lung disease.

[26] [2001] QB 351 (noted, Weir 2001b).

badly performed that he was blinded in that eye. In the aftermath of these experiences, the claimant developed a psychiatric illness. The Court of Appeal held, on the basis of 'expert' evidence, that the claimant's psychiatric illness could be divided up – the court held that part of the claimant's psychiatric illness would have been suffered anyway even if the defendants had not been negligent and so the defendants could only be held liable for that part of the claimant's psychiatric illness that he would not have suffered had the defendants not been negligent. It seems unlikely that it was possible to divide up the claimant's psychiatric illness in this way. A better way of deciding the case would have been to find that the claimant would not have developed his (indivisible) psychiatric illness *in the way he did* but for the defendant's negligence and therefore hold the defendant liable for the *whole* of the psychiatric illness suffered by the claimant. However, in assessing the damages payable to the claimant to compensate him for that illness, it would have been legitimate to knock something off to take account of the fact that when the claimant went into hospital, he was probably 'doomed' anyway to suffer some form of psychiatric illness – even if he had been treated impeccably by the defendants.

Difficulties of proof

It is sometimes difficult, for the purposes of applying the 'but for' test, to determine what would have happened had a tort not been committed. That is, if A has committed a tort in relation to B and B has subsequently suffered some kind of loss, it is sometimes difficult to determine whether B would have suffered that loss anyway in the way she did had A not committed his tort. How the courts handle these cases depends on the type of loss that B has suffered.

(1) *Physical injury cases.* Suppose that A has committed a tort in relation to B and B subsequently developed cancer. Suppose further that it is claimed that A's tort caused B to develop cancer. Suppose finally that it is hard to tell whether B would have developed cancer in the way she did had A not committed his tort. In this sort of case, the courts determine whether the 'but for' test is satisfied by using a *balance of probabilities* test. They ask: Is it more likely than not that B would not have developed cancer in the way she did had A not committed his tort?[27] If the answer is 'yes' then the courts will find that B would not have developed her cancer but for A's tort and A will usually be held liable to compensate B for the fact that she has developed cancer. If the answer is 'no' then the courts will find that B would have developed her cancer in the way she did even if A had not committed his tort, with the result that A will usually not be held liable to compensate B for her cancer.[28]

For instance, in *Hotson* v *East Berkshire Health Authority*,[29] the claimant fell when climbing a tree and one of his hips sustained an acute traumatic fracture. He was taken to hospital but the defendants (in breach of the duty of care they owed him) failed to diagnose his injury and sent him home. After five days the claimant was taken back to the hospital and this time his injury was correctly diagnosed. As things turned out the hip

[27] In other words: Is the probability that B would not have developed cancer in the way she did had A not committed his tort over 50%?

[28] Though there is an exception to this, dealt with below, at pp. 552–9.

[29] [1987] AC 750.

fracture resulted in the claimant being permanently disabled. The claimant claimed that the defendants' failure to treat him properly caused him to be permanently disabled. It was impossible to tell with any certainty whether or not the claimant would have been permanently disabled even if the defendants had correctly diagnosed and treated his injury when he first went to the hospital. If the claimant's fall had damaged a certain proportion – call it *x* per cent – of the blood vessels in his hip then the claimant would have been permanently disabled whatever the defendants had done when he first went to hospital. If the fall had damaged less than *x* per cent of the blood vessels in his hip then the defendants would have been able to prevent the claimant becoming permanently disabled had they acted promptly when the claimant first went to hospital. No one could tell with any degree of certainty what proportion of blood vessels in the claimant's hip were damaged by his fall and therefore no one could tell with any degree of certainty whether or not the claimant would have been permanently disabled even if the defendants had treated his injuries when he first came to the hospital.

The courts in *Hotson* resolved this uncertainty by asking – Was it more likely than not that the claimant's fall damaged less than *x* per cent of the blood vessels in his hip? If the answer was 'yes' then they would have held that the claimant would not have become permanently disabled but for the defendants' negligence. But if the answer was 'no' then the courts would have held that the claimant would have become permanently disabled in the way he did even if the defendants had not been negligent. As things turned out, the answer was 'no'. It was found that the probability that the claimant's fall damaged less than *x* per cent of the blood vessels in his hip was only 25 per cent. It was therefore more likely than not that the claimant's fall damaged at least *x* per cent of the blood vessels in his hip and therefore more likely than not that the defendants' negligence made no difference to the claimant's becoming permanently disabled. The claimant's claim for damages therefore failed: he could not show that the defendants' negligence caused him to become permanently disabled.

Some academics have suggested that the claimant in *Hotson* should have been allowed to sue the defendants for depriving him, through their negligence, of the *chance of being cured*.[30] But did the defendants' negligence actually deprive the claimant of a chance of being cured? It is important to remember that in *Hotson* it was *possible* that when the claimant went into hospital, he had a (very good) chance of being cured. But it was *also possible* that when he went into hospital, he had *no chance* of being cured: that is, it was *also possible* that he was *doomed* to become permanently disabled. So it was uncertain whether or not the defendants' negligence actually deprived the claimant of a chance of being cured. Again, we resolve this uncertainty by applying a balance of probabilities test and ask – when the claimant went into hospital, was it more likely than not that he was *doomed* to become permanently disabled? The answer is 'yes' – it was 75 per cent likely that when the claimant went into hospital more than *x* per cent of the blood vessels in his hip had been damaged and he was therefore doomed to be permanently disabled. So *Hotson* was not a case where a claim for a loss of a chance of being cured could have been brought:[31] the claimant in

[30] See, for example, Peel 2003b, 627, and references contained therein.

[31] Contra, M&D, 262; Porat & Stein 2003, 679; Tettenborn 2003, 580; Weir 2004, 214–15, all of whom seem to suggest that the fact that the House of Lords awarded the claimant in *Hotson nothing* means that *Hotson* is authority for the proposition that damages for loss of a chance of avoiding physical injury cannot be claimed in

Hotson simply could not have established that the defendants' negligence caused him to lose a chance of avoiding injury.

Students generally seem to find it hard to understand this point, but the following analogy may help. Suppose that Bob is a gambling addict. He is playing Monopoly with his wife, Sarah, and her friend Mary, and Mary's husband, Carl. Bob asks Mary to pass him the dice they have been using. Bob tells Mary he will give her his Ferrari if, after he throws the dice, the sum of the numbers that are face up on the dice come to seven. Bob puts the dice in a throwing cup, rattles the cup a bit, and then turns it upside down flat on a table so the dice are resting on the table inside the cup. Before Bob can remove the cup to allow everyone to see the sum of the numbers that are face up on the dice, Sarah – horrified at Bob's recklessness – dashes the cup, and the dice inside, to the ground. As a result, no one will ever know whether the sum of the numbers that were face up on the dice came to seven. Now – did Sarah's actions deprive Mary of a chance of winning Bob's Ferrari?

In our experience, most students would say, 'Yes – before Sarah did what she did, Mary had a 1 in 6 chance[32] of winning the Ferrari.' In fact, the truth is that Sarah's actions did not deprive Mary of a *chance* of winning Bob's Ferrari. Once Bob had rolled the dice, either Mary was *certain* to win Bob's Ferrari (if the sum of the numbers that were face up on the dice came to 7) or Mary was *certain* not to win Bob's Ferrari (if the sum of the numbers that were face up on the dice came to any number other than 7). Now – we do not know whether Mary was *certain* to win the Ferrari, or whether Mary was *certain not* to win the Ferrari, but what we do know is that once Bob put the throwing cup face down on the table, the destiny of the Ferrari was no longer a matter of chance: its fate had already been settled. So it would be wrong here to say that Sarah's actions deprived Mary of a chance of winning the Ferrari. Either Sarah's actions deprived Mary of the Ferrari, or they deprived her of nothing. To decide which is the case here, we apply a 'balance of probabilities' test and ask: was it more likely than not that Mary had won the Ferrari when Sarah dashed the throwing cup and the dice inside to the ground? As the answer is 'no' – it was only 17 per cent likely that the sum of the numbers that were face up on the dice came to seven – we cannot say that Sarah's actions deprived Mary of the Ferrari.

So we cannot say in this case *either* that Sarah's actions deprived Mary of Bob's Ferrari, *or* that they deprived Mary of a *chance* of winning the Ferrari. Similarly, in *Hotson*, when the claimant was carried into hospital, he was either certainly going to get better (with better treatment) or he was doomed not to get better (however much treatment he was given). There was no chance about what would happen to him: his fate had already been decided as soon as he hit the ground after he fell out of the tree. Of course, we do not know what fate had in store for the claimant in *Hotson* because his doctors failed to do the tests on him that would have revealed whether or not his injury was curable. But we make up for this lack of knowledge by asking: was it more likely than not that the claimant's leg was

negligence. As the majority of the Court of Appeal recognised in *Gregg* v *Scott* [2002] EWCA Civ 1471 (at [39], per Latham LJ and at [78], per Mance LJ) this is incorrect – the facts of the case in *Hotson* were such that the claimant simply could not bring a claim for loss of a chance against the defendants. See, to the same effect, Reece 1996; also Hill 1991. Fleming 1997 puts the point quite well (at 69): '[A] 25% probability that there was a chance [of avoiding injury cannot] be conflated into a 25% chance [of avoiding injury].'

[32] This is based on the fact that there are (6 × 6 =) 36 different combinations of numbers that could have come up when Bob rolled the dice, and 6 of those combinations add up to 7 (6+1, 1+6, 2+5, 5+2, 3+4, 4+3).

doomed when he fell out of the tree? As the answer is 'yes', we find that the claimant in *Hotson* had no chance of getting better when he was first taken into hospital, and that he would have suffered a permanent leg injury even if his doctors had not been negligent in the way they treated him.

So the *Hotson* case was not one where damages for loss of a chance of being cured could have been awarded, and so the issue of whether such damages can be awarded in a medical negligence case never arose. However, that issue was squarely raised in the recent case of *Gregg v Scott*,[33] which we will discuss later on in this chapter.[34]

(2) *Economic loss cases.* The courts adopt a different approach in cases where it is uncertain whether or not the victim of a tort would have obtained a particular amount of money had that tort not been committed.

Suppose that Gary and Ian were two professional footballers and that when they were playing football together, Ian negligently injured Gary with the result that Gary became permanently disabled. Suppose that, at the time of the accident, a big club was interested in signing Gary. The transfer would have earned Gary a large amount of money in signing on fees and publicity deals and so on – let's say that if Gary had been transferred he would have made £1,000,000 in all. Of course, after Gary's accident, the big club in question lost interest in signing him.

In this sort of case, it is difficult to tell whether or not Gary would have earned £1,000,000 but for Ian's negligence. Had Ian not injured Gary, the big club might have decided not to sign Gary anyway. In this sort of case, the courts will *not* find that Ian's negligence caused Gary to lose £1,000,000. And this is so even if the probability that Gary's transfer would have gone ahead was 80 per cent – making it more likely than not that Gary would have earned £1,000,000 had he not been injured by Ian.[35] Instead, the courts will find that Ian's negligence deprived Gary of a chance to make £1,000,000 and will award Gary damages designed to compensate Gary for that loss of a chance.[36] So if the probability that the transfer would have gone through was 80 per cent then Gary will be awarded £800,000 in damages; if the probability was 20 per cent, £200,000.[37]

[33] [2005] 2 AC 176.

[34] See below, pp. 559–63.

[35] See now *Brown* v *Ministry of Defence* [2006] EWCA Civ 546 (claimant who suffered an ankle injury that meant she could no longer pursue a career in the army – eight weeks after her career began – was not entitled to sue the army for the *full* loss of the pension rights that she would have acquired if she had continued serving in the army for 22 more years, as she probably would have but for her injury. She was only entitled to sue for compensation for a proportion of that loss, reflecting the probability that she would have continued serving in the army for 22 more years).

[36] The availability of damages to compensate someone for the loss of a chance is discussed in more detail below, at pp. 594–6.

[37] *Important note.* Note that even if the probability of the transfer going through was only 20%, one would *not* say that it was more likely than not that the transfer was *doomed* not to go through. Clearly there *was* a (smallish) chance that the transfer would go through, for which Gary can be compensated. Because the football club that was thinking about buying Gary when he was injured possessed free will – and was therefore free to choose to buy Gary – we would always say that there *was* a *chance* that the transfer would go through.

The 'material increase in risk' test for causation

The mere fact that B would not have suffered some kind of loss but for a tort committed by A does *not* establish that A's tort materially contributed to B's suffering that loss. B will still have to show that A's tort *materially increased the risk* that B would suffer the kind of loss that she did. This is the 'material increase in risk' test for causation. A couple of hypothetical examples demonstrate how this test works.

First, suppose that Tom beats Lara up so badly that she is hospitalised. Lara's injuries are treated in hospital over a couple of weeks and she is finally judged fit enough to go home. As Lara is walking through the hospital car park, she is carelessly run over by Nita, with the result that Lara suffers a broken leg. In this case, it would be wrong to say that Tom's beating Lara up caused her to suffer a broken leg. This is so even though Lara's leg would not have been broken had she not been beaten up by Tom. (Had Lara not been beaten up by Tom, Lara would never have been in the hospital car park when she was run over by Nita.) The reason why we cannot say that Tom's beating Lara up caused her to suffer a broken leg is that Tom's beating Lara up did not materially increase the risk that she would be run over a couple of weeks later.

Secondly, suppose that at 11.55 am Tom is driving along a very long, twisting country road at the reckless speed of 60 mph. He does this for five minutes (covering five miles in the process) before coming to his senses and reducing his speed to the much more sensible 15 mph. Five seconds elapse after Tom does this and then Tom's car hits Lara, and Lara suffers a broken leg as a result. There was nothing Tom could have done to avoid the collision. At the time of the collision, he was driving sensibly and it was entirely Lara's fault that she was run over: she had tried to cross the road at a sharp bend in the road, making it impossible for Tom to see her in time to avoid hitting her. Obviously, Tom owed Lara – as a pedestrian using the road Tom was driving on – a duty of care not to drive dangerously, and let's assume that we can say that he breached that duty when he drove down the road at 60 mph. Now – Tom would not have hit Lara had he not been driving so fast between 11.55 am and 12 noon. Had Tom been driving at a sensible speed during this time, Tom's car would have been nowhere near Lara when she tried to cross the road; it would have been almost four miles away. So there is a 'but for' link between Tom's negligence in driving at 60 mph down the road, and Lara's being run over by Tom's car. But it would still be wrong to say that Tom's negligence caused Lara to suffer a broken leg. This is because Tom's negligence did not materially increase the risk that Lara would suffer a broken leg in the way she did – that is, as a result of being hit by a car that was being driven at 15 mph, and by a driver who could not have seen Lara in time to avoid hitting her.

These examples demonstrate the validity of the 'material increase in risk' test for causation. But students should be wary of invoking it too often to deny that there was a causal link between a tort and some loss suffered by the victim of that tort. It will be rare for this test not to be satisfied, and it will only really come into play to deny that A's tort caused B to suffer some kind of loss where the occurrence of that loss was a freak or coincidental result of A's having committed the tort in question. Having said that, the recent case law does provide us with one example of a real life situation where the 'material increase in risk' test for causation was not satisfied. That

situation arose in the case of *Chester v Afshar*,[38] which we will discuss later on in this chapter.[39]

Break in the chain of causation

Suppose that A committed a tort in relation to B. Suppose further that B suffered some kind of loss as a result[40] of A's tort. Even if this is true, it may be wrong to say that A's tort *caused* B to suffer that loss.

To take an obvious example, suppose that Paul beat Mary up and Mary was so angered by this that she burned down the offices where Paul worked. Mary was subsequently imprisoned for committing arson. Now – here Mary has suffered a loss (being imprisoned) which she would not have suffered but for Paul's beating her up, but no one would say that Paul's beating Mary up caused her to be imprisoned. In this sort of situation, we say that there has been a *break in the chain of causation* between the tort committed by Paul in beating Mary up and Mary's being imprisoned.[41]

So – when will we be able to say that there was a break in the chain of causation between someone's tort and a loss suffered by the victim of that tort? To clear the ground, we can immediately identify three kinds of events that could *never* break the chain of causation between someone's tort and a loss suffered by the victim of that tort.

(1) *Events preceding a tort.* Suppose that Carl's wife beat him up so badly that he underwent a personality change and developed an obsessive hatred of women. As a result, one day Carl attacked Karen in the street and this caused Karen to develop a psychiatric illness. In this case, the beating Carl received from his wife could not possibly have broken the chain of causation between the tort committed by Carl in attacking Karen and Karen's developing her psychiatric illness. This is because Carl's wife beat him up *before* Carl attacked Karen. For an event to break the chain of causation between someone's committing a tort and the victim of that tort's suffering some kind of loss, that event *must* occur between the time that tort was committed and the time the victim of the tort suffered that loss.

(2) *Events that make no difference.* Suppose that Tom raped Dawn and Dawn developed a psychiatric illness as a result. Suppose further that after Dawn had been raped but before her psychiatric illness developed, she went to the police to complain that she had been raped and was treated in an insensitive manner by the police. Suppose finally that the manner in which Dawn was treated by the police had nothing to do with her developing her psychiatric illness, which was entirely attributable to the rape. In this case, the manner in which the police treated Dawn could not possibly have broken the chain of causation

[38] [2005] 1 AC 134.

[39] See below, pp. 563–5.

[40] From here on *in this chapter*, a loss will be said to have been suffered 'as a result of' a tort having been committed if that loss would not have been suffered in the way it was *but for* that tort having been committed *and* that tort's being committed *materially increased the risk* that that loss would be suffered in the way it was.

[41] See, however, Stapleton 2001, arguing (at 166) that the rules dealt with in this section should not be presented as part of the law on causation, and that to do so gives a 'misleadingly factual flavour to a collection of rules based on normative concerns'. Against this, one could observe that someone approaching Paul's case without any normative concerns at all (such as a concern to protect Paul from being subjected to excessive liabilities) would still find it odd to say that Paul's assault *caused* Mary to be imprisoned.

between Tom's rape of Dawn and Dawn's developing a psychiatric illness. The reason is the police's treatment of Dawn did not contribute towards her developing her psychiatric illness. For an event to break a chain of causation between someone's committing a tort and the victim of that tort's suffering some kind of loss as a result, that event *must* have contributed in some way to the victim's suffering that loss.

(3) *Omissions*. Suppose that Vijay was driving at a very high speed down the road and as a result he negligently knocked Ruth, a little girl, off the bike that she was riding in the road. Ignoring her wails, Vijay drove off. Ruth made her way home and told her mother, Lara, that she had been hit by a car and that her head felt 'funny'. Lara told Ruth not to make a fuss and packed her off to bed. During the night, Ruth suffered a brain haemorrhage. She survived the haemorrhage – she was immediately rushed to hospital as soon as the problem become obvious – but suffered permanent brain damage as a result. Had Lara taken Ruth to hospital as soon as Ruth came in complaining that she had been hit by a car, then the brain haemorrhage and consequent brain damage could have been avoided.

In this situation, Lara's failure to take Ruth to hospital could not possibly have broken the chain of causation between Vijay's negligence in knocking Ruth down and the brain damage suffered by Ruth as a result of being knocked down. The reason is that *omissions do not break chains of causation*.[42] So Vijay's negligence will be held to have caused Ruth's brain damage. But Lara has also committed a tort here. As Ruth's mother, she owed Ruth a duty to take reasonable steps to see that Ruth did not come to any physical harm[43] and she breached that duty when she failed to take Ruth to hospital when Ruth told her that she had been knocked down. Lara's negligence *also* caused Ruth's brain damage because Ruth would not have suffered her brain damage had Lara not been negligent.

So Vijay *and* Lara will *each* be held in this case to have committed a tort in relation to Ruth which caused Ruth to become permanently brain-damaged. The result is that Ruth will be entitled to sue either Vijay or Lara or both for compensation for her brain damage. If she chooses to sue Vijay (the obvious choice), Vijay will be entitled to make a claim in contribution against Lara to make her share some of the burden of compensating Ruth for her brain damage.

The same point about omissions not breaking chains of causation also applies in cases where the victim of a tort fails to take steps to save herself suffering some loss which she was put in danger of suffering as a result of that tort's being committed. Her failure to save herself from suffering that loss will not break the chain of causation between that loss and the tort that was committed in relation to her. However, she will probably be prevented from suing for compensation for that loss on the ground that she only suffered it because she *failed to mitigate* the losses flowing from the tort that was committed in relation to her.[44]

42 One case which seems to contradict this is *Mann* v *Coutts & Co.* [2004] 1 All ER (Comm) 1. In that case the claimants suffered loss as a result of acting on a letter supplied by the defendants relating to an agency with whom the claimants had dealings. Their claim in negligence for compensation for that loss was dismissed on the ground that they would not have suffered that loss had they not failed to investigate the agency and that failure broke the chain of causation between the loss suffered by the claimants and the letter supplied by the defendants. However, the decision was at first instance and the judge seems not to have realised that the same result could have been reached by reference to the law on mitigation of damage, dealt with below, at pp. 590–2.

43 See above, p. 184.

44 The victim of a tort's so-called 'duty to mitigate' the losses suffered by her as a result of that tort's being committed is discussed further below, at pp. 590–2.

For example, in *McAuley* v *London Transport Executive*,[45] the claimant suffered an accident at work as a result of the defendants' negligence. The claimant's left wrist was cut in the accident. The claimant was taken to hospital but he refused to have an operation on his wrist which would have gone some way towards restoring the claimant's left hand and wrist to full working order. Without an operation, the condition of the claimant's left wrist deteriorated and he lost the use of his left hand. In this case, the defendants' negligence caused the claimant to lose the use of his left hand: the claimant's failure to agree to the operation that would have saved his hand did not break the chain of causation between the defendants' negligence and the claimant's losing the use of his left hand. However, the claimant was still barred from suing for compensation for the loss of the use of his left hand: he only lost the use of his left hand because he failed to mitigate the losses suffered by him as a result of the defendants' negligence.

Now that we have clarified what sort of events will *not* amount to a break in a chain of causation, we can go on to discuss what kind of event – known in the legal literature as a *novus actus interveniens* – *will* give rise to a break in a chain of causation. Two kinds of event will have this effect. First, an unexpected and natural event. Second, a deliberate and unreasonable act. Let's now look at each in turn.

Unexpected and natural events

The standard example of an unexpected and natural event is a lightning strike. So: suppose that Alan beats Eric up with the result that Eric needs to be taken to hospital in an ambulance. On the way to the hospital, the ambulance is struck by lightning and Eric is electrocuted. We would not say here that Alan's beating Eric up caused Eric to be electrocuted. The lightning strike, which occurred after Alan's beating Eric up and contributed to Eric's being electrocuted, broke the chain of causation between Alan's beating Eric up and Eric's being electrocuted.

In *Carslogie Steamship Co. Ltd* v *Royal Norwegian Government*,[46] the claimants' ship, the *Heimgar*, was damaged in a collision with the *Carslogie*, which was owned by the defendants. The collision occurred because of the defendants' negligence. The *Heimgar* was on its way to port to have the damage it had suffered in the collision with the *Carslogie* repaired permanently when it was involved in a violent storm which rendered the *Heimgar* unseaworthy. The *Heimgar* limped into port where it spent 30 days having both the storm damage and the damage done in the collision with the *Carslogie* repaired simultaneously. If the *Heimgar* had not suffered any storm damage it would have taken ten days to repair the damage done in the collision with the *Carslogie*. It was held that the defendants' negligence did not cause the *Heimgar* to suffer the storm damage which resulted in its being detained in port for 30 days. While the *Heimgar* would not have suffered that storm damage had the defendants' not been negligent, the violent storm – an unexpected and natural event – broke the chain of causation between the defendants' negligence and the storm damage suffered by the *Heimgar*. Given this, the defendants did not cause the *Heimgar* to be detained in port for the 30 days that it was detained and they were therefore

[45] [1958] 2 Lloyd's Rep 500.
[46] [1952] AC 292.

not liable for the profits which the claimants could have made had the *Heimgar* been available to them in that period.

Free, deliberate and unreasonable acts

It is well established that, as a general rule, *free, deliberate and unreasonable acts break chains of causation*. We have already seen this with the example of Mary's burning down the offices in which Paul worked to get revenge on him for beating her up. Paul's beating Mary up did not cause her to be imprisoned because her free, deliberate and unreasonable act in burning down the offices where Paul worked broke the chain of causation between Paul's beating Mary up and Mary's being imprisoned. Let's now look at a number of cases that illustrate this principle at work.

In *Haynes* v *Harwood*,[47] it will be recalled, the defendant left some horses unattended in a street. The horses bolted and the claimant, a policeman, dashed out and attempted to stop the horses. He was injured in doing so. It was held that the defendant's negligence in leaving the horses unattended in the street had caused the claimant to be injured. True, the claimant was only injured as a result of the defendant's negligence because he deliberately ran out and attempted to stop the defendant's horses bolting. However, it had been reasonable for the claimant to do this.

In *Hyett* v *Great Western Railway Company*,[48] a fire broke out in a train wagon which had been left by the defendants – the wagon's owner – in a railway siding. The fire broke out because of the defendants' negligence in leaving a number of leaking paraffin drums in the wagon. The claimant – who was employed to do work on the wagons in the railway siding – saw the fire and tried to deal with it. While a friend of his went for assistance, the claimant attempted to remove a number of the paraffin drums from the wagon. While he was doing so one of the drums exploded and the claimant was injured. It was held that the defendants' negligence had caused the claimant to be injured. While the claimant was only injured as a result of the defendants' negligence because he deliberately chose to try to remove some of the paraffin drums in the wagon, as it was reasonable for the claimant to do this, this deliberate act of his did not break the chain of causation between the defendants' negligence and his being injured.

In *Lagden* v *O'Connor*,[49] the claimant's car was damaged as a result of the defendant's negligence and needed to be repaired. While his car was out of action, the claimant hired a replacement car. The claimant could not afford to hire a car from a normal car hire firm. Instead he hired a car from a credit hire company called Helphire which – crucially – did not charge him anything upfront for the hire of the car. Instead, Helphire allowed him to hire the car on credit – the idea being that when the claimant succeeded in his claim against the defendant, the damages payable to the claimant would cover the cost of renting a car from Helphire, and the defendant would be able to pay off his debt to Helphire out of that portion of the damages. The claimant ended up owing £659 to Helphire for the hire of their car; and he sought to recover that sum from the defendant. Now – a normal car hire firm would have charged the claimant a lot less to use one of their cars for an

[47] [1935] 1 KB 146.
[48] [1948] 1 KB 345.
[49] [2004] 1 AC 1067.

equivalent period of time: Helphire's rates were a lot higher because they were hiring their cars out on credit and their hire charges included charges designed to cover the cost of helping the claimant to sue the defendant for damages and the cost of taking out an insurance policy to pay off the claimant's debt to Helphire should his claim against the defendant fail. A majority of the House of Lords held that the claimant was allowed to recover damages from the defendant to cover the cost of renting a car from Helphire. The fact that he had chosen to rent a car from Helphire rather than a normal car hire firm did not break the chain of causation between the defendant's negligence and the claimant's owing Helphire £659 for the use of one of their cars. This is because – given the claimant's impecuniosity – the claimant had acted quite reasonably in hiring a replacement car from Helphire rather than a normal car hire firm, despite the fact that Helphire's rental charges were a lot higher than a normal car hire firm's would have been.[50] Of course, it would have been different if the claimant had been rich enough to afford to hire a replacement car from a normal car hire company. Had this been the case, his decision to hire a replacement car from Helphire would have been unreasonable and would have broken the chain of causation between the defendant's negligence and the claimant's owing Helphire £659 for the use of one of their cars.[51]

In *Knightley* v *Johns*,[52] the defendant drove his car dangerously down a tunnel, in breach of the duty of care he owed other users of the tunnel. As a result, the car overturned near the exit to the tunnel. The police turned up but failed to close the entrance to the tunnel to oncoming traffic. A police inspector at the exit to the tunnel realised the omission and told the claimant – a police constable on a motorcycle – to ride through the tunnel to the entrance and close off the entrance to oncoming traffic. The claimant did so, travelling against the traffic coming through the tunnel, and was hit by a car as he came round a bend in the tunnel. It was held that the defendant's dangerous driving did not cause the claimant's accident, even though the accident would not have happened but for the defendant's dangerous driving. The defendant's dangerous driving only resulted in the claimant being injured because the police inspector deliberately and unreasonably instructed the claimant to ride back through the tunnel against the flow of the traffic. Given this, the defendant's dangerous driving did not cause the claimant's injury – the police inspector's instruction broke the chain of causation between the defendant's dangerous driving and the claimant's accident. It would have been different, of course, if the inspector's instruc-

[50] It was suggested in *The Liesbosch* [1933] AC 449 that damages could not be recovered by the victim of a tort in respect of economic losses incurred by him because of his impecuniosity. However, this was not followed by the House of Lords in *Lagden* v *O'Connor*; and quite rightly too.

[51] This was the majority's (surprising) explanation of the House of Lords' decision in *Dimond* v *Lovell* [2002] 1 AC 384. The facts in *Dimond* were identical to those in *Lagden* v *O'Connor* except for the fact that the claimant in *Dimond* 'could have found the money needed to hire a replacement car until she was reimbursed by [the defendant in that case] or his insurers' (*Lagden* v *O'Connor* [2004] 1 AC 1067, at [5], per Lord Nicholls). It was held that the defendant could not recover anything from the defendant for the cost of hiring a replacement car from a credit hire company because her credit agreement with the credit hire company was not binding under the Consumer Credit Act 1974. However, the majority of the House of Lords went on to observe that even if the agreement had been binding, the claimant would *not* have been entitled to sue the defendant for more than whatever a normal car hire firm would have charged her to hire a replacement car from them. For an explanation of the majority's reasoning in *Dimond* that actually reflects what was said by the majority in *Dimond*, see either McBride & Bagshaw 2001, 516–18, or Lord Scott's powerful dissenting judgment in *Lagden* v *O'Connor*.

[52] [1982] 1 WLR 349.

tion had been a reasonable one to give: in that case, the giving of the instruction would not have broken the chain of causation between the defendant's dangerous driving and the claimant's accident.

In *The Oropesa*[53] two steam vessels, *The Manchester Regiment* and *The Oropesa* collided. The collision was, in part, due to the negligence of the defendants, who were in charge of *The Oropesa*. Although *The Manchester Regiment* was badly damaged in the collision, its master thought it could be salved and set out in a boat with 16 men to go to *The Oropesa* and to discuss what could be done to rescue *The Manchester Regiment*. Before the boat could reach *The Oropesa* it capsized in rough weather and nine of the men in the boat were drowned. It was held that the collision between *The Manchester Regiment* and *The Oropesa* had caused the death of the nine men in the boat. While the defendants' negligence only resulted in the nine men dying because the master of *The Manchester Regiment* voluntarily set out to sea with those nine men – and seven more – the master acted reasonably in doing so and therefore his voluntarily setting out to sea did not break the chain of causation between the negligence of the defendants and the men's deaths.

In *Wieland* v *Cyril Lord Carpets Ltd*,[54] the claimant was injured in a traffic accident caused by the defendant's negligence. She was taken to hospital where a collar was fitted to her neck. The collar made it difficult for the claimant to move her head and as a result she was unable to use her bifocal glasses with her normal skill. The result was that shortly afterwards, when she was descending some stairs with the assistance of her son, she became confused as to the position of the stairs and fell. Her ankles were damaged in the fall. It was held that the defendant's negligence had caused the damage to the claimant's ankles. Admittedly, the defendant's negligence only resulted in the claimant's ankles being fractured because: (1) the hospital put a collar on the claimant which made it difficult for the claimant to use her bifocals; and (2) the claimant chose to walk down a flight of steps while it was difficult for her to use her bifocals. However, it was obviously reasonable for the hospital to do (1) and it was reasonable for the claimant to do (2) given that she walked down the stairs with the assistance of her son and so there was no break in the chain of causation between the defendant's negligence and the claimant's ankles being fractured.

It was different in *McKew* v *Holland & Hannen & Cubitts (Scotland) Ltd*.[55] In that case, the claimant was employed by the defendants. The claimant suffered certain injuries as a result of the defendants' negligence. The claimant's injuries meant, among other things, that his left leg was prone to give way suddenly. A few days later the claimant and a few members of his family inspected a flat which he was thinking of renting. On leaving the flat, the claimant, unassisted, walked down some steep stairs which had no handrail. The claimant's left leg suddenly gave way and he fell down the stairs with the result that he fractured one of his ankles. The House of Lords held that the defendants' negligence did not cause the claimant's ankle fracture. The defendant's negligence only resulted in the claimant suffering an ankle fracture because the claimant chose to walk down a steep staircase which had no handrail without any assistance. This was an unreasonable thing to do and so the claimant's decision to walk down the staircase without any assistance broke the chain of causation between the defendant's negligence and the claimant's ankle fracture.

[53] [1943] P 32.
[54] [1969] 3 All ER 1006.
[55] [1969] 3 All ER 1621.

In *Lynch* v *Knight*,[56] the defendant warned the claimant's husband that the claimant was a 'notorious liar', that she took 'delight in causing disturbances' wherever she went and that her behaviour could be attributed to one Dr Casserley who 'all but seduced' the claimant. The claimant's husband reacted to these words by divorcing the claimant. The claimant sued the defendant in slander for compensation for the fact that her husband had divorced her. It was admitted that the defendant's words amounted to slander, but it was held that the husband's decision to divorce the claimant had broken the chain of causation between the defendant's words and the break-up of the claimant's marriage: it had not been reasonable for the claimant's husband to react to the defendant's words in the way he did.

In a number of cases, the courts have made it clear that if B develops a mental illness as a result of A's tort, and under the influence of that mental illness B kills herself, then A's tort will have caused B's death.[57] B's decision to kill herself will not break the chain of causation between A's tort and B's death: B's decision, while deliberate and unreasonable, cannot be said to have been freely taken given that it was taken under the influence of a mental illness.

One further point needs to be made about this kind of *novus actus interveniens*. Suppose that Beth negligently injured John and John chose to pay someone to treat his injuries. Beth's negligence will have caused John to incur this expenditure if it was reasonable for John to incur that expense. In attempting to establish that it was *unreasonable* for John to incur this expense, Beth will *not* be able to argue that as John could have had his injuries treated free on the National Health Service it was unreasonable for John to 'go private' and pay someone to treat his injuries. Section 2(4) of the Law Reform (Personal Injuries) Act 1948 provides that in 'an action for damages for personal injuries . . . there shall be disregarded, in determining the reasonableness of any expenses, the possibility of avoiding those expenses or part of them by taking advantage of facilities available under the National Health Service . . .'.

SOME EXCEPTIONAL CASES

In this section, we will look at a number of cases where the courts have held that a defendant's tort caused a claimant to suffer some kind of loss even though the defendant's tort did *not* materially contribute to the claimant's suffering that loss. We will also consider the recent case of *Gregg* v *Scott*,[58] in which the House of Lords considered whether a cancer patient should be allowed to recover damages from the defendant doctor on the ground that the defendant's negligence caused him to lose a *chance* of being cured of cancer.

Baker

In *Baker* v *Willoughby*,[59] the claimant was crossing the main highway when he was struck by the defendant's car. The accident happened due to the defendant's negligence. As a result

[56] (1861) 9 HLC 577, 11 ER 854.
[57] *Pigney* v *Pointer's Transport Services Ltd* [1957] 1 WLR 1121; *Kirkham* v *Chief Constable of the Greater Manchester Police* [1990] 2 QB 283; *Corr* v *IBC Vehicles Ltd* [2007] QB 46.
[58] [2005] 2 AC 176.
[59] [1970] AC 467.

of the accident the claimant suffered fairly severe injury to his left leg and ankle. The accident occurred in 1964. The claimant sued the defendant so as to be compensated for the fact that the defendant's negligence had caused him to lose the use of his left leg. In 1967 – before the claimant's case against the defendant had been tried – the claimant was shot in the left leg during an armed robbery and the claimant's left leg had to be amputated immediately. The House of Lords awarded damages against the defendant on the basis that the defendant's negligence had caused the claimant to lose the use of his left leg *for the rest of his life*. This is puzzling. Had the defendant not been negligent, the claimant would have only enjoyed the use of his left leg for three more years, until 1967 when his left leg would have been amputated. So the defendant's negligence only caused the claimant to lose the use of his left leg for *three years* – the three years between 1964 and 1967.

Why then did the House of Lords proceed on the basis that the defendant's negligence had caused the claimant to lose the use of his left leg for the rest of his life? One explanation goes as follows. *Had* the House of Lords held that the defendant's negligence only caused the claimant to lose the use of his left leg for the three years between 1964 and 1967, the claimant would not have been entitled to sue *anyone* for compensation for the loss of the use of his left leg experienced by him from 1967 onwards. Even if the criminals who had shot the claimant were found, he could not have claimed – for the purpose of suing them for damages – that their shooting him in the leg caused him to lose the use of his left leg between 1967 and the rest of his life because his left leg was already useless at the time of the shooting. But it would have been unjust if the claimant had only been entitled to sue for the loss of the use of his left leg between 1964 and 1967. The criminals and the defendant *together* robbed the claimant of the use of his left leg from 1964 to the end of his life. The claimant should therefore have been entitled to sue *someone* – either the criminals or the defendant – for compensation for the fact that between 1967 and the end of his life he would have to get along without a left leg. So, the argument goes, the House of Lords held that the defendant's negligence caused the claimant to lose the use of his left leg for the rest of his life so as to ensure that the claimant would be able to sue *someone* – in this case, the defendant – for compensation for the loss of the use of his left leg that he would experience post-1967. No injustice was done to the defendant by the House of Lords in so holding: if the claimant had not been shot in the armed robbery, the claimant would have been entitled to sue the defendant on the basis that the defendant's negligence had caused him to lose the use of his left leg for the rest of his life.

The decision in *Baker* is to be confined to its own facts. It has no application to the situation presented in *Jobling* v *Associated Dairies Ltd*,[60] where – it will be recalled – the defendants' negligence in 1973 resulted in the claimant's back becoming disabled and then three years later the claimant developed a condition which would have disabled the claimant's back anyway. The House of Lords held that the defendants' negligence only caused the claimant's back to become disabled between 1973 and 1976 and assessed the damages payable by the defendants to the claimant on that basis. No injustice was done to the claimant as a result of the House of Lords' decision: this was not a case where two tortfeasors, working independently of each other, caused the claimant to lose the use of his back from 1973 onwards and applying the rules on causation strictly would result in the

[60] [1982] AC 794.

claimant only having a remedy against them for the loss of his back between 1973 and 1976. It may be noted, by the way, that while the House of Lords in *Jobling* subjected the House of Lords in *Baker* to some criticism for the *way* in which they reached their decision, their Lordships overall seemed to think the House of Lords in *Baker* reached the right *result*. So, for example, Lord Edmund-Davies said in *Jobling* that he could 'formulate no convincing juristic or logical principles supportive of the decision' in *Baker* but at the same time conceded that the decision in *Baker* might have been 'acceptable on its own facts'.[61]

Fairchild

Fairchild v *Glenhaven Funeral Services Ltd*[62] concerned three cases. In each of them an employee (C) was 'employed at different times and for differing periods by both A and B ... A and B were both subject to a duty to take reasonable care to prevent C inhaling asbestos dust because of the known risk that asbestos dust (if inhaled) might cause a [form of cancer called] mesothelioma ... [Both] A and B [breached] that duty ... during the periods of C's employment by each of them with the result that during both periods C inhaled excessive quantities of asbestos dust.'[63] C subsequently developed mesothelioma and sought to recover damages from either A or B for his mesothelioma. It was impossible to tell who C was working for when C inhaled the fatal dust that triggered his mesothelioma. Moreover, C could not show that it was more likely than not that he developed his mesothelioma as a result of either A or B's breach of the duty of care they owed him to see that he did not inhale asbestos dust.[64] So he could not show that either A or B's negligence caused him to develop his mesothelioma.

Despite this, the House of Lords held that C *would* be entitled to sue A and B for compensation for his mesothelioma. Why was this? Two arguments seem to have led the House of Lords to reach this conclusion.

The first – which we can call the *fairness argument* – goes as follows. If we applied the strict rules on causation to cases such as C's, then it seems that employees who worked for *one* bad employer and contracted mesothelioma as a result would be much better off than employees who worked for *two or more* bad employers and contracted mesothelioma as a result. An employee who worked for one bad employer would have no problem establishing that it was his employer's negligence that triggered his mesothelioma and would therefore have no problem obtaining full compensation for his mesothelioma from that employer. An employee who worked for two or more bad employers would find it very difficult to establish which of his employers' negligence caused his mesothelioma and would therefore find it very difficult to identify anyone whom he was entitled to sue for compen-

[61] Ibid., 808–9.

[62] [2003] 1 AC 32 (discussed, Stapleton 2002b, Morgan 2003).

[63] Ibid., at [2] (per Lord Bingham).

[64] This is because we have *no idea* how asbestos dust triggers mesothelioma. It could be that mesothelioma is triggered by long exposure to asbestos dust; or it could be that mesothelioma is triggered by one fatal fibre being inhaled. So even if C worked for A for 10 years and for B for one year, it is not possible to say that it was more probable than not that C's working for A triggered C's mesothelioma. It could *equally* well be the case that the year that C worked for B tipped the balance and caused his mesothelioma to develop. We simply do not know. See, further, Stapleton 2002b, 280–1, 299.

sation for his mesothelioma. This is unfair: why should an employee who worked for one bad employer be in a much better position to obtain compensation for his mesothelioma than an employee who worked for two or more bad employers?[65] To avoid this unfairness, we have to waive the strict rules on causation in the case where an employee who has contracted mesothelioma worked for two or more employers and allow the employee to sue his employers for compensation for his mesothelioma even though we cannot establish *which* of his employers' negligence caused that mesothelioma to develop.[66]

The second argument – which we can call the *sanction argument* – goes as follows. If we do not allow C to sue A and B for compensation for his mesothelioma in this sort of case, then the duties that employers owe their employees to take reasonable steps to see that they do not inhale asbestos dust will become essentially empty. An employer will know that if he breaches that duty and one of his employees subsequently develops mesothelioma, he will not be held liable so long as he can show that that employee was also exposed to asbestos dust during the course of his working life while working for someone else.[67] We have to ensure that employers do not feel free to breach the duties of care that they owe their employees – and so in this sort of case we have to make it clear that an employer who has negligently exposed an employee to asbestos dust will be held liable to pay that employee compensation if the employee subsequently develops mesothelioma and this is so even if it cannot be shown that it was the employer's negligence that caused the employee to develop his mesothelioma, because the employee was also exposed to asbestos dust while working for other people.[68]

65 [2003] 1 AC 32, at [36]: '[Holding that C could not obtain compensation for his mesothelioma] would be deeply offensive to instinctive notions of what . . . fairness demands' (per Lord Nicholls).

66 It could be argued against this that it is unfair to hold a negligent employer liable for mesothelioma developed by a claimant when it was more likely than not that his negligence did not cause that mesothelioma to develop. However, their Lordships were able to overcome this objection, arguing that if they had a choice between being unfair to an innocent claimant and being unfair to a negligent employer, they would rather be unfair to the wrongdoing employer: ibid., at [33] (per Lord Bingham), [39]–[42] (per Lord Nicholls), [155] (per Lord Rodger).

67 Ibid., at [33]: 'Were the law [not to allow C's claim in the kind of case we are considering], an employer exposing his employee to asbestos dust could obtain complete immunity against mesothelioma . . . claims by employing only those who had previously been exposed to excessive quantities of asbestos dust. Such a result would reflect no credit on the law' (per Lord Bingham); at [62]: 'a rule requiring proof of a link between the defendant's asbestos and the claimant's disease would, with the arbitrary exception of single-employer cases, empty the duty of content. If liability depends upon proof that the conduct of the defendant was a necessary condition of the injury, it cannot effectively exist' (per Lord Hoffmann); at [155]: 'if the law did [here] impose a standard of proof that no [one claiming compensation for mesothelioma] could ever satisfy, then, so far as the civil law is concerned, employers could with impunity negligently expose their workmen to the risk of . . . mesothelioma. The substantive duty of care would be emptied of all practical content so far as victims are concerned' (per Lord Rodger).

68 This argument is actually quite weak in this context. This is for two reasons. First, the argument's success in this context depends on a verbal sleight of hand. The argument only works in this context if one says that the duty of care that C's employers owed him, and breached, was a duty to take reasonable steps to see that he did not inhale asbestos dust – the argument being that if C were not allowed to sue A and B here, then employers generally would be left free to breach this duty of care. But if one characterises the duty of care that C's employers owed him, and breached, in wider terms – as a duty to take reasonable steps to see that he did not come to any physical harm in working for him – then not allowing C to sue *in this situation* would not mean that employers generally would be free to breach this wider duty of care. Secondly, even if *Fairchild* had gone the other way, employers would hardly have had *carte blanche* to expose their employees to excessive amounts of asbestos dust. An employer acting in this way would be: (1) subject to criminal sanctions; and (2) held liable to an employee who contracted asbestosis after working for him (the idea being that the employer's negligence in exposing the employee to asbestos will have either caused the employee to develop asbestosis or made the asbestosis 'worse'

So, in the situation we have been considering – where C developed mesothelioma as a result of being exposed to asbestos dust while working for both A and B – the House of Lords' decision in *Fairchild* established that C could sue both A and B for compensation for his mesothelioma. In the subsequent case of *Barker* v *Corus UK Ltd*,[69] the House of Lords considered whether that meant that:

(1) A and B were *each* individually liable to compensate C *in full* for his mesothelioma. If that were the case, then C could obtain full compensation for his mesothelioma by suing *either* A *or* B. So if B were insolvent, C could still recover full compensation for his mesothelioma by suing A.

or

(2) A and B were *each* only liable to compensate C for a proportion of his mesothelioma. If that were the case, then C could only recover full compensation for his mesothelioma by suing *both* A *and* B. So if B were insolvent, C would *not* be able to recover full compensation for his mesothelioma by suing A but would only be able to recover compensation for the proportion of his mesothelioma for which A was liable.

Obviously, claimants in the position of C were hoping that the House of Lords would rule in favour of option (1), as that was more favourable for them. However, the House of Lords ruled in favour of option (2), holding that each of A and B should only be liable to compensate C for a proportion of his mesothelioma, with the proportion that A (or B) should be liable for being assessed according to how much A (or B) did to expose C to the risk of developing mesothelioma.[70]

The decision in *Barker* was severely criticised by trade unions and MPs who represented the interests of employees who had developed mesothelioma as a result of being exposed to asbestos dust at work. The Labour government immediately responded to this criticism by enacting s 3 of the Compensation Act 2006. This provides that if: (1) C has contracted mesothelioma as a result of being exposed to asbestos dust, and (2) A is liable under *Fairchild* to compensate C for the fact that he has contracted mesothelioma, then (3) A will be liable to compensate C *in full* for his mesothelioma, though the damages payable may be reduced for any contributory negligence on C's part. It should be noted that s 3 has absolutely no effect on cases not involving mesothelioma. It follows that in any case not involving mesothelioma where *Fairchild* is applied to allow a claimant to sue a defendant for compensation for a loss that she has suffered even though she cannot prove that the defendant's tort caused her to suffer that loss, the House of Lords' decision in *Barker* will still apply and the defendant will only be held liable to compensate the claimant for a proportion of the loss that she has suffered.

So – how far does *Fairchild* go in releasing the victim of a tort from the necessity of

– in which case the employer will be held liable to compensate the employee for that 'part' of the asbestosis which is attributable to the employer's negligence: see above, pp. 538–9).

69 [2006] 2 AC 572.

70 See *Barker* v *Corus UK Ltd* [2006] 2 AC 572, at [48] (per Lord Hoffmann): 'The damages which would have been awarded against a defendant who actually caused the disease must be apportioned to the defendants according to their contributions to the risk. It may be that the most practical method of apportionment will be according to the time of exposure for which each defendant is responsible, but allowance may have to be made for the intensity of exposure and the type of asbestos.'

proving that that tort caused her to suffer a particular loss? Five situations can be considered.

(1) *Innocent exposure/self-exposure.* So far we have been considering a case where C developed mesothelioma after having been negligently exposed to asbestos dust by both A and B. In *Barker* v *Corus UK Ltd*,[71] the House of Lords considered whether *Fairchild* would also apply in the cases where:

(i) C developed mesothelioma after: (1) C was negligently exposed to asbestos dust by A; and (2) C was innocently exposed to asbestos dust by B.
(ii) C developed mesothelioma after: (1) C was negligently exposed to asbestos dust by A; and (2) C exposed himself to asbestos dust by working either at home or on a self-employed basis in conditions where he would encounter quantities of asbestos dust.

All five of the judges who decided *Barker* agreed that justice demanded that *Fairchild* should be applied in both cases (i) and (ii), with the result that A would be held liable to compensate C for his mesothelioma in both of these cases.[72] However, at least three of those judges made it clear that they only agreed to this on the basis that A's liability to pay compensation to C would be proportionate to the degree to which his actions had contributed to C's being exposed to a risk of contracting mesothelioma.[73] Now that s 3 of the Compensation Act 2006 has been enacted that condition can no longer be satisfied – if A is held liable *at all*, he will be held liable *in full*. (Unless, that is, it can be shown in case (ii) that C was careless in exposing himself to asbestos dust, in which case the damages payable to C by A in case (ii) will be reduced to take into account C's contributory negligence.) Given this, it is now uncertain whether a majority of the judges who decided *Barker* would have been willing to find A liable *at all* in either case (i) or case (ii). As a result, the question of whether A is now liable *at all* in either case (i) or case (ii) must be regarded as still to be settled. Having said that, this point may be regarded as too subtle and it may be that in practice practitioners will proceed on the basis that the combined effect of the House of Lords' decision in *Barker* and s 3 of the Compensation Act 2006 is that A *will* be held liable to compensate C *in full* for his mesothelioma in both cases (i) and (ii), subject to the possibility of the damages payable in case (ii) being reduced for contributory negligence.

(2) *The two hunters.* In the Canadian case of *Cook* v *Lewis*,[74] two hunters negligently fired their guns in the direction of the claimant. The claimant was hit and injured by a pellet fired from one of the hunters' guns – but it was impossible to tell from whose gun the pellet had come. The Supreme Court of Canada held that in this situation, each of the hunters should have been held liable to compensate the claimant for his injury.[75] It is clear that the House of Lords in *Fairchild* thought that the same conclusion should be reached under English law[76] – though, presumably, following the decision of the House of Lords in *Barker*,

[71] [2006] 2 AC 572.
[72] Ibid., at [16]–[17] (per Lord Hoffmann), [59] (per Lord Scott), [97]–[99] and [101] (per Lord Rodger), [117] (per Lord Walker), [128] (per Baroness Hale).
[73] Ibid., at [101] (per Lord Rodger, considering case (ii)), [117] (per Lord Walker), [128] (per Baroness Hale).
[74] *Cook* v *Lewis* [1951] SCR 830.
[75] The Supreme Court of California reached an identical conclusion in *Summers* v *Tice*, 199 P 2d 1 (1948). See GS&Z, 257–62.
[76] [2003] 1 AC 32, at [39] (per Lord Nicholls), [169] (per Lord Rodger).

under English law each hunter would only be liable to compensate the claimant for 50 per cent of his injuries. A finding of liability on the part of both hunters in this case can probably be justified by the fairness argument.[77] If a claimant was hit by a pellet negligently fired from a gun, he would have no problem suing for compensation for his injuries if only one gun was fired in his direction just before he was hit – so it would seem unfair to deprive him of a remedy if two guns were fired in his direction just before he was hit.

(3) *The dangerous drug.* In the American case of *Sindell* v *Abbott Laboratories*,[78] the claimant's mother was given a drug called diethylstilbesterol (DES for short) while she was pregnant with the claimant. The drug was designed to prevent her having a miscarriage. After the claimant was born, she developed a cancerous tumour in her bladder as a result of being exposed to DES while she was in her mother's womb. Whoever manufactured the DES taken by the claimant's mother knew or ought to have known that there was a danger that taking DES would have this effect, and was therefore liable in negligence to compensate the claimant for the cancer she had developed as a result of her mother's taking that DES.

Unfortunately, the claimant could not identify *who* had manufactured the DES taken by her mother – there were about 200 companies that manufactured DES at the time her mother was pregnant and the DES taken by the claimant's mother could have come from any one of them. The Supreme Court of California overcame this difficulty by holding that the claimant was entitled to sue *all* the manufacturers of DES at the relevant time for compensation for her cancer, with each manufacturer being held liable to compensate the claimant for her cancer in proportion to the share of the market for DES that it enjoyed at the time the claimant's mother was pregnant.[79]

In his judgment in the *Fairchild* case, Lord Hoffmann sought to distinguish the *Sindell* case from *Fairchild* by saying that, in *Fairchild*, A and B each *increased* the risk that C would develop mesothelioma by exposing him to excessive quantities of asbestos dust. In contrast, in *Sindell*, all the other manufacturers of DES who did not manufacture the DES taken by the claimant's mother did nothing to increase the risk that the claimant would develop cancer.[80] This, Lord Hoffmann thought, was the reason why an English court would not apply *Fairchild* in a *Sindell*-type case.[81] Whether this is correct or not, it *is* doubtful whether

[77] The sanction argument will not apply here: if a claimant were not allowed to sue in a two hunters situation, it is unlikely that people firing guns would feel free to fire them wherever they wanted.

[78] 607 P 2d 924 (1980).

[79] A manufacturer who could affirmatively prove that it was not his DES that triggered the claimant's cancer would, however, not be held liable. See, generally, GS&Z, 900–13.

[80] [2003] 1 AC 32, at [78].

[81] *Important note.* In *Barker* v *Corus UK Ltd* [2006] 2 AC 572, Lord Hoffmann argued (at [31] and [35]–[36]) that in a typical *Fairchild* situation – where C has developed mesothelioma, having been negligently exposed to asbestos by both A and B – A and B are *not* held liable to compensate C for his mesothelioma because their negligence is deemed to have *caused* him to develop mesothelioma. Instead, he argued, A and B are held liable to compensate C for his mesothelioma because their negligence *increased the risk* that C would develop mesothelioma. This is why, Lord Hoffmann said, A and B should only be held liable to compensate C for a proportion of his mesothelioma, assessed according to how far their negligence increased the risk that C would develop mesothelioma. So, on this view of the decision in *Fairchild*, *Fairchild* only applies in cases where a defendant has done something to *increase the risk* that the claimant would suffer the loss for which she is seeking to be compensated. With respect to Lord Hoffmann – and the other judges who agreed with him in *Barker* on this point (see Lord Scott at [61] and Lord Walker at [103]) – this view of the decision in *Fairchild* simply cannot be correct. As Lord Rodger pointed out in *Barker* (at [79]), if this were right then if C *died* of his mesothelioma,

an English court would go as far as the Supreme Court of California did in *Sindell*. Neither the fairness argument nor the sanction argument require that *all* the manufacturers of a dangerous drug should be held liable for the harm done by that drug to a claimant if the company that manufactured that drug cannot be identified.[82]

(4) *The dirty cleaner*. In *McGhee* v *National Coal Board*,[83] the claimant was employed by the defendants to clean out some brick kilns. This was hot and dirty work which exposed the claimant to clouds of abrasive brick dust. The defendants (in breach of the duty of care they owed the claimant as his employers) failed to provide the claimant with any on-site washing facilities which would allow him to wash off the brick dust as soon as he knocked off work. Instead, the claimant had to cycle home and wash there. After some days of working in the brick kilns, the claimant was found to be suffering from dermatitis. The claimant claimed that the defendants' breach of the duty of care they owed him had caused him to develop dermatitis. To make out this claim he normally would have had to have shown that he would not have developed dermatitis had the defendants provided him with on-site washing facilities. This was impossible to show. Despite this, the House of Lords found that the defendants' failure to provide the claimant with on-site washing facilities did cause the claimant to develop dermatitis and allowed the claimant's claim.

The House of Lords in *Fairchild* clearly thought that *McGhee* was correctly decided. (Though, presumably, following the decision in *Barker*, a defendant in a *McGhee*-type situation would now only be held liable for a proportion of the claimant's dermatitis.) Indeed, their Lordships relied heavily on *McGhee* as authority in favour of the view that, on the facts of *Fairchild*, C was entitled to sue A and B for compensation for his mesothelioma.[84] The decision in *McGhee* can probably be justified by reference to the sanction argument.[85] If the claimant had not been allowed to sue in *McGhee* on the ground that he could not prove that the defendants' negligence caused him to develop dermatitis, an employer who, in breach of the duty of care he owed his employees, did not guard against the risk that his employees would develop dermatitis in working for

---

C's dependants would not be able to sue either A or B under the Fatal Accidents Act 1976. This is because if C's dependants wanted to bring a claim for (say) loss of support against A under the 1976 Act, they would have to show that A's negligence *caused* C to die. They would not be able to do this if *Fairchild* has the effect Lord Hoffmann argues that it does. They would not be able to use *Fairchild* to establish that A's negligence caused C to develop mesothelioma, and thereby caused C's death. Now: the claim in *Barker* was a claim for loss of support under the 1976 Act, and nobody – least of all Lord Hoffmann – argued that it should be thrown out on the ground that the claimant could not establish that any of the defendants' acts of negligence caused her husband to die of cancer. The fact that the claim in *Barker* was not thrown out – and nobody suggested it should be – shows that Lord Hoffmann's view of the effect of the decision in *Fairchild* must be wrong.

82 The point is, though, somewhat academic. A claimant who was harmed by a dangerous drug could bring an action for compensation under the Consumer Protection Act 1987 and if the manufacturer of that drug could not be identified, the last identifiable person who was involved in the chain of supply of that drug would normally be held liable: see below, p. 776.

83 [1973] 1 WLR 1 (discussed, Hope 2003).

84 [2003] 1 AC 32, at [33] (per Lord Bingham), [44] (per Lord Nicholls), [64]–[66] (per Lord Hoffmann), [151]–[153] (per Lord Rodger).

85 [1973] 1 WLR 1, at 9: '[Not to hold for the claimant] would mean that the [defendants] were under a legal duty which they could, in the present state of medical knowledge, with impunity ignore' (per Lord Simon of Glaisdale); and at 12: '[Not to hold for the claimant] would mean that in the present state of medical knowledge and in circumstances such as these (which are by no means uncommon) an employer would be permitted by the law to disregard with impunity his duty to take reasonable care for the safety of his employees' (per Lord Salmon).

him by providing his employees with showering facilities would never face any sanction for his negligence. Even if one or more of his employees developed dermatitis, they would never be able to prove that the failure to provide showering facilities caused them to develop dermatitis.

(5) *The premature baby*. In *Wilsher* v *Essex Area Health Authority*,[86] the claimant was a baby that was born prematurely. Shortly after he was born, he developed a serious eye condition called retrolental fibroplasia (RLF for short) and was blinded as a result. The claimant may have developed RLF because he was exposed to excess oxygen by the defendants. However, the claimant also suffered from four medical conditions that could have accounted for his developing RLF. Given this, he could not show that it was more likely than not that he developed RLF because he was given too much oxygen by the defendants. The House of Lords held that the claimant's action against the defendants in negligence for compensation for the fact that he was blind could not succeed: he could not show that the defendants' actions had caused him to go blind.

Four of the five Law Lords in *Fairchild* thought that *Wilsher* was correctly decided.[87] Why is this case so different from *Fairchild*? Three of those four Law Lords drew a formalistic distinction between *Wilsher* and *Fairchild*, arguing that in *Fairchild* there was only one possible agent which could have caused the claimant to develop mesothelioma: asbestos dust. In contrast, in *Wilsher* there were five different agents that could have caused the claimant to develop RLF.[88] In *Fairchild*, Lord Hoffmann criticised this way of distinguishing *Wilsher* from *Fairchild*, arguing that the suggested distinction was unprincipled: 'What if [one of the claimants in *Fairchild*] had been exposed to two different agents – asbestos dust and some other dust – both of which created a material risk of the same cancer and it was equally impossible to say which had caused the fatal cell mutation? I cannot see why this should make a difference.'[89] However, in the subsequent *Barker* case, Lord Hoffmann recanted, admitting that his objections in *Fairchild* to the way the majority in that case distinguished *Wilsher* from *Fairchild* had been 'wrong'.[90] He went on to reformulate that distinction as resting on the fact that *Fairchild* only applied in cases where 'the impossibility of proving that the defendant caused the damage arises out of the existence of another potential causative agent which operated in the same way. It may have been different in some causally irrelevant respect [such as in Lord Hoffmann's example in *Fairchild* of the 'asbestos dust and some other dust'], but the mechanism by which it caused the damage, whatever it was, must have been the same.'[91]

We are less convinced of the merit of the single-agent/multiple-agent distinction between *Fairchild* and *Wilsher*. A better way of distinguishing the two cases, it seems to us, is to observe that the reasons why the defendants were held liable in *Fairchild* simply did not apply in *Wilsher*. In particular, the sanction argument did not apply in *Wilsher*: it could

[86] [1988] AC 1074.
[87] [2003] 1 AC 32 at [22] (per Lord Bingham), [70] (per Lord Hoffmann), [118] (per Lord Hutton), [149] (per Lord Rodger). The fifth judge, Lord Nicholls, expressed no opinion on the matter.
[88] Ibid., at [22] (per Lord Bingham), [118] (per Lord Hutton), [170] (per Lord Rodger).
[89] Ibid., at [72].
[90] [2006] 2 AC 572, at [23].
[91] Ibid., at [24].

not be said that if the defendants were not held liable in *Wilsher* then doctors would be free to breach the duties of care that they owed their patients.[92]

Gregg v *Scott*

In *Fairchild*, there was no doubt that *someone's* negligence *had* caused the claimant to suffer physical harm. In *Gregg* v *Scott*[93] the best that could be said of the claimant was that the defendant's negligence had caused him to lose a chance of avoiding physical harm.

In order to understand the facts of *Gregg* v *Scott*, it is first necessary to understand some points of terminology relating to the treatment of cancer patients. Someone suffers from cancer if they have at least one malignant tumour in their body. A cancer patient is said to go into remission if all the malignant tumours that were in his body have been killed. A cancer patient who is in remission is said to have suffered a relapse if a new malignant tumour is detected in his body. This new tumour will almost always have developed from a cancer cell that was secreted by one of the tumours that was formerly in the cancer patient's body. A cancer cell can take years to develop into a tumour, so a cancer patient who is in remission can suffer a relapse some years after he went into remission. A cancer patient is said to be 'cured' if he has been in remission for 10 years. The reason for this is that if a cancer patient has been in remission for 10 years it is unlikely that he is still carrying any cancer cells that were secreted by the tumours that were in his body 10 years ago: if he were, one would expect them to have developed into tumours by now, thus causing the patient to suffer a relapse.

Now we can make sense of the facts of *Gregg* v *Scott*. In 1994, the claimant developed a lump under his left arm. He consulted his doctor, the defendant, and the defendant told him not to worry about it. Had the defendant treated the claimant with a reasonable degree of skill and care, he would have referred the claimant to hospital, where they would have discovered the lump was cancerous, and treatment of the lump would have started in April 1995. Had the lump been treated at that stage there was a 42 per cent chance that the claimant's cancer would have been 'cured'. However, the lump went untreated and the claimant's cancer spread. A year later, the claimant consulted another doctor, the cancer was detected and treatment started in January 1996. However, because the cancer was more advanced, the treatment that the claimant underwent was much more intensive, and his chances of being 'cured' were now only 25 per cent. The claimant did go into remission after treatment commenced, but he subsequently suffered two relapses. However, he went into remission after the second relapse, and by the time the House of Lords heard the claimant's claim for damages against the defendant – that is, in May 2004 – he had been in remission for six years.

[92] [2003] 1 AC 32 at [69] (per Lord Hoffmann). However, if one characterised the duty of care owed, and breached, in *Wilsher* more narrowly as being a duty to take reasonable steps not to expose the premature baby to excess oxygen the sanction argument might apply. One could argue that if hospitals are not held liable in *Wilsher*-type situations, then they will be free to breach the duties of care that they owe premature babies in their care not to expose them to excess oxygen. Whether this argument works or not will depend on whether exposing a premature baby to excess oxygen might cause the baby any ill effects – other than developing RLF – which could not also be attributed to medical complications arising out of the baby's premature birth.

[93] [2005] 2 AC 176 (discussed, Reid 2005).

The claimant could not establish that had the defendant doctor not been negligent he would have been 'cured'. Had the defendant doctor not been negligent, and treatment of the claimant's cancer commenced in April 1995, it was still more likely than not at that stage that the claimant's cancer would not be 'cured'. So, on the balance of probabilities, the claimant's cancer would not have been 'cured' even if the defendant doctor had not been negligent. Instead, then, of suing the defendant doctor for damages for the fact that he had not been 'cured', the claimant sought to sue the defendant for damages to compensate him for the fact that, as a result of the defendant doctor's negligence, his chances of being 'cured' had gone down from 42 per cent to 25 per cent – he had lost a 17 per cent chance of being 'cured'.

By a majority of 3:2, the House of Lords dismissed the claimant's claim for damages. Only Lord Nicholls was in favour of allowing the claimant to make a claim for a 'pure' loss of a chance of being cured. He advanced three basic arguments in favour of his position:

(1) *The sanction argument.* If claims for the loss of a chance of being cured cannot be brought under English law, then a doctor who is presented with a patient with a very poor chance of being cured will have no incentive to treat the patient properly.[94] If he fails to treat the patient properly and the patient's condition worsens, he will always be able to argue that he should not be held liable to the patient because it was more likely than not that the patient's condition would have got just as bad had he treated the patient with a reasonable degree of care and skill.

(2) *The argument from fairness.* If claims for the loss of a chance of being cured are not allowed in English law, then the law will unfairly discriminate between different kinds of patients.[95] For example, suppose that Beth and John both independently consult Mary, a doctor, because they have been feeling unwell. In fact, both of them are – without knowing it – HIV+. John's condition is more advanced than Beth's and he has only a 45 per cent chance of avoiding developing AIDS, even if he receives proper treatment. Beth, on the other hand, has a 55 per cent chance of avoiding developing AIDS, if she receives proper treatment. Unfortunately, neither of them receive proper treatment because Mary negligently fails to diagnose that they are HIV+. John and Beth both subsequently develop AIDS. In this situation, Beth will be able to claim *full* compensation from Mary for the fact that she has developed AIDS.[96] She will be able to argue that it was more likely than not that had Mary not been negligent she would not have developed AIDS and so Mary's negligence caused her to develop AIDS. In contrast, John will not be able to argue that Mary's negligence caused him to develop AIDS because it was more likely than not that he would still have developed AIDS even if Mary had treated him properly. Now – if John is not allowed here to sue Mary for damages for the fact that as a result of her negligence he lost a 45 per cent chance of avoiding developing AIDS, then the result is that Beth will be allowed to sue for full compensation for the fact that she has developed AIDS, and John will not be allowed to sue for anything. And this is so even though the difference between Beth's

[94] Ibid., at [4].
[95] Ibid., at [3].
[96] Though the courts will reduce the compensation somewhat to take account of the possibility that Beth would have developed AIDS anyway even if Mary had not been negligent.

and John's chances of avoiding developing AIDS with proper treatment was only 10 per cent.

(3) *The argument from authority*. The law already allows claims for pure losses of a chance in other contexts.[97] For example, if a court throws out A's claim for damages because his solicitor negligently failed to file the claim in time, A will be able to sue his solicitor in negligence for compensation for the loss of the chance that he might have won his case. So why not allow a claim for the pure loss of a chance here? Why should doctors be treated more favourably than solicitors?

Lord Hoffmann and Baroness Hale advanced the following arguments against awarding damages for the pure loss of a chance of being cured:

(1) *The* Hotson[98] *problem*. In cases such as *Gregg* v *Scott*, it may well be that the claimant *never had a chance* of being cured, and if this is the case it would be inappropriate to award him damages on the basis that his doctor's negligence deprived him of a chance of being 'cured'.[99] The statisticians tell us that of 100 patients presenting with a lump like the claimant's in *Gregg* v *Scott*, 42 will be 'cured' if they are treated immediately. One way of interpreting this statistic is to say that *each* of those 100 patients has a 42 per cent chance of being 'cured'. If this is right, then it would be correct to say that the claimant in *Gregg* v *Scott* had a 42 per cent chance of being 'cured' when he saw the defendant doctor. But there is a different way of reading the statistics. It may be that of 100 patients presenting with a lump like the claimant's in *Gregg* v *Scott*, the varying genetic make-ups of the 100 patients mean that 42 of them are *certain* to be 'cured' so long as the lump is treated immediately, and 58 of them have *no chance* of being 'cured' no matter how much treatment they receive. If this is right, then it was more likely than not that the claimant in *Gregg* v *Scott* had no chance of being 'cured' and it would therefore be inappropriate to award him damages on the basis that he *did* have a chance of being cured.

(2) *Administrative difficulties*. Even if this problem could be overcome, and the claimant in *Gregg* v *Scott* did genuinely have a chance of being 'cured' when he saw the defendant doctor – though it is hard to know how that could be established – allowing claimants to bring claims for the pure loss of a chance of being cured would create a number of administrative difficulties.

First, the number of claims that could be brought against doctors would be hugely increased, with 'enormous consequences for insurance companies and the National Health Service'.[100] Doctors would, in effect, become liable to pay damages to their patients every time it was established that they had failed to treat their patients with reasonable skill and care. This is because in every such case the doctor's patient would be able to argue that his or her doctor's negligence had diminished his or her chances of being cured and that he or she was therefore entitled to compensation for the loss of that chance of being cured.[101]

97 [2005] 2 AC 176, at [15]–[19].

98 See above, pp. 539–42.

99 [2005] 2 AC 176, at [79]–[81] (per Lord Hoffmann).

100 Ibid., at [90] (per Lord Hoffmann).

101 Ibid., at [215] (per Baroness Hale).

Secondly, personal injury claims arising out of medical negligence would become much more complicated to process. In the case of John, Beth and Mary, discussed above, if John were allowed to sue Mary for the fact that her negligence deprived him of a chance of avoiding developing AIDS, the law could no longer justifiably hold Mary liable to compensate Beth *in full* for the fact that she had developed AIDS based only on the fact that Beth had a 55 per cent chance of avoiding developing AIDS with proper treatment when she saw Mary. Beth would instead be confined to suing Mary for the loss of the 55 per cent chance of avoiding AIDS that she was deprived of as a result of Mary's negligence. So all personal injury claims arising out of medical negligence would become loss of a chance claims, involving 'expert evidence [that] would have to be far more complex than it is at present. Negotiations and trials would be a great deal more difficult. Recovery would be much less predictable . . .'.[102]

(3) *Lord Nicholls's arguments*. Finally, none of Lord Nicholls's arguments in favour of allowing recovery for a pure loss of a chance in *Gregg* v *Scott* stand up.

First, as to the sanction argument, it is not necessary to allow claims for a pure loss of a chance of being cured to be made against doctors in order to encourage them to treat patients who have poor prospects of recovering properly. The doctor's natural desire to do his or her best for his or her patients, the General Medical Council, and the criminal law provide sufficient encouragement.[103]

Secondly, as to the fairness argument, any unfairness in the way the law currently treats patients in terms of the remedies they are provided with when their doctors let them down is justified on the grounds of the administrative difficulties, described above, that would arise under any other remedial regime.

Thirdly, as to the argument from authority, there may be a difference between a case like *Gregg* v *Scott* and cases where the law currently allows claims for a pure loss of a chance to be made.[104] The law currently allows claims for a pure loss of a chance to be made in cases where A has hired B to make him money, and due to B's negligence A has lost a chance to make money. In contrast, in *Gregg* v *Scott*, the claimant consulted the defendant doctor to make him physically better, and due to the doctor's negligence the claimant lost a chance of getting better. It may be that there is something special about 'money' cases which accounts for why the law allows claims for a pure loss of a chance in those cases, but not in medical negligence cases. For example, a pure loss of a chance may count in the law's eyes as a form of pure economic loss – it cannot, after all, be classified as a form of physical injury or property damage – and is thus only claimable in cases where A has hired B to safeguard or promote his economic welfare.

As to the other two judges who decided *Gregg* v *Scott*:

(1) *Lord Hope* would have allowed the claimant's claim for damages, not on the ground that it was a claim for a pure loss of a chance, but on the basis that the defendant doctor's negligence had caused the claimant to suffer a physical injury – the spreading of his cancer. The claimant, Lord Hope argued, was entitled to be compensated for this injury, and such com-

102 Ibid, at [225] (per Baroness Hale).
103 Ibid., at [217] (per Baroness Hale).
104 Ibid., at [218]–[220] (per Baroness Hale).

pensation would include a sum for the chance that, because of the spread in the cancer, the claimant's cancer would not be cured in future. (In the same way, if A has tortiously caused B to suffer a hip injury, A will not only be held liable to compensate B for the hip injury, but also for the chance that B will develop arthritis in the future as a result of the hip injury.) The problem with this approach is that it assumes that the defendant's negligence *caused* the claimant's cancer to spread – but, on the balance of probabilities, it is far from clear that the claimant's cancer would not have spread in any case, even if the defendant had not been negligent.

(2) *Lord Phillips MR* indicated that he would be willing to allow a claim for damages for a loss of a chance in a case – such as John's, discussed above – where a patient has suffered an 'adverse outcome' and there was a chance that it could have been avoided had the patient been treated with a reasonable degree of care and skill by his or her doctor.[105] However, it was not clear whether the claimant in *Gregg* v *Scott had* suffered an 'adverse outcome' – which in this case would mean not being 'cured'. Given that at the time of the House of Lords' hearing, the claimant had been in remission for six years, and the fact that the official definition of being 'cured' of cancer is being in remission for ten years, there was every chance that the claimant would in fact finally be 'cured'. So Lord Phillips concluded that *Gregg* v *Scott* was simply not an appropriate case in which damages for the loss of a chance of avoiding an 'adverse outcome' could be awarded.

Chester v *Afshar*

In *Chester* v *Afshar*,[106] Chester was suffering from back pain. She consulted the defendant doctor, Afshar. Afshar recommended that she have an operation to remove three discs from her back. Unfortunately, he failed to warn her that there was a very small risk (1–2 per cent) that she would suffer nerve damage in her back as a result of the operation. Chester agreed that Afshar could operate on her and three days later, on 21 November 1994, Afshar carried out the operation. Although Afshar carried out the operation with all due care and skill, Chester suffered nerve damage and was partially paralysed as a result of the operation. Chester sued Afshar in negligence for compensation for the harm she had suffered.

There was no doubt in this case that Afshar had breached the duty he owed Chester, as her doctor, to treat her with reasonable skill and care. Afshar should have told Chester of the risk of nerve damage associated with the operation he was proposing to carry out on her. But did Afshar's breach cause Chester to suffer the harm that she had suffered in this case?

The 'but for' test for causation was satisfied in this case. It was established that had Afshar told Chester of the risk of nerve damage associated with the operation, Chester would have taken a few days to think over whether she should go ahead with the operation. As a result, the operation would probably have taken place on something like the 25 November 1994. Had the operation been carried out *then*, it was more likely than not (in fact 98–99 per cent likely) that the operation would have passed off without incident, and Chester would not have suffered any nerve damage or paralysis in her back. So – had Afshar

105 Ibid., at [190].
106 [2005] 1 AC 134 (noted, Stevens 2005).

not breached the duty of care he owed Chester to treat her with a reasonable degree of skill and care, she almost certainly would not have suffered the nerve damage and paralysis for which she was seeking compensation.

However, the problem with Chester's case was that the 'material increase in risk' test for causation was not satisfied. Afshar's breach of duty in failing to tell Chester of the risk of nerve damage associated with her operation did not materially increase the risk that Chester would suffer that kind of harm when she had the operation. The risk was always constant, and could not be affected by what Afshar had or had not told Chester in his consulting room. So Afshar's breach of the duty of care that he owed Chester did *not* cause Chester to suffer the harm for which she was seeking compensation.[107]

Despite this, the House of Lords held – by a 3:2 majority – that Afshar should be held liable to compensate Chester for the nerve damage and consequent paralysis that she had suffered as a result of being operated on by Afshar. The majority so ruled because they were concerned that, if Afshar were not held liable, then every time a doctor advised a patient to have an operation and failed – in breach of the duty of care he owed the patient – to inform her of the risks associated with the operation, his breach of duty would go unsanctioned by tort law. If the patient agreed to have the operation and suffered harm as a result, even though the operation was carried out impeccably, the doctor could argue that he should not be held liable for that harm because his breach of duty in failing to inform the patient of the risks associated with that operation had not caused the harm suffered by the patient. The doctor's duty to inform his patient of the risks associated with a particular operation would then become empty – the doctor would be free to breach that duty with impunity. In order, then, to vindicate the patient's 'right to know', the majority felt[108] that it was necessary to create a special exception to the rules on causation in *Chester* v *Afshar* and hold that: (1) if a doctor wrongfully failed to inform a patient of a risk associated with an operation that it was proposed the patient undergo; and (2) had the patient been informed of this risk, she would probably have either refused to undergo the operation or delayed having the operation so as to think it over whether she should undergo it;[109] and (3) in the course of the operation, this risk materialised with the result that the patient suffered harm; then (4) the doctor should be held liable in negligence to compensate the patient for that harm.

In dissent, Lord Hoffmann held that if (1), (2) and (3) were established, then there might be a case for awarding the patient a 'modest solatium'[110] to compensate her for the fact that her right to know the risks associated with her operation so as to make an informed decision whether or not to undergo the operation had been violated. However, he failed to see why the compensation payable to a patient whose 'right to know' had been violated should depend on whether the risk which the patient was not informed of had

[107] Ibid., at [13]–[22] (per Lord Steyn); [30]–[32] (per Lord Hoffmann); and [61] and [81] (per Lord Hope).

[108] Ibid., at [22]–[24] (per Lord Steyn); [56] and [87] (per Lord Hope); and [101] (per Lord Walker).

[109] *Important note*. There is an issue as to whether this requirement has to be satisfied in order for an award of damages to be made under *Chester* v *Afshar*. The argument is that if the object of such an award of damages is to vindicate a patient's 'right to know' such damages should be available even if telling the patient of the risks associated with her operation would have had no effect on the timing of her operation. However, of the majority judges, both Lord Steyn (at [19]) and Lord Hope (at [61] and [81]) attached importance to the fact that had Chester been told of the risk of nerve damage associated with her operation, her operation probably would not have gone ahead when it did. In light of this, it seemed to us correct to say that damages will only be awarded to a patient under *Chester* v *Afshar* if requirement (2) is satisfied.

[110] [2005] 1 AC 134, at [34].

materialised, and how much harm had been suffered by the patient as a result of that risk's materalising.[111] Lord Bingham also dissented. He dismissed the majority's justification for allowing Chester's claim on the ground that 'in the current legal and social climate' few doctors would 'consciously or deliberately violate' a patient's 'right to be appropriately warned' of the risks associated with her operation. He saw no reason why 'the law should seek to reinforce that right by providing for the payment of very large damages by a defendant whose violation of that right is not shown' to have caused the claimant to suffer the injury for which she is seeking compensation.[112]

Reeves

In *Reeves* v *Commissioner of Police of the Metropolis*,[113] a man named Lynch hanged himself while in the defendants' custody. Lynch was known to be a suicide risk and the defendant police force therefore owed him a duty to take reasonable steps to ensure that he did not commit suicide. The defendant police force breached this duty. Lynch – who was of sound mind and knew what he was doing – took advantage of the defendants' negligence to hang himself. The claimant sued the defendants under the Fatal Accidents Act 1976, claiming that their negligence had caused Lynch's death and that the defendants were therefore liable to compensate her for the loss of support that she and her child by Lynch suffered as a result of Lynch's death. It was argued that the defendants' negligence had not caused Lynch's death: there was a break in the chain of causation between the defendants' negligence and Lynch's death because Lynch freely, deliberately and unreasonably took advantage of the defendants' negligence by hanging himself.

The House of Lords refused to find that the defendants' negligence had not caused Lynch's death: '[If] the law [has imposed] a duty [on someone] to guard against loss caused by the free, deliberate and informed act of a human being . . . [it] would make nonsense of the existence of this duty if the law were to hold that the occurrence of the very act which ought to have been prevented negatived [the existence of a] causal connection between the breach of duty and the loss.'[114] In other words, if the normal rules on when there will be a break in the chain of causation were applied in this case, then the defendants could never have been held liable for breaching the duty of care they owed Lynch to take reasonable steps to see that he did not kill himself. If Lynch took advantage of their breach of duty to kill himself, the defendants would always be able to argue that their breach did not cause Lynch's death because his free, deliberate and unreasonable decision to kill himself broke the chain of causation between their breach and Lynch's death.[115]

[111] Ibid., at [35].
[112] Ibid., at [9].
[113] [2000] 1 AC 360.
[114] Ibid., at 367 (per Lord Hoffmann).
[115] For the same reason, a plea that there was a break in the chain of causation between the defendant's breach of duty and the claimant's loss could not have succeeded in *Stansbie* v *Troman* [1948] 2 KB 48 (defendant decorator was employed by claimant to decorate her house and was held liable for theft of property from the house that occurred when he negligently left the claimant's front door open) or in *Dorset Yacht Co. Ltd* v *Home Office* [1970] AC 1004 (defendants held liable for deliberate criminal damage done by Borstal boys under the defendants' control). To allow such a plea would have allowed the defendants in these cases to breach the duties of care they owed the claimants with impunity: whenever some harm resulted from their breach, they could argue that their breach did not cause the harm because there was a break in the chain of causation between the breach and the harm.

PRESUMPTION OF LOSS

Before we leave the topic of causation, we should note that if A has committed a tort in relation to B, the courts will sometimes *presume* that A's tort caused B to suffer some kind of loss.[116]

So, for example, we have already seen that if A has committed the tort of libel in relation to B, the courts will presume that A's libel caused B to suffer some kind of loss.[117] In contrast, it will be recalled, if A has committed the tort of slander in relation to B, the courts will only presume that A's slander caused B to suffer some kind of loss if: (1) A slandered B by publishing to another words that suggested B had committed a criminal offence; *or* (2) A slandered B by publishing to another words that suggested B had a contagious or infectious disease; *or* (3) A slandered B by publishing to another words that were calculated to disparage B in an office, profession, calling, trade or business held or carried on by B at the time of the publication; *or* (4) A slandered B by publishing to another words that suggested B was unchaste or adulterous (though this will only hold true if B is a woman).

Similarly, as we have already seen,[118] if A has committed the tort of malicious falsehood in respect of B, the courts will presume that A's falsehood caused B to suffer some kind of loss if: (1) A's falsehood was calculated to cause pecuniary damage to B and was published in writing or other permanent form; *or* (2) A's falsehood was calculated to cause pecuniary damage to B in respect of any office, profession, calling, trade or business held or carried on by him at the time of the publication of the falsehood. Again, if A caused B to suffer some kind of personal injury by committing a tort in relation to B, the courts will naturally presume that the infliction of that injury caused B to suffer some kind of pain and suffering.

Visit **http://www.mylawchamber.co.uk/mcbride** to access updates on recent cases, as well as model answers and tips for answering tort problem questions.

Use **Case Navigator** to read in full some of the key cases referenced in this chapter:

- **Gregg** *v* **Scott**
- **Chester** *v* **Afshar**
- **Fairchild** *v* **Glenhaven Funeral Services Ltd**

[116] Damages which are awarded to compensate the victim of a tort for a loss which he is *presumed* to have suffered as a result of that tort being committed are known as 'general damages'. Damages which are awarded to compensate the victim of a tort for a loss which he had to prove that he suffered as a result of that tort being committed are known as 'special damages'.

[117] See above, p. 309.

[118] See above, p. 460.

28 Actionability

Suppose that A has committed a tort in relation to B and that tort caused B to suffer some kind of loss. B will only be entitled to sue A for compensation for that loss if it is *actionable*. This chapter explains when this condition will be satisfied.

However, before we can set out the rules governing when a loss will be actionable, we must first make a distinction between the kinds of losses that might be suffered by the victim of a tort. All these losses can be divided up into *primary losses* and *secondary losses*. Suppose, for example, that A has committed a tort in relation to B and B has suffered various losses as a result.[1] If we take one of the losses suffered by B as a result of A's tort, that loss will be a primary loss if she did *not* suffer that loss because she suffered some other kind of loss as a result of A's tort; in contrast, that loss will be a *secondary* loss if B's suffering that loss was a consequence of B's suffering some other kind of loss as a result of A's tort.[2] (See Figure 28.1.)

So, for example, suppose that A negligently crashed into B's car. B's car was badly damaged in the collision and she had to spend £1,000 having it repaired. B's leg was also broken in the crash. At the time of the crash, B was on her way to a job interview but was unable to make the interview as she had to be taken to hospital to have her leg treated; the job went to someone else. B's heart was so set on getting this job that she became extremely depressed. In this situation B has suffered six losses. First, property damage: her car was damaged. Secondly, economic loss: B had to spend £1,000 having her car repaired. Thirdly, physical injury: B's leg was broken. Fourthly, distress: B will have suffered a great deal of pain as a result of her leg being broken. Fifthly, economic loss, again: B lost the chance of getting a job as a result of A's crashing into her car. Sixthly, distress, again: B became extremely depressed as a result of losing the chance to get the job she had set her heart on. The property damage and physical injury suffered by B here will count as *primary* losses: B did not suffer those losses because she some other kind of loss as a result of A's tort. The other losses suffered by B will count as *secondary* losses: they were all suffered because B suffered some other kind of loss as a consequence as a result of A's tort. The money B spent on having her car repaired was spent because her car was damaged. The pain B suffered in the aftermath of the crash was suffered because her leg was broken. The chance B lost to get the job she wanted was lost because her leg was broken. And the depression B went through was suffered because she lost the chance of getting that job.

Now that we are familiar with the distinction between primary and secondary losses, we are in a good position to understand the rules governing when a loss suffered by the victim of a tort as a result of that tort's having been committed will be actionable. Basically, if A

[1] From now on in this book, a loss suffered by the victim of a tort will be said to have been suffered 'as a result of' that tort having been committed if the commission of that tort *caused* the victim of that tort to suffer that loss.

[2] An alternative term for 'secondary losses' which enjoys some popularity is *consequential losses*.

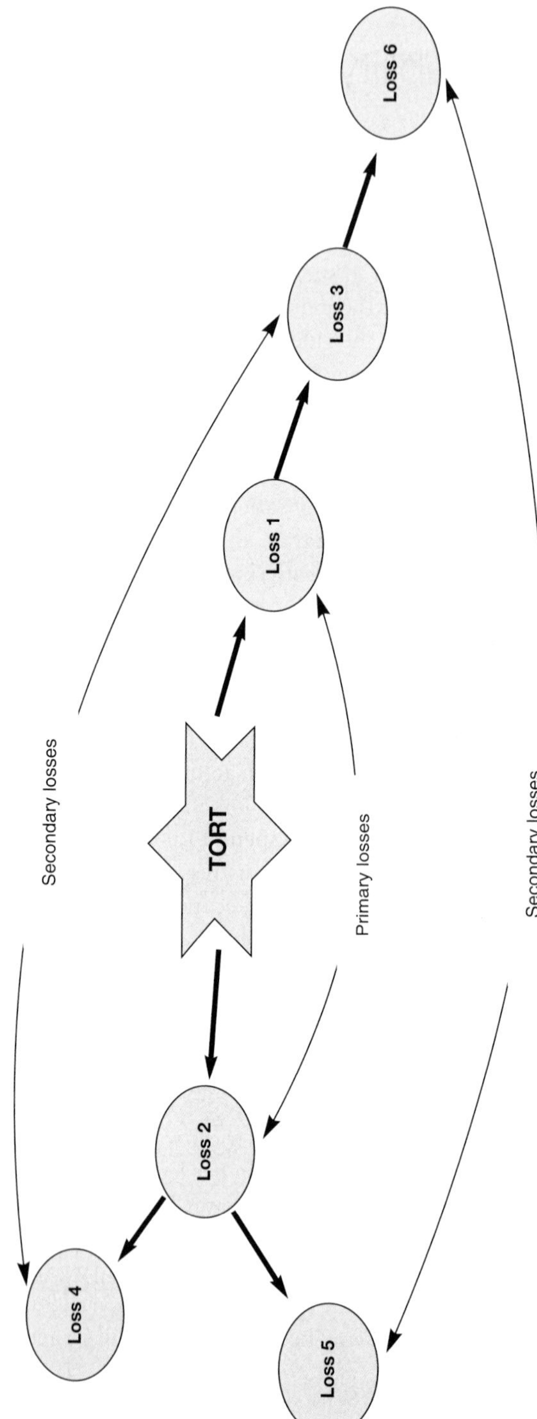

Figure 28.1 The distinction between primary and secondary losses (the thick straight arrows indicate chains of causation)

has committed a tort in relation to B and B has suffered some kind of loss as a result, that loss will be non-actionable if:

(1) it was a *remote* consequence of A's tort;[3] *or*
(2) it is a *primary* loss and is the *wrong kind of loss*; *or*
(3) it would be contrary to *public policy* to allow B to sue A for compensation for that loss; *or*
(4) it is regarded as being *automatically non-actionable* for some reason.

If none of these things are true of the loss that B has suffered, then that loss will be actionable. Let's now look at these four different reasons why a loss might be non-actionable.

REMOTENESS

The foreseeability test

Suppose A has committed a tort in relation to B and B has suffered some kind of loss as a result. *Normally* that loss will count as a remote consequence of A's tort if it was *not* reasonably foreseeable at the time A committed his tort that *someone like B would suffer that kind of loss as a result of A's committing that tort.*[4] Let's call this the *foreseeability test* for determining whether a loss suffered by the victim of a tort was a remote consequence of that tort.[5] The foreseeability test may seem straightforward to apply, but it is not. The reason is that whether or not the foreseeability test is satisfied in a given case depends a great deal on how we describe what kind of loss it was that the claimant suffered. And in a lot of cases there will be room for dispute as to what is the appropriate way of describing what kind of

[3] *Important note.* There is a paper, or even a monograph, to be written on the mania for unification that afflicts most lawyers and causes them to try and unify what are in fact disparate legal rules or doctrines, with invariably disastrous results. We have seen, and will see, many examples of this. For example: the idea that the various torts recognised in English law can be reduced to one or two or three 'master torts' (see above, pp. 18–20); Lord Atkin's insistence that there *must* exist *one* principle or test which accounts for the existence of *all* the duties of care recognised in English law (see above, pp. 72–3); the popular misconception that *all* cases where a claimant may sue another in negligence for pure economic loss fall under the 'principle in *Hedley Byrne*' (see above, pp. 142–4); the continual hankering after a rule or principle that would unify the 'economic' torts dealt with in Chapters 20–23 of this book (see above, pp. 405–6; also Weir 1997 and Bagshaw 1998); the insistence of some restitution scholars that in *all* cases where restitutionary damages are awarded against a defendant who has committed a tort, he is *always* stripped of the gains he has made by committing that tort (see below, pp. 707–8); and the insistence, recently endorsed for no good reason by the House of Lords in *Transco plc* v *Stockport MBC* [2003] 3 WLR 1467, that the rule in *Rylands* v *Fletcher* is an outgrowth, or part, of the law on private nuisance (see below, pp. 756–7). This mania for unification has caused many tort scholars to treat the law on remoteness of damage as being part of the law on causation: see, for example, Murphy 2003, 299f, GS&Z, 265f. Increasingly, it is being recognised that this is a mistake and that the law on remoteness of damage has *nothing to do* with the law on causation: the law on causation determines what losses can be said to have been caused by a defendant's committing a tort; the law on remoteness of damage helps to determine for which of those losses the defendant will be held liable. See, for example, Stapleton 2003a, at 389, congratulating the authors of the *Restatement (Third) of Torts: Liability for Physical Harm (Basic Principles)* for taking the 'bold and necessary' step of clearly distinguishing between the law on causation and the law on the 'scope of liability for consequences', of which the law on remoteness of damage forms part.

[4] *Hughes* v *Lord Advocate* [1963] AC 837.

[5] Cases in which the foreseeability test was adopted to determine whether a loss suffered by the victim of a tort was a remote consequence of that tort include: *Overseas Tankship (UK) Ltd* v *Morts Dock & Engineering Co. Ltd, The Wagon Mound* [1961] AC 388 (a negligence case); *Overseas Tankship (UK) Ltd* v *Miller Steamship Co. Pty, The Wagon Mound (No. 2)* [1967] 1 AC 617 (private nuisance); and *Slipper* v *British Broadcasting Corpn* [1991] 1 QB 283 (libel).

loss it was that the claimant suffered – especially as, *in this context*, we describe *what* kind of loss it was that a claimant suffered by reference – in part – to *how* that loss was suffered.[6]

For example, in *Jolley* v *Sutton London Borough Council*,[7] a council owned a piece of amenity land near a block of flats. A boat had been left lying on this land for about two years. The boat was in a poor condition and anyone playing about on the boat was liable to put a foot through the rotten timbers of the boat and suffer an injury. Given this – and given the fact that children playing on the amenity land were liable to clamber onto the boat and run the risk of being injured – the council owed children going onto the amenity land a duty under the Occupiers' Liability Act 1957 to take reasonable steps to remove the boat from the land. The council breached this duty when they did nothing about the boat for two years. In that time, the claimant and a friend of his – both children – saw the boat and decided to repair it so they could go sailing in it. They used a car jack to elevate one side of the boat and, crawling underneath, repaired some of the holes in the hull of the boat. Unfortunately, one day when the claimant was working under the boat, the car jack gave way and the boat fell on the claimant's back, causing him severe spinal injuries. The claimant sued the council for damages. The case turned on whether the claimant's injuries were a remote consequence of the council's admitted negligence under the foreseeability test.

Now whether or not you think that the foreseeability test was satisfied here will depend a great deal on how you describe what kind of loss it was that the claimant suffered. Remembering that in this context, we describe what kind of loss it was that the claimant suffered by reference – in part – to how it was suffered, you might say that the kind of loss suffered by the claimant here was 'Physical injury resulting from meddling with the boat'. If you say *that* then the foreseeability test was plainly satisfied here. It was reasonably foreseeable that if the defendants did not remove the boat from their land, someone like the claimant would 'meddle' with the boat and would suffer physical injury as a result. However, you could adopt a narrower description and say that the kind of loss suffered by the claimant here was 'Physical injury resulting from the boat falling on him'. But if you say *that* then it is unlikely that you will conclude that the foreseeability test was satisfied here: it was not really reasonably foreseeable that if the defendants left the rotten boat on their land that it would *fall* on someone like the claimant. The trial judge and the House of Lords adopted the first description of what kind of loss it was that the claimant suffered here and accordingly found that the foreseeability test was satisfied. In contrast, the Court of Appeal adopted the second description of what kind of loss it was that the claimant suffered here

[6] *Important note*. For example, in *Doughty* v *Turner* [1964] 1 QB 518, the claimant was very badly burned in an explosion that occurred at the defendants' factory when a cement cover was carelessly knocked into a cauldron of molten liquid. The claimant sued the defendants in negligence for compensation for his injuries but his claim was dismissed. One of the grounds for doing so was that the kind of loss suffered by the claimant here was *burns caused in an explosion* and it was not reasonably foreseeable at the time that knocking a cement cover into the molten liquid would result in the claimant suffering *that* kind of loss. (It was not known at the time that putting cement into the molten liquid in the cauldron would trigger an explosive reaction.) It would have been different had some of the molten liquid escaped from the coverless cauldron and splashed onto the claimant's skin, burning it. In that case, the kind of loss suffered by the claimant would have been *burns caused by splashing* – and the claimant would have been able to show that it was reasonably foreseeable at the time the cover was knocked into the cauldron that doing this would result in the claimant suffering *that* kind of loss.

[7] [2000] 1 WLR 1082 (noted, Nolan 2001).

and dismissed his claim on the basis that his injuries were a remote consequence of the council's negligence.[8] What accounts for the difference? It is impossible to say for certain but it is hard to resist the impression that sympathy for the claimant and the fact that the council was a 'deep pockets' defendant must have influenced the way the trial judge and the House of Lords approached the case.

So the foreseeability test is not a self-executing test. In some cases, such as the *Jolley* case, it will allow an imaginative judge room for manouevre. This, and the fact that any finding as to whether the foreseeability test is satisfied in a given case will always turn on a detailed scrutiny of the facts of that case,[9] means there is little point in our going through the decided cases where the foreseeability test has been applied to determine whether or not a loss suffered by a victim of a tort was a remote consequence of that tort or not.[10] Instead, we will note a number of exceptions that exist to the foreseeability test.

Exceptions to the foreseeability test

There seem to be five exceptions to the foreseeability test for determining whether a loss suffered by the victim of a tort was a remote consequence of that tort.

[8] [1998] 1 WLR 1546.

[9] An example of a situation where this was true is provided by the *Wagon Mound* litigation. The litigation arose out of a fire that started when the defendants negligently allowed a lot of oil to spill into Sydney Harbour. The oil spread and drifted close to the first claimants' wharf, where the first claimants were doing some welding work on a ship called the *Corrimal*, which belonged to the second claimants. A piece of molten metal from the welding work dropped into the oil and set it on fire. The wharf and the *Corrimal* suffered severe fire damage. The first claimants sued the defendants in negligence for compensation for the fire damage done to their wharf in *Overseas Tankship (UK) Ltd* v *Morts Dock & Engineering Co. Ltd, The Wagon Mound* [1961] AC 388. Their claim failed because it was held that it was not reasonably foreseeable at the time that if the defendants spilled any oil into the harbour it would ignite and set the first claimants' wharf on fire. (Why then did the defendants owe the first claimants a duty to take care that they did not spill any oil into the harbour? The reason is that it *was* reasonably foreseeable that if the defendants spilled any oil into the harbour it would spread and foul the first claimants' wharf.) When the second claimants subsequently sued the defendants for compensation for the fire damage done to the *Corrimal* (in *Overseas Tankship (UK) Ltd* v *Miller Steamship Co. Pty, The Wagon Mound (No. 2)* [1967] 1 AC 617) they introduced a lot of scientific evidence to show that it *was* reasonably foreseeable at the time the defendants negligently spilled the oil into Sydney Harbour that it could ignite and start a fire and convinced the courts that the fire damage to the *Corrimal* was a reasonably foreseeable consequence of the defendants' spilling oil into Sydney Harbour. Why didn't the first claimants press this evidence on the courts in the original *Wagon Mound* case? Two reasons can be given. First, they did not think that they had to: they assumed that if they showed that the defendants were negligent, the defendants would be held liable for *all* the losses that were a *direct* result of the defendants' negligence, however unforeseeable. This was the rule laid down by the Court of Appeal in *Re Polemis* [1921] 3 KB 560. This rule was, however, overturned in the first *Wagon Mound* case, with the Privy Council ruling that a negligent defendant could not be held liable for a loss suffered by a claimant if that loss was not a reasonably foreseeable consequence of the defendant's negligence. Secondly, it would have harmed the first claimants' claim for compensation if they had admitted that it was reasonably foreseeable that the oil that the defendants spilled into Sydney Harbour could ignite. If it *was* reasonably foreseeable, then the first claimants would have been partly to blame for the fire damage done to their wharf, having carried on doing welding work on the *Corrimal* while oil was lapping around their wharf. And if the first claimants were partly to blame for the fire damage done to their wharf, the damages payable to compensate them for that fire damage would have been reduced on the grounds of contributory negligence.

[10] See Lord Steyn's observation in *Jolley* v *Sutton London Borough Council* [2000] 1 WLR 1082, 1089: '[In] this corner of the law the results of decided cases are inevitably very fact-sensitive. Both counsel nevertheless at times invited your Lordships to compare the facts of the present case with the facts of other decided cases. That is a sterile exercise.' The leading cases applying the foreseeability test include, in addition to *Jolley* and the *Wagon Mound* cases: *Hughes* v *Lord Advocate* [1963] AC 837, *Doughty* v *Turner Manufacturing Co.* [1964] 1 QB 518 (discussed above, n. 6) and *Tremain* v *Pike* [1969] 1 WLR 1556. For a detailed account of these cases, see McBride & Bagshaw 2001, 493–4.

(1) *The eggshell skull rule.* The *eggshell skull rule* says that if A has committed a tort in relation to B and it was reasonably foreseeable that B would suffer some kind of physical injury if A committed that tort but – because B suffered from a pre-existing condition – B actually suffered a very different and much worse form of physical injury as a result of A's tort, the injury suffered by B will *not* have been a remote consequence of A's tort, however unforeseeable it might have been that someone like B would suffer that kind of injury as a result of A's tort.[11]

The eggshell skull rule will also apply in cases where A commits a tort in relation to B and B develops a psychiatric illness as a result. If it was reasonably foreseeable that B would develop some kind of psychiatric illness as a result of A's tort, but – because B suffered from some pre-existing condition – B in fact developed a very different and much more serious psychiatric illness as a result of A's tort, B's psychiatric illness will not have been a remote consequence of A's tort, however unforeseeable it might have been that B would develop that kind of mental illness in the aftermath of A's tort.[12]

(2) *Economic loss consequent on physical injury.* A rule analogous to the eggshell skull rule says that if A has committed a tort in relation to B, and B has suffered some kind of physical injury as a result, if B can recover compensation for the physical injury that she has suffered as a result of A's tort, she will be able to sue A for compensation in respect of the economic losses that she has suffered as a result of sustaining that injury without having to prove that it was reasonably foreseeable at the time A committed his tort that she would suffer those economic losses as a result. Scrutton LJ made the point graphically in *The Arpad*: 'In the cases of claims in tort, damages are constantly given for consequences of which the defendant had no notice. You negligently run down a shabby-looking man in the street, and he turns out to be a millionaire engaged in a very profitable business which the accident disables him from carrying on [. . . you will be held liable for the economic loss so caused].'[13]

The same rule will *not* apply if A commits a tort and B suffers some damage to *property* of hers which causes her to suffer various consequential economic losses. If B wants to recover compensation for those economic losses, she will have to show that it was reasonably foreseeable at the time A committed his tort that if A committed that tort she would

[11] See *Smith* v *Leech Brain* [1962] 2 QB 405, where the claimant's husband was struck on the lip by a piece of molten metal as a result of his employer's negligence. The ensuing burn caused the tissues in the husband's lip to turn cancerous and the husband eventually died from the cancer. It was, of course, *not* reasonably foreseeable that the defendants' negligence would cause the claimant's husband to develop cancer but the Court of Appeal still held that the cancer was not a remote consequence of the defendant's negligence: the eggshell skull rule applied.

[12] See *Brice* v *Brown* [1984] 1 All ER 997, where the claimant was involved in a car accident with her daughter; the accident was caused by the defendants' negligence. The claimant had suffered from a hysterical personality disorder from early childhood and developed a severe mental illness as a result of the accident, in which the claimant was slightly injured and the daughter more seriously so, though she made a swift recovery. Stuart Smith J held that the claimant's illness was not a remote consequence of the defendants' negligence even though it had not been reasonably foreseeable that the claimant would suffer a psychiatric illness as severe as the one she developed as a result of the accident in which she and her daughter were involved. It was enough that it had been reasonably foreseeable that the claimant would develop *a* psychiatric illness as a result of being involved in the car accident. (It should be noted that nowadays the claimant would not even need to show that it was reasonably foreseeable that she would suffer a psychiatric illness as a result of being involved in the accident: it would be enough for her to show that it was reasonably foreseeable that she would suffer some kind of physical injury as a result. See *Page* v *Smith* [1996] AC 155, discussed below, pp. 573–5.)

[13] [1934] P 189, 202. To the same effect, see *Smith* v *London and South Western Railway Co.* (1870) LR 6 CP 14, 22–3 (per Blackburn J).

suffer those kinds of losses as a result.[14] So, for example, suppose Fred negligently ran down and killed Rover, a dog which belonged to Nita. Suppose further that a film company was going to pay Nita £50,000 to use Rover in one of its films. Nita will not be able to sue Fred for compensation for the loss of this £50,000 unless it was reasonably foreseeable at the time Fred ran over and killed Rover that his doing so would prevent Nita making money by hiring Rover out to the film company. However, Nita *will* be entitled to sue Fred for compensation for the fact that Rover has been killed – and this compensation will equal Rover's market value at the time he was killed.[15] So if Rover was especially valuable because he was trained to perform all kinds of tricks, Fred *will* be held liable to pay more to Nita by way of compensatory damages than he would have had Rover been a normal dog.

(3) Page *v* Smith.[16] In this case, the defendant negligently ran into the claimant's car while the claimant was in it. As a result,[17] the claimant developed chronic fatigue syndrome (CFS).[18] The House of Lords held, by a bare majority, that the claimant's CFS was *not* a remote consequence of the defendant's negligence. Two of the Law Lords who made up the majority in *Page* v *Smith* held that it was reasonably foreseeable at the time the defendant negligently ran into the claimant's car that if he did so the claimant would develop a psychiatric illness as a result.[19] But they *also* expressed their agreement with the opinion of Lord Lloyd, the third member of the majority, and *he* said that the claimant would be entitled to recover for his psychiatric illness even if it was *not* reasonably foreseeable at the time the defendant crashed into the claimant's car that the claimant would suffer a psychiatric illness as a result.[20]

Lord Lloyd's view is hard to justify. He seemed to take the view that even if the claimant's psychiatric illness was not a reasonably foreseeable consequence of the defendant's negligence, the claimant's psychiatric illness would *not* count as a remote consequence of the defendant's negligence under the foreseeability test because psychiatric illness counts as a form of physical injury[21] and it *was* reasonably foreseeable that the claimant would suffer *that kind of loss* if the defendant crashed into the claimant's car.[22] However, it is hard to see why we should treat psychiatric illnesses and physical injuries as being the same kind of loss in this context when in almost every other context we recognise that there is a distinction

[14] Scrutton LJ disagreed with this in *The Arpad* [1934] P 189, at 202–3; but he was in a minority on this issue and his views have not been followed since. See, for example, *Saleslease Ltd* v *Davis* [1999] 1 WLR 1664.

[15] Cf. *Horne* v *Midland Railway* (1873) LR 8 CP 131, 140 (per Blackburn J). See below, pp. 607–8.

[16] [1996] AC 155.

[17] It was found in *Page* v *Smith (No. 2)* [1996] 1 WLR 855 that the claimant's CFS was indeed attributable to his being involved in the crash.

[18] The collision was quite trivial but the claimant – having suffered from CFS in the past – was liable to develop CFS again as a results of incidents such as these.

[19] [1996] AC 155, 170 (per Lord Ackner), 181–2 (per Lord Browne-Wilkinson).

[20] Though he too thought that at the time the defendant crashed into the claimant's car, it was reasonably foreseeable that the claimant would develop a psychiatric illness as a result: ibid., at 197. The two dissenting Law Lords in *Page* v *Smith* thought that the crash had not been serious enough as to make it reasonably foreseeable that the claimant would suffer a psychiatric illness as a result: ibid., at 169–70 (per Lord Keith of Kinkel), 180 (per Lord Jauncey of Tullichettle).

[21] Ibid., at 197: 'There is no justification for regarding physical and psychiatric injury as "different kinds of damage".'

[22] That was after all the main reason why the defendant owed the claimant a duty to take care not to run into his car in the first place.

between them.[23] Perhaps recognising this, the courts seem to be very unwilling to apply *Page* v *Smith* outside the area of traffic accidents.[24]

For example, in *Rothwell* v *Chemical & Insulating Co. Ltd*,[25] the claimants in that case were negligently exposed to asbestos fibres by their employers, the defendants. Each of the claimants developed 'pleural plaques' – areas of thickening on the walls of the lungs – as a result but as pleural plaques are completely innocuous, it was held that they did not amount to a physical injury. One of the claimants – one Mr Grieves – developed a psychiatric illness when he was told that he had been exposed to asbestos fibres because he was worried that he might eventually develop an asbestos-related disease. It was accepted that this was not a reasonably foreseeable consequence of Grieves's being exposed to asbestos fibres. However, Grieves sought to argue that because it *was* reasonably foreseeable that he would suffer a physical injury as a result of being exposed to asbestos fibres, the House of Lords' decision in *Page* v *Smith* applied in his case to say that he could still recover damages for his psychiatric illness.

The House of Lords rejected this contention and held that Grieves's psychiatric illness was too remote a consequence of his employer's negligence to be actionable. Four of the Law Lords who decided the case seemed to agree that the reason why *Page* v *Smith* did not apply in Grieves's case was that his psychiatric illness did not arise as an *immediate* result of his being exposed to asbestos fibres, but arose because he worried so much about what the consequences might be of his being exposed to those fibres.[26] Lord Hoffmann gave a different reason as to why *Page* v *Smith* did not apply in Grieves's case. He said that in *Page* v *Smith* there

[23] For example, a duty of care will normally be owed if it is reasonably foreseeable that someone else will suffer a form of physical injury as a result of your actions – but the same is not necessarily true if it reasonably foreseeable that someone else will suffer a form of psychiatric illness as a result of your actions: see above, pp. 92–3.

[24] Though see *Essa* v *Laing* [2004] ICR 746, where the defendant committed the statutory tort of racial discrimination (discussed above, pp. 493–6) in relation to the claimant and the claimant suffered a psychiatric illness as a result. Held, on the basis of *Page* v *Smith*, that the claimant could sue for damages in respect of his psychiatric illness even if it was not a foreseeable consequence of the defendant's tort: it was enough that it was reasonably foreseeable that the claimant would suffer distress as a result of the defendant's tort. Rix LJ dissented on this point. Also see *Donachie* v *Chief Constable of Greater Manchester* [2004] EWCA Civ 405, where *Page* v *Smith* was applied to allow a claimant police officer to sue for the hypertension that he had suffered as a result of being made by the defendants to make nine trips to a suspect's car to attach a tagging device to the underside of the car (the tagging device was faulty and it took nine trips to make it work). It was held that the defendants had owed the claimant a duty of care not to make him make so many trips to the car because it was reasonably foreseeable that he would suffer some kind of physical injury at the hands of the suspect if he were made to do so. It was held that the claimant could sue for the psychiatric illness that he had suffered as a result of the defendants' breach of this duty of care even though it was not foreseeable that he would suffer such an illness as a result of the defendants' breach; it was enough that it was reasonably foreseeable that the claimant would suffer some kind of physical injury as a result of the defendants' carelessness.

[25] [2007] 3 WLR 876.

[26] Ibid., at [55] (per Lord Hope), [77] (per Lord Scott), [95] (per Lord Rodger), and [104] (per Lord Mance). See also *Group B Plaintiffs* v *British Medical Council* [2000] Lloyd's Rep Med 161 (discussed, O'Sullivan 1999) where the claimants were negligently injected with human growth hormone (HGH) that might have contained a virus that could trigger Creutzfeld-Jakob Disease (CJD). Here it was reasonably foreseeable that the claimants would suffer a physical injury as a result of being given the HGH (that was why the defendants who injected the claimants owed them a duty in the first place not to give them the HGH) but the claimants developed psychiatric illnesses instead as a result of worrying about whether they would develop CJD in the future. The claimants were allowed to recover compensation for their psychiatric illnesses but Morland J held that they would *not* have been entitled to recover if their psychiatric illnesses had not been a reasonably foreseeable consequence of the defendants' negligence: in other words, he did not think *Page* v *Smith* applied in this kind of case.

> was a foreseeable event (a collision) which, viewed in prospect, was such as might cause physical injury or psychiatric injury or both. [When the event occurred] and caused psychiatric injury ... it [was] unnecessary to ask whether it was foreseeable that what *actually happened* would have that consequence ... In [Grieves's] case, the foreseeable event was that [he] would contract an asbestos-related disease [and that event] could no doubt cause psychiatric as well as physical injury. But the event has not occurred.[27]

We would submit that Lord Hoffmann's approach to the scope of *Page* v *Smith* is too clever by half. One could easily recharacterise the foreseeable event in *Rothwell*, that could have occurred as a result of the defendants' negligence and could well have caused the claimants to suffer either physical injury or psychiatric illness or both, as 'being exposed to excessive quantities of asbestos fibres'. Now, this event did actually occur in Grieves's case and did cause him to suffer a psychiatric illness. So Lord Hoffmann's interpretation of *Page* v *Smith* does not actually provide a convincing basis for explaining why *Page* v *Smith* did not apply in Grieves's case.

(4) *Intentional torts.* The foreseeability test for determining whether the loss suffered by the victim of a tort was a remote consequence of that tort does not seem to apply to cases where someone commits an *intentional tort*.

We should explain that an intentional tort is *not* a tort that is committed intentionally. An intentional tort is a tort that can *only* be committed intentionally – that is, by someone who knows what he or she is doing. So most of the torts we have studied – such as negligence, battery, false imprisonment, defamation and private nuisance – are examples of *non-intentional torts*. All these torts can be committed unintentionally or inadvertently.[28] In contrast, malicious falsehood is an example of an intentional tort: it can only be committed intentionally – by *maliciously* making a false statement about someone to a third party which results in that someone suffering loss. Other examples of intentional torts are: the intentional infliction of harm using unlawful means, conspiracy, deceit and malicious prosecution.

It seems the remoteness rule that applies to intentional torts goes as follows. If A has committed an intentional tort in relation to B and B has suffered some kind of loss as result, that loss will not have been a remote consequence of A's tort if it was a *direct*[29] consequence of A's tort.[30] So A may be held liable to compensate B for the loss she has suffered even if it was *not* reasonably foreseeable at the time A committed his tort that B would suffer that kind of loss as a result. Why is this? Why do the courts treat people who commit unintentional torts more favourably than they do people who commit intentional torts?

The reason must be that the courts recognise that people can commit non-intentional

[27] [2007] 3 WLR 876, at [32]–[33] (emphasis added).

[28] Though of course they can also be committed intentionally. See above, pp. 48–9 for a discussion of whether the tort of negligence can be committed intentionally.

[29] 'Direct' here probably means 'without the intervention of any other cause'. So the fire damage that resulted from the defendant's parking his car without authority in the claimants' car park in *Mayfair Ltd* v *Pears* [1987] 1 NZLR 459 (discussed above, p. 360 n. 6) was not a direct consequence of the defendant's intentional trespass on the claimants' land: the defendant's trespass only resulted in the claimants' car park suffering fire damage because the car caught on fire.

[30] *Doyle* v *Olby (Ironmongers) Ltd* [1969] 2 QB 158 and *Smith New Court* v *Scrimgeour Vickers (Asset Management) Ltd* [1997] AC 254 confirm that this is the position in relation to the tort of deceit. Lord Lindley confirmed that this is the position in regard to conspiracy in *Quinn* v *Leathem* : [1901] AC 495, 527.

torts quite innocently, and accordingly attempt to ensure that the liability of someone who commits a non-intentional tort does not get out of all proportion to his fault for committing that tort. They attempt to do this by holding someone who has committed a non-intentional tort liable only for the reasonably foreseeable consequences of his tort. In contrast, someone who commits an intentional tort will always be very wicked and there is no reason why we should try to put a limit on such a person's liabilities. Accordingly, someone who commits an intentional tort will be held liable for all the losses that were suffered by the victim of his tort as a direct result of that tort being committed – however unforeseeable those losses were.[31]

(5) *Statutory torts.* In *Essa* v *Laing*,[32] the Court of Appeal held that if A has committed a tort by breaching a statutory duty owed to B and B has suffered some kind of loss as a result, the foreseeability test will not necessarily apply to determine whether the loss suffered by B was a remote consequence of A's tort. To see whether the test will apply or not, one simply has to interpret the Act or Regulations that created the statutory duty breached by A.[33] In *Essa*, the defendant committed a tort under the Race Relations Act 1976 by racially abusing the claimant. The claimant developed a psychiatric illness as a result of the abuse he had suffered. Pill and Clarke LJJ held that – given the language of, and policy underlying, the 1976 Act – the foreseeability test should *not* be applied to determine whether the claimant's psychiatric illness was a remote consequence of the defendant's tort. It seems that Pill LJ might have taken a different view had the defendant's tort been committed unintentionally,[34] whereas Clarke LJ took the view that the foreseeability test should *never* apply in race discrimination cases. The third judge in the *Essa* case – Rix LJ – thought that the foreseeability test should apply in race discrimination cases: there was no reason to adopt a more relaxed remoteness rule given that a tort can be committed under the 1976 Act even if one has no intention of doing so.[35] Taken together, the judgments in the *Essa* case are deeply unsatisfactory. They have created a great deal of uncertainty over what remoteness rules will apply in respect of the various statutory torts recognised in English law – and, because each of the judges in *Essa* took a different view on the issue, they do not even have the merit

[31] *Important note.* Of course, if A has *deliberately* committed a non-intentional tort, it is hard to see why the courts should treat him any more indulgently than it does people who commit intentional torts. Given this, there is a strong case for saying that the remoteness rule which applies to people who commit intentional torts should also be applied to people who deliberately commit non-intentional torts. (To the same effect, see Gordley 1998.) Under this approach, if A has deliberately committed a non-intentional tort in relation to B and B has suffered some kind of loss as a direct result of A's committing that tort, that loss would not be a remote consequence of A's tort – even if it was not reasonably foreseeable that B would suffer that kind of loss when A committed his tort. There is some authority in favour of the view that the remoteness rule that applies to people who commit intentional torts should also be applied to people who intentionally commit non-intentional torts. Lord Nicholls indicated he thought that a defendant who intentionally converted another's goods should be held liable for all the losses suffered by that other as a direct result of the defendant's act of conversion in *Kuwait Airways Corpn* v *Iraqi Airways Co. (Nos 4 & 5)* [2002] 2 AC 883, at [103]–[104]; and the New Zealand Court of Appeal held in *Mayfair Ltd* v *Pears* [1987] 1 NZLR 459 that a defendant who intentionally trespasses on another's land should be held liable for all the losses suffered by that other as a direct result of the defendant's trespass. See also Pill LJ's judgment in *Essa* v *Laing* [2004] ICR 746, discussed below.

[32] [2004] ICR 746.

[33] Ibid., at [46], [48] (per Clarke LJ)

[34] Ibid., at [39].

[35] Ibid., at [98], [105]. Rix LJ was unenthusiastic about the idea that the foreseeability test should apply in cases of non-intentional racial discrimination but not in cases of intentional race discrimination: ibid., at [106].

of establishing once and for all what remoteness rule will apply in race discrimination cases.

WRONG KIND OF LOSS

The basic principle

Suppose A has committed a tort by breaching a duty owed to B. Suppose further that the duty breached by A was imposed on him in order to help ensure that B did not suffer a certain kind of loss. Suppose finally that one of the *primary losses* suffered by B as a result of A's tort was a different kind of loss from the loss which the duty breached by A was imposed on him in order to avoid. If this is true then it seems that that primary loss will be non-actionable on the ground that it amounts to the *wrong kind of loss*.[36]

Examples of the principle at work

A number of cases show this principle – which we can call the *wrong kind of loss principle* – in action.

(1) *Breach of a statutory duty owed to another*.[37] In *Gorris* v *Scott*,[38] the claimant's sheep were transported to a foreign port on the defendant's ship. Under the Contagious Diseases (Animals) Act 1869, the defendant had a statutory duty to ship the claimant's sheep in pens. However, he did not bother doing this. As a result, the claimant's sheep were swept out to sea when a wave crashed onto the defendant's ship; had they been placed in pens at the time, the sheep would have been perfectly safe. The claimant sued the defendant for compensation for the loss of his sheep but his claim was dismissed.

The duty breached by the defendant in this case was imposed on him *not* in order to stop the claimant's sheep from drowning but in order to help ensure that if some of the claimant's sheep contracted some kind of disease mid-voyage, the disease would not spread to the rest of the claimant's sheep; if the claimant's sheep were kept separated in pens the sheep in one pen would not be able to pass on any disease they were suffering from to the sheep in the other pens. So the primary loss suffered by the claimant in this case – the loss

[36] While academics are only now starting to take seriously the idea that a loss suffered by the victim of a tort will not be actionable if it is the wrong kind of loss (thanks mainly to Lord Hoffmann's judgment in *South Australia Asset Management Corporation* v *York Montague Ltd* [1997] AC 191) there is good reason to think that this idea underlies the existence of the foreseeability test for remoteness of damage in negligence. See, for example, Machin 1954 and Stauch 2001, both of whom advance wrong kind of loss-type arguments in favour of a foreseeability test of remoteness in negligence. (The idea being that if A owes B a duty of care because it is foreseeable that B will suffer loss X if A is careless, then if A is careless and B suffers a different and unforeseeable loss Y as a result of A's carelessness, B should not be allowed to sue for compensation for loss Y: it is the wrong kind of loss, not the kind of loss that A's duty of care was imposed on him in order to avoid.) Machin's article was truly ahead of its time, anticipating by seven years the Privy Council's decision in *The Wagon Mound* [1961] AC 388.

[37] See Stanton 2003, 303–5.

[38] (1874) LR 9 Ex 125. See also *Nicholls* v *F Austin (Leyton) Ltd* [1946] AC 493 (claimant was hit and injured by a piece of wood flying out of a piece of machinery that had been inadequately fenced, in breach of s 14(1) of the Factories Act 1937; held, the claimant could not sue her employer for damages because s 14(1) was designed to prevent the claimant coming into contact with dangerous machinery, not to prevent her being hit by something that had been ejected from a machine); and *Bretton* v *Hancock* [2006] PIQR 1 (above, p. 480 n. 2).

of his sheep through drowning – was non-actionable because it was the wrong kind of loss; not the kind of loss which the duty breached by the defendant in this case was imposed on him in order to avoid.

(2) *Dangerously defective buildings.* Suppose that Karen commissioned Tom to build a house for her. Tom built the house but he carelessly failed to ensure that the house was built on adequate foundations. However, when the house was built it seemed to be fine and Karen was very happy with it. After a few years, she sold the house to Eric, who subsequently sold the house to Wendy. A few months after Wendy moved in, the problem with the foundations became apparent and it soon became clear that the house was actually dangerous to live in. Wendy spent £10,000 on having the foundations strengthened, thereby making the house safe to live in again. Can Wendy sue Tom for compensation for the £10,000 she has spent on making the house save to live in?

Now – there is no doubt that in this situation, Tom owed Wendy a duty to take care not to build the house in such a manner that it would become physically dangerous to live in it.[39] There is no doubt either that he breached this duty and that his breach caused Wendy to lose £10,000.[40] Moreover, the economic loss suffered by Wendy was not a remote consequence of Tom's negligence – it was eminently foreseeable at the time Tom built the house that if he built the house in such a way that it would become dangerous to live in, a future occupant of the house down the line would have to spend money having the house repaired. But the decisions of the House of Lords in *D & F Estates* v *Church Commissioners*[41] and *Murphy* v *Brentwood DC*[42] make it clear that Wendy will *not* be entitled to sue Tom in negligence for compensation for the economic loss she has suffered here.[43]

One explanation why Wendy will not be entitled to sue Tom here is that she has suffered the wrong kind of loss. The duty of care that Tom breached here was imposed on him in order to help ensure that people like Wendy would not be *physically injured* as a result of

39 The existence of this duty can be justified under the physical danger principle set about above, pp. 73–4.

40 Wendy acted perfectly reasonably in spending £10,000 on having the house made safe to live in so her decision to spend that money did *not* amount to a *novus actus interveniens*, breaking the chain of causation between Tom's negligence and the economic loss suffered by Wendy.

41 [1989] AC 177.

42 [1991] 1 AC 398.

43 *Important note.* The position taken by the House of Lords is not without its critics (see, for example, Cooke 1991; Fleming 1997, 59–60) and it is clear that in other common law jurisdictions Wendy *would* be entitled to sue Tom in negligence for compensation for the economic loss she has suffered: see *Bryan* v *Moloney* (1995) 182 CLR 609 (Australia); *Winnipeg Condominium Corporation No. 36* v *Bird Construction Co. Ltd* [1995] 1 SCR 85 (Canada). It may be that the criticism of the House of Lords' stance rests on a false premise. The critics say that in the situation we are considering Wendy *ought* to be able to sue Tom for the money she has spent on making her house safe; *therefore* she ought to be able to sue Tom in *negligence*. But this assumes that the *only* cause of action available to Wendy in this situation is a claim in negligence. There is no reason to think that this is true. See Moran 1997 for an interesting argument that Wendy would be able to bring a claim in *restitution* against Tom to recover the money she has spent in making her house safe to live in; also Stevens 2007, 30–1. There are a number of American cases which support Moran's argument: see *City of New York* v *Keene Corp.*, 505 NYS 2d 782 (1986) (aff'd, 513 NYS 2d 1004 (1987)) (claimants allowed to sue defendants in restitution for cost of removing potentially toxic asbestos which defendants had installed in claimants' schools); *Adams-Araphoe School District No. 28-J* v *Celotex Corp.*, 637 F Supp 1207 (1986) (ditto); *Drayton Public School District No. 19* v *WR Grace & Co.*, 728 F Supp 1410 (1989) (ditto); *City of New York* v *Lead Industries Ass'n, Inc.*, 644 NYS 2d 919 (1996) (claimants allowed to sue manufacturers of potentially toxic paint in restitution for cost of removing paint from their city buildings).

living in the house built by Tom. But in this situation the only loss that Wendy has suffered as a result of Tom's breach was that she had to spend money on having her house repaired – a completely different kind of loss from the kind of loss which the duty breached by Tom was imposed on him in order to avoid. It would therefore have been different if – after Wendy moved in – the problem with the foundations caused part of the house to fall down and Wendy was injured as a result. In such a case, Wendy would have suffered the right kind of loss as a result of Tom's breach of the duty of care that he owed her and would therefore have no problem suing Tom for compensation for her injury.[44]

Similarly, a different result would have been reached in Tom and Wendy's case if Tom had owed Wendy a duty under s 1 of the Defective Premises Act 1972 to ensure that his work was done in a workmanlike manner and with proper materials so that the house built by him would be fit for habitation. If Tom had owed Wendy such a duty, she *would* have been able to sue him under the 1972 Act for the £10,000 she spent on repairing her house. This is because the duty imposed on those undertaking work in connection with the provision of a house is not just imposed on them in order to help ensure that future occupants of the house will not be injured; the duty is also imposed in order to help ensure that the future occupants of the house will not have to spend money making the house safe to live in. So the £10,000 spent by Wendy on making the house safe would *not* have counted as the wrong kind of loss.

(3) *Power cut*. In *Spartan Steel & Alloys Ltd* v *Martin & Co. (Contractors) Ltd*,[45] the defendants negligently damaged an electric power cable that supplied electricity to the claimants' factory, thus causing the claimants' factory to be shut down for about 14 hours. The claimants manufactured stainless steel in that factory. Among other things they would melt metal in furnaces in order to turn it into stainless steel ingots. The power cut caused the claimants to suffer two primary losses. First of all, the 'melts' that were being processed at the time of the power cut were damaged. Secondly, because the defendants could not operate their factory, they suffered an economic loss of £1,767: this was the profit they would have made if they had been allowed to work for the 14 hours the factory was out of action. The claimants were allowed to sue the defendants in negligence for compensation in respect of the first loss, but not the second. The wrong kind of loss principle explains why.

The defendants had owed the claimants a duty to take care not to cut the power off to their factory because it was reasonably foreseeable that if they did so the claimants' property would be damaged.[46] So the duty of care that the defendants breached in this case was imposed on them in order to help ensure that the claimants did not suffer any harm to their property. As a result, the damage to the 'melts' that the claimants suffered as a result of the defendants' negligence in *Spartan Steel* counted as the right kind of loss and was therefore actionable: it was the kind of loss which the duty breached by the defendants had been imposed on them in order to avoid. By contrast, the loss of profits suffered by the claimants in *Spartan Steel* as a result of their factory being shut down counted as the wrong kind of loss and was therefore non-actionable: the duty breached by the defendants was not

[44] See *Rimmer* v *Liverpool City Council* [1985] QB 1; *Targett* v *Torfaen Borough Council* [1992] 3 All ER 27.
[45] [1973] QB 27.
[46] See above, pp. 116–17.

imposed on them in order to help ensure that the claimants did not experience any interruption in the running of their business.

(4) *Negligently inflicted pure distress.* The wrong kind of loss principle helps explain when negligently inflicted pure distress (that is, distress not occasioned by physical injury or property damage) will and will not be actionable.

So – pure distress caused by the breach of a duty of care arising under the physical danger principle[47] will not be actionable, as the duty of care in question was imposed to prevent physical injury, rather than pure distress. For example, in *Hicks* v *Chief Constable of South Yorkshire Police*,[48] the estates of Sarah and Victoria Hicks were not allowed to sue in negligence for compensation for the anxiety and then pain and suffering they went through before they were crushed to death in the Hillsborough tragedy. While the police in that case had owed Sarah and Victoria a duty to take care not to cause the spectator pens where they were standing to become overcrowded, that duty was imposed on the police to safeguard spectators like Sarah and Victoria from suffering physical injury, not pure distress.[49]

Similarly, the claimants in *Rothwell* v *Chemical & Insulating Co. Ltd*[50] were negligently exposed to asbestos fibres by their employers. As a result, the claimants started worrying that they might develop an asbestos-related disease in the future. When the case was heard by the Court of Appeal, the court held that the claimants were not allowed to recover for this anxiety – which counted as a form of pure distress as it was not consequent on the claimants actually having suffered any kind of physical injury as a result of their exposure to asbestos. The duties of care that the employers had breached in the *Rothwell* case were imposed to help ensure that the claimants did not suffer physical injury, not pure distress.[51]

In contrast, pure distress that has been caused by the breach of a duty of care arising under the extended principle in *Hedley Byrne*[52] *will* be actionable so long as one of the reasons why that duty was imposed – or rather, in this context, one of the reasons why that duty was *assumed* – was to save the claimant from suffering that kind of pure distress.[53] So, for example, in *Gregg* v *Scott*[54] the claimant's doctor breached the duty he owed him to treat

[47] See above, pp. 73–4.

[48] [1992] 2 All ER 65.

[49] The anxiety and other suffering that Victoria and Sarah went through before they died counted as pure distress because – the House of Lords found – Victoria and Sarah did not actually suffer any physical injury before the moment they died (ibid., 68–9).

[50] [2006] 1 ICR 1458.

[51] Both the Court of Appeal and, subsequently, the House of Lords ([2007] 3 WLR 876) found that the claimants had not suffered any kind of physical injury as a result of being exposed to the asbestos fibres.

[52] See above, pp. 132–9.

[53] See, in addition to the case cited in the main text, *Farley* v *Skinner* [2002] 2 AC 732 (*not* a tort case). In that case, the claimant was thinking of buying a house in Sussex which was 15 miles away from Gatwick Airport. He paid the defendant surveyor to tell him whether the house would be unduly affected by the noise of aircraft taking off and landing. The surveyor reported back that, essentially, the claimant had nothing to worry about and the claimant subsequently bought the house. He then discovered that the house was substantially affected by aircraft noise because it was located near a beacon that planes would circle while they were waiting to land. The claimant brought an action for breach of contract against the defendant surveyor, claiming damages designed to compensate him for the fact that the time he spent in the house was made miserable through the amount of aircraft noise he had to endure. The claim was allowed. It is hard to imagine that the result would have been any different had the claimant sued the defendant in *negligence*, claiming that his distress was a result of the defendant's breach of a duty of care that the defendant owed the claimant under the extended principle in *Hedley Byrne*.

[54] [2005] 2 AC 176.

him with reasonable skill and care by failing to diagnose that a lump under his left arm was cancerous. As a result, the cancer went untreated for ten months. While it could not be shown – on the balance of probabilities – that the claimant's physical condition would have been any better had his cancer been treated properly,[55] Baroness Hale made it clear that if the delay in treating the claimant meant that he underwent any *extra* pain and suffering that he would not have endured had his cancer been treated properly – because, for example, the delay in treating the cancer meant that it had to be treated with more aggressive chemotherapy to eliminate it – then the claimant should be entitled to recover damages for this pure distress.[56] This is compatible with the wrong kind of loss principle. Part of the reason why a doctor agrees to treat a patient is to stop the patient undergoing pain and suffering – so part of the reason why a doctor owes his patient a duty to treat him with reasonable skill and care is to stop that patient suffering pure distress.

(5) SAAMCO *principle*. The *SAAMCO* principle[57] says that a loss arising out of the breach of a duty of care arising under the basic or extended principle in *Hedley Byrne* will be non-actionable unless part of the reason why that duty was assumed was to save the victim of the breach of that duty from suffering that loss. It very much looks like the *SAAMCO* principle is a subset of the wrong kind of loss principle. Given this, where a loss has been suffered as a result of the breach of a duty of care arising under *Hedley Byrne*, we would be doing the same thing twice if we asked first whether the loss is actionable under the *SAAMCO* principle, and then proceeded to ask whether the law is actionable under the wrong kind of loss principle. It should be sufficient simply to ask whether the loss is actionable under the *SAAMCO* principle.

(6) *Private nuisance*. Adapting the facts of *Malone* v *Laskey*[58] somewhat, suppose that Dawn and Gary are neighbours. Suppose further that Gary committed a tort of private nuisance in relation to Dawn by running an engine on his land to produce electricity which was so noisy and produced such large vibrations that Dawn's use and enjoyment of her land was seriously interfered with. Suppose finally that one day while Gary's engine was running, the walls of Dawn's house began to shake with the result that a shelf fell off one of the walls of Dawn's house and hit her on the head.

Now in this case, Dawn has suffered two primary losses as a result of Gary's committing the tort of private nuisance – and let us suppose that both of them were equally foreseeable consequences of Gary's tort. First of all, she suffers a form of economic loss: Gary's running of his engine on his land diminishes the value of her land. Secondly, Dawn suffered a physical injury: the injury to her head. Now Dawn will be entitled to sue Gary in private nuisance for damages in respect of the interference with the value of her land that she has suffered as a result of his tort. But what about the physical injury she has sustained? In *Hunter* v *Canary Wharf Ltd*, Lords Hoffmann and Lloyd made it clear that they thought that Dawn would *not* be entitled to sue Gary in private nuisance for compensation in respect of the injury to her head.[59]

[55] See above, pp. 559–60.
[56] [2005] 2 AC 176, at [206].
[57] Discussed above, pp. 139–42 and p. 537, n. 22.
[58] [1907] 2 KB 141.
[59] [1997] AC 655, 696D (per Lord Lloyd), 707H (per Lord Hoffmann).

The wrong kind of loss principle explains why this is. The duty breached by Gary in committing the tort of private nuisance here was imposed on him in order to help ensure that the use value of Dawn's land was not unreasonably interfered with – so the diminution in the value of Dawn's land that has resulted from Gary's running his engine counts as the right kind of loss, the kind of loss that the duty breached by Gary here was imposed on him in order to avoid. That loss is therefore actionable in private nuisance. In contrast, the physical injury suffered by Dawn here counts as the wrong kind of loss: the duty breached by Gary in committing the tort of private nuisance was *not* imposed on him in order to help ensure that Dawn would not be physically injured. So that loss is not actionable in private nuisance.

Of course it is probable that Gary, in running his engine, also committed the tort of negligence. If it was reasonably foreseeable that Dawn would be injured as a result of Gary's running his engine, then Gary would almost certainly have owed Dawn a duty not to run that engine.[60] If he did then then Dawn *would* be entitled to sue Gary in *negligence* for compensation for the head injury she suffered as a result of his running his engine. That injury would count as a foreseeable consequence of Gary's negligence and, moreover, no wrong kind of loss objection could be made to Dawn's suing Gary in negligence for compensation in respect of her head injury because the duty of care that Gary breached in this case *was* imposed on him in order to help ensure that Dawn would not be physically injured.

Two important points

Two important points remain to be made about the wrong kind of loss principle.

(1) *Secondary losses*. It is important to remember that the wrong kind of loss principle only applies to determine whether a *primary* loss suffered by the victim of a tort is actionable. It does not apply to *secondary* losses.[61]

So, for example, in *Attia* v *British Gas*,[62] the defendants negligently burned down the claimant's house when they did work on her house. The claimant came home to see her house burning down and suffered a psychiatric illness as a result. In this case, the claimant suffered a primary loss (damage to her house) and a secondary loss (psychiatric illness) that flowed from this primary loss. The primary loss was actionable under the wrong kind of loss principle: the duty of care breached by the defendants in this case had been imposed on them in order to help ensure that the claimant's house was not damaged or destroyed. The fact that the duty of care breached by the defendants was not imposed on them in order to save the claimant from suffering a psychiatric illness did not stand in the way of the claimant's suing for that psychiatric illness: because the psychiatric illness was a secondary loss, flowing from the damage to her house, the wrong kind of loss principle did not apply to her claim for compensation for that illness. So the claimant's psychiatric illness counted as actionable loss – provided, of course, that it was a non-remote consequence of the defendants' negligence.[63]

[60] This is under the physical danger principle discussed above, at pp. 73–4.

[61] Though any secondary losses suffered by a claimant because she suffered a primary loss which is non-actionable under the wrong kind of loss principle will themselves be non-actionable: see below, pp. 596–7.

[62] [1988] QB 304.

[63] The other two tests for determining whether a loss is actionable did not apply here: it would not have been contrary to public policy to allow the claimant to recover for her psychiatric illness and there was no reason why the claimant's psychiatric illness was automatically non-actionable.

(2) *A rogue case.* We should note one case in which a claimant was allowed to recover compensation in respect of a primary loss suffered by him as a result of the defendant's tort even though that loss was non-actionable under the wrong kind of loss principle.[64]

In *Morrison Steamship Co. Ltd* v *Greystoke Castle (Cargo Owners)*,[65] two ships – the *Greystoke Castle* and the *Cheldale* – collided. The collision was due in part to the negligence of the defendants who were in charge of the *Cheldale*. As a result of the collision the *Greystoke Castle* had to put into port to be repaired. Before the *Greystoke Castle* could be repaired, its cargo had to be unloaded. After the *Greystoke Castle* was repaired, its cargo was reloaded onto the ship. The claimants were owners of cargo on board the *Greystoke Castle* and the owners of the *Greystoke Castle* charged the claimants – as they were entitled to do under the terms of the contract of carriage between them and the claimants – for some of the expense they had incurred (called a 'general average expenditure') in unloading and reloading the claimant's goods. The claimants successfully sued the defendants in negligence so as to be compensated for the pure economic loss that this charge caused them to suffer.

No complaints can be made about the court's finding that the defendants had owed the claimants a duty to take care not to collide with the *Greystoke Castle*; or that the defendants breached that duty; or that the defendants' negligence caused the claimants to incur the economic loss for which they were suing; or that that economic loss was a non-remote consequence of the defendants' negligence. However, the economic loss suffered by the claimants was non-actionable under the wrong kind of loss principle. The duty of care breached by the defendants in this case was imposed on them in order to help ensure that the claimants' property was not damaged: a completely different kind of loss from the loss that the claimants suffered here. It is therefore a bit of a puzzle why the claimants were allowed to sue the defendants in this case. However, it should be noted that only a bare majority (3:2) of the Law Lords who decided the *Greystoke Castle* case were in favour of holding the defendants liable to compensate the claimants and subsequent judicial reaction to the *Greystoke Castle* case has been tepid to say the least.[66]

PUBLIC POLICY

Suppose that A has committed a tort in relation to B and B suffered some kind of loss as a result. Obviously, the courts will hold that that loss is not actionable if it would be contrary to public policy to allow B to sue A for compensation in respect of that loss.

[64] *Important note.* There are also a couple of rogue *dicta* which indicate that if A carelessly creates a danger to other people's health and B is compelled by law to spend money eliminating that danger, then B will be entitled to sue A in negligence for compensation for the fact that she has had to spend that money: see *Murphy* v *Brentwood DC* [1991] 1 AC 398, 495 (per Lord Bridge); *The Orjula* [1995] 2 Lloyd's Rep 395, 403 (per Mance J). These *dicta* are inconsistent with the wrong kind of loss principle: even if A breached a duty of care owed to B in creating the danger in question, that duty was imposed on A to save B from being physically harmed, not in order to save her from having to incur the expense of cleaning up the danger created by A. It may be that the judges in these cases got their causes of action mixed up and instead of saying that B could sue A in *negligence* for the cost of eliminating the danger created by A, they should have said that B could sue A in *restitution*: see above, n. 43.

[65] [1947] AC 265.

[66] See *Murphy* v *Brentwood DC* [1991] 1 AC 398, 468 (per Lord Keith of Kinkel): '[The *Greystoke Castle*] case, which was decided by a narrow majority, may . . . be regarded as turning on specialities of maritime law concerned in the relationship of joint adventurers at sea.'

In *Pritchard* v *J H Cobden Ltd*,[67] the claimant was severely injured in a road traffic accident caused by the defendant's negligence. He suffered brain damage which meant he experienced a complete change in personality. As a result, his marriage broke down and his wife divorced him. The claimant sued the defendant, seeking to be compensated for the economic loss that he had suffered when his assets were divided up between him and his wife in the divorce. The Court of Appeal held that the economic loss suffered by the claimant in *Pritchard* was not actionable. The reason was that it would be contrary to public policy to allow the claimant to sue the defendant so as to be compensated for this loss of wealth.

There were a number of reasons why this was so. First, allowing this sort of claim could lead to abuse. Suppose Vijay and Sarah were a married couple who were going to divorce when Vijay was involved in an accident negligently caused by Ian. If the sort of claim made by the claimant in *Pritchard* were allowed, Vijay and Sarah could easily collude with each other and claim that, when they divorced each other, they did so because of the effects of the accident. Vijay would then be allowed to recover from Ian, and split with Sarah, the value of the assets that he lost in the divorce.

Secondly, allowing this sort of claim could undermine marriages. Suppose that Fred was happily married to Beth when he was involved in an accident that was negligently caused by Paul, and that the injuries sustained by Fred in the accident had a damaging effect on his personality. If the sort of claim made by the claimant in *Pritchard* were allowed then Fred would know that if Beth divorced him because of his change in personality he would suffer no financial prejudice whatsoever: he would be able to claim the value of any assets he lost in the divorce. He would then have less incentive to try and moderate the effect of the accident on his personality for the sake of preserving his marriage.

Thirdly, if this sort of claim were allowed, then in the case we have just been considering – where Fred was happily married to Beth when he was negligently injured by Paul – if Beth wanted to divorce Fred because of the effect that his injuries have had on his personality, *Paul* would be entitled to be represented in any proceedings dealing with how Fred and Beth's assets should be divided. This is because such proceedings would have an effect on his legal liabilities. So the divorce court dealing with Fred and Beth's divorce would have to have regard not only to their interests, but also to Paul's interests, in deciding how Fred and Beth's assets should be divided between them.

Another case where public policy was invoked as a reason for finding that a loss suffered by the victim of a tort was non-actionable was *Meah* v *McCreamer (No. 2)*.[68] We have already come across the first *Meah* v *McCreamer* case.[69] In *that* case, it will be recalled, the defendant negligently crashed a car that he was driving. The claimant was a passenger in the car and suffered severe head injuries as a result. The claimant's injuries caused his personality to change for the worse. Before the accident, he had been involved in various scrapes with the law but did not have a history of being violent. After the accident, he developed a tendency to attack women. As a result, he sexually assaulted two women and was sent to prison.

[67] [1988] Fam 22.
[68] [1986] 1 All ER 943.
[69] [1985] 1 All ER 367. See above, p. 520 n. 71; 532.

In the first *Meah* v *McCreamer* case, the claimant sued the defendant for compensation for the fact that he had been sent to prison and Woolf J allowed his claim, awarding the claimant £45,500 in damages. This decision caused something of a public outcry, which had the useful side effect of letting the two women who had been attacked by the claimant know that the claimant now had some money and was worth suing. Accordingly, they sued the claimant in tort for compensation in respect of the harm they had suffered when he attacked them and between them they obtained £17,000 in damages.[70] The claimant then sued the defendant again in *Meah* v *McCreamer (No. 2)*, arguing that the defendant was liable to compensate him for the damages he had had to pay out to the women he had attacked.

This time round, Woolf J – perhaps wary of the outcry that had attended his first decision[71] – dismissed the claimant's claim. He held that it would be contrary to public policy to allow the claimant to sue the defendant for the £17,000 he had had to pay in damages to the victims of his sexual assaults.[72] Why would it have been contrary to public policy to allow the claimant to sue the defendant here? Woolf J did not say much in support of his finding on this issue, remarking only that it would be 'distasteful' to allow the claimant to sue.[73] However, it can be inferred from other parts of his judgment that he was concerned that if the claimant's claim was allowed here, then the defendant's liability to the claimant might become unlimited in nature – with the defendant being held liable for any harm caused by the claimant's personality disorder.

A third case in which public policy was invoked to explain why a loss suffered by the victim of a tort was non-actionable was *Spartan Steel & Alloys Ltd* v *Martin & Co. (Contractors) Ltd*.[74] In that case, it will be recalled, the claimants were not allowed to sue for compensation in respect of the loss of profits they experienced when the power to their factory was negligently cut off by the defendants. The finding that the claimants' loss of profits was non-actionable can be justified by reference to the wrong kind of loss principle, but Lord Denning MR also thought it would be contrary to public policy to allow the claimants to recover for their loss of profits.[75]

He had three reasons for thinking that it would be contrary to public policy to allow this element of the claimants' claim. First, allowing claims such as the claimants' to succeed could lead to abuse. Someone whose business was disrupted by a negligently caused power cut would be tempted to exaggerate the profits he could have made had his business not

[70] *W* v *Meah, D* v *Meah* [1986] 1 All ER 935.

[71] In *Meah* v *McCreamer (No. 2)* [1986] 1 All ER 943, Woolf J – somewhat defensively – attempted to justify his decision in the first *Meah* v *McCreamer* case on the ground that the claimant had a wife and child who had suffered a loss of support as a result of the claimant's being locked up. So allowing the claimant to recover compensation for his being imprisoned would help him support his wife and child while he was in prison: ibid., 951f–h. (Dependants of the victim of a tort who have suffered a loss of support as a result of that tort are entitled to sue the tortfeasor for compensation in respect of the loss of support that they have experienced, but only if the tort caused the victim of the tort to die: see below, pp. 631–7.)

[72] He also found that the payout to the victims of the claimants' sexual assaults was a remote consequence of the defendant's negligence ([1986] 1 All ER 943, 950d) but that finding is impossible to reconcile with his decision in *Meah* v *McCreamer* [1985] 1 All ER 367: if the claimant's imprisonment was *not* a remote consequence of the defendant's negligence in that case then the claimant's being sued for damages for the things he did which got him imprisoned could not have been a remote consequence of the defendant's negligence either.

[73] [1986] 1 All ER 943, 950h–j.

[74] [1973] QB 27, discussed above, pp. 116–17, 579–80.

[75] Ibid., 38E–39A.

had its power cut off if he knew that he could claim compensation for the profits he would have made if his business had not been disrupted. Secondly, allowing claims such as the claimants' to succeed could sap people's capacity for self-reliance. Someone whose business was disrupted by a negligently caused power cut would have less incentive to make up the profits he could have made had the power cut not occurred if he knew that he could claim compensation for the loss of those profits from whoever was responsible for the occurrence of the power cut. Moreover, someone running a business would have less incentive to take steps to guard against having his business disrupted by a negligently caused power cut (by, for example, installing a back-up power system) if he knew that should his business be disrupted by a negligently caused power cut he could recover compensation for the profits he would have made had his business not been disrupted. Thirdly, allowing claims such as the claimants' to succeed would result in the courts being clogged with claims for compensation for losses suffered as a result of power cuts, thus making it harder for more important and more deserving cases to be dealt with speedily.

LOSSES THAT ARE AUTOMATICALLY NON-ACTIONABLE

Some kinds of losses that might be suffered by the victim of a tort are automatically regarded as being non-actionable. They are as follows.

The cost of bringing up a child

Suppose A committed a tort in relation to B and B ended up giving birth to a child that she would not otherwise have had.[76] It is well established that in this situation B will be entitled to sue A for compensation in respect of the inconvenience that she suffered in the run-up to giving birth, the pain and suffering that she went through in labour, any economic losses that she suffered before giving birth as a result of taking time off work, having to spend money on new clothes to fit her as she grew larger, and so on.[77] But if B attempts to sue A for compensation in respect of the money she is going to have to spend on bringing up the child, she will usually find that that loss is regarded as being automatically non-actionable by the courts.[78] In order to understand *when* this loss will be held to be non-actionable, we have to distinguish between the case where B's child is healthy and the case where B's child is born disabled.

[76] The two most common situations where this will happen are as follows. (1) B's partner, C, asks A to perform a vasectomy on him; A fails to carry out the vasectomy properly; B and C, not knowing this, have unprotected sex; B becomes pregnant as a result and chooses to carry the baby to term (in this situation, A will have owed *B* a duty to perform the vasectomy with a reasonable degree of care and skill under the principle in *White* v *Jones* [1995] 2 AC 207: see above, pp. 153–4). (2) B becomes pregnant and A, B's doctor, negligently fails to tell B that B's baby will be seriously disabled when it is born when had B known this she would have chosen to have an abortion (s 1(1)(d) of the Abortion Act 1967 allows an abortion to be performed 'if there is a serious risk that if the child were born it would suffer from such physical or mental abnormalities as to be seriously handicapped'); as a result B gives birth to a baby that she would not have had but for A's negligence.

[77] *McFarlane* v *Tayside Health Board* [2000] 2 AC 59, 74A–E (per Lord Slynn), 81F–G (per Lord Steyn), 87B–E (per Lord Hope), 102F–H (per Lord Clyde). It is unclear why, in a type (2) (see n. 76, above) situation, B will be entitled to sue A for compensation in respect of these losses – it could be argued that she willingly took the risk that she would suffer these losses when she became pregnant. See, on this, Mason 2002, 50.

[78] The cost of bringing up B's child will be regarded as actionable in Australia: *Cattanach* v *Melchior* (2003) 215 CLR 1 (noted, Cane 2004).

(1) *Healthy child.* The House of Lords ruled in *McFarlane* v *Tayside Health Board*[79] that if B and her child are both healthy then the cost of bringing up the child will be automatically non-actionable.[80] In a subsequent case – *Rees* v *Darlington Memorial Hospital NHS Trust*[81] – the House of Lords placed a 'gloss' on the ruling in *McFarlane*, holding that while B would not be entitled to sue A for damages representing the cost of bringing up her child, B *would* be entitled to sue A for a fixed sum of £15,000 to compensate her for the disruption to her life that bringing up her child will involve. Two issues arise out of this: (1) Why is B *not* allowed to sue A for the cost of bringing up her child? (2) Why *is* B allowed to sue A for a fixed sum of £15,000 to compensate her for the disruption to her life that bringing up her child will involve?

On the first issue, a number of reasons were advanced by the Law Lords in both *McFarlane* and *Rees* as to why the cost of bringing up B's child should be held to be non-actionable. First, it would be wrong, in assessing the damages payable to B for the fact that she had given birth to an unwanted child, to disregard the benefits B would reap from bringing that child up. It would be morally offensive to think that those benefits are worth less than the cost of bringing B's child – to think that would be to think that bringing up B's child up is more trouble than it is worth. Given this, it must be taken that the benefits of bringing B's child up outweigh the costs and therefore no claim can be made for the cost of bringing up that child.[82] Secondly, the benefits B will reap from bringing her child up are incalculable, but they must be taken into account in judging how much B should be paid by way of damages. The only fair way of taking these benefits into account is to assume that they at least equal the cost of bringing up B's child and therefore no claim can be brought for damages in respect of the cost of bringing up B's child.[83] Thirdly, to make A liable for the cost of bringing up B's child would impose on A a liability far out of proportion to his fault in causing B to conceive in the first place.[84] Fourthly, if A were required to compensate B for the cost of bringing up her child, the funds would in all probability come out of the hard-pressed coffers of the National Health Service; and the general public would think it wrong for that money to be used to subsidise the upbringing of B's child as opposed to

[79] [2000] 2 AC 59 (henceforth, '*McFarlane*').

[80] For criticisms of this ruling, see Hoyano 2002. An attempt to get round this ruling was made in *Greenfield* v *Irwin* [2001] 1 WLR 113, where the claimant – who had given birth to a baby that she would not have had but for the defendants' negligence – did not sue the defendants for the cost of bringing up the baby, but rather sued to be compensated for the loss of income she had experienced as a result of giving up work to look after the baby full time. The claim was dismissed on the ground that if it were allowed, a coach and horses would be driven through the House of Lords' ruling in *McFarlane*. Another attempt to get round *McFarlane* was made in *Rees* v *Darlington Memorial Hospital NHS Trust* [2004] 1 AC 309, where a woman who was near-blind decided that she would be incapable of bringing up a baby properly and as a result had the defendants perform a sterilisation operation on her. The defendants performed the operation incompetently and the claimant subsequently conceived, and gave birth, to a healthy baby boy. It was argued that while the claimant's boy was perfectly healthy, the fact that the *claimant* was disabled meant that *McFarlane* did not apply, and that the claimant should at the very least be allowed to recover the *extra* cost of bringing up the boy that was attributable to the fact that *she* was disabled. The House of Lords rejected this claim by 4:3, holding that *McFarlane* applies across the board to *all* cases where someone gives birth to a healthy child as a result of another's negligence.

[81] [2004] 1 AC 309 (henceforth, '*Rees*').

[82] *McFarlane*, at 82 (per Lord Steyn), 111 (per Lord Millett); *Rees*, at [28] (per Lord Steyn), [112] (per Lord Millett).

[83] *McFarlane*, at 97 (per Lord Hope); *Rees*, at [51] (per Lord Hope), [138] (per Lord Steyn).

[84] *McFarlane*, at 91 (per Lord Hope); *Rees*, at [16] (per Lord Nicholls).

using it to treat patients.[85] Fifthly, were B to be compensated for the cost of bringing up her child, then the amount payable to B would depend on how rich she is – the richer she is, the more she could be expected to spend on bringing her child up and therefore the greater the damages that would be payable to B. It would be 'unseemly' for the law to allow B's award to depend on how rich or poor she is.[86]

Moving on to the second issue, why will B be allowed to sue A for a fixed sum of £15,000 in the situation we are considering? The House of Lords divided 4:2 in *Rees* over the issue of whether B should be allowed to make such a claim against A.[87] The majority thought that it would be wrong if the law did nothing to compensate B for the 'loss of autonomy' that she had suffered as a result of giving birth to a child.[88] They thought that awarding B £15,000 would afford her some compensation for this 'loss of autonomy'.[89] Lords Steyn and Hope criticised the majority ruling on this issue. Lord Steyn took the view that the courts simply did not have the power to make awards designed to compensate individuals for intangible fancies such as 'loss of autonomy' – let alone to rule that such awards would be fixed across the board at £15,000, whatever the circumstances of a claimant who gave birth to an unwanted healthy baby as a result of someone else's negligence.[90] Lord Hope criticised the majority ruling on this issue on the basis that he could not understand why the majority was proposing to compensate for the 'loss of autonomy' suffered by a claimant who gave birth to an unwanted healthy baby as a result of someone's negligence through the award of a *fixed* sum of £15,000. If such an award is meant to be compensatory, then why should such a claimant not be entitled to say, 'The value of *my* loss of autonomy comes to much more than £15,000, and so I should be awarded much more than the fixed sum the majority in *Rees* said I should be given.'[91]

(2) *Disabled child.* Let's now consider what the position is if, in the situation we are considering, the child that B has given birth to is *disabled.* The House of Lords' decision in *McFarlane* did not deal with that issue at all – it was purely concerned with what the position would be if a claimant such as B gave birth to a healthy child. After *McFarlane* was decided, the Court of Appeal ruled in *Parkinson* v *St James and Seacroft University Hospital NHS Trust* that if, in the situation we are considering, B gave birth to a disabled baby, B would be entitled to sue A for the *extra cost of raising the child that is attributable to the fact he was born disabled.*[92] So, on this view, the normal costs of raising B's child, that B would have incurred whether or not the child was disabled, would still be non-actionable. But any extra expenses that B would have to incur in raising her child because he is disabled would be actionable.

In *Rees*, the House of Lords found themselves split on the issue of what the position should be in the case where B gives birth to a disabled child. Lords Steyn, Hope and Hutton

[85] *Rees*, at [6] (per Lord Bingham).
[86] *McFarlane*, at 82 (per Lord Steyn).
[87] Lord Hutton, sitting in *Rees*, did not express an opinion on the issue.
[88] *Rees*, at [8] (per Lord Bingham), [17] (per Lord Nicholls), [123] (per Lord Millett); [148] (per Lord Scott).
[89] Though confusingly Lord Bingham took the view that the award of £15,000 is not designed to *compensate* B for any loss that she has suffered: ibid., at [8]. But, as Lord Hope pointed out in dissent at [74], if the award is not compensatory in nature, what is it?
[90] Ibid., at [45].
[91] Ibid., at [71]–[73].
[92] [2002] QB 266 (henceforth, '*Parkinson*').

took the view that *Parkinson* was correctly decided.[93] Lords Bingham and Nicholls took the view that *Parkinson* was wrongly decided and that in the situation we are considering, A's liability to B should not depend on whether B's child was born healthy or disabled. In *both* cases, B should not be allowed to claim *anything* for the cost of bringing up the child: instead, all she will be entitled to sue A for (in addition to damages for the pain of pregnancy and so on) is a fixed sum of £15,000 to compensate her for her 'loss of autonomy'.[94] Lord Scott took the view that we may have to distinguish between: (1) the case where A was employed to stop B becoming pregnant because she was fearful that any baby she had would be disabled; and (2) the case where A was employed to stop B becoming pregnant because she did not want to have another baby. He thought that the Court of Appeal's ruling in *Parkinson* should only be allowed to apply in case (1). So he thought that if (2) were true, B should not be allowed to sue for *anything* in respect of the cost of bringing up her child.[95] As the issue of whether *Parkinson* was rightly decided did not arise for decision in *Rees*, Lord Millett preferred to leave the question 'open'.[96] He went on to observe that while in 'strict logic', a claimant who gave birth to a disabled child should not be allowed to claim anything for the cost of bringing up the child,[97] he himself did not think that the Court of Appeal's ruling in *Parkinson* was 'morally offensive'. At the same time, he expressed himself fearful that allowing B to sue for the extra cost of bringing up her child that was attributable to the fact that her child was born disabled might 'prove difficult to achieve without introducing nice distinctions and unacceptable refinements of a kind which tend to bring the law into disrepute'.[98]

What a mess! However, as *Parkinson* was not overruled in *Rees*,[99] *Parkinson* will remain binding on all courts up to and including the Court of Appeal until the House of Lords readdresses the issue of whether *Parkinson* was correctly decided. As this is not likely to happen any time soon, we can safely assume that for the foreseeable future, the Court of Appeal's decision in *Parkinson* will determine how much a claimant is entitled to sue a defendant for in a disabled child case. So if B gives birth to a child as a result of A's negligence, and that child proves to be disabled, B will be entitled to sue A for compensation in respect of any extra expenses that she will have to incur in raising the child because he is disabled.[100] This ruling gives rise to a couple of complications that need to be addressed.

First of all, what is the difference between a disabled child and a healthy child? Suppose, for example, that due to Carl's negligence Ruth gives birth to a baby boy, Alan. As Alan grows up, it becomes clear that he is short-sighted and will need to wear glasses. Will Ruth be able to sue Carl for the cost of providing those glasses? It depends on whether Alan

93 *Rees*, at [35] (per Lord Steyn), [57] (per Lord Hope), [91] (per Lord Hutton).

94 Ibid., at [9] (per Lord Bingham), [18] (per Lord Nicholls).

95 Ibid., at [145].

96 Ibid., at [112].

97 Because – following the logic underlying Lord Millett's judgments in *McFarlane* and *Rees* on the issue of whether a claim for the cost of bringing up a healthy child should be allowed – if one did allow such a claim to be made in the case where a claimant gave birth to a disabled child, one *would* be saying that bringing up a disabled child *is* more trouble than it is worth; which can hardly be right.

98 *Rees*, at [112].

99 Nor could it have been as the correctness of the Court of Appeal's ruling in *Parkinson* was not at issue in *Rees*.

100 Though this point was not addressed by any of the Law Lords in *Rees*, it is presumably the case that B would *also* be entitled to sue A for a fixed sum of £15,000 to compensate her for the 'loss of autonomy' suffered by her as a result of A's negligence.

counts as being 'disabled' or not: if he is a 'healthy' child, then Ruth will not be able to recover *any* of the costs of raising him, including the cost of providing him with spectacles. In the *Parkinson* case, Hale LJ suggested that a child will be held to be disabled if 'he is blind, deaf or dumb or suffers from mental disorder of any kind or is substantially and permanently handicapped by illness, injury or congenital deformity . . .'.[101] On this definition, Alan would probably not count as being disabled and so Ruth would not be able to sue Carl for the cost of providing him with glasses.

Secondly, what is the position in the following case? Dawn negligently performs a vasectomy on Lara's husband, Tom. Thinking (incorrectly) that the operation has been a success, Lara and Tom have unprotected sex. As a result Lara becomes pregnant. She decides to carry the child to term but six months into her pregnancy, she is involved in a car accident due to the negligence of the driver of another car, Eric. Lara survives the car accident but her doctors tell her that, as a result of the accident, her baby is liable to be severely brain-damaged when he is born. Nevertheless Lara decides to carry on with the pregnancy and three months later she gives birth to a baby boy, John, who suffers from severe brain damage.[102] Will Dawn be liable for the extra cost that Lara will have to incur in raising John that is attributable to the fact that he has been born brain-damaged? One would have thought not, but in *Parkinson* the Court of Appeal held that Dawn *would* be liable so long as Eric's negligence did not break the chain of causation between Dawn's negligence and Lara's giving birth to John.[103] As Eric's negligence did not have that effect, Dawn will be liable.[104]

Avoidable losses

The duty to mitigate

Suppose that A has committed a tort in relation to B and B has suffered some kind of loss as a result. That loss will be non-actionable if B could have done something after A committed his tort to avoid suffering that loss but she unreasonably failed to do so. B has a 'duty to mitigate'[105] the losses suffered by her as a result of A's tort and will be barred from suing

[101] *Parkinson*, at [91] (quoting s 17(11) of the Children Act 1989).

[102] In this situation, Eric will be liable to compensate John for the fact that he was born disabled under the Congenital Disabilities (Civil Liability) Act 1976: see below, pp. 641–2.

[103] *Parkinson*, at [53] (per Brooke LJ) and [92] (per Hale LJ).

[104] Eric's negligence was not a *novus actus interveniens* because it was not deliberate. Could it be argued that Lara's failure to have an abortion when she was told that John would be born severely brain-damaged broke the chain of causation between Dawn's negligence and Lara's giving birth to John? No – it must be remembered that omissions do not break chains of causation (see above, pp. 545–6). Could it be argued, alternatively, that Lara is barred from suing Dawn for the extra cost of raising John that is attributable to the fact that he has been born with brain damage because by failing to have an abortion she failed to mitigate the losses suffered by her as a result of Dawn's negligence? The answer is 'no' – see below, pp. 591–2.

[105] This is, of course, not a real duty – B cannot be compelled to mitigate the losses suffered by her as a result of A's tort or sued if she fails to mitigate those losses.

[106] It seems, in light of the decision of the Privy Council in *Geest plc* v *Lansiquot* [2002] 1 WLR 3111, that the burden of proving that B has breached this 'duty' will fall on A. So if B has suffered some kind of loss as a result of A's tort that she could have avoided, B will still be able to claim compensation for that loss unless A can show that B acted *unreasonably* in failing to avoid that loss. In an earlier case, the Privy Council took the opposite view, holding that in the situation just described, B would not be able to claim compensation for the loss that she has suffered unless *she* could show that she acted *reasonably* in failing to avoid that loss:

A for damages in respect of any losses that she has only suffered as a result of A's tort because she breached that 'duty'.[106]

We have already seen an example of this principle at work in the case of the workman who unreasonably refused to have an operation which would have saved his left hand, the hand having been originally injured by the defendants' negligence.[107] He was not allowed to sue the defendants for compensation in respect of the loss of his left hand because the loss of that hand was attributable to his failure to mitigate the losses suffered by him as a result of the defendants' negligence.

Avoidable births and the duty to mitigate

What is the position in the following case? Suppose Lara and Gary were married, and they asked Paul, a surgeon, to carry out a vasectomy on Gary so that Lara and Gary could have sexual relations without using contraceptives. Paul performed the operation but (in breach of the duty of care he owed Lara and her husband) he failed to carry it out properly and the operation was as a result ineffective. Thinking, however, that the operation had been a success, Lara and her husband began to have unprotected sexual intercourse and Lara eventually fell pregnant. Nine months later, Lara gave birth, experiencing a lot of pain and suffering in doing so. Lara also had to take time off work during the pregnancy and spent money on new clothes that would fit her in the latter stages of her pregnancy. Suppose she wants to sue Paul for damages in respect of these forms of economic loss and the pain and suffering experienced by her in labour, arguing that Paul's negligence caused her to suffer these forms of loss.

Could Paul argue that Lara is barred from suing him for damages in respect of these losses on the ground that she could have avoided these losses by having an abortion? Obviously, the answer is 'no'. It cannot be argued that Lara acted *unreasonably* in not having an abortion – so it cannot be said that her failure to have an abortion put her in breach of her 'duty to mitigate' the losses suffered by her as a result of Paul's negligence. Astonishingly, in *Emeh* v *Kensington Area Health Authority*,[108] Park J, at first instance, took the opposite line and suggested that in the case we are considering, Lara *might* be barred from suing Paul for damages in respect of the losses that her pregnancy caused her to suffer on the ground that she could have avoided those losses by having an abortion. Fortunately, good sense has prevailed in the courts: Park J's views have been firmly rejected by both the Court of Appeal in *Emeh*'s case and by the House of Lords in *McFarlane* v *Tayside Health Board*.[109]

Having said that, in the case of *Richardson* v *LRC Products Ltd*,[110] Ian Kennedy J suggested that if Lara was warned by Paul that Gary's vasectomy had been unsuccessful the day after Gary impregnated her, then Lara might be barred from suing Paul for damages in

Selvanayagam v *University of West Indies* [1983] 1 WLR 585. There is something to be said for the position taken by the Privy Council in *Selvanayagam*: it will surely be easier for B to demonstrate that she acted reasonably in failing to avoid the loss in question than it will be for A to show that B acted unreasonably in failing to avoid that loss.

107 *McAuley* v *London Transport Executive* [1958] 2 Lloyd's Rep 500, discussed above, p. 546.

108 [1985] 1 QB 1012.

109 *McFarlane*, 74 (per Lord Slynn), 81 (per Lord Steyn), 104 (per Lord Clyde), 112–13 (per Lord Millett).

110 [2000] Lloyd's Rep Med 280.

respect of the losses suffered by her as a result of her pregnancy if she failed to bring that pregnancy to a halt by taking a 'morning-after' pill. In such a case he thought it could be said that Lara had failed to mitigate the losses suffered by her as a result of Paul's negligence.[111]

White *v* Jones *and the duty to mitigate*[112]

An unusual case which raised a 'duty to mitigate' point – though it was not argued as such in the case – was *Gorham* v *British Telecommunications plc*.[113] That case, it will be recalled, concerned a man, G, who was given some bad pensions advice by the defendants. As a result, the claimants, G's wife and two young children, were left worse off after G's death then they would have been had the defendants advised G properly. Had the defendants advised G properly, G would have joined his employer's pension scheme, instead of taking out a pension plan with the defendants. And had G joined his employer's pension scheme, the claimants would have obtained a lump sum on his death.

The claimants sued the defendants for compensation and it was held that the defendants had owed them a duty of care in advising G under the principle in *White* v *Jones* and that the defendants had breached that duty of care. However, it was held that the claimants could not sue for the lump sum that they would have received on G's death had he been properly advised by the defendants. The reason was that some time after being badly advised by the claimants, G discovered that his employer's pension scheme was superior to the pension plan that he had taken out with the defendants, but he then failed to join his employer's pension scheme. Had he done so, the claimants would have received the lump sum on G's death that they were suing the defendants for not receiving. In other words, G failed to mitigate the loss that the defendants' negligence caused the claimants to suffer on G's death.

It is not surprising that G's failure to mitigate the claimants' loss should have been held against the claimants. If the principle in *White* v *Jones* is (as we contend)[114] concerned with situations where A has been *prevented* by B's actions from conferring a benefit on C no action should be available to C under *White* v *Jones* if B's actions did not actually *prevent* A from conferring that benefit on C.

[111] The case actually concerned a claim under the Consumer Protection Act 1987: a married couple claimed that the wife had become pregnant as a result of their using a defective condom which split while they were making love. Ian Kennedy J rejected the claim that the condom was defective but held that even if it were, the claimants still had no case because the wife – knowing that the condom had split – could have easily avoided suffering any loss as a result by taking a 'morning-after' pill. The decision is not easy to reconcile with the views expressed by the Court of Appeal in *Emeh* and the House of Lords in *McFarlane*. Is there a distinction between taking a 'morning-after' pill and having an abortion? Munby J thought there was in *R (Smeaton)* v *Secretary of State for Health* [2002] 2 FLR 146 (*not* a tort case), ruling that the 'morning-after' pill was not an abortifacient under the Abortion Act 1967.

[112] For a straightforward *White* v *Jones* case which raised a duty to mitigate point, see *Walker* v *Medlicott & Son* [1999] 1 WLR 727, where the defendant firm of solicitors failed to draft a will properly with the result that the claimant was not left a house in the will which the testatrix had intended to leave to the claimant; the claimant's claim for compensation was dismissed because he could have applied to have the will rectified under s 20(1) of the Administration of Justice Act 1982 and so had failed to mitigate the loss suffered by him as a result of the defendants' negligence.

[113] [2000] 1 WLR 2129 (discussed above, p. 153).

[114] See below, pp. 153–4.

Losses caused in the course of a rescue

In *The Tojo Maru*, Lord Reid considered what would be the position in the following situation: 'Suppose a house is on fire. It contains a valuable collection of, say, china. There is little or no hope of saving the collection but a passer-by, with or without the consent of the owner, goes in and brings most of the collection to safety. But owing to some gross negligence on his part some of the china is smashed.'[115]

In principle, one would have thought that the passer-by could be sued for the loss of the smashed china: when he went into the house, he owed the owner of the china a duty to take care not to smash it, he breached that duty, and the china was destroyed as a result of that breach. However, subject to a couple of qualifications that we will set out below, Lord Reid thought the loss of the china in this case would be non-actionable: he said it would be 'most unjust'[116] if the passer-by were held liable for the destruction of the china.

In this sort of situation we can say that the passer-by is entitled to take advantage of a 'I did more good than harm' defence[117] to being sued for the loss of the china.[118] What are the limits on this defence? Lord Reid said that the passer-by should not be allowed the defence if he deterred other people from rescuing the china by rushing in to rescue it himself or if there was no immediate emergency requiring the china to be saved.[119] It is also doubtful whether the passer-by could take advantage of the defence if he – having seized the china in an attempt to rescue it – deliberately smashed one cup to see what noise it would make when it broke.

Losses associated with the destruction or damage of property

It seems that the following losses – each of which might be suffered by the victim of a tort if that tort causes his property to be destroyed or damaged – will be automatically non-actionable.

(1) *Distress.* Suppose that A negligently runs over B's cat and B suffers a great deal of distress as a result. Will B's distress be actionable? The question has not been much addressed but it seems implicit in *Attia* v *British Gas*[120] that the answer is 'no'.[121] After all, if B could

[115] [1972] AC 242, 268.

[116] Ibid.

[117] The name we have given the defence is a bit of a misnomer because the loss of the china would still be non-actionable under Lord Reid's principle even if the passer-by did more harm than good, by – for example – destroying a complete set of dinner plates while managing to save one teacup. And in fact the loss of the china would not be actionable under Lord Reid's principle if the passer-by did no good whatsoever: which would be the case if he picked up the china, and then smashed it all carelessly and walked out of the house with nothing.

[118] Notice that the passer-by could not argue that his liability should be very small because the destroyed china was 'doomed' anyway (see above, pp. 535–6 and below, pp. 607–8). It was not: had the passer-by not been negligent, the china would have been saved. Notice also that the passer-by could not argue either that his liability to compensate for the loss of the china should be reduced to take account of the benefits obtained by the owners of the china as a result of his negligence (see below, pp. 611–14). The owners of the china obtained no benefit from his carelessly smashing the china – they only obtained a benefit from his rushing in and rescuing the china (in the course of which he smashed some of it).

[119] [1972] AC 242, 268.

[120] [1988] QB 304 (discussed above, p. 582).

[121] Of course, distress suffered by the victim of a tort who has been *physically injured* as a result of that tort's being committed will be actionable as a matter of routine so long as the victim's physical injury is actionable. So if

sue for compensation in respect of her distress here, it is hard to see why the claimant's claim in *Attia* v *British Gas*[122] for compensation in respect of the psychiatric illness that she developed as a result of seeing her house burn down was thought to be problematic.[123]

(2) *Cost of repair.* Though the point is not made anywhere, it seems to us that if A has committed a tort in relation to B and in doing so caused B's property to be damaged and B has spent money on repairing that property, then the economic loss suffered by B in having the property repaired will *not* be actionable. The reason is that if it *were* actionable then B would be able, other things being equal, to sue A for compensation in respect of (1) the damage done to her property; *and* (2) the money she spent on repairing that property. But if B were allowed to sue A for (1) *and* (2), she would be overcompensated. This is because the courts, in awarding B damages for the damage done to her property, will customarily give her damages equal to the cost of repairing that property.[124] So if B is allowed to sue A for (1) *and* (2) she will recover the cost of repairing the property that A damaged twice over. This cannot be right. This possibility is avoided if we say that the money spent by B on repairing the damage done to her property is non-actionable.

(3) *Cost of replacement.* For the same reason, if A has tortiously destroyed B's property and B has spent money buying a replacement item of property, it seems to us that the money spent on the replacement will be non-actionable. If it were actionable then B would be entitled to sue A for compensation for the loss of her property *and* the cost of its replacement, and in so doing would recover the cost of replacing the item of property in question twice over (giving B the replacement cost of the item of property being the standard way of compensating B for the loss of that property). This possibility is avoided if we say that the money B actually laid out in obtaining a replacement for the item of property that A's tort destroyed will be non-actionable.

Loss of a chance/incurring a chance

It is well established that if A's tort has caused B to suffer a physical injury or property damage and as a result B has either lost a chance to obtain some benefit or has incurred a chance of suffering some kind of harm in the future, there is no reason in principle why that loss should not be actionable. Three examples can be given:

A negligently ran over *B* and B suffered pain and suffering as a result, B would have little difficulty in recovering for compensation for that pain and suffering. Moreover, if B was so badly injured as a result of A's hitting him that his expectation of life was shortened, B would be able to recover damages for the distress suffered by him as a result of knowing that he did not have long to live: Administration of Justice Act 1982, s 1(1)(b).

122 [1988] QB 304.

123 See *Essa* v *Laing* [2004] EWCA Civ 2, at [40]–[42] (per Pill LJ), [54]–[55] (per Clarke LJ), [112]–[116] (per Rix LJ), considering what the position would be if: (1) A committed a tort in relation to B; (2) B suffered a psychiatric illness as a result; and (3) had B suffered pure distress as a result of A's tort, she would have been entitled to sue A for damages in respect of that distress. Pill and Clarke LJJ thought – on the basis of the decision in *Page* v *Smith* [1996] AC 155 – that B would be able to sue A for damages in respect of her psychiatric illness *without* having to show that her *psychiatric illness* was a foreseeable consequence of A's tort: it is enough that it was reasonably foreseeable that B would suffer pure distress as a result of A's tort. Rix LJ dissented on this point.

124 See below, pp. 607–8.

(1) *Chance of future physical injury.* If A has tortiously injured B's hip and as a result there is a chance that B will develop arthritis in the future, so long as B's hip injury is an actionable consequence of A's tort, B will normally be allowed to claim damages for the chance that he will develop arthritis in the future.[125]

(2) *Loss of employment prospects.* If A has tortiously injured B with the result that B may find it hard to find work in the future, so long as B's injury is an actionable consequence of A's tort, B will normally be allowed to claim damages for the chance that, as a result of A's tort, he may suffer a prolonged period of unemployment in the future.[126]

(3) *Loss of chance to sell land.* If A has tortiously contaminated B's land with the result that B has lost the chance to sell that land on to a developer at a very good price, so long as the contamination is an actionable consequence of A's tort, B will normally be entitled to claim damages for the loss of the chance of selling his land at a lucrative price that he suffered as a result of A's tort.[127]

In cases where A's tort has caused B to suffer a pure loss of a chance of obtaining some kind of benefit or has caused B to incur a pure chance of suffering some harm in the future, the law is more complex. It seems at the moment that the loss suffered by B in such a case will be automatically non-actionable unless A was under a duty to safeguard B's financial welfare.

This requirement was satisfied in *Allied Maples Group Ltd* v *Simmons & Simmons.*[128] In that case, the claimants bought the share capital of K, a subsidiary of G, in order to acquire leases held by K. The claimants' solicitors – the defendants – conducted the negotiations with G over the terms of the share deal. The defendants negligently failed to tell the claimants that the terms of the share deal did not protect them against the risk that they would have to meet any liabilities incurred by K's subsidiaries. The claimants successfully argued that had they been told this, there was a chance they would have successfully renegotiated the deal with G to obtain such protection. As a result, they were allowed to sue the defendants for damages to compensate them for the fact that they lost that chance to renegotiate the deal with G as a result of the defendants' negligence.

The 'financial welfare' requirement was not satisfied in *Gregg* v *Scott,*[129] where – as we have seen[130] – a cancer patient was not allowed to sue his doctor in negligence for the fact

125 See above, pp. 562–3.

126 See below, pp. 598–9.

127 See *Blue Circle Industries plc* v *Ministry of Defence* [1999] Ch 289. The claimants owned land next to land owned by the Atomic Weapons Establishment (AWE). The claimants were in negotiations to sell the land for about £10.5m to a third party when it was discovered that the land was contaminated with nuclear waste from the AWE's land. The third party broke off negotiations and the claimants set about cleaning up their land. The property market collapsed in the meantime and once the claimants' land was cleaned up and marketable again, it was only worth £5m. The claimants sued the defendants for damages, claiming that the defendants had committed a tort in contaminating their land. The trial judge found that there was a 75% chance that had the defendants not committed their tort, the third party would have bought the claimants' land for £10.5m and therefore that there was a 75% chance that but for the defendants' tort, the claimants would have been £5.5m better off than they were. Consequently, he awarded the claimants 75% of £5.5m as compensation for the fact that the defendants' tort deprived the claimants of the chance of selling their land for £5.5m more than they ended up obtaining for it.

128 [1995] 1 WLR 1602.

129 [2005] 2 AC 176.

130 See above, pp. 559–63.

that the doctor's negligent failure to diagnose his cancer caused his prospects of being cured of cancer to diminish. Nor was it satisfied in *Rothwell* v *Chemical & Insulating Co. Ltd*,[131] where the Court of Appeal ruled that the claimants – who had been negligently exposed to asbestos fibres by their employers, the defendants – were not allowed to sue the defendants for damages to compensate them for the chance that they might develop asbestos-related diseases in the future as a result of the defendants' negligence. It was crucial to the Court of Appeal's reasoning in this case that the defendants' negligence had not so far caused the claimants to suffer any kind of physical injury.[132] So the claimants had incurred a *pure* chance of developing an asbestos-related disease in the future, and the Court of Appeal ruled that that chance was automatically non-actionable.

Losses suffered as a result of the infliction of a non-actionable loss

Suppose that A has committed a tort in relation to B and B suffered some kind of loss as a result of A's tort. Suppose further that because B suffered that loss, she went on to suffer a further loss. If the first loss suffered by B is non-actionable then the second loss suffered by B – which proceeded from the first – will also be non-actionable.

The point is perhaps too obvious to require support. Suppose, for example, that Ian negligently ran down Helen's cat and Helen was so grief-stricken by this that she was unable to go to work for a year and suffered a consequent loss of income. If Helen's grief is non-actionable,[133] then nobody would suggest that the loss of income suffered by Helen as a result of her being grief-stricken *is* actionable. So we will move on to mention one possible exception to the rule stated above.

In *Dulieu* v *White & Sons*,[134] the defendants carelessly drove a van into a pub. The claimant was serving behind the bar. The claimant was not hit by the van but she received such a fright at the sight of the van crashing into the pub that she fell ill. The claimant sued the defendants in negligence for compensation in respect of her illness. In principle, one would have expected the court to have ruled that the claimant's illness was non-actionable. There was no doubt that the defendants owed the claimant a duty to take care not to drive the van into the pub where she was working[135] and that they breached that duty. However, the claimant suffered two losses as a result of the defendant's breach: shock and fright (which counted as a primary loss); and physical illness (which counted as a secondary loss flowing from the shock and fright suffered by the claimant).

There is no doubt that the shock and fright suffered by the claimant was non-actionable[136] under the wrong kind of loss principle: the duty breached by the defendants in this

131 [2006] 1 ICR 1458.

132 The claimants had developed what are called 'pleural plaques' – small, smooth plates – on their lungs as a result of being exposed to the asbestos fibres, but both the Court of Appeal and, subsequently, the House of Lords ([2007] 3 WLR 876) ruled that these were not serious enough to count as a physical injury.

133 Which is our view: see above, pp. 593–4.

134 [1901] 2 KB 669.

135 This is justified under the physical danger principle set out above at pp. 73–4: it was plainly foreseeable that someone like the claimant would be injured if the defendants drove the van into the pub.

136 One can test this by asking: what would have happened if the claimant had not fallen ill in the aftermath of the defendants' crashing the van into the pub but had merely been shaken up by the experience? Would she have been entitled to sue the defendants for compensation in respect of the pure distress that she had suffered as a result of the defendants' negligence? The answer is 'no': see above, p. 580.

case was imposed on them in order to help ensure that the claimant was not physically injured, not in order to help ensure that she did not become frightened. However, the claimant was still allowed to sue the defendants for compensation in respect of her illness – that loss was declared to be actionable, even though it flowed from the claimant's suffering a loss that was in itself non-actionable. In reaching its conclusion, the court was probably influenced by the fact that if the defendants' van had *hit* the claimant when it crashed into the pub, she would have been entitled to sue the defendants in respect of the injuries suffered by her as a result. The court may have thought that it should make no difference to the claimant's right to recover that the physical injury suffered by the claimant here was suffered by her not because she was *hit* by the defendant's van but because she thought that she was *going to be hit* by the defendant's van.

Visit **http://www.mylawchamber.co.uk/mcbride** to access updates on recent cases, as well as model answers and tips for answering tort problem questions.

Use **Case Navigator** to read in full some of the key cases referenced in this chapter:

- **Gregg** *v* **Scott**
- **Chester** *v* **Afshar**
- **Fairchild** *v* **Glenhaven Funeral Services Ltd**
- **Hunter** *v* **Canary Wharf Ltd**

29 Quantification of loss

Suppose that A has committed a tort in relation to B and A's tort has caused B to suffer at least one actionable loss. So B is entitled to sue A for compensatory damages. But how much will B be entitled to sue A for? This chapter and the next are concerned with that question. In this chapter we explain *how much* B will normally be entitled to sue A for – what we can call the *prima facie measure of liability*. In the next chapter we will explain when the damages payable to B will be *reduced* below this *prima facie* level.

THE LUMP SUM RULE

The *prima facie* measure of liability is assessed in the following way. The courts will aim – in awarding damages to B – to award B a *lump sum* sufficient to compensate B for the losses[1] that A's tort *has caused* her to suffer and the losses that A's tort *may* cause B to suffer in the future.

So suppose that John negligently runs Mary over and one of Mary's legs has to be amputated as a result. Mary currently works in an office and her terms of employment are unaffected by the fact that she has lost one leg, though she did of course have to take some time off work to have her injuries treated. In this situation John's tort *has caused* Mary to suffer three kinds of losses. First, physical injury – Mary was injured in the accident caused by John's negligence and one of her legs had to be amputated. Secondly, distress – Mary will have experienced a great deal of pain and suffering as a result of being injured in the accident, as well as distress at the fact that she will now have to live with having only one leg. Thirdly, economic loss – as a result of the fact that she had to take time off work to have her injuries treated, Mary will have suffered some kind of diminution in income. However, in this situation, John's tort *may cause* Mary to suffer a further kind of loss *in the future*. If Mary loses her current job in the future, the fact that she has only one leg may make it difficult for her to find alternative employment. So Mary may suffer economic loss in the future as a result of John's tort.

So the lump sum payable to Mary in this situation will be designed to compensate her for: (1) the fact that John's tort has *caused* her to suffer physical injury, distress and economic loss; *and* (2) the fact that John's tort *may* cause her to suffer economic loss in the future because her capacity to find alternative employment if she loses her current job has been diminished.[2] Inevitably, in awarding damages designed to compensate Mary for (2),

[1] By 'losses' we mean here and from now on, *actionable* losses.

[2] Damages that are designed to compensate the victim of a tort for the fact that she may suffer economic losss in future because the tort has reduced her capacity to find alternative employment are known as damages for 'loss of earning capacity' or '*Smith* v *Manchester* damages' after one of the cases in which such damages were awarded: *Smith* v *Manchester* (1974) 17 KIR 1. In the situation we are considering, such damages will only be awarded to Mary if there is in fact a *real or substantial* risk that she will lose her job in the future and that her disability will make it difficult for her to find alternative employment: *Moeliker* v *Reyrolle* [1977] 1 All ER 9.

she will not be awarded damages equal to the *full* amount of money she would lose if she lost her job and found it difficult, because of her disability, to find alternative employment. Because there is a chance that she will not lose her job, the damages payable to Mary will be *discounted* to take account of that chance. However, this creates a problem.

The problem arises out of the fact that once Mary is awarded a lump sum in damages that is designed to compensate her for (1) and (2), that is it. If the lump sum proves inadequate to cover the losses that Mary has suffered as a result of John's tort, she will not be able to go back to court to obtain a larger amount. Similarly, if it proves that John has overpaid and the lump sum award turns out in fact to be larger than was necessary to compensate Mary for the losses that she has suffered as a result of John's tort, then John will not be able to go back to court to claw back the overpayment.

Now – because the lump sum payable to Mary in this case will be designed in part to compensate her for (2), that lump sum will *inevitably* either undercompensate or overcompensate Mary for the losses she has suffered as a result of John's tort.[3] Either Mary will at some stage in the future lose her job and find it difficult to find alternative employment because she has only one leg – in which case the lump sum award will undercompensate her because that part of the award which was designed to compensate her for the fact that this might happen was discounted to take account of the possibility that Mary might *not* lose her job. Or Mary will never lose her current job and will sail on to retirement, with her earning capacity undisturbed by the fact that she has only one leg – in which case Mary will be overcompensated, because the lump sum paid to her included an element designed to compensate her for the possibility that she might suffer a loss that, as things turned out, she never did.

Given this problem, the law has started to move towards different systems of awarding damages:

(1) *Provisional damages.* Under an award of provisional damages, the victim of a tort is awarded a sum designed to compensate her for the losses that she *has* suffered as a result of that tort being committed; and then, if it turns out that that tort has caused her to suffer some futher losses, she is able to go back to court and sue for further damages, designed to compensate her for those losses. Section 32A of the Senior Courts Act 1981[4] allows[5] the courts in a personal injury case to make a provisional award of damages which would be later topped up with further awards of damages if 'there is proved or admitted to be a

[3] See Lord Scarman's remarks in *Lim* v *Camden Area Health Authority* [1980] AC 174, at 182H–183B: '[There are] insuperable problems implicit in a system of compensation for personal injuries which (unless the parties agree otherwise) can yield only a lump sum assessed by the court at the time of judgment. Sooner or later ... if the parties do not settle, a court (once liability is admitted or proved) has to make an award of damages. The award, which covers past, present, and future injury and loss, must, under our law, be of a lump sum assessed at the conclusion of the legal process. The award is final; it is not susceptible to review as the future unfolds, substituting fact for estimate. Knowledge of the future being denied to mankind, so much of the award as is to be attributed to future loss and suffering – in many cases the major part of the award – will almost surely be wrong. There is really only one certainty: the future will prove the award to be either too high or too low.' See also Lord Steyn in *Wells* v *Wells* [1999] 1 AC 345, at 384.

[4] As amended by s 6 of the Administration of Justice Act 1982.

[5] Under rule 25.7 of the Civil Procedure Rules 1998, the courts are only allowed to exercise this power in cases where the defendant is insured or is a public authority – the idea being that in such cases, there is no real injustice to the defendant in having the possibility of a further award of damages being made against him sometime in the future hanging over his head.

chance that at some definite or indefinite time in the future the injured person will, as a result of the act or omission which gave rise to the cause of action, develop some serious disease or suffer some serious deterioration in his physical or mental condition'.

(2) *Periodical payments.*[6] An award of periodical payments is designed to deal with the following kind of situation: David has tortiously injured Karen and she is disabled and unable to work as a result. She needs to be compensated for the future loss of income that she will suffer as a result of David's tort, but no one can be certain how much longer Karen will live. Under the lump sum system, the courts simply have to make a guess as to how much longer Karen is likely to live and award her a lump sum that – when properly invested – will yield her an annual income over her remaining (estimated) lifespan equivalent to the money she would have earned each year but for David's tort. But if Karen dies earlier than expected, the lump sum awarded her to compensate her for her future loss of income will prove to have been too much; and if she dies later than expected, the lump sum awarded her will prove to have been too little. An award of periodical payments solves this problem: David is simply required to pay Karen a regular sum to cover her loss of income for as long as she lives. Section 2(1) of the Damages Act 1996[7] now provides that 'A court awarding damages for future pecuniary loss in respect of personal injury ... may order that the damages are wholly or partly to take the form of periodical payments.' Under s 2(3): 'A court may not make an order for periodical payments unless satisfied that the continuity of payment under the order is reasonably secure.'

(3) *Flexible periodical payments.* Suppose that in the above case Karen's injuries were such that she was unable to continue working as a high-flying legal executive, but she is still able, despite her injuries, to take a lower paid, but far less stressful, job teaching A-Level Law in a school. Suppose further that there is a chance that Karen's injuries might get worse in the future and she might be unable to carry on teaching. In such a case regular periodical payments designed to compensate Karen for the difference in her current income teaching A-Level Law and the income she would have been earning but for David's tort might end up seriously undercompensating or overcompensating her. They will undercompensate her if her condition gets worse and she has to give up teaching: she will not be compensated for the loss of the income from teaching that David's tort has caused her to suffer. They will overcompensate her if she suddenly gets a lot better and she can go back to work as a high-flying legal executive: David will continue having to pay Karen a regular sum to cover a loss of income that she is no longer experiencing. To cover this possibility, the Damages (Variation of Periodical Payments) Order 2005[8] provides that:

> If there is proved to be a chance that at some definite or indefinite time in the future the claimant will –
>
> (a) as a result of the act or omission which gave rise to the cause of action, develop some serious disease or suffer some serious deterioration, or
>
> (b) enjoy some significant improvement in his physical or mental condition, where that condition had been adversely affected as a result of that act or omission,

[6] See Lewis 2007.

[7] As amended by the Courts Act 2003, s 100.

[8] SI 2005/841.

> the court may, on the application of a party, with the agreement of all the parties, or of its own initiative, provide in an order for periodical payments that it may be varied.

So in the case we are imagining, when the initial order for periodical payments is made against David, provision can be made for the payments to go up or down in the future depending on what happens in the future.

Despite the advantages involved in making awards of damages in these new and more flexible ways, it should be noted that there are some disadvantages involved in making awards of damages in these ways.

First, all the parties to litigation will have an interest in not letting litigation 'drag on'. The victim of a tort's ability to get on with her life will be impeded if she is left in constant uncertainty as to how much compensation she will get in respect of the losses suffered by her as a result of that tort being committed. At the same time, the tortfeasor (or his insurer) will have an interest in knowing as soon as possible what his total liability to the victim of his tort is going to be for the purpose of financial planning.

Secondly, the victim of a tort may well have other reasons for preferring to receive a lump sum award designed to compensate her for *all* the losses that she has suffered as a result of that tort being committed and the losses that she may suffer in the future as a result of that tort being committed, rather than receiving small periodic payments designed to compensate her for the losses that, it turns out, she has suffered as a result of that tort being committed. She will be able to do more things with a lump sum: for instance, armed with a lump sum award of damages, she could purchase a business which would be out of her financial reach if she received her damages in small periodic payments over a number of years.[9]

Let's now look at some typical cases where the victim of a tort might sue the person who committed that tort for compensatory damages and see how the courts assess how large the lump sum that is payable to the victim of the tort should be.

PHYSICAL INJURY CASES

The standard case

Let us consider first a standard case where A negligently caused a car crash in which B was injured. B's injuries were such that she has become permanently disabled and, as a result, she has had to take a job which pays less than the job she was working in before the crash. B had to take six months off work so as to have her injuries treated with the result that she did not receive any wages for those six months. B opted to have her injuries privately treated and as a result she incurred substantial medical bills.

[9] At the same time, the victim of a tort who has suffered large losses as a result of that tort being committed might not want to shoulder the burden of managing the large lump sum that she will be awarded to compensate her for her losses. If this is the case *and* liability is undisputed *and* the person who committed the tort in question is insured, the victim of the tort will have the option of entering into what is called a 'structured settlement' with the tortfeasor's insurer. Under this arrangement, a proportion of the damages that would be paid to the victim of the tort in a lump sum if she went to court are paid over to the victim of the tort upfront and the rest is invested by the tortfeasor's insurer in annuities that will produce a regular, tax-free, yearly income for the victim of the tort.

So A's negligence will have caused B to suffer the following losses:

(1) *Physical injury*: B was injured in the car crash caused by A.
(2) *Distress*: B will have suffered pain and suffering as a result of being injured in the car crash.
(3) *Inconvenience*: now that B is disabled, it is more difficult for her to get around and cope with life generally.
(4) *Loss of amenity*: B's disability will almost certainly mean that B now gets less enjoyment out of life than she used to.
(5) *Economic loss*: A's negligence caused B to suffer two kinds of economic loss. First, B had to take six months off work to have her injuries treated and suffered a loss of income as a result. Secondly, B opted to have her injuries privately treated and thereby incurred substantial medical bills.
(6) *Future economic loss*. A's negligence will also almost certainly cause B to suffer a further economic loss in the future: B's disabilities mean that she has had to take a job which will pay her less in the future than the job she was working in before she was injured.

Now, how do we assess how much of a lump sum B should be paid to compensate her for the fact that she has suffered losses (1)–(5) and for the fact that she will almost certainly suffer loss (6) in the future?

Non-pecuniary losses

Let us deal first with the non-pecuniary losses suffered by B: that is, losses (1)–(4), above. The courts will normally take these items of loss together in determining how much compensation should be paid to B for the fact that B has suffered them.

Inevitably, the process of determining how much B should be paid to compensate her for the fact that she has suffered losses (1)–(4) is arbitrary in the sense that there is no demonstrably correct answer as to how much B should be awarded so as to compensate her for the fact that she has suffered these losses. We could easily award B £10,000 or we could award her £20,000; neither figure seems more appropriate. In assessing the figure payable, the courts will merely seek to be *consistent*. So if someone in a previous case who suffered a similar injury to B was awarded £15,000 in respect of that injury and consequential non-pecuniary loss, then the courts will almost certainly award the same amount to B. Moreover, if someone in a previous case who suffered a much more serious injury than B was awarded £20,000 in respect of that injury and consequential non-pecuniary loss, the courts will not give B more than that. In this way, a body of case law has been built up on how much will be customarily awarded to compensate people who suffer certain 'standard' injuries and consequential non-pecuniary losses, details of which can be found in advanced works on damages. At the prompting of the Law Commission, the Court of Appeal has sought to update this case law, finding that in the past personal injury victims have been undercompensated by the courts for the non-pecuniary losses suffered by them as a result of their injuries. From now on, if the victim of a tort who has suffered a personal injury as a result of a tort being committed would have been entitled – under the old case law – to sue for more than £10,000 in respect of that injury and consequential non-pecuniary losses, her award should be increased by up to one-third, depending on what she would have obtained under the old case law.[10]

Whatever sum is payable to B to compensate her for the fact that she has suffered losses (1)–(4), it will normally be discounted somewhat to take account of the possibility that had B not become disabled as a result of A's negligence, she might have become disabled at some stage in the future. So if B was 'doomed' to become disabled even if A had not been negligent, then the damages payable to B to compensate her for the fact that she has suffered losses (1)–(4) will be substantially reduced.[11]

Pecuniary losses

In considering how much B should be paid so as to compensate her for the pecuniary losses that she has suffered or may suffer in the future as a result of A's negligence, we should draw a distinction between the pecuniary losses that B *has* suffered as a result of A's negligence – that is, loss (5) – and the pecuniary losses that B will almost certainly suffer in the future as a result of A's negligence – that is, loss (6).

(1) *Past loss.* It is quite easy to determine how much B should be paid to compensate her for the loss of wages suffered by her when she had to take time off work to have her injuries treated. She should be paid a sum equivalent to the *net* loss suffered by her: that is, a sum equal to how much B would have taken home after tax had she not had to take time off work. Again, it is not difficult to determine how much B should be paid to compensate her for the fact that she incurred medical bills as a result of having her injuries treated. She should be paid a sum equivalent to the amount she was charged for medical treatment.[12]

(2) *Future loss.* Assessing the amount payable to B in respect of the future loss of income that she will probably suffer as a result of A's negligence is much more problematic. Let us suppose that before she was injured, B was earning £20,000 a year net of tax. B's disability means that she is now in a job where she earns £12,000 a year net of tax. Let us further assume that B was 40 when she was injured.

It is *not* possible to say that had B not been injured she would probably have earned £8,000 a year more than she is currently earning up until retirement age (65) and that she should therefore be awarded (£8,000 × (65−40) =) £200,000 to compensate her for the future loss of income that she will probably suffer as a result of A's negligence. This is for three reasons.

First, B might not live until 65. If B's medical health is such that an actuary would predict that B will not survive beyond 60, then the damages payable to B in respect of the loss of income that she will probably suffer in the future as a result of A's negligence should be assessed on the basis that B will die at 60.

Secondly, B might not have continued to earn £20,000 a year net of tax but for A's negligence for the rest of her expected working lifespan. B might have been sacked, or been

[10] *Heil* v *Rankin* [2001] QB 272.

[11] *Jobling* v *Associated Dairies Ltd* [1982] AC 794. For an exceptional situation where the damages payable to the victim of a tort who was injured as a result of that tort being committed will not be reduced, even though she was 'doomed' to suffer those injuries anyway at some stage in the future, see above, pp. 550–2.

[12] Though the sum payable will be reduced if the medical bills covered the cost of food and laundry: see below, pp. 611–12.

made redundant and found it difficult to find alternative employment. The damages payable to B to compensate her for the loss of income that she will probably suffer in the future as a result of A's negligence should be adjusted to take account of these possibilities.

Thirdly, suppose that we estimate that B will probably work for 20 more years and that, but for A's negligence, B would have earned £8,000 a year more over those years than she actually will. The damages paid to B *now* in respect of the loss of income that she will probably suffer in the future as a result of A's negligence should not equal the total amount of extra income B would probably have earned over her expected working lifespan, that is, (£8,000 × 20 =) £160,000. If they did, then B could invest the damages and earn a yearly income with them – made up of interest plus yearly withdrawals of portions of the capital sum invested – which would exceed the yearly income loss suffered by her as a result of A's negligence. So awarding B damages equal to the total amount of extra income B would have obtained over her expected lifespan had A not negligently injured her would overcompensate B: it would make B better off than she would have been had A not been negligent. To avoid this possibility, the damages payable to B should amount to a capital sum which, when properly invested, will yield B an annual income – made up of interest plus a proportion of the capital sum – equivalent to £8,000 a year for 20 years; at the end of which 20 years the capital sum will be used up. This capital sum will be considerably smaller than £160,000.

So one way of assessing how much B should be paid to compensate her for the loss of income that she will probably suffer in the future as a result of A's negligence would be to proceed as follows. First, ask: What is the difference between what B is earning now net of tax and what she would have been earning now net of tax had A not been negligent? (Say this is £8,000.) Then ask: How much of a working life has B probably got left to her? (Say this is 20 years.)

Next, multiply £8,000 by 20 to get a rough idea of how much the total loss of income will be that B will suffer over the rest of her working life as a result of A's negligence: this gives us £160,000. Next, discount that sum to take account of the possibility that had A not been negligent, B would have been sacked or made redundant and might not have earned as much as £8,000 more over the rest of her working life than she will now earn over the rest of her working life. So if we discount it by 25 per cent, this gives us a figure of £120,000, equivalent to a loss of income of £6,000 a year over the rest of B's expected working life.

Then we assess what sort of capital sum, properly invested, would produce a yearly income stream – made up of interest plus a proportion of the capital sum – of £6,000 a year over 20 years. Obviously this depends a lot on how we might expect B to invest the capital sum awarded. If we can expect B to invest the money only in very safe investments which produce a low rate of interest, then more of a capital sum must be awarded to B to produce the necessary income stream. If, on the other hand, we can expect B to invest her money in more risky investments which produce a higher rate of interest, then less of a capital sum must be awarded to B to produce the necessary income stream. In *Wells* v *Wells*,[13] the House of Lords ruled that in assessing the damages payable in respect of future loss of income it must be assumed that the payee will invest the damages in very safe, low-interest investments such as government index-linked bonds. The capital sum we finally come up with

[13] [1999] AC 345.

(say £112,000) is the sum B should be paid to compensate her for the loss of income that she will probably suffer in the future as a result of A's negligence.

Instead, the courts adopt a slightly different method of assessing how much B should be paid by way of damages to compensate her for the loss of income that she will probably suffer in the future as a result of A's negligence. This method is known as the *multiplier method*. What the courts do is assess the difference between what B now earns net of tax and what she would have been earning now net of tax had A not been negligent. This figure (here £8,000) is known as the *multiplicand*. They then multiply the multiplicand by a figure (known as the *multiplier*) which takes into account: (*a*) the number of years that B can be expected to suffer that yearly loss of income; (*b*) the possibility that B would not actually have earned as much in the future as she was earning at the time A injured her; and (*c*) the fact that B is being awarded damages *now* in respect of future income loss and can therefore be expected to earn interest with those damages which will help to cover that future income loss.

The end result is exactly the same as is yielded by the approach suggested in the above paragraph (the courts might be expected to apply a multiplier of about 14 in the above case,[14] resulting in a damages award of £112,000). The multiplier approach simply represents a slightly different way of going about assessing the damages payable to B in respect of the loss of income that she will probably suffer in the future as a result of A's negligence.

The case where an injury results in a loss of life expectancy

Suppose A has negligently injured B. Suppose further that B was 35 when she was injured and before she was injured she could have been expected to live to 70. However, B's injury now means that she can only be expected to live to 45.

B will, of course, be entitled to sue A for damages in respect of: her injury and any consequential non-pecuniary losses suffered by her as a result of that injury; any medical expenses incurred by her as a result of being injured; and any loss of income that she has suffered or is likely to suffer as a result of A's injuring her between the date of her injury and the date of her death (now anticipated to occur at 45).

It is, however, well established that B will *also* be entitled to sue A for damages in respect of the money she could have earned during the years that are now 'lost' to her as a result of A's negligence.[15] This is a bit puzzling: what earthly good would awarding B such damages do her? However, the point of awarding B such damages is *not* actually to compensate B but to ensure that any dependants of B – who would have been supported by B in the years that are now 'lost' to her – do not lose out as a result of B's expectation of life being reduced.[16]

[14] Of course, if B had been younger when she was injured, a higher multiplier would be used to assess the damages payable to her. In practice, the courts will rarely apply a multiplier greater than 17 or 18 in assessing how much should be paid to compensate someone for a future loss of income.

[15] *Pickett* v *British Rail Engineering Ltd* [1980] AC 126, overruling *Oliver* v *Ashman* [1962] 2 QB 210. Section 1(1)(a) of the Administration of Justice Act 1982 prevents victims of torts who have suffered a 'loss of expectation of life' suing for damages to compensate them for that fact (so no action for loss of amenity can be brought in respect of the pleasures that a victim of a tort would have enjoyed in the years that are now 'lost' to her as a result of that tort being committed). However, s 1(2) of the same Act provides that s 1(1)(a) does not apply to actions for 'damages in respect of loss of income'.

[16] However, B will be entitled to sue A for damages in respect of the money she would have earned in the years that are now lost to her even if she has no dependants who would have been supported by her in those years.

B can sue for damages in respect of the money she would have earned in the years that are now lost to her and thereby create a fund that will help to support her dependants after she dies.[17]

How do we assess how much B should be entitled to recover in respect of this loss of income? The courts again use a 'multiplier' approach. They first assess how much B could have been expected to earn per year net of tax in the years that are now 'lost' to her: say this is £50,000. They then deduct from that the yearly amount B would have spent on supporting herself in the years that are now 'lost' to her: call this £35,000.[18] Thus, £15,000 (the difference between £50,000 and £35,000) is the multiplicand used by the courts to determine how much B should be paid in damages. The courts then arrive at a multiplier, which takes into account the following factors: (1) the fact that B could have been expected to earn money for 20 of the 25 years that are now 'lost' to her as a result of A's negligence; (2) the fact that had B not been injured she might not have earned £50,000 per year in the years that are now 'lost' to her: she might have been made redundant and found it difficult to find alternative employment; (3) the fact that any damages awarded to B can be invested and produce an income stream which will help replace the yearly net amount that B would have earned and not spent on herself in the years that are now 'lost' to her. They then multiply the multiplier and multiplicand together to arrive at the figure B should be awarded in damages to compensate her for the money she would have made in the years that are now 'lost' to her.

PROPERTY DAMAGE CASES

Let us now consider what the position is if A commits a tort in relation to B and thereby causes property belonging to B to be destroyed or damaged. Assuming that this loss is actionable, how do we go about determining how much B should be paid so as to compensate her for the fact that she has suffered this loss?

[17] *Important note.* See Lord Diplock's explanation of the decision in *Pickett* v *British Rail Engineering Ltd* in *Gammell* v *Wilson* [1982] AC 27, at 64–5; also Lord Phillips MR in *Gregg* v *Scott* [2005] 2 AC 176, at [177]–[181]. An alert student might raise the following objection to this explanation. 'Surely after B dies, B's dependants will be entitled in any case to bring a claim for loss of support against A under the Fatal Accidents Act 1976? So why would the law go to such lengths to allow B to protect her dependants while she is still alive?' However, if B sues A for damages before she dies, B's dependants will lose any rights they might otherwise have had to sue A under the 1976 Act – and B will almost certainly want and need to sue A before she dies in order to get some compensation for the losses that she is *currently* suffering as a result of A's negligence. However, on this point, see: (1) Lord Phillips MR in *Gregg* v *Scott* [2005] 2 AC 176, arguing at [182] that 'It would be much better if [B] had no right to recover for such loss of earnings [that would have been made in the 'lost years'] and the dependants' right to claim under [s] 1(1) of the Fatal Accidents Act 1976 subsisted despite the claimants' recovery of damages for his injury. I am not persuaded that this result could not be achieved by a purposive construction of that section.' (2) Section 3 of the Damages Act 1996, which provides that 'The award of provisional damages [to the victim of a tort] shall not operate as a bar to an action in respect of that person's death under the Fatal Accidents Act 1976', though the award may be taken into account in judging how much a claimant bringing a claim under the 1976 Act has in fact lost by way of a loss of support.

[18] This is consistent with the reason why B is allowed to sue A for damages in respect of the money she would have earned in the years that are now 'lost' to her. As the object of awarding her such damages is really to compensate B's dependants, if any, for the loss of support that they will suffer on B's premature death, there is no reason to allow B to claim damages in respect of any income that she would have earned in the years that are now 'lost' to her that she would merely have spent on supporting herself.

Damage to property

Suppose first that A has negligently damaged B's property and that the damage done to B's property amounts to an actionable loss. How much should B be paid so as to compensate her for the fact that her property has been damaged? The courts' answer is: *As a general rule*, B should be paid damages equal to the amount of money it would have cost B to repair the property in question had she repaired that property at the time it was first reasonable for her to do so.

So, for example, in *Dodd Properties (Kent) Ltd* v *Canterbury City Council*,[19] the defendants built a multi-storey car park beside a building owned by the claimants. The building work took place in 1968. Due to the defendants' negligence in carrying out pile-driving operations for the foundations, serious structural damage was done to the claimants' building. The earliest time the claimants could have repaired the building was in 1970 when it would have cost £11,375 to repair the building. However, the claimants could not easily raise the funds to do the repairs at that date and were in any case uncertain as to whether or not they would be able to claim back the cost of the repairs from the defendants. Given this, they decided to hold off doing any repairs until they had sued the defendants. The claimants' case was heard in 1978, by which time the cost of doing the repairs had risen to £30,327. The Court of Appeal held that the claimants had acted reasonably in delaying repairing their building until they had sued the defendants and therefore held that the claimants should be awarded damages in respect of the damage done to their property equal to the cost of repairing the building in 1978. The Court of Appeal therefore awarded the claimants £30,327 in damages.[20]

The general rule set out above is subject to three exceptions.

(1) *Cheaper to replace*. If, when B's property was damaged, it would have been cheaper to replace it rather than repair it then the compensation for the damage done to B's property will *usually* be assessed by reference to the cost of replacing it rather than repairing it. The cost of repair measure of compensation will still be used if the property in question was so special to B that it would have been unreasonable to expect her to have replaced it rather than repaired it.

So in *O'Grady* v *Westminster Scaffolding Ltd*,[21] the defendant negligently damaged the claimant's 1938 MG motor car. The claimant could have bought a replacement car for about £185 but his MG was his 'pride and joy' and so he decided to keep it and spent about £250 repairing it. It was held that the claimant was entitled to damages for the damage done to his car assessed according to the cost of repair measure: given his special attachment to his car, it would have been unreasonable to expect him to have scrapped it and bought a replacement car.

It was different in *Darbishire* v *Warran*.[22] In that case, the claimant's car was badly damaged in a collision caused by the defendant's negligence. The claimant had owned the car for about four years and it had always proved reliable. Rather than look for a replacement

19 [1980] 1 WLR 433.

20 See also the Privy Council decision in *Alcoa Minerals of Jamaica Inc.* v *Broderick* [2002] 1 AC 371, which endorsed the decision in *Dodd Properties*.

21 [1962] 2 Lloyd's Rep 238.

22 [1963] 1 WLR 1067.

– which would have cost about £80 – the claimant chose, more out of inertia than anything, to have the car repaired instead. The repairs cost him about £192. The court held that the claimant was entitled to damages for the damage done to his car assessed according to the cost of replacement measure: it would not have been unreasonable to expect the claimant to have bought a new car rather than have his old, damaged, one repaired. So the claimant was awarded £80 as compensation for the damage done to his car, with the result that he was left out of pocket by £112.

(2) *Valueless property.* The second qualification to the general rule stated above is that if the property that was damaged by A's negligence was valueless to B – for example, B was going to scrap it – then B will, of course, not be entitled to recover the cost of repairing that property from A.

(3) *Property in need of repair.* The third qualification is that if the property that was damaged by A's negligence was in need of repair anyway and performing that repair work would at the same time repair the damage done by A's negligence, B will not be entitled to recover anything for the damage done to his property by A's negligence.

So in *Performance Cars Ltd* v *Abraham*,[23] the defendant negligently drove his car into the claimant's Rolls-Royce. The front wing of the claimant's Rolls-Royce was damaged as a result. It was agreed that in order to repair the damage the whole of the lower part of the Rolls-Royce would need to be resprayed. However, at the time of the collision, the rear wing of the Rolls-Royce was already damaged and *that* damage could only be repaired by respraying the whole of the lower part of the Rolls-Royce. The Court of Appeal held that the claimant was not entitled to sue the defendant for anything by way of damages: at the time of the accident, the Rolls-Royce was already in need of a respray and carrying out that respray would, as well as repairing the damage to the rear wing of the Rolls-Royce, at the same time repair the damage done by the defendant to the front wing of the Rolls-Royce.

Destruction of property

Now suppose that A has negligently destroyed B's property. Again, we can assume that the destruction of B's property amounts to an actionable loss. How much should B be paid so as to compensate her for the fact that her property has been destroyed? The courts' answer is: B should be paid damages equal to how much it would have cost her to replace the property that was destroyed if she had obtained such a replacement at the time it was first reasonable for her to do so.[24]

DEFAMATION CASES

Suppose that A has libelled or slandered B and it is found (or presumed) that A's libel/slander caused B to suffer some damage to her reputation. This damage will of course be an actionable consequence of A's libel/slander. How do we determine how much B

[23] [1962] 1 QB 33.

[24] Though of course if the property in question was valueless to B at the time it was destroyed, then very little will be awardable in respect of its destruction.

should be paid so as to compensate her for the fact that she has suffered this damage to her reputation?

Normally a jury will have the job of determining how much B should be paid – an action for libel or slander will be tried in front of a jury if either party wishes it to be.[25] If a jury *is* given the job of determining how much B should be paid then its first problem – in the case where it is presumed that B has suffered some damage to her reputation as a result of A's libel/slander – will be to determine how much damage it is willing to presume has been done to B's reputation. Because juries do not have to justify their decisions, it is hard to tell what they take into account in doing this, but it seems to follow as a matter of common sense that the worse the libel/slander in question, the more damage it will be presumed was done to B's reputation as a result of A's publishing that libel/slander. But if B was generally of low reputation anyway, the jury will be entitled to find that little damage was done to B's reputation on the grounds that she had little reputation to lose in the first place.[26] And if only a few of the people to whom the libel/slander in question was published actually knew that it referred to B, then it can be presumed that little damage was done to B's general reputation as a result of the publication of that libel/slander.[27]

Having determined how much damage (real or presumed) was done to B's reputation as a result of the publication of A's libel/slander, the jury's next task will be to determine how much B should be paid so as to compensate her for that damage. Again, as juries do not have to justify their decisions, it is hard to know what factors a jury will take into account in determining how much the victim of a libel or slander should be paid so as to compensate her for the damage (real or presumed) that has been found to have been done to her reputation. Juries have tended to put a high value on reputation and have in the past awarded damages for loss of reputation which are far in excess of the damages that someone could hope to recover for a broken leg or the loss of an eye.

To take some examples from previous cases: Lord Aldington was awarded £1.5m by a jury when he sued the authors of a pamphlet which suggested that he had participated in a war crime at the end of the Second World War;[28] the wife of the Yorkshire Ripper was awarded £600,000 by a jury when *Private Eye* published a story which suggested that she had known of her husband's guilt before he was arrested;[29] Esther Rantzen was awarded £250,000 by a jury when the *Daily Mirror* suggested that she had knowingly shielded a child abuser from prosecution;[30] and Elton John was awarded £350,000 by a jury when the *Daily Mirror* accused him of being bulimic.[31]

[25] Though the Senior Courts Act 1981, s 69(1) provides that a jury trial should not be allowed if 'the court is of the opinion that the trial [will require] any prolonged examination of documents or accounts or any scientific or local investigation which cannot conveniently be made with a jury'.

[26] *Plato Films Ltd* v *Speidel* [1961] AC 1090. The damages payable in such a case are known as 'derisory' or 'contemptuous' (*not* 'nominal': see below, pp. 679–80) because the fact that they are so low indicates that the jury thought that the claimant had very little reputation to lose.

[27] *Morgan* v *Odhams Press* [1971] 1 WLR 1239.

[28] *Tolstoy Miloslavsky* v *United Kingdom* (1995) 20 EHRR 442 (the European Court of Human Rights held that the award – being disproportionately large – violated the authors' rights of freedom of expression under Art 10 of the European Convention on Human Rights).

[29] *Sutcliffe* v *Pressdram Ltd* [1991] 1 QB 153.

[30] *Rantzen* v *MGN (1986) Ltd* [1994] QB 670.

[31] *John* v *MGN Ltd* [1997] QB 586. Admittedly, a large proportion of this award (£275,000) was made up of exemplary damages, damages designed to punish the *Daily Mirror* for the way it acted in publishing the story about Elton John.

Both Parliament and the courts have acted on mounting concerns that juries tend to award excessive amounts to compensate the victims of libels and slanders for the damage done to their reputation. First, s 8 of the Courts and Legal Services Act 1990 gives the Court of Appeal the power to reduce a jury's award in a libel or slander case if they think it 'excessive', a power which was exercised in the *Rantzen* case (damages reduced to £110,000) and in the Elton John case (damages reduced to £50,000).[32] Secondly, in *John* v *MGN Ltd*,[33] the Court of Appeal developed the law on what guidance a trial judge could give a jury in a libel or slander case to help them in their deliberations as to what amount of damages should be awarded. The position now is that while a trial judge cannot tell the jury of awards that other juries have made in other cases, he can tell them of awards that have been approved or substituted by the Court of Appeal. He may also tell them of how much would be awarded in different kinds of personal injury case. Furthermore, he may tell them how much he thinks it might be appropriate to award for the damage done to the claimant's reputation.[34]

OTHER CASES

It is beyond the scope of this book to explain how we determine how much the victim of a tort should be paid by way of damages to compensate him for the fact that the commission of a tort has caused him to suffer some kind of loss other than the types of loss dealt with above, for example, a temporary loss of liberty. The interested reader should consult detailed works on the law of damages for such an explanation.

Visit **http://www.mylawchamber.co.uk/mcbride** to access updates on recent cases, as well as model answers and tips for answering tort problem questions.

[32] The decision of the Court of Appeal in *Kiam* v *MGN Ltd* [2003] QB 281 provides the latest guidance as to when the courts will exercise this power. The following points emerge from the decision in that case: (1) The question of whether an award was 'excessive' will be determined by asking whether 'a reasonable jury could have thought the award necessary to compensate the claimant and re-establish his reputation' (ibid., at [48], per Simon Brown LJ). (2) The fact that a claimant in a libel case has been made an award which is much greater than he might be awarded were he to suffer a serious physical injury does not necessarily indicate that it is 'excessive' (ibid., at [60], per Waller LJ; see also *The Gleaner Co. Ltd* v *Abrahams* [2004] 1 AC 628, at [50]–[56], per Lord Hoffmann). (3) In judging whether an award is 'excessive' the courts should show great deference to the decision of the jury ([2003] QB 281, at [53], per Simon Brown LJ; and [60], per Waller LJ). (4) Even if an award is judged to be 'excessive', it should only be set aside if it 'substantially [exceeds] the most that any jury could reasonably have thought appropriate' (ibid., at [49], per Simon Brown LJ).

[33] [1997] QB 586.

[34] Ibid., 611–16.

30 Reduction in liability

We are concerned in this chapter with the situation where A has committed a tort in relation to B and B is entitled to sue A for compensatory damages. Let's say that A's *prima facie* measure of liability in this case is £10,000 – that is, other things being equal, B will be entitled to sue A for £10,000 in compensatory damages. In certain situations, the damages payable to B will be reduced below this level. In this chapter we explain what those situations are.

RECEIPT OF BENEFIT

If, in the situation, we are considering, B obtained some kind of benefit as a result of A's tort, the damages payable to B by A may be reduced to take account of that fact.[1] However, it is important to emphasise that the damages payable *may* be reduced: they will not always be. It is hard to formulate a principle which will tell us when a benefit that has been received by the victim of a tort as a result of that tort being committed will be taken into account in determining the damages payable to the victim. Perhaps all that can be said is that receipt of a benefit by the victim of a tort as a result of that tort being committed will operate to reduce the damages payable to the victim unless there is a good reason why the damages payable should not be reduced.

Situations where the receipt of a benefit will be taken into account

In the following situations, the fact that the victim of a tort received some benefit as a result of that tort being committed will be taken into account in assessing the damages payable to him or her.

Savings on food and other necessities

Suppose that Dawn negligently injured Eric, with the result that Eric had to stay for a few weeks in a private hospital, having his injuries treated. Suppose further that while he was in the hospital, the hospital provided him with meals. Dawn will of course be *prima facie*

[1] There is a difficult line to be drawn between this kind of case and cases where we determine how much of a loss has been suffered by B as a result of A's tort. For example, suppose B was employed on a job which paid £50,000 a year when she was negligently injured by A. As a result, B had to leave her job and obtained alternative employment which paid a salary of £30,000 a year. No one would treat this as a reduction of liability case – that is, no one would say that A is *prima facie* liable to compensate B for the fact that she no longer earns £50,000 a year but A's liability is reduced to take account of the fact that as a result of A's negligence, B is now earning £30,000 a year. Instead, we simply say that B has suffered and will suffer in the future a drop in salary of £20,000 a year for which loss A is *prima facie* liable to compensate her. It is hard to see why this isn't treated as a reduction of liability case – but the convention is to treat it as a quantification of loss case.

liable to pay Eric a sum sufficient to compensate him for the medical bills he has incurred in being treated.

However, in this situation Dawn's negligence will have resulted in Eric receiving a benefit: while he was in hospital, he did not have to buy his own food. Dawn's liability will be reduced to take account of this saving that Eric has made.[2] So suppose that Eric's medical bills came to £10,000; but in the time Eric was in hospital, he would have spent £500 on buying food for himself. On these figures, Dawn will only be liable to pay Eric £9,500 in compensatory damages – Dawn's *prima facie* liability to pay Eric £10,000 in damages will be reduced to take account of the fact that Eric saved £500 that he would otherwise have spent on buying food for himself while he was in hospital.[3]

The same point will apply if, had Eric not been in hospital, he would have spent money on necessities that were provided by the hospital, such as washing Eric's clothes. The damages payable to Eric will be reduced to take account of this saving.

Compensation payments from other defendants liable in tort

Suppose that A committed a tort in relation to B and B suffered losses worth £10,000 as a result of that tort being committed. Suppose further that C was also liable *in tort* to compensate B for the fact that she suffered these losses. Suppose finally that C made a compensation payment to B – that is, a payment designed to compensate B in full or in part for the losses that she suffered in this situation.[4] In this situation the damages payable by A to B will be reduced: the compensation payment will count as a benefit that B received as a result of A's tort.

The difficult question is by how much A's liability to B will be reduced. Obviously, if C's compensation payment to B came to £10,000, then A will not be liable to pay B anything. B will be fully compensated for the losses that she suffered as a result of A's tort and will therefore not be entitled to sue A for anything.[5] But what if C's compensation payment came to only £7,000? The normal rule is that B will be entitled to sue A for £3,000 – the balance of the uncompensated loss that she suffered as a result of A's tort. However, there are two situations in which C's compensation payment to B of £7,000 will have the effect of extinguishing *entirely* A's liability to B.

(1) *Joint liability.* It used to be the case that if A and C were *jointly liable*[6] to compensate B for the losses suffered by her, then C's compensation payment to B would have had the effect of discharging A's liability to B. However, the position nowadays is a bit more complicated.

2 *Shearman* v *Folland* [1950] 2 KB 43.

3 Of course, Eric's medical bills will almost certainly include a charge for the food Eric received while he was in hospital but that is immaterial. At the same time as Eric was paying the hospital for the food that the hospital served him, he was saving money which he would have spent had Dawn not injured him on buying food for himself.

4 The payment could have been made either in order to settle B's claims against C or because a court ordered C to make that payment to B.

5 However, C will be entitled to make a claim in contribution against A, forcing A to shoulder a 'just and equitable' share of the burden of compensating B for the losses she has suffered: see above, pp. 24–5.

6 *Important note.* A and C will be *jointly* liable in respect of the losses suffered by B *if*: (1) C is liable as an accessory for A's tort because he persuaded or authorised A to commit that tort with the result that C is regarded as having committed A's tort and is liable to compensate B for the losses suffered by her as a result of A's tort (see below, pp. 644–6); *or* (2) C is vicariously liable for A's tort, with the result that C is treated as though he committed A's tort and is liable to compensate B for the losses suffered by her as a result of A's tort (see below,

If C's compensation payment was made because B won a judgment against C, then C's payment will not have the effect of extinguishing B's rights to sue A for compensation: A will therefore be liable to pay B £3,000 in damages.[7] If, on the other hand, C's compensation payment was made to B under a settlement that he reached with B, then the old rule will apply – and A's liability to B will be extinguished – *unless* B's settlement with C preserved her rights to sue A for damages in respect of the losses suffered by her:[8] in which case, A will again be liable to pay B £3,000 in damages.

(2) *Payment treated by the claimant as fully compensating her.* Even if A and C were *jointly and severally* liable to compensate B for the losses suffered by her, C's compensation payment to B will have the effect of extinguishing A's liability to B if B treated C's payment of £7,000 to her as fully compensating her for the losses she has suffered.[9]

Redundancy payments

Suppose that Fred negligently injured Ruth and as a result Ruth was unable to continue in her job and was made redundant. Any redundancy payment received by Ruth on leaving her job will operate to reduce the damages payable by Fred to Ruth.[10]

---

pp. 647–73). If neither of these conditions are satisfied then A and C will be *jointly and severally* liable to compensate B for the losses suffered by her. An example of joint and several liability is provided by *The Koursk* [1924] P 140. In that case, two ships – the *Clan Chisholm* and the *Koursk* – collided with each other. The collision occurred as a result of the negligence of both the owners of the *Clan Chisholm* and the negligence of the defendants, the owners of the *Koursk*. As a result of the collision, the *Clan Chisholm* collided with the claimants' vessel, the *Itria*, which sank. In this case the owners of the *Clan Chisholm* and the defendants, the owners of the *Koursk*, were each liable in tort to compensate the claimants for the loss of the *Itria*: each of them committed the tort of negligence in relation to the claimants and the *Itria* would not been sunk had not each of them been negligent. However, as their negligent acts were unconnected, the owners of the *Clan Chisholm* and the defendants were not *jointly* liable to compensate the owners of the *Itria* for the loss of the *Itria*; they were jointly an severally liable. So when the owners of the *Clan Chisholm* made a compensation payment to the owners of the *Itria*, that did not have the effect of extinguishing the liability of the defendants to the owners of the *Itria*. The defendants were still liable to compensate the owners of the *Itria* for the balance of the uncompensated loss that they had suffered as a result of the sinking of the *Itria*.

7 Civil Liability (Contribution) Act 1978, s 3: 'Judgment recovered against any person liable in respect of any . . . damage shall not be a bar to an action . . . against any other person who is . . . jointly liable with him in respect of the same . . . damage.'

8 *Gardiner* v *Moore* [1969] 1 QB 55.

9 *Jameson* v *CEGB* [2000] 1 AC 455. That case concerned the following situation. A and C each committed a tort in relation to B and B was injured as a result. A and C were *jointly and severally* liable to compensate B for that injury. A made a compensation payment to B which did not have the effect of fully compensating B for that injury but was treated by both parties as fully compensating B for his injury. B then died of his injury and B's widow brought an action against C for loss of support under the Fatal Accidents Act 1976, arguing that C committed a tort that caused B to die and at the time B died, he was entitled to sue C for compensation in respect of the injury suffered by him as a result of C's tort. Now: if C were held liable to compensate B for her loss of support here, he would have been entitled to bring a claim in contribution against A, thereby making A shoulder some of the burden of compensating B's widow for her loss of support. It was thought that this would be unfair on A because A had already made a compensation payment to B and that payment would not be taken into account in assessing the damages payable to B's widow to compensate her for the loss of support she had experienced. (Although that compensation payment passed to B's widow on B's death, s 4 of the Fatal Accidents Act 1976 provides that 'In assessing damages in respect of a person's death in an action under this Act, benefits which have accrued . . . to any person from his estate . . . as a result of his death will be disregarded.') In order to avoid this unfairness, it was held that A's compensation payment to B had had the effect of extinguishing B's rights to sue C for compensation in respect of his injury because A's payment was treated by B as fully compensating him for his injury. The decision is hardly principled and as a result may not survive being tested in the courts.

10 *Colledge* v *Bass Mitchells & Butlers Ltd* [1988] 1 All ER 536.

Social security payments

Suppose that Carl negligently injured Beth and Beth was incapacitated as a result. Suppose that as a result of her being incapacitated, Beth received quite a lot of money in social security payments. The Social Security (Recovery of Benefits) Act 1997 establishes that the social security payments that Beth received as a result of her being incapacitated in the first *five* years after Carl injured her will be taken into account in determining the damages payable to Beth; however, any subsequent social security payments will be disregarded. At first sight, the Act seems to work in Carl's favour. However, the Act also provides that if Carl makes a compensation payment to Beth, he will be liable to compensate the State for *all* the social security payments that Beth received as a result of her being incapacitated in the first five years after Carl injured her. This can cause injustice if Carl is not wholly to blame for the fact that Beth was injured.

Situations where the receipt of a benefit will not be taken into account

There are many situations where the damages payable to the victim of a tort will *not* be reduced even though she received a benefit as a result of that tort being committed.

Gifts

Suppose that Sarah negligently injured Tom and as a result Tom was laid up for a while. Tom's friend, Nita, heard his bad news and sent him £100 'to help you out until you are back on your feet'. Nita's gift will *not* have the effect of reducing the damages payable to Tom by £100. There are two reasons for this.

First, if the damages payable to Tom *were* reduced, then Nita's gift would end up benefiting Sarah and not Tom. As Nita intended her gift to be for Tom's sole benefit, this would be unfair. Secondly, if the damages payable to people like Tom were reduced to take account of any gifts that he received as a result of being injured, then people like Nita would be discouraged from helping out people like Tom: if Nita knew any gift she gave Tom would simply benefit Sarah and not Tom, she would see little point in making a donation.[11]

Insurance payments

In *Bradburn* v *Great Western Railway Co.*,[12] the defendant railway company's negligence caused the claimant to be injured while he was travelling on the defendants' line. The claimant sued the defendants for compensatory damages. Compensation for the actionable losses suffered by the claimant as a result of his injuries was assessed at £217. However, the claimant had received, on account of his injuries, £31 from his insurance company, the Accidental Insurance Company. The question was whether the claimant was entitled to recover £217 or (£217 − £31 =) £186 in compensatory damages from the defendants. It was held that even though the £31 received by the claimant was a benefit which he received as a result of the defendants' negligence – had the defendants not been negligent he would

[11] See *Parry* v *Cleaver* [1970] AC 1, 14A–D (per Lord Reid).
[12] (1874) LR 10 Ex 1.

never have received that £31 – the claimant was still entitled to recover £217 from the defendants in compensatory damages.[13]

Why didn't the court hold that the claimant could only sue the defendants for £186? The reason is that had they done this all the premiums paid by the claimant on his insurance policy with the Accidental Insurance Company would have gone to waste. He would have obtained no benefit from them. Instead, the defendants would have been the ones who benefited from the insurance premiums paid by the claimant. As the claimant paid those premiums for his benefit and not for the benefit of anyone else, this would have been unfair. As Asquith LJ remarked in *Shearman* v *Folland*: 'If the wrongdoer were entitled to set-off what the wrongdoer was entitled to recoup or had recouped under his policy, he would, in effect, be depriving the claimant of all benefit from the premiums paid by the latter and appropriating that benefit to himself.'[14]

Three points may be made about this. First, there could have been no objection if the Court in *Bradburn* had held that the claimant would only be entitled to recover £186 in compensatory damages from the defendants *if* the defendants repaid all the premiums paid by the claimant on his insurance policy with the Accidental Insurance Company.[15] However, it probably did not occur to the court to decide the *Bradburn* case in this way.

Secondly, what would have been the position if the *defendants* had paid the insurance premiums on the claimant's insurance policy with the Accidental Insurance Company? Say, for example, that the claimant had been an employee of the defendants and they had taken out the insurance policy for his benefit to protect him against the risk of being killed or injured while he worked for them. Recent authority indicates that if this had been the case, then the claimant would have been limited to suing the defendants for £186.[16] This is quite right: in the case just described, no injustice would have been done to anyone if the defendants had been allowed to take advantage of the premiums paid on the claimant's insurance policy – after all, they paid those premiums in the first place.

Thirdly, what would have been the position if someone other than the claimant or the defendants – call him John – had paid the premiums on his insurance policy with the Accidental Insurance Company for him? If this had been the case, should the court have held that the claimant could only sue the defendants for £186? Subsequent authorities seem

13 The claimant – having obtained those damages – would have been entitled to keep the damages for himself. What is the position if A negligently destroys B's property, B obtains the value of the property from his property insurer, and then sues A for damages equal to the value of the property? B will be entitled to recover the full value of the property from A – for the reasons set out below, the damages payable to B will not be reduced to take account of the insurance payment that B has already obtained in respect of the destruction of his property – but B's insurance company will then have a charge over those damages for the value of the insurance money it paid out to B: *Lord Napier and Ettrick* v *Hunter* [1993] AC 713. The reason why B's insurance company will have a charge over the damages is to prevent double recovery. (For the same reason, if A tortiously causes B to suffer some kind of pure economic loss that B was insured against, B will be entitled to claim on her insurance policy but will then hold any damages obtained against A subject to a charge for the insurance company.) The reason why contracts of insurance against physical injury – such as the contract of insurance in *Bradburn* – are 'different' is that the concern to prevent double recovery will not apply in the cases where a claimant suffers physical injury as a result of someone's committing a tort in relation to her. The courts acknowledge that it is impossible to determine what would amount to an 'adequate' level of compensation for the physical injury suffered by the claimant – so people should be left free to insure their persons so as to 'boost' the amount of money they will be able to recover if someone physically injures them.

14 [1950] 2 KB 43, 46.

15 *Bristol & West Building Society* v *May, May & Merrimans (No. 2)* [1998] 1 WLR 336, 356.

16 *Gaca* v *Pirelli General plc* [2004] 1 WLR 2683.

to say that the answer to this question is 'yes'.[17] However, it is more complex than that. We can imagine two variations on the situation we are now imagining obtained in *Bradburn*, where John paid the insurance premiums on the claimant's policy with the Accidental Insurance Company. In the first case, John intended, when he paid the premiums, that the claimant and no one else should get the benefit of those premiums. If this had been the case, it would have been unfair – unfair on John – for the court to allow the defendants to take advantage of the payment of those premiums and hold that the claimant was only entitled to recover £186 in compensatory damages from the defendants. The right decision would have been to hold that the claimant could sue the defendants for £217. In the second case, John paid the premiums because he was contractually obliged to do so under an arrangement with the claimant – say John was the claimant's employer – and, in paying the premiums, had no intention one way or the other as to who should benefit from the payment of those premiums. If this had been the case, it would *not* have been unfair for the court to allow the defendants to take advantage of the payment of those premiums and hold that the claimant could sue the defendants for £186. Given this, that is what the court should have held.

Pension payments[18]

In *Parry* v *Cleaver*,[19] the claimant was prevented from carrying on working as a police constable as a result of injuries he sustained in a traffic accident caused by the defendant's negligence. At the time of the accident the claimant was 35 years old and had worked as a police constable for 12 years. Throughout his time in the force the claimant had made a weekly contribution to the police pension fund. On being invalided out of the force, the claimant obtained an invalidity pension of £204 a year. It was found that had the claimant not been injured, he would have continued working as a police constable until the age of 48 and would then have retired on a pension of £515 a year and found work in the civilian sector. As it was, the claimant's injury meant he had to find work in the civilian sector at the age of 35 and he did not receive a retirement pension at all.

So the defendant's negligence caused the claimant to suffer two losses: (1) the loss of the extra money the claimant would have earned net of tax between the ages of 35 and 48 had he continued working for the police and not been forced to work in the civilian sector (say this loss was worth £5,000); (2) the loss of the extra pension money the claimant would have received from the age of 48 until the end of his life had he not been invalided out of the police force (this was worth £311 a year: the difference between the retirement pension that the claimant would have received had he stayed on in the police force until he was 48 and the invalidity pension that the claimant actually did receive as a result of being invalided out of the police force).

However, the defendant's negligence also meant that the claimant would receive a benefit between the ages of 35 and 48: an invalidity pension payment of £204 a year. Had the defendant not been negligent, the claimant would not have received that payment. The House of Lords held that this benefit should not be taken into account in determining the

[17] *Hussain* v *New Taplow Paper Mills* [1988] 1 AC 514, 527G–H; *Hodgson* v *Trapp* [1989] 1 AC 807, 819H; *Bristol & West Building Society* v *May, May & Merrimans (No. 2)* [1998] 1 WLR 336, 358–9.

[18] See Lewis 1999, 81–6.

[19] [1970] AC 1.

damages payable to the claimant, on the ground that if it were then the claimant would lose the benefit of his 12 years' worth of contributions to the police pension fund that he made before he was injured.[20]

Parry v *Cleaver* was followed in *Smoker* v *London Fire Authority*.[21] In that case, the claimant was employed as a firefighter by the defendants. Under the terms of his employment, he was a member of a pension scheme to which he contributed approximately 11 per cent of his wages. The defendants contributed twice as much as the claimant towards his pension. In 1985 the claimant was disabled as a result of the defendants' negligence and his disability meant he had to retire from the force in December 1985. Had the defendants not been negligent, the claimant would have continued to work as a firefighter until December 1987, when he was due to retire.

The defendants' negligence therefore resulted in the claimant suffering a loss of income: the money the claimant would have earned in the two years between December 1985 and December 1987 had he been allowed to continue to work for the defendants. This loss was worth about £13,500. At the same time the defendants' negligence resulted in the claimant obtaining a benefit during those two years. The claimant received about £10,000 in invalidity pension payments in the two years between December 1985 and December 1987. These payments were made out of the claimant's pension scheme in consideration of the contributions that he and the defendants made to that pension scheme.

The House of Lords held, following *Parry* v *Cleaver*, that the invalidity pension payments made to the claimant between December 1985 and December 1987 were not to be taken into account in calculating the damages payable to the claimant. So the claimant was entitled to recover £13,500 in compensatory damages from the defendants in respect of the loss of income suffered by him between December 1985 and December 1987: no deduction would be made to take account of the fact that the claimant had in fact received a benefit of about £10,000 in invalidity pension payments as a result of the defendants' negligence during those two years. This decision can be criticised. The pension payments that the claimant received between December 1985 and December 1987 could be split into two. One third of those payments (approximately £3,300) were attributable to the contributions that the claimant made to his pension scheme. Two thirds (approximately £6,700) were attributable to the contributions that the defendants made to the claimant's pension scheme.

Now it might be conceded that the £3,300 that the claimant received in pension payments between December 1985 and December 1987 and that were attributable to the claimant's contributions to his pension scheme should not have been taken into account in determining the damages payable to the claimant, on the ground that if they were that would be unfair on the claimant. However, it would not have been unfair – on the claimant or the defendants – to deduct the remaining pension payments, that were attributable to

[20] This is not quite true. The claimant was allowed to sue the defendant for the extra pension money he would have received after the age of 48 had he not been invalided out of the police force and that extra pension money would have been payable in part because of the 12 years' worth of contributions that the claimant made to the police pension fund. So the claimant would still have obtained something for those 12 years' worth of contributions even if the damages payable to him had been reduced to take account of the invalidity pension payments he was going to receive between the ages of 35 and 48 as a result of the defendant's negligence.

[21] [1991] 2 AC 502.

the *defendants*' contributions to the claimant's pension scheme, from the damages payable to the claimant.

The House of Lords recognised the strength of this point in the case of *Hussain* v *New Taplow Paper Mills Ltd*.[22] In that case the claimant was injured in an accident due to the negligence of the defendants, his employers, and was unable, due to his injuries, to continue working for the defendants. For 15 months after the accident, the defendants continued to pay the claimant his full pay – even though he was not doing any work for them – under their 'permanent health insurance scheme'. This scheme was paid for by the defendants: the defendants' employees, including the claimant, made no contribution to this scheme. The claimant sued the defendants in negligence for damages to compensate him for the loss of income that he had suffered as a result of the defendants' negligence.

The House of Lords held that the health insurance payments that the claimant had received for 15 months after he had stopped work should be taken into account in determining the damages payable to the claimant. The House of Lords held that deducting these payments from the damages payable to the claimant would not be unfair on the claimant. The claimant could not claim that making such a deduction would result in him receiving no benefit from the contributions he had made to the defendants' health insurance scheme: the claimant made no such contributions.

Windfall payments

In *Needler Financial Services Ltd* v *Taber*,[23] the defendants negligently advised the claimant to switch pension schemes. The claimant did so and lost out as a result: the pension scheme that he switched into (with the Norwich Union) was not as profitable as his original pension scheme. He sued the defendants for damages. The defendants admitted liability but claimed that the damages payable to the claimant should be reduced because the claimant received a windfall payment of about £7,800 when the Norwich Union demutualised. Sir Andrew Morritt V-C held that this benefit – which the claimant had received as a result of the defendants' negligent advice – should *not* be taken into account in determining the damages payable to the claimant. It is hard to understand why it should not have been. However, one possible explanation is that the claimant might have already spent the windfall payment that he received from the Norwich Union. If he had, then taking that windfall payment into account in determining the damages payable to the claimant would have made him, through no fault of his own, worse off overall – which would have been unfair to the claimant.

Gains made through the exercise of skill and judgment

In *Hussey* v *Eels*[24] the defendants fraudulently induced the claimants to buy their house. The house was, to the defendants' knowledge, affected by subsidence but the defendants told the claimants that to their knowledge the property had not been subject to subsidence. The claimants purchased the defendants' house for approximately £53,000. The true value of the house was about £36,000 as repairing it would have cost in excess of £17,000. So the

[22] [1988] 1 AC 514.
[23] [2002] 3 All ER 501.
[24] [1990] 2 QB 227.

defendants' fraud caused the claimants to lose £17,(
covered the problem with subsidence, then began t
to have the house repaired. Instead, they demolish(
build two bungalows on the vacant plot. This was
land to a developer with the planning permission

So – having initially lost £17,000, the claimants
of £42,500 on selling the land on which their h(
£78,500 in return for an asset which was origin
claimants then sued the defendants for the origina
defendants' house. The defendants claimed that tl
on selling the land on which the house was built
the damages payable to the claimants. So in effect
liable to the claimants at all. The Court of Appea
quite right: had the claimants' profit been taken into account, ...
they did in improving the value of their land would have redounded to the benefit of the defendants. So the defendants were correctly held liable to pay the claimants £17,000 in damages.

Psychic benefits

In *Wise* v *Kaye*, Sellers LJ remarked that: 'The complete loss of sight may bring, and I think often does, a serenity and calm of life which might lead to a happiness hitherto unknown, but I cannot think that a defendant is entitled to pray that in aid in order to reduce the damages he has to pay to the sufferer. [Similarly if] [i]nfirmity which cripples and incapacitates a man ... [brings] him a sympathy and attention which reveals in him an inward comfort which he has never previously known [making him] happier than he has ever been.'[25]

CONTRIBUTORY NEGLIGENCE

Section 1(1) of the Law Reform (Contributory Negligence) Act 1945 provides that where 'any person suffers damage as the result partly of his own fault and partly of the fault of any other person or persons ... the damages recoverable in respect thereof shall be reduced to such extent as the court thinks just and equitable having regard to the claimant's share in the responsibility of the damage'. Section 4 of the 1945 Act provides that '"fault" means negligence, breach of statutory duty or other act or omission which gives rise to liability in tort or would, apart from this Act, give rise to a defence of contributory negligence'.

The basic effect of the 1945 Act is this. Suppose A has committed a tort in relation to B. Suppose further that B suffered losses worth £50,000 as a result of A's tort and she wants to sue A for compensation in respect of those losses. A will usually have a defence of *contributory negligence* to B's claim if B was partly to blame for the fact that she suffered the losses that she has suffered.[26] B will be partly to blame for the fact that she suffered those losses if

[25] [1962] 1 QB 638, 651.

[26] Although the defence is known as the defence of *contributory negligence*, there is no reason to think that the defence will not be available in the case where B *deliberately* did something that resulted in her suffering the losses that she suffered as a result of A's tort. In such a case, the losses suffered by B will still be partly her fault.

ed those losses had she not acted unreasonably[27] in some way.[28] e of a defence of contributory negligence in meeting B's claim, the B will be reduced to take account of the fact that B was partly to blame he suffered those losses. So B will not be able to claim £50,000 from A by es: she will only be entitled to claim some lesser amount.

er of points need to be made about the scope and effect of the defence of con-y negligence.[29]

Assessment of reduction: two-party cases. If A has committed a tort in relation to B but can raise a defence of contributory negligence to reduce the damages payable to B in respect of the losses suffered by B as a result of A's tort, the courts determine by how much the damages payable to B should be reduced by assessing the *comparative blameworthiness* of A and B for the losses suffered by B. So if they were equally to blame for the fact that B suffered those losses, the damages payable will be reduced by 50 per cent;[30] if A was four times as much to blame as B for the losses suffered by B, the damages will be reduced by 20 per cent.[31]

(2) *Assessment of reduction: three-party cases.* The position is a bit more complicated in a case which involves two tortfeasors. Suppose that A and B each committed a tort in relation to C and C suffered various losses as result but C was partly to blame for the fact that he suffered those losses. We determine by how much the damages payable to C should be reduced by lumping A and B together and asking: as compared to C, how much to blame were A and B *together* for the losses suffered by C?

The House of Lords ruled that the defence of contributory negligence would cover cases where a victim of a tort's deliberate act contributed to her suffering the losses she did in *Reeves* v *Commissioner of Police of the Metropolis* [2000] 1 AC 360, at 370 (per Lord Hoffmann), 377 (per Lord Jauncey), 383 (per Lord Hope), 385 (per Lord Hobhouse).

27 *Important note.* In judging whether B acted reasonably, one asks whether a reasonable person of B's age (*Yachuk* v *Oliver Blais Co. Ltd* [1949] AC 386; *Gough* v *Thorne* [1966] 1 WLR 1387) and in B's physical condition (*Daly* v *Liverpool Corporation* [1939] 2 All ER 142) would have acted in the way B did. Although there is authority to the contrary (*Baxter* v *Woolcombers Ltd* (1963) 107 SJ 553), it is hard to believe that B's mental condition will not also be taken into account in judging whether B acted unreasonably – so that if a reasonable person with B's mental condition would have acted in the same way, B will *not* be found to have acted unreasonably. So, for example, if B kills himself while in police custody because he is mentally ill, it would not be appropriate to reduce any damages payable to B's dependants for contributory negligence. (So far as we know, no such reduction has ever been made in a case where a mentally ill person killed himself in police custody.)

28 Of course if A's tort only resulted in B suffering the losses she did because B deliberately and unreasonably did *x after* A committed his tort then B will usually be *barred* from suing A for damages in respect of those losses, either on the ground that B's deliberate and unreasonable act broke the chain of causation between A's tort and the losses suffered by B or on the ground that B had a duty to mitigate the losses suffered by her as a result of A's tort and she only suffered the losses she did because she breached that duty. So A will only really need to take advantage of the defence of contributory negligence in the following cases: (1) where B only suffered the losses she did because B did something unreasonable *before* A committed his tort; (2) where B only suffered the losses she did because she did something unreasonable *after* A committed his tort but she did not act deliberately when she acted as she did; (3) where B only suffered the losses she did because she deliberately did something unreasonable *after* A committed his tort but there is some policy reason why B's act should not be held to have broken the chain of causation between A's tort and B's suffering those losses.

29 On which, see, generally, Gravells 1977.

30 The deduction made in *Reeves* v *Commissioner of Police of the Metropolis* [2000] 1 AC 360 (prisoner took advantage of defendants' negligence to commit suicide).

31 The deduction made in *Froom* v *Butcher* [1976] QB 286 (claimant's failure to wear seat belt contributed to the injuries she suffered in car accident caused by defendant's negligence).

So in *Fitzgerald* v *Lane*,[32] the claimant walked across a road when the lights were against him. He was struck by a motor car being negligently driven by the first defendant. While he was lying in the road he was struck by a motor car which was negligently driven by the second defendant. It was held that the first defendant and second defendant both caused the claimant to suffer the injuries he suffered as a result of the second collision[33] and so the claimant was entitled to sue either the first defendant or the second defendant or both for compensation for the fact that he received those injuries. However, the claimant was partly to blame for the fact that he suffered those injuries: he would not have suffered those injuries had he not acted unreasonably by walking across the road when the lights were against him. Given this, the damages payable to the claimant were liable to be reduced for contributory negligence. It was found that the claimant in this case was twice as much to blame as each of the defendants for the injuries that he suffered in the second collision. It followed that he was just as much to blame for the injuries that he suffered as the two defendants *together*. The damages payable to the claimant were therefore reduced by 50 per cent.

(3) *One-hundred per cent reduction?* Could the defence of contributory negligence have the effect of reducing the damages payable to the victim of a tort to *zero*? The Court of Appeal doubted in *Pitts* v *Hunt*[34] whether the 1945 Act could ever have this effect. After all, if A has committed a tort in relation to B and B has suffered various losses as a result, it is hard to imagine that B could ever be 100 per cent to blame for the fact that she suffered those losses – after all they were triggered in part by A's committing a tort.

However, in *Reeves* v *Commissioner of Police of the Metropolis*, one judge in the Court of Appeal found that a prisoner who hanged himself while in the custody of the police was 100 per cent to blame for his death and held as a result that if the prisoner had survived his suicide attempt, he would not have been entitled to sue the police for anything.[35] When *Reeves* went to the House of Lords, their Lordships found that the police and the prisoner were equally to blame for the prisoner's death and accordingly reduced the damages payable to the prisoner's dependants by 50 per cent.[36] But they did not go so far as to say that it would never be possible to find that the victim of a tort was 100 per cent to blame for the losses that she suffered as a result of that tort being committed. The point must therefore be regarded as still open to argument.

(4) *Torts to which the defence is inapplicable.* The defence of contributory negligence will not be available in *all* cases where A commits a tort in relation to B and B suffers losses as

[32] [1989] AC 328.

[33] How was it that the *first* defendant's negligence caused the claimant to suffer the injuries that he suffered in the *second* collision? The claimant would not have suffered those injuries but for the first defendant's negligence and the second defendant's negligence did not break the chain of causation between the first defendant's negligence and the injuries suffered by the claimant in the second collision: while the second defendant acted unreasonably in running over the claimant, he did not *deliberately* run over the claimant. He was careless, not malicious.

[34] [1991] 2 QB 24.

[35] [1999] QB 169, 195 (per Morritt LJ). Of the other two judges, Buxton LJ did not think the defence of contributory negligence was available (ibid., 182–3), and Lord Bingham CJ thought that the damages payable should be reduced by 50%, but in order to produce a result with which at least two members of the court agreed, he held that the damages payable should not be reduced at all (ibid., 198).

[36] [2000] 1 AC 360.

a result for which B was partly to blame. If the tort committed by A was conversion or amounted to an intentional trespass to B's goods, then the defence will not apply;[37] nor will it if the tort committed by A was deceit[38] or involved dishonesty of any kind[39] (as will be the case if the tort committed by A was conspiracy or inducing a breach of contract). In *Standard Chartered Bank* v *Pakistan National Shipping Corporation (Nos 2 and 4)*, Lord Rodger of Earlsferry stated that 'contributory negligence [has] never been a defence open to a defendant who . . . intended to harm the [claimant]'.[40] However, this may be too wide.

(5) *Contributory negligence and* Hedley Byrne. Two problems need to be addressed under this heading. First, will a defendant who has breached a duty of care owed to another under one of the principles in *Hedley Byrne* be entitled to rely on the defence of contributory negligence to reduce the damages payable to that other? Secondly, if he is, how does the defence of contributory negligence interact with the limit placed by the *SAAMCO* principle on what damages can be sued for in a *Hedley Byrne* case?

On the first question, suppose that A advised B that a car that she was thinking of buying was in good condition and that he indicated to her that she could safely rely on his advice. Suppose further that she did rely on A's advice and bought the car. However, the car later proved to be so defective that it was not worth repairing and had to be given away to some scrap metal merchants. If B sues A in negligence, can A attempt to raise a defence of contributory negligence to B's claim on the basis that she was partly to blame for the fact that she lost the money she spent on the car because it was very foolish of her to rely on his advice? It is unlikely that A would be allowed to make such an argument.[41] Having earlier indicated to B that she could safely rely on his advice, it is likely that A would be prevented (estopped) from subsequently arguing that B was foolish to rely on his advice for the purpose of raising a defence of contributory negligence to her claim for damages.

However, if the *extent* of the losses suffered by B as a result of acting on A's advice was partly B's fault, then there is no reason why A should not be allowed to raise a defence of contributory negligence to reduce the damages payable to B. This was what happened in *Platform Home Loans* v *Oyston Shipways Ltd*,[42] a case which also dealt with the interaction between the *SAAMCO* principle and the defence of contributory negligence. Simplifying the facts of the case slightly, the claimant lent £1m to a Mr Hussain secured by a mortgage of Hussain's home. The home was negligently valued by the defendant as being worth £1.5m: it was in fact worth only £1m. Four years later, Hussain defaulted on repaying the loan and the claimant sought to recoup the money he had lent by selling Hussain's house,

[37] Section 11 of the Torts (Interference with Goods) Act 1977 provides that 'Contributory negligence is no defence in proceedings founded on conversion, or on intentional trespass to goods.'

[38] *Alliance & Leicester Building Society* v *Edgestop Ltd* [1993] 1 WLR 1462; *Standard Chartered Bank* v *Pakistan National Shipping Corporation (Nos 2 and 4)* [2003] 1 AC 959.

[39] *Corporacion Nacional de Cobre* v *Sogemin* [1997] 1 WLR 1396.

[40] [2003] 1 AC 959, at [45], querying whether Lord Denning MR was right to think in *Murphy* v *Culhane* [1977] QB 94 that the defence would be available in a case where A beat B up in response to provocation from B (ibid., at 98–9).

[41] See *Gran Gelato Ltd* v *Richcliff (Group) Ltd* [1992] Ch 560, 574 (per Sir Donald Nicholls V-C), doubting whether the damages payable to a claimant in a *Hedley Byrne* case could be reduced for contributory negligence where it was alleged that the claimant was contributorily negligent because she should not have done the very thing that she was advised to do by the defendant.

[42] [2000] 2 AC 190.

which was worth only £400,000 at that stage. So the claimant lost £600,000 as a result of the defendant's negligence.[43] But two points complicated the case.

The first was that under the *SAAMCO* principle, the defendant should only have been entitled to sue the claimant for £500,000 – that was the loss which the defendant had suffered that was attributable to the fact that it had loaned money to Hussain on inadequate security.[44] The second point was that the claimant was – as compared with the defendant – 20 per cent to blame for the fact that he lost the money he did on the loan to Hussain. The reasons for this were: (1) he had failed to check whether or not Hussain was a credit risk; and (2) he had loaned Hussain more than was reasonable given the defendant's valuation of Hussain's house. So the defendant was entitled to raise a defence of contributory negligence to reduce the damages that he had to pay the claimant.

The problem faced by the courts in the *Platform Home Loans* case was – how did these two points relate to each other? Do you say that the defendant was *prima facie* liable to pay the claimant £600,000, deduct 20 per cent for contributory negligence, turning the defendant's liability into one to pay the claimant £480,000, and then allow the claimant to claim for the whole of that on the basis that doing so would not violate the *SAAMCO* principle (under which the most the claimant could have sued the defendant for was £500,000)? Or do you say that the *SAAMCO* principle means that the defendant was *prima facie* liable to pay the claimant £500,000 and then knock 20 per cent off *that* figure, turning the defendant's liability into one to pay the claimant £400,000? The Court of Appeal preferred the latter approach;[45] but the House of Lords ruled that the former approach was correct. In so doing, the House of Lords reinterpreted the *SAAMCO* principle as one which does not determine *which* of the losses suffered by a claimant in a *Hedley Byrne* case can be sued for by that claimant, but as one which places a 'cap' on the potential liability of a defendant to a claimant in a *Hedley Byrne* case. It is, however, doubtful whether that interpretation of the *SAAMCO* principle is reconcilable with the reasons for its adoption by Lord Hoffmann in the *SAAMCO* case.

(6) *Contributory negligence and* White v Jones. Suppose that A asked C to prepare a will for him under which B would inherit £9,000. C prepared the will but only had one person witness A's signing the will, thus making the will invalid. A – who had some knowledge of the law relating to wills – thought that more than one witness was required but did not raise any objections because he thought C 'knew best'. Shortly afterwards, A died and his will was declared to be invalid with the result that B did not receive her legacy. B will, of course, be able to sue C for damages under the principle in *White* v *Jones*,[46] but will C be able to raise a defence of contributory negligence to her claim on the basis that *A* was partly

[43] It was established that if the defendant had taken care in his valuation, he would have accurately valued the house as being worth only £1m; as a result, the claimants would have offered to lend Mr Hussain only £700,000 and he would have declined the loan.

[44] Had the claimant lent the £1m to Hussain on adequate security – that is, in return for a mortgage of a house worth £1.5m – when Hussain defaulted, the security would have been worth £900,000 and the claimant would have lost £100,000 on the loan. So £100,000 of the £600,000 loss suffered by the claimant would have been suffered by the claimant anyway, even if he had lent Hussain money on adequate security. Therefore, £500,000 of the money lost by the claimant was lost by the claimant because he lent money to Hussain on inadequate security.

[45] [1998] Ch 466.

[46] [1995] 2 AC 207.

to blame for the fact that B did not receive her legacy? The question was raised in *Gorham* v *British Telecommunications plc*.[47] Of the three members of the Court of Appeal who decided that case, Pill and Schiemann LJJ preferred to leave the matter to be decided another day,[48] though Pill LJ thought the argument that a defence of contributory negligence should be available in this kind of case had its 'attractions'.[49] Sir Murray Stuart-Smith thought that the defence *would* be available in this kind of case.[50]

(7) *One final limit*. Suppose that A has committed a tort in relation to B and B has suffered various losses as a result, for which she was partly to blame – she would not have suffered those losses had she not acted unreasonably in some way. It seems to be the case that if the reason why B suffered those losses has nothing to do with the reason why it was unreasonable for B to act in the way she did, A will not be able to raise a defence of contributory negligence to B's claim to be compensated for those losses.

So, for example, in *Jones* v *Livox Quarries Ltd*,[51] Denning LJ considered whether the defence would be available in the following case. A negligently fires a gun and the bullet fired from the gun happens to hit and injure B while she was dangerously perched on the back of a moving lorry. Now – it was clearly unreasonable for B to stand on the back of the lorry and had she not done this she would not have been hit by the bullet: it was because she was on the lorry that she was in the wrong place at the wrong time. Does this mean that A can raise a defence of contributory negligence to any claim B makes against him for damages? Denning LJ thought not.[52] But the only explanation as to why the defence would not be available here is that the reason why it was unreasonable for B to perch on the back of the lorry had nothing to do with the reason why B was hit by the bullet.

In *Westwood* v *The Post Office*,[53] the claimant worked for the Post Office at a telephone exchange. His place of work was a three-storey building with a flat roof. Workers at the exchange, including the claimant, would frequently take short breaks on the roof although they were not authorised to do so and not permitted to gain access to the roof. While on his way back from one such break on the roof, the claimant fell through a defective trapdoor and was injured. The claimant sued the Post Office for damages in respect of his injuries, claiming that he had been injured because the Post Office had breached the duty it owed him under s 16 of the Offices, Shops and Railway Premises Act 1963 to ensure that the floors in the claimant's workplace were of sound construction. The Post Office admitted liability but sought to raise a defence of contributory negligence to the claimant's claim. The Post Office argued that the claimant was partly to blame for his injuries because he would not have been injured had he not acted unreasonably in trespassing on the flat roof of the telephone exchange. The House of Lords held that no defence of contributory negligence could be raised here: the reason why the claimant was injured (he trod on a trapdoor which was not soundly constructed) had nothing to do with the reason why it was

47 [2000] 1 WLR 2129.
48 Ibid., 2144 (per Pill LJ), 2145 (per Schiemann LJ).
49 Ibid., 2144.
50 Ibid., 2149.
51 [1952] 2 QB 608.
52 Ibid., 616.
53 [1974] AC 1.

unreasonable for the claimant to trespass on the flat roof of the telephone exchange (he had no business being up there).

LIMITATION CLAUSE

We have already come across the concept of an exclusion clause – a clause in a contract which provides that someone will not be held liable if he commits a tort in relation to someone else. A limitation clause is a clause in a contract which provides that if someone commits a tort, the most he can be held liable for is a certain sum of money. So if A has committed a tort in relation to B and B has suffered losses worth £50,000 as a result, A's liability to B will be reduced to £5,000 if there exists a limitation clause which he is entitled to rely on which provides that A's liability to B in the event of his committing a tort in relation to B will be limited to £5,000. The same rules that apply to determine whether a tortfeasor can rely on an exclusion clause to escape being held liable to the victim of his tort[54] also apply to determine whether a tortfeasor can rely on a limitation clause to limit his liability to the victim of his tort, so we need say no more about the validity of limitation clauses here.

Visit http://www.mylawchamber.co.uk/mcbride
to access updates on recent cases, as well as model answers and tips for answering tort problem questions.

[54] Discussed above, pp. 511–14.

B.

Compensatory damages: Third parties

Introduction

We are concerned in this section of the book with two questions:

(1) When will a third party to a tort[1] be able to obtain compensation for a loss that he has suffered as a result of that tort being committed?
(2) If a tort has been committed, when will a third party to the tort be held liable to compensate those who suffered loss as a result of that tort being committed?

Let's briefly look at how the law answers these two questions.

THE FIRST QUESTION

Occasionally, the law will allow the victim of a tort to sue for damages that are essentially designed to compensate a third party for a loss that she has suffered because that tort was committed. We have already seen an example of this.

If A has committed a tort in relation to B and B has been so badly injured as a result that her expectation of life has been reduced, she will be allowed to sue A for damages in respect of the money she would have earned and not spent on herself in the years that are now 'lost' to her.[2] The point of allowing B to sue for such damages is essentially to ensure that any dependants that B has, who would have been supported by her in the years that are now 'lost' to her, do not lose out as a result of A's tort. By allowing B to sue A for damages in respect of the money she would have earned in the years that are now 'lost' to her, the law enables B to set up a fund which will look after her dependants after she has died.

Another example is provided by what we can call the principle in *Donnelly* v *Joyce*.[3] This principle applies in the following kind of situation. Suppose that A negligently injured B and B, as a result, was incapacitated and needed to be looked after. Suppose further that C – a friend[4] of B's – looked after B without charging her anything for the work done by him

[1] Someone will be a 'third party' to a tort if he neither committed the tort in question nor was he the victim of that tort.

[2] See above, pp. 605–6. Though no such damages will be awarded if B is so young that any estimate as to how much she earned in the years that are now 'lost' to her would be purely speculative: *Gammell* v *Wilson* [1982] AC 27, 78E–G (per Lord Scarman, suggesting there might be an exception in the case where a child was already earning money at the time her expectation of life was cut short as a result of someone's negligently injuring her; which would be the case if the child was a movie star).

[3] [1974] QB 454.

[4] The principle will equally apply if C was a relative of B's. It is uncertain whether the principle in *Donnelly* v *Joyce* will apply in the situation where a complete stranger looks after the victim of a tort without charging her anything for doing so. In Scotland, only care provided by a relative is covered by their version of the principle in *Donnelly* v *Joyce*: Administration of Justice Act 1982, s 8. It seems implicit in *Islington LBC* v *University College London Hospital NHS Trust* [2005] EWCA Civ 596 that the position is the same in England. In that case, the claimant local authority sought to sue the defendant hospital in negligence for the money it had spent providing residential care to Mrs J, a woman who had had a stroke as a result of the defendant's negligence. The claim was dismissed – the defendant had not owed the claimant a duty of care. It seemed to be assumed that

in looking after her.[5] The principle in *Donnelly* v *Joyce* says that in this situation, B will be entitled to sue A for damages equal to the value of the work that C did in looking after B.[6] That such damages are designed to compensate C for the effort he put in looking after B is shown by two things. First, the damages payable will depend on what sort of sacrifices were incurred by C in looking after B; the greater the sacrifices, the greater the damages payable.[7] Secondly, if B does sue A for damages equal to the value of the work done by C in looking after her, she will hold those damages on trust[8] for C.[9] (It is a difficult question whether B will also hold her *right to sue* A for those damages on trust for C; if she does, then C will be allowed to *compel* B to sue A for those damages.[10])

There are other situations where the victim of a tort will be entitled to sue for damages in respect of losses suffered by third parties to that tort – though it must be emphasised that these situations are exceptional in nature; the normal rule is that the victim of a tort is confined to suing for compensatory damages in respect of the losses that *she* has suffered as a result of that tort being committed. So: if A negligently injures a housewife with the result that she can no longer do any housework, she will be entitled to sue A for damages in respect of the work done by any members of her family

suing in negligence was the only way for the claimant to recover the money it had spent caring for Mrs J; that is, she could not have sued herself for the costs of her care by the claimant. But, on the other hand, Clarke LJ wondered (at [45]) whether if Mrs J had been looked after by a friend, the friend could have compelled Mrs J to have made a claim for the cost of her care by the friend, and if so, whether Islington LBC could have done so as well.

5 If C had *charged* B for looking after her, then A would of course be liable to compensate B for the money she spent on getting C to look after her – so long, of course, as the money she paid C for looking after her was reasonable.

6 So – in *Donnelly* v *Joyce* [1974] QB 454 itself, the claimant was a child who was negligently injured by the defendant and as a result needed to spend six months at home having his injuries treated. The claimant's mother took time off work to look after the claimant. The claimant was allowed to sue the defendant for damages equal to the value of the work done by the claimant's mother in looking after him.

7 *Housecroft* v *Burnett* [1986] 1 All ER 332, 343e–f. However, the damages payable will not be allowed to exceed the going market rate for the kind of services that C provided B: ibid. So, for example, suppose Paul negligently injured Mary and Mary's injuries were so serious that she needed to be looked after 24 hours a day for six months. Mary's husband – who earned £400 a hour working as a lawyer – decided to quit his legal practice to look after Mary full time for the six months she was laid up, thereby forgoing roughly £400,000. Mary would not be able to sue Paul for that £400,000; instead she will be limited to suing Paul for the market value of the services provided by her husband in looking after. The reason why Mary will not be able to sue Paul for £400,000 under the principle in *Donnelly* v *Joyce* is that by having her husband look after her, she and her husband failed to mitigate the loss suffered by them as a result of Paul's tort: it would have been much cheaper to hire a nurse to look after Mary and have Paul carry on working.

8 Property is held 'on trust' for another when the legal owner of that property is under an obligation – equitable in nature – to apply that property for the benefit of another. In such a case, we say that the property is held on trust for that other, who is known as a *beneficiary* or a *cestui que trust*.

9 *Hunt* v *Severs* [1994] 2 AC 350 (the defendant in that case negligently injured his girlfriend in a car crash and then spent a lot of time looking after her; when she sued him for damages (which would, in effect, have been paid by the defendant's liability insurer), it was held that she could not recover damages in respect of the work the defendant had done in looking after her because if such damages were awarded her, they would have to be paid straight back to the defendant. The logic of the decision is impeccable, but it has been criticised on the ground that its effect is to encourage a husband who has negligently injured his wife to contract out her care to a complete stranger rather than looking after her himself. The Law Commission has accordingly recommended that the result in *Hunt* v *Severs* be reversed: Law Commission No. 262, *Damages for Personal Injury* (1999), paras 3.67–3.76.

10 Degeling 2003 takes the view that, as the law stands, C will not be able to compel B to sue. However, she goes on to argue that C *should* be subrogated to B's rights to sue A for damages in respect of the cost of caring for her – which would allow C to sue A for such damages in B's name.

in filling in for her.[11] Similarly, if B regularly looked after C, a family member, but is now no longer able to do so because she was negligently injured by A, with the result that another family member has to look after C, B will be entitled to sue A for damages equal to the value of the work she used to do in looking after C.[12] If A negligently damages B's car and C – a friend of B's – lends B a replacement car while his car is being repaired, then B may be entitled to sue A for damages equal to the rent that he would normally have had to pay to rent that kind of replacement car.[13]

These are all cases where the victim of a tort will be entitled to sue the person who committed that tort for damages in respect of the losses suffered by a third party to that tort as a result of that tort being committed. When will a third party to a tort be entitled to sue *in her own right* for compensation in respect of the losses she has suffered because that tort was committed? *Normally*, she never will be.[14] However, there are some exceptions to this rule and they are set out in the next chapter.

THE SECOND QUESTION

Not much needs to be said at this stage on this issue. If A has committed a tort in relation to B, and B has suffered various losses as a result, B will normally only be allowed to sue *A* for compensation in respect of those losses. However, there are two major exceptions to this rule.

First, if C procured or authorised A to commit his tort, then C will be an accessory to A's tort, with the result that the courts will hold that A's tort was committed by A *and C*, thus opening the door to B's being allowed to sue C for damages. We deal with the issue of when someone will be an accessory to a tort committed by someone else in Chapter 32.

Secondly, if C is vicariously liable in respect of A's tort, then if B is entitled to sue A for compensation for the losses that she has suffered as a result of A's tort, she will be entitled to sue C for such compensation as well.[15] We explain in Chapter 33 when someone will be held vicariously liable in respect of a tort committed by someone else.

[11] *Daly* v *General Steam Navigation Co. Ltd* [1981] 1 WLR 120. But if A negligently injures a businessman and as a result the businessman can no longer run his business and has his wife fill in for him, he will not be able to sue A for damages in respect of the work done by his wife running the business for him: *Hardwick* v *Hudson* [1999] 1 WLR 1770.

[12] *Lowe* v *Guise* [2002] QB 1369. Rix LJ suggested in that case (at [38]) that the damages, once paid over, 'may' be held on trust for the family member who took B's place in looking after C. What if C responded to B's being incapacitated by paying someone else to look after him, C? Presumably in that case the damages payable to B might then be held on trust for C.

[13] The point was left open in *Giles* v *Thompson* [1994] 1 AC 142, at 166G–167A. However, it is implicit in the House of Lords' decision in *Dimond* v *Lovell* [2002] 1 AC 384 that such a claim will be available to B, and may even be available where C was not a friend but a complete stranger. No such claim could be made on the facts of *Dimond* v *Lovell*, however – where the replacement car was provided by a finance company under a hire agreement that was void under the Consumer Credit Act 1974 – because to allow such a claim would have subverted the 1974 Act.

[14] See above, at pp. 20–1, 480–1, for examples of situations where a claimant sued for compensation in respect of losses suffered by her because a tort was committed, but her claim was thrown out because she was a third party to that tort.

[15] Of course, she cannot recover twice over for the losses that she has suffered: she will lose all her rights to sue once A or C has fully compensated her for the losses that she has suffered.

31 Liability to third parties

Suppose A has committed a tort in relation to B. Suppose further that C, a third party, has suffered some kind of loss as a result. As a general rule, C will *not* be entitled to sue A[1] for compensatory damages in respect of the loss he has suffered as a result of A's tort. However, there are some exceptions to this rule.

THE FATAL ACCIDENTS ACT 1976

The major exception is created under the Fatal Accidents Act 1976. That Act covers the situation where A has committed a tort in relation to B, B has died as a result and a dependant of B's has suffered loss as a result. In such a case, that dependant *may* be entitled to sue A for damages under the 1976 Act. Whether he will or not depends on the principles set out below.

General conditions for bringing a claim under the 1976 Act

If A has committed a tort in relation to B, and C wants to bring a claim against A under the 1976 Act, C will only be entitled to sue A if:

(1) A's tort caused B to die; *and*
(2) B's death was not a remote consequence of A's tort;[2] *and*
(3) C was a 'dependant' of B's; *and*
(4) had B not died, she would have been entitled to sue A for compensatory damages; *and*
(5) the limitation period for C's bringing a claim against A under the 1976 Act has not elapsed.

We have already looked at the law on causation and remoteness; but requirements (3), (4) and (5) deserve some further consideration.

Who is a dependant?

It is common for students to think that C will have been a dependant of B's if he was financially dependent on her. However, the definition of 'dependant' set out in the 1976 Act is quite different.

1 Or anyone who is vicariously liable in respect of A's tort.

2 The Act does not explicitly state that this is a condition of C's being entitled to bring an action against A under the 1976 Act: s1(1) of the Act merely says that 'If death is *caused* by any wrongful act . . . the person who would have been liable had death not ensued shall be liable to an action for damages . . .' (emphasis added). However, it has been accepted by both the Law Commission (Law Com. No. 263, *Claims for Wrongful Death* (1999), para 2.4) and the Court of Appeal (*Corr* v *IBC Vehicles Ltd* [2007] QB 46) that C will not be entitled to bring an action against A under the 1976 Act if B's death was a remote consequence of A's tort.

Section 1(3) of the Act provides that if someone commits a tort that causes another to die, the deceased's dependants will be: (1) the wife or husband or former wife or husband of the deceased; (2) any person who was living with the deceased at the time of the deceased's death as the deceased's husband or wife and had been living with the deceased in such a capacity for at least two years before the deceased's death; (3) any parent or other ascendant of the deceased; (4) any person who was treated by the deceased as being his or her parent; (5) any child or other descendant of the deceased; (6) if the deceased was married to someone else and had started a family with that someone else, any person who was treated by the deceased as being a member of that family; *and* (7) anyone who was, or was the issue of, the deceased's brother, sister, uncle or aunt.[3]

The parasitical nature of claims under the Act

Suppose that A committed a tort in relation to B and A's tort caused B to die and B's death was not a remote consequence of A's tort. Suppose further that C was a dependant of B's. C will only be entitled to bring a claim against A under the 1976 Act *if* had B not died she would have been entitled to sue A for compensatory damages. In this sense, C's right to sue A for damages under the Act is parasitical on B's right: if B would not have been able to sue A for damages had she survived his tort, then C will have no right to sue A for damages under the Act. This limit on C's right to sue A under the Act covers – somewhat uneasily – two entirely different situations, which need to be considered separately.

(1) *Instantaneous death.* Suppose that A's tort caused B to die instantaneously. Suppose, for example, that A shot B in the head. In order to see whether C is entitled to sue A under the 1976 Act, we have to ask: had B survived the shooting and merely been injured by it, would she have been entitled to sue A for compensatory damages? The answer will usually be 'yes' – in which case, C will be entitled to bring a claim against A under the 1976 Act. However, it may be 'no' – in which case, C will not be able to bring a claim against A under the 1976 Act. This will be the case if, had B merely been injured, A would have been able to raise a defence of illegality to any claim B might have brought against him for damages.[4]

(2) *Tort causing injury which results in death some time after.* Suppose that A's tort caused B to suffer some kind of injury and B died some time after that because she suffered that

[3] The most notable omission from this list is people who were involved in a stable homosexual relationship with the deceased and it may be that the definition of 'dependant' needs updating to eliminate this omission. The Law Commission has recommended that the definition of 'dependant' under the 1976 Act be altered to cover anyone who was being maintained on a non-business basis by the deceased at the time of his or her death and was likely to have continued being maintained on that basis by the deceased had he or she not died: Law Com. No. 263, para 7.7.

[4] See *Murphy* v *Culhane* [1977] QB 94. In that case, Culhane struck Murphy on the head with a plank of wood and killed him. Murphy's widow brought an action against Culhane, seeking to recover compensation for the loss of support that she had experienced as a result of Murphy's death. Her claim could not succeed if, had Murphy survived Culhane's attack, Murphy would not have been entitled to sue Culhane for damages. It was alleged that Culhane had struck Murphy only after Murphy, along with some other men, had attempted to attack Culhane. The Court of Appeal held that if that allegation were made out then the widow's claim would fail. On the facts as they were alleged to be, had Murphy survived Culhane's attack and merely been injured by it, he would *not* have been allowed to sue Culhane for damages: had he attempted to do so, Culhane would have been able to raise a defence of illegality to defeat Murphy's claim. Presumably the court thought in this case that there would have existed a sufficiently close connection between Murphy's threatening to beat Culhane up and Culhane's attacking Murphy: see above, pp. 518–20.

injury. In order to see whether C is entitled to sue A under the 1976 Act we have to ask: had B not died when she did but had lived a little longer, would she have been entitled to sue A for damages in respect of her injury? So – if before she died, B had already obtained a compensation payment from A in respect of her injury, then the answer will be 'no' and C will not be entitled to bring a claim against A under the 1976 Act.[5] Because A had already compensated B once for the injury suffered by her as a result of his tort, she could not have gone to court to try to sue him for more compensation.[6]

If B did *not* obtain a compensation payment from A before she died, then we simply look to see whether B could have sued A at the time she died for damages in respect of the injury she suffered as a result of A's tort. If she could have, then C might be able to bring a claim against A under the 1976 Act. If she could not – because, for example, B's injury was a non-actionable consequence of A's tort or because, before she died, B obtained a compensation payment from someone else in respect of her injury which had the effect of extinguishing A's liability to compensate B for the fact that she suffered that injury[7] – then C will not be able to bring a claim against A under the 1976 Act.

Limitation period

Section 12(2) of the Limitation Act 1980 provides that, in the case where the victim of a tort has died as a result of that tort having been committed, a claimant will not be able to bring an action under the 1976 Act more than three years after the *later* of the following two dates: (1) the date the victim of the tort died; (2) the date the claimant first learned, or could have reasonably been expected to learn, that the victim of the tort had died. Section 33 of the Limitation Act 1980 creates an exception to this rule: it provides that a claimant who attempts to bring a claim under the 1976 Act outside the limitation period set out in s 12(2) may be allowed to do so if it would be 'equitable' to do so.

The sort of claims that can be brought under the 1976 Act

There are basically three kinds of claims that can be brought under the 1976 Act by a dependant who has suffered loss as a result of a victim of a tort's death: (1) a claim for loss of support; (2) a claim for bereavement; (3) a claim for funeral expenses.

Loss of support

Suppose that A committed a tort in relation to B and B died as a result. Suppose further that C was a dependant of B's. In this case, C will be entitled to bring a claim for *loss of support* against A under the 1976 Act *if*:

[5] See, for example, *Read v The Great Eastern Railway Company* (1868) LR 3 QB 555. In that case, the claimant's husband was injured as a result of the defendant railway company's negligence. The claimant's husband died of his wounds but not before he accepted a sum of money from the defendants in full and final settlement of all his claims against the defendants. Once the claimant's husband died the claimant brought a claim for loss of support against the defendants. Her claim was dismissed: at the time of her husband's death, he was not entitled any more to sue the defendants for damages.

[6] See above, pp. 598–9. This is assuming that A's compensation payment did not take the form of a payment of provisional damages, in which case s 3 of the Damages Act 1996 provides that A's compensation payment will not bar anyone from bringing a claim against A under the Fatal Accidents Act 1976.

[7] Which was the case in *Jameson* v *CEGB* [2000] 1 AC 455, discussed above, p. 613 n. 9.

(1) the basic conditions that have to be satisfied before C can sue A under the 1976 Act are satisfied; *and*
(2) C can show that there was a *reasonable prospect* that had B not died, he would have obtained some kind of financial benefit in the future; *and*
(3) C would have obtained that benefit by virtue of the fact that he was B's dependant.

The following cases demonstrate the above rule in action.

In *Franklin* v *The South Eastern Railway Company*,[8] the claimant's son was killed as a result of the defendants' negligence. At the time his son was killed, the claimant was getting old and infirm but was not receiving any assistance from his son, who was earning 3s 6d a week at the time he was killed. It was held that had the son not been killed there was a reasonable prospect that as the claimant grew older and weaker, the son would have paid the claimant some money so as to assist him financially. As a result the claimant was held entitled to bring an action for loss of support against the defendants.

In *Barnett* v *Cohen*,[9] the claimant's four-year-old son was killed as a result of the defendant's negligence. The claimant brought an action for loss of support against the defendant, claiming that had his son not been killed and had instead grown up to earn a living, his son would have paid him some money to assist him financially. The claim was dismissed: the claimant had not established that there was a reasonable prospect he would have received such assistance from his son had his son not been killed and grown up instead. This was for two reasons. First, the age of the claimant's son when he was killed made it impossible to predict what would have happened had he not been killed as a result of the defendant's negligence. Secondly, the claimant was a very wealthy man (earning £1,000 a year at the time of his son's death) and it was therefore hardly likely that the claimant's son would have had any reason to give the claimant anything by way of financial assistance if he had been allowed to grow up.

In *Davies* v *Taylor*,[10] the claimant's husband was killed in a road accident that was caused by the defendant's negligence. At the time the claimant's husband died, the claimant and her husband were separated and the claimant's husband was in the process of divorcing the claimant for adultery. The claimant brought an action for loss of support against the defendant, claiming that had her husband not been killed, there was a reasonable prospect her husband would have spent money on her. The claimant's claim was dismissed: had the claimant's husband not been killed, the claimant's husband would only have spent money on the claimant if they had been reconciled and the claimant had not established that there was a reasonable prospect that she and her husband would have been reconciled had he not been killed as a result of the defendant's negligence. While it was *possible* that they would have been reconciled had the claimant's husband not been killed, the chances of their being reconciled were not so high as to make it reasonable to think that the claimant and her husband would have been reconciled had her husband not been killed.

In *Berry* v *Humm*,[11] the defendant negligently knocked down and killed the claimant's wife. At the time of her death, the claimant's wife stayed at home and did all the domestic

[8] (1858) 3 H & N 211, 157 ER 448.
[9] [1921] 2 KB 461.
[10] [1972] 1 QB 286.
[11] [1915] 1 KB 627.

chores while her husband worked in the docks. Had the claimant's wife not been killed there was every prospect that the claimant's wife would have continued to do work around the claimant's house for free, thereby conferring a financial benefit on the claimant. As a result, the claimant was held entitled to bring a claim for loss of support against the defendant.

In *K* v *JMP Co. Ltd*,[12] a man and a woman lived together and had three illegitimate children. The father covered all the family expenses on things such as rent, food, electricity and holidays. The father was killed as a result of the defendants' negligence. The children were, of course, entitled to sue the defendants for damages in respect of the money their father would have spent on them had he not been killed. It was held that in assessing how much money the father would have spent on his children had he not been killed, account should be taken of the money the father would have spent enabling the mother to come on holiday with him and the children: this money could fairly be regarded as money the father would have spent *on the children* as the point of spending money to enable the mother to come on holiday would have been to enhance the children's enjoyment of their holidays.

In *Burgess* v *Florence Nightingale Hospital for Gentlewomen*,[13] the claimant and his wife were professional dance partners. The claimant's wife was killed as a result of the defendant's negligence. There was a reasonable prospect that had the wife not been killed the claimant and his wife would have continued to dance together and would have earned a certain amount of prize money. It was held that the claimant – in bringing a claim against the defendant for loss of support – could not sue for the prize money he would have earned in the future had his wife not been killed. The reason was that the prize money that the claimant would have earned if his wife had not been killed would not have been obtained by him by virtue of the fact that he was one of his wife's dependants. That money would have been obtained by him because he was his wife's *dancing partner*, not because he was *married* to her.[14] The claimant *was*, however, entitled, in bringing a claim for loss of support against the defendant, to sue the defendant for damages in respect of the money his wife would have given him as a contribution towards their household expenses had she not been killed. *That* money *would* have been obtained by him as a result of the fact that he was married to his wife and therefore one of his wife's dependants.

In *Malyon* v *Plummer*,[15] the claimant and her husband ran a business selling and distributing portable electrical machinery to builders and farm machinery suppliers in East Anglia. The business was run through a company which paid the claimant a salary of about £600 a year. The claimant did not do much work for the company in return for her salary; the claimant's husband did most of the work drumming up business and collecting and processing orders. In fact, the value of the work done by the claimant for the company came to only about £200 a year: the remaining £400 a year paid to the claimant essentially amounted to a gift to the claimant. When the claimant's husband was killed in a car crash

[12] [1976] QB 85.

[13] [1955] 1 QB 349.

[14] See also *Cox* v *Hockenhull* [2000] 1 WLR 750. The claimant's wife was killed in a car accident that the defendant negligently caused. The claimant's wife was disabled and at the time of the accident the claimant was her full-time carer and as such received an invalidity care allowance. Held: the claimant could not sue the defendant for the loss of the invalidity care allowance that he experienced after his wife's death as that allowance had not been received by the claimant because he was his wife's husband but because he was his wife's carer.

[15] [1964] 1 QB 330.

caused by the defendant's negligence, the business collapsed. The company through which the business was run went into insolvency and the claimant lost her £600 a year salary.

Of course, had the claimant's husband not been killed there was every prospect that the family business would have flourished and the claimant would have continued to draw a salary of £600 a year from their company, but £200 of that £600 a year salary would have been obtained by the claimant by virtue of the work done by her for the company she and her husband owned; only £400 of that £600 a year salary would have been paid to her by virtue of, or in recognition of, the fact that the claimant was married to her husband and therefore one of her husband's dependants. The claimant could therefore only bring a claim for loss of support against the defendant in respect of two-thirds of the £600 a year salary she would have continued to draw had her husband not been killed. In other words, she could only sue the defendant for damages in respect of that proportion of the salary she would have continued to draw had her husband not been killed which was attributable to the fact that she was married to her husband and therefore one of her husband's dependants.

Two limits on a dependant's ability to bring a claim for loss of support under the 1976 Act should be noted.

(1) *Illegality*. In the case we are considering, C will be barred from bringing an action for loss of support against A if the financial benefit that he would have received had B not died have represented the proceeds of crime.

In *Burns* v *Edman*,[16] the claimant's husband was killed in a motor accident caused by the defendant's negligence. The claimant's husband had never had a job and what money he gave her (£20 a week) invariably represented the proceeds of crime. The claimant brought an action for loss of support against the defendant but her claim was dismissed. While there was more than a reasonable prospect that the claimant would have received a weekly allowance of £20 a week from her husband had he not been killed, there was no prospect that that weekly allowance would have represented anything but the proceeds of crime.

(2) *No loss of benefit*. In the case we are considering, C will of course be barred from bringing a claim for loss of support against A if B's death did not actually prevent C receiving the financial benefit that he would have received had B not died.

In *Auty* v *National Coal Board*,[17] the claimant's husband was killed due to the defendants' negligence. Her husband was 55 when he died. When he died the claimant received a widow's pension under the Mineworkers' Pension Scheme. Had the claimant's husband not been killed, there was a reasonable prospect that he would have died before retiring at 65 and the claimant would have received a widow's pension. The claimant brought an action for loss of support against the defendants and included in her claim a claim for the fact that had her husband not been killed as a result of the defendant's negligence there was a reasonable prospect he would have been killed before retiring and she would have received a widow's pension. This element of her claim was thrown out: her husband's death had not actually prevented her from receiving a widow's pension as when he died as a result of the defendants' negligence, she received a widow's pension.

16 [1970] 2 QB 541.
17 [1985] 1 WLR 784.

In light of this, the decision of the Court of Appeal in *Hay* v *Hughes*[18] is difficult to understand. In that case, the parents of two boys were killed in a motor accident caused by the defendant's negligence. Had the parents not been killed the boys would have received a financial benefit: they would have been cared for until the age of their majority. But in fact the parents' deaths did not prevent the boys obtaining that benefit: the boys' grandmother took them in and looked after them. Despite this, the boys were still held entitled to bring a claim for loss of support against the defendant to compensate them for the loss of the free of charge care that they would have received from their parents until the age of their majority.

Perhaps the best explanation of the result in this case (and others similar to it)[19] is that if A has committed a tort in relation to B and B has died as a result, B's children (if any) will *not* be entitled to bring a claim for bereavement against A so as to console them for the loss of B.[20] So in *Hay* v *Hughes* the two boys were not entitled to claim any damages for bereavement from the defendant so as to console them for the loss of their parents. This might have seemed unfair to the Court of Appeal in *Hay* v *Hughes* and allowing the boys to sue the defendant for damages equivalent to the value of the care they would have received from their parents until the age of their majority might have seemed to the Court of Appeal an acceptable way of giving the boys something to console them for the loss of their parents.

Section 3(3) of the 1976 Act creates an exception to the rule that, in a case where the victim of a tort has died as a result of that tort being committed, a claimant cannot bring a claim for loss of support under the Act if the victim's death has not actually prevented him receiving a financial benefit that he would have received had the victim not died. Section 3(3) provides that if in 'an action under this Act . . . there fall to be assessed damages payable to a widow in respect of the death of her husband there shall not be taken into account the re-marriage of the widow . . .'. So suppose Carl was married to Lara and Carl supported Lara: he would pay for all the common household expenses as well as paying for Lara's clothes and so on. Suppose further that John committed a tort in relation to Carl and Carl died as a result. Suppose finally that shortly after Carl's death, Lara remarried and her new husband supported her to the same extent as Carl used to. In such a case, John's tort will not have caused Lara to suffer any loss of support but Lara will still be able to bring a claim for loss of support against John: the fact that Lara has remarried and is being supported by her new husband will be disregarded and Lara will be able to sue John on the basis that John's tort *did* cause her to suffer a loss of support.

This aspect of the law, it should be noted, discriminates between widows and widowers in favour of widows. If you cause a married woman to die by committing a tort in relation to her and her husband remarries shortly afterwards and consequently suffers no loss of support as a result of your tort, the husband will have no action against you under the 1976 Act: s 3(3) does not instruct the courts to disregard the husband's remarriage in assessing the damages payable to him as a result of his first wife's death.

[18] [1975] 1 QB 790.

[19] See *Regan* v *Williamson* [1976] 1 WLR 305; *Mehmet* v *Perry* [1977] 2 All ER 529; *Creswell* v *Eaton* [1991] 1 WLR 1113; *Corbett* v *Barking Havery and Brentwood Health Authority* [1991] 2 QB 408; *R* v *Criminal Injuries Compensation Board, ex parte Kavanagh* [1998] 2 FLR 1071.

[20] See below, p. 638.

Bereavement

The second kind of action that can be brought under the 1976 Act is a claim for bereavement. Section 1A of the Fatal Accidents Act 1976 provides that – so long as the general conditions that have to be satisfied before a claim can be brought under the 1976 Act are satisfied – this sort of claim can be made in two kinds of situations.

The first is where A commits a tort in relation to B, B dies as a result, and at the time B died she was married. In such a case, B's spouse will be able to bring a claim for bereavement against A.[21] The second kind of case where a claim for bereavement can be brought is where the victim of a tort who has died as a result of that tort being committed was not married and was a minor at the time he or she died. In such a case, the victim's parents (if the victim was legitimate) or the victim's mother (if the victim was illegitimate) will be entitled to bring an action for bereavement under the 1976 Act against whoever committed that tort.[22]

The damages payable for bereavement are fixed at £10,000:[23] if A has committed a tort in relation to B and B has died as a result, and C is entitled to claim damages for bereavement, the damages payable to C will not be increased if he was especially upset by B's death and they will not be reduced if C was indifferent to the fact that B died. This leads Tony Weir to argue that the damages payable for bereavement are 'not designed as compensation for grief but [are] simply...a replacement in money for a life lost. The lump sum is standard because people are equal, not because they are equally regrettable.'[24] However, it may be argued that these damages *are* designed to compensate for grief but the damages payable are fixed so as to avoid the courts having to make intrusive and distasteful inquiries into *how* grief-stricken a particular claimant is. Thus, £10,000 is the maximum someone can be held liable to pay by way of damages for bereavement; so if more than one person is entitled to claim such damages,[25] the lump sum has to be shared out between them.[26]

Funeral expenses

Section 3(5) of the 1976 Act provides that 'If the dependants [of the victim of a tort who was killed as a result of that tort being committed] have incurred funeral expenses in respect of the deceased, damages may be awarded in respect of those expenses.' Such a claim will of course be available only if the conditions that have to be satisfied before a claim can be brought under the 1976 Act are satisfied.

Reduction in liability

Suppose that A has committed a tort in relation to B, B has died as a result and C – a dependant of B's – is entitled to bring some kind of claim against A under the 1976 Act.

The damages payable to C will be reduced if B was partly to blame for the fact that she died. Section 5 of the Fatal Accidents Act 1976 provides that where 'any person dies as the

[21] Section 1A(2)(a).
[22] Section 1A(2)(b).
[23] Damages for Bereavement (Variation of Sum) (England and Wales) Order 2002 (SI No. 644).
[24] Weir 2006, 215.
[25] This will only be the case where a legitimate minor has been killed as a result of someone else's tort: in such a case both parents will be entitled to sue for damages for bereavement.
[26] Fatal Accidents Act 1976, s 1A(4).

result partly of his own fault and partly of the fault of any other person or persons, and accordingly if an action were brought for the benefit of the estate under the Law Reform (Miscellaneous Provisions) Act 1934 the damages recoverable would be reduced under s 1(1) of the Law Reform (Contributory Negligence) Act 1945, any damages recoverable in an action ... under this Act shall be reduced to a proportionate extent'.[27]

However, the damages payable to C will *not* be reduced to take account of any benefit that he might have received as a result of B's death. Section 4 of the Fatal Accidents Act 1976 provides that 'In assessing damages in respect of a person's death in an action under this Act, benefits which have accrued or will or may accrue to any person from his estate or otherwise as a result of his death shall be disregarded.'[28]

So – in *Pidduck* v *Eastern Scottish Omnibuses Ltd*[29] the claimant's husband was killed as a result of the defendants' negligence. Before the claimant's husband was killed he received money from a pension scheme, two-thirds of which he spent on the claimant. The payments under the pension scheme ceased when the claimant's husband was killed but the claimant started to receive a widow's allowance instead. The claimant brought an action for loss of support against the defendants on the basis that had her husband not been killed there was a reasonable prospect that he would have continued to receive a pension for a good few years and would have spent two-thirds of that pension money on the claimant.

The defendants argued that the damages payable to the claimant should be reduced to take account of the fact that as a result of her husband's death she was now in receipt of a widow's allowance. The defendants' argument was rejected and no reduction in the damages payable to the claimant was made. The result was that the claimant was left better off (financially) than she would have been had her husband not died; she not only obtained from the defendants damages equivalent to the value of all the pension money she would have received had her husband not been killed, she also enjoyed the benefit of the widow's allowance that she would *not* have received had her husband not been killed.

In two situations, the courts have shown themselves willing to disregard the rule set out in s 4 of the 1976 Act:

(1) *Receipt of benefit from defendant.* If, in the situation we are considering, C received a benefit worth £5,000 from *A* as a result of B's death, the damages payable to C under the 1976 Act will be reduced by £5,000. The reason is that the benefits conferred by A on C as a result of B's death are regarded as partially compensating C for the losses suffered by him as a result of B's death.

[27] This was the position in *Reeves* v *Commissioner of Police of the Metropolis* [2000] 1 AC 360 (damages payable under 1976 Act to partner of deceased who committed suicide in custody – when police in breach of the duty of care they owed the deceased failed to take reasonable steps to prevent him committing suicide – were reduced by 50% because the deceased was partly to blame for his own death).

[28] The Social Security (Recovery of Benefits) Act 1997 (discussed above, p. 614) does not seem to apply to actions brought under the Fatal Accidents Act 1976. So: suppose Eric committed a tort in relation to Wendy and Wendy died as a result. Suppose further that had Wendy not died, Sarah – a dependant of Wendy's – would have received a financial benefit worth £14,000 which she is not now going to receive. Suppose also that because Wendy died, Sarah was paid social security benefits worth £10,000. It seems that so long as the conditions that have to be satisfied before Sarah can bring a claim for loss of support against Eric under the 1976 Act are satisfied, Sarah will be entitled to sue Eric for £14,000 in damages; the 1997 Act will not reduce the damages payable to Eric to £4,000.

[29] [1990] 1 WLR 993.

So, in *Hayden* v *Hayden*[30] the claimant's mother was killed because of the negligence of the defendant, the claimant's father, in driving a car in which the claimant's mother was a passenger. The defendant gave up his job to look after the claimant. The claimant brought an action for loss of support against the defendant (in reality, the defendant's liability insurer), claiming that had his mother not been killed as a result of the defendant's negligence, his mother would have looked after him free of charge until he was 18. The damages payable to the claimant were reduced to take account of the value of the care the claimant had received from the defendant as a result of his mother's death.

(2) *Adoption*. In *Watson* v *Willmott*,[31] the claimant's mother was killed in a car accident caused by the defendant's negligence. The claimant's father, depressed at the death of his wife, committed suicide and the claimant was adopted. The claimant brought an action for loss of support against the defendant, seeking to obtain compensation for the fact that he would not now, thanks to the defendant's negligence, be looked after free of charge by his father and mother until he was 18.

The damages payable to the claimant were reduced to take account of the value of the benefit he had received and would receive as a result of the defendant's negligence: the value of the care he had received and would receive from his adoptive parents. The court felt it was authorised to depart from the rule set out in s 4 of the 1976 Act by virtue of para 3 of Sch 1 of the Children Act 1975 under which '[a]n adopted child shall be treated in law ... where the adopters are a married couple, as if he had been born as a child of the marriage'. As such, the decision in *Watson* v *Willmott* is to be confined strictly to the case where a child's parents have been killed as a result of a tort committed in relation to them and the child has been subsequently adopted.

RECOVERY OF LOSSES SUFFERED BY THE STATE

In two situations, the State is allowed to sue someone who has committed a tort for compensation in respect of the losses that it has suffered as a result of that tort being committed.

(1) *The Social Security (Recovery of Benefits) Act 1997. Roughly speaking*, this Act provides that someone who has made a compensation payment to the victim of a tort will be held liable to the State for the value of *all* the social security payments that have been made to the victim of that tort as a result of her being a victim of that tort.[32]

(2) *The Health and Social Care (Community Health and Standards) Act 2003*. Section 150 of this Act covers the situation where B, the victim of a tort, has suffered some kind of injury ('physical or psychological')[33] as a result of that tort being committed. If B has received treatment on the National Health Service (NHS) for that injury, or has been provided with an ambulance service on the NHS as a result of suffering that injury, then anyone who

[30] [1992] 1 WLR 986.
[31] [1991] 1 QB 140.
[32] Space does not allow us to say more than this. For a *very* detailed treatment of the Act, see Lewis 1999, 113–222.
[33] Section 150(5) provides that '"Injury" does not include any disease.'

makes a compensation payment to B in respect of that injury will be liable to pay charges to the NHS for the treatment, or ambulance services, received by B. If B was partly to blame for her injury so that the compensation payable to her is liable to be reduced for contributory negligence, the charges payable in respect of the NHS services received by B will be reduced by a corresponding amount.[34]

THE CONGENITAL DISABILITIES (CIVIL LIABILITY) ACT 1976

The basic idea

This Act is primarily designed to cover the situation where A committed a tort in relation to B while she was pregnant and as a result her child was born disabled *when it would otherwise have been born healthy*. In this situation, B's child will normally be entitled to sue A under the Congenital Disabilities (Civil Liability) Act 1976 for compensation for the fact that it was born disabled.[35]

Torts committed before conception

The Act also covers two other situations:

(1) *Torts affecting a woman's ability to bear a healthy child.* If A commits a tort in relation to B before she gets pregnant which affects her ability to have a healthy child and, as a result, she gives birth to a disabled child, that child will normally be able to sue A for damages under the 1976 Act. However, there is one limit on this. If B knew that A's tort had affected her ability to have a healthy child but she nonetheless went on to get pregnant and carried the child to term, the child – if born disabled – would not be able to sue A for damages under the 1976 Act.[36]

(2) *Torts committed in the course of fertility treatment.* If B went to A for fertility treatment, and A breached the duty of care that he owes B as his patient by implanting in her a defective embryo or defective sperm or defective eggs and – as a result – the child that B subsequently gave birth to was disabled, that child will be entitled to sue A for damages under the 1976 Act.[37] There is, again, one limit on this. If B willingly took the risk that the embryo, sperm or eggs implanted inside her would turn out to be defective – and therefore willingly took the risk that she would, as a result of being given that embryo, sperm or eggs, give birth to a disabled child – then B's child will not be able to sue A for damages under the 1976 Act.

[34] Section 153(3).

[35] The baby's right to sue A is parasitic on B's. So if A would be able to rely on an exclusion clause to defeat any claim for damages that B might make against him in respect of his tort, then he will similarly be entitled to rely on that clause to defeat any claim that B's baby makes against him under the 1976 Act: s 1(6). Similarly, if A would be entitled to raise a defence of contributory negligence to any claim B might make against him for damages in respect of his tort, A will also be entitled to rely on that defence if B's baby sues him for damages under the 1976 Act: s.1(7).

[36] Section 1(4).

[37] Section 1A(1), (2).

Actions for wrongful birth

The 1976 Act does not cover situations where a child *that was always going to be born disabled* was born as a result of someone's committing a tort in relation to the child's mother before she gave birth to the child.

For example, in *McKay* v *Essex Area Health Authority*[38] the claimant was born disabled because her mother suffered rubella (or German measles) while the claimant was in her womb. The defendant doctor had – in breach of the duty of care he owed the claimant's mother in treating her – failed to inform the claimant's mother that she had been infected with rubella. Had he told her that she had been infected with rubella, she would probably have had an abortion. While the 1976 Act was not in force at the time of these events, the Court of Appeal unanimously held that had the 1976 Act been in force at the time these events occurred, the claimant would *not* have been entitled to sue the defendant doctor for damages designed to compensate her for the fact that she was born disabled.[39]

Why does the 1976 Act not cover this kind of situation – which we can call a 'wrongful birth' case?[40] The answer is simple. In a case like *McKay* any damages award made to the claimant would be designed to compensate her for the losses she suffered as a result of the defendant's tort. But what losses has she suffered as a result of his tort? Had he not committed his tort, the claimant would never have been born. As a result of his tort, the claimant was born and not aborted. So to award the claimant damages here would be to say that she suffered a loss as a result of being born. In other words, to award the claimant damages here would be to say that she would have been better off dead. Understandably, the courts are unwilling to accept that anyone would be 'better off dead' on the grounds that to do so would undermine the sanctity of human life. In any case, an 'I would have been better off dead' argument could only have any plausibility in the case of a claimant who was born with such severe disabilities that she was constantly racked in pain and unable to garner any enjoyment from life whatsoever – and not many claimants in a 'wrongful birth' case would be able to satisfy this requirement.

THE LATENT DAMAGE ACT 1986

Section 3 of the Latent Damage Act 1986 covers the situation where A committed a tort in relation to B and B's property was damaged as a result, but before the damage was discovered B transferred the property to C. In such a case, s 3 provides that if B would have been entitled to sue A for damages in respect of the damage done to his property had he discovered it in time, C will be entitled to sue A for damages in respect of the damage done to that item of property.

THE PRINCIPLE OF TRANSFERRED LOSS

In *The Aliakmon*, it will be recalled, Leigh & Sillavan Ltd suffered a loss as a result of Aliakmon Shipping Co. Ltd's breaching a duty of care owed to Kinso-Mataichi Corp.[41] They had agreed to buy some steel coils from Kinso-Mataichi. The coils were to be

[38] [1982] 1 QB 1166.

[39] Ibid., 1178A–C (per Stephenson LJ), 1186H–1187B (per Ackner LJ), 1192C (per Griffiths LJ).

[40] 'Wrongful birth' because the claimant in *McKay* would not have been born but for the defendant's wrong.

[41] *Leigh & Sillavan Ltd v Aliakmon Shipping Co. Ltd, The Aliakmon* [1986] AC 785 (discussed above, pp. 121–2).

shipped to them by Aliakmon Shipping. During shipment the coils still belonged to Kinso-Mataichi. The coils were damaged during shipment due to Aliakmon Shipping's negligence and Leigh & Sillavan suffered loss as a result; they ended up paying far more for the coils than they were, in their damaged state, actually worth.

In the Court of Appeal, Robert Goff LJ, dissenting, held that Leigh & Sillavan *were* entitled to sue Aliakmon Shipping for compensatory damages sufficient to compensate them for the loss they had suffered as a result of Aliakmon Shipping's negligence, even though that negligence had consisted in the breach of a duty of care owed not to Leigh & Sillavan but rather to Kinso-Mataichi. Robert Goff LJ suggested that English law should recognise a 'principle of transferred loss' according to which if 'A owes a duty of care in tort not to cause physical damage to B's property, and commits a breach of that duty in circumstances in which the loss of or physical damage to the property will ordinarily fall on B but (as is reasonably foreseeable by A) such loss or damage, by reason of a contractual relationship between B and C, falls upon C, then C will be entitled, subject to the terms of any contract restricting A's liability to B, to bring an action in tort against A in respect of such loss or damage to the extent that it falls on him, C'.[42]

When *The Aliakmon* fell to be decided by the House of Lords they roundly rejected the idea that English law should give effect to this principle of transferred loss. Lord Brandon of Oakbrook remarked: 'With the greatest possible respect to Robert Goff LJ, the principle of transferred loss . . . is not only not supported by authority, but is on the contrary inconsistent with it.'[43] In *White* v *Jones* (*not* a case which was covered by the principle of transferred loss)[44] Lord Goff (as he had by then become) did not renew the attempt he made in *The Aliakmon* to introduce the principle of transferred loss into English law, beyond observing that recognition of such a principle might serve to fill some lacunae in English law.[45] Subsequently, in the case of *Alfred McAlpine Construction Ltd* v *Panatown Ltd*, Lord Goff seemed to disown the principle of transferred loss entirely, remarking that the principle 'is not an easy one for a common lawyer to grasp' and observing that he did not feel 'sufficiently secure' in his understanding of how it would apply to employ it in deciding the case at hand.[46] With Lord Goff now retired from the bench, it must be doubted whether anyone else will attempt to introduce the principle of transferred loss into English law and thereby create another exception to the general rule that if A has committed a tort in relation to B and a third party, C, has suffered loss as a result, C will *not* be entitled to sue A for damages in respect of that loss.

Visit http://www.mylawchamber.co.uk/mcbride to access updates on recent cases, as well as model answers and tips for answering tort problem questions.

[42] [1985] QB 350, 399E–G. For discussion of this principle and how it works, see Cane 1996, 327–9.

[43] [1986] AC 785, 820E–F.

[44] In *White* v *Jones* [1995] 2 AC 207, it will be recalled, a father instructed his solicitor to make a will under which his daughters would receive £9,000 each. The solicitor was unacceptably tardy in drawing up the will and it was not signed and witnessed by the time the father died. As a result the father's daughters did not receive their bequests. In this case, the father did *not* suffer any loss as a result of his solicitor's negligence which was then passed on to his daughters.

[45] Ibid., 264–6.

[46] [2001] 1 AC 518, 557.

32 Accessory liability

We have already seen that A1 will commit the tort of private nuisance if he authorises A2 to create a state of affairs that unreasonably interferes with B's use and enjoyment of her land.[1] This rule seems to be an application of a wider rule, which says that if A commits a tort in relation to B, then the courts will hold that C *also* committed A's tort if C was an *accessory* to that tort. So if C was an accessory to A's tort, the courts will hold that A *and* C committed A's tort,[2] with the result that A and C will be held *jointly* liable to compensate B for the harm she suffered as a result of A's tort.[3]

So – when will the courts find that a third party to a tort was an accessory to that tort?[4]

(1) *Procuring*. In *John Hudson & Co. Ltd* v *Oaten*,[5] Oliver LJ said, 'A man who procures the commission by another person of a tortious act becomes liable because he then becomes principal in the commission of the act. It is his tort.'

In *CBS Songs* v *Amstrad*,[6] Lord Templeman made it clear that 'A defendant may procure [someone to commit a tort] by inducement, incitement or persuasion.'[7] He then went on to observe that 'Generally speaking, inducement, incitement or persuasion to [commit a tort] must be by a defendant to an individual tortfeasor and must identifiably procure a particular [tort] in order to make the defendant liable as a joint [tortfeasor].'[8] Two points need to be made about this way of becoming an accessory to a tort.

First, if A has committed a tort by doing *x*, C can only be held to have procured A to commit that tort if his words of inducement, incitement or persuasion played some part in A's decision to do *x*. It would be going too far to demand that it be shown that A would not have done *x* but for C's words, but it must be shown that A took C's words into account in deciding to do *x*.

Secondly, if something C said to A led A to commit a tort by doing *x*, C can only be held to have procured A to commit that tort if C intended to encourage A to do *x* when he spoke to A. So, for example, suppose Fred told John that John's wife was having an affair with Carl. As a result, John beat Carl up, thereby committing the tort of battery. Fred can only be said to have procured John to commit the tort of battery if, when he told John of his wife's affair, he intended to encourage John to beat Carl up.

1 See above, pp. 386–7.

2 If C was an accessory to A's tort, lawyers commonly say that A and C committed A's tort as *joint tortfeasors*.

3 See above, pp. 612–13, for an explanation of the significance of two people being *jointly* liable to compensate a claimant for a loss that she has suffered.

4 See, on this, Carty 1999; Stevens 2007, 246–8, 253–4.

5 19 June 1980 (unreported), quoted by House of Lords in *Credit Lyonnais NV* v *ECGD* [2000] 1 AC 486, 497–8.

6 [1988] AC 1013.

7 Ibid., at 1058.

8 Ibid.

(2) *Authorisation.* If A commits a tort by doing *x*, and C has granted A permission to do *x* then C will be held to be an accessory to A's tort.[9]

It does not have to be shown that A would not have committed his tort but for C's giving him permission. For example, in a case where C has let his house to A and has agreed in the lease that A can use the house for A's band to rehearse in, it is no defence – when C is sued by C's neighbours for private nuisance – for C to argue that had he not given his permission, A would still have used the house for band rehearsals.

However, if A has committed a tort by doing *x*, C can only be held to have been an accessory to A's tort under this head if C had the authority, or purported to have the authority, to permit A to do *x*.[10] So if Nita produces an illegal copy of a CD or a DVD on her computer, the manufacturer of that computer cannot be said to have 'authorised' Nita to commit this breach of copyright because the manufacturer does not have, and does not pretend to have, the authority to permit Nita to produce illegal CDs and DVDs on her computer.[11]

(3) *Ratification.* If A commits a tort by doing *x*, and C subsequently treats A as though A did *x* on C's behalf, then C will be held to be an accessory to A's tort.

For example, in *Hilbery* v *Hatton*,[12] a ship called *John Brooks* was stranded off the coast of Africa. A man called Ward – who owned cargo on board the ship – unlawfully took charge of the ship and sold it to the defendants' agent, a man called Thompson, who was principally employed by the defendants to buy palm oil for them. Thompson subsequently wrote to the defendants announcing that he had purchased *John Brooks* for them; presumably, he thought the defendants could use the ship in their business. The defendants wrote back, approving the purchase. It was held that Thompson had committed the tort of conversion in buying, and taking possession, of the ship, and that the defendants also committed the tort of conversion when they approved the purchase of the ship on their behalf.

(4) *Common design.* In *The Koursk*,[13] the Court of Appeal endorsed the proposition that 'Persons are said to be joint tortfeasors when their respective shares in the commission of the tort are done in furtherance of a common design.'[14] So if A commits a tort by doing *x*, and in doing *x*, he was carrying out a plan of action agreed on between him and C, then C will be an accessory to A's tort.

Some have argued that liability for committing the tort of unlawful means conspiracy[15] has its origins in this rule of accessory liability. However, it is not clear that this is correct.[16] Suppose that Tom and Eric agree to imprison Beth, a famous opera singer, so as to disrupt

[9] For further discussion of this point in relation to the tort of private nuisance, see above, pp. 386–7.

[10] See *CBS Inc* v *Ames Records & Tapes Ltd* [1982] Ch 91, at 106 (per Whitford J): 'authorisation can only come from somebody having or purporting to have authority . . . an act is not authorised by somebody who . . . does not purport to have any authority which he can grant to justify the doing of the act.'

[11] *CBS Songs* v *Amstrad plc* [1988] AC 1013, 1053–5.

[12] (1864) 2 H & C 822, 159 ER 341.

[13] [1924] P 140 (discussed above, p. 612, n. 6).

[14] Ibid., 151, 156, 159.

[15] Discussed above, pp. 450–3.

[16] For arguments that the tort of unlawful means conspiracy is rooted in this rule of accessory liability, see Sales 1990; Carty 2001, 24–6; and Stevens 2007, 249.

a performance of *Le Nozze di Figaro* which Vijay is putting on. Tom subsequently kidnaps Beth and the opera performance has to be cancelled.

It is well established that in this situation Vijay can bring a claim for unlawful means conspiracy against both Tom and Eric. It is not clear how Vijay's claim can be rationalised as being based on a form of accessory liability. Clearly, Tom committed the tort of false imprisonment in kidnapping Beth, and Eric will be liable for Tom's tort as an accessory. But that does not explain the basis of *Vijay*'s claims against Eric and Tom as it was *Beth* who was the victim of Tom's act of false imprisonment, not Vijay.

It is possible to argue that in kidnapping Beth, Tom committed the tort of intentional infliction of harm by unlawful means[17] in relation to Vijay, and that Eric is an accessory to that tort. Given this, one could argue that the real reason why the courts allow Vijay to sue Tom and Eric for unlawful means conspiracy is that Tom committed the tort of intentional infliction of harm by unlawful means in relation to Vijay, and Eric is an accessory to that tort. However, this seems implausible – the tort of unlawful means conspiracy existed long before the tort of intentional infliction of harm by unlawful means was explicitly recognised by the courts.

(5) *Assistance*. The decision of the House of Lords in *CBS Songs* v *Amstrad plc* makes it clear that merely assisting someone to commit a tort will *not* make you an accessory to that tort.[18] So in the *Amstrad* case, CBS Songs argued that Amstrad were liable for all the breaches of copyright that were committed by people who used stereos manufactured by Amstrad to produce copies of music tapes bought in the shops. The House of Lords held that this would only be the case if Amstrad had procured or authorised people to make these copies, or that these copies were produced as part of a common design between Amstrad and their customers. The mere fact that Amstrad was helping its customers commit breaches of copyright by manufacturing their stereos was not enough to make it liable as an accessory for those breaches of copyright.

[17] Discussed above, pp. 423–33.

[18] See also *Credit Lyonnais NV* v *ECGD* [2000] 1 AC 486, discussed below, pp. 672–3.

33 Vicarious liability

THE NATURE OF VICARIOUS LIABILITY

Suppose that Mary has committed a tort in relation to Fred. We say that Lara is *vicariously liable* in respect of Mary's tort if the law treats Lara *as though* she committed that tort along with Mary. So although Lara did not actually do anything wrong,[1] she is treated as though she did. The result is that if Fred is entitled to sue *Mary* for compensation in respect of the losses that he has suffered as a result of Mary's tort, Fred will also be entitled to sue *Lara* for such compensation.[2] Four points about the nature of vicarious liability need to be emphasised:

(1) *Joint liability*. To say that Lara is *vicariously* liable in respect of Mary's tort is slightly misleading because it suggests that Mary's liability to pay damages to Fred is shifted[3] onto Lara.[4] The reality is that *both* Mary *and* Lara will be liable to pay damages to Fred and he will be free to choose to sue one or the other or both of them. Because Lara is treated as though she committed Mary's tort along with Mary, they will be *jointly liable* to compensate Fred for the losses suffered by him as a result of Mary's tort.[5] So if Fred releases Mary from liability, all his rights to sue Lara for compensation will usually also be extinguished.[6]

(2) *Distinction between vicarious liability and personal liability*. In the above case, Mary is personally liable to compensate Fred for the losses that he has suffered because *she* committed a tort in relation to Fred and thereby caused him to suffer those losses. Lara's liability is merely vicarious in nature because she herself did not commit a tort in the

[1] See *Dubai Aluminium Co Ltd* v *Salaam* [2003] 2 AC 366, at [155] (per Lord Millett): '[In a vicarious liability case] [t]he employer is not a wrongdoer; he is not liable in respect of his own conduct. He is answerable for his employee's wrongdoing, and his liability is coextensive with that of his employee. He is personally innocent, but he is liable because his employee is guilty.' To the same effect, see also *Majrowski* v *Guy's and St Thomas's NHS Trust* [2007] 1 AC 224, at [7] and [15] (per Lord Nicholls), and [68] (per Baroness Hale). Stevens 2007 (at 259–67) makes a powerful case that if Lara is held vicariously liable in this situation, it is because she *has* committed a tort *herself*. (See also, to the same effect, Williams 1956a.) The argument is that Lara's vicarious liability arises out of the fact that the law *attributes* Mary's actions to Lara. The end result is that Lara will be held to have committed whatever tort it was that Mary committed in acting as she did, and Lara will be held liable in the normal way for committing that tort. However, the weight of authority is heavily against this theory of vicarious liability.

[2] Likewise, if a third party has suffered loss as a result of Mary's tort for which he is entitled to sue Mary, he will also be entitled to sue *Lara* for compensation for that loss.

[3] See Birks 1995, 41: 'A "vicarious" liability is a liability which one person takes over from another, and as such [is] not his but that other's, just as a "vicar" was originally a person in holy orders who occupied a place which was not his but the rector's whose substitute he was.'

[4] Some commentators use the term 'secondary liability' instead of 'vicarious liability' to describe Lara's liability here, but that is also misleading because it suggests that Lara is only liable if Fred has no effective remedy against Mary.

[5] See above, pp. 612–13.

[6] Ibid.

situation we are considering. Lara is held liable to Fred because she is treated *as though* she committed a tort in this situation – the same tort that Mary committed.

So suppose Wendy entrusted her mink coat to Karen's care and Karen gave the coat to Paul to look after. Suppose further that Paul stole the coat. It is well established in this situation that Wendy will be entitled to sue Karen for compensation for the loss of her coat.[7] At first sight, this looks like an example of vicarious liability.[8] Karen, it may be argued, is liable to compensate Wendy for her coat because Karen is vicariously liable in respect of the tort of conversion that Paul committed when he stole Wendy's coat. But appearances mislead. The real reason that Karen is liable to Wendy here is that she owed Wendy a non-delegable duty[9] to take reasonable steps to safeguard Wendy's coat and Paul's actions put her in breach of this duty.[10] So as Karen has acted wrongfully in this situation, she is *personally*, not vicariously, liable to compensate Wendy for the loss of her coat.

Again, suppose that XYZ plc runs a nuclear power plant. Suppose further that, in order to save money, the managing directors of XYZ decide not to pay for their employees to have regular medicals so as to detect at an early stage whether any of them are showing signs that they are developing cancer as a result of working in the power plant. Suppose further that Nita develops cancer as a result of working in XYZ's power plant and she can show that had she had a regular medical in all probability her cancer would have been detected early enough to have been treated successfully. In this situation Nita will be able to sue XYZ for compensation. Again, this is not an example of vicarious liability. XYZ are personally liable here to compensate Nita for her injuries because XYZ – acting through those representing its 'guiding mind or will' – did something wrong and Nita suffered injury as a result. XYZ owed Nita a duty to take reasonable steps to see that she would be reasonably safe working for XYZ[11] and it breached that duty when it failed to arrange regular medicals for Nita.

Sticking with the same company, suppose that Carl was employed by XYZ and he was racially abused by his fellow employees while he was working with them. In this case, Carl will be entitled to sue XYZ for damages under Part III of the Race Relations Act 1976.[12] Again, this may look like an example of vicarious liability – we may suppose that Carl's fellow employees did something wrong in racially abusing him and that XYZ is held vicariously liable in respect of that wrong. But, again, appearances mislead. Whether or not Carl's fellow employees did anything wrong in racially abusing him is immaterial. XYZ are held liable here because the 1976 Act provides that when XYZ's employees racially abused Carl they put XYZ in breach of the duty it owed Carl not to subject him to unfavourable treatment because of his race.[13] So XYZ's liability to Carl here is personal in nature. XYZ is held liable here because *it* did something wrong – not because it is vicariously liable in

[7] *Morris* v *C.W. Martin & Sons Ltd* [1966] 1 QB 716.

[8] It was assumed that this is an example of vicarious liability in *Lister* v *Hesley Hall Ltd* [2002] 1 AC 215, at [19] (per Lord Steyn), [46] (per Lord Clyde), [57] (per Lord Hobhouse), [75]–[76] (per Lord Millett). See also *Dubai Aluminium Co. Ltd* v *Salaam* [2003] 2 AC 366, at [129] (per Lord Millett).

[9] Any reader currently unacquainted with the concept of a non-delegable duty of care should read pp. 230–6, above, before proceeding further.

[10] See Weir 2006, 111–12. Also *New South Wales* v *Lepore* (2003) 212 CLR 511, at [127] (per Gaudron J) and at [147], [161] (per McHugh J).

[11] See above, pp. 236–9.

[12] See above, pp. 493–6.

[13] Section 32(1). See above, pp. 494–5.

respect of any wrongs that its employees might have committed in relation to Carl when they racially abused him.

(3) *Distinction between vicarious liability and liability for breach of a non-delegable duty of care.* Let's go back to the example above where Wendy entrusted her mink coat to Karen's care and Karen gave the coat to Paul to look after. We have already seen that if Paul steals the coat Karen will be held liable to pay damages to Wendy on the basis that Paul's theft of the coat put Karen in breach of the non-delegable duty of care that she owed Wendy to look after Wendy's coat. It is sometimes said that Karen's liability to pay Wendy damages in this situation is *really* an example of vicarious liability – Karen is being held liable to compensate Wendy for the loss she has suffered as a result of Paul's tort in stealing Wendy's coat. So, for example, Gleeson CJ, of the High Court of Australia, urged in *Leichhardt Municipal Council* v *Montgomery*[14] that the law should 'frankly acknowledge' that in cases where someone is held liable for breaching a non-delegable duty of care owed to another, 'what is involved is not the breach by the defendant of a special kind of duty, but an imposition upon a defendant of a special kind of vicarious [liability].'[15]

With all due respect to Gleeson CJ, and those who think like him,[16] the law on when someone will be held liable for breaching a non-delegable duty of care *cannot* be subsumed within the law on vicarious liability.[17] This is shown by considering the position where Wendy entrusted her mink coat to Karen's care, and Karen asked Paul to look after the coat for her without telling Paul that it belonged to someone else. Now – let us assume that Paul carelessly allowed *someone else* to steal the coat. What is the position? Karen will be liable to pay Wendy damages because Paul's carelessness put her in breach of the non-delegable duty of care she owed Wendy to look after the coat. Now – this liability *cannot* be recharacterised as a form of vicarious liability. The reason is that when Paul carelessly allowed someone else to steal Wendy's coat, he did *not* commit a tort in relation to *Wendy*. He only owed *Karen* a duty of care to look after the coat.[18] So Paul committed a tort in relation to Karen in carelessly allowing someone to steal Wendy's coat, but not Wendy. But if Paul did not commit a tort in relation to Wendy in this situation, we cannot say that Karen's liability to pay Wendy damages is a form of vicarious liability. Paul has not committed a tort in relation to Wendy for which Karen can be held vicariously liable.

(4) *Distinction between vicarious liability and accessory liability.* Let's suppose that Mary committed the tort of battery by beating Fred up, and that Mary beat Fred up with Lara's encouragement. As we saw in the previous chapter, Lara will be an accessory to Mary's tort. As a result, Mary and Lara will be held jointly liable to compensate Fred for the harm he suffered as a result of being beaten up. How is this situation different from one where Lara is held vicariously liable for Mary's beating Fred up?

The main difference seems to be that in the first situation – that of accessory liability – the courts will find that *Lara*, as well as Mary, committed the tort of battery. In the second situation – where Lara is merely held vicariously liable for Mary's tort in beating Fred up –

[14] [2007] HCA 6.
[15] Ibid., at [24].
[16] See, for example, Williams 1956b; Fleming 1998, 434.
[17] Stevens 2007, 118.
[18] *The Pioneer Container* [1994] 2 AC 324, 342 (per Lord Goff); see above, p. 182, n. 75.

Lara will *not* be held to have committed the tort of battery. She will merely be treated *as though* she committed that tort. It may be thought that it makes little difference whether the courts find that Lara actually *did* commit the tort of battery, or whether the courts merely treat Lara *as though* she committed the tort of battery, but in some situations the distinction can be crucial.

First, in the case where Lara is an accessory to Mary's battery, Lara is a wrongdoer and as a result it might be that a court would award exemplary damages – damages designed to punish Lara for her conduct – against her. In the situation where Lara is vicariously liable for Mary's battery, it would be much more controversial to award exemplary damages against Lara. After all, if Lara is not actually a wrongdoer – but merely treated as though she were one – how can it be legitimate to punish her for what she has done?

Secondly, in the case where Lara is an accessory to Mary's battery, because Lara will be held to have actually committed the tort of battery in that case, there is a possibility that someone else might be held vicariously liable for the tort committed by *Lara*, with the result that Fred will have *three* people to sue for damages – Mary (as a principal wrongdoer), Lara (as a principal wrongdoer) and whoever is vicariously liable for Lara's actions. In the case where Lara is merely vicariously liable for Mary's battery, the courts will not find that Lara has *actually* done something wrong herself and as a result there will be no possibility of anyone else being held vicariously liable for Lara's actions. If Lara did not *herself* commit a tort in acting as she did, no one else can be held vicariously liable for her actions.[19]

SITUATIONS OF VICARIOUS LIABILITY

There are many different[20] situations in which one person will be vicariously liable in respect of a tort committed by another:

(1) *Employment.* If A is B's *employer*, A will be vicariously liable in respect of a tort committed by B if that tort is committed by B 'in the course of his employment'.[21] On the other hand, if A gets B to do some work for him as an *independent contractor*, A will *never* be

[19] See *Credit Lyonnais Bank Nederland NV* v *Export Credit Guarantee Department* [2000] 1 AC 486 (discussed below, pp. 672–3).

[20] It should be noted that the Supreme Court of Canada takes the view that these situations are not so different and that there is a general rule underlying all these instances of vicarious liability, namely that A may be held vicariously liable for a tort committed by B if the relationship between A and B at the time B committed his tort was 'sufficiently close as to make a claim for vicarious liability appropriate': see *KLB* v *British Columbia* [2003] 2 SCR 403, at [18] (per McLachlin CJ). In order to judge whether this requirement is satisfied, we must determine whether B was '"acting on his own account" or acting on behalf of [A]' at the relevant time (ibid., at [21]) – and this in turn will depend, in part, on how much 'control' A exerted over B at the relevant time (ibid., at [22]). Accordingly, it was held in the *KLB* case (Arbour J dissenting) that the government could not be held vicariously liable for various assaults that a foster parent committed on a child placed in his care by the government: foster families do not operate under 'close government control' and, as a result, while they do 'indeed [act] in the service of a public goal, their actions are too far removed from the government in the sense necessary to justify vicarious liability' (ibid., at [23], [25]).

[21] It used to be the case that if an employee of the Crown committed a tort in the course of his employment, the Crown would not be held vicariously liable in respect of that tort. That rule has now been abolished by s 2(1)(a) of the Crown Proceedings Act 1947.

vicariously liable in respect of a tort committed by B, even if B commits that tort in the course of doing the work that A has hired him to do.[22]

(2) *Police*. If A is the chief police officer in charge of an area in which B, a police officer, is working, A will be vicariously liable in respect of a tort committed by B in performing his functions as a police officer.[23]

(3) *Agency*. If A appoints B to act as his agent,[24] and B commits a tort while acting within the actual or ostensible scope of her authority as A's agent, A will be vicariously liable in respect of B's tort.[25]

(4) *Car owners*. Suppose that A requested B to perform some task for him which required B to drive A's car. Suppose further that in performing that task B negligently crashed A's car and in so doing injured C. It has been held – perhaps by analogy to the above rule dealing with vicarious liability for the acts of one's agents – that in this situation, A will be vicariously liable in respect of B's negligence.[26]

(5) *Partnership*. Under s 10 of the Partnership Act 1890, the partners in a firm will be vicariously liable in respect of a tort committed by one of the partners in that firm so long as the partner in question was acting 'in the ordinary course of the business of the firm'.[27]

(6) *Joint venture*. If A and B embark on a joint venture, and B commits a tort in the course of furthering that venture, then A will be vicariously liable in respect of B's tort.

So in *Brooke* v *Bool*,[28] the defendant let to the claimant a shop on the ground floor of a house next door to the defendant's home. The claimant agreed that each day the defendant could enter the shop after the claimant had left it to check that it was securely locked up. One night a lodger in the defendant's home told the defendant that he thought he could smell gas coming from the claimant's shop. The defendant and the lodger both went to

22 Of course, if A was subject to a non-delegable duty and he gave B – an independent contractor – the job of discharging that duty, then B might put A in breach of that duty and A might incur some sort of liability as a result. However, as has already been made clear, that liability will be personal in nature, not vicarious.

23 Police Act 1996, s 333.

24 An 'agent' is someone who acts as someone else's representative for legal purposes.

25 *Lloyd* v *Grace, Smith & Co.* [1912] AC 716 (for an alternative explanation of the decision in this case, see above, pp. 233–4); *Uxbridge Permanent Benefit Building Society* v *Pickard* [1939] 2 KB 248; *Armagas Ltd* v *Mundogas Ltd, The Ocean Frost* [1986] AC 717. For a full discussion, see Fridman 1996, 315–25.

26 See *Ormrod v Crosville Motor Services Ltd* [1953] 1 WLR 1120 (criticised, Brooke-Smith 1954). The defendant asked O to drive his car down to Monte Carlo so that the defendant could drive it in a motor rally there. In doing so, O negligently crashed the car into a bus. It was held that the defendant was vicariously liable in respect of O's negligence. *Ormrod* did *not* apply in *Klein* v *Caluori* [1971] 1 WLR 619, where F borrowed the defendant's car without his consent; when the defendant discovered this, he told F to bring the car back. As F was driving the car back, he negligently crashed into the claimant's car. Held, the defendant was not vicariously liable in respect of F's negligence because F was not performing a task for the defendant in bringing the car back – the job of bringing the car back was always F's to perform, not the defendant's. Neither did it apply in *Morgans* v *Launchbury* [1973] AC 127, where the defendant's husband went to the pub in the defendant's car. Realising he was too drunk to drive himself home, he had C drive him home in the defendant's car. On the way home, C drove the car so negligently that the claimants were injured. It was held that the defendant was not vicariously liable in respect of C's negligence as the defendant did not ask C to drive her husband home. See also *Nelson* v *Raphael* [1979] RTR 437.

27 It is worth noting that vicarious liability used to arise in the context of a very different kind of partnership: a husband used to be held vicariously liable in respect of any torts committed by his wife, but that rule was abolished by s 3 of the Law Reform (Married Women and Joint Tortfeasors) Act 1935.

28 [1928] 2 KB 578.

investigate. They inspected a gas pipe which passed down a wall in the claimant's shop, the defendant inspecting the lower half of the pipe and the lodger the upper half. The lodger used a naked light to inspect his half of the gas pipe. Unfortunately, the upper half of the gas pipe was leaking gas and when the gas came into contact with the lodger's light there was an explosion which damaged the claimant's goods. The lodger had been negligent in using a naked light to inspect the gas pipe and the defendant was held to be vicariously liable in respect of the lodger's negligence: he and the lodger had been engaged in a joint venture (checking for a gas leak) and the lodger had been attempting to further that venture when he acted as he did.[29]

Of these six situations in which one person will be held vicariously liable in respect of a tort committed by someone else, the most important by far is the first, which we will now discuss in detail.

VICARIOUS LIABILITY FOR EMPLOYEES' TORTS

It is well established that an employer will be vicariously liable in respect of a tort committed by one of his employees if that tort was committed 'in the course' of the employee's employment. This rule raises three questions. First of all, *why* does this rule exist? Secondly, when can we say that someone is another's *employee*? Thirdly, when can we say that an employee who has committed a tort did so in the *course* of his employment?

Rationale of the law

Suppose that A employs B and B commits a tort in the course of his employment by A. Nobody really understands why A will be held vicariously liable in respect of B's tort in this situation.[30] A number of different explanations of the law in this area have been advanced[31] but none of them really stand up to even the mildest critical scrutiny.[32]

(1) *Deep pockets.* It has been argued that A will be held vicariously liable in respect of B's tort because B is not likely to be worth suing. So making A vicariously liable in respect of B's tort will help to ensure that those who have suffered loss as a result of B's tort will be

[29] Stevens 2007, at 248–9, seems to treat this case as an example of accessory liability, but as there was no agreement between the defendant and the lodger that the lodger should use a naked light to inspect the pipe (and no encouragement from the defendant that the lodger should do so), we would prefer to see it as an example of vicarious liability. Even Carty 1999 (at 500) concedes that if *Brooke* v *Bool* is an example of accessory liability, it is 'probably at the outer limits' of such liability.

[30] Cf. *Hollis* v *Vabu Pty Ltd* (2001) 207 CLR 21, at [35] (per Gleeson CJ, Gaudron, Gummow, Kirby and Hayne JJ): 'a fully satisfactory rationale for the imposition of vicarious liability ... has been slow to appear ...'; also *New South Wales* v *Lepore* (2003) 212 CLR 511, at [106] (per Gaudron J, remarking on the 'absence of a satisfactory and comprehensive jurisprudential basis for the imposition of liability on a person for the harmful acts or omissions of others'), and [299] (per Kirby P: 'The history of the imposition of vicarious liability demonstrates that the foundation of such liability has been uncertain and variable').

[31] See, generally, Fleming 1998, 410; Neyers 2005, 291–301; Stevens 2007, 257–9. Both Neyers 2005 and Stevens 2007 propose interesting alternative rationales of the law on vicarious liability; but their attempts to explain the law are fatally flawed by the fact that many of the cases on vicarious liability simply do not fit their explanations and they are forced to argue that those cases were wrongly decided or reasoned.

[32] Which is not to say that the law on vicarious liability should not be reformed so that it gives effect to one of the rationales identified below. We personally are in favour of the law on vicarious liability being reformed so it gives effect to the 'enterprise risk' rationale set out below, at pp. 653–4.

able to sue someone of substantial means for compensation for their losses.[33] But this does not explain why A's liability in respect of B's tort is dependent on it being shown that B's tort was committed *in the course of his employment*. The 'deep pockets' rationale of an employer's vicarious liability for the torts committed by his employees justifies his being held liable for *all* the torts committed by his employees, whether they were committed within or without the course of their employment.[34]

(2) *Deterrence*. It is also said that holding A vicariously liable in respect of B's tort here will encourage him to take steps to see that his employees do not act wrongfully while they work for him.[35] But if this is correct, one would expect the law to say that A will be held vicariously liable in respect of B's tort if A could possibly have done something to prevent that tort being committed. But it does not say this and it has never said this.

(3) *Enterprise risk*. Another explanation as to why A will be vicariously liable in respect of B's tort goes as follows. Elementary fairness dictates that if you seek to make money from engaging in some activity and other people suffer loss as a result of your engaging in that activity, you should compensate them for that loss – if you want to obtain the gains resulting from engaging in that activity, then you should bear the losses as well.

This principle of fairness applies here:[36] A set up in business for himself and as a result of his doing so, other people – the people who were harmed by B's tort – have suffered loss as a result. It is only fair that A should compensate those people for the loss they have suffered and the law's way of ensuring that A does so is to make A vicariously liable in respect of B's tort.[37]

But if this is right, it is hard to understand why someone who carries on his business

[33] Cf. *Limpus* v *London General Omnibus Company* (1862) 1 H&C 526, 529; 158 ER 995, 998: 'It is well-known that there is virtually no remedy against the driver of an omnibus, and therefore it is necessary that, for injury resulting from an act done by him in the course of his master's service, the master should be responsible; for there ought to be a remedy against some person capable of paying damages to those injured by improper driving' (per Willes J). Also Baty 1916, 152; Atiyah 1967, 22; Feldthusen 1998, 224–5.

[34] Fleming 1998 argues (at 410) that the law does not hold employers liable for torts committed by their employees outside the course of their employment because it does not want to 'foist an undue burden on business enterprise'. But there is more than a whiff of *ex post facto* rationalisation about this explanation.

[35] Cf. *Bazley* v *Curry* [1999] 2 SCR 534, at [32]–[33]: 'Fixing the employer with responsibility for the employee's wrongful act, even where the employer is not negligent, may have a deterrent effect. Employers are often in a position to reduce accidents and intentional wrongs by efficient organization and supervision ... Beyond the narrow band of employer conduct that attracts direct liability in negligence lies a vast area where imaginative and efficient administration and supervision can reduce the risk [of wrongdoing by the employer's employees]. Holding the employer vicariously liable for the wrongs of its employee may encourage the employer to take such steps and, hence, reduce the risk of future harm' (per McLachlin J). Also *New South Wales* v *Lepore* (2003) 212 CLR 511, at [305] (per Kirby P); Pollock 1882, 130.

[36] It may also underlie the Consumer Protection Act 1987, in so far as it makes a manufacturer who manufactures goods for profit liable for the harm caused by any of his goods being defective. See Stapleton 1994a, 185–217; Waddams 1998, 124–5. The 1987 Act is discussed in detail below, in Chapter 43. The rule in *Rylands* v *Fletcher* (discussed below, at pp. 754–64), might also be said to rest on this principle of fairness: Cane 1999, 202.

[37] Cf. *Dubai Aluminium* v *Salaam* [2003] 2 AC 366, at [21]: 'The ... legal policy [underlying the law on vicarious liability] is based on the recognition that carrying on a business enterprise necessarily involves risks to others. It involves the risk that others will be harmed by wrongful acts committed by the [employees] through whom the business is carried on. When those risks ripen into loss, it is just that the business should be responsible for compensating the person who has been wronged' (per Lord Nicholls). See also *Lister* v *Hesley Hall Ltd* [2002] 1 AC 215, at [65] (per Lord Millett); *Bazley* v *Curry* [1999] 2 SCR 534, at [22], [30] (per McLachlin J); *New South Wales* v *Lepore* (2003) 212 CLR 511, at [303] (per Kirby P); *Majrowski* v *Guy's and St Thomas's NHS Trust* [2007] 1 AC 224, at [9] (per Lord Nicholls); Pollock 1882, 122; W&J, 882–3.

using independent contractors to work for him is not held vicariously liable in respect of the torts committed by those independent contractors in the course of working for him. Moreover, this explanation does not explain why the law on vicarious liability applies as much to government agencies and private foundations that do not seek to make money from their activities as it does to people who set up businesses to earn money.[38]

(4) *Relative blame.* In *Hern* v *Nichols*, Holt CJ explained that an employer will be vicariously liable in respect of a tort committed by an employee in the course of his employment because 'seeing somebody must be a loser [as a result of a tort committed by an employee] it is more reason that he that employs and puts a trust and confidence in [the employee] should be a loser than a stranger'.[39] But if this is right it is again hard to see why someone who engages someone else to work for him as an independent contractor should not be vicariously liable in respect of any torts committed by that contractor in doing the work he is engaged to do.

(5) *Loss-spreading.* Finally, it has been said that A will be held vicariously liable in respect of B's tort because doing this will allow the losses caused by B's tort to be effectively spread among the community at large. If A is held vicariously liable in respect of B's tort, the losses caused by B's tort will be shifted onto A's shoulders and A will then be able to spread the losses – either by charging his customers slightly higher prices or by making a claim on his liability insurance.[40]

But this does not explain why an employer will not be held vicariously liable in respect of a tort committed by one of his employees if that tort was not committed in the course of the employee's employment. In such a case, there is just as much of a need to spread the losses caused by the employee's tort as there would be if he committed it in the course of his employment, but the law does not respond to this need by making the employer vicariously liable in respect of his employee's tort. Why not?

Employee

Basic principles

Suppose that A commits a tort while working for B. When can we say that A is an employee

[38] However, it could be argued (as Kirby P did in *New South Wales* v *Lepore* (2003) 212 CLR 511, at [303]) that as the *community as a whole* seeks to profit from the activities of government agencies, the community as a whole should bear the losses caused by someone who committed a tort while working for a government agency if it was predictable that the person doing that kind of work would commit that kind of tort. One way of doing this is to hold the government agency vicariously liable in respect of the tortfeasor's tort: the government can then spread the cost of paying compensation for the losses caused by the tort among the community as a whole through higher taxes or increased borrowing. This argument will not work to justify holding private foundations that do not seek to make money from their activities vicariously liable for torts committed by their employees as they cannot pass any losses resulting from their being held vicariously liable onto the community. Despite this, the Supreme Court of Canada refused to find that such foundations should be given any special exemption from the rules on vicarious liability in *Bazley* v *Curry* [1999] 2 SCR 534, at [47]–[56].

[39] (1700) 1 Salk 289, 91 ER 256. See also *Bazley* v *Curry* [1999] 2 SCR 534, at [50] and [54] (per McLachlin J).

[40] Cf. *Bazley* v *Curry* [1999] 2 SCR 534, at [31]: 'the employer is often in the best position to spread the losses [caused by an employee's tort] through mechanisms like insurance and higher prices, thus minimizing the dislocative effect of the tort within society' (per McLachlin J).

of B's? The basic answer is – A will be an employee of B's if A contracts[41] to do work for B under a *contract of service*, as opposed to a *contract for services*.

The distinction between a contract of service and a contract for services is easy to grasp but hard to express. We can grasp the distinction by looking at two cases. In the first, A contracts to build a greenhouse for B in B's back garden. In the second, A contracts to work in B's factory making glass panes for greenhouses. In the first case, A's contract with B is a contract for services. So, in the first case, B will not be A's employer, or, to put it another way, A will not be B's servant or employee; rather, he will be an independent contractor vis-à-vis B. In the second case, A's contract with B will be a contract of service. So, in the second case, B will be A's employer and A will be B's employee or servant.

It is far harder to put one's finger on what makes a given contract to do work for another a contract of service or a contract for services.[42] Traditionally, the courts adopted a 'control test' to differentiate between contracts of service and contracts for services. According to the 'control test', if A contracts to do work for B, that contract will be a contract of service if B has the power under the contract to dictate *how* A will do his work; if, on the other hand, B does not have the power under the contract to dictate how A will do his work but merely specifies *what* work is to be done by A and leaves it up to A to determine how he will do that work, then that contract will be a contract for services.[43]

In *Performing Right Society Ltd* v *Mitchell & Booker (Palais de Danse) Ltd*,[44] the defendants owned a dance hall and engaged a band to play in it. On one occasion the band performed some dance music which was protected by copyright. The copyright on the music in question belonged to the claimants and the band did not have the claimants' permission to play that music when they did so. The claimants sued the defendants, claiming that the defendants were vicariously liable in respect of the band's violation of the claimants' copyright. The case turned on whether the band were employees of the defendants when they played in the dance hall or whether they were in fact independent contractors. The court applied the control test and found that the band were employees of the defendants when they played in the defendants' dance hall: 'the contract [gave] to the defendants the right of continuous, dominant and detailed control on every point, including the nature of the music to be played [by the band].'[45]

More recently, the courts have rejected the 'control test' as an unsatisfactory means of differentiating between contracts of service and contracts for services.[46] For example,

41 Obviously, if A is at a given time under no contractual obligation to do any work for B then A cannot be an employee of B's at that time: *Carmichael* v *National Power plc* [1999] 1 WLR 2042 (tour guides who worked for defendant on casual basis, turning up for work as and when they were required to do so, could not claim to be employees of the defendant as they were under no obligation to turn up for work when they were asked to do so).

42 See Kidner 1995.

43 Cf. *Yewens* v *Noakes* (1880) 6 QBD 530, 532–3: 'A servant is a person who is subject to the command of his master as to the manner in which he shall do his work' (per Bramwell LJ). See also *Honeywill and Stein Ltd* v *Larkin Brothers Ltd* [1934] 1 KB 191, 196: 'The determination whether [someone] is a servant . . . on the one hand or an independent contractor on the other depends on whether or not the employer not only determines what is to be done, but retains control of the actual performance, in which case the doer is a servant . . .; but if the employer, while prescribing the work to be done, leaves the manner of doing it to the control of the doer, the latter is an independent contractor' (per Slesser LJ).

44 [1924] 1 KB 762.

45 Ibid., 771.

46 Which is not to say that considerations of control are not sometimes taken into account by the courts in

suppose that A contractually undertakes to do work for B and the work which A is supposed to do for B is of such a technical character that B – in his ignorance as to how that work should be done – is in no position to dictate to A how that work should be done. In such a case, under the control test, it will be impossible to find that A is employed by B. But this is counter-intuitive: there are plenty of cases where we would say that B is A's employer even though the work to be done by A under the contract between him and B is of such a complex character that B is in no position to tell him how to do it. For example, the master of a ship is plainly employed by the owners of the ship even though the owners are in no position to dictate to him how he should navigate the ship.[47] Similarly, a surgeon may well be employed by the hospital at which he works even though the hospital authorities are in no position to dictate to him how he should conduct his operations.[48] If the 'control test' is no longer a useful test for differentiating between contracts of service and contracts for services, what test should we adopt in its place? The courts have suggested a variety of alternative tests.

(1) *Ordinary person.* In *Cassidy* v *Ministry of Health*, Somervell LJ suggested that a given contract to do work for another would be a contract of service if an ordinary person would regard it as being a contract of service and that it would be a contract for services if an ordinary person would regard it as being a contract for services.[49]

This test for differentiating between contracts of service and contracts for services – which we can call the 'ordinary person' test – is of severely limited usefulness. There are many instances of contracts to do work for another which an ordinary person would be hard-pressed to classify as being contracts of service or contracts for services. For instance, in *Argent* v *Minister of Social Security*[50] a drama school engaged Argent to work for them as a part-time teacher. Argent was paid on an hourly basis. The school did not dictate to Argent what he should do in his classes. Occasionally, Argent would cease giving classes at the school in order to work full-time as an actor in various theatre productions. Would an ordinary person say that Argent's contract with the drama school was a contract of service or a contract for services? It is difficult to imagine he would have any firm view on the matter.[51] Given this, it is doubtful whether the 'ordinary person' test provides much of a guide as to whether a given contract to do work for another amounts to a contract of service or a contract for services.

(2) *Integration.* In *Stephenson Jordan & Harrison Ltd* v *MacDonald & Evans*, Denning LJ suggested that 'under a contract of service, a man is employed as part of the business and his work is done as an integral part of the business: whereas under a contract for services his work, although done for the business, is not integrated into it but is only accessory to it'.[52] Shortly afterwards, in *Bank voor Handel en Scheepvart NV* v *Slatford*, Denning LJ

---

judging whether someone is an employee or not. See, for example, *Montgomery* v *Johnson Underwood Ltd* [2001] ICR 819 (held, a temp is not employed by the employment agency which places her with various employers on a temporary basis because the employment agency had no control over how she did her work).

47 *Gold* v *Essex County Council* [1942] 2 KB 293, 305 (per Mackinnon LJ).

48 *Cassidy v Ministry of Health* [1951] 2 KB 343.

49 Ibid., 352–3.

50 [1968] 1 WLR 1749.

51 In fact, it was found that he was not an employee but was employed under a contract for services.

52 (1951) 69 RPC 10, 22.

rephrased this test – which we can call the 'integration' test – for differentiating between contracts of service and contracts for services. In that case, he suggested 'the test of being a servant does not rest nowadays on submission to orders. It depends on whether the person is part and parcel of the organisation.'[53]

The integration test for differentiating between contracts of service and contracts for services is again, because of its vagueness, of very limited usefulness. MacKenna J criticised the test in *Ready Mixed Concrete (South East) Ltd* v *Minister of Pensions and National Insurance*, arguing that it 'raises more questions than I know how to answer. What is meant by being "part and parcel of an organisation"? Are all persons who answer this description servants? If only some are servants, what distinguishes them from the others . . .?'[54]

(3) *Four indicia*. In *Short* v *J W Henderson Ltd*, Lord Thankerton suggested that a contract under which A undertakes to do work for B will amount to a contract of service if: (1) B selected A to do work for him; (2) under the contract A is to be paid wages for the work done by him; (3) B has the right under the contract to control the way in which A does the work contracted for; (4) B has the right to suspend or dismiss A.[55]

This test for determining whether or not a contract to do work for another is a contract of service or a contract for services – which we can call the 'four *indicia*' test – is not particularly helpful. First of all, the fact that (1) and (4) are true of a particular contract to do work for another does not indicate that that contract is a contract of service: (1) and (4) may well be satisfied even if the contract in question is a contract for services. Secondly, as we have seen, if (3) is not true of a particular contract to do work for another that does not necessarily mean that that contract is not a contract of service. However, the 'four *indicia*' test does highlight *a* difference between a contract of service and a contract for services. A person who does work for another under a contract of service is usually paid *wages* or a *salary* for the work done by him. A person who does work for another under a contract for services is usually paid a *fee* for the work done by him.

(4) *Principal obligation*. In *WHPT Housing Association Ltd* v *Secretary of State for Social Services*, Webster J suggested that 'the difference between a contract of service and one for services must reside, essentially, in the terms of the principal obligation agreed to be undertaken by the employee – a word which I use without begging the question. In a contract of service . . . the principal obligation undertaken by the employee is to provide himself to serve: whereas in a contract for services the principal obligation is not to provide himself to serve the employer but his services for the use of the employer.'[56]

This test – which we can call the 'obligation' test – seems to capture *a* difference between a contract of service and a contract for services. If A enters into a contract for services with B, the contract will *normally* specify that A must do a specific piece of work for B; how long A takes over the work is left up to A.[57] If A enters into a contract of service with B, the

[53] [1953] 1 QB 248, 295.
[54] [1968] 2 QB 497, 524.
[55] (1946) 62 TLR 427, 429.
[56] [1981] ICR 737, 748.
[57] There are obvious exceptions to this point. For example, if B hires A to clean his house for four hours a week, the contract will still be a contract for services even though A's contractual obligation is to work for a certain amount of time for B.

contract will normally specify that A must work a certain number of hours for B doing a particular kind of work and A will have no flexibility over how long he can take working for B.

Related to this is another difference that seemingly exists between contracts of service and contracts for services. A contract of service is *personal*: if A enters into a contract of service with B, A will not be able to discharge his obligations under the contract by getting C to fill in for him and fulfil his duties under his contract with B. As a general rule, a contract for services is *impersonal*: if A enters into a contract for services with B, A will – as a general rule[58] – be able to discharge his obligations under the contract through other people.[59] So, for example, if A contracts to build a greenhouse in B's back garden, he will discharge his obligation to build that greenhouse in B's back garden if he gets C to build the greenhouse requested by B.

(5) *Independence.* In *Market Investigations Ltd* v *Minister of Social Security*, Cooke J suggested that 'the fundamental test to be applied [to determine whether a given contract is a contract of service or a contract for services] is this: "Is the person who has engaged himself to perform these services performing them as a person in business on his own account?" If the answer to that question is "yes" then the contract is a contract for services. If the answer is "no" then the contract is a contract of service.'[60]

We can call this the 'independence' test for differentiating between contracts of service and contracts for services. Cooke J then went on to say that a variety of factors would have to be taken into account in judging whether or not someone who has engaged himself to perform services for another will perform them in business on his own account: 'control will no doubt always have to be considered, although it can no longer be regarded as the sole determining factor; ... factors which may be of importance are such matters as whether the man performing the services provides his own equipment, whether he hires his own helpers, what degree of financial risk he takes, what degree of responsibility for investment and management he has, and whether and how far he has an opportunity of profiting from sound management in the performance of his task.'[61] In *Lee Ting Sang* v *Chung Chi-Keung*, the Privy Council explicitly endorsed Cooke J's approach in the *Market Investigations* case to the question of whether a given contract is a contract of service or a contract for services, holding that the appropriate approach to this question had 'never been better put than by Cooke J in *Market Investigations Ltd* . . .'[62]

Again, this test does capture *a* difference between a contract of service and a contract for services. If A works for B under a contract of service, to some extent A's economic welfare is bound up with B's: if B does not do well, then that imperils A's economic welfare. On the other hand, if A works for B under a contract for services, then A's economic welfare is relatively independent of B's. Instead, A's economic welfare is bound up with the quality of the

[58] Again, there are some obvious exceptions to this point. If B hires A to paint her portrait, the contract will be a contract for services even though it is personal in nature; A will not be able to discharge his obligations to B under the contract by getting a third party to paint B's portrait.

[59] This is why when B hires a company to do some work for him, one could never say that the company does that work as B's employee. The company – being incapable of doing the work itself – will always do that work through other people; that is, its own employees.

[60] [1969] 2 QB 173, 184.

[61] Ibid., 185.

[62] [1990] 2 AC 374, 382.

work he does for B: if his work is bad, he will not be paid; if it is good, then he will be paid. In other words, if A works for B under a contract of service, A and B's interests will coincide: A will have an interest in seeing that B's interests are promoted. If A works for B under a contract for services, A will not necessarily have an interest in seeing that B's interests are promoted.

In light of the above, we can propose a 'five *indicia*' test for determining whether a given contract to do work for another amounts to a contract of service or a contract for services. Under this test, if A has entered into a contract with B under which he undertakes to do work for B, that contract will be a contract *of service* if *most* of the following five requirements are met: (1) Under the contract, B has the power to control how A does his work; (2) A is required under the contract to work for B for a set period of time; (3) A is due to be paid wages or a salary for the work done by him under his contract with B; (4) A's obligations under his contract with B are personal to him and cannot be discharged by having a third party perform them; (5) the terms of A's contract with B indicate that A, in working for B, is not engaged in some business on his own account. If *most* of these requirements are *not* met then A's contract with B will be a contract for services.

The problem of 'borrowed' employees

In a 'borrowed' employee situation, the problem is not so much determining whether someone who has committed a tort was an employee – there is no question about that – but *whose* employee he was at the time he committed his tort. The basic situation we are concerned with is this: A is an employee of B's, and then A is sent by B to work for C. While A was working for C, A committed a tort in relation to D. A is not worth suing, so D wants to sue whoever was A's employer at the time A committed his tort, arguing that A's employer is vicariously liable for A's tort. So the question is: When A committed his tort, whose employee was he? Was he B's employee, or was he C's, or was he, perhaps, employed by *both* B *and* C at the time he committed his tort?

Two recent Court of Appeal decisions have provided some guidance as to how we determine who will be said to have been A's employer at the time he committed his tort.[63] The following propositions can be extracted from the cases:

(1) *Initial presumption.* For the purposes of the law on vicarious liability, the initial presumption will be that when A was working for C, he was still employed solely by B. This presumption will be difficult to displace.[64]

(2) *Shifting the presumption.* However, this initial presumption – which will be difficult to displace[65] – will be displaced if A was so much under C's control while he was working for C that we can say that C had the power and responsibility to stop A committing the tort that he committed.[66]

(3) *Settling the question.* If the initial presumption that A was B's employee at the time he

[63] See *Viasystems (Tyneside) Ltd* v *Thermal Transfer (Northern) Limited* [2006] QB 510 ('*Viasystems*'); *Hawley* v *Luminar Leisure Ltd* [2006] IRLR 817 ('*Hawley*').
[64] *Hawley*, at [28].
[65] Ibid.
[66] *Viasystems*, at [16] (per May LJ); *Hawley*, at [28].

committed his tort can be displaced, then we find out who was A's employer at the time he committed his tort by asking – Who had the power and responsibility to stop A committing that tort? If the answer is: 'C, and no one else' then we should say that A was C's employee, and not B's, at the time A committed his tort. If, on the other hand, the answer is: 'B and C *both* had the power and responsibility to stop A committing his tort' then we should say that A was employed by *both* B *and* C at the time he committed his tort.

So – in *Mersey Docks & Harbour Board* v *Coggins & Griffith (Liverpool) Ltd*,[67] A was a crane operator, B was a harbour authority that owned the crane operated by A, and C was a firm of stevedores that had hired the crane to help unload a ship. A was negligent in operating the crane, and as a result the claimant was injured. The House of Lords held that in this case the initial presumption that A was B's employee when he was working for C was not displaced. When A went to work for C, C obtained no kind of control over how A did his work. All they could do was direct him what to do. They had no power over *how* A operated the crane.

In contrast, in *Hawley* v *Luminar Leisure Ltd*,[68] A was a nightclub 'bouncer', B was a firm that supplied bouncers to nightclubs, and C was a firm that operated a nightclub. A was sent by B to work at C's nightclub. One evening, a fracas broke out outside C's nightclub, and in the course of dealing with the fracas, A punched the claimant in the face. The Court of Appeal found that C exercised a great deal of control over how A discharged his duties as a bouncer at C's nightclub. So the initial presumption that A was B's employee at the time he hit the claimant was displaced. The Court of Appeal went on to find that C exercised so much control over how A did his job as a bouncer at C's nightclub compared with B that the sole power and responsibility of stopping A beating up customers outside C's nightclub rested with C. Given this, the Court of Appeal found that when A hit the claimant, he was employed solely by C. It followed that only C could be held vicariously liable for the tort A committed in hitting the claimant.

Finally, in *Viasystems (Tyneside) Ltd* v *Thermal Transfer (Northern) Limited*,[69] A was an apprentice metalworker, learning his trade under the supervision of a 'fitter'. B was a firm that supplied metalworkers to help out on building sites. C was a firm that had been engaged to install some airducts in the claimants' factory. B supplied C with a fully trained 'fitter' to work on the installation job, and sent A along with the 'fitter' to help out. While A was fetching some equipment, he carelessly set off the factory sprinkler system, which caused a flood. The Court of Appeal found that C exercised enough control over how A did his work to displace the initial presumption that A was B's employee when he negligently damaged the claimants' factory. The Court of Appeal went on to find that the power and responsibility of stopping A being negligent was shared between C and B. (In the case of B, the fully trained 'fitter' supplied by B to C had the task of supervising A's work.) So the Court of Appeal found that at the time A was negligent, he was employed by *both* B *and* C, with the result that both B and C could be held vicariously liable for A's negligence.

[67] [1947] AC 1.
[68] [2006] IRLR 817.
[69] [2006] QB 510.

Course of employment

Suppose that A was an employee of B's when he committed a tort. When can we say that A committed that tort 'in the course of his employment' by B? The law on this question has undergone a dramatic transformation in recent years.

The Salmond test

Before the decision of the House of Lords in *Lister* v *Hesley Hall Ltd*,[70] one would use the *Salmond test* to determine whether an employee's tort was committed in the course of his employment. Under this test – set out by the great tort lawyer Sir John Salmond in the first edition of his *Law of Torts* – an employee's tort will have been committed in the course of his employment if it was:

> either (a) a wrongful act authorised by [the employee's employer], or (b) a wrongful and unauthorised mode of doing some act authorised by [the employee's employer][71]

To put the test another way, under the Salmond test, an employee's tort will have been committed in the course of his employment if *the employee did something he was employed to do by committing that tort.*

So suppose that Gary, who was employed by Ruth, drove a car from point A to point B at 100 mph, thereby breaking the speed limit. And suppose further that Ian was injured as a result of Gary's dangerous driving. Under the Salmond test, Ruth would be vicariously liable in respect of Gary's negligence if Gary was employed by her to drive from point A to point B.[72] If he was, then he did something he was employed to do by driving the car at 100 mph. It may be that he was not authorised to break the speed limit in driving from point A to point B but that is immaterial under the Salmond test: the only thing that counts is whether Gary was employed to drive from point A to point B. If he was not, then Ruth would not be vicariously liable in respect of Gary's negligence under the Salmond test.[73] Gary would not have done anything he was employed to do by driving from point A to point B at 100 mph.

Similarly, suppose Gary intentionally hit Ian while he, Gary, was employed by Ruth. Under the Salmond test, Ruth would only be vicariously liable in respect of the tort

[70] [2002] 1 AC 215.

[71] Salmond 1907, 83. It should be pointed out that an employer will be held liable as an accessory for an employee's tort if the tort was committed with the employer's authority (see above, p. 645), and so there is no need in this kind of case (situation (a) in the Salmond test) to say that the employer will be held vicariously liable in respect of his employee's tort.

[72] See *Limpus* v *London General Omnibus Company* (1862) 1 H&C 526; 158 ER 995 (bus company vicariously liable for bus driver's breaking of speed limit while driving buses on route); also *Rose* v *Plenty* [1976] 1 WLR 141 (defendant employers vicariously liable in respect of milkman's negligent driving in driving milk float on his round).

[73] See *Storey* v *Ashton* (1869) LR 4 QB 476 (two employees of defendant's went by horse and cart to deliver some wine to a customer of the defendant's; on the way back, one employee persuaded the other to make a diversion and pick up a cask of wine from the first employee's brother-in-law; held, defendant not vicariously liable in respect of negligent way in which second employee drove horse and cart on the way to the home of the first employee's brother-in-law as second employee not employed to drive horse and cart to that destination); also *Conway* v *George Wimpey & Co. Ltd* [1951] 2 KB 266 (defendant building contractor appointed to do work at airport; had employee drive lorry around perimeter of airport and pick up and drop off any of defendant's employees who were working in the airport and wanted a lift to a different part of the airport; employee gave a lift to someone who was not working for defendant and drove lorry so negligently that the passenger was injured; held, defendant not vicariously liable in respect of employee's negligent driving as employee did not do anything he was employed to do by giving passenger a lift).

committed by Gary in hitting Ian if Gary did something he was employed to do by hitting Ian. So suppose Gary was employed by Ruth to work in a bar and was charged with the general responsibility of keeping order in the bar. If Ian was making a nuisance of himself in the bar and Gary hit him to shut him up, then Gary would have done something he was employed to do by hitting Ian and Ruth would be vicariously liable in respect of Gary's tort under the Salmond test.[74] If, on the other hand, Gary – in hitting Ian – was merely taking revenge on him for some slight which Gary suffered at Ian's hands in the past, then, under the Salmond test, Ruth would not have been vicariously liable in respect of the tort committed by Gary in hitting Ian.[75] Gary would not have done anything he was employed to do by hitting Ian.

A difficulty in applying the Salmond test

For the most part, the Salmond test for determining whether or not an employer would be vicariously liable in respect of a tort committed by one of his employees was straightforward to apply. However, in certain marginal cases there were difficulties – arising out of the fact that it is not always clear how widely or narrowly we should characterise what an employee was employed to do. For example, in *London County Council* v *Cattermoles (Garages) Ltd*,[76] the defendants employed one Preston to work in their garage. One of Preston's duties was to move cars that had been left at the garage when they were in the way of other cars using the garage. He was told to move any cars by hand as he did not have a driving licence. Preston was instructed to move a van which was obstructing access to the defendants' petrol pumps. Preston got into the van and drove it into the road. However, he did not keep a proper lookout in driving the van into the road and it collided with the claimant's vehicle. The claimant sued the defendants claiming that they were vicariously liable in respect of Preston's negligence.

[74] See *Poland* v *John Parr & Sons* [1927] 1 KB 236 (carter employed by defendants to accompany wagon of sugar as it travelled through Liverpool; carter hit claimant schoolboy who he mistakenly thought was trying to steal some sugar off the wagon; held, defendants vicariously liable in respect of carter's battery as carter did something he was employed to do – defend the wagon from theft – by hitting the claimant); *Bernard* v *Attorney General of Jamaica* [2004] UKPC 47 (policeman wanted to use a public payphone to call for assistance but the claimant – who was using the payphone at the time – refused to hang up; the policeman then shot the claimant; the defendants were held vicariously liable for the policeman's shooting the claimant as the policeman was acting on police business in attempting to get the claimant to give up the phone); *Brown* v *Robinson* [2004] UKPC 56 (in an attempt to maintain order in a crowd of people waiting to get into a football stadium, a security guard got into an altercation with the claimant which resulted in his shooting the claimant; held that defendant employers of security guard were vicariously liable for the shooting as the security acted as he did to maintain some discipline in the crowd).

[75] See *Warren* v *Henleys Ltd* [1948] 2 All ER 935 (a petrol pump attendant struck a customer in the course of an altercation about whether or not the customer had paid for petrol taken from the petrol pump; held, that the employers of the attendant were not vicariously liable in respect of the battery committed by the attendant as the attendant did not do anything he was employed to do by striking the passenger); *Keppel Bus Co.* v *Sa'ad bin Ahmed* [1974] 1 WLR 1082 (bus conductor swore at passenger and then hit him when the passenger protested; held, bus company not vicariously liable in respect of conductor's battery as he did not do anything he was employed to do in hitting the passenger); *Aldred* v *Nacanco* [1987] IRLR 292 (defendant employer not vicariously liable for tort committed by employee in trying to startle fellow employee; first instance decision in *Harrison* v *Michelin Tyre Co. Ltd* [1985] 1 All ER 918, holding defendant employer vicariously liable in respect of tort committed by employee in causing fellow employee to lose footing and fall, disapproved); *Deatons Pty Ltd* v *Flew* (1949) 79 CLR 370 (defendant hotel owners not vicariously liable in respect of tort committed by employee tending bar in hotel when she reacted to lewd suggestion by a patron of the bar by throwing beer, and subsequently an empty glass, in his face).

[76] [1953] 1 WLR 997.

The case turned on the question: What was Preston employed to do? If he was employed to move cars in the defendants' garage *by hand* then Preston did *not* do anything he was employed to do by *driving* the van into the road without keeping a proper lookout. If he was simply employed to *move* cars in the defendants' garage, then Preston *did* do something he was employed to do by driving the van into the road without keeping a proper lookout. The Court of Appeal took a wide view of what Preston was employed to do in this case and found that Preston was employed to move cars in the defendants' garage. So the court concluded that Preston *was* acting in the course of his employment when he drove the van into the road without keeping a proper lookout.

Other cases are more difficult. For example, suppose Alan was an employee of Acme Co. and one day he drove to work at 100 mph, with the result that he negligently crashed into Dawn's car. Could we say – for the purposes of applying the Salmond test to determine whether Acme are vicariously liable in respect of Alan's negligence – that Alan was doing something he was employed to do when he drove to work at 100 mph? The House of Lords addressed this issue in the case of *Smith* v *Stages*.[77] Lord Lowry sought to deal with it by setting out some guidelines which are worth setting out in full:

1. An employee travelling from his ordinary residence to his regular place of work, whatever the means of transport and even if it is provided by the employer is not on duty and is not acting in the course of his employment, but, if he is obliged by his contract of service to use the employer's transport, he will normally, in the absence of an express condition to the contrary, be regarded as acting in the course of his employment while doing so.
2. Travelling in the employer's time between workplaces (one of which may be the regular workplace) or in the course of a peripatetic profession, whether accompanied by goods or tools or simply in order to reach a succession of workplaces . . . will be in the course of the employment.
3. Receipt of wages (though not receipt of a travelling allowance) will indicate that the employee is travelling in the employer's time and for his benefit and is acting in the course of his employment, and in such a case the fact that the employee may have discretion as to the mode and time of travelling will not take the journey out of the course of his employment.
4. An employee travelling in the employer's time from his ordinary workplace to a workplace other than his regular workplace or in the course of a peripatetic profession or to the scene of an emergency (such as a fire, an accident or mechanical breakdown of plant) will be acting in the course of his employment.
5. A deviation from or interruption of a journey undertaken in the course of employment (unless the deviation or interruption is merely incidental to the journey) will for the time being (which may include an overnight interruption) take the employee out of the course of his employment.
6. Return journeys are to be treated as on the same footing as outward journeys.[78]

Estoppel and the Salmond test

It should also be noted that the application of the Salmond test in particular cases to determine whether an employer was vicariously liable in respect of a tort committed by one of his employees was sometimes affected by the following legal rule: In any proceedings between a claimant and an employer of an employee who has committed a tort, the employer will be *estopped* (or prevented) from denying that the employee in question was

[77] [1989] 1 AC 928.
[78] Ibid., 955–6.

employed to do *x* if the employer led the claimant to believe that the employee was employed to do *x* and the claimant relied on that belief.

So, in *Conway* v *George Wimpey & Co. Ltd*,[79] the defendant building company took on some construction work at an airport and to help out their employees they had some of their employees drive lorries around the perimeter of the airport – the idea being that if any of the defendants' employees wanted a lift to another area of the airport, they could hitch a lift on one of these lorries. The claimant – who was not one of the defendants' employees – hitched a ride on one of these lorries and was injured as a result of the fact that the driver was negligent in driving the lorry. The Court of Appeal applied the Salmond test and held that the defendants were *not* vicariously liable in respect of their driver's negligence because he was not employed to give rides to people like the claimant: he was only employed to give rides to the defendants' employees of the defendant company who were working at the airport.

But it would have been different if the defendants had led the claimant to believe that their drivers were employed to give rides to *anyone* working in the airport and the claimant had relied on that belief by hitching a ride on one of the defendants' lorries. In such a case – when the claimant sued the defendants on the basis that they were vicariously liable in respect of their driver's negligence – the defendants would have been estopped (or prevented) from denying that their driver was employed to give rides to people like the claimant. The defendants would therefore have been unable to deny that their driver was acting in the course of his employment when he drove the claimant to his chosen destination in a negligent fashion. As it happened, the defendant company had done nothing to induce the claimant to believe that its lorry driver was employed to pick up people like him and give them lifts to where they wanted to go and so the defendant company was not estopped from denying that its lorry driver was employed to pick up people like the claimant.

This principle of estoppel is often said[80] to underlie the decision of the House of Lords in *Lloyd* v *Grace, Smith & Co.*[81] In that case, the claimant owned two cottages. She was dissatisfied with the income she received from her assets and consulted the defendant firm of solicitors for advice. Her case was handled by one Sandles, the managing clerk of the firm. He tricked her into transferring the two cottages to him. The House of Lords held that the defendants were liable to compensate the claimant for the losses suffered by her as a result of Sandles's deceit. It is possible to argue that the source of the defendants' liability in this case was that they were vicariously liable in respect of Sandles's deceit – and the reason why they were vicariously liable in respect of Sandles's deceit was that they were estopped from denying that Sandles did something he was employed to do when he persuaded the claimant to sign over her cottages to him. After all, the defendants did lead the claimant to believe that Sandles was acting with their authority in *whatever* he did in relation to the claimant's affairs and the claimant relied on that belief by allowing Sandles to handle her affairs.

[79] [1951] 2 KB 266. See above, n. 73.

[80] See *Dubai Aluminium Co. Ltd* v *Salaam* [2003] 2 AC 366, at [28] (per Lord Nicholls); *New South Wales* v *Lepore* (2003) 212 CLR 511, at [108] – [111] (per Gaudron J) and [232] (per Gummow and Hayne JJ).

[81] [1912] AC 716. For an alternative explanation of the case, see above, pp. 233–4.

The Lister *decision*

We are now in a position to understand the radical change in the law that was brought about by the decision of the House of Lords in *Lister* v *Hesley Hall Ltd*.[82] In that case, the defendants ran a boarding house for children who attended a nearby school. The defendants employed a married couple, Mr and Mrs Grain, to run the boarding house and maintain discipline. Unfortunately, Mr Grain used his position to sexually abuse a number of the children staying at the boarding house. The claimant sued the defendants for compensation, claiming that the defendants were vicariously liable in respect of the torts committed by Grain when he sexually abused them.

Had the Salmond test been applied to determine whether or not Grain was acting in the course of his employment when he sexually abused the claimants, the claimants' claims for compensation would certainly have been dismissed. There was no way it could be said that Grain did something he was employed to do by sexually abusing the claimants. Indeed, in an earlier case the Court of Appeal had applied the Salmond test to determine whether a local education authority was vicariously liable in respect of the torts committed by a deputy headmaster in sexually assaulting a student when they were on a school trip together, and had concluded that the deputy head had not been acting in the course of his employment when he sexually assaulted the student.[83]

However, the Salmond test was *not* applied in the *Lister* case to determine whether or not Grain was acting in the course of his employment when he sexually abused the claimants. The House of Lords swept that test away. In its place, the House of Lords adopted a quite different test for determining whether or not an employee was acting in the course of his employment when he committed a tort. This test was first adopted by the Supreme Court of Canada in the cases[84] of *Bazley* v *Curry*[85] and *Jacobi* v *Griffiths*.[86] Under this test, an employee will be held to have acted in the course of his employment when he committed a tort if that tort was 'so closely connected with his employment that it would be fair and just to hold the [employee's employer] vicariously liable [in respect of that tort]'.[87] The House of Lords held that under *this* test – what we might call the 'sufficiently close connection' test, Grain *had* acted in the course of his employment when he sexually abused the claimants.[88] Their main reason for so finding was that the defendants had owed the claimants a duty to look after them; that they tried to discharge that duty by having Grain

[82] [2002] 1 AC 215 (noted, Giliker 2002).

[83] *Trotman* v *North Yorkshire County Council* [1999] LGR 584.

[84] Noted, Cane 2000a.

[85] [1999] 2 SCR 534.

[86] [1999] 2 SCR 570.

[87] *Lister* v *Hesley Hall Ltd* [2002] 1 AC 215, at [28] (per Lord Steyn). See also [70] (per Lord Millett: 'What is critical is . . . the closeness of the connection between the employee's duties and his wrongdoing'). An alternative formulation of the same test was offered by Lord Nicholls in *Dubai Aluminium Co. Ltd* v *Salaam* [2003] 2 AC 366, at [23]: 'the wrongful conduct must be so closely connected with acts the . . . employee was authorised to do that, for the purpose of the liability of the . . . employer to third parties, the wrongful conduct *may fairly and properly be regarded* as done by the [employee] while acting in the ordinary course of the . . . employee's employment' (emphasis in original).

[88] They also found that under this test the deputy headmaster in the *Trotman* case (see above, n. 83) *had* been acting in the course of his employment when he sexually assaulted the student in that case and, accordingly, the House of Lords overruled the Court of Appeal's decision in that case that the local education authority was not vicariously liable in respect of the torts committed by the deputy head in sexually assaulting the student.

look after the claimants; and Grain conspicuously failed to look after the claimants when he sexually abused them.[89]

Critique of the decision in Lister

Three criticisms may be made of the House of Lords' decision in *Lister*:

(1) *Constitutionality.* It may be wondered whether the House of Lords acted entirely constitutionally in sweeping aside a test for determining whether an employee acted in the course of his employment when he committed a tort that had stood the test of time for almost a century. It was surely a job for Parliament, acting in conjunction with the Law Commission, to bring about such a radical change in the law on vicarious liability.[90]

Perhaps recognising this, their Lordships in *Lister* attempted to argue that there was nothing *new* about the 'sufficiently close connection' test that they adopted in *Lister*.[91] They argued that there were plenty of cases where this test had *already* been used to determine whether an employee acted in the course of his employment in committing a tort. Unfortunately, it could be argued that two of the cases mentioned – *Morris* v *C W Martin & Sons Ltd*[92] and *Photo Production* v *Securicor*[93] – are not vicarious liability cases at all but cases where the defendant was put in breach of a non-delegable duty of care by the acts of one of his employees.[94] A similar analysis could be made of the third case mentioned by their Lordships – *Lloyd* v *Grace, Smith & Co.*[95] But even if that case *is* regarded as a vicarious liability case, the decision in that case is compatible with the Salmond test for determining whether an employee acted in the course of his employment in committing a tort and cannot be read as supporting the 'sufficiently close connection' test adopted by their Lordships in *Lister*.

(2) *Necessity.* Had the House of Lords wanted to rule in favour of the claimants in *Lister*, they had no need to alter the law on vicarious liability to do so. They could have easily found that the defendants in *Lister* were *personally* liable to compensate the claimants for the harm they suffered as a result of being sexually abused by Grain. Their Lordships could have reached this conclusion using the device of a non-delegable duty of care. They could have ruled that: (1) the defendants owed the claimants a non-delegable duty of care to look after them; (2) the defendants gave Grain the job of looking after the claimants; and (3) Grain put the defendants in breach of the non-delegable duty of care that they owed the claimants when, by sexually abusing the claimants, he failed to look after the claimants properly. It is hard to understand why the House of Lords did not decide *Lister* in this way

[89] [2002] 1 AC 215, at [25]–[28] (per Lord Steyn), [50] (per Lord Clyde), [59]–[61] (per Lord Hobhouse), [82]–[83] (per Lord Millett).

[90] It was argued by counsel for the defendants that 'Any radical expansion or development of liabiliy in this area of law should be left to Parliament' (ibid., at 218) but that argument was ignored by their Lordships.

[91] Ibid., at [15] (per Lord Steyn), [69] (per Lord Millett). Cf. *New South Wales* v *Lepore* (2003) 212 CLR 511, at [319]: '[The House of Lords] did not depart from precedent in establishing the "close connection" analysis. They merely developed and elaborated the traditional approach' (per Kirby P). Academic support for this line can be found in W&J, 902 (expressing surprise that the Court of Appeal refused to find vicarious liability in *Lister*).

[92] [1966] 1 QB 716.

[93] [1980] AC 827.

[94] For such an explanation, see above, pp. 232–3.

[95] [1912] AC 716. See above, pp. 233–4.

– particularly as these were the *very* reasons why the House of Lords found that there *was* a 'sufficiently close connection' between the torts committed by Grain in the *Lister* case and what he was employed to do so as to make the defendants *vicariously* liable in respect of those torts.[96]

(3) *Certainty*. The third criticism that may be made of the House of Lords' decision in *Lister* is that the 'sufficiently close connection' test is so vague and open-ended that it is now very hard to tell when exactly an employee will be held to have committed a tort in the course of his employment.[97] As Lord Nicholls observed in *Dubai Aluminium Co. Ltd* v *Salaam*,

> the 'close connection' test ... affords no guidance on the type or degree of connection which will normally be regarded as sufficiently close to prompt the legal conclusion that the risk of the wrongful act occurring, and any loss resulting from the wrongful act, should fall on the firm or employer rather than the third party who was wronged ... [Under the 'sufficiently close connection' test, the] crucial feature or features, either producing or negativing vicarious liability, [will] vary widely from one case or type of case to the next. Essentially the court makes an evaluative judgment in each case, having regard to all the circumstances ...[98]

It is not clear that the judges who decided *Lister* would regard the lack of certainty inherent in the 'sufficiently close connection' test as a problem; they might even regard it as a virtue. It is obvious that in the *Lister* case, their Lordships wanted to come up with a test for when an employee would be held to have acted in the course of his employment in committing a tort that would allow them to do 'practical justice'[99] in individual cases.[100] But, as Lord Millett observed in *Lister*, it is doubtful whether anyone can come up with a test that is sufficiently flexible as to allow the courts to do 'practical justice' in individual cases but at the same time sufficiently precise so as 'to enable the outcome of a particular case to be predicted'.[101] Any test which did work in a predictable fashion would be 'rigid and possibly inappropriate ... as a test of liability' in particular cases.[102]

However, in their desire to do 'practical justice' in individual cases, the Law Lords who decided *Lister* forgot or disregarded the primary responsibility that they owe the public at large, which is to ensure that the law is stated in clear and certain terms, so that we can all

96 See Glofcheski 2004, 27; also *New South Wales* v *Lepore* (2003) 212 CLR 511, at [208]: 'The analyses of Lord Hobhouse and Lord Millett [in *Lister*] have strong echoes of non-delegable duties' (per Gummow and Hayne JJ).

97 Cf. Callinan J's criticisms of the 'sufficiently close connection' test for determining whether an employee committed a tort in the course of his employment in *New South Wales* v *Lepore*: '[If such a test were to be adopted in Australia] [d]istinguishing between [cases where there was a "sufficiently close connection" between an employee's tort and what he was employed to do and cases where there was not] would be very difficult. Cases would, as a practical matter, be decided according to whether the judge ... thought it "fair and just" to hold the employer liable. Perceptions of fairness vary greatly. The law in consequence would be thrown into a state of uncertainty. I would not therefore be prepared to adopt their Lordships' or any like test' (ibid., at [345]). Only one of the seven judges who decided *New South Wales* v *Lepore* in the High Court of Australia expressed any enthusiasm for the 'sufficiently close connection' test (Kirby P). Callinan, Gaudron, Gummow, Hayne JJ and (less clearly) Gleeson CJ all held that Australian courts should continue to use the Salmond test to determine whether an employee committed a tort in the course of his employment. McHugh J declined to express an opinion on the issue.

98 [2003] 2 AC 366, at [25]–[26].

99 [2002] 1 AC 215, at [16] per Lord Steyn.

100 For a fine critique of judicial attempts to do 'practical justice' in individual cases, see Beever 2003b.

101 [2002] 1 AC 215, at [66].

102 Ibid.

know where we stand when we get involved in disputes with other people. For this reason, it is to be hoped that a future House of Lords will abandon the 'sufficiently close connection' test for determining whether an employee committed a tort in the course of his employment in favour of another test which will work in a more predictable fashion.[103]

How will the new test work in practice?

Until that day comes, in any case where an employee has committed a tort the courts will have to determine whether the employee committed that tort in the course of his employment by asking – Was there a sufficiently close connection between the employee's tort and what he was employed to do so as to make it 'fair and just' that the employer should be held vicariously liable in respect of the employee's tort? When are the courts likely to find that this test is satisfied? The available case law on the matter offers the following guidance.

(1) *The Salmond test.* It seems clear that if an employer would have been held vicariously liable in respect of a tort committed by one of his employees under the old Salmond test, then the courts will hold that there is a 'sufficiently close connection' between the employee's tort and what he was employed to do.[104]

(2) *Delegation.* It seems to follow from the *Lister* decision that if an employer was under a duty to do *x*, and he instructed one of his employees to discharge that duty, then if the employee failed to follow instructions and in so doing committed a tort, there will exist a 'sufficiently close connection' between the employee's tort and what he was employed to do.[105]

In order to show a 'sufficiently close connection' under this head, it is crucial to show that the employee in question was entrusted with the job of discharging a duty of his employer's. So it was vital that the employee in the *Lister* case was employed to discharge

[103] *Important note.* Such a test would have to identify exactly *when* it is 'fair and just' to hold an employer vicariously liable in respect of a tort committed by one of his employees in terms which make it possible to predict with a fair degree of success in any given case whether an employer will be held vicariously liable in respect of a tort committed by one of his employees. The Supreme Court of Canada attempted to come up with such a test in *Bazley* v *Curry* [1999] 2 SCR 534, holding that 'the policy purposes underlying the imposition of vicarious liability on employers are served *only* where the wrong *is so connected with the employment that it can be said that the employer has introduced the risk of the wrong* (and is thereby and usefully charged with its management and minimization)' (at [37], per McLachlin J, emphasis added). However, members of the High Court of Australia expressed themselves doubtful in *New South Wales* v *Lepore* (2003) 212 CLR 511 whether that test was expressed in sufficiently clear terms as to make its application predictable: see [126] (per Gaudron J) and [212] (per Gummow and Hayne JJ). If it is not possible to identify in clear and certain terms *when* it would be 'fair and just' to hold an employer vicariously liable in respect of a tort committed by one of his employees (and Lord Millett seemed to think in *Lister* that it was not: see above, p. 667), a 'second-best' test would have to be formulated which worked in a predictable fashion *and* served to make employers vicariously liable for their employees' torts in *most* situations where it it would be 'fair and just' to make them so liable. It may be that the only such 'second-best' test on offer is the Salmond test.

[104] It can hardly be supposed that for nearly 100 years before *Lister* was decided, the courts acted unfairly or unjustly by holding employers vicariously liable for their employees' torts when the Salmond test was satisfied. But see Lord Millett's observation in *Dubai Aluminium Co. Ltd* v *Salaam* [2003] 2 AC 366 that 'the Salmond test is only that – a test. It is not a conclusive definition of the circumstances in which vicarious liability arises. *Even if it is satisfied, the facts, taken as a whole, may nevertheless show that the employee was not acting in the course of his employment*' (at [128], emphasis added).

[105] See [2002] 1 AC 215, at [50] (per Lord Clyde), [59] (per Lord Hobhouse), [82] (per Lord Millett). The House of Lords did not feel it necessary to explain *why* it is 'fair and just' to hold an employer vicariously liable in respect of a tort committed by one of his employees in this situation: Lord Steyn thought that it was a clear case where vicarious liability should be imposed (at [28]).

the duty that the defendants were under to look after the children staying at their boarding house. Had the claimants in *Lister* been abused by a handyman who was employed by the defendants merely to do odd jobs around the boarding house, then it is unlikely that the House of Lords would have found a 'sufficiently close connection' between the torts committed by the handyman in abusing the claimants and what he was employed to do.[106] It could not have been said that the defendants employed the handyman to discharge the duty they were under to look after the children staying at their boarding house.

(3) *Opportunity*. It seems well acknowledged that if an employee was given the opportunity to commit a tort by virtue of his being employed to do a certain kind of work, that fact *on its own* will *not* be enough to establish that there was a 'sufficiently close connection' between the employee's tort and what he was employed to do.[107]

So in *Jacobi* v *Griffiths*,[108] the defendants set up a club for children. They employed a Harry Griffiths to act as programme director at the club. His job was to organise recreational activities at the club and the occasional outing. Griffiths used his position to befriend a couple of the children who used the club and he ended up inviting them to his home, where he sexually assaulted them. The Supreme Court of Canada held, by four to three, that there was *not* a 'sufficiently close connection' between what Griffiths was employed to do and the torts that he committed in sexually assaulting the children. The fact that Griffiths had been employed to work at the club had of course given him the opportunity to sexually assault the children, but that was not enough to establish the requisite connection between his torts and what he was employed to do.[109]

(4) *Special risk*. In the *Lister* case, Lord Steyn made clear that the decisions of the Supreme Court of Canada in *Bazley* v *Curry* and *Jacobi* v *Griffiths* should form the 'starting point' of any inquiry into whether there was a 'sufficiently close connection' between what an employee was employed to do and a tort committed by the employee.[110] Those decisions indicate that if an employee is employed to do a particular job and there is a *special risk*[111] associated with that job that he will commit a particular kind of tort, then if the employee in question commits that tort, there will be a 'sufficiently close connection' between the employee's tort and what he was employed to do.[112]

106 See *Jacobi* v *Griffiths* [1999] 2 SCR 570, at [45] (per Binnie J); also *EDG* v *Hammer* [2003] 2 SCR 459, at [36] (per Arbour J).

107 *Lister* v *Hesley Hall Ltd* [2002] 1 AC 215, at [45] (per Lord Clyde), [59] (per Lord Hobhouse), [65] (per Lord Millett). Also *Bazley* v *Curry* [1999] 2 SCR 534, at [40] (per McLachlin J); and *Jacobi* v *Griffiths* [1999] 2 SCR 570, at [81] (per Binnie J).

108 [1999] 2 SCR 570.

109 If the same case occurred in the United Kingdom, could a court find the defendants vicariously liable for the programme director's acts of sexual abuse using the 'delegation' idea set out above? It depends on whether it could be said that the programme director in *Jacobi* v *Griffiths* was employed by the defendants in that case to discharge the duty they owed the children at the club to take reasonable steps to see that they were reasonably safe in using the club.

110 [2002] 1 AC 215, at [27].

111 The decisions actually talk in terms of an 'increased or materially enhanced ... risk' (*Bazley* v *Curry* [1999] 2 SCR 534, at [39] (per McLachlin J)) but we prefer to use the term 'special risk'.

112 The Supreme Court thought that the enterprise risk and deterrence rationales for vicarious liability set out above, at pp. 653–4, implied that it would be 'fair and just' to hold an employer vicariously liable in respect of a tort committed by one of his employees in this situation. See, to the same effect, Feldthusen 1998.

This requirement was held to be satisfied in *Bazley* v *Curry*, where the defendants unknowingly employed a paedophile to work in a home for disturbed children and the paedophile used his position to sexually abuse some of the children in the home. It was held that there was a special risk that people who work in children's homes will sexually assault the children there. This is because, McLachlin J explained, people who work in children's homes occupy a position of 'power and intimacy' in relation to the children at the homes – as a result, if they have paedophiliac tendencies, they will feel emboldened to sexually abuse the children in their care and the children in their care will be more likely to submit to being assaulted without complaint.[113]

In contrast, the special risk requirement was held not to be satisfied in *Jacobi* v *Griffiths* where, as we have seen, the programme director at a children's club used his position to sexually abuse the children at the club. There was no special risk that someone employed in such a capacity would sexually abuse children who used the club because there was no special reason to think that someone employed to work as a programme director at a children's club would develop a relationship of 'power and intimacy' with the children at the club that might embolden him to assault the children at the club and lead them to submit to the assaults without complaint.[114]

The fact that the Supreme Court of Canada divided four to three in *Jacobi* over whether the special risk requirement was satisfied in that case indicates that it will often be very difficult to tell – in a given case where an employee has committed a tort – whether or not there was a special risk associated with what he was employed to do that he would commit that kind of tort. For example, in *Heasmans* v *Clarity Cleaning Co.*,[115] the claimants engaged the defendant cleaning company to clean its offices. One of the cleaners employed by the defendants to clean the claimants' offices made a number of long-distance telephone calls on the claimants' telephones while cleaning their offices, thereby committing the tort of conversion. The claimants sued the defendants, claiming that they were vicariously liable in respect of their cleaner's acts of conversion. The claim was dismissed on the ground that, under the Salmond test, the cleaner did not act in the course of his employment when he made his international telephone calls.[116] But were the same case to occur today, could it be argued that there was a special risk that the cleaner would make international telephone calls while cleaning the claimants' offices and that there was therefore a 'sufficiently close connection' between the cleaner's acts of conversion and what he was employed to do so as

[113] [1999] 2 SCR 534, at [44]. See also *New South Wales* v *Lepore* (2003) 212 CLR 511, at [216] (per Gummow and Hayne JJ). The result in *Weir* v *Chief Constable of Merseyside Police* [2003] EWCA Civ 111 may also be justified in this way. The defendant chief constable in that case was held vicariously liable in respect of an assault committed by an off-duty police officer on the claimant in a police van which the officer had borrowed in order to help a friend move some belongings. (The police officer suspected that the claimant had attempted to pilfer some of the friend's belongings while they were awaiting removal.) The Court of Appeal's main reason for finding the defendant vicariously liable in respect of the officer's assault was that, before he took the claimant into the police van and assaulted him, 'he . . . confirmed to, and the [claimant] understood, that he was a police officer' (at [12], per Rt Hon Sir Denis Henry). It may be that there is a special risk that police officers will commit assaults on ordinary citizens whenever they act in their capacity as police officers: they may feel that they are more likely to 'get away' with assaulting people when they act in their official capacity.

[114] [1999] 2 SCR 570, at [79]–[86] (per Binnie J).

[115] [1987] ICR 949.

[116] This was obviously right: the cleaner did not do anything he was employed to do by making the telephone calls.

to make the defendants vicariously liable in relation to the cleaner's acts of conversion? It is very hard to tell.

(5) *Revenge attacks.* Until recently, it seemed well acknowledged in the cases dealing with the 'sufficiently close connection' test that the test would not be satisfied in the case of an employee who attacks someone else in revenge for some perceived slight or harm.[117]

However, in *Mattis* v *Pollock*,[118] the claimant was stabbed by a nightclub bouncer employed by the defendants; the bouncer had earlier had an altercation with the claimant and was seeking to take revenge on him for this. The Court of Appeal held that the defendants *were* vicariously liable in respect of the bouncer's attack on the claimant. The court held that a 'close and direct' connection was established between the bouncer's attack and what he was employed to do because: (1) using violence on other people was part of his job; *and* (2) the earlier altercation between the bouncer and the claimant had arisen out of the bouncer's doing what he was employed to do and the bouncer's stabbing the claimant was directly linked to the earlier altercation. It is suggested that the decision is to be confined to its own facts,[119] and that the general rule remains that the 'sufficiently close connection' test will *not* be satisfied where an employee carries out a revenge attack on someone who has annoyed him or her.

FURTHER POINTS

A couple of further points about the law on vicarious liability remain to be made:

(1) *Contribution and indemnity.* Suppose that Beth has committed a tort and John is vicariously liable in respect of that tort. Suppose further that John is held liable to compensate someone who has suffered loss as a result of that tort. In such a case John will be entitled to bring a claim in contribution against Beth under the Civil Liability (Contribution) Act 1978 because they were both liable to make the compensation payment that John made. This will allow John to recover from Beth a 'just and equitable' *proportion* of the compensation payment that he made.

However, if the reason why John was vicariously liable in respect of Beth's tort was that Beth was his employee and she committed her tort in the course of her employment by John, then John will be entitled to bring a claim for breach of contract against Beth as she will have invariably breached her contract of employment in committing her tort. If he does bring a claim for breach of contract against Beth, he will be allowed to sue Beth for

117 *Bazley* v *Curry* [1999] 2 SCR 534, at [21] and [42] (per McLachlin J); *Lister* v *Hesley Hall Ltd* [2002] 1 AC 215, at [81] (per Lord Millett, endorsing the result in *Deatons Pty Ltd* v *Flew* (1949) 79 CLR 370, summarised above at n. 75); *Attorney-General for the British Virgin Islands* v *Hartwell* [2004] 1 WLR 1273, at [16]–[17] (police officer saw his ex-girlfriend in a bar with her new lover; he fired four shots into the bar with a gun issued to him by the police authority for whom he worked; one of the shots hit the claimant; 'clear-cut' that police authority not vicariously liable for police officer's actions).

118 [2003] 1 WLR 2158 (reversing the decision of Judge Seymour QC at [2002] EWHC 2177).

119 For a similar case where a finding of vicarious liability was also made by the Court of Appeal, see *Fennelly* v *Connex South Eastern Ltd* [2001] IRLR 390 (an initial altercation between a passenger and a ticket inspector over the passenger's failure to produce his ticket escalated and the ticket inspector ended up putting the passenger into a headlock; held, the inspector's employers were vicariously liable in respect of the tort committed by the inspector in laying his hands on the passenger).

damages equal to the *entire* compensation payment that he has had to make as this payment will count as a loss that John has suffered as a result of Beth's breach of contract.

So – in *Lister* v *Romford Ice and Cold Storage Co. Ltd*,[120] Lister, who was employed by the claimants as a lorry driver, drove his lorry into a slaughterhouse yard to pick up some waste. Lister's father accompanied him and got out of the lorry before Lister had parked it. In parking the lorry, Lister negligently knocked down and injured his father. Lister's father sued the claimants, claiming that they were vicariously liable in respect of his son's negligence, and recovered £1,600 from the claimants in compensatory damages. The claimants then sued Lister, claiming that he had breached his contract of employment when he negligently knocked down his father and that they were therefore entitled to sue him for damages equal to the £1,600 that they had to pay out to Lister's father as a result of Lister's negligence. The House of Lords allowed the claim, agreeing that Lister had breached his contract of employment in negligently knocking down his father: they found that there was an implied term in Lister's contract of employment with the claimants that he would perform his duties under his contract of employment with reasonable skill and care and that when Lister negligently knocked down his father he breached that implied term.

(2) *Vicarious liability for the acts of accessories.* We noted above that if A has committed a tort in relation to B, and C is an accessory to A's tort with the result that the courts will hold that A's tort was committed by both A *and C*, then it may be possible for someone else to be vicariously liable in respect of the tort that the courts will hold C has committed. The decision of the House of Lords in *Credit Lyonnais* v *Export Credit Guarantee Department* emphasises that if, in this situation, C's employer is to be held vicariously liable for C's tort, then *all* of the actions that made C an accessory to A's tort have to have been committed in the course of C's employment.

In the *Credit Lyonnais*[121] case, the claimants were defrauded of a substantial amount of money by one Mr Chong. The fraud worked like this. Chong forged some bills of exchange – promises to pay for goods received – and offered them for sale to the claimants. Obviously the claimants wanted some assurance that they would be paid under the bills of exchange before they bought them. This is where Chong's accomplice, a man called Mr Pillai, came in. Pillai was employed by the defendants, a government agency called the Export Credit Guarantees Department. Pillai – who knew very well that Chong's bills of exchange were forged – arranged for the defendants to guarantee that they would pay the claimants 90 per cent of the value of the bills of exchange if they were not paid. Encouraged by this guarantee, the claimants paid Chong £10m for the bills of exchange. Chong then disappeared. The bills of exchange were worthless. So was the defendants' guarantee: it was conditional on the claimants' having taken reasonable steps to assure themselves that the bills of exchange were genuine, and the claimants had not done this. The claimants sued the defendants for damages, claiming that Pillai had committed a tort in acting as he did, and that the defendants were vicariously liable for that tort.

But what tort had Pillai committed? Pillai had not committed the tort of deceit through his own actions because the claimants had not been deceived by the defendants' guarantee. Chong *had* committed the tort of deceit in relation to the claimants. Was Pillai an acces-

[120] [1957] AC 555.

[121] [2000] 1 AC 486.

Introduction

We saw much earlier in the book that many people believe – wrongly – that the function of tort law is to determine when one person will be entitled to sue another for compensation in respect of some loss that he has suffered.[1] Let's say that Paul is one such person. Paul will find it difficult to understand the areas of law that we are going to look at in the next few chapters. For these areas of law allow a claimant to sue a defendant in tort for damages that are *not* designed to compensate the claimant for a loss that she has suffered, but instead serve some other function. So these areas of law represent a problem for Paul, a problem which he will characteristically react to in one of three ways.

First, Paul might attempt to ignore or minimise these areas of law, to brush over them as not very important.

Secondly, Paul might attempt to distort these areas of law – to argue that the kinds of damages that are awarded to claimants under these areas of law are *really* compensatory in nature. One sees this reaction in, for example, the Law Commission's analysis of aggravated damages, according to which aggravated damages are designed to *compensate* the victim of a tort for any *distress* she might feel at the way the tort was committed.[2] Again one sees this reaction among academics who argue that when B – whose property has been used by A without B's permission – is allowed to sue A for *gain-based damages* designed to make A account for the gain he has obtained by using her property, those damages are really designed to *compensate* B for the fact that A wrongfully deprived B of the *right to bargain* with A for a fee for using her property.[3] And you again see this reaction in Lord Nicholls's analysis of what is happening when B – whose property has been converted by A – is allowed to sue A for damages equal to the value of that property at the time it was converted. According to him, the damages payable to B here are really *compensatory* in nature, designed to compensate B for the fact that A did not return B's property to her, instead of converting it.[4]

Thirdly, Paul might condemn these areas of law as 'anomalous' and call for their abolition. One sees this reaction in Lord Scott's speech in *Kuddus* v *Chief Constable of Leicestershire*, which called for the abolition of awards of exemplary damages in tort cases on the ground that 'the function of an award of damages in our civil justice system is to compensate the claimant for a wrong done to him. The wrong may consist of a breach of contract, or a tort, or an interference with some right of the claimant under public law. But whatever the wrong may consist of the award of damages should be compensatory in its

[1] See above, pp. 30–1.

[2] Law Com. No 247, *Aggravated, Exemplary and Restitutionary Damages*, para 2.1; Tettenborn 2003, 30. Beever 2003a contends, alternatively, that aggravated damages are designed to compensate the victim of a tort for any injury to his moral dignity that he suffered as a result of the way that tort was committed.

[3] Sharpe & Waddams 1982; also Tettenborn 2003, 48–9.

[4] *Kuwait Airways Corpn* v *Iraqi Airways Company (Nos 4 and 5)* [2002] 2 AC 883, at [67] (per Lord Nicholls).

intent. Measured by this fundamental principle of damages, an award of exemplary damages, the intention of which is not to compensate the victim of a wrong but to punish its perpetrator, is an anomaly.'[5]

Whichever way Paul reacts to the areas of law dealt with in the following chapters, he will fail to do them justice. These areas of law are important: they cannot be brushed under the carpet. Moreover, the kinds of damages awarded to tort claimants under these areas of law cannot be explained away on the basis that they are really compensatory in nature: to say that is fundamentally to misunderstand their nature and rationale. Finally, to call for the abolition of – say – awards of exemplary damages on the ground that they do not fit with the speaker's preconceived vision of what tort law says or does is to condemn them for no good reason whatsoever.

The only way to avoid falling into this trap that Paul has fallen into is to recognise that the function of tort law is *not* to determine when one person can sue another for compensation in respect of some loss that he has suffered. Rather, tort law serves two functions: it helps determine what duties we owe each other; and it determines what remedies will be available when someone breaches one of those duties.[6] Once you realise this, you will be able to do justice to these areas of law – to appreciate their importance, to understand them correctly, and to take a reasoned view as to how, if at all, these areas of law should be reformed. That is what we will try to do in the following chapters.

[5] [2002] 2 AC 122, at [95]. Weir 2006 (at 221) rightly criticises Lord Scott's argument as 'a fine example of question-begging, that is, assuming what you are setting out to prove, otherwise known as *petitio principii* . . .'.

[6] See above, p. 30.

34 Nominal damages

Suppose A has committed a tort in relation to B but B has not suffered any actionable loss as a result of A's tort. Obviously, in this situation, B will not be entitled to recover anything by way of compensatory damages from A. However, B may be entitled to sue A for *nominal damages*, that is a nominal sum equal to £5.[1] Whether B will be entitled to sue A for such damages will depend on whether the tort committed by A is 'actionable *per se*'.

The following torts are actionable *per se*: torts involving a trespass to someone's person;[2] trespass to land; private nuisances involving an interference with someone's right to light or other rights attached to his land.[3] The classic example of a tort that is *not* actionable *per se* is negligence. So if A drives recklessly down the street and almost runs over a nearby pedestrian, that pedestrian will not be entitled to sue A for nominal damages. Private nuisances not involving an interference with someone's right to light or other rights attached to his land do not seem to be actionable *per se*. It is unclear whether the tort of trespass to goods is actionable *per se*, but what authority there is on the matter indicates that it is not.[4] The House of Lords has recently made it clear that the tort of misfeasance in public office is not actionable *per se*.[5] It seems that it will be very rare for the breach of a statutory duty owed to another to be actionable *per se*.[6]

Libel is often said to be a tort that is actionable *per se*. This is because if A publishes to C a statement referring to B that is defamatory of B, B will still be entitled to sue A for a small sum in damages even if she cannot show that she suffered any loss as a result of A's publication. However, the damages payable to B in such a case will often be much smaller than £5, the sum which is normally recoverable by the victim of a tort that is actionable *per se* who has not suffered any actionable loss as a result of that tort being committed.[7] The better analysis of what is going on in a libel case such as B's is that B does not have to *prove* that she has suffered any loss as a result of A's libel. Instead, it will be *presumed* that she did

1 £5 is currently the conventional figure awarded in making an award of nominal damages: see, for example, *Brandeis Goldschmidt & Co.* v *Western Transport* [1981] QB 864, 874A; *Watkins* v *Secretary of State for the Home Department* [2004] EWCA Civ 966, at [61]. Until the 1980s, the conventional sum awarded in making an award of nominal damages was £2: see, for example, *Child* v *Stenning* (1879) 11 Ch D 82; *Sykes* v *Midland Bank Executor & Trustee Co.* [1971] 1 QB 113.

2 That is, assault, battery and false imprisonment.

3 See *Nicholls* v *Ely Beet Sugar Factory Ltd (No. 2)* [1936] 1 Ch 343, 348–9.

4 *Slater* v *Swann* (1730) 2 Stra 872, 93 ER 906.

5 *Watkins* v *Secretary of State for the Home Department* [2006] 2 AC 395.

6 In *Cullen* v *Chief Constable of the Royal Ulster Constabulary* [2003] 1 WLR 1763 (discussed above, pp. 488–9), Lord Hutton held that the breach of a statutory duty owed by A to B might be actionable *per se* if the statutory duty was contained in a written constitution, but if the duty in question was imposed by an ordinary statute, A's breach of that duty would only be actionable if it caused B to suffer 'loss or injury of a kind for which the law awards damages': ibid., at [47], quoting *Pickering* v *Liverpool Daily Post* [1991] 2 AC 370, at 420 (per Lord Bridge).

7 In *Newstead* v *London Express Newspaper* [1940] 1 KB 377, the claimant was awarded one farthing. In *Reynolds* v *Times Newspapers Ltd* [2001] 2 AC 127, the claimant was awarded one penny.

suffer some loss as a result of A's libel and it will be up to a jury or a judge to put a figure on how much of a loss she suffered.[8] If the loss suffered by B seems to the jury or judge to be very small because, for example, C did not believe A's statement or because B was of such bad character that she had no reputation to lose, then B will not be awarded very much by way of damages[9] – but the damages paid to her will still be *compensatory* in nature, not *nominal.*

Why, it might be wondered, would the victim of a tort ever sue the person who committed that tort for nominal damages? Three reasons may be given.

(1) *Setting the record straight.* If A has committed a tort that is actionable *per se* in relation to B but B has suffered no actionable loss as a result, B might want to sue A for nominal damages in order to have it publicly established that A committed a tort in acting as he did. This is why, for example, if A defames B, B might want to sue A even though she has suffered no loss as a result of A's defaming her: she will want it to be publicly established that whatever A said about her was untrue.[10]

(2) *Assertion of right.* If A has committed a tort that is *actionable per se* in relation to B by doing *x* but B has suffered no actionable loss as a result, B might still want to sue A for nominal damages because if she does not sue him for doing *x*, he might acquire a *licence* to do *x* in the future.

Suppose, for example, that A regularly walks across B's land without her permission but she does not suffer any loss as a result of his walking across her land. Because A's conduct amounts to the tort of trespass to land, B will be entitled to sue A for nominal damages here. Now: B will have an incentive to sue A for such damages, because if she does not A might – if he continues to walk across her land – acquire a *right by prescription* to walk across B's land.

Similarly, in *Bower* v *Hill*,[11] the defendant blocked a drain which lay between the claimant's land and a nearby river. In so doing he committed a tort: the claimant had a right of way over the drain. The claimant did not suffer any loss as a result of the defendant's blocking the drain as it was already choked with mud. However, the claimant still sued the defendant for nominal damages (as he was entitled to do as the tort committed by the defendant in blocking the drain was actionable *per se*) because, as Tindal CJ noted, if '[the claimant] acquiesced in [the blockage of the drain] for twenty years, [that] would become evidence of a renunciation and abandonment of the [claimant's] right of way'[12] and everyone would, after that time, be free to block the drain.

(3) *Punishment.* If A commits a tort that is actionable *per se* in relation to B but B has suffered no actionable loss as a result, B might want to sue A for nominal damages as a way of punishing A for committing that tort. The punishment would not of course consist in

[8] To the same effect, see Mitchell 2005, 53.

[9] If the damages payable to B are extremely small because she had no reputation to lose when A libelled her, they will be known as *contemptuous* or *derisory* damages.

[10] Of course, a finding of liability in a defamation case does not indicate that what the defendant said about the claimant was untrue; it merely indicates that the defendant could not prove that what he said about the claimant was true (see above, pp. 311–12).

[11] (1835) 1 Bing NC 549, 131 ER 1229.

[12] Ibid., 555, 1231.

having to pay B £5 in nominal damages; the punishment would consist in having to repay the legal costs incurred by B in bringing her case against A – which would, obviously, come to a lot more than £5. However, such a plan might well backfire on B: if the courts thought that B's sole motivation in suing A for nominal damages was to inflict a bill for her legal costs on him, then they might well refuse to award B costs and she would have to bear those costs herself.[13]

Visit **http://www.mylawchamber.co.uk/mcbride** to access updates on recent cases, as well as model answers and tips for answering tort problem questions.

[13] See Devlin J's remarks in *Anglo-Cyprian Agencies* v *Paphos Industries* [1951] 1 All ER 873, at 874D–G doubting whether a claimant who has obtained nominal damages from a defendant should always be entitled to recover the costs incurred by him in suing the defendant for such damages.

35 Aggravated damages

THE NATURE OF AGGRAVATED DAMAGES

Suppose that A has committed a tort in relation to B and B is entitled to sue A as a result for either compensatory damages or nominal damages. In such a case, B will *also* be entitled to sue A for *aggravated damages* if: (1) A acted in an arrogant and high-handed way in committing his tort or in dealing with B's claims to be compensated for the actionable losses that she suffered as a result of A's committing that tort; *and* (2) the tort committed by A is the sort of tort in respect of which aggravated damages may be claimed.

What are aggravated damages? There is some dispute over this question. The dominant view is that aggravated damages are designed to compensate the victim of a tort, who has been treated in an arrogant and high-handed way by the person who committed that tort, for the distress suffered by her as a result of being treated in that way.[1] On this view, aggravated damages are a form of compensatory damages, though they are unusual in that they can sometimes be awarded to the victim of a tort not to compensate her for the actionable losses suffered by her as a result of that tort being committed but to compensate her for losses suffered by her as a result of the way the person who committed the tort in question treated her *after* he committed that tort.[2]

The better view, we would submit, is that aggravated damages are awarded in order to assuage the anger and outrage felt by the victim of a tort who has been treated in an arrogant and high-handed way by the person who committed that tort. On this view, aggravated damages are not a form of compensatory damages; they are not awarded in order to compensate the victim of a tort for any distress suffered by her but in order to pacify her.[3] There is some support for this view in the

[1] *Rookes* v *Barnard* [1964] AC 1129, 1221 (per Lord Devlin); *McCarey* v *Associated Newspapers Ltd (No. 2)* [1965] 2 QB 86, 104G–105A (per Pearson LJ); *Broome* v *Cassell & Co. Ltd* [1972] AC 1027, 1124 (per Lord Diplock); *Archer* v *Brown* [1985] QB 401, 424–5 (per Peter Pain J); *Thompson* v *Commissioner of Police of the Metropolis* [1998] QB 498, 512; Scott 2006. Windeyer J criticised this view of aggravated damages in the Australian case of *Uren* v *John Fairfax & Sons Pty Ltd* (1965–66) 117 CLR 118, 151: 'The theory is that [aggravated] damages are . . . compensatory because the more insulting or reprehensible the defendant's conduct the greater the indignity that the claimant suffers and the more he should receive for the outrage to his feelings . . . This . . . explanation is convenient, but not altogether convincing. Two objections may be made. First, the satisfaction that the claimant gets is that the defendant has been made to pay for what he did . . . Secondly, conceding an indignity suffered must be paid for, why is the degree of indignity that the claimant suffers to be measured by considering what was in the mind of the defendant, the malice or motive that moved him?'

[2] This may be why Birks 1996a argues that in aggravated damages cases, *two* torts have been committed – the primary tort committed by the tortfeasor and a secondary tort, committed by insulting the victim of the primary tort.

[3] In *Merest* v *Harvey* (1814) 5 Taunt 442, 128 ER 761, the claimant was shooting game on his land when the defendant, who was drunk and happened to be passing by the claimant's land, asked the claimant if he could join the claimant's shooting party. The claimant refused and warned the defendant not to trespass on his land or shoot his game. The defendant took umbrage at this and walked onto the claimant's land and started shooting at the claimant's game. The claimant sued the defendant for trespass and was awarded £500 damages by a jury. The £500 award was clearly intended to punish the defendant for his conduct, the actual loss suffered

cases.[4] In *Duffy* v *Eastern Health and Social Services Board*,[5] the defendants acted unlawfully in failing to appoint one of their employees, the claimant, to a permanent position because she was Catholic. The claimant was awarded £15,000 in compensation for the distress she suffered as a result of the defendant's conduct. But she was *also* awarded £5,000 in aggravated damages because of the high-handed and arrogant way she had been treated by the defendants in, first of all, blatantly discriminating against her on grounds of her religion and, secondly, in defending her claim to be compensated for the actionable losses that she had suffered as a result of their discrimination.

Clearly, the aggravated damages awarded to the claimant in *Duffy* were not awarded to her in order to compensate her for the distress suffered by her as a result of the way in which she was treated by the defendants: the award of £15,000 fully compensated her for that distress. Rather, aggravated damages were awarded to the claimant in *Duffy* in order to assuage the anger she felt towards the defendants as a result of the way they treated her both in discriminating against her and in attempting to frustrate her attempts to obtain some redress in respect of that discrimination.[6]

In *AB* v *South West Water Services Ltd*,[7] the Court of Appeal addressed the question: can aggravated damages be awarded in a negligence case? Answering this question in the negative, Sir Thomas Bingham MR remarked: 'I know of no precedent for awarding damages for indignation aroused by a defendant's conduct [where the defendant has merely acted negligently or committed some other non-intentional tort].'[8] Clearly, Sir Thomas Bingham MR took the view that when aggravated damages are awarded to the victim of a tort, they are awarded to her in recognition of the anger felt by her at the way she was treated by the person who committed the tort in question.

---

by the claimant as a result of the defendant's trespass was minimal. The jury's award was upheld on appeal. Heath J remarked: 'It goes to prevent the practice of duelling if juries are permitted to punish insult by [making awards of exemplary] damages' (ibid.). On the view of aggravated damages taken here, he could have said the same of awards of aggravated damages.

4 See, in addition to the authorities mentioned in the text, *Deane* v *Ealing London Borough Council* [1993] ICR 329, where it was conceded that aggravated damages are entirely distinct from damages awarded to the victim of a tort in order to compensate her for any distress suffered by her as a result of that tort being committed: ibid., 335C.

5 [1992] IRLR 251.

6 See also *Prison Service* v *Johnson* [1997] ICR 275 where the claimant, who was the victim of unlawful racial discrimination by the defendants, was awarded £20,000 to compensate him for the distress suffered by him as a result of the defendants' conduct *and* £7,500 in aggravated damages.

7 [1993] QB 507.

8 Ibid., 532. It is necessary to insert the passage in square brackets because otherwise Sir Thomas Bingham's remarks may be read as indicating that aggravated damages may *never* be awarded to the victim of a tort. Cf. Smith J's remarks in *Prison Service* v *Johnson* [1997] ICR 275, at 286H–287B: '[It has been suggested] that Sir Thomas Bingham MR was [in *AB* v *South West Water Services Ltd*] making a statement of general application that there is not or should not be any such thing as an award of aggravated damages . . . [However it must be] realised that those remarks were made in the context of a claim for damages . . . based upon the torts of negligence, non-intentional nuisance and non-intentional breach of statutory duty . . . [Sir Thomas Bingham MR's] dicta were not [therefore] of general application and were not intended to change the law relating to aggravated damages . . .'

THE AVAILABILITY OF AGGRAVATED DAMAGES

To recap: if A has committed a tort in relation to B and B is entitled to sue A for either compensatory damages or nominal damages as a result, then B will also be entitled to sue A for aggravated damages if: (1) A acted in an arrogant and high-handed way in committing his tort or in dealing with B's claims to be compensated for the actionable losses suffered by her as a result of A's committing that tort; *and* (2) the tort committed by A is the kind of tort in respect of which aggravated damages may be claimed. These two requirements need some explanation.

Arrogant and high-handed conduct

In discussing when a tortfeasor will be held to have acted in an arrogant and high-handed way towards the victim of his tort, we have to distinguish between cases where the tortfeasor is alleged to have acted in an arrogant and high-handed way *in committing his tort* and cases where a tortfeasor is alleged to have acted in an arrogant and high-handed way *after committing his tort.*

(1) *Conduct in committing the tort.* Suppose A has committed a tort in relation to B. When can we say that A acted in an arrogant and high-handed way in committing that tort? The available authorities provide some guidance.

They indicate that someone who has *knowingly* committed a tort can be said to have acted in an arrogant and high-handed way in committing that tort. So – in *Thompson* v *Hill*,[9] the claimant's business as a tailor was disrupted when the defendant built some extra floors on his house, thus blocking off the light to the premises in which the claimant conducted his business. The defendant knew that his building the extra floors on his house would prevent the claimant's premises receiving any light and he also knew that the claimant had a right to receive such light. He therefore knew when he built the extra floors on his house that his doing so would amount to a private nuisance. Aggravated damages were awarded against the defendant and the award was upheld on appeal. Again, in *McMillan* v *Singh*[10] the claimant was a tenant of the defendant's, paying £16 a week rent. The defendant realised that if the claimant left, he could rent out the claimant's room for £26 a week. As a result the defendant threw the claimant out along with his belongings. The defendant knew that he had no right to do this and therefore knew that in throwing the claimant and his belongings out of his room, he was committing a tort. Aggravated damages were awarded against the defendant.

The authorities also indicate that someone who has unknowingly committed a tort can still be said to have acted in an arrogant and high-handed way in committing that tort if he humiliated or insulted the victim of that tort in committing the tort in question. So, for example, in *Thompson* v *Commissioner of Police of the Metropolis*,[11] the Court of Appeal held that police officers who commit the tort of false imprisonment by arresting someone when they are not entitled to do so can be sued for aggravated damages if, in making the

[9] (1870) LR 5 CP 564.
[10] (1984) 17 HLR 120.
[11] [1998] QB 498.

arrest, they humiliated the person being arrested or otherwise behaved in a 'high-handed, insulting, malicious or oppressive manner [in conducting] the arrest',[12] and this is so even if the police officers thought they were entitled to make the arrest in question and therefore did not knowingly commit the tort of false imprisonment in making the arrest.

(2) *Conduct after the tort was committed*. Again, suppose A has committed a tort in relation to B. When can we say that A acted in an arrogant and high-handed manner in dealing with B's claims to be compensated for the actionable losses suffered by her as a result of A's tort? Again, the authorities provide some guidance.

In *Sutcliffe* v *Pressdram Ltd*,[13] the Court of Appeal held that if A has wrongfully defamed B, A will act in an arrogant and high-handed manner in dealing with B's claims to be compensated for the actionable losses suffered by her as a result of A's defaming her if: (1) he fails to make any or sufficient apology for and withdrawal of his defamatory statement; (2) he repeats the statement; (3) he tries to deter B from proceeding with her claim against A; (4) he tries to defeat B's claims by persisting, 'by way of a prolonged or hostile cross-examination of [B] or in turgid speeches to the jury, in a plea of justification which is bound to fail';[14] (5) he tries to give wider publicity to his defamatory statement in the preliminaries to the trial of B's action against A or in the trial itself; (6) he engages in a general persecution of B.[15]

In *Ley* v *Hamilton*,[16] the claimant libelled the defendant by publishing to some business partners of the defendant a letter which alleged that the defendant had embezzled money. This was completely untrue. When the claimant sued the defendant for libel, the defendant unsurprisingly did not seek to rely in his pleadings on a defence of justification but instead claimed that his statement to the claimant's business partners was protected by qualified privilege. However, when the case came to trial and the defendant was cross-examined, he persisted in claiming that the claimant *had* embezzled money. The claimant won his case and was awarded aggravated damages as well as damages to compensate him for the actionable losses suffered by him as a result of the defendant's libel. The award of aggravated damages was upheld by the House of Lords.

In *Alexander* v *Home Office*,[17] the Court of Appeal held that if A commits a tort by unlawfully discriminating against B on grounds of her race, A will act in an arrogant and high-handed way in dealing with B's claims to be compensated for the actionable losses suffered by her as a result of A's discrimination if: (1) he makes untrue and injurious allegations about B in an attempt to establish that his acts of discrimination against B were not racially motivated; *or* (2) he conspicuously fails to acknowledge that his acts of discrimination against B were unjustified.[18] Similarly, if A commits the tort of false imprisonment by arresting B when he had no right to do so, he will act in an arrogant and high-handed way in dealing with B's claims to be compensated for the losses suffered by

[12] Ibid., 516.
[13] [1991] 1 QB 153.
[14] Ibid., 184E–F.
[15] Ibid., 184D-G.
[16] (1935) 153 LT 384.
[17] [1988] 1 WLR 968.
[18] Ibid., 979C.

her as a result of A's falsely imprisoning her if he attempts, through making untrue allegations about B, to justify his arrest of B.[19]

The torts in respect of which aggravated damages may be awarded

It has been established that aggravated damages may be awarded against someone who has committed one of the following torts: assault or battery, false imprisonment, libel or slander, trespass to land, private nuisance, using unlawful means to harm another, deceit, malicious falsehood, malicious prosecution, unlawfully discriminating against another on grounds of race contrary to the Race Relations Act 1976 and unlawfully discriminating against another on grounds of sex contrary to the Sex Discrimination Act 1975.[20]

It has also been established that aggravated damages may *not* be awarded in a negligence case.[21] There seems no good reason why this should be so. In *Kralj* v *McGrath*, Woolf J explained that

> it would be wholly inappropriate to introduce into claims ... for ... negligence, the concept of aggravated damage. [Making such damages available in negligence cases would] be wholly inconsistent with the general approach to damages in this area, which is to compensate the [claimant] for the loss that she has actually suffered, so far as it is possible to do so, by the award of monetary compensation and not to treat those damages as being a matter which reflects the degree of negligence ... of the defendant.[22]

This is, of course, no explanation at all.[23]

Further points

A couple of further points need to be made about the circumstances in which one person will be entitled to sue another for aggravated damages:

(1) *Aggravated damages and artificial legal persons.* Suppose that A has committed a tort in relation to B and A acted in an arrogant and high-handed manner in committing that tort. Suppose further that B is a company or some other kind of artificial legal person such as a local authority. Because B is an artificial legal person, it will be incapable of feeling anger or distress at the way it was treated by A. Given this, it would seem strange to allow B to sue A for aggravated damages, whatever view one takes as to the nature of aggravated damages.

[19] *Thompson* v *Commissioner of Police of the Metropolis* [1998] QB 498, 518.

[20] Assault or battery: *W* v *Meah* [1986] 1 All ER 935. False imprisonment: *Thompson* v *Commissioner of Police of the Metropolis* [1998] QB 498. Libel or slander: *Ley* v *Hamilton* (1935) 153 LT 384; *Sutcliffe* v *Pressdram Ltd* [1991] 1 QB 153. Trespass to land: *Drane* v *Evangelou* [1978] 1 WLR 455, 461H, 462E; *McMillan* v *Singh* (1984) 17 HLR 120. Private nuisance: *Thompson* v *Hill* (1870) LR 5 CP 564. Intentionally inflicting harm on another using unlawful means: *Messenger Newspapers Group Ltd* v *National Graphical Association* [1984] IRLR 397. Deceit: *Archer* v *Brown* [1985] QB 401, 426D–G. Malicious falsehood: *Khodaparast* v *Shad* [2000] 1 WLR 618. Malicious prosecution: *Thompson* v *Commissioner of Police of the Metropolis* [1998] QB 498. Discriminating against another on grounds of race: *Prison Service* v *Johnson* [1997] ICR 275. Discriminating against another on grounds of sex: *Ministry of Defence* v *Meredith* [1995] IRLR 539.

[21] *Kralj* v *McGrath* [1986] 1 All ER 54; *AB* v *South West Water Services Ltd* [1993] QB 507.

[22] [1986] 1 All ER 54, 61e–g.

[23] Cf. Lord Scott's 'explanation' (set out above, pp. 677–8) why exemplary damages should not be awarded in tort cases in *Kuddus* v *Chief Constable of Leicestershire* [2002] 2 AC 122, at [95].

However, in *Messenger Newspapers Group Ltd* v *National Graphical Association*[24] Caulfield J remarked 'aggravated damages can be awarded against inanimate legal entities like limited companies, and I cannot see any reason why the same legal entities cannot be awarded aggravated ... damages'.[25] On the other hand, in *Columbia Picture Industries Inc.* v *Robinson*,[26] the defendants wrongfully and arrogantly seized a number of video tapes which were on sale in a video shop run by one Robinson and a company controlled by him. Scott J held that Robinson and the company were entitled to sue the defendants for damages. Robinson was allowed to sue the defendants for compensatory damages and aggravated damages. The company was only allowed to sue the defendants for compensatory damages. The reason why the company was only allowed to sue the defendants for compensatory damages but not aggravated damages was that 'contumely and affront affect individuals, not inanimate corporations'.[27]

(2) *Lack of awareness of arrogant and high-handed conduct.* Suppose that A has committed a tort in relation to B and A acted in an arrogant and high-handed manner in committing that tort. If B is unaware that A acted in an arrogant and high-handed manner in committing the tort in question then there will be no reason to award her aggravated damages.[28] In such a case, B will not feel angry or distressed at the manner in which A acted.

In *Ministry of Defence* v *Meredith*,[29] the defendants unlawfully sacked the claimant when she became pregnant. The claimant sued the defendants for compensatory *and* aggravated damages. As part of her case, she sought to obtain discovery of documents that would indicate whether or not the defendants had known they were acting unlawfully in sacking her because she was pregnant. The Employment Appeal Tribunal held that the claimant was not entitled to discovery of those documents as they had no relevance to her claim. They obviously had no relevance to her claim for compensatory damages; and they had no relevance to her claim for aggravated damages as she would only have been entitled to claim such damages from the defendants if she *already* knew that the defendants had acted in an arrogant and high-handed manner in sacking her.

Visit **http://www.mylawchamber.co.uk/mcbride** to access updates on recent cases, as well as model answers and tips for answering tort problem questions.

[24] [1984] IRLR 397.
[25] Ibid., at [77].
[26] [1987] 1 Ch 38.
[27] Ibid., 88H.
[28] Again, this will be true whatever view one takes as to the nature of aggravated damages.
[29] [1995] IRLR 539.

36 Exemplary damages

THE AVAILABILITY OF EXEMPLARY DAMAGES

Suppose that A has committed a tort in relation to B and B is entitled to sue A for compensatory damages or nominal damages. In this situation, B may also be entitled to sue A for *exemplary damages*[1] – that is, damages that are designed to *punish* A for committing his tort.

B will only be allowed to sue A for such damages if three conditions are fulfilled.[2] First, it must be shown that A deserves to be punished for committing his tort. Secondly, it must be shown that if exemplary damages were not awarded against A, he would not be adequately punished for committing his tort. Thirdly, it must be shown that awarding exemplary damages against A would not fall foul of the limits that the House of Lords' decision in *Rookes* v *Barnard*[3] placed on when such awards could be made.[4] Let's now look at each of these conditions in turn.

[1] Another name for exemplary damages is *punitive damages*. English courts refer to the kind of damages discussed here as 'exemplary damages': see *Broome* v *Cassell & Co. Ltd* [1972] AC 1027, 1073–1074 (per Lord Hailsham LC)). Courts in the United States and Canada refer to the kind of damages discussed here as 'punitive damages'. The American usage is preferable because it makes clearer why the kind of damages discussed here are awarded: to punish someone who has committed a tort for committing that tort. However, we will refer to the kind of damages discussed here as 'exemplary damages' in order to avoid any confusion.

[2] See, generally, Ghandi 1990.

[3] [1964] AC 1129.

[4] *Important note*. It used to be that a *fourth* condition had to be fulfilled before an award of exemplary damages could be made against A. It had to be shown that the tort committed by A was the *right kind of tort* – that is, the kind of tort in respect of which exemplary damages could be awarded. However, that condition was abolished by the House of Lords in *Kuddus* v *Chief Constable of Leicestershire* [2002] 2 AC 122. For reasons that are best forgotten, the Court of Appeal ruled in *AB* v *South West Water Services Ltd* [1993] QB 507 that a tort would only count as the right kind of tort if there existed some case pre-dating the decision of the House of Lords in *Rookes* v *Barnard* in which exemplary damages were awarded against a defendant who had committed that tort. This meant, for example, that exemplary damages could *not* be awarded against a public servant who committed the tort of misfeasance in public office as there was no case decided before 1964 in which exemplary damages were awarded against someone who committed that tort. *Kuddus* was a misfeasance in public office case in which exemplary damages *were* claimed. The House of Lords refused to follow the decision of the Court of Appeal in the *AB* case and held that the claim for exemplary damages could not be struck out on the basis that there was no case decided before 1964 in which exemplary damages were awarded against a defendant who committed the tort of misfeasance in public office. Subject to one doubt, it seems then that there is now no limit on the kinds of torts in respect of which exemplary damages can be awarded: for confirmation of this point see, for example, [2002] 2 AC 122, at [45] (per Lord Mackay), [60] (per Lord Nicholls), [120] (per Lord Scott). The one doubt arises in the case where a tort involved the breach of a statutory duty owed to another. In *Kuddus*, Lord Mackay thought (at [46]) that exemplary damages could only be awarded against someone who breached a statutory duty owed to another if the statute that created that duty expressly authorised exemplary damages to be awarded against someone who breached that duty. However, it is not clear whether the other Law Lords who decided *Kuddus* agreed with him on that point.

The tortfeasor must deserve to be punished

One might think that all tortfeasors deserve to be punished for their behaviour because they have acted unlawfully. However, this is an extreme view. For example, suppose that a police officer arrests someone thinking that he is entitled to do so. However, he was not in fact entitled to make the arrest and his arrest was therefore wrongful. It is hard to argue in this case that the police officer deserves to be punished: while he acted wrongfully, he also acted with the best intentions and attempted to stay the right side of the law.[5]

So the fact that someone has acted wrongfully does not necessarily mean that he or she deserves to be punished for acting as he or she did. Something more is required before we can conclude that punishment is deserved.[6] What that 'something more' must be divided the Privy Council in *A* v *Bottrill*.[7] The claimant in that case had four cervical smear tests over four years. In each case, the smear test was examined by the defendant pathologist and in each case he gave the claimant a clean bill of health. However, the defendant failed in each case to inspect the claimant's smear test with a proper degree of care and skill. Had the defendant done so, he would have spotted that the claimant was in danger of developing cervical cancer and the claimant would have received treatment that would have prevented the cancer developing. However, because the claimant's smear tests were not properly examined, the claimant's condition went untreated and she developed cervical cancer.

The claimant sued the defendant for exemplary damages.[8] Now it was possible that the defendant was not aware at the time he examined the claimant's smear test that he was doing anything improper or negligent in examining the claimant's smear test in the way he did. At the same time, the method used by the defendant to examine smear tests such as the claimant's resulted in his having a spectacularly high error rate in examining smear tests: on average, for every two smear tests that he received which revealed signs that the patient from whom the smear test was taken was in danger of developing cervical cancer, he would report one of them as 'normal'. So it was possible that the defendant was not *conscious* at the time he examined the claimant's smear test that he was doing anything wrong in examining the smear test. At the same time, the defendant's conduct in examining the claimant's smear test fell so far below the standard expected of people in the claimant's position that it was *outrageous* for him to behave in the way he did.

The majority in the Privy Council thought that an award of exemplary damages could properly be made against a tortfeasor such as the defendant whose conduct was so outrageous as to call for condemnation. Lords Millett and Hutton dissented, arguing that exemplary damages should only be awarded against a tortfeasor who consciously acted unlawfully: they therefore thought exemplary damages should only be awarded against the

[5] See *Holden* v *Chief Constable of Lancashire* [1987] 1 QB 380, 388E.

[6] The criminal law acknowledges this point. To commit a criminal offence – and thereby render yourself liable to be punished under the criminal law – it is usually not enough for you to commit a wrongful act (an *actus reus*); you usually also have to have committed that wrongful act with a guilty mind (a *mens rea*).

[7] [2003] 1 AC 449.

[8] As the case occurred in New Zealand, she was not allowed to sue the defendant for compensation for the fact that she developed cervical cancer: that was covered under the New Zealand Accident Compensation Scheme (summarised below, pp. 806–7). However, s 396 of the Accident Insurance Act 1998 preserved the powers of the courts in New Zealand to award exemplary damages against defendants in personal injury cases.

defendant if he was aware when he was examining the claimant's test that the method employed by him in examining that test fell short of the standards expected of him.

Decisions of the Privy Council are not binding on the English courts, but there is no reason to think that the majority's approach in *Bottrill* will not be adopted by the English courts in deciding whether or not an award of exemplary damages is warranted in a particular case. So if A has committed a tort in relation to B, the first thing B is likely to have to establish if she wants to sue A for exemplary damages is that A's conduct was so outrageous that it deserves condemnation. If that is true, then A will deserve to be punished for his behaviour.

An award of exemplary damages must be required

Even if A does deserve to be punished for his behaviour, exemplary damages will not be awarded against him if it is not necessary to award such damages against him to ensure that he is adequately punished for his behaviour.

So, for example, if A has already been criminally punished for committing his tort, then exemplary damages will not be awarded against him. In *Archer* v *Brown*,[9] for instance, a defendant defrauded the claimant of £30,000, thereby committing the tort of deceit in relation to the claimant. Peter Pain J held that exemplary damages could not be awarded against the defendant because he had already been sent to prison for defrauding the claimant.[10] Similarly, if A has lost his job or incurred disciplinary proceedings from his employer for committing his tort, it is unlikely that an award of exemplary damages will be made against him.[11] Even if none of these things have happened to A, exemplary damages will still not be awarded against A if allowing B to sue A for compensatory damages and – if available – aggravated damages – would adequately punish A for committing his tort.[12]

Rookes v Barnard

Suppose that A has committed a tort in relation to B, that A deserves to be punished for committing that tort and that if B is not allowed to sue A for exemplary damages, A will

[9] [1985] QB 401.

[10] In light of this, it is doubtful whether the case of *Ashgar* v *Ahmed* (1984) 17 HLR 120 was correctly decided. In that case, the Court of Appeal held that the claimant – a tenant who was unlawfully evicted by his landlord, the defendant – was entitled to sue the defendant for £1,000 in exemplary damages even though the defendant had already been punished under the Protection from Eviction Act 1977 for evicting the claimant. (The defendant was fined £750 for evicting the claimant.) In *Borders* v *Commissioner of Police of the Metropolis* [2005] EWCA Civ 197, £100,000 in exemplary damages was awarded against a book thief who had already been sentenced to 30 months in prison for his activities. However, it is pretty clear that the award of exemplary damages in that case was actually designed both to compensate the claimants' bookstores for the losses that they had suffered as a result of the book thief's activities and to strip the book thief of the gains he had made as a result of his activities: ibid., at [8], [11], [13], [25]–[27], [39], [47]. In other words, while the courts *said* that they were awarding exemplary damages against the thief, what they were really awarding were either compensatory damages or disgorgement damages; and the fact that the defendant has already been punished for his conduct is no bar to either of those kinds of damages being awarded.

[11] *Thompson* v *Commissioner of Police of the Metropolis* [1998] QB 498, 518.

[12] See Lord Devlin's speech in *Rookes* v *Barnard* [1964] AC 1129, at 1228 (jury is only allowed to award exemplary damages against a defendant in a tort case if 'the sum which they have in mind to award as compensation (which may, of course, be a sum aggravated by the way in which the defendant has behaved . . .) is inadequate to punish him for his outrageous conduct . . .').

not be adequately punished for committing that tort. Even if all this is established, B will still not be allowed to sue A for exemplary damages if she is not allowed to do so under the decision of the House of Lords in *Rookes* v *Barnard*.[13]

In that case, the House of Lords set very tight limits on when exemplary damages may be awarded against a defendant in a tort case. They[14] held that if A has committed a tort, exemplary damages can *only* be awarded against him if:

(1) A was a 'servant of the government' at the time he committed his tort and he acted in an 'oppressive, arbitrary or unconstitutional' manner in committing that tort;[15] *or*
(2) A committed his tort because he figured that he would make more money committing that tort than he would have to pay out in damages to the victim of that tort; *or*
(3) statute law authorises an award of exemplary damages to be made against someone who has committed the kind of tort that A committed. If A's case does not fall into one of these categories, then exemplary damages cannot be awarded against him.

Let's now look at each of these categories in turn.

The first category

Two points need to be made under this heading.

First, it is clear from the judgments in *Broome* v *Cassell & Co. Ltd* that the phrase 'servant of the government' should be construed broadly: it covers anyone 'purporting to exercise powers of government, central or local, conferred on them by statute or at common law'.[16] So the police would be counted for these purposes as being servants of the government; as would officials of a local authority. In *AB* v *South West Water Services Ltd*, the Court of Appeal held that a nationalised corporation which supplied water to the inhabitants of Camelford was not a 'servant of the government' for the purpose of determining whether or not it could be sued for exemplary damages; it did not exercise any governmental powers but was merely a commercial operation.[17]

Secondly, suppose that A – a 'servant of the government' – has committed a tort in relation to B. The decision of the Court of Appeal in *Holden* v *Chief Constable of Lancashire*[18] makes it clear that A will have committed his tort in an 'oppressive, arbitrary or unconstitutional' manner if he acted oppressively in committing that tort *or* if he acted arbitrarily in committing that tort *or* if he acted unconstitutionally in committing that tort. In other words, it is not necessary, for the purposes of establishing that A acted in an 'oppressive, arbitrary or unconstitutional' manner in committing his tort, to show that A acted oppressively in committing that tort. In the *Holden* case itself, a police officer wrongfully arrested the claimant for 20 minutes. He did not act oppressively in doing so: he merely held on to the claimant's arm for 20 minutes. The Court of Appeal held that it could

13 Ibid.
14 Or rather Lord Devlin: he was the only Law Lord in *Rookes* v *Barnard* to address the issue of when exemplary damages could be awarded against a defendant in a tort case. The other Law Lords were content to indicate that they agreed with this aspect of Lord Devlin's judgment.
15 Ibid., 1226.
16 [1972] AC 1027, 1130 (per Lord Diplock). See also 1077–8 (per Lord Hailsham LC) and 1087–8 (per Lord Reid).
17 [1993] QB 507, 525 (per Stuart-Smith LJ), 532 (per Sir Thomas Bingham MR).
18 [1987] 1 QB 380.

be argued that the police officer acted in an 'oppressive, arbitrary or unconstitutional' manner in wrongfully arresting the claimant. The fact that the defendant wrongfully arrested the claimant established that he acted unconstitutionally in arresting the claimant.

The second category

Lord Devlin made it clear in his judgment in *Rookes* v *Barnard* that this category does not just cover cases where someone deliberately commits a tort because he thinks that he will make more money by committing that tort than he will have to pay the victim of the tort in compensatory damages: 'It extends to cases in which [someone deliberately commits a tort in order] to gain . . . some object – perhaps some property which he covets – which either he could not obtain at all or not obtain except at a price greater than he wants to put down.'[19]

So – in *Drane* v *Evangelou*,[20] the defendant let some premises to the claimant. He then unlawfully evicted the claimant from the premises so that they could be occupied by his in-laws. It was held that the case fell within *Rookes* v *Barnard*'s second category of situations where exemplary damages could be awarded: the defendant deliberately committed the tort of trespass because he thought he would gain more by committing that tort – possession of the premises occupied by the claimant – than he would have to pay the claimant in damages.

Suppose that A has committed a tort in relation to B and we want to establish that A committed that tort because he figured he could make more money by committing that tort than he would have to pay out in damages to B. In order to establish this, we do *not* have to show that A did a precise calculation before he committed his tort of how much he would gain by committing that tort and how much he would have to pay out to B in damages if he committed that tort.[21] It is enough to show that when A committed his tort he did so because he knew or hoped he would obtain some kind of material gain from committing that tort: from this it can be inferred that A calculated that he would gain more by committing that tort than he would have to pay B in damages.[22] So if the *Daily Herald* deliberately libels Karen in order to boost its sales, Karen may well be allowed under *Rookes* v *Barnard* to sue the *Daily Herald* for damages. But, on the other hand, if the *Daily Herald* deliberately libels Karen for non-mercenary reasons – say, because it wants to victimise Karen – Karen will *not* be able to sue the *Daily Herald* for exemplary damages. Her case will fall foul of the *Rookes* v *Barnard* limits on when an award of exemplary damages may be made.

The Court of Appeal suggested in *Borders* v *Commissioner of Police of the Metropolis*[23] that exemplary damages that are awarded under this second category really function as disgorgement damages.[24] That is – exemplary damages awarded under the second category are designed to strip a wrongdoer of the profits he has made from committing his wrong.

[19] [1964] AC 1129, 1227.
[20] [1978] 1 WLR 455.
[21] *Broome* v *Cassell & Co. Ltd* [1972] AC 1027, 1078–9 (per Lord Hailsham LC), 1094 (per Lord Morris).
[22] *John* v *Mirror Group Newspapers Ltd* [1997] QB 586, 619A.
[23] [2005] EWCA Civ 197.
[24] Ibid., at [25]–[27] (per Sedley LJ).

There are two problems with this view – both of which become obvious if we consider the situation where the *Daily Herald* deliberately libelled Karen.

First, if Karen wants to sue the *Daily Herald* for exemplary damages under the second category in *Rookes* v *Barnard* all she has to show is that the *Daily Herald* acted as it did because it *thought* it would make more money by libelling Karen than it would have to pay her in compensatory damages. Karen does *not* have to show that the *Daily Herald* actually *did* make any money from libelling her. So exemplary damages can be awarded under the second category in *Rookes* v *Barnard* against a wrongdoer who has not actually made any profit from his wrong.

Secondly, even if the *Daily Herald* did make some money out of running its story about Karen, there is no reason to think that in judging how much to make the *Daily Herald* pay Karen by way of exemplary damages, the courts will simply confine itself to making the *Daily Herald* cough up the money it made by libelling Karen. Instead, the damages will be assessed according to how much is required to *punish* the *Daily Herald* for its conduct towards Karen. The sum required to make the *Daily Herald* 'smart' for the way it acted towards Karen could well far exceed the actual profit that the *Daily Herald* made from its conduct. Indeed, it is hard to see how simply awarding disgorgement damages against the *Daily Herald* could work effectively to punish it for its conduct and discourage it from doing the same thing in the future. Simply making a wrongdoer hand over the profits he has made from his wrong will not discourage him from acting in the same way in the future:[25] next time, he will think that the worst that can happen is that he will not be allowed to profit from his wrong, so why not take a chance and commit the wrong and see if anyone tries to strip him of his gains? So – when exemplary damages are awarded under the second category in *Rookes* v *Barnard* against a wrongdoer who has made a profit from his wrong, the amount payable in damages will rarely, if ever, simply equal the profit the wrongdoer has made from his wrong.

Statutory authorisation

There are very few examples of statutes which authorise the victim of a tort to sue the person who committed that tort for exemplary damages. Perhaps the only example is provided by s 13(2) of the Reserve and Auxiliary Forces (Protection of Civil Interests) Act 1951, which provides that exemplary damages may be awarded against someone who converts goods that are covered by the Act.

FURTHER POINTS

Some further points need to be made about this area of the law.

Assessment of damages

Suppose A has committed a tort in relation to B and B is – according to the principles set out above – entitled to sue A for exemplary damages. How much will A be required to pay B by way of exemplary damages? As a general rule, the answer is: just enough to bring the

[25] Contra, Edelman 2006, at 149.

entire amount of damages A has to pay B up to a level sufficient to punish A for committing his tort.[26]

So, for example, in *Duffy* v *Eastern Health and Social Services Board*[27] the defendants unlawfully discriminated against the claimant on grounds of her religion. The claimant was entitled to sue the defendants for £15,000 in compensatory damages and for £5,000 in aggravated damages. The court held that the claimant was entitled to sue the defendant for exemplary damages and found that the defendants would only be sufficiently punished for behaving in the way they did if they were made to pay the claimant £25,000 in damages. So they held that the claimant was entitled to sue the defendant for £5,000 in exemplary damages.

This general rule is subject to two qualifications.

(1) *Contributory negligence.* In *Holden* v *Chief Constable of Lancashire* the Court of Appeal held that the exemplary damages payable to the victim of a tort might be reduced if he or she provoked the person who committed that tort into committing that tort.[28]

(2) *Mass torts.* Suppose that Carl's doing x means that he has committed a tort in relation to Nita, Lara and Wendy. Suppose further that Nita, Lara and Wendy are each – according to the principles set out above – entitled to sue Carl for exemplary damages. The decision of the Court of Appeal in *Riches* v *News Group Newspapers*[29] says that one should use the following method to determine how much Carl must pay Nita, Lara and Wendy in exemplary damages. One first adds up the sums Nita, Lara and Wendy are each entitled to sue Carl for compensatory and aggravated damages. Say that Nita is entitled to sue Carl for £1,000; that Lara is entitled to sue Carl for £2,000; and that Wendy is entitled to sue Carl for £5,000. Added up, these sums come to £8,000. One then works out what sort of sum Carl should be made to pay to punish him for doing x – say that this is £11,000. Thus £3,000 (the difference between £11,000 and £8,000) will therefore represent the *total* amount of exemplary damages that Carl should be made to pay to Nita, Lara and Wendy *together*. Nita, Lara and Wendy will *each* be entitled to a third of this lump sum, so Carl will be liable to pay each of them £1,000 in exemplary damages.[30]

Standard of proof

Suppose that events X, Y and Z are alleged to have occurred and if they did occur, then B would be entitled to sue A for exemplary damages under the principle set out above. As this is a civil case, the courts will find that events X, Y and Z occurred if it is *more probable than not* that those events occurred.[31] They will *not* require it to be proved *beyond a reasonable doubt* that those events occurred. But this is very odd. If it were alleged that events X, Y and

[26] What level of damages will be sufficient to punish A for committing his tort will, of course, depend on his means and how badly he behaved in committing his tort: *Rookes* v *Barnard* [1964] AC 1129, 1228.

[27] [1992] IRLR 251.

[28] [1987] 1 QB 380, 388 (per Purchas LJ).

[29] [1986] 1 QB 256.

[30] Notice that if Carl's doing x had not affected Lara and Wendy, Carl would have had to pay Nita £10,000 in exemplary damages – £9,000 more than he is liable to pay her under the facts assumed above.

[31] For another example of a situation where the courts apply a 'balance of probabilities' test to resolve what happened, see above, pp. 539–42.

Z occurred for the purpose of establishing that A committed a criminal offence, and is therefore liable to be punished criminally, the courts *would* require it to be proved beyond a reasonable doubt that those events occurred. So why is a lower standard of proof required in a case where establishing that events X, Y and Z occurred will result in an award of exemplary damages being made against A? The same standard of proof should apply in both cases.[32]

Vicarious liability

Suppose that A committed a tort in relation to B and, on the principles set out above, B is entitled to sue A for exemplary damages. Suppose further that A's employer, C, is vicariously liable in respect of A's tort. Could B sue *C* for exemplary damages? One would have thought the answer must be 'no': why on earth would we punish C for something that A did?[33]

However, there are some authorities that indicate that B may well be able to sue C for exemplary damages in this situation.[34] For example, in *Lancashire County Council* v *Municipal Mutual Insurance Ltd*[35] the question arose: could a local authority insure against the possibility that it would be held liable to pay someone exemplary damages? The Court of Appeal held that the answer was 'yes'. Its reason for so finding was that if the local authority were ever held liable to pay someone exemplary damages, that would be because it was vicariously liable in respect of a tort committed by one of its employees. So allowing the local authority to insure against the risk that it would be held liable to pay someone exemplary damages would not offend against the general principle of law that no one should be allowed to insure himself against the risk of being held liable for engaging in criminal conduct. The significance of the decision here lies in the fact that the Court of Appeal clearly assumed that the victim of a tort committed by a local authority employee in the course of his employment might be able to sue the local authority for exemplary damages, depending on whether he is entitled to sue the employee for such damages.

The same assumption was made by the Court of Appeal in *Thompson* v *Commissioner of Police of the Metropolis*.[36] In that case, the court went so far as to hold that in the situation we are considering, the exemplary damages payable by C could *exceed* the damages payable by A. The reason for this is that as exemplary damages are designed to punish a defendant for his behaviour, how much the defendant will be held liable to pay the claimant by way

[32] The OJ Simpson saga in the United States provides a graphic illustration of this point. OJ Simpson was charged with murdering his ex-wife, Nicole Brown Simpson and her friend, Ron Goldman. He was acquitted on the ground that it could not be proved beyond a reasonable doubt that he murdered Nicole Brown Simpson and Ron Goldman. Ron Goldman's estate then sued OJ Simpson in tort. It was found that it was more probable than not that OJ Simpson had murdered Ron Goldman and Ron Goldman's estate was held to be entitled to sue OJ Simson for $33.5m, most of which was exemplary damages.

[33] Under the criminal law, of course, an employer would *not* be held criminally liable if one of his employees committed a crime in the course of his employment.

[34] See, in addition, to the authorities cited below, *New South Wales* v *Ibbett* [2006] HCA 57, where the High Court of Australia upheld an award of exemplary damages against the State of New South Wales on the ground that it was vicariously liable for two police officers' torts (trespass to land and assault), holding (at [51]) that the award was necessary to bring home to the State that police officers employed by the State had to be trained not to engage in the sort of conduct that the police officers in *Ibbett* had engaged in.

[35] [1997] QB 897.

[36] [1998] QB 498.

of exemplary damages will depend a great deal on his means. If the defendant is very wealthy, then the exemplary damages awardable against him will have to be correspondingly large to ensure that they 'smart'. If he is very poor, then not much need be awarded against him by way of exemplary damages to ensure that he is punished for what he did. Now – the Court of Appeal made it clear in *Thompson* that if, in the situation we are considering, B made a claim for exemplary damages against *C*, then the damages payable should be assessed by reference to *C*'s means, not *A*'s.[37] So C – who is presumably much wealthier than A – may be held liable to pay B a sum in exemplary damages that far exceeds what B would have been able to recover from A had she sued him for exemplary damages.

In *Kuddus* v *Chief Constable of Leicestershire*,[38] the claimant called the police, complaining that some of his property was stolen. The police constable who dealt with the case later falsely reported that the claimant had withdrawn his complaint. He committed the tort of misfeasance in public office in so doing. The claimant was entitled to sue the police constable for exemplary damages.[39] Instead, he sued the chief constable for such damages on the basis that he was vicariously liable for the police constable's tort.[40] The House of Lords invited counsel to address them on the issue of whether exemplary damages could be awarded against someone who was merely vicariously liable in respect of a tort committed by someone else. However, counsel declined the opportunity,[41] preferring instead to concentrate on the issue of whether exemplary damages could ever be awarded in a misfeasance in public office case.[42] As a result, all but one of the Law Lords who decided *Kuddus* declined to express a view on whether exemplary damages could properly be awarded in a vicarious liability case. The exception was Lord Scott who expressed the strong view – which we share – that it is improper to award such damages against someone who is vicariously liable for another's tort.[43]

Death

Suppose that A has committed a tort in relation to B and B is entitled to sue A for exemplary damages. Section 1(2)(a)(i) of the Law Reform (Miscellaneous Provisions) Act 1934 provides that if B dies before she has had a chance to sue A for damages, her right to sue A for exemplary damages will die with her. Her estate will not be able to sue A for such damages.[44] This is puzzling. If A's conduct is worthy of punishment, then it is still worthy of punishment even after B has died. So why should B's death have the effect of letting him

[37] Ibid., 517. Lord Mackay doubted whether this could be correct in *Kuddus* v *Chief Constable of Leicestershire* [2002] 2 AC 122, at [47], but as the point was not argued, he expressed 'no concluded view upon it'.

[38] [2002] 2 AC 122.

[39] The case fell into the first *Rookes* v *Barnard* category of situations where exemplary damages may be awarded against a defendant in a tort case.

[40] See above, p. 651.

[41] [2002] 2 AC 122, at [125].

[42] To which the answer was 'yes' – see above, n. 4.

[43] [2002] 2 AC 122, at [137]. Interestingly, in a subsequent misfeasance in public office case, which involved prison officers interfering with the claimant's right of access to court, counsel for the claimant did *not* seek an award of exemplary damages against the Home Office, but only against the prison officers. When the case came before the Court of Appeal, that court said that counsel had acted 'prudently' in not pursuing a claim for exemplary damages against the Home Office: *Watkins* v *Secretary of State for the Home Department* [2005] QB 883, at [54].

[44] Though it will be able to sue A for damages in respect of the actionable losses suffered by B before she died: see above, p. 503.

off the hook? What makes the law in this area even more puzzling is that it seems that if B has a right to sue A for *aggravated* damages, then that right *will* survive her death. But there is no reason why her estate should be allowed to sue A for aggravated damages. The whole point of awarding aggravated damages is to pacify the victim of a tort – so if B is no longer around to be pacified, there is no reason for aggravated damages to be awarded against A anymore. So the law in this area has got things completely backwards – it allows B's right to sue A for exemplary damages to die with her, when it should survive her death; and it allows B's right to sue A for aggravated damages to survive her death, when it should die with her.

OPTIONS FOR REFORM

It is likely that the law on exemplary damages will be reformed in one way or the other in the next few years. While the government has declined the opportunity to reform the law on exemplary damages through statutory means,[45] it is plain that the House of Lords in the *Kuddus* case was keen to take a fresh look at the law on exemplary damages and was only prevented from making some radical changes to the law in this area because counsel in that case declined to invite them to do so. So it may be worth spending some time canvassing the various options for reform that are available.

(1) *Abolish exemplary damages.* The first option is to abolish the availability of exemplary damages in tort cases.[46] Clearly, Lord Devlin was in favour of doing this in *Rookes* v *Barnard*.[47] However, he felt constrained by precedent from doing so and instead sought – as a second best solution – to confine awards of exemplary damages to situations where there was clear precedent for their being awarded: hence the *Rookes* v *Barnard* limits on when exemplary damages may be awarded.[48] Lord Scott also announced a clear preference for abolishing exemplary damages in *Kuddus* v *Chief Constable of Leicestershire*.[49]

If we can get past non-arguments[50] in favour of the abolition of exemplary damages (for

45 Hansard (HC Debates), 9 November 1999, col. 502.

46 For a fuller discussion of the case for and against abolishing exemplary damages, see Burrows 1996 and McBride 1996.

47 [1964] AC 1129.

48 See Lord Reid's remarks in *Broome* v *Cassell & Co. Ltd* [1972] AC 1027, 1088: 'I freely admit that [saying that exemplary damages may be awarded against a "servant of the government" who has acted in an "oppressive, arbitrary or unconstitutional" manner in committing a tort but that exemplary damages may not be awarded against a private individual who has acted in a similar manner in committing a tort] is illogical. The real reason for the distinction was, in my view, that the cases showed that it was firmly established with regard to servants of "the government" that damages could be awarded against them beyond any sum justified as compensation, whereas there was no case except one which was overruled where damages had been awarded against a private bully or oppressor to an amount that could not be fairly regarded as compensatory . . . Again I freely admit there is no logical reason [for saying that exemplary damages may be awarded against someone who has deliberately committed a tort if he committed that tort because he thought he would make more money by committing that tort than he would have to pay out in compensatory damages but not if he committed that tort out of malice towards the victim of the tort]. The reason for [this] is simply that firmly established authority required us to accept [that exemplary damages could be awarded against someone who deliberately committed a tort in order to make a gain] however little we might like it, but did not require us to go further.'

49 [2002] 2 AC 122, at [111].

50 These are non-arguments because they assume the very thing they are trying to show, namely that awards of exemplary damages should not be made in tort cases.

example, that awards of such damages are 'anomalous'[51] or that they confuse the respective functions of the criminal law and the civil law[52]) the primary[53] argument against such awards being made is that if the victim of a tort is ever allowed to sue the person who committed that tort for exemplary damages, that person may be punished for his behaviour without being afforded any of the protections that we would normally accord to someone who is subject to criminal punishment.[54] This is not only objectionable in principle; it might also be argued that a consequence of this is that awarding exemplary damages against tortfeasors will violate their rights under Article 1 of the Second Protocol to the European Convention on Human Rights.[55] If that is true, then the courts would be duty bound under the Human Rights Act 1998 to cease awarding exemplary damages in tort cases. However, the fact that tortfeasors who are sued for exemplary damages are not given as much protection as people who are prosecuted for committing criminal offences does not mean that we should not award exemplary damages in tort cases – rather, it suggests that we should do more than we do now to protect defendants who are sued for exemplary damages.[56]

So there is no very strong argument *in favour* of the *complete abolition* of awards of exemplary damages. There is, on the other hand, a very strong argument *against* the complete abolition of such awards. If the law were changed so that it said that the victim of a tort can never sue the person who committed that tort for exemplary damages, people would have less incentive to abide by the law and the rule of law would be correspondingly weakened.[57] As Lord Devlin observed in *Rookes* v *Barnard*, 'an award of exemplary damages

[51] [2002] 2 AC 122, at [95] (per Lord Scott).

[52] See Lord Reid's remark in *Broome* v *Cassell & Co. Ltd* [1972] AC 1027, 1086: 'I . . . think that [allowing the victim of a tort to sue the person who committed that tort for exemplary damages] is highly anomalous. It is confusing the function of the civil law which is to compensate with the function of the criminal law which is to inflict deterrent and punitive penalties.' For a more sophisticated version of this argument see Beever 2003a, 105–10.

[53] Another argument is that awarding exemplary damages to a claimant confers an undeserved windfall on him. But what is wrong with giving someone a windfall if doing so serves some valuable social purpose (here, ensuring that people who flagrantly breach the law are punished)? Is that not what happens every time someone wins on the National Lottery?

[54] *Broome* v *Cassell & Co. Ltd* [1972] AC 1027, at 1087 (per Lord Reid): 'I think that the objections to allowing juries to go beyond compensatory damages are overwhelming. To allow pure punishment in this way contravenes almost every principle which has been evolved for the protection of offenders. There is no definition of the offence except that the conduct punished must be oppressive, high-handed, malicious, wanton or its like – terms too vague to be admitted to any criminal code worthy of the name. There is no limit to the punishment except that it must not be unreasonable . . . [T]here is no effective appeal against sentence . . .'

[55] This provides that 'Every natural or legal person is entitled to the peaceful enjoyment of his possessions. No one shall be deprived of his possessions except in the public interest and subject to the conditions provided for by law . . .' Lord Scott hinted in the *Kuddus* case that awards of exemplary damages might violate Art 6 of the ECHR: [2002] 2 AC 122, at [110], but it is hard to see that Art 6 extends this far. Article 6(3) sets out various minimum rights which those charged with a criminal offence are to enjoy – but of course, in a case where exemplary damages are awarded, no one is charged with a criminal offence. Article 5 provides that 'No one shall be deprived of his liberty save . . . in accordance with a procedure prescribed by law' and Art 7 provides that 'No one shall be held guilty of any criminal offence on account of any act or omission which did not constitute a criminal offence under national or international law at the time when it was committed' – but neither of these Arts seem apt to cover the case where exemplary damages are awarded against a defendant in a tort case.

[56] For a discussion of when a defendant in the United States will be able to argue that an award of exemplary damages has violated his constitutional rights, see GS&Z, 970–84.

[57] Zipursky 2005 (at 151–61) also defends awards of exemplary damages on the ground that, on occasion, the victim of a tort has a 'right to be punitive' towards the person who committed that tort, because of the manner in which it was committed. See Stevens 2007, at 85–7, and Sebok 2007 for similar arguments.

can serve a useful purpose in vindicating the strength of the law'.[58] In the *Kuddus* case, Lord Nicholls also pointed to the useful role awards of exemplary damages make in helping to ensure that the rule of law is maintained:

> The availability of exemplary damages has played a significant role in buttressing civil liberties, in claims for false imprisonment and wrongful arrest ... On occasion conscious wrongdoing by a defendant is so outrageous, his disregard of the plaintiff's rights so contumelious, that something more is needed to show that the law will not tolerate such behaviour. Without an award of exemplary damages, justice will not have been done.[59]

Lord Hutton agreed: 'the power to award exemplary damages ... serves to uphold and vindicate the rule of law because it makes clear that the courts will not tolerate such conduct.'[60]

Given this, it is hard to see that there is any case for pursuing the first option for reform.[61]

(2) *Overrule* Rookes *v* Barnard. If this second option for reform were pursued, exemplary damages would be awarded if a tortfeasor deserved to be punished for committing his tort and he would not be adequately punished for committing that tort if an award of exemplary damages were not made against him. The *Rookes* v *Barnard* limits on when exemplary damages may be awarded would be abolished.

The attractions of reforming the law on exemplary damages in this way are obvious. Everyone agrees that the *Rookes* v *Barnard* limits on when exemplary damages may be awarded are 'illogical'.[62] This was the major criticism made of *Rookes* v *Barnard* by the Court of Appeal in *Broome* v *Cassell & Co. Ltd*.[63] Lord Denning MR observed that 'If exemplary damages for libel can be awarded against the greedy seeker after profit, surely they should be able to be awarded against the wicked inventor of calumnies.'[64] And Salmon LJ asked:

> Why should exemplary damages be recoverable only for outrageous conduct by servants of the Crown? The public equally requires protection against such conduct if it is perpetrated by ... nationalised industries ..., trade unions, large corporations and indeed by anyone, especially if in a position of power ... There is ... no sensible reason why the defendant's precise standing should be the criterion of his legal liability to pay exemplary damages. There exists an even more serious objection ... The doctrine that the executive is subject to extraordinary legal liabilities is dangerous. It is but a short and natural step from that doctrine to the doctrine that the executive may

[58] [1964] AC 1129, 1226.

[59] [2002] 2 AC 122, at [63].

[60] Ibid., at [79].

[61] Which is *not* to say that the courts will *not* abolish awards of exemplary damages in the future. They may be required to do so by the European Court of Human Rights. Moreover, some of our more *communautaire*-minded judges may take the view that as awards of exemplary damages are unheard of in France and Germany, they should not be allowed here. Certainly, any attempt to bring English private law more into line with private law on the Continent would see exemplary damages being jettisoned.

[62] *Broome* v *Cassell & Co. Ltd* [1972] AC 1027, 1088 (per Lord Reid). It is noticeable that no other common law jurisdiction has followed *Rookes* v *Barnard*.

[63] [1971] 2 QB 354.

[64] Ibid., 381. See also Taylor J's criticism of this aspect of *Rookes* v *Barnard* in the Australian case of *Uren* v *John Fairfax & Sons Pty Ltd* (1965–66) 117 CLR 118, 138: 'I am quite unable to see why the law should look with less favour on wrongs committed with a profit-making motive than upon wrongs committed with the utmost degree of malice or vindictively, arrogantly or high-handedly with a contumelious disregard for the claimant's rights.'

> enjoy corresponding legal rights. This is entirely contrary to one of the fundamental principles of the common law, namely that it regards all men indifferently. The cabinet minister by virtue of his office has no greater legal rights or liabilities than his humblest constituent. All are equal before the law.[65]

This criticism was revived by Lord Nicholls in the *Kuddus* case. He was 'respectfully inclined to doubt the soundness of [the] distinction[s]' drawn in *Rookes* v *Barnard* between the cases where exemplary damages could be awarded and the cases where they could not be.[66]

The case for abolishing the *Rookes* v *Barnard* limits on when exemplary damages may be awarded seems unanswerable. However, a word of caution is in order. *In the current climate* it seems likely that abolishing the *Rookes* v *Barnard* limits would result in an undesirable explosion in litigation, most of it frivolous and unmeritorious. Given this, it might be that the third option for reform discussed below might prove a better choice.

(3) *Incremental reform*. This third option for reform would involve removing some of the existing patent defects in the law on exemplary damages that have already been identified above – such as the fact that (seemingly) exemplary damages can be awarded against people who are vicariously liable for other people's torts and the fact that the death of the victim of a tort will extinguish any right she held while she was alive to sue the tortfeasor for exemplary damages. However, the *Rookes* v *Barnard* limits on when exemplary damages may be awarded would *not* be abolished until there was some assurance that the dramatic expansion in the range of situations where exemplary damages may be awarded that that would entail would not trigger an undesirable explosion in unmeritorious litigation. Until that time, the existing law on when exemplary damages may be awarded would remain basically unchanged.

Visit **http://www.mylawchamber.co.uk/mcbride** to access updates on recent cases, as well as model answers and tips for answering tort problem questions.

[65] [1971] 2 QB 354, 386.
[66] [2002] 2 AC 122, at [66].

37 Gain-based damages

THE NATURE OF GAIN-BASED DAMAGES

Gain-based damages are designed to make a wrongdoer (here, a tortfeasor) account for a gain that he has obtained as a result of committing his wrong (here, a tort).[1] There are two kinds of gain that a tortfeasor can obtain as a result of committing a tort:

(1) *Money*. A tortfeasor may have received or saved money as a result of committing his tort. So, for example, if A is paid £200 for beating up B, then he has obtained £200 as a result of committing a tort – battery – in relation to B.

(2) *Freedom*. The second kind of gain that a tortfeasor can obtain as a result of committing a tort is *freedom*. Every tortfeasor obtains this kind of gain as a result of committing his tort. By definition, if A commits a tort in relation to B by doing *x*, then A has enjoyed the freedom to do *x*. So, for example, if A converts B's horse by taking it for a ride, then A has enjoyed the freedom of riding on B's horse.

Corresponding to these two types of gain that a tortfeasor can obtain as a result of committing a tort, there are two kinds of gain-based damages that may be awarded against someone who has committed a tort:

(1) *Disgorgement damages*. The first type of gain-based damages is directed at a tortfeasor who has obtained or saved money as a result of committing his tort. These damages are designed to make a tortfeasor *give up* the money he has obtained or saved. There is widespread agreement nowadays that these damages should be called *disgorgement damages* – because they are designed to make a tortfeasor *disgorge* the money he has obtained or saved as a result of committing his tort.[2]

(2) *Licence fee damages*. The second type of gain-based damages is targeted at making a tortfeasor account for the freedom he has enjoyed as a result of committing his tort. It would be wrong to call these damages 'disgorgement damages' because the freedom that a tortfeasor enjoyed as a result of committing his tort is in the past. Being in the past, this gain cannot now be handed over to someone else. For example, if A converted B's horse by riding on it, the freedom that A enjoyed in converting B's horse was enjoyed by A while he was riding on the horse. Once he stopped riding the horse, that freedom disappeared into the past and cannot now be recalled to be handed over to someone else.

1 Some dislike the term 'gain-based damages', thinking that the word 'damages' denotes an award which is *compensatory* in function: see *Attorney-General* v *Blake* [2001] 1 AC 268, 284 (per Lord Nicholls, who prefers to use the term 'account of profits' to describe what are usually now known as 'disgorgement damages') and McGregor 1996, 203. But no one objects to using the term 'exemplary *damages*' to describe a money award which is punitive in function. Given this, it is hard to see what is so objectionable about using the term 'gain-based damages' to describe a money award which is designed to make a wrongdoer account for a gain that he has made as a result of committing that wrong.

2 Smith L 1992; Edelman 2002b.

The second type of gain-based damages is not, then, concerned to make a tortfeasor give up any gain he has obtained as a result of committing his tort. Instead, these damages are intended to make the tortfeasor *pay a reasonable sum* for the fact that he enjoyed that gain in the past. There is no widespread agreement on what name should be given to these damages. Dr James Edelman – who must now be recognised as being the leading scholar on gain-based damages – calls this second type of gain-based damages, *restitutionary damages*.[3] We cannot accept this suggestion. It implies that these damages are designed to make a tortfeasor *give back* a gain that he has obtained from the victim of his tort by committing his tort. But if – as we have seen – the gain that is the target of the second type of gain-based damages cannot be given *up*, it is hard to see how it can be given *back*. The gain is in the past and cannot be now recalled to be handed over to someone else. Instead, we will call this second type of gain-based damages, *licence fee damages*.[4] As the name suggests, these damages are concerned to make a tortfeasor pay a fee for the licence he has enjoyed as a result of committing his tort.

THE AVAILABILITY OF GAIN-BASED DAMAGES

Disgorgement damages

Disgorgement damages may be awarded against someone who has obtained or saved money as a result of committing one of the following torts.

(1) *Conversion*. In *Kuwait Airways Corpn* v *Iraqi Airways Co. (Nos 4 & 5)*, Lord Nicholls remarked that 'all those who convert [someone else's goods] should be accountable for the *benefits* they receive';[5] and indeed it has long been established that disgorgement damages may be claimed against someone who commits the tort of conversion.

So, for example, in *Oughton* v *Seppings*[6] the defendant, a sheriff's officer, received a warrant authorising him to seize the property of one Winslove and sell it in order to pay off a debt which Winslove owed. The defendant met Winslove driving a pony cart. The defendant seized the pony cart and the pony and sold both items of property. In selling the pony, the defendant committed the tort of conversion as the pony belonged to the claimant, Winslove's landlord, and not Winslove, at the time it was sold. The claimant was held entitled to sue the defendant for the money he obtained in return for the claimant's pony.

In *Oughton*, the defendant converted the claimant's property by selling it. May disgorgement damages be awarded against a defendant who converts another's property by *using* it? There is no English authority where disgorgement damages have been awarded against someone who has converted another's property by using it.[7] However, there is an American

[3] Edelman 2002b.

[4] See Jaffey 2007, 100.

[5] [2002] 2 AC 883, at [79] (emphasis added).

[6] (1830) 1 B & Ad 241, 109 ER 776. See also *Lamine* v *Dorrell* (1701) 2 Ld Raym 1216, 92 ER 303 (defendant who committed the tort of conversion by selling debentures belonging to claimant's estate held liable to hand over money he had received for the debentures to estate); and *Powell* v *Rees* (1837) 7 Ad & E 426, 112 ER 530 (defendant who committed tort of conversion by selling claimant's coal held liable for money made by selling the coal).

[7] See McInnes 2003, at 712: '[The] precedents consistently indicate that while the defendant is required to give up his entire gain if he wrongfully *sells* the claimant's property, he merely is required to pay a hiring fee [i.e. licence fee damages] for improper *usage*' (at 712). See also, to the same effect, Mason & Carter 1995, 649–52.

case where such damages were awarded. In *Olwell* v *Nye & Nissen*,[8] the defendant converted a machine belonging to the claimant by using it in his factory. It was held that the claimant was entitled to sue the defendant for the profits the defendant had made by using that machine.

(2) *Passing off.* Disgorgement damages may be awarded against someone who has *deliberately* committed the tort of passing off.[9] So in *My Kinda Town* v *Soll*,[10] the defendants deliberately dressed up their restaurant in such a way that people would be deceived into thinking that the defendants' restaurant was a branch of a chain of restaurants run by the claimants. Slade J held that the claimants were entitled to sue the defendants for the money they had made by passing off their restaurant as being one of the claimants' restaurants. But the claimants were only entitled to sue the defendants for the money they had made by deceiving people into believing that their restaurant was run by the claimants: the claimants were not entitled to sue the defendants for the money they had made from customers who had not entered the defendants' restaurant in the belief that it was run by the claimants. Quantifying how much money the claimants could sue the defendants for therefore proved a very difficult exercise: the court had to estimate how many of the defendants' customers had walked into the restaurant in the belief that it was run by the claimants and what the profits were on the meals sold to those customers.

(3) *Infringement of intellectual property rights.* Disgorgement damages may be awarded against someone who infringes another's copyright[11] or someone who infringes another's design right.[12] In the case where a defendant has infringed another's patent, disgorgement damages may be awarded if the defendant knew or ought to have known of the existence of the patent at the time he infringed it.[13]

(4) *Invasion of privacy.* The equivalent of disgorgement damages are routinely awarded against defendants who commit equitable wrongs such as a breach of trust, a breach of fiduciary duty, or a breach of confidence.[14] The fact that the new tort of wrongful disclosure of private information has its origins in the equitable wrong of breach of confidence makes it likely that disgorgement damages will be routinely awarded against defendants who commit this tort. Indeed, in *Douglas* v *Hello! Ltd (No. 3)*,[15] the Court of Appeal accepted that if the defendants in that case had made a profit from publishing unauthorised photographs of the claimants' wedding celebrations, then the claimants would have been entitled to sue the defendants for a sum equal to that profit.[16] However, it was found

[8] 173 P 2d 652 (1946).
[9] *Edelsten* v *Edelsten* (1863) 1 De G J & S 185, 46 ER 72.
[10] [1982] FSR 147 (rev'd on other grounds, [1983] RPC 407).
[11] Copyright, Designs and Patents Act 1988, s 96(2). It is not thought that s 97(1) of the 1988 Act affects this point. That subsection provides that: 'Where in action for infringement of copyright it is shown that at the time of the infringement the defendant did not know, and had no reason to believe, that copyright subsists in the work to which the action relates, the claimant is not entitled to damages against him, but without prejudice to any other remedy.' It is thought that the reference to *damages* in this section is a reference to *compensatory* damages.
[12] Section 229(2). Again, it is not thought that s 233(1) of the 1988 Act – which provides that the owner of a design right which has been infringed will not be entitled to sue the person who infringed the design right for damages if he did not know of, and had no reason to know of, the existence of the design right infringed by him – affects this point.
[13] Patents Act 1977, s 62(1).
[14] See, for example, *Attorney-General* v *Guardian Newspapers Ltd (No. 2)* [1990] 1 AC 109.
[15] [2006] QB 125.
[16] Ibid., at [249].

that the defendants had paid so much for the photographs, they did not in the end make a profit from the extra sales of their magazine that resulted from their publishing the photographs.[17]

(5) *Other torts*. It is not clear whether disgorgement damages will be awardable against a defendant who commits any other kind of tort. The question of whether such damages may be awarded against someone who commits a tort such as trespass to land,[18] battery, negligence, or defamation has simply not been addressed by the courts. In *Stoke-on-Trent County Council* v *Wass*,[19] the Court of Appeal refused to award disgorgement damages against a trader who had committed the tort of private nuisance by running a market in an area where the claimants had the exclusive right to run a market.[20]

In *Halifax BS* v *Thomas*,[21] the Court of Appeal refused to award disgorgement damages against someone who had committed the tort of deceit to obtain a mortgage to buy a house which had subsequently risen in value. However, it may be that a different result would be reached nowadays.[22] In the subsequent case of *Dubai Aluminium Co. Ltd* v *Salaam*,[23] a firm of solicitors, A, paid $10m to D to compensate them in part for the loss D had suffered as a

[17] Ibid., at [245].

[18] *Important note*. But see the American case of *Edwards* v *Lee's Administrators*, 96 SW 2d 1028 (1936), which concerned a long cave that contained some very interesting rock formations. The entrance to the cave was on the defendants' land and they would charge people to enter the cave and look around. Unfortunately, a third of the cave stretched under the claimants' land. So the defendants committed the tort of trespass to land whenever they allowed customers to view that part of the cave that was under the claimants' land. The claimants were held entitled to sue the defendants for damages equal to the money the defendants had made by allowing people to look at that part of the cave that was under the claimants' land. McInnes 2003 is, however, doubtful whether this authority would be followed in England: '[It] is quite likely that an English claimant, in the same circumstances, would be limited to reasonable rental value [i.e. licence fee damages]' (at 712); to the same effect, Cooke 1994, 428–9; also *Severn Trent Water Ltd* v *Barnes* [2004] EWCA Civ 570 (disallowing anything but an award of licence fee damages against a defendant who had trespassed on the claimant's land by laying a water mains under the land). Edelman 2006, at 147, instances *Livingstone* v *Rawyards Coal Company* (1880) 5 App Cas 25 as authority for the proposition that if A *deliberately and in bad faith* trespasses on B's land and makes a gain as a result, he will be liable to pay disgorgement damages to B. However, the only statement in the case that can be taken as supporting that proposition is Lord Hatherley's (at 34): 'There is no doubt that if a man furtively and in bad faith robs his neighbour of property . . . the person [will be held liable for] the value of the whole of the property which he has so furtively taken, and . . . no allowance [will be made] in respect of what he has so done as would have been justly made to him if the parties had been working by agreement, or if, as in the present case, they had been the one working and the other permitting the working through a mistake.' But there he is considering the case where A has stolen B's property (a case of conversion), rather than the case where A trespasses on B's land and makes a profit for himself as a result without actually stealing anything from B.

[19] [1988] 1 WLR 1406. The private nuisance in this case took the anomalous form of an interference with the claimant's monopoly right to hold a market in a particular area.

[20] Restitution scholars sometimes point to *Carr-Saunders* v *Dick McNeil Associates Ltd* [1986] 1 WLR 922 as authority for the proposition that disgorgement damages may be awarded against someone who commits the tort of private nuisance: see, for example, Birks 1989, 471; Edelman 2002b, 136. However, that case was one where the claimant was denied an injunction to stop the defendant committing a nuisance and was awarded damages *in lieu*. It well established that in awarding such damages, the courts will take into account any profits that the defendant has or will make from engaging in the conduct which the claimant wanted to be enjoined. See below, p. 729.

[21] [1996] Ch 217.

[22] Having said that, see *Renault UK Ltd* v *Fleetpro Technical Services Ltd* [2007] EWHC 2541, refusing to award disgorgement damages against a defendant who, by deceit, persuaded the claimant to manufacture and sell to him some cars that he then sold on at a profit.

[23] [2003] 2 AC 366.

result of a fraud carried out on it by S and T, with the assistance of one of the partners in A. S and T obtained $20.3m and $16.5m from the fraud respectively. A made a claim in contribution against S and T, and the House of Lords held S and T liable *in full* to cover the payment that A made to D. The House of Lords made it clear that the reason they were doing this was to strip S and T of as much of the profits of their fraud as was possible.[24] Given that the House of Lords was willing to manipulate the law on contribution to strip S and T of the profits they had made from their fraud, it seems unlikely that they would have baulked at the suggestion that D should have been allowed to sue S and T directly for those profits.

Licence fee damages

The availability of licence fee damages

Licence fee damages may be awarded against a defendant who has committed one of the following torts.

(1) *Conversion*. It is well established that licence fee damages may be awarded against someone who has committed the tort of conversion.[25]

So, for example, if A has converted B's property by using it, B will be entitled to sue A for damages designed to make A pay B a reasonable sum for the use he has made of B's property.[26] What if A did not *use* B's property but converted it by doing something to prevent B getting hold of it? It does not matter: B will still be entitled to sue A for damages designed to make A pay B a reasonable sum for the *dominion* he has enjoyed over B's property.[27]

(2) *Trespass to land*. It is also well established that licence fee damages may be awarded against someone who has committed the tort of trespass to land.

So – if A occupies a house leased by B and then stays in the house beyond the term of the lease, B will be entitled to sue A for a reasonable sum – known as *mesne profits* – for the use A made of B's house by staying in it beyond the term of his tenancy.[28] More generally, if A commits the tort of trespass to land by using B's land without his consent for some purpose, B will be entitled to sue A for damages designed to make A pay B a reasonable sum for the use he has made of B's land.[29]

24 Ibid., at [59] (per Lord Nicholls), [76] (per Lord Hobhouse), [164] (per Lord Millett).

25 See *Kuwait Airways Corpn* v *Iraqi Airways Co. (Nos 4 and 5)* [2002] 2 AC 883, at [87] (per Lord Nicholls).

26 See, for example, *Strand Electric Engineering Co. Ltd* v *Brisford Entertainments* [1952] 2 QB 246 (defendants converted claimants' switchboards by using them in various theatre productions staged at the defendants' theatre; they were held liable to pay the claimants a reasonable sum for the use they had made of the switchboards).

27 So if A takes one of B's chairs away for a year but does not use it, B will be entitled to sue A for damages designed to make A pay B a reasonable sum for the dominion he has enjoyed over the chair for a year – and this is so even if B did not miss the chair at all in the year A had it: *Mediana (Owners of Steamship)* v *Comet (Owners of Lightship)* [1900] AC 113, 117 (per Earl of Halsbury LC).

28 *Swordheath Properties* v *Tabet* [1979] 1 WLR 285; *Ministry of Defence* v *Ashman* [1993] 2 EGLR 102; *Ministry of Defence* v *Thompson* [1993] 2 EGLR 107.

29 See *Whitwham* v *Westminster Brymbo Coal & Coke Company* [1896] 2 Ch 538 (defendants who committed the tort of trespass to land by tipping refuse from their colliery onto the claimants' land held liable to pay the claimants a reasonable sum for the use they had made of the claimants' land); and *Penarth Dock Engineering Co.* v *Pounds* [1963] 1 Lloyd's Rep 359 (defendant committed the tort of trespass to land by keeping his boat tied up in the claimants' docks; he was held liable to pay the claimants a reasonable sum for the use he had made of their land).

What if A commits the tort of trespass to land not by using B's land but by preventing B gaining access to his land? A will still have to pay B a reasonable sum for the dominion he has enjoyed over B's land while B was kept out. So in *Inverugie Investments Ltd* v *Hackett*,[30] the claimant leased 30 apartments in a hotel in the Bahamas but was then kept out of them for 15 years by the defendants, who owned the hotel. During those 15 years, the defendants let the apartments out to guests but at any one time only about 40 per cent of the apartments were let out. So the defendants used only about 40 per cent of the claimant's apartments during the 15 years they kept him out of them. However, during those 15 years they enjoyed dominion over all the claimant's apartments, 365 days a year. Accordingly, it was held that the claimant was entitled to sue the defendant for damages designed to make the defendants pay the claimant the going rate for renting apartments like the claimant's 365 days a year for 15 years.

(3) *Inducing a breach of contract.* It seems that licence fee damages may be awarded against someone who commits the tort of inducing a breach of contract. So, for example, in *Lightly* v *Clouston*[31] the defendant persuaded the claimant's apprentice to work as a mariner on his ship instead of working on board the claimant's ship. Mansfield CJ held that the claimant was entitled to compel the defendant to pay him a reasonable sum for the work that his apprentice did for the defendant.[32]

(4) *Other torts.* Again, it is unclear whether licence fee damages may be awarded against a defendant who has committed any other kind of tort.

The nature of licence fee damages

Many scholars would deny that licence fee damages exist as an independent category of damages.

Some say that licence fee damages are really just an example of compensatory damages and not gain-based at all.[33] So – the argument goes – if A converts B's horse by going for a ride on it without her permission, B is entitled to sue A for a reasonable sum for the ride he has enjoyed on the horse because by taking the horse without permission, A deprived B of the chance to charge him a reasonable sum for the use of the horse, and she should be compensated for the fact that A's tort deprived her of that money-making opportunity. On this view, licence fee damages are simply designed to compensate B for the loss of the chance to make some money off A that she suffered as a result of A's tort.

Others say that licence fee damages are really an example of disgorgement damages.[34] So – the argument goes – in the case where A converts B's horse by going for a ride on it without her permission, A will have saved money by committing his tort. The money he will have saved is the money he would have had to pay B to obtain her permission to go for a ride on her horse. So when the law allows B to sue A for a reasonable sum for the ride he has enjoyed on her horse, it is really stripping A of the money he saved by tortiously going for a ride on the horse without B's permission.

30 [1995] 1 WLR 713.
31 (1808) 1 Taunt 112, 127 ER 774.
32 See also *Foster* v *Stewart* (1814) 3 M & S 191, 105 ER 582.
33 See, for example, Sharpe & Waddams 1982; Scott 2006; Giglio 2007; *WWF* v *WWF* [2006] EWHC 184, at [137] (per Peter Smith J).
34 See, for example, Burrows 2002a, 455–62; Cane 1996, 298–300.

We cannot accept either of these alternative analyses of the basis of awards of licence fee damages.[35] This is for two reasons.

First, in the case where A converted B's horse by going for a ride on it without her permission, licence fee damages will be awarded to B even if, had A asked B's permission to ride on her horse beforehand, B would have refused her permission and refused to accept any amount of money from A to go for a ride on her horse. In this situation, it is difficult to say either that A's going for a ride on B's horse without her permission deprived B of a money-making opportunity for which she should be compensated, or that A saved money by not asking B for her permission to go for a ride on her horse.

Secondly, the amount payable in licence fee damages to a claimant will often *exceed* how much she would have charged the defendant to give her permission for whatever it was that the defendant was seeking to do. As we have already seen, in *Inverugie Investments Ltd* v *Hackett*,[36] the defendants committed a tort in relation to the claimant by taking over 30 hotel apartments that the claimant had leased. The defendants were held liable as a result to pay the claimant whatever was the going rate for renting those apartments 365 days a year. Lord Lloyd – who gave the judgment in the case – was quite explicit that this award was neither designed to compensate the claimant for the loss he had suffered as a result of being kept out of his apartments, nor was it designed to strip the defendants of the money they had made by taking over those apartments.[37] Had the award of damages in this case been designed to do either of these things, the claimant would have been awarded *far less* by way of damages. This is because had the defendants gone to the claimant and asked his permission for them to take over his apartments, if the claimant had been willing to negotiate to allow the defendants to do this, there is simply no way the claimant and the defendants would have agreed that the defendants should pay the claimant the going market rate for renting the claimant's apartments 365 days a year. This is for two reasons: (1) the defendants could not have expected to be able to rent out every single one of the claimant's apartments 365 days a year; and (2) even if the defendants could have done this, they would have made no money from renting out the claimant's apartments if they were simultaneously paying the claimant the going market rate for renting his apartments 365 days a year. So if the award of damages in *Inverugie Investments* had been designed to compensate the claimant for the loss of a money-making opportunity, or to strip the defendants of the money they saved by not paying the claimant to take over his apartments, the damages awarded to the claimant would definitely not have been as high as they were.

Given this, we see no alternative but to contend that licence fee damages are not compensatory, and neither are they designed to make a defendant disgorge the gains he has made from his wrong. They stand on their own two feet and are independent of those other two heads of damages.

Four points

Four points remain to be made about the availability of these two kinds of awards.

[35] To the same effect, see Dagan 1997, 13–14; Edelman 2002b, 65–87; McInnes 2003, 710, 712; Tettenborn 2003, 48–50; Edelman 2006, 153–8; Jaffey 2007, 100–1.

[36] [1995] 1 WLR 713.

[37] Ibid., at 718, saying that the award of damages in this case 'need not be characterised as exclusively compensatory, or exclusively restitutionary, it combines elements of both'. (By 'restitutionary', Lord Lloyd meant here – 'designed to make the defendants disgorge the gains they had made from their trespass'.)

(1) *Change of position.* Suppose that B acquired title to money that belonged to A; but the money was transferred to B under a mistake or some other kind of vitiating factor. In this case, A will be entitled to sue B for that money back.[38] However, A's right to sue B may be subject to a defence of *change of position.*

This defence works in the following way. First of all, find out how much money was received by B – say it was £100. Next, see by how much B was enriched as a result of receiving that £100 *when she first found out that that money was transferred to her under a vitiating factor*. Call this amount £*x*. If £*x* is higher than £100 then A will be entitled to sue B for £100. But if £*x* is lower than £100 then A will only be entitled to sue B for £*x*; B will have a defence of change of position to A's claim for the remaining £$(100 - x)$. The effect of this defence is to ensure that if A sues B for his money back, B will normally not be made worse off than she would have been had she never received A's money.[39]

Now – will the defence of change of position operate to protect someone who would otherwise be liable to pay disgorgement damages to the victim of his tort?[40] For example, take the sheriff in *Oughton* v *Seppings*. Could he have argued, 'I know that I converted the claimant's pony and obtained £10 [say] for it. But I then handed the £10 over to Winslove's creditor. So holding me liable to pay the claimant £10 here will make me, someone who has acted throughout in complete good faith, worse off than I would have been had I not sold the claimant's horse.'

It might be thought that such an argument could not succeed because the sheriff in *Oughton* v *Seppings* was a wrongdoer: as Lord Goff remarked in *Lipkin Gorman* v *Karpnale*, 'it is commonly thought that the defence [of change of position] should not be open to a wrongdoer'.[41] However, in *Kuwait Airways Corpn* v *Iraqi Airways Co. (Nos 4 & 5)*, Lord Nicholls suggested that the defence of change of position *would* be open to someone who converted another's property and was as a result held liable for the benefits he obtained by converting that property.[42] If this is right then were *Oughton* v *Seppings* to be decided today, the sheriff might well not have been held liable to pay the claimant anything by way of disgorgement damages.[43] However, he would of course still have been held liable to compensate the claimant for the loss of her pony.

(2) *Assessment of licence fee damages.* As we have seen, if A – a tenant of B's – has stayed on B's land beyond the expiry of his tenancy, then B will be entitled to compel A to pay him a

[38] A's right to sue B does not of course arise out of a tort but out of the fact that if B does not give the money – or its equivalent – back, she will be *unjustly enriched*.

[39] The exception arises if B squandered the amount by which she was enriched as a result of receiving the £100 *after* she found out that that money was transferred to her under a vitiating factor.

[40] For a good discussion of the various academic views on this matter, see Burrows 2002a, 524–7.

[41] [1991] 2 AC 548, 580.

[42] [2002] 2 AC 883, at [79]. Though, presumably, he did not think that the defence should be open to someone who *knowingly* converted another's property and then squandered the enrichment that he obtained by converting that property.

[43] Though see *Foskett* v *McKeown* [2001] 1 AC 102, denying that the defence of change of position is available in a property-based claim, where someone is suing another person for their property or its value. The same case makes it clear that the House of Lords would regard the claim in *Oughton* v *Seppings* as being property-based – the idea being that the money obtained by selling the claimant's horse belonged to the claimant, being the product of the claimant's property. (See Burrows 2001 for criticism of this aspect of the decision in *Foskett* v *McKeown*; though his arguments have been dismissed as 'unconvincing and unsustainable': Grantham & Rickett 2003, 173, n. 59.)

reasonable sum for the use he made of B's land in staying on that land beyond the expiry of his tenancy. But how do we assess what amounts to a reasonable sum?

The usual approach is to assess what the going market rate would have been to rent B's land for the period on which A stayed on it.[44] However, the Court of Appeal departed from this approach in *Ministry of Defence* v *Ashman*.[45] In that case, Flight Sergeant Ashman, his wife – the defendant – and their two children took up accommodation in married quarters made available by the Ministry of Defence to members of services stationed at RAF Hulton. They were charged £95.41 a month for the accommodation, a rate far below what they would have had to pay for equivalent accommodation on the open market. It was made clear to Ashman that he was only entitled to remain in the married quarters so long as he remained a serving member of the RAF, living with his wife, and that he would be required to remove his family from the accommodation if he separated from his wife. On 14 February 1991 Ashman deserted the defendant and his children. Having nowhere else to go – the defendant was too impecunious to move out and rent accommodation on the open market – Ashman's family stayed on in the married quarters until 26 April 1992 when they were found alternative local authority accommodation.

The claimants, the Ministry of Defence, sued the defendant, seeking to obtain a reasonable sum for the use of the claimants' accommodation that the defendant and her children had enjoyed between 14 February 1991 and 26 April 1992. There was no question that the claimants were entitled to claim such a sum from the defendant; the question was how that reasonable sum should be assessed. The claimants claimed that the defendant should be made to pay them a sum equivalent to the rent she would have had to pay had she rented equivalent accommodation on the open market between 14 February 1991 and 26 April 1992, that is, £435.72 a month. However, the Court of Appeal thought that it would be inappropriate to make the defendant pay that much. To make her pay that much for the use of the claimants' accommodation that the defendant and her children had enjoyed between 14 February 1991 and 26 April 1992 would have been to punish the defendant for the fact that the local authority could not promptly rehouse the defendant and her children: had the local authority been able to offer her and her children alternative accommodation, she would have moved out into that accommodation and paid the going rate for that accommodation. In order to ensure that the defendant was not disadvantaged as a result of the local authority's failure to rehouse the defendant and her children promptly, the Court of Appeal held that the claimants were only entitled to sue the defendant for a sum equivalent to the rent the defendant would have paid the local authority between 14 February 1991 and 26 April 1992 had she and her children been rehoused by the local authority as soon as Ashman deserted them.

(3) *Election.* In *Strand Electric Engineering Co. Ltd* v *Brisford Entertainments*,[46] the defendants used some electrical switchboards belonging to the claimants when they were not entitled to do so and were held liable to pay the claimants a reasonable sum for the use of the switchboards that they had enjoyed. Now – suppose that the claimants could have rented out those switchboards had they been returned to the claimants when they should have been. If this is right, then the defendants' act of conversion in using the switchboards caused

[44] *Swordheath Properties Ltd* v *Tabet* [1979] 1 WLR 285.

[45] [1993] 2 EGLR 102. See also *Ministry of Defence* v *Thompson* [1993] 2 EGLR 107.

[46] [1952] 2 QB 246.

the claimants to suffer an actionable loss – the rent that the claimants could have obtained for the switchboards had the defendants not converted them. Could the claimants have sued the defendants for compensatory damages in respect of this loss *and* licence fee damages on top? The answer is 'no': the claimants would have had to *choose* which remedy to pursue.[47]

This rule – namely, that you cannot sue for both gain-based damages and compensatory damages – only seems to apply in cases where the victim of a tort suffered an actionable loss that was an *inevitable* result of that tort being committed. This was true in the case we have just been considering. Once the defendants decided to keep the switchboards and use them, it was inevitable that the claimants would not be able to rent them out to anyone else and would suffer loss as a result. But if the victim of a tort is entitled to sue the person who committed that tort for gain-based damages, she will also be entitled *on top of that* to sue him for compensatory damages in respect of any actionable losses suffered by her as a result of that tort being committed that were *not* an inevitable consequence of that tort being committed. So, for example, if one of the switchboards in the *Strand Electric* case had been damaged while it was being used by the defendants, the claimants would have been entitled to sue the defendants for compensation in respect of that damage *in addition to* suing the defendants for licence fee damages: the damage was not an inevitable result of the defendants' keeping and using the switchboards.[48]

(4) *Restitution without wrongdoing?* Daniel Friedmann raises an interesting question – could someone obtain an award analogous to an award of disgorgement damages or licence fee damages *without being the victim of a wrong*?[49] In other words, can one have gain-based damages without wrongdoing?

How you answer this question will depend on why you think tortfeasors are sometimes held liable to pay gain-based damages to the victims of their torts. If you think that when the law holds a tortfeasor liable to pay gain-based damages it does so in order to give effect to the principle that 'no man shall profit from his wrong',[50] then you will find it difficult to understand why anyone would think that an award analagous to the kind of awards under discussion here could ever be made against someone who has *not* committed a wrong.

But it may be that the law in this area is *not* actually based on the principle that 'no man shall profit from his wrong'.[51] It may be that the law in this area is designed to give effect to

[47] The claimants would of course have opted to pursue the most lucrative remedy. In a situation where the victim of a tort has to choose between suing the person who committed a tort for compensatory or gain-based damages, the law goes out of its way to ensure that she makes the 'right' choice and does not elect to sue the defendant for gain-based damages when she would have been better off suing for compensatory damages or *vice versa*. So she is allowed to sue the defendant for both kinds of damages and put off the moment of choosing which kind of damages she wants to recover from the defendant until she knows how much she will be allowed to recover from the defendant under each measure: *United Australia Ltd* v *Barclays Bank Ltd* [1941] AC 1. And if she – not knowing that she would be better off suing the defendant for gain-based damages – successfully sues the defendant for compensatory damages, she will be allowed to reverse her decision and sue him for gain-based damages instead (though the damages already paid will be taken into account in judging how much more the defendant should pay under the gain-based measure): *Tang Man Sit* v *Capacious Investments* [1996] AC 514.

[48] *Strand Electric Engineering Co. Ltd* v *Brisford Entertainments* [1952] 2 QB 246, 254 (per Denning LJ).

[49] He thinks the answer is 'yes': see Friedmann 1998. (For criticisms, see Andrews 1998.)

[50] See Burrows 2002a, 480.

[51] Jackman 1989 attempts to explain the fact that this area of law is mainly concerned with proprietary torts by arguing (at 304) that gain-based damages are awarded when it is necessary to do so to protect 'facilitative institutions' such as 'contracts, trusts and private property'. But it is not clear why the law would regard such institutions as worthy of greater protection than people's persons or reputations.

moral principles such as 'An owner of property is entitled to the fruits of that property' and 'You should not use another man's property without paying him for it.' This explains why, if A sells B's car without her permission for £1,000, B will be entitled to sue A for that £1,000 – as the £1,000 represents the 'fruits' of B's property, B is entitled to it.[52] Similarly, this explains why if A uses B's land without her permission, B will be entitled to sue A for a reasonable sum for the use he has made of her land – A, having used B's land, has a moral obligation to pay B something for the use he has made of her land.[53]

If this latter analysis of the cases gathered together in this chapter is correct, it may well be that the courts *could* make an award analogous to an award of gain-based damages against someone who has not actually committed a wrong.[54] Take, for example, the facts of *Vincent* v *Lake Erie Transportation Co.*[55] In that case, the defendants kept their ship moored to the claimants' dock against the claimants' will during a storm which repeatedly threw the defendants' ship against the dock. The dock sustained a great deal of damage as a result and the claimants sued the defendants for compensation. It was held that while the defendants did nothing wrong in keeping their ship moored to the defendants' dock,[56] they were still liable to compensate the claimants for the damage done to the dock. This could be interpreted as a case where the courts allowed gain-based damages without wrongdoing in order to give effect to the moral principle that 'You should not use another man's property without paying him for it.' The defendants used the claimants' dock here and therefore had a moral obligation to pay them a reasonable sum for the use they had made of it – which sum, naturally, took into account the damage the defendants did to the claimants' dock by using it.[57]

52 See Weinrib 2000, 12. Arguably, the decision of the House of Lords in *Foskett* v *McKeown* [2001] 1 AC 102, in rejecting the view that B's right to the £1,000 arises out of 'unjust enrichment' but is instead property-based, can be read as supporting this analysis of the basis of B's right.

53 See Weinrib 2000, 16; Jaffey 2007, 103. See also the Court of Appeal's attempted synthesis in *Stoke-on-Trent County Council* v *Wass* [1988] 1 WLR 1406 of the authorities on when licence fee damages could be awarded against a tortfeasor as being based on a 'user principle'; which principle did not apply on the facts of the *Wass* case because the defendants in that case did not *use* anything belonging to the claimants: Worthington 1999, 229–30. See also Grantham & Rickett 2003's analysis (at 174) of *Edwards* v *Lee's Administrators* (discussed above, n. 18): 'The characterisation of trespass [the tort committed in *Edwards*] as a wrong must not displace the focus of Lee's claim, [which was] *that his property was being used*' (emphasis added).

54 To the same effect, see Jaffey 2007, at 103 and 105–6.

55 124 NW 221 (1910).

56 While the defendants would normally have committed a trespass to land in keeping their ship moored to the claimants' dock against the claimants' wishes, it could be argued that they had a defence of necessity in this case which meant that they were allowed to keep their ship moored to the claimants' dock even though the claimants had objected to its being kept there: see above, p. 366.

57 On the other hand, we should note the existence of a significant anti-gain-based damages without wrongdoing case in *McKenna & Armistead Pty Ltd* v *Excavations Pty Ltd* (1957) 57 SR (NSW) 483. In that case the defendant sold three earth-moving machines to the claimant and then, before he was due to deliver them to the claimant, he continued to use them in his business. The claimant sued the defendant for a reasonable sum for the use he had made of the machines after selling them to the claimant. The New South Wales Court of Appeal held that as the defendant had not committed a tort in using the machines after he sold them to the claimant (there was no conversion because the claimant did not have possession of, or an immediate right to possess, the machines as soon as they had been sold to him), the claimant's claim could not be allowed.

OPTIONS FOR REFORM

Let's now canvass two options for reforming this area of the law.

(1) *Abolish gain-based damages.* So far as we know no one is in favour of this option: unlike exemplary damages, the place of gain-based damages in the firmament of remedies for wrongs is assured. Indeed, the courts have started to liberalise the rules on when such damages may be awarded.[58]

(2) *Make disgorgement damages available for all torts that are committed intentionally.* This is the view advanced in Goff and Jones's *Law of Restitution.*[59] The case for expanding the range of situations where disgorgement damages may be awarded is that doing so will help discourage people from breaching the duties they owe other people: anyone planning to wrong someone else in order to make some kind of gain will know that he will not be allowed to retain that gain.[60] Moreover, there seems little reason why disgorgement damages should not be made more widely available. For example, expanding the range of situations where disgorgement damages may be awarded would not – we think – trigger an explosion in frivolous and unmeritorious litigation.

Visit **http://www.mylawchamber.co.uk/mcbride** to access updates on recent cases, as well as model answers and tips for answering tort problem questions.

[58] In *Attorney-General* v *Blake* [2001] 1 AC 268, the House of Lords held that gain-based damages could be awarded against someone who committed a breach of contract, though only in 'exceptional cases, where [the normal] remedies [for breach of contract] are inadequate' (ibid., at 285, per Lord Nicholls). Lord Nicholls went on to observe that in judging whether an award of gain-based damages is appropriate in a breach of contract case, '[the courts] will have regard to all the circumstances, including the subject matter of the contract, the purpose of the contractual provision which has been breached, the circumstances in which the breach occurred, the consequences of the breach and the circumstances in which relief is being sought. A useful general guide, although not exhaustive, is whether the [claimant] had a legitimate interest in preventing the defendant's profit-making activity and, hence, in depriving him of his profit' (ibid.).

[59] Jones 2007, 809; see also Birks 1989, 328–9.

[60] *Important note.* Some scholars make a different case for expanding the range of situations where gain-based damages may be awarded against a tortfeasor. They argue that the law as it stands is incoherent and illogical: that it makes no sense, for example, for the law to allow someone whose property has been converted to sue another for disgorgement damages while it does not allow such damages to be claimed by someone whose character has been unjustly defamed. This kind of argument was made by Lord Nicholls in *Attorney-General* v *Blake* [2001] 1 AC 268 in support of his ruling that gain-based damages should be available in the case where someone has committed a breach of contract: 'it is not easy to see why, as between the parties to a contract, a violation of a party's contractual rights should attract a lesser degree of remedy than a violation of his property rights' (ibid., 283); 'it would be only a modest step for the law to recognise openly that, exceptionally, an account of profits may be the most appropriate remedy for breach of contract. It is not as though this step would contradict some recognised principle applied consistently throughout the law to the grant or withholding of the remedy of an account of profits. No such principle is discernible' (ibid., 285). However, this argument only works if one assumes that the law in this area, *as it currently stands*, seeks to discourage people from committing torts. But, as we have noted, it is at least as arguable that the law in this area attempts to give effect to certain moral precepts applying to the ownership of property. If this is right, then the law in this area *as it stands* is not at all illogical or incoherent.

38 Damages for conversion

GENERAL PRINCIPLES

The normal rule

If A has converted B's property,[1] B will *normally* be entitled to sue A for:

(1) damages equal to the value of B's property at the time it was converted;[2] *and*
(2) damages sufficient to compensate B for any actionable losses – other than the loss of her property – that B has suffered as a result of A's converting her property.[3]

Let's call the first set of damages, 'market value damages'; let's call the second set of damages, 'damages for consequential loss'. This chapter is mainly concerned with when someone whose property has been converted by another will be entitled to sue that other for market value damages.

Are market value damages compensatory?

Lord Nicholls has made it clear that he thinks damages for conversion are compensatory in nature. In *Kuwait Airways Corpn* v *Iraqi Airways Co. (Nos 4 & 5)*, he said:[4]

> The fundamental object of an award of damages in respect of this tort,[5] as with all wrongs, is to award just compensation for loss suffered. Normally ('prima facie') the measure of damages is the market value of the goods at the time the defendant expropriated them. This is the general rule, because generally this measure represents the amount of the basic loss suffered by the defendant. He has been dispossessed of his goods by the defendant. Depending on the circumstances some other measure, yielding a higher or lower amount, may be appropriate.

If this is right then market value damages are compensatory – if A has converted B's property, then B will only be entitled to sue A for market value damages if A's act of conversion caused B to lose the property that was converted by A. But is this true?

Take the facts of the *Kuwait Airways* case. In that case, Iraq took possession of four

[1] As in Chapter 16, the term 'B's property' will be used as shorthand for 'property which was in B's possession or which B had an immediate right to possess'.

[2] If the property in question was a cheque, the value of the property converted by A is assessed by reference to the value of the cheque *not* the value of the paper on which the cheque was written: *Morison* v *London County Westminster Bank* [1914] 3 KB 356.

[3] *Bodley* v *Reynolds* (1846) 8 QB 779, 115 ER 1066; *Re Simms* [1934] 1 Ch 1.

[4] See [2002] 2 AC 883, at [67].

[5] Lord Nicholls is referring here to the tort of 'wrongful interference with goods' (ibid.), but there is in fact no such tort in English law. Section 1 of the Torts (Interference with Goods) Act 1977 uses the term 'wrongful interference with goods' to refer to conversion, trespass to goods, acts of negligence that result in damage to goods and 'any other tort [that] results in damage to goods' but this was merely for convenience: the 1977 Act did not purport to subsume all these different torts within a 'master tort' of 'wrongful interference with goods'.

planes belonging to the claimants (the Kuwait Airways Corporation) when it invaded Kuwait in 1990. The planes were then handed over to the defendants (the Iraqi Airways Company) and became part of its fleet. The planes were subsequently destroyed in coalition bombing of Iraq. The House of Lords held that had those events happened in England, the defendants would have been held liable for converting the claimant's aircraft and would have been held liable for the market value of the planes at the time the defendants converted them by incorporating them into their fleet.[6]

But it is hard to understand why market value damages would have been awarded in this case *if* damages for conversion are genuinely compensatory. It could hardly be said that the defendants' incorporating the claimants' planes into their fleet caused the claimants to lose those planes. Had the defendants not converted the claimants' planes, they would still have been destroyed in coalition bombing. Lord Hoffmann thought this point was 'irrelevant'.[7] However, that just raises the question of why, *if* awards of market value damages are designed to be compensatory, is it not relevant to consider what would have happened to the claimants' property had it not been converted by the defendants?

Lord Nicholls sought to get round this point by saying that the wrong involved in conversion is 'wrongfully [excluding] the owner from possession of his goods'.[8] So the damages awardable in a conversion case are assessed by asking – what position would the claimant have been in had the defendant not wrongfully excluded the claimant from posssession of his goods?[9] Now: if the defendants in the *Kuwait Airways* case had not wrongfully excluded the claimants from their planes – that is, if the defendants had given the claimants their planes back, rather than incorporating them into their fleet – the claimants would obviously not have lost their planes. So, on this view, the market value damages awarded to the claimants in the *Kuwait Airways* case *were* compensatory in nature – the damages compensated the claimants for the loss that they suffered as a result of the defendants' wrongfully excluding them from their planes.

However, it is not at all clear that one can say here that the defendants *excluded* the claimants from their planes *by accepting them*. The fact is the defendants *never had the option* of returning the claimants' planes to them. No doubt they happily accepted the planes when they did – and that is why they were liable for converting the planes[10] – but had they not been happy to accept the planes and attempted to return them to the claimants, the Iraqi government would not have allowed them to do so.

So we remain to be convinced that *as the law stands* market value damages are genuinely compensatory in nature – hence the location of this chapter in the book. It may be that the stand taken by their Lordships' in the *Kuwait Airways* case over the nature of damages for conversion will in due course mean that market value damages will only be awarded to

[6] Iraq actually took ten of the claimants' planes and handed them over to the defendants. The other six – that we have ignored in the main text – were not destroyed. They were smuggled into Iran and eventually returned to the claimants in return for $20m. Market value damages could not be claimed in respect of these planes because one of the established exceptions to the normal rule set out above is that market value damages will not be payable to a claimant whose property has been converted by someone else if that property has been returned to her: see below, pp. 715–16.

[7] [2002] 2 AC 883, at [129].

[8] Ibid., at [82].

[9] Ibid., at [83].

[10] Had they been forced at gunpoint to accept the planes, no doubt they might have been able to raise a defence of necessity to being sued for conversion.

someone whose property has been converted if it can be shown that she lost her property as a result of that act of conversion. However, the *result* in the *Kuwait Airways* case shows that that remains a remote prospect.

So – as the law stands at the moment, someone whose property has been converted by another will normally be entitled to sue that other for market value damages; and this is so even if she cannot show that that act of conversion caused her to lose the item of property in question. However – recognising the anomalous and perhaps unjustifiable[11] nature of this rule – the courts have created many exceptions to it. It is to these that we now turn.

SPECIAL CASES

If A has converted B's property, B will sometimes *not* be entitled to sue A for market value damages. This will be the case in the following situations.

Return of the property

Subject to what is said below, if A has converted B's property, but that property was subsequently returned to B, B will only be entitled to sue A for damages equal to the difference between the value of the property at the time it was converted and its present value.

For example, in *BBMB Finance (Hong Kong) Ltd* v *Eda Holdings Ltd*,[12] the defendants came into possession of shares belonging to the claimants and sold them for $5.75 a share when they had no lawful justification or excuse for doing so; it should be noted, though, that the defendants never received any money for the shares. When they realised what they had done, they bought an equivalent number of shares to replace the shares they had sold and gave them to the claimant. The market in the shares in question had collapsed so the defendants had to pay only $2.40 per share to replace the shares that they had sold. The claimants were held entitled to sue the defendants for damages equal to the difference between the value of the shares at the time they were sold by the defendants (assessed at $5.75 a share) and the value of the replacement shares the claimants got back from the defendants (assessed at $2.40 a share).[13]

[11] *Important note.* Tettenborn 1993 canvasses a variety of explanations of the rule discussed here but finds all of them wanting. Weir 2004 argues (at 483–6) that this whole area of law is based on a historical accident. As he sees it, conversion started off as a tort which allowed B to sue A if A had her goods. Liability was strict because if A has B's goods, and B is suing A for them, it is no defence for A to say 'But it's not my fault I've got your goods!' If A had B's goods – and had no defence to B's claim against him – then B would naturally be entitled to sue A for the value of her goods (though if money damages were not as good as the goods themselves, specific restitution could be ordered: see Chapter 40, below). At some point, the law lost touch with the idea that A had to *have* B's goods if he was to be held liable to her in conversion; instead, the law substituted a requirement that A had to have dealt with B's goods in such a way as to 'deny B's title' to the goods. But while the conditions of liability changed, the nature of the liability – irrationally – remained the same. Liability for conversion remained strict, and it remained the case that if A were liable to B for converting her goods, B would be entitled to sue A for the value of her goods.

[12] [1990] 1 WLR 409.

[13] Note that in this case the claimants suffered no loss as a result of the defendants' converting their shares, but the claimants were still entitled to sue the defendants for substantial damages. Lord Nicholls sought to distinguish this case in the *Kuwait Airways* case, arguing that the defendants in the *BBMB* case were *really* held liable to pay the claimants disgorgement damages: [2002] 2 AC 883, at [89]. This is unconvincing as it is not clear that the defendants benefited in any way from selling the claimants' shares.

Similarly, suppose Paul steals Mary's car and sells it to Eric. Suppose further that Eric crashes the car and as a result its value drops from £5,000 to £500. Suppose finally that police investigating Eric's car crash find out that the car is stolen and return it to Mary. Mary will be entitled to sue Paul for £4,500 in damages: the difference between the market value of her car when it was stolen and its present market value.

Unlawful detention

If A has converted B's property by refusing to hand it over to B when he had no lawful justification or excuse for doing so, B will only be entitled to sue A for damages sufficient to compensate her for the actionable losses she suffered as a result of A's unlawfully detaining her goods.

For example, in *Brandeis Goldschmidt & Co. Ltd* v *Western Transport Ltd*,[14] the defendants wrongfully refused to hand over the claimants' copper to them. The defendants eventually relented and handed over the copper to the claimants. By that time the copper had diminished in value. The claimants sued the defendants but it was held that they could only sue the defendants for damages sufficient to compensate them for the actionable losses that the defendants' wrongful detention of the copper had caused them to suffer. As the claimants could not show that the detention had caused them any kind of loss – there was no evidence, for example, that had the defendants not unlawfully detained that copper, they would have sold the copper before it declined in value – they could not sue the defendants for anything by way of compensatory damages.[15]

Limited interest

In *Wickham Holdings Ltd* v *Brooke House Motors Ltd*,[16] the claimants let a car to one Mr Pattinson under a hire-purchase agreement. The car was sold without their authority when they had received £615 for the car under the hire-purchase agreement: the total hire-purchase price was £889. The claimants sued the purchasers of the car, claiming damages equal to the value of the car when it was sold: £415. The Court of Appeal held that the claimants were only entitled to sue for the actionable losses that they had suffered as a result of the car being sold without their authority: £274.[17] The expressed basis for the decision was that as the claimants had only a 'limited interest' in the car when it was sold, they were not entitled to claim market value damages; they could only sue for compensation in respect of the actionable losses that they had suffered because their car was sold.[18] However, a more straightforward explanation of the decision is that had the claimants been allowed to recover damages equal to the value of the car at the time it was sold, they would have been unjustly enriched: they would have received, in all, £1,030[19] for a car which was only ever worth £889.

[14] [1981] QB 864.

[15] The claimants were, however, entitled to sue the defendants for nominal damages: conversion is a tort that is actionable *per se*.

[16] [1967] 1 WLR 295.

[17] Had the car not been sold without their authority, Pattinson would have continued paying the hire purchase instalments and they would have received £274 more for the car than they had at the time it was sold.

[18] [1967] 1 WLR 295, 299H–310A (per Lord Denning MR).

[19] The sum of £615 and £415.

Receipt of benefit

If A has converted B's property and as a result of A's converting his property, B has obtained some benefit, the damages payable to B will *sometimes* be reduced to take account of this fact. For example, in *Plevin* v *Henshall*,[20] the defendant converted goods worth £947 that belonged to the claimant. He converted them by detaining them on premises let by T, a landlord. The claimant was liable for the rent on these premises. T seized the goods detained by the defendant, claiming that he was owed £118 in unpaid rent. The defendant, in order to get the goods back, paid the rent owed. It was held that the claimant could only sue the defendant for £829 in damages – the market value of the goods converted by the defendant (£947) *minus* the value of benefit that the claimants indirectly received as a result of the defendants' detaining their goods on T's premises (£118).

Improvement

Suppose Dawn stole a car worth £500 from Vijay and sold it to Gary, who purchased it in good faith. Gary then made a number of improvements to the car, thereby increasing its market value to £750, and sold the car to Wendy for that amount. If Vijay sues Gary on the ground that he converted Vijay's car when he sold it to Wendy, Vijay will *not* be entitled to sue Gary for £750, the value of Vijay's car when it was sold to Wendy. Section 6(1) of the Torts (Interference with Goods) Act 1977 provides that 'If in proceedings for [conversion] against a person (the "improver") who has improved the goods, it is shown that the improver acted in the mistaken but honest belief that he had a good title to them, an allowance shall be made for the extent to which, at the time as at which the goods fall to be valued in assessing damages, the value of the goods is attributable to the improvement.' So, in the situation we are considering, Vijay will only be entitled to sue Gary for £500 in damages: while it was worth £750 when Gary converted it by selling it to Wendy, £250 of the car's worth was attributable to the fact that Gary improved it.[21]

Bailment

If Alan converts goods that Nita held on a bailment at will for Lara, Alan will have committed the tort of conversion in relation to both Nita and Lara.[22] Now – if Nita sues Alan for damages equal to whatever Lara's goods were worth when they were converted by Alan, Lara will be barred from suing Alan for such damages.[23] The same is true if Lara sues Alan

[20] (1853) 10 Bing 24, 131 ER 814.

[21] What if Vijay sues *Wendy* for converting his car by buying it? In principle, if he sues Wendy, he should be entitled to sue her for the value of the car at the time she bought it: £750. Once he recovers that from Wendy, will Gary be entitled to bring a claim against Vijay, arguing that £250 of the £750 that Vijay has recovered from Wendy is attributable to the work that Gary did on Vijay's car? Lord Denning MR thought that Gary could: see *Greenwood* v *Bennett* [1973] QB 195, at 202. Phillimore LJ in the same case seemed to agree with Lord Denning MR (ibid., at 202–3) but Cairns LJ disagreed: ibid., at 203.

[22] See above, p. 345.

[23] *The Winkfield* [1902] P 42, 61. No injustice will be done to Lara as a result of this rule – Nita will hold the damages she has recovered from Alan on trust for Lara: ibid., 55.

for market value damages; in such a case, Nita will be barred from bringing a similar claim against Alan.[24]

Multiple claimants

Suppose goods belonging to Karen were stolen from her by Tom. Suppose further that Tom abandoned Karen's goods and they were found by Ruth, who took them. Suppose finally that they were then stolen from Ruth by John. In such a case, John will have committed the tort of conversion in relation to Ruth *and* Karen.[25] Ruth and Karen will not *each* be allowed to sue John for market value damages. This is the effect of ss 7 and 8 of the Torts (Interference with Goods) Act 1977.

If Ruth and Karen both sue John *at the same time* for converting Karen's goods, John's *total* liability to Ruth and Karen *together* will not exceed the value of Karen's goods at the time they were converted by John.[26] The courts will decide how to apportion that liability between Ruth and Karen.[27]

If Ruth – but not Karen – sues John in conversion for market value damages, Ruth will be required under Rules of Court to give particulars of her title to the goods at the time they were converted by John and disclose any information she has as to who else had a claim to the goods at the time they were converted by John.[28] If it becomes evident that the goods were Karen's when they were converted, then John can ask the court to direct that Karen be joined to Ruth's action. If his application is successful and Karen joins Ruth's action, John's liability to Karen and Ruth will be assessed as above. If his application is successful and Karen for some reason *fails* to join Ruth's action, Karen may be stripped of any right she might otherwise have had to sue John for converting her goods.[29]

If it is not evident that the goods converted by John belonged to someone other than Ruth at the time they were converted,[30] Ruth will be entitled to sue John for market value damages.[31] However, Karen will then be entitled to sue Ruth for whatever proportion of the damages recovered by Ruth that Karen would have been awarded had she and Ruth sued John together for converting Karen's goods.[32] The 1977 Act clearly contemplates that Karen

[24] *O'Sullivan* v *Williams* [1992] 3 All ER 385.

[25] At the time John stole the goods, Ruth was in possession of them and Karen had an immediate right to possession of them.

[26] Torts (Interference with Goods) Act 1977, s 7(2): 'In proceedings to which any two or more claimants are parties, the relief shall be such as to avoid double liability of the wrongdoer as between those claimants.'

[27] Presumably, the courts will award Karen market value damages and give Ruth nothing. But what is the position if, after John stole Karen's goods, Karen recovered them? In such a case, Karen would not be entitled to sue John for market value damages (see above, pp. 715–16) and it would be open to the courts to award *Ruth* market value damages instead (as happened in *Wilson* v *Lombank Ltd* [1963] 1 WLR 1294). But this would give Ruth an undeserved windfall.

[28] Torts (Interference with Goods) Act 1977, s 8(2).

[29] In such a case, will Ruth be entitled to sue John for market value damages? It is unclear: see W&J, 766. On the one hand, s 8(1) of the 1977 Act says that a defendant in a conversion case may raise as a defence the fact that someone else had a better title than the claimant to the goods that were converted (the defence of *ius tertii*). On the other hand, this seems inconsistent with s 7, which clearly contemplates that, in the right circumstances, Ruth will be entitled to sue John for market value damages: see, for example, s 7(4).

[30] Say, for example, that Ruth can make out a plausible case for thinking that the goods converted by John were abandoned when she found them.

[31] This point is unaffected by s 8(1) because John will not be able to establish in this case that someone other than Ruth had a better title to the goods that he converted.

[32] Torts (Interference with Goods) Act 1977, s 7(3).

will, alternatively, be allowed to sue John but it is unclear what will happen if she does. The better view, we would submit, is that Karen will not be allowed to recover more from John by way of damages than she would have recovered if she had sued John with Ruth for converting her goods. If Karen's claim against John is successful, then John will be entitled to recoup from Ruth whatever he has had to pay out to Karen by way of damages.[33]

Successive conversions

Suppose Sarah stole Fred's goods and sold them to Carl. To keep things simple, let us assume the goods were never returned to Fred. In such a case, both Sarah and Carl will have committed the tort of conversion in relation to Fred.[34]

If Fred sues *Sarah* for market value damages, Fred will *not* then be entitled to sue *Carl* for such damages. This is because of s 5 of the Torts (Interference with Goods) Act 1977, which provides that if Fred recovers damages in conversion from Sarah, Fred's title to his goods will be extinguished – presumably, from the date that Sarah converted Fred's goods. So once Fred sues Sarah in conversion for market value damages, history is rewritten: the goods that Sarah sold to Carl are treated as though they were Sarah's when they were sold; the result is that Carl can no longer be said to have converted *Fred*'s goods when he bought them. So Fred will no longer have any right to sue Carl for converting his property.

What if Fred sues Carl first and then Sarah? Section 5 will not work to prevent Fred doing this. However, it is submitted that if Fred sues Carl first and recovers market value damages from him, Fred will be barred from bringing a similar claim against Sarah. Instead, Fred will only be entitled to sue Sarah for damages equal to the depreciation in value, if any, that his goods experienced between the time they were stolen by Sarah and the time they were sold to Carl. In this way, Fred will be allowed to recover damages equal to whatever his goods were worth at the time they were stolen from him but no more than that – if he were allowed to recover more, he would obtain an undeserved windfall.

[33] Section 7(4).
[34] See above, pp. 342–5.

D.
Remedies designed to prevent the commission of a tort

Introduction

Those who take the view that the function of tort law is to determine when one person will be held liable to compensate another for some loss that that other has suffered usually have the grace, and the intelligence, to acknowledge that this view of tort law is not wholly accurate.[1] So, for example, the legal historian David Ibbetson observes that 'tort [law] … is *primarily* reactive to events that have occurred in the past … [it is] *hardly at all* concerned with facilitating the orderly regulation of individuals' affairs …'.[2] The qualifiers 'primarily' and 'hardly at all' are inserted here because of the existence of the remedies dealt with in the next two chapters of this book. These remedies are not at all concerned with *loss-compensation*. They are concerned, rather, with *wrong-prevention*:[3] they are awarded in order to stop someone committing a tort. These remedies *are* therefore concerned with facilitating the orderly regulation of individuals' affairs; they *do* look to determine what will happen in the future, not to unpick a mess that has been created in the past.

The existence of these remedies establishes definitively that committing a tort involves breaching a duty owed to another.[4] It is this fact that sets a natural limit to tort law's jurisdiction: if committing a tort involves breaching a duty owed to another, it follows that *no one* can be held liable *in tort* to compensate A for some loss that A has suffered if no *civil wrong* was committed in causing A to suffer loss. It is therefore wrong to think that tort law is concerned *generally* to determine when one person will be held liable to compensate another for some loss that that other has suffered: if that loss was not wrongfully inflicted, tort law has nothing to say on the issue, one way or the other. And if this is right, it is wrong to think that the function of tort law is to determine when one person will be held liable to compensate another for a loss that that other has suffered. Rather, the function of tort law is to help determine what specific duties we owe each other and to determine what remedies will be available when one of those duties is breached.[5]

[1] Of course, a statement that is not *wholly* accurate is not accurate *at all*.

[2] Ibbetson 2003, 475 (emphasis added).

[3] *Important note*. Some would prefer to say 'loss-prevention' at this point: see Jones 2002, 1; W&J, 2; S&H, 13. But if it is not legally wrong for A to cause B loss in a certain situation, why on earth would the courts try to prevent A causing B loss in that situation? Why would they not allow A to inflict the loss and then, if it is appropriate to do so, require A to compensate B for that loss? The *only* possible reason why the remedies dealt with in the next two chapters might be awarded against a given defendant is that the defendant proposes to commit a civil wrong; that is, he proposes to do something that involves the breach of a duty owed to another.

[4] See above, n. 3.

[5] To the same effect, see GS&Z, 3: 'tort law articulates legal responsibilities or duties that persons owe to one another, and provides victims of conduct breaching those duties with redress against those who have wronged them.'

39 Injunction

Suppose that A will commit a tort in relation to B if he does *x*. Suppose further that A is likely to do *x* unless he is prevented from doing so. In such a case, B may be able to obtain an injunction[1] against A, requiring him not to do *x*.[2] If such an injunction were issued against A and he ignored it then he would commit a contempt of court and render himself liable to be punished.

CLASSIFICATION OF INJUNCTIONS

Mandatory and prohibitory injunctions

If an injunction instructs someone to take positive action, for example, to repair a wall, then the injunction is called a *mandatory* injunction. On the other hand, if an injunction instructs someone to cease behaving in a particular way the injunction is called a *prohibitory* injunction. The distinction is one of substance rather than form. A good rule of thumb is that if fulfilling an injunction requires the expenditure of money then the injunction is, in substance, *mandatory*. English courts are more cautious about granting mandatory injunctions than prohibitory injunctions.[3]

Quia timet injunctions

Most injunctions will instruct someone either not to *continue* committing a tort or to undo the consequences which followed the commission of a tort. It is also possible, however, for someone to obtain an injunction if she can establish that she is *about* to be the victim of a tort to be committed by A. Such an injunction, known as a *quia timet* injunction, will order A not to commit the tort. For example, in *Litchfield-Speer* v *Queen Anne's Gate Syndicate (No. 2) Ltd*,[4] Lawrence J held that the claimants were entitled to an injunction to restrain the defendants from erecting a new building, which, had it been built, would have amounted to a private nuisance because its presence would have unreasonably interfered with the claimants' right to light.

Interim and final injunctions

Injunctions granted as a remedy at the conclusion of a trial are referred to as *final* or *perpetual* injunctions. English civil procedure also allows a party to seek an injunction to

[1] An injunction is 'a court order prohibiting a person from doing something or requiring a person to do something', Civil Procedure Rules, glossary.

[2] The general authority of the High Court to grant injunctions is found in Senior Courts Act 1981, s 37(1).

[3] The reasons for this are explained below, pp. 727–8.

[4] [1919] 1 Ch 407.

protect his or her position before trial. Such injunctions are referred to as *interim* (formerly *interlocutory*) injunctions.

WHEN WILL AN INJUNCTION BE GRANTED?

Interim injunctions

Interim injunctions are particularly important where A proposes to do something – *x* – which will cause damage to B *before* there is any opportunity to hold a trial to determine whether A's doing *x* will be a tort to B, and the damage which will be caused is of a type which could not be properly reversed by a payment of damages. In such a case, B may be able to obtain an *interim* injunction against A, requiring him not to do *x* until some future time.

The 'balance of convenience' test[5]

The general rule is that B will be required to do three things before an interim injunction will be granted:

(1) B must establish that there is a serious question to be tried as to whether if A does *x* he will commit a tort to B.[6]
(2) B will have to undertake that if an interim injunction is granted against A and it is later found that *x* would not have involved A committing a tort to B, she will compensate A for any losses suffered by him as a result of that injunction's being granted.[7]
(3) B will have to convince the court that the 'balance of convenience' favours granting an interim injunction.

The 'balance of convenience' is determined by balancing B's need to be protected against any harm that she might suffer if A were allowed to do *x* for which she could not be adequately compensated in damages recoverable against A's need to be protected against any harm that he might suffer as a result of being prevented from doing *x* for which he could not be adequately compensated in damages under the claimant's undertaking.

Thus if Vijay wanted to cut down an old tree, and Beth claimed that the old tree was on her land so cutting it down would be a tort to her, then the court would balance the extent to which Beth would be adequately compensated if the tree was cut down and it turned out to be her tree, against the extent to which Vijay could be adequately compensated by damages if he was prevented from cutting down the tree until trial and it turned out that

[5] This test was set out by Lord Diplock in *American Cyanamid* v *Ethicon Ltd* [1975] AC 396, and is commonly referred to as 'the *American Cyanamid* test'. For its detailed application, and some of the criticisms that have been made of it, the reader is advised to consult a specialist book on civil procedure.

[6] This is not a high hurdle. In *American Cyanamid* v *Ethicon Ltd* [1975] AC 396, Lord Diplock explained (at 407) that there was a 'serious question to be tried' if the court was satisfied that the claim was not 'frivolous or vexatious'. He also stated that, 'It is no part of the court's function at this stage of the litigation to try to resolve conflicts of evidence on affidavit as to facts on which the claims of either party may ultimately depend nor to decide difficult questions of law which call for detailed argument and mature considerations. These are matters to be dealt with at the trial.' Zuckerman 2006, 9.45, suggests that many judges are reluctant to use such a *low* hurdle when they feel able to reach a preliminary view on the merits and that there is a 'widespread but unstated practice' of using a *higher* hurdle: 'as every lawyer should know, a clear probability of success on the merits is bound to figure in judges' calculations when they come to decide whether to grant interim relief.'

[7] Civil Procedure Rules, Practice Direction 25, 5.1(1).

cutting the tree down would not involve a tort to Beth. In such circumstances a pivotal issue would be what harm, if any, Vijay might suffer if he had to delay cutting down the tree.

Exceptions

There are three situations which commonly arise in tort cases where the courts will *not* use the 'balance of convenience' test:

(1) *Time is of the essence.* In some situations ordering A not to do something until trial will effectively preclude him from ever doing it, since he may only want to do it at a particular time. Consequently, in some tort cases the question whether an interim injunction will be granted effectively determines the whole dispute. An example might be where Carl seeks an order that Nita should not organise some industrial action. By the time of any trial the dispute which generated the threat of industrial action may have been resolved, and neither party may have much desire to determine whether the previously proposed action would have been lawful. In such an exceptional case a judge who is asked to grant an interim injunction should not consider merely whether there is a serious question to be tried, but whether Carl would have been likely to obtain a *final* injunction if the case had been fully tried.[8]

(2) *Defamation cases.* '[T]he importance of leaving free speech unfettered is a strong reason in cases of libel for dealing most cautiously and warily with the granting of interim injunctions.'[9] This caution is reflected in the rule[10] that interim injunctions will not generally be granted in cases where B claims that a proposed publication by A will libel or slander her[11] but A intends to argue at trial that his statement is not defamatory,[12] or intends to put forward a defence of justification,[13] fair comment on a matter of public interest,[14] or privilege.[15] If, however, it is clear that the defence is doomed to fail, an interim injunction may still be granted.[16]

Section 12(3) of the Human Rights Act 1998 provides that 'No such relief [affecting the exercise of the Convention right to freedom of expression] is to be granted so as to restrain publication before trial unless the court is satisfied that the applicant is likely to establish that publication should not be allowed.' This provision has not altered the common law rule discussed in the previous paragraph, which applies in cases of libel and slander.[17] But the

[8] *NWL Ltd* v *Woods* [1979] 1 WLR 1294, 1306–7.
[9] *Bonnard* v *Perryman* [1891] 2 Ch 269, 284 (per Lord Coleridge).
[10] Commonly referred to as 'the rule in *Bonnard* v *Perryman*'.
[11] Similar rules probably apply to the tort of malicious falsehood, and courts will be careful not to allow the rules to be evaded by claims that the publication may amount to some other tort, such as lawful means conspiracy (discussed in Chapter 22, above): see *Gulf Oil (Great Britain) Ltd* v *Page* [1987] Ch 327, 333–4; *Femis-Bank* v *Lazar* [1991] Ch 391.
[12] *Coulson* v *Coulson* [1887] 3 TLR 846.
[13] *Bonnard* v *Perryman* [1891] 2 Ch 269.
[14] *Fraser* v *Evans* [1969] 1 QB 349, 360.
[15] *Quartz Hill Consolidated Mining Co.* v *Beal* (1882) 20 Ch D 501; *Harakas* v *Baltic Mercantile and Shipping Exchange Ltd* [1982] 1 WLR 958.
[16] *Holley* v *Smyth* [1998] QB 726, holding that a claimant is allowed to adduce evidence to show that a defence of justification is bound to fail; *Herbage* v *Pressdram* [1984] 1 WLR 1160, 1164, discussing a situation where there was overwhelming evidence of malice which would negate a defence of qualified privilege.
[17] *Greene* v *Associated Newspapers Ltd* [2005] QB 972.

statutory provision means that the 'balance of convenience' will *also* not apply in other situations where an interim injunction is sought to prevent the commission of a wrong involving publication, such as the wrongful disclosure of private information.[18] In *Cream Holdings Ltd* v *Banerjee*[19] the House of Lords noted the difficulty of defining 'likely' in this provision because the test must be applied in such a wide range of situations. In some cases (for instance, those involving allegedly confidential information about the dealings of a company) the claimant might be seeking to protect a financial interest and the defendant relying on the public interest, but in others (for instance, those involving the new identity of a released criminal) the claimant might be seeking to protect his right to life. Lord Nicholls solved this difficulty by holding that Parliament intended the word 'likely' to be able to change meaning: 'The intention of Parliament must be taken to be that "likely" should have an extended meaning which sets as a normal perquisite to the grant of an injunction before trial a likelihood of success at the trial higher than the commonplace *American Cyanamid* standard of "real prospect" but permits the court to dispense with the higher standard where particular circumstances make this necessary.'[20] Later in his speech he identified the degree of likelihood that an applicant would have to establish in a normal case (that is, not one involving particularly severe potential consequences, and not one involving a very brief injunction pending the judge being able to read the papers or an appeal being considered) as being that his claim would 'more likely than not' succeed at trial.[21]

The approach under s 12(3) is distinct from that under the ordinary 'balance of convenience' test not only because it asks whether the claimant is 'likely to establish that publication should not be allowed' instead of whether there is 'a serious question to be tried', but also because under s 12(3) the court must reach a provisional view on disputes of fact and questions of law in order to reach a view on the merits of the claim. In considering the merits the court must consider not merely the likelihood of the claimant establishing the defendant's *liability* but also the likelihood of the claimant convincing the court that a *final* injunction is appropriate.

(3) *Trade disputes.* The third exception is where A claims that his proposed course of action will be performed in contemplation or furtherance of a trade dispute. In such a case, before granting an interim injunction a court must consider the likelihood that A will be able to establish the defence of trade union immunity[22] at trial.[23]

Final injunctions

The general rule

The general rule is that courts will grant a *final* injunction to prevent the continuation or repetition of any tort where there is a sufficient basis for believing that without an injunc-

[18] Discussed in Chapter 15, above. In *A* v *B* [2003] QB 195, [11], the Court of Appeal set out guidelines for judges asked to decide whether an interim injunction should be granted to prevent commission of this tort.

[19] [2005] 1 AC 253.

[20] Ibid., [20].

[21] Ibid., [22].

[22] The immunity is found in Trade Union and Labour Relations (Consolidation) Act 1992, ss 219–220. These provisions are discussed above, at p. 504.

[23] Trade Union and Labour Relations (Consolidation) Act 1992, s 221(2).

tion there will be a continuation or repetition of that tort. In practice this means that injunctions are far more common where certain types of tort are alleged. Torts which are usually committed by isolated impacts, such as negligence, are unlikely to give rise to claims for injunctions,[24] while torts which are often committed by interference over a longer period with someone's interests, such as private nuisance, commonly give rise to such claims. It is worth noting, however, that because injunctions are intended to deal with future continuation or repetition of the wrongful behaviour, a claimant seeking an injunction will often *also* claim damages for past injury – and where a court finds that A has committed and is committing a tort by engaging in a continuous course of conduct, it will often award *both* an injunction against A to prevent the tort being committed in the future *and* damages for any past injury caused by A's tort.

The remedy of injunction was initially developed in the Courts of Equity and consequently it conforms to general equitable principles about remedies. The central general principle is that remedies developed by the Courts of Equity (known as 'equitable remedies') are discretionary. What this means is that even where a claimant has established the conditions sufficient to be awarded a remedy the courts will not necessarily grant it – they can still refuse. In practice, the courts' choices as to whether or not to grant someone an equitable remedy are usually directed by well-developed rules. Thus an injunction will not be awarded where justice can be done by ordering the defendant to pay damages to the claimant,[25] where granting the injunction would be oppressive,[26] where the claimant seeking the injunction does not have 'clean hands',[27] where the claimant seeking the injunction is unwilling to 'do equity',[28] where the claimant initially allowed the defendant to do what she is now seeking an injunction against,[29] or where there has been unacceptable delay on the part of the claimant in seeking an injunction against the defendant. But even beyond these rules there exists a degree of residual flexibility.

Courts are generally more cautious about granting mandatory injunctions than prohibitory injunctions for two principal reasons. First, if a mandatory injunction is awarded against a defendant, the court must specify what the defendant must do to comply with it.

[24] Cf Lord Denning MR's remark in *Miller* v *Jackson* [1977] QB 966, 980: 'there is no case, so far as I know, where [an injunction] has been granted to stop a man being negligent.' This is disputed, however, in McBride 2004, pointing to the American cases of *Shimp* v *New Jersey Bell Telephone Co.*, 368 A 2d 408 (1976) and *Smith* v *Western Electric Co.*, 643 SW 2d 10 (1982), where in each case an injunction was granted against an employer, compelling him to comply with the duty of care he owed his employees to take reasonable steps to see that they would be reasonably safe in working for him.

[25] Damages are generally not thought to be adequate where the harm caused is to non-pecuniary interests, such as health or amenity, or where the damages would be hard to quanitfy. Consequently, this basis for refusing an injunction is rarely relied on in tort cases.

[26] This concept is discussed in detail below, pp. 729–32.

[27] This basis for refusing an injunction allows a court to take account of any misconduct by a claimant seeking an injunction. Of course, the courts will not refuse to grant an injunction because of a trivial act of misconduct by the claimant.

[28] This basis for refusing an injunction allows a court to consider whether the claimant is willing to perform any duties that she owes the defendant.

[29] An injunction might be refused on this basis if, for instance, B stood by and watched A expend money on a project before objecting to it and seeking an injunction. In *Jaggard* v *Sawyer* [1995] 1 WLR 269 the claimant warned the defendant that the defendant's proposed action was wrongful but did not seek an interim injunction. The Court of Appeal treated this failure to seek an interim injunction as relevant to the decision whether to grant a final injunction: 283 (Sir Thomas Bingham MR), 289 (Millett LJ).

Where it is impossible to state clearly what it is that the defendant is being required to do a mandatory injunction will be refused.[30]

Secondly, there is a concern that if a mandatory injunction is awarded against A for B's benefit, A may be compelled to spend more money complying with that injunction than B will gain from that injunction being complied with. This might be regarded as wasteful. Consequently, it is necessary to pay particular attention to whether damages will be an *adequate* remedy for any future harm, and how much it will cost a defendant to obey a mandatory injunction.[31] However, if the cost to A of complying with the injunction that B is seeking far outweighs whatever benefits B will reap from that injunction being awarded against A, an injunction may still be awarded against A if A has acted with wanton disregard of B's interests.

Injunctions affecting freedom of expression

Where a court is considering whether to grant any relief which, if granted, might affect the exercise of the Convention right to freedom of expression then:

> The court must have particular regard to the importance of the Convention right to freedom of expression and, where the proceedings relate to material which the respondent claims, or which appears to the court, to be journalistic, literary or artistic material (or to conduct connected with such material), to –
>
> (a) the extent to which –
>
> (i) the material has, or is about to, become available to the public; or
>
> (ii) it is, or would be, in the public interest for the material to be published;
>
> (b) any relevant privacy code.[32]

Clearly an injunction may affect freedom of expression to a greater extent than an award of damages. Thus before granting an injunction which will interfere with freedom of expression a court will want to be convinced that the proposed interference is supported by 'relevant and sufficient grounds', will respond to a 'pressing social need' and will not interfere to any extent greater than necessary to meet the legitimate aim pursued. The Court of Appeal has held that s 12(4) does not require a court to attribute *extra* weight to the listed factors but 'does no more than underline the need to have regard to contexts in which [the European Court of Human Rights'] jurisprudence has given particular weight to freedom of expression, while at the same time drawing attention to considerations which may none the less justify restricting that right'.[33] Equally, s 12(4) is not intended to give one Convention right (Article 10, freedom of expression) pre-eminence in a case where another Convention right (e.g. Article 8, privacy) is also involved.[34]

30 *Redland Bricks Ltd* v *Morris* [1970] AC 632.

31 Ibid.

32 Human Rights Act 1998, s 12(4).

33 *Ashdown* v *Telegraph Group Ltd* [2002] Ch 149, [27].

34 The court should not give either right precedence over the other, should focus intensely 'on the comparative importance of the specific rights being claimed in the individual case', should take account of 'the justifications for interfering with or restricting each right' and should apply the proportionality test to each right: *In re S (A Child)(Identification: Restrictions on Publication)* [2005] 1 AC 593, at [17].

Damages in lieu of final injunctions

If B applies to a court for a final injunction which would require A not to commit a particular tort in relation to B, the choice for the court which is considering B's application is not a straightforward one between granting an injunction and leaving B without any remedy. The court may refuse to award B an injunction but at the same time award B damages *in lieu of* (instead of) an injunction.[35]

The effect of such an award will be to leave A free to commit the tort complained of by B. In return, A is made to pay B a reasonable sum for the privilege of being allowed to commit that tort. If the court dealing with B's application does decide to award B damages in lieu of an injunction it will assess how much B should be paid by way of damages in lieu by asking: How much would a reasonable person in B's shoes charge A for the privilege of being allowed to commit the tort complained of by B?[36] The figure the court comes up with will be the amount it awards B by way of damages in lieu. So suppose the court dealing with B's application has decided to deny her application for an injunction and decided to award her damages in lieu of an injunction instead. In determining how much B should be paid by way of damages in lieu, the court will take into account how much B stands to lose if A is allowed to commit the tort complained of by B *and* how much money A will make if he is allowed to commit the tort complained of by B.[37] A reasonable man in B's shoes would take both matters into account in determining how much to charge A for the privilege of being allowed to commit the tort complained of by B.[38]

So an award of damages in lieu of an injunction in effect amounts to a forced sale of B's rights against A. Consequently, the courts have traditionally been cautious about using their power to award damages in lieu of injunctions. In the leading case of *Shelfer* v *City of London Electric Lighting Co.*,[39] A.L. Smith LJ stated,

> In my opinion it may be stated as a good working rule that – (1) If the injury to the claimant's legal rights is small, (2) And is one which is capable of being estimated in money, (3) And is one which can be adequately compensated by a small money payment, (4) And the case is one in which it would be oppressive to the defendant to grant an injunction: – then damages in substitution for an injunction may be given.[40]

A.L. Smith LJ then went on to suggest that regardless of the four factors, a defendant who had acted in reckless disregard of the claimant's rights would be unable to ask the court to award damages in lieu of injunction.[41]

[35] The Chancery Amendment Act 1858, better known as Lord Cairns's Act, allowed the Court of Chancery to award damages in lieu of an injunction. This statute has been repealed, but s 50 of the Senior Courts Act 1981 preserves the court's jurisdiction to award damages in lieu of an injunction.

[36] *Jaggard* v *Sawyer* [1995] 1 WLR 269.

[37] *Carr-Saunders* v *Dick McNeil Associates Ltd* [1986] 1 WLR 922.

[38] In *Tamares Ltd* v *Fairpoint Properties Ltd (No. 2)* [2007] 1 WLR 2167, Gabriel Moss QC held that where a court refused to grant a party an injunction to protect its right to light against a development on neighbouring land the owner of the right should normally be awarded some part of the likely profit from the development, but not so much as would have been likely to prevent the development from taking place (at [22]). In the particular case he awarded the claimant £50,000, which was slightly less than a third of the developer's expected profit and considerably *more* than the claimant's loss of amenity (assessed at no more than £3,030).

[39] [1895] 1 Ch 287.

[40] Ibid., 322–3.

[41] Ibid., 323. In *Ketley* v *Gooden* (1996) 73 P & CR 305, the Court of Appeal awarded damages in lieu of an injunction despite the fact that the defendant had recklessly disregarded the claimant's rights because of delay by the claimant in starting proceedings and the minor nature of the damage.

In *Jaggard* v *Sawyer*,[42] the Court of Appeal treated A.L. Smith LJ's list of four factors as having 'stood the test of time'.[43] Indeed, Lord Bingham MR favoured a narrow interpretation of the fourth factor and said, 'It is important to bear in mind that the test is one of oppression, and the court should not slide into application of a general balance of convenience test.'[44] Millett LJ did not doubt the utility of A.L. Smith LJ's four factors, but he also observed that they were not to be treated as an exhaustive list of the situations when it would be appropriate to award damages in lieu of an injunction.[45] Most probably he was referring here to the general equitable principles, which may make a court reluctant to grant an injunction.

It is worth drawing attention to the fact that A.L. Smith LJ's four factors do not make any reference to the question whether awarding an injunction will be contrary to the *public interest*. The question whether the claimant should be able to obtain an injunction which might close down an enterprise operating in the public interest is controversial. In *Shelfer*, Lindley LJ expressed the strong view that,

> the Court has always protested against the notion that it ought to allow a wrong to continue simply because the wrongdoer is able and willing to pay for the injury he may inflict. Neither has the circumstance that the wrongdoer is in some sense a public benefactor (e.g., a gas or water company or a sewer authority) ever been considered a sufficient reason for refusing to protect by injunction an individual whose rights are being persistently infringed.[46]

Thus the court was willing to grant an injunction against the Bankside power station in London. Similarly, in *Manchester Corporation* v *Farnworth*,[47] an injunction was granted closing one of Manchester's main power stations.

A contrasting view was adopted by the majority of the Court of Appeal in *Miller* v *Jackson*.[48] The action in *Miller* was brought by owners of a new house bordering a cricket field in County Durham seeking an injunction ordering the village cricket club not to conduct games without first taking adequate steps to prevent balls being struck out of the ground. Such an order would effectively have prevented cricket being played, since the club had already erected a 15-foot-high chain-link fence (they could not build a higher one

42 [1995] 1 WLR 269.

43 Ibid., 287 (per Millett LJ). In *Regan* v *Paul Properties DPF No. 1 Ltd* [2007] Ch 135, the Court of Appeal held that the same approach – based on *Shelfer* – applied in 'right to light' cases.

44 [1995] 1 WLR 269, 283.

45 Ibid., 287.

46 [1895] 1 Ch 287, 315–6.

46 [1930] AC 171. In this context it is also common to cite the Irish case of *Bellew* v *Cement Ltd* [1948] IR 61 where the quarry which provided 80% of the cement in the Republic of Ireland was stopped from blasting by injunction at a time of national rebuilding. It is important to note, however, that while under the ordinary law injunctions may be granted against such activities as power stations and sewage works this has not meant that such activities have had to cease. Rather, operators of such works have had to seek statutory authority for causing the disturbance that they inevitably cause. Such statutory authority effectively renders such activities immune from tort claims arising from such inevitable disturbance, but it is often a condition of the grant of such authority that compensation must be paid to those worst affected. From this perspective, the question whether courts should take the public interest into account when deciding whether to grant injunctions is really a question about the appropriate forum and procedure for deciding what is in the public interest: Parliament or the courts.

48 [1977] QB 966.

because of the wind) and even that was insufficient to prevent half a dozen balls a season escaping onto the new estate.[49]

A majority of the Court of Appeal found that the club's activities constituted a private nuisance, with Lord Denning MR dissenting. But Cumming-Bruce LJ then joined Denning MR to form a majority in favour of taking into account the interests of the public generally when deciding whether to grant an injunction. Cumming-Bruce LJ said, 'a court of equity must seek to strike a fair balance between the right of the claimants to have quiet enjoyment of their house and garden without exposure to cricket balls occasionally falling like thunderbolts from the heavens and the opportunity of the inhabitants of the village in which they live to continue to enjoy the manly sport which constitutes a summer recreation for adults and young persons, including one would hope and expect the [claimants'] son'.[50] Striking this balance, the injunction was refused. The trial judge had awarded £174.14 for past damages as well as granting an injunction. The Court of Appeal substituted an award of £400 to cover both past and future loss.

This decision understandably attracted criticism from those who shared the views expressed by Lindley LJ in *Shelfer*. When a similar point arose four years later, in *Kennaway* v *Thompson*,[51] the Court of Appeal returned to the orthodox view. In that case, the claimant owned a house next to a lake. A motor boat racing club frequently held races on the adjoining lake, and the noise disturbed the claimant's enjoyment of her house. She brought a claim against the club in private nuisance for an injunction and damages. The trial judge held that the races held by the club on the lake were so frequent that they amounted to a nuisance but denied an injunction on the ground that it was in the public interest for the club to be allowed to carry on with its activities. On appeal, the Court of Appeal reversed the trial judge and granted the claimant an injunction.

Lawton LJ said, 'We are of the opinion that there is nothing in *Miller* v *Jackson*, binding on us, which qualifies what was decided in *Shelfer*. Any decisions before *Shelfer's* case (and there were some at first instance . . .) which give support to the proposition that the public interest should prevail over the private interest must be read subject to *Shelfer*'s case.'[52] The Court of Appeal therefore held that the trial judge should have granted an injunction restricting the noise made by the motor boat racing club. Importantly, however, the Court of Appeal in *Kennaway* stressed that the injunction should be carefully drafted to deal with the nuisance, and should not outlaw the whole activity. The injunction which the court drafted recognised that while motor boat racing every weekend from March to November was a nuisance, a reasonable inhabitant of a lakeside house could be expected to tolerate some motor boat racing. The injunction thus allowed the club to have one three-day international event, two two-day national events and three one-day club events each year, with a further rule that no boat emitting more than 75 decibels was to be used at any event.

In the United States, the American Law Institute's Restatement 2d of Torts, §936(1)

[49] The club had offered to take other measures, such as putting a net over the Jacksons' garden, or fitting their windows with shutters and unbreakable glass, but those offers were rejected by the Jacksons on the ground that they were measures which would not prevent the nuisance in the garden but would merely limit the resulting damage.

[50] [1977] QB 966, 988G–H.

[51] [1981] QB 88.

[52] Ibid., 93G.

advocates an approach somewhere between those adopted in *Miller* and *Kennaway*. Thus the Institute recommends determining the appropriate remedy by taking into account a list of factors including the nature of the claimant's interest, the relative adequacy of damages and injunction, the relative hardship involved in granting or refusing an injunction and the effects on the interest of third parties and the public generally.

In England, however, it seems that in almost all cases since *Kennaway* the courts have reverted to applying *Shelfer*. For instance, in *Elliott* v *London Borough of Islington*,[53] a case involving private nuisance by encroaching tree roots, Lord Donaldson MR said,

> I would only be echoing the authorities, and in particular *Shelfer*'s case, if I say that it is not the function of the courts to licence breaches of the rights of citizens. Compulsory purchase under statute is a well-known concept and is subject to well-known protections, but it is not for the courts to add to that burden on the citizen a system whereby, as in this case, they will grant, for a fee [i.e. damages in lieu of injunction] payable to the claimant, a compulsory lease of land to accommodate the roots of this tree in addition to putting up with the nuisance it creates.[54]

Where there is a risk that an injunction will harm the public interest, however, it is very common for the injunction to be *suspended* for a period sufficient to give the defendant time to make alternative arrangements.

Alternatives to injunctions other than damages

Damages are not the only alternative to awarding an injunction. In situations where there is no doubt that the defendant will voluntarily comply with the law as soon as it has been clarified the court may choose to make a declaration rather than granting an injunction. Similarly, the defendant may volunteer to give a formal undertaking that he will behave in a particular way rather than the court having to order him to do so.

One other situation where a court might refuse an injunction is where future damage can reasonably be eliminated by the defendant providing the victim of his tort with some form of protection. The best illustration of this is the unusual New Zealand case of *Bank of New Zealand* v *Greenwood*.[55] In that case, the defendant had built a shopping centre with a glass-roofed walkway. Unfortunately, the angle of the glass roof was such that it reflected the glare of the sun in the windows of the Bank of New Zealand, to the discomfort of staff and customers. The judge found that this amounted to a private nuisance, but that the defendant did not have to alter the roof, which would have cost the defendant $20,000. Instead, the defendant could provide 'venetian blinds' for the Bank.

The precise nature of this remedy is not easy to classify. Hardie Boys J insisted that he was not awarding damages in lieu of an injunction, but was merely pointing out a way in which the defendant could leave the claimant without a claim. It is probably best to treat the case as exemplifying a principle that an injunction can be refused when the defendant has offered to provide the victim of his tort with a reasonable way of eliminating future damage and the victim of his tort has refused this offer.

This principle will only be applied, however, where it would be wholly unreasonable for the victim to reject the offer and insist on an injunction. In *Elliott* v *London Borough of*

53 [1991] 1 EGLR 167.
54 Ibid., 168K.
55 [1984] 1 NZLR 525.

Islington,[56] the owners of a tree with encroaching roots offered to rebuild the claimant's wall on a pre-cast concrete bar raised above the ground, so that the roots could pass underneath it without causing any damage.[57] This solution, however, would not have eliminated the private nuisance by encroachment, but merely reduced its effects, and the Court of Appeal held that Elliott was still entitled to an injunction.

Reform of the law concerning the availability of final injunctions

It is important to note that a court's decision to grant a final injunction to B ordering A not to do *x* does not necessarily determine whether *x* will eventually be done. If A believes that it will be profitable for him to do *x*, then even if B has obtained an injunction against him, ordering him not to do *x*, he can still try to reach an accommodation with B and buy the right to do what would otherwise be a tort.

One question which has excited legal economists is whether the approach of courts to questions of remedies is likely to lead to *x* being done when it is efficient to do *x* rather than *y* (some activity which the doing of *x* prevents), and *x* not being done when it is *not* efficient to do *x* rather than *y*. For instance, it has been asked whether the law concerning remedies for the tort of private nuisance is likely to lead to land being used as productively as possible.

Professor Coase argued in a famous article[58] that if 'bargaining costs' were ignored, then the initial decision in a private nuisance case would have no effect on how land was actually used. Whatever the decision, the parties would end up using their land in the most profitable way.[59] All the decision would determine is how the profits garnered from using the land in that way would be shared between them.[60] In the real world, however, there are

[56] [1991] 1 EGLR 167.

[57] Lord Donaldson MR described this as 'the arborial equivalent of a cat-flap' (ibid., 168B).

[58] Coase 1960.

[59] It may be worth spelling this out. Suppose that if A does *x* on his land then B will be prevented from doing *y* on her land. Suppose further that A will make £10,000 if he is allowed to do *x* on his land while B will make only £3,000 if she is allowed to do *y* on her land. If this is the case, then if the courts decide that A's doing *x* on his land will *not* amount to a private nuisance, A will end up doing *x* on his land: B will only be prepared to pay A up to £2,999 not to do *x* on his land, but A will need to be offered more than £10,000 to make it worth his while not to do *x*. If, on the other hand, the courts decide that A's doing *x* on his land *will* amount to a private nuisance and award an injunction against A, A will still end up being allowed to do *x* on his land. The money A stands to make from doing *x* on his land is such that he will be able to pay B enough money to convince B to agree to allow him to do *x* and still turn a profit.

Now suppose that B's doing *y* on her land will actually be more profitable than A's doing *x* on his: B will make £10,000 if she is allowed to do *y* on her land while A will make only £3,000 if he is allowed to do *x* on his land. If this is the case, then if the courts decide that A's doing *x* on his land will *not* amount to a private nuisance, A will not, in the end, do *x* on his land and B will as a result be allowed to do *y* on her land. The reason for this is that the money B stands to make from doing *y* on her land exceeds the money A will make from doing *x* on his land. So B will be able to afford to pay A enough money to get him to agree not to do *x* on his land and still turn a profit. If, on the other hand, the courts decide that A's doing *x* on his land *will* amount to a private nuisance and award an injunction against A, A will not in the end be allowed to do *x* on his land and B will as a result be left free to do *y* on her land. A will not be able to afford to pay B enough money to persuade her to release him from the injunction. B would have to be offered more than £10,000 to release A from his injunction, while it is not in A's interests to offer her more than £2,999. So *whatever the courts decide*, if A's doing *x* on his land will be more profitable than B's doing *y* on hers, then A will end up doing *x* on his land. Similarly, if B's doing *y* on her land will be more profitable than A's doing *x* on his land: *whatever the courts decide*, A will not in the end do *x* on his land and B will as a result be allowed to do *y* on her land.

[60] Of course, the fairness of the distribution of the profits is a perfectly legitimate concern for English law. It is worth remembering throughout this section that economic efficiency is not all-important.

'bargaining costs', and these make it important whether a court dealing with a dispute chooses to grant an injunction or merely damages in lieu.

Suppose, for example, that Tom wants to hold very noisy concerts on his land and Wendy wants to run a hotel on her land, which is next to Tom's. Suppose further that if Tom holds concerts on his land, no one will want to stay at Wendy's hotel and so Wendy will have to close it down. Suppose further that Tom will commit the tort of private nuisance in relation to Wendy if he holds concerts on his land. If the courts grant an injunction to Wendy – requiring Tom not to hold concerts on his land – then if Tom wants to hold concerts on his land, he will have to pay Wendy to release him from the injunction that she has obtained against him. Now if the costs of bargaining with Wendy are high, then Tom may be unable to reach an agreement with Wendy to obtain the right to be allowed to hold concerts on his land even if he stands to make more money by holding concerts on his land than Wendy will make if she is allowed to run a hotel on her land.

Now suppose, instead, that the courts grant damages in lieu of an injunction to Wendy. In assessing how much Wendy should be paid by way of damages in lieu the courts will, of course, take into account how much money Wendy will lose if Tom is allowed to hold concerts on his land. If it really is more profitable for Tom to hold concerts on his land than it is for Wendy to run a hotel on her land, then Tom will pay the damages in lieu and get on with holding concerts on his land: the right result from the point of view of economic efficiency. Holding concerts on his land will give Tom enough money to pay Wendy her damages in lieu – damages which will at least cover the losses that Wendy will suffer – and still have something left over. If, on the other hand, the money Wendy would make if she were allowed to run a hotel on her land exceeds the money Tom will make by holding concerts on his land, then Tom will decline to hold any concerts on his land: again, the right result from the point of view of economic efficiency. Tom will not make enough money out of holding concerts on his land to cover the damages in lieu that he will have to pay Wendy if he presses ahead.

Now – it costs time and money for a court to calculate, for the purpose of determining how much Wendy should be awarded by way of damages in lieu of an injunction.[61] So a court will only want to do this if it is necessary. Taking these matters together, legal economists[62] commonly argue that if 'bargaining costs' between Tom and Wendy are low, an injunction against Tom should be granted. This way, the courts will not have to spend time calculating how much Wendy will lose if Tom is allowed to hold concerts on his land. If Tom will really make more money holding concerts on his land than Wendy will make if she runs a hotel on her land, Tom will have little difficulty in buying the right to hold concerts on his land from Wendy anyway. If, however, 'bargaining costs' are high, it may be better to refuse to grant Wendy an injunction and instead award her damages in lieu of an injunction. As long as these damages are calculated correctly, Tom will only end up holding concerts on his land if he will make more money holding concerts on his land than Wendy would make if she were able to run a hotel on her land. If this is not the case, then Tom will undertake not to hold concerts on his land.

So legal economists commonly suggest that unless 'bargaining costs' are low between

[61] For how such damages are calculated see above, p. 729.

[62] See, for instance, Ogus & Richardson 1977; Tromans 1982.

parties in private nuisance cases, English law should not be so willing to grant injunctions in such cases: the granting of injunctions in private nuisance cases will sometimes give rise to economically inefficient results if the 'bargaining costs' between parties in private nuisance cases are high. Unfortunately, what evidence there is suggests that 'bargaining costs' between parties in private nuisance cases *are* high. A careful study of 20 American nuisance cases found that there was no serious bargaining after judgment in any of them.[63] This was in part because the litigation seemed to have resulted in animosity between the parties; also, winning claimants often seemed unwilling to treat their rights – for example, to freedom from noise, or freedom from smell – as things which could be commodified and sold. Consequently, there is some basis for suggesting that English courts should be more willing to grant damages in lieu of injunctions in private nuisance cases.

[63] Farnsworth 1999.

40 Specific restitution of goods

As we have seen, if A is in possession of certain goods and B has an immediate right to possess those goods, A will commit a tort – the tort of conversion – if he refuses to hand those goods over to B.[1] If A refuses to hand those goods over to B, s 3(2)(a) of the Torts (Interference with Goods) Act 1977 gives the courts the power to order A to do what he ought to do and hand those goods over to B.

One would have thought that if A is in possession of B's goods and has unlawfully refused to hand those goods over to B, the courts would *automatically* order A to hand those goods over to B. In fact, the courts will only order A to hand those goods over to B if those goods are unique or are of some special value. If they are not, then the courts will simply order A to hand over the goods *or* pay B damages equal to the value of the goods unlawfully detained by him, and it will be up to A to decide whether or not he will give B his goods back.[2] As Swinfen Eady MR observed in *Whiteley Limited* v *Hilt*: 'the power vested in the Court to order the delivery up of a particular chattel is discretionary and ought not to be exercised when the chattel is an ordinary article of commerce and of no special value or interest, and not alleged to be of any special value to the [claimant], and where damages would fully compensate.'[3]

In *Howard E Perry & Co. Ltd* v *British Railways Board*,[4] it will be recalled, the defendant board was in possession of steel belonging to the claimants. Industrial action prevented the defendant board from transporting the steel to the claimants' customers. At the same time the defendant board did not want to hand the steel over to the claimants for fear that doing so would trigger more industrial action. The defendants had no right to withhold the claimants' steel from the claimants and the claimants asked the courts to order the defendants to hand over the steel. The order was granted. The industrial action that obtained at the time the case was heard meant that steel was a very rare commodity. As a result, awarding the claimants damages equal to the market value of the steel detained by the defendants would not have allowed the claimants to purchase substitute supplies of steel that they could use instead of the steel detained by the defendants. Given this, the courts thought that the only appropriate remedy was to order the defendants to hand the claimants' steel over to the claimants.

It was argued that as the claimants merely wanted the steel to sell it to their customers, they should simply be awarded damages equal to the money they would have made by selling the steel. However, this argument was rejected on the ground that awarding the claimants such damages and nothing more would not adequately safeguard the claimants' interests. The claimants had an interest in keeping their customers supplied with steel

[1] See above, pp. 343–4.

[2] Torts (Interference with Goods) Act 1977, s 3(2)(b).

[3] [1918] 2 KB 808, 819. See also *IBL Ltd* v *Coussens* [1991] 2 All ER 133, 137h–j (per Neill LJ).

[4] [1980] 1 WLR 1375.

because their customers would become insolvent if they did not receive regular supplies of steel, and if the claimants' customers became insolvent, they would be in no position to do business with the claimants in future. This interest of the claimants' in keeping their customers supplied with steel would therefore not have been served at all if the claimants had merely been awarded damages designed to compensate them for the money they would have made if they had sold the steel detained by the defendants.

Visit **http://www.mylawchamber.co.uk/mcbride** to access updates on recent cases, as well as model answers and tips for answering tort problem questions.

Part IV

Alternative sources of compensation

Introduction

In this part of the book we leave tort law behind and explore some other areas of law which someone who wants to obtain compensation for some loss that he has suffered might be able to take advantage of. If he's entitled to bring such a claim for compensation under one of these areas of law, we can say that he's entitled to bring a *non-tortious claim for compensation*. The mark of a non-tortious claim for compensation is that whether or not someone is entitled to bring such a claim does *not* depend on whether a tort has been committed. In contrast, if someone wants to sue in tort for compensation for some loss that she has suffered, she will only be entitled to make such a claim – a *claim in tort* – if a tort has been committed.

Tortious and non-tortious claims for compensation can overlap: there are occasions when someone who has suffered a loss will be entitled to bring both a tortious claim for compensation in respect of that loss and a non-tortious claim. For example, suppose that A, a police officer, falsely imprisoned B for some considerable period of time. B will, of course, be entitled to bring a claim in tort against A for compensation for the loss that she suffered when she was locked up.[1] But B may also be entitled under the Human Rights Act 1998 to make a non-tortious claim against A for compensation for the loss that she suffered as a result of her being falsely imprisoned.[2] B may be able to argue that: (1) When A imprisoned me, he acted inconsistently with my right to liberty under Article 5 of the European Convention on Human Rights; (2) A was a 'public authority' at the time he unlawfully imprisoned me; (3) A's conduct in imprisoning me was therefore unlawful under s 6 of the Human Rights Act 1998 which provides that it 'is unlawful for a public authority to act in a way which is incompatible with a Convention right'; (4) I am therefore entitled, under s 8 of the 1998 Act, to sue A for damages sufficient to compensate me for the loss that I suffered as a result of A's locking me up.[3]

Again – to take an extreme example – suppose that B was walking round A's zoo when she was savaged by a tiger which had escaped from its cage when one of A's employees carelessly left it open. B will, of course, be entitled to bring a claim in tort against A for compensation for the losses – pain and suffering, loss of salary, cost of medical treatment – that she suffered as a result of being mauled by A's tiger. She will be able to establish that A's employee was negligent in relation to her in acting as he did and that A is vicariously liable in respect of that employee's negligence. But B will also be entitled under the Animals

[1] See Chapter 12, above.

[2] B will have a free choice as to which claim – the claim in tort or the non-tortious claim under the Human Rights Act 1998 – to pursue. Section 11 of the 1998 Act provides that 'A person's reliance on a Convention right does not restrict . . . his right to make any claim or bring any proceedings which he could make or bring apart from ss 7 to 9.'

[3] In fact, s 8 of the 1998 Act places strict limits on when damages may be awarded against a public authority that has acted inconsistently with someone's rights under the European Convention on Human Rights. See below, pp. 750–2.

Act 1971 to bring a non-tortious claim against A for compensation for the loss that she suffered as a result of being mauled by B's tiger. Section 2(1) of the 1971 Act provides that '[where] any damage is caused by an animal which belongs to a dangerous species, any person who is a keeper of the animal is liable for the damage . . .'.

We have just noted that the same set of facts can give rise to a claim in tort and a non-tortious claim for compensation. However, there are occasions when the only remedy available to someone who has suffered loss of some kind is to bring a non-tortious claim for compensation in respect of that loss. For example, suppose that the police knew that Fred, a criminal on the loose, was very likely to attack Sarah if he were not apprehended and, due to the police's carelessness, they did not manage to arrest Fred before he attacked Sarah. Suppose further that Sarah wants to sue the police for compensation for the losses suffered by her as a result of her being attacked by Fred. (Fred will probably not be worth suing.)

As the law currently stands, Sarah will not be able to bring a claim in tort against the police: the police will not have owed her a duty to take reasonable steps to arrest Fred before he attacked Sarah.[4] However, Sarah may be able to make a non-tortious claim against the police under the Human Rights Act 1998 for the compensation she wants. She may be able to argue that: (1) the police acted inconsistently with my right to liberty and security under Article 5 of the European Convention on Human Rights when they carelessly failed to apprehend Fred before he attacked me; (2) the police are a 'public authority' under the Human Rights Act 1998; (3) the police therefore acted unlawfully under s 6 of the 1998 Act when they carelessly failed to apprehend Fred before he attacked me; (4) I am therefore entitled under s 8 of the 1998 Act to sue the police for damages sufficient to compensate me for the losses that I suffered as a result of Fred attacking me.

Again, suppose that John was injured when he used a product manufactured by Lara that was dangerously defective. Suppose further that Lara took all reasonable steps to ensure that the product in question would not be dangerously defective – say Lara had a very strict quality control regime in her factory but somehow the product that injured John managed to slip through the net and into general circulation. John will obviously want to sue Lara for compensation for his injuries but he will not be able to bring a claim in tort against her for such compensation. This is because he will not be able to show that Lara was negligent in manufacturing the product that harmed him. At the same time he *will* be able to bring a non-tortious claim against Lara for compensation for his injuries under the Consumer Protection Act 1987.

[4] See above, pp. 54–5.

41 The Human Rights Act 1998

Section 6(1) of the Human Rights Act 1998 makes it unlawful for a 'public authority to act in a way which is incompatible with a Convention right', except where s 6(2) applies. If A, a public authority, acts in a way which is incompatible with a 'Convention right' in circumstances where s 6(2) does not apply and B suffers loss as a result, B may be able to claim damages from A under s 8 of the 1998 Act in respect of that loss. In making such a claim B will not have to allege that A committed a tort; as we have already seen, acting incompatibly with a 'Convention right' will not, of and in itself, amount to a tort.[1] All this raises four issues which we will deal with in this chapter:

(1) What is a public authority?
(2) When will a public authority be held to have acted in a way which was incompatible with a 'Convention right'?
(3) When will s 6(2) apply?
(4) If A, a public authority, acts in a way which is incompatible with a 'Convention right' and B suffers loss as a result, when will B be able to claim damages in respect of that loss?

WHAT IS A PUBLIC AUTHORITY?

The Human Rights Act 1998 does not define 'public authority'. It states that courts and tribunals *are* 'public authorities',[2] and that neither of the Houses of Parliament, nor any person exercising functions in connection with proceedings in Parliament, is a 'public authority'.[3] Beyond these classes, however, the Act merely provides that the term 'public authority' *includes* 'any person certain of whose functions are functions of a public nature'[4] *but* that such a person will not be a 'public authority' by virtue only of this provision when carrying out an act of a private nature.[5]

After reading this provision it might be thought that the question whether A is a 'person certain of whose functions are functions of a public nature' is the principal test for whether A is a 'public authority'. This, however, is not what Parliament intended.[6] Parliament intended that there should be two classes of 'public authorities'. First, *core* or *pure* public authorities, such as government departments, local authorities, the police and the armed

[1] See above, p. 9.
[2] Human Rights Act 1998, s 6(3)(a). The special problems arising from liability for judicial acts are discussed below, p. 753.
[3] Section 6(3)(b).
[4] Ibid.
[5] Section 6(5).
[6] When interpreting a statute it is Parliament's intention which is crucial. Here, however, the best evidence of Parliament's intentions is the statements of government ministers who were involved in steering the Human Rights Act 1998 onto the statute book.

forces,[7] which are treated as 'public authorities' for *all* activities. Secondly, *hybrid* or *functional* authorities, which are only treated as 'public authorities' with regard to acts which are part of their public functions.[8] In the parliamentary debates concerning the 1998 Act, Railtrack plc[9] was regularly used as an example of a *hybrid* or *functional* authority. Thus the Lord Chancellor suggested that Railtrack would have to act compatibly with 'Convention rights' when carrying out its *public* functions in relation to safety, but not when carrying out its *private* functions as a property developer.[10] The Home Secretary identified the churches and the governing bodies of certain sports as further authorities which might be treated as *hybrid*.[11] Another example might be a private security company which provided services to corporate clients and also ran a 'private' prison.

How do the courts determine whether a body is a *core* or *pure* 'public authority'? In *Aston Cantlow* v *Wallbank*,[12] Lord Nicholls said that the 'nature' of such bodies was 'governmental', and that factors leading to such a classification were likely to include 'the possession of special powers, democratic accountability, public funding in whole or in part, an obligation to act only in the public interest, and a statutory constitution'.

The courts have found it more difficult to agree how to determine whether a body is a *hybrid* public authority because some of its functions are 'of a public nature'. In *Aston Cantlow* v *Wallbank*,[13] Lord Nicholls concluded that 'there is no single test of universal application' which can determine whether a particular function is 'of a public nature' because of 'the diverse nature of governmental functions and the variety of means by which these functions are discharged today'. He went on, however, to identify several *relevant* factors, and subsequent cases have also adopted a 'factor-based' approach. Within such an

[7] These are the examples given by Lord Nicholls in *Aston Cantlow and Wilmcote with Billesley Parochial Church Council* v *Wallbank* (henceforth '*Aston Cantlow* v *Wallbank*') [2004] 1 AC 546, at [7].

[8] In *Aston Cantlow* v *Wallbank* [2004] 1 AC 546 the two classes are referred to (at [11]) as 'core public authorities' and 'hybrid public authorities'. But in its reports the Joint Committee on Human Rights, *The Meaning of Public Authority under the Human Rights Act, Seventh Report of the Session 2003–4* (HL Paper 39, HC 382) and *The Meaning of Public Authority under the Human Rights Act, Ninth Report of the Session 2006–7* (HL Paper 77, HC 410), prefers the terms 'pure' and 'functional'. For evidence that two classes were intended see, for example, Lord Irvine of Lairg LC, Hansard (HL Debates), 24 November 1997, col. 784, 'There are obvious public authorities . . . which are covered in relation to the whole of their functions by [s 6(1)]. Then there are some bodies some of whose functions are public and some private. If there are some public functions the body qualifies as a public authority but not in respect of acts which are of a private nature.' See also Jack Straw MP, Home Secretary, Hansard (HC Debates), 16 February 1998, col. 775.

[9] The private company in which the infrastructure of the railway system was vested after privatisation. In 2001, Railtrack was put into administration, changed its name, and was purchased by Network Rail Ltd.

[10] Hansard (HL Debates), 24 November 1997, col. 784. Many of Railtrack's duties relating to the *regulation* of safety were removed by the Railways (Safety Case) Regulations 2000 (SI 2000/2688) and in *Cameron* v *Network Rail Infrastructure Ltd* [2007] 1 WLR 163 Sir Michael Turner held that the company was not *thereafter* a 'public authority' under the Human Rights Act.

[11] Hansard (HC Debates), 20 May 1998, col. 1020. At col. 1017 he stated that 'the two most obvious examples' of churches carrying out *public* functions 'relate to marriages and to the provision of education in Church schools'. Despite pressure Parliament did not exclude churches from the scope of s 6 but instead sought to allay concerns by accepting the amendment which became s 13 Human Rights Act 1998. In *Aston Cantlow* v *Wallbank* [2004] 1 AC 546 the House of Lords confirmed that parochial church councils, an emanation of the Church of England, were a hybrid body.

[12] [2004] 1 AC 546, [7]. He drew attention to Oliver 2000, where it is suggested (at 492) that the test for a *core* public authority should 'place emphasis on whether it enjoys special powers and authority, and whether it is under constitutional duties to act only in the public interest which are "enforceable", *inter alia*, via mechanisms of democratic accountability'.

[13] [2004] 1 AC 546, [12].

approach '[a] number of factors may be relevant, but none is likely to be determinative on its own and the weight of different factors will vary from case to case'.[14]

What factors are relevant? In order to answer this question it is necessary to look in detail at the case of *YL* v *Birmingham City Council*,[15] where the House of Lords had to decide whether Southern Cross Healthcare Ltd (SCH), an independent company, was performing a function 'of a public nature' by providing YL, an elderly sufferer from Alzheimer's disease, with residential care in one of its care homes. Most of the fees for this care were being paid by Birmingham City Council, which had a statutory duty to 'make arrangements for providing' residential care for YL. Thus the case raised the more general question of whether private companies and charities delivering services under contracts with pure public authorities, particularly local government bodies, are *functional* 'public authorities'.[16] A majority of the House of Lords held that SCH, when caring for YL, was not carrying out 'functions of a public nature'.[17]

One factor which Lord Nicholls identified as relevant in *Aston Cantlow* v *Wallbank* was 'the extent to which in carrying out the relevant function the body is publicly funded'.[18] But while the majority in the *YL* case accepted that 'public funding' was relevant, they thought that it was important to distinguish between a company which was seeking to make a profit receiving a commercial fee under a contract with a public authority and a company receiving a 'subsidy' from public funds.[19]

The majority in the *YL* case also agreed with Lord Nicholls that a second relevant factor was 'the extent to which in carrying out the relevant function the body ... is exercising statutory powers'.[20] Indeed the majority treated the *absence* of special powers as particularly significant in the *YL* case because SCH provided similar residential care for both publicly-funded and privately-funded clients, and it would be anomalous if the nature of its function changed from client to client.[21]

Further factors identified by Lord Nicholls in *Aston Cantlow* v *Wallbank*[22] were 'the extent to which in carrying out the relevant function the body ... is taking the place of central government or local authorities, or is providing a public service'. The majority in the *YL* case, however, were cautious about how these factors might be understood. In particular they thought that very little weight could be attached to the fact that a function had previously been performed by a *core* public authority, or could have been performed by a

14 *YL* v *Birmingham City Council* [2007] 3 WLR 112, [5] (per Lord Bingham). Although Lord Bingham was in the minority with regard to the outcome of this appeal his general description of a 'factor-based' approach is *not* what divided the House of Lords. The matters which did divide the court are discussed in the next paragraphs of the text.

15 [2007] 3 WLR 112.

16 Important cases *before* the *YL* case included *Poplar Housing and Regeneration Community Association Ltd* v *Donoghue* [2002] QB 48 and *R (Heather)* v *Leonard Cheshire Foundation* [2002] 2 All ER 936. These were criticised in Craig 2002 and by the Joint Committee on Human Rights, *The Meaning of Public Authority under the Human Rights Act, Seventh Report of the Session 2003–4* (HL Paper 39, HC 382), para 16–17: 'A serious gap has opened in the protection which the Human Rights Act was intended to offer.'

17 The majority comprised Lord Scott, Lord Mance and Lord Neuberger. Lord Bingham and Baroness Hale dissented.

18 [2004] 1 AC 546, [12].

19 [2007] 3 WLR 112, [27] (per Lord Scott), [105] (per Lord Mance), [165] (per Lord Neuberger).

20 [2004] 1 AC 546, [12] (per Lord Nicholls); [2007] 3 WLR 112, [28] (per Lord Scott), [102] (per Lord Mance), [160] (per Lord Neuberger).

21 [2007] 3 WLR 112, [117]–[119] (per Lord Mance), [151] (per Lord Neuberger).

22 [2004] 1 AC 546, [12].

core public authority instead of being 'contracted out'. Lord Mance argued that the fact that a function was sometimes performed by *core* public authorities did not establish that it was a '*public* function' because the Human Rights Act 1998 applies to *all* functions, public or private, performed by *core* public authorities,[23] whilst Lord Neuberger drew attention to the wide range of functions undertaken by *core* public authorities.[24] In contrast, the minority in the *YL* case attached considerable importance to whether the State had 'assumed responsibility' for seeing that a particular task was performed[25] and to whether it was in the public interest for it to be performed, something that might be demonstrated by the task being regulated by the State. The majority, however, doubted the significance of both regulation[26] and 'the public interest' in a service being performed.[27] The minority also attached more significance than the majority to whether the improper performance of a function was likely to lead to the violation of an individual's 'Convention rights'.[28]

Standing back, we think that it is possible to describe the majority in the *YL* case as having concentrated on how a function might appear from the perspective of the person performing it, while the minority focused on the perspective of the person whose 'Convention rights' were at stake. Thus SCH probably would have described its function as to provide a service under a contract for a commercial fee, whilst YL's relatives probably would have described her as a vulnerable person receiving the necessary care which it is the State's responsibility to provide. For the time being[29] the majority's approach is the law, so, the most important factors in identifying a function as 'of a public nature' are 'public funding' (in the form of a subsidy rather than a commercial fee) and the grant of special powers (such as the power to regulate a particular field of activity or the sort of powers granted to the operator of a private prison).

[23] [2007] 3 WLR 112, [110] (per Lord Mance), 'it is a fallacy to regard all functions and activities of a core public authority as inherently public in nature', citing Oliver 2004.

[24] Ibid., [144] (per Lord Neuberger), 'Apart from anything else, there must be scarcely an activity which cannot be carried out by some core public authority.' See also [30] (per Lord Scott).

[25] Ibid. [7], [15] (per Lord Bingham), [66] (per Baroness Hale).

[26] Ibid., [116] (per Lord Mance), 'Regulation by the state is no real pointer towards the person regulated being a state or governmental body or a person with a function of a public nature, if anything perhaps the contrary.' See also [134] (per Lord Neuberger). To the contrary, [9] (per Lord Bingham).

[27] Ibid., [134] (per Lord Neuberger): 'The fact that a service can fairly be said to be to the public benefit cannot mean, as a matter of language, that it follows that providing the service itself is a function of a public nature. Nor does it follow as a matter of logic or policy. Otherwise, the services of all charities, indeed, it seems to me, of all private organizations which provide services which could be offered by charities, would be caught by section 6(1).' To the contrary, [67] (per Baroness Hale).

[28] Ibid. [11] (per Lord Bingham), [71] (per Baroness Hale).

[29] The UK Parliament's Joint Committee on Human Rights has been critical in the past of the position adopted by the majority in the *YL* case (see its reports *The Meaning of Public Authority under the Human Rights Act, Seventh Report of the Session 2003–4* (HL Paper 39, HC 382) and *The Meaning of Public Authority under the Human Rights Act, Ninth Report of the Session 2006–7* (HL Paper 77, HC 410)) and subsequent to the case the Committee's Chairman presented a Human Rights Act 1998 (Meaning of Public Function) Bill (Hansard (HC Debates), 18 December 2007, col. 741–4) and persuaded a Minister to announce the Government's intention to legislate to reverse the decision (Hansard (HC Debates), 13 November 2007, col. 526–7). For an impressive academic analysis of the issues from a comparative perspective see Donnelly 2007.

WHEN WILL A PUBLIC AUTHORITY ACT INCOMPATIBLY WITH A 'CONVENTION RIGHT'?

The scope of this book does not allow us to deal with this issue in detail; the interested reader should consult a standard work on the Human Rights Act 1998. However, a few preliminary points may be made here.

Convention rights

The term 'Convention rights' refers to the rights and fundamental freedoms set out in Articles 2 to 12 and 14 of the Convention for the Protection of Human Rights and Fundamental Freedoms ('the European Convention on Human Rights') and in Articles 1 to 3 of the First Protocol and Articles 1 to 2 of the Sixth Protocol.[30]

These include: the right to life (Article 2), the right not to be subjected to torture or to inhuman and degrading treatment (Article 3), the right not to be enslaved or compelled to perform forced labour (Article 4), the right to liberty and security of person (Article 5), the right to a fair trial (Article 6), the right not to be retrospectively convicted of committing an offence (Article 7), the right to respect for private and family life (Article 8), the right to freedom of thought, conscience and religion (Article 9), the right to freedom of expression (Article 10), the right to freedom of peaceful assembly and freedom of association (Article 11), the right to marry (Article 12), the right not to be discriminated against in the enjoyment of the other rights and freedoms (Article 14), the right to peaceful enjoyment of possessions (First Protocol, Article 1), the right to education (First Protocol, Article 2), and the right to free elections (First Protocol, Article 3).

Many of these 'Convention rights' stretch beyond the interests currently protected by the law of tort. To pick one example, there is no tort designed to protect directly a person's right to a fair trial (Article 6) or a person's right to marry (Article 12). Further, some of the 'Convention rights' offer greater protection for particular interests than is provided by the law of tort.[31] Consequently, it seems likely that there will be attempts to claim damages under s 8 of the Human Rights Act 1998 for violations of many, if not all, of these 'Convention rights'.[32]

It is important to bear in mind that not all of these rights are *absolute*. Many of the rights *expressly* permit restrictions, provided that such restrictions can be demonstrated to be 'prescribed by law' and 'necessary in a democratic society' in order to fulfil certain listed purposes. Where a public authority's act goes no further than a permitted restriction or interference it will not be incompatible with a 'Convention right'.

[30] These articles are all set out in Sch 1 to the Human Rights Act 1998.

[31] A good example is provided by Art 2, the right to life. In *Osman* v *United Kingdom* [1999] 1 FLR 193, the European Court of Human Rights suggested that Art 2 puts a broader duty on police to take steps to deal with threats to life by criminals than is imposed on the police by the common law. This has been relied on to bring a claim against the police for failing to take appropriate steps to protect the life of a witness in circumstances where a claim relying on the tort of negligence would have failed: *Van Colle* v *Chief Constable of the Hertfordshire Police* [2007] 1 WLR 1821. See also *Savage* v *South Essex Partnership NHS Foundation Trust* [2007] EWCA Civ 1375 (failure by an NHS hospital to take reasonable steps to prevent a patient detained pursuant to s 3 of the Mental Health Act 1983 from absconding and committing suicide).

[32] Of course, in practice, some of the 'Convention rights' are violated by public authorities far more often than others.

Acts and omissions

'Failures to act' by a public authority are treated as 'acts' for the purpose of determining whether it has acted in a way which is incompatible with a 'Convention right'.[33] This provision is particularly important in those contexts where it has been held that the Convention imposes a *positive* obligation on states to protect 'Convention rights'.

For instance, in *Osman* v *United Kingdom*[34] the European Court of Human Rights ruled that Article 2 imposed a positive obligation on a state to protect an individual whose life was at risk from criminal acts, and that this included an obligation on the police to 'do all that could be reasonably expected of them to avoid a real and immediate risk to life of which they have or ought to have knowledge'.[35] Similarly, in *Z* v *United Kingdom*,[36] the European Court of Human Rights held that there was a parallel positive obligation under Article 3 on local authorities to take all steps that could reasonably be expected of them to avoid a real and immediate risk of ill-treatment of children of which they knew or ought to have had knowledge.[37] In *Anufrijeva* v *Southwark LBC*[38] the Court of Appeal accepted that Article 8 also imposed a positive obligation which extended beyond the obligation under Article 3 where a family unit was involved.[39] The Court offered the following guidance on when inaction would constitute a lack of respect for private and family life:

> [T]here must be some ground for criticising the failure to act. There must be an element of culpability. At the very least there must be knowledge that the claimant's private and family life were at risk ... Where the domestic law of a state imposes positive obligations in relation to the provision of welfare support, breach of those positive obligations of domestic law may suffice to provide the element of culpability necessary to establish a breach of article 8, provided that the impact on private or family life is sufficiently serious and was foreseeable.[40]

Although the Human Rights Act 1998 generally covers omissions as well as acts, s 6(6) makes it clear that a failure to introduce a proposal for legislation or to make a remedial order cannot be treated as an unlawful 'act'.

WHEN WILL SECTION 6(2) APPLY?

Section 6(2) of the 1998 Act provides that a public authority will not be liable for an act which violates a 'Convention right' if '(a) as the result of one or more provisions of primary legislation, the authority could not have acted differently; or (b) in the case of one or more provisions of, or made under, primary legislation which cannot be read or given effect in a

33 Human Rights Act 1998, s 6(6).
34 [1999] 1 FLR 193.
35 Ibid., 223G–H. On the facts, though, the European Court of Human Rights found that there had not been a violation of Art 2.
36 *Z* v *United Kingdom* [2001] 2 FLR 612.
37 Ibid., at [73].
38 *Anufrijeva* v *Southwark London Borough Council* [2004] QB 1124.
39 Ibid., at [43]. The Court suggested that where only an individual's welfare was involved it was unlikely that Art 8 would require the State to provide positive support unless the individual's predicament was sufficiently severe to engage Art 3.
40 Ibid., at [45]. This passage clearly involves a jumble of conditions. It seems that the Court of Appeal intended that three elements should be relevant (the degree to which the public authority was at fault, whether the inaction breached a statutory duty, and the effect on the claimant) and that a decision whether there had been a breach of Art 8 should turn on the combined effect of these three elements.

way which is compatible with the Convention rights, the authority was acting so as to give effect to or enforce those provisions.' This provision means that a public authority cannot be liable for performing a statutory duty, even if this leads to a violation of a 'Convention right'. In such circumstances the most that an English court will be able to do is to declare that the statutory provision is incompatible with a 'Convention right'.[41] Similarly, a public authority will not be liable for enforcing or giving effect to an incompatible statute or delegated legislation, where that legislation cannot be given effect to in any way which is compatible.

THE AVAILABILITY OF COMPENSATORY DAMAGES

The 'victim' requirement[42]

If B has suffered loss as a result of a public authority's acting incompatibly with a 'Convention right', B will not be able to claim damages in respect of that loss unless he was a 'victim' of the public authority's unlawful act.[43] The Human Rights Act 1998 expressly relies on the definition of 'victim' developed in individual claims to the European Court of Human Rights under Article 34 of the European Convention on Human Rights.[44] A person will have no difficulty in establishing that she is a 'victim' if she has been 'directly affected' by the public authority's unlawful act. In certain circumstances, however, the European Court of Human Rights has also allowed claims by 'indirect victims', for instance, close relatives of a person whose right to life was violated.[45] Companies and other associations with legal personality can be 'victims',[46] but *core* public authorities cannot be.[47]

Courts able to award damages

Where a court finds that a public authority has acted incompatibly with a 'Convention right' it may only award damages if it is a type of court which can award damages in civil proceedings.[48]

Principles relevant to awards of damages[49]

Section 8(3) of the Human Rights Act 1998 states that a court should not award damages unless, taking account of all the circumstances of the case, it 'is satisfied that the award is

41 Human Rights Act 1998, s 4.
42 See, generally, Miles 2000.
43 Human Rights Act 1998, s 7(1).
44 Section 7(7).
45 *Mrs W* v *United Kingdom* (1983) 32 D&R 10. In *Van Colle* v *Chief Constable of the Hertfordshire Police* [2007] 1 WLR 1821, [114], the Court of Appeal left open for 'future consideration' the question whether an 'indirect victim' can recover damages for his or her *own* losses, as opposed to obtaining an award as a representative of the 'direct victim'. The point is of some importance because in several recent cases, for instance *Cameron* v *Network Rail Infrastructure Ltd* [2007] 1 WLR 163, relatives of a person who has been killed have brought claims under the Human Rights Act 1998 in circumstances where they could not have successfully obtained damages under the Fatal Accidents Act 1976. For discussion of the relevant provisions of the Fatal Accidents Act 1976 see above, pp. 631–40.
46 Provided that the right that they are asserting is one which can be enjoyed by such a body.
47 *Aston Cantlow* v *Wallbank* [2004] 1 AC 546 at [8], 'A core public authority seems inherently incapable of satisfying the Convention description of a victim' (per Lord Nicholls).
48 Human Rights Act 1998, s 8(1). This is thought to prevent awards by magistrates and the Crown Court. The position of the Court of Appeal (Criminal Division) is unclear.
49 See, generally, Fairgrieve 2001; also McGregor 2003, 1541–9.

necessary to afford just satisfaction to the person in whose favour it is made'. In considering whether it is necessary to make such an award, and, if so, the amount, courts are instructed to 'take into account the principles applied by the European Court of Human Rights in relation to the award of compensation under Art 41 of the Convention'.[50] This instruction might seem relatively loose, since it is an instruction 'to take into account', not 'to follow'; and it refers to 'principles', not 'detailed practice'. But in *R (Greenfield)* v *Secretary of State for the Home Department*[51] a unanimous House of Lords held that domestic courts should follow the Strasbourg court's guidance with regard to both *when* an award should be made and the *amount* because 'the purpose of incorporating the Convention in domestic law through the 1998 Act was not to give victims better remedies at home than they could recover in Strasbourg but to give them the same remedies without the delay and expense of resort to Strasbourg'.

Before the Human Rights Act 1998 came into force the Law Commission carried out a survey of the 'principles' applied by the European Court of Human Rights.[52] It found that 'the only principle which is clearly stated in the Strasbourg case-law is that of *restitutio in integrum*'.[53] That is: the victim should be returned, as far as possible, to the position that he or she would have been in had there not been a breach of a 'Convention right'. The Court of Appeal has described this as 'the fundamental principle' and has derived from it the proposition that 'where the breach of a Convention right has clearly caused significant pecuniary loss, this will usually be assessed and awarded'. Despite describing the *restitutio in integrum* principle as 'fundamental' the Court of Appeal has also emphasised the further principle that, 'in considering whether to award compensation and, if so, how much, there is a balance to be drawn between the interests of the victim and those of the public as a whole'.[54] This means that the claimant's interest in receiving compensation must be weighed against the interest of the wider public in the continued funding of public services.

The Law Commission identified five specific factors which seem to have been regularly taken into account by the European Court of Human Rights in determining whether or not to make an award of damages.[55]

(1) *A finding of a violation may constitute 'just satisfaction'*. Where an applicant has not suffered pecuniary loss as a result of a breach, the European Court of Human Rights has often concluded that the mere decision that there was a violation is sufficient to constitute 'just satisfaction'. This factor has been most influential in cases where convicted criminals have claimed that while they were being investigated or tried there were violations of a procedural type.[56]

(2) *The degree of loss suffered must be sufficient to justify an award of damages*. Although the European Court of Human Rights has generally been more willing to award damages for

[50] Section 8(4).
[51] [2005] 1 WLR 673, [19].
[52] Law Com. No. 266, *Damages Under the Human Rights Act 1998* (2000).
[53] Ibid., para 3.78.
[54] *Anufrijeva* v *Southwark LBC* [2004] QB 1124 at [56].
[55] Law Com. No. 266, para 4.44.
[56] In *R (Greenfield)* v *Secretary of State for the Home Department* [2005] 1 WLR 673, the House of Lords decided that no damages should be awarded to a prisoner whose Art 6 'Convention right' was violated when a deputy controller, who was not an independent and impartial tribunal, decided that he had committed a prison disciplinary offence. The court concluded, however, a procedural violation could lead to an award of damages if the violation led to the claimant being 'deprived of a real chance of a better outcome' (see, [14]–[15]) or caused 'anxiety and frustration' (see, [16]).

non-pecuniary losses than English courts dealing with tort claims, it has also usually insisted that something beyond mere annoyance or frustration must be shown before an award of damages will be appropriate.[57] In *R (KB)* v *London and South and West Region Mental Health Review Tribunal*,[58] Stanley Burnton J concluded that mental health patients who had suffered frustration and distress because of inordinate delay in processing their claims to mental health review tribunals in violation of Article 5(4) were only entitled to compensation for significant distress, which he took to be distress at the level that might be recorded in clinical notes.

(3) *The seriousness of the violation will be taken into account.* Generous awards have been made for both pecuniary and non-pecuniary losses where there has been a serious violation, for instance, deliberate torture.[59] At the same time, however, the European Court of Human Rights has expressly refused to award 'aggravated damages'[60] and 'exemplary damages'.[61] It seems that despite this refusal the European Court of Human Rights does take account of 'aggravating features' in assessing damages, particularly for distress, anxiety and injury to feelings.

(4) *The conduct of the public authority may be taken into account.* This may include both the conduct giving rise to the application and a record of previous violations by the State. Although the European Court of Human Rights has expressly refused to award 'exemplary damages' in cases where someone's Convention rights have been violated it tends to be more generous in compensating for non-pecuniary loss when the behaviour of the public authority in question has been particularly reprehensible[62] or forms part of a pattern of violations.[63] In *Anufrijeva* v *Southwark LBC*[64] the Court of Appeal treated the wording of s 8 as precluding an award of exemplary damages.[65]

The question has been asked whether a claimant will have to show that a breach of Convention rights was the result of a public authority's carelessness in order to claim damages.[66] The simple answer to this question must be 'no'. The more detailed answer will add the qualifications that *in some circumstances* the claimant will have to show fault on the

57 *Silver* v *United Kingdom* (1991) 13 EHRR 582. In *R (Greenfield)* v *Secretary of State for the Home Department* [2005] 1 WLR 673, the House of Lords did not suggest that feelings of 'anxiety and frustration' had to reach any particular pitch before an award of damages could be made *but* nonetheless refused to make an award to the claimant in the case confronting them. The court apparently attached weight to the facts that although the claimant had demonstrated 'structural bias' the conduct of the adjudication was exemplary and he was not treated in an unexpected way or differently from anyone else (see, [29]).

58 [2004] QB 936.

59 *Aksoy* v *Turkey* (1997) 23 EHRR 553.

60 Discussed in Chapter 35, above.

61 Discussed in Chapter 36, above.

62 Two cases involving the United Kingdom provide good examples of this factor in action: *Halford* v *United Kingdom* (1997) 24 EHRR 523 (£10,000 awarded for stress caused by phone-tapping); *Smith and Grady* v *United Kingdom* (2000) 29 EHRR 493 (£19,000 awarded for non-pecuniary loss suffered as a result of investigation and dismissal from the armed forces because of sexual orientation).

63 Cases involving excessive length of legal proceedings in Italy provide the best example of this factor in action: Law Com. No. 266, paras 3.52–3.53.

64 [2004] QB 1124.

65 Ibid. at [55]. The House of Lords has suggested, however, that one reason why an award of damages may be appropriate, rather than a finding of a violation being held to be just satisfaction, is if 'there is felt to be a need to encourage compliance [with their duties under the Convention] by individual officials or classes of official: *R (Greenfield)* v *Secretary of State for the Home Department* [2005] 1 WLR 673, [19].

66 Fairgrieve 2001, 698.

part of the public authority in order to establish that the authority acted incompatibly with a particular Convention right,[67] and *in some circumstances* the fault of the public authority may be decisive in demonstrating that an award of compensation is necessary as 'just satisfaction' and reflects the appropriate balance between the interests of the victim and those of the public as a whole.

(5) *The conduct of the applicant will be taken into account.* An award will be reduced where the applicant's conduct made a violation more likely or contributed to the damage suffered as a result of a violation.[68] There is some evidence of a general reluctance to compensate criminals for violations of their 'Convention rights'.[69]

Quantification of damages[70]

With regard to the quantification of damages the Law Commission concluded that 'in many cases – probably the majority of cases – the terms of section 8, read in the light of our review of the Strasbourg case-law, will not require [a court] awarding damages under the [Human Rights Act 1998] to apply measures which are significantly different to those it would reach were the claim one in tort'.[71] And in an early case under s 8, Lord Woolf instructed courts making awards for kinds of harm not commonly compensated for by common law damages to consider the level of awards for such harm commonly made by the Parliamentary Ombudsman and Local Government Ombudsman.[72] But in *R (Greenfield)* v *Secretary of State for the Home Department*,[73] as we noted above, the House of Lords suggested that courts should look instead primarily to awards made by the European Court of Human Rights and 'should not aim to be significantly more or less generous than [that] court might be expected to be'.[74] This guidance may prove difficult to follow since the European Court of Human Rights maintains a broad and flexible discretion in assessing damages which 'takes account of a range of factors including the character and conduct of the parties, to an extent which is hitherto unknown in English law'.[75]

Before the Human Rights Act 1998 came into force Lord Woolf expressed the view, extra-judicially, that awards made by English courts under s 8 for non-pecuniary losses should be 'moderate',[76] and this comment has been judicially endorsed.[77]

[67] For instance, where the Convention right imposes a positive obligation to take *reasonable* steps, a claimant will only be able to show that an omission to take steps was incompatible if it would have been *reasonable* to take such steps. Similarly, it seems that simple negligence in the care and treatment of a patient in hospital resulting in the patient's death is not sufficient in itself to amount to a breach of the State's positive obligations under Art 2 to protect life (*Powell* v *United Kingdom* (2000) 30 EHRR CD 152) but gross negligence, sufficient to sustain a charge of manslaughter, may be: see, *Savage* v *South Essex Partnership NHS Foundation Trust* [2007] EWCA Civ 1375.

[68] In *McCann* v *United Kingdom* (1996) 21 EHRR 97, the European Court of Human Rights found a violation of Art 2 (right to life) with respect to three IRA terrorists suspected of planning a bomb attack on Gibraltar, but refused to award compensation because of the applicants' behaviour.

[69] Law Com. No. 266, para. 3.57 discusses the different views on this matter.

[70] See, generally, McGregor 2003, 1549–72.

[71] Law Com. No. 266, para 4.97.

[72] *Anufrijeva* v *Southwark LBC* [2004] QB 1124, [74].

[73] [2005] 1 WLR 673.

[74] Ibid., [19].

[75] Law Com. No. 266, para 4.96.

[76] Woolf 2000, 434.

Liability for judicial acts

Section 9(3) of the Human Rights Act 1998 states that 'In proceedings under this Act in respect of a judicial act done in good faith, damages may not be awarded otherwise than to compensate a person to the extent required by Art 5(5) of the Convention'. Article 5(5) provides that 'Everyone who has been the victim of arrest or detention in contravention of the provisions of this Art [5] shall have an enforceable right to compensation.' In practice, the European Court of Human Rights has not interpreted Article 5(5) as requiring that every victim of a violation of Article 5 must be awarded compensation. Indeed, the Strasbourg Court has often ruled that the finding that Article 5 was violated is itself sufficient 'just satisfaction'.

Section 9(3) may be important, however, in that it precludes an award of damages for a good faith violation by a judge of, for instance, Article 6 (right to a fair trial) or Article 8 (right to respect for private or family life). To an extent, it may be possible to circumvent this by attributing the violation to the act of some other public authority, for instance, a public prosecutor. This will not always be possible, however, because s 9(5) defines 'judicial act' as including 'an act done on the instructions, or on behalf, of a judge'.

Liability for legislative acts

For the avoidance of doubt it is worth stating that because 'public authority' does not include 'either House of Parliament or a person exercising functions in connection with proceedings in Parliament'[78] there will be no liability under s 8 of the Human Rights Act 1998 for legislation which violates a 'Convention right'. Further, because 'act' does not include 'a failure to (a) introduce in, or lay before, Parliament a proposal for legislation, or (b) make any primary legislation or remedial order',[79] there will be no liability under s 8 of the Human Rights Act 1998 for a ministerial failure to correct legislation which violates a 'Convention right'.

Visit **http://www.mylawchamber.co.uk/mcbride** to access updates on recent cases, as well as model answers and tips for answering tort problem questions.

[77] *Anufrijeva* v *Southwark LBC* [2004] QB 1124, [73]. Lord Woolf also stated extra-judicially that awards should be 'normally on the low side by comparison to tortious awards', but in the same paragraph that endorsed his view that awards should be 'moderate' the Court of Appeal said that the 'on the low side' comment 'should in future be ignored'. In *R (Greenfield)* v *Secretary of State for the Home Department* [2005] 1 WLR 673, [19], the House of Lords suggested that damages under the Human Rights Act 1998 might seem modest alongside tort awards because in Human Rights Act cases the finding of a violation would always be 'an important part' of a claimant's remedy.

[78] Human Rights Act 1998, s 6(3)(b).

[79] Section 6(6).

42 Liability for dangerous things

If A keeps, stores or uses a dangerous thing that escapes from A's control with the result that B suffers some kind of harm, B may be entitled to bring a non-tortious claim against A so as to be compensated for the harm that she has suffered under: (1) the rule in *Rylands* v *Fletcher*; (2) some liability rule analogous to the rule in *Rylands* v *Fletcher*; or (3) the Animals Act 1971.[1]

THE RULE IN *RYLANDS* v *FLETCHER*

There is continuing debate over the scope of the rule in *Rylands* v *Fletcher*. However, the recent decision of the House of Lords in *Transco plc* v *Stockport Metropolitan Borough Council*[2] seems to establish that the rule applies where A has brought onto, or kept on, some land an *exceptionally dangerous or mischievous thing in extraordinary or unusual circumstances*. Let's call the thing in question 'T' and the land which that thing was brought onto, or kept on, 'Blackacre'. The rule in *Rylands* v *Fletcher* – as interpreted by the House of Lords in *Transco* – says that if:

(1) T *escapes* from Blackacre and
(2) T consequently *damages B's land*[3] then
(3) B will be entitled to sue A for compensation for that damage unless
(4) A can raise a *defence* to B's claim.[4]

Importantly, in order to sue A for compensation under the rule in *Rylands* v *Fletcher*, B will *not* have to prove that A was at fault for the fact that T escaped from Blackacre.

Rylands v *Fletcher*: the litigation[5]

In the 1860s John Rylands was the leading textile manufacturer in England. He arranged for contractors to build a reservoir to provide water for the steam engines which powered

[1] B's claim for damages under any of these heads of liability will be non-tortious in nature because, in order to succeed in bringing a claim for damages under any of these heads, she will *not* have to prove that A committed any kind of legal wrong in relation to her either in keeping, storing or using the dangerous thing which harmed her or in failing to ensure that that dangerous thing did not harm her.

[2] [2004] 2 AC 1 (noted, Bagshaw 2004b). We will refer to this case hereafter as '*Transco*'.

[3] When we use the phrase 'B's land' in this context we intend the word 'land' to include not just the earth itself but also things attached to it, such as buildings, which count as real property. The statement that the land must be 'B's' is shorthand for the fact that in order to claim B must have a particular relationship with the land. The precise nature of that necessary relationship is discussed below, pp. 757–8. At this stage, an adequate summary is that the land will count as 'B's land' if B has a legally-recognised interest in the land, and in certain circumstances it may be sufficient that B has exclusive possession of the land.

[4] This statement of the rule is based on the formulation of Lord Bingham in *Transco*, at [11].

[5] The crucial judgments in this litigation are those of Blackburn J for the Court of Exchequer Chamber (at (1866) LR 1 Ex 265) and of the House of Lords (at (1868) LR 3 HL 330).

the looms in one of his mills. The reservoir was built over old mine shafts which had been filled with earth, but one of these plugs of earth gave way and water escaped from the reservoir into the mine workings. It flowed through some abandoned mine workings and flooded a mine worked by Thomas Fletcher.

In the Court of Exchequer Martin B found that Rylands was not liable to compensate Fletcher for the flooding to his mine.[6] He stated that 'the making of a pond for holding water is a nuisance to no one'.[7] This must be correct: a pond does not *in itself* interfere unreasonably with the interests of neighbours. But Martin B went on to say that even when the water in a pond escaped the owner of the land on which it was built should not be liable, because 'To hold the defendants liable would . . . make them insurers against the consequences of a lawful act upon their own land when they had no reason to believe or suspect that any damage was likely to ensue.'[8] As it was not reasonably foreseeable that building a reservoir on Rylands' land would result in Fletcher suffering any harm, it could not be argued that Rylands owed Fletcher a duty not to build a reservoir on his land. So it was not possible to argue that Rylands committed any kind of wrong – let alone a tort – in building the reservoir on his land.

On appeal, however, the Court of Exchequer Chamber decided the case in favour of the claimant, Fletcher. Blackburn J said,

> We think the rule of law is, that the person who, for his own purposes, brings on his land and collects and keeps there anything likely to do mischief if it escapes, must keep it in at his peril; and if he does not do so, is *prima facie* answerable for all the damage which is the natural consequence of its escape. He can excuse himself by showing that the escape was owing to the claimant's default; or perhaps that the escape was the consequence of *vis major*, or the act of God.

He went on to explain the justice of this rule:

> It seems but reasonable and just that the neighbour who has brought something onto his own property (which was not naturally there), harmless to others so long as it is confined to his own property, but which he knows will be mischievous if it gets on his neighbour's, should be obliged to make good the damage which ensues if he does not succeed in confining it to his own property.[9]

In the House of Lords Lord Cairns LC quoted the rule and the explanation for it then stated, 'I must say I entirely concur.'[10] Lord Cranworth similarly supported Blackburn J's exposition of the law.[11] However, Lord Cairns LC suggested that the rule of liability formulated by Blackburn J would *only* apply to someone who had in the course of a *non-natural use* of his land brought onto or stored on his land something which was liable to do damage if it escaped.[12] This limit on the application of the rule in *Rylands* v *Fletcher* – as originally formulated by Blackburn J – has been followed ever since.

[6] *Rylands* v *Fletcher* (1865) 3 H & C 774, 159 ER 737.
[7] Ibid., 792, 745.
[8] Ibid., 793, 745.
[9] (1866) LR 1 Ex 265, 279–80.
[10] (1868) LR 3 HL 330, 340.
[11] Ibid. Three Law Lords heard the appeal in *Rylands* v *Fletcher* but there is some mystery as to who the third Law Lord was. See, generally, Heuston 1970.
[12] (1868) LR 3 HL 330, 339.

The rationale of the rule in *Rylands* v *Fletcher*

Lord Hoffmann has explained that 'it is tempting to see, beneath the surface of the rule, a policy of requiring the costs of a commercial enterprise to be internalised; to require the entrepreneur to provide, by insurance or otherwise, for the risks to others which his enterprise creates'.[13] But in most contexts English law has rejected this policy and has insisted that entrepreneurs (and others) should only be liable for damage caused by their *wrongs*. Thus, quoting Lord Hoffmann again, 'with hindsight, *Rylands* v *Fletcher* can be seen as an isolated victory for the internalisers. The following century saw a steady refusal to treat it as laying down any broad principle of liability.'[14]

Given that the policy beneath the rule has been rejected in most contexts we might ask why the House of Lords has resisted calls to abolish the rule. One explanation is simply that to overturn a case which has been part of English law for so long is 'too radical a step' for judges to take.[15] A second explanation, however, is that the fairness of liability without the need to prove fault where a defendant has created an extraordinary risk still appeals to some judges.[16]

The combination of the refusal to abolish the rule in *Rylands* v *Fletcher* with the 'refusal to treat it as laying down any broad principle of liability' has led to the rule being restricted within narrow limits. These limits, however, have proved difficult to define with any precision. The High Court of Australia castigated them as so uncertain that 'the practical application of the rule in a case involving damage caused by the escape of a substance is likely to degenerate into an essentially unprincipled and *ad hoc* subjective determination'.[17] One of the principal aims of the speeches in the House of Lords in *Transco* was to 'restate [the rule] so as to achieve as much certainty and clarity as attainable'.[18]

Current scope of the rule

The relationship with private nuisance

Many of the limits on the scope of the rule in *Rylands* v *Fletcher* flow from the supposed relationship between that rule and the tort of private nuisance. In *Transco* a majority of the House of Lords classified the rule as 'a sub-species of nuisance',[19] 'an aspect of the law of private nuisance'[20] or 'a species, or special case, of nuisance'.[21] This followed the earlier opinion that *Rylands* was part of the law concerning 'the mutual duties of adjoining or neighbouring landowners'.[22] If this classification is correct then it is one which will deter-

13 *Transco*, at [29].

14 Ibid. Oliphant 2005 suggests (at 118) that although the facts of *Rylands* v *Fletcher* provided an ideal testing ground for a fledgling theory of enterprise liability, an examination of the judgments gives 'no reason to believe that ideas of loss-distribution, deterrence, etc., were in the minds of the judges who participated in the decision'.

15 Ibid., at [43] (per Lord Hoffmann).

16 For instance, ibid. at [6] (per Lord Bingham) and [110] (per Lord Walker). Nolan 2005 (at 449) remains unconvinced: '[T]he best way forward appears to be abolition.'

17 *Burnie Port Authority* v *General Jones Pty Ltd* (1994) 179 CLR 520, 540 (per Mason CJ, Deane, Dawson, Toohey and Gaudron JJ)

18 *Transco*, at [8] (per Lord Bingham).

19 Ibid., at [9] (per Lord Bingham).

20 Ibid., at [52] (per Lord Hobhouse).

21 Ibid., at [92] (per Lord Walker).

22 *Read* v *J. Lyons & Co. Ltd* [1947] AC 156, 173 (per Lord Macmillan).

mine who can be liable, who can claim, and what types of damage can be claimed for under the rule.

We have three reasons for believing that this classification was misguided.[23] First, private nuisance is a tort. In contrast, liability under the rule in *Rylands* v *Fletcher* does not arise in response to someone's committing a tort: a defendant does not have to commit any kind of legal *wrong* in order to be held liable under the rule in *Rylands* v *Fletcher*.[24] Secondly, the original rationale behind *Rylands* – internalisation of costs to commercial enterprises[25] – provides no justification for distinguishing between costs from damage to neighbouring land and costs from other types of damage, for instance personal injuries. Instead this rationale suggests that the rule has more in common with the other liability rules discussed in this chapter, most of which cover types of damage beyond damage to neighbouring land. Thirdly, the reasons recently provided by the House of Lords for preserving the rule in *Rylands* v *Fletcher*[26] provide no justification for limiting its operation to compensating for damage to land. Unfortunately, it seems that the erroneous classification is too firmly woven into the speeches of a majority of their Lordships in *Transco* for any court below the House of Lords to ignore it. Consequently in the paragraphs that follow we will assume that the erroneous classification is the current law.

Who can be held liable under the rule?

The proposition that *Rylands* is part of the law concerning 'the mutual duties of adjoining or neighbouring landowners'[27] might be taken to mean that only *an owner* of land from which a dangerous thing escapes can be held liable. Weighing against this suggestion, however, are several cases where defendants who neither owned the land, nor were tenants of it, were held liable.[28] These cases suggest that liability can attach to any *occupier* of land from which the dangerous thing escaped.[29] Some *dicta* seem to go further and suggest that the person responsible for storing or collecting the mischievous substance can be liable regardless of his relation to the land.[30] Our view, consistent with our view as to who can be liable in private nuisance,[31] is that it is these *dicta* which correctly express the law.

Who can claim under the rule?

The conclusion that liability under *Rylands* arises out of the law on private nuisance means that the question of who can claim under the rule should be answered in line with the way that the House of Lords answered the question who can sue in private nuisance in *Hunter*

[23] We are not alone in believing this classification to have been misguided. See Murphy 2004 and Nolan 2005.
[24] See above, pp. 26–7.
[25] See above, p. 756.
[26] Ibid.
[27] *Read* v *J. Lyons & Co. Ltd* [1947] AC 156, 173 (per Lord Macmillan).
[28] *Eastern & South African Telegraph Co.* v *Cape Town Tramways Co.* [1902] AC 381; *West* v *Bristol Tramways Co.* [1908] 2 KB 14; *Charing Cross Electricity Supply Co.* v *Hydraulic Power Co.* [1914] 3 KB 772; *Rainham Chemical Works Ltd* v *Belvedere Fish Guano Co. Ltd* [1921] 2 AC 465; *Shiffman* v *Order of St John* [1936] 1 All ER 557.
[29] In *Transco*, at [11], Lord Bingham's restatement uses the phrase 'occupier of land' to refer to the potential defendant.
[30] In *Rainham Chemical Works* v *Belvedere Fish Guano Co. Ltd* [1921] 2 AC 465, Lord Sumner said (at 479) 'they cannot escape any liability which otherwise attaches to them on *storing it* [explosives] there merely because they have no tenancy or independent occupation' (emphasis added). In *Powell* v *Fall* (1880) 5 QBD 597 the escape was from the highway.
[31] See above, pp. 384–5.

v *Canary Wharf*.[32] Thus to sue under *Rylands*[33] a claimant must have a legally-recognised interest in the land[34] or must be in exclusive possession of the land,[35] and such a claimant can only sue for physical harm caused to the land, harm to its amenity value and consequential damage to chattels, not for personal injuries.[36]

A claimant cannot therefore rely on *Rylands* to recover compensation for pure economic losses that he has suffered as a result of a dangerous thing's escaping onto a third party's land. In *Cattle* v *Stockton Waterworks Co.*, Blackburn J was clear that in the *Rylands* case a claim could not have been made 'by every workman and person employed in the mine, who in consequence of its stoppage made less wages than he would otherwise have done'.[37] This should not be taken to mean, however, that *all* economic losses are irrecoverable under the rule in *Rylands* v *Fletcher*. Compensation for any diminution in the amenity value of land and compensation for economic losses *consequential on* physical damage to the claimant's land may be recovered under the rule in *Rylands* v *Fletcher*.[38]

An exceptionally dangerous or mischievous thing

Blackburn J spoke of the rule in *Rylands* v *Fletcher* as covering 'anything likely to do mischief if it escapes'. For a time, however, courts seemed to insist that this meant that the rule only extended to things which were 'inherently dangerous'. Thus in *Hale* v *Jennings Bros*[39] the Court of Appeal discussed whether a fairground 'chair-o-plane' was inherently dangerous, and concluded that it was because it was intended for use by 'ignorant people' who would be unaware of the dangers of fooling about in flying chairs.

It is difficult to disagree, however, with Professor Stallybrass who exhaustively examined the cases and concluded that a condition of 'inherent dangerousness' was unhelpful because 'just as there is nothing which is at all times and in all circumstances dangerous so it seems that there is scarcely anything which is in all circumstances safe'.[40]

In *Transco* Lord Bingham reasserted the importance of the 'dangerousness' condition. He said that:

> It must be shown that the defendant has done something which he recognized, or judged by the standards appropriate at the relevant place and time, he ought reasonably to have recognized, as

32 [1997] AC 655 (discussed above, pp. 393–8).

33 This would have caused problems for the claimant in *Eastern & South African Telegraph Co.* v *Cape Town Tramways Co.* [1902] AC 381 because it was claiming for damage done to its submarine cable.

34 Such as a fee simple in possession, a tenancy, or a reversionary interest. A more detailed presentation of what interests in land the law recognises is to be found in the chapter on the tort of private nuisance, above, pp. 394–5.

35 Exclusive possession will be sufficient *unless* the defendant has the right to possess the land, or acted with the authority of the person with the right to possess. But exclusive possession is not necessary because, for instance, a reversioner may be able to sue. Unfortunately, in *Transco*, [9] and [11], Lord Bingham seems to have oversimplified when he stated that the claimant only had to be an 'occupier' of the land.

36 A majority in *Transco* expressly states that claims cannot be brought for personal injuries under the rule in *Rylands* v *Fletcher*: see [9] (Lord Bingham), [35] (Lord Hoffmann), and [52] (Lord Hobhouse).

37 (1875) LR 10 QB 453, 457.

38 The claimants' claim in *Cambridge Water Co.* v *Eastern Counties Leather* [1994] 2 AC 264 was a claim to be compensated for economic loss suffered by them as a result of their land suffering some kind of physical damage: see below, pp. 762–3.

39 [1938] 1 All ER 579.

40 Stallybrass 1929, 387.

> giving rise to an exceptionally high risk of danger or mischief if there should be an escape, however unlikely an escape may have been thought to be.[41]

Moreover, he stated that he did not think that 'the mischief or danger test should be at all easily satisfied'.[42] However, while Lords Hoffmann and Walker agreed with Lord Bingham that 'creation of an exceptional risk' was a relevant factor in the application of the rule, they both treated the matter as more relevant to the requirement of 'an extraordinary use of land'.[43]

Extraordinary use

The rule in *Rylands* v *Fletcher* as originally formulated by Blackburn J applied only to cases where someone brought onto land or kept on land something 'which was not naturally there'. As we have seen, in the House of Lords, Lord Cairns LC built on this statement and drew a distinction between defendants who use their land 'for any purpose for which it might in the ordinary course of the enjoyment of land be used . . . what I may term the natural user of land' and those who 'not stopping at the natural use of their close, had desired to use it for any purpose which I may term a non-natural use'.[44] So Lord Cairns LC seemed to think: (1) that liability under the rule in *Rylands* v *Fletcher* was limited to cases where someone used his land in a 'non-natural' way; *and* (2) that someone would use his land in a 'non-natural' way if he used it in an *extraordinary* way.

The early cases do not provide any clear answer as to the original meaning of 'non-natural user'. Since the House of Lords upheld the decision in favour of Fletcher their Lordships must have concluded that a reservoir was a sufficiently non-natural use of land. Moreover, the reasoning in Blackburn J's judgment suggested that the rule would also cover straying cattle and an escape of sewage.[45] Other early cases treated the rule as covering poisonous yew trees,[46] creosote,[47] and large quantities of electricity.[48] In *Wilson* v *Waddell*,[49] however, Lord Blackburn (as he had by then become) stated that use of land for ordinary mining operations was a natural use.

In *Rickards* v *Lothian*[50] the Privy Council held that an escape of water from ordinary plumbing[51] did not fall within the scope of the rule in *Rylands* v *Fletcher*. Lord Moulton

41 *Transco*, at [10].
42 Ibid.
43 Ibid., at [49] (per Lord Hoffmann), [103] (per Lord Walker).
44 (1868) LR 3 HL 330, 339.
45 In *Smeaton* v *Ilford Corp.* [1954] Ch 450, Upjohn J stated that 'To collect into a sewer a large volume of sewage, inherently noxious and dangerous and bound to cause great damage if not properly contained, cannot be described, in my judgment, as a natural use of land' (ibid., 472).
46 *Crowhurst* v *Amersham Burial Board* (1878) 4 CPD 5. The rule does not, apparently, cover thistles which are 'the natural growth of the soil': *Giles* v *Walker* (1890) 24 QBD 656, 657.
47 *West* v *Bristol Tramways Co.* [1908] 2 KB 14.
48 *Eastern & South African Telegraph Co.* v *Cape Town Tramways Co.* [1902] AC 381.
49 (1876) 2 App Cas 95.
50 [1913] AC 263.
51 The line is not easy to draw between ordinary and extraordinary plumbing but it seems to lie somewhere between *Western Engraving Co.* v *Film Laboratories Ltd* [1936] 1 All ER 106, where the Court of Appeal held that the use of large quantities of water for film-washing was a non-natural user, and *Peters* v *Prince of Wales Theatre* [1943] KB 73 where a differently constituted Court of Appeal suggested that connection of water to a sprinkler system in a theatre was an ordinary and usual user. In *Transco* [2004] 2 AC 1 a water pipe carrying sufficient water for 66 flats was treated as 'entirely normal and routine' (at [13]) and thus not an 'extraordinary use', though Lord Bingham complicated the matter somewhat by stating that in his opinion the volume of water in a domestic plumbing system was also insufficient to amount to a sufficiently dangerous thing (at [10]).

said, 'It is not every use to which land is put that brings into play that [rule]. It must be some special use bringing with it increased danger to others, and must not merely be the ordinary use of land or such a use as is proper for the general benefit of the community.'[52] The last portion of this statement – 'not merely ... such a use as is proper for the general benefit of the community' – can be interpreted to suggest that only *improper* uses of land should fall within the scope of the rule in *Rylands* v *Fletcher*. By adopting such an interpretation those who disliked the rule in *Rylands* v *Fletcher* could severely restrict its scope. Thus in *Read* v *J. Lyons & Co.*[53] two members of the House of Lords suggested that use of land for a munitions factory in wartime might not be a 'non-natural user',[54] and in *Cambridge Water* v *Eastern Counties Leather* the trial judge held that the use of chemical solvents by a tannery in an industrial village was not a non-natural user given the benefits for local employment.

Shortly before the judgment of the House of Lords in *Cambridge Water* we could have described the meaning of 'non-natural user' as having shifted from 'not naturally there' to 'improper', via 'extraordinary'. But in his judgment in that case Lord Goff spoke against any broad reading of Lord Moulton's phrase. Four points made by Lord Goff in this part of his judgment are worth particular attention. First, he made clear that in his opinion 'the storage of substantial quantities of chemicals on industrial premises should be regarded as an almost classic case of non-natural use'.[55] Secondly, he stated that the creation of employment could not be sufficient of itself to establish that a particular use of land was 'natural or ordinary'.[56] Thirdly, he suggested that because in the same case the House of Lords was deciding that there could be no liability under the rule in *Rylands v Fletcher* for unforeseeable consequences of escapes, it would be less necessary *in future* to interpret the phrase 'non-natural user' narrowly in order to limit the scope of liability.[57] Fourthly, he thought that the historic relationship between the rule in *Rylands* v *Fletcher* and the tort of private nuisance meant that in future the concept of 'non-natural user' might develop alongside the concept of 'reasonable user' in private nuisance.[58] The fourth point is particularly important because it suggests that the main activities which should be excluded from the scope of 'non-natural user' are those which create risks which are generally accepted as part of ordinary social give-and-take.

In *Transco* Lord Bingham confirmed that a defendant's use of land does not have to be 'unreasonable' or 'improper' in order to fall within the scope of the rule:

> I think it is clear that ordinary user is a preferable test to natural user, making it clear that the rule in *Rylands v Fletcher* is engaged only where the defendant's use is shown to be extraordinary and unusual. This is not a test to be inflexibly applied: a use may be extraordinary and unusual at one time or in one place but not so at another time or in another place ... I also doubt whether a test of reasonable user is helpful, since a user may well be quite out of the ordinary but not unreason-

52 [1913] AC 263, 280.

53 [1947] AC 156, 169–70 (per Viscount Simon), 173–4 (per Lord Macmillan).

54 In the earlier case of *Rainham Chemical Works* v *Belvedere Fish Guano Co. Ltd* [1921] 2 AC 465, the House of Lords had shown no hesitation in finding that making munitions during the First World War was 'certainly not the common and ordinary use of the land': ibid., 471 (per Lord Buckmaster).

55 [1994] 2 AC 264, 309.

56 Ibid.

57 Ibid.

58 Ibid., 299.

> able, as was that of *Rylands*, *Rainham Chemical Works* or the tannery in *Cambridge Water*. Again, as it seems to me, the question is whether the defendant has done something out of the ordinary in the place and at the time when he does it. In answering that question, I respectfully think that little help is gained (and unnecessary confusion perhaps caused) by considering whether the use is proper for the general benefit of the community.[59]

While Lord Bingham cast doubt on the utility of tests asking whether particular uses were unreasonable or improper he offered little guidance on how to draw the line between the ordinary and extraordinary. Indeed Lord Hoffmann seemed to regard a test based around 'ordinary uses of land' as 'rather vague'.[60] He offered 'a use creating an increased risk' as the 'converse' of 'natural use',[61] stated that 'the criterion of exceptional risk must be taken seriously',[62] and, contentiously, asserted that a 'useful guide in deciding whether the risk has been created by a "non-natural" user of land is . . . to ask whether the damage which eventuated was something against which the [claimant] occupier could reasonably be expected to have insured himself'.[63]

An approach which distinguishes between ordinary and extraordinary uses of land in terms of the degree of risk posed to neighbours in the event of an escape seems as easy to apply and attractive as any. But we cannot offer any support for Lord Hoffmann's extraordinary proposition about insurability. It seems to us that insurability of the claimant's property is *irrelevant* to the correct classification of the defendant's activitiy. When a property owner insures a terraced house against destruction such insurance generally does not distinguish between a car swerving into the front wall or the local fireworks factory exploding, but that surely cannot make the local fireworks factory into an ordinary use of land in the locality?

Furthermore, in many situations, as Lord Hoffmann noted,[64] *both* the person responsible for the activity *and* the neighbouring property owners will be insured. In such circumstances it is doubtful whether leaving losses with the property owners will be economically efficient.[65] Moreover, as Lord Hobhouse pointed out, the issue is not solely about efficiency but also about whether it is fair to make potential claimants pay the insurance premiums which cover the risk of damage as a result of such incidents. Lord Hoffmann's argument that most property losses should be dealt with by self-insurance rather than by claims against those responsible for the activity looks remarkably like an argument *against*

59 *Transco*, at [11]. Lord Scott agreed with Lord Bingham's judgment. Lord Walker expressly commended Lord Bingham's discussion of this requirement, but also commended the different approach of Lord Hoffmann!

60 Ibid., at [37].

61 Ibid., at [44].

62 Ibid., at [49].

63 Ibid., at [46].

64 Ibid., at [39].

65 Leaving the potential claimant to bear the loss might be efficient if *either*: (*a*) the claimant was better placed to avoid the harm caused by an escape than the defendant to prevent the escape; *or* (*b*) the claimant was better placed to evaluate and insure against the risk of his suffering loss as a result of an escape from the defendant's land and *only* he carried insurance to guard against that loss. Neither of these conditions is likely to be satisfied. One might think that by leaving the loss with the potential claimant at least the legal costs of determining whether the defendant is liable will be saved. But because a *negligence* claim can certainly be brought when a careless escape has caused personal injury or damage to personal property, and probably *can* be brought if a careless escape has caused damage to land, the costs saved by preventing claims under the rule in *Rylands* v *Fletcher* where land has been damaged by an escape will be small. To spell the point out, the costs saved in not pursuing a claim under the rule in *Rylands* v *Fletcher* will often be spent instead determining whether there is a good claim in negligence.

internalisation of costs to the activity, and thus an argument against the existence of *Rylands* v *Fletcher* liability, rather than a criterion for determining *when* costs should be internalised.

It is worth briefly making two further points about the 'extraordinary use' requirement. First, it seems that where statute has authorised a particular use of land that use will be considered as 'natural and ordinary' unless there has been negligence.[66] Secondly, Blackburn J's original formulation of the rule stated that the collection of the dangerous thing had to be 'for his own purposes'.[67] A court would be unlikely to use this phrase to protect a defendant whose activity was intended to benefit the public generally, but might use it to protect a defendant whose activity was intended to benefit both himself and the claimant. In such circumstances, however, there is often an overlap with the defence of consent.

Escape

In *Read* v *J. Lyons & Co.*[68] the claimant was an inspector at a munitions factory who was injured by an exploding shell. The House of Lords determined that the rule in *Rylands* v *Fletcher* did not apply in these circumstances because the explosive had not escaped from the defendant's premises, but merely from its control. An escape from the defendant's land was treated as logically necessary because, in the words of Lord Macmillan, 'the doctrine of *Rylands* v *Fletcher*, as I understand it, derives from a conception of mutual duties of adjoining or neighbouring landowners, and its cogenors are trespass and [private] nuisance'.[69] A requirement of an escape from the defendant's premises ensures that the *Rylands* rule does not become entangled with the rules concerning the liability of an occupier to his or her visitors.

Transco involved an escape of water from one part of the defendant's premises to another part of the premises where it threatened to damage a gas pipe which the claimant had a right to run across the defendant's premises. Lord Scott was adamant that even if the claimant's right to run the pipeline across the defendant's land was a proprietary right, an easement, the claimant still could not sue the defendant because there had been no escape from the defendant's land.[70]

Reasonable foreseeability

Suppose A brought a dangerous thing, T, onto his land in the course of an extraordinary use of his land and T then escaped off A's land with the result that B suffered some kind of damage to his land. In *Rylands* v *Fletcher*, Blackburn J seemed to be of the opinion that B would be entitled to sue A for compensation for the harm suffered by her so long as her suffering that harm was a 'natural' consequence of T's escaping from A's land.[71] However, the House of Lords made it clear in *Cambridge Water Co.* v *Eastern Counties Leather*[72] that, in the case we are considering, B will *only* be entitled to sue A under the rule in *Rylands* v

[66] *Transco*, at [30]–[31] (per Lord Hoffmann), [89] (per Lord Scott).
[67] See quotation above, p. 755.
[68] [1947] AC 156.
[69] Ibid., 173.
[70] *Transco*, at [78]–[80].
[71] (1866) LR 1 Ex 265, 279–80.
[72] [1994] 2 AC 264.

Fletcher for compensation for the harm that she suffered as a result of T's escaping from A's land if it was *reasonably foreseeable* that someone like B would suffer *that kind of harm* if T escaped from A's land.

The facts of the *Cambridge Water* case illustrate the point. The defendants ran a tanning business which used large quantities of chemicals. Some of these chemicals got spilled from time to time on the defendants' factory floor and they seeped through the factory floor and into the ground beneath the defendants' factory. The chemicals then flowed along impermeable strata until they reached a borehole owned by the claimants which was located over a mile away from the defendants' factory. The claimants used this borehole to obtain water which they would then supply to nearby residents. The chemicals from the defendants' factory contaminated this borehole with the result that the claimants were forbidden to extract any more water from the borehole.[73] The claimants sued the defendants under the rule in *Rylands* v *Fletcher* for compensation for the costs incurred by them in creating a new borehole.[74] The House of Lords dismissed the claimants' claim on the ground that no one could have foreseen that the claimants' borehole would be contaminated if the chemicals that the defendants used escaped from their land.

It should be noted that in the case we are considering, B will not have to show that it was reasonably foreseeable that T *would escape* from A's land in order to bring a claim under the rule in *Rylands* v *Fletcher*. All B will have to show is that it was reasonably foreseeable that *if* T escaped, someone like her would suffer the kind of harm for which she wants compensation. So suppose that Alan kept some chemicals on his land. Suppose further that Alan used elaborate precautions to ensure that the chemicals would not escape from his land and as a result it was not reasonably foreseeable that the chemicals would escape from his land. Suppose further that the chemicals – against all expectation – managed to escape and damaged Betty's neighbouring land.

In such a case, the fact that it was not reasonably foreseeable that the chemicals would escape from Alan's land would not be fatal to Betty's claim under the rule in *Rylands* v *Fletcher* to be compensated for the harm suffered by her. All Betty would have to show – for the purposes of satisfying the requirement of reasonable foreseeability of damage under the rule in *Rylands* v *Fletcher* – is that it was reasonably foreseeable that someone like her would suffer damage to her land *if* the chemicals escaped from Alan's land. This was, of course, eminently foreseeable.[75]

Defences

Suppose something that A brought onto his land escaped from that land and harmed B. If B sues A for compensation for that harm under the rule in *Rylands* v *Fletcher*, there are a number of different defences that A may be able to raise to B's claim.

[73] The water may have been drinkable despite the contamination, but it fell foul of legislation that had been introduced pursuant to an EC Directive, banning the supply of water which contained even the slightest traces of the kind of chemicals that had contaminated the claimants' borehole.

[74] This claim did not fall foul of the rule in *Cattle* v *Stockton Waterworks* (1875) LR 10 QB 453 that compensation for pure economic loss may not be recovered under the rule in *Rylands* v *Fletcher*. The economic loss for which the claimants wanted to be compensated in *Cambridge Water* was consequential on the claimant's property (their borehole) being damaged.

[75] However, Betty's claim under the rule in *Rylands* v *Fletcher* for compensation for the damage suffered may still be defeated if a defence is available to Alan.

(1) *Act of a stranger.* A will have a defence to B's claim for compensation under the rule in *Rylands* v *Fletcher* if the escape resulted from the act of a person whom A could not control.[76] It seems to be assumed that a landowner has a sufficient degree of control over the anticipated activities[77] of independent contractors who he engages to bring the dangerous thing onto his premises or to store it there.[78] A defendant will not be liable, however, for an escape resulting from the deliberate and malicious act of a stranger, unless such an act ought to have been anticipated and guarded against. So in *Perry* v *Kendricks Transport Ltd*[79] a couple of boys threw a lighted match into the petrol tank of a motor coach that was standing on the defendants' land. The coach blew up and the claimant, who was standing outside the defendants' land at the time of the explosion, was injured. The defendants were not held liable to compensate the claimant for his injuries under the rule in *Rylands* v *Fletcher*.[80]

(2) *Act of God.* In the situation we are considering, A will have a defence to B's claim for compensation under the rule in *Rylands* v *Fletcher* if the escape resulted from a wholly extraordinary natural event.[81]

(3) *Fault of the claimant.* In the situation we are considering, A will have a defence to B's claim for compensation under the rule in *Rylands* v *Fletcher* if B was wholly at fault for the fact that she suffered the harm for which she is seeking compensation.[82]

(4) *Consent.* In *Peters* v *Prince of Wales Theatre*[83] the Court of Appeal held that where a tenant took premises knowing that a particular water system was installed in the landlord's adjoining premises the tenant consented to the existence of the system and could not complain if water escaped from it. An analogy was drawn with the rule that if A has granted possession of a parcel of land to B, and it is contemplated at the time of the grant that A will continue to use adjoining property for a particular purpose, B will not be able to complain that A's using the adjoining premises for that purpose will amount to a nuisance.[84]

[76] *Box* v *Jubb* (1879) 4 Ex D 76; *Rickards* v *Lothian* [1913] AC 263; *Perry* v *Kendricks Transport Ltd* [1956] 1 WLR 85.

[77] Where the independent contractor behaves in a wholly unanticipated way A may be able to avoid liability. This has certainly been the position in the analogous cases involving fire. See below, pp. 765–7.

[78] In *Rylands* v *Fletcher* itself the escape seems to have been caused by the carelessness of the independent contractors who built the reservoir.

[79] [1956] 1 WLR 85.

[80] It is now clear that the claimant's claim under the rule in *Rylands* v *Fletcher* should also have failed because the rule does not apply in personal injury cases: see above, pp. 766–7.

[81] *Nichols* v *Marsland* (1876) 2 Ex D 1, where a rainstorm was said to have been the heaviest in human memory. A different heavy storm was judged insufficiently unusual in *Greenock Corporation* v *Caledonian Railway Co.* [1917] AC 556. In *Transco*, at [59], Lord Hobhouse stated that the phrase 'Acts of God' was 'used to describe those events which involved no human agency and which it was not realistically possible for a human to guard against: an accident which the defendant can show is due to natural causes, directly and exclusively, without human intervention and could not have been prevented by any amount of foresight, pains and care, reasonably to be expected of him'.

[82] *Rylands* v *Fletcher* (1868) LR 1 Ex 265, 280.

[83] [1943] KB 73.

[84] *Vanderpant* v *Mayfair Hotel Co. Ltd* [1930] 1 Ch 138, 162–3; *Thomas* v *Lewis* [1937] 1 All ER 137.

LIABILITY RULES ANALOGOUS TO THE RULE IN *RYLANDS* v *FLETCHER*

Fire

It is commonly believed that the ancient common law made an occupier of premises liable for any damage caused by fire escaping from those premises. This stern rule was altered by statute and s 86 of the Fire Prevention (Metropolis) Act 1774 now states that no action can be brought 'against any person in whose house, chamber, stable, barn or other building, or on whose estate any fire shall . . . accidentally begin'. But the interpretation and application of this provision is not straightforward.

In order to explain the current pattern of an occupier's liability for the spread of fire it may be helpful to distinguish three types of situation:

(1) *A fire is negligently started on A's property and then spreads to B's property.* It has been held that the 1774 Act does not protect the occupier from liability when the fire has been started 'negligently' rather than 'accidentally'.[85] Importantly, this applies even when the negligence was not the negligence of the occupier or his employee but of a guest or independent contractor. Thus a claimant who wishes to sue the occupier for damage done by a fire negligently started by a guest or independent contractor will be able to sue the occupier under the ancient common law rule and not have to rely on the tort of negligence.[86] The 1774 Act will protect the occupier from being sued under the ancient common law rule, however, if the fire was started by the negligence of a *stranger*. In this context 'a "stranger" is anyone who in lighting a fire . . . acts contrary to anything which the occupier could anticipate that he would do'.[87] In rare circumstances a guest or independent contractor may become a 'stranger' for the purposes of this rule 'if his conduct in lighting a fire is so alien to your invitation that he should *qua* the fire be regarded as a trespasser'.[88]

By way of illustration, in *Ribee* v *Norrie*,[89] the defendant owned a hostel and rented out bedrooms in it to various people. A fire started in the hostel's sitting room, probably as a result of a tenant dropping a smouldering cigarette onto the settee. The fire spread and damaged the adjoining house which belonged to the claimant. The defendant was held liable for the fire damage done to the claimant's house. He was held to have been in occupation of the hostel's sitting room when the fire started. The fire was negligently started in the sitting room by a tenant who had permission from the defendant to use the sitting room. Finally, the tenant's conduct was not 'so alien' that he could '*qua* the fire be regarded as a trespasser' because the defendant could reasonably have anticipated that a tenant using the sitting room 'might inadvertently drop a smouldering cigarette onto the settee eventually setting it on fire'.[90]

(2) *A fire is deliberately started on A's property and then spreads to B's property.* Liability in this situation depends on the *type* of fire involved and *why it spread*. The *type* of fire

[85] *Balfour* v *Barty-King* [1957] 1 QB 496.
[86] The claimant can, of course, seek to sue the guest or the contractor in negligence.
[87] *H & N Emmanuel Ltd* v *GLC* [1971] 2 All ER 835, 839a (per Lord Denning MR).
[88] Ibid.
[89] (2001) 33 HLR 777.
[90] Ibid., at [26] (per Ward LJ).

involved is relevant because it has been held that some deliberate fires involve the 'extraordinary use' of land and potentially fall within the ambit of the rule in *Rylands* v *Fletcher*. If the type of fire does fall within the ambit of this rule then the occupier may be liable for its escape even if the escape was not a result of anyone's negligence. But lighting an ordinary domestic fire in a fireplace is not an 'extraordinary use', so there will be no liability for the accidental escape of such a fire.[91] The reasons *why the fire spread* are relevant because where the fire spread because of the *negligence* of the occupier, his employee, his guest or his independent contractor, it has been held that the 1774 Act does not protect the occupier against liability.[92] Again, the occupier's liability is broader than ordinary vicarious liability for negligence, but does not stretch to cover liability for the negligence of a 'stranger'.[93]

(3) *Natural forces start a fire on A's property and it then spreads to B's property*. Where natural forces (or, indeed a 'stranger') start a fire on the occupier's premises and it subsequently escapes to damage B's neighbouring premises, it seems that the 1774 Act will prevent A being held liable for the damage to B's premises *unless* the claim can be brought under the rule in *Rylands* v *Fletcher* or the rule in *Goldman* v *Hargrave*.[94] In order to show that the rule in *Rylands* applies here, it would have to be shown that the fire started on the occupier's premises because he used those premises in an extraordinary way. This requirement would probably be satisfied if the occupier stored large quantities of inflammable chemicals on his land which accidentally caught fire.[95] But the 'extraordinary use' requirement will probably not be satisfied if what happened was that A parked his car on his land and the petrol in the tank accidentally caught fire.[96] *Goldman* v *Hargrave*[97] may assist a neighbour in claiming against an occupier for damage caused by the spread of a natural fire from his land if he failed to take reasonable steps to stop the fire spreading onto the neighbour's property. Whether the occupier will be held to have taken such reasonable steps will depend on factors such as his interests and resources, and the relative interests and resources of anyone imperilled by the fire.[98]

91 *Sochacki* v *Sas* [1947] 1 All ER 344; *J Doltis Ltd* v *Issac Braithwaite & Sons (Engineers) Ltd* [1957] 1 Lloyd's Rep 522; *Johnson* v *BJW Property Developments Ltd* [2002] 3 All ER 574, at [31].

92 *H & N Emmanuel Ltd* v *GLC* [1971] 2 All ER 835. This seems to be the opinion of Lord Denning MR (ibid., at 838b–g; though he later evinces a reluctance to classify the liability rule at 839d–e) and also the opinion of Phillimore LJ (ibid., at 842). See also *Johnson* v *BJW Property Developments Ltd* [2002] 3 All ER 574.

93 *H & N Emmanuel Ltd* v *GLC* [1971] 2 All ER 835, 838–9 (per Lord Denning MR).

94 *Goldman* v *Hargrave* [1967] 1 AC 645. See above, pp. 177–9.

95 In *Mason* v *Levy Auto Parts* [1967] 2 QB 530, MacKenna J found that the storage of a large number of motor spares coated in oil or wrapped in waxed paper was a non-natural user of land. Similarly, in *LMS International Ltd* v *Styrene Packaging and Insulation Ltd* [2005] EWHC 2065 (TCC) HHJ Peter Coulson QC held that the use in the defendant's factory of several tonnes of inflammable expanded polystyrene beads, pentane, and hot-wire cutting machines, amounted to a non-natural use of land. The fact that it is not the inflammable material which escaped in these cases but a fire is not legally important. In cases of explosion courts have similarly not treated it as important whether the explosive chemicals *themselves* escaped (as opposed to mere shockwaves). See, for example, *Rainham Chemical Works Ltd* v *Belvedere Fish Guano Co. Ltd* [1921] 2 AC 465.

96 Admittedly, in *Musgrove* v *Pandelis* [1919] 2 KB 43, the Court of Appeal held that a motor car and its petrol tank were a 'dangerous thing' to which the rule in *Rylands* v *Fletcher* could apply, but paid less attention to the question whether storage of a car in a garage was an extraordinary user. The better view, which accords with the opinion of Romer LJ in *Collingwood* v *Home & Colonial Stores Ltd* [1936] 3 All ER 200, 209, must be that parking a car in a garage attached to residential property is not an extraordinary use of land. Indeed in *Transco*, [107] Lord Walker used the *Musgrove* case to illustrate how the 'extraordinary use' test changes though time. It might still be arguable that to park a petrol tanker on land is an 'extraordinary user': see *Perry* v *Kendricks Transport Ltd* [1956] 1 WLR 85.

97 *Goldman* v *Hargrave* [1967] AC 645.

98 See above, pp. 221–5, 387–9.

We should finally consider how far the liability rules that we have summarised above are 'analogous to the rule in *Rylands* v *Fletcher*' since this may determine questions such as who can claim and what types of damage they can claim for.[99] Straightforwardly, we can say that those cases where it is necessary to prove that the type of fire involved or the collection of inflammable material was an 'extraordinary use' of land actually fall within the rule in *Rylands* and do not depend on a special analogous rule relating to fire at all. Further, the rule in *Goldman* v *Hargrave* seems to form part of both the tort of negligence and the tort of private nuisance and need not be treated as analogous to the rule in *Rylands*. What remains to be classified is that remnant of the ancient common law rule relating to the escape of fire which has survived the 1774 statute.

From one perspective this remnant is analogous to the rule in *Rylands* because it makes an occupier liable for escapes of fire which were the consequence of the negligence of a guest or independent contractor. But two distinctions may also be worth mentioning. First, under the remnant the occupier will avoid liability if he can prove that the escape was 'accidental', in the sense of not involving negligence. This is a broader defence than any available under the rule in *Rylands*.[100] Secondly, it is not clear that the ancient common law rule *only* protects neighbours against damage to their land.[101] One of the best known ancient authorities for the rule involves a claim for damage to chattels[102] and more recent judgments have also assumed that such claims were possible.[103]

Cattle trespass

Under s 4 of the Animals Act 1971, if livestock[104] belonging[105] to any person stray[106] onto land in the ownership or occupation of another, the person to whom the livestock belongs is liable for any damage[107] caused by the livestock to the land and property on it and for expenses reasonably incurred in impounding the livestock,[108] tracing who owns it and keeping it pending return. There is no defence covering escapes of livestock caused by malicious strangers or Acts of God. However, s 5(1) of the 1971 Act provides that a 'person [will not be] liable under [s 4] for any damage which is due wholly to the fault of the person suffering it'.[109]

[99] For these matters under the rule in *Rylands* v *Fletcher* see above, pp. 757–8.

[100] For defences under the rule in *Rylands* v *Fletcher* see above, pp. 763–4.

[101] See above, pp. 757–8, for the limits on who can sue and for what under the rule in *Rylands* v *Fletcher*.

[102] *Beaulieu* v *Finglam* (1401) YB 2 Hen IV fo 18, pl 6.

[103] *Sochacki* v *Sas* [1947] 1 All ER 344, 345A, 'If I happen to be on somebody else's land at a time when a fire spreads to that land and my motor car or property is destroyed, I have just as much right against the person who improperly allows the fire to escape from his land as the owner of the land on which I happen to be' (per Lord Goddard CJ).

[104] This is broadly defined in s 11. It includes cattle, horses, sheep, pigs and poultry.

[105] Animals Act 1971, s 4(2): 'For the purposes of this section any livestock belongs to the person in whose possession it is.'

[106] There is no liability where livestock strays from a highway which it was being driven along or across: Animals Act 1971, s 5(5), following the common law rule in *Tillett* v *Ward* (1882) 10 QBD 17. There could be liability in negligence if the drovers were careless, or under s 2 of the Animals Act 1971 if the livestock in question was known to have an unusual and dangerous tendency.

[107] Not limited to damage to land.

[108] See Animals Act 1971, s 7.

[109] Damages can also be reduced for contributory negligence: s 10.

Someone who has suffered harm as a result of straying livestock may not have to rely on s 4 of the Animals Act 1971 to obtain compensation for that harm: he may be entitled to bring a claim in tort for such compensation. So if A sends livestock onto B's land, he will commit the tort of trespass to land and B will be entitled to sue A in trespass for compensation for the harm caused by the livestock while it was on her land. Again, if A carelessly allows livestock to stray when it is reasonably foreseeable that they will do harm to B if they are allowed to stray, A will commit the tort of negligence and if B suffers foreseeable harm as a result of the livestock straying, B will be entitled to sue A in negligence for damages sufficient to compensate her for that harm.[110]

Escape of water from the mains

Where an escape of water, however caused,[111] from a pipe vested in a water undertaker causes loss or damage, the undertaker shall be liable for the loss or damage.[112]

Nuclear installations

The licensee of a nuclear installation is liable for injuries to persons and damage to the property of others caused by occurrences involving nuclear matter or the escape of ionising radiation.[113] Licensees cannot escape liability by showing that the occurrence was the result of an Act of God or of an uncontrollable third party, though there is a defence for incidents caused by 'hostile action in the course of armed conflict'.[114] The courts, however, have defined the forms of damage covered by the statutory liability narrowly,[115] and some claimants seeking to rely on it have been unable to prove causation.[116]

THE ANIMALS ACT 1971

Antecedents of the Act

Under the common law the keeper of an animal which had a tendency to do harm would be liable for any damage that it caused if he knew that that animal had a tendency to do harm.[117] Animals were divided by species into two classes. If an animal belonged to a

[110] In this context the tort of negligence will straightforwardly allow B to claim for personal injury or property damage.

[111] There is an exception where the escape was due wholly to the fault of the person who sustained the loss or damage: Water Industry Act 1991, s 209(2).

[112] Water Industry Act 1991, s 209(1). There are some exceptions to this liability in s 209(3) and (6). Claims are not limited to claims for damage to land.

[113] Nuclear Installations Act 1965, ss 7 and 12. Thus for there to be liability under the Act there does not have to be an escape from the land occupied by the licensee.

[114] Nuclear Installations Act 1965, s 13(4).

[115] In *Merlin* v *BNFL* [1990] 2 QB 557, Gatehouse J held that a fall in the value of a house as a result of radioactive contamination was not 'damage' to property, and suggested *obiter* that 'the presence of alpha-emitting radionuclides in the human airways or digestive system or even in the bloodstream merely increases the risk of cancer to which everyone is exposed from both natural and artificial radioactive sources. They do not *per se* amount to injury' (ibid., 572–3).

[116] *Reay* v *BNFL*, *Hope* v *BNFL* [1994] PIQR P171.

[117] *Important note.* In this context 'harm' covers both personal injury and property damage.

dangerous species, it would be conclusively presumed to have a tendency to do harm, its keeper would be conclusively presumed to know that it had a tendency to do harm,[118] and its keeper would be held liable for any damage that it caused. If, on the other hand, the animal which caused harm belonged to a species that was by nature harmless or generally tamed or domesticated, then its keeper would only be held liable for the harm under the above liability rule if it could be specifically proved that the animal had a tendency to do such harm and that its keeper knew that it had a tendency to do such harm. The Animals Act 1971 abolished these common law rules[119] and replaced them with the following set of liability rules.

The Animals Act 1971

The liability rules created by the Act

The liability rules created by the 1971 Act can be summarised as follows:

(1) *Liability of the keeper of an animal belonging to a dangerous species.* Section 2(1) of the 1971 Act provides that the keeper of an animal which belongs to a dangerous species is liable for the damage that it causes unless a relevant defence applies.

(2) *Liability of the keeper of an animal that does not belong to a dangerous species.* Section 2(2) of the 1971 Act provides that the keeper of an animal which does not belong to a dangerous species will be liable for damage that has been caused by that animal if three conditions are satisfied and no relevant defence applies. The three conditions are as follows.

First, *either* the animal, unless restrained, must have been likely[120] to cause that kind of damage *or* it must have been likely that if the animal ever caused that kind of damage, it would do so to a severe degree.

Secondly, *either* the likelihood of the damage or of its being severe[121] must have been attributable to the animal having characteristics not normally found in animals of the same species *or* the likelihood of the damage or of its being severe must have been attributable to the animal having characteristics not normally found except at particular times or in particular circumstances.

118 Thus for the purposes of the common law, elephants were treated as wild and dangerous, even if individual elephants were docile and tame: *Behrens* v *Bertram Mills Circus Ltd* [1957] 2 QB 1.

119 Section 1 of the Animals Act 1971 provides that the 'provisions . . . of this Act replace . . . the rules of the common law imposing a strict liability . . . for damage done by an animal on the ground that the animal is regarded as ferae naturae or that its vicious or mischievous propensities are known or presumed to be known.'

120 In *Mirvahedy* v *Henley* [2003] 2 AC 491, at [95]–[97], Lord Scott suggested that in this context damage would only be 'likely' if it was 'to be reasonably expected'. But the other Law Lords did not express an opinion on this point.

121 The statute says that it is 'the likelihood of the damage or of its being severe' which must be 'due to' the abnormal characteristics of the animal, but in *Curtis* v *Betts* [1990] 1 WLR 459, the Court of Appeal suggested that the provision should be treated as if it read 'the damage' must be 'attributable to' the abnormal characteristics. But while this rewording makes clear that a court should consider whether an unusual characteristic *caused* the damage – not merely whether such a characteristic made such damage *likely* – the rewording has the disadvantage that it obscures the relationship between the first and second conditions: see *Bowlt* v *Clark* [2006] EWCA Civ 978, discussed below, pp. 771–2.

Thirdly, the keeper of the animal must have known that the animal had these characteristics.[122]

(3) *Liability of the keeper of a dog that has killed or injured livestock.* Section 3 of the 1971 Act provides that the keeper of a dog is liable for damage it causes by killing or injuring livestock unless a relevant defence applies.

(4) *Liability of person in possession of livestock for the damage done by that livestock.* Section 4 of the 1971 Act provides that the possessor of livestock is liable for certain types of damage and expenses caused by that livestock straying onto land in the ownership or occupation of another person unless a relevant defence applies.[123]

Interpretation

Certain terms in this summary require further discussion.

(1) *Keeper.* The keeper of an animal that has caused harm may be held liable for that harm under ss 2 and 3 of the 1971 Act. Who counts as being a keeper of an animal? Section 6(3) of the 1971 Act provides that 'a person is a keeper of an animal if – (a) he owns the animal or has it in his possession; or (b) he is the head of a household of which a member under the age of sixteen owns the animal or has it in his possession'. Section 6(4) of the 1971 Act qualifies this by providing that someone who takes an animal into his possession 'for the purpose of preventing it from causing damage or of restoring it to his owner' will not thereby become a keeper of that animal. Section 6(3) goes on to provide that 'if at any time an animal ceases to be owned by or to be in the possession of a person, any person who immediately before that time was a keeper thereof by virtue of the preceding provisions of this subsection [will continue] to be a keeper of the animal until another person becomes a keeper thereof by virtue of those provisions'.

(2) *Dangerous species.* For the purposes of applying s 2(1) of the 1971 Act, an animal belongs to a dangerous species if two conditions are met. The conditions are that the species is not commonly domesticated in the British Isles and that fully grown animals of that species have characteristics making it likely that they will cause severe damage, or that if they cause damage it is likely to be severe.

(3) *Knowledge of abnormal characteristics.* The second liability rule set out above summarises the effect of s 2(2) of the 1971 Act. Several judges have complained about the difficulty of interpreting this provision. It has been described by Lord Denning MR as 'very cumbrously worded',[124] by Ormrod LJ as 'remarkably opaque',[125] and by Slade LJ as 'somewhat tortuous'.[126] In *Mirvahedy* v *Henley*[127] the House of Lords split 3:2 over how to interpret the second condition in s 2(2), that dealing with abnormal characteristics.

[122] It is sufficient to prove that the characteristics were known to someone who had charge of the animal as the keeper's servant, or to someone under 16 years old who was a member of the keeper's household and was also a keeper: Animals Act 1971, s 2(2)(c).

[123] This provision replaces the old common law rules on liability for cattle trespass and is discussed above, pp. 767–8.

[124] *Cummings* v *Grainger* [1977] QB 397, 404.

[125] Ibid, 407.

[126] *Curtis* v *Betts* [1990] 1 WLR 459, 462F–G.

[127] [2003] 2 AC 491. This followed the approach of the Court of Appeal in *Cummings* v *Grainger* [1977] QB 397

In the *Mirvahedy* case the claimant had been injured by a horse which had escaped onto a dual carriageway. The horse had apparently stampeded out of its field, pushing through an electric fence, because it had been subjected to a severe fright.[128] The parties agreed that such behaviour was unusual for a horse, but that it was not wholly unusual for a horse that had been subjected to a severe fright. This made it necessary to interpret s 2(2)(b) – the second condition – which requires that: 'the likelihood of the damage or of its being severe was due to characteristics of the animal which are not normally found in animals of the same species or are not normally so found except at particular times or in particular circumstances.' The crucial issue was whether the phrase 'or are not normally so found except at particular times or in particular circumstances' was intended to create strict liability when an animal behaved in an unusual way even though that behaviour was usual in the particular circumstances of the case (as would be the case, for example, if a normally docile bitch bit a stranger to protect its pups) or was intended only to prevent keepers of animals that they knew were abnormally vicious trying to escape being held liable under the Act by arguing that all such animals are vicious in some circumstances (as would be the case, for example, if a keeper of a dog which bit all strangers argued that this characteristic was not abnormal for a dog because all dogs will bite strangers that poke them with sticks). A bare majority of the House of Lords favoured the first interpretation of the phrase, and thus held that the keeper of the escaped horse was liable, because the horse's behaviour was unusual (horses do not usually stampede), even though it was usual in the particular circumstances (having been terrified).

The strongest objection to this reading of the statute is the argument that almost any circumstances in which a domesticated animal causes harm can be presented as involving a 'characteristic' only exhibited in 'particular circumstances', thus potentially leading to liability. Lord Scott gave the example of a police horse which kicked an innocent passer-by after a miscreant jabbed a sharp instrument into its rump. Lord Scott believed that on the majority's approach 'kicking out' would be a characteristic not normally displayed by horses, but it would be normal in the 'particular circumstances' of being jabbed in the rump, and the keeper would be likely to know this.[129] But Lord Nicholls, who was in the majority, suggested that this objection was exaggerated and that liability would not attach if, for instance, a cow slipped and fell on someone, because the dangerous characteristic (its weight) would *not* be one found only in particular circumstances.[130]

Lord Nicholls's response raises the difficult question of the relationship between the first and second conditions on liability arising under s 2 of the Act. In *Bowlt* v *Clark*[131] the claimant was injured as a result of a horse asserting its will against its rider and moving into the road in front of his car. The trial judge found that the first condition for liability was satisfied by the weight of the horse – it was of such a weight that if it ever collided with a car it was likely to cause *severe* damage – and that the second condition was satisfied by the horse's tendency 'to assert an inclination to move otherwise than as directed' at particular

and *Curtis* v *Betts* [1990] 1 WLR 459, and rejected the opinions of Lloyd and Oliver LJJ in *Breeden* v *Lampard*, 21 March 1985, unreported.

128 It was never discovered what caused the horse to panic.

129 *Mirvahedy* v *Henley* [2003] 2 AC 491, at [115].

130 Ibid., [46].

131 [2006] EWCA Civ 978.

times or in particular circumstances, and that the third condition was satisfied by the keeper's knowledge of this tendency. The Court of Appeal, however, held that such findings involved a 'muddle' because the second condition on liability arising under s 2 of the Act for harm done by an animal required that 'the likelihood of the [animal's doing] damage or of [any damage done by the animal] being severe' be due to the animal having some kind of abnormal characteristic.[132] Thus if 'the weight of the horse' was used to establish that the horse was likely to do damage, or that any damage done by the horse was likely to be severe, then the second condition could not be satisfied because 'the weight of the horse' was not due to any *abnormal* characteristic. And reference to the characteristic 'to assert an inclination to move otherwise than as directed' at particular times or in particular circumstances could not help the claimant because neither 'the likelihood of the damage' nor 'the likelihood . . . of its being severe' was due to this characteristic. If this interpretation of the relationship between the first and second conditions is correct[133] then it means that Lord Scott was *incorrect* to say that there would be liability if a police horse kicked an innocent passer-by after a miscreant jabbed a sharp instrument into its rump. This is because while it is true to say that if the horse kicked the passer-by the damage done by the kick was likely to be severe, the likelihood of that damage being severe had nothing to do with the police horse having the characteristic (shared by other horses only under certain circumstances) of 'being liable to kick out' but was instead a consequence of the police horse having a powerful kick (a characteristic that is shared by all horses, under all circumstances, and therefore not abnormal).

Even if the decision in the *Mirvahedy* case has not extended the potential scope of liability for injuries caused by animals which are normally domesticated to the degree feared by Lord Scott, the effect of the House of Lords' ruling has been to make it easier to establish liability in some cases. Consequently, attention will be focused more often on the possible defences.

Defences

There are a number of defences open to someone who is sued under the 1971 Act.

(1) *Wholly at fault.* If B sues A for compensation for harm suffered by her under any of the liability rules set out above, A will have a defence to B's claim if B was wholly at fault for the fact that she suffered that harm.[134]

(2) *Voluntary assumption of risk; trespass.* If B has been harmed by an animal and seeks to sue A for compensation for that harm under s 2(1) or s 2(2) of the 1971 Act, A will have a defence to B's claim if B voluntarily took the risk that she would be harmed by that animal.[135] A will also have a defence if:

132 The wording of the two conditions is: '(a) the damage is of a kind which the animal, unless restrained, was likely to cause or which, if caused by the animal, was likely to be severe; and (b) the likelihood of the damage or of its being severe was due to characteristics of the animal which are not normally found in animals of the same species or are not normally so found except at particular times or in particular circumstances'.

133 It has been criticised by Burnett 2007, 21–9.

134 Animals Act 1971, s 5(1). The defence of contributory negligence also applies: s 10.

135 Section 5(2).

(i) the animal in question harmed B while she was trespassing on premises on which that animal was kept; *and*

(ii) *either* that animal was *not* kept on the premises for the protection of persons or property *or* that animal *was* kept on the premises for the protection of persons or property and the keeping of the animal on those premises for that purpose was not unreasonable.[136]

The question whether a trespasser injured by an animal might be able to sue the occupier of the premises (rather than the animal's keeper) under the Occupiers' Liability Act 1984 is not straightforward, and depends on the scope of that Act.[137]

(3) *Straying livestock.* Suppose livestock belonging to B strayed onto land belonging to someone else and was attacked there by a dog. If B sues A – the dog's keeper – for compensation for the damage done to her livestock by the dog under s 3 of the 1971 Act, A will have a defence to B's claim if: (i) the dog belonged to the occupier of the land on which the livestock was attacked; *or* (ii) the dog was authorised to be on the land on which the livestock was attacked.[138]

(4) *No defences of act of a stranger and Act of God.* If an animal has caused B to suffer some kind of harm, and B seeks to sue A – the keeper of that animal – for compensation for that harm under the Animals Act 1971, it seems that the fact that the animal acted in the way it did because of the malicious act of a stranger or an Act of God will afford A no defence to B's claim. Consequently, the potential liability of the keeper of a dangerous animal is wider than the potential liability of the keeper of an inanimate dangerous thing.

Visit **http://www.mylawchamber.co.uk/mcbride** to access updates on recent cases, as well as model answers and tips for answering tort problem questions.

Use **Case Navigator** to read in full some of the key cases referenced in this chapter:

- **Rylands *v* Fletcher**
- **Transco plc *v* Stockport Metropolitan Borough Council**
- **Read *v* J Lyons & Co**
- **Cambridge Water *v* Eastern Counties Leather**

136 Animals Act 1971, s 5(3). In *Cummings* v *Grainger* [1975] 1 WLR 1330, O'Connor J thought that it was unreasonable for a scrap metal dealer to keep an untrained Alsatian with a known propensity to attack black people as protection for his yard, but the Court of Appeal disagreed: [1977] QB 397. It is worth noting, however, that the case arose before the Guard Dogs Act 1975 made it unlawful to keep an uncontrolled guard dog.

137 On which see above, pp. 171–5.

138 Animals Act 1971, s 5(4).

43 The Consumer Protection Act 1987

ANTECEDENTS OF THE ACT

If you suffer some kind of harm as a result of a product being defective, you may be entitled to sue the 'producer' of that product for compensation under the Consumer Protection Act 1987.[1] Your claim for compensation under the 1987 Act will be non-tortious in character: in order to make out your claim, you will not have to show that the producer of the product committed any kind of legal wrong in manufacturing the product that harmed you.

The Consumer Protection Act 1987 has a European origin. It was passed to give effect to Council Directive 85/374/EEC ('the Directive') which required each Member State of the European Union to take steps to ensure that under their national laws the producer of a defective product would be held liable on a 'no-fault' basis for the damage done by that product – that is, would be held liable without the necessity of showing that the producer was at fault for the existence of the defect in the product in question. On its face, the object of the Directive was to harmonise the laws on product liability across the European Union because 'existing divergences may distort competition and affect the movement of goods within the [European Union's] common market'.[2] The idea was that producers of products in a particular country might gain an unfair competitive advantage if they were subject to products liability rules that were less harsh than those applied to producers of similar products in other countries within the European Union.[3] The Directive has signally failed to achieve this objective for three reasons:

(1) *Non-applicability to commercial property*. The Directive sought to harmonise only the laws on when the producer of a defective product would be held liable in respect of damage done by that product to people or property 'intended for private use or consumption'.[4] National laws on when the manufacturer of a defective product would be held liable in respect of damage done by that product to *commercial property* were left untouched by the Directive.

(2) *Opt-outs*. European Union governments did not have to implement *all* aspects of the Directive; they had some latitude to pick and choose which parts of the Directive they would implement. For example, the Directive provides that the producer of a defective product should not be held liable as a result of that product being defective if 'the state of

[1] The Act has now been amended by the Consumer Protection Act 1987 (Product Liability) (Modification) Order 2000 (SI No. 2771).

[2] Preamble to Council Directive 85/374/EEC.

[3] For this reason, the European Court of Justice has ruled that the Directive is a 'maximum harmonisation' directive – that is, national governments are not allowed to give effect to a products liability regime which is *stricter* than that contemplated by the Directive. See *EC* v *Greece*, C-154/00, 25 April 2002; *EC* v *France*, C-52/00, 25 April 2002; *Sanchez* v *Medicina Asturiana* SA, C-183/00, 25 April 2002.

[4] Directive, Art 9.

scientific and technical knowledge at the time when he put the product into circulation was not such as to enable the existence of the defect to be discovered'.[5] However, national governments were allowed, in implementing the Directive, to choose whether or not to implement this particular provision: Article 15(1)(b) of the Directive gives national governments the power to provide 'that the producer [of a defective product] shall be liable even if he proves that the state of scientific and technical knowledge at the time when he put the product into circulation was not such as to enable the existence of [the] defect to be discovered'. Again, Article 16(1) of the Directive provides that '[any] Member State *may* provide that a producer's total liability for damage resulting from a death or personal injury and caused by identical items with the same defect shall be limited to an amount which may not be less than 70 million ECU'.[6] So national governments were free to choose, in passing legislation which implemented the Directive, whether or not to put a cap on the liability that might be incurred by a manufacturer of a defective product under that legislation.

(3) *Remedies*. The Directive did nothing to harmonise the remedies that would be available if someone was killed or injured as a result of a product being defective; for instance, the Directive did nothing to harmonise the law on whether – if someone was killed as a result of a product being defective – the deceased's dependants would be able to bring an action for damages in respect of the loss of support suffered by them as a result of the deceased's death.

Given this, it may be suspected that the real reason for the 1985 Directive was *not* to harmonise the law on products liability across the European Union; rather, the Directive was adopted in order to help ensure that a 'citizen' of the European Union who suffered harm to his person or property as a result of a product being defective would be able to recover compensation for that harm without having to prove: (1) that anyone was at fault for the fact that he suffered that harm; or (2) that that harm was suffered by him as a result of someone's committing a legal wrong in relation to him.[7] Whatever the objectives that were sought to be achieved by adopting the 1985 Directive, as the Consumer Protection Act 1987 was enacted in order to implement that Directive the courts are required to take the Directive into account in interpreting the provisions of the 1987 Act and to interpret those provisions in such a way as will give effect to the Directive and promote its objectives.[8] It is to the provisions of the 1987 Act that we now turn.

[5] Directive, Art 7(e). This is known as the 'development risks defence'. On which, see below, pp. 786–7.

[6] Emphasis added.

[7] Given this, the European Court of Justice's ruling that national governments are not allowed to introduce products liability regimes which are *more favourable* to an injured consumer than that contemplated by the Directive (see above, n. 3) may represent something of an own-goal. Significantly, the Council of the European Union has reacted to this ruling by calling for an assessment as to whether the Directive should be amended so as to allow national governments to hold *suppliers* of defective products liable for the harm done by those products *outside* the situations where the Directive currently contemplates suppliers of defective products may be held liable: Council Resolution of 19 December 2002, 2003/C 26/02.

[8] Consumer Protection Act 1987, s 1(1).

THE BASIC RULE

Section 2 of the Consumer Protection Act 1987 sets out the basic rule which underlies the Act. It provides that if 'any damage is caused wholly or partly by a defect in a product'[9] then, as a general rule, 'the producer of the product'[10] *and* 'any person who, by putting his name on the product or by using a trade mark or other distinguishing mark in relation to the product, has held himself out to be the producer of the product'[11] *and* 'any person who has imported the product into a member State from a place outside the member States in order, in the course of any business of his, to supply it to another'[12] will be held jointly and severally[13] 'liable for the damage'.[14]

The supplier of the product will also be 'liable for the damage' if: '(a) the person who suffered the damage requests the supplier to identify one or more of the persons (whether still in existence or not) [mentioned in the previous sentence]; (b) that request is made within a reasonable period after the damage occurs and at a time when it is not reasonably practicable for the person making the request to identify all those persons; and (c) the supplier fails, within a reasonable period after receiving the request, either to comply with that request or to identify the person who supplied that product to him.'[15] All this needs more explanation.

Product

Section 1(2) of the 1987 Act provides that '"product" means any goods or electricity and includes a product which is comprised in another product, whether by virtue of being a component part or raw material or otherwise'. So the term 'product' covers not only *manufactured products* (like cars, radios and computers)[16] but also *natural products* (like coal, flowers and animals).

There is some debate over whether body parts and blood count as 'products' under the Act. It seems likely that they do – 'goods' is defined in the Act as including 'substances',[17] which would cover body parts and blood products; and Article 2 of the Directive defines the term 'product' as covering 'all moveables', which again would cover body parts and blood products. Indeed, it was conceded in the important case of *A* v *National Blood Authority* that contaminated blood did count as a 'product' under the Act.[18]

Opinion is more divided on the issue of whether an inaccurate map or some faulty software will count as a defective product under the 1987 Act.[19] The problem is that the map or software *qua* physical item will not be deficient in any respect. It is the information *on*

9 Section 2(1).
10 Section 2(2)(a).
11 Section 2(2)(b).
12 Section 2(2)(c).
13 Section 2(5).
14 Section 2(1).
15 Section 2(3).
16 But not buildings: s 46(3).
17 Section 45(1).
18 [2001] 3 All ER 289, at [17]. Blood and other human body parts and tissues are not generally regarded as 'products' under American products liability laws: see GS&Z, 842.
19 See, generally, Whittaker 1989, and Nolan 2007. For a negative view, see Stapleton 1994a, 333–4.

the map or *in* the software that is deficient and that information does not seem to count as a 'substance' or a 'moveable'. This question has yet to be settled by the courts. It would seem an arbitrary result if, for example, an inaccurate map was not counted as being a defective product under the 1987 Act while, for example, a faulty pair of boots was regarded as defective under the Act: the danger posed by each to a mountaineer is the same. However, it may be that the language of the 1987 Act and the Directive will leave the courts with little choice but to reach such a conclusion.

Producer

Section 1(2) of the 1987 Act also specifies who the 'producer' of a product will be. If the product was manufactured, the 'producer' of that product will be the person who manufactured it. If the product in question was not manufactured but was instead 'won or abstracted' – say the product in question was coal – 'the person who won or abstracted it' will be the producer of the product.[20] The 1987 Act goes on to specify that 'in the case of a product which has not been manufactured, won or abstracted but essential characteristics of which are attributable to an industrial or other process having been carried out (for example, in relation to agricultural produce), the person who carried out that process' will be the 'producer' of that product.

Defect

Certainly the most important and difficult provision in the 1987 Act is s 3, which explains when a product will count as being defective under the Act.

The legitimate expectations test

Section 3 follows the Directive[21] in adopting a 'legitimate expectations' test for determining whether a given product is defective. It provides that:

> (1) . . . there is a defect in a product . . . if the safety of the product is not such as persons generally are entitled to expect . . .
> (2) In determining . . . what persons generally are entitled to expect in relation to a product all the circumstances shall be taken into account, including –
> (a) the manner in which, and purposes for which, the product has been marketed, its get-up, the use of any mark in relation to the product and any instructions for, or warnings with respect to, doing or refraining from doing anything with or in relation to the product;
> (b) what might reasonably be expected to be done with or in relation to the product; and
> (c) the time when the product was supplied by its producer to another . . .'

This definition is far from easy to understand or apply. How, for example, do we determine whether a product's safety is such as persons 'generally are *entitled* to expect'? Fortunately,

[20] What is the position if John dies and a surgeon, Wendy, takes out his heart for transplantation purposes and the heart is given to Fred in a heart transplant operation? If the heart proves to be defective (say, for example, it is cancerous), who will count as being the 'producer' of the heart? Stapleton 1994a suggests (at 310–11) that John will be the producer because he 'manufactured' the heart. However, this seems unreal: a heart is not a manufactured product but a natural product. The better view is that Wendy is the producer because she 'won or abstracted' the heart.

[21] See Art 6(1).

there is a growing body of case law which provides a good deal of guidance as to how the 'legitimate expectations' test will operate in practice.[22] But before we look at this case law, it might be helpful to distinguish between six different types of product that *might* be regarded as defective under the 1987 Act. We will then be able to look at when each type of product *will* be regarded as defective under the Act.

A typology of products that may be defective under the Act

The six types of product are as follows:

(1) A manufactured product that does not conform to its intended design and as a result is more dangerous to use than would otherwise be the case. It is customary to say that such a product suffers from a *manufacturing defect*.[23] An example of such a product is a tin of food where the inner lining of the tin is scratched, making the food inside dangerous to eat.

(2) A manufactured product that conforms to its intended design but it could be designed to a higher safety standard. It is customary to say that such a product suffers from a *design defect*. An example of such a product is a car that is not fitted with airbags.

(3) A manufactured product that is dangerous to use but which cannot be made any safer than it is. We can say that such a product is *inherently dangerous*. An example of such a product is a cigarette.

(4) A natural product that is contaminated or infected with some dangerous substance or otherwise diseased in some way. As the product is natural, and therefore not designed or manufactured, it would be inappropriate to say that it suffers from a *manufacturing defect*, though it is analogous to such a product. Instead, we will say that such a product is *dangerously abnormal*. An example of such a product is a cancerous kidney or a dog that is infested with fleas.

(5) A product that does not carry a warning as to how it should be used. We can say that such a product suffers from a *marketing defect*. An example of such a product is a box of paracetamol that does not warn that the paracetamol should not be taken in conjunction with other medicine or by those who suffer kidney problems.

(6) A product that *may* be dangerous to use but it is impossible to tell whether it is or is not. We can say that such a product is *potentially harmful*. An example of such a product is a bag of blood that may or may not carry a virus that will trigger Creutzfeld-Jakob Disease (CJD) in a patient who is given the blood. The blood may be perfectly safe or it may be deadly; but it is impossible to tell which it is.[24]

[22] See also the useful discussion in Stoppa 1992.

[23] Note that we use the term 'defect' here and below without prejudice to the issue of whether this kind of product is *actually* defective under the 1987 Act.

[24] Of course, if we give the blood to a patient and he subsequently develops symptoms of CJD, we will know that the blood was dangerous. In such a case, the blood that was given to the patient will have been *both* potentially harmful (it was impossible to tell at the time the blood was given to the patient whether it was dangerous) *and* dangerously abnormal (it was a natural product that was contaminated with a CJD-triggering virus). This example shows that a given product may well fall into more than one of the categories of product listed above. So a cup of coffee served in a restaurant may suffer from a design defect (it could have been made safer by serving it at a lower temperature); at the same time it may also suffer from a marketing defect (it did not carry a warning that it was hot or that harm might be caused if the cup was spilled). In order to determine whether

Doubtless there are other types of product that may be regarded as defective under the Act, but it is these six that we will concentrate on in discussing the case law that deals with the ambit of s 3 of the 1987 Act.

The case law

The most important case dealing with the issue of whether a product will be defective under the Act is *A* v *National Blood Authority*.[25] The claimants were people who had been infected with the hepatitis C virus as a result of receiving blood transfusions containing blood donated by people who had hepatitis C. At the time the claimants were infected, no test existed to detect whether a given bag of blood contained the hepatitis C virus. The claimants sued the National Blood Authority (the NBA) for compensation under the 1987 Act, claiming that the blood that they were given was defective under the 1987 Act.

Counsel for the NBA must have thought they had a good case for arguing that the blood given to the claimants was *not* defective under the 'legitimate expectations' test set out in s 3. After all, at the time the claimants were infected, there was no way of ensuring that the bags of blood given to the claimants were free of the hepatitis C virus. Given this, how could it be said that 'persons generally were *entitled* to expect' that the bags of blood given to the claimants would be free of hepatitis C? Surely they could not be entitled to expect the impossible? However, if this argument were accepted, then it would seem to follow that a product that suffered from a manufacturing defect would not be defective if it was not possible to detect the existence of that manufacturing defect. But such a finding would be inconsistent with the intentions of the framers of the Directive who clearly intended that producers of products that suffer from manufacturing defects should be held liable for the harm done by those defects irrespective of whether those defects could be discovered or not.

Faced with this problem, Burton J brushed aside the arguments of counsel for the NBA and held that the 'avoidability' of the harm suffered by a claimant in a products liability case is not to be taken into account in judging whether the product that harmed the claimant was defective or not under the Act.[26] Burton J went on to hold that the blood given to the claimants was defective under the Act. His reasoning went as follows. He held that the bags of blood given to the claimants were 'non-standard products ... They were different from the norm which the producer intended for use by the public.'[27] He further held that 'Where, as here, there is a harmful characteristic in a non-standard product, a decision that it is defective is likely to be straightforward, and I ... make my decision accordingly.'[28] However, Burton J conceded that the result might have been different had the public been generally aware at the time the claimants were infected that there was a risk that someone receiving a blood transfusion might contract hepatitis C. In such a case, it might have been difficult to contend that at the time the claimants were infected 'persons

---

such a cup of coffee is defective under the Act, it is necessary first to ask whether it is defective because it suffered from a design defect; and if the answer is no, then ask whether it is defective because it suffered from a marketing defect.

[25] [2001] 3 All ER 289 (noted, Howells & Mildred 2002).

[26] Ibid., at [63].

[27] Ibid., at [65].

[28] Ibid., at [66].

generally were entitled to expect' that supplies of blood were free of hepatitis C.[29] However, that was not the case here. At the time the claimants were infected, people generally did *not* know that there was a risk they might contract hepatitis C if they were given a blood transfusion.

Burton J's judgment represents the outcome of a struggle to reconcile the 'legitimate expectations' test for defectiveness that is set out in the Act with the policy objectives which underlie the Act – in particular, the objective of ensuring that producers of products that suffer from manufacturing defects are held liable for the harm caused by their products on a 'no-fault' basis. The policy behind the Act was allowed to trump the 'legitimate expectations' test when Burton J ruled that 'avoidability' of harm was not to be taken into account in judging whether a product is defective under the Act. But the 'legitimate expectations' test was reintroduced into the equation when Burton J acknowledged that had there been widespread public knowledge of the risk that blood supplies might be contaminated with hepatitis C, a bag of blood which was contaminated with hepatitis C might not have counted as a defective product under the Act.

So, Burton J's judgment in *A* v *National Blood Authority* seemed to establish in relation to products (1) and (4), above – that is, manufactured products that suffer from a manufacturing defect and natural products that are abnormally dangerous – that such products, being non-standard in nature, would *always* be regarded as defective under the Act unless the possibility of such products being non-standard is widely acknowledged and accepted.

However, this statement of the law has now been qualified by the decision of the Court of Appeal in *Tesco Stores Ltd* v *Pollard*.[30] In that case, a 13-month-old child was made sick eating some dishwasher powder that was in a bottle. The bottle – which was manufactured by the defendants – was fitted with a childproof lock but there was some evidence that the lock was not as strong as it was intended to be. The Court of Appeal rejected the claim that this meant the bottle of dishwasher powder was automatically defective: to accept this would mean that 'every producer of a product whose use causes injury effectively warrants to the general public that the product fulfils its design standards ... It is quite impossible to get such a result out of the terms of the 1987 Act.'[31] The Court of Appeal went on to find that all that persons generally were entitled to expect of the child-resistant lock was that it make the 'bottle ... more difficult to open than if it had an ordinary screwtop'[32] and that as the child-resistant lock in this case did make the bottle difficult to open, then the bottle was not defective. It may be that the Court of Appeal thought that finding that the bottle in this case was defective would result in the defendants being penalised for *aiming* to make their product much safer than people generally would have expected it to be. So long as a defendant's product was safe enough according to people's general expectations, that product should not be held to be defective merely because a manufacturing defect meant that that product was not quite as safe as the defendant intended it to be.

In light of the above discussion, we can say that: (1) A natural product that is abnormally dangerous will always be defective under the 1987 Act. (2) A product that suffers from a manufacturing defect that introduces a *new* danger into the product that would not other-

[29] Ibid., at [65].
[30] [2006] EWCA Civ 393.
[31] Ibid., at [17].
[32] Ibid., at [18].

wise have been there will always be defective under the 1987 Act. (3) A product that suffers from a manufacturing defect that reduces the effectiveness of some safety device that forms part of the product will only be defective under the 1987 Act if the manufacturing defect means that the product is not as safe as people generally expect it to be.

What of the other types of product in our typology?

(1) *Design defect.* When will a product that suffers from a design defect be regarded as defective under the Act? The 'legitimate expectations' test indicates that a product that purports to be designed to a higher safety standard than it actually is will be defective under the Act – it will not be as safe as 'persons generally are entitled to expect' given the product's 'get-up' and the way it 'has been marketed'. So a coat which has been marketed as 'suitable for all weathers' will be defective under the Act if it turns out not to be waterproof and its wearer catches influenza as a result; and this is so even if it was not actually designed to be waterproof.

What is the position if the product does not purport to be designed to a higher safety standard than it actually is? For example, what if a car obviously does not come with an airbag equipped? Or what if the packaging of a condom – that has been designed in such a way that there is a 0.01 per cent chance that it will split – does not promise that the condom will be 100 per cent effective but warns the user that it is liable to split? When will such a product be held to be defective under the Act? Common sense indicates that such products cannot *automatically* be held to be defective under the Act. Otherwise every car would have to be equipped with every conceivable safety feature in order to avoid being held to be defective under the Act. Instead, it is suggested, such a product should be held to be defective under the Act if it was *unreasonable* not to design that product to a higher safety standard, given the costs and benefits involved.[33]

The available case law seems to adopt this line of thinking. In *Abouzaid* v *Mothercare (UK) Ltd*,[34] it will be recalled, the claimant was injured when he attempted to fit a sleeping bag onto a pushchair. The sleeping bag was to be attached to the pushchair by passing two elasticated straps attached to the sleeping bag around the back of the pushchair and buckling them together. Unfortunately, the claimant let go of one of the elasticated straps and the buckle at the end of the strap hit him in the eye. He sued the defendants who marketed the sleeping bag under their name for compensation in negligence and under the 1987 Act. The sleeping bag was held to be defective under the Act. The sleeping bag suffered from a design defect: it could have been designed to a higher safety standard, either by making the straps attached to the sleeping bag non-elasticated or by having one continuous elasticated strap stretch from one side of the sleeping bag to the other. And it was unreasonable not to design the sleeping bag to such a higher safety standard: it would have been quite easy to make the sleeping bag safer to use at no added cost.[35]

[33] *Important note.* It might be objected that questions of reasonableness should be irrelevant under a 'no fault' products liability regime. However, the point is that it is impossible *not* to attend to questions of reasonableness in determining whether a product that suffers from a design defect is defective – otherwise we end up with a liability regime which condemns almost all but the most expensive, top quality cars as being defective. So a pure 'no fault' liability regime is an impossibility – in certain cases, some fault-related considerations will *have* to be taken into account in judging whether or not a given product is defective.

[34] The Times, 20 February 2001. See above, pp. 81–2.

[35] The fact that no one had any reason to know that there was any need to modify the sleeping bag was highly relevant to the claim against the defendants in negligence; but was irrelevant to the question of whether the

In contrast, in *B (a child)* v *McDonald's Restaurants Ltd*,[36] the claimants sued McDonald's for compensation under the 1987 Act when they were scalded by McDonald's coffee that was spilled on them. The coffee suffered from a design defect: it would not have scalded the claimants so badly had it been served at 55 °C rather than the 90 °C that it was actually served at. However, Field J refused to find that the coffee was defective under the Act. He held that the costs involved in serving the coffee at this lower temperature – in the shape of a loss in custom – outweighed the benefits: 'coffee served at between 55 °C and 60 °C would not have been acceptable to McDonald's customers. Indeed, on the evidence, I find that the public want to be able to buy . . . coffee served hot, that is to say at a temperature of at least 65 °C [the temperature at which coffee will cause a severe burn if spilled on skin] even though they know . . . that there is a risk of a scalding injury if the drink is spilled.'[37]

(2) *Inherently dangerous*. It might be thought that a product that is inherently dangerous *cannot* be defective under the 'legitimate expectations' test – how can persons generally be entitled to expect an average cigarette to be safer to use or consume when such a cigarette cannot possibly be made any safer to use or consume? However, Burton J in the *A* case ruled that if 'avoidability' of harm was not something to be taken into account in judging whether a 'non-standard' product is defective under the Act, then 'avoidability' cannot be taken into account either in judging whether a 'standard' product is defective under the Act.[38] So it seems that a product that is inherently dangerous may be defective under the Act. Whether it will be or not may depend on whether persons generally are aware that the product is inherently dangerous. If they are then it will be difficult to argue that the product's safety is not such as 'persons generally are entitled to expect'. But if they are not – if persons generally think that the product in question is safer than it actually is – then a finding that the product is defective under the Act should be straightforward. So cigarettes nowadays would almost certainly not count as being defective under the Act – though it might have been different 70 years ago, when the risks attached to cigarette smoking were less well understood.

(3) *Marketing defect*. If a product does not carry a warning as to how it should be used, it *cannot* be the law that it is *automatically* defective under the Act. Otherwise, we would be in the ridiculous position of saying that a knife will be defective if it does not carry a

sleeping bag was defective under the 1987 Act. So even in a design defect case, a defendant's fault is not *entirely* relevant to the question of whether he will be held liable under the Act.

36 [2002] EWHC 490.

37 Ibid., at [33]. For another design defect case where it was held that the offending product was not defective under the Act, see *Richardson* v *LRC Products Ltd* [2000] Lloyd's Rep Med 280 where the claimant fell pregnant after having sex with her husband using a condom that split. The claimant sued the defendant manufacturers of the condom for compensation under the 1987 Act. However, the condom was held not to be defective. An attempt to argue that the condom was defective because it suffered from a manufacturing defect failed: it was argued that the condom was unusually brittle because it was exposed to too much sunlight in the factory, but it could not be proved that the signs of excessive exposure to sunlight were not attributable to the claimant having stored the condom near a window after it split. And it was held that the fact that the condom could have been designed in such a way as to make it less liable to split did not make it defective under the Act. It did not purport to be more reliable than it was and making it less liable to split would have adversely affected its quality and marketability to little benefit.

38 [2001] 3 All ER 289, at [71].

warning that it is sharp and that a cup of coffee is defective if it does not carry a warning that it is hot. Something more must be required before a product that does not carry a warning as to how it should be used will be held to be defective under the Act. It must be shown, we would suggest, that it was *reasonable to expect* that product to carry a warning as to how it should be used, given the purposes for which the product might have been used, who might have been expected to use the product or get their hands on it, and the extent of the damage that might have been suffered had the product been misused. Under this test, a failure to give a warning of an obvious danger attached to the use of a product will not make the product defective under the Act – it is not reasonable to expect the producer of a product to spend time and trouble warning people against dangers which are obvious to everyone.[39]

(4) *Potentially harmful.* In *A* v *National Blood Authority*, it was argued that at the time the claimants contracted hepatitis C, *every* bag of blood in the UK was defective under the Act because at that time any given bag of blood was potentially harmful – any given bag of blood might have contained the hepatitis C virus and it was impossible to tell which ones did and which ones did not. However, Burton J rejected this argument, holding that only bags of blood which *did* contain the hepatitis C virus were defective under the Act.[40]

If this is right, then a product which is merely potentially harmful will not count as being defective under the Act. So, for example, in the case of *Group B Plaintiffs* v *Medical Research Council*,[41] the claimants were all treated with human growth hormone (HGH) that, they subsequently discovered, might have been contaminated with a virus that triggers CJD in adults. Each of the claimants developed a psychiatric illness as a result of worrying about the fact that they might develop CJD in the future. Had the 1987 Act been in force at the time they were injected with the human growth hormone, could they have sued for compensation for their psychiatric illnesses under the Act?[42] On Burton J's approach, the answer is 'no.' In the absence of any evidence that the HGH that they were given was *actually* contaminated with a CJD-triggering virus, they would not have been able to establish that that HGH was defective. The fact that HGH was potentially harmful would not have been enough to establish that it was defective under the Act.

Complex products

Suppose that Eric was driving along in his new car when one of the tyres on the car blew out with the result that Eric crashed the car and suffered severe injuries. In this situation, Eric will be able to sue the producer of the car *and* the producer of the tyre under the 1987 Act for compensation for his injuries. Eric can sue the producer of the car because the car was defective under the 1987 Act – it was not as safe as persons generally are entitled to expect (persons generally are entitled to expect when they buy a new car that the tyres on the car will not be faulty) – and Eric sustained his injuries because the car was defective.

[39] *B (a child)* v *McDonald's Restaurants Ltd* [2002] EWHC 490, at [66] (McDonald's failure to warn its customers that its coffee is hot and liable to scald if spilled does not make it defective as 'its customers [can] be taken to know that the coffee they [are] buying [is] hot and could cause a nasty scalding injury if spilled on someone').

[40] [2001] 3 All ER 289, at [65].

[41] [2000] Lloyd's Rep Med 161.

[42] Note that psychiatric illnesses are actionable under the Act: see below, n. 43.

Similarly, Eric can sue the producer of the tyre which blew out because the tyre was defective under the 1987 Act and sustained his injuries because the tyre was defective.

It should be noted that the person who sold the car to Eric – Mary – will only be treated as having supplied the *car* and not the *tyre* to Eric. Section 1(3) of the 1987 Act makes it clear that 'a person who supplies any product in which products are comprised ... shall not be treated by reason only of his supply of that product as supplying any of the products so comprised'. So Mary will *not* be held liable under s 2(3) of the 1987 Act to compensate Eric for the injuries sustained by him if she is unable to tell Eric who manufactured the *tyre* on Eric's car or who supplied that *tyre* to her. This is, of course, something which Mary may well not be in a position to know. Eric will only be entitled to request Mary to tell him who manufactured Eric's *car* and so Mary will only be held liable under s 2(3) of the 1987 Act to pay Eric damages in respect of his injuries if she does not tell Eric who manufactured Eric's car or who supplied that car to him.

Damage

Section 5(1) of the 1987 Act provides that '"damage" means death or personal injury or any loss of or damage to any property (including land)'. So only harm to someone's person or property is actionable under the Act.[43] However, s 5 goes on to set out three situations in which someone will not be entitled to recover compensation under the 1987 Act for harm done to his property by a defective product.

First, s 5(2) provides that a 'person shall not be liable [under the Act] in respect of any defect in a product for the loss of or any damage to the product itself or for the loss of or any damage to the whole or any part of the product which has been supplied with the product in question comprised in it'. So, returning to the example we considered above – where Eric was involved in a car crash because a tyre blew out on his new car while he was driving it – Eric will be able to sue the manufacturer of the car and the manufacturer of the tyre for compensation in respect of the injuries suffered by him in the car crash. On the other hand, s 5(2) means that Eric will not be able to sue them for compensation for the damage done to his car in the crash.

What is the position if Karen bought a car and then later refitted the car with new tyres, one of which suffered from a manufacturing defect which caused it to blow out while Karen was out driving with the result that Karen crashed the car and suffered various injuries? Karen will *not* be able to sue the manufacturer of the *car* for compensation for her injuries or the damage done to her car: the manufacturer will have a defence to any claim brought by Karen on the ground that the car was not defective when it left his hands.[44] But Karen *will* be able to sue the manufacturer of the *tyre* for damages to compensate her for the injuries that she sustained in the car crash *and* the damage done to her car. As the defective tyre was not supplied *with* the car Karen will not be barred by s 5(2) from suing the tyre manufacturer for damages in respect of the damage done to her car by that tyre: that

43 *Important note.* 'Personal injury', as defined in the Act, not only covers physical injury but also psychiatric illness. See s 45(1): '"personal injury" includes any disease and any other impairment of a person's physical *or mental condition* ...' (emphasis added).

44 See below, p. 785.

damage will not amount to damage done to a product which was supplied with the tyre *comprised in it*.

Secondly, s 5(3) provides that a 'person shall not be liable [under the Act] for any loss of or damage to any property which, at the time it is lost or damaged, is not – (a) of a description of property ordinarily intended for private use, occupation or consumption; and (b) intended by the person suffering the loss or damage mainly for his own private use, occupation or consumption'. So if a defective product damages a lathe in a factory, damages will not be recoverable under the 1987 Act in respect of the damage done to the lathe: lathes are not ordinarily intended for private (as opposed to commercial) use and the lathe here was not intended for private use. What if a defective product damages a company car? Could the company sue under the 1987 Act for damages in respect of the damage done to its car? It cannot: while the car counts as property that is *ordinarily* intended for private use, occupation or consumption, the car is *in fact* not intended by the company which has suffered the loss of the car to be privately used.

Thirdly, s 5(4) provides that no 'damages shall be awarded to any person [under this Act] in respect of any loss of or damage to any property if the amount which would fall to be so awarded to that person . . . does not exceed £275'.

DEFENCES

Let us suppose that A has suffered some kind of actionable 'damage' as a result of a product being defective and B was the producer of that product. As a general rule, A will be entitled under the 1987 Act to sue B for damages in respect of the harm suffered by him. However, A will not be entitled to sue B for such damages if B can raise a *defence* to A's claim. Someone who is sued in respect of a defect in a product will have a defence if he can show:

(1) *That the defect was attributable to compliance with any requirement imposed by or under any enactment or with any Community obligation.*[45]

(2) *That he did not put the product into circulation.*[46] So say Lara manufactures a car which is then stolen from Lara's factory before it is shipped out. The car is then sold to Gary who is injured because the car suffers from some manufacturing defect. If Gary attempts to sue Lara for damages in respect of his injuries under the 1987 Act, Lara will have a defence to Gary's claim: she did not put the car into circulation.

(3) *That he did not supply the product to another in the course of business and he did not produce, brand or import it with a view to profit.*[47] So if Dawn bakes some cakes for a school fair and Ian, having bought them at the fair, is poisoned by them, Ian will not be entitled to sue Dawn for damages under the 1987 Act: Dawn did not supply the cakes to the fair organisers in the course of a business of hers and she did not supply those cakes for profit.

(4) *That the defect did not exist in the product at the time he supplied the product to someone else.*[48]

[45] Section 4(1)(a); Art 7(d).
[46] Section 4(1)(b); Art 7(a).
[47] Section 4(1)(c); Art 7(c).
[48] Section 4(1)(d); Art 7(b).

(5) *That the state of scientific and technical knowledge at the time when he put the product into circulation was not such as to enable the existence of the defect to be discovered.*[49] The classic case where this defence – known as the 'development risks defence' – will be available is where A puts into circulation some drug that has an dangerous side-effect which no one[50] could have known about at the time the drug was marketed. Those who have suffered harm as a result of the drug's having that side effect will not be able to sue A for compensation under the 1987 Act.

It is now clear from the decision in *A* v *National Blood Authority* that the defence may also be available in a manufacturing defect case. Suppose A manufactures a product that suffers from some kind of manufacturing defect and B suffers some kind of actionable damage as a result. If it was simply not possible at the time the product was manufactured to detect the existence of this manufacturing defect, then A may be able to take advantage of the development risks defence to defeat B's claim for compensation under the Act.

However, Burton J placed one very important limit on the availability of the defence in this case. He held that A will not be able to take advantage of the defence if *he was aware at the time he manufactured the product that there was a risk that it might not conform to its intended design in the way it did.*[51] This limit severely curtails the availability of the development risks defence in manufacturing defect cases. For example, suppose that Eric manufactures tyres on a mass scale. Suppose further that he knows that his manufacturing process is imperfect and as a result it is likely to produce one faulty tyre in 10,000 – however, there is no way he can detect which of his tyres are faulty. Suppose finally that Eric's manufacturing process produces a faulty tyre which is then fitted on Wendy's car; and because the tyre was faulty it blew out when Wendy was driving her car at high speed and she was injured as a result. If Wendy sues Eric for compensation under the Act, Eric will *not* be able to take advantage of the development risks defence to defeat Wendy's claim. While it was not possible to detect beforehand that the tyre was faulty, Eric was aware that there was a risk that one in every 10,000 tyres manufactured by him would suffer from such a fault.[52]

[49] Art 7(e). The equivalent provision in the 1987 Act – s 4(1)(e) – might appear to be somewhat narrower. That provides that someone who is sued in respect of a defect in a product under the Act will have a defence if the 'state of scientific and technical knowledge at the relevant time was not such that a *producer or producers of products of the same description as the product in question might be expected to have discovered the defect* . . .' (emphasis added). This led the European Commission to bring an action against the UK, claiming that the UK had failed in s 4(1)(e) correctly to implement the Directive. However, the European Court of Justice expressed itself content with the wording of s 4(1)(e), holding that 'there is nothing . . . to suggest that the courts in the United Kingdom, if called upon to interpret s 4(1)(e), would not do so in light of the wording and purpose of the Directive so as to achieve the result it has in view': *European Commission* v *UK* [1997] All ER (EC) 481, at [33].

[50] If, at the time A put the drug into circulation, an academic had published a paper in Manchuria revealing that the drug had this side effect, that – it seems – would not be enough to deprive A of the development risks defence: see the opinion of the Advocate-General in [1997] All ER (EC) 481, at [24]. It has to be shown that the state of *accessible* scientific and technical knowledge at the time the drug was circulated was not such as to allow the existence of the side-effect to be discovered: ibid., at [23].

[51] [2001] 3 All ER 289, at [74].

[52] It would be different if, at the time Eric manufactured the faulty tyre on Wendy's car, he believed that his manufacturing process was perfect and that every single tyre manufactured by him would be fault-free. In such a case, Eric would be allowed to take advantage of the development risks defence to defeat Wendy's claim against him for compensation (provided, of course, that he could show that the state of scientific and technical knowledge at the time he manufactured the tyre was such that he could not have detected that the tyre was faulty).

Burton J's limit on the applicability of the development risks defence also meant that it was unavailable to the defendants in the *A* case. They sought to argue that the defence was available to them because the state of scientific and technical knowledge at the time the claimants contracted hepatitis C was not such as to enable them to detect which of their bags of blood were contaminated with hepatitis C. Burton J held that even if this were true, the defence was unavailable because the defendants were aware at the time the claimants contracted hepatitis C that there was a risk that the blood supplied by them to people like the claimants might be contaminated with hepatitis C.

(6) *That the defect – (i) constituted a defect in a product ('the subsequent product') in which the product in question was comprised; and (ii) was wholly attributable to the design of the subsequent product or to compliance by the producer of the product in question with instructions given by the producer of the subsequent product.*[53] It is often said that this defence will cover the case where, say, a lorry manufacturer fits tyres on one of his lorries which are completely unsuitable for that lorry with the result that when the lorry is driven the tyres blow out and an accident is caused. It is said that the tyre manufacturer will be able to take advantage of this defence if he is sued by the people involved in the accident under the 1987 Act. But it is difficult to see how he could be sued in any case by the people involved in the accident: surely his tyres were never defective?

It is worth mentioning two defences that are *not* available to the producer of a defective product:

(1) *Voluntary assumption of risk.* Suppose that Helen goes to her doctor for some botox injections into her face. Helen's doctor warns her against having the operaton, telling her that he has heard 'on the grapevine' that there are some stocks of botox that are infected with CJD-triggering viruses. Helen insists on going ahead with the operation. If the botox injected into Helen's face *is* contaminated with CJD-triggering viruses and Helen develops CJD as a result then Helen will be entitled to sue the manufacturer of the botox for compensation under the 1987 Act. It will be no defence for the manufacturer to say that Helen voluntarily took the risk that she would contract CJD when she had her injections.

(2) *More good than harm.* As we have seen,[54] there is some authority that a negligent defendant will in certain circumstances be able to take advantage of an 'I did more good than harm' defence. But no such defence is available to an action under the 1987 Act. So suppose that Nita is admitted to hospital in desperate need of a heart transplant. A donor heart is tracked down and is transplanted into Nita. Unfortunately, and unknown to everyone, the heart is cancerous and Nita develops cancer as a result of the heart transplant operation. Nita wants to sue the 'producers' of the heart for compensation. It seems likely that her claim will succeed: the heart was defective under the 1987 Act (it was cancerous) and Nita suffered actionable damage as a result of the heart being defective (she developed cancer). The producers of the heart will not be able to defeat Nita's claim for compensation by pointing out that her having the heart transplant operation did her more good than harm – that is, had she not had the operation, she would be dead by now.

[53] Section 4(1)(f); Art 7(f).

[54] See above, p. 593.

REMEDIES

A number of points may be made here about the remedies that will be available under the 1987 Act to someone who has suffered some actionable 'damage' as a result of a product being defective.

(1) *Consumers and third parties.* Although the title of the 1987 Act is the *Consumer* Protection Act, the Act operates to protect *anyone* who has suffered actionable 'damage' as a result of a product being defective. So say John drives a car and one of the tyres on the car blows out because it suffers from some kind of manufacturing defect. Suppose further that the blow out causes John to crash the car with the result that both John and a passer-by, Mary, are injured. Both John and Mary will be entitled to sue the tyre manufacturer for damages under the 1987 Act to compensate them for their injuries: the fact that John is a consumer and Mary a third party is irrelevant.

(2) *Range of liability.* Having said that, the 1987 Act is completely silent on the issue of whether any limits should be drawn on the range of third parties who will be entitled to sue for damages under the 1987 Act. Suppose, for example, that in the above example, John's car crash had an adverse effect on his personality with the result that he eventually raped Wendy. Will Wendy be able to sue the manufacturer of the defective tyre that caused John's car crash for damages under the 1987 Act to compensate her for the fact that she was raped by John? There is nothing in the Act to guide us one way or the other on this issue. Suppose, alternatively, that John was so severely injured in the car crash that his wife, Ruth, had to give up her job and look after John. She was eventually so worn down by the strain of looking after John that she suffered a nervous breakdown. If she sued the tyre manufacturer in negligence for compensation for her breakdown, she would lose: she would not be able to establish that the tyre manufacturer owed her a duty of care in manufacturing the tyre.[55] But could she instead sue the tyre manufacturer for compensation for her breakdown under the 1987 Act? Again, there is nothing in the Act to give us any guidance on this issue.

(3) *Fatal accidents.* Section 6(1) of the 1987 Act provides that any 'damage for which a person is liable under [the Act] shall be deemed to have been caused – (a) for the purposes of the Fatal Accidents Act 1976, by that person's wrongful act, neglect or default'. So, if Paul has been killed by a defective product and, had he not been killed but merely injured by that product, he would have been entitled to sue its producers for damages under the 1987 Act, Paul's dependants may be entitled to sue those producers for damages under the Fatal Accidents Act 1976. Whether they will or not depends on who they are and what sort of loss they have suffered as a result of Paul's death.

(4) *Exclusion/limitation clauses.* If A has suffered some actionable 'damage' as a result of a product being defective, A will be entitled to sue B – the 'producer' of that product – for damages under the 1987 Act. This is so even if there exists a contract between A and B which purports to exclude or limit B's liability to A under the 1987 Act. Section 7 of the 1987 Act provides that the 'liability of a person [under this Act] to a person who has suf-

[55] See above, p. 96.

fered damage caused wholly or partly by a defect in a product, or to a dependant or relative of such a person, shall not be limited or excluded by any contract term . . .'.

(5) *Assessment of liability*. If A has suffered some actionable 'damage' as a result of a product being defective, the 1987 Act is almost completely silent on the issue of how the damages payable in respect of that damage should be assessed. Presumably, A will not just be entitled to recover damages in respect of the damage suffered by him: he will also be entitled to recover damages in respect of the consequential losses suffered by him as a result of his sustaining that damage. So if A's leg is broken by a defective ski, A will not just be entitled to sue the manufacturer for damages to compensate him for the bare fact that his leg has been broken; he will also be entitled to sue him for damages in respect of the medical bills and loss of earnings, if any, incurred by him as a result of his leg being broken. But will A be entitled to sue the manufacturer for all the *foreseeable* losses suffered by him as a consequence of his leg being broken; or will he be entitled to sue the manufacturer for *all* the losses suffered by him as a consequence of his leg being broken? Presumably the answer is the former – subject, of course, to the 'egg-shell skull' rule. After all, this would be the rule if the manufacturer were negligent in manufacturing the ski; there seems little reason why he should be treated more harshly under the 1987 Act.

(6) *Contributory negligence*. If A has suffered some actionable 'damage' as a result of a product being defective with the result that he is *prima facie* entitled to sue B, the producer of that product, for £100,000 in compensatory damages, the damages payable to A may be reduced if A was partly to blame for the fact that he suffered the damage in question. Similarly, if A has been killed as a result of a product being defective, the damages, if any, payable to A's dependants by the producer of that product under the Fatal Accidents Act 1976 may be reduced if A was partly to blame for the fact that he was killed as a result of that product being defective. This is the effect of s 6(4) of the 1987 Act, which provides that where 'any damage is caused partly by a defect in a product and partly by the fault of the person suffering the damage, the Law Reform (Contributory Negligence) Act 1945 and section 5 of the Fatal Accidents Act 1976 (contributory negligence) shall have effect as if the defect were the fault of every person liable by virtue of [this Act] for the damage caused by the defect'.

(7) *Contribution*. Suppose A has suffered some actionable 'damage' as a result of a product being defective. Suppose further that A recovers damages in respect of that damage from B, when A could also have sued C for such damages under the 1987 Act. In such a case, B may well be entitled to bring a claim in contribution against C under the Civil Liability (Contribution) Act 1978 and recoup some of the money he paid out to A to compensate him for the damage suffered by him.

So, for example, suppose Tom developed dermatitis as a result of wearing a T-shirt which, due to a flaw in the way it was manufactured, contained trace elements of some dermatitis-causing chemical. The T-shirt was imported into the United Kingdom by Sarah from China. The T-shirt was then sold to Beth who put her mark on it and held herself out to be the manufacturer of the T-shirt. Beth then sold the T-shirt in her store to Tom. Tom successfully sues Beth for damages under the 1987 Act to compensate him for the fact that he has developed dermatitis as a result of wearing the T-shirt. In such a case, Beth will be entitled to bring a claim in contribution against Sarah on the ground that Sarah imported the T-shirt into the European Union and was therefore liable under the 1987 Act to compensate Tom for the harm suffered by him in wearing that T-shirt.

Visit **http://www.mylawchamber.co.uk/mcbride**
to access updates on recent cases, as well as model answers and tips for answering tort problem questions.

44 Public nuisance

INTRODUCTION

A will commit a public nuisance if he creates, authorises, adopts or continues a state of affairs which unreasonably interferes with a public right or with the comfort, convenience or safety of the public, and he knew, or ought to have known (because the means of knowledge were available to him), that would be the consequence of what he did or omitted to do.

If A commits a public nuisance, he commits a crime – the crime of public nuisance – and can therefore be prosecuted, convicted and punished as a criminal. But this is not the only way in which A can be dealt with. Where it is necessary to prevent the continuance or recurrence of a public nuisance a public official or body may seek an injunction.[1] The public official or body may seek such an injunction of its own volition, or there is a procedure which allows the Attorney-General to lend his name to an action which is in reality controlled by a private individual.[2] More important, however, for the purposes of this book is the fact that a private individual may bring an action for damages (and/or an injunction) in her own name if the public nuisance has caused her 'special damage', that is, damage over and above that suffered by the public in general. Claims for public nuisance brought by private individuals who have suffered 'special damage' *resemble* claims in tort, and are sometimes brought alongside tort claims for damages such as claims in private nuisance or in negligence. Strictly speaking, however, public nuisance is *not* a tort. This is because the duty which is broken by A when he commits a public nuisance is not a duty owed to other individuals but a duty owed *to the public at large*; hence the fact that violations of the duty are usually dealt with by actions brought by public officials.[3]

It is difficult to define what a public nuisance is in any helpful way.[4] Most books rely on Archbold's definition, according to which A will commit the crime of public nuisance if he 'commits an act not warranted by law, or omits to discharge a legal duty, where the effect of the act or omission is to endanger the life, health, property, [morals,] or comfort of the public or to obstruct the public in the exercise of rights common to all Her Majesty's subjects'.[5] But this definition is very vague.

[1] For instance, a local authority is empowered to bring such an action by s 222(1) Local Government Act 1972, and a highway authority by s 130 Highways Act 1980.

[2] Called a 'relator' action.

[3] In practice, public officials probably do not bring many claims which specifically allege public nuisance. Rather they rely on statutory provisions which allow them to deal with *all* types of nuisance; see, for example, the Environmental Protection Act 1990, ss 79 and 80. Criminal prosecutions for public nuisance are also uncommon. Ormerod 2005 states at 991 that 'the major importance of public nuisance today is in the civil remedy which it affords.'

[4] For a vigorous critique see Spencer 1989.

[5] Archbold's definition was approved by the House of Lords in *R* v *Rimmington, R* v *Goldstein* [2006] 1 AC 459, subject to removal of the reference to morals (per Lord Bingham at [36], per Lord Rodger at [45]), which is

What, for instance, is 'an act not warranted by law'?[6] The Second US Restatement of Torts notes that English judicial decisions have held that public nuisance covers, 'interference with the public health, as in the keeping of diseased animals . . .; with the public safety, as in the case of storage of explosives in the midst of a city . . .; with the public morals, as in houses of prostitution . . .; with the public peace, as by loud and disturbing noises; with the public comfort, as in the case of widely disseminated bad odors, dust, and smoke; with the public convenience, as by obstruction of a public highway or navigable stream; and with a wide variety of miscellaneous public rights of a similar kind'.[7]

This catalogue usefully illustrates the width of public nuisance in practice. But it is also misleading so far as it suggests that *any* interference with these public interests will be sufficient. This is incorrect. If we take the example of storage of explosives and inflammable substances, it is not the law in England that someone will commit public nuisance whenever he stores the slightest amount of these.[8] Similarly, A will not commit a public nuisance whenever he obstructs the highway to a minor extent.[9] What is crucial is whether the substances are stored to an unreasonable extent or in an unreasonable way, and whether the highway is obstructed to an unreasonable extent.[10] Thus we think that someone who commits a public nuisance breaches one or both of the following two overlapping duties:

(1) a duty not to create, authorise, adopt or continue a state of affairs which interferes unreasonably with a public right; and
(2) a duty not to create, authorise, adopt or continue a state of affairs which interferes unreasonably with the comfort, convenience or safety of the public.

---

why we have put that word in square brackets. Archbold's definition follows *Stephen's Digest of the Criminal Law*, 9th edn (1900), p. 184: 'A common nuisance is an act not warranted by law or an omission to discharge a legal duty, which act or omission obstructs or causes inconvenience or damage to the public in the exercise of rights common to all His Majesty's subjects.'

6 In *R* v *Rimmington*, *R* v *Goldstein* [2006] 1 AC 459, the House of Lords held that the definition of public nuisance is not so vague that it violates human rights standards because it is (at [36]): 'clear, precise, adequately defined and based on a discernible rational principle. A legal adviser asked to give his opinion in advance would ascertain whether the act or omission contemplated was likely to inflict significant injury on a substantial section of the public exercising their ordinary rights as such: if so, an obvious risk of causing a public nusance would be apparent; if not, not.'

7 Restatement of Torts 2d, §821B, comment b.

8 *R* v *Lister* (1856–7) 7 Dears & B 209, 169 ER 979; *R* v *Chilworth Gunpowder Co.* (1888) 4 TLR 557.

9 *Trevett* v *Lee* [1955] 1 All ER 406, CA (temporarily placing a hosepipe across a country lane).

10 Support for this proposition can be found in the Court of Appeal decision of *Harper* v *G.N. Haden & Sons Ltd* [1933] Ch 298 concerning whether builders' scaffolding which obstructed a pavement amounted to a public nuisance. Lord Hanworth MR said, at 302, 'A temporary obstruction to the use of the highway or to the enjoyment of adjoining premises does not give rise to a legal remedy where such obstruction is reasonable in quantum and in duration.' Romer LJ drew an express parallel with the standard of unreasonableness in private nuisance cases and stated, at 317, 'The law relating to the user of the highway is in truth the law of give and take.' However, in the recent case of *Westminster City Council* v *Ocean Leisure Ltd* [2004] EWCA Civ 970, the Court of Appeal treated Lord Hanworth's dictum as too wide: ibid., at [24]. The Court preferred the view that a limited restriction on the ability of the public to use the highway will be lawful if the restriction is a consequence of a reasonable incident of use of the highway, for instance parking, or of reasonable access to or maintenance of premises alongside the highway: ibid., at [42].

INTERFERENCE WITH PUBLIC RIGHTS

Claims based on a breach of duty (1) raise the question of what counts as a public *right*. Some of the uncertainties as to the scope of public nuisance flow from the fact that it is easy to use the word *right* in a loose sense. It is important not to assume that there is a *right* to all benefits which are widely enjoyed. The rights which are most often relied on in public nuisance cases are the right to free passage along public highways and the right to free navigation along a public river. As an example of the law in action we discuss unreasonable interference with the right to free passage along public highways in detail in the next section.

Unreasonable interference with public highways

A will commit this form of public nuisance if he creates, authorises, adopts or continues a state of affairs which interferes unreasonably with free passage along a public highway. Free passage will be unreasonably interfered with if the highway is unreasonably obstructed or users of the highway are unreasonably endangered.

Unreasonable obstruction

Whether an obstruction to the highway will amount to an unreasonable obstruction depends on the degree of interference created by the obstruction and the reasonableness of causing that degree of interference. Where the obstruction is not such as is likely to inconvenience the public, such as a lamp-post on a pavement, the court will probably hold that there is no unreasonable obstruction.[11] Further, even when an obstruction does cause inconvenience, the person creating the obstruction may be able to demonstrate that there was no unreasonable obstruction because it was reasonable to use the highway in the way that he did. 'No member of the public has an exclusive right to use the highway. He has merely a right to use it subject to the reasonable user of others, and if that reasonable user causes him to be obstructed he has no legal cause of complaint.'[12] Thus it is not a public nuisance to block a highway with a cart in order to unload it.[13] But it is a public nuisance to block a highway so regularly as effectively to prevent it from being used by others.[14] Similarly, it is a public nuisance to block a highway for some reason other than reasonable use of the highway for passage, incidents of passage, access to premises alongside the highway, or building work on premises alongside the highway.[15] In such cases the interferences cannot be defended by appealing to some advantage that might flow to the public

11 *W.H. Chaplin & Co. Ltd v Mayor of Westminster* [1901] 2 Ch 329.

12 *Harper* v *G.N. Haden & Sons Ltd* [1933] Ch 298, 317 per Romer LJ. See also, *Herring* v *Metropolitan Board of Works* (1865) 19 CB NS 510, 144 ER 886.

13 *R* v *Jones* (1812) 3 Camp 230, 231, 170 ER 1364, 1365: 'A cart or wagon may be unloaded at a gateway; but this must be done with promptness' (per Lord Ellenborough).

14 *R* v *Cross* (1812) 3 Camp 224, 227, 170 ER 1362, 1363: 'No one can make a stable yard of the king's highway' (per Lord Ellenborough, finding against the proprietors of the Greenwich stagecoach which made two 45-minute stops each day near Charing Cross). But it seems that in rare circumstances even this may be reasonable: *Dwyer* v *Mansfield* [1946] 1 KB 437, where the obstruction was caused by queues at a greengrocer's shop during wartime rationing.

15 *Westminster City Council* v *Ocean Leisure Ltd* [2004] EWCA Civ 970, where the state of affairs that would have been a public nuisance had it not been authorised by statute involved obstruction of the highway in order to build a new footbridge across the River Thames.

interest from such an obstruction continuing.[16] An unreasonable obstruction does not always have to be physical. Thus in *Wandsworth LBC* v *Railtrack PLC*[17] the obstruction took the unusual form of users being discouraged from using a particular footpath by the risk of falling pigeon excrement. Gibbs J held that this state of affairs amounted to a public nuisance even without consideration of the possible health risks.

No right to persist with an obstruction of the highway can be obtained by long use,[18] but if an obstruction pre-dates dedication of the road as a highway then the dedication may be treated as subject to the reservation of the obstruction being continued.[19]

Unreasonable endangering

A state of affairs which unreasonably endangers users of the highway will amount to an unreasonable interference with free passage. It might be thought that in a situation where a claimant alleges that he was unreasonably endangered *and then injured* by a state of affairs which the defendant created, authorised, continued or adopted, the claimant ought really to allege that the defendant committed the tort of negligence.[20] After all, this is the tort which is – in large part – built around the existence of duties to avoid creating unreasonable risks of others suffering physical injury.[21] The fact that such claims are conventionally treated as falling within public nuisance probably stems from the high number of cases where there is both an obstruction *and* an endangering. This overlap has increased over time because users of the highway have attained greater speeds, consequently increasing the danger posed by unanticipated obstructions.

INTERFERENCE WITH THE PUBLIC'S COMFORT AND CONVENIENCE

Claims based on a breach of duty (2) raise the difficult question of how we draw the line between situations where we say 'this has interfered with the comfort, convenience or safety of *some individuals*' and those where we say 'this has interfered with the comfort, convenience or safety of *the public*'.

In *Attorney-General* v *PYA Quarries*, Denning LJ proposed that this question should be answered by considering whether the nuisance was 'so widespread in its range or so indiscriminate in its effect that it would not be reasonable to expect one person to take proceedings

[16] In *R* v *Train* (1862) 2 B & S 640, 121 ER 1129, the King's Bench ruled that a tramway in Lambeth was a public nuisance since it withdrew part of the highway from ordinary use. As Crompton J pointed out, the effect of such a ruling was merely to insist that those who wanted to promote such projects had to obtain a private Act of Parliament. Some 'technical' obstructions may, however, be held to be reasonable because they 'enable the public to exercise their right with greater facility and more convenience', such as a barrier preventing unauthorised vehicles from using a towpath: *A-G* v *Wilcox* [1938] 3 All ER 367, 372 (liability found on the facts).

[17] [2001] 1 WLR 368. The conclusion that the state of affairs amounted to a public nuisance was not challenged when the case was heard before the Court of Appeal: [2002] QB 756.

[18] *R* v *Cross* (1812) 3 Camp 224, 227, 170 ER 1362, 1363: 'It is immaterial how long the practice may have prevailed, for no length of time will legitimate a nuisance' (per Lord Ellenborough).

[19] *Fisher* v *Prowse* (1862) 2 B & S 770, 121 ER 1258. This explains the legality of maintaining, for instance, stone steps leading down from an old house onto a pavement, and the cellar-flaps of an ancient public house.

[20] See *Hunter* v *Canary Wharf* [1997] AC 655, 692. The question whether public nuisance *should* be restricted to exclude claims for personal injuries is discussed in detail below, pp. 802–3.

[21] For an account of the 'physical danger principle' which underlies the existence of a large number of duties of care in negligence, see above, pp. 73–4.

on his own responsibility to put a stop to it, but that it should be taken on the responsibility of the community at large'.[22] This statement has been regularly cited and has made its way into almost all the tort textbooks. But our opinion is that it must be treated with caution.

Our main quarrel with Denning LJ's statement is that it seems to assume that a public nuisance is also a private nuisance to a large number of claimants.[23] This overlooks the fact that the public interest (protected by public nuisance) is not simply a conglomeration of private interests in land (protected by private nuisance[24]). Many cases of public nuisance do not involve interference with private interests in land at all. For instance, in *R* v *Vantandillo*[25] the defendant created a public nuisance by carrying a child with smallpox through the streets and it is unlikely that this was an interference with the interests in land of a substantial number of citizens. Similarly, in *R* v *Madden*[26] the Court of Appeal stated that the crime of public nuisance could be committed by making a hoax bomb threat if a considerable number of persons was affected, but there was no suggestion that there had to be any possibility of those affected being able to sue for private nuisance.

Thus our view is that it would be better if Denning LJ had made no reference to the reasonableness or otherwise of expecting *individuals* to sue. We think that the appropriate test should be whether the interference was so widespread in its range or so indiscriminate in its effect that it is reasonable for proceedings to be taken on behalf of the community at large.[27] For the avoidance of doubt we should add that where it would be reasonable for proceedings to be taken on behalf of the community at large, individuals who have suffered 'special damage' as a result of the interference in question will still be able to make claims for compensation for that damage. Moreover, if the interference in question has at the same time caused a claimant to suffer an unreasonable interference with land in which he has an interest, then that claimant could still make a claim in *private nuisance* against anyone who created, authorised, adopted or continued the interference in question. Claims in public nuisance and private nuisance are not exclusive.[28]

But we still have to face the question of *how many* people, in practice, must be inconvenienced or discomforted before a defendant will be held to have committed a public

22 [1957] 2 QB 169, 191.

23 This assumption can best be seen by going through the following steps. (1) Denning LJ's test for a public nuisance depends on whether it *would be reasonable to expect* an individual to sue. (2) The question whether it is *reasonable to expect* an individual to sue assumes that the individual *could sue*. (3) The most obvious thing individuals could be suing for is private nuisance.

24 We explain in Chapter 18 how the courts have treated the tort of private nuisance as protecting private interests in land.

25 (1815) 4 M & S 73, 105 ER 762. See also *R* v *Henson* (1852) Dears 24, 169 ER 621 (taking a horse with an infectious disease into a public place).

26 [1975] 1 WLR 1379.

27 Repeatedly engaging in behaviour which harms people *individually* will not amount to a *public* nuisance. For instance, in *R* v *Rimmington, R* v *Goldstein* [2006] 1 AC 459 the House of Lords held that a defendant did not commit the crime of public nuisance by sending 538 letters and packages containing racially offensive material to a large number of people. Similarly, the House of Lords held that making obscene telephone calls to a large number of different people will not amount to a public nuisance.

28 For example, in the case of *Jan de Nul (UK) Ltd* v *AXA Royale Belge SA* [2000] 2 Lloyd's Rep 700 (upheld on appeal, [2002] 1 Lloyd's Rep 583) Jan de Nul (UK) Ltd conducted dredging operations in Southampton Water in such a way as to cause silt to be deposited elsewhere in the estuary. Some of the users who were inconvenienced by this *possessed* parts of the river bed and could have sued in private nuisance, while others could only have sued for public nuisance by interference with the public right of navigation or the public right to take fish.

nuisance by breaching duty (2).[29] Our view is that the most useful discussion of how many people must be affected before the effects will be sufficiently widespread is found in Romer LJ's judgment in *Attorney-General* v *PYA Quarries*.[30] He suggests that a judge should ask whether 'the neighbourhood' is affected by the defendant's activity and should then consider whether 'the local community within that sphere comprises a sufficient number of persons to constitute a class of the public'. These issues are described by Romer LJ as 'questions of fact', which seems to mean that they are matters for the judgment of trial judges rather than for appellate rules. On the particular facts of the *PYA Quarries* case the Court of Appeal held that there were no grounds for interfering with the trial judge's conclusions that flying rocks which disturbed 30 petitioners and vibrations which prompted fewer complaints were both sufficiently widespread. It is common to cite *R* v *Lloyd*[31] as a case on the other side of the line. In this case it was held that the defendant did not create a public nuisance when he created a noise which disturbed only three houses in Clifford's Inn.

It is important to note that the number of people affected does not provide an exhaustive answer to the question whether duty (2) has been breached. Denning LJ's test states that A's behaviour can also amount to a public nuisance if its effect is indiscriminate. It seems to us, however, that the purpose of this addition to the test is to catch cases where A's behaviour has interfered unreasonably with a public *right* which only a small number of people made use of. Thus Denning LJ could have defined duty (2) more simply if he had recognised the separate existence of duty (1).

ISOLATED INCIDENTS

The question has sometimes been raised as to whether an isolated incident can amount to a public nuisance. In *Stone* v *Bolton*, Oliver J stated that 'an isolated act of hitting a cricket ball on to a road, cannot, of course, amount to a nuisance ... nuisance must be a state of affairs'.[32] Oliver J's opinion was supported by Professor Newark, though he seems to have been chiefly motivated by the fear that if this opinion was rejected then a skidding bus might constitute a public nuisance.[33] If Oliver J's opinion represents the law,[34] then it is

[29] Where the defendant breaks duty (1) – that is, 'interferes unreasonably with a public right' – there is no need for any minimum number of people to be effected. As Denning LJ said in *Attorney-General* v *PYA Quarries* [1957] 2 QB 169, 191, 'Take the blocking up of a public highway or the non-repair of it. It may be a footpath very little used except by one or two householders. Nevertheless, the obstruction affects everyone indiscriminately who may wish to walk along it.'

[30] [1957] 2 QB 169, 184–5.

[31] (1802) 4 Esp 200, 170 ER 691.

[32] [1949] 1 All ER 237, 238e. This point was not discussed when the case reached the House of Lords: [1951] AC 850.

[33] Newark 1949, 486, 488. There are more convenient ways of avoiding inconsistency with the tort of negligence in road accident cases. Thus it could be argued that (1) it is not an unreasonable use of the highway to drive a reasonably safe bus on it, (2) such buses sometimes skid without anyone having been careless, and (3) consequently, the non-careless skidding of a bus is not an unreasonable interference with the safety of other road users.

[34] It is not clear that the case law supports Oliver J. Thus public nuisance can cover situations where a mass of snow suddenly falls off a roof onto a claimant (*Slater* v *Worthington's Cash Stores (1930) Ltd* [1941] 1 KB 488, decided by Oliver J!), where a building next to the highway suddenly collapses (see, for instance, *Wringe* v *Cohen* [1940] 1 KB 229 and *Mint* v *Good* [1951] 1 KB 517) and where an isolated incident, such as the discharge of oil, creates a longer term interference (see, for example, *Southport Corporation* v *Esso Petroleum Co. Ltd* [1954] 2 QB 182, 197 per Denning LJ). It may be that the first two situations can be explained on the basis that the mass of snow and buildings were public nuisances even before they collapsed because of the *danger* they posed to users of the highway (see above, p. 794).

necessary to determine: (1) how long a single incident must last in order to amount to a 'state of affairs'; *and* (2) whether, and, if so when, a series of single incidents can amount to a 'state of affairs'. In our opinion there is no good reason of principle for getting enmeshed in such arcane questions. Rather courts should concentrate on the central question whether there was an unreasonable interference or not.

KNOWLEDGE

R v *Goldstein*[35] involved a defendant who enclosed a small amount of salt in a letter which he posted. This was intended as a harmless joke but some of the salt leaked from the envelope in a postal sorting office and because of fears that it might be anthrax the building was evacuated and the police called in. The House of Lords held that a defendant is only responsible for a public nuisance which 'he knew, or ought to have known (because the means of knowledge were available to him), would be the consequence of what he did or omitted to do'.[36] Applying this test, the House of Lords held that Goldstein should not have been convicted because it had not been proved that he ought to have known that the salt would escape.

The House of Lords adopted this test from the Court of Appeal in *R* v *Shorrock*,[37] which had itself adopted it from Lord Wright in *Sedleigh-Denfield* v *O'Callaghan*. The relevant passage in Lord Wright's speech states:[38]

> Though the rule has not been laid down by this House, it has I think been rightly established in the Court of Appeal that an occupier is not prima facie responsible for a nuisance created without his knowledge and consent. If he is to be liable a further condition is necessary, namely, that he had knowledge or means of knowledge, that he knew or should have known of the nuisance in time to correct it and obviate its mischievous effects. . . . The responsibility which attaches to the occupier because he has possession and control of the property cannot logically be limited to the mere creation of the nuisance. It should extend to his conduct if, with knowledge, he leaves the nuisance on his land. The same is true if the nuisance was such that with ordinary care in the management of his property he should have realised the risk of its existence. This principle was affirmed in *Barker* v *Herbert*[39] . . . Though the nuisance [in *Barker* v *Herbert*] was a public nuisance, and though a public nuisance in many respects differs or may differ from a private nuisance, yet there is in my opinion no difference, in the respect here material, which is that if the defendant did not create the nuisance he must, if he is to be held responsible, have continued it, which I think means simply neglected to remedy it when he became or should have become aware of it.

In this passage Lord Wright was only purporting to discuss what had to be proved as to the defendant's state of mind in order to establish liability in cases where the defendant was an occupier of land *who had not created (or consented to the creation of)* the nuisance. *Sedleigh-Denfield* involved a flood arising from work done on the defendant's land by a trespasser and earlier in his speech Lord Wright had bluntly stated that: 'If the work had been done by or on behalf of the [defendant], the conditions requisite to constitute a cause of action

35 *R* v *Rimmington, R* v *Goldstein* [2006] 1 AC 459.
36 Ibid., at [39] (per Lord Bingham) and [56] (per Lord Rodger).
37 [1994] QB 279.
38 [1940] AC 880, 904–5.
39 [1911] 2 KB 633.

for damages for a private nuisance, would be beyond question complete.'[40] Similarly, *R* v *Shorrock*[41] involved potential liability of an occupier for a public nuisance caused by the acts of others on his land. In this case the event that amounted to a public nuisance was an 'acid house party' attended by between 3,000 and 5,000 people, and the defendant was the farmer whose field had been the venue. The farmer had been convicted despite testifying that he had gone to Harrogate for the weekend to celebrate his anniversary after allowing an acquaintance to use the field for what the acquaintance had described as a 'disco' to raise money for charity. The farmer appealed against his conviction on the grounds that the judge ought to have directed the jury that actual knowledge had to be proved, but the Court of Appeal held that the trial judge's direction in accordance with Lord Wright's speech had been correct.

This suggests that the House of Lords *changed the law* in *Goldstein*'s case by extending the requirement of knowledge to cases where defendants have *created* the conditions giving rise to a public nuisance.

Two further points must be made. First, it is important to emphasise that a defendant who had 'means of knowledge' will be treated in the same way as a defendant who actually knew that his behaviour would cause a public nuisance. Lord Wright treated the phrase 'means of knowledge' as equivalent to what an occupier should have realised 'with ordinary care in the management of his property'. We have noted above, that the test will in future have to be applied to classes of defendants *beyond* occupiers. But the general guidance that 'means of knowledge' refers to 'the capacity to know through the exercise of reasonable care' is likely to be useful.

Secondly, where a defendant is alleged to have committed public nuisance by *endangering* the public it seems unlikely that the defendant will have to be proved to have known exactly how and when people would be injured. For instance, if an owner of a building fails to take any action when he becomes aware that a wall is 'bowing' he should not be able to avoid liability for an injury caused by its collapse by saying that a full investigation would only have disclosed a *risk* of injury rather than *knowledge* that it was about to collapse.

CREATING, AUTHORISING, ADOPTING OR CONTINUING

Where A *creates* a state of affairs, or *authorises* someone else to create it, in circumstances where he knows, or ought to know, that it will cause a public nuisance, it seems straightforward to hold him responsible for that nuisance. But what if A engages a contractor to perform some task which involves obstruction of the highway or endangers users of the highway, and the *contractor* creates an unreasonable obstruction or unreasonably endangers other users of the highway? In such a case, there is a rule that A will be responsible for the public nuisance created by the contractor unless the contractor's behaviour was collateral to what he was instructed to do.[42] This rule has been relied on principally against bodies with special statutory powers allowing them to arrange for the digging up of the highway. In *Rowe* v *Herman*, the Court of Appeal suggested that the rule would not make

40 [1940] AC 880, 902.

41 [1994] QB 279.

42 *Hardaker v Idle DC* [1896] 1 QB 335; *Penny v Wimbledon Urban District Council* [1899] 2 QB 72; *Holliday v National Telephone Co.* [1899] 2 QB 392.

a householder liable if builders she engaged failed to put lights on a skip which they placed in the road.[43] Thus it seems possible that this rule applies only to those with special statutory powers.

Someone can also be held liable for an interference caused by a state of affairs which she did not create or authorise. This will be the case if the state of affairs in question arose on land *owned*[44] or *occupied*[45] by her and she *continued* or *adopted* the state of affairs in question. She will be held to have continued or adopted the state of affairs in question if it arose through her careless failure to prevent it arising or through her careless failure to deal with it once she had realised it had arisen.

Owners and occupiers are often held to have *continued* or *adopted* a state of affairs directly caused by the workings of nature. For instance, if a tree on A's land falls into the highway, A may be held liable for the interference with the highway so caused if he carelessly failed to inspect that tree to determine whether or not it was likely to fall into the road or otherwise obstruct the highway.[46] Similarly, in *Wandsworth LBC* v *Railtrack PLC*,[47] the defendant, which owned a railway bridge over Balham High Road, was held liable for failing to take reasonable steps to prevent pigeons roosting under the bridge and inconveniencing passing pedestrians.

Owners and occupiers can also be held to have continued or adopted a state of affairs directly caused by trespassers, provided that a reasonable owner or occupier would have discovered the state of affairs and dealt with it.[48] Thus in *Attorney-General* v *Tod Heatley*[49] the owner of a building site in Westminster was held to have continued a public nuisance by failing to take sufficient steps to remove from the site dead dogs, cats, fish and offal which had been dumped by unknown trespassers.

The rules concerning when owners and occupiers will be held to have continued or adopted a state of affairs directly caused by a *building* falling into a state of disrepair are relatively stringent. Thus courts tend to take the robust view that 'there must be some fault on the part of someone or other for that to happen'.[50] Further, if A is aware of the disrepair, or ought to be, her duty to take reasonable steps to deal with the problem will be non-delegable; as a result, if contractors appointed by A carelessly fail to deal with the problem, A will still be held liable.[51] A will avoid liability, however, if she can establish that the danger was purely the result of 'latent defects'. Historically, the non-delegable duty owed by an owner or occupier which allows claims by those injured by a thing falling from the owner's or occupier's land onto the highway, was probably related to the rule in *Rylands* v

43 [1997] 1 WLR 1390, 1394H.

44 In *Mint* v *Good* [1951] 1 KB 517 the Court of Appeal held that the rule set out in the text applied to owners who were not in possession as well as to occupiers.

45 For instance, a tenant at will can be held liable under this rule: *R* v *Watts* (1703) 1 Salk 357, 91 ER 311.

46 *Noble* v *Harrison* [1926] 2 KB 332; *Caminer v Northern & London Investment Trust Ltd* [1951] AC 88; *British Road Services* v *Slater* [1964] 1 WLR 498.

47 [2002] QB 756.

48 *Barker* v *Herbert* [1911] 2 KB 633.

49 [1897] 1 Ch 560. A decision which was approved by the House of Lords in *Sedleigh-Denfield v O'Callaghan* [1940] AC 880, and was held still to represent the law by the Court of Appeal in *Wandsworth LBC v Railtrack PLC* [2002] QB 756, at [26].

50 *Mint* v *Good* [1951] 1 KB 517, 526–7, per Denning LJ. Though in *Wringe* v *Cohen* [1940] 1 KB 229, 233, the Court of Appeal suggested that where premises were undermined by 'a secret and unobservable operation of nature, such as subsidence under or near the foundations' the owner or occupier might not be liable.

51 *Tarry* v *Ashton* (1876) 1 QBD 314.

Fletcher.[52] Now, however, only an extraordinary or unusual use of land falls within the ambit of the rule in *Rylands* v *Fletcher*, while public nuisance covers a far broader range of uses of land. The public nuisance duty is also distinct in that where the complaint is of an unreasonable interference with the highway users of neighbouring highways will be able to make claims, while claims under the rule in *Rylands* v *Fletcher* must be made by persons with interests in neighbouring land.[53]

SPECIAL DAMAGE

If A has created a public nuisance and B has suffered some harm as a result, B will only be entitled to sue A for damages in respect of that harm if that harm counts as 'special damage'. For these purposes 'special damage' means damage which is different in nature or extent to that suffered by the other members of the public affected by the nuisance. Thus if A creates a public nuisance by unreasonably obstructing a highway, if all that B suffers as a result is the inconvenience of having to go round by another route or being delayed then B probably will not have suffered 'special damage'. But if B trips on the obstruction and is injured, or damages her personal property, then she will have suffered 'special damage'. The difficulty comes with deciding how to deal with cases that fall between these extremes. Four situations which have caused difficulty will be discussed.

Special costs from obstruction

In some cases courts have decided that a particular person suffered 'special damage' because the obstruction suffered by all was, in practice, far more inconvenient for that person. The best example of this is provided by *Rose* v *Miles*[54] where the defendant was alleged to have moored a barge across a public navigable creek and the claimant had to incur the expense of unloading goods from his barges and conveying them by land. The court seems to have thought that the claimant 's damage was 'special' to him because he had already loaded his goods before the time of the obstruction and consequently he was unable to avoid the extra expenses. Dampier J said, 'If this be not a particular damage, I scarcely know what is'.[55]

A similar approach was taken in *Jan de Nul (UK) Ltd* v *AXA Royale Belge SA*,[56] where Moore-Bick J considered the liability of a dredging company responsible for siltation inter-

[52] See Chapter 42 for a discussion of this rule. It will be noted that Blackburn J played a pivotal role in both *Rylands* v *Fletcher* and *Tarry* v *Ashton*, and that both cases involved independent contractors carrying out operations on the defendants' land.

[53] In *Wringe* v *Cohen* [1940] 1 KB 229 the Court of Appeal held that the non-delegable duty only attached to 'premises on a highway' but that both passers-by and owners of adjoining property could take advantage of the duty. It seems to us, however, that it would be implausible for an adjoining owner to claim that he had been a victim of unreasonable interference with the public right to use the highway. Consequently, we think that if the owner of adjoining property has a claim at all it certainly is not a claim for *public* nuisance. Instead it may be a claim for continuing a *private* nuisance (see above, pp. 387–9). In *Mint* v *Good* [1951] 1 KB 517, 527, Denning LJ stated that the decision in *Wringe* v *Cohen* was 'clearly correct in regard to the responsibility of an occupier to *passers-by*' (emphasis added).

[54] (1815) 4 M & S 101, 105 ER 773. See also *Walsh* v *Ervin* [1952] VLR 361.

[55] (1815) 4 M & S 101, 104; 105 ER 773, 774. 'Particular damage' is a phrase that some judges and authors use instead of 'special damage'.

[56] [2000] 2 Lloyd's Rep 700.

fering with freedom of navigation in an estuary. He held that in such circumstances, 'any significant interference with an individual's commercial operations or the enjoyment of private rights resulting from the obstruction to navigation would in my judgment represent damage over and above that suffered by the public at large and would be sufficient to support an action'.[57]

Interference with customers

Where an obstruction is particularly harmful to B because it interferes with his ability to receive customers it seems that B will be able to establish 'special damage'. In *Iveson* v *Moore*[58] the claimant alleged that he had lost customers and the profits of his colliery because of the obstruction of the highway near his colliery. The Court of King's Bench split 2:2 on whether this was sufficiently 'special damage'. But it seems that the case was later argued before all the judges of the Common Pleas and Exchequer, and their opinions unanimously supported the claimant 's claim.[59] Similarly, in *Wilkes* v *Hungerford Market Co.*[60] a bookseller successfully claimed that the loss he suffered through his customers being inconvenienced by an obstructed highway was sufficiently distinct to constitute 'special damage'. The correctness of *Wilkes* was doubted by Lord Chelmsford LC in the case of *Ricket* v *Metropolitan Railway*.[61] But the case was treated as correct by the Court of Appeal in *Blundy, Clark & Co. Ltd* v *London North Eastern Railway*.[62] In that case Greer LJ stated that, 'Where a [claimant] has property near a highway which he uses for the purposes of his business, and the highway ... is unlawfully obstructed, and he is thereby put to greater expense in the conduct of his business, or suffers loss by the diminution of his business, he is entitled to recover damages as a person who has suffered special or peculiar damage beyond that which has been suffered by other members of the public wanting to use the highway.'[63]

[57] Ibid., [44]. This point was not challenged on appeal: [2002] 1 Lloyd's Rep 583.

[58] *Iveson* v *Moore* (1699) 1 Ld Raym 486, 91 ER 1224.

[59] It is worth noting that in this case the defendant was a rival colliery owner and it was alleged that he obstructed the road with the aim of harming the claimant. In such a situation a modern claimant might prefer to rely on the tort of intentional infliction of harm by unlawful means (discussed in Chapter 21) rather than alleging public nuisance. Such a claimant would have to establish that the means used were 'unlawful' (as defined in Chapter 21) and that the defendant was 'aiming at' causing harm to him. It would not be necessary, however, to demonstrate 'special damage'.

[60] (1835) 2 Bing NC 281, 132 ER 110.

[61] (1867) LR 2 HL 175, 188.

[62] [1931] 2 KB 334.

[63] Ibid., 369. See also *Lyons, Sons & Co.* v *Gulliver* [1914] 1 Ch 631; *Walsh* v *Ervin* [1952] VLR 361. Stevens 2007, 186–8, objects to *Wilkes* because he believes that the bookseller's claim was not based on interference with *his own* right to use the highway but interference with the rights of his *customers*. This assumes, however, that a person's right to use the highway does not include a right to use it as a way of *being reached* by customers, guests, etc. Similarly, courts have allowed the occupiers of piers and those with businesses at the water's edge to bring cases based on interference with public rights of navigation when the difficulty was in *being reached* by others: *Jan de Nul (UK) Ltd* v *AXA Royale Belge SA* [2000] 2 Lloyd's Rep 700 (upheld on appeal, [2002] 1 Lloyd's Rep 583).

Costs of removing the public nuisance

In *Winterbottom* v *Lord Derby*[64] the Court of Exchequer held that the claimant could not rely on the expense he had incurred in removing an obstruction as 'special damage' since otherwise any person could give to himself the opportunity to sue. But in *Tate & Lyle Industries Ltd* v *GLC*,[65] the House of Lords held that the claimant could claim for the expense it had incurred in dredging the River Thames in order to remove the obstruction to free navigation for which the defendant was responsible. The majority of the House of Lords seems to have held that the 'special damage' was not the cost of dredging itself, but the special loss that the claimant suffered because ships of particular dimensions were unable to progress up the channel. This is important, because it clarifies that the claimant had suffered 'special damage' *before* the dredging was undertaken, and thus does not conflict with the decision in *Winterbottom*. Lord Diplock, however, disagreed with the majority and argued that 'special damage' arising from the claimant's choice about how it used public rights could not be the basis for a claim for public nuisance.[66] We think, however, that Lord Diplock's dissent was out of line with the cases discussed in the previous two sections. It is clear that the fact that a claimant has *chosen* to make use of a particular highway or river for delivering goods or receiving customers does not prevent an action against someone responsible for an unreasonable obstruction. Further, there is no obvious reason for distinguishing between choosing to use a highway for making deliveries and choosing to use a river for receiving supplies.

The position is different where the body which incurs costs to remove the public nuisance is fulfilling a statutory function by doing so. In *Jan de Nul (UK) Ltd* v *AXA Royale Belge SA*[67] the Court of Appeal held that where a dredging company had caused quantities of silt to be deposited in such a way as to interfere with the public right of navigation in a river, a harbour authority could sue that company in public nuisance for the cost of dredging the river bed, if either it was its duty to dredge the river bed or it had a statutory power to do so.[68]

Personal injuries

There is no real dispute over whether personal injuries can be sufficiently 'special' to an individual claimant. Instead, the debate is over whether personal injuries should be recoverable in public nuisance claims at all. In Chapter 19 we discussed the question whether personal injuries should be recoverable in the tort of private nuisance and noted that the House of Lords has recently suggested that the answer is 'no'.[69] An important step in the

64 (1867) LR 2 Ex 316.
65 [1983] 2 AC 507.
66 Ibid., 547F.
67 [2002] 1 Lloyd's Rep 583.
68 Ibid., at [60]. For a similar case involving a highway authority see *Louth District Council* v *West* (1896) 65 LJ (QB) 535.
69 In *Hunter* v *Canary Wharf* [1997] AC 655, at 692, Lord Goff drew attention 'to the fact that although, in the past, damages for personal injury have been recovered at least in actions of public nuisance, there is now developing a school of thought that the appropriate remedy for such claims as these should lie in our now fully developed law of negligence, and that personal injury claims should be altogether excluded from the domain of nuisance'.

reasoning towards this answer was the opinion that the tort of negligence sets the appropriate conditions for redress for unintentionally inflicted personal injuries. It is difficult, however, to extend this answer over into public nuisance cases because there is a long line of precedents where damages were awarded for personal injuries.[70] Moreover, some of the other reasons given by the House of Lords for excluding personal injury claims from the scope of the tort of private nuisance are not relevant to the scope of public nuisance; for instance, the desirability of facilitating agreements to tolerate a certain level of disturbance[71] and the difficulty of defining who has a sufficient interest in 'a home',[72] do not apply directly to public nuisance. Consequently, although the House of Lords may in future bring public nuisance into line with private nuisance,[73] it seems that under the current law a claim for damages for personal injuries caused by public nuisance may succeed even where a claim in negligence would have failed.[74]

[70] See, for example, *Castle* v *St Augustine's Links* (1922) 38 TLR 615, and, more recently, *Mistry* v *Thakor* [2005] EWCA Civ 953.

[71] Such agreements are easier to secure if only a small number of people have private law rights which must be accommodated.

[72] If private nuisance claims could be brought by people who did not have interests in land (or exclusive possession) then some other limit would have to be defined. In public nuisance 'special damage' defines who can claim.

[73] The House of Lords has already extended the limits on the tort of private nuisance developed in *Hunter* v *Canary Wharf* [1997] AC 655 to liability under the rule in *Rylands* v *Fletcher*: *Transco plc* v *Stockport MBC* [2004] 2 AC 1.

[74] *Dymond* v *Pearce* [1972] 1 QB 496. Sachs and Stephenson LJJ both expressly accepted that a claim in public nuisance could succeed where a claim in negligence would have failed (ibid., 502A–C, 508F–G). Edmund-Davies LJ was more cautious (at 504H–507A), but seems only to have insisted that the risk of damage had to be reasonably foreseeable before a claim for damages could be made in public nuisance. This opinion is consistent with *The Wagon Mound (No. 2)* [1967] 1 AC 617, and is not equivalent to saying that the defendant must have been negligent.

45 Loss compensation schemes

In this part of the book, we have been looking so far at situations where a claimant who has suffered loss will be entitled to bring a non-tortious claim for compensation against the person who *caused* her to suffer that loss. But the claimant may be able to bring a claim for compensation against a *third party*, such as the State. This will be the case if the claimant's loss is covered by a *loss compensation scheme*. It is impossible in a book of this size to describe all the loss compensation schemes that have been set up to assist people who have suffered loss either at other people's hands or through nobody's fault. We will simply try to set out the key features of such schemes, describe some examples of schemes which either exist or have been proposed, and evaluate their advantages and disadvantages.

THE VARIABLE FEATURES IN LOSS COMPENSATION SCHEMES

The dominant model for a loss compensation scheme involves the State compelling contributions to a fund, with the fund then paying compensation to a defined range of claimants. A variety of schemes can be based on this simple model, but there are five principal variables.

Conditions for entitlement

First, there is a range of options as to the conditions for entitlement to claim against the fund. A common feature of all schemes is that the claimant's ability to prove that a particular defendant was at fault is *not* a condition for entitlement. Thus such schemes are often referred to as *no-fault compensation schemes*. But beyond this common feature there are many possibilities. An ambitious *general* scheme might attempt to assist all victims of serious adverse events, including illness, a less ambitious *general* scheme might attempt to assist all victims of *accidents*, and a sector-limited scheme might attempt to assist only victims of a particular type of accident or adverse event, e.g. road accidents or adverse events during medical treatment. Schemes might be further refined by making particular categories of people ineligible, e.g. victims of self-inflicted injury or drivers who were drunk when injured.

Contributors and their contributions

Secondly, there is a range of options as to who is compelled to contribute to the fund and in what proportions. For instance, a State could seek to compel contributions by risk creators in proportion to the risks that they create, or it could seek to compel contributions from potential claimants in proportion to the potential benefits that they might claim, or it could add the cost to the burden of general taxation, or it could adopt some combination of these approaches.

Level of compensation

Thirdly, there is scope for defining the level of compensation to be paid by the fund. Some schemes involve the payment of compensation at a level equivalent to what would be awarded in a successful tort claim, while others award more limited payments (e.g. only 80 per cent of lost earnings). Some more complicated schemes, particularly those which involve contributions from potential claimants, allow contributors to select their own possible level of compensation when their contributions are calculated.[1]

Relationship to tort claims

The fourth variable is the relationship between the scheme and tort claims. In some jurisdictions where a loss compensation scheme has been set up it operates parallel to tort law[2] while in others tort law has been abolished for incidents falling within the scope of the scheme. A more complicated option involves the scheme as the exclusive way of dealing with minor injuries, but the scheme being supplemented by the possibility of tort claims for more serious injuries.[3]

Who administers the fund

The fifth variable is the question of who administers the fund. Although such funds are usually created by statute[4] they can be operated either by a public body or by private organisations such as insurance companies. More complicated possibilities are also sometimes used. For instance, where contributions are paid by potential injurers (for instance, employers) to a scheme which will cover possible injuries to a fixed class (for instance, their employees) it is possible that a public body will operate the scheme for small employers and large employers can choose to opt out, and take full responsibility themselves for providing benefits equivalent to those under the scheme.[5]

The interdependence of the five factors

Clearly when it comes to designing or evaluating a scheme these five variables cannot be considered in isolation. For instance, the wider the scope of entitlement to claim, and in

1 A greater contribution is demanded in exchange for the promise of a higher level of compensation.

2 Where a loss compensation scheme operates parallel to tort law it will be necessary to define the relationship between the two types of claims. One possibility would be to reduce the tort claim by any amount recovered under the scheme. But an alternative would not reduce the tort claim but would i nstead allow the operators of the scheme to recoup any tort damages paid to compensate for loss that the scheme had already compensated. The Criminal Injuries Compensation Scheme, which pays compensation to those suffering personal injuries as a result of being a victim of crime, or seeking to prevent a crime or apprehend a criminal, is an example of a scheme which is supplementary to tort law. Such victims are entitled to sue the perpetrators in tort if such a course is likely to be worthwhile.

3 For an example of a scheme like this see the discussion of road traffic accident schemes in use in some American states, below, pp. 807–8.

4 Of course operators of activities may also set up contractual insurance pools as a supplement to tort rights. Many climbing gyms, for instance, require users to purchase insurance which will cover all accidents and mishaps.

5 A variation on this model is used in New Zealand.

particular the further that the entitled group extends beyond the range of those who might be able to claim in tort, the greater the pressure to cap the level of payments and the greater the pressure to raise some proportion of the contributions from the potential beneficiaries. As a second example, it is where the entitled group is limited to the victims of a particular type of accident that it may be most practical to compel contributions from risk creators, to quantify awards in line with tort, and to abolish tort claims.

The interrelationship of the five factors may become clearer by considering some specific schemes.

FOUR LOSS COMPENSATION SCHEMES

The New Zealand Accident Compensation Scheme

The New Zealand Accident Compensation Scheme came into operation on 1 April 1974, though it has been regularly amended since then. The 1974 scheme covered all personal injuries suffered in accidents and tort law claims were abolished for injuries falling within it.[6] Contributions were raised from three groups: employers paid a levy on wages (and the self-employed made similar payments) to cover the costs of injuries to earners (other than in road accidents); owners of motor vehicles paid a levy to cover the costs of injuries in road accidents; and the government funded the costs of injuries to non-earners, such as students, the unemployed, the retired and visitors from abroad. The level of compensation was reasonably close to tort law. The scheme covered a victim's medical expenses, 80 per cent of their loss of earnings after the first week, and also provided a lump sum for pain, suffering and loss of amenity.

One criticism of the 1974 scheme was that it was unfair to make employers pay contributions to cover the cost of all accidental injuries suffered by their employees, including those not associated with work. A second criticism was that it was unfair not to distinguish between employers with good and bad safety records when setting contribution levels. A third criticism was that it was unfair to treat the victims of accidents more generously than victims of illness and those born disabled.

The scheme has been amended to respond to the first and second criticisms. Thus employees now pay a special contribution towards the cost of non-work injuries which is collected from them by the Inland Revenue and there are schemes which allow employers to reduce their contributions by participating in promoting workplace safety. The third criticism has proved more difficult to meet, however, and the only significant move in that direction has been the extension of the scheme to cover injuries caused by medical 'treatment injuries'.[7]

Some other significant changes to the scheme have also been tried but then reversed. Thus at one stage lump sum payments were abolished and replaced by 'independence allowances'. This, however, has now been reversed, and other attempts are being made to

6 Claims for exemplary damages can still be brought.

7 'Treatment injuries' are adverse medical events causally linked to treatment (including non-treatment and diagnosis) by a registered health professional, as opposed to adverse events which are a necessary part or ordinary consequence of treatment. Thus injury caused by an allergic reaction to a medicine will be covered, but an ordinary side effect will not be.

encourage rehabilitation. A second experiment was 'privatisation' of the scheme by allowing private insurance companies to compete to provide scheme-style cover to employers. This, however, has also been reversed and the scheme is once again administered by the Accident Compensation Corporation,[8] a Crown entity.

Road traffic accident schemes in use in some American states[9]

It is often argued that there are strong reasons for introducing a limited scheme covering personal injuries suffered in road accidents because: (1) drivers are already used to paying for insurance which covers the cost of some[10] such personal injuries; (2) the class of people who create the risk of road accidents and might be expected to pay for them (that is, drivers) are also by-and-large those who might make most claims from a compensation scheme;[11] but (3) it is costly and slow to sort out road accidents through the tort system, and (4) there are significant classes of victims who excite sympathy but are left uncompensated by tort (for example, children who unpredictably run into the road). Given these factors any scheme which will cost drivers no more than current insurance premiums while offering a better protection for victims could gain popular support.

The model scheme which is most common in the United States involves contributions from road users and is administered by private insurance companies. Under the scheme all victims of road accidents are entitled to compensation even if they cannot prove that another driver was at fault, but in exchange for this wider-than-tort scope of entitlement the level of compensation is reduced to below the tort level for victims of *minor* accidents. Usually tort claims are abolished for minor accidents. Private insurance companies sell membership of these schemes and pay out benefits, and treat them alongside other insurance policies.[12] Thus drivers pay to their insurers amounts covering the risk that they will be injured in a road accident (and the risk that they will injure a person who is not a driver and will consequently not have a policy of his own), while claims are made by injured drivers against their insurers, and by injured non-drivers against the insurers of the driver who injured them.

Two arguments are commonly raised against such schemes. The first objection is that it seems unfair that where a victim was undoubtedly injured by the negligence of another the scheme leaves her with less compensation than tort law would have provided. This first objection is often augmented by the fact that when it is a driver who was undoubtedly

8 Details of the history and operation of the New Zealand scheme can be found at http://www.acc.co.nz/

9 We concentrate on American schemes because they are well established and have been carefully studied. Similar schemes are also in place, however, in several Canadian provinces, Australian states, and European countries, e.g. France.

10 Not all. Currently it is not compulsory in England and Wales for a driver to insure against injury to *himself* or *herself*, though it is compulsory to insure against the possibility of *negligently* injuring a *third party*. Nonetheless, many drivers purchase insurance against injury to themselves.

11 To spell this out the risk of road accidents is created by drivers and people injured in road accidents are generally also drivers (even though they may be travelling as passengers or be pedestrians at the time when they are injured).

12 Indeed, often insurers sell to drivers a 'package' which includes (1) scheme membership, which is often called 'personal injury protection' (PIP); (2) liability insurance, covering the risk of being held liable in tort for causing personal injuries not covered by the scheme; and (3) insurance covering property damage, which is usually outside the scheme.

injured by the negligence of another then the scheme adds insult to injury by making the innocent victim claim on her own policy (perhaps forfeiting a no-claims bonus).

The first objection is partially met by preserving the possibility of a tort claim if the injury suffered goes above a certain level of seriousness. This means that no victim suffering a *serious* injury will be left significantly worse off by the scheme. Unfortunately, however, the use of seriousness hurdles, especially if seriousness is measured by the cost of medical treatment, creates an incentive for fraud, in the form of exaggerated medical bills.[13]

The second objection is that drivers who drive badly, and know that this is the case, will still be able to claim compensation for their own injuries if they cause an accident and will not have to pay damages to other motorists, except those suffering serious injuries. Given this, the incentive to drive carefully may be reduced, and accident rates may rise. Studies trying to determine whether the introduction of no-fault schemes has led to an increase in accident rates have yielded mixed results, and are discussed in the final section of this chapter.

Currently, 12[14] American states have no-fault road accident schemes. All of these allow tort claims to be brought if the victim's injury exceeds a particular threshold of severity, with seven expressing that threshold in terms of the medical bills ($1,000 in Kentucky, $4,000 in Minnesota) and five using a phrase such as 'serious injury' (New York) or 'permanent injury' (Florida). Usually such a threshold is sufficient to keep most claims out of tort law.[15] When the claim is below the threshold then the schemes differ as to the level of compensation provided. In New York, for instance, the scheme covers up to $50,000 in total by way of hospital and medical expenses and 80 per cent of lost wages up to a maximum of $2,000 per month for a period not exceeding three years. In Florida, by contrast, the scheme covers only 80 per cent of hospital and medical expenses up to a maximum of $10,000. Moreover, it is only if any of the $10,000 is left that a claim can be made for loss of earnings, and then only for 60 per cent. Michigan is the only state which has extended its no-fault scheme beyond personal injuries: it also covers up to $1 million of damage to the property of others, with the exception of moving or improperly-parked cars.

Vaccine damage schemes

Many vaccines that are routinely administered have a small risk of very serious adverse consequences. The Vaccine Damage Payments Act 1979 set up a scheme under which people who have been left severely disabled[16] by vaccination are awarded a lump sum, currently £120,000. This is clearly far less than such a child might expect to be awarded if the

[13] After Massachusetts raised its tort threshold from $500 to $2,000 in 1988, the median number of treatment visits rose from 13 to 30 per auto injury claim: Marter & Weisberg 1992, 488.

[14] January 2008. In nine of these states the no-fault scheme is mandatory, while in three a driver can choose whether to participate in the no-fault scheme (in which case her insurance premium will be lower) or to keep full tort rights. At the peak of the popularity of no-fault road schemes during the late 1970s, 16 states had some form of no-fault scheme.

[15] Estimated to be kept out of tort law in 1997, 58% of claims in Kentucky, 70% in Colorado, 78% in New York and 66% in Florida: Insurance Research Council 1999.

[16] This requires at least 60% disability: Vaccine Damage Payments Act 1979, s 1(4), as amended by the Regulatory Reform (Vaccine Damage Payments Act 1979) Order 2002 (SI 2002/1592). The sum of £120,000 was set by the Vaccine Damage Payments Act 1979 Statutory Sum Order 2007 (SI 2007/1931).

disability was caused by a tort, but an award does not preclude a tort claim. The scheme is funded by the State from general revenue and administered by the Department for Work and Pensions. The justification for such a scheme was explained by the Pearson Commission: 'There is a special case for paying compensation for vaccine damage where vaccination is recommended by a public authority and is undertaken to protect the community.'[17]

The United Kingdom scheme is far less generous than the scheme operating in the United States. In the United States, the National Childhood Vaccine Injury Act of 1986 established a Federal *no-fault* scheme to compensate those injured by certain listed childhood vaccines, whether administered in the private or public sector. Awards under the scheme are substantial, covering medical and rehabilitative expenses, and in certain cases, pain and suffering and future lost earnings.[18] Eligibility and appropriate compensation are decided by the US Federal Court of Claims[19] but legal fees are covered provided that there was a reasonable basis for the claim and it was made in good faith, and many hearings are simplified by the statutory presumption that the victim is eligible if he suffered an 'adverse event' appearing in the 'Vaccine Injury Table'.[20] The scheme is funded by an excise tax of 75 cents on each dose of covered vaccine. One of the reasons why a generous scheme exists is that before its creation tort claims led to vaccine prices soaring and several manufacturers halted production. A vaccine shortage resulted and public health officials became concerned about the return of epidemic disease. The statute requires victims to file claims for compensation under the *no-fault* scheme before commencing tort litigation, and if a claimant accepts an award under the scheme he is precluded from pursuing a tort claim.

Professor Atiyah's first-party insurance scheme

Patrick Atiyah has suggested that 'the personal injury tort system should be abolished, but *not* replaced by a universal state compensation system. Instead, we should be willing to leave its replacement largely to the operation of the free market.'[21] He predicted that many people would choose to go into the market to buy insurance covering themselves against income lost as a result of non-trivial accidents (regardless of who, if anyone, was at fault) but usually would not buy coverage for pain and suffering or medical costs. Moreover, such people would consider carefully how far they needed protection for loss of income.[22] Perhaps the government would have to intervene to compel people to buy at least a minimum level of coverage against common types of serious accidents, such as road accidents, but in other spheres of life, for instance the workplace, institutions such as unions might arrange convenient mass cover.

It is worth representing Atiyah's proposals in terms of the five factors which we have used when describing loss compensation schemes. Under Atiyah's proposals the contributions

17 Pearson 1978, para.1398.

18 The average award is currently (January 2008) just over US $1 million (with a maximum of $250,000 in cases of death).

19 At first instance by 'special masters' appointed by the Court.

20 This lists particular 'adverse events' and 'time windows' for each vaccine covered by the scheme.

21 Atiyah 1996, 35. See also Atiyah 1997, ch 8.

22 For example, professional footballers might conclude that if they were injured in an accident they could 'get by' in future on less than £75,000 per week.

are paid by potential victims in proportion to the degree of risk that they face, and such potential victims choose for themselves what events they want to be covered against and what level of compensation they want should such events occur; these choices will be made at the time of buying a policy from a private insurance company and tort law will be abolished for personal injuries.

Many students' first reaction to Atiyah's proposals is that it is unfair to make potential victims pay for their own protection, and indeed many could not afford to do so. But it may be the case that the costs of liability policies (that is, of potential tort claims) are already passed on to potential victims in the form of higher prices for products and services, and that the cost of choosing a low level of general coverage under one of Atiyah's insurance policies will be *cheaper* than the total of all these passed-on costs.[23] Moreover, it is generally assumed that Atiyah's scheme would be cheaper to administer and claimants would get their payments more quickly.

This should not suggest, however, that we think that Atiyah's proposals should be accepted without further debate. At the very least we think that there are major practical issues to be thought through concerning the position of those who could not reasonably be expected to buy policies, such as children and the insane, and those who foolishly failed to buy any cover, or bought less cover than they later turned out to need. We also think that there are broader issues to be considered when evaluating loss compensation schemes which are intended to replace tort law, and these are considered in the next section.

EVALUATION OF LOSS COMPENSATION SCHEMES

In evaluating a particular scheme we recommend considering it from five perspectives.

First, the *fairness of the funding arrangements* should be considered. It is commonly argued that there are justifications for internalising the costs associated with particular risks to those that create the risks, and this could support a particular approach to funding. But other approaches might also be justified, for instance, by a person who believes that it is fair to redistribute resources from profit-making enterprises to potential victims of the industrial society.

Secondly, the *cost of administering the scheme* should be considered. This should include consideration of the costs of collecting contributions and of deciding whether claimants are entitled to claim. Clearly with a sector-limited scheme, such as one covering only the

[23] In particular, it may be cheaper for a low earner to buy an *Atiyah*-policy which offers him better coverage than to buy an ordinary *liability*-policy. For instance, imagine that the chance for all drivers of being involved in a serious collision with another car is 1 in 1,000 per year; and that the chance of that accident being caused by your own negligence is 40%, by the other driver's negligence 40%, and by nobody's negligence 20%. Imagine further, that in such accidents both drivers have to take one year off work. Now let us consider the position of A, who earns £10,000 per year, which is less than the £30,000 per year earned by the average driver. The cost of an *Atiyah*-policy for A will reflect his risk of being a victim, which is £10 (1/1,000 x £10,000). The cost of a *liability*-policy for A will reflect his risk of negligently injuring another, which is £12 (40% x 1/1,000 x £30,000). Of course, the average driver's *Atiyah*-policy will be more expensive (£30) than a *liability*-policy (£12), but that is because an *Atiyah*-policy will compensate him for his loss of earnings in 100% of accidents, while a liability-policy will only help him in 40% of accidents. Moreover, the example has been kept artificially simple by considering *only* loss of earnings. Currently a *liability*-policy also has to cover possible claims for pain and suffering and private medical care. If we added to the example the extra fact that all such accidents involve £20,000 of pain and suffering and £25,000 of medical bills then the average driver's earnings-only-*Atiyah*-policy would be the same price (£30) as his current *liability* policy (40% × 1/1,000 × £75,000).

victims of road accidents, there may be costs involved in determining which claims properly fall within the scheme and which do not.

Thirdly, the *fairness of the definition of those qualified to claim* should be considered. Here an important issue may be whether there is any sufficient reason for distinguishing between those qualified to claim and other people suffering similar injuries or disabilities who are not entitled to assistance from the fund.

Fourthly, the *effect of the scheme on accident rates* should be considered. Many defenders of tort law argue that it plays a role in reducing the number of accidents to an efficient minimum, or (to put the same point a different way) in deterring inefficient risk-creating behaviour.[24] Consequently, if a scheme is promoted with the intention that tort law is abolished it will be necessary for the scheme's supporters to explain whether they believe that the scheme will continue to provide such incentives (as might be the case if contributions to the scheme are truly proportionate to risk created), whether such incentives will be sufficiently provided by some other area of law (e.g. criminal law), or whether they believe that the beneficial effect of tort law on accident rates was always exaggerated and will not be much missed.

Fifthly, it must be considered whether *tort law performs any irreplaceable tasks* which a loss compensation scheme would not perform.

Fairness of the funding arrangements

Some of the questions concerning the fairness of funding arrangements, such as whether it is fair to redistribute the cost of accidental injuries from the rich to the poor, require deeper analysis of competing models of justice than is appropriate in a tort book. That said, many of the proposals for schemes which have failed to attract support have been unpopular because their funding arrangements did not actually achieve what the proponents of the scheme thought that they would achieve. For instance, at one time advocates of road-accident schemes proposed that contributions should be funded by a levy on petrol, a so-called 'pay-at-the-pump' scheme.[25] These advocates thought that it would be fair for those who drove further to pay more since they would be likely to be involved in more accidents. In fact this was a false premise, since accident rates are more closely related to traffic density than to mileage,[26] and if the scheme had ever been put into practice it would have led to those driving long distances in rural areas subsidising the accident costs of those making short journeys in busy cities!

24 In Chapter 3 we explained why we believe that it cannot be plausibly argued that the tort compensation rule exists *in order to* deter wrongful behaviour: see above, p. 35. Our intention here is merely to consider what effect a switch to a loss compensation scheme might have on incentives to behave reasonably.

25 The Pearson Commission recommended a 'pay-at-the-pump' scheme (Pearson 1978, paras 1054, 1057) though this was intended as a supplement to tort law rather than an alternative.

26 Though there are more fatalities per mile driven on rural roads, perhaps because of the speed of collisions and the distance to hospitals.

Cost of administration

It has sometimes been suggested that the main problem with ambitious State-run schemes, such as the New Zealand scheme, is that they create massive bureaucracies which cost too much to operate. But, in fact, the bureaucracies that are created are many times less costly than the networks of professionals and officials who are required to operate the tort system. The real problem with ambitious State-run schemes is that the *total* cost of achieving their goals is high. Let us imagine (for the sake of argument) that the tort system compensates only 20 per cent of accident victims, that the total compensation bill is £n per year, and that the administration costs are a further 40 per cent on top of the total compensation bill. Given these figures we can say that the tort system costs £1.4n per year. So what might an accident compensation scheme cost by comparison? Let us assume that such a scheme will compensate 90 per cent of accident victims, will pay them each only 75 per cent of what they would have received had they successfully sued in tort and will cost only 10 per cent on top of the total compensation bill to administer. Such a compensation scheme requires £3.7n per year.[27] So it requires more than two-and-a-half times as much as the tort system in total despite the fact that it is paying less per claimant and is more efficient.

Some people find it baffling that a more efficient system which pays less per claimant ends up being more expensive. But the key to avoiding bafflement is to realise that the current tort system leaves such a high proportion of accident victims uncompensated.[28] Currently members of this large group obtain medical care through the NHS, but beyond that are left to struggle through life as best as they can with assistance from savings, family, friends, charities and the social security safety net. One major cost of an ambitious loss compensation scheme is that many in this group will now qualify for the far better benefit of an award at 75 per cent of tort levels and such awards add up. Of course, a good case can be made for conferring such a benefit on this group. But the proposition, 'we should pay more tax to ensure better provision for those injured in accidents which they cannot demonstrate were caused by anyone else's fault' is not uncontroversial.

Fairness of qualification

Those who have advocated loss compensation schemes have often relied on the argument that because claimants can only obtain remedies in tort law if they prove that the defendant's breach of a duty caused them compensatable damage, and because the breach and causation elements of such claims are often difficult to prove in practice, many claimants who were *in fact* victims of torts are *in practice* unable to obtain remedies. Thus some of the beneficiaries of loss compensation schemes are persons who *ought to have been* compensated in tort law.[29]

[27] This figure is derived in the following way: If compensating 20% of victims at tort law levels costs £n, then compensating 90% of victims at 75% of tort law levels will cost £3.38n (n × 4.5 × 0.75). Add to that administration costs of 10% (£0.338n) and the total is £3.7n (£3.38n + £0.338n).

[28] Harris 1984 found that tort damages were recovered by 19% of work accident victims, 29% of road accident victims, and 2% of victims of other accidents: ibid., 51. Because accidents in the home make up such a high proportion of all accidents the overall figure was that 12% of accident victims obtain tort compensation.

[29] We explained above, pp. 30–4, why it is an error to treat the compensation of accident victims as the function of tort law. But we also explained how requiring wrongdoers to compensate the victims of their wrongs might be justified. Depending on the funding arrangement and the qualification rules a loss compensation scheme may achieve a similar purpose more efficiently.

It is usually impossible, however, to define those entitled to claim so as to include *only* persons who *ought to have been* compensated in tort law; any attempt to do so is likely to make it costly to determine whether any particular individual is entitled or not. Consequently, it is common to define the class of those entitled to claim in terms of the type of accident which *caused* their injuries, such as 'victims of road accidents' or 'victims of vaccine'. It is not easy to explain why accident victims generally, or victims of specific types of accidents, should be treated better than those who succumb to illness or who are born with disabilities. But, as the discussion under the previous sub-heading suggests, one of the major problems with compensation schemes has been their total cost. Consequently, any proposal to extend qualification far beyond accident victims would probably cost more than most governments would be willing to raise by way of taxation.[30]

Effect on accident rates

Some studies have suggested that no-fault road accident schemes lead to higher accident rates.[31] For instance, Cummins, Weiss and Phillips modelled the effect of road accident schemes in the United States and concluded that no-fault is associated with higher fatality rates than tort: two models yielded estimates of 12.8–13.8 per cent and 7.2–7.5 per cent higher than tort.[32] A subsequent empirical study by Cohen and Deheija estimated that no-fault led to a 10 per cent increase in fatalities.[33] These effects seem severe, but are actually more moderate than McEwin's estimate of 16 per cent higher fatalities in Australia and New Zealand.[34] By contrast Loughran concluded that his comparison of fatal accident, car damage and negligence rates in tort and no-fault states cast 'serious doubts on contentions that no-fault auto insurance as implemented in the United States has led to greater driver negligence and higher accident rates'.[35] Loughran pointed out that most people avoid driving negligently because they do not want to risk being injured, that if they thought that *others* were driving *less* safely they might alter their *own* behaviour so as to drive *more* safely, and that because most road accidents involve damage to cars and most no-fault schemes do not cover property damage tort law still provides some incentives.

Effect on tort law's functions

Does tort law perform any tasks that a loss compensation scheme cannot perform? It will be recalled that tort law is made up of two parts, each of which performs a different function. The duty-imposing part of tort law helps to determine what duties we owe each

[30] In 1989 the New Zealand government (Labour) announced that the compensation scheme would be extended to cover those incapacitated by sickness or disease, but the Labour Party lost the election in 1990 to the National Party and no such change was made when the scheme was reformed in 1992.

[31] There is less evidence available as to the effect that schemes might have on accident rates in sectors other than road accidents. Rubin and Shepherd 2007, have suggested that several reforms aimed at *reducing* tort damages in the United States have led to a *reduction* in death rates. Their explanation for this effect is that many tort claims are directed at defendants who are in the business of reducing risks, for instance medical professionals and the producers of pharmaceuticals and safety devices, and reforms which reduce the exposure of such defendants to heavy liability bills may lead to their services and products becoming both cheaper and more widely available.

[32] Cummins, Weiss & Phillips 2001, 455.

[33] Cohen & Deheijia 2004, 360, 382.

[34] McEwin 1989.

[35] Loughran 2001.

other; while the remedial part of tort law determines what remedies will be available when one of these duties is breached.[36] Obviously no loss-compensation scheme could perform the first function – that of helping to determine what duties we owe each other. So if tort law were abolished outright in favour of a loss-compensation scheme, the task of determining what duties we owe each other would be shouldered by the criminal law and contract law. Whether this would be a good thing or a bad thing is too complex a question to be addressed in this book.

What of the remedial part of tort law? *As this part of tort law currently stands*, the remedial part of tort law performs a number of different tasks. (1) By giving effect to the compensation rule, the remedial part of tort law helps prevent potential flashpoints arising between tortfeasors and the victims of their torts.[37] (2) By allowing the victim of a tort that has been committed in an arrogant or high-handed way to sue the person who committed that tort for aggravated damages, the remedial part of tort law helps assuage the victim of the tort's outrage at the way she has been treated.[38] (3) By allowing the victim of a tort to sue the person who committed that tort for gain-based damages *in the situations it currently does*, the remedial part of tort law gives effect to moral principles such as 'The owner of property is entitled to the fruits of that property' and 'Don't use someone else's property without paying for the use of it.'[39] (4) By awarding injunctions against people who are committing, or who are proposing to commit, a tort, the remedial part of tort law forces people to abide by the duties they owe other people.[40] (5) By allowing the victim of a tort to sue the person who committed that tort in certain circumstances for exemplary damages, the remedial part of tort law helps to deter people from committing torts.[41]

The existence of a loss-compensation scheme would mean that the law no longer needed to give effect to the compensation rule in respect of losses covered by that loss-compensation scheme. The existence of the loss-compensation scheme would eliminate the potential for a flashpoint arising between the victim of a tort and the person who committed that tort as effectively as giving effect to the compensation rule presently does. This is because if A has wrongfully caused B to suffer some kind of loss that has been fully compensated by a loss-compensation scheme, A no longer needs to do anything to 'make up for his wrong'. So if he fails to do *anything* for B in this situation he will not necessarily signal to B that he does not think he did anything wrong, thereby aggravating B. So a loss-compensation scheme can perform exactly the same task as the remedial part of tort law currently does in giving effect to the compensation rule. But a loss-compensation scheme cannot perform any of the other tasks that the remedial part of tort law currently performs. Given this, we would suggest that any proposal to abolish tort law *altogether* in favour of a loss-compensation scheme would be seriously defective. Before such a proposal could be countenanced, some other mechanism would need to be found to perform tasks (2)–(5), above.

Visit **http://www.mylawchamber.co.uk/mcbride** to access updates on recent cases, as well as model answers and tips for answering tort problem questions.

[36] See above, p. 30.
[37] See above, p. 37.
[38] See above, pp. 682–3.
[39] See above, p. 711.
[40] See above, p. 722.
[41] See above, pp. 698–9.

Appendix: Professor Stapleton's criticisms of the traditional view of tort law

In a recent article,[1] Professor Jane Stapleton – who can fairly claim to be the most intelligent and knowledgeable exponent of what we have called the 'modern view of tort law' in the world today – set out a number of criticisms of the traditional view of tort law. So far as we know, this is the first time an adherent of the modern view of tort law has attempted to address the traditional view of tort law at an intellectual level, as opposed to simply dismissing the traditional view of tort law as 'absurd' or 'ridiculous'. Given this, we thought it might be worthwhile to set out Professor Stapleton's arguments against the traditional view of tort law and see if any of her arguments stand up to scrutiny.

Professor Stapleton advances five arguments against the traditional view of tort law:

(1) *Discrimination*. To say that a tort claimant is allowed to sue a defendant for damages because her rights have been violated is 'callous',[2] 'distasteful',[3] 'unpleasant'[4] and 'odious'[5] because it suggests that tort claimants who are not allowed to sue for damages enjoy fewer rights than their more successful counterparts. So, for example, if B injures herself putting her foot through a defective stair in A's house, it is much more likely that B will be able to sue A in tort for compensation for her injury if she were a guest in A's house than if she were a burglar. Professor Stapleton claims it is 'callous' etc. etc. to say that the reason for this is that if B were a guest of A's, she would be far more likely to be able to establish that she had a right that A protect her from being harmed going up his staircase than she would if she were burgling A's house.

Against this, it must be observed that most forms of morality do distinguish between different classes of people. For example, most forms of morality require us to do more for our children than for other people's children – it is wrong, for instance, not to feed one's children; but it is not wrong not to feed the child up the road. No one regards this as 'callous'. Similarly, we are required by most forms of morality to do more for our parents, for our friends, for our employees, for our spouses, than we are for people who have nothing to do with us. Again, no one regards this as 'callous'. Most people, if asked, would see nothing wrong in saying that a householder should do more for his visitors than he should for someone who is attempting to steal his possessions. They certainly would not regard the law as 'callous' if they were informed that A's visitors enjoy more rights against him than his burglars do – indeed, they would be astonished if the law said anything else.

So this argument against the traditional view of tort law simply does not work. There is nothing wrong or distasteful in acknowledging that some people have more rights against

[1] Stapleton 2006.
[2] Ibid., 1530, 1544, 1546, 1549, 1550, 1551.
[3] Ibid., 1531, 1549, 1550, 1555, 1561.
[4] Ibid., 1549.
[5] Ibid., 1549.

us than other people. Those closer to us enjoy more rights against us than people who are complete strangers to us. No one regards this as at all strange or difficult to accept.

(2) *Strict liability*. Professor Stapleton argues that the traditional view of tort law finds it hard to account for instances of strict liability – that is, liability without fault – within tort law.[6]

For example, suppose that A brings a dangerous thing onto his land in the course of using his land in a non-natural way. If – without any fault on A's part – that thing escapes from A's land and damages B's land, A will be held liable to compensate B for the damage done under what is known as the rule in *Rylands* v *Fletcher*.[7] We accept that it is impossible to say in this case that A's liability arises out of the fact that he has done something to violate B's rights.[8] Similarly, suppose that C manufactures computer chips, and without any fault on C's part, one of those chips leaves the production line with a defect in it. The chip is used in the manufacture of an aircraft and because the chip is defective, the aircraft crashes and D – the sole person on board the aircraft at the time of the crash – is injured. In this situation, D will be entitled to sue C for compensation for his injuries under the Consumer Protection Act 1987. Again, we accept that it is impossible to say in this case that C's liability arises out of the fact that he violated D's rights in putting into circulation a defective computer chip.[9]

So here we have two examples of strict liability that cannot be rationalised as arising out of the fact that someone has violated someone's rights. But are these forms of liability genuinely examples of tort liability? Most tort lawyers would regard as laughable the idea that the rule in *Rylands* v *Fletcher* and the Consumer Protection Act 1987 have nothing to do with tort law. After all, all the tort textbooks – including this one – discuss *Rylands* v *Fletcher* and the 1987 Act in great detail. But let's stop to reflect for a second. Most tort lawyers would *not* say that A or C committed a *tort* in the situations set out above. Instead, a tort lawyer would simply say that 'A is liable under the rule in *Rylands* v *Fletcher*' or 'C is liable under the Consumer Protection Act 1987'. It is very rare for someone to talk about 'the tort in *Rylands* v *Fletcher*' or 'the tort of manufacturing a defectively dangerous product'.[10] So, for example, a professional, educated lawyer would very rarely say something like, 'A will probably be liable to B here for committing the tort in *Rylands* v *Fletcher*.' The way we use language, then, shows that we do not seriously think that either A or C have committed a tort here. But does that not then show that A and C's liabilities are not *in fact* forms of tort liability, and that the only reason they are normally treated as forms of tort liability is the current prevalence of the modern view of tort law, under which any liability to pay compensation to someone else is treated as a form of tort liability?

If this is right, then Professor Stapleton's second argument against the traditional view

[6] Ibid., 1530, 1542.

[7] See above, pp. 754–64.

[8] See above, pp. 26–7.

[9] See above, pp. 27–8.

[10] A search of the JUSTIS database yielded 113 hits for 'the rule in Rylands v Fletcher'; in contrast, a search of the same database for 'the tort in Rylands v Fletcher' yielded zero hits. An identical search of the Butterworths LexisNexis database resulted in 270 hits for 'the rule in Rylands v Fletcher' and zero hits for 'the tort in Rylands v Fletcher'. Googling 'the rule in Rylands v Fletcher' gives 1,160 hits, while Googling 'the tort in Rylands v Fletcher' gives 3 hits, all of them of academic origin.

of tort law is circular. It tries to establish that the traditional view of tort law is incorrect by pointing to forms of liability that are only treated as instances of tort liability because so many academics assume that the modern view of tort law is correct.

(3) *Public nuisance.* The same criticism can be made of Professor Stapleton's third argument against the traditional view of tort law – that the 'tort' of 'public nuisance' does not fit this view of tort law.[11] Again, the language is odd – most people do not talk about 'the *tort* of public nuisance'. Public nuisance – which, for our present purposes, we can take as being synonymous with unreasonably obstructing the highway – is a *crime.* If A commits this crime and B suffers special damage as a result, then B will be entitled to sue A for compensation. We accept that it is impossible to argue that A's liability in this situation arises out of the fact that A has violated B's rights.[12] However, we do not accept that this form of liability is a form of tort liability, and would argue that it has only been treated as such because of the prevalence of the modern view of tort law and the fact that a genuine form of tort liability – liability for committing the tort of *private nuisance* – shares half a name with this form of liability.

(4) *The basis of liability in negligence.* No one doubts that liability in negligence is a form of tort liability. Indeed, it is the primary form of tort liability and negligence is the tort that tort law students spend most of their time studying. If liability in negligence does not arise out of the fact that someone has wronged someone else – or, in other words, if liability in negligence does not arise out of the fact that someone has violated someone else's rights – then the traditional view of tort law must be wrong.

On the face of it, liability in negligence *is* wrong-based. A cannot be held liable in negligence to pay damages to B unless it is first shown that A breached a *duty* of care owed to B in acting as he did. However, those who reject the traditional view of tort law attempt to argue that when the courts *say* that 'A owes B a duty of care not to do *x*' they are not *really* telling A to take care not to do *x*. Instead, they are simply warning A, 'If you carelessly do *x* and B suffers harm as a result, you will have to pay B compensation.' On this view, if A does carelessly do *x* and B suffers harm as a result, A's liability to pay compensation to B is not based on the fact that he wronged B in acting as he did – for A was never under a *real* duty to take care not to do *x* – but instead rests on a complex mix of 'policy considerations'.

In her recent article on the traditional view of tort law, the only argument Professor Stapleton advances for endorsing this view of duties of care in negligence is that if A owes B a duty of care not to do *x*, B will not be able to get an injunction to compel A to take care not to do *x*.[13] Professor Stapleton does not cite a single authority in favour of this proposition and no consideration is given to the possibility that the dearth of authority on whether an injunction can be granted to compel someone to comply with a duty of care is accounted for by the fact that duties of care tend to be breached suddenly and without warning, leaving no opportunity to seek an injunction to stop the duty being breached.

[11] Stapleton 2006, 1544, 1545.
[12] See above, p. 28.
[13] Stapleton 2006, 1538, 1541.

Someone who is carelessly run over by a motorist driving at 100 mph tends never to get the chance to go to court first to ask the court to order the motorist to slow down.

So if the courts say that A owes B a duty of care not to do *x*, it is unrealistic to test for whether the courts mean what they say by asking whether B could get an injunction to compel A to take care not to do *x*. In real life, it is highly unlikely that B would ever seek such an injunction. A better test is to ask – If A blatantly disregards his duty of care and deliberately does *x*, will the courts punish A for his conduct? If the answer is 'yes' then that tends to indicate that when the courts say that A owes B a duty of care not to do *x*, they actually *are* telling A to take care not to do *x*, and not just warning him that he can do what he wants, but if he carelessly does *x* and B suffers harm as a result, he will have to compensate B. And in fact the answer to our question *is* 'yes': there are plenty of authorities that indicate that punitive damages – damages designed to punish someone for his conduct – may be awarded against someone who blatantly breaches a duty of care owed to someone else.[14]

It follows that Professor Stapleton's fourth argument against the traditional view of tort law fails. There is no reason to think that liability in negligence is not wrong-based, as the traditional view of tort law tells us it is.

(5) *Normative, not descriptive.* Finally, Professor Stapleton argues that the traditional view of tort law is really *normative*, rather than descriptive in nature.[15] What this means is that people who advance the traditional view of tort law and reject the modern view of tort law are really saying that the law *should* concentrate on remedying wrongs, and *not* take on a more wide-ranging role of requiring compensation to be paid in every case where it would be 'fair, just and reasonable' for A to compensate B for some loss that he has caused her to suffer. If this is right, then it is incumbent on those who advance the traditional view of tort law to explain why precisely the law should confine itself to remedying wrongs, and shut its doors to those deserving of compensation who cannot show that they have been the victim of a wrong. And until such an explanation is offered, the traditional view of tort law cannot be accepted.

This fifth argument against the traditional view of tort law fails because the traditional view of tort law is avowedly *descriptive* in nature, and not normative at all. It is simply concerned to describe what is going on when the courts decide whether or not to hold someone liable in tort. It is perfectly possible for someone to take the view that tort law *is* concerned to remedy wrongs – a descriptive claim – while at the same time taking the view – a normative view – that the law should *not* concern itself with remedying wrongs, and that it should rather encourage people to 'turn the other cheek' when they suffer injustice at another's hands.[16] There is a world of difference between what the law *says* and what the law *should say*, just as there is a world of difference between describing what someone *is* doing and talking about what someone *should* do. The traditional view of tort law is simply concerned to clarify what the law *says*, and not concerned at all with what the law *should say*.

[14] See McBride 2004.
[15] Stapleton 2006, 1532, 1562.
[16] Matthew 5:39.

So none of Professor Stapleton's arguments against the traditional view of tort law stand up to scrutiny. This does not of course prove that the traditional view of tort law is correct. It may be that there is a 'killer' argument out there against the traditional view of tort law that Professor Stapleton did not make. But this is not likely. If there were a strong argument to be made against the traditional view of tort law, we would have expected Professor Stapleton to have made it. The flimsiness of the arguments that Professor Stapleton *did* make against the traditional view of tort law is powerful evidence that the traditional view of tort law adopted in this book is in fact correct.

Bibliography

Table of abbreviations

C&L Dugdale & Jones 2006.
GS&Z Goldberg, Sebok & Zipursky 2004.
M&D Deakin, Johnston & Markesinis 2008.
S&H Heuston & Buckley 1996.
W&J Rogers 2006.

Secondary literature

Abel, R. 1994. 'A critique of torts' *Tort Law Review* 2:99.

Allen, C.K. 1931. *Legal Duties and Other Essays in Jurisprudence*. Clarendon Press.

Ames, J.B. 1908. 'Law and morals' *Harvard Law Review* 22:97.

Andenas, M. and Fairgrieve, D. 2000. eds. *Judicial Review in International Perspective: II*. Kluwer Law International.

Andrews, N.H. 1998. 'Civil disgorgement of wrongdoer's gains: the temptation to do justice' in Cornish 1998, 155–62.

Armour, J. 1999. 'Corporate personality and asssumption of responsibility' *Lloyd's Maritime and Commercial Law Quarterly* [1999]:246.

Atiyah, P.S. 1967. *Vicarious Liability in the Law of Torts*. Butterworths.

——. 1996. 'Personal injuries in the twenty-first century: thinking the unthinkable' in Birks 1996b, 1–46.

——. 1997. *The Damages Lottery*. Hart Publishing.

Bagshaw, R. 1998. 'Can the economic torts be unified?' *Oxford Journal of Legal Studies* 18:729.

——. 1999. 'The duties of care of emergency service providers' *Lloyd's Maritime and Commercial Law Quarterly* [1999]:71.

——. 2000. 'Inducing breach of contract' in Horder 2000, 131–50.

——. 2004a. 'Private nuisance and the defence of the realm' *Law Quarterly Review* 120:37.

——. 2004b. 'Rylands confined' *Law Quarterly Review* 120:388.

Bailey, S.H. and Bowman, M.J. 2000. 'Public authority negligence revisited' *Cambridge Law Journal* 59:85.

Barendt, E. 1999. 'What is the point of libel law?' *Current Legal Problems* [1999]:110.

Barker, K. 1993. 'Unreliable assumptions in the law of negligence' *Law Quarterly Review* 109:461.

Baty, T. 1916. *Vicarious Liability*. Clarendon Press.

Beever, A. 2003a. 'The structure of aggravated and exemplary damages' *Oxford Journal of Legal Studies* 23:87.

——. 2003b. 'Particularism and prejudice in the law of tort' *Tort Law Review* 11:146.

——. 2007. *Rediscovering the Law of Negligence*. Hart Publishing.

Bell, A. 1998. 'The place of bailment in the modern law of obligations' in Palmer and McKendrick 1998, 461–89.

Bell, J. 2002. 'Introduction' in Fairgrieve, Adenas and Bell 2002, xv–xxvi.

Benson, P. 1995. 'The basis for excluding liability for economic loss in tort law' in Owen 1995, 427–58.

Bernstein, R. 1998. *Economic Loss*. 2nd edn. Sweet & Maxwell.

Birks, P.B.H. 1983. 'Obligations: one tier or two?' in Stein and Lewis 1983, 18–38.

——. 1989. *Introduction to the Law of Restitution*, revised edn. Clarendon Press.

——. 1994. ed. *The Frontiers of Liability: Volume 2*. Oxford University Press.
——. 1995. 'The concept of a civil wrong' in Owen 1995, 31–51.
——. 1996a. *Harassment and Hubris: The Right to an Equality of Respect*. University College, Dublin.
——. 1996b. ed. *Wrongs and Remedies in the 21st Century*. Clarendon Press, Oxford.
——. 1997a. 'Definition and division: a meditation on Institutes 3.13' in Birks 1997b, 1–35.
——. 1997b. ed. *The Classification of Obligations*. Clarendon Press.
——. 1997c. ed. *Privacy and Loyalty*. Clarendon Press.
——. 2000a. ed. *English Private Law, Vol II*. Oxford University Press.
——. 2000b. 'Rights, wrongs and remedies' *Oxford Journal of Legal Studies* 20:1
Bitensky, S. 1998. 'Spare the rod, embrace our humanity: towards a new legal regime prohibiting corporal punishment of children' *University of Michigan Journal of Law Reform* 31:353.
Bix, B. 1998. ed. *Analyzing Law: New Essays in Legal Theory*. Clarendon Press.
Bloustein, E. 1964. 'Privacy as an aspect of human dignity: an answer to Dean Prosser' *New York University Law Review* 39:962.
Bohlen, C. 1926. 'Incomplete privilege to inflict intentional invasions of property and personality' *Harvard Law Review* 39:307.
Bowman, M.J. and Bailey, S.H. 1984. 'Negligence in the realm of public law – a positive obligation to rescue?' *Public Law* [1984]:277.
Bright, S. 2000. 'The third party's conscience in land law' *Conveyancer and Property Lawyer* 64:398.
——. 2001. 'Liability for the bad behaviour of others' *Oxford Journal of Legal Studies* 21:311.
Brooke-Smith, B.J. 1954. 'Liability for the negligence of another' *Law Quarterly Review* 70:253.
Burnett, D. 2007. 'Torts involving animals' in Oliphant 2007, 1085–110.
Burrows, A. 1983. 'Contract, tort and restitution – a satisfactory division of the law of obligations or not?' *Law Quarterly Review* 99:217.
——. 1996. 'Reforming exemplary damages' in Birks 1996b, 153–74.
——. 1998. *Understanding the Law of Obligations*. Hart Publishing.
——. 2001. 'Proprietary restitution: unmasking unjust enrichment' *Law Quarterly Review* 117:412.
——. 2002a. *The Law of Restitution*, 2nd edn. Butterworths.
——. 2002b. 'We do this at common law but that in equity' *Oxford Journal of Legal Studies* 22:1.
Burrows, A. and Peel, E. 2003. eds. *Commercial Remedies: Current Issues and Problems*. Oxford University Press.
Burrows, A. and Rodger, Lord 2006. eds. *Mapping the Law: Essays in Memory of Peter Birks*. Oxford University Press.
Butler, D. 2002. 'An assessment of competing policy considerations in cases of psychiatric injury resulting from negligence' *Torts Law Journal* 10:13.
Butler, R. 2003. 'SAAMCO in practice' in Burrows and Peel 2003, 71–90.
Butler, S. 2006. ed. *Discovering the Law*. Law Matters Publishing.
Calnan, A. 2005. 'In defense of the liberal justice theory of torts: a reply to Professors Goldberg and Zipursky' *New York University Journal of Law & Liberty* 1:1023.
Cane, P. 1996. *Tort Law and Economic Interests*, 2nd edn. Clarendon Press, Oxford.
——. 1998. 'Retribution, proportionality and moral luck in tort law' in Cane and Stapleton 1998, 141–74.
——. 1999. 'Fault and strict liability for harm in tort law' in Swadling and Jones 1999, 171–206.
——. 2000a. 'Vicarious liability for sexual abuse' *Law Quarterly Review* 116:21.
——. 2000b. 'Consequences in judicial reasoning' in Horder 2000, 41–59.
——. 2001a. 'The temporal element in law' *Law Quarterly Review* 117:5.
——. 2001b. 'Distributive justice and tort law' *New Zealand Law Review* 4:401.
——. 2002. *Responsibility in Law and Morality*. Hart Publishing.
——. 2004. 'The doctor, the stork and the court: a modern morality tale' *Law Quarterly Review* 120:23.
——. 2006. *Atiyah's Accidents, Compensation and the Law*, 7th edn. Cambridge University Press.

Cane, P. and Gardner, J. 2001. eds. *Relating to Responsibility*. Hart Publishing.
Cane, P. and Stapleton, J. 1998. eds. *The Law of Obligations: Essays in Honour of John Fleming*. Oxford University Press.
Cane, P. and Tushnet, M. 2003. eds. *The Oxford Handbook of Legal Studies*. Oxford University Press.
Carty, H. 1999. 'Joint tortfeasance and assistance liability' *Legal Studies* 19:489.
——. 2001. *An Analysis of the Economic Torts*. Oxford University Press.
Coase, R. 1960. 'The problem of social cost' *Journal of Law and Economics* 3:1.
Cohen, A. and Dehejia, R. 2004. 'The effect of automobile insurance and accident liability laws on traffic fatalities' *The Journal of Law and Economics* 47:357.
Coleman, J. 1993. *Risks and Wrongs*. Cambridge University Press.
——. 1998. 'Second thoughts and other first impressions' in Bix 1998, 257–322.
——. 2001. *The Practice of Principle*. Clarendon Press, Oxford.
Coleman, J. and Shapiro, S. 2002. eds. *The Oxford Handbook of Jurisprudence and Philosophy of Law*. Oxford University Press.
Conaghan, J. and Mansell, W. 1999. *The Wrongs of Tort*, 2nd edn. Pluto Press.
Cooke, E. 1994. 'Trespass, mesne profits and restitution' *Law Quarterly Review* 110:420.
Cooke, Lord. 1991. 'An impossible distinction' *Law Quarterly Review* 107:46.
——. 1998. 'The right of Spring' in Cane and Stapleton 1998, 37–57.
Cornish, W. 1998. et al. eds. *Restitution: Past, Present and Future – Essays in Honour of Gareth Jones*. Hart Publishing.
Craig, P. 2002. 'Contracting out, the Human Rights Act and the scope of judicial review' *Law Quarterly Review* 118:551.
Cross, G. 1995. 'Does only the careless polluter pay? A fresh examination of the nature of private nuisance' *Law Quarterly Review* 111:445.
Cummins, J.D., Weiss, D. and Phillips, M. 2001. 'The incentive effects of no-fault automobile insurance' *Journal of Law and Economics* 44:427.
Dagan, H. 1997. *Unjust Enrichment: A Study of Private Law and Public Values*. Cambridge University Press.
Dalphond, P. 2002. 'Duty of care and the supply of alcohol' *Supreme Court Law Review (2d)* 17:97.
Davies, D. 1993. 'Equitable compensation: causation, foreseeability and remoteness' in Waters 1993, 297–324.
Davis, J.L.R. 1998. 'Farewell to the action for breach of statutory duty?' in Mullany and Linden 1998, 69–83.
——. 2000. 'Liability for careless acts or omissions causing purely economic loss: *Perre* v *Apand Pty Ltd*' *Torts Law Journal* 8:123.
Deakin, S., Johnston, A. and Markesinis, B. 2008. *Markesinis and Deakin's Tort Law*, 6th edn. Oxford University Press.
Degeling, S. 2003. *Restitutionary Rights to Share in Damages: Carers' Claims*. Cambridge University Press.
Dietrich, J. 2000. 'Lawful coercive threats and the infliction of harm' *Torts Law Journal* 8:187.
Donaldson, L. 2003. *Making Amends: A Consultation Paper Setting out Proposals for Reforming the Approach to Clinical Negligence in the NHS*. HMSO.
Donnelly, C. 2007. *Delegation of Governmental Power to Private Parties: A Comparative Perspective*. Oxford University Press.
D'Souza, D. 2002. *Letters to a Young Conservative*. Basic Books.
Duff, R.A. and Marshall, S.E. 2006. 'How offensive can you get?' in Von Hirsch and Simester 2006, 57–90.
Dugdale, T. 2000. 'The impact of SAAMCO' *Professional Negligence* 16:203.
Dugdale, T. and Jones, M. 2006. et al. *Clerk and Lindsell on Torts*. 19th edn. Sweet & Maxwell.
Duncan Wallace, I. 2000. '*Donoghue* v *Stevenson* and "complex structures": *Anns* revisited?' *Law Quarterly Review* 116:530.

Dziobon, S. and Tettenborn, A. 1997. 'When the truth hurts: the incompetent transmission of distressing news' *Professional Negligence* 13:70.
Economides, K. 2000. et al. eds. *Fundamental Values*. Hart Publishing.
Edelman, J. 2002a. 'Equitable torts' *Torts Law Journal* 10:64.
——. 2002b. *Gain-Based Damages*. Hart Publishing.
——. 2006. 'Gain-based damages and compensation' in Burrows and Rodger 2006, 141–60.
Eekelaar, J. 2003. 'Corporal punishment, parent's religion and children's rights' *Law Quarterly Review* 119:370.
Elvin, J. 2003a. 'Liability for negligent refereeing of a rugby match' *Law Quarterly Review* 119:560.
——. 2003b. 'The duty of schools to prevent bullying' *Tort Law Review* 11:168.
Epstein, R.A. 1973. 'A theory of strict liability' *Journal of Legal Studies* 2:151.
Evans, H. 2001. 'The scope of the duty revisited' *Professional Negligence* 17:147.
Fairgrieve, D. 2001. 'The Human Rights Act 1998, damages and tort law' *Public Law* [2001]:695.
Fairgrieve, D., Adenas, M. and Bell, J. 2002. eds. *Tort Liability of Public Authorities in Comparative Perspective*. BIICL.
Farnsworth, W. 1999. 'Do parties to nuisance cases bargain after judgment? A glimpse inside the cathedral' *University of Chicago Law Review* 66:373.
Feldman, D. 1997. 'Privacy-related rights and their social value' in Birks 1997c, 15–50.
Feldthusen, B. 1991. 'Economic loss in the Supreme Court of Canada: yesterday and tomorrow' *Canadian Business Law Journal* 17:356
——. 1997. 'Failure to confer discretionary public benefits: the case for complete negligence immunity' *Tort Law Review* 5:17.
——. 1998. 'Vicarious liability for sexual torts' in Mullany and Linden 1998, 221–43.
Finnis, J. 1995. 'Intention in tort law' in Owen 1995, 229–48.
——. 2002. 'Natural law: the classical tradition' in Coleman and Shapiro 2002, 1–60.
Fischer, D. 1992. 'Causation in fact in omission cases' *Utah Law Review* 41:1335.
Fleming, J. 1997. 'Preventive damages' in Mullany 1997, 56–71.
——. 1998. *The Law of Torts*, 9th edn. LBC Information Services.
Fridman, G.H.L. 1963. 'Compensation of the innocent' *Modern Law Review* 26:481.
——. 1993. 'Interference with trade or business – part 2' *Tort Law Review* 1:99.
——. 1996. *Law of Agency*, 7th edn. Butterworths.
Fried, C. 1968. 'Privacy' *Yale Law Journal* 77:475.
Friedmann, D. 1997. 'Rights and remedies' *Law Quarterly Review* 113:424.
——. 1998. 'Restitution for wrongs – the basis of liability' in Cornish 1998, 133–54.
Fuller, L. 1964. *The Morality of Law*. Yale University Press.
Gardner, J. 2002. 'Obligations and outcomes in the law of tort' in Cane and Gardner 2001, 111–43.
Gearty, C. 1989. 'The place of private nuisance in a modern law of torts' *Cambridge Law Journal* 48:214.
Ghandi, P.R. 1990. 'Exemplary damages in the English law of tort' *Legal Studies* 10:182.
Gibbons, T. 1996. 'Defamation reconsidered' *Oxford Journal of Legal Studies* 16:587.
Giglio, F. 2007. 'Restitution for wrongs: a structural analysis' *Canadian Journal of Law and Jurisprudence* 20:5.
Giliker, P. 2000. '*Osman* and police immunity in the English law of torts' *Legal Studies* 20:372.
——. 2002. 'Rough justice in an unjust world' *Modern Law Review* 65:269.
Giliker, P. and Beckwith, G. 2004. *Tort*, 2nd edn. Sweet & Maxwell.
Gilligan, C. 1982. *In a Different Voice: Psychological Theory and Women's Development*. Harvard University Press.
Glofcheski, R. 1999. 'Plaintiff's illegality as a bar to recovery of personal injury damages' *Legal Studies* 19:6.
——. 2004. 'A frolic in the law of tort: expanding the scope of employers' vicarious liability' *Tort Law Review* 12:18.

Goldberg, J. 2000. 'Duty and the structure of negligence' *Kansas Journal of Law and Public Policy* [2000]:149.
——. 2002. 'Unloved: tort law in the modern legal academy' *Vanderbilt Law Review* 55:1501.
——. 2003a. 'Tort' in Cane and Tushnet 2003, 21–47.
——. 2003b. 'Twentieth-century tort theory' *Georgetown Law Journal* 91:513.
——. 2003c. 'Rethinking injury and proximate cause' *San Diego Law Review* 40:1315.
Goldberg, J., Sebok, A. and Zipursky, B. 2004. *Tort Law: Responsibilities and Redress*. Aspen Publishers.
Goldberg, J. and Zipursky, B. 1998. 'The moral of *MacPherson*' *University of Pennsylvania Law Review* 146:1733.
——. 2001. 'The Restament (Third) and the place of duty in negligence law' *Vanderbilt Law Review* 54: 657.
——. 2002. 'Unrealized torts' *Virginia Law Review* 88:1625.
——. 2006. 'Seeing tort law from the internal point of view: Holmes and Hart on legal duties' *Fordham Law Review* 75:1563.
Goodhart, A.L. 1938. 'The foundations of tortious liability' *Modern Law Review* 2:1.
Goodin, R.E. 1989. 'Theories of compensation' *Oxford Journal of Legal Studies* 9:56.
Gordley, J. 1995. 'Tort law in the Aristotelian tradition' in Owen 1995, 131–58.
——. 1998. 'Responsibility in crime, tort and contract for the unforeseeable consequences of an intentional wrong: a once and future rule?' in Cane and Stapleton 1998, 175–208.
Grantham, R.B. and Rickett, C.E.F. 2003. 'Disgorgement for unjust enrichment?' *Cambridge Law Journal* 62:159.
Gravells, N. 1977. 'Three heads of contributory negligence' *Law Quarterly Review* 93:581.
Gray, K. 1991. 'Property in thin air' *Cambridge Law Journal* 50:255.
Gray, N. and Edelman, J. 1998. 'Developing the law of omissions: a common law duty to rescue?' *Torts Law Journal* 6:240.
Gronow, M. 1995. 'Conspiracy: the tort that failed?' *Torts Law Journal* 3:255.
Guest, A.G. 1961. ed. *Oxford Essays in Jurisprudence 1st Series*. Clarendon Press.
Haberfield, L. 1998. '*Lowns* v *Wood* and the duty to rescue' *Tort Law Review* 6:56.
Handley, E. and Davis, G. 2001. 'Defamation and satire: *Hanson* v *Australian Broadcasting Corporation*' *Torts Law Journal* 9:1.
Harris, D. 1984. et al. *Compensation and Support for Illness and Injury*. Oxford University Press.
Harris, J. 1961. 'The concept of possession in English law' in Guest 1961, 69–106.
——. 1986. 'Who owns my body?' *Oxford Journal of Legal Studies* 16:55.
Hart, H.L.A. and Honoré, A.M. 1985. *Causation in the Law*, 2nd edn. Oxford University Press.
Hedley, S. 2006. *Tort*. 5th edn. Oxford University Press.
Hedley, S. and Halliwell, M. 2002. eds. *The Law of Restitution*. Butterworths.
Hepple, B. 1997. 'Negligence: the search for coherence' *Current Legal Problems* [1997]:69.
Heuston, R.F.V. 1970. 'Who was the third Law Lord in *Rylands* v *Fletcher*?' *Law Quarterly Review* 86:160.
——. 1986. 'Judicial prosopography' *Law Quarterly Review* 102:90.
Heuston, R.F.V. and Buckley, R.A. 1996. *Salmond and Heuston on the Law of Torts*. 21st edn. Sweet & Maxwell.
Hill, T. 1991. 'A lost chance for compensation in the tort of negligence by the House of Lords' *Modern Law Review* 54:511.
Hoffmann, Lord. 2005. 'Causation' *Law Quarterly Review* 121:592.
Holmes, O.W. 1873. 'The theory of torts' *American Law Review* 7:652.
Hope, Lord. 2003. 'James McGhee – a second Mrs Donoghue?' *Cambridge Law Journal* 62:587.
Horder, J. 2000. ed. *Oxford Essays in Jurisprudence 4th Series*. Clarendon Press.
Howarth, D. 1995. *Textbook on Tort*. Butterworths.
——. 2004. 'Public authority non-liability: spinning out of control?' *Cambridge Law Journal* 63: 546.

——. 2005a. 'Poisoned wells: "proximity" and "assumption of responsibility" in negligence' *Cambridge Law Journal* 64:23.
——. 2005b. 'Against *Lumley* v *Gye*' *Modern Law Review* 68:195.
——. 2006. 'Many duties of care – or a duty of care? Notes from the underground' *Oxford Journal of Legal Studies* 26:449.
——. 2007. 'Duty of care' in Oliphant 2007, 629–729.
Howarth, D. and O'Sullivan, J. 2000. *Hepple, Howarth and Matthews' Tort: Cases and Materials*, 5th edn. Butterworths.
Howells, G. and Mildred, M. 2002. 'Infected blood' *Modern Law Review* 65:95.
Hoyano, L. 1999. 'Policing flawed police investigations: unravelling the blanket' *Modern Law Review* 62:912.
——. 2002. 'Misconceptions about wrongful conception' *Modern Law Review* 65:883.
Hunt, M. 1998. 'The "horizontal" effect of the Human Rights Act' *Public Law* [1998]:422.
Hyman, D. 2005. 'Rescue without law: an empirical perspective on the duty to rescue' *Texas Law Review* 84:653.
Ibbetson, D. 1999. *A Historical Introduction to the Law of Obligations*. Oxford University Press.
——. 2003. 'How the Romans did for us: ancient roots of the tort of negligence' *University of New South Wales Law Journal* 26:475.
Insurance Research Council. 1999. *Injuries in Auto Accidents: An Analysis of Auto Insurance Claims*. Insurance Research Council.
Jackman, I. 1989. 'Restitution for wrongs' *Cambridge Law Journal* 48:302.
Jaffey, A.J.E. 1985. 'Volenti non fit injuria' *Cambridge Law Journal* 44:87.
Jaffey, P. 2007. *Private Law and Property Claims*. Hart Publishing.
Jones, G. 2007. *Goff and Jones' Law of Restitution*. 7th edn. Sweet & Maxwell.
Jones, M. 2002. *Textbook on Torts*, 8th edn. Oxford University Press.
Keeton, R. 1984. et al. *Prosser and Keeton on the Law of Torts*, 5th edn. West Publishing Co.
Kelley, P.J. 1990. 'Who decides? Community safety conventions at the heart of tort liability' *Cleveland State Law Review* 38:315.
Kelly, R. 1967. 'The inner nature of the tort action' *Irish Jurist (New Series)* 2:279.
Kennedy, I. 2001. *Final Report of the Bristol Royal Infirmary Inquiry*. HMSO.
Kessler, D.P. and McClellan, M. 1996. 'Do doctors practise defensive medicine?' *Quarterly Journal of Economics* 111:353.
Kidner, R. 1991. 'The variable standard of care, contributory negligence and volenti' *Legal Studies* 11:1.
——. 1995. 'Vicarious liability: for whom should the "employer" be held liable?' *Legal Studies* 15:47.
Klar, L. 1998. 'Downsizing torts' in Mullany and Linden 1998, 305–20.
Koenig, T.H. and Rustad, M.L. 2001. *In Defense of Tort Law*. New York University Press.
Koziol, H. and Steininger, B. 2005. eds. *European Tort Law 2004: Tort and Insurance Yearbook*. Springer.
Landes, W.M. and Posner, R.A. 1987. *The Economic Structure of Tort Law*. Harvard University Press.
Lee, M. 2003. 'What is private nuisance?' *Law Quarterly Review* 119:298.
Lewis, R. 1999. *Deducting Benefits from Damages for Personal Injury*. Oxford University Press.
——. 2007. 'Tort law in practice: appearance and reality in reforming periodical payments of damages' in Neyers, Chamberlain and Pitel 2007, 487–508.
Loughran, D. 2001. *The Effect of No-Fault Automobile Insurance on Driver Behaviour and Automobile Accidents in the United States*. Rand Corporation.
Loveland, I. 2000. *Political Libels*. Hart Publishing.
Lunney, M. and Mitchell, P. 2007. 'Intentional interference with the person' in Oliphant 2007, 437–84.
Lunney, M. and Oliphant, K. 2008. *Tort Law: Text and Materials*. 3rd edn. Oxford University Press.
MacDonald, A. 1936–1938. '*Hollywood Silver Fox Farm* v *Emmett*' *Alberta Law Quarterly* 2:99.
Machin, E.A. 1954. 'Negligence and interest' *Modern Law Review* 17:405.

Macneil, I. 1982. 'Efficient breach of contract: circles in the sky' *Virginia Law Review* 68:947.

Madden, M.S. 2005. *Exploring Tort Law*. Cambridge University Press.

Mahoney, F. 1997. 'Defamation law – time to rethink' in Mullany 1997, 261–73.

Markesinis, B. 1999. et al. *Tortious Liability of Statutory Bodies: A Comparative and Economic Analysis of Five English Cases*. Hart Publishing.

Markesinis, B., Johnston, A. and Deakin, S. 2003. *Markesinis & Deakin's Tort Law*. 5th edn. Oxford University Press.

Marter, S. and Weisberg, H. 1992. 'Medical expenses and the Massachusetts automobile Tort Reform Law: a first review of 1989 bodily injury liability claims' *Journal of Insurance Regulation* 10:462.

Mason, J.K. 2002. 'Wrongful pregnancy, wrongful birth and wrongful terminology' *Edinburgh Law Review* 6:46.

Mason, K. and Carter, J.W. 1995. *Restitution Law in Australia*. Butterworths.

Matthews, P. 1983. 'Whose body? People as property' *Current Legal Problems* [1983]:193.

Matula, M.L. 1996. 'Manufacturers' post sale duties in the 1990s' *Tort and Insurance Law Journal* 32:87.

McBride, N.J. 1995. 'A case for awarding punitive damages in response to deliberate breaches of contract' *Anglo-American Law Review* 24:369.

——. 1996. 'Punitive damages' in Birks 1996b, 175–202.

——. 2000. 'On the conceptual and philosophical foundations of tort law' in Horder 2000, 219–36.

——. 2004. 'Duties of care: do they really exist?' *Oxford Journal of Legal Studies* 24:417.

——. 2006a. 'Tort law' in Butler 2006, 26–35.

——. 2006b. 'Negligence liability for omissions – some fundamental distinctions' *Cambridge Student Law Review* 2:10.

McBride, N.J. and Bagshaw, R. 2001. *Tort Law*, 1st edn. Pearson Education.

——. 2003. *Tort Law*, 2nd edn. Pearson Education.

McBride, N.J. and Hughes, A. 1995. '*Hedley Byrne* in the House of Lords: an interpretation' *Legal Studies* 15:376.

McEwin, I.R. 1989. 'No-fault and road accidents: some Australasian evidence' *International Review of Law and Economics* 9:13.

McGregor, H. 1996. 'Restitutionary damages' in Birks 1996b, 203–16.

——. 2003. *McGregor on Damages*, 17th edn. Sweet & Maxwell.

McInnes, M. 2003. 'Interceptive subtraction, unjust enrichment and wrongs – a reply to Professor Birks' *Cambridge Law Journal* 62:697.

Meagher, R.P, Heydon, J.D. and Leeming, M.J. 2002. *Meagher, Gummow and Lehane's Equity: Doctrines and Remedies*, 4th edn. Butterworths.

Miles, J. 2000. 'Standing under the Human Rights Act 1998: theories of rights enforcement and the nature of public law adjudication' *Cambridge Law Journal* 59:133.

Mitchell, P. 1999. 'Malice in qualified privilege' *Public Law* [1999]:328.

——. 2005. *The Making of the Modern Law of Defamation*. Hart Publishing.

Monti, G. 1999. '*Osman* v *UK* – transforming English negligence law into French public law' *International and Comparative Law Quarterly* 48:757.

Moran, M. 1997. 'Rethinking *Winnipeg Condominium*: restitution, economic loss, and anticipatory repairs' *University of Toronto Law Journal* 47:115.

——. 2003. *Rethinking the Reasonable Person*. Oxford University Press.

Morgan, J. 2003. 'Lost causes in the House of Lords: *Fairchild* v *Glenhaven Funeral Services*' *Modern Law Review* 66:277.

——. 2004. 'Tort, insurance and incoherence' *Modern Law Review* 67:384.

——. 2006. 'The rise and fall of the general duty of care' *Professional Negligence* 22:206.

Mullany, N. 1997. ed. *Torts in the Nineties*. LBC Information Services.

Mullany, N. and Linden, A.M. 1998. eds. *Torts Tomorrow: A Tribute to John Fleming*. LBC Information Services.

Mullender, R. 2000. 'Negligence, the personal equation of defendants and distributive justice' *Tort Law Review* 8:211.

Murphy, J. 1996. 'Expectation losses, negligent omissions and the tortious duty of care' *Cambridge Law Journal* 55:43.

——. 2003. *Street on Torts*, 11th edn. Butterworths.

——. 2004. 'The merits of *Rylands* v *Fletcher*' *Oxford Journal of Legal Studies* 24:643.

——. 2007. 'Juridical foundations of common law non-delegable duties' in Neyers, Chamberlain and Pitel 2007, 369–91.

Newark, F.H. 1949. 'The boundaries of nuisance' *Law Quarterly Review* 65:480.

Neyers, J. 2002. 'Distilling duty: the Supreme Court of Canada amends *Anns*' *Law Quarterly Review* 118:221.

——. 2005. 'A theory of vicarious liability' *Alberta Law Review* 43:287.

Neyers, J., Chamberlain, E. and Pitel, S. 2007. eds. *Emerging Issues in Tort Law*. Hart Publishing.

Nolan, D. 2001. 'Risks and wrongs – remoteness of damage in the House of Lords' *Tort Law Review* 9:101.

——. 2005. 'The distinctiveness of *Rylands* v *Fletcher*' *Law Quarterly Review* 121:421.

——. 2007. 'Product liability' in Oliphant 2007, 975–1031.

Ogus, A. and Richardson, G. 1977. 'Economics and the environment – a study of private nuisance' *Cambridge Law Journal* 36:284.

Oliphant, K. 2005. '*Rylands* v *Fletcher* and the emergence of enterprise liability in the common law' in Koziol and Steininger 2005, 81–120.

——. 2007. ed. *The Law of Tort*. 2nd edn. LexisNexis Butterworths.

Oliver, D. 2000. 'The frontiers of the State: public authorities and public functions under the Human Rights Act' *Public Law* [2000]:476.

——. 2004. 'Functions of a Public Nature under the Human Rights Act' *Public Law* [2004]:329.

Ormerod, D. 2005. *Smith and Hogan Criminal Law*. 11th edn. Oxford University Press.

Orr, G. 1995. 'Is an innkeeper her brother's keeper? The liability of alcohol servers' *Torts Law Journal* 3:239.

O'Sullivan, J. 1997. 'Negligent professional advice and market movements' *Cambridge Law Journal* 56:19.

——. 1999. 'Liability for fear of the onset of future medical conditions' *Professional Negligence* 15:96.

Owen, D. 1995. ed. *Philosophical Foundations of Tort Law*. Clarendon Press.

Palmer, N. 2000. 'Bailment' in Birks 2000a, 357–406.

Palmer, N. and McKendrick, E. 1998. eds. *Interests in Goods*, 2nd edn. Lloyd's of London Press.

Pearson, Lord. 1978. *Royal Commission on Civil Liability and Compensation for Personal Injury*. HMSO.

Pedain, A. 2005. 'Requiem for a fairytale' *Cambridge Law Journal* 64:11.

Peel, E. 2003a. 'SAAMCO revisited' in Burrows and Peel 2003, 55–70.

——. 2003b. '"Loss of a chance" revisited: *Gregg* v *Scott*' *Modern Law Review* 66:623.

Perlman, H. 1982. 'Interference with contract and other economic expectancies: a clash of tort and contract doctrine' *University of Chicago Law Review* 49:61.

Perry, S. 1992. 'Protected interests and undertakings in the law of negligence' *University of Toronto Law Journal* 42:247.

Pollock, F. 1882. *Essays in Jurisprudence and Ethics*. Macmillan, London.

Porat, A. and Stein, A. 2003. 'Indeterminate causation and apportionment of damages: an essay on *Holtby*, *Allen* and *Fairchild*' *Oxford Journal of Legal Studies* 23:667.

Posner, R.A. 2003. *Economic Analysis of Law*. 6th edn. Aspen.

Prosser, W. 1960. 'Privacy' *California Law Review* 48:383.

Reece, H. 1996. 'Losses of chance in the law' *Modern Law Review* 59:188.

Reed, A. 1996. 'The professional liability of agents in tort' *Tort Law Review* 4:62.

Reid, G. 2005. '*Gregg* v *Scott* and lost chances' *Professional Negligence* 21:78.

Ripstein, A. 2002. 'Philosophy of tort law' in Coleman and Shapiro 2002, 656–86.
Rogers, W.V.H. 2006. *Winfield & Jolowicz on Tort*. 17th edn. Sweet & Maxwell.
Rotherham, C. 2002. 'Subrogation' in Hedley and Halliwell 2002, 131–55.
Rubin, P.H. and Shepherd, J.M. 2007. 'Tort reform and accidental deaths' *The Journal of Law and Economics* 50:221.
Rudden, B. 1991–1992. 'Torticles' *Tulane Civil Law Forum* 6/7:105.
Sales, P. 1990. 'The tort of conspiracy and civil secondary liability' *Cambridge Law Journal* 49: 491.
Sales, P. and Stilitz, D. 1999. 'Intentional infliction of harm by unlawful means' *Law Quarterly Review* 115:411.
Salmond, J. 1907. *Law of Torts*. Sweet & Maxwell.
Scott, Lord. 2006. 'Damages' *Lecture at Chancery Bar Association Conference*.
Sebok, A. 2007. 'Punitive damages: from myth to theory' *Iowa Law Review* 92:957.
Seneviratne, M. 2001. 'The rise and fall of advocates' immunity' *Legal Studies* 21:644.
Sharpe, R.J. and Waddams, S.M. 1982. 'Damages for lost opportunity to bargain' *Oxford Journal of Legal Studies* 2:290.
Sherwin, E. 2003. 'Compensation and revenge' *San Diego Law Review* 40:1387.
Simester, A. and Chan, W. 2004. 'Inducing breach of contract: one tort or two?' *Cambridge Law Journal* 63:132.
Simpson, A.W.B. 1995. *Leading Cases in the Common Law*. Oxford University Press.
Smith, J.C. and Burns, P. 1983a. '*Donoghue* v *Stevenson* – the not so golden anniversary' *Modern Law Review* 46:147.
——. 1983b. 'The good neighbour on trial: good neighbours make bad law' *University of British Columbia Law Review* 17:93.
Smith, L. 1992. 'The province of the law of restitution' *Canadian Bar Review* 71:672.
Smith, R. 1977. 'The economic torts: their impact on real property' *Conveyancer and Property Lawyer* 41:318.
——. 2006. *Property Law*. 5th edn. Pearson Education.
Smith, S. 1997. 'Rights, remedies and normal expectancies in tort and contract' *Law Quarterly Review* 113:426.
Solomon, R. and Payne, J. 1996. 'Alcohol liability in Canada and Australia: sell, serve and be sued' *Tort Law Review* 4:188.
Spencer, J. 1989. 'Public nuisance – a critical examination' *Cambridge Law Journal* 48:55.
Stallybrass, W.T.S. 1929. 'Dangerous things and non-natural user of land' *Cambridge Law Journal* 3:376.
Stanton, K. 1997. 'Incremental approaches to the duty of care' in Mullany 1997, 34–55.
——. 2003. et al. *Statutory Torts*. Sweet & Maxwell.
Stapleton, J. 1991. 'Duty of care and economic loss: a wider agenda' *Law Quarterly Review* 107:249.
——. 1994a. *Product Liability*. Butterworths.
——. 1994b. 'In restraint of tort' in Birks 1994, 83–102.
——. 1995. 'Duty of care: peripheral parties and alternative opportunities for deterrence' *Law Quarterly Review* 111:301.
——. 1997. 'The normal expectancies measure in tort damages' *Law Quarterly Review* 113:257.
——. 1998. 'Duty of care factors: a selection from the judicial menus' in Cane and Stapleton 1998, 59–95.
——. 2001. 'Unpacking causation' in Cane and Gardner 2001, 145–85.
——. 2002a. 'Comparative economic loss: lessons from case-law-focused "middle theory"' *University of California, Los Angeles Law Review* 50:531.
——. 2002b. 'Lords a-leaping evidentiary gaps' *Torts Law Journal* 10:276.
——. 2003a. 'Cause-in-fact and the scope of liability for consequences' *Law Quarterly Review* 119:388.

——. 2003b. 'The golden thread at the heart of tort law: protection of the vulnerable' *Australian Bar Review* 24:135.

——. 2006. 'Evaluating Goldberg and Zipursky's civil recourse theory' *Fordham Law Review* 75:1529.

Stauch, M. 2001. 'Risk and remoteness of damage in negligence' *Modern Law Review* 64:191.

Steele, J. 2007. *Tort Law: Text, Cases and Materials*. Oxford University Press.

Stein, P.G. and Lewis, A.D.E. 1983. eds. *Studies in Justinian's Institutes*. Sweet & Maxwell.

Stevens, R. 2005. 'An opportunity to reflect' *Law Quarterly Review* 121:189.

——. 2007. *Torts and Rights*. Oxford University Press.

Stone, J. 1946. *The Province and Function of Law*. Associated General Publications.

Stoppa, A. 1992. 'The concept of defectiveness in the Consumer Protection Act 1987: a critical analysis' *Legal Studies* 12:210.

Sugarman, S. 2002. 'A new approach to tort doctrine: taking the best from the civil law and common law of Canada' *Supreme Court Law Review (2d)* 17:375.

Swadling, W. and Jones, G. 1999. eds. *The Search for Principle: Essays in Honour of Lord Goff of Chieveley*. Oxford University Press.

Taggart, M. 2002. *Private Property and Abuse of Rights in Victorian England*. Oxford University Press.

Tan, K.F. 1981. 'A misconceived issue in the tort of false imprisonment' *Modern Law Review* 44:166.

Teff, H. 1996. 'The requirement of "sudden shock" in liability for negligently inflicted psychiatric damage' *Tort Law Review* 4:44.

——. 1998. 'Liability for negligently inflicted psychiatric harm: justifications and boundaries' *Cambridge Law Journal* 57:91.

Tettenborn, A. 1993. 'Damages in conversion – the exception or the anomaly?' *Cambridge Law Journal* 52:128.

——. 1996. 'Trust property and conversion: an equitable confusion' *Cambridge Law Journal* 55:36.

——. 2000a. 'Professional negligence: free riders and others' in Economides 2000, 295–311.

——. 2000b. 'Components and product liability: damage to "other property"' *Lloyd's Maritime and Commercial Law Quarterly* [2000]:338.

——. 2003. et al. *The Law of Damages*. Butterworths.

Todd, S. 2007. 'Policy issues in defective property cases' in Neyers, Chamberlain and Pitel 2007, 199–232.

Tomlinson, E.A. 2000. 'The French experience with duty to rescue: a dubious case for criminal enforcement' *New York Law Journal of International and Comparative Law* 20:451.

Treiger-Bar-Am, L.K. 2000. 'Defamation law in a changing society: the case of *Youssoupoff* v *Metro-Goldwyn-Mayer*' *Legal Studies* 20:291.

Treitel, G.H. 1999. 'Bills of lading and bailment on terms' in Swadling and Jones 1999, 115–42.

——. 2003. *The Law of Contract*. 11th edn. Sweet & Maxwell.

Trindade, F. 1982. 'Intentional torts: some thoughts on assault and battery' *Oxford Journal of Legal Studies* 2:211.

Tromans, S. 1982. 'Private nuisance – prevention or payment' *Cambridge Law Journal* 41:87.

Tugendhat, M. and Christie, I. 2002. eds. *The Law of Privacy and the Media*. 2nd ed. Oxford University Press.

——. 2006. eds. *The Law of Privacy and the Media, Second Cumulative Supplement*. Oxford University Press.

Van Gerven, W., Lever, J. and Larouche, P. 2000. *Tort Law and Scope of Protection: Cases, Materials and Text*. Hart Publishing.

Von Hirsch, A. and Simester, A. 2006. *Incivilities*. Hart Publishing.

Waddams, S. 1998. 'New directions in products liability' in Mullany and Linden 1998, 119–29.

——. 2001. 'Johanna Wagner and the rival opera houses' *Law Quarterly Review* 117:431.

——. 2003. *Dimensions of Private Law: Categories and Concepts in Anglo-American Legal Reasoning*. Cambridge University Press.

Waters, D.W.M. 1993. ed. *Equity, Fiducaries and Trusts*. Carswell.

Wedderburn, Lord. 1983. 'Rocking the torts' *Modern Law Review* 46:224.
Weinrib, E. 1980. 'The case for a duty to rescue' *Yale Law Journal* 90:247.
——. 1995. *The Idea of Private Law*. Harvard University Press.
——. 2000. 'Restitutionary damages as corrective justice' *Theoretical Inquiries in Law* 1:1.
——. 2005. 'The disintegration of duty' in Madden 2005, 143–86.
Weir, J.A. 1964. 'Chaos or cosmos? *Rookes, Stratford* and the economic torts' *Cambridge Law Journal* 23:225.
——. 1995. 'A damnosa hereditas' *Law Quarterly Review* 111:357.
——. 1997. *Economic Torts*. Clarendon Press.
——. 1998a. 'The staggering march of negligence' in Cane and Stapleton 1998, 97–138.
——. 1998b. 'Suicide in custody' *Cambridge Law Journal* 57:241.
——. 2001a. *Tort Law*. 1st edn. Clarendon Law Series.
——. 2001b. 'The maddening effect of consecutive torts' *Cambridge Law Journal* 60:237.
——. 2004. *A Casebook on Tort*. 10th edn. Sweet & Maxwell.
——. 2006. *An Introduction to Tort Law*. 2nd edn. Clarendon Law Series, Oxford.
Weston, C.A.R. 1999. 'Suing in tort for loss of computer data' *Cambridge Law Journal* 58:67.
Whittaker, S. 1989. 'European product liability and intellectual products' *Law Quarterly Review* 105:125.
——. 1997. 'The application of the "broad principle of *Hedley Byrne*" as between parties to a contract' *Legal Studies* 17:169.
Williams, G. 1939–1941. 'The foundation of tortious liability' *Cambridge Law Journal* [1939-41]:111.
——. 1956a. 'Vicarious liability: tort of the master or servant?' *Law Quarterly Review* 72:122.
——. 1956b. 'Liability for independent contractors' *Cambridge Law Journal* 15:180.
Williams, K. 2000. 'Defaming politicians: the not so common law' *Modern Law Review* 63:748.
——. 2001. 'Medical Samaritans: is there a duty to treat?' *Oxford Journal of Legal Studies* 21:393.
Winfield, P. 1926. 'The history of negligence in the law of torts' *Law Quarterly Review* 42:184.
——. 1927. 'The foundation of liability in tort' *Columbia Law Review* 27:1.
——. 1931. *The Province of the Law of Tort*. Cambridge University Press.
——. 1934. 'Duty in tortious negligence' *Columbia Law Review* 34:41.
Witting, C. 2000a. 'Negligent inspectors and flying machines' *Cambridge Law Journal* 59:544.
——. 2000b. 'Liability to third parties for negligent misstatements' *Oxford Journal of Legal Studies* 20:615.
——. 2001. 'Distinguishing between property damage and pure economic loss in negligence: a personality thesis' *Legal Studies* 21:481.
Wolfe, J. 1995. 'Casinos and the compulsive gambler: is there a duty to monitor the gambler's wagers?' *Mississippi Law Journal* 64: 687.
Woolf, Lord. 2000. 'The Human Rights Act 1998 and remedies' in Andenas and Fairgrieve 2000, 429–36.
Worthington, S. 1999. 'Reconsidering disgorgement for wrongs' *Modern Law Review* 62:218.
Wright, C. 1944. 'Introduction to the law of torts' *Cambridge Law Journal* 8:238.
——. 1961. 'The English law of torts – a criticism' *University of Toronto Law Journal* 11:84.
Wright J. 2001. *Tort Law and Human Rights*. Hart Publishing.
Wright, R. 1985. 'Causation in tort law' *California Law Review* 73:1735.
——. 1988. 'Causation, responsibility, risk, probability, naked statistics and proof: pruning the bramble bush by clarifying the concepts' *Iowa Law Review* 73:1001.
——. 2001. 'Once more into the bramble bush: duty, causal contribution, and the extent of legal responsibility' *Vanderbilt Law Review* 53:1071.
Young, A.L. 2000. 'Fact, opinion and the Human Rights Act 1998' *Oxford Journal of Legal Studies* 20:89.
Zipursky, B. 1998a. 'Rights, wrongs and recourse in the law of torts' *Vanderbilt Law Review* 51:1.
——. 1998b. 'Legal malpractice and the structure of negligence law' *Fordham Law Review* 67:649.

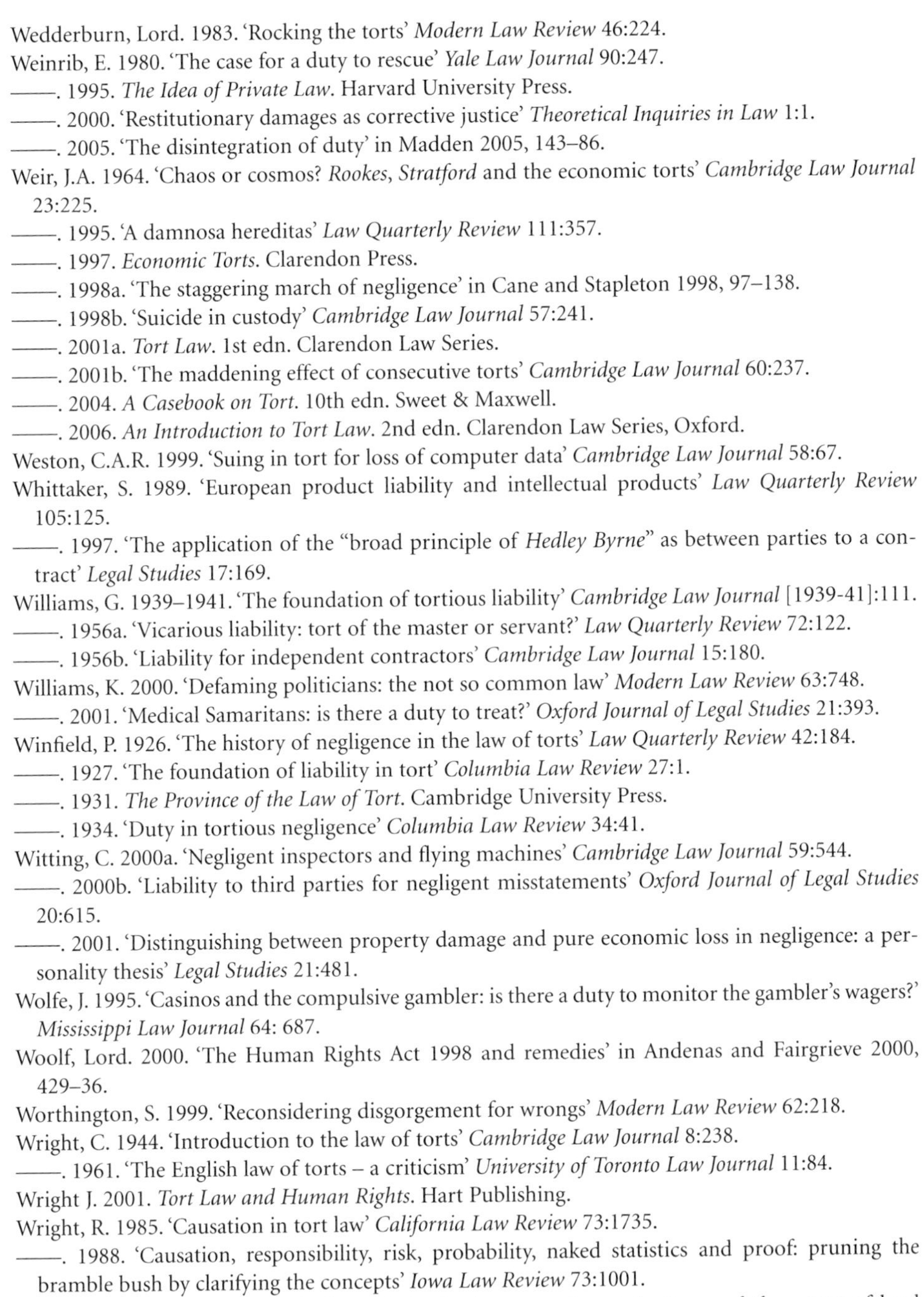

——. 2002. 'Philosophy of private law' in Coleman and Shapiro 2002, 623–55.
——. 2003. 'Civil recourse, not corrective justice' *Georgetown Law Journal* 91:695.
——. 2005. 'A theory of punitive damages' *Texas Law Review* 84:105.
Zuckerman, A. 2006. *Zuckerman on Civil Procedure – Principles of Practice*. 2nd edn. Sweet & Maxwell.
Zweigert, K. and Kötz, H. 1998. *An Introduction to Comparative Law*. 3rd rev'd edn. (trans Weir, J.A.). Oxford University Press.

Index